ECONOMIC TIMES

TABLE OF CONTENTS

THE ECONOMICS OF CRIME

BY DONALD H. DUTKOWSKY

Reducing crime continues to be one of the fundamental challenges to society. In arguing for passage of President Clinton's proposed crime bill, Senator Joseph Biden echoed the view of many when he said, "Crime is the most serious problem facing America." The heated debate surrounding this legislation indicates that we are far from a general consensus regarding how to effectively lower the incidence of crime.

How has the United States fared in recent years? The table presented below compares the levels of crime in 1983 and 1992. From the first row, observe that total crime has risen in the United States by approximately 10 percent. This increase has not come from greater homicide, as the murder rate has barely nudged upward. Drug abuse, aggravated assault, simple assault, and motor vehicle theft registered the largest percentage increases. Crime rates actually declined for certain violations such as driving under the influence, burglary, and gambling.

This issue of *Economic Times* addresses the ways in which the thinking and tools of economics can be applied to the problem of crime. It begins with an interview with Isaac Ehrlich, one of the leading researchers in this area. Professor Ehrlich discusses how the perspective of economics can generate insights into the study of crime in a variety of ways.

Why do people commit crime? What benefits and costs do they face? How can we decrease crime by changing the incentives involved with undertaking criminal action? And what are the costs of doing so? Articles in this issue examine how economics can be used to answer these questions with regard to income tax evasion, exceeding the 55-mph speed limit, and sentencing convicted criminals.

As the table indicates, illegal drug use represents a growing problem. Many people contend that costly programs designed to eliminate drug use have failed to produce significant gains. They argue that, like alcohol, drugs should be legalized and even taxed. Several articles examine the problem of drug use from an economic point of view, examining the effects of drug prohibition, economics of the illegal drug trade, and the opportunity costs of a drug war.

Crime is costly. A *Reading Between the Lines* feature applies the concepts of production to determining the effect of shoplifting on the firm's cost and output decision within the music industry. Governments also incur costs in trying to enforce laws and deter crime. Two features look at issues involved in government allocation of resources to criminal justice. Another *Economics in the News* piece examines the cost of crime to the general economy.

Crime has other macroeconomic effects as well. A considerable amount of total production and expenditure does not appear in the macroeconomic statistics. An article in this issue explores the underground economy in the United States—what it is, how it comes about, and what can be done to reduce its magnitude. A *Reading Between the Lines* feature looks at the smuggling of cigarettes into Canada to avoid excise taxes. Finally, another *Reading Between the Lines* piece examines the effects of the recently enacted crime bill on the economy.

Crime in the United States: 1983 and 1992
(arrests per 100,000 people)

Type of Crime	1983	1992
Total	5,198.7	5,703.9
Murder and nonnegligent manslaughter	9.1	9.8
Drug abuse violations	320.8	460.4
Driving under the influence	831.8	621.6

Source: Computed from Federal Bureau of Investigation, *Crime in the United States, 1992*, Table 32.

Talking with Isaac Ehrlich

Professor Isaac Ehrlich holds the Melvin H. Baker Chair of American Enterprise at the State University of New York at Buffalo, where he is also Leading Professor of Economics and Director of the Institute for the Study of Free Enterprise Systems. He is also an associate member of the Institute for Policy Analysis at the University of Toronto.

Professor Ehrlich is one of the most cited economists in the United States. Although best known for his pioneering work on the economics of crime and criminal behavior, he has also published numerous articles in leading journals on health economics, law and economics, uncertainty and insurance, information and advertising, the economics of life protection, longevity and economic growth, and productivity growth and firm ownership. He has been a recipient of numerous research grants and awards concerning these research topics.

His current research concerns the economics of social security, corruption and economic growth, income growth and income equality, a book of readings on the economics of crime, and a book of his collected essays on crime and punishment.

You have done considerable research on applying economics to crime. What prompted your interest in this area?

I was looking for a dissertation topic in the late 1960s and was fascinated by the idea that offenders could be treated as rational agents. Criminal behavior did not seem to be an issue economists could say much about, despite the important contributions by Belton Fleisher, Simon Rottenberg, Gordon Tullock, and, especially, Gary Becker. Becker's path-breaking work concentrated mainly on optimal law enforcement strategies by the government and related welfare implications, but there was a need to explore more fully the supply side of the market for criminal activity. I decided to apply the full force of the economic methodology in addressing the issue of participation in illegitimate activity.

In addition, crime had grown into a serious social problem in the late 1960s, but we had little knowledge about the extent to which it could be reduced through specific law enforcement instruments and other policy tools, and whether we were spending an optimal amount of resources to combat crime. My early work on participation in illegitimate activity therefore combined both a theoretical analysis of the supply decisions of actual and would-be offenders and an empirical investigation of the effects of some key determinants of supply on the actual incidence of crime in the United States. Later on I sought to extend my approach to the problem by bringing into the analysis the complex demand side of the market, including the roles of consumers and potential victims, thus treating the incidence of crime as a reflection of market equilibrium, where supply and demand forces are brought to balance partly (but not exclusively) through government intervention.

What insights can be gained in looking at crime from an economic perspective, as opposed to the more traditional psychological or sociological point of view?

Criminologists have by and large treated criminal activity as an outcome of biological and psychological aberrations or exceptional social pressures that drive people to commit crime. Economists do not necessarily disagree with such explanations. But by treating offenders as responsive to incentives, they are in a position to identify actual or shadow prices, pecuniary rewards, alternative employment prospects, and specific market conditions that contribute to the *incentive* to commit crime.

This is not to say that a person's moral character, preference for risk, or proclivity to violence does not play an important part in explaining criminality. But economists stress the effect of objective opportunities *given* preferences, while criminologists focus on the latter.

To economists, the problem of crime is largely the challenge of explaining the observed *diversity* in the incidence of crime: why is crime more prevalent in some states and countries than in others; why has reported crime increased dramatically in the U.S. in recent decades; why is corruption seemingly more prevalent in less developed countries than it is in countries experiencing robust economic growth?

By pursuing such issues from a positive perspective, economists are also in a position to offer some useful policy recommendations—e.g., what should be the optimal severity of punishment for different crimes, and what types of penalties should be imposed; what role can rehabilitation and intermediate punishment play in reducing crime relative to fines and imprisonment; should a greater effort be made to increase the probability of apprehension or the severity of punishments imposed on those convicted; should law enforcement be exclusively public, or could it be partially privatized as well?

It may be difficult to understand the connection between economics and crime. While crime is generally regarded as the rash actions of irrational individuals, economics assumes rational behavior. Can a criminal act be viewed as rational in the economic sense? How?

Economics is best defined as the study of the allocation of scarce resources to meet competing ends. Criminal activity involves the use of scarce resources (individual time and effort and other factors of production) and a choice between violating the law and pursuing a legitimate alternative. Illegal parking and nonreckless speeding are two relatively innocuous examples of such choices that most people face at one point or another during their lifetime. Violating Prohibition in the 30s and smoking pot in more recent years are other examples.

Participation in illegitimate activity can be viewed as an outcome of rational choice because it generally involves some benefits to the perpetrator, and these can be balanced against the various costs involved. The benefits need not be monetary; they may include psychic benefits, even such that most people would find bizarre or reprehensible. Similarly, the costs of engaging in criminal activity involve opportunity costs from forgoing legitimate employment or consumption alternatives, the costs of prospective penalties, as well as psychological, or moral, costs. Fortunately, these costs are high enough for most people, who therefore never engage in serious crime. But the way to understand under what conditions some people violate specific laws, or the frequency with which they do it, is by viewing their decision as a consequence of changes in incentives set by potential victims (or customers), general economic conditions, and public law enforcement. The latter constitute the demand side of the market.

> But even people with deviant tastes, strong risk preferences, or few moral inhibitions are capable of making self-serving choices, and this is the fundamental principle of rational behavior. ■

The decision to commit crime involves risk. But many legitimate employment opportunities, and most investment decisions, involve idiosyncratic risks as well. The more peculiar characteristic of criminal activities is that they involve unethical, immoral, and even reprehensible conduct. But even people with deviant tastes, strong risk preferences, or few moral inhibitions are capable of making self-serving choices, and this is the fundamental principle of rational behavior.

Can even a violent crime, such as murder, reflect rational behavior? How?

Just because assault, rape, and murder are defined as crimes of passion does not mean that they are uncontrollable. Passion does not rule out the ability to choose. The question is "at what price passion?" Would proclivity to violence or passion automatically lead to the commission of crime independently of the ease or difficulty of carrying it out? Most victims of physical or sexual assault are the very young and the very old or women—i.e., people substantially weaker than their attackers—and most murders occur "within the family," broadly defined to include friends and relatives. To the extent that motive and opportunity play a role in murder, robbery, assault, and other violent crimes, these crimes obey the basic laws of rational behavior.

The only group of people who could be considered immune to the laws of economics on a-priori grounds are those who are mentally deficient. But empirical evidence does not support the view that offenders—even the minority of actual offenders who are caught and prosecuted—are mentally sick.

President Clinton and Congress have passed several laws to deal with the crime problem in the United States. Measures include increased police enforcement combined with tougher penalties. Is greater law enforcement the direction to pursue?

The economic approach predicts that offenders respond to incentives, and by that is meant both negative and positive ones. Law enforcement by police and courts is a critical means of generating *negative* incentives, and a large body of empirical evidence assembled by economists indicates that these incentives exert a significant deterrent effect in reducing crime. An increase in the probability of detecting, apprehending, and punishing offenders, combined with stiffer penalties, raises the social tax on crime and can therefore be expected to reduce it.

This by no means implies that positive incentives won't work, but prudent public choice requires the balancing of the marginal returns from the various incentives under government control with the marginal cost of producing them. We do not currently have a systematic analysis that compares the marginal return on the last dollar of public resources spent on "crime deterrence" with the marginal return on what President Clinton's administration calls "crime prevention."

If "positive" alternatives—such as employment opportunities—are those that raise the opportunity cost for illegal behavior, then some parts of the bill are better than others. Midnight basketball programs, for example, are likely to prove a weak preventive measure. First, their efficacy as an alternative to the lure of financial gains from car theft or drug dealing is questionable. Also, such games encourage nightly gatherings of youth with relatively low opportunity cost of time, which may therefore lead to disorderly conduct and other illegal acts, absent sufficient police supervision. But with police occupied in maintaining law and order on the basketball courts, their effectiveness in deterring burglaries and car thefts can actually fall.

One problem with positive incentives is that the government generally lacks effective tools to create them without direct and costly intervention in private economic activity, and even successful rehabilitation of convicted offenders has no deterrent value for those at large. In contrast, the threat of monetary fines, imprisonment, and other penalties is a deterrent to crime for all offenders, regardless of their personal circumstances or legitimate employment opportunities.

The crime legislation includes the "three strikes and you're out" rule of sentencing, where a mandatory lifetime prison sentence results from the third conviction for a class of crimes. Does this measure make sense from an economic perspective?

The economic approach to optimal law enforcement identifies several principles that should guide an optimal structure of penalties: (1) the penalty must "fit the crime"—by which I mean the *severity* of the offense as judged by its marginal social harm; (2) the *marginal* penalty should be such that it generates a marginal deterrent effect on the incentive to commit more serious offenses; (3) the penalty should be linked to the actual probability that the offensive behavior is detected and punished; and (4) it should be least costly from a social point of view relative to alternatives of equal efficacy.

> The principle is simple: Crime is motivated by the prospective gain from crime over and above legitimate earning alternatives. ■

For repeat offenders, the desired social objective is to make the price they are required to pay for a more intensive participation in criminal activity higher than that for a less intensive one. If the penalty on the last offense were the same as that on the first offense, this would increase the likelihood that offenders would become specialized in criminal activity. Also, if offenders get more skilled at committing serious (socially costly) offenses or better at avoiding apprehension and conviction as they gain experience from greater involvement, the marginal penalty for them should be higher to constitute an efficient deterrent. By these arguments, "three strikes and you're out" makes economic sense.

Applying such a rule uniformly to all offenses, however, regardless of their severity, would be inconsistent with the first principle I mentioned. In Oregon, a person has recently been sentenced to life imprisonment without parole after being convicted of writing bad checks (a felonious activity) for the third time! The problem with applying the rule uniformly to all offenses is not just that it seems unjust, but also that imposing the most severe punishment on the least severe crime, for example, creates an incentive for offenders to shift from the former to the latter. By the same token, one may argue that for the most severe crime—murder—"three strikes and you're out" is *not* a sufficiently severe rule, and that two strikes should be sufficient to incarcerate the offender for life.

There has also been pressure in states such as New York to legalize capital punishment. Does capital punishment serve as an effective deterrent to crime?

There hasn't been a question more controversial than this one in the literature, largely because of the very intense and emotional reactions the application of capital punishment evokes. Many are opposed to capital punishment on moral, ethical, and esthetic grounds, while others are strongly in favor of a wide application of the penalty as a means of preventing or avenging heinous crime. Much literature on the subject has been motivated more by the wish to influence public policy than by the interest in testing specific scientific hypotheses.

When I first set out to explore this question, an overwhelming number of studies by criminologists argued unequivocally that capital punishment did not deter murder and should therefore be abolished. Applying my model of the "supply of offenses" against time series data on murder in the United States over the period 1933–1968, I could not reject the hypothesis that the *conditional* probability of execution—given apprehension and conviction for murder and given the age composition and the rate of unemployment and labor force participation in the population—does deter murder. While the effect was not sizable, it was found to be statistically significant at the standard confidence levels. In a sequel to this paper, using cross-state data from the United States in 1940 and 1950, I found independent support for these findings.

My original time series analysis has been both vigorously challenged and defended. Looking back at the debate today, however, I can say that the statistics are more consistent with the hypothesis that the death penalty is an effective deterrent to murder than with the alternative hypothesis that it is not.

One reason is that earlier studies that reported no such effect have often focused on the legal status of the penalty rather than on its actual application. But the economic approach suggests that what exerts a deterrent effect is the probability that the death penalty will actually be applied.

Capital punishment, however, is not a panacea. It certainly will not eradicate the crime of murder, as proponents may naively believe. To be used effectively, it must also be used *selectively*. Indeed, the tendency in many countries where the death penalty is actually practiced has been to apply it sparingly, against only a narrow subset of all murders—for example, when the crime is premeditated or includes multiple murders. Moreover, even if capital punishment is a more effective deterrent than, say, imprisonment, this does not automatically justify its selection if imprisonment is considered less costly from a social point of view. The United States has proscribed the use of torture, hard labor, and exile as means of punishing offenders not because of a conviction that they do not exert a deterrent effect, but because of a consensus that application of such penalties would be in conflict with more fundamental values that define civilized societies.

Indeed, the economic approach suggests that to be a deterrent, punishment need not be cruel or inhumane. Economic theory, as well as my own empirical findings, indicates that raising the probability of apprehending and convicting murderers will have a substantially higher deterrent effect on the incidence of murder than raising the conditional probability of capital punishment.

> The argument that freer trade may result in importing (or exporting) more crime is patently false. ■

From an economic point of view, how can rehabilitation be employed effectively to reduce crime?

Recall that the economic approach suggests that offenders respond to both negative and positive incentives. To the extent that rehabilitation involves raising the legitimate earning opportunities available to offenders upon release from prison, it would reduce their incentive to go back to crime. This suggests that successful rehabilitation programs should focus largely on teaching offenders marketable skills, which would lower the differential gain to them from engaging in criminal activity and raise the opportunity costs of future incarcerations, rather than concentrate exclusively on "therapy."

There are, however, a few caveats. Having a criminal record lowers the range of labor market options available to offenders, and thus the potential return from any given investment in a legitimate skill. Moreover, while an effective training program may prove to be an unmitigated blessing for the rehabilitated offender, its effect on would-be offenders is different. To the extent that prisons provide a free educational subsidy to inmates, they reduce the potential cost of punishment for crime and thus increase the willingness of potential offenders to enter a criminal activity. In this sense, rehabilitation, while desirable from the point of view of service to the offender, may not be an effective means of reducing aggregate crime.

Some have argued that greater crime in the United States has resulted from increased inequality in income distribution. They assert that poor people have more incentive to commit crime. Does your research support this contention?

My model of participation in illegitimate activities has given this argument both theoretical and empirical support. The principle is simple: Crime is motivated by the prospective gain from crime over and above legitimate earning alternatives. Since payoffs on property crimes such as robbery, burglary, and theft do not require high legitimate skills and are determined largely by the material possessions of the surrounding population, the differential gains from crime would be higher for those with the poorest legitimate earning opportunities. Also, if the price of crime to the offender is a prison term, then the opportunity cost of imprisonment for those with relatively low earning opportunities will be low. Relative poverty can therefore be expected to increase the incentive to participate in crimes against both persons and property.

I have subjected this proposition to empirical tests using cross-state data in the United States in 1940, 1950, and 1960. My measure of inequality was the percentage of families with income below one-half of the median family income, which was designed to capture inequality in earning opportunities especially at the lower tail of the earning distribution. While this is hardly a perfect measure of the "differential gross gain from illegitimate over legitimate activity," the results were statistically significant and highly compatible with the underlying hypothesis. After controlling for the effect of deterrence variables and demographic factors, higher income inequality was found to increase the frequency of robbery, burglary, larceny, and auto theft, and even of murder and assault, across states in all three census years.

Should the United States do more to address crime in its education of young people? What, if anything, have you found to be the connection between education and crime?

My comments concerning the impact of income inequality on crime suggest that education may play a critical role in affecting incentives, largely because of its well-documented effect on legitimate earning opportunities. Also, good education inculcates and strengthens values.

In the case of crimes such as burglary and theft, or receiving and buying stolen property, which require low legitimate skills, education increases mainly the returns from legitimate market alternatives. One would expect it to be an effective deterrent to these crimes. The same may be true for white-collar crimes, such as fraud, embezzlement, counterfeiting, and gambling, but here education may enhance criminal payoffs as well.

What are some ways to effectively reduce business fraud, or white-collar crime?

One way is to ensure a competitive market environment in which various forms of implicit fraud, such as shoddy merchandise and fraudulent advertising, can be challenged by competitors. Firms can also reduce white-collar crimes such as embezzlement, business theft by employees, and shoplifting by customers by engaging in private self-protection. In this sense, the firm becomes a private enforcement mechanism, which sets up optimal probabilities of detecting and charging the violators or punishing them privately through loss of bonuses and gratuity payments or dismissal. Optimal *public* enforcement would take such private enforcement measures into account in pursuing complementary efforts.

Since business fraud and related white-collar crimes are typically committed by profit-making enterprises, the feasibility of using fines as sanctions is much higher here than in the case of indigent offenders. Since fines are relatively less costly socially than any efforts to raise the probability of apprehension and punishment, and because a given level of deterrence can be produced by alternative mixtures of probability and severity of punishment, the optimal strategy would be to set very high fines but only modest probabilities of detecting and apprehending violators. This seems to be the way law enforcement activity works in practice.

Will the increased trend toward free trade, as in NAFTA, tend to increase or decrease crime in the United States? Will the United States be literally importing more crime, or will NAFTA reduce the incentive to undertake Illegal trade?

The argument that freer trade may result in importing (or exporting) more crime is patently false. The elimination of protective tariffs and quotas would tend to equalize the market prices of traded goods and services across borders, thus eliminating the incentive to engage in cross-border smuggling and related violations of customs regulations. Open borders essentially expand the marketplace and thus enhance competition among producers and consumers, which reduces the likelihood of collusion and the potential gains from business fraud.

What suggestions do you have for students who wish to apply economic principles in their daily lives?

Bernard Shaw said that economics is the art of making the most out of life. The methodology of economics offers a systematic approach to human behavior in all of its colorful manifestations, so when applied skillfully (as by Shaw) it can be penetrating and even amusing.

Many people, even some economists, may be tempted to exclude large subsets of human behavior from the range of activities amenable to economic analysis. Traditional applications of economics concern production, investment, and business decisions. Would we say that individuals cease to be rational once they take off their business suits and don their leisure outfits?

Most advances in economics in recent decades have come about by recognizing the applicability of economic principles to problems that have not traditionally been considered economic problems. Family decisions—including fertility, investments in children, and intrafamily or intergenerational transfers—for example, may sound like topics that are outside the mainstream of traditional economics, but they are being fast recognized as potentially the most important determinants of economic growth and development.

Applying economic principles relentlessly may not necessarily make you rich or win you many friends, especially among students of competing social sciences, but it will hopefully keep you intellectually (and otherwise) honest.

The Economic Effects of Drug Prohibition

BY JEFFREY A. MIRON

The use of illegal drugs is widely viewed as one of the most important problems of modern societies. Accordingly, government policy toward drugs is the subject of heated debate. The most common view is that governments should prohibit the production, sale, and use of the currently illegal drugs. A small but vocal minority, however, suggests that prohibition causes many of the problems associated with illegal drugs. This minority believes that legalization—repeal of prohibition—would eliminate or reduce the problems associated with illegal drugs.

Economic analysis can shed considerable light on this debate. This analysis suggests that prohibition discourages drug consumption but that the magnitude and desirability of this reduction are open to debate. The analysis also suggests that prohibition has many additional effects, mostly undesirable. In particular, prohibition generates both violent crime and income-generating crimes such as theft and prostitution. Thus, the analysis largely substantiates the claims of legalization proponents.[1]

The Supply and Demand for Drugs Under Prohibition

The analysis of drug prohibition starts from the observation that legal prescriptions against the production, distribution, or possession of drugs do not necessarily eliminate these activities. If substantial demand for a prohibited commodity exists (whether drugs, alcohol, or toaster ovens), prohibition leads instead to the creation of a black market. This market operates similarly to a legal market, with several important exceptions.

Supply Effects

Prohibition decreases the supply of drugs from where it would be in a free market. Enforcement and potential legal punishment effectively raise the supply costs of drugs. These added costs take several forms. Suppliers face jail sentences and fines if apprehended. Additionally, suppliers incur costs attempting to avoid detection. Supply costs also increase because drug suppliers cannot use the official legal and judicial system to enforce contracts or resolve disputes.

Demand Effects

Prohibition also decreases the demand for drugs from where it would be in a free market. Prohibition imposes legal penalties for possession of drugs, so consumers demand less at any given price. Prohibition also makes it difficult for consumers to determine the quality of the drugs they purchase or to seek redress against sellers when purchased drugs are not the quality represented; this again lowers demand for any given price. Prohibition might also discourage consumption because consumers exhibit "respect for the law."

Changes in Equilibrium Price and Quantity

These effects are summarized in Figure 1. The downward-sloping line, D_0, is the demand curve for drugs. It slopes downward because at higher prices consumers substitute away from drugs toward other goods, such as alcohol, cigarettes, or prescription drugs. The upward-sloping line, S_0, is the supply curve for drugs. It slopes upward because as the quantity produced increases, some factors of production (e.g., land suitable for growing opium, coca, or marijuana) become scarce and increase in price, implying higher per-unit costs of production. Also, the costs per unit of smuggling large amounts of drugs might be greater than those of smuggling small amounts of drugs. The equilibrium quantity of drugs produced and consumed is Q_0, and the equilibrium price is P_0.

FIGURE 1

Effects of Prohibition on the Demand and Supply for Drugs

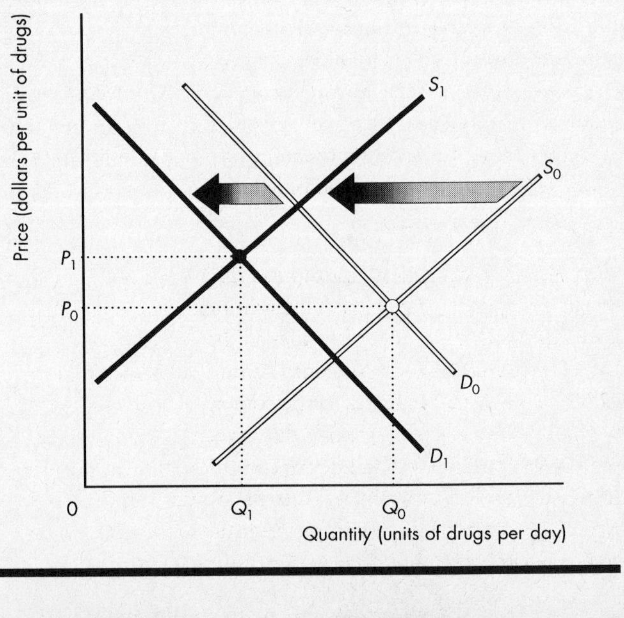

[1] This article draws heavily on my joint paper with Jeffrey Zwiebel, "An Economic Analysis of Drug Prohibition," *Journal of Economic Perspectives,* forthcoming. For additional discussion of drug prohibition, see Ethan A. Nadelmann, "Drug Prohibition in the United States: Costs, Consequences, and Alternatives," *Science,* September 1989, **245**, 939–947; Rod L. Evans and Irwin M. Berent, eds., *Drug Legalization: For and Against,* La Salle, IL: Open Court Press, 1992; Mark A. Kleiman, *Against Excess: Drug Policy for Results,* New York: Basic Books, 1992; Melvyn B. Krauss and Edward P. Lazear, eds., *Searching for Alternatives: Drug-Control Policy in the United States,* Stanford, CA: Hoover Institution Press, 1991.

As discussed above, prohibition is likely to cause both a decrease in supply and a decrease in demand. Thus, the demand curve shifts to D_1 and the supply curve shifts to S_1. The new equilibrium quantity, Q_1, is lower as a result, but the resulting price level is ambiguous and may increase or decrease depending on the magnitude of the shifts in demand, *D*, and supply, *S*. In Figure 1, the resulting price level is higher because the effect of the supply shift is greater than the effect of the demand shift.

Whether the decrease in supply dominates the decrease in demand depends on a number of factors. As a rule, the shift in demand is likely to be small relative to the shift in supply. The legal prescriptions and realized punishments for possession of drugs are generally far less extreme than those for production and distribution. Similarly, increased transaction costs associated with an illegal trade are likely to be smaller for consumers than for suppliers. Respect for the law seems unlikely to play a substantial role in discouraging demand, given the widespread violations of parking and speeding laws, certain tax laws, sodomy laws, and blue laws. Indeed, prohibition might glamorize drug use in the eyes of some consumers, tending to shift the demand curve upward.

Assuming this characterization of the shifts in supply and demand is correct, prices generally increase under prohibition, say from P_0 to P_1. This characterization is consistent with widespread empirical evidence that prices of restricted goods—be they drugs, alcohol, prostitution, or tires—are higher under prohibition. Both the shift in supply and the shift in demand also imply that equilibrium consumption falls under prohibition, say from Q_0 to Q_1.

The Effects of Prohibition on Economic Welfare

The analysis of prohibition's effects on economic welfare begins with a proposition that is trivial yet radical when evaluated in the light of widespread assumptions about drugs. If consumer preferences over drug consumption satisfy standard rationality assumptions and generate no externalities, prohibition unambiguously lowers consumer welfare. As with any good, the higher prices caused by prohibition mean that the difference between the utility received by consumers and the price they pay is lower than it would be in the absence of prohibition.

The Rationality of Addiction

The possibility that drug consumption might be "addictive" does not invalidate this conclusion. Under rationality, consumers understand and deliberately consider all the possible consequences of their actions, taking into account all relevant and readily available information. In the context of addictive goods, this means that consumers realize that current consumption might lower the utility of future consumption, but they take this into account when deciding whether to consume an addictive good. If the current benefits from consumption of this good are large, consumers might still wish to consume it even though the future consequences of current consumption are undesirable (e.g., experiencing withdrawal).

Many would argue that drug consumption is not rational, but this view is problematic. No doubt some individuals make a mistake in consuming drugs. Yet information on the negative potential consequences of drugs is pervasive; indeed, current drug "education" often overstates the costs of drug use. Despite such messages, many individuals voluntarily use drugs, and drug users speak of great short-run enjoyment from consumption.

Externalities

If drug consumption generates externalities, then the laissez-faire level of consumption might be too high. The question in formulating policy, however, is how the externalities from consumption under laissez-faire compare with those under prohibition. Policies designed to reduce drug consumption are likely to cause substitutions to products that also generate externalities (e.g., alcohol and tobacco), and existing evidence suggests that alcohol and tobacco can generate externalities as great as those from illegal drugs. For example, medical researchers have identified alcohol as a leading cause of fetal brain damage, and the deleterious effects of alcohol on driving ability appear at least as great as those of marijuana.

Health Effects

In addition, prohibition might *increase* the extent to which consumers use publicly funded health care. By making quality difficult to determine, prohibition raises the frequency of accidental poisonings and overdoses from drug consumption. By raising drug prices, prohibition encourages the injection of drugs (since this increases the bang for the buck), which contributes to the spread of AIDS via dirty needles. Prohibition also discourages the medicinal use of marijuana (for relieving the nausea of chemotherapy) and of narcotics (for relieving pain). The net impact of these effects on public funding is confounded by the fact that dying early (before receiving much Social Security or Medicare) often yields a net inflow to public coffers. These examples show, however, that prohibition might increase, not decrease, the magnitude of "health-care externalities."

Drug Prohibition and Crime

The effects of drug prohibition go far beyond those discussed so far. Arguably the most important effects are the increased economic incentives for crime.

Because participants in the illegal drug trade cannot use the official legal and judicial system, prohibition increases violent crime. Violence is an obvious substitute for the legal remedies not available to resolve commercial disputes, and since drug suppliers must conceal their identities from law enforcement officials in their primary activity, it is relatively easy for them to escape identification as perpetrators of violent acts. More generally, the evasive actions necessary to operate an illegal industry likely lower the marginal costs of violence. Further, participants in an illegal enterprise require protection because they have no recourse to the law. Hiring a security force then lowers the marginal cost of initiating violent acts.

The claim that drug *prohibition* promotes violence contrasts sharply with the usual claim that drug *consumption* promotes violence. A host of historical examples, however, indicate that the production and distribution of various goods is associated with violence only when those goods are prohibited. Violence has occurred in the illegal drug trade only since 1914, when drugs were first prohibited in the United States. Similarly, violence was employed in the alcohol trade only during the years of prohibition. The supply of many goods is associated with violence in centrally planned economies but not in market economies.

These examples confirm that prohibition increases the use of violence in the *production and distribution* of illegal commodities, including drugs. They do not mean that *consumption* of drugs has no effect in producing violence. They do suggest that the violent effects resulting from the consumption of drugs are often overstated because many observers fail to note that the correlation between the drug trade and violence has an alternative explanation.

In addition to promoting violent crime, prohibition encourages income-generating crimes such as theft or prostitution. Because prohibition raises drug prices, it encourages consumers with highly inelastic demand and little discretionary spending both to substitute from consumption of "essentials" and to increase income-generating crime. Comparisons between consumers of illegal drugs and consumers of alcohol and tobacco support this view, as opposed to the view that drug consumption causes criminal activity. Medical evidence suggests that alcohol is among the most potent drugs at lowering inhibitions and that the physical demands of nicotine withdrawal are more severe than those of many illegal drugs. Nonetheless, the great majority of alcohol and cigarette consumers do not commit crimes.

Historical Evidence on Prohibition

To the extent that any foundation for prohibition exists, it is the ability of prohibition to reduce drug use, especially irrational or externality-producing drug use. A critical empirical question is therefore whether drug prohibition produces a large or small effect in this direction.

As a starting point, consider the pre-1914 period in the United States. Although drug prohibition is almost universally practiced by governments of the modern world, it is a recent phenomenon by historical standards. In the United States, federal prohibition of opium, heroin, and cocaine dates only from 1914 and of marijuana only from 1937. Before these dates, currently prohibited drugs were not only legal but widely available from drug stores, street vendors, and mail-order catalogs. They were also dispensed by pharmacists and physicians for a host of medical problems, particularly the alleviation of pain.

For current discussions of drug prohibition, the lessons from this period are instructive. First and foremost, although drugs were legal and widely available, the United States was not a country of addicts. Many individuals used opium, heroin, cocaine, and other drugs without significant ill effects. For example, many individuals consumed opiates for the alleviation of pain, yet most such individuals did not become addicts.

Second, in the absence of substantial government prohibitions, opium use declined significantly over the period from about 1895 to 1914, and opium use fluctuated significantly from year to year during the sample for which data exist. These changes in opium consumption suggest that forces other than government policy, such as demographics, urbanization, the price of alcohol, and unemployment rates, are important determinants of drug use.

Finally, to the extent that drug use was associated with negative out-

FIGURE 2

Estimated Alcohol Consumption

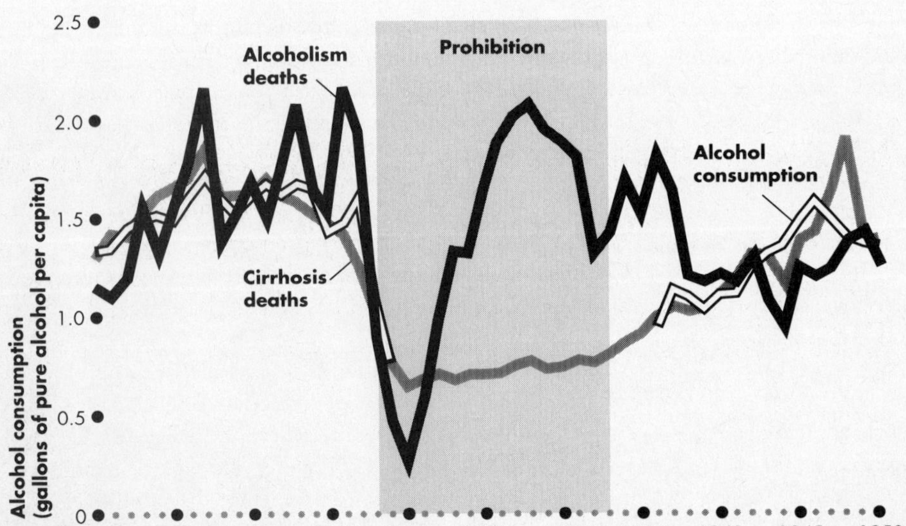

comes, these were mainly confined to users. Society was not afflicted with the drug-related social ills that are commonly attributed to drug use today.

This historical episode does not prove that drug prohibition is undesirable or that laissez-faire is a superior policy. It does support much of the analysis above, however. Perhaps as importantly, it suggests that the most dire predictions of prohibitionists—namely, that legalization would produce a boom in the number of "addicts"—were not borne out prior to prohibition restrictions.

A second crucial piece of evidence comes from alcohol prohibition in the United States, which was in effect from 1918 through 1933.[2] Although no official data exist on alcohol consumption during Prohibition, data are available on a number of closely related series. These include the death rate from cirrhosis of the liver, the death rate from alcoholism, the drunkenness arrest rate, and the number of first admittances to mental hospitals for alcoholic psychosis. In the periods before and after Prohibition, each of these measures is an accurate proxy for the consumption of alcohol per capita. Figure 2 illustrates how alcoholism deaths and cirrhosis deaths relate to alcohol consumption before and after Prohibition.

The different proxies tell a similar story about alcohol consumption during Prohibition. Taken together, they indicate that initially consumption declined significantly, to approximately 30 percent of its pre-Prohibition level. In the early 1920s, however, alcohol consumption increased sharply, rising to about 60–70 percent of the pre-Prohibition level. Consumption grew slightly over the last few years of Prohibition and stayed approximately constant after repeal. One interpretation is that it took several years for illegal supply networks to organize, but by the early 1920s they were sufficiently well developed that the return to a legal market did not have a significant effect on availability.

The data described above do not *per se* indicate the magnitude of Prohibition's effect on consumption, since other factors may have influenced consumption. The data do suggest that prohibitions have modest effects on consumption of the prohibited commodity. The absence of a substantial increase in alcohol consumption upon repeal is particularly relevant. Just as by the late 1920s illegal liquor supply was well developed, in the 1990s illegal drug supply is pervasive.

[2] See Jeffrey A. Miron and Jeffrey Zwiebel "Alcohol Consumption During Prohibition," *American Economic Review*, 1991, **81**, 242–247.

Conclusion

The prohibition of drugs is a controversial topic, with participants on both sides of the debate often making strong statements about the likely effects of legalizing drugs. Economic analysis, combined with evidence, can help determine the validity of many of these claims. The analysis offered here suggests that prohibition has substantial costs with few demonstrable benefits. The economic analysis of prohibition therefore shifts the burden of proof onto those who advocate this policy.

◆ *Jeffrey A. Miron is Professor and Chairman of the Economics Department at Boston University, and Research Associate at the National Bureau of Economic Research. He received his BA in Economics from Swarthmore College in 1979 and his Ph.D. in Economics from the Massachusetts Institute of Technology in 1984. He has served on the faculties of the University of Michigan and the Sloan School of Management, and as a consultant to the Federal Reserve Board. Professor Miron has published extensively on topics such as the theory and practice of monetary policy, the quality of government statistics, the seasonal fluctuations in aggregate activity, the seasonality of births, and the economics of illegal drugs.*

SEE ALSO

Chapter 1 What is Economics?
Chapter 4 Demand and Supply
Chapter 6 Markets in Action
Chapter 11 Competition
Chapter 19 Market Failure

ECONOMY WATCH

- The fiscal year in the United States runs from October 1 to September 30. Most of the high-profile political action in the budget process takes place in the fall, as Congress and the administration attempt to agree on a budget. But the budget process begins in January. Watch for the following events:

  February 6 — Congress receives the president's budget for fiscal year 1996.
  February 15 — Congressional Budget Office reports to the Budget Committees on the president's budget.
  April 1 — Senate Budget Committee reports concurrent resolution on the budget.
  April 15 — Congress completes its action on the concurrent resolution.

- The Chairman of the Federal Reserve Board reports to Congress regularly. Watch for the next report in February 1995.
- The Federal Open Market Committee (FOMC) meets approximately every 6 weeks (the exact schedule varies), and its minutes are released about 6 weeks after a meeting. Watch the Wall Street Journal for reports of the FOMC meetings.

Scarcity, Choice, and Opportunity Cost

Crime Costs

Philip K. Way

Preview

- Crime in America is leading governments at all levels to spend considerable sums on the criminal justice system.
- Private households and businesses spend a lot of money on protection.
- Costs related to crime itself are also incurred by households, business, and society.
- Such costs include lower productivity, lost wages, higher health-care costs, a reduced quality of life, and costs arising from theft and improper financial dealings.

◆ *Philip K. Way earned a Ph.D. from the University of Warwick and is Associate Professor of Economics at the University of Cincinnati. Way has published widely on current issues in the field of labor.*

Resources are scarce, so choices have to be made between competing alternatives. When all resources are fixed and employed, devoting more resources to one use necessarily involves an opportunity cost—that is, less of other goods can be produced. This consideration is relevant whether we are talking about society as a whole or an individual household.

The maximum combinations of goods that it is possible to produce with a given amount of resources can be represented diagrammatically in terms of a production possibility frontier. The slope of the frontier shows the opportunity cost of producing more of one good in terms of another good.

The accompanying article refers to the costs that governments, households, and individuals incur because of crime. It also shows the choices that governments and households have made concerning the allocation of resources to various anti-crime measures.

After studying your text, reading the article, and answering the questions, you should be able to:

- ◆◆ Cite examples of opportunity costs for various goods and services.
- ◆◆ Recognize that opportunity costs may differ for different economic actors.
- ◆◆ Apply the concept of opportunity cost to the value of a human life.
- ◆◆ Represent resource allocation decisions in terms of a production possibility frontier.
- ◆◆ Recognize that spending more on one activity involves opportunity costs.
- ◆◆ Demonstrate the principle of opportunity cost using the production possibility frontier

SEE ALSO
Chapter 3 Production, Specialization, and Exchange

U.S. NEWS & WORLD REPORT, January 17, 1994

Cost of Crime: $674 Billion

COMPILED BY SARA COLLINS

THE CRIMINAL JUSTICE SYSTEM • $78 BILLION
Federal, state, and local governments in America spend nearly $39 billion on police protection every year. An additional $29 billion is spent on the sprawling prison system. Legal and judicial costs for criminal cases drain an estimated $10 billion more annually.

PRIVATE PROTECTION • $64 BILLION
The private sector in America currently spends 64 percent more on security measures—alarm systems, locks, guards and armored vehicles, for example—than federal, state and local governments spend on police protection.

LOSS OF LIFE & WORK • $202 BILLION
The medical and mental health costs stemming from violent crimes like murder, rape, assault, robbery and arson total about $11 billion each year. Less visible are the lost wages and the costs of pain and suffering by victims, which come to $191 billion.

CRIMES AGAINST BUSINESS • $120 BILLION
Despite soaring expenditures on private security devices like closed-circuit television, businesses across the country are losing billions of dollars each year from such crimes as retail pilferage and shoplifting, bribery, kickbacks and embezzlement schemes.

STOLEN GOODS & FRAUD • $60 BILLION
The price tag for stolen property resulting form theft crimes such as robbery and burglary is estimated at $20 billion. Non-corporate fraud may cost Americans up to $40 billion.

DRUG ABUSE • $40 BILLION
Excluding outlays for police protection and incarceration, drug abuse in America levies costs on society in the form of medical and mental health care as well as lost wages and productivity. Drug abuse has also significantly reduced the quality of life.

DRIVING WHILE INTOXICATED • $110 BILLION
Drunk driving costs the United States $6 billion in medical expenses, $25 billion in lost wages and $79 billion as a result of the pain and suffering endured by individuals.

Questions

1. a) What is the opportunity cost of governments' spending a greater portion of their budgets on criminal justice?

   b) What is the opportunity cost of consumers' buying more security devices?

2. What is the opportunity cost to each of the following of a death through violent crime?
   a) The decedent (the deceased person)

   b) The decedent's family

   c) Society in general

3. a) Draw a production possibility frontier showing the maximum combinations of criminal justice and other, non-criminal justice goods and services that could be provided given the budgets of governments at federal, state, and local levels. Place a point on the frontier representing the combination of goods that, in your judgment, was provided ten years ago. Label it *a*.

   b) Assuming a stable budget, draw a point *b* on your diagram representing the position of the governments today. Justify your positioning of *b*.

   c) What has been the opportunity cost of the governments' reallocation of spending? Explain your answer in terms of your diagram.

   d) Has the opportunity cost of each extra unit of criminal justice provided from government budgets increased, decreased, or stayed the same? Explain your answer with reference to your diagram.

   e) On your diagram, show where governments would be if they were to reduce overall public expenditure, but maintain the current level of spending on criminal justice programs. Label this point *c*.

   f) On a new diagram, show what happens to the production possibility frontier when the unit cost of providing criminal justice increases, assuming that public expenditure is held constant.

4. Given your responses to the above question, how might the production of criminal justice be increased without decreasing the production of other services, assuming that costs are unchanged?

The Opportunity Cost of Crime

BY BRUCE L. BENSON AND
DAVID W. RASMUSSEN

What Does It Cost to Wage Drug War?

Frank Potts was released from the Florida prison system in 1988, after serving six years of a 15-year sentence for molesting an 11-year-old girl. He was released even though a parole examiner warned that Potts was not a good candidate for parole "now or in the future" and predicted that Potts would commit more crimes if he was released. Today Potts is charged with molesting another 11-year-old girl; but in addition, an intensive investigation is under way to determine whether Potts is guilty of at least 13 murders in six states. What does this tragic series of events have to do with the cost of a drug war?

Most people think of the cost of something as the money paid for it, but the real costs, or *opportunity costs*, are the alternative uses of scarce resources that must be forgone when the resources are used for a particular purpose. When costs are viewed in terms of forgone opportunities, it is clear that a decision to use resources in a particular way may have consequences, or costs, that were not anticipated by policymakers.

Asked why Frank Potts was released in 1988, a representative of the Florida Department of Corrections recently explained, "The agency is bound by mandates from the courts and the legislature. In the mid-1980s, the prison system was inundated with inmates carrying minimum mandatory sentences during the country's initial skirmishes in the war on drugs."

Florida was building prisons during the 1980s, but the number of criminals being sentenced to imprisonment was increasing even faster than the prison capacity was expanding. Drug criminals in particular were flowing into prison faster than space was being added. During fiscal year 1983–84, there were 1,620 admissions to Florida's prisons for drug offenses, accounting for 12.9 percent of the 12,516 total admissions. By 1989–90, drug admissions had risen by 875 percent to 15,802, or 36.4 percent of the 43,387 total (nondrug admissions increased by a comparatively small 153 percent, from 10,896 to 27,585). At the same time, the legislature passed an array of longer minimum mandatory sentences for drug criminals.

Getting tough on drug offenders by sentencing more of them to longer prison terms resulted in leniency for other offenders. Because the supply of criminals to be punished—in terms of numbers of prison admissions and lengths of prison sentences—was increasing faster than prison space was being added, the cost to the criminal of committing crimes in Florida was falling. The decline in the cost of crime to criminals occurred when Florida had to implement an "administrative gain time program" in February of 1987. This program was established to determine when prisoners would be released. It granted prisoners "gain time awards" assigned by the administrative authority (the Florida Department of Corrections) rather than the courts. The consequences were dramatic. Prior to 1987, prisoners in Florida typically served 50 percent or more of their sentences; by the end of 1989, the average prisoner was serving only 33 percent of his or her sentence. Some prisoners could not be released early, so many served even less than 33 percent of their sentences; in fact, about 37 percent of the prisoners released in December 1989 had served less than 25 percent of their sentences, and some had served less than 15 percent. Therefore, the actual punishment that criminals in Florida could expect if they were convicted of a crime was falling dramatically. The cost of committing crimes had become lower for criminals.

While the cost of producing crimes was declining for criminals, Florida citizens were being exposed to more and more convicted criminals, who were being released earlier and earlier. The extra crimes committed by Frank Potts and many of the thousands of others like him who were released early constitute one of the opportunity costs of the war on drugs. To see some of the other opportunity costs of allocating scarce criminal justice resources to wage a drug war, we have to consider how the criminal justice system influences the decision to commit crimes.

The Criminal Justice System and Decisions to Commit Crimes

The Criminal's Decision

Many factors influence the decision to commit crimes, of course. But determinants of crime such as psychological makeup and economic opportunity cannot be influenced directly by the criminal justice system. Let us focus on how the criminal justice system influences the level of criminal activity.

Most criminal offenders are like other people in one important way: they respond to incentives. This is why deterrence works. Considerable evidence suggests that, by and large, criminals implicitly weigh the expected benefits of an offense against the expected costs when they are choosing to commit a crime. One potentially important cost of committing a crime is the punishment the criminal *expects*. We can think of this expected cost as the expected price society charges for crimes, and it is the criminal justice system that establishes this expected price.

Law Enforcement Decisions

All valuable criminal justice resources are scarce, so law enforcement decision making is a resource allocation problem. Legislators must decide how many resources to allocate to law enforcement (e.g., sworn officers, jails, courts and prosecutors, prisons, parole systems), given alternative uses of tax revenues (e.g., schooling, highways). After that, the resources purchased to enforce the law must be allocated among competing uses (e.g., solving robberies and burglaries; traffic control; crime prevention efforts; solving of rapes, assaults and murders; control of drug markets). Prosecutors and judges decide how to allocate punishment resources as they sentence criminals to prison, probation, and so on. Corrections officials decide what portion of the prison sentence will be served by each prisoner and who will be released early, within the confines of legislative mandates regarding minimum mandatory sentences. These allocation decisions result in a set of expected prices of crimes in the form of expected punishments that the criminal justice system sets for various criminal acts. Potential criminals compare these expected prices to the benefits they anticipate from criminal acts as they make their decisions to commit crimes.

The Expected Price of Crime

The expected price of crime is not the actual sentence given to a convicted criminal, or even the portion of that sentence served. Rather, the expected price is determined by the probabilities of a series of events.

- *Reporting of the Crime.* First, the crime must be reported to or observed by police. According to the Bureau of Justice Statistics' most recent victimization survey, only about 39 percent of all Index I crimes (murder and manslaughter, sexual offenses, aggravated assault, robbery, burglary, larceny, and auto theft) are reported in the United States, although reporting varies by crime type from 92 percent for motor vehicle theft to 15 percent for larceny resulting in losses of less than $50.
- *Arrest.* Second, the police must arrest the criminal. The probability of arrest for a particular crime depends on many circumstances specific to the crime, of course: the skill of the criminal, luck, how observant the victim and/or witnesses are, the response time of police, and so on. Clearance rates (the proportion of total crimes in a particular category that are considered solved) provide an estimate of the probability of arrest for reported crimes. In 1992 in Florida, clearance rates ranged from a high of 68 percent for murder to a low of 15 percent for motor vehicle theft and burglary.
- *Prosecution.* Third, the offender must be charged and prosecuted after being arrested. Many people who are arrested are not prosecuted because of insufficient evidence, mistakes in arrests (e.g., arresting the wrong person, violation of due process rules by police), charges being dropped by the victim (as in many assault cases involving family members), or delays in the processing of the case. A comparison of the number of persons accused to the number arrested, using 1992 Florida data, suggests that chances of prosecution given arrest are 68 percent for robbery and 82 percent for burglary.
- *Conviction.* Fourth, the prosecution must be successful before a sentence is imposed. The probability of conviction can be approximated by the ratio of convictions to the number of persons accused. The very high probability of conviction in Florida during 1992, ranging from 0.84 for murder up to 0.92 for burglary, suggests that this is one area in which the criminal justice system may be working well. Offsetting this impression is the fact that prosecutors probably have a good idea of the chances of conviction before they actually file accusations. Perhaps more significantly, about 98 percent of these Florida convictions were obtained by plea or charge bargaining, a practice dictated by the shortage of court resources. Since offenders will agree to a plea bargain only if they have something to gain—a reduced expected punishment—many of these convictions are for lesser crimes and/or fewer crimes than were actually committed.
- *Imprisonment.* Fifth, given a conviction, the criminal must be sentenced to one of a number of punishments. Possible alternatives include capital punishment (a highly unlikely outcome except for the most heinous murders), a prison term, supervised release including probation (the largest number of sentences are for probation), immediate release with credit for time already served in jail, and a fine. Debate on criminal justice policy focuses on imprisonment, which is assumed to be a more onerous punishment and clearly incapacitates the offender for the duration of the sentence actually served. For Florida in 1992, the probability of imprisonment after conviction is estimated to be 26 percent for burglary and 46 percent for robbery.
- *Prison Sentence.* Sixth, when a criminal is sentenced to imprisonment, a specific prison term must be established. Average prison sentences vary by crime, ranging in Florida during 1992 from 21.8 years for murder to 4.1 years for theft and fraud.
- *Portion of Sentence Served.* Finally, the actual time served by a prisoner must be determined by corrections officials. Most prisoners can expect to serve only a portion of their full sentences, as explained above. Recent additions to capacity, combined with a reduction in the portion of felons sentenced to prison and a relaxing of minimum mandatory sentences for some types of crimes (particularly some drug felonies), has increased the average portion of a prison sentence served in Florida from 33 percent in 1989 up to approximately 43 percent in July 1993.

Figure 1 summarizes the points made above. It shows that the expected time in prison for a criminal is equal to the probability that a victim or witness will report the crime, times the probability of arrest given that the crime is reported, times the probability of prosecution given arrest, times the probability of conviction given prosecution, times the probability of imprisonment given conviction, times the expected prison sentence. The expected prison sentence can be approximated by the average sentence handed down by judges times the average portion of the sentence served before early release.

FIGURE 1

The Price of Crime: Calculating Expected Prison Terms

EXPECTED TIME IN PRISON =												
1		**2**		**3**		**4**		**5**		**6**		**7**
Probability of victim reporting	X	Probability of arrest	X	Probability of prosecution	X	Probability of conviction	X	Probability of imprisonment	X	Average prison sentence	X	Portion of sentence served

Using 1992 Florida data, we can make a rough approximation of the calculation described in Figure 1 for some crimes. Figure 2 provides such estimates for robbery and burglary. The numbers (1) through (7) labeling the columns in Figure 2 refer to the seven factors used to calculate the expected time in prison as detailed in Figure 1. Burglars (with an average prison sentence of 5.5 years) can expect to spend about 13 days in prison per burglary committed, while robbers (with an average prison sentence of 8.6 years) can expect the cost of their crimes to be roughly 66 days in prison. These numbers are approximations of the expected price the criminal justice system is charging for committing these crimes. Similar calculations suggest that violent crimes against persons have relatively high expected penalties: a murderer can expect to spend roughly 2.99 years in prison, and a sexual offender can expect about 338 days. Property offenses may be common in Florida because there is a very low expected penalty to deter potential offenders. Those engaged in theft face about 4.5 days in prison, while auto thieves can expect about 10 days. Clearly, the expected prices of most crimes committed in Florida are very low. That is one reason for the high level of crime in Florida. During the peak years of the drug war, many of these expected prison terms were even lower.

The War on Drugs and the Expected Price of Property Crimes

Property crime rates in Florida were falling in the early 1980s, from 74.65 reported crimes per 1,000 population in 1981 to 62.60 in 1984. Nonetheless, in 1984, Florida law enforcement joined the war on drugs declared by the Reagan administration, because the war was seen as a way to solve Florida's crime problem: drug use was widely believed to be a primary cause of crime, as users would steal to support their habits. Research on the drug-crime relationship suggests that, in reality, only about 25 to 35 percent of drug users are active property criminals, but drug arrests rose dramatically over the next 5 years anyway, from a 1984 level of 38.76 per 10,000 population to 66.83 in 1989. What were the consequences?

Our research demonstrates that the diversion of scarce police resources to fighting drug crime is a primary factor in explaining the 16.3-percent increase in Florida's property crime rates, from their recent low in 1984 to their historic maximum of 80.19 per 1,000 population in 1989. The consequences of the drug war can be seen in Figure 3, which shows the direct relationship between drug enforcement by Florida police and the state's property crime rate. As police efforts against drugs increased, efforts against property crime fell, and property crime rates rose.

The reallocation of police resources to making drug arrests meant that fewer police resources were available for controlling property crime. For example, in 1983, police made 3 times as many property arrests as drug arrests, but by 1989 this figure had fallen to 1.8. The probability of arrest for property crime, the second factor in the calculation of expected price in Figure 1, fell as a result. We estimate that a 1-percent increase in drug enforcement in Florida relative to enforcement directed at reported crimes led to a 0.20-percent to 0.34-percent decrease in the probability of arrest for property crime.

Drug enforcement relative to property crime enforcement actually increased by about 40 percent in Florida, so the reduction in the probability of arrest for property crimes, and therefore in the expected price of such crimes, was dramatic. Not surprisingly, as

FIGURE 2

Expected Prison Terms for Robbery and Burglary in Florida in 1992

	1	X	2	X	3	X	4	X	5	X	6	X	7	=	Expected prison time
Robbery	0.70	X	0.25	X	0.68	X	0.85	X	0.46	X	3139 days	X	0.45	=	65.7 days
Burglary	0.60	X	0.15	X	0.82	X	0.92	X	0.26	X	2008 days	X	0.37	=	13.1 days

FIGURE 3

Drug Arrests and Property Crime in Florida, 1984–89

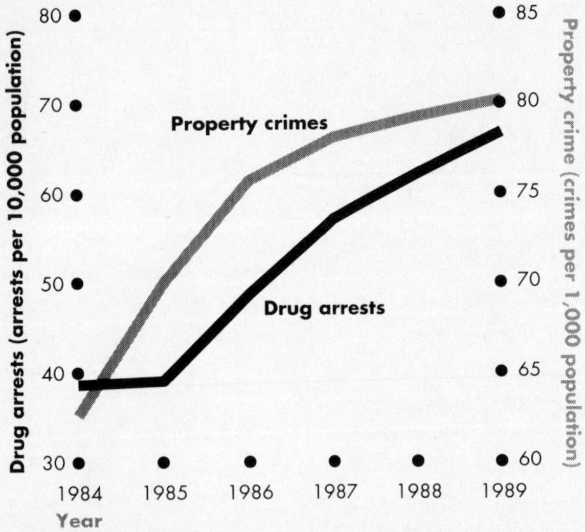

Sources: The Florida Department of Law Enforcement, and *The Uniform Crime Reports*, Federal Bureau of Investigation.

the expected price of property crime fell, property crime rose. Many factors influence the level of property crime, of course, but by controlling for these other factors, our research shows that the reallocation of police resources to fighting drug crime, and the resulting reduction in the probability of arrest for property crimes, explains an estimated 40 to 50 percent of the increase in property crime rates in Florida over the 1984–89 period.

The prison crowding discussed earlier, which occurred in large part because of the increase in the number of drug offenders going to prison, also had an impact on criminal behavior. The average portion of sentence served, the last component of the calculation in Figure 1, fell from over 50 percent to less that 33 percent between 1987 and 1989, lowering the expected price of crime even more. This was probably another significant factor in the increase in property crime in Florida. Clearly, this increased level of property crime was one important opportunity cost of increasing drug enforcement.

The situation reversed itself after 1989. The political backlash against the consequences of the drug war had begun to materialize. Drug arrests fell by 17.3 percent in Florida between 1989 and 1992. This freed up some police resources, which could be refocused on other crimes. The result apparently has been an increase in the probability of arrest for property crimes and a higher expected price of such crimes: property crime rates fell by 7.4 percent. The direct relationship between drug enforcement and property crime—depicted in Figure 3 for the period when drug enforcement was increasing—also holds when drug enforcement decreases.

The number of drug offenders sentenced to Florida prisons fell from 4,014 in the second quarter of 1989 to 2,304 in the last quarter of 1992 (the most recent published data), and the legislature revoked or reduced several of its minimum mandatory sentences for drug offenders in 1993. By mid-1993, prisoners were serving 43 percent of their sentences. Still drug admissions accounted for 25 percent of total admissions, so considerably more can be done.

Conclusions

The federal expenditures of some $70 billion on the 1980s drug war are frequently cited as the cost of that effort, but state and local resources are the primary "forces" in such an offensive, and there is no total accounting of the expenditures for all of these resources. Even if the dollar costs could be calculated, they would hide many of the real costs of the drug war. A portion of those costs have been borne by the victims of Frank Potts and other criminals released early from prisons all over the United States to make way for drug criminals, and by the victims of the robbers and burglars who were less effectively deterred because police were not focusing on property crime.

None of this implies that police should ignore drug market activities. Rather, it demonstrates that one of the costs of a war on drugs is higher than generally recognized, so policymakers deciding to engage in such a policy should consider these costs. After all, there are alternatives for combatting drug use. In fact, a recently released study by the Rand Corporation estimates that treatment is, on the margin, about 7 times more cost effective at reducing cocaine use than is traditional law enforcement, suggesting that diverting many of the drug offenders from prisons to alternative programs could save money while simultaneously increasing the portion of sentences served by nondrug criminals.

◆ *Bruce L. Benson was named Distinguished Research Professor at Florida State University in 1993. He has published widely in law and economics, the economics of crime, public choice, and spatial economics. Benson's books include* The Enterprise of Law: Justice Without the State (1990) *and* The Economic Anatomy of a Drug War: Criminal Justice in the Commons (1994), *co-authored with David W. Rasmussen. Rasmussen is a Professor of Economics and Director of the Policy Sciences Center at Florida State University. He has published numerous articles and books focusing on public policy considerations in the areas of urban and regional economics, labor economics, and the economics of crime.*

SEE ALSO

Chapter 1	What is Economics?
Chapter 3	Production, Specialization, and Exchange
Chapter 17	Uncertainty and Information

Statute Revision: Economical Approaches to Crime Reduction

BY PHILIP E. GRAVES

There are a number of possible approaches to reducing crime in the United States. Many social workers, guidance counselors, psychologists, and teachers have argued for programs designed to educate and rehabilitate those committing crimes as a means of reducing the amount of crime. For example, the recently proposed House Crime Bill would spend almost $10 billion on programs for young criminals designed to "increase . . . self esteem," "provide . . . life skills," fund "cultural programs, arts and crafts, health education and dance programs," and so on.

The Economist's Approach

The economist's way of thinking about crime reduction is like the economist's way of thinking about any resource allocation problem: those engaging in socially undesirable behavior perceive their private benefits of doing so as exceeding their private costs—hence *effective* policy must either raise the costs or lower the benefits facing those making the decision. Some of the policies mentioned above might be consistent with the economist's approach; for example, expanding job-training centers could conceivably increase the opportunity cost of criminal activity. Some of the other policies, however, take the view that criminals do not know that what they are doing is "bad," and if only they could be rehabilitated, society would be spared further criminal activity. The economist views this attitude as naive—it is unlikely that people exceed the 55 mph speed limit, to focus on the example emphasized here, because of low self-esteem, poor guidance, lack of rehabilitative activities, and the like. The economist takes criminal activity as the outcome of a rational comparison of benefits and costs—hence the emphasis on altering either benefits or costs in an effective policy approach.

A number of economic approaches designed to reduce crime have been advocated and put into place in recent years:

- reductions in crime benefits (e.g., "driver has no more than $20 after eleven o' clock," "store clerk does not know the safe's combination")
- increases in costs through raising the probability of apprehension (e.g. more police or patrol cars)
- increases in costs through raising the probability of conviction (e.g., more resources devoted to prosecution)
- increases in costs through raising the probability and severity of penalties (e.g., mandatory prison sentences, large fines)

The problem with the preceding approaches is that they all increase personal cost or decrease benefits of crime to the criminal by methods that involve higher real resource costs. Almost three decades ago Gary Becker[1] recognized that a society could most efficiently reduce crime (get a given reduction in criminal activity at least cost) by setting extremely high fines. Becker's important observation was that, on efficiency grounds, fines should be set as high as possible (equal, for serious crimes, to the entire wealth of the criminal), for this would enable society to achieve a given level of crime reduction at least social resource cost. Were a low fine assessed for criminal activity, greater real resource costs would be required to achieve the same level of crime (with fines lower, probability of capture, conviction, and incarceration must be higher to achieve the same end). Thus large fines raise the cost of crime to the criminal without raising the real cost of crime prevention to society; hence we can all have a larger economic pie with greater reliance on this method of criminal deterrence. In the spirit of the original Becker contribution, I focus here primarily on the important role of statute revision (say, going from 65 to 55 miles per hour) as a means of reducing average highway speeds, although other contexts will be considered.

Statutes versus Enforcement Effort

As noted above, many approaches to the reduction of crime require a great deal of society's scarce resources if they are to be effective. For example, reducing a store's or taxicab's cash balance to lower the benefit of robbing it may require more frequent trips to locations where cash can be safely stored (raising labor and other costs). Increasing the probability of apprehension will require more labor and capital; again, this labor and capital could otherwise be used to produce goods that we care about. Mandatory prison sentences provide perhaps the clearest example of the high real cost to society of discouraging criminal behavior.

The central point is, of course, that merely declaring an activity illegal will have little impact on crime—society's scarce real resources (labor, capital, materials, and energy) must be used to enforce any law restricting activities that are perceived by those engaging in them as having benefits greater than their costs. The recognition that enforcement activity is not costless suggests that the search should be expanded for economic approaches to crime that (like setting high fines) reduce crime without great reliance on costly enforcement activity.

Revision of existing statutes fits this line of reasoning—merely rewriting our laws can offer real resource cost savings to society.[2]

---

[1] Gary S. Becker, "Crime and Punishment: An Economic Approach," *Journal of Political Economy*, **76**, March/April 1968, pp. 169–217.

[2] A formal statement of this approach in the transportation setting can be found in Philip E. Graves, Dwight R. Lee, and Robert L. Sexton, "Statutes Versus Enforcement: The Case of the Optimal Speed Limit," *American Economic Review*, **79**, September 1989, pp. 932–936.

FIGURE 1

The Decision to Speed

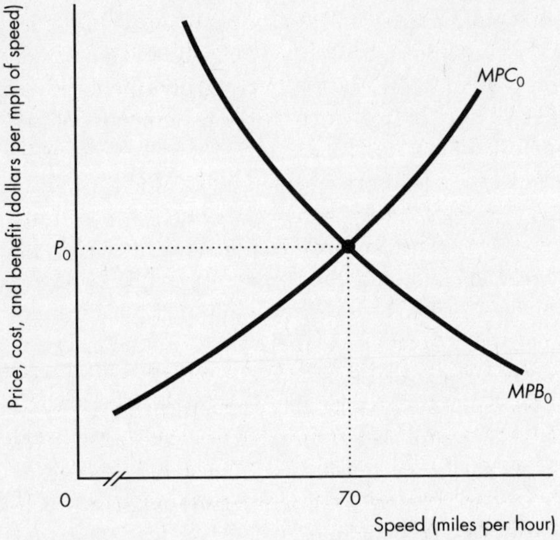

For example, an average speed of 70-odd mph on highways where a speed of 65 mph is posted might be reduced to perhaps 65 mph by merely posting a speed limit of 55 instead of 65. Achieving the same reduction with rigorous enforcement of the 65-mph limit would require many more police, police cars, and so on. Although the reduction in the speed limit from 65 mph to 55 mph was initiated as a fuel conservation measure (and later viewed as a safety measure), the clear benefit in the present context is that the average speed was reduced without the need for the extensive policing effort that otherwise would have been necessary. Note that a lower cost method of achieving reduced speeds is better than a higher cost approach, regardless of how one feels about whether average speeds should be reduced.

These thoughts can be clarified further with reference to the model shown in Figure 1. For simplicity we will deal with the average speed of the representative driver (damages associated with speed variance could be handled similarly, however). The horizontal axis depicts the average speed chosen by the typical driver—"speed" is a good like any other. The marginal benefits and costs of speed *from the driver's perspective* are given on the vertical axis. As with any good, there is a diminishing marginal benefit to pay for speed as one drives faster (indeed, driving "uncomfortably fast" would correspond to the marginal private benefits curve's dipping below the *x*-axis at, say, 100 mph!). Similarly, increasing average speed results in increasing marginal costs in the form of reduced gas mileage, reduced safety, and greater risk of speeding tickets for a given speed limit. The initial situation, shown with curves MPB_0 and MPC_0, reflects what drivers will do when the speed limit is 65 mph—namely, drive at 70 mph.

In light of obvious "externalities" (collisions with other drivers and property damage, which are greater at higher speed and are unlikely to be fully considered by any given driver), society may wish to achieve a lower average speed—say, 65 mph. This can be done by either reducing the benefits of speed (shifting the *MPB* curve downward) or increasing the costs of speed (shifting the *MPC* curve upward). One example of an upward shift in the *MPC* curve is more stringent enforcement of the 65-mph speed limit, but, as already suggested, this would be very costly in terms of labor and capital. The alternative recommended here is statute revision: lowering the stated speed limit from 65 to 55. Lowering the speed limit can be thought of either as raising the cost of any given level of speed or as lowering the demand by law-abiding citizens for any given speed. The downward shift in the benefits curve, to MPB_1 shown in Figure 2, takes the latter view. Note that the same result, a 65 mph average speed, can be obtained either with costly enforcement efforts or with much less costly statute revision.

It is not difficult to think of other contexts in which the statute-revision approach offers cost savings—and hence more of other goods we desire—in achieving social goals. In the past several years, drunken driving has become of increasing concern in the United States. A recommended approach along the lines pursued here would be to define "drunk driving" as occurring when blood alcohol levels exceed, say, .05 rather than the current .10 or more. This redefinition would no doubt reduce the average level of blood alcohol among drivers in much the way it has in Scandinavia where any positive blood alcohol reading is considered an

FIGURE 2

The Impact of a Statute Revision: Changing the Speed Limit from 65 to 55 mph

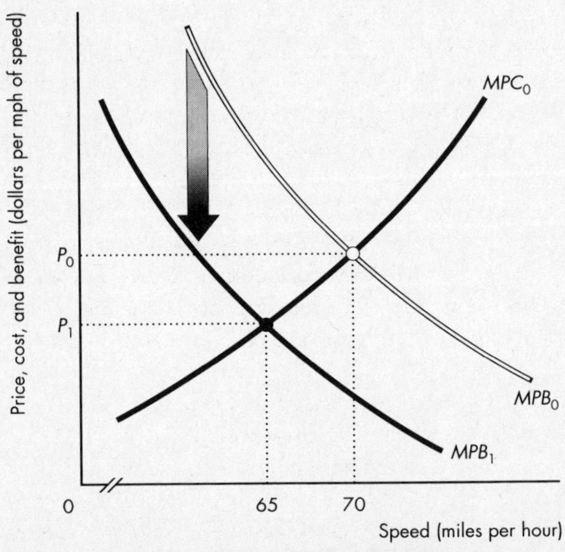

indicator of "drunken driving." Many boating and industrial accidents and deaths occur each year because of excessive blood alcohol, yet the statute approach recommended here is virtually ignored on our waterways and in our workplaces.

Much of both violent and property crime in this country is attributable to young offenders. Juvenile crime could be greatly reduced, without the use of additional scarce resources, by lowering the age at which one is no longer defined as a "juvenile." Many older criminals actively recruit youths below the cut-off age to engage in crimes with high adult penalties. The current, but infrequent, practice of trying those accused of particularly heinous crimes as adults could readily be expanded.

Most of the world's fisheries have become seriously depleted because of overfishing in the last two decades. The appropriate solution to this problem from an economist's standpoint would be to charge a usage fee for "nature's" scarce fish. The result would be much like that of paying farmers for cattle or chickens—we economize on cattle and chicken as demanders, while at the same time providing an incentive for farmers to continue providing these goods. As an interim measure, setting more restrictive "catch limits" would, as with the speed limit, reduce overfishing at lower social cost than that required for greater enforcement of current limits.

Some Drawbacks to the Statute-Revision Approach

There are some potential objections to the approach recommended here. These will be illustrated for the case of a lower speed limit, but they apply with appropriate revision to the other examples. First, a lower speed limit with less enforcement to obtain the same average speed would lead to more violators of the *posted* speed, each having a lower probability of being caught. This might result in considerable sympathy for those arbitrarily singled out for punishment. In the extreme, a speeding ticket could come to be viewed as "cruel and unusual punishment." Moreover, a mistaken conviction (although no doubt much less likely than at present) would be received with great resentment. Further, since relying extensively on this approach would convert many more of our citizens into law-breakers at the more stringent limits set, there might be a general—and undesirable—loss in respect for the law, even in those circumstances where this approach was not being used. Finally, rapid development of enforcement technology (e.g., photographic techniques in the speeding context) is likely to soften the policy implications of this approach by reducing the enforcement cost.

To the extent that these criticisms are valid, however, they merely reduce the degree to which we would want to rely on the substitution of more restrictive statutes for enforcement effort—they do not eliminate a role for the method. These arguments effectively raise the marginal cost of statute revision from zero to something positive and increasing, but it is still likely that some reliance on this method will have lower cost than the enforcement alternative. Statutes are currently set by one group of people largely without consideration of the costs of enforcement, conducted by another group of people; hence some gains from substituting more stringent statutes for costly enforcement will probably remain. The large fines for littering our highways (raised recently in many places from $500 to $2,000 or more) are virtually never enforced but probably do contribute importantly to litter reduction, in spite of the fact that all of the preceding criticisms could be leveled at litter laws. It must be emphasized, though, that the objections suggest that considerable caution be exercised in moving to a revised legal system incorporating the tradeoff between statute stringency and enforcement costs.

◆ *Philip E. Graves, Ph.D. Northwestern University, 1973, is Professor of Economics at the University of Colorado. His interests currently lie in urban/regional and environmental economics, and his recent research emphasizes the role of amenities in the location (and relocation) decisions of households and firms. A member of several professional associations, Graves has published six books and more than thirty refereed journal articles in the last decade.*

SEE ALSO

Chapter 10 Output and Costs
Chapter 19 Market Failure

By permission of Chip Bok and Creators Syndicate

Macroeconomic Effects of the Crime Bill

Donald H. Dutkowsky

THE NEW YORK TIMES, July 29, 1994

Accord Reached on Sweeping Bill to Battle Crime

BY KATHERINE Q. SEELYE
SPECIAL TO THE NEW YORK TIMES

WASHINGTON, July 28—House and Senate negotiators today approved a sweeping $30.2 billion anti-crime bill providing for 100,000 new police officers, a ban on some assault weapons and the death penalty for scores of crimes.

President Clinton hailed the bill as "the toughest, largest, smartest Federal attack on crime in the history of our country." But critics, including some law enforcement officials, called it a social-welfare boondoggle and, in the words of Representative Henry J. Hyde, Republican of Illinois, "the whole Emerald City of Oz."

The bill, which is about seven inches thick, would spend roughly equal amounts of money on prevention, punishment and new prisons. It provides money for drug courts and to fight violence against women. It pays for sports leagues and provides anti-gang grants to give young people positive alternatives to crime.

It also helps states pay for the cost of incarcerating illegal aliens, and it would expand application of the death penalty to about 60 Federal crimes, including carjacking. What it would not do is allow death-row inmates to challenge their sentences as racially motivated.

After a marathon session that started on Wednesday morning and broke up at 2:15 AM today in a dispute over money for prisons, Senator Joseph R. Biden Jr., the Democratic chairman of the Judiciary Committee, called his colleagues at 5:30 AM to meet before the full conference was to resume at 8 this morning.

When the negotiators reconvened, they zipped through the remaining hurdles and forwarded the bill to the two chambers. The House is expected to act on it next week, and the Senate shortly thereafter.

Despite some misgivings over the bill, most Democrats and some Republicans appear eager to pass anti-crime legislation in this election year, and the President is anxious to sign it. The bill represents one of the few major promises he made as a candidate in 1992 that he has been able to turn into law.

The money for the bill, an extraordinary amount at a time when Federal spending is stagnant, is supposed to come from a trust fund specifically to fight crime. "These are real dollars," Senator Biden said today at the news conference with Mr. Clinton. "This isn't funny money."

The Administration says the trust fund will not increase the deficit because nearly the same amount of money—about $30 billion—will be saved by the anticipated retirement of 285,000 Federal workers over the next six years. But the Congressional Budget Office has said the Administration vastly overestimates its savings from the work-force reductions, and some Republicans remain dubious of the financing.

The trust fund sets aside a total of $30.2 billion for crime programs through the year 2000.

The bill also authorizes programs that would cost an additional $3.1 billion, money that would not come from the trust fund. The programs would have to be financed, if at all, at the expense of other appropriations.

An example would be a police corps proposed in the bill, a program that would provide partial college scholarships for students who agreed to serve as law-enforcement officers after graduation. The bill says it would cost $400 million for an unspecified number of students, but since the plan would not be financed from the trust fund, its implementation would depend on President Clinton or a member of Congress seeking money for it from the general budget.

The Essence of the Story

A wide-ranging bill to fight crime in the United States passed House and Senate Subcommittees and was headed for a formal vote in Congress.

President Clinton supported the bill and said he would sign the legislation if it was approved.

Measures included provisions to increase the number of police, construct more prisons, expand crime prevention and rehabilitation programs, and offer college scholarships to students who agreed to serve as law-enforcement officers. The law also banned assault weapons and expanded situations where the death penalty could be applied.

The bill called for $33.3 billion in federal expenditures to fight crime. Programs were to be financed in part by a $30.2 billion trust fund created with money saved through the anticipated retirement of federal employees. Congressional Budget Office estimates indicated that the administration may have overestimated the actual size of the trust fund.

Many criticized the proposed legislation. Representative Hyde referred to the bill as a social-welfare boondoggle. Republicans were particularly dubious regarding the financing.

Despite legislators' misgivings about the bill, it was expected to pass in this election year.

Background and Analysis

The expenditures in the Crime Bill represent *government purchases of goods and services* (*G*), as defined within real gross domestic product (GDP). Constructing prisons is an example of a government purchase of goods; increasing the number of police, expanding rehabilitation programs, and offering scholarships are considered purchases of services.

The legislation calls for a net increase in *G* of at least $3.1 billion. From a macroeconomic point of view, this is an example of fiscal policy.

To examine the policy's effect on output, we need to convert the above increase into real terms. Given that the GDP deflator for 1994 equals 125.0 (1987 = 100), the proposed government purchases of goods and services equal approximately $2.5 billion in 1987 dollars.

Figure 1 describes the effect of the increase in expenditure within the short-run aggregate demand–aggregate supply model. The rise in government spending increases aggregate demand, shifting the curve from AD_0 to AD_1. This raises the equilibrium price level from 125.0 to 126.5 and raises real GDP from $5,300 billion to $5,306 billion. Real GDP does not increase as much as the aggregate expenditure model predicts ($5,310), since a higher price level also results from the policy. The effect of the rise in government purchases on aggregate expenditure assumes that the price level remains at 125.0. Nevertheless, the increase in government spending will work to expand the macroeconomy.

FIGURE 1

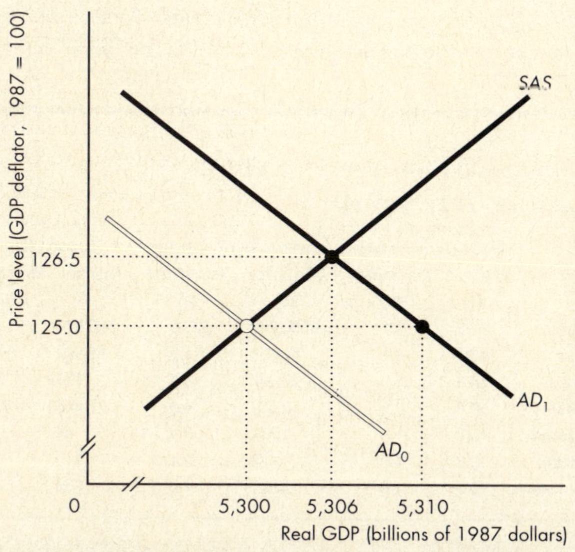

The $3.1 billion also represents an increase in the *federal deficit*, since it constitutes a net increase in government expenditure without any change in taxes.

Some members of Congress were concerned about expanding an already large federal deficit, estimated to be $234.8 billion in fiscal year 1994 (*Economic Indicators*, June 1994). The increase in the deficit could even exceed $3.1 billion if the trust fund estimate overstated the actual cost savings.

People tend to view economic expansion as favorable, since increases in real GDP generally result in lower unemployment. In an election year, the state of the economy generally plays a significant role in whether voters decide to reelect the incumbent. Along with the bill's intent to fight crime, the positive economic effects made it likely that Congress would support passage.

On the other hand, the legislation might be defeated because of concerns about the increased federal deficit and other controversial provisions (e.g., the ban on assault rifles).

Note: A modified version of the Crime Bill passed both Houses of Congress and became law. The revised legislation cut back the increase in government purchases to approximately $30 billion. If estimates of the trust fund are correct, the federal deficit will not undergo major change.

◆ *Donald H. Dutkowsky is Associate Professor of Economics at Syracuse University. His primary teaching and research interests are in macroeconomic theory and policy as well as money and banking. His current research involves investigating the mechanism of how economic policy changes aggregate output. Another line of research examines bank borrowing from the Federal Reserve.*

SEE ALSO

Chapter 22	Inflation, Unemployment, Cycles, and Deficits
Chapter 24	Aggregate Demand and Aggregate Supply
Chapter 25	Expenditure Decisions and GDP
Chapter 26	Expenditure Fluctuations and Fiscal Policy
Chapter 34	The Deficit

Criminal Sentences: Are They Just or Efficient?

BY JOEL WALDFOGEL

Criminal sentencing seems an odd application for economic analysis. Unlike the rational, calculating world of commerce to which economics is customarily applied, criminal sentencing seems to be a moral enterprise with utterly non-economic rationales. Or is it? What explains the sentences that we observe for different crimes? Why is larceny typically punished with 10.3 months in prison, while the typical amount of time served in prison for murder is 81.0 months[1]? Is the observed pattern of punishments consistent with some notion of justice, or does it correspond more closely to an economic notion of efficiency?

A philosopher could no doubt discourse at length on the meaning of justice, but we employ a simple and tractable definition. The notion of proportional justice is that sentences are proportional to harms. For example, if robbery is twice as harmful as larceny, then the robbery sentence is twice the larceny sentence if the sentencing system is proportionally just.

Efficiency, by contrast, means that sentences serve to minimize the combined costs of crime and punishment. In the familiar language of economics, an efficient sentence sets the marginal cost for punishing a crime through imprisonment equal to the marginal benefit of doing so.

Economic Benefits of Sentencing

To see the marginal costs and benefits of sentencing concretely, consider what happens when policymakers lengthen the sentence for an offense. The increase in the penalty generates a social benefit by preventing some prospective offenders from committing offenses. This reduction in crime in response to punishment depends both on incapacitation (additional offenders cannot commit crimes against the general public while imprisoned) and deterrence (fewer offenders will choose to seek illegal gains in the face of higher penalties). Collectively, the effects of sentencing on crime are summarized in the *elasticity* of crime with respect to sentencing. Of course, because individuals contemplating different offenses do so under different circumstances, the overall levels of different crimes will have different elasticities with respect to sentencing.

To translate the reductions in crime caused by sentences into benefits that may be quantified in dollars, we must attach a dollar figure to the occurrence of each crime. These dollar figures must answer the question "What dollar value do we attach to one occurrence of an offense?"

Although associating dollar harms with crime is difficult, it can be done.[2] Table 1, column 3, shows Mark Cohen's estimates of the dollar harm of crime to its victims. These dollar harm estimates include components for economic loss, pain and suffering, and risk of death. The economic benefit of sentencing is the reduction in the dollar amount of harm experienced by victims. We will return to these figures below.

Economic Costs of Sentencing

At the same time that lengthening a sentence engenders a benefit by reducing the dollar harm imposed on potential victims, it also increases the social cost of running the criminal justice system by expanding the prison population. The prison population at any point may be approximated by the number of inmates admitted to prison each year (equal to the number of crimes committed times the probability of being convicted and sentenced to prison) times the average time served for each offense. The following example illustrates determination of the prison population: If a crime is committed 1,000 times per year and 5 percent of the commissions result in convictions with prison sentences, then 50 offenders will be admitted to prison each year. If the average time that these offenders serve in prison is 1.5 years and they are sentenced steadily throughout the year, the prison population will be 75.

Increasing sentences has both a direct and an indirect effect on the prison population. The direct effect of keeping imprisoned offenders behind bars longer is an increase in the prison population. However, the deterrent and incapacitative effects of longer sentences reduce the amount of crime committed in the first place, indirectly reducing prison populations. On balance, longer sentences increase prison populations and the attendant costs of

TABLE 1
Absolute and Normalized Monetized Harm and Time Served

	Time Served (months)		Cohen's Harm Estimates		Implicit Harms	
Crime	Absolute	Normalized	Absolute	Normalized	Absolute	Normalized
	(1)	(2)	(3)	(4)	(5)	(6)
Murder	81.0	7.7	2,000,000	629.6	329,574	910.1
Rape	43.3	4.1	51,058	16.3	18,900	52.2
Assault	18.6	1.8	12,028	3.8	186	0.5
Robbery	30.8	2.9	12,594	4.0	5,478	15.1
Burglary	15.2	1.5	1,372	0.4	48	0.1
Larceny	10.3	1.0	179	0.1	113	0.3
Auto theft	10.5	1.0	3,127	1.0	362	1.0

Source: Joel Waldfogel, "Criminal Sentences as Endogenous Taxes: Are They "Just" or Efficient," *Journal of Law and Economics,* **36** (1993), pp. 139–151. Normalizations are relative to auto theft.

[1] In this essay the term "sentence" refers to time served in prison.

[2] See Mark Cohen, "Pain, Suffering, and Jury Awards: A Study of the Cost of Crime to its Victims," *Law and Society Review,* **22** (1988), pp. 537–556.

operating prisons. The increase in the dollar cost of operating the prison system with longer sentences is the per-inmate cost of holding prisoners (about $27,350 per year) multiplied by the change in the prison population.

Setting Marginal Benefits Equal to Marginal Costs

We achieve an efficient, or *optimal*, sentence for an offense at the sentence length where the marginal benefit to society from prevented harm equals the marginal cost to society of operating the prison system. Figure 1 illustrates a model for the determination of optimal sentences. The downward-sloping curve labeled *MSB* shows the marginal social benefit of sentencing. The slope of the *MSB* curve reflects the responsiveness of the dollar harm from crime to sentencing, while the position of the curve depends on the harmfulness of the crime. The curve for assault, for example, lies above the curve for the less serious crime of burglary. The marginal social cost curve (labeled *MSC* in Figure 1) reflects the responsiveness of imprisonment cost to sentencing.[3] The optimal sentence, Q_0, is located at the intersection of *MSB* and *MSC*, or the point where marginal social costs and benefits of sentencing are equal.

Like just sentences, optimal sentences are higher for crimes that are more harmful. Figure 2 illustrates that the optimal sentence is higher for an offense with a greater harm, all else being constant. Remember that the position of the *MSB* curve depends on the harmfulness of the crime. If MSB_0 represents burglary and MSB_1 represents the more harmful crime of assault, the optimal sentence for assault, Q_1, is higher.

In contrast to just sentences, however, optimal sentences are higher for crimes that are more responsive to punishment, or that are supplied more elastically. To see this, imagine a crime that is completely unresponsive to punishment. Because the marginal benefit of sentencing is zero, the sentence should be zero as well. Note that some serious but impulsive violent crimes may be difficult or impossible to deter with the threat of imprisonment and thus, ironically may have small efficient punishments, all other things being equal.

Optimal sentences are lower, the higher is the cost of incarceration, as illustrated in Figure 3. When increased incarceration cost shifts the marginal social cost of punishment curve up, the new equilibrium results in a reduced efficient punishment, Q_2. Increases in the probability of incarceration make any sentencing policy more expensive to implement and therefore reduce the optimal sentence.

Evaluating Existing Sentencing Policy

In addition to using this framework to calculate optimal sentences, we can also use it "in reverse" to infer the harm that existing policy implicitly attaches to an occurrence of a crime. For example, the amount that we spend, at the margin, to prevent one murder through sentencing shows the harm that our society implicitly attaches to murder.

How can we determine whether existing sentencing policy is efficient? If our sentencing policy is efficient, then the harms

[3] The *MSC* curve is drawn upward-sloping for ease of exposition. The existence of optimal sentences requires only that *MSC* intersect *MSB*.

FIGURE 1

Determining an Optimal Sentence for a Crime

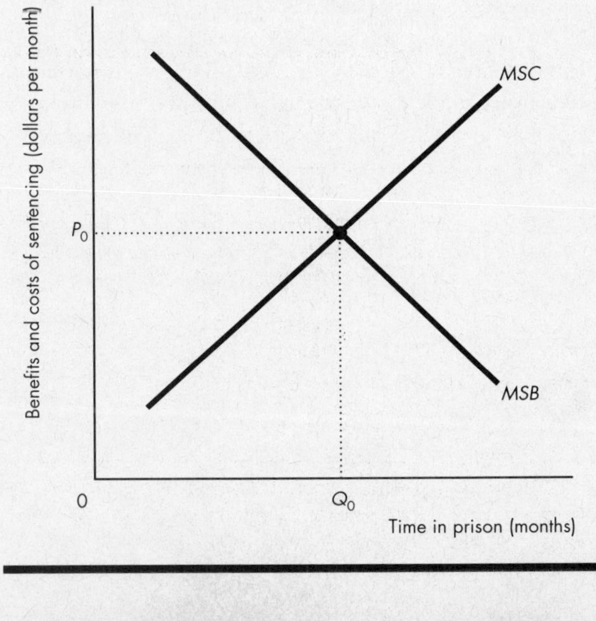

FIGURE 2

Relation of Optimal Sentence to Harm Value of Crime

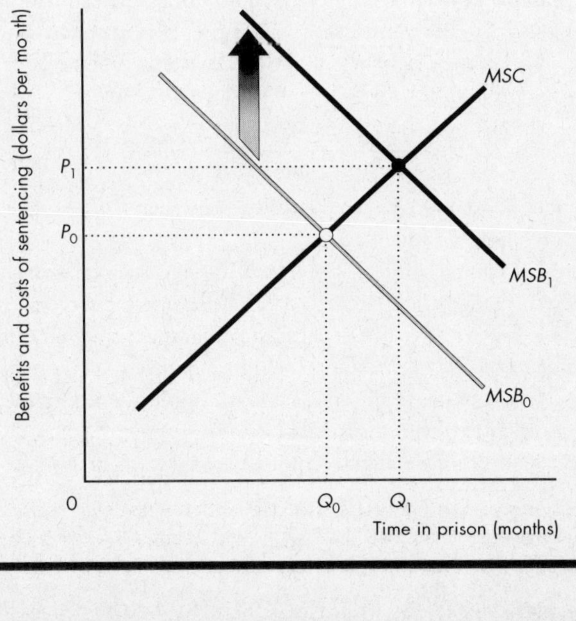

FIGURE 3

Relation of Optimal Sentence to Cost of Incarceration

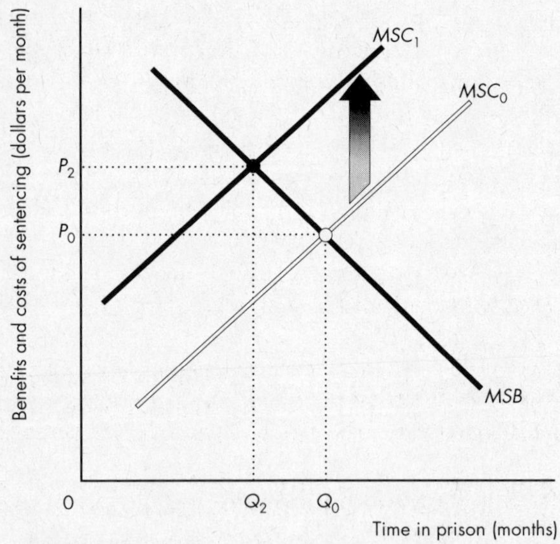

implicitly attached to crimes by sentencing policy will be close to the crimes' actual harms. We may calculate the implicit harm for each crime as

$$\frac{-spb(E+1)}{E}$$

where s is the sentence, p is the probability of imprisonment (given commission of the crime), b is the per-inmate annual imprisonment cost, and E is the elasticity of the crime rate with respect to sentencing.[4]

For example, the time served in prison (s) for murder is 81 months, the probability of incarceration (p) is 43 percent, and the elasticity of the murder rate with respect to the murder sentence (E) has been estimated to be -0.19. Hence, the implicit harm for murder is

$$\frac{-81(0.43)(\$27{,}350/12)(-0.19+1)}{-0.19}$$

or about $330,000. We can calculate the implicit harm for the other offenses in similar fashion.

Table 1 contains information relevant to the evaluation of current sentencing policy. For each of seven major offense types, Table 1 displays three pieces of information: the average amount of time served in prison, Cohen's estimate of the dollar harm from an occurrence of the crime, and the implicit harm for the crime, calculated with the method described above. Each of these three pieces of information is reported in two ways: in absolute levels (months for time served and dollars for the other two measures) and normalized for comparison.

Do sentences appear to be proportionally just? That is, are existing sentences proportional to actual harms? Table 1, column 1 shows the average amounts of time served in state prison, in months, for each of seven offenses, roughly in decreasing order of severity: murder, rape, assault, robbery, burglary, larceny, and auto theft. Note that these figures refer to the time actually served in prison for these offenses, rather than the sentences imposed, which are typically two to three times longer.

At first glance, the figures on time served lend some support to the justice hypothesis: the more severe the offense, the longer the average time served. On closer inspection, however, it becomes clear that existing sentences cannot possibly be proportionally just. The time served in prison for the most serious crime, murder, is just 7.7 times as long as the time served in prison for the least serious crime, auto theft. Yet, a murder seems far more than 7.7 times as serious as an auto theft. Compare columns 1 and 2, showing the absolute and normalized prison sentences with columns 3 and 4, reflecting Cohen's actual and normalized estimates of the actual harm from crime. The absolute dollar harm figure for murder of $2,000,000 is over 500 times the figure for auto theft. Because column 2 is clearly not proportional to column 4, existing sentences are not proportionally just.

If not "just," then are the sentences efficient? To answer this question, examine the absolute and normalized implicit harm figures in columns 5 and 6. The implicit harm figures show the dollars spent at the margin to prevent an occurrence of each crime; they therefore show the value that policy implicitly places on an occurrence of each offense. Although the figures must be viewed as very approximate, it is nevertheless clear that column 4 is closer to column 6 than to column 2. Hence, the pattern of implicit harms is much closer to the pattern of actual harms than the pattern of sentences is to the pattern of actual harms.

On this basis, it appears that sentences are better described as efficient than as proportionally just. As with many areas of empirical study in economics, more research is needed before firm conclusions may be reached. Still, perhaps surprisingly, economics helps to explain the pattern of observed criminal sentences.

◆ *Joel Waldfogel received his Ph.D. in economics at Stanford University in 1990 and is currently Assistant Professor of Economics at Yale University. His research interests include law and economics and public finance.*

SEE ALSO

Chapter 5 Elasticity
Chapter 10 Output and Costs
Chapter 11 Competition
Chapter 19 Market Failure

[4] For a derivation of this formula, see Joel Waldfogel, "Criminal Sentences as Endogenous Taxes: Are They "Just" or Efficient," *Journal of Law and Economics*, **36** (1993), pp. 139–151.

Aggregate Demand and Aggregate Supply

A Weight on Well-Being: Crime

Saul Pleeter

Aggregate demand and aggregate supply are important tools for understanding real-world events. The *aggregate demand curve* represents the inverse relationship between real gross domestic product (GDP) demanded and the aggregate price level. *GDP* is the value of all the final goods and services produced in the economy in a given year. Along the aggregate demand curve, the interest rate, expected inflation, the foreign exchange rate, the quantity of money, and taxes are held constant. The *short-run aggregate supply curve* gives a direct relationship between the quantity of real GDP supplied and the price level, assuming the prices of factors of production are constant. The *long-run aggregate supply curve* shows the full-employment level of real GDP and is independent of the price level. The interaction of aggregate demand and short-run aggregate supply determines a *macroeconomic equilibrium*—that is, a level of real GDP and a price level.

The following article uses the concepts of aggregate demand and aggregate supply to analyze the effects of crime on the macroeconomy.

After studying your text, reading this article, and answering the questions, you should be able to:

◆◆ Explain the determinants of the aggregate demand curve and the short-run and long-run aggregate supply curves.

◆◆ Distinguish between a shift in the curves and movements along the curves.

◆◆ Distinguish between a shift in the short-run aggregate supply curve and a shift in both aggregate supply curves.

◆◆ Analyze the effects of crime and expenditures related to criminal punishment and crime avoidance on the macroeconomy.

SEE ALSO

Chapter 23 Measuring Output and the Price Level

Chapter 24 Aggregate Demand and Aggregate Supply

Chapter 29 Fiscal and Monetary Influences on Aggregate Demand

Preview

- According to recent estimates, the direct costs of crime are in excess of $163 billion each year.
- Indirect costs are also substantial, as crime leads to higher prices and higher insurance rates.
- Expenditures on violence-related health care amounted to $13.5 billion in 1992. Since many victims do not have health insurance, the cost of their treatment is passed on to others.
- The criminal justice system employs 1.65 million people and spends about $25 billion annually on incarceration of criminals.
- Another cost of crime is consumers' spending for goods such as security systems, metal bars, and anti-theft devices.

◆ *Saul Pleeter received his Ph.D. from the University of Buffalo in 1970, has taught at the University of Cincinnati and Indiana University, and was chief economist for the city of Cincinnati. Dr. Pleeter is now affiliated with American University and the Department of Defense.*

THE WASHINGTON POST, July 5, 1994

Beyond Grief and Fear Is Crime's Bottom Line

BY PIERRE THOMAS
WASHINGTON POST STAFF WRITER

Each year the country is spending or losing in excess of $163 billion because of the consequences of crime, according to the Justice Department, the insurance industry and academic researchers. This is more than five times as much as the federal government spends on education.

Crime costs include better than $31.8 billion at the state and federal level for police, $24.9 billion for corrections, $36.9 billion in retail losses, $20 billion in insurance fraud, and $17.6 billion for individual property losses and medical expenses. Still $15 billion more is spent on private security, $9.3 billion on court costs and $7.2 billion on prosecution and public defense.

Moreover, crime is costing Americans more through higher prices, as companies and individuals seek to make up losses from theft and other unlawful acts.

Consider:

• Violence boosted the nation's health care costs by $13.5 billion in 1992, White House officials said. About 85 percent of hospital costs for firearms and stabbing victims is not covered by insurance and is eventually passed on to paying consumers.

For example, the medical expenses for the preliminary treatment, surgery and recovery for the typical trauma victim at D.C. General is $15,675, the District budget office states. Gunshot victims are often more costly. A June 15 shooting victim—in this instance with insurance—has already racked up bills of $103,033.25, according to hospital officials.

• Insurance fraud and motor vehicle theft cost $28 billion, according to the National Insurance Crime Bureau. "With at least 10 cents of every premium dollar going to cover fraud and crime, it's the policy holder who is the true victim," the bureau said.

• Shoplifting, internal pilferage and other losses cost retailers about $36.9 billion each year, retail analysts said. Two percent to 4 percent of the price on an item is a built-in cost for such losses. "It's a hidden cost you don't think about when you walk out of the store with your merchandise," said John Ronzetti, vice president of the National Retail Federation. The costs of guards, security cameras and the electronic devices that stores employ to thwart thieves also are passed on to customers.

• As of 1990, there were 1.65 million people employed in the nation's criminal justice system and 900,000 working as security guards, according to Justice Department statistics and those from Hallcrest Systems Inc., a Northern Virginia-based security industry analyst firm.

As a result of the fear, security and corrections have emerged as leading growth industries.

Americans are buying metal bars for their homes, anti-theft devices for their cars and alarm systems. Prisons are being constructed at a faster pace than universities.

"The perception of threat is at an all-time high," said John Galante, executive director of the Security Industry Association. "Even though property crime is down, some categories of violent crime are up and there is a change in the nature of violence. It seems more random, as if it can happen to any of us."

There are 15 million active accounts for monitoring systems or alarm systems for residences and businesses, producing $2.15 billion in revenue for companies providing such services, according to a recent security market overview by Galante's association.

"We are willing to spend a lot of tax dollars and private money to feel safer," said William Cunningham, of Hallcrest Systems. "It's amazing what we've expended."

In 1990, the country spent about $25 billion to house inmates in state and federal prisons. The number of inmates has tripled since 1980 to 948,881, at a cost of about $25,000 per prisoner. Corrections spending is almost certain to rise as more states rush to adopt "three strikes" bills that mandate life imprisonment without parole for any person convicted of three violent felonies. The hope is that the prison spending eventually will reduce overall crime because repeat offenders would be removed from society.

"The fastest growing segment of state budgets in (fiscal) 1994 is corrections," according to a study by the National Conference of State Legislatures. "For the third year in a row, corrections received more new state dollars than higher education."

"In Texas, the state prison population grew from 28,543 in 1980 to 69,054 at the end of 1993. During the same time, the number of inmates in Florida grew from 19,881 to 50,448; the number of prisoners in Maryland rose from 7,779 to 19,958; and in Virginia the inmate population increased from 8,270 to 17,019.

California had the biggest growth, from 23,511 in 1980 to 119,242 by December 1993. In fiscal 1994, even though California cut its overall budget, it increased its corrections budget by 15 percent, the conference of state legislatures said: "California illustrates the fact that the growth in prison populations has been expensive for states, and it shows no sign of easing."

A California General Assembly Ways and Means committee review found that in recent years corrections spending has grown "twice as fast as total state spending . . . at the expense of other programs, primarily higher education."

The District of Columbia has seen its adult prison population level off to 11,159 after peaking at 12,355 in 1990, or nearly double the 6,576 recorded in 1983.

But although the District of Columbia prison population and resulting spending remained steady, individual inmates are becoming costlier. Eighty percent of District prisoners have a history of substance abuse. Nearly 63 percent haven't completed high school when they are incarcerated. At least 20 percent are believed to be HIV positive.

"Prison systems are becoming full-service providers," said Walter Hill, D.C. corrections spokesman. "We're not just a jail, we are providing everything from health care to education and employment services."

Yet for all the billions of dollars spent, neither the District nor the nation will declare victory over the crime problem in the foreseeable future.

"Right now the system simply isn't working," said Rep. Bill McCollum (R-Fla.). "There are no easy answers."

The "American dream is rooted in a sense of security and I think that it is our first obligation to provide that security; and I believe that as a society we are trying hard, but we have failed at it so far," said Deputy Attorney General Jamie S. Gorelick in a recent interview.

Crime is the "single most serious problem facing America," said Sen. Joseph R. Biden Jr. (D-Del.), chairman of the Senate Judiciary Committee. The current federal crime bill, which may add as much as $30 billion in spending over six years, reflects the realization that no one has a monopoly on the answer, he said.

The prospect of curbing the spending in the near future is not good, said U.S. Attorney Eric H. Holder Jr. "In the short term, the expenditure of money has to increase," Holder said. "We need more and better cops, more prosecutors" although more enforcement is not the final solution and serves only to keep crime from becoming unbearable.

Ultimately, the public and government must confront the social ills contributing to crime, Holder said. That will require individual and community efforts, but also more government spending in the long term "on the social end, which hopefully will eventually lessen the need for short-term money."

Either way, the result is the same.

"It's a shame," he said. "But, we are going to have to spend more."

Questions

1. a) Draw an aggregate demand curve and a short-run aggregate supply curve. Label the equilibrium price level and the level of real GDP.

   b) According to the article, the direct costs of crime are estimated to be $163 billion a year. Those costs results in part from the purchase of goods like metal bars and anti-theft devices that attempt to deter crime. If crime were to vanish overnight, how would these purchases be affected? What would be the effect of this change on the aggregate demand curve, the aggregate supply curve, real GDP, and the price level?

   c) The article indicates that another component of the cost of crime is the increased prices that result from shoplifting and pilferage. According to the article, 2 to 4 percent of the cost of an item is a built-in adjustment for these losses. Which curve would be affected by a dramatic decline in shoplifting and theft? Show on your diagram the resulting change in macroeconomic equilibrium.

   d) What would be the simultaneous impact on the price level and the level of real GDP of the reduction in prices and consumer purchases of crime deterrence devices? Could GDP fall? Would that be bad?

2. a) Why is the long-run aggregate supply curve drawn as a vertical line? What determines the position of the long-run aggregate supply curve?

   b) Almost 1 million persons are incarcerated in U.S. prisons. Compare the long-run supply curve today with the long-run aggregate supply curve that would exist if crime had disappeared a long time ago so the prison population was zero. Should this factor be included in a listing of the costs of crime? What does this cost do to the short-run supply curve? Explain.

   c) According to the article, spending on corrections amounted to $25 billion in 1990 and is one of the fastest rising components of state spending. In part, the increase in corrections spending is made at the expense of spending on education. If crime were to disappear, how would the long-run aggregate supply curve be affected by a transfer of spending from corrections to education? Should this factor be included in a listing of the costs of crime?

3. The federal and state governments spend billions of tax dollars investigating crimes, prosecuting criminals, and maintaining prisons. If crime were to disappear, the need for these expenditures would also disappear.

   a) Assuming that the governments reduced their spending and passed the savings on to taxpayers by lowering taxes, can you tell what would happen to the aggregate demand curve? On what does this depend?

   b) Suppose that instead of reducing taxes, the governments reallocated these expenditures to education. What would happen to the aggregate demand curve? Why?

4. GDP is a measure of economic activity. It is also used as a measure of our standard of living and the current performance of the economy. It too is affected by the presence of crime and the criminal justice system. What is the impact on GDP as a measure of economic activity and standard of living of the following:

   a) The elimination of the underground economy

   b) The transfer of resources from the criminal justice system to education

   c) A reduction in crime and consequent reduction in criminal deterrence expenditures

How to Reduce Juvenile Crime?

Kari Battaglia

THE DALLAS MORNING NEWS, August 10, 1994

Youth crime budget questioned

BY TRACY EVERBACH
STAFF WRITER OF THE DALLAS MORNING NEWS

Dallas County commissioners on Tuesday questioned a request for an additional $5 million to deal with young offenders, leaving the county Juvenile Department's new director frustrated about how to fix its problems.

A visibly fatigued Rose Washington, who is undergoing her first Dallas County budget process, said after the hearing that if her request is denied, juvenile crime will continue to spiral out of control.

"There's a serious problem here, and I was brought in to manage this problem," she said, her voice breaking. "I've laid out the plan to the best of my ability, and that plan is cost-effective. . . .

"If a CEO is hired to run a company, he is not nickel-and-dimed about how to run it. I feel I have everyone questioning almost everything I proposed."

Ms. Washington and commissioners are at least $4 million apart in their recommendations for the fiscal 1995 budget, which covers the year that begins Oct. 1.

"The resources in this department are inadequate," she said. "I suggest they do what they think they need to do best as commissioners. The ball is in their court."

Minutes earlier, commissioners had scrutinized Ms. Washington's budget request, with some saying it asked for too much. The county budget office has said that commissioners will have only about $2 million available for raises and new programs in *all* county departments. That's if they stick with their plan to keep the budget balanced and don't raise taxes. . . .

Even now, Ms. Washington said, the department's emergency shelter and detention center have been cited by state agencies as not meeting standards.

The problem, she told commissioners, is reflected in juvenile crime statistics: Felony referrals of juvenile delinquents to the department increased from 5,000 in 1989 to 8,000 in 1993. In the last four years, juvenile drug offenses increased 96 percent, felony thefts 73 percent, aggravated assaults 56 percent and robberies 41 percent.

But commissioners appeared lukewarm to her requests. The county's budget office recommended accepting $1 million in programs. It called for approving four of 22 new programs she proposed, partially approving eight others, and deferring or refusing 10.

County Commissioner Jim Jackson noted that Dallas County spends more than any other county in Texas on its juvenile department: $19 million last year. The county also has the highest juvenile crime rate in the state.

Commissioner Nancy Judy said: "It would be foolish to approve all these changes until they can be proven to be a success.". . .

"In this day and age, we can't simply throw money at the problem," [Ron Davis, co-chairman of a watchdog group called the African-American Advisory Council for Juveniles,] told commissioners.

Claude Watson, director of Right Alternatives for People, a program to rehabilitate juvenile offenders, praised Ms. Washington's proposals.

"If I'm asked as a citizen if I'm willing to shoulder the load—to have my taxes raised—I give an unequivocal yes," he told commissioners. "If we don't address these problems now, we're going to have to pay a higher price."

The Essence of the Story

Juvenile crime in the city of Dallas and surrounding suburbs is soaring; the incidence of violent crime and drug offenses among the youth population has increased significantly over the past five years.

To better manage the problem, Dallas County hired a new Director of the Juvenile Department, Rose Washington. Ms. Washington believes the department's physical and financial resources are inadequate to deal effectively with the problem of youth crime.

The cost of the new programs proposed in Ms. Washington's budget far exceeds the funds currently available to finance them. The county cannot meet her requests and still balance the budget, an objective the county commissioners are committed to attaining. Other new programs and raises would have to be forgone or taxes would have to be increased in order to channel the additional funds to the Juvenile Department.

The county budget office recommends accepting only about 20 percent of Ms. Washington's proposals, citing the fact that Dallas County spends more than any other county in Texas to fight juvenile crime, yet has the highest juvenile crime rate in the state. Under this recommendation, the Juvenile Department would receive $1 million in additional funds rather than the $5 million requested.

There are many outside of the county commissioners' office who are supportive of Ms. Washington's proposals, even to the extent of being willing to pay more taxes to implement them. If the problem is not dealt with today, the county may well have to pay more to deal with it in the future.

Background and Analysis

Like household budgets, government budgets are *constrained* by limited income and market prices. Governments must make choices regarding the use of public funds and resources in the face of limited tax revenue.

A *budget line* can be used to analyze the effects of the budget limitations. To simplify the analysis, Figure 1 is drawn assuming that the budget available to fund all new projects is \$2 million, the price of an additional unit of juvenile crime–fighting activity (P_{JC}) is \$1,000, and the price of an additional unit of activity in all other departments (P_{OD}) is also \$1,000. Some possible combinations of additional crime-fighting activity and other county government activity are given in Table 1; these combinations are shown on the budget line in Figure 1. Any combination on or inside the budget line is affordable given the current budget and market prices.

The county budget office's recommendation to allocate \$1 million to additional juvenile crime fighting and \$1 million to all other departments exactly exhausts the \$2 million budget and is represented by point *b* in Figure 1. The request for \$5 million in additional funds for the Juvenile Department is given by point *d* in Figure 1; point *d* lies outside of the budget line and is unaffordable given the current budget and market prices.

Three possible avenues for achieving point *d* are as follows:

- Raise taxes to increase the funds available for government activity. Assuming prices are constant, if taxes are increased by \$4 million, then 5,000 units of crime-fighting activity and 1,000 units of other government activity can be added with the total of \$6 million in new funding. BL_1 parallel shifts out to the right to BL_3, as shown in Figure 2.
- Take funds away from existing government programs to increase the budget available for new programs. Taking \$4 million away from programs already in place also results in a parallel shift from BL_1 to BL_3, as shown in Figure 2.
- Reduce prices for crime prevention, (e.g., decrease the wages paid to law enforcement officers), allowing the same budget to purchase a greater amount of juvenile crime-fighting activity. All other things being equal, if the price of 1 unit of crime fighting activity falls to \$200, then a \$2 million budget can purchase 10,000 units of the activity and the budget constraint moves out along the horizontal axis to BL_2 in Figure 2.

TABLE 1

Consumption Possibilities, Given P_{JC} = \$1,000 and P_{OD} = \$1,000 and a \$2 million budget

	Juvenile Department		All Other Departments	
Possibility	**Quantity**	**Expenditure**	**Quantity**	**Expenditure**
a	0	0	2,000	\$2,000,000
b	1,000	\$1,000,000	1,000	\$1,000,000
c	2,000	\$2,000,000	0	0

The third possibility is highly unlikely. Government will have to either raise taxes, or take funds away from other programs. Like households, governments face tough choices. Unfortunately, government spending on crime prevention is undertaken to reduce the *negative utility* (disutility) associated with crime rather than to add to satisfaction by purchasing something that enhances well-being. Resources spent to reduce an economic bad, such as crime, cannot simultaneously be used to increase the availability of an economic good, such as education.

◆ *Kari Battaglia is Associate Director of the Center for Economic Education and a Lecturer in Economics at the University of North Texas. Economic education is Battaglia's special research interest.*

SEE ALSO
Chapter 8 Possibilities, Preferences, and Choices

FIGURE 1

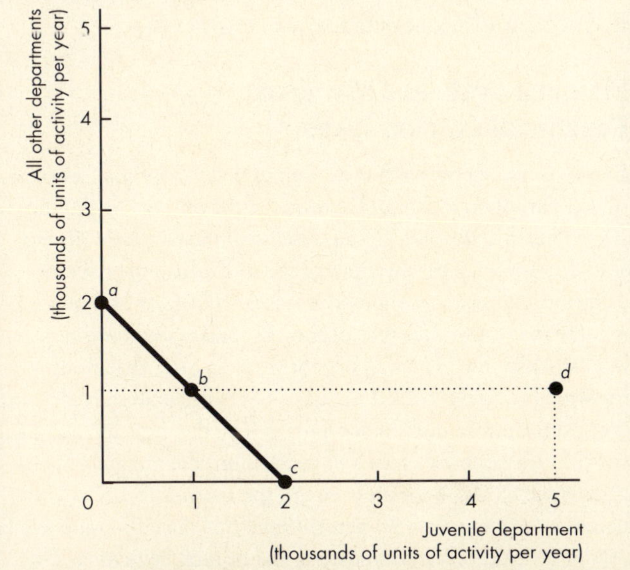

FIGURE 2

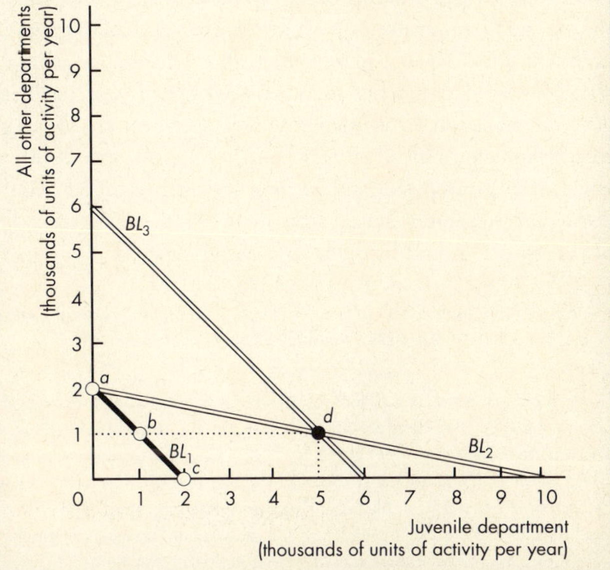

Who Doesn't Pay on April 15th?

BY DIANE LIM ROGERS

Tax evasion, or the failure to pay taxes owed, is one of the most prevalent forms of illegal activity in the United States. Although it is not clear what proportion of the evasive actions are willful versus unintentional, the Internal Revenue Service (IRS) estimates that nearly half of all individual taxpayers, and nearly 90 percent of those who itemize, fail to comply fully with the tax system.[1] Most of the individual noncompliance involves fairly small amounts, but because the activity is so widespread, the aggregate dollar value of the uncollected taxes is large. The **tax gap**, defined as uncollected taxes on legally earned personal and corporate income, has been estimated to be equal to over 20 percent of federal taxes collected and over 40 percent of the budget deficit.[2] Policies designed to reduce tax evasion and encourage tax compliance thus have potentially important effects on the structure of the overall tax system and the condition of the macroeconomy. For example, increases in the *tax base* through increased compliance would allow either a reduction in statutory *tax rates* or an increase in tax revenues.

Economists traditionally have used the term "tax evasion" to refer to the illegal failure to pay taxes due. They contrast this term with **tax avoidance**, which refers to the legal reduction of tax burdens through substitution away from taxed activities. For example, an individual might reduce his or her consumption of beer (and perhaps consume more soft drinks) if the tax rate on beer were increased; this is a perfectly legal way for the consumer to reduce taxes paid. Or a working mother might respond to higher income tax rates by choosing to reduce the hours she spends in the labor market (and increase the time spent on child care). While policymakers see tax avoidance as inevitable, tolerable, and sometimes even desirable behavior, willful evasion and accidental noncompliance are viewed as undesirable and somewhat avoidable, justifying government action. In an attempt to reduce evasion, the IRS has recently initiated a broad strategy known as Compliance 2000, which emphasizes positive reinforcement of compliant behavior during tax-preparation stages, rather than negative reinforcement of case-by-case evasive behavior after taxes go unpaid. A large part of Compliance 2000 involves research into what determines taxpayer behavior, with an emphasis on thinking about the factors influencing compliance and how they might differ across certain taxpayer categories. The basic, microeconomic theory of consumer behavior is a frequently used framework for examining why and how much people evade taxes.

Why Do People Evade Taxes?

The *marginal utility theory* of consumer behavior states that individuals maximize utility subject to budget constraints by consuming different goods up to the point where the marginal utility per dollar spent is equal across goods. For the simple case of just two goods, *X* and *Y*, the condition is written as

$$\frac{MU_X}{P_X} = \frac{MU_Y}{P_Y}$$

where MU indicates marginal utility and P indicates the price. If we rearrange this condition (by multiplying both sides by P_X and dividing both sides by MU_Y), we obtain the following:

$$\frac{MU_X}{MU_Y} = \frac{P_X}{P_Y}$$

This equation can be interpreted as saying that the relative *marginal benefit* (MB) from consuming X should equal the relative *marginal cost* (MC) of purchasing X, or

$$MB_X = MC_X,$$

in order to maximize the *net benefit* (total benefit minus total cost) of X, measured in terms of the *opportunity cost* of forgone consumption of Y. The general criterion of $MB = MC$ for optimal decisions shows up over and over again in economic theory. For example, the theory of the firm states that a producer maximizes profits at a level of output where *marginal revenue* (the marginal benefit the firm receives from selling the output) equals marginal cost.

Marginal Costs and Marginal Benefits of Evading Taxes

In the context of tax payments, we can define "optimal" evasion on the part of an individual in terms of the optimal level of unreported **taxable income**. Because many of the factors in the evasion decision may be uncertain to the individual, the relevant values are expected, as opposed to actual. The level of unreported income that maximizes the consumer's total *expected utility* is the level at which the perceived benefit from an extra dollar not reported (i.e., the expected marginal benefit) equals the perceived cost from an extra dollar not reported (i.e., the expected marginal cost). In the simplest models of tax evasion, the marginal benefit of unreported income simply equals the *marginal tax rate*, because, for example, a 20-percent marginal tax rate would imply 20¢ of tax paid on an additional dollar of taxable income. The

[1] Jeffrey A. Roth, John T. Scholz, and Ann Dryden Witte, eds., *Taxpayer Compliance,* Volume I: An Agenda for Research, University of Pennsylvania Press, 1989, pp. 2–3.

[2] The estimated "gross tax gap" for federal corporate and personal taxes in fiscal year 1992 (FY92) was between $110.1 billion and $127.0 billion (Internal Revenue Service, *Income Tax Compliance Research: Net Tax Gap and Remittance Gap Estimates,* Publication 1415 (4-90), Washington, DC). The federal budget deficit for FY92 was $290 billion, and total personal and corporate taxes collected were $576.7 billion (Advisory Commission on Intergovernmental Relations, *Significant Features of Fiscal Federalism,* Vol. 2, 1993).

marginal cost of unreported income is more complicated, as it depends on the expected value of penalties and eventual taxes paid, as well as the extent to which the individual is averse to risk. The expected value reflects the fact that there is some probability that the evader will not be caught (and will thus pay nothing) and some probability that he or she will be caught (and will thus pay taxes owed plus some penalty). The marginal cost associated with evasion is thus increased when either the probability of detection or the level of penalties increases. The translation from mathematical expected values to subjective utility values depends on individual preferences, however, and two taxpayers facing the same probabilities of detection and the same expected values of taxes and penalties may nevertheless choose to evade to different extents, because of differences in their attitudes about risk.

Tastes Toward Risk Matter

A simple numerical example will illustrate the distinction between objective values and expected utility. Suppose that an individual in a 20 percent marginal-tax-rate bracket is contemplating a $5,000 understatement of his or her taxable income, which would allow a $1,000 reduction in tax liability (0.20 x $5,000). Suppose further that the individual believes there is a 30-percent probability of the evasion's being detected, and that if it is detected, he or she will have to pay the $1,000 in taxes owed plus a $1,000 penalty. Then the evasive activity has a mathematical expected value of payments equal to (0.30 x $2,000) + (0.70 x $0) = $600.

If the individual complies, on the other hand, tax payments equal $1,000 with 100 percent probability. Now, if the individual is not at all averse to risk (i.e., is **risk neutral,**) the perceived expected cost of evasion will just equal the mathematical expected value of $600. Since the benefit of the $5,000 understatement is a savings of $1,000 in taxes, a risk-neutral individual would choose to evade, because the expected benefit from evasion ($1,000) exceeds the expected cost of evasion ($600). On the other hand, an individual who is **risk averse**, would assign a **risk premium** to the value of any uncertain outcome, so the uncertainty associated with the probability of being caught would cause expected cost (in terms of the individual's subjective valuation) to exceed the $600 mathematical expected value. Depending on the degree of risk aversion, the expected cost could rise above the $1,000 benefit of evasion, and under such circumstances an individual would not find it worthwhile to evade.

"Optimal" Evasion

The above numerical example was phrased as a discrete decision—whether or not to hide $5,000 in taxable income. The basic theory of consumer behavior assumes that continuous decisions are possible, and in such a case the issue becomes finding the optimal level of evasion. Marginal analysis tells us that an individual will evade up to the point where the marginal benefit from not reporting income equals the marginal cost. Marginal benefit should be expected to decline with the level of unreported income because of the graduated structure of rates in the federal income tax system, where marginal tax rates rise with income. The larger the amount of unreported income, the more likely the taxpayer is to fall into lower tax-rate brackets. Expected marginal

FIGURE 1

An Evader's Optimal Level of Evasion

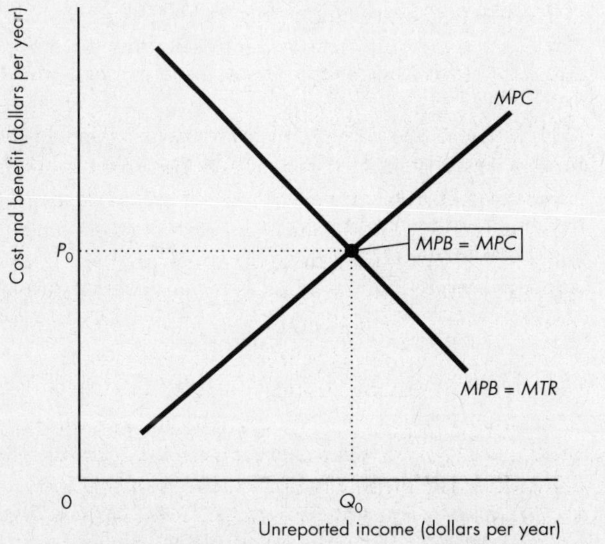

FIGURE 2

When Zero Evasion is Optimal *(MPC > MPB)*

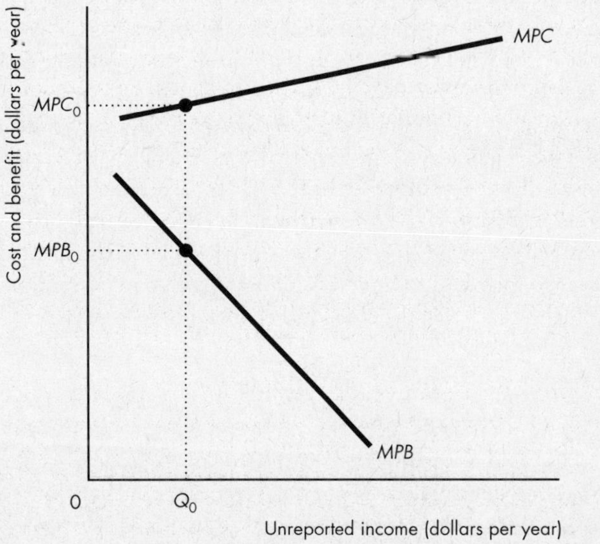

FIGURE 3

The Effect of a Decrease in Tax Rates

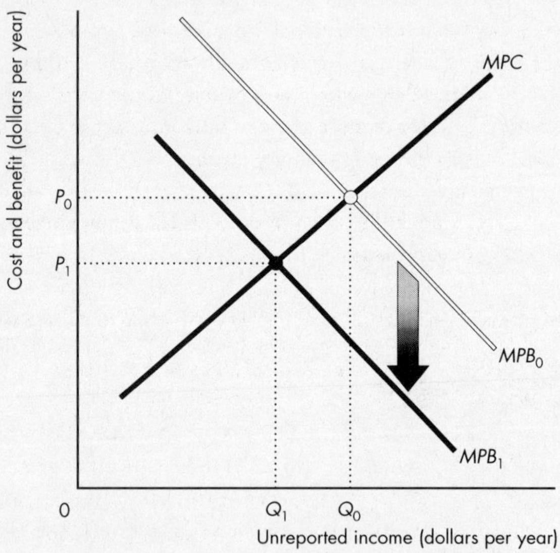

FIGURE 4

The Effect of an Increase in Penalties

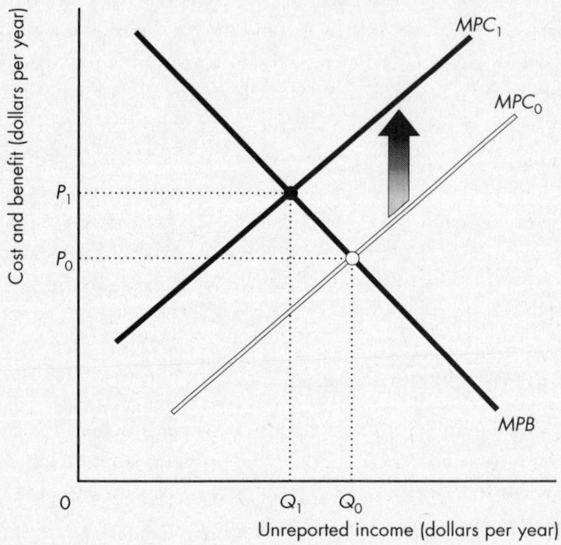

cost might rise with unreported income if either (perceived) penalty rates or (perceived) probabilities of detection increase with the extent of evasion.

Figure 1 illustrates a case of decreasing *marginal private benefit, MPB,* and increasing *marginal private cost, MPC,* where the optimal level of evasion (unreported taxable income) from the individual's perspective, Q_0, is positive. (These marginal costs and benefits are "private" costs and benefits—i.e., they reflect the values affecting the individual alone, because we are discussing an individual's decision making. The social costs and benefits may differ from the private values, however; so what is an optimal level of tax evasion for the individual may not be optimal for society as a whole.) The marginal private benefit equals the marginal tax rate, *MTR,* because (for example) with a 25-percent marginal tax rate the individual would save 25¢ for each additional dollar of income not reported. Figure 2 illustrates a case where marginal private cost exceeds marginal private benefit at every positive level of evasion; that is, the perceived marginal costs are sufficiently high—either the person is sufficiently risk averse or penalties and/or probabilities of detection are sufficiently high—such that the individual chooses not to evade taxes.

Effects of Government Policies

This simple model suggests how different types of government policy could, theoretically, affect the level of tax evasion. As illustrated in Figure 3, decreases in the marginal tax rate would reduce the marginal private benefit of evasion from MPB_0 to MPB_1 (since $MPB = MTR$), and hence reduce the optimal level

TABLE 1

Who Evades and How? Some Empirical Findings

- When noncompliance is defined as including both overreporting and underreporting, a 1979 sample indicates that nearly half of individual taxpayers are noncompliant; among itemizers, noncompliance rises to 88 percent. Of taxpayers who misreport income, about 12 percent overreport. Of those who misreport subtractions, about one-third fail to claim all to which they are entitled.
- The 1987 distribution of individual noncompliance in terms of dollar value of taxes uncollected is as follows: 76 percent due to unreported income, 11 percent due to overstated subtractions (exemptions, deductions, and credits), 11 percent due to nonfiling, and the remaining 2 percent due to arithmetic errors.
- Most incidents of noncompliance involve small amounts. From a 1982 sample of taxpayers, 70 percent of returns had reported taxable income accurate within $50 and 90 percent were within $1,000.
- Income that is more visible to the IRS (through withholding or information reporting) is more likely to be fully reported than other forms of income.
- There is some evidence that personal experience of an audit in the past or higher-than-average audit rates in local geographic areas increase compliance when the taxpayer feels the audit process is fair.
- There is only scanty or mixed evidence that higher penalty rates or lower marginal tax rates encourage compliance. Part of the problem in estimating tax-rate effects lies in trying to disentangle those effects from income effects.
- Compliance is greater among older taxpayers and among female taxpayers.

Source: Results are summarized from Jeffrey A. Roth, John T. Scholz, and Ann Dryden Witte, eds., *Taxpayer Compliance, Volume. I: An Agenda for Research,* University of Pennsylvania Press, 1989, and from Internal Revenue Service, *Income Tax Compliance Research: Gross Tax Gap Estimates and Projections for 1973–1992,* Publication 7285 (March 1988), Washington, DC.

of evasion from Q_0 to Q_1. As shown in Figure 4, increases in the size of penalties imposed on evaders would increase marginal private cost from MPC_0 to MPC_1 and hence decrease evasion from Q_0 to Q_1. The same would be true of increases in the probabilities of detection. The theoretical model can predict these qualitative results, but the quantification of such effects requires data and empirical analysis.

Lessons from the Data

Measuring the extent of tax evasion, let alone the effects of various policies on evasion, is a huge challenge. The secretive nature of the activity implies that any available data will be limited and/or unreliable. Even so, economists and other policy analysts have attempted to quantify noncompliance and its determinants using a variety of empirical approaches. The most frequent strategy involves statistical and econometric analyses of historical data gathered through IRS audits. Based on detected failures to pay taxes, researchers have learned something about what types of taxpayers and forms of income are most likely to be involved in noncompliant behavior. Some of these findings are summarized in Table 1. Other quantitative approaches include the use of surveys to assess taxpayer attitudes and the use of controlled experiments in laboratory settings ("experimental economics").[3]

Much of this empirical work has challenged the basic theoretical model of tax evasion outlined above. For example, there is some indication that penalties and probabilities of detection have only small negative—and sometimes even positive—effects on evasion, despite their central theoretical role in affecting marginal cost. This puzzling result might be explained in part by the fact that evaders may not know actual penalty levels and/or probabilities with perfect certainty, as is assumed in the simple theoretical model. In addition, the basic model postulates that the marginal benefit of evasion is simply the marginal tax rate, but survey data suggest that general attitudes toward government and the overall structure of the tax system (not just the marginal tax rate) can influence the willingness or ability of taxpayers to comply with the tax laws. Some experimental work suggests that taxpayers may be more responsive to positive incentives than to negative ones. Evasion could actually increase with increases in penalties and probabilities of detection, if the IRS's enforcement activities fuel negative attitudes toward government.

The lessons learned from recent research have spawned a new and different way of thinking about tax administration that emphasizes the encouragement of compliance rather than the punishment of evasion. While the traditional theory of tax evasion stresses the potential importance of enforcement activity, the IRS's Compliance 2000 focuses on a kinder and gentler strategy of determining how government can reduce the costs of compliance through such methods as simplifying the tax laws and forms and providing taxpayer assistance. Compliance 2000 also examines to what extent government can promote positive attitudes toward compliance by personalizing the tax-collection process and reminding taxpayers of social commitments. It may be that going after cheaters is a less effective means of collecting taxes due than is encouraging people to comply in the first place.

This article reflects the views of the author and does not necessarily represent those of the Congressional Budget Office.

◆ *Diane Lim Rogers received her Ph.D. in Economics from the University of Virginia in 1991. She is currently Assistant Professor of Economics at The Pennsylvania State University and Visiting Scholar with the U.S. Congressional Budget Office. Her research focuses on the distributional and incentive effects of U.S. taxes.*

MINI-GLOSSARY:

Risk averse: used to describe individuals who have a dislike for uncertain outcomes and thus are willing to pay some amount of money to reduce the uncertainty of an outcome.

Risk neutral: used to describe individuals whose decisions about utility are based only on expected values and not on the riskiness of outcomes.

Risk premium: amount of money a person is willing to pay to remove the uncertainty associated with an outcome.

Tax avoidance: (legal) change in behavior to reduce tax liability, through responses to the changes in relative prices caused by taxes.

Tax evasion: noncompliance with the tax laws by failing to pay taxes that are legally due.

Tax gap: amount of tax owed for a given year but not voluntarily paid; does not account for income earned in the underground (illegal) economy.

Taxable income: portion of income earned by individuals that is subject to the personal income tax; equals gross income minus the value of exemptions and deductions.

SEE ALSO

Chapter 7	Utility and Demand (Household Consumption Choices)
Chapter 17	Uncertainty and Information
Chapter 20	Public Choice

[3] Some of the most recent empirical research on tax evasion and compliance can be found in Joel Slemrod, ed., Why People Pay Taxes, University of Michigan Press, 1992. Research is also summarized in Roth, Scholz, and Witte, Taxpayer Compliance, op. cit.

The Underground Economy

BY JEFFREY WRASE

It goes by many names. It is difficult to detect, since the reason it exists is to escape detection. It includes garage sales, children's lemonade stands, tutors, and recent Attorney General–designate Zoë Baird. It is the *underground economy*, also known as the subterranean, shadow, unofficial, informal, irregular, and off-the-books economy.

A variety of definitions have been assigned to the underground economy, associated with various methods used to estimate its size and growth. According to all estimates, the underground economy is too large to be ignored. Most agree that the scale of underground economic activity involving only legal activities is larger than 10 percent of reported GDP. Many activities within the underground economy are legal, aside from not being reported to tax authorities. Examples are easy to think of, such as babysitting services, garage sales, and lemonade stands. More significant is unreported income of workers from their main or secondary jobs. Adding illegal activities, such as drug dealing, cigarette smuggling, and prostitution, could push the scale of underground activities up an additional 1 to 5 percent of reported GDP.

The underground economy provides a large number of jobs. It also distorts major economic indicators, on which monetary and fiscal policies are based. Economic activity, as measured by GDP, net domestic income at factor cost, or labor productivity, is understated because of unreported activities. Unemployment is overstated, as time spent producing unreported income escapes measures of labor market activities. Another adverse effect of the underground economy is that it leads to lost public revenue. The Internal Revenue Service, (IRS), for example, estimates that tax revenue not collected because of underreported income and overstated deductions in 1992 was over one-third of the $300 billion federal budget deficit of that year.[1]

In order to assign structure to the concept of an underground economy, we shall, in what follows, ask and answer the following questions. What defines the underground economy? What gives rise to underground economic activities? How is the underground economy measured and what is its size? What are benefits and costs of underground activities? What can be done to reduce the size of the underground economy?

What Defines the Underground Economy?

To the IRS, the underground economy means income that is not reported to tax authorities and that may or may not show up in estimates of national income. Suppose, for example, that you arrange for someone to paint your house in return for a cash payment. Your house-painting expenditure may show up in estimated GDP as consumption, yet the painter may not report as income to the tax authorities the cash you paid.

To most, the underground economy refers to economic activities that are unreported to tax authorities or to government agencies that gather data on economic activities. If reported income is the component of total income captured in the National Income and Product Accounts (NIPA), then total unreported income consists of income produced in illegal activities or in legal market activities that escape NIPA measurement. Income from illegal activities escapes formal NIPA measurement for the obvious reason that participants in such activities do not report their infractions. Income produced in legal market activities may not show up in NIPA accounts because participants withhold information to evade taxes or regulations. For example, your house painter may not report income in order to evade income taxes. A retired individual may not report income receipts in order to avoid Social Security benefit reductions. You may wish to pay cash for painting or, perhaps, babysitting services to evade payment of taxes as an employer. (See inset.)

What Gives Rise to Underground Economic Activities?

The incentives to not report income receipts or expenditures are simple to understand. Participants in the underground economy wish to evade taxes, regulations, or detection of illegal activities. According to a detailed study by Carl Simon and Ann Witte, nonreporting of legal income primarily to evade taxes or loss of public benefits such as Social Security constitutes the dominant sector of the underground economy.[2] Tax and benefit-loss evasion, according to the study, is the incentive behind roughly one-half of all income produced in underground economic activities. Escaping detection of illegal transactions and avoiding regulations provide the incentive for the remaining half of underground income.

Prominent historical examples of tax evasion and attempts to circumvent regulations or statutes occurred during the Prohibition era and World War II. During Prohibition, income-producing activities associated with alcohol trading went unreported. During World War II, attempts to evade wage and price controls and rationing constraints gave rise to unreported economic trades. In 1958, Phillip Cagan estimated that at the end of World War II there was close to $13 billion of currency outstanding in excess of what was required for normal, legal transactions.[3] This currency, used to facilitate price control violations and transactions that cir-

[1] K. Pennar, and C. Farrel, "Notes from the Underground Economy," *Business Week*, February 15, 1993, pp. 98–101.

[2] C. P. Simon, and A. D. Witte, *Beating the System: The Underground Economy*, Boston, MA: Auburn House Publishing, 1982.

[3] P. Cagan, "The Demand for Currency Relative to Total Money Supply," *National Bureau of Economic Research Occasional Paper 62*, 1958.

cumvented rationing constraints, was associated with unreported income of $21 to $25 billion, or 12.4 to 14.7 percent of reported personal income, according to Cagan's estimates.

How Is the Underground Economy Measured and What Is Its Size?

A variety of methods have been devised to estimate the size of the underground economy. Estimating the scale of underground economic activities is inherently difficult given that these activities exist to avoid detection. Methods used to estimate underground economic activity are survey methods, discrepancy methods, and currency methods.

Survey methods are based on microeconomic data from individual surveys, tax returns, unemployment records, or similar sources. The IRS, for example, periodically undertakes anonymous taxpayer opinion surveys on tax evasion. The IRS also, in its Taxpayer Compliance Measurement Program, subjects a random sample of approximately 50,000 individual income tax returns to extensive audit examinations. Using the audit results, along with a complex set of estimates from other data sources, the IRS arrives at estimates of taxpayer compliance with tax codes.

Discrepancy methods utilize discrepancies between independent estimates of a common quantity to arrive at measures of underground activities. For example, independent measures of personal income can be compared to arrive at an estimate of unreported income. Personal income, which corresponds roughly to individuals' taxable incomes, is estimated by the Bureau of Economic Analysis (BEA) independently of income statistics compiled by the IRS from individual income tax returns. Comparing the BEA estimates of personal income to the IRS statistics from tax returns reveals that the BEA figures are significantly higher than the IRS figures. The discrepancy can be considered income earned but not reported for tax purposes, which is one measure of underground economic activity.

The most widely cited estimates of the size of the underground economy are derived from **currency methods**. Currency methods measure underground economic activity indirectly based on currency (cash), deposit (checking and saving accounts), and transactions (GDP, for example) data. An influential study utilizing the currency method attracted media and IRS attention in 1977.[4] Peter Gutmann estimated the ratio of the amount of currency in circulation to the amount of money in checking accounts for each year from the late 1930s to 1977. He used the growth of this ratio to estimate that the GNP of the underground economy was $176 billion in 1976 and $195 billion in 1977. These amounts were above 10 percent of officially reported GNP.

Gutmann's Currency Method

To calculate underground economic activity, Gutmann made several assumptions. First, he assumed that no underground

[4] P. Gutmann, "The Subterranean Economy," *Financial Analysts Journal*, Nov./Dec., 1977.

A Choice: Pay The Nanny Tax or Enter the Underground

Recent publicity about Attorney General–designate Zoë Baird's hiring of illegal aliens to work off the books has brought one aspect of the underground economy into the headlines. To get a perspective on incentives to participate in the underground economy, consider the options facing Baird and others.

Suppose that you have children and hire a nanny to look after them while you work or attend school. If your nanny is an employee in the eyes of the IRS, then you are legally an employer. You have the following options. You could simply pay your nanny cash, "off-the-books," and not report the payments to tax authorities. This option is illegal, but simple and convenient. Alternatively, you could abide by the law, which may not make life simple.

As a law-abiding employer, you must first verify that your nanny is eligible to work in the United States. It is illegal to hire illegal aliens. If your nanny can work in the United States, then you face many of the same requirements for tax filing as any other employer. This means that you must file about a dozen forms per year. First, you need to file an Application for Employer Identification Number (Form SS-4) with the IRS to obtain an ID number. Then, each year you must list wages paid during any quarter in excess of $50 on a Wage and Tax Statement (Form W-2). If you paid over $1,000 of wages in any quarter of the calendar year, you also need to file an annual Federal Unemployment Tax Return (Form 940 or 940EZ). Next, on a quarterly basis you are required to file an Employer's Quarterly Tax Return for Household Employees (Federal Form 942). This is where you pay Social Security and Medicare taxes for your nanny. You will also probably need to file quarterly state unemployment tax forms and may need to obtain worker's compensation insurance coverage.

The options provided above point out incentives to participate in the underground economy. Paying your nanny cash and not reporting the payments saves a lot of time, energy, paperwork, and maybe even money. There are risks, however, in going off the books. If your illegal nonreporting of payments is detected, you will pay taxes that were owed, penalties, and interest. In addition, you may not be able to serve as Attorney General.

activity existed during the period from 1937 to 1941 (when the ratio of cash to checking accounts was the lowest in his sample). Second, he assumed that the amount of currency needed for legal transactions in either 1976 or 1977 was the same proportion of checking account balances as in 1937. Currency outstanding in excess of the amount needed for legal transactions was considered to have been used for underground activities. A third assumption was that the volume of transactions supported by a given amount of currency and checking accounts was the same for both reported and underground activities. Using data on reported transactions and money balances, Gutmann arrived at his estimates.

A basic premise of Gutmann's work on estimating the underground economy was that underground transactions primarily involve cash. This premise was challenged by Edgar Feige, who also used the currency method to estimate the underground economy.[5] Using an analysis based on a ratio of estimated total transactions in the economy to observed income, Feige derived his own estimates for the size of the underground economy.

Feige's Currency Method

Specifically, Feige calculated the ratio of total transactions in the economy to GNP for 1939, 1976, and 1978. Total transactions were defined as the volume of checking transactions (checking balances times the velocity of those balances) plus the volume of currency transactions (currency in circulation times the velocity of currency in transactions). Velocity here refers to the *velocity of circulation,* which is the number of times a dollar or deposit balance is used in a period in transactions. Feige found that the ratio of transactions to GNP had been rising. He assumed that there was no underground economic activity in 1939 and reasoned that the volume of transactions in the economy should bear the same relation to GNP in the 1970s as in 1939. He attributed increases in the ratio of transactions to GNP to underground activity. Feige's calculations yielded estimates of the GNP of the underground economy that were larger than those obtained by Gutmann. In particular, Feige estimated that underground GNP was $225 to $369 billion in 1976, or 13 to 22 percent of reported GNP, and $542 to $704 billion in 1978.

It is instructive to note that the conceptual root for Feige's approach to estimating unrecorded monetary transactions is the *equation of exchange*. The equation of exchange specifies the equality between the total volume of payments (the quantity of money, M, times the velocity of circulation, V) and the total volume of transactions (the price level, P, times real GNP, Y). That is, the equation of exchange is $MV = PY$. If some GNP transactions are recorded, say Y_R, and some unrecorded, say Y_U, then we can also write that $MV = PY_R + PY_U$. If we have an estimate of MV and of recorded transactions PY_R, then any difference between MV and recorded transactions represents an estimate of the volume of unrecorded transactions, PY_U. This was the basis for Feige's calculations.

The IRS's Estimation

In response to publicity given to Gutmann's and Feige's currency method estimates, which suggested a sizable underground economy, the IRS in 1979 undertook its own investigation. The investigation was of the extent of underreporting on federal income tax returns.[6] The IRS study of noncompliance with income tax rules utilized a somewhat complicated mixture of assumptions and discrepancy and survey methods. The study provided estimates that in 1976 $75 to $100 billion of income in the legal sector and $25 to $35 billion of income in the illegal sector were not reported to the IRS. The resulting loss of federal tax revenue was $19 to $26 billion.

More recently, the IRS has estimated that the amount of tax revenue that was not collected because of underreporting of income and overstating of deductions may have been as high as $127 billion in 1992.[7] The federal *budget deficit,* measured as total expenditure of the government sector minus total revenue of that sector in a period, was approximately $300 billion in 1992. Had the $127 billion of revenue been collected, the 1992 government deficit would have been reduced by about 42 percent.

Common Ground

All of the studies mentioned above point toward an underground economy with a scale of over 10 percent of reported GNP in the late 1970s. A more recent calculation by Feige is that unreported income in 1993 was at least $800 billion, which is approximately eight times the amount calculated for 1974 without adjusting for inflation.[8] All indications are that the scale of underground economic activity is too large to be overlooked, at least by the IRS.

What Are Benefits and Costs of Underground Activities?

There are clearly private benefits associated with participation in underground activities. These are discussed in detail in "Who Doesn't Pay on April 15th?" on pp. 32–35 of this issue of the *Economic Times*. On the cost side, there are at least three factors to consider. First, if illegal activities involving violations of private property rights are included as part of the underground economy, then social costs due to crime arise.

Second, even if we exclude illegal activities from consideration, underground economic activities that are legal but not reported lead to substantial revenue losses to taxing authorities. This

[5] E. L. Feige, "The Irregular Economy: Its Size and Macroeconomic Implications," Social Science Research Institute, University of Wisconsin-Madison, May 1979.

[6] U.S. Department of the Treasury, Internal Revenue Service, "Estimates of Income Unreported on Individual Income Tax Returns," U.S. Government Printing Office, 1979.

[7] Pennar and Farrel, op.cit.

[8] *Fortune Magazine,* April 4, 1994, p. 30.

implies that those who report income are assigned a larger burden of taxation.

Third, underground economic activity leads to distortions of measures of economic activity. GDP and unemployment measurements, for example, do not perfectly reflect conditions in goods and labor markets partly because some goods trades and employment occur in the underground, unmeasured economy. *Real GDP* measures the value of the output of final goods and services in a period, using prices that prevailed in some base period. Clearly, output in the underground economy that does not show up in GDP is excluded from data that policymakers and analysts use to gauge the volume of productive activity in the economy. Since some government policies are based on movements in measures of activity such as GDP, distorted measures can give rise to suboptimal policies.

Like GDP, data on labor market activities are distorted by the existence of underground economic activities. Recall that the *unemployment rate* is the number of people unemployed expressed as a percentage of the *labor force*. The labor force consists of those with jobs and those who do not have jobs but are actively seeking work at prevailing wages. Unemployment is measured by the Bureau of Labor Statistics based on the Current Population Survey (CPS), which is a survey of households' labor market experiences. One way individuals are counted as unemployed is if their responses to survey questions reveal that they were without work, but actively seeking employment, within a four-week period preceding the survey.

The unemployment rate will overstate the amount of idle productive labor resources if respondents to the CPS survey assert that they are unemployed when, in fact, they work in underground activities. If the unemployment rate is significantly overstated because of the underground economy, then monetary or fiscal polices designed to reduce unemployment by stimulating aggregate demand and employment can be misguided. Moreover, such polices may generate unnecessary inflation, as strengthened aggregate demand exerts upward pressure on prices.

Aside from the overall unemployment rate, there is also concern over the distribution of unemployment across various types of workers. An often cited feature of labor markets is the high incidence of unemployment for minority teenagers. While not denying the costs of unemployment, some argue that teenage unemployment is overstated since relatively large numbers of young people find employment in the underground economy.[9]

What Can Be Done to Reduce the Size of the Underground Economy?

Reducing the scale of underground economic activity requires reducing or eliminating incentives to not report underground activities. Reducing illegal activities obviously requires crime prevention. Reducing activities that, aside from nonreporting, are legal requires increased compliance with reporting requirements, which could be brought about by reductions in regulations and taxes. The IRS works to increase compliance with existing tax codes. Existing codes, which rely primarily on taxation of income, may not, however, provide the best incentives available for the reporting of economic activities. Reductions in regulations and taxes have been featured in the rhetoric of recent political administrations. With given levels of compliance, reductions in current and future taxes cannot occur without reductions in government expenditure.

◆ *Jeffrey Wrase is Assistant Professor at Brigham Young University. His research interests include international macroeconomics and monetary economics.*

SEE ALSO

Chapter 22	Inflation, Unemployment Cycles, and Deficits
Chapter 23	Measuring Output and the Price Level
Chapter 27	Money, Banking, and Prices
Chapter 29	Fiscal and Monetary Influences on Aggregate Demand

ECONOMY WATCH

Index of Leading Indicators

Each month the U.S. Department of Commerce releases its index of leading indicators, which combines data on 11 indicators of economic performance. The Index of Leading Indicators is released about one month after the data month. The items that make up the index are:

1. Average work week
2. Average weekly initial state unemployment claims
3. Vendor performance
4. Stock prices
5. Contracts and orders for plant and equipment
6. Change in manufacturers' unfilled orders for durable goods
7. Change in sensitive material prices
8. Index of consumer expectations
9. Money supply
10. Building permits issued
11. Manufacturers' new orders for consumer goods and materials

You can get the latest data on the *Index of Leading Indicators* and its components from a U.S. Department of Commerce recording by calling (202) 606-5361.

[9] This claim and references to support it can be found in Simon and Witte, op. cit., p. 292.

Canada Cuts Cigarette Taxes to Fight Smuggling

M. Shawn Carter and Dennis W. Jansen

THE NEW YORK TIMES, February 9, 1994

Canada Cuts Cigarette Taxes to Fight Smuggling

BY CLYDE FARNSWORTH
SPECIAL TO THE NEW YORK TIMES

TORONTO, Feb. 8—Against protests from health groups, Prime Minister Jean Chrétien announced today that Canada was slashing taxes on cigarettes to try to stamp out widespread smuggling from the United States, where taxes are currently about one-fifth as high.

A carton of cigarettes on which all taxes are paid costs upward of $44 in Canada, against as little as $15 to $20 for the contraband product. Hundreds of millions of dollars worth of illegal cigarettes enter Canada every month, chiefly through Mohawk reservations that straddle the border with the United States in Ontario and Quebec.

According to law enforcement officials, the smuggling has attracted organized-crime gangs in the area. It has also led to losses of millions of dollars of revenues from provincial and federal treasuries and created hardships for corner store operators whose livelihood depends to a large degree on the cigarette trade.

The main elements of the Chrétien plan are: to reduce the current $16 a carton federal tax to $11; invite Canada's provinces, which like states in the United States levy their own taxes, to match the federal cut; set an $8 a carton export levy on Canadian-manufactured cigarettes that briefly enter the United States and then are usually spirited back into Canada, and strengthen enforcement of smuggling laws. The tax cuts go into effect at midnight tonight.

The antismuggling force to the Royal Canadian Mounted Police will be doubled to 700 officers, and special marine patrols along the St. Lawrence and Great Lakes will be increased.

Health Officials Angry

Although Mr. Chrétien linked the plan with some measures of health promotion, including a new tax on the tobacco industry to finance a more active anti-smoking campaign, many health officials and some provincial leaders expressed displeasure.

"The Canadian Cancer Society is appalled that the Federal Government would even consider a tax rollback to control smuggling without first trying other options," said Dr. Jacques Cantin, president of the cancer society and a prominent surgeon in Montreal. Ken Kyle, the society's director of public issues, called today's action "a public health disaster."

British Columbia's Health Minister, Paul Ramsey, said the tax cut would encourage smoking, drive up healthcare costs and increase smuggling between provinces. The province said it will not cut its own tobacco taxes.

But smuggling is nowhere near as big a problem in British Columbia as in Quebec and Ontario. Three quarters of all cigarettes sold in Quebec are estimated to be contraband. In Ontario the proportion is about one in three.

Quebec's new Premier, Daniel Johnson, a Liberal like Mr. Chrétien, facing elections later this year against the separatist Parti Québécois, lobbied hard for the cigarette tax cut. The Parti Québécois had been citing the lack of action on smuggling as another example of why federalism doesn't work in Quebec.

Minutes after Mr. Chrétien spoke in the House of Commons, Mr. Johnson called a news conference in Quebec city to announce the province was slashing its tobacco tax by $11 a carton, also effective at midnight. As the Chrétien plan calls for federal tax cuts to match provincial cuts up to $10, Quebec's move means the average price of a carton of cigarettes will drop to around $23 from around $44 and according to Mr. Johnson, should end most of the smuggling in the province.

As the Canadian Government and Quebec acted today to lower their taxes, President Clinton served notice in his budget message to Congress on Monday that he will ask for a dramatic increase in American cigarette taxes.

Under the Clinton plan, a pack of 20 cigarettes, costing an average of $1.75 would be taxed an additional 75 cents, or $7.50 a carton, on top of the existing Federal levy of 52 cents. An American dollar is worth about $1.30 in Canadian currency.

American health officials lamented the Canadian decision.

"The U.S. tobacco industry is salivating over what's going on in Canada," said John Bloom, the American Cancer Society's policy director, and will try to convince the American public that "tobacco taxes don't work when, in fact Canada has proven that tobacco taxes save lives and raise revenue."

Kerrie B. Wilson, national vice president for government relations for the cancer society, said, "Low U.S. taxes are the chief cause of the smuggling problem Canada faces, and raising U.S. taxes is the best solution."

The Essence of the Story

The sales tax imposed on cigarettes is about five times higher in Canada than in the United States. Exports of cigarettes are not taxed. This policy results in organized-crime gangs' purchasing hundreds of millions of dollars' worth of Canadian cigarettes that were legally exported to the United States and then smuggling them back into Canada, where they are sold on the black (illegal) market.

The illegal smuggling has cost the Canadian government millions of dollars in tax revenues. In an effort to end the illegal smuggling, the Canadian government is cutting its tax on cigarettes and setting an export levy on Canadian cigarettes entering the United States. Smuggling laws are also being enforced more stringently, adding an additional cost to the smugglers.

Canadian health officials are angry because they believe that making legal cigarettes cheaper will lead to more smoking and impose a heavier cost on the nation's health care system by increasing expenditures for treating smoking-related illnesses.

Canada's national vice president for government relations for the cancer society, Kerrie B. Wilson, believes the best solution is for the United States to raise its cigarette tax.

◆ M. Shawn Carter is a Ph.D. candidate at Texas A&M University. His dissertation research is concerned with how industrial structures impact stock price valuation. Dennis W. Jansen is Professor and Director of the Graduate Program in Economics at Texas A&M University. His research interests are in macroeconomics.

Background and Analysis

Canadian cigarette taxes were raised 167 percent between 1984 and 1992. These taxes account for up to 75 percent of the retail price of a pack of cigarettes. While the tax rate for Canadian cigarettes has increased, the number of cigarettes made in Canada, shipped to the United States, and sold tax-free to distributors has grown astronomically. It has been estimated that up to 90 percent of the Canadian cigarettes shipped legally to the United States are then illegally smuggled back into Canada in order to avoid Canadian taxes.

An analysis of the effects of the cigarette tax on the Canadian cigarette market can be conducted using the supply and demand model shown in Figure 1. Assuming there is no black market activity, the demand curve for cigarettes in Canada is D_0 and the supply curve is S_0. We have drawn the supply curve as perfectly elastic, assuming that Canadian cigarette manufacturers will supply all the cigarettes demanded at the price P_0. With no tax on cigarettes, the quantity consumed is Q_0 and the price is P_0. When a tax is imposed, the supply curve shifts upward the amount of the tax and becomes $S_0 + tax$. The equilibrium quantity is reduced to Q_1 at price P_1. The shaded area represents the tax revenue collected by the government.

Organized-crime gangs smuggle cigarettes into Canada through Mohawk Indian reservations along the U.S.-Canadian border. These gangs sell to consumers who decide to purchase the less expensive smuggled cigarettes to avoid the Canadian tax. This reduces the demand for cigarettes in the legal market. Therefore, fewer legally taxed cigarettes are sold, decreasing the government's tax revenue.

The Canadian government is now lowering the tax on cigarettes in an effort to stop the illegal smuggling. The lower price of legal cigarettes decreases the incentive for consumers to buy illegal cigarettes. An analysis of the illegal market is demonstrated with the supply and demand model shown in Figure 2. The demand curve for cigarettes in the black market is D_1, and the supply curve is S_1. The equilibrium quantity consumed is Q_2, and the price is P_2. The tax cut lowers the price of legal cigarettes—a substitute—thus lowering the black market's demand to D_2. The quantity of illegally sold cigarettes falls to Q_3.

The export levy raises the cost of first exporting cigarettes to the United States and then smuggling them back into Canada. In addition, strengthening the enforcement of smuggling laws creates a cost to the smugglers, which must be added to their other costs. In Figure 2, the cost of breaking the law (*CBL*) represents increased costs of smuggling, shifting the supply curve to $S_1 + CBL$. With demand at D_2, the price increases to P_3 and the quantity falls to Q_4. The amount the price increases depends on how severe the penalty for smuggling cigarettes into Canada is and how effectively the law is enforced. The higher price decreases the incentive for consumers to purchase smuggled cigarettes.

The ultimate impact depends on the ability of the smugglers to continue to profit. The tax reduction along with the added export levy—a tax on exports—will allow the Canadian government to continue to receive large revenues while decreasing the incentive to smuggle. Cigarette manufacturers can profit as much from selling lightly taxed legal cigarettes as they can from exporting cigarettes destined for the black market. However, the export levy does cut into profits and might encourage manufacturers to move production to the United States, costing thousands of Canadian jobs.

If the U.S. government substantially increases its cigarette tax, as Kerrie Wilson suggested, the smuggling of cheaper cigarettes into Canada can be stopped. However, there will be no barrier to prevent duty-free cigarettes from being exported to Mexico and then smuggled back into the United States, possibly creating a problem for the United States similar to the problem experienced by Canada.

FIGURE 1

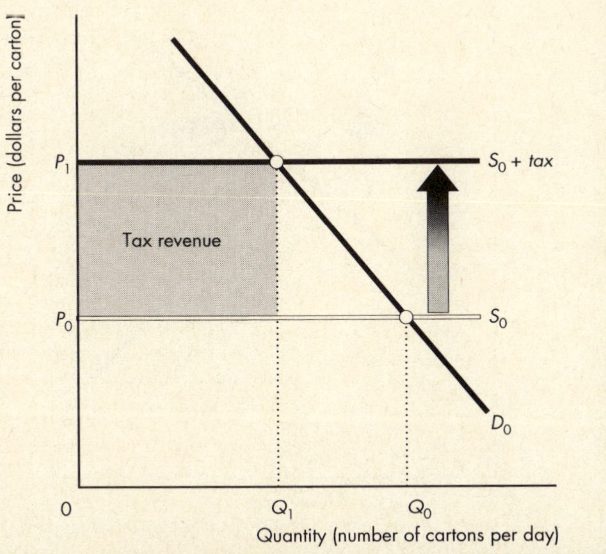

FIGURE 2

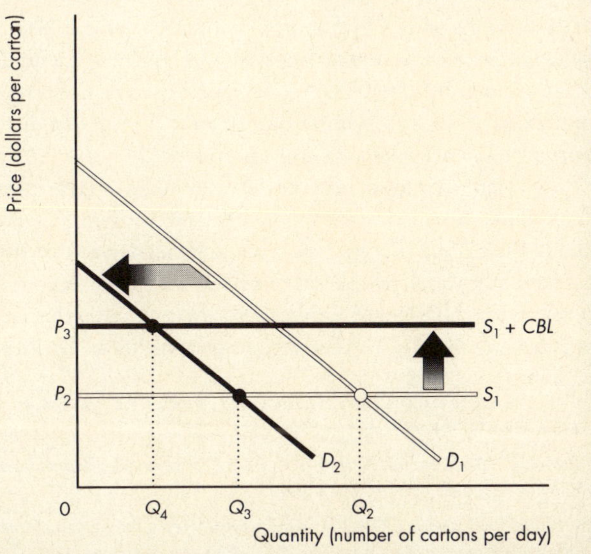

Some Economics of the Illegal Drug Trade

BY MARTIN RICHARDSON

What do Kurt Schmoke (mayor of Baltimore), Milton Friedman (Nobel Prize-winning economist), Richard Cohen (arch-liberal newspaper columnist), and William Buckley Jr. (arch-conservative newspaper columnist) have in common? Probably very little, except that all have suggested that the United States might seriously consider legalizing drugs such as cocaine. While some proponents of legalization take their position for ethical reasons, for others it is a purely practical matter: they contemplate a never-ending, increasingly costly but inevitably futile "war on drugs" and see legalization as a means of both reducing the costs of policing and reducing the violence involved in the distribution of drugs. Opponents of legalization, however, fear that drug use would increase dramatically, with consequent individual and social problems. A big issue, then, is the likely response of demand to legalization.

Demand Effects of Prohibition

There are two reasons why the quantity of drugs demanded might increase, and they are quite separate. As Miron notes in this issue and Parkin notes in Chapter 6, prohibition shifts the supply curve up, so legalization, by shifting it back down, would bring down the price of drugs—and the quantity demanded, like that of any good whose price falls, would increase. Second, prohibition shifts the demand curve down, so legalization would be expected to shift it back up. Using Miron's Figure 1 on page 8, you can see the effects of legalization as a shift in supply from S_1 to S_0 and a shift in demand from D_1 to D_0.

Parkin notes on p. 144 that prohibition sends a signal that may influence preferences. Interestingly, Milton Friedman has argued that there may be a "forbidden fruit" aspect to some drug consumption, which is an example of such an effect, but one that is working to increase demand under prohibition!

How might one try to estimate the magnitudes of these effects? Economists have made some serious efforts recently to get some idea of these effects, but the task is very difficult. Given that the entire trade is illegal, reliable data are hard to come by. Accordingly, researchers have looked at other addictive substances that are legal in order to see if the same arguments apply there. One study of cigarette consumption[1] found a short-run (one-year) price elasticity of demand of -0.4 but a long-run elasticity of between -0.7 and -0.8, which is substantially larger. Another study[2] looked at gambling behavior at U.S. horse racetracks, taking "consumption" to be the real amount bet per person at the track and "price" to be the fraction of the total amount bet that is retained by the track. This study also found a long run elasticity of around -0.7, more than double the short-run elasticity of -0.3. Similar results have been obtained regarding alcohol consumption.

These studies can tell us something about the steepness or flatness of a given demand curve. But what about the shift of the entire curve? This shift might seem impossible to measure but again, we can learn by considering similar episodes in similar markets. A recent study of alcohol consumption during Prohibition[3] is interesting in this regard, as it seems to lend some support to Friedman's "forbidden fruit" hypothesis. The initial effect of Prohibition in 1920 was a very sharp decrease in per-capita alcohol consumption. However, consumption then increased steadily every year until Prohibition was repealed in 1933. Interestingly, repeal itself seems to have had little impact on consumption levels: the average over the period 1937–40 was about the same as it was during the last years of Prohibition. This behavior can be described by the demand and supply for alcohol, illustrated in Figure 1. Prohibition decreases the supply of alcohol, shifting the supply curve from S_0 to S_1 and changing the equilibrium from point *a* to point *b*. This results in a decrease in quantity consumed, from Q_a to Q_b; and an increase in price, from P_a to P_b.

FIGURE 1

The Effect of Prohibition on the Demand and Supply for Alcohol

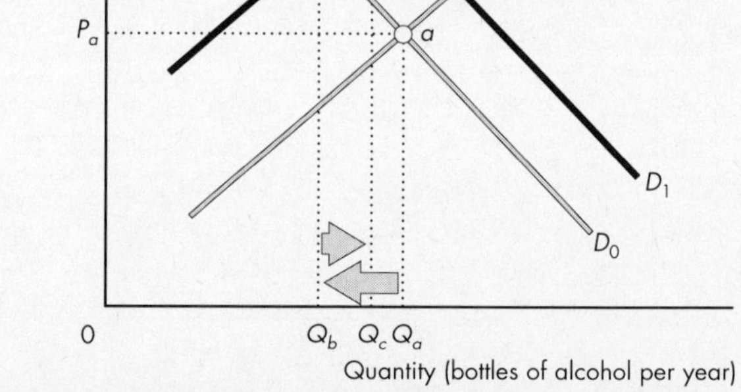

[1] G. Becker, M. Grossman, and K. Murphy, "An Empirical Analysis of Cigarette Addiction," NBER Working Paper No. 3322, 1990.

[2] P. Mobilia, "An Economic Analysis of Addictive Behavior: The Case of Gambling," Ph.D. dissertation, CUNY, 1990.

[3] J. Miron and J. Zwiebel, "Alcohol Consumption During Prohibition," *American Economic Review,* 81 (2), pp. 242–247, 1991.

However, "forbidden fruit" behavior increases the demand for alcohol, shifting the demand curve from D_0 to D_1, with a new equilibrium at point *c*. An even higher price level (P_c) results, but the quantity consumed (Q_c) becomes only slightly smaller than before Prohibition. Empirical evidence from the period supports this account. The authors calculate that if all changes in the quantity of alcohol consumed were due solely to price changes (movement along a given demand curve), the elasticity would have a very small value of -0.1. In light of the other studies mentioned above, it is implausible that the demand curve would be so steep.

The Market Structure for Illegal Drugs

Estimates of demand elasticities can also tell us something about supply conditions in a market. Suppose that demand elasticities of -0.7 to -0.8 are accurate estimates for currently illegal drugs. Although these numbers might be higher than initially thought, a demand curve with an elasticity of -0.8 is still termed "inelastic." Accordingly, we know that the market for illegal drugs must be fairly competitive. How? Well, suppose it were monopolized (or operated by a very collusive cartel). We know that a profit-maximizing monopolist equates *marginal revenue* and *marginal cost* to determine the quantity to sell and the price to charge. This profit-maximizing point occurs on the elastic portion of the demand curve (i.e., where the absolute value of the elasticity is greater than 1). Thus an elasticity of -0.8 is inconsistent with monopoly behavior.

Indeed, at the street level the distribution of drugs seems quite competitive (as opposed to the middleman tier, which is more or less cartelized), and it's this competition that leads to one of the most obvious social problems of the drug business: violence. While there are many instances where this violence claims innocent victims and the lives of law enforcement officers, most of the violence is between dealers or dealers' gangs. In economic terms it stems from *rent-seeking* behavior, which is behavior motivated by efforts to capture *economic rents*. Rent seeking is observed in many areas of economic activity and is generally considered to be socially wasteful in that it draws real resources away from productive activities, but it is doubly bad in the illicit drug market because of its extreme nature. Artificial restriction of the supply of a good raises its price and creates economic rents in the market for that good. In the case of drugs, the restriction is their prohibition, and we observe nonprice competition between dealers in the form of violence, so a part of the monetary return to drug dealing can be thought of as compensation for the risk of being a victim of this violence. If entry into dealing were totally free, we would expect to see the economic profit of dealers driven to zero once the costs of violence were allowed for. Of course, we see nonprice competition in many industries, and one might wonder why its form is so extreme in the case of illegal drugs. The answer is simply that other forms (such as advertising) are unavailable, for obvious reasons! One of the gains of legalization, proponents argue, is that by removing economic rents from dealing, legalization would remove rent-seeking behavior and thus remove the incentive for a lot of the violence currently endemic in many of our cities.

Legalization and Regulation of Cocaine

One final issue is of some interest from an economist's perspective. Whereas an economist's solution to the legalization debate would generally involve a compromise that trades off costs and benefits of legalization, the public debate and the U.S. position of "zero tolerance" clearly do not admit such a trade-off. One possible solution, is to legalize drugs but tax and regulate them so heavily as to mitigate the undesirable effect of increased drug use. The question then arises of whether we can find a combination of legalization and taxation that leaves consumption *unchanged* from its prohibition levels, and so involves no tradeoff between greater use and decreased enforcement. Although in the context of the analysis of the textbook in Chapter 6 the answer to this question is "yes," if we modify that model to allow for the continuing incentive to pursue illegal trade (and so avoid taxes) the answer becomes "no": there is no legalization policy and non-trivial regulation that can abolish all illegal trade!

Of course, evasion is a problem with any form of restriction in any market. Very often it is not dealt with explicitly, the supposition being that it is minor. However, in the issue of drug legalization it is a major concern. Illicit channels for drug dealing are well established, and the apparent gains are large. So we must consider the incentives to operate illegally that still exist after legalization. A simple economic model will illustrate the situation.

Supply and Demand for Cocaine

Let's think about the market for cocaine. We start by noting that the government undertakes some efforts to prevent illegal cocaine flows, and so it incurs some costs of enforcement. The greater are such expenditures, presumably the greater is the proportion of illegal drugs that the government intercepts, *ceteris paribus,* but it is likely that this effort suffers diminishing returns in that increased success comes at higher and higher cost as expenditures rise. That is, it might be quite easy to capture a small percentage of illegal drugs, but increasing the capture rate becomes increasingly expensive as more difficult routes must be exposed, and so on.

It also seems reasonable to suppose that the likelihood of detection of illicit drugs increases with the total volume of unlawfully trafficked drugs and at an increasing rate. That is, for a given level of enforcement, if very few drugs are traded, they are unlikely to be detected, but as the volume increases, an increasing percentage will be intercepted. If we denote by x the fraction of illegal drugs actually detected, then x depends positively both on the total volume of unlawfully trafficked drugs and on enforcement expenditures. Only the fraction $1-x$ of any illegally trafficked drugs actually reach consumers.

The demand curve for cocaine determines the total quantity consumed as a function of the price paid by the final user of the cocaine. Let's suppose that consumers are willing to pay prices shown by demand curve *D* in Figure 2; this curve corresponds to curve *D* in Figure 6.9 of the Parkin text. On the supply side, the profit-maximizing dealer will choose the volume of trade so that the marginal cost of smuggling another gram equals the marginal revenue. We are used to thinking of competitive behavior as meaning price-taking behavior, as each producer is too small to affect the price of the good, which depends on total sales. In this context, the same presumption also implies that each producer takes the risk of detection, *x*, as given, as it too depends on total sales. If traffickers are caught, not only is their cocaine confiscated but they also incur an additional penalty for every gram intercepted. Furthermore, smugglers will not earn any revenue on the confiscated fraction *x*, and this forgone revenue is an opportunity cost. The marginal cost of smuggling another gram, then, is the cost of production, which we shall assume to be constant per unit at *ATC*, *plus x* (the fraction of smuggled units that are detected by the authorities) times both the price of a gram of cocaine and the fine on units detected. For a price-taking firm, the marginal revenue is simply the price of a gram of cocaine.

Figure 2 shows this industry supply curve for the total quantity of cocaine trafficked as S_T, which is upward-sloping because *x* increases as the volume of trade rises: dealers are willing to supply more only if the price rises, because the risk of interception increases with the volume of trade. Recall however, that for any quantity shipped illegally, only a fraction $1-x$ will reach consumers. The actual supply to consumers, then, is a fraction $1-x$ of S_T, which is represented by the curve labeled S_C. This curve corresponds to the supply curve *S* in the text's Figure 6.9.

To find our overall equilibrium, consider the present case in which all trade is illegal. Equlibrium occurs at point *b*, where the demand for cocaine equals the supply that reaches consumers. Consumers pay a price P_0 and consume Q_b grams of cocaine. Note that at price P_0, Q_a grams are actually produced and trafficked, corresponding to point *a*. However, only $Q_b = (1-x)Q_a$ goes undetected by authorities. The price is just sufficiently in excess of the production cost per unit, *ATC*, to compensate sellers for the costs of detection.

Legalizing and Taxing Cocaine

Now consider legalization of the trade combined with a tax designed to maintain the same quantity of drugs reaching final users. Legalization alone would mean that producers face the demand curve *D* and have a marginal cost of *ATC* only. Thus, in Figure 3 below, point *c* becomes the equilibrium. The price would fall to P_c and consumption would increase to Q_c. Now consider the effects of no illegal trade but a tax of $(P_0 - P_c)$ per gram, described by the supply curve S_C. At point *b* the quantity consumed decreases to Q_b and the consumer price increases to P_0. The producer price remains at $P_c = ATC$.

However, this cannot be an equilibrium, as there is still an incentive to pursue illegal trade to avoid the tax. If enforcement expenditures remained unchanged, then a supplier would perceive that selling 1 unit of the good illegally, on top of the exist-

FIGURE 2

Equilibrium in the Cocaine Market under Prohibition

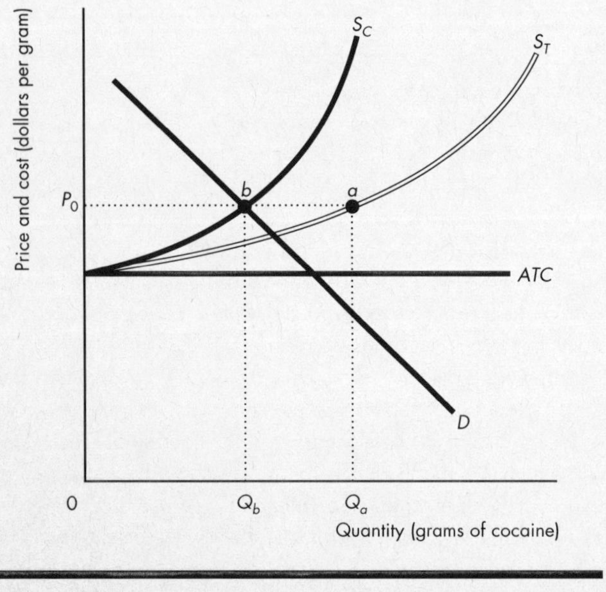

FIGURE 3

Equilibrium with Legalization and Taxation of Cocaine

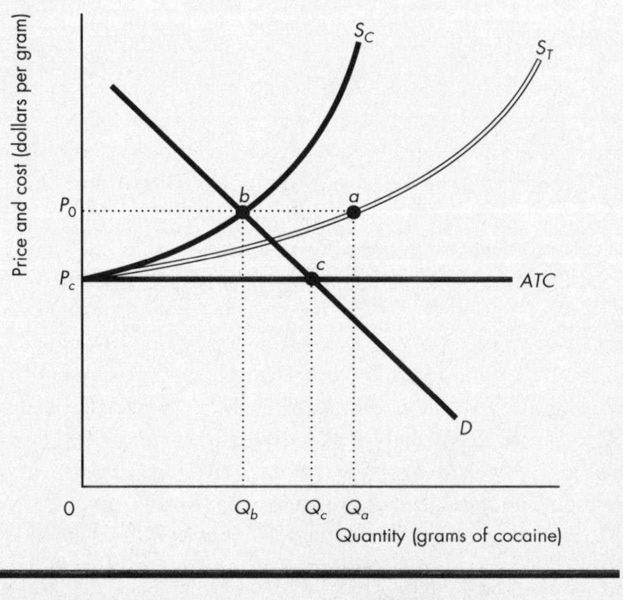

ing legal trade, would earn a price P_0 but would cost only a little over P_c. When there's only 1 illegal unit, the probability of detection is very small so the expected costs of detection are also very small. This trade is profitable, then, so illegal trade would continue. In fact, if the tax were left at $P_0 - P_c$, we would observe no legal trade at all! The reason is that illegal trade drives down the consumer price, making legal trade, subject to tax, loss-making. With the tax in place, we'd get exactly the same outcome as before the tax—total illegal trade of Q_a, with Q_b reaching consumers at a price P_0—and no incentive to operate any legal trade.

Legalizing and Licensing Cocaine

Let's consider one final policy option: licensing. Suppose that cocaine is legalized but the legal quantity is restricted by the issuance of licenses. In order to sell a gram of cocaine, say, a seller needs a license, and licenses are restricted in number. Can we control total consumption by only issuing licenses for a quantity Q_b? Well, the problem of illegal sales will still be with us in this case.

On the supply side, if Q units are sold overall, of which Q_b are sold legally, then x, the chance of detection, depends now on $Q - Q_b$, the volume of illegal sales. So penalties are incurred only when the total trade exceeds Q_b, the legal amount, and the *overall* supply curve of cocaine will be given by the curve S_{TL} in Figure 4, rather than S_T in Figures 2 and 3. We have left S_T out of Figure 4 to avoid cluttering the diagram, but note that S_{TL} is just S_T shifted horizontally to the right by the amount of legal trade. Of course, only a fraction $1 - x$ of amounts in excess of Q_b will actually reach consumers, so the effective supply to consumers is now S_{CL}. (Again, S_C has been left out of the diagram, but S_{CL} is just S_C shifted to the right by the amount of legal trade.) Equating the marginal cost (S_{CL}) with the price (from D), we get a total quantity delivered to consumers of Q_d of which $Q_d - Q_b$ is illegal. Consumers are willing to pay a price P_d for this quantity, and so this is the equilibrium price for all sales, legal or not.

Thus the license policy is even less effective at controlling total consumption than the tax policy. Note, finally, that the lucky sellers who are given licenses to sell legally will make an economic rent equal to $P_d - ATC$ on each legal unit sold. Alternatively, if the government were to auction off these licenses, it might be surprised to find that, instead of receiving a price $P_0 - ATC$ for each one, it would receive $P_d - ATC$; the existence of illegal trade has made legal trade less rewarding.

FIGURE 4

Equilibrium with Legalization and Licensing of Cocaine

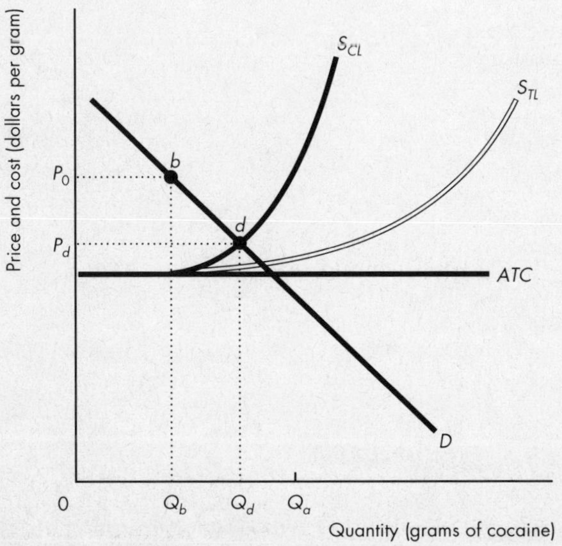

◆ *Martin Richardson, Assistant Professor of Economics at Georgetown University, received his Ph.D. from Princeton University. His fields of interest include international trade theory (political economy of protection, commercial policy, and preferential trading areas) and public finance.*

SEE ALSO

Chapter 4	Demand and Supply
Chapter 5	Elasticity
Chapter 6	Markets in Action
Chapter 10	Output and Costs
Chapter 12	Monopoly
Chapter 13	Monopolistic Competition and Oligopoly

Record Shrinkage Rate

Philip K. Way

BILLBOARD, March 12, 1994

Shrinkage Rising at Music Stores, NRSS Study Says

BY TERRI HORAK

NEW YORK—Recorded music/video retailers have the third-highest percentage rate of shrinkage to sales among all retailers, according to the 1993 National Retail Security Survey.

The study found that the percentage of shrinkage to sales for music/video retailers rose to 2.67% for 1992 from 2% in 1991.

Correspondingly, recorded music/video retailers applied just 0.53% of their total sales in 1992 to loss prevention. This figure is down from 0.84% in the previous year's study.

For companies with more than $100 million in sales, the NRSS study found that music/video retailers employed 18.1 people in loss prevention. This is considerably higher than the average of 12.7 employees for all retailers. In 1991, music/video retailers employed an average of 28 employees in their loss-prevention departments.

Retailers across all categories reported that 1.88% of their annual sales were lost to shrinkage, over 1.91% in 1991.

A similar study by the National Association of Recording Merchandisers found that music/video retailers with more than $20 million in annual sales had a 2.4% average of shrinkage to sales in 1992. The same year, companies with $1 million–$20 million in sales reported shrinkage of 1.4%, and companies with under $1 million in sales had shrinkage of 1.31%, according to the NARM study.

The NRSS study found that the prosecution rate for shoplifters apprehended in the music/video category was 60.3% in 1992. Less than half of the shoplifters apprehended were prosecuted in the previous year. The prosecution rate for employees caught stealing was 26.6% in 1992.

While music/video retailers had the third-highest rate of shrinkage to sales, jewelry/optical was the highest category, with 4.93%; auto parts stores had the second-highest percentage, 3.07%. The retailer category with the lowest percentage of shrinkage to sales was cameras/photos, at 0.55%.

Respondents believed internal theft to be the largest source of shrinkage, accounting for 40.7%.

Shoplifting was the next highest source, at 33.7%. Administrative errors accounted for 18.2%, and 7.4% of the shrinkage was attributed to vendor fraud.

The study also examined 52 loss-prevention strategies, which were grouped into four classifications: pre-employment integrity screening measures, employee awareness programs, asset control policies, and loss-prevention systems.

Asset control policies were the most frequently used strategy, with more than 75% of the firms requiring at least three specific types (refund controls, void controls, and merchandise receiving).

Less than half of the potential integrity screening methods were used by more than one-third of the survey respondents. Further, there were considerable differences in the use of these measures, depending on the position being filled.

A considerable number of respondents said they would be increasing pre-employment integrity screening measures this year. The top screening methods expected to increase this year are criminal conviction checks, past employment checks, credit checks, and multiple interviews.

The survey of 386 companies was directed by the University of Florida Center for Retailing Education and Research, with additional research provided by the National Retail Federation and Loss Prevention Specialists. The study was sponsored by Sensormatic Electronics Corporation.

The Essence of the Story

Shrinkage in the music/video retailing industry is caused mainly by internal theft, shoplifting, administrative error, and vendor fraud.

Music/video retailers had a ratio of shrinkage to sales of 2.67 percent in 1992, an increase over 1991, and the third highest in the retail sector. The shrinkage rate tended to increase as sales increased.

Although music/video retailers employed more loss prevention staff than did other retailers, their loss prevention expenditures relative to sales declined in 1992. Asset control measures were the most popular method of loss prevention.

FIGURE 1

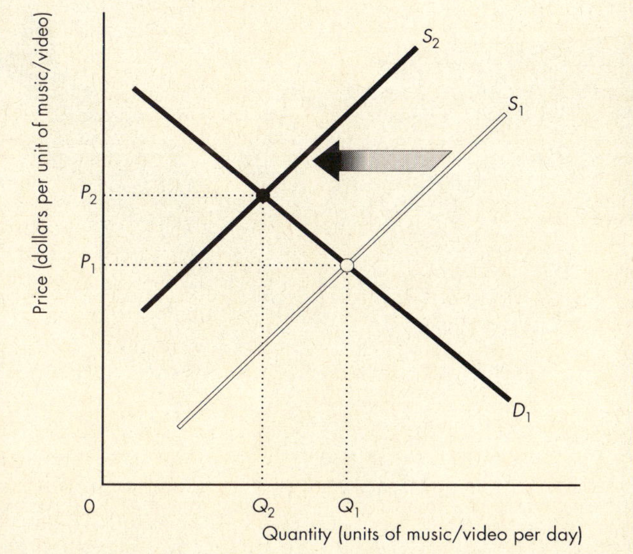

FIGURE 2

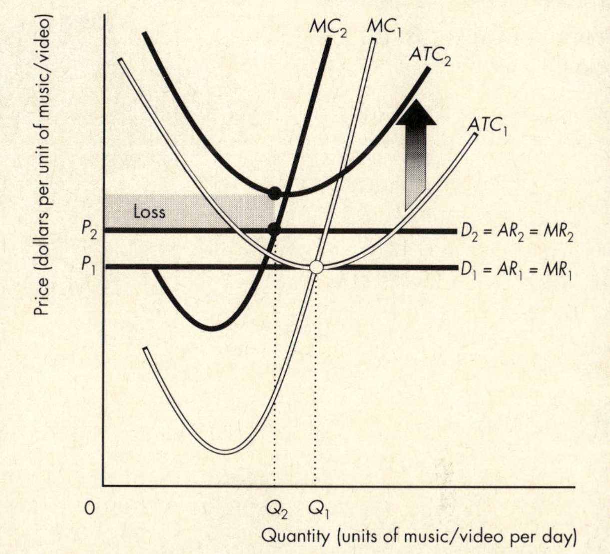

Background and Analysis

The music/video retail industry is best approximated by perfect competition because there are many retailers and consumers, the selection of music sold is quite similar, there is reasonably good information about the prices charged by each retailer, and entry and exit are not abnormally difficult as fixed costs are relatively low.

In the diagram of the music/video retail industry in Figure 1, the 1991 demand (D_1) and supply (S_1) curves are shown, and the equilibrium price and quantity of music/videos traded are marked as P_1 and Q_1.

Figure 2 shows the marginal cost (MC_1) and average total cost (ATC_1) curves of a typical store for 1991, as well as the demand (D_1), marginal revenue (MR_1), and average revenue (AR_1) curves, assuming that no profits were earned. Since the store is a price-taker, the store's equilibrium price, P_1, is the same as the industry price. The store's profit-maximizing output, Q_1, occurs where the marginal cost of production equals the marginal revenue.

Shrinkage costs vary with store sales, so they impact both marginal and average costs. In 1992, when retailers incurred higher shrinkage costs, there was a leftward shift in the supply curve to S_2, shown in Figure 1, with the vertical displacement representing the unit cost increase. This shift raised price to P_2 and reduced output to Q_2. The price increased by less than costs, owing to the slope of the demand curve.

In the representative store, both cost curves shifted up because of the higher variable costs, as shown in Figure 2. The price increased to P_2, reflecting the change in the industry price. Marginal and average revenue therefore rose. The output of the store declined to Q_2.

For stores that were breaking even in 1991, a loss resulted in 1992 because the higher price failed to cover the higher costs: average total cost was greater than average revenue. Some stores shut down in the short run because the price was less than their average variable cost.

To reduce average and variable costs, retailers cut back on their spending on loss prevention. This had the opposite effect, however, of bringing about the higher shrinkage costs cited above.

◆ *Philip K. Way earned a Ph.D. from the University of Warwick and is Associate Professor of Economics at the University of Cincinnati. Way has published widely on current issues in the field of labor.*

SEE ALSO

Chapter 4 Demand and Supply

Chapter 10 Output and Costs

Chapter 11 Competition

Property Crime Rate, 1991

(estimated number of offenses known to police per 100,000 population)

Property crimes are offenses of burglary, larceny-theft, and motor vehicle theft. Data for the property crime of arson are not included.

- Under 4000
- 4000–5000
- Over 5000

Source: Crime in the United States, 1991, U.S. Department of Justice, Federal Bureau of Investigation (Washington, D.C.: USPGO, 1992).

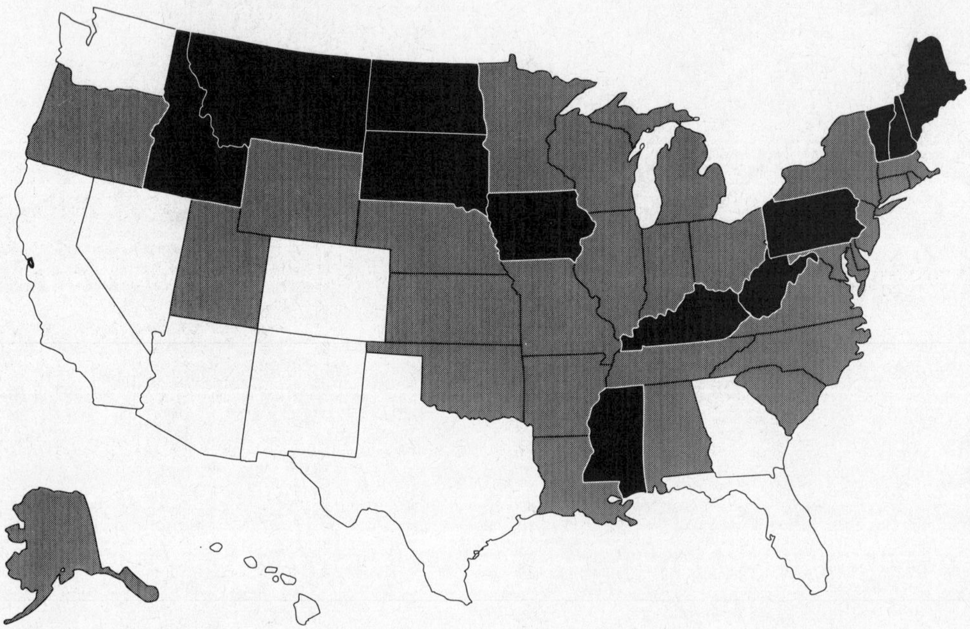

State and Local Justice System Expenditures, 1990

(dollars per capita)

- Under $200
- $200–$300
- Over $300

Source: Justice Expenditure and Employment in the U.S., 1990, U.S. Department of Justice, Bureau of Justice Statistics (Washington, D.C.: USPGO, forthcoming).

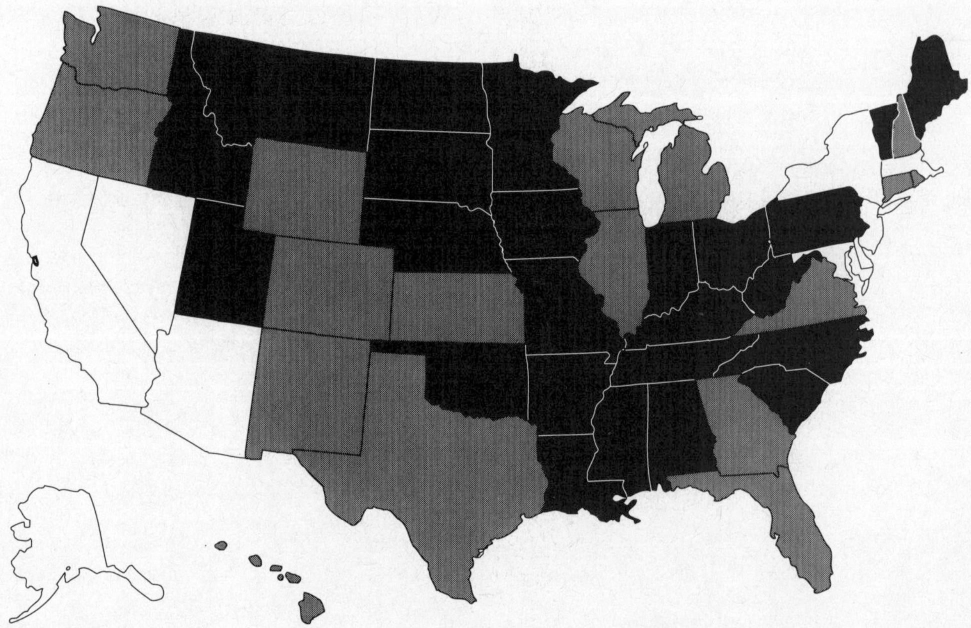

MACROECONOMICS

SECOND EDITION

UPDATED EDITION

MACROECONOMICS

SECOND EDITION

MICHAEL PARKIN

UNIVERSITY
OF
WESTERN ONTARIO

ADDISON-WESLEY
PUBLISHING COMPANY

READING, MASSACHUSETTS ◆ MENLO PARK, CALIFORNIA ◆ NEW YORK
DON MILLS, ONTARIO ◆ WOKINGHAM, ENGLAND ◆ AMSTERDAM
BONN ◆ SYDNEY ◆ SINGAPORE ◆ TOKYO
MADRID ◆ SAN JUAN ◆ MILAN ◆ PARIS

Library of Congress Cataloging-in-Publication Data

Parkin, Michael, 1939–
Macroeconomics / Michael Parkin.—Updated 2nd ed.
p. cm.
Includes index.
ISBN 0-201-50033-7
1. Macroeconomics. I. Title.
HB172.5.P36 1994
339—dc20 93-46052
CIP

Executive Editor: **Barbara Rifkind**
Senior Sponsoring Editor: **Marjorie Williams**
Senior Development Editor: **Marilyn R. Freedman**
Production Supervisor: **Loren Hilgenhurst Stevens**
Managing Editor: **Kazia Navas**
Cover Design Director: **Peter M. Blaiwas**
Cover Design Associate: **Eileen R. Hoff**
Cover and Interior Designer: **Karen Gourley-Lehman**
Art and Design Coordinator: **Meredith Nightingale**
Art Development Editor: **Kelley Hersey, Focus Design**
Technical Art Supervisor: **Joseph Vetere**
Technical Art Consultants: **Loretta Bailey and Dick Morton**
Art Coordinators: **Janice Alden Mello and Connie Hulse**
Illustrators: **TSI Graphics**
Electronic Vignettes: **Frank Mazzola, Jr., Raffaele Delicata Design, and Thomas Vanin-Bishop, Ampersand Studios**
Photo Researchers: **Pembroke Herbert and Sandi Rygiel, Picture Research Consultants**
Prepress Services Manager: **Sarah McCracken**
Assistant Editor: **Kari Heen**
Special Project Manager: **Cindy Johnson**
Copyeditor: **Barbara Willette**
Production Services: **Jane Hoover, Lifland et al., Bookmakers, and Sarah Hallet Corey**
Layout Artists: **Jane Hoover and Karen Gourley-Lehman**
Permissions Editor: **Mary Dyer**
Indexer: **Alexandra Nickerson**
Manufacturing Supervisor: **Roy Logan**
Senior Marketing Manager: **David Theisen**
Creative Services Manager: **Eileen Spingler**
Compositor: **Black Dot Graphics**
Color Separator: **Black Dot Graphics**
Printer: **R. R. Donnelley & Sons Company**

Printed in the United States of America.
3 4 5 6 7 8 9-DO-97969594

Text and photo credits appear on page xvii, which constitutes a continuation of the copyright page.

To Robin

About Michael Parkin

Michael Parkin received his training as an economist at the Universities of Leicester and Essex in England. Currently in the Department of Economics at the University of Western Ontario, Canada, Professor Parkin has held faculty appointments at Brown University, the University of Manchester, and the University of Essex. He has served on the editorial boards of the *American Economic Review* and the *Journal of Monetary Economics* and as managing editor of the *Canadian Journal of Economics*. He is the author of *Macroeconomics* (Prentice-Hall). Professor Parkin's research on macroeconomics, monetary economics, and international economics has resulted in 160 publications in journals and edited volumes, including the *American Economic Review*, the *Journal of Political Economy*, the *Review of Economic Studies*, the *Journal of Monetary Economics*, and the *Journal of Money, Credit and Banking*. It became most visible to the public with his work on inflation that discredited the use of wage and price controls. Michael Parkin also spearheaded the movement toward European monetary union. Professor Parkin is an experienced and dedicated teacher of introductory economics.

PREFACE

TO CHANGE THE WAY STUDENTS SEE THE world—this is my purpose in teaching economics and has remained my goal in preparing this revision. There is no greater satisfaction for a teacher than sharing the joy of students who have come to understand the powerful lessons of the economic approach. But these lessons are not easy to master. Every day in my classroom, I relearn the challenges of gaining the insights that we call the economist's way of thinking and recall my own early struggles to master this discipline. In preparing this revision, I have been able to draw on the experiences not only of my own students, but also of hundreds of users of the first edition, both instructors and their students.

Three assumptions have guided the choices that faced me in writing this book. First, students are eager to learn, but they are overwhelmed by the seemingly endless claims on their time and energy. Therefore they want to know why they are being asked to study a particular body of material and require demonstration of its relevance to their own everyday experience. Second, students expect thoughtful and straightforward explanations, so they can begin to apply the principles they are learning. Third, today's students are more interested in the present and the future than in the past. They want to learn the economics of the 1990s so that, as they enter the twenty-first century, they will be equipped with the principles that will help them understand apparently unpredictable events.

Approach

The core of the principles course has been around for more than 100 years, and other important elements, especially parts of the theory of the firm and Keynesian macroeconomics, have been with us for more than 50 years. But economics has also been developing and changing rapidly during the past few decades. All principles texts pay some attention to these more recent developments, but none has succeeded in integrating the new and traditional. My goal has been to incorporate new ideas—game theory, the modern theory of the firm, information, and public choice—into the body of timeless principles.

The presence of modern topics does not translate into "high level"; nor does it translate into "bias." At every point, I have striven to make recent developments accessible to beginning students. Where these theories are controversial, alternative approaches are presented, evaluated, and compared.

But this book does have a point of view. It is that economics is a serious, lively, and evolving science—a science that seeks to develop a body of theory powerful enough to explain the economic world around us and that pursues its task by building, testing, and rejecting economic models. Where matters are settled, I present what we know; where controversy persists, I present the alternative viewpoints.

The Second Edition Update

Consistent with my desire to keep pace with rapid change in the economic landscape, I have made many changes to bring this special updated edition closer to the student's "real time." For instance, eight of the second edition's "Reading Between the Lines" features have been replaced. Statistics have been updated through 1992. And the Clinton administration's first steps in formulating policy have been included.

Macroeconomics and Changes in the Second Edition

My goals in revising the macroeconomics coverage have been to extend and improve the positive, fact-driven approach of the first edition. I have changed the balance of the coverage of national income accounting (Chapter 6), giving greater prominence to a discussion of the validity of the GDP as a measure of economic well-being. Since the aggregate demand–aggregate supply model is inherently more subtle than the microeconomic demand and supply model, it needs to be explained carefully and clearly. I have simplified and streamlined the initial presentation of aggregate demand–aggregate supply model (Chapter 7) so that students can make effective and immediate use of it. I have also clarified the discussion of the components and workings of the aggregate demand model (in Chapters 8 and 9). In light of the 1991 recession and the ongoing federal deficit, it has become increasingly apparent that an understanding of both fiscal and monetary policy is essential. The role of fiscal policy is thoroughly discussed throughout the text (especially in Chapters 7, 9, 12, and 15) and is illustrated through issues drawn from the 1991 recession. And the role of financial deregulation in the macroeconomy is given enhanced prominence in Chapter 10. The extended coverage of aggregate supply issues has also been thoroughly revised. Today's students care about the issues of productivity and growth, and they will find information on these in Chapter 13. The discussion of inflation as an issue and subject of analysis is now separate from the thorough discussion of expectations (Chapter 14). The coverage of stabilization policy has been revised and extended to include a discussion of the political business cycle. Finally, the coverage of economies in transition has necessarily been completely revised. Chapter 21 provides a framework for understanding events in Eastern Europe, the former Soviet Union, and China as these countries change their economic systems and open their markets to international influences.

Special Features

This second edition, like its predecessor, is packed with special features designed to enhance the learning process.

Art Program

A highly successful innovation in the first edition was the outstanding art program. The art not only was visually attractive and engaging but also communicated the economic principles unambiguously and clearly. We received enormously positive feedback on the art program, confirming our belief that one of the most important tools for economists is graphical analysis and also that this is precisely an area that gives many students much difficulty. In the second edition, we have further refined the data-

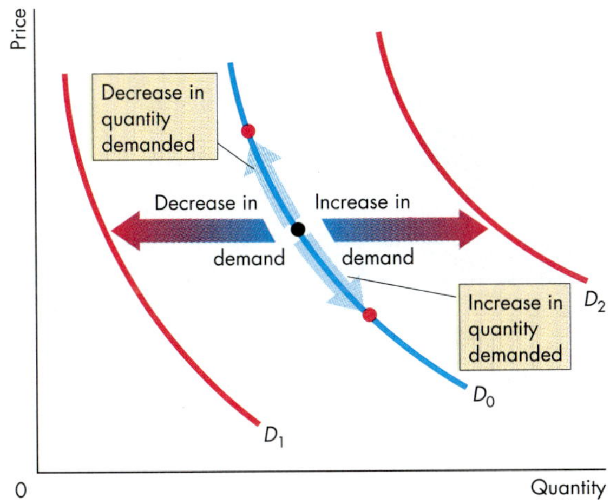

based art by deriving a style that clearly reveals the data and trends. In addition, diagrams that illustrate economic processes now consistently distinguish key economic players (firms, households, governments, and markets).

Our goal is to show clearly "where the economic action is." To achieve this, we observe a consistent protocol in style, notation, and use of color:

- Highlighting shifted curves, points of equilibrium, and the most important features in red
- Using arrows in conjunction with color to lend directional movement to what are usually static presentations
- Pairing graphs with data tables from which the curves have been plotted
- Using color consistently to underscore the content and referring to such use of color in the text and captions
- Labeling key pieces of information in graphs with boxed notes
- Rendering each piece electronically so that precision is achieved

The entire art program has been developed with the study and review needs of the student in mind. We have retained the following features:

- Marking the most important figures and tables with a red key ◆ and listing them at the end of the chapter under "Key Figures and Tables"
- Using complete, informative captions that encapsulate major points in the graph so that students can preview or review the chapter by skimming through the art

The Interviews

Substantive interviews with famous economists constituted another popular feature in the first edition. I am continuing the tradition and have included all new interviews—seven in total—each with an economist who has contributed significantly to advancing the thinking and practice in our discipline. One of the interviews is with Nobel laureate Franco Modigliani. The interviews encourage students to participate in the conversations as the economists discuss their areas of specialization, their unique contributions to economics, and also their general insights that are relevant to beginning students.

Each interview opens one of the book's seven parts and has been carefully edited to be self-contained. Since each interview discusses topics that are introduced formally in the subsequent chapters, students can use it as a preview to some of the terminology and theory they are about to encounter. A more careful reading afterwards will give students a fuller appreciation of the discussion. Finally, the whole series of interviews can be approached as an informal symposium on the subject matter of economics as it is practiced today.

Reading Between the Lines

Another feature of the previous edition that was well received was "Reading Between the Lines." These news article spreads help students to build critical thinking skills and to interpret daily news events (and their coverage in the media) using economic principles. I have updated all of the news articles in this edition and have selected topics that appeal to students, such as falling SAT scores, Nintendo rentals, and the environmental debate over the spotted owl. Each "Reading Between the Lines" spread contains three passes at a story. It begins with a facsimile (usually abbreviated) of an actual newspaper or magazine article. It then presents a digest of the article's essential points. Finally, it provides an economic analysis of the article, based on the economic methods presented in that chapter.

Our Advancing Knowledge

The fully revised "Our Advancing Knowledge" features help students trace the evolution of pathbreaking economic ideas and recognize the universality of their application, not only to the past but to the present. For example, Adam Smith's powerful ideas about the division of labor apply to the creation of a computer chip as well as to the pin factory of the eighteenth century. And Dionysius Lardner's 1850s application of demand and supply theory to railroad pricing applies equally to airline pricing today. A new visual design brings excitement and vitality to these inserts, much in the way that the ideas have brought excitement and vitality to economics.

Learning Aids

We have refined our careful pedagogical plan to ensure that this book complements and reinforces classroom learning. Each chapter contains the following pedagogical elements:

Objectives Each chapter opens with a list of objectives that enable students to set their goals as they begin the chapter.

Chapter Openers Intriguing puzzles, paradoxes, or metaphors frame the important questions that are unraveled and resolved as the chapter progresses.

Highlighted In-Text Reviews Succinct summaries for review are interspersed throughout the chapter at the ends of sections.

Key Terms Highlighted within the text, these concepts form the first part of a three-tiered review of economic vocabulary. These terms are repeated with page references at chapter ends and compiled in the end-of-book glossary.

Key Figures and Tables The most important figures and tables are identified with the red key and listed at chapter end.

End-of-Chapter Study Material Chapters conclude with summaries organized around major headings, lists of key terms with page references, lists of key figures and tables with page references, review questions, and problems. In the second edition, we have added many new problems.

Flexibility

I have tried to accommodate a wide range of teaching approaches by building flexibility and optionality into the book. There are several optional sections, which are indicated by footnote. These may be omitted with no loss of continuity.

The Teaching and Learning Package

Our fully integrated text and supplements package provides students and professors with a seamless teaching and learning experience. The authors of the components are outstanding educators and scholars and have brought their own human capital (and that of their students!) to the job of improving the quality and value of the ancillaries for the second edition.

Study Guide Now available in microeconomics and macroeconomics split versions, the revised Study Guide was prepared by David Spencer of Brigham Young University. Carefully coordinated with the main textbook, each chapter of the Study Guide contains: Chapter in Perspective; Learning Objectives; Helpful Hints; Self-Test (concepts review, true/false, multiple-choice, and short-answer questions, and problems) and Answers to Self-Test; and Key Figures and Tables.

Economics in the News with Video Selections Updated with all new articles, this unique workbook extends the "Reading Between the Lines" feature of the textbook. Prepared by Saul Pleeter (U.S. Department of Defense) and Philip Way of the University of Cincinnati, the supplement includes eighty-five recent news articles organized according to the topical outline of the textbook. An introductory paragraph, learning objectives, and preview precede a facsimile of each article, which is accompanied by analytical questions that give students practice in developing their ability to think like economists. In this edition we have also incorporated ten video excerpts from the MacNeil-Lehrer Business Reports. Just as for the print articles, Pleeter and Way provide a series of probing questions to help students dissect the economic principles that underlie the issues illustrated in the video news clips.

Instructor's Manual for Economics in the News The solutions to questions and problems in Economics in the News are available to instructors upon request from the Business and Economics Group at Addison-Wesley.

Test Item File Thoroughly revised test items were prepared by David Denslow of the University of Florida and Barbara Haney Martinez of the Center for Economic Education at the University of Alaska, Fairbanks. The file includes over 4,000 multiple choice questions, about half of which are new to this edition. All questions have been reviewed carefully for accuracy by Robert Horn and Sharon O'Hare at James Madison University. Each chapter includes a section of questions that are directly from the Study Guide and a section of questions that parallel those in the Study Guide.

Computerized Test Item File Testing software with graphics capability for IBM-PC and compatible microcomputers or Macintosh microcomputers is available to qualified adopters.

Instructor's Manual A brand new Instructor's Manual has been prepared by Mark Rush of the University of Florida. It includes detailed chapter outlines and teaching suggestions; cross-references to the color acetates, videos, and software; answers to all review questions and problems in the textbook; additional discussion questions; information on material new to the second edition; explanations of how each chapter relates to the rest of the book; and a flexibility guide for different course sequences.

Acetates and Overlays Key figures from the text are rendered in full color on the acetates. There are 180 acetates, of which 70 have overlays. The acetates are available to qualified adopters of the textbook (contact your Addison-Wesley sales representative).

MacNeil-Lehrer Business Reports Videos An exclusive from Addison-Wesley, these videos illustrate economic principles in action via highly topical news stories. Ten video selections, split evenly between macroeconomic and microeconomic concepts, can be used in conjunction with either the textbook or the Economics in the News supplement. The videos are free to adopters.

Video Guide to MacNeil-Lehrer Business Reports Helpful teaching notes and discussion questions for using videos in the classroom, as well as relevant graphics prepared as transparency masters, are provided free to adopters.

"Economics in Action" Software New to this edition is truly interactive tutorial software available for both IBM-compatible and Macintosh computers. This software was created specifically for this text by Douglas McTaggart (co-author of the Australian edition of this book) and David Gould of Bond University, Paul Davies of the University of Melbourne, and myself, with a great deal of help from the many people thanked below. The software includes modules on core concepts such as graphing, production possibilities and opportunity cost, demand and supply, elasticity, utility and demand, product curves and cost curves, perfect competition, monopoly, macroeconomic performance, aggregate demand and aggregate supply, expenditure multipliers, money and banking, and international trade.

Three interactive modes take full advantage of the computer's capability to facilitate critical thinking skills. First, a tutorial mode walks students through the central concepts. Second, a quiz mode enables guided self-testing. Third, a free mode allows students and professors to interact with economic models by changing parameters and observing the effects on the graphs. For professors, a special disk is available that extends this capability to generating electronic transparencies for dynamic use in the classroom.

In addition to its emphasis on interaction, the software is also closely integrated with the text. The art style is the same, the terminology is consistent, and supporting material in the text is cross-referenced in the software.

The software has its own authoring language that enables professors to customize tutorials, quizzes, and graphs to fit their own course material. The software has been fully tested and reviewed for accuracy. An Economics in Action Instructor's Guide is available.

Acknowledgments

The endeavor of creating a principles textbook involves the creative collaboration and contribution of many individuals. Although the extent of my debts cannot be fully acknowledged here, it is nevertheless a joy to record my gratitude to the many people who have helped, some without realizing just how helpful they were.

I want to thank those of my colleagues at the University of Western Ontario who have taught me a great deal that can be found in these pages: Jim Davies, Jeremy Greenwood, Ig Horstmann, Peter Howitt, Greg Huffman, David Laidler, Phil Reny, Chris Robinson, John Whalley, and Ron Wonnacott. I want to extend a special thanks to Glenn MacDonald, who worked well beyond the call of duty discussing this project with me from its outset, helping me develop many of the pedagogical features and reading and commenting in detail on all the micro chapters. Special thanks also go to Doug McTaggart of Bond University and Christopher Findlay of the University of Adelaide, co-authors of the Australian edition, and David King, co-author of the European edition. Their suggestions arising from their adaptations of the first edition have been extremely helpful in fine-tuning this edition. More than that, Doug and I worked together on the early drafts of the new chapter on uncertainty and information in the perfect Queensland winter of 1991.

I also want to acknowledge my debt to those who have had a profound influence on my whole view of and approach to economics and whose influence I can see in these pages. Although I never sat in their classrooms, they are in a very real sense my teachers. I am especially grateful to John Carlson (Purdue University), Carl Christ (Johns Hopkins University), Robert Clower (University of South Carolina), Ed Feige (University of Wisconsin at Madison), Herschel Grossman (Brown University), and Sam Wu (University of Iowa). I also want to place on record my enormous debt to the late Karl Brunner. The energy, drive, and entrepreneurship of this outstanding economist provided me and my generation of economists with incredible opportunities to interact and learn from each other in a wide variety of conference settings, in both the United States and Europe.

It is also a pleasure to acknowledge my debt to the several thousand students to whom I have been privileged to teach introductory economics. The instant feedback that comes from the look of puzzlement or enlightenment has taught me, more than anything else, how to teach economics.

Producing a text such as this is a team effort, and the members of the Addison-Wesley "Parkin Team" are genuine co-producers of this book. I am especially grateful to and have been truly inspired by Barbara Rifkind, an extraordinary editor who, as executive editor, created and directed the team with whom it has been a privilege to work. I am also deeply indebted to my development editor, Marilyn Freedman. The personal dedication and professional skill that she brought to the task of crafting the book's broad thrust and fine details and her commitment to making the book as interesting, effective, and error-free as possible were extraordinary. High praise and great thanks go to Loren Hilgenhurst Stevens, who, as production supervisor, coordinated the entire production process, coping calmly and decisively with the cascading crises that daily crossed her desk as she brought all the many complex elements together. Sincere thanks also to Marjorie Williams, who, as senior economics editor, managed and coordinated all the interviews and devised the weekly workload memo that kept my nose pointed firmly in the desired direction; Dave Theisen, business and economics marketing manager, who devised and managed the marketing plan; Kari Heen, assistant editor, whose cheery voice and friendly faxes lifted the sagging spirits in just the right way at just the right time; and especially Cindy Johnson, project manager of the supplements, whose outstanding editorial and managerial skills and personal commitment have brought together a state-of-the-art teaching and learning package. Great thanks go to Loretta Bailey, Janice Mello, Sherry Berg, Sharon Cogdill, Phyllis Coyne, Kelley Hersey, Jane Hoover, Karen Lehman, Stephanie Magean, Dick Morton, Kazia Navas, Meredith Nightingale, and Barbara Willette.

I also wish to express my gratitude to Bob McGough, a superb financial and economics journalist, who provided a thorough and creative edit of an early draft of the first edition and who taught me a great deal about how to write more clearly and effectively. Mark Rush, David Denslow, Barbara Haney Martinez, David Spencer, Saul Pleeter, Phillip Way, Paul Davis, and David Gould were the primary authors of the supplements package and graciously shared their professional insights and teaching expertise with me. I also want to thank my secretary, Barbara Craig, who helped at various stages of this book, typing and retyping its countless drafts and redrafts.

I have left until last four people to whom I want

to give special thanks. First, my wife, colleague, best friend, and co-author of the Canadian edition, Robin Bade, has been almost a co-author of this work. She has read every word that I have written, commented in detail on every draft, and helped manage the project from its conception to its conclusion. Without the anticipation of her help and its availability, I could not have contemplated embarking on this project. Finally, I want to acknowledge the help and inspiration of my children, Catherine, Richard, and Ann. Through the years when I was developing and writing the first edition, they were going through various stages of high school and college. They forced me to craft a book that they could understand and found interesting. In preparing this edition, I have been especially helped by Richard, who became a Harvard Graphics wizard and created the entire art manuscript.

The empirical test of this textbook's value continues to be made in the classroom. I would appreciate hearing from instructors and students about how I might continue to improve the book in future editions.

Michael Parkin
Department of Economics
University of Western Ontario
London, Ontario N6A 5C2

Reviewers

Update Reviews

Gerald McDougall, Southeast Missouri State University
Mark Rush, University of Florida

Manuscript Reviews

Ronald M. Ayers, University of Texas at San Antonio
Mohsen Bahmani-Oskooee, University of Wisconsin–Milwaukee
Charles L. Ballard, Michigan State University
Vanessa Craft, Bentley College
Ronald E. Crowe, University of Central Florida
Shirley J. Gedeon, The University of Vermont
James Robert Gillette, Texas A&M University
John W. Graham, Rutgers—The State University of New Jersey, Newark Campus
James H. Holcomb, The University of Texas at El Paso
Robert N. Horn, James Madison University
Noreen E. Lephardt, Marquette University
Steven J. Matusz, Michigan State University
J. M. Pogodzinski, San Jose State University
James E. Price, Syracuse University
Jonathan B. Pritchett, Tulane University
Christine Rider, St. John's University
Richard Rosenberg, Pennsylvania State University
Peter Rupert, State University of New York at Buffalo

Planning Reviews

Mary E. Allender, University of Portland
Philip J. Grossman, Wayne State University
Bruce Herrick and members of the Department of Economics, Washington and Lee University
Andrew Kliman, New York Institute of Technology
M. L. Livingston, University of Northern Colorado
Nan Maxwell, California State University–Hayward
Henry McCarl, University of Alabama at Birmingham
Augustus Shackelford, El Camino College
Eleanor T. von Ende, Texas Tech University
Larry Wimmer, Brigham Young University
Gary Zinn, East Carolina University

Accuracy Reviews

William Aldridge, Shelton State Community College
Donald H. Dutkowsky, Syracuse University
Mark Rush, University of Florida
David Spencer, Brigham Young University

Telephone Interviews

David Abel, Mankato State University
Richard Adelstein, Wesleyan University
Marjorie Baldwin, East Carolina University
Maurice Ballabon, City University of New York, Bernard M. Baruch College
Scott Benson, Jr., Idaho State University
Steven Berry, Yale University
Scott Bloom, North Dakota State University
Mary O. Borg, University of North Florida
Michael Boyd, University of Vermont
Jim Bradley, University of South Carolina
Habtu Braha, Coppin State College
Michael Brun, Illinois State University
Gregory Bush, Suffolk County Community College
Rupert Caine, Onondaga Community College
Fred Carstensen, University of Connecticut

Shirley Cassing, University of Pittsburgh
Cleveland A. Chandler, Sr., Howard University
Larry Chenault, Miami University
Edward Christ, Cabrini College
Donald Coffin, Indiana University
Walter Coleman, Shaw University
James Perry Cover, University of Alabama
Anthony Davies, State University of New York at Albany
Edward A. Day, University of Central Florida
Larry DeBrock, University of Illinois at Urbana-Champaign
David Denslow, University of Florida
Johan Deprez, Texas Tech University
Frances Durbin, University of Delaware
John Eastwood, Northern Arizona University
David H. Feldman, College of William and Mary
David Ferrell, Central College
Warren Ford, North Shore Community College
Joseph Fosu, Western Illinois University
Alwyn Fraser, Atlantic Union College
Arthur Friedberg, Mohawk Valley Community College
Joseph Fuhrig, Golden Gate University
Ena Garland, Babson College
Gasper Garofalo, University of Akron
Maria Giuili, Diablo Valley College
Marsha Goldfarb, University of Maryland, Baltimore County
Mary Goldschmid, College of Mount Saint Vincent
Lawrence Gwinn, Wittenberg University
Anthony Gyapong, Wayne State University
Ahsan Habib, Adrian College
Steven Henson, Western Washington University
Carter Hill, Louisiana State University
Basawaraj Hiremath, Fisk University
Chris W. Holmes, Bainbridge College
Soloman Honig, Montclair State College
Esmail Hossein-zadeh, Drake University
Sheng Hu, Purdue University
M. G. Inaba, Hofstra University
Wasfy B. Iskander, Rhodes College
Rebecca Janski, Indiana State University
Nancy Jianakoplos, Colorado State University
Holorin Jones, Empire State College
Allen Kelly, Duke University
Jyoti Khanna, Cleveland State University
Shin Kim, Chicago State University
John J. Klein, Georgia State University
Ghanbar Kooti, Albany State College
Julia Lane, American University
Stanley J. Lawson, St. John's University
Dennis Patrick Leyden, University of North Carolina
Y. Joseph Lin, University of California–Riverside
Colin Linsley, St. John Fisher College
Ashley Lyman, University of Idaho
Kathryn Marshall, Ohio University
Robert Marshall, Duke University
Therese McCarty, Union College
David Mirza, Loyola University
Richard Moss, Ricks College
Archontis Pantsios, State University of New York at Binghamton
Sanjay Paul, State University of New York at Buffalo
Richard Payne, Boise State University
Pegg Pelt, Gulf Coast Community College
Robert Pugh, Surry Community College
Jack Railey, Illinois Central College
Victor Rieck, Miami Dade Community College
Debra Rose, Gordon College
Gary Santoni, Ball State University
Phillip Sarver, University of Southern Colorado
George Sawdy, Providence College
Ralph Scott, Hendrix College
Chiqurupati Rama Seshu, State University of New York at New Paltz
Michael Sesnowitz, Kent State University
Larry G. Sgontz, University of Iowa
Steve Shapiro, University of North Florida
B. Ted Stecker, North Hennepin Community College
Andrew Stern, California State University–Long Beach
Gerard Stockhauser, Creighton University
Sue Stockly, University of Texas at Austin
Michael Stoller, State University of New York at Plattsburgh
Scot Stradley, University of North Dakota
Fredrick Tiffany, Wittenberg University
James Vincent, University of St. Thomas
Arthur Welsh, Pennsylvania State University
Bert Wheeler, Liberty University
Chuck Whiteman, University of Iowa
Peter Wilanoski, University of Portland
Patricia Wiswell, Columbia-Greene Community College
Craig Witt, University of Louisville

Credits *(continued from p. iv)*

Part 1: Robert Solow (pp. 1–4), © **L. Barry Hetherington.**

Chapter 1: Pin factory (p. 22), **Culver Pictures.** Woman holding silicon wafer (p. 23), **Tony Stone Worldwide.** Adam Smith (p. 23), **The Bettmann Archive.**

Chapter 4: The railroad suspension bridge near Niagara Falls, anonymous (p. 86), **gift of Maxim Karolik for the M. and M. Karolik Collection of American Paintings, 1815–1865; courtesy Museum of Fine Arts, Boston.** Crowded airport (p. 87), **Steve Proehl/The Image Bank.** Antoine-Augustin Cournot (p. 87), **Historical Pictures/Stock Montage.** Alfred Marshall (p. 87), **Historical Pictures/Stock Montage.**

Part 2: Franco Modigliani (pp. 97–100), © **L. Barry Hetherington.**

Chapter 5: Four teens washing car (p. 151), **Jeffrey Meyers/Stock Boston.** Automatic car wash (p. 151), **Lightstream.** William Petty (p. 151), **The Bettmann Archive.**

Part 3: Allan Meltzer (pp. 184–187), **AP/Wide World Photos.**

Chapter 8: Young couple in kitchen (p. 194), **Peter Menzel/Stock Boston.** College students buying CDs (p. 195), © **John Coletti/The Picture Cube.** John Maynard Keynes (p. 195), **Historical Pictures/Stock Montage.**

Chapter 10: Woman burning marks (p. 268), **UPI/Bettmann.** Woman at ATM (p. 269), **Stock Boston © Doug Cooke.** David Hume (p. 269), **The Bettmann Archive.**

Part 4: Edmund Phelps (pp. 332–335), **Joe Pineiro/Columbia University.**

Chapter 15: NYT headlines, March 6, 1933 (p. 412), **The New York Times.** Crowd outside bank (p. 412), **Franklin D. Roosevelt Library Collection/UPI (ACME)/The Bettmann Archive.** Boarded-up contemporary businesses (p. 413) **Lightstream.** Robert Lucas (p. 413), **Marshall Henrichs/Addison-Wesley.**

Part 5: Andrew F. Brimmer (pp. 417–418), **Brooks Photographers.**

Chapter 16: Kennedy and economic advisors (p. 438), **Walter Bennett/TIME Magazine.** Richard Darman and chart (p. 439), **AP/Wide World Photos.** Milton Friedman (p. 439), **Marshall Henrichs/Addison-Wesley.**

Part 6: Laura Tyson (pp. 469–470), **Jane Scherr/University of California.**

Chapter 18: Nineteenth-century clipper ship card (p. 484), **Museum of the City of New York.** Container ship (p. 485), **Sea-Land Corporation.** David Ricardo (p. 485), **Historical Pictures/Stock Montage.**

Part 7: Jeffrey Sachs (pp. 527–529), **Hank Morgan.**

Chapter 21: Chinese peasant farmers (p. 558), **Mark Riboud/Magnum.** Affluent contemporary Chinese couple (p. 559), **Owen Franken/Stock Boston.** Karl Marx (p. 559), **The Bettmann Archive.**

BRIEF CONTENTS

CONTENTS

PART 1

INTRODUCTION

PART 2

INTRODUCTION TO MACROECONOMICS

PART 3

AGGREGATE DEMAND FLUCTUATIONS

PART 4

Aggregate Supply, Inflation, and Recession

PART 5
MACROECONOMIC POLICY

PART 6

INTERNATIONAL ECONOMICS

PART 7

GROWTH, DEVELOPMENT, AND REFORM

MACROECONOMICS

SECOND EDITION

PART 1

INTRODUCTION

Talking with Robert Solow

Robert M. Solow was born in New York City in 1924. He was an undergraduate and graduate student at Harvard University, where he obtained his Ph.D. in 1951. Professor Solow is an Institute Professor at MIT and has received all the honors possible for his outstanding contributions, including the John Bates Clark Medal (awarded to the best economist under 40) in 1961, President of the Econometrics Society, and President of the American Economics Association. In 1987, he was awarded the Nobel Memorial Prize in Economics. Professor Solow has studied a wide range of problems, including the links between unemployment and inflation, the theory of long-run economic growth, and the role of nonrenewable natural resources. Michael Parkin talked with Professor Solow about some of these issues and the economic landscape of the 1990s.

Professor Solow, why and how did you get into economics?

I grew up during the Depression of the 1930s and went to college in 1940 just before the outbreak of the Second World War. Our economy and our society were functioning badly, so it was hard *not* to be interested in economics. As a freshman and sophomore, I studied a little of all the social sciences. Then I joined the Army. When I came back to the university, I had to choose an area of study. I chose economics because it combined analytical precision with a focus on what seemed the central social problems.

Today there is a lot of anxiety about the prospects for income growth in the United States in the 1990s. Is the anxiety justified?

There is plenty of reason to be anxious about income growth in the 1990s. You only have to look at the 1970s and 1980s to understand why. So far nothing has happened to suggest that the near stagnation of the past two decades will give way to something better. There are no signs of greater investment and no partic-

"It is a fantasy . . . that a handful of space-age engineers simply have to apply themselves . . . to revolutionize civilian technology."

ular reasons to expect the rate of technological progress to improve. Perhaps we will be able to release much of the first-class science and engineering talent that has been used in weapons systems and divert it to advancing civilian technology. But that hasn't happened yet; and when it does happen, there will not be some instantaneous golden age. Good people will eventually produce good results, but it is a fantasy to believe that a handful of space-age engineers simply have to apply themselves in order to revolutionize civilian technology. They will have some old habits to unlearn and new ones to acquire. My guess is that we will scrape along in the 1990s.

Does the same prediction hold true for jobs in the 1990s?

Jobs present an altogether more complicated question. An economy can grow slowly and generate plenty of jobs, and I expect that our economy will do so. There is a lot of talk about whether it will produce "good" jobs. In a sense, the answer is no, if by good jobs one means jobs with good wages and rising wages. On average, incomes will follow productivity. For example, if productivity rises only very slowly, then incomes will also rise only very slowly on the average. I doubt that the range of unemployment rates will be very different from the recent past. So there will be about the usual number of jobs, paying about what productivity will permit.

Remember that it is not quite right to speak of "jobs" as if they are all the same. In the 1980s, Americans with good education and advanced skills did well, even if not quite as well as earlier. It is the uneducated with limited skills who find themselves falling behind, forced to compete with low-wage labor elsewhere.

Does creating jobs inevitably create more inflation? Or can we have steady growth *and* stable prices?

We can probably have reasonably steady growth and reasonably stable prices. The harder question is whether we can do it with a low unemployment rate. I am something of a pessimist here. It seems to me that no one has yet found a way to achieve price stability in an economy that runs along with very little unemployment and excess industrial capacity. Japan may be an exception, but I don't pretend to understand how the Japanese economy works in this respect. Anyway, there is no guarantee that the Japanese secret, if there is one, could be transferred elsewhere. The tendency of modern macroeconomics is to define the problem away, I fear: "low unemployment" *is* whatever is compatible with stable prices. To my mind, the "natural rate of unemployment" is an analytically and empirically flimsy concept. There is room for different models of the way the labor market works, with quite different implications for the understanding of inflation. This is an active subject of research right now.

How should we view international competition from Japan?

I think there are two sides to the Japan problem. The important thing to keep in mind is that no one is forced to buy a Japanese car or VCR. Many Americans do so because they prefer the combination of price and quality. North American manufacturing can get a lot better. It has already started to do so. From that point of view, competition from Japan and Europe is a good thing. Eliminate it and there is danger that our own producers will backslide. Between exchange rate movements and productivity improvements at home, we will come to an equilibrium.

"The various scenarios in which the world economy runs out of resources and then falls into a tailspin are neither valid nor helpful."

I also think that evidence suggests that the Japanese do not play completely by the free-trade rules. I suspect that Japanese institutions, policies, and habits contribute to the large Japanese trade surplus. Of course, a country that saves a lot more than it can invest at home is bound to have a current-account surplus. We should keep pressuring Japan, hard, to abide by the norms. But we should not kid ourselves: the main part of the problem and its solution lie at home.

Has the federal government deficit got in the way of using tax cuts to stimulate our economy?

It certainly has. You can make a case that the Reagan administration intended the massive tax cuts of 1981–1983 to do just that, to leave the federal government without the resources to undertake any positive action at all. There is no doubt that the Congress today feels that there is no elbow room. Some may think that was a good idea. I have no doubt that micromanagement by government is a loser. But I think that passive macroeconomic policy will occasionally get us what we have now—three years of stagnation, apparently to be followed by a period of weak growth.

What is an appropriate goal of macroeconomic policy?

Prolonged budget deficits that persist even when the economy is doing well present a real problem. They are a drain on the national saving, and they imply some combination of low investment and large current-account deficits. So it should be a goal of macroeconomic policy to move toward budget balance or even a surplus, depending on how much we value investment and growth compared with current consumption. But when the economy is weak, when there is plenty of idle labor and capacity, the situation is different. There is no need for investment to displace consumption. There is room for both, and consumption spending stimulates investment. Both fiscal and monetary policy stimuli would be a good thing, even at the expense of a temporary increase in the deficit.

Are there any limits to economic growth? Are we going to run Spaceship Earth out of fuel?

Finding a route to sustainable growth or sustainable development or even to a sustainable state will not be easy. First of all, I think the various scenarios in which the world economy runs

"It may be a mistake to think in terms of Great Unsolved Problems and Sensational Breakthroughs."

out of resources and then falls into a tailspin are neither valid nor helpful. My reading is that they are poor science and poor economics. We are more likely to experience rising costs of fuel and materials than to run out. We simply cannot know what tastes and technology will be like 50 or 100 years from now.

There are, however, plenty of things that people and policy should be concerned with now. Ensure that full environmental costs are reckoned into economic decision making. Impose the taxes or regulations that are needed for efficient long-run use of fish stocks and other renewable resources. Subsidize scientific and technological research that can find or create new materials and energy sources. Help and induce poor countries to control their populations. I really don't think that Doomsday scenarios move us in these directions.

What are the most important economic questions that have not been answered and that the next generation of economists will work on and possibly solve?

It may be a mistake to think in terms of Great Unsolved Problems and Sensational Breakthroughs. Instead, the next generation of economists would be wise to direct themselves toward slowly coming to understand the way the economy works. I have already mentioned the behavior of the labor market as a fertile field for research: flows into and out of employment, how they and the stocks of employed and unemployed workers relate to the level of wages. Those are traditional questions. But more and more data accumulate, and models are improved. A lot of purely technical finger exercises get done on the way.

Another, less traditional, set of questions emerges from growth theory. Once upon a time, it was customary to treat technological change as exogenous. No one believed that, of course, but economics seemed to have little to say about the pace and direction of invention and innovation. It is now fashionable to go a step further and try to understand the allocation of resources to research and development and the payoff to resources invested. It is far from clear that this work will get very far. But it is obviously important, so the effort has to be made.

How would you advise a student to prepare for a career in economics today? What subjects are the most important to study while an undergraduate? Math? History? Politics?

Certainly an undergraduate interested in economics has no choice but to learn a little mathematics. Better to get it done before graduate school. Then some probability, statistics, and econometrics. Those are indispensable research tools. Then what? Almost anything, I would say. These days you meet too many economists who don't seem to know anything else—not history, not literature, not anything. I think anyone would be a better economist for knowing that there are other things in the world. My own favorite, I will admit, is history, especially social history and economic history. What I am hoping for is some grasp of the many ways in which people have managed to organize themselves and their societies, to give some insight into our own.

CHAPTER 1

What Is Economics?

After studying this chapter, you will be able to:

- State the kinds of questions that economics tries to answer
- Explain why all economic questions and economic activity arise from scarcity
- Explain why scarcity forces people to make choices
- Define opportunity cost
- Describe the function and the working parts of an economy
- Distinguish between positive and normative statements
- Explain what is meant by an economic theory and how economic theories are developed by building and testing economic models

I F YOU WANTED TO WATCH A MOVIE IN YOUR HOME IN 1975, you had to rent a movie projector and screen—as well as the movie itself. The cost of such entertainment was as high as that incurred by a theater showing the same movie to several hundred people. Only the rich chose to watch movies in the comfort of their own homes. ◆◆ In 1976, the video cassette recorder (VCR) became available to consumers. Its typical price tag was $2,000 ($4,000 in today's dollars). Even at such a high price, the VCR slashed the cost of home movie watching. Since that time, the price of VCRs has steadily fallen so that today you can buy a reliable machine for $200. A video can be rented for a dollar a day and can be bought for less than $30. In just a few years, watching a movie at home changed from a luxury available to the richest few to an event enjoyed by millions. ◆◆ Advances in technology affect the way we consume. We now watch far more movies at home than we did a decade ago because new technologies have lowered the cost. ◆◆ We hear a great deal these days about lasers. Their most dramatic use is in weapons systems such as those used in "Desert Storm" in 1991. They are also used to guide the machines that bore tunnels and lay pipelines and to align the jigs that build the wings and bodies of modern jet aircraft. But lasers affect us every day. They scan prices at the supermarket checkout. They create holograms on credit cards, making them harder to forge. Neurosurgeons and eye surgeons use them in our hospitals. These advances in technology affect the way we produce.

Choice and Change

Ever-changing technology raises the first big economic question:

How do people choose what to consume and how to produce and how are these choices affected by the discovery of new technologies?

Wages and Earnings

On a crisp, bright winter day on the ski slopes at Aspen, a bronzed 23-year-old instructs some beginning skiers in the snowplow turn. For this pleasant and uncomplicated work, the young man, who quit school after eleventh grade, is paid $10 an hour.

In a lawyer's office in the center of a busy city, a 23-year-old secretary handles a large volume of correspondence, filing, scheduling, and meetings. She arrives home most evenings exhausted. She has a bachelor's degree in English and has taken night courses in computer science and word processing. She receives $8 an hour for her work.

On September 12, 1993, Pete Sampras and Cedric Pioline played a superb tennis match in the men's final of the U.S. Open. At the end of the hard-fought match, the winner—Sampras—received $500,000; Pioline collected only half that amount. A similar phenomenon can be seen in the headquarters of large corporations. Chief executive officers who work no harder (and in some cases even less hard) than the people immediately beneath them receive far higher salaries than their subordinates.

Situations like these raise the second big economic question:

What determines people's incomes and why do some people receive much larger rewards than others whose efforts appear to be similar?

Government, Environment, and Economic Systems

The federal government has grown. At the beginning of this century, it provided law and order and national defense. Today, it provides education, interstate highways, and social security; it regulates the production of food, drugs, and nuclear energy; and it puts satellites into orbit. Tomorrow, if President Clinton is able to implement one of his major campaign promises, it will expand its role even further to provide affordable health care for everyone.

The environment is fragile. Chlorofluorocarbons (CFCs), used as coolants in refrigerators and air conditioners and as cleaning solvents for computer circuits, are believed to damage the atmosphere's protective ozone layer. The burning of coal and oil adds carbon dioxide and other gases to the atmosphere, which prevent infrared radiation from escaping and result in a gradual warming of the planet—the greenhouse effect. The long-term consequences of these two processes might be devastating.

The global economic order is changing dramatically. In Russia and the other countries of Eastern Europe, governments have abandoned central economic planning and begun to sell off or give away state-owned farms and factories. At the same time, these countries have introduced democratic forms of government. The immediate result of these changes was economic chaos. Production and employment fell, and prices increased rapidly. But the goal and hope of these countries is to establish an open and democratic system of government and a type of economic system similar to what we have in the United States.

These facts about government, the environment, and the dramatic changes taking place in Eastern Europe raise the third big economic question:

What is the most effective role for government in economic life and can government help us protect our environment and do as effective a job as private enterprise at producing goods and services?

Unemployment

During the Great Depression, the four years from 1929 to 1933, unemployment afflicted almost one fifth of the labor force in the industrial world. For months and in some cases years on end, many families had no income other than meager payments from the government or from private charities. In the 1950s and 1960s, unemployment rates stayed below 5 percent in most countries and, in some, below 2 percent. During the 1970s and early 1980s, unemployment steadily increased so that by late 1982 and early 1983 almost 11 percent of the U.S. labor force was looking for work. But in 1989, the U.S. unemployment rate had fallen to 5 percent.

Unemployment hurts different groups unequally. When the average unemployment rate in the United States was 7 percent—as it was in 1992—the unemployment rate among young people 16 to 19 years old was 19 percent. But for young black males it was 36 percent. These facts raise the fourth big economic question:

What are the causes of unemployment and why are some groups more severely affected than others?

Inflation

Between August 1945 and July 1946, prices in Hungary rose by an average of 20,000 percent per month. In the worst month, July 1946, they rose 419 quadrillion percent (a quadrillion is the number 1 followed by 15 zeros).

In 1992, the cost of living in Brazil rose by 1,000 percent. This meant that in downtown Rio de Janiero a sandwich that cost 25,000 cruzeiros on January 1 cost 250,000 cruzeiros by the end of the year. That same year, prices rose only 3 percent in the United States. But in the late 1970s, prices in the United States were rising at a rate well in excess of 10 percent a year. These facts raise the fifth big economic question:

Why do prices rise and why do some countries sometimes experience rapid price increases while others have stable prices?

International Trade

In the 1960s, almost all the cars and trucks on the highways of the United States were Fords, Chevrolets, and Chryslers. By the 1980s, Toyotas, Hondas, Volkswagens, and BMWs were a common sight on these same highways. As a matter of fact, in 1990, more than one third of all new cars sold in the United States were imported; in 1950, less than 1 percent were.

Cars are not exceptional. The same can be said of television sets, clothing, and computers.

Governments regulate international trade in cars and in most other commodities. They impose taxes on imports, called tariffs, and also establish quotas, which restrict the quantities that may be imported. These facts raise the sixth big economic question:

What determines the pattern and the volume of trade between nations and what are the effects of tariffs and quotas on international trade?

Wealth and Poverty

At the mouth of the Canton River in southeast China is a small rocky peninsula and a group of islands with virtually no natural resources. But this bare land supports more than five million people who, though not excessively rich, live in rapidly growing abundance. They produce much of the world's fashion goods and electronic components. They are the people of Hong Kong.

On the eastern edge of Africa, bordering the Red Sea, a tract of land a thousand times larger supports a population of 34 million people—only seven times that of Hong Kong. Its people suffer such abject poverty that in 1985 rock singers from Europe and North America organized one of the most spectacular worldwide fund-raising efforts ever seen—Live Aid—to help them. These are the desperate and dying people of Ethiopia.

Hong Kong and Ethiopia, two extremes in income and wealth, are not isolated examples. The poorest two thirds of the world's population consumes less than one fifth of all the things produced. A middle income group accounts for almost one fifth of the world's population and consumes almost one fifth of the world's output. A further one fifth of the world's population—living in rich countries such as the United States, Canada, Western Europe, Japan, Australia, and New Zealand—consumes two thirds of the world's output.

These facts raise the seventh big economic question:

What causes differences in wealth among nations, making the people in some countries rich and those in other countries poor?

These seven big questions provide an overview of economics. They are *big* questions for two reasons. First, they have an enormous influence on the quality of human life. Second, they are hard questions to answer. They generate passionate argument and debate, and just about everybody has an opinion about them. One of the hardest things for students of economics, whether beginners or seasoned practitioners, is to stand clear of the passion and emotion and to approach their work with the detachment, rigor, and objectivity of a scientist.

Later in this chapter, we'll explain how economists try to find answers to economic questions. But before doing that, let's go back to the big questions.

What do these questions have in common? What makes them *economic* questions? What distinguishes them from non-economic questions?

Scarcity

All economic questions arise from a single and inescapable fact: you can't always get what you want. We live in a world of scarcity. An economist defines **scarcity** to mean that wants always exceed the resources available to satisfy them. A child wants a 75¢ can of soft drink and a 50¢ pack of gum but has only $1.00 in her pocket. She experiences scarcity. A student wants to go to a party on Saturday night but also wants to spend that same night catching up on late assignments. He also experiences scarcity. The rich and the poor alike face scarcity. The U.S. government with its $1.4 trillion budget faces scarcity. The total amount that the federal government wants to spend on defense, health, education, welfare, and other services exceeds what it collects in taxes. Even parrots face scarcity—there just aren't enough crackers to go around.

Wants do not simply exceed resources; they are unlimited. People want good health and a long life, material comfort, security, physical and mental recreation, and, finally, an awareness and understanding of themselves and their environment.

None of these wants are satisfied for everyone; and everyone has some unsatisfied wants. While many Americans have all the material comfort they want, many do not. No one feels entirely satisfied with his or her state of health and length of life. No one feels entirely secure, even in this post–Cold War era, and no one—not even the wealthiest person—has the time to enjoy all the travel, vacations, and art that he or she would like. Not even the wisest and most knowledgeable philosopher or scientist knows as much as he or she would like to know.

"Not only do I want a cracker—we all want a cracker!"

Drawing by Modell; © 1985 The New Yorker Magazine, Inc.

We can imagine a world that satisfies people's wants for material comfort and perhaps even security. But we cannot imagine a world in which people live as long and in as good a state of health as they would like. Nor can we imagine people having all the time, energy, and resources to enjoy all the sports, travel, vacations, and art that they would like. Natural resources and human resources—in the form of time, muscle-power, and brain-power—as well as all the dams, highways, buildings, machinery, tools, and other equipment that have been built by past human efforts amount to an enormous heritage, but they are limited. Our unlimited wants will always outstrip the limited resources available to satisfy them.

Economic Activity

The confrontation of unlimited wants with limited resources results in economic activity. **Economic activity** is what people do to cope with scarcity. And **economics** is the study of how people use their limited resources to try to satisfy unlimited wants. Defined in this way, economic activity and economics deal with a wide range of issues and problems. The seven big questions posed earlier are examples of the more important problems that economists study. Let's see how those questions could not arise if resources were infinitely abundant and scarcity did not exist.

With unlimited resources there would be no need to devise better ways of producing more goods. Studying how we all spend our time and effort would not be interesting because we would simply do what we enjoyed without restriction. We would do only the things that we enjoyed because there would be enough goods and services to satisfy everyone without effort. Unemployment would not be an issue because no one would work—except for people who wanted to work simply for the pleasure that it gave them. There would be no wages. Inflation—rising prices—would not be a problem because no one would care about prices. Questions about government intervention in economic life would not arise because there would be no need for government-provided goods and no taxes. We would simply take whatever we wanted from the infinite resources available. There would be no international trade since, with complete abundance, it would be pointless to transport things from one place to another. Finally, differences in wealth among nations would not arise because we would all have as much as we wanted. There would be no such thing as rich and poor countries—all countries would be infinitely wealthy.

You can see that this science fiction world of complete abundance would have no economic questions. It is the universal fact of scarcity that produces economic questions.

Choice

Faced with scarcity, people must make *choices*. When we cannot have everything that we want, we have to choose among the available alternatives. Because scarcity forces us to choose, economics is sometimes called the science of choice—the science that explains the choices that people make and predicts how changes in circumstances affect their choices.

To make a choice, we balance the benefits of having more of one thing against the costs of having less of something else. The process of balancing benefits against costs and doing the best within the limits of what is possible is called **optimizing**. There is another word that has a similar meaning—*economizing*. **Economizing** is making the best use of the resources available. Once people have made a choice and have optimized, they cannot have more of *everything*. To get more of one thing means having less of something else. Expressed in another way: in making choices, we face costs. Whatever we choose to do, we could always have chosen to do something else instead.

Opportunity Cost

Economists use the term *opportunity cost* to emphasize that making choices in the face of scarcity implies a cost. The **opportunity cost** of any action is the best alternative forgone. If you cannot have everything that you want, then you have to choose among the alternatives. The best thing that you choose not to do—the forgone alternative—is the cost of the thing that you choose to do.

Dollar Cost We often express opportunity cost in terms of dollars. But this is just a convenient unit of measure. The dollars spent on a book are not available for spending on a CD. The opportunity cost of the book is not the dollars spent on it, but the CD forgone.

Time Cost The opportunity cost of a good includes the value of the time spent obtaining it. If it takes an hour to visit your dentist, the value of that hour must be added to the amount you paid your dentist. We can convert time into a dollar cost by using a person's hourly wage rate. If you take an hour off work to visit your dentist, the opportunity cost of that visit (expressed in units of dollars) is the amount that you paid to your dentist plus the wages that you lost by not being at work. Again, it's important to keep reminding yourself that the opportunity cost is not the dollars involved but the goods that you could have bought with those dollars.

External Cost Not all of the opportunity costs that you incur are the result of your own choices. Sometimes others make choices that impose opportunity costs on you. And your own choices can impose opportunity costs on others. For example, when you enjoy a cold drink from your refrigerator, part of its opportunity cost (borne by others) is the increased carbon dioxide in the atmosphere resulting from burning coal to generate the electricity that powers the refrigerator.

Best Alternative Forgone In measuring opportunity cost, we value only the *best* alternative forgone. To make this clear, consider the following example. You are supposed to attend a lecture at 8:30 on a Monday morning. There are two alternatives to attending this lecture: stay in bed for an hour or go jogging for an hour. You cannot stay in bed *and* go jogging for that same hour. The opportunity cost of attending the lecture is not the cost of an hour in bed *and* the cost of jogging for an hour. If these are the only two alternatives that you would contemplate, then you have to decide which one you would do if you did not go to the lecture. The opportunity cost of attending a lecture for a jogger is an hour of exercise; the opportunity cost of attending a lecture for a late sleeper is an hour in bed.

Scarcity implies cost—opportunity cost. It also implies one other fundamental feature of human life—competition.

Competition and Cooperation

Competition If wants exceed resources, wants must compete against each other for what is available. **Competition** is a contest for command over scarce resources. In the case of the child with $1.00 in pocket money who wants a soft drink and gum that add up to $1.25, the soft drink and gum compete for the $1.00 in her pocket. For the student who has allowed assignments to accumulate, the party and the assignments compete with each other for Saturday night. For the government, defense and social services compete with each other for limited tax dollars.

Scarcity also implies competition between people. Because it is not possible to have everything that you want, you must compete with others for what is available. In modern societies, competition has been organized within a framework of almost universally accepted rules that have evolved. This evolution of rules is itself a direct response to the problem of scarcity. Not all societies, even modern societies, employ identical rules to govern competition. For example, the way in which economic life is organized in the United States differs greatly from that in the former Soviet Union. In the final chapter, we examine these differences and compare alternative economic systems. For now, we'll focus on the rules that govern competition in the United States.

A key rule of economic competition in the United States is that people own what they have acquired through voluntary exchange. People can compete with each other by offering more favorable exchanges—for example, selling something for a lower price or buying something for a higher price. But they cannot compete with each other by simply taking something from someone else.

Cooperation Perhaps you are thinking that scarcity does not make competition inevitable and that cooperation would better solve economic problems. **Cooperation** means working with others to achieve a common end. If instead of competing with each other we cooperated, wouldn't that solve our economic problems? Unfortunately, cooperation does not eliminate economic problems, because it does not eliminate economic scarcity. But cooperation is part of the solution to scarcity. We cooperate, for example, when we agree to rules of the game that limit competition to avoid violence and when we agree to participate in an economic system based on the rule of law and voluntary exchange.

Other examples of solving economic problems through cooperation abound. Marriage partners cooperate. Most forms of business also entail cooperation. Workers cooperate with each other on the production line; members of a management team cooperate with each other to design, produce, and market their products; management and workers cooperate; business partners cooperate.

Common as it is, cooperative behavior neither solves the economic problem nor eliminates competition. Almost all cooperative behavior implies some prior competition to find the best individuals with whom to cooperate. Marriage provides a good example. Although marriage is a cooperative affair, unmarried people compete intensely to find a marriage partner. Similarly, although workers and management cooperate with each other, firms compete for the best workers and workers compete for the best employers. Professionals such as lawyers and doctors compete with each other for the best business partners.

Competition does not end when a partner has been found. Groups of people who cooperate together compete with other groups. For example, although a group of lawyers may have formed a partnership and may work together, they will be in competition with other lawyers.

REVIEW

Scarcity is the confrontation of unlimited wants with limited resources. Scarcity forces people to make choices. To make choices, people evaluate the costs of alternative actions. We call these opportunity costs, to emphasize that doing one thing removes the opportunity to do something else. Scarcity also implies that people must compete with each other. Economics studies the activities arising from scarcity. ◆

You now know the types of questions that economists try to answer and that all economic questions and economic activity arise from scarcity. In the following chapters, we are going to study economic activity and discover how a modern economy such as that of the United States works. But before we do that, we need to stand back and take an overview of the economy.

The Economy

What do we mean by "the economy"? How does an economy work? Rather than trying to answer these questions directly, let's begin by asking similar questions about a more familiar subject. What is an airplane? How does an airplane work?

Without delving into the detail that would satisfy an aeronautical engineer, most of us could take a shot at answering these two questions. We would describe an airplane as a flying machine that transports people and cargo. To explain how an airplane works, we would describe its key components—fuselage (or body), wings, and engines, and also perhaps its flaps, rudder, and control and navigation systems. We would also explain that as powerful engines move the machine forward, its wings create an imbalance in air pressure that lifts it into the air.

This example nicely illustrates four things. First, it is hard to explain what something is without saying what it does. To say that an airplane is a machine does not tell us much. We have to go beyond that and say what the machine is for and how it works.

Second, it is hard to explain how something works without being able to divide it up into components. Once we have described something in terms of its components, we can explain how those components work and how they interact with each other.

Third, it is hard to explain how something works without leaving out some details. Notice that we did not describe an airplane in all its detail. Instead, we isolated the most important parts in order to explain how the whole works. We did not mention the in-flight movie system, the seat belts, or the color of the paint on the wings. We supposed that these things were irrelevant to an explanation of how an airplane works.

Fourth, and finally, there are different levels of understanding how something works. We gave a superficial account of how an airplane works. An aeronautical engineer would have given a deeper explanation, and experts in the individual components—engines, navigation systems, control system, and so on—would have given even more detailed and precise explanations than a general engineer.

Now let's return to questions about the economy. What is the economy? How does it work?

What Is the Economy?

The **economy** is a mechanism that allocates scarce resources among competing uses. This mechanism achieves three things:

- What
- How
- For whom

1. *What* goods and services will be produced and in *what* quantities? Will more VCRs be made or will more movie theaters be built? Will young professionals vacation in Europe or live in large houses? Will more high-performance sports cars or more trucks and station wagons be built?
2. *How* will the various goods and services be produced? Will a supermarket operate with three checkout lines and clerks using laser scanners or six checkout lines and clerks keying in prices by hand? Will workers weld station wagons by hand or will robots do the job? Will farmers keep track of their livestock feeding schedules and inventories by using paper and pencil records or personal computers? Will credit card companies use computers to read charge slips in New York or ship paper records to Barbados for hand processing?
3. *For whom* will the various goods and services be produced? The distribution of economic benefits depends on the distribution of income. People with high incomes are able to consume more goods and services than people with low incomes. Who gets to consume what thus depends on income. Will the ski instructor consume more than the lawyer's secretary? Will the people of Hong Kong consume more than the people of Ethiopia?

FIGURE 1.1
A Picture of the Economy

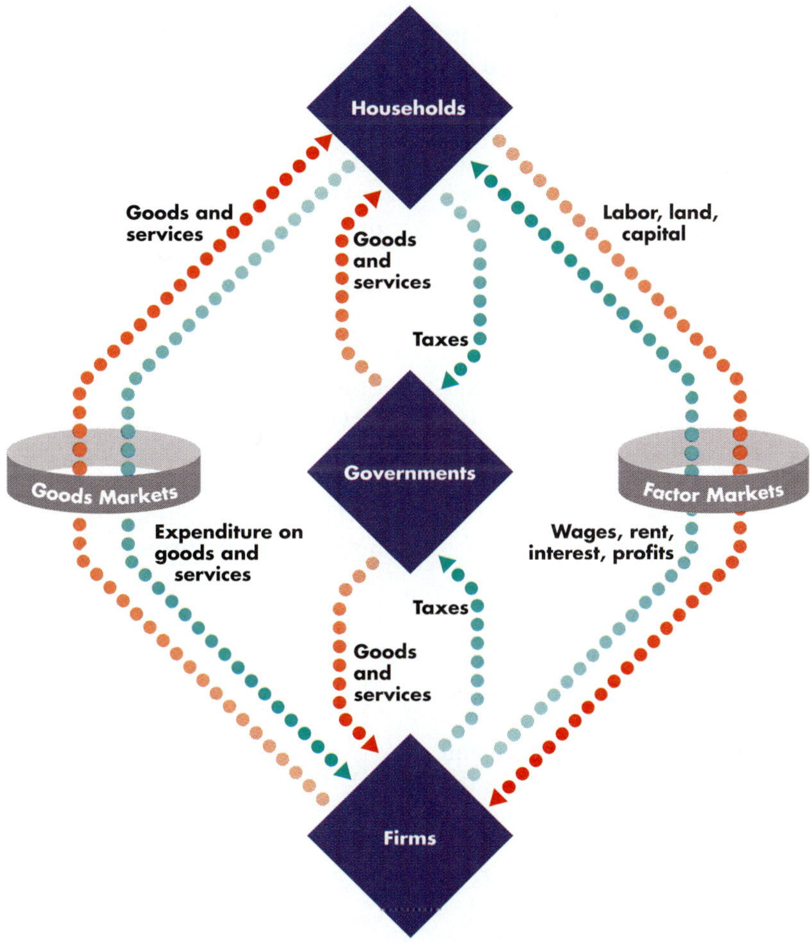

Households, firms, and governments make economic decisions. Households decide how much of their labor, land, and capital to supply in exchange for wages, rent, interest, and profits. They also decide how much of their income to spend on the various types of goods and services available. Firms decide how much labor, land, and capital to hire and how much of the various types of goods and services to produce. Governments decide which goods and services they will provide and the taxes that households and firms will pay.

These decisions by households, firms, and governments are coordinated in markets—the goods markets and factor markets. In these markets, prices constantly adjust to keep buying and selling plans consistent.

To understand how an economy achieves its objectives, we must identify its main components and then study the way in which these components interact with each other. Figure 1.1 shows a picture of the economy. It contains two types of components:

- Decision makers
- Markets

Decision Makers

Decision makers are the economic actors. They make the economizing choices. Figure 1.1 identifies three types of decision makers:

1. Households
2. Firms
3. Governments

A **household** is any group of people living together as a decision-making unit. Every individual in the economy belongs to a household. Some households consist of a single person, while others consist either of families or of groups of unrelated individuals, such as two or three students sharing an apartment. Each household has unlimited wants and limited resources.

A **firm** is an organization that uses resources to produce goods and services. All producers are called firms, no matter how big they are or what they produce. Car makers, farmers, banks, and insurance companies are all firms.

A **government** is an organization that provides goods and services and redistributes income and wealth. The most important of the services provided by government is a framework of laws and a mechanism for their enforcement (courts and police forces). But governments also provide such services as national defense, public health, transportation, and education.

Markets

In ordinary speech, the word *market* means a place where people buy and sell goods such as fish, meat, fruits, and vegetables. In economics, *market* has a more general meaning. A **market** is any arrangement that facilitates buying and selling. An example is the market in which oil is bought and sold—the world oil market. The world oil market is not a place. It is the arena in which the many firms—oil producers, oil users, wholesalers, and brokers—who buy and sell oil interact. In this market, decision makers do not meet physically. They make deals by telephone, fax, and direct computer link.

Figure 1.1 identifies two types of market: goods markets and factor markets. **Goods markets** are those in which goods and services are bought and sold. **Factor markets** are those in which factors of production are bought and sold.

Factors of production are the economy's productive resources. They are classified under three headings:

1. Labor
2. Land
3. Capital

Labor is the brain-power and muscle-power of human beings; **land** includes natural resources of all kinds; **capital** is all the equipment, buildings, tools, and other manufactured goods that can be used in production.

Decisions

Households and firms make decisions that result in the transactions in the goods markets and factor markets shown in Fig. 1.1. Households decide how much of their labor, land, and capital to sell or rent in factor markets. They receive incomes in the form of wages, rent, interest, and profit from these factors of production. Households also decide how to spend their incomes on goods and services produced by firms.

Firms decide the quantities of factors of production to hire, how to use them to produce goods and services, what goods and services to produce, and in what quantities. They sell their output in goods markets.

The flows resulting from these decisions by households and firms are shown in Fig. 1.1. The red flows are the factors of production that go from households to firms and the goods and services that go from firms to households. The green flows in the opposite direction are the payments made in exchange for these items.

Governments decide what goods and services to provide to households and firms, as well as the rates of taxes that create the funds to pay for them. These actions by governments are also shown in Fig. 1.1.

Coordination Mechanisms

Perhaps the most striking thing about the choices made by households, firms, and governments is that they surely must come into conflict with each other. For example, households choose how much work to do and what type of work to specialize in, but firms choose the type and quantity of labor to employ in the production of various goods and services. In other words, households choose the types and quantities of labor to sell, and firms choose the types and quantities of labor to buy. Similarly, in markets for goods and services, households choose the types and quantities of goods and services to buy, while firms choose the types and quantities to sell. Government choices regarding taxes and the provision of goods and services also enter the picture. Taxes taken by the government affect the amount of income that households and firms have available for spending. Also, decisions by firms and households depend on the types and quantities of goods and services that governments make available. For example, if the government provides excellent highways but a dilapidated railroad system, households will allocate more of their income to buying motor vehicles and less to buying train rides.

How is it possible for the millions of individual decisions made by households, firms, and governments to be consistent with each other? What makes households want to sell the same types and quantities of labor that firms want to buy? What happens if the number of households wanting to work as economics professors exceeds the number that universities want to hire? How do firms know what to produce so that households will buy their output? What happens if firms want to sell more hamburgers than households want to buy?

Markets Coordinate Decisions Markets coordinate individual decisions through price adjustments. To see how, think about the market for hamburgers in your local area. Suppose that the quantity of hamburgers being offered for sale is less than the quantity that people would like to buy. Some people who want to buy hamburgers will not be able to do so. To make the choices of buyers and sellers compatible, buyers will have to scale down their appetites and more hamburgers will have to be offered for sale. An increase in the price of hamburgers will produce this outcome. A higher price will encourage producers to offer more hamburgers for sale. It will also curb the appetite for hamburgers and change some lunch plans. Fewer people will buy hamburgers and more will buy hot dogs (or some other alternative to hamburgers). More hamburgers (and more hot dogs) will be offered for sale.

Now imagine the opposite situation. More hamburgers are available than people want to buy. In this case, the price is too high. A lower price will discourage the production and sale of hamburgers and encourage their purchase and consumption. Decisions to produce and sell, and to buy and consume, are continuously adjusted and kept in balance with each other by adjustments in prices.

In some cases, prices get stuck or fixed. When this happens, some other adjustment has to make the plans and choices of individuals consistent. Customers waiting in lines and inventories of goods operate as a temporary safety valve when the market price is stuck. If people want to buy more than the quantity that firms have decided to sell, and if the price is temporarily stuck, then one of two things can happen. Sometimes, firms wind up selling more than they would like and their inventories shrink. At other times, lines of customers develop and only those who get to the head of the line before the goods run out are able to make a purchase. The longer the line or the bigger the decline in inventories, the more prices adjust to keep buying and selling decisions in balance.

We have now seen how the market solves the question of *what* quantity to produce—how many hamburgers to make. The market also solves the question of *how* to produce in similar fashion. For example, hamburger producers can use gas, electric power, or charcoal to cook their hamburgers. Which fuel is used depends in part on the flavor that the producer wants to achieve and on the cost of the different fuels. If a fuel becomes very expensive, as did oil in the 1970s, less of it is used and more of other fuels are used in its place. By substituting one fuel for another as the costs of the different fuels change, the market solves the question of how to produce.

Finally, the market helps solve the question of *for whom* to produce. Skills, talents, and resources that are in very short supply command a higher price than those in greater abundance. The owners of rare resources and skills obtain a larger share of the output of the economy than the owners of resources that are in abundant supply.

Alternative Coordination Mechanisms The market is one of two alternative coordination mechanisms. The other is a command mechanism. A **command mechanism** is a method of determining *what, how,* and *for whom* goods and services are produced, using an hierarchical organization structure in which people carry out the instructions given to them. The best example of an hierarchical organization structure is the military. Commanders make decisions requiring actions that are passed down a chain of command. Soldiers and marines on the front line take the actions they are ordered to take.

An economy that relies on a command mechanism is called a **command economy.** Examples of command economies in today's world are China, North Korea, Vietnam, and Cambodia. Before they embarked on programs of reform in the late 1980s, the former Soviet Union and other countries of Eastern Europe also had command economies.

In a command economy, a central planning bureau makes decisions about *what, how,* and *for whom* goods and services are to be produced. We will study command economies and compare them with other types of economies at the end of our study of economics, in the last chapter.

An economy that determines *what, how,* and *for whom* goods and services are produced by coordinating individual choices through markets is called a **market economy.** But most real-world economies use both markets and commands to coordinate economic activity. An economy that relies on both markets and command mechanisms is called a **mixed economy.**

The U.S. economy relies extensively on the market as a mechanism for coordinating the decisions of individual households and firms. But the U.S. economy also uses command mechanisms. The economy of the armed forces is a command economy. Command mechanisms are also employed in other government organizations and also within large firms. There is also a command element in our legal system. By enacting laws and establishing regulations and agencies to monitor the market economy, governments influence the economic decisions of households and firms and change our economic course.

Thus *what, how,* and *for whom* goods and services are produced in the United States depends mainly on the market mechanism, but also partly on a command mechanism, so the U.S. economy is a mixed economy.

FIGURE 1.2

International Linkages

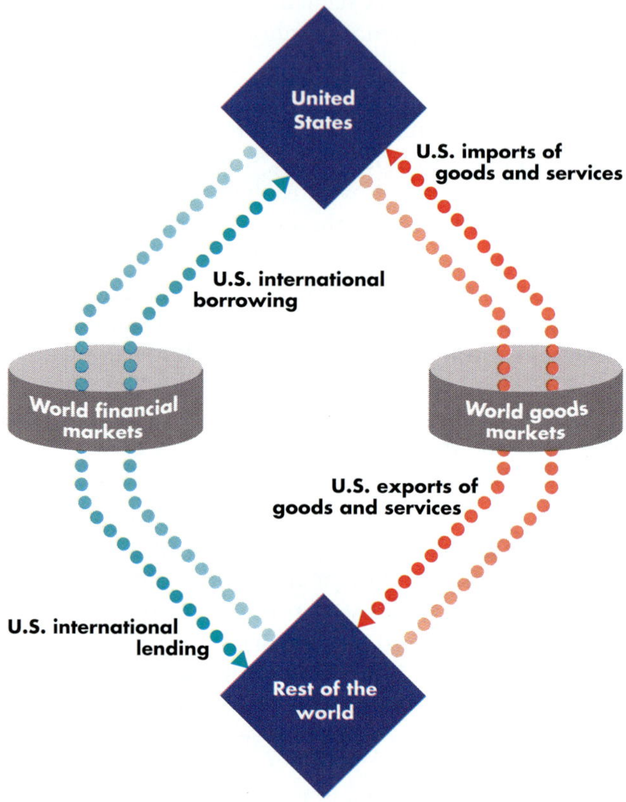

The U.S. economy buys and sells goods and services in world goods markets. What it buys are U.S. imports, and what it sells are U.S. exports. The U.S. economy also borrows from and lends to the rest of the world. These transactions take place in the world financial markets.

The Global Economy

A **closed economy** is one that has no links with any other economy. The only closed economy is that of the entire world. The U.S. economy is an **open economy,** an economy that has economic links with other economies.

The economic links between the U.S. economy and the rest of the world are illustrated in Fig. 1.2. Firms in the open U.S. economy sell some of their production to the rest of the world. These sales are U.S. exports of goods and services. Also, firms, households, and governments in the United States buy goods and services from firms in other countries. These purchases are U.S. imports of goods and services. Both types of transactions take place in world goods markets and are illustrated in the figure.

The total values of exports and imports are not necessarily equal to each other. When U.S. exports exceed U.S. imports, we have a surplus. When U.S. imports exceed U.S. exports, we have a deficit. A country with a surplus lends to the rest of the world, and a country with a deficit borrows from the rest of the world. These international lending and borrowing transactions take place in the world financial markets and are also illustrated in Fig. 1.2.

The United States has had an international deficit in recent years. As a consequence, by the mid-1980s, foreigners had larger investments in the United States than we had in the rest of the world. Other countries, notably those of the European Community and Japan, have international surpluses and are using those surpluses to invest in businesses in the United States.

During the 1980s, the global economy became a highly integrated mechanism for allocating scarce resources and deciding *what* will be produced, *how* it will be produced, and *for whom* it will be produced. It is also a mechanism deciding *where* the various goods and services will be produced and consumed.

REVIEW

An economy is a mechanism that determines what is produced, how it is produced, and for whom it is produced. Choices are made by households, firms, and government, that are coordinated through markets—markets for goods and services and markets for factors of production—or by command mechanisms. The U.S. economy relies mainly on markets but to a degree on command mechanisms. The U.S. economy and the global economy became highly integrated during the 1980s. ◆

We have now described an economy in about as much detail as we described an airplane. But we're about to become the economic equivalent of aeronautical engineers! We're going to build economies that fly! To do that, we have to understand the principles of economics as thoroughly as aeronautical engineers understand the principles of flight. To discover these principles, economists approach their work with the rigor and objectivity of natural scientists—they do economic science.

Economic Science

Economic science, like the natural sciences (such as physics and biology) and the other social sciences (such as political science, psychology, and sociology), is an attempt to find a body of laws. All sciences have two components:

1. Careful and systematic observation and measurement
2. Development of a body of theory to direct and interpret observations

All sciences are careful to distinguish between two types of statements:

- Statements about what *is*
- Statements about what *ought* to be

What Is and What Ought To Be

Statements about what *is* are **positive statements.** Statements about what *ought* to be are **normative statements.** Let's illustrate the distinction between positive and normative statements with two examples.

First, consider the controversy over global warming. Some scientists believe that the burning of coal and oil is increasing the carbon dioxide content of the earth's atmosphere and leading to higher temperatures that eventually will have devastating consequences for life on this planet. "Our planet is warming because of an increased carbon dioxide buildup in the atmosphere" is a positive statement. "We ought to cut back on our use of carbon-based fuels such as coal and oil" is a normative statement. Second, consider the economic controversy over tax cuts and cutbacks on social programs. "Lower taxes and less generous social programs will make people work harder" is a positive statement. "Taxes and social programs should be cut" is a normative statement.

Positive statements may be true or false. It is the task of science—whether natural, social, or economic—to discover and catalog positive statements that are true, that is, consistent with what we observe in the world. Normative statements are matters of opinion. You agree or disagree with them. Science is silent on normative questions. It is not that such questions are unimportant. On the contrary, they are often the most important questions of all. Nor is it that scientists as people do not have opinions on such questions. It is simply that the activity of doing science cannot settle a normative matter, and the possession of scientific knowledge does not equip a person with superior morals or norms. A difference of opinion on a positive matter can ultimately be settled by careful observation and measurement. A difference of opinion on a normative matter cannot be settled in that way. In fact, there are no well-defined rules for settling a normative dispute, and sometimes reasonable people simply have to agree to disagree. When they cannot, political and judicial institutions intervene so that decisions can be made. We settle normative disagreements in the political, not the scientific, arena. The scientific community can, and often does, contribute to the normative debates of political life. But science is a distinct activity. Even though scientists have opinions about what ought to be, those opinions have no part in science itself.

Now let's see how economists attempt to discover and catalog positive statements that are consistent with their observations and that enable them to answer economic questions.

Observation and Measurement

Economic phenomena can be observed and measured in great detail. We can catalog the amounts and locations of natural and human resources. We can describe who does what kind of work, for how many hours, and how they are paid. We can catalog the things that people produce, consume, and store and their prices. We can describe in detail who borrows and who lends and at what interest rates. We can also catalog the things that government taxes and at what rates, the programs it finances and at what cost.

These are examples of the array of things that economists can describe through careful observation and measurement of economic activity.

In today's world, computers have given us access to an enormous volume of economic description. Government agencies around the world, national statistical bureaus, private economic consultants, banks, investment advisors, and research economists working in universities generate an astonishing amount of information about economic behavior.

But economists do more than observe and measure economic activity, crucial as that is. Describing something is not the same as understanding it. You can describe your digital watch in great detail, but that does not mean you can explain what makes it work. Understanding what makes things work requires the discovery of laws. That is the main task of economists—the discovery of laws governing economic behavior. How do economists go about this task?

Economic Theory

We can describe in great detail the ups and downs, or cycles, in unemployment, but can we explain *why* unemployment fluctuates? We can describe the fall in the price of a VCR or a pocket calculator and the dramatic increase in its use, but can we explain the low price and popularity of such items? Did the fall in the price lead more people to use pocket calculators, or did their popularity lower the costs of production and make it possible to lower the price? Or did something else cause both the fall in the price and the increase in use?

Questions like these can be answered only by developing a body of economic theory. An **economic theory** is a general rule or principle that enables us to understand and predict the economic choices that people make. We develop economic theories by building and testing economic models. What is an economic model?

Economic Model

You have just seen an economic model. To answer the question "What is an economy and how does it work?" we built a model of an economy. We did not describe in all their detail all the economic actions that take place in the United States. We concentrated our attention only on those features that seemed important for understanding economic choices, and we ignored everything else. You will perhaps better appreciate what we mean by an economic model if you think about more familiar models.

We have all seen model trains, cars, and airplanes. Although we do not usually call dolls and stuffed animals "models," we can think of them in this way. Architects make models of buildings, and biologists make models of DNA (the double helix carrier of the genetic code).

A model is usually smaller than the real thing that it represents. But models are not always smaller in scale (think of a biologist's model of the components of cells), and in any case, the scale of a model is not its most important feature. A model also shows less detail than its counterpart in reality. For example, all the models that we have mentioned resemble the real thing in *appearance,* but they are not usually made of the same substance, nor do they work like the real thing that they represent. The architect's model of a new high-rise shows us what the building will look like and how it will conform with the buildings around it—but it does not contain plumbing, telephone cables, elevator shafts, air conditioning plants, and other interior workings.

All the models that we have discussed (including those that are typically used as toys) represent something that is real, but they lack some key features and deliberately so. The model abstracts from the detail of the real thing. It includes only those features that are needed for the purpose at hand. It leaves out the inessential or unnecessary. What a model includes and leaves out is not arbitrary; it results from a conscious and careful decision.

The models that we have just considered are all physical models. We can see the real thing and we can see the model. Indeed, the purpose of those models is to enable us to visualize the real thing. Some models, including economic models, are not physical. We cannot look at the real thing and look at the model and simply decide whether the model is a good or bad representation of the real thing. But the idea of a model as an abstraction from reality still applies to an economic model.

An economic model has two components:

1. Assumptions
2. Implications

Assumptions form the foundation on which a model is built. They are propositions about what is important and what can be ignored. **Implications** are the outcome of a model. The link between a model's assumptions and its implications is a process of logical deduction.

Let's illustrate these components of a model by building a simple model of your daily journey to school. The model has three assumptions:

1. You want to be in class when it begins at 9:00 A.M.
2. The bus ride to school takes 30 minutes.
3. The walk from the bus to class takes 5 minutes.

The implication of this model is that you will be on the bus no later than 8:25 A.M. With knowledge of the bus timetable, we could use this model to predict the bus that you would catch to school.

The assumptions of a model depend on the model's purpose. The purpose of an economic model is to understand how households, firms, and governments make choices in the face of scarcity. Thus in building an economic model, we abstract from the rich detail of human life and focus only on behavior that is relevant for coping with scarcity. Everything else is ignored. Economists know that people fall in love and form deep friendships, that they experience great joy and security or great pain and anxiety. But economists assume that in seeking to understand economic behavior, they may build models that ignore many aspects of life. They focus on one and only one feature of the world: people have wants that exceed their resources and so, by their choices, have to make the best of things.

Assumptions of an Economic Model Economic models are based on four key assumptions:

1. *People have preferences.* Economists use the term **preferences** to denote likes and dislikes and the intensity of those likes and dislikes. People can judge whether one situation is better, worse, or just as good as another one. For example, you can judge whether, for you, one loaf of bread and no cheese is better, worse, or just as good as a half a loaf of bread and four ounces of cheese.
2. *People are endowed with a fixed amount of resources and a technology that can transform those resources into goods and services.* Economists use the term **endowment** to refer to the resources that people have and the term **technology** to describe the methods of converting those endowments into goods and services.
3. *People economize.* People choose how to use their endowments and technologies in order to make themselves as well-off as possible. Such a choice is called a rational choice. A **rational choice** is one which, among all possible choices, best achieves the goals of the person making the choice. Each choice, no matter what it is or how foolish it may seem to an observer, is interpreted, in an economic model, as a rational choice. Choices are made on the basis of the information available. With hindsight, and with more information, people may well feel that some of their past choices were bad ones. This fact does not make such choices irrational. Again, a rational choice is the best possible course of action, from the point of view of the person making the choice, given that person's preferences and *given the information available when the choice is made.*
4. *People's choices are coordinated.* One person's choice to buy something must be matched by another person's choice to sell that same thing.

One person's choice to work at a particular job must be matched by another person's choice to hire someone to do that job. The coordination of individual choices is made by either a market mechanism or a command mechanism.

Implications of an Economic Model The implications of an economic model are the equilibrium values of various prices and quantities. An **equilibrium** is a situation in which everyone has economized—that is, all individuals have made the best possible choices in the light of their own preferences and given their endowments, technologies and information—and in which those choices have been coordinated and made compatible with the choices of everyone else. Equilibrium is the solution or outcome of an economic model.

The term *equilibrium* conjures up the picture of a balance of opposing forces. For example, a balance scale can be said to be in equilibrium if a pound of butter is placed on one side of the balance and a one-pound weight is placed on the other side. The two weights exactly equal each other and so offset each other, leaving the balance arm horizontal. A soap bubble provides another excellent physical illustration of equilibrium. The delicate spherical film of soap is held in place by a balance of forces of the air inside the sphere and the air outside it.

This second physical analogy illustrates a further important feature of an equilibrium. An equilibrium is not necessarily static but may be dynamic—constantly changing. By squeezing or stretching the bubble, you can change its shape, but its shape is always determined by the balance of the forces acting upon it (including the forces that you exert upon it).

An economic equilibrium has a great deal in common with that of the soap bubble. First, it is in a constant state of motion. At each point in time, each person makes the best possible choice, given the endowments and actions of others. But changing circumstances alter those choices. For example, on a busy day in Manhattan, there are more cars looking for parking spaces than the number of spaces available. But people do get to park. Individual cars are leaving and arriving at a steady pace. As soon as one car vacates a parking space, another instantly fills it. In this situation, the equilibrium number of free spaces is zero. But being in equilibrium does not mean that everyone gets to park instantly. There is an equilibrium amount of time spent finding a

"And now a traffic update: A parking space has become available on Sixty-fifth Street between Second and Third. Hold it! A bulletin has just been handed me. That space has been taken."

vacant space. People hunting for a space are frustrated and experience rising blood pressure and increased anger. But there is still an equilibrium in the hunt for available parking spaces.

Similarly, an economic equilibrium does not mean that everyone is experiencing economic prosperity. The constraints may be such that some people are very poor. Nevertheless, given their preferences, their endowments, the available technologies, and the actions of everyone else, each person has made the best possible choice and sees no advantage in modifying his or her current action.

Microeconomic and Macroeconomic Models

Economic models fall into two categories: microeconomic and macroeconomic. **Microeconomics** is the branch of economics that studies the decisions of individual households and firms. Microeconomics also studies the way in which individual markets work and the detailed way in which regulation and taxes affect the allocation of labor and of goods and services.

Macroeconomics is the branch of economics that studies the economy as a whole. It seeks to understand the big picture rather than the detailed individual choices. In particular, it studies the determination of the overall level of economic activity—of unemployment, aggregate income, average prices, and inflation.

Of the seven big economic questions, those dealing with technological change, production and consumption, and wages and earnings are microeconomic. Those dealing with unemployment, inflation, and differences in wealth among nations are macroeconomic.

Model, Theory, and Reality

People who build models often get carried away and start talking as if their model *is* the real world—as if their model is reality. No matter how useful it is, there is no sense in which a model can be said to be reality.

A model is abstract. It lists assumptions and their implications. When economists talk about people who have made themselves as well-off as possible, they are not talking about real people. They are talking about artificial people in an economic model. Do not lose sight of this important but easily misunderstood fact.

Economic theory is the bridge between economic models and the real world. Economic theory is a catalog of models that seem to work—that seem to enable us to understand and interpret the past and to predict some aspects of the future. Economic theory evolves from a process of building and testing economic models.

To test an economic model, its implications are matched against actual events in the real world. That is, the model is used to make predictions about the real world. The model's predictions may correspond to or be in conflict with the facts. It is by comparing the model's predictions with the facts that we are able to test a model. The process of developing economic theories by using models is illustrated in Fig. 1.3. We begin by building a model. The model's implications are used to generate predictions about the world. These predictions and their test form the basis of a theory. When predictions are in conflict with the facts, either a theory is discarded in favor of a superior alternative or we return to the model-building stage, modifying our assumptions and creating a new model. Economics itself provides guidance on how we might discover a better model. It prompts us to look for some aspect

FIGURE 1.3

How Theories Are Developed

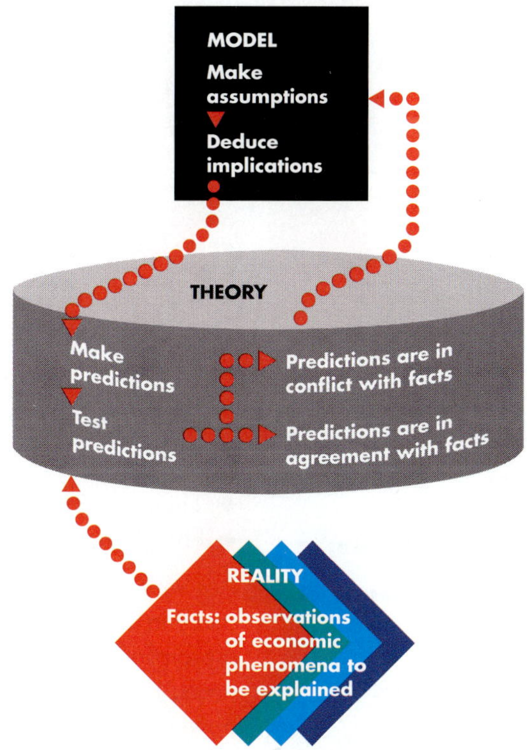

Economic theories are developed by building and testing economic models. An economic model is a set of *assumptions* about what is important and what can be ignored and the *implications* of those assumptions. The implications of a model form the basis of *predictions* about the world. These predictions are tested by being checked against the facts. If the predictions are in conflict with the facts, the model-building process begins again with new assumptions. Only when the predictions are in agreement with the facts has a useful theory been developed.

of preferences, endowments, technology, or the coordination mechanism that has been overlooked.

Economics is a young science and a long way from having achieved its goal of explaining and understanding economic activity. Its birth can be dated fairly precisely in the eighteenth century with the publication of Adam Smith's *The Wealth of Nations* (see Our Advancing Knowledge, pp. 22–23). In the closing years of the twentieth century, economic science has managed to discover a sizable

UNDERSTANDING the Sources of ECONOMIC WEALTH

In 1776, new technologies were being invented and applied to the manufacture of cotton and wool, iron, transportation, and agriculture in what came to be called the "Industrial Revolution."

Adam Smith was keenly interested in these events. He wanted to understand the sources of economic wealth, and he brought his acute powers of observation and abstraction to bear on this question. His answer:

- The division of labor
- Free domestic and international markets

Smith identified the division of labor as the source of "the greatest improvement in the productive powers of labor." The division of labor became even more productive when applied to creating new technologies. Scientists and engineers, trained in extremely narrow fields, became specialists at inventing. Their powerful skills speeded the advance of technology so that by the 1850s we could make machines that could make consumer goods and other machines by performing repetitive operations faster, more accurately, and for longer than people.

But, said Smith, the fruits of the division of labor are limited by the extent of the market. To make the market as large as possible, there must be no impediments to free trade both within a country and among countries. Smith argued that when each person makes the best possible economic choice based on self-interest, that choice leads as if by "an invisible hand" to the best outcome for society as a whole.

"It is not from the benevolence of the butcher, the brewer, or the baker, that we expect our dinner, but from their regard to their own interest."

ADAM SMITH
The Wealth of Nations

Adam Smith speculated that one person, working hard, using the hand tools available in the 1770s, might possibly make 20 pins a day. Yet by using those same hand tools but breaking the process into a number of individually small operations in which people specialize—by the division of labor—he observed that ten people could make a staggering 48,000 pins a day. One draws out the wire, another straightens it, a third cuts it, a fourth points it, a fifth grinds it. Three specialists make the head and a fourth attaches it. Finally, the pin is polished and wrapped in paper.

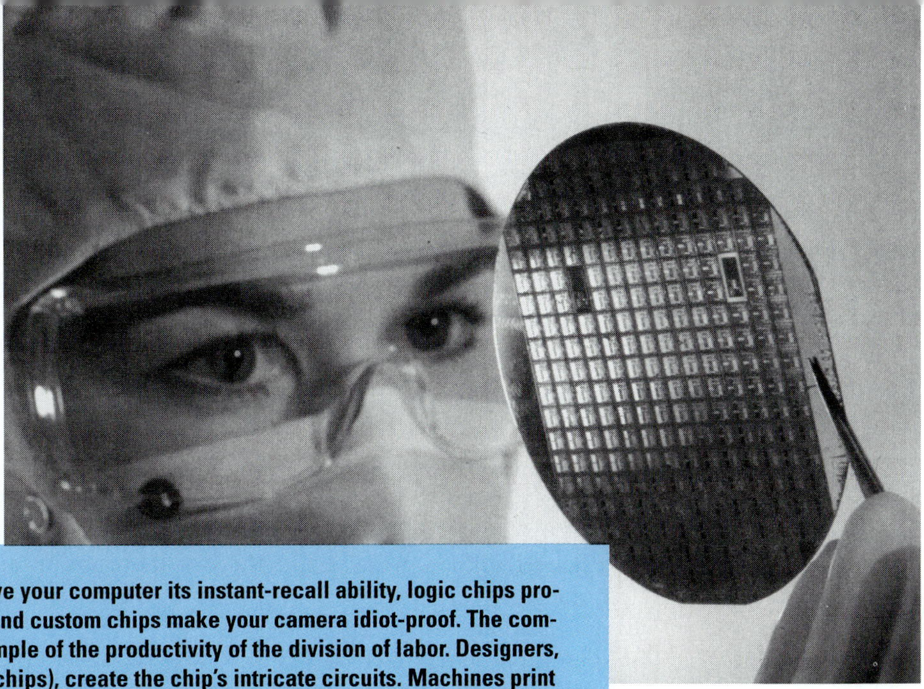

Memory chips give your computer its instant-recall ability, logic chips provide its number-crunching power, and custom chips make your camera idiot-proof. The computer chip is an extraordinary example of the productivity of the division of labor. Designers, using computers (made from microchips), create the chip's intricate circuits. Machines print the design on paper and photograph it on glass plates called masks that work like stencils. Workers prepare silicon wafers on which the circuits are printed. Some slice the wafers, others polish them, others bake them, and yet others coat them with a light-sensitive chemical. Technicians put masks and wafers into a machine that shines light through the mask, imprinting a copy of the circuit onto the wafer. Chemicals eat the unexposed portion of the wafer. A further series of passes through gas-filled ovens deposits atoms that act as transistors. Aluminum is deposited on the wafer to connect the transistors. Finally, a diamond saw or laser separates the hundreds of chips on the wafer.

ADAM SMITH AND *THE Wealth of Nations*

Adam Smith, born in 1723 in Kirkcaldy, a small fishing town near Edinburgh, Scotland, and only child of the town's customs officer (who died before his son was born), was a giant of a scholar who made extraordinary contributions in ethics and jurisprudence as well as economics.

His first academic appointment, at age 28, was as Professor of Logic at the University of Glasgow. He subsequently became tutor to a wealthy Scottish duke whom he accompanied on a two-year European grand tour, following which he received a pension of £300 a year—ten times the average income at that time.

With the financial security of his pension, Smith devoted ten years to writing the treatise that founded economic science, *An Inquiry into the Nature and Causes of The Wealth of Nations,* which was published to great acclaim in 1776.

Many had written on economic issues before Adam Smith, but it was he who made economics a science. His account of what was then known was so broad and authoritative that no subsequent writer on economics could advance his own ideas while ignoring the state of general knowledge.

number of useful generalizations. In many areas, however, we are still going around the circle—changing assumptions, performing new logical deductions, generating new predictions, and getting wrong answers yet again. The gradual accumulation of correct answers gives most practitioners some faith that their methods will eventually provide usable answers to the big economic questions.

As we make progress, though, more and more things become clearer and seem to fit together. Theoretical advances lead to deeper understanding. This feature of economics is shared with scientists in all fields. As Albert Einstein, the great physicist, said, "Creating a new theory is not like destroying an old barn and erecting a skyscraper in its place. It is rather like climbing a mountain, gaining new and wider views, discovering new connections between our starting point and its rich environment. But the point from which we started still exists and can be seen, although it appears smaller and forms a tiny part of our broad view gained by the mastery of the obstacles on our adventurous way up."[1]

◆ ◆ ◆ ◆ In the next chapter, we will study some of the tools that economists use to build economic models. Then, in Chapter 3, we will build an economic model and use that model to understand the world around us and to start to answer some of the seven big economic questions.

[1] These words are attributed to Einstein in a letter by Oliver Sacks to *The Listener,* 88, No. 2279, November 30, 1972, 756.

Summary

Scarcity

All economic questions arise from the fundamental fact of scarcity. Scarcity means that wants exceed resources. Human wants are effectively unlimited, but the resources available to satisfy them are finite.

Economic activity is what people do to cope with scarcity. Scarcity forces people to make choices. Making the best choice possible from what is available is called optimizing or economizing. To make the best possible choice, a person weighs the costs and benefits of the alternatives—optimizes.

Opportunity cost is the cost of one choice in terms of the best forgone alternative. The opportunity cost of any action is the best alternative action that could have been undertaken in its place. Attending class instead of staying in bed has an opportunity cost—the cost of one hour of rest.

Scarcity forces people to compete with each other for scarce resources. People may cooperate in certain areas, but all economic activity ultimately results in competition among individuals acting alone or in groups. (pp. 9–11)

The Economy

People have unlimited wants but limited resources or factors of production—labor, land, and capital. The economy is a mechanism that allocates scarce resources among competing uses, determining *what, how,* and *for whom* the various goods and services will be produced.

The economy's two key components are decision makers and markets. Economic decision makers are households, firms, and governments. Households decide how much of their labor, land, and capital to sell or rent and how much of the various goods and services to buy. Firms decide what factors of production to hire and which goods and services to produce. Governments decide what goods and services to provide to households and firms and how much to raise in taxes.

The decisions of households, firms, and governments are coordinated through markets in which prices adjust to keep buying plans and selling plans consistent. Alternatively, coordination can be achieved by a command mechanism. The U.S. economy relies mainly on markets, but there is a command element in the actions taken by governments that also influences the allocation of scarce resources. The U.S. economy is therefore a mixed economy. (pp. 12–17)

Economic Science

Economic science, like the natural sciences and the other social sciences, attempts to find a body of laws. Economic science makes only *positive* statements—statements about what is. It does not make *normative* statements—statements about what ought to be. Economists try to find economic laws by developing a body of economic theory, and economic theory, in turn, is developed by building and testing economic models. Economic models are abstract, logical constructions that contain two components: assumptions and implications. An economic model has four key assumptions:

1. People have preferences.
2. People have a given endowment of resources and technology.
3. People economize.
4. People's choices are coordinated through market or command mechanisms.

The implications of an economic model are the equilibrium values of various prices and quantities that result from each individual doing the best that is possible, given the individual's preferences, endowments, information, and technology and given the coordination mechanism. (pp. 17–24)

KEY ELEMENTS

Key Terms

Key Figure

REVIEW QUESTIONS

1 Give two examples, different from those in the chapter, that illustrate each of the seven big economic questions.

2 Why does scarcity force us to make choices?

3 What do we mean by "rational choice"? Give examples of rational and irrational choices.

4 Why does scarcity force us to economize?

5 Why does optimization require us to calculate costs?

6 Why does scarcity imply competition?

7 Why can't we solve economic problems by cooperating with each other?

8 Name the main economic decision makers.

9 List the economic decisions made by households, firms, and governments.

10 What is the difference between a command mechanism and a market?

11 Distinguish between positive and normative statements by listing three examples of each type of statement.

12 What are the four key assumptions of an economic model?

13 Explain the difference between a model and a theory.

PROBLEMS

1 You plan to go to school this summer. If you do, you won't be able to take your usual job that pays $6,000 for the summer and you won't be able to live at home for free. The cost of your tuition will be $2,000, textbooks $200, and living expenses $1,400. What is the opportunity cost of going to summer school?

2 On Valentine's Day, Bernie and Catherine exchanged gifts: Bernie sent Catherine red roses and Catherine bought Bernie a box of chocolate. They each spent $15. They also spent $50 on dinner and split the cost evenly. Did either Bernie or Catherine incur any opportunity costs? If so, what were they? Explain your answer.

3 Nancy asks Beth to be her maid-of-honor at her wedding. Beth accepts. Which of the following are part of her opportunity cost of being Nancy's maid-of-honor? Explain why they are or are not.

- **a** The $200 Beth spent on a new outfit for the occasion
- **b** The $50 she spent on a party for Nancy's friends
- **c** The money she spent on a haircut a week before the wedding
- **d** The weekend visit she missed for her grandmother's 75th birthday—the same weekend as the wedding
- **e** The $10 she spent on lunch on the way to the wedding

4 The local mall has free parking, but the mall is always very busy, and it usually takes 30 minutes to find a parking space. Today when you found a vacant spot, Harry also wanted it. Is parking really free at this mall? If not, what did it cost you to park today? When you parked your car today, did you impose any costs on Harry? Explain your answers.

5 Which of the following statements are positive and which are normative?

- **a** A cut in wages will reduce the number of people willing to work.
- **b** High interest rates prohibit many young people from buying their first home.
- **c** No family ought to pay more than 25 percent of its income in taxes.
- **d** The government should reduce the number of minorities in the military and increase the number of whites.
- **e** The government ought to supply a medical insurance scheme for everyone free of charge.

6 You have been hired by Soundtrend, a company that makes and markets tapes, records, and compact discs (CDs). Your employer is going to start selling these products in a new region that has a population of 10 million people. A survey has indicated that 50 percent of people buy only popular music, 10 percent buy only classical music, and no one buys both types of music. Another survey suggests that the average income of a pop music fan is $10,000 a year and that of a classical fan is $50,000 a year. Based on a third survey, it appears that, on the average, people with low incomes spend one quarter of 1 percent of their income on tapes, records, and CDs, while people with high incomes spend 2 percent of their income on these products.

Build a model to enable Soundtrend to predict how much will be spent on pop music and classical music in this region in one year. In doing so:

- **a** List your assumptions.
- **b** Work out the implications of your assumptions.
- **c** Highlight the potential sources of errors in your predictions.

CHAPTER 2

Making and Using Graphs

After studying this chapter, you will be able to:

- Make and interpret a scatter diagram and a time-series graph
- Distinguish between linear and nonlinear relationships and relationships that have a maximum and a minimum
- Define and calculate the slope of a line
- Graph relationships among more than two variables

BENJAMIN DISRAELI, BRITISH PRIME MINISTER IN THE LATE nineteenth century, is reputed to have said that there are three kinds of lies: lies, damned lies, and statistics. One of the most powerful ways of conveying statistical information is in the form of a picture—a graph. Thus graphs, too, like statistics, can tell lies. But the right graph does not lie. Indeed, it reveals data and helps its viewer to see and think about relationships that would otherwise be obscure. ◆◆ Graphs are a surprisingly modern invention. The first graphs appeared in the late eighteenth century, long after the discovery of mathematically sophisticated ideas such as logarithms and calculus. But today, especially in the age of the personal computer and the video display, graphs have become almost more important than words. The ability to make and use graphs is as important as the ability to read and write. ◆◆ How do economists use graphs? What are the different types of graphs that economists use? What do economic graphs reveal and what can they hide? What are the main pitfalls that can result in a graph that lies? ◆◆ The seven big questions that you studied in Chapter 1—the problems that economics seeks to solve—are difficult ones. They involve relationships among a large number of variables. Hardly anything in economics has a single cause. Instead, a large number of variables interact with each other. It is often said that in economics, everything depends on everything else. Well, maybe not everything else, but lots of things. Variations in the quantity of ice cream consumed are caused not merely by variations in the air temperature or in the price of cream, but by at least these two

Three Kinds of Lies

factors and probably several others as well. How can we draw graphs of relationships that involve several variables, all of which vary simultaneously? How can we interpret such relationships?

◆ ◆ ◆ ◆ In this chapter, we are going to look at the different kinds of graphs that are used in economics. We are going to learn how to make them and read them. We are going to look at examples of useful graphs as well as misleading graphs. We are also going to study how we can calculate the strength of the effect of one variable on another. ◆ ◆ There are no graphs or techniques used in this book that are more complicated than those explained and described in this chapter. If you are already familiar with graphs, you may want to skip or at least only skim this chapter. Whether you study this chapter thoroughly or give it a quick pass, you should regard it as a handy reference chapter to which you can return if you feel that you need additional help understanding the graphs that you encounter in your study of economics.

FIGURE 2.1

Graphing a Single Variable

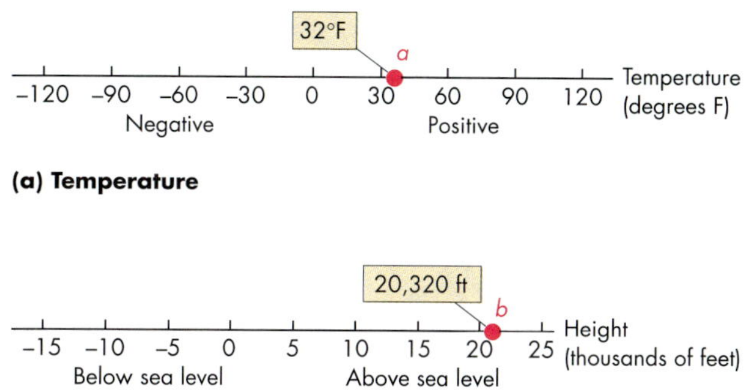

(a) Temperature

(b) Height

All graphs have a scale that measures a quantity as a distance. The two scales here measure temperature and height. Numbers to the right of zero are positive. Numbers to the left of zero are negative.

Graphing Data

Graphs represent a quantity as a distance. Figure 2.1 gives two examples. Part (a) shows temperature, measured in degrees Fahrenheit, as the distance on a scale. Movements from left to right represent increases in temperature. Movements from right to left represent decreases in temperature. The point marked 0 represents zero degrees Fahrenheit. To the right of zero, the temperatures are positive. To the left of zero, the temperatures are negative (as indicated by the minus sign in front of the numbers).

Figure 2.1(b) provides another example. This time altitude, or height, is measured in thousands of feet above sea level. The point marked 0 represents sea level. Points to the right of zero represent feet above sea level. Points to the left of zero (indicated by a minus sign) represent depths below sea level. There are no rigid rules about the scale for a graph. The scale is determined by the range of the variable being graphed and the space available for the graph.

The two graphs in Fig. 2.1 show just a single variable. Marking a point on either of the two scales indicates a particular temperature or a particular height. Thus the point marked *a* represents 32°F, the freezing point of water. The point marked *b* represents 20,320 feet, the height of Mount McKinley, the highest mountain in North America.

Graphing a single variable as we have done does not usually reveal much. Graphs become powerful when they show how two variables are related to each other.

Two-Variable Graphs

To construct a two-variable graph, we set two scales perpendicular to each other. Let's continue to use the same two variables as those in Fig. 2.1. We will measure temperature in exactly the same way, but we will turn the height scale to a vertical position. Thus temperature is measured exactly as it was before, but height is now represented by movements up and down a vertical scale.

The two scale lines in Fig. 2.2 are called **axes.** The vertical line is called the ***y*-axis,** and the horizontal line is called the ***x*-axis.** The letters x and y appear on the axes of Fig. 2.2. Each axis has a zero point that is shared by the two axes. The zero point, common to both axes, is called the **origin.**

FIGURE 2.2

Graphing Two Variables

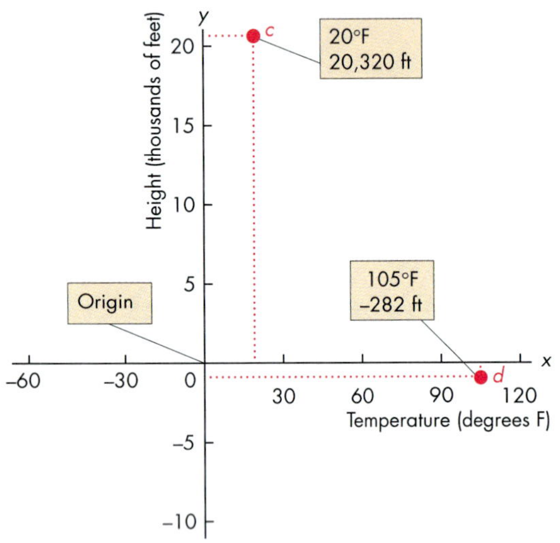

The relationship between two variables is graphed by drawing two axes perpendicular to each other. Height is measured here on the *y*-axis and temperature on the *x*-axis. Point *c* represents the top of Mt. McKinley, 20,320 feet above sea level (measured on the *y*-axis), with a temperature of 20°F (measured on the *x*-axis). Point *d* represents Death Valley, 282 feet below sea level, with a temperature of 105°F.

To represent something in a two-variable graph, we need two pieces of information. For example, Mount McKinley is 20,320 feet high and, on a particular day, the temperature at its peak is 20°F. We can represent this information in Fig. 2.2 by marking the height of the mountain on the *y*-axis at 20,320 feet and the temperature on the *x*-axis at 20°F. We can now identify the values of the two variables that appear on the axes by marking point *c*.

Two lines, called coordinates, can be drawn from point *c*. **Coordinates** are lines running from a point on a graph perpendicularly to an axis. The line running from *c* to the *x*-axis is the ***y*-coordinate,** because its length is the same as the value marked off on the *y*-axis. Similarly, the line running from *c* to the vertical axis is the ***x*-coordinate,** because its length is the same as the value marked off on the *x*-axis.

Now let's leave the top of Mount McKinley, at 20,320 feet and 20°F, and go to Death Valley in the Mojave Desert, the lowest point in the United States at 282 feet *below* sea level. Death Valley is represented by point *d*, which shows that we are 282 feet below sea level (the *y*-coordinate) and the temperature is 105°F (the *x*-coordinate).

Economists use graphs similar to this one in a variety of ways. Let's look at two examples.

Scatter Diagrams

Economists use graphs to reveal and describe the relationship between two economic variables. The most important type of graph used for these purposes is the scatter diagram, an example of which is shown in Fig. 2.3. A **scatter diagram** plots the value of one economic variable associated with the value

FIGURE 2.3

A Scatter Diagram: Consumption and Income

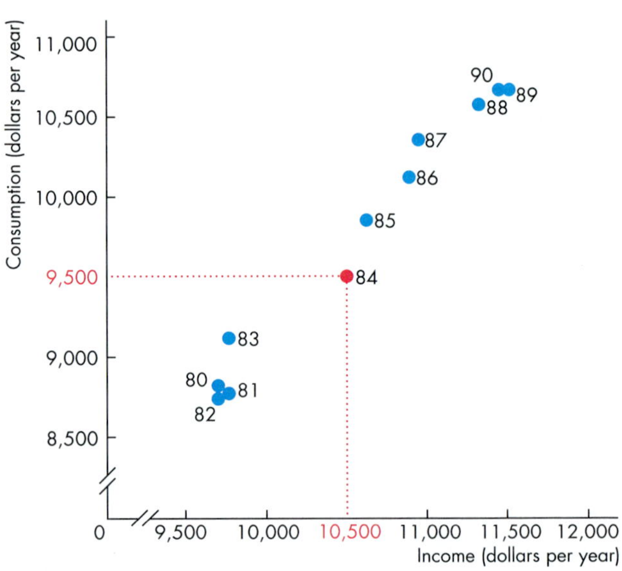

A scatter diagram shows the relationship between two variables. This scatter diagram shows the relationship between average consumption and average income during the years 1980 to 1990. Each point shows the values of the two variables in a specific year, and the year is identified by the two-digit number. For example, in 1984 average consumption was $9,500 and average income was $10,500. The pattern formed by the points shows that as income increases, so does consumption.

of another. It measures one of the variables on the x-axis and the other variable on the y-axis.

The Relationship Between Consumption and Income Figure 2.3 uses a scatter diagram to show the relationship between consumption and income. The x-axis measures average income, and the y-axis measures average consumption. Each point represents average consumption and average income in the United States in a given year between 1980 and 1990. The points for all eleven years are "scattered" within the graph. Each point is labeled with a two-digit number that tells us its year. For example, the point marked 84 tells us that in 1984, average consumption was \$9,500 and average income was \$10,500.

This graph reveals that a relationship *does* exist between average income and average consumption. The pattern formed by the points in Fig. 2.3 tells us that when income increases, consumption also increases.

Breaks in the Axes Notice that each axis in Fig. 2.3 has a break in it—illustrated by the small gaps. The breaks indicate that there are jumps from the origin, 0, to the first values recorded. The breaks are used because in the period covered by the graph average consumption was never less than \$8,500 and average income was never less than \$9,500. With no breaks in the axes of this graph, there would be a lot of empty space, all the points would be crowded into the top right corner, and we would not be able to see whether a relationship existed between these two variables. By using axis breaks, we are able to bring the relationship into view. In effect, we use a zoom lens to bring the relationship into the center of the graph and magnify it so that it fills the graph.

The range of the variables plotted on the axes of a graph are an important feature of a graph, and it is a good idea to get into the habit of always looking closely at the axis values—and labels—before you start to interpret a graph.

Other Relationships Figure 2.4 shows two other scatter diagrams. In part (a), the x-axis shows the percentage of households owning a video cassette recorder, and the y-axis shows its average price. Each point with its two-digit number represents a year. Thus the point marked 81 tells us that the

FIGURE 2.4

More Scatter Diagrams

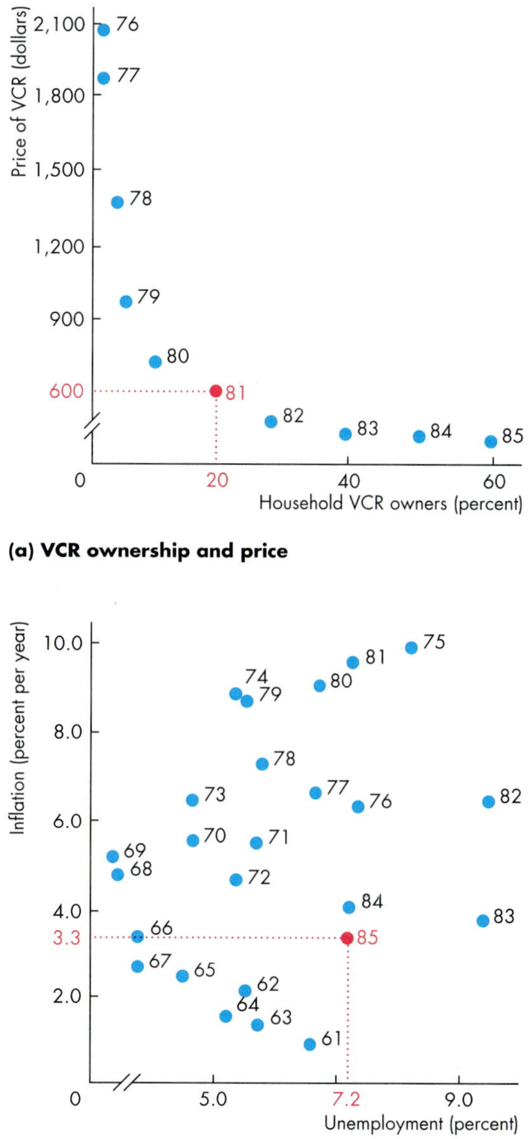

(a) VCR ownership and price

(b) Unemployment and inflation

Part (a) is a scatter diagram showing the relationship between the percentage of households owning a VCR and the average price of a VCR. It shows that as the price of a VCR has fallen, the percentage of households owning a VCR has increased. Part (b) is a scatter diagram showing inflation and unemployment. It shows that there is no clear relationship between these two variables.

average price of a VCR in 1981 was $600 and that VCRs were owned by 20 percent of all households. The pattern formed by the points in part (a) tells us that as the price of a VCR falls, a larger percentage of households own one.

In part (b), the x-axis measures unemployment in the United States, and the y-axis measures inflation. Again, each point with its two-digit number represents a year. The point marked 85 tells us that in 1985 unemployment was 7.2 percent and inflation was 3.3 percent. The pattern formed by the points in part (b) does not reveal a clear relationship between the two variables. The graph thus informs us, by its lack of a distinct pattern, that there is no relationship between these two variables.

A scatter diagram enables us to see the relationship between two economic variables. But it does not give us a clear picture of how those variables evolve over time. To see the evolution of economic variables, we use a different but common kind of graph—the time-series graph.

Time-Series Graphs

A **time-series graph** measures time (for example, years or months) on the x-axis and the variable or variables in which we are interested on the y-axis.

Figure 2.5 illustrates a time-series graph. Time is measured in years on the x-axis. The variable that we are interested in—the U.S. unemployment rate (the percentage of the labor force unemployed)—is measured on the y-axis. The time-series graph conveys an enormous amount of information quickly and easily:

1. It tells us the *level* of the unemployment rate—when it is *high* and *low*. When the line is a long way from the x-axis, the unemployment rate is high. When the line is close to the x-axis, the unemployment rate is low.
2. It tells us how the unemployment rate *changes*—whether it *rises* or *falls*. When the line slopes upward, as in the early 1930s, the unemployment rate is rising. When the line slopes downward,

FIGURE 2.5

A Time-Series Graph

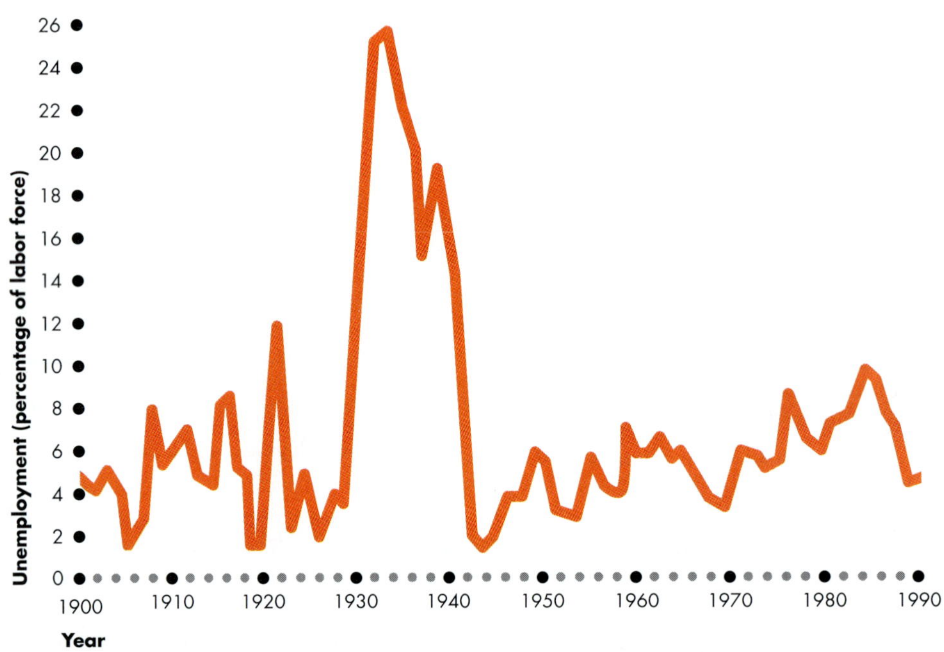

A time-series graph plots the level of a variable on the y-axis against time (day, week, month, or year) on the x-axis. This graph shows the U.S. unemployment rate each year from 1900 to 1990.

Source: Economic Report of the President.

as in the early 1940s, the unemployment rate is falling.

3. It tells us the *speed* with which the unemployment rate is *changing*—whether it is rising or falling *quickly* or *slowly*. If the line rises or falls very steeply, then unemployment is changing quickly. If the line is not steep, unemployment is rising or falling slowly. For example, unemployment rose very quickly between 1930 and 1932. Unemployment went up again in 1933 but more slowly. Similarly, when unemployment was falling in the early 1950s, it fell quickly between 1950 and 1951, but then it began to fall much more slowly in 1952 and 1953.

A time-series graph can also be used to depict a trend. A **trend** is a general tendency for a variable to rise or fall. You can see that unemployment had a general tendency to rise from the mid-1940s to the mid-1980s. That is, although there were ups and downs in the unemployment rate, there was an upward trend.

Graphs also allow us to compare different periods quickly. It is apparent, for example, that the 1930s were different from any other period in the twentieth century because of exceptionally high unemployment. You can also see that unemployment fluctuated more violently in the years before 1920 than it did in the years after 1950. The sawtooth pattern is more jagged in the period from 1900 to 1930 than it is in the period after 1950.

Thus we can see that Fig. 2.5 conveys a wealth of information, and it does so in much less space than we have used to describe only some of its features.

Misleading Time-Series Graphs Although time-series graphs are powerful devices for conveying a large amount of information, they can also be used to distort data and to create a misleading picture. The two most commonly used ways of distorting data are stretching and squeezing the scales on the *y*-axis and omitting the origin—the zero point—on the *y*-axis.

Figure 2.6 illustrates the first of these devices. It contains exactly the same information as Fig. 2.5, but the information is packaged in a different way. In part (a) the scale on the *y*-axis has been compressed; in part (b) it has been expanded. When we look at these two parts as a whole, they suggest that unemployment was pretty stable during the first half of this century, but that it has trended upward dramatically in the last 40 years or so.

You might think that this graphical way of distorting data is so outrageous that no one would ever

FIGURE 2.6

Misleading Graphs: Squeezing and Stretching Scales

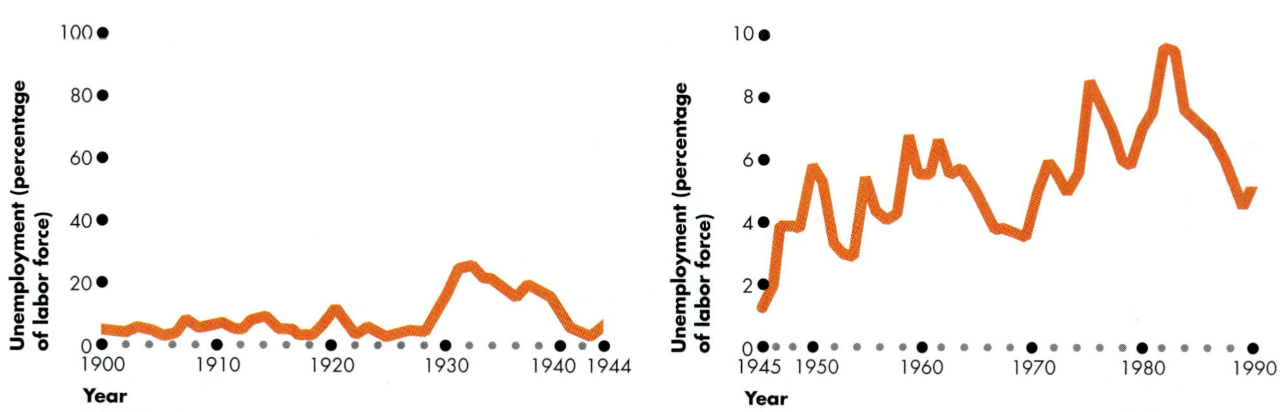

(a) 1900–1944

(b) 1945–1990

Graphs can mislead by squeezing and stretching the scales. These two graphs show exactly the same thing as Fig. 2.5—U.S. unemployment from 1900 to 1990. Part (a) has squeezed the *y*-axis, while part (b) has stretched that axis. The result appears to be a low and stable unemployment rate before 1945 and a rising, highly volatile unemployment rate after that date. Contrast the lie of Fig. 2.6 with the truth of Fig. 2.5.

attempt to use it. If you scrutinize the graphs that you see in newspapers and magazines, you will be surprised how common this device is.

Figure 2.7 illustrates the effect of omitting the origin on the *y*-axis. Sometimes, omitting the origin is precisely the correct thing to do, as it enables the graph to reveal its information. But there are also times when omitting the origin is misleading. In parts (a) and (b), you can see a graph of the unemployment rate between 1970 and 1990. Part (a) includes the origin, and part (b) does not. The graph in part (a) provides a clear account of what hap-

FIGURE 2.7

Omitting the Origin

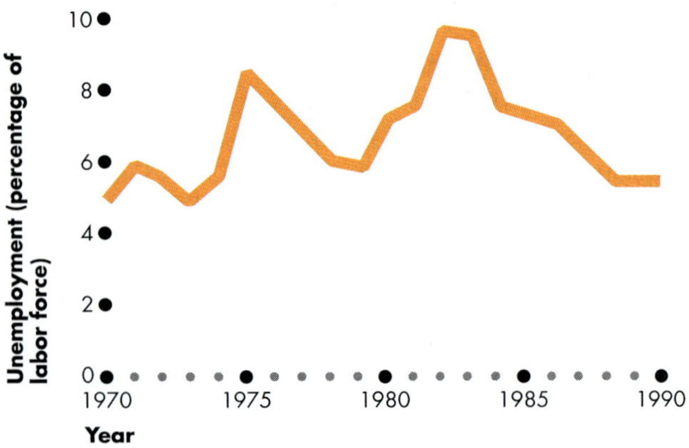

(a) Revealing graph with origin

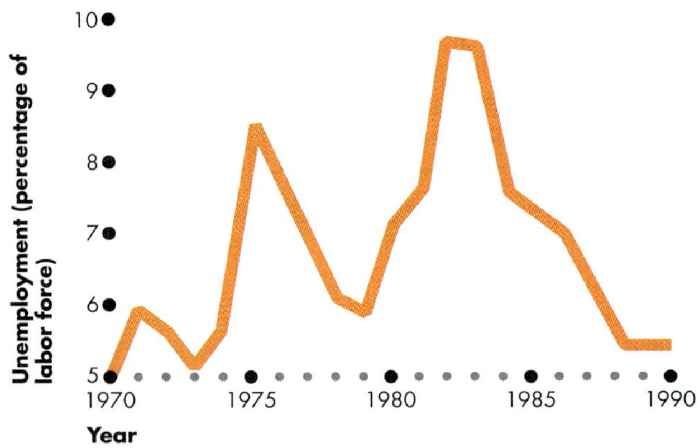

(b) Misleading graph with origin omitted

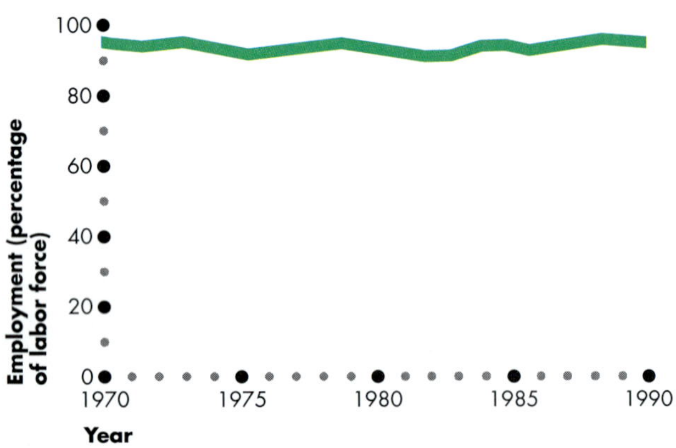

(c) Uniformative graph with origin

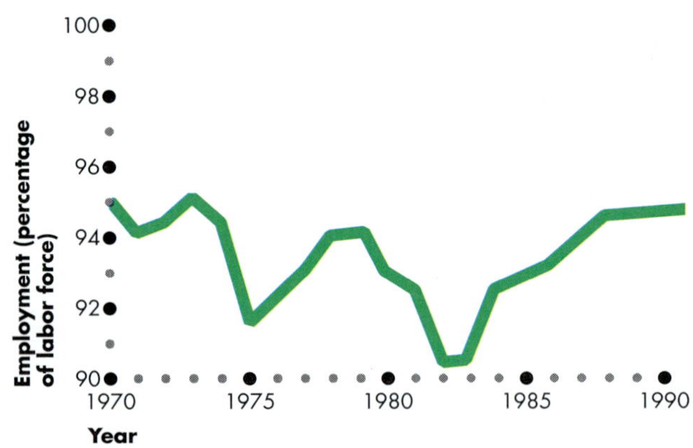

(d) Revealing graph with origin omitted

Sometimes the origin is omitted from a graph. This practice can be either revealing or misleading, depending on how it is used. Parts (a) and (b) graph the U.S. unemployment rate between 1970 and 1990. Part (a) is graphed with the origin on the *y*-axis, and part (b) without it. Part (a) reveals a large amount of information about the level and changes in the unemployment rate over this time period. Part (b) overdramatizes the rises and falls in unemployment and gives no direct visual information about its level.

Parts (c) and (d) graph the employment rate. Part (c) contains an origin on the *y*-axis, and part (d) does not. In this case the graph in part (c) with the origin on the *y*-axis is uninformative and shows virtually no variation in the employment rate. The graph in part (d) gives a clear picture of fluctuations in the employment rate and is more informative than part (c) about those fluctuations.

pened to unemployment over the time period in question. You can use that graph in the same way that we used Fig. 2.5 to describe all the features of unemployment during that time period. But the graph in part (b) is less revealing and distorts the picture. It fails to reveal the *level* of unemployment. It focuses only on, and exaggerates, the magnitude of the increases and decreases in the unemployment rate. In particular, the increases in the unemployment rate in 1974–1975 and in 1981–1982 look enormous when compared with the increases that appear in part (a). With the origin omitted, small percentage changes in unemployment look like many hundredfold changes. Another example of this device is shown in Reading Between the Lines, on pp. 36–37.

Parts (c) and (d) of Fig. 2.7 graph the employment rate—the percentage of the labor force employed. Part (c) includes the origin, and part (d) omits it. As you can see, the graph in part (c) reveals very little about movements in the employment rate. It seems to suggest that the employment rate was pretty constant and lying between 90 and 95 percent. The main feature of part (c) is an enormous amount of empty space and an inefficient use of the space available. Part (d) shows the same information but with the origin omitted. The scale begins at 90 percent. In this case, we can see very clearly the ups and downs in the employment rate. This graph does not provide a visual impression of the level of employment, but it does provide a clear picture of variations in its rate.

The decision about whether to include or exclude the origin of the graph depends on what the graph is designed to reveal. To convey information about the level of employment and unemployment and variations in their rates, the graphs in parts (a) and (d) of Fig. 2.7 are almost equally revealing. By comparison, the graphs in parts (b) and (c) convey almost no information.

Comparing Two Time Series Sometimes we want to use a time-series graph to compare two different variables. For example, suppose you wanted to know how the balance of the government's budget—its surplus or deficit—fluctuated and how those fluctuations compared with fluctuations in the unemployment rate. You can examine two such series by drawing a graph of each of them in the manner shown in Fig. 2.8(a). The scale for the unemployment rate appears on the left side of the figure, and

FIGURE 2.8

Time-Series Relationships

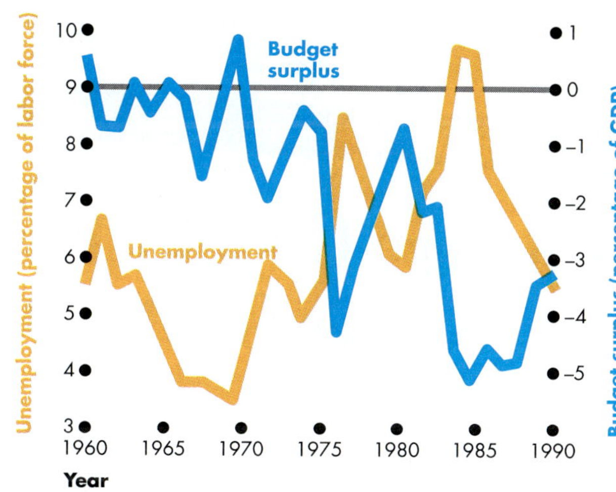

(a) Unemployment and budget surplus

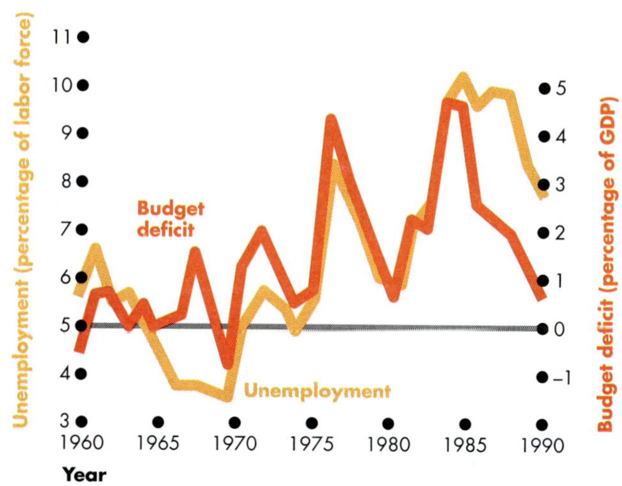

(b) Unemployment and budget deficit

A time-series graph can be used to reveal relationships between two variables. These two graphs show the unemployment rate and the balance of the government's budget between 1960 and 1990. The unemployment line is identical in the two parts. In part (a), the budget balance is shown measuring surpluses upward and deficits downward (as negative numbers) on the right scale. It looks as if the budget goes into a bigger deficit when unemployment rises, but not much else is shown by part (a). Part (b) inverts the scale on which the budget is measured. Now a deficit is measured in the up direction and a surplus in the down direction on the right scale. The relationship between the budget deficit and unemployment is now easier to see.

Graphs in Action

The Wall Street Journal, August 27, 1991

Concern Goes Up as SAT Scores Go Down

By Gary Putka

Scholastic Aptitude Test scores declined despite increased course loads and higher grades in U.S. high schools, suggesting that efforts to reform education are being hampered by falling academic standards. . . .

The average composite score on the SAT, the most-taken college-admissions test, fell to 896 from 900 out of a maximum 1,600. The average score has fallen four years in a row and is at its lowest point since 1983's 893. The verbal score, which fell two points to 422, is the lowest on record at the College Board, the New York organization that gives the test on behalf of U.S. colleges. The score in mathematics, the test's other part, slipped two points to 474, also the lowest since 1984. . . .

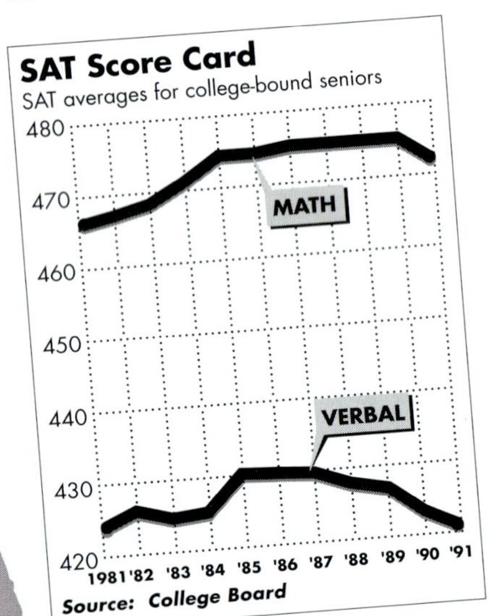

Need for a New Strategy

"You either have to say it's too early and reforms haven't been in place long enough, or all the things we put in the schools were wrong and we need a radical new strategy," said Albert Shanker, president of the American Federation of Teachers. "My own view is the latter is the case." . . .

Mr. Shanker said that his analysis of federal test scores indicate that only 4% of high-school graduates "really know algebra," although 96% of those who took the SAT reported taking an algebra class. Ninety-three percent took geometry. Yet on the math section of the SAT, which is largely a test of algebra and geometry, students got an average of only 26 of 60 questions correct. . . .

Not all of the SAT data pointed to educational setbacks. The total number of test takers, which stayed about flat at one million, represented 42% of this year's high-school graduates, up from 40% in 1990 and an indication of rising educational aspirations. . . .

The Essence of the Story

The average composite SAT score has fallen for four years in a row.

The verbal score in 1991 was the lowest on record, and the mathematics score in 1991 was at its lowest level since 1984.

The 1980s have been years of major reforms in education and of large increases in expenditure on education.

Many people read these facts as a sign of "falling academic standards" and of the failure of the reforms.

The percentage of high school graduates taking the SAT increased from 40 percent in 1990 to 42 percent in 1991.

This last fact is seen as a sign of "rising educational aspirations."

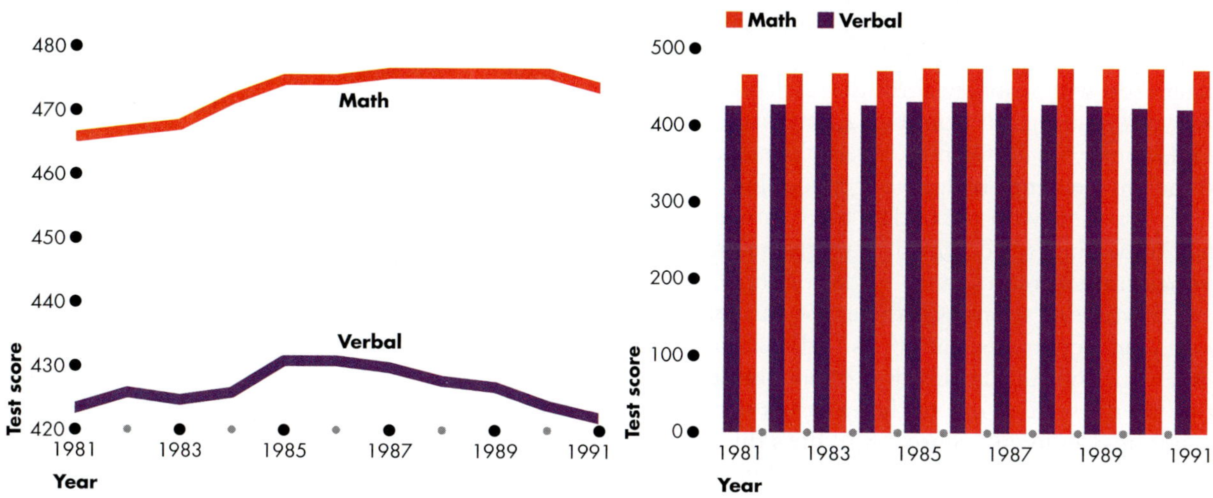

(a) Verbal score dives and math sags in 1991

(b) Verbal score steady and math gets better

Figure 1

Background and Analysis

A 2 percent fall in the SAT verbal score is shown in both parts of Fig. 1, but the false impression of a large fall is created in part (a)—as in the news story—by omitting thc origin.

During the 1980s, the number of students taking the SAT increased and the college entry age population decreased. The percentage of the college entry age population taking the SAT increased from 23 percent in 1981 to 29 percent in 1991.

Other things being equal, the larger the percentage of the population taking *any* test, the lower the average score.

Figure 2 gives a third view of the falling SAT scores that shows the relationship between the SAT scores and the percentage of the college entry age population taking the test.

Despite the increased percentage taking the test, the math score increased throughout the 1980s and dipped only in 1991. These facts suggest remarkable improvements in mathematical achievement.

The verbal score increased between 1981 and 1985 but declined as the percentage taking the test increased after 1985. It continued to decline in 1990 and 1991, even though the percentage of the population taking the test stabilized.

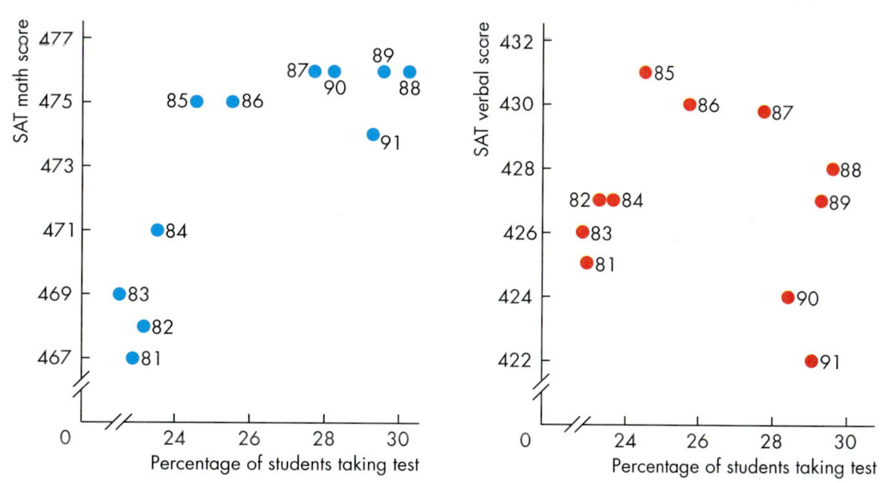

(a) SAT math score and percentage taking test

(b) SAT verbal score and percentage taking test

Figure 2

the scale for the government's budget surplus appears on the right. The purple line shows unemployment, and the blue line shows the government's budget. You will probably agree that it is pretty hard work figuring out from Fig. 2.8(a) just what the relationship is between the unemployment rate and the government's budget. But it does look as if there is a tendency for the budget to go into a bigger deficit (blue line goes downward) when the unemployment rate increases (purple line goes upward). In other words, it seems as if these two variables have a tendency to move in opposite directions.

In a situation such as this, it is often more revealing to flip the scale of one of the variables over and graph it upside-down. Figure 2.8(b) does this. The unemployment rate in part (b) is graphed in exactly the same way as in part (a). But the government's budget has been flipped over. Now, instead of measuring the deficit (a negative number) in the down direction and the surplus (a positive number) in the up direction, we measure the deficit upward and the surplus downward. You can now "see" very clearly the relationship between these two variables. There is indeed a tendency for the government's deficit to get bigger when the unemployment rate gets higher. But the relationship is by no means an exact one. There are significant periods, clearly revealed in the graph, when the deficit and the unemployment rate move apart. You can "see" these periods as those in which the gap between the two lines widens.

Now that we have seen how we can use graphs in economics to represent economic data and to show the relationship between variables, let us examine how economists use graphs in a more abstract way to construct and analyze economic models.

Graphs Used in Economic Models

Although you will encounter many different kinds of graphs in economics, there are some patterns that, once you have learned to recognize them, will instantly convey to you the meaning of a graph. There are graphs that show each of the following:

- Things that go up and down together
- Things that move in opposite directions
- Things that have a maximum or a minimum
- Things that are not related to each other at all

Let's look at these four cases.

Things That Go Up and Down Together

Graphs that show the relationship between two variables that move up and down together are shown in Fig. 2.9. The relationship between two variables that move in the same direction is called a **positive relationship.** Such a relationship is shown by a line that slopes upward.

Part (a) shows the relationship between the number of miles traveled in 5 hours and speed. For example, the point marked *a* tells us that we will travel 200 miles in 5 hours if our speed is 40 miles an hour. If we double our speed and travel at 80 miles an hour, we will cover a distance of 400 miles in 5 hours. The relationship between the number of miles traveled in 5 hours and speed is represented by an upward-sloping straight line. A relationship depicted by a straight line is called a **linear relationship.**

Part (b) shows the relationship between distance sprinted and exhaustion (exhaustion being measured by the time it takes the heart rate to return to normal). This relationship is an upward-sloping one depicted by a curved line that starts out with a gentle slope but then becomes steeper as we move along the curve away from the origin.

Part (c) shows the relationship between the number of problems worked by a student and the amount of study time. This relationship is illustrated by an upward-sloping curved line that starts out with a steep slope but then becomes more gentle as we move away from the origin.

There are three types of upward-sloping lines in the graphs in Fig. 2.9: one straight and two curved. But they are all called curves. Any line on a graph—no matter whether it is straight or curved—is called a **curve.**

Things That Move in Opposite Directions

Figure 2.10 shows relationships between things that move in opposite directions. A relationship between variables that move in opposite directions is called a **negative relationship.**

FIGURE 2.9

Positive Relationships

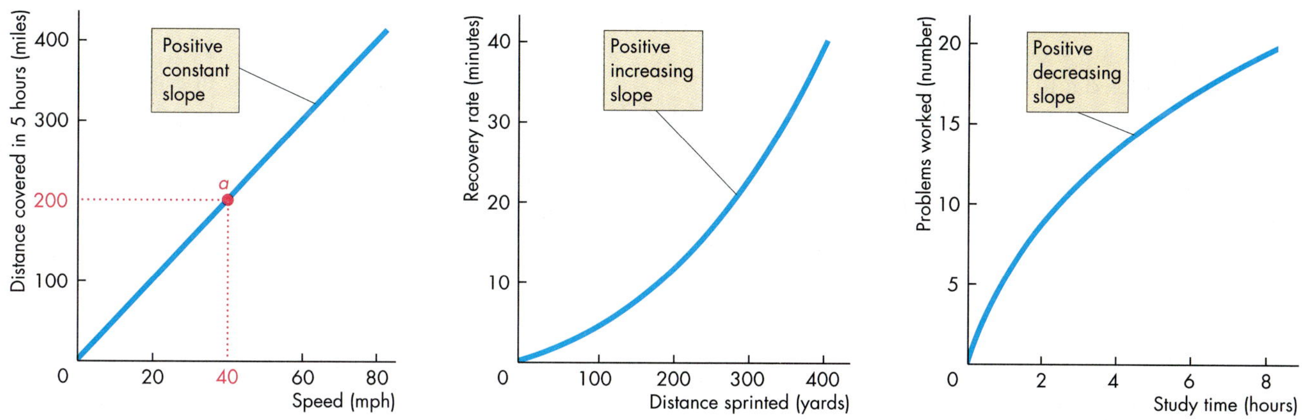

(a) Positive constant slope **(b) Positive increasing slope** **(c) Positive decreasing slope**

Each part of this figure shows a positive relationship between two variables. That is, as the value of the variable measured on the *x*-axis increases, so does the value of the variable measured on the *y*-axis. Part (a) illustrates a linear relationship—a relationship whose slope is constant as we move along the curve. Part (b) illustrates a positive relationship whose slope becomes steeper as we move along the curve away from the origin. It is a positive relationship with an increasing slope. Part (c) shows a positive relationship whose slope becomes flatter as we move away from the origin. It is a positive relationship with a decreasing slope.

FIGURE 2.10

Negative Relationships

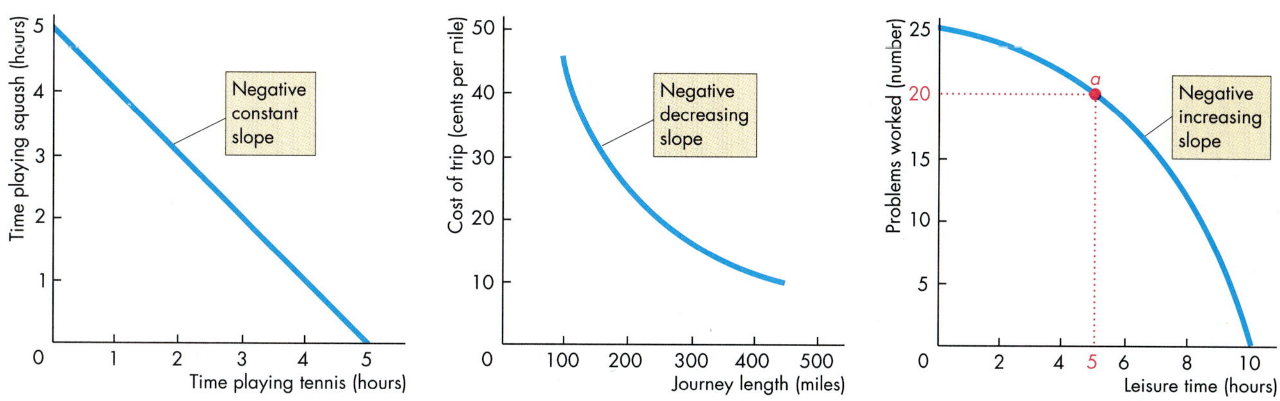

(a) Negative constant slope **(b) Negative decreasing slope** **(c) Negative increasing slope**

Each part of this figure shows a negative relationship between two variables. Part (a) shows a linear relationship—a relationship whose slope is constant as we travel along the curve. Part (b) shows a negative relationship of decreasing slope. That is, the slope of the relationship gets less steep as we travel along the curve from left to right. Part (c) shows a negative relationship of increasing slope. That is, the slope becomes steeper as we travel along the curve from left to right.

Part (a) shows the relationship between the number of hours available for playing squash and the number of hours for playing tennis. One extra hour spent playing tennis means one hour less playing squash and vice versa. This relationship is negative and linear.

Part (b) shows the relationship between the cost per mile traveled and the length of a journey. The longer the journey, the lower is the cost per mile. But as the journey length increases, the cost per mile decreases at a decreasing rate. This feature of the relationship is illustrated by the fact that the curve slopes downward, starting out steep at a short journey length and then becoming flatter as the journey length increases.

Part (c) shows the relationship between the amount of leisure time and the number of problems worked by a student. If the student takes no leisure, 25 problems can be worked. If the student takes 5 hours of leisure, only 20 problems can be worked (point *a*). Increasing leisure time beyond 5 hours produces a large reduction in the number of problems worked, and if the student takes 10 hours of leisure a day, no problems get worked. This relationship is a negative one that starts out with a gentle slope at a low number of leisure hours and becomes increasingly steep as leisure hours increase.

Things That Have a Maximum and a Minimum

Economics is about optimizing, or doing the best with limited resources. Examples of optimizing include making the highest possible profits and achieving the lowest possible costs of production. Economists make frequent use of graphs depicting relationships that have a maximum or a minimum. Figure 2.11 illustrates such relationships.

Part (a) shows the relationship between rainfall and wheat yield. When there is no rainfall, wheat will not grow, so the yield is zero. As the rainfall increases up to 10 days a month, the wheat yield also increases. With 10 rainy days each month, the wheat yield reaches its maximum at 40 bushels an acre (point *a*). Rain in excess of 10 days a month starts to lower the yield of wheat. If every day is rainy, the wheat suffers from a lack of sunshine and the yield falls back almost to zero. This relationship

FIGURE 2.11

Maximum and Minimum Points

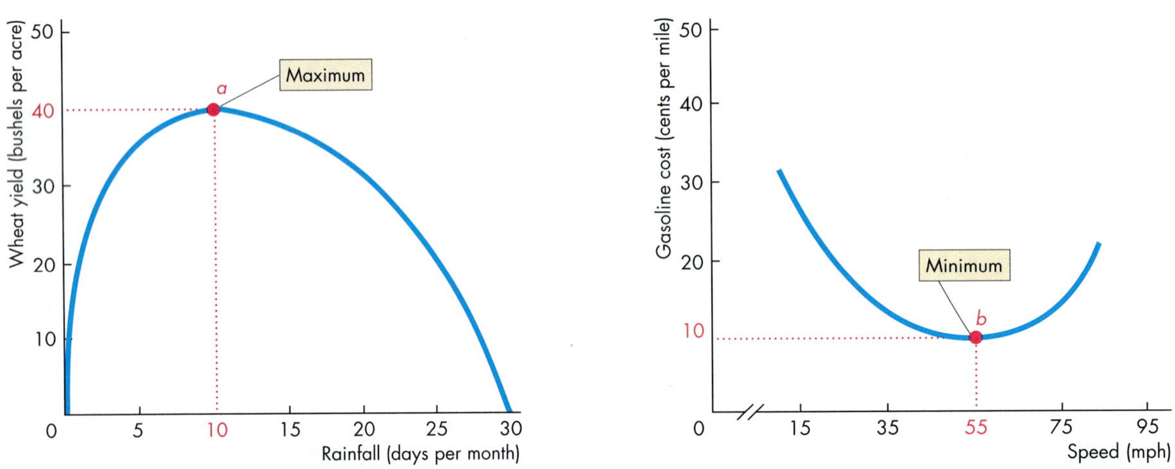

(a) Maximum

(b) Minimum

Part (a) shows a relationship that has a maximum point, *a*. The curve rises at first, reaches its highest point, and then falls. Part (b) shows a relationship with a minimum point, *b*. The curve falls to its minimum and then rises.

is one that starts out positive, reaches a maximum, and then becomes negative.

Part (b) shows the reverse case—a relationship that begins with a negative slope, falls to a minimum, and then becomes positive. An example of such a relationship is the gasoline cost per mile as the speed of travel varies. At low speeds, the car is creeping along in a traffic snarl-up. The number of miles per gallon is low, so the gasoline cost per mile is high. At very high speeds, the car is operated beyond its most efficient rate, and again the number of miles per gallon is low and the gasoline cost per mile is high. At a speed of 55 miles an hour, the gasoline cost per mile traveled is at its minimum (point *b*).

Things That Are Independent

There are many situations in which one variable is independent of another. No matter what happens to the value of one variable, the other variable remains constant. Sometimes we want to show the independence between two variables in a graph. Figure 2.12 shows two ways of achieving this. In part (a), your grade in economics is shown on the vertical axis against the price of bananas on the horizontal axis. Your grade (75 percent in this example) does not depend on the price of bananas. The relationship between these two variables is shown by a horizontal straight line. In part (b), the output of French wine is shown on the horizontal axis and the number of rainy days a month in California is shown on the vertical axis. Again, the output of French wine (3 billion gallons a year in this example) does not change when the number of rainy days in California changes. The relationship between these two variables is shown by a vertical straight line.

Figures 2.9 through 2.12 illustrate ten different shapes of graphs that we will encounter in economic models. In describing these graphs, we have talked about curves that slope upward or slope downward and slopes that are steep or gentle. The concept of slope is an important one. Let's spend a little time discussing exactly what we mean by slope.

FIGURE 2.12

Variables with No Relationship

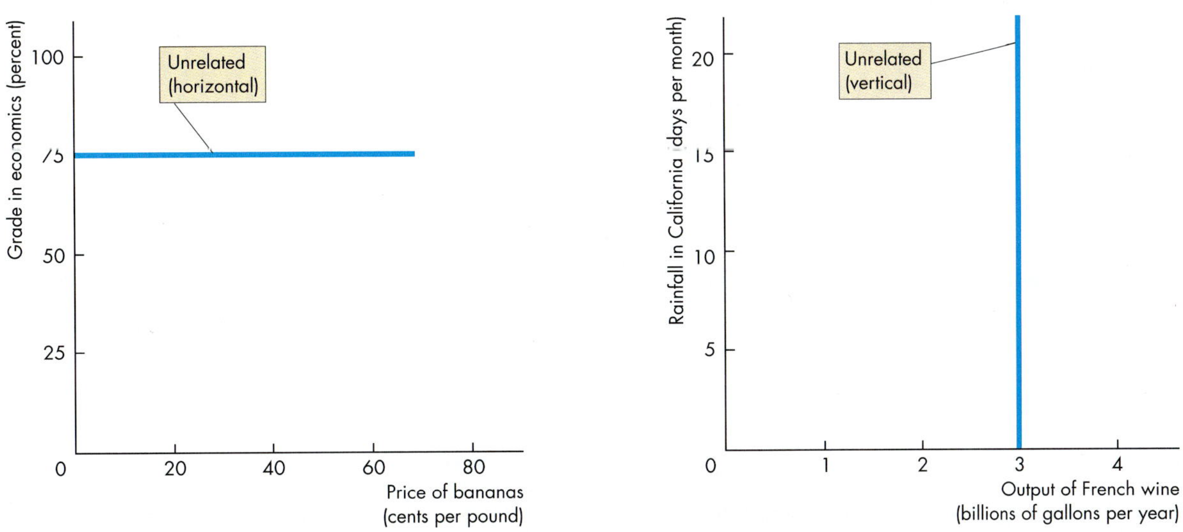

(a) Unrelated: horizontal

(b) Unrelated: vertical

This figure shows how we can graph two variables that are unrelated to each other. In part (a), a student's grade in economics is plotted at 75 percent regardless of the price of bananas on the *x*-axis. In part (b), the output of the vineyards of France does not vary with the rainfall in California.

The Slope of a Relationship

The **slope** of a relationship is the change in the value of the variable measured on the y-axis divided by the change in the value of the variable measured on the x-axis. We use the Greek letter Δ to represent "change in." Thus Δy means the change in the value of the variable measured on the y-axis, and Δx means the change in the value of the variable measured on the x-axis. Therefore the slope of the relationship is

$$\Delta y/\Delta x.$$

If a large change in the variable measured on the y-axis (Δy) is associated with a small change in the variable measured on the x-axis (Δx), the slope is large and the curve is steep. If a small change in the variable measured on the y-axis (Δy) is associated with a large change in the variable measured on the x-axis (Δx), the slope is small and the curve is flat.

We can make the idea of slope sharper by doing some calculations.

Calculating Slope of a Straight Line

The slope of a straight line is the same regardless of where on the line you calculate it. Thus the slope of a straight line is constant. Let's calculate the slopes of the lines in Fig. 2.13. In part (a), when x increases from 2 to 6, y increases from 3 to 6. The change in x is +4—that is, Δx is 4. The change in y is +3—that is, Δy is 3. The slope of that line is

$$\frac{\Delta y}{\Delta x} = \frac{3}{4}.$$

FIGURE 2.13

The Slope of a Straight Line

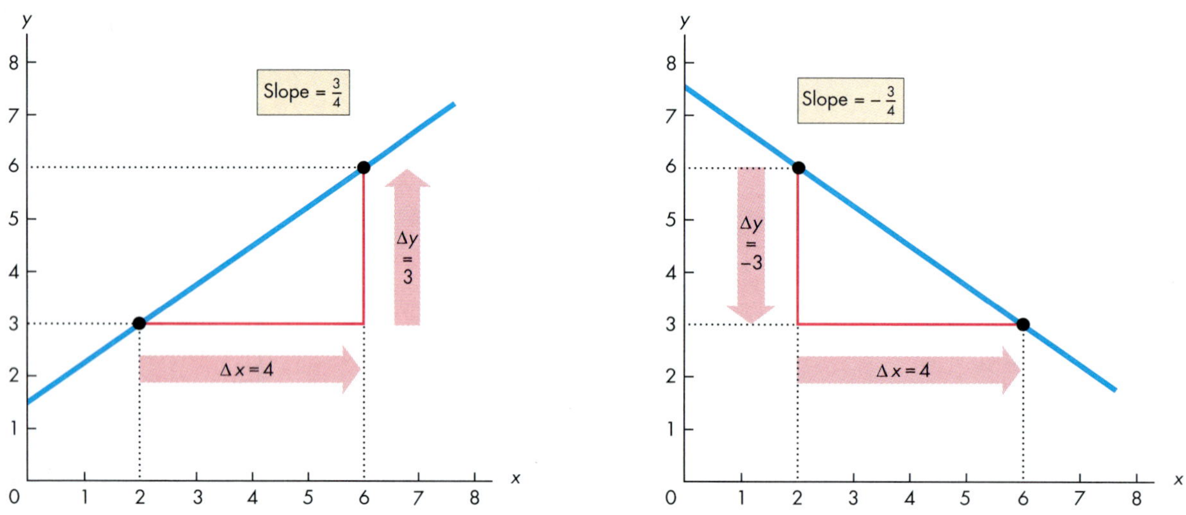

(a) Positive slope **(b) Negative slope**

To calculate the slope of a straight line, we divide the change in the value of the variable measured on the y-axis by the change in the value of the variable measured on the x-axis. Part (a) shows the calculation of a positive slope (when x goes up, y goes up). When x goes up from 2 to 6, the change in x is 4—that is, Δx equals 4. That change in x brings about an increase in y from 3 to 6, so Δy equals 3. The slope ($\Delta y/\Delta x$) equals 3/4. Part (b) shows a negative slope (when x goes up, y goes down). When x goes up from 2 to 6, Δx equals 4. That change in x brings about a decrease in y from 6 to 3, so Δy equals −3. The slope ($\Delta y/\Delta x$) equals −3/4.

In part (b), when x increases from 2 to 6, y decreases from 6 to 3. The change in y is *minus* 3—that is, Δy is –3. The change in x is *plus* 4—that is, Δx is +4. The slope of the curve is

$$\frac{\Delta y}{\Delta x} = \frac{-3}{4}.$$

Notice that the two slopes have the same magnitude (3/4), but the slope of the line in part (a) is positive (+3/+4 = 3/4), while that in part (b) is negative (–3/+4 = –3/4). The slope of a positive relationship is positive; the slope of a negative relationship is negative.

Calculating Slope of a Curved Line

Calculating the slope of a curved line is trickier. The slope of a curved line is not constant. Its slope depends on where on the line we calculate it. There are two ways to calculate the slope of a curved line: you can calculate the slope at a point on the line, or you can calculate the slope across an arc of the line. Let's look at the two alternatives.

Slope at a Point To calculate the slope at a point on a curved line, you need to construct a straight line that has the same slope as the curve at the point in question. Figure 2.14 shows how such a calculation is made. Suppose you want to calculate the

FIGURE 2.14

The Slope of a Curve

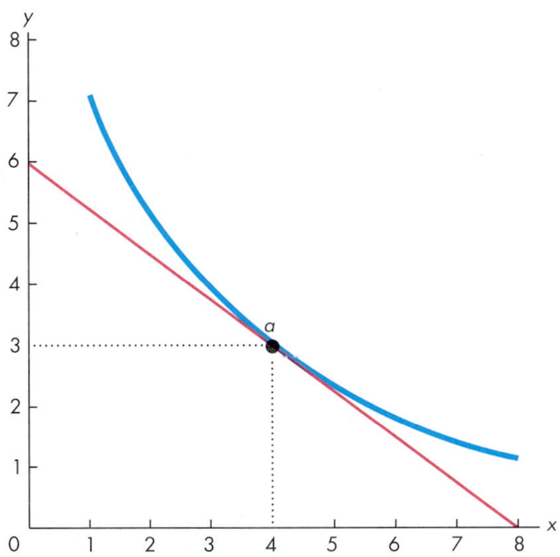

(a) Slope at a point

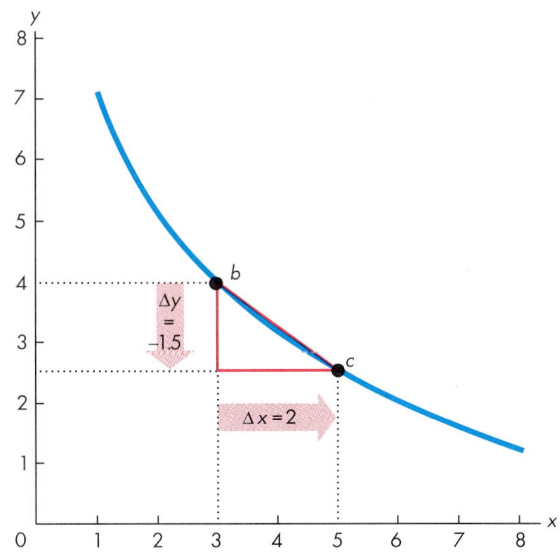

(b) Slope across an arc

The slope of a curve can be calculated either at a point, as in part (a), or across an arc, as in part (b). The slope at a point is calculated by finding the slope of a straight line that touches the curve only at one point. One such straight line touches the curve at point *a*. The slope of that straight line is calculated by dividing the change in *y* by the change in *x*. When *x* increases from 0 to 8, Δx equals 8. That change in *x* is associated with a fall in *y* from 6 to 0, so Δy equals –6. The slope of the line is –6/8, or –3/4.

To calculate the slope across an arc, we place a straight line across the curve from one point to another and then calculate the slope of that straight line. One such line is that from *b* to *c* in part (b). The slope of the straight line *bc* is calculated by dividing the change in *y* by the change in *x*. In moving from *b* to *c*, *x* goes up by 2, Δx equals 2, and *y* goes down by 1½, Δy equals –1½. The slope of the line *bc* is –1½ divided by 2, or –3/4.

slope of the curve at the point marked *a*. Place a ruler on the graph so that it touches point *a* and no other point on the curve; then draw a straight line along the edge of the ruler. The straight red line in part (a) is such a line. If the ruler touches the curve only at point *a*, then the slope of the curve at point *a* must be the same as the slope of the edge of the ruler. If the curve and the ruler do not have the same slope, the line along the edge of the ruler will cut the curve instead of just touching it.

Having now found a straight line with the same slope as the curve at point *a*, you can calculate the slope of the curve at point *a* by calculating the slope of the straight line. We already know how to calculate the slope of a straight line, so the task is straightforward. In this case, as x increases from 0 to 8 ($\Delta x = 8$), y decreases from 6 to 0 ($\Delta y = -6$). Therefore the slope of the straight line is

$$\frac{\Delta y}{\Delta x} = \frac{-6}{8} = \frac{-3}{4}.$$

Thus the slope of the curve at point *a* is –3/4.

Slope across an Arc Calculating a slope across an arc is similar to calculating an average slope. In Fig. 2.14(b), we are looking at the same curve as in part (a), but instead of calculating the slope at point *a*, we calculate the slope for a change in x from 3 to 5. As x increases from 3 to 5, y decreases from 4 to 2½. The change in x is +2 ($\Delta x = 2$). The change in y is –1½ ($\Delta y = -1\frac{1}{2}$). Therefore the slope of the line is

$$\frac{\Delta y}{\Delta x} = \frac{-1\frac{1}{2}}{2} = \frac{-3}{4}.$$

This calculation gives us the slope of the line between points *b* and *c*. In this particular example, the slope of the arc *bc* is identical to the slope of the curve at point *a* in part (a). Calculating the slope does not always work out so neatly. You might have some fun constructing counterexamples.

Graphing Relationships among More Than Two Variables

We have seen that we can graph a single variable as a point on a straight line and we can graph the relationship between two variables as a point formed by the x- and y-coordinates in a two-dimensional graph. You might be suspecting that although a two-dimensional graph is informative, most of the things in which you are likely to be interested involve relationships among many variables, not just two.

Examples of relationships among more than two variables abound. For example, consider the relationship between the price of ice cream, the air temperature, and the amount of ice cream eaten. If ice cream is expensive and the temperature is low, people eat much less ice cream than when ice cream is inexpensive and the temperature is high. For any given price of ice cream, the quantity consumed varies with the temperature; for any given temperature, the quantity of ice cream consumed varies with its price.

Other Things Being Equal

Figure 2.15 illustrates such a situation. The table shows the number of gallons of ice cream that will be eaten each day at various temperatures and ice cream prices. How can we graph all these numbers? To graph a relationship that involves more than two variables, we consider what happens if all but two of the variables are held constant. This device is called ceteris paribus. **Ceteris paribus** is a Latin phrase that means "other things being equal." For example, in Fig. 2.15(a), you can see what happens to the quantity of ice cream consumed when the price of ice cream varies while the temperature is held constant. The line labeled 70°F shows the relationship between ice cream consumption and the price of ice cream when the temperature stays at 70°F. The numbers used to plot that line are those in the third column of the table in Fig. 2.15. For example, when the temperature is 70°F, 18 gallons are consumed when the price is 30¢ a scoop and 13 gallons are consumed when the price is 45¢. The curve labeled 90°F shows the consumption of ice cream when the price varies and the temperature is 90°F.

Alternatively, we can show the relationship between ice cream consumption and temperature while holding the price of ice cream constant, as is shown in Fig. 2.15(b). The curve labeled 30¢ shows how the consumption of ice cream varies with the temperature when ice cream costs 30¢, and a second curve shows the relationship when ice cream costs 15¢. For example, at 30¢ a scoop, 12 gallons are

FIGURE 2.15

Graphing a Relationship among Three Variables

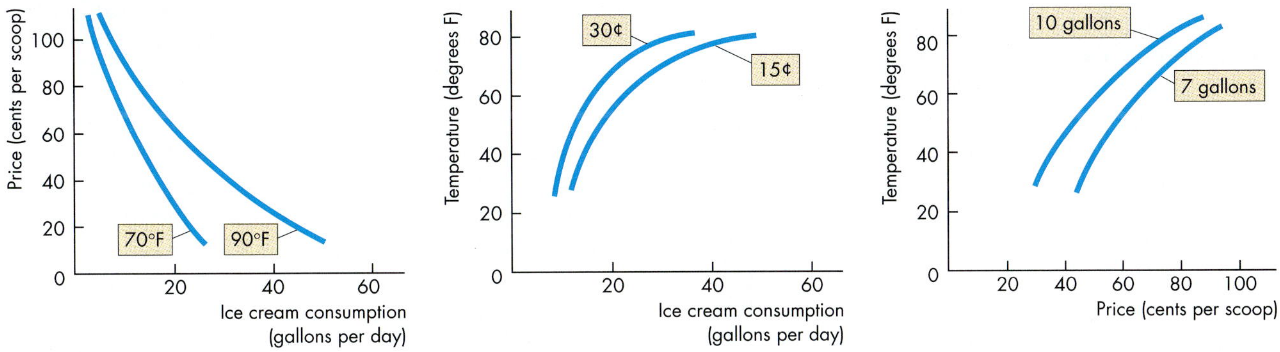

(a) Price and consumption at a given temperature

(b) Temperature and consumption at a given price

(c) Temperature and price at a given consumption

Price (cents per scoop)	Ice cream consumption (gallons per day)			
	30°F	50°F	70°F	90°F
15	**12**	**18**	**25**	**50**
30	**10**	**12**	**18**	**37**
45	**7**	**10**	**13**	**27**
60	**5**	**7**	**10**	**20**
75	**3**	**5**	**7**	**14**
90	**2**	**3**	**5**	**10**
105	**1**	**2**	**3**	**6**

The quantity of ice cream consumed (one variable) depends on its price (a second variable) and the air temperature (a third variable). The table provides some hypothetical numbers that tell us how many gallons of ice cream are consumed each day at different prices and different temperatures. For example, if the price is 45¢ per scoop and the temperature is 50°F, 10 gallons of ice cream will be consumed. To graph a relationship among three variables, the value of one variable must be held constant.

Part (a) shows the relationship between price and consumption, holding temperature constant. One curve holds temperature constant at 90°F and the other at 70°F. Part (b) shows the relationship between temperature and consumption, holding price constant. One curve holds the price at 30¢ and the other at 15¢. Part (c) shows the relationship between temperature and price, holding consumption constant. One curve holds consumption constant at 10 gallons and the other at 7 gallons.

consumed when the temperature is 50°F and 18 gallons when the temperature is 70°F.

Figure 2.15(c) shows the combinations of temperature and price that result in a constant consumption of ice cream. One curve shows the combination that results in 10 gallons a day being consumed, and the other shows the combination that results in 7 gallons a day being consumed. A high price and a high temperature lead to the same consumption as a lower price and lower temperature. For example, 7 gallons are consumed at 30°F and 45 cents per scoop and at 70°F and 75 cents per scoop.

◆ ◆ ◆ ◆ With what you have now learned about graphs, you can move forward with your study of economics. There are no graphs in this book that are more complicated than those that have been explained here.

SUMMARY

Graphing Data

There are two main types of graphs used to represent economic data: scatter diagrams and time-series graphs. A scatter diagram plots the value of one economic variable associated with the value of another. Such a diagram reveals whether or not there is a relationship between two variables and, if there is a relationship, its nature.

A time-series graph plots the value of one or more economic variables on the vertical axis (y-axis) and time on the horizontal axis (x-axis). A well-constructed time-series graph quickly reveals the level, direction of change, and speed of change of a variable. It also reveals trends. Graphs sometimes mislead, especially when the origin is omitted or when the scale is stretched or squeezed to exaggerate or understate a variation. (pp. 29–38)

Graphs Used in Economic Models

Graphs are used in economic models to illustrate relationships between variables. There are four cases: positive relationships, negative relationships, relationships that have a maximum or a minimum, and variables that are not related to each other. Examples of these different types of relationships are summarized in Figs. 2.9 through 2.12. (pp. 38–41)

The Slope of a Relationship

The slope of a relationship is calculated as the change in the value of the variable measured on the y-axis divided by the change in the value of the variable measured on the x-axis, that is, $\Delta y/\Delta x$. A straight line has a constant slope, but a curved line has a varying slope. To calculate the slope of a curved line, we calculate the slope either at a point or across an arc. (pp. 42–44)

Graphing Relationships among More Than Two Variables

To graph a relationship among more than two variables, we hold constant the values of all the variables except two. We then plot the value of one of the variables against the value of another. Holding constant all the variables but two is called the ceteris paribus assumption—the assumption of other things being equal. (pp. 44–45)

KEY ELEMENTS

Key Terms

Axes, 29
Ceteris paribus, 44
Coordinates, 30
Curve, 38
Linear relationship, 38
Negative relationship, 38
Origin, 29
Positive relationship, 38
Scatter diagram, 30
Slope, 42
Time-series graph, 32
Trend, 33
x-axis, 29
x-coordinate, 30
y-axis, 29
y-coordinate, 30

Key Figures

REVIEW QUESTIONS

1 Why do we use graphs?

2 What are the two scale lines on a graph called?

3 What is the origin on a graph?

4 What do we mean by the y-coordinate and the x-coordinate?

5 What is a scatter diagram?

6 What is a time-series graph?

7 List three things that a time-series graph shows quickly and easily.

8 What do we mean by trend?

9 Sketch some graphs to illustrate the following:

- **a** Two variables that move up and down together
- **b** Two variables that move in opposite directions
- **c** A relationship between two variables that has a maximum
- **d** A relationship between two variables that has a minimum

10 Which of the relationships in question 9 is a positive relationship and which a negative relationship?

11 What is the definition of the slope of a relationship?

12 What are the two ways of calculating the slope of a curved line?

13 How do we graph relationships among more than two variables?

PROBLEMS

1 The inflation rate in the United States between 1970 and 1990 was as follows:

Year	Inflation rate (percent per year)
1970	5.7
1971	4.4
1972	3.2
1973	6.2
1974	11.0
1975	9.1
1976	5.8
1977	6.5
1978	7.6
1979	11.3
1980	13.5
1981	10.3
1982	6.2
1983	3.2
1984	4.3
1985	3.6
1986	1.9
1987	3.6
1988	4.1
1989	4.8
1990	5.4

Draw a time-series graph of these data, and use your graph to answer the following questions:

- **a** In which year was inflation highest?
- **b** In which year was inflation lowest?
- **c** In which years did inflation rise?
- **d** In which years did inflation fall?
- **e** In which year did inflation rise/fall the fastest?
- **f** In which year did inflation rise/fall the slowest?
- **g** What have been the main trends in inflation?

2 Interest rates on treasury bills in the United States between 1970 and 1990 were as follows:

Year	Interest rate (percent per year)
1970	6.5
1971	4.3

Year	Interest rate (percent per year)
1972	4.1
1973	7.0
1974	7.9
1975	5.8
1976	5.0
1977	5.3
1978	7.2
1979	10.0
1980	11.5
1981	14.0
1982	10.7
1983	8.6
1984	9.6
1985	7.5
1986	6.0
1987	5.8
1988	6.7
1989	8.1
1990	7.5

Use these data together with those in problem 1 to draw a scatter diagram showing the relationship between inflation and the interest rate. Use this diagram to determine whether there is a relationship between inflation and the interest rate and whether it is positive or negative.

3 Use the following information to draw a graph showing the relationship between two variables x and y:

x	0	1	2	3	4	5	6	7	8
y	0	1	4	9	16	25	36	49	64

a Is the relationship between x and y positive or negative?

b Does the slope of the relationship rise or fall as the value of x rises?

4 Using the data in problem 3:

a Calculate the slope of the relationship between x and y when x equals 4.

b Calculate the slope of the arc when x rises from 3 to 4.

c Calculate the slope of the arc when x rises from 4 to 5.

d Calculate the slope of the arc when x rises from 3 to 5.

e What do you notice that is interesting about your answers to (b), (c), and (d) compared with your answer to (a)?

5 Calculate the slopes of the following two relationships between two variables x and y:

a

x	0	2	4	6	8	10
y	20	16	12	8	4	0

b

x	0	2	4	6	8	10
y	0	8	16	24	32	40

6 Draw a graph showing the following relationship between two variables x and y:

x	0	1	2	3	4	5	6	7	8	9
y	0	2	4	6	8	10	8	6	4	2

a Is the slope positive or negative when x is less than 5?

b Is the slope positive or negative when x is greater than 5?

c What is the slope of this relationship when x equals 5?

d Is y at a maximum or at a minimum when x equals 5?

7 Draw a graph showing the following relationship between two variables x and y:

x	0	1	2	3	4	5	6	7	8	9
y	10	8	6	4	2	0	2	4	6	8

a Is the slope positive or negative when x is less than 5?

b Is the slope positive or negative when x is greater than 5?

c What is the slope of this relationship when x equals 5?

d Is y at a maximum or at a minimum when x equals 5?

CHAPTER 3

PRODUCTION, SPECIALIZATION, AND EXCHANGE

After studying this chapter, you will be able to:

- Define the production possibility frontier
- Calculate opportunity cost
- Explain why economic growth and technological change do not provide free gifts
- Explain comparative advantage
- Explain why people specialize and how they gain from trade
- Explain why property rights and money have evolved

Making the Most of It

WE LIVE IN A STYLE THAT MOST OF OUR GRANDPARENTS could not even have imagined. Advances in medicine have cured diseases that terrified them. Most of us live in better and more spacious homes. We eat more, we grow taller, we are even born larger than they were. Our parents are amazed at the matter-of-fact way in which we handle computers. We casually use products—microwave ovens, graphite tennis rackets, digital watches—that didn't exist in their youth. Economic growth has made us richer than our parents and grandparents. ◆◆ But economic growth and technological change, and the wealth they bestow, have not liberated us from scarcity. Why not? Why, despite our immense wealth, do we still have to face costs? Why are there no "free lunches"? ◆◆ We see an incredible amount of specialization and trading in the modern world. Each one of us specializes in a particular job—as lawyer, car maker, homemaker. Countries and regions also specialize—Florida in orange juice, Idaho in potatoes, Detroit in cars, and the Silicon Valley in computer-related products. We have become so specialized that one farm worker can feed 100 people. Only one in five of us works in manufacturing. More than half of us work in wholesale and retail trade, banking and finance, other services, and government. Why do we specialize? How do we benefit from specialization and exchange? ◆◆ Over many centuries, institutions and social arrangements have evolved that today we take for granted. One of them is private property rights, together with the legal system that protects them. Another is money. Why have these institutions evolved? And how do they extend our ability to specialize and increase production?

◆ ◆ ◆ ◆ These are the questions that we tackle in this chapter. We will begin by making the idea of scarcity more precise. Then we will go on to see how we can measure opportunity cost. We will also see how, when each individual tries to get the most out of scarce resources, specialization and exchange occur. That is, people specialize in doing what they do best and exchange their products with other specialists. We are also going to see why such institutions as private property and money exist and how they arise from people's attempts to make the most of their limited resources.

The Production Possibility Frontier

What do we mean by production? **Production** is the conversion of *land, labor,* and *capital* into goods and services. We defined the factors of production in Chapter 1. Let's briefly recall what they are.

Land is all the gifts of nature. It includes the air, the water, and the land surface, as well as the minerals that lie beneath the surface of the earth. *Labor* is all the muscle-power and brain-power of human beings. The voices and artistry of singers and actors, the strength and coordination of athletes, the daring of astronauts, the political skill of diplomats, as well as the physical and mental skills of the many millions of people who make cars and cola, gum and glue, wallpaper and watering cans are included in this category.

Capital is all the goods that have been produced and can now be used in the production of other goods and services. Examples include the interstate highway system, the fine buildings of great cities, dams and power projects, airports and jumbo jets, car production lines, shirt factories, and cookie shops. A special kind of capital is called human capital. **Human capital** is the accumulated skill and knowledge of human beings, which arise from their training and education.

Goods and services are all the valuable things that people produce. Goods are tangible—cars, spoons, VCRs, and bread. Services are intangible—haircuts, amusement park rides, and telephone calls. There are two types of goods: capital goods and consumption goods. **Capital goods** are goods that are used in the production process and can be used many times before they eventually wear out. Examples of capital goods are buildings, computers, automobiles, and telephones. **Consumption goods** are goods that can be used just once. Examples are dill pickles and toothpaste. **Consumption** is the process of using up goods and services.

Our limited resources and the technologies available for transforming those resources into goods and services limit what can be produced. That limit is described by the production possibility frontier. The **production possibility frontier** (PPF) marks the boundary between those combinations of goods and services that can be produced and those that cannot. It is important to understand the production possibility frontier in the real world, but to achieve that goal more easily, we will first study an economy that is simpler than the one in which we live—a model economy.

A Model Economy

Instead of looking at the real-world economy with all its complexity and detail, we will build a model of an economy. The model will have features that are essential to understanding the real economy, but we will ignore most of reality's immense detail. Our model economy will be simpler in three important ways:

1. Everything that is produced is also consumed so that in our model, capital resources neither grow nor shrink. (Later we will examine what happens if we consume less than we produce and add to capital resources.)
2. There are only two goods, corn and cloth. (In the real world we use our scarce resources to produce countless goods and services.)
3. There is only one person, Jane, who lives on a deserted island and has no dealings with other people. (Later we will see what happens when Jane's island economy has links with another economy. Also, we'll extend our view to the real world with its five billion people.)

Jane uses all the resources of her island economy to produce corn and cloth. She works 10 hours each day. The amount of corn and cloth that Jane produces depends on how many hours she devotes to

TABLE 3.1

Jane's Production Possibilities

Hours worked (per day)		Corn grown (pounds per month)		Cloth produced (yards per month)
0	**either**	**0**	**or**	**0**
2	**either**	**6**	**or**	**1**
4	**either**	**11**	**or**	**2**
6	**either**	**15**	**or**	**3**
8	**either**	**18**	**or**	**4**
10	**either**	**20**	**or**	**5**

If Jane does no work, she produces no corn or cloth. If she works for 2 hours per day and spends the entire amount of time on corn production, she produces 6 pounds of corn per month. If that same time is used for cloth production, 1 yard of cloth is produced but no corn. The last four rows of the table show the amounts of corn or cloth that can be produced per month as more hours are devoted to each activity.

producing them. Table 3.1 sets out Jane's production possibilities for corn and cloth. If she does no work, she produces nothing. Two hours a day devoted to corn farming produces 6 pounds of corn per month. Devoting more hours to corn increases the output of corn, but there is a decline in the extra amount of corn that comes from extra effort. The reason for this decline is that Jane has to use increasingly unsuitable land for growing corn. At first, she plants corn on a lush, flat plain. Eventually, when she has used all the arable land, she has to start planting on the rocky hills and the edge of the beach. The numbers in the second column of the table show how the output of corn rises as the number of hours devoted to cultivating it rises.

To produce cloth, Jane gathers wool from sheep that live on the island. As she devotes more hours to collecting wool and making cloth, her output rises. The numbers in the third column of Table 3.1 show how the output of cloth rises as the number of hours devoted to this activity rises.

If Jane devotes all her time to growing corn, she can produce 20 pounds of corn in a month. In that case, however, she cannot produce any cloth. Conversely, if she devotes all her time to making cloth, she can produce 5 yards a month but will have no time left for growing corn. Jane can devote some of her time to corn and some to cloth but not more than 10 hours a day total. Thus she can spend 2 hours growing corn and 8 hours making cloth or 6 hours on one and 4 hours on the other (or any other combination of hours that add up to 10 hours).

We have defined the production possibility frontier as the boundary between what is attainable and what is not attainable. You can calculate Jane's production possibility frontier by using the information in Table 3.1. These calculations are summarized in the table in Fig. 3.1 and graphed in that figure as Jane's production possibility frontier. To see how we calculated that frontier, let's concentrate first on the table in Fig. 3.1.

Possibility *a* shows Jane devoting no time to cloth and her entire 10-hour working day to corn. In this case, she can produce 20 pounds of corn per month and no cloth. For possibility *b*, she spends 2 hours a day making cloth and 8 hours growing corn, to produce a total of 18 pounds of corn and 1 yard of cloth a month. The pattern continues on to possibility *f*, where she devotes 10 hours a day to cloth and no time to corn. These same numbers are plotted in the graph shown in Fig. 3.1. Yards of cloth are measured on the horizontal axis and pounds of corn on the vertical axis. Points *a*, *b*, *c*, *d*, *e*, and *f* represent the numbers in the corresponding row of the table.

Of course, Jane does not have to work in blocks of 2 hours, as in our example. She can work 1 hour or 1 hour and 10 minutes growing corn and devote the rest of her time to making cloth. All other feasible allocations of Jane's 10 hours enable her to produce the combinations of corn and cloth described by the line that joins points *a*, *b*, *c*, *d*, *e*, and *f*. This line shows Jane's production possibility frontier. She can produce at any point on the frontier or inside it, within the orange area. These are attainable points. Points outside the frontier are unattainable. To produce at points beyond the frontier, Jane needs more time than she has—more than 10 hours a day. By working 10 hours a day producing both corn and cloth, Jane can choose any point she wishes on the frontier. And by working less than 10 hours a day, or by not putting her resources to their best possible use—by wasting some of her resources—she can produce at a point inside the frontier.

FIGURE 3.1

Jane's Production Possibility Frontier

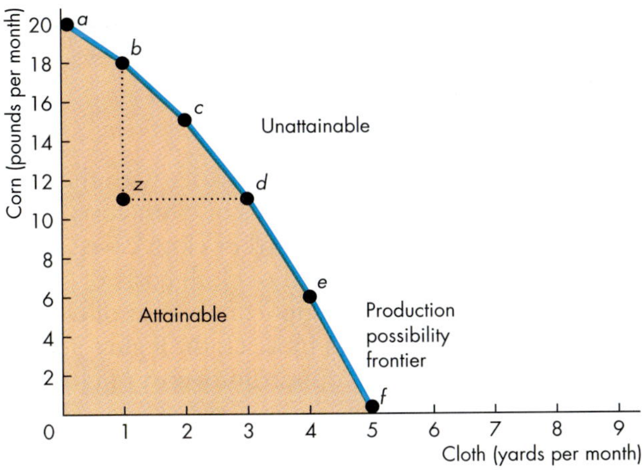

Possibility	Corn (pounds per month)		Cloth (yards per month)
a	20	and	0
b	18	and	1
c	15	and	2
d	11	and	3
e	6	and	4
f	0	and	5

The table lists six points on Jane's production possibility frontier. Row *e* tells us that if Jane produces 6 pounds of corn, the maximum cloth production that is possible is 4 yards. These same points are graphed as points *a*, *b*, *c*, *d*, *e*, and *f* in the figure. The line passing through these points is Jane's production possibility frontier, which separates the attainable from the unattainable. The attainable orange area contains all the possible production points. Jane can produce anywhere inside this area or on the production possibility frontier. Points outside the frontier are unattainable. Jane prefers points on the frontier to any point inside. She prefers points between *b* and *d* on the frontier to point *z* inside the frontier because they give her more of both goods.

Jane's Preferences

Jane produces corn and cloth not for the fun of it, but so that she can eat and keep warm. She wants much more corn and cloth than she can produce, and the more of each she has, the better she likes it. Because Jane wants as much as possible of both corn and cloth, the best she can do is to produce—and therefore consume—at a point *on* her production possibility frontier. To see why, consider a point such as *z* in the attainable region. At point *z*, Jane is wasting resources. She may be taking time off work, but leisure time on the island is not worth anything to Jane. Or she may not be using her sheep and her cornfields as effectively as possible. Jane can improve her situation at *z* by moving to a point such as *b* or *d* or to a point on the frontier between *b* and *d*, such as point *c*. Jane can have more of both goods on the frontier than at points inside it. At point *b*, she can consume more corn and no less cloth than at point *z*. At point *d*, she can consume more cloth and no less corn than at point *z*. At point *c*, she can consume more corn and more cloth than at point *z*. Jane will never choose points such as *z* because preferred points, such as *b*, *c*, and *d*, are available to her. That is, Jane prefers some point on the frontier to a point inside it.

We have just seen that Jane wants to produce at some point on her production possibility frontier, but she is still faced with the problem of choosing her preferred point. In choosing between one point and another, Jane is confronted with opportunity costs. At point *c*, for example, she has less cloth and more corn than at point *d*. If she chooses point *d*, she does so because she figures that the extra cloth is worth the corn forgone. Let's go on to explore opportunity cost more closely and see how we can measure it.

REVIEW

The production possibility frontier is the boundary between the attainable and the unattainable. There is always a point on the frontier that is preferred to any point inside it. But moving from one point on the frontier to another involves an opportunity cost—having less of one good to get more of another.

Opportunity Cost

We've defined opportunity cost as the best alternative forgone: for a late sleeper, the opportunity cost of attending an early morning class is an hour in bed; for a jogger, it is an hour of exercise. The concept of opportunity cost can be made more precise by using a production possibility frontier such as the one shown in Fig. 3.1. Let's see what that curve tells us.

The Best Alternative Forgone

The production possibility frontier in Fig. 3.1 traces the boundary between attainable and unattainable combinations of corn and cloth. Since there are only two goods, there is no difficulty in working out what is the best alternative forgone. More corn can be grown only by paying the price of having less cloth, and more cloth can be made only by bearing the cost of having less corn. Thus the opportunity cost of an additional yard of cloth is the amount of corn forgone, and the opportunity cost of producing an additional pound of corn is the amount of cloth forgone. Let's put numerical values on the opportunity costs of corn and cloth.

Measuring Opportunity Cost

We are going to measure opportunity cost by using Jane's production possibility frontier. We will calculate how much cloth she has to give up to get more corn and how much corn she has to give up to get more cloth.

If all Jane's time is used to produce corn, she produces 20 pounds of corn and no cloth. If she decides to produce 1 yard of cloth, how much corn does she have to give up? You can see the answer in Fig. 3.2. To produce 1 yard of cloth, Jane moves from *a* to *b* and gives up 2 pounds of corn. Thus the opportunity cost of the first yard of cloth is 2 pounds of corn. If she decides to produce an additional yard of cloth, how much corn does she give up? This time, Jane moves from *b* to *c* and gives up 3 pounds of corn to produce the second yard of cloth.

These opportunity costs are set out in the table of Fig. 3.2. The first two rows set out the opportunity costs that we have just calculated. The table also lists the opportunity costs of moving between points *c*, *d*, *e*, and *f* on Jane's production possibility frontier of Fig. 3.1. You might want to work out another example on your own to be sure that you understand what is going on. Calculate Jane's opportunity cost of moving from *e* to *f*.

Increasing Opportunity Cost

As you can see, opportunity cost varies with the quantity produced. The first yard of cloth costs 2 pounds of corn. The next yard of cloth costs 3 pounds of corn. The last yard of cloth costs 6 pounds of corn. Thus the opportunity cost of cloth increases as Jane produces more cloth. Figure 3.2(a) illustrates the increasing opportunity cost of cloth.

The Shape of the Frontier

Pay special attention to the shape of the production possibility frontier in Fig. 3.1. When a large amount of corn and not much cloth is produced—between points *a* and *b*—the frontier has a gentle slope. When a large amount of cloth and not much corn is produced—between points *e* and *f*—the frontier is steep. The whole frontier bows outward. These features of the production possibility frontier are a reflection of increasing opportunity cost. You can see the connection between increasing opportunity cost and the shape of the production possibility frontier in Fig. 3.2(b). Between points *a* and *b*, 1 yard of cloth can be obtained by giving up a small amount of corn. Here the opportunity cost of cloth is low, and the opportunity cost of corn is high. Between points *e* and *f*, a large amount of corn must be given up to produce 1 extra yard of cloth. In this region, the opportunity cost of cloth is high, and the opportunity cost of corn is low.

Everything Has an Increasing Opportunity Cost

We've just worked out the opportunity cost of cloth. But what about the opportunity cost of corn? Does it also increase as more of it is produced? You can see the answer in Fig. 3.2. By giving up 1 yard of

FIGURE 3.2

Jane's Opportunity Costs of Corn and Cloth

The table records Jane's opportunity cost of cloth. The first yard of cloth costs 2 pounds of corn. The next yard of cloth costs 3 pounds of corn. The opportunity cost of cloth rises as Jane produces more cloth, with the last yard of cloth costing 6 pounds of corn. Part (a) of the figure shows the increasing opportunity cost of cloth, and part (b) shows increasing opportunity cost as Jane moves along her outward-bowed production possibility frontier, increasing her production of cloth and decreasing her production of corn.

As Jane increases her cloth production:

First **1** yard of cloth costs **2** pounds of corn
Next **1** yard of cloth costs **3** pounds of corn
Next **1** yard of cloth costs **4** pounds of corn
Next **1** yard of cloth costs **5** pounds of corn
Last yard of cloth costs **6** pounds of corn

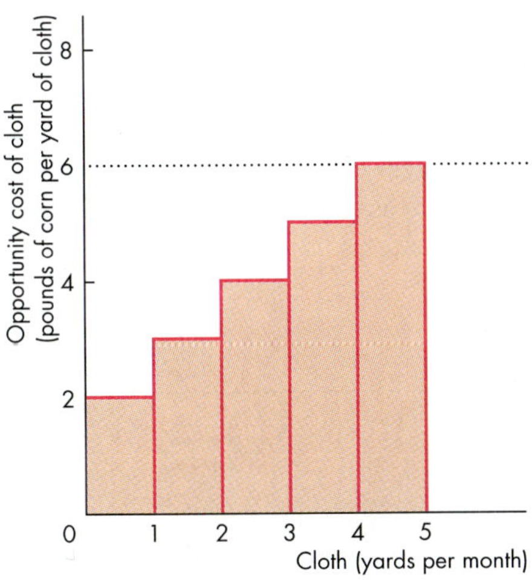

(a) Opportunity cost of cloth

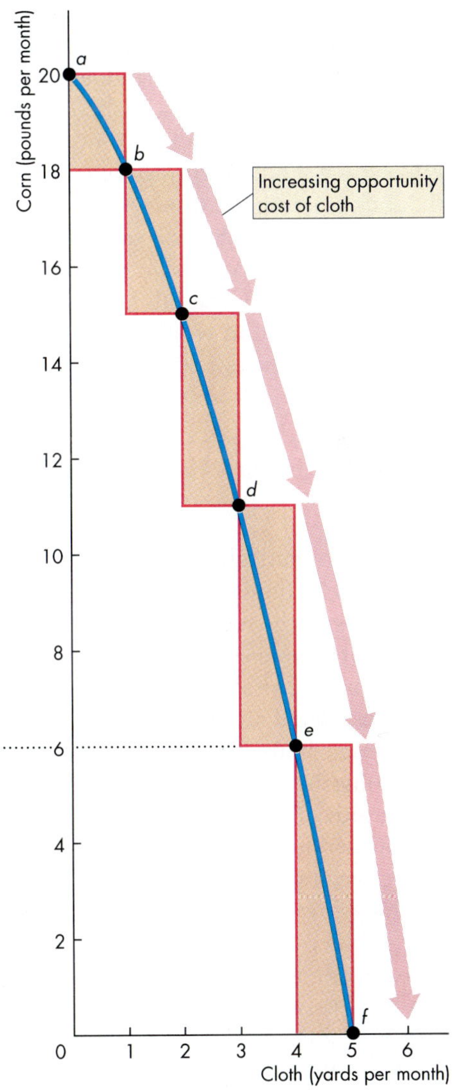

(b) Opportunity cost along the PPF

cloth to produce some corn, Jane moves from *f* to *e* and produces 6 pounds of corn. Thus the opportunity cost of the first 6 pounds of corn is 1 yard of cloth. Moving from *e* to *d*, you can see that the next 5 pounds of corn cost 1 yard of cloth. Thus the opportunity cost of corn also increases as Jane makes more corn.

Increasing opportunity cost and the outward bow of the production possibility frontier arise from the fact that scarce resources are not equally useful in all activities. For instance, some of the land on Jane's island is extremely fertile and produces a high crop yield, while other land is rocky and barren. The sheep on the island, however, prefer the rocky, barren land.

Jane uses the most fertile land for growing corn and the most barren areas for raising sheep. Only if she wants a larger amount of corn does she try to cultivate relatively barren areas. If she uses all her time to grow corn, she has to use some very unsuitable, low-yielding land. Devoting some time to making cloth, and reducing the time spent growing corn by the same amount, produces a small drop in corn production but a large increase in the output of cloth. Conversely, if Jane uses all her time to make cloth, a small reduction in woolgathering yields a large increase of corn production.

Production Possibilities in the Real World

Jane's island is dramatically different from the world that we live in. The fundamental lesson it teaches us, however, applies to the real world. The world has a fixed number of people endowed with a given amount of human capital and limited time. The world also has a fixed amount of land and capital equipment. These limited resources can be employed, using the available but limited technology to produce goods and services. But there is a limit to the goods and services that can be produced, a boundary between what is attainable and what is not attainable. That boundary is the real-world economy's production possibility frontier. On that frontier, producing more of any one good requires producing less of some other good or goods.

For example, a presidential candidate who promises better welfare and education services must at the same time, to be credible, promise either cuts in defense spending or higher taxes. Higher taxes mean less money left over for vacations and other consumption goods and services. The cost of better welfare and educational services is less of other goods. On a smaller scale but equally important, each time you decide to rent a video, you decide not to use your limited income to buy soda, popcorn, or some other good. The cost of one more video is one less of something else.

On Jane's island, we saw that the opportunity cost of a good increased as the output of the good increased. Opportunity costs in the real world increase for the same reasons that Jane's opportunity costs increase. Consider, for example, two goods vital to our well-being: food and health care. In allocating our scarce resources, we use the most fertile land and the most skillful farmers to produce food. We use the best doctors and the least fertile land for health care. If we shift fertile land and tractors away from farming and ask farmers to do surgery, the production of food drops drastically and the increase in the production of health care services is small. The opportunity cost of health care services rises. Similarly, if we shift our resources away from health care toward farming, we have to use more doctors and nurses as farmers and more hospitals as hydroponic tomato factories. The drop in health care services is large, but the increase in food production small. The opportunity cost of producing more food rises.

This example is extreme and unlikely, but these same considerations apply to any pair of goods that you can imagine: guns and butter, housing for the needy and diamonds for the rich, wheelchairs and golf carts, television programs and breakfast cereals. We cannot escape from scarcity and opportunity cost. Given our limited resources, more of one thing always means less of something else, and the more of anything that we have or do, the higher is its opportunity cost.

REVIEW

Opportunity cost is the value of the best alternative forgone. It is measured along the production possibility frontier by calculating the number of units of one good that must be given up to obtain one more unit of the other good. The production possibility frontier is bowed outward because not all resources are equally useful for producing all goods. The most useful resources are employed first. Because the frontier is bowed outward, the opportunity cost of each good increases as more of it is produced. ◆

Economic Growth

Although the production possibility frontier defines the boundary between what is attainable and what is unattainable, that boundary is not static. It is constantly changing. Sometimes the production possibility frontier shifts *inward,* reducing our production possibilities. For example, droughts or other extreme climatic conditions shift the frontier inward. Sometimes the frontier moves outward. For example, excellent growing and harvest conditions have this effect. Sometimes the frontier shifts outward because we get a new idea. It suddenly occurs to us that there is a better way of doing something that we never before imagined possible—we invent the wheel.

Over the years, our production possibilities have undergone enormous expansion. The expansion of our production possibilities is called **economic growth.** As a consequence of economic growth, we can now produce much more than we could a hundred years ago and quite a bit more than even ten years ago. By the late 1990s, if the same pace of growth continues, our production possibilities will be even greater. By pushing out the frontier, can we avoid the constraints imposed on us by our limited resources? That is, can we get our free lunch after all?

The Cost of Economic Growth

We are going to discover that although we can and do increase our production possibilities, we cannot have economic growth without incurring costs. The faster the pace of economic growth, the less we can consume at the present time. Let's investigate the costs of growth by examining why economies grow and prosper.

Two key activities generate economic growth: capital accumulation and technological progress. **Capital accumulation** is the growth of capital resources. **Technological progress** is the development of new and better ways of producing goods and services. As a consequence of capital accumulation and technological progress, we have an enormous quantity of cars and airplanes that enable us to produce more transportation than when we had only horses and carriages; we have satellites that make transcontinental communications possible on a scale much larger than that produced by the earlier cable technology. But accumulating capital and developing new technology are costly. To see why, let's go back to Jane's island economy.

Capital Accumulation and Technological Change

So far, we've assumed that Jane's island economy can produce only two goods, corn and cloth. But let's now suppose that while pursuing some of the sheep, Jane stumbles upon an outcrop of flint stone and a forest that she had not known about before. She realizes that she can now make some flint tools and start building fences around the corn and sheep, thereby increasing production of both of these goods. But to make tools and build fences, Jane has to devote time to these activities. Let's continue to suppose that there are only 10 hours of working time available each day. Time spent making tools and building fences is time that could have been spent growing corn and making cloth. Thus to expand her future production, Jane must produce less corn and cloth today so that some of her time can be devoted to making tools and building fences. The decrease in her output of corn and cloth today is the opportunity cost of expanding her production of these two goods in the future.

Figure 3.3 provides a concrete example. The table sets out Jane's production possibilities for producing capital—tools and fences—as well as current consumption goods—corn and cloth. If she devotes all her working hours to corn and cloth production (row *e*), she produces no capital—no tools or fences. If she devotes enough time to producing one unit of capital each month (row *d*), her corn and cloth production is cut back to 90 percent of its maximum possible level. She can devote still more time to capital accumulation, and as she does so, her corn and cloth production falls by successively larger amounts.

The numbers in the table are graphed in Fig. 3.3. Each point, *a* through *e*, represents a row of the

FIGURE 3.3

Economic Growth on Jane's Island

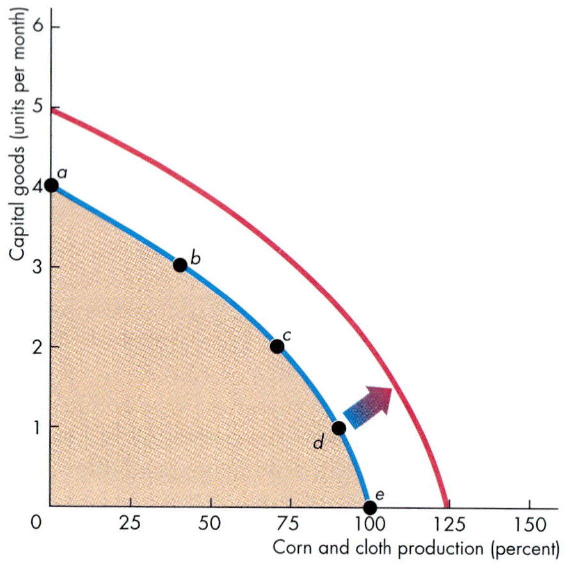

Possibility	Capital (units per month)	Corn and cloth production (percent)
a	4	0
b	3	40
c	2	70
d	1	90
e	0	100

If Jane devotes all her time to corn and cloth production, she produces no capital equipment (row *e* of the table). If she devotes more time to capital accumulation, she produces successively smaller amounts of corn and cloth. The curve *abcde* is Jane's production possibility frontier for capital and consumption goods (tools and fence versus corn and cloth). If Jane produces no capital (point *e*), her production possibility frontier remains fixed at *abcde*. If she cuts her current production of corn and cloth and produces one unit of capital (point *d*), her future production possibility frontier lies outside her current frontier. The more time Jane devotes to accumulating capital and the less to producing corn and cloth, the farther out her frontier shifts. The decreased output of corn and cloth is the opportunity cost of increased future production possibilities.

table. Notice the similarity between Fig. 3.3 and Fig. 3.1. Each shows a production possibility frontier. In the case of Fig. 3.3, the frontier is that between producing capital equipment—tools and fences—and producing current consumption goods—corn and cloth. If Jane produces at point *e* in Fig. 3.3, she produces no capital goods and remains stuck on the production possibility frontier for corn and cloth shown in Fig. 3.1. But if she moves to point *d* in Fig. 3.3, she can produce one unit of capital each month. To do so, Jane reduces her current production of corn and cloth to 90 percent of what she can produce if all her time is devoted to those activities. In terms of Fig. 3.1, Jane's current production possibility frontier for corn and cloth shifts to the left as less time is devoted to corn and cloth production and some of her time is devoted to producing capital goods.

By decreasing her production of corn and cloth and producing tools and building fences, Jane is able to increase her future production possibilities. An increasing stock of tools and fences makes her more productive at growing corn and producing cloth. She can even use tools to make better tools. As a consequence, Jane's production possibility frontier shifts outward as shown by the shift arrow. Jane experiences economic growth.

But the amount by which Jane's production possibility frontier shifts out depends on how much time she devotes to accumulating capital. If she devotes no time to this activity, the frontier remains at *abcde*—the original production possibility frontier. If she cuts back on current production of corn and cloth and produces one unit of capital each month (point *d*), her frontier moves out in the future to the position shown by the red curve in Fig. 3.3. The less time she devotes to corn and cloth production and the more time to capital accumulation, the farther out the frontier shifts.

But economic growth is not a free gift for Jane. To make it happen, she has to devote more time to producing tools and building fences and less to producing corn and cloth. Economic growth is no magic formula for abolishing scarcity.

Economic Growth in the Real World

The ideas that we have explored in the setting of Jane's island also apply to our real-world economy. If we devote all our resources to producing food, clothing, housing, vacations, and the many other consumer goods that we enjoy and none to research, development, and accumulating capital, we will have no more capital and no better technologies in the future than we have at present. Our production possibilities in the future will be exactly the same as those we have today. If we are to expand our production possibilities in the future, we must produce fewer consumption goods today. The resources that we free up today will enable us to accumulate capital and to develop better technologies for producing consumption goods in the future. The cut in the output of consumption goods today is the opportunity cost of economic growth.

The recent experience of the United States and Japan provides a striking example of the effects of our choices on the rate of economic growth. In 1965, the production possibilities per person in the United States were much larger than those in Japan (see Fig. 3.4). The United States devoted one fifth of its resources to producing capital goods and the other four fifths to producing consumption goods, as illustrated by point *a* in Fig. 3.4(a). But Japan devoted one third of its resources to producing capital goods and only two thirds to producing consumption goods, as illustrated by point *a* in Fig. 3.4(b). Both countries experienced economic growth, but the growth in Japan was much more

FIGURE 3.4

Economic Growth in the United States and Japan

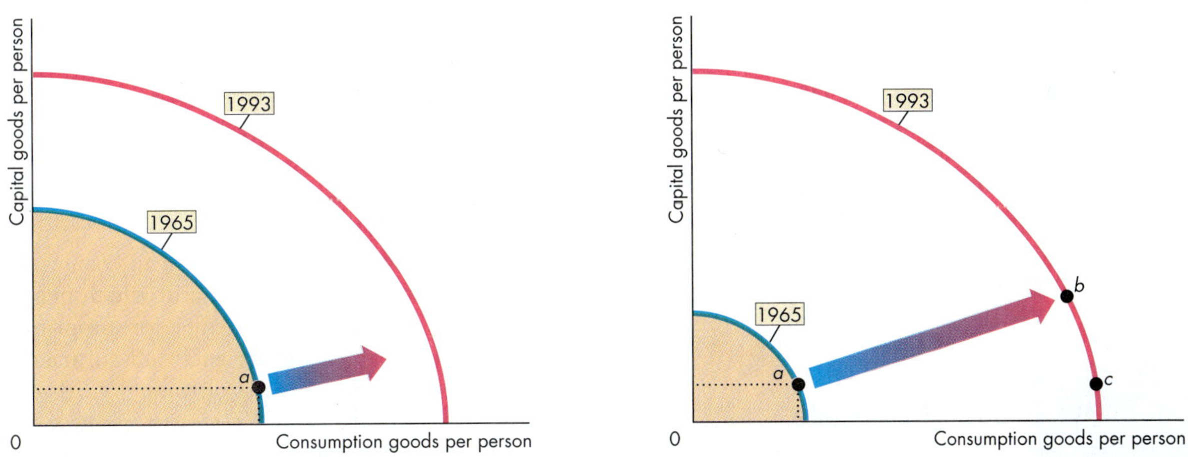

(a) United States

(b) Japan

In 1965, the production possibilities per person in the United States, part (a), were much larger than those in Japan, part (b). But Japan devoted one third of its resources to producing capital goods, while the United States devoted only one fifth—point *a* in each part of the figure. Japan's more rapid increase in capital resources resulted in its production possibility frontier shifting out more quickly than that of the United States. The two production possibilities per person in 1993 are similar. If Japan produces at point *b* on its 1993 frontier, it will continue to grow more quickly than the United States. If Japan increases consumption and produces at point *c* on its 1993 frontier, its growth rate will slow down to that of the United States.

rapid than the growth in the United States. Because Japan devoted a bigger fraction of its resources to producing capital goods, its stock of capital equipment grew more quickly than ours, and its production possibilities expanded more quickly. As a result, Japanese production possibilities per person are now so close to those in the United States that it is hard to say which country has the larger per person production possibilities. If Japan continues to devote a third of its resources to producing capital goods (at point *b* on its 1993 production possibility frontier), it will continue to grow much more rapidly than the United States, and its frontier will move out beyond our own. If Japan increases its production of consumption goods and reduces its production of capital goods (moving to point *c* on its 1993 production possibility frontier), then its rate of economic expansion will slow down to that of our own.

REVIEW

Economic growth results from the accumulation of capital and the development of better technologies. To reap the fruits of economic growth, we must incur the cost of fewer goods and services for current consumption. By cutting the current output of consumption goods, we can devote more resources to accumulating capital and to the research and development that lead to technological change—the engines of economic growth. Thus economic growth does not provide a free lunch. It has an opportunity cost—the fall in the current output of consumption goods. ◆

Gains from Trade

No one excels at everything. One person is more athletic than another; another person has a quicker mind or a better memory. What one person does with ease, someone else finds difficult.

Comparative Advantage: Jane Meets Joe

Differences in individual abilities mean that there are also differences in individual opportunity costs of producing various goods. Such differences give rise to **comparative advantage**—we say that a person has a comparative advantage in producing a particular good if that person can produce the good at a lower opportunity cost than anyone else.

People can produce for themselves all the goods that they consume, or they can concentrate on producing one good (or perhaps a few goods) and then exchange some of their own products for the output of others. Concentrating on the production of only one good or a few goods is called **specialization.** We are going to discover how people can gain by specializing in the good at which they have a comparative advantage and trading their output with others.

Let's return again to our island economy. Suppose that Jane has discovered another island very close to her own and that it too has only one inhabitant—Joe. Jane and Joe each have access to a simple boat that is adequate for transporting themselves and their goods between the two islands.

Joe's island, too, can produce only corn and cloth, but its terrain differs from that on Jane's island. While Jane's island has a lot of fertile corn-growing land and a small sheep population, Joe's island has little fertile corn-growing land and plenty of hilly land and sheep. This important difference between the two islands means that Joe's production possibility frontier is different from Jane's. Figure 3.5 illustrates these production possibility frontiers. Jane's frontier is labeled "Jane's PPF," and Joe's frontier is labeled "Joe's PPF."

Jane and Joe can be self-sufficient in corn and cloth. **Self-sufficiency** is a situation in which people produce only enough for their own consumption. Suppose that Jane and Joe are each self-sufficient. Jane chooses to produce and consume 3 yards of cloth and 11 pounds of corn a month, point *d*. Joe chooses to produce and consume 2 yards of cloth and 7 pounds of corn a month, point *b*'. These choices are identified on their respective production possibility frontiers in Fig. 3.5. (Each could have chosen any other point on his or her own production possibility frontier.) Total production of corn and cloth is the sum of Jane's and Joe's production: 18 pounds of corn and 5 yards of cloth. Point *n* in the figure represents this total production.

FIGURE 3.5

The Gains from Specialization and Exchange

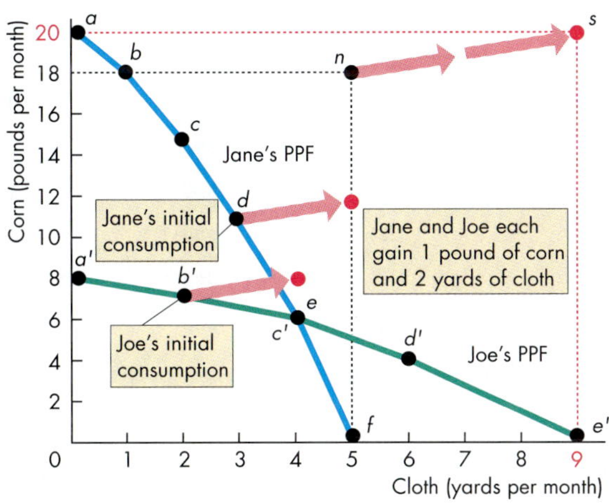

When Jane and Joe are each self-sufficient, Joe consumes 7 pounds of corn and 2 yards of cloth (point *b´*), and Jane consumes 11 pounds of corn and 3 yards of cloth (point *d*). Their total production is 18 pounds of corn and 5 yards of cloth (point *n*). Joe and Jane can do better by specialization and exchange. Jane, whose comparative advantage is in corn production, specializes in that activity, producing 20 pounds a month (point *a*). Joe, whose comparative advantage is in cloth production, specializes in that activity, producing 9 yards of cloth a month (point *e´*). Total production is then 20 pounds of corn and 9 yards of cloth (point *s*). If Jane gives Joe 8 pounds of corn in exchange for 5 yards of cloth, they each enjoy increased consumption of both corn and cloth. They each gain from specialization and exchange.

Jane's Comparative Advantage In which of the two goods does Jane have a comparative advantage? We have defined comparative advantage as a situation in which one person's opportunity cost of producing a good is lower than another person's opportunity cost of producing that same good. Jane, then, has a comparative advantage in producing whichever good she produces at a lower opportunity cost than Joe. What is that good?

You can answer the question by looking at the production possibility frontiers for Jane and Joe in Fig. 3.5. At the points at which they are producing and consuming, Jane's production possibility frontier is much steeper than Joe's. To produce one more pound of corn, Jane gives up less cloth than Joe. Hence Jane's opportunity cost of a pound of corn is lower than Joe's. This means that Jane has a comparative advantage in producing corn.

Joe's Comparative Advantage Joe's comparative advantage is in producing cloth. His production possibility frontier at his consumption point is flatter than Jane's. This means that Joe has to give up less corn to produce one more yard of cloth than Jane does. Joe's opportunity cost of a yard of cloth is lower than Jane's, so Joe has a comparative advantage in cloth production.

Achieving the Gains from Trade

Can Jane and Joe do better than be self-sufficient? In particular, what would happen if each were to specialize in producing the good at which each has a comparative advantage and then trade with the other?

If Jane, who has a comparative advantage in corn production, puts all her time into growing corn, she can grow 20 pounds. If Joe, who has a comparative advantage in cloth production, puts all his time into making cloth, he can make 9 yards. By specializing, Jane and Joe together can produce 20 pounds of corn and 9 yards of cloth (the amount labeled *s* in the figure). Point *s* shows the production of 20 pounds of corn (all produced by Jane) and 9 yards of cloth (all produced by Joe). Clearly, Jane and Joe produce more cloth and corn at point *s* than they were producing at point *n*, when each took care of only his or her own requirements. Jane and Joe prefer point *s* to point *n* because, between them, they have more of both corn and cloth at point *s* than at point *n*. They have an additional 2 pounds of corn and 4 yards of cloth.

To obtain the gains from trade, Jane and Joe must do more than specialize in producing the good at which each has a comparative advantage. They must exchange the fruits of their specialized production. Suppose that Jane and Joe agree to exchange 5 yards of cloth for 8 pounds of corn. Jane has 20 pounds of corn, and Joe has 9 yards of cloth before any exchange takes place. After the exchange takes place, Joe consumes 8 pounds of corn and Jane 12 pounds of corn; Joe consumes 4 yards of cloth and Jane 5 yards of cloth. Compared to the time when they were each self-sufficient, Jane now has 1 extra pound of corn and 2 extra yards of cloth, and Joe has 1 extra pound of corn and 2 extra yards of cloth. The gains from trade are represented by the increase in consumption of both goods that each obtains. Each consumes at a point outside their individual production possibility frontier.

Productivity and Absolute Advantage

Productivity is defined as the amount of output produced per unit of inputs used to produce it. For example, Jane's productivity in making cloth is measured as the amount of cloth she makes per hour of work. If one person has greater productivity than another in the production of all goods, that person is said to have an **absolute advantage.** In our example, neither Jane nor Joe has an absolute advantage. Jane is more productive than Joe in growing corn, and Joe is more productive than Jane in making cloth.

It is often suggested that people and countries that have an absolute advantage can outcompete others in the production of all goods. For example, it is often suggested that the United States cannot compete with Japan because the Japanese are more productive than we are. This conclusion is wrong, as you are just about to discover. To see why, let's look again at Jane and Joe.

Suppose that a volcano engulfs Jane's island, forcing her to search for a new one. And suppose further that this disaster leads to good fortune. Jane stumbles onto a new island that is much more productive than the original one, enabling her to produce twice as much of either corn or cloth with each hour of her labor. Jane's new production possibilities appear in Table 3.2. Notice that she now has an absolute advantage.

We have already worked out that the gains from trade arise when each person specializes in producing the good in which he or she has a comparative advantage. Recall that a person has a comparative advantage in producing a particular good if that person can produce it at a lower opportunity cost than anyone else. Joe's opportunity costs remain exactly the same as they were before. What has happened to Jane's opportunity costs now that she has become twice as productive?

You can work out Jane's opportunity costs by using exactly the same calculation that was used in the table of Fig. 3.2. Start by looking at Jane's opportunity cost of corn. The first 12 pounds of corn that Jane grows cost her 2 yards of cloth. So the opportunity cost of 1 pound of corn is $\frac{1}{6}$ of a yard of cloth—the same as Jane's original opportunity cost of corn. If you calculate the opportunity costs for Jane's production possibilities *a* through *f*, you will discover that each of them has remained the same.

TABLE 3.2

Jane's New Production Possibilities

Possibility	Corn (pounds per month)		Cloth (yards per month)
a	40	and	0
b	36	and	2
c	30	and	4
d	22	and	6
e	12	and	8
f	0	and	10

Since the opportunity cost of cloth is the inverse of the opportunity cost of corn, Jane's opportunity costs of cloth also have remained unchanged. Let's work through one example. If Jane moves from *a* to *b* to make 2 yards of cloth, she will have to reduce her corn production by 4 pounds—from 40 to 36 pounds. Thus the first 2 yards of cloth cost 4 pounds of corn. The cost of 1 yard of cloth is therefore 2 pounds of corn—exactly the same as before.

When Jane becomes twice as productive as before, each hour of her time produces more output, but her opportunity costs remain the same. One more unit of corn costs the same in terms of cloth forgone as it did previously. Since Jane's opportunity costs have not changed and Joe's have not changed, Joe continues to have a comparative advantage in producing cloth. Both Jane and Joe can have more of both goods if Jane specializes in corn production and Joe in cloth production.

The key point to recognize is that it is *not* possible for a person having an absolute advantage to have a comparative advantage in everything.

REVIEW

Gains from trade come from comparative advantage. A person has a comparative advantage in producing a good if that person can produce the good at a lower opportunity cost than anyone else. Thus differences in opportunity cost are the source of gains from specialization and exchange. Each person specializes in producing the good in which he or she has a comparative advantage and then exchanges some of that output for the goods produced by others. ◆◆ If a person can produce a good with fewer inputs than someone else—is more productive—that person has an absolute advantage but not necessarily a comparative advantage. Even a person with an absolute advantage gains from specialization and exchange. ◆

Exchange in the Real World

In the real world, countries can gain by specializing in the production of those goods and services in which they have a comparative advantage. An example is given in Reading Between the Lines on pp. 64–65. But to obtain the gains from trade in the real world, where billions of people specialize in millions of different activities, trade has to be organized. To organize trade, we have evolved rules of conduct and mechanisms for enforcing those rules. One such mechanism is private property rights. Another is the institution of money. In the island economy of Jane and Joe, direct exchange of one good with another is feasible. In the real-world economy, direct exchange of one good for another would be very cumbersome. To lubricate the wheels of exchange, societies have created money—a medium that enables indirect exchange of goods for money and money for goods. Let's examine these two aspects of exchange arrangements in more detail.

Property Rights

Property rights are social arrangements that govern the ownership, use, and disposal of property. **Property** is anything of value: it includes land and buildings—the things that we call property in ordinary speech; it also includes stocks and bonds, durable goods, and plant and equipment; it also includes intellectual property. **Intellectual property** is the intangible product of creative effort, protected by copyrights and patents. This type of property includes books, music, computer programs, and inventions of all kinds.

What if property rights did not exist? What would such a social science fiction world be like?

A World Without Property Rights Without property rights, people could take possession of whatever they had the strength to obtain for themselves. In such a world, people would have to devote a good deal of their time, energy, and resources to protecting what they had produced or acquired.

In a world without property rights, it would not be possible to reap all the gains from specialization and exchange. People would have little incentive to specialize in producing those goods at which they each had a comparative advantage. In fact, the more of a particular good someone produced, the bigger the chance that others would simply help themselves to it. Also, if a person could take the goods of others without giving up something in exchange, then there would be no point to specializing in producing something for exchange. In a world without property rights, no one would enjoy the gains from specialization and exchange, and everyone would specialize only in unproductive acts of piracy.

It is to overcome the problems that we have just described that property rights have evolved. Let's examine these property rights as they operate to govern economic life in the United States today.

Property Rights in Private Enterprise Capitalism

The U.S. economy operates for the most part on the principles of private enterprise capitalism. **Private enterprise** is an economic system that permits individuals to decide on their own economic activities. **Capitalism** is an economic system that permits private individuals to own the capital resources used in production.

The Gains from Specialization and Exchange

The New York Times, February 21, 1991

Bush Asserts Need for Foreign Oil

BY MATTHEW L. WALD

Saying he was committed to "the power of the marketplace," President Bush presented an energy policy today that he asserted would save energy, increase domestic production of fuels and improve the environment without new taxes or harsh Government edicts. . . .

The plan gives considerable attention to oil. In contrast to the energy policy initiatives undertaken by Presidents Richard Nixon and Jimmy Carter in the oil crises that occurred during their terms, the Bush proposal asserts that the United States will have to live with a high level of dependence on foreign oil. . . .

The Energy Secretary, James D. Watkins, defended the policy's approach to energy efficiency, saying that its critics "want Government control of how you run your life."

FORTUNE, DECEMBER 31, 1990

America's Hottest Export: Pop Culture

BY JOHN HUEY

Industrial hard guys like Henry Ford, Andrew Carnegie, and George Westinghouse probably wouldn't take much heart from what we're about to report, but there is good news for the U.S. these days on the export front. Around the globe, folks just can't get enough of America. They may not want our *hardware* any more—our cars, steel, or television sets. But when they want a jolt of popular culture—and they want more all the time—they increasingly turn to American *software*—our movies, music, TV programming, and home video, which together now account for an annual trade surplus of some $8 billion. Only aerospace—aircraft and related equipment—outranks pop culture as an export.

Like it or not, Mickey Mouse, Michael Jackson, and Madonna—her overseas sales are 2½ times her domestic numbers—prop up what's left of our balance of trade. Radio Free Europe and Radio Moscow are out; international broadcasts of CNN and MTV are in.

Essence of the Stories

The Bush Administration energy policy is one that relies on a large amount of oil imports from other countries.

The Energy Secretary claims this approach delivers energy efficiently.

One of the major U.S. exports is pop culture—movies, music, TV programming, and home videos.

Only aerospace equipment outranks pop culture as an export.

Madonna's overseas sales are 2½ times her domestic sales.

Background and Analysis

Holding the production of all other goods and services constant, the United States can produce pop culture and oil along the production possibility frontier, U.S. PPF in the figure.

With no specialization and exchange, we could consume 3 million hours of pop culture and 6 billion barrels of oil a day at point *a* in the figure (the numbers are hypothetical).

By specializing in the production of pop culture and cutting back our domestic production of oil, we can produce 8 million hours of fun a day and 3 billion barrels of oil at point *b* in the figure.

We can exchange pop culture for oil with the rest of the world along the red line in the figure. This line shows our international trading possibilities.

At point *b*, our opportunity cost of producing oil—the hours of fun we must give up to produce one more barrel—exceeds its opportunity cost in the rest of the world—the amount of fun we must give up to get one more barrel of foreign oil. By specializing in pop culture and selling it to the rest of the world in exchange for oil, we can increase our consumption of both pop culture and oil and consume at point *c* in the figure.

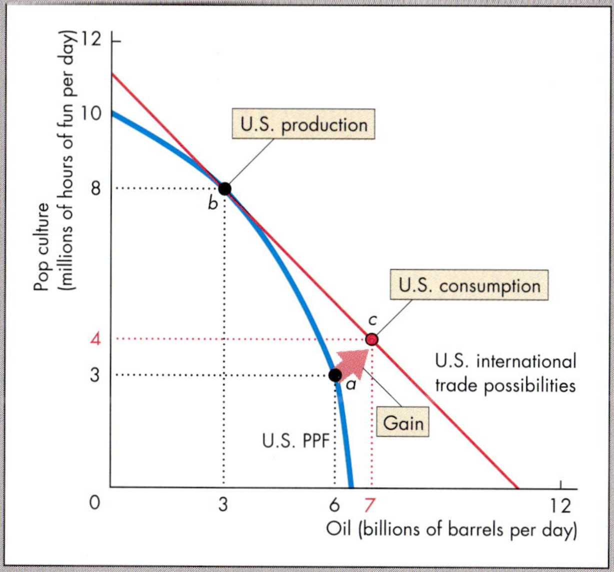

Under the property rights in such an economic system, individuals own what they have made, what they have acquired in a voluntary exchange with others, or what they have been given. Any attempt to remove someone's property against that person's will is considered theft, a crime that is punished by a sufficiently severe penalty to deter most people from becoming thieves.

It is easy to see that property rights based on these ideas can generate gainful trade: people can specialize in producing those goods that, for them, have the least opportunity cost. Some people will specialize in enforcing and maintaining property rights (for example, politicians, judges, and police officers), and all individuals will have the incentive to trade with each other, offering the good in which they have a comparative advantage in exchange for the goods produced by others.

The U.S. economic system is based on private property rights and voluntary exchange. But there are important ways in which private property rights are modified in our country.

Taxes Modify Private Property Rights Taxes on expenditure, income, and wealth transfer property from individuals to governments. Such transfers limit people's efforts to create more property and reduce their gains from specialization and exchange. But the taxes themselves are not arbitrary. Everyone faces the same rules and can calculate the effects of their own actions on the taxes for which they will be liable.

Regulation Modifies Private Property Rights Some voluntary exchanges are prohibited or regulated. For example, food and drug manufacturers cannot place a product on the market without first obtaining approval from a government agency. The government controls or prohibits the sale of many types of drugs and also restricts trading in human beings and their component parts—that is, it prohibits the selling of slaves, children, and human organs.

These restrictions on the extent of private property and on the legitimacy of voluntary exchange, though important, do not, for the most part, seriously impede specialization and gainful trade. Most people take the view that the benefits of regulation—for example, prohibiting the sale of dangerous drugs—far outweigh the costs imposed on the sellers.

Let's now turn to the other social institution that permits specialization and exchange—the development of an efficient means of exchange.

Money

We have seen that well-defined property rights based on voluntary exchange allow individuals to specialize and exchange their output with each other. In our island economy, we studied only two people and two goods. Exchange in such a situation was a simple matter. In the real world, however, how can billions of people exchange the millions of goods that are the fruits of their specialized labor?

Barter Goods can be simply exchanged for other goods. The direct exchange of one good for another is known as **barter.** However, barter severely limits the amount of trading that can take place. Imagine that you have roosters but you want to get roses. First, you must look for someone with roses who wants roosters. Economists call this a **double coincidence of wants**—when person A wants to sell exactly what person B wants to buy, and person B wants to sell exactly what person A wants to buy. As the term implies, such occurrences are coincidences and will not arise frequently. A second way of trading by barter is to undertake a sequence of exchanges. If you have oranges and you want apples, you might have to trade oranges for plums, plums for pomegranates, pomegranates for pineapples, and then eventually pineapples for apples.

Cumbersome though it is, quite a large amount of barter trade does take place. For example, when British rock star Rod Stewart played in Budapest, Hungary, in 1986, he received part of his $30,000 compensation in Hungarian sound equipment, electrical cable, and the use of a forklift truck. And before the recent changes in Eastern Europe, hairdressers in Warsaw, Poland, obtained their barbershop equipment from England in exchange for hair clippings that they supplied to London wigmakers.

Although barter exchange does occur, it is an inefficient means of exchanging goods. Fortunately, a better alternative has been invented.

Monetary Exchange An alternative to barter is **monetary exchange**—a system in which some commodity or token serves as the medium of exchange.

A **medium of exchange** is anything that is generally acceptable in exchange for goods and services. **Money** can also be defined as a medium of exchange—something that can be passed on to others in exchange for goods and services.

Money lowers the cost of transacting and makes millions of transactions possible that simply would not be worth undertaking by barter. Can you imagine the chain of barter transactions you'd have to go through every day to get your coffee, Coke, textbooks, professor's time, video, and all the other goods and services you consume? In a monetary exchange system, you exchange your time and effort for money and use that money to buy the goods and services you consume, cutting out the incredible hassle you'd face each day in a world of barter.

Metals such as gold, silver, and copper have long served as money. Most commonly, they serve as money by being stamped as coins. Primitive societies have traditionally used various commodities, such as seashells, as money. During the Civil War and for several years after, people used postage stamps as money. Prisoners of war in German camps in World War II used cigarettes as money. Using cigarettes as a medium of exchange should not be confused with barter. When cigarettes play the role of money, people buy and sell goods by using cigarettes as a medium of exchange.

In modern societies, governments provide paper money. The banking system also provides money in the form of checking accounts. Checking accounts can be used for settling debts simply by writing an instruction—writing a check—to the bank requesting that funds be transferred to another checking account. Electronic links between bank accounts, now becoming widespread, enable direct transfers between different accounts without any checks being written.

◆ ◆ ◆ ◆ You have now begun to see how economists go about the job of trying to answer some important questions. The simple fact of scarcity and the associated concept of opportunity cost allow us to understand why people specialize, why they trade with each other, why they have social conventions that define and enforce private property rights, and why they use money. One simple idea—scarcity and its direct implication, opportunity cost—explains so much!

SUMMARY

The Production Possibility Frontier

The production possibility frontier is the boundary between what is attainable and what is not attainable. Production can take place at any point inside or on the production possibility frontier, but it is not possible to produce outside the frontier. There is always a point on the production possibility frontier that is better than a point inside it. (pp. 51–53)

Opportunity Cost

The opportunity cost of any action is the best alternative action forgone. The opportunity cost of acquiring one good is equivalent to the amount of another good that must be given up. The opportunity cost of a good increases as the quantity of it produced increases. (pp. 54–56)

Economic Growth

Although the production possibility frontier marks the boundary between the attainable and the unattainable, that boundary does not remain fixed. It changes over time, partly because of natural forces (for example, changes in climate and the accumulation of ideas about better ways of producing) and partly because of the choices that we make (choices about consumption and saving). If we use some of today's resources to produce capital goods and for research and development, we will be able to produce more goods and services in the future. The economy will grow. But growth cannot take place without incurring costs. The opportunity cost of more goods and services in the future is consuming fewer goods and services today. (pp. 57–60)

Gains from Trade

A person has a comparative advantage in producing a good if that person can produce the good at a lower opportunity cost than anyone else. People can gain from trade if each specializes in the activity at which he or she has a comparative advantage. Each person produces the good for which his or her opportunity cost is lower than everyone else's. They then exchange part of their output with each other. By this activity, each person is able to consume at a point *outside* his or her individual production possibility frontier.

When a person is more productive than another person—is able to produce more output from fewer inputs—that person has an absolute advantage. But having an absolute advantage does not mean that there are no gains from trade. Even if someone is more productive than other people in all activities, as long as the other person has a lower opportunity cost of some good, then gains from specialization and exchange are available. (pp. 60–63)

Exchange in the Real World

Exchange in the real world involves the specialization of billions of people in millions of different activities. To make it worthwhile for each individual to specialize and to enable societies to reap the gains from trade, institutions and mechanisms have evolved. The most important of these are private property rights, with a political and legal system to enforce them, and a system of monetary exchange. These institutions enable people to specialize, exchanging their labor for money and their money for goods, thereby reaping the gains from trade. (pp. 63–67)

KEY ELEMENTS

Key Terms

Absolute advantage, 62
Barter, 66
Capital accumulation, 57
Capital goods, 51
Capitalism, 63
Comparative advantage, 60
Consumption, 51
Consumption goods, 51
Double coincidence of wants, 66
Economic growth, 57
Goods and services, 51
Human capital, 51
Intellectual property, 63
Medium of exchange, 67
Monetary exchange, 66
Money, 67
Private enterprise, 63
Production, 51
Production possibility frontier, 51
Productivity, 62
Property, 63
Property rights, 63
Self-sufficiency, 60
Specialization, 60
Technological progress, 57

Key Figures

Figure 3.1 Jane's Production Possibility Frontier, 53
Figure 3.2 Jane's Opportunity Costs of Corn and Cloth, 55
Figure 3.3 Economic Growth on Jane's Island, 58

REVIEW QUESTIONS

1 How does the production possibility frontier illustrate scarcity?

2 How does the production possibility frontier illustrate opportunity cost?

3 Explain what shifts the production possibility frontier outward and what shifts it inward.

4 Explain how our choices influence economic growth. What is the cost of economic growth?

5 Why does it pay people to specialize and trade with each other?

6 What are the gains from trade? How do they arise?

7 Why do social contracts such as property rights and money become necessary?

8 What is money? Give some examples of money. In the late 1980s, people in Rumania could use Kent cigarettes to buy almost anything. Was this monetary exchange or barter? Explain your answer.

9 What are the advantages of monetary exchange over barter?

PROBLEMS

1 Suppose that there is a change in the weather conditions on Jane's island that makes the corn yields much higher. This enables Jane to produce the following amounts of corn:

Hours worked (per day)	Corn (pounds per month)
0	0
2	60
4	100
6	120
8	130
10	140

Her cloth production possibilities are the same as those that appeared in Table 3.1.

- **a** What are six points on Jane's new production possibility frontier?
- **b** What are Jane's opportunity costs of corn and cloth? List them at each of the five levels of output.
- **c** Compare Jane's opportunity cost of cloth with that in the table in Fig. 3.2. Has her opportunity cost of cloth gone up, gone down, or remained the same? Explain why.

2 Amy lives with her parents and attends the local college. The college is operated by the state government, and tuition is free. Jobs that pay $7 an hour are available to high school graduates in the town. Amy's mother, a high school graduate, takes a part-time job so that Amy can go to school. Amy's textbooks cost $280, and Amy gets an allowance of $140 a month from her mother. List the items that make up the opportunity cost of Amy attending college.

3 Suppose that Leisureland produces only two goods—food and suntan oil. Its production possibilities are

Food (pounds per month)		Suntan oil (gallons per month)
300	and	0
200	and	50
100	and	100
0	and	150

Busyland also produces only food and suntan oil, and its production possibilities are

Food (pounds per month)		Suntan oil (gallons per month)
150	and	0
100	and	100
50	and	200
0	and	300

- **a** What are the opportunity costs of food and suntan oil in Leisureland? List them at each output given in the table.
- **b** Why are the opportunity costs the same at each output level?
- **c** What are the opportunity costs of food and suntan oil in Busyland? List them at each output given in the table.

4 Suppose that in problem 3 Leisureland and Busyland do not specialize and trade with each other—each country is self-sufficient. Leisureland produces and consumes 50 pounds of food and 125 gallons of suntan oil per month. Busyland produces and consumes 150 pounds of food per month and no suntan oil. The countries then begin to trade with each other.

- **a** Which good does Leisureland export, and which good does it import?
- **b** Which good does Busyland export, and which good does it import?
- **c** What is the maximum quantity of food and suntan oil that the two countries can produce if each country specializes in the activity at which it has the lower opportunity cost?

5 Suppose that Busyland becomes three times as productive as in problem 3.

- **a** Show, on a graph, the effect of the increased productivity on Busyland's production possibility frontier.
- **b** Does Busyland now have an absolute advantage in producing both goods?
- **c** Can Busyland gain from specialization and trade with Leisureland now that it is twice as productive? If so, what will it produce?
- **d** What are the total gains from trade? What do these gains depend on?

6 Andy and Bob work at Mario's Pizza Palace. In an 8-hour day, Andy can make 240 pizzas or 100 ice cream sundaes, and Bob can make 80 pizzas or 80 ice cream sundaes. Who does Mario get to make the ice cream sundaes? Who makes the pizzas? Explain your answer.

CHAPTER 4

DEMAND AND SUPPLY

After studying this chapter, you will be able to:

- Construct a demand schedule and a demand curve
- Construct a supply schedule and a supply curve
- Explain how prices are determined
- Explain how quantities bought and sold are determined
- Explain why some prices rise, some fall, and some fluctuate
- Make predictions about price changes using the demand and supply model

Slide, Rocket, and Roller Coaster

SLIDE, ROCKET, AND ROLLER COASTER—DISNEYLAND rides? No. Commonly used descriptions of the behavior of prices. There are lots of examples of price slides. One particular example is probably very familiar to you. In 1979, Sony began to market a pocket-sized cassette player that delivered its sound through tiny earphones. Sony named its new product the Walkman and gave it a price tag of around $300—more than $500 in today's money. Today Sony has been joined by many other producers of Walkman clones, and you can buy a Walkman (or its equivalent) that's even better than the 1979 prototype for less than one tenth of the original price. During the time that the Walkman has been with us, the quantity bought has increased steadily each year. Why has there been a long and steady slide in the price of the Walkman? Why hasn't the increase in the quantity bought kept its price high? ◆◆ Rocketing prices are also a familiar phenomenon. An important recent example is that of rents paid for apartments and houses, especially in central locations in big cities. Huge increases in rents and house prices have not deterred people from living in the centers of cities—on the contrary, their numbers have increased slightly in recent years. Why do people continue to seek housing in city centers when rents have rocketed so sharply? ◆◆ There are lots of price roller coasters—cases in which prices rise and fall from season to season or year to year. Prices of coffee, strawberries, and many other agricultural commodities fit this pattern. Why does the price of coffee roller-coaster even when people's taste for coffee hardly changes at all? ◆◆ Though amusement park rides provide a vivid description of the behavior of prices, many of the things that we buy have remarkably steady prices. The audiocassette tapes that we play in a Walkman are an example. The price of a tape has barely changed over the past ten years. Nevertheless, the number of tapes bought has risen steadily year after year. Why do firms sell more and more tapes, even though they're not able to get higher prices for them, and why do people willingly buy more tapes, even though their price is no lower than it was a decade ago?

◆ ◆ ◆ ◆ We will discover the answers to these and similar questions by studying the theory of demand and supply. This powerful theory enables us to analyze many important economic events that affect our lives. It even enables us to make predictions about future prices.

Demand

The **quantity demanded** of a good or service is the amount that consumers plan to buy in a given period of time at a particular price. Demands are different from wants. **Wants** are the unlimited desires or wishes that people have for goods and services. How many times have you thought that you would like something "if only you could afford it" or "if it weren't so expensive"? Scarcity guarantees that many—perhaps most—of our wants will never be satisfied. Demand reflects a decision about which wants to satisfy. If you demand something, then you've made a plan to buy it.

The quantity demanded is not necessarily the same amount as the quantity actually bought. Sometimes the quantity demanded is greater than the amount of goods available, so the quantity bought is less than the quantity demanded.

The quantity demanded is measured as an amount per unit of time. For example, suppose a person consumes one cup of coffee a day. The quantity of coffee demanded by that person can be expressed as 1 cup per day or 7 cups per week or 365 cups per year. Without a time dimension, we cannot tell whether a particular quantity demanded is large or small.

What Determines Buying Plans?

The amount that consumers plan to buy of any particular good or service depends on many factors. Among the more important ones are

- The price of the good
- The prices of related goods
- Income
- Expected future prices
- Population
- Preferences

The theory of demand and supply makes predictions about prices and quantities bought and sold. Let's begin by focusing on the relationship between the quantity demanded and the price of a good. To study this relationship, we hold constant all other influences on consumers' planned purchases. We can then ask: how does the quantity demanded of the good vary as its price varies?

The Law of Demand

The law of demand states:

Other things being equal, the higher the price of a good, the lower is the quantity demanded.

Why does a higher price reduce the quantity demanded? The key to the answer lies in *other things being equal.* Because other things are being held constant, when the price of a good rises, it rises *relative* to the prices of all other goods. Although each good is unique, it has substitutes—other goods that serve almost as well. As the price of a good climbs higher, relative to the prices of its substitutes, people buy less of that good and more of its substitutes.

Let's consider an example—blank audiocassette tapes, which we'll refer to as "tapes." Many different goods provide a service similar to that of a tape; for example, records, compact discs, prerecorded tapes, radio and television broadcasts, and live concerts. Tapes sell for about $3 each. If the price of a tape doubles to $6 while the prices of all the other goods remain constant, the quantity of tapes demanded will fall. People will buy more compact discs and prerecorded tapes and fewer blank tapes. If the price of a tape falls to $1 while the prices of all the other goods stay constant, the quantity of tapes demanded will rise, and the demand for compact discs and prerecorded tapes will fall.

Demand Schedule and Demand Curve

A **demand schedule** lists the quantities demanded at each different price when all the other influences on consumers' planned purchases—such as the prices of related goods, income, expected future prices, population, and preferences—are held constant.

The table in Fig. 4.1 sets out a demand schedule for tapes. For example, if the price of a tape is $1, the quantity demanded is 9 million tapes a week. If the price of a tape is $5, the quantity demanded is 2 million tapes a week. The other rows of the table show us the quantities demanded at prices between $2 and $4.

A demand schedule can be illustrated by drawing a demand curve. A **demand curve** graphs the relationship between the quantity demanded of a good and its price, holding constant all other influences on consumers' planned purchases. The graph in Fig. 4.1 illustrates the demand curve for tapes. By convention, the quantity demanded is always measured on the horizontal axis, and the price is measured on the vertical axis. The points on the demand curve labeled *a* through *e* represent the rows of the demand schedule. For example, point *a* on the graph represents a quantity demanded of 9 million tapes a week at a price of $1 a tape.

Willingness to Pay

There is another way of looking at the demand curve: it shows the highest price that people are willing to pay for the last unit bought. If a large quantity is available, that price is low; but if only a small quantity is available, that price is high. For example, if 9 million tapes are available each week, the highest price that consumers are willing to pay for the 9 millionth tape is $1. But if only 2 million tapes are available each week, consumers are willing to pay $5 for the last tape available.

FIGURE 4.1

The Demand Curve and the Demand Schedule

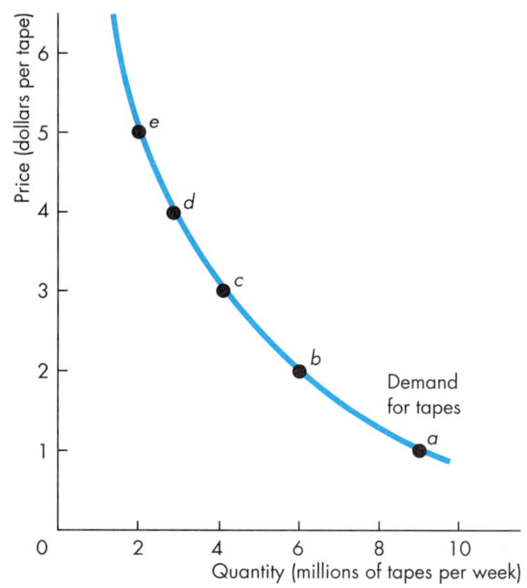

	Price (dollars per tape)	Quantity (millions of tapes per week)
a	**1**	**9**
b	**2**	**6**
c	**3**	**4**
d	**4**	**3**
e	**5**	**2**

The table shows a demand schedule listing the quantity of tapes demanded at each price if all other influences on buyers' plans are held constant. At a price of $1 a tape, 9 million tapes a week are demanded; at a price of $3 a tape, 4 million tapes a week are demanded. The demand curve shows the relationship between quantity demanded and price, holding everything else constant. The demand curve slopes downward: as price decreases, the quantity demanded increases. The demand curve can be read two ways. For a given price, it tells us the quantity that people plan to buy. For example, at a price of $3 a tape, the quantity demanded is 4 million tapes a week. For a given quantity, the demand curve tells us the maximum price that consumers are willing to pay for the last tape bought. For example, the maximum price that consumers will pay for the 6 millionth tape is $2.

This view of the demand curve may become clearer if you think about your own demand for tapes. If you are given a list of possible prices of tapes, you can write down alongside each price your planned weekly purchase of tapes—your demand schedule for tapes. Alternatively, if you are told that there is just one tape available each week, you can say how much you are willing to pay for it. If you are then told that there is one more tape available, you can say the maximum price that you will be willing to pay for that second tape. This process can continue—you are told that there is one more tape available, and you say how much you are willing to pay for each extra tape. The schedule of prices and quantities arrived at is your demand schedule.

A Change in Demand

The term **demand** refers to the entire relationship between the quantity demanded and the price of a good. The demand for tapes is described by both the demand schedule and the demand curve in Fig. 4.1. To construct a demand schedule and demand curve, we hold constant all the other influences on consumers' buying plans. But what are the effects of each of those other influences?

1. Prices of Related Goods The quantity of tapes that consumers plan to buy does not depend only on the price of tapes. It also depends in part on the prices of related goods. These related goods fall into two categories: substitutes and complements.

A **substitute** is a good that can be used in place of another good. For example, a bus ride substitutes for a train ride; a hamburger substitutes for a hot dog; a pear substitutes for an apple. As we have seen, tapes have many substitutes—records, prerecorded tapes, compact discs, radio and television broadcasts, and live concerts. If the price of one of these substitutes increases, people economize on its use and buy more tapes. For example, if the price of compact discs doubles, fewer compact discs are bought, and the demand for tapes increases—there is much more taping of other people's compact discs. Conversely, if the price of one of these substitutes decreases, people use the now cheaper good in larger quantities, and they buy fewer tapes. For example, if the price of prerecorded tapes decreases, people play more of these tapes and make fewer of their own tapes—the demand for blank tapes falls.

The effects of a change in the price of a substitute occur no matter what the price of a tape. Whether tapes have a high or a low price, a change in the price of a substitute encourages people to make the substitutions that we've just reviewed. As a consequence, a change in the price of a substitute changes the entire demand schedule for tapes and shifts the demand curve.

A **complement** is a good that is used in conjunction with another good. Some examples of complements are hamburgers and french fries, party snacks and drinks, spaghetti and meat sauce, running shoes and jogging pants. Tapes also have their complements: Walkmans, tape recorders, and stereo tape decks. If the price of one of these complements increases, people buy fewer tapes. For example, if the price of a Walkman doubles, fewer Walkmans are bought and, as a consequence, fewer people are interested in buying tapes—the demand for tapes decreases. Conversely, if the price of one of these complements decreases, people buy more tapes. For example, if the price of the Walkman halves, more Walkmans are bought, and a larger number of people buy tapes—the demand for tapes increases.

2. Income Another influence on demand is consumer income. Other things remaining the same, when income increases, consumers buy more of most goods, and when income decreases, they buy less of most goods. Consumers with higher incomes demand more of most goods. Consumers with lower incomes demand less of most goods. Rich people consume more food, clothing, housing, art, vacations, and entertainment than do poor people.

Although an increase in income leads to an increase in the demand for most goods, it does not lead to an increase in the demand for all goods. Goods that do increase in demand as income increases are called **normal goods.** Goods that decrease in demand when income increases are called **inferior goods.** Examples of inferior goods are rice and potatoes. These two goods are a major part of the diet of people with very low incomes. As incomes increase, the demand for these goods declines as more expensive meat and dairy products are substituted for them.

3. Expected Future Prices If the price of a good is expected to rise, it makes sense to buy more of the good today and less in the future, when its price is higher. Similarly, if its price is expected to fall, it pays to cut back on today's purchases and buy more later, when the price is expected to be lower. Thus the higher the expected future price of a good, the larger is today's demand for the good.

4. Population Demand also depends on the size of the population. Other things being equal, the larger the population, the greater is the demand for all goods and services, and the smaller the population, the smaller is the demand for all goods and services.

5. Preferences Finally, demand depends on preferences. *Preferences* are an individual's attitudes toward goods and services. For example, a rock music fanatic has a much greater preference for tapes than does a tone-deaf workaholic. As a consequence, even if they have the same incomes, their demands for tapes will be very different.

There is, however, a fundamental difference between preferences and all the other influences on demand. Preferences cannot be directly observed. We can observe today's price of a good and the prices of its substitutes and complements. We can observe income and population size. We can observe economic forecasts of future prices. But we cannot observe people's preferences. Economists assume that *changes* in preferences occur only slowly and so are not an important influence on *changes* in demand.

A summary of influences on demand and the direction of those influences is presented in Table 4.1.

TABLE 4.1

The Demand for Tapes

THE LAW OF DEMAND

The quantity of tapes demanded

Decreases if:	*Increases if:*
◆ The price of a tape rises	◆ The price of a tape falls

CHANGES IN DEMAND

The demand for tapes

Decreases if:	*Increases if:*
◆ The price of a substitute falls	◆ The price of a substitute rises
◆ The price of a complement rises	◆ The price of a complement falls
◆ Income falls*	◆ Income rises*
◆ The price of a tape is expected to fall in the future	◆ The price of a tape is expected to rise in the future
◆ The population decreases	◆ The population increases

*A tape is a normal good

Movement along the Demand Curve versus a Shift in the Curve

Changes in the influences on buyers' plans cause either a movement along the demand curve or a shift in it. Let's discuss each case in turn.

Movement along the Demand Curve If the price of a good changes but everything else remains the same, there is a movement along the demand curve. For example, if the price of a tape changes from $3 to $5, the result is a movement along the demand curve, from point *c* to point *e* in Fig. 4.1.

A Shift in the Demand Curve If the price of a good remains constant but some other influence on buyers' plans changes, we say that there is a change in demand for that good. We illustrate the change in demand as a shift in the demand curve. For example, a fall in the price of the Walkman—a complement of tapes—increases the demand for tapes. We illustrate this increase in demand for tapes with a new demand schedule and a new demand curve. Consumers demand a larger quantity of tapes at each and every price.

The table in Fig. 4.2 provides some hypothetical numbers that illustrate such a shift. The table sets out the original demand schedule when the price of a Walkman is $200 and the new demand schedule when the price of a Walkman is $50. These numbers record the change in demand. The graph in Fig. 4.2 illustrates the corresponding shift in the demand

FIGURE 4.2

A Change in the Demand Schedule and a Shift in the Demand Curve

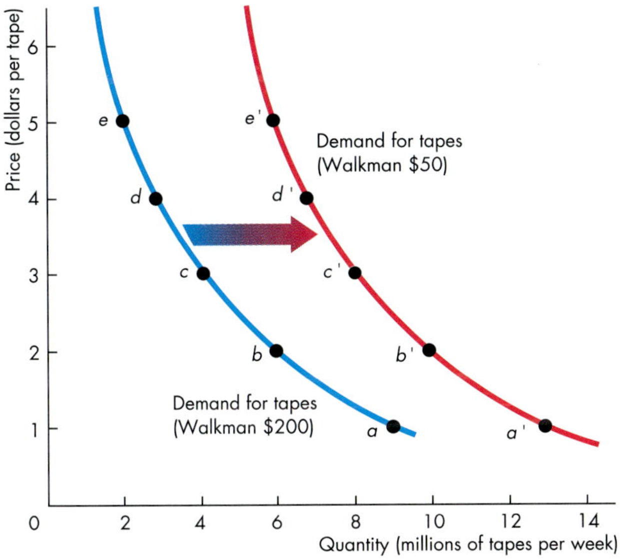

	Original demand schedule (Walkman $200)			New demand schedule (Walkman $50)	
	Price (dollars per tape)	Quantity (millions of tapes per week)		Price (dollars per tape)	Quantity (millions of tapes per week)
a	**1**	**9**	***a′***	**1**	**13**
b	**2**	**6**	***b′***	**2**	**10**
c	**3**	**4**	***c′***	**3**	**8**
d	**4**	**3**	***d′***	**4**	**7**
e	**5**	**2**	***e′***	**5**	**6**

A change in any influence on buyers other than the price of the good itself results in a new demand schedule and a shift in the demand curve. Here, a fall in the price of a Walkman—a complement of tapes—increases the demand for tapes. At a price of $3 a tape (row *c* of table), 4 million tapes a week are demanded when the Walkman costs $200 and 8 million tapes a week are demanded when the Walkman costs only $50. A fall in the price of a Walkman increases the demand for tapes. The demand curve shifts to the right, as shown by the shift arrow and the resulting red curve.

curve. When the price of the Walkman falls, the demand curve for tapes shifts to the right.

A Change in Demand versus a Change in Quantity Demanded A point on the demand curve shows the quantity demanded at a given price. A movement along the demand curve shows a **change in the quantity demanded.** The entire demand curve shows demand. A shift in the demand curve shows a **change in demand.**

Figure 4.3 illustrates and summarizes these distinctions. If the price of a good falls but nothing else

FIGURE 4.3

A Change in Demand versus a Change in the Quantity Demanded

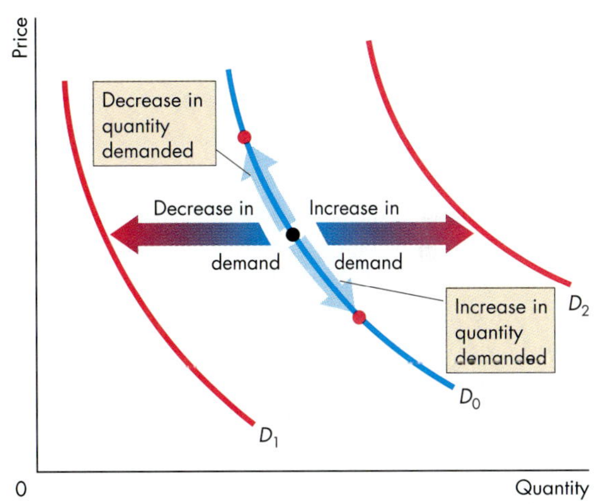

When the price of a good changes, there is a movement along the demand curve and a *change in the quantity of the good demanded.* For example, if the demand curve is D_0, a rise in the price of the good produces a decrease in the quantity demanded and a fall in the price of the good produces an increase in the quantity demanded. The blue arrows on demand curve D_0 represent these movements along the demand curve. If some other influence on demand changes, which increases the quantity that people plan to buy, there is a shift in the demand curve to the right (from D_0 to D_2) and an *increase in demand.* If some other influence on demand changes, which reduces the quantity people plan to buy, there is a shift in the demand curve to the left (from D_0 to D_1) and a *decrease in demand.*

changes, then there is an increase in the quantity demanded of that good (a movement down the demand curve D_0). If the price rises but nothing else changes, then there is a decrease in the quantity demanded (a movement up the demand curve D_0). When any other influence on buyers' planned purchases changes, the demand curve shifts and there is a *change* (an increase or a decrease) *in demand.* A rise in income (for a normal good), in population, in the price of a substitute, or in the expected future price of the good or a fall in the price of a complement shifts the demand curve to the right (to the red demand curve D_2). This represents an *increase in demand.* A fall in income (for a normal good), in population, in the price of a substitute, or in the expected future price of the good or a rise in the price of a complement shifts the demand curve to the left (to the red demand curve D_1). This represents a *decrease in demand.* For an inferior good, the effects of changes in income are in the opposite direction to those described above.

REVIEW

The quantity demanded is the amount of a good that consumers plan to buy in a given period of time. Other things being equal, the quantity demanded of a good increases if its price falls. Demand can be represented by a schedule or curve that sets out the quantity demanded at each price. Demand describes the quantity that consumers plan to buy at each possible price. Demand also describes the highest price that consumers are willing to pay for the last unit bought. Demand increases if the price of a substitute rises, if the price of a complement falls, if income rises (for a normal good), or if the population increases; demand decreases if the price of a substitute falls, if the price of a complement rises, if income falls (for a normal good), or if the population decreases. ◆◆ If the price of a good changes but all other influences on buyers' plans are held constant, there is a change in the quantity demanded and a movement along the demand curve. All other influences on consumers' planned purchases shift the demand curve. ◆

Supply

The **quantity supplied** of a good is the amount that producers plan to sell in a given period of time at a particular price. The quantity supplied is not the amount a firm would like to sell but the amount it definitely plans to sell. However, the quantity supplied is not necessarily the same as the quantity actually sold. If consumers do not want to buy the quantity a firm plans to sell, the firm's sales plans will be frustrated. Like quantity demanded, the quantity supplied is expressed as an amount per unit of time.

What Determines Selling Plans?

The amount that firms plan to sell of any particular good or service depends on many factors. Among the more important ones are

- The price of the good
- The prices of factors of production
- The prices of related goods
- Expected future prices
- The number of suppliers
- Technology

Because the theory of demand and supply makes predictions about prices and quantities bought and sold, we focus first on the relationship between the price of a good and the quantity supplied. To study this relationship, we hold constant all the other influences on the quantity supplied. We ask: how does the quantity supplied of a good vary as its price varies?

The Law of Supply

The law of supply states:

Other things being equal, the higher the price of a good, the greater is the quantity supplied.

Why does a higher price lead to a greater quantity supplied of a good? It is because the cost of producing an additional unit of the good increases (at least eventually) as the quantity produced increases. To induce them to incur a higher cost and increase production, firms must be compensated with a higher price.

Supply Schedule and Supply Curve

A **supply schedule** lists the quantities supplied at each different price when all other influences on the amount firms plan to sell are held constant. Let's construct a supply schedule. To do so, we examine how the quantity supplied of a good varies as its price varies, holding constant the prices of other goods, the prices of factors of production used to produce it, expected future prices, and the state of technology.

The table in Fig. 4.4 sets out a supply schedule for tapes. It shows the quantity of tapes supplied at each possible price. For example, if the price of a tape is $1, no tapes are supplied. If the price of a tape is $4, 5 million tapes are supplied each week.

A supply schedule can be illustrated by drawing a supply curve. A **supply curve** graphs the relationship between the quantity supplied and the price of a good, holding everything else constant. Using the numbers listed in the table, the graph in Fig. 4.4 illustrates the supply curve for tapes. For example, point *d* represents a quantity supplied of 5 million tapes a week at a price of $4 a tape.

Minimum Supply Price

Just as the demand curve has two interpretations, so too does the supply curve. So far we have thought about the supply curve and the supply schedule as showing the quantity that firms will supply at each possible price. But we can also think about the supply curve as showing the minimum price at which the last unit will be supplied. Looking at the supply schedule in this way, we ask: what is the minimum price that brings forth a supply of a given quantity? For firms to supply the 3 millionth tape each week, the price has to be at least $2 a tape. For firms to supply the 5 millionth tape each week, they have to get at least $4 a tape.

A Change in Supply

The term **supply** refers to the entire relationship between the quantity supplied of a good and its

FIGURE 4.4

The Supply Curve and the Supply Schedule

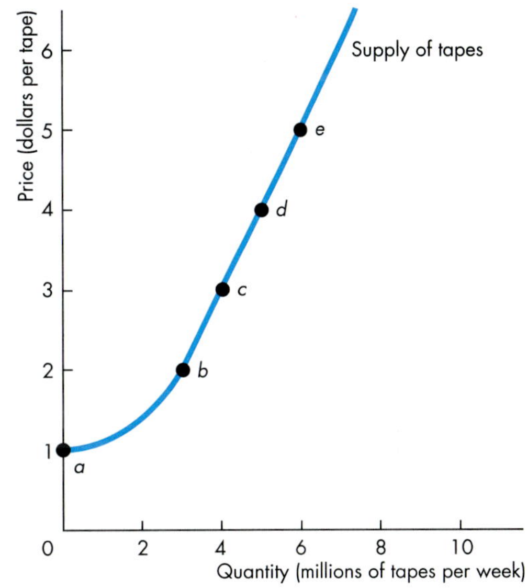

	Price (dollars per tape)	Quantity (millions of tapes per week)
a	**1**	**0**
b	**2**	**3**
c	**3**	**4**
d	**4**	**5**
e	**5**	**6**

The table shows the supply schedule of tapes. For example, at $2 a tape, 3 million tapes a week are supplied; at $5 a tape, 6 million tapes a week are supplied. The supply curve shows the relationship between the quantity supplied and price, holding everything else constant. The supply curve usually slopes upward: as the price of a good increases, so does the quantity supplied. A supply curve can be read in two ways. For a given price, it tells us the quantity that producers plan to sell. For example, at a price of $3 a tape, producers plan to sell 4 million tapes a week. The supply curve also tells us the minimum acceptable price at which a given quantity will be offered for sale. For example, the minimum acceptable price that will bring forth a supply of 4 million tapes a week is $3 a tape.

price. The supply of tapes is described by both the supply schedule and the supply curve in Fig. 4.4. To construct a supply schedule and supply curve, we hold constant all the other influences on suppliers' plans. Let's now consider these other influences.

1. Prices of Factors of Production The prices of the factors of production used to produce a good exert an important influence on its supply. For example, an increase in the prices of the labor and the capital equipment used to produce tapes increases the cost of producing tapes, so the supply of tapes decreases.

2. Prices of Related Goods The supply of a good can be influenced by the prices of related goods. For example, if an automobile assembly line can produce either sports cars or sedans, the quantity of sedans produced will depend on the price of sports cars and the quantity of sports cars produced will depend on the price of sedans. These two goods are *substitutes in production.* An increase in the price of a substitute in production lowers the supply of the good. Goods can also be complements in production. *Complements in production* arise when two things are, of necessity, produced together. For example, extracting chemicals from coal produces coke, coal tar, and nylon. An increase in the price of any one of these by-products of coal increases the supply of the other by-products.

Tapes have no obvious complements in production, but they do have substitutes in production: prerecorded tapes. Suppliers of tapes can produce blank tapes and prerecorded tapes. An increase in the price of prerecorded tapes encourages producers to increase the supply of prerecorded tapes and decrease the supply of blank tapes.

3. Expected Future Prices If the price of a good is expected to rise, it makes sense to sell less of the good today and more in the future, when its price is higher. Similarly, if its price is expected to fall, it pays to expand today's supply and sell less later, when the price is expected to be lower. Thus, other things being equal, the higher the expected future price of a good, the smaller is today's supply of the good.

4. The Number of Suppliers Other things being equal, the larger the number of firms supplying a good, the larger is the supply of the good.

5. Technology New technologies that enable producers to use fewer factors of production will lower the cost of production and increase supply. For example, the development of a new technology for tape production by companies such as Sony and Minnesota Mining and Manufacturing (3M) has lowered the cost of producing tapes and increased their supply.

A summary of influences on supply and the directions of those influences is presented in Table 4.2. Over the long term, changes in technology are the most important influence on supply.

TABLE 4.2
The Supply of Tapes

THE LAW OF SUPPLY	
The quantity of tapes supplied	
Decreases if:	***Increases if:***
◆ The price of a tape falls	◆ The price of a tape rises
CHANGES IN SUPPLY	
The supply of tapes	
Decreases if:	***Increases if:***
◆ The price of a factor of production used to produce tapes increases	◆ The price of a factor of production used to produce tapes decreases
◆ The price of a substitute in production rises	◆ The price of a substitute in production falls
◆ The price of a complement in production falls	◆ The price of a complement in production rises
◆ The price of a tape is expected to rise in the future	◆ The price of a tape is expected to fall in the future
◆ The number of firms supplying tapes decreases	◆ The number of firms supplying tapes increases
	◆ More efficient technologies for producing tapes are discovered

Movement along the Supply Curve versus a Shift in the Curve

Changes in the influences on producers cause either a movement along the supply curve or a shift in it.

Movement along the Supply Curve If the price of a good changes but everything else influencing suppliers' planned sales remains constant, there is a movement along the supply curve. For example, if the price of tapes increases from \$3 to \$5 a tape, there will be a movement along the supply curve from point *c* (4 million tapes a week) to point *e* (6 million tapes a week) in Fig. 4.4.

A Shift in the Supply Curve If the price of a good remains constant but another influence on suppliers' planned sales changes, then there is a change in supply and a shift in the supply curve. For example, as we have already noted, technological advances lower the cost of producing tapes and increase their supply. As a result, the supply schedule changes. The table in Fig. 4.5 provides some hypothetical numbers that illustrate such a change. The table contains two supply schedules: the original, based on "old" technology, and one based on "new" technology. With the new technology, more tapes are supplied at each price. The graph in Fig. 4.5 illustrates the resulting shift in the supply curve. When tape-producing technology improves, the supply curve of tapes shifts to the right, as shown by the shift arrow and the red supply curve.

A Change in Supply versus a Change in Quantity Supplied A point on the supply curve shows the quantity supplied at a given price. A movement along the supply curve shows a **change in the quantity supplied.** The entire supply curve shows supply. A shift in the supply curve shows a **change in supply.**

Figure 4.6 illustrates and summarizes these distinctions. If the price of a good falls but nothing else changes, then there is a decrease in the quantity supplied of that good (a movement down the supply curve S_0). If the price of a good rises but nothing else changes, there is an increase in the quantity supplied (a movement up the supply curve S_0). When any other influence on sellers changes, the supply curve

FIGURE 4.5

A Change in the Supply Schedule and a Shift in the Supply Curve

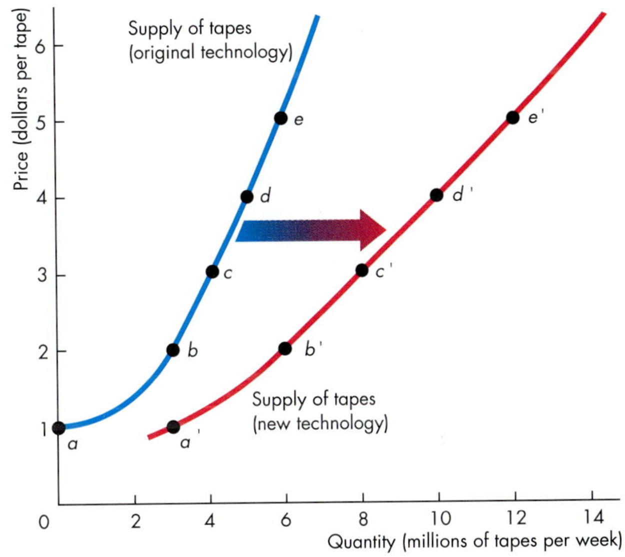

	Original technology			New technology	
	Price (dollars per tape)	Quantity (millions of tapes per week)		Price (dollars per tape)	Quantity (millions of tapes per week)
a	1	0	*a*′	1	3
b	2	3	*b*′	2	6
c	3	4	*c*′	3	8
d	4	5	*d*′	4	10
e	5	6	*e*′	5	12

If the price of a good remains constant but another influence on its supply changes, there will be a new supply schedule and the supply curve will shift. For example, if Sony and 3M invent a new, cost-saving technology for producing tapes, the supply schedule changes, as shown in the table. At \$3 a tape, producers plan to sell 4 million tapes a week with the old technology and 8 million tapes a week with the new technology. Improved technology increases the supply of tapes and shifts the supply curve for tapes to the right.

FIGURE 4.6

A Change in Supply versus a Change in the Quantity Supplied

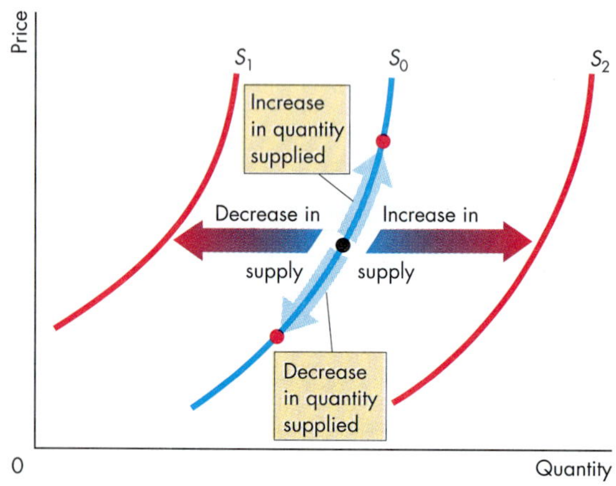

When the price of a good changes, there is a movement along the supply curve and a *change in the quantity of the good supplied.* For example, if the supply curve is S_0, a rise in the price of the good produces an increase in the quantity supplied, and a fall in the price produces a decrease in the quantity supplied. The blue arrows on curve S_0 represent these movements along the supply curve. If some other influence on supply changes, increasing the quantity that producers plan to sell, there is a shift in the supply curve to the right (from S_0 to S_2) and an *increase in supply.* If some other influence on supply changes, reducing the quantity the producers plan to sell, there is a shift to the left in the supply curve (from S_0 to S_1) and a *decrease in supply.*

shifts and there is a *change in supply.* If the supply curve is S_0 and there is, say, a technological change that reduces the amounts of the factors of production needed to produce the good, then supply increases and the supply curve shifts to the red supply curve S_2. If production costs rise, supply decreases and the supply curve shifts to the red supply curve S_1.

REVIEW

The quantity supplied is the amount of a good that producers plan to sell in a given period of time. Other things being equal, the quantity supplied of a good increases if its price rises. Supply can be represented by a schedule or a curve that shows the relationship between the quantity supplied of a good and its price. Supply describes the quantity that will be supplied at each possible price. Supply also describes the lowest price at which producers will supply the last unit. Supply increases if the prices of the factors of production used to produce the good fall, the prices of substitutes in production fall, the prices of complements in production rise, the expected future price of the good falls, or technological advances lower the cost of production. If the price of a good changes but all other influences on producers' plans are held constant, there is a change in the quantity supplied and a movement along the supply curve but *no change in supply.* A change in any other influence on producers' plans changes supply and shifts the supply curve. Changes in the prices of factors of production, in the prices of substitutes in production and complements in production, in expected future prices, or in technology shift the supply curve and are said to change supply. ◆

Let's now bring the two concepts of demand and supply together and see how prices are determined.

Price Determination

We have seen that when the price of a good rises, the quantity demanded decreases and the quantity supplied increases. We are now going to see how adjustments in price coordinate the choices of buyers and sellers.

Price as a Regulator

The price of a good regulates the quantities demanded and supplied. If the price is too high, the quantity supplied exceeds the quantity demanded. If the price is too low, the quantity demanded exceeds the quantity supplied. There is one price, and only one price, at which the quantity demanded equals the quantity supplied. We are going to work out what that price is. We are also going to discover that natural forces operating in a market move the price toward the level that makes the quantity demanded equal the quantity supplied.

The demand schedule shown in the table in Fig. 4.1 and the supply schedule shown in the table in Fig. 4.4 appear together in the table in Fig. 4.7. If the price of a tape is $1, the quantity demanded is 9 million tapes a week, but no tapes are supplied. The quantity demanded exceeds the quantity supplied by 9 million tapes a week. In other words, at a price of $1 a tape, there is a shortage of 9 million tapes a week. This shortage is shown in the final column of the table. At a price of $2 a tape, there is still a shortage but only of 3 million tapes a week. If the price of a tape is $5, the quantity supplied exceeds the quantity demanded. The quantity supplied is 6 million tapes a week, but the quantity demanded is only 2 million. There is a surplus of 4 million tapes a week. There is one price and only one price at which there is neither a shortage nor a surplus. That price is $3 a tape. At that price the quantity demanded is equal to the quantity supplied—4 million tapes a week.

The market for tapes is illustrated in the graph in Fig. 4.7. The graph shows both the demand curve of Fig. 4.1 and the supply curve of Fig. 4.4. The demand curve and the supply curve intersect when the price is $3 a tape. At that price, the quantity demanded and supplied is 4 million tapes a week. At each price *above* $3 a tape, the quantity supplied exceeds the quantity demanded. There is a surplus of tapes. For example, at $4 a tape, the surplus is 2 million tapes a week, as shown by the blue arrow in the figure. At each price *below* $3 a tape, the quantity demanded exceeds the quantity supplied. There is a shortage of tapes. For example, at $2 a tape, the shortage is 3 million tapes a week, as shown by the red arrow in the figure.

Equilibrium

We defined *equilibrium* in Chapter 1 as a situation in which opposing forces balance each other and in which no one is able to make a better choice given the available resources and actions of others. In an equilibrium, the price is such that opposing forces exactly balance each other. The **equilibrium price** is the price at which the quantity demanded equals the

FIGURE 4.7

Equilibrium

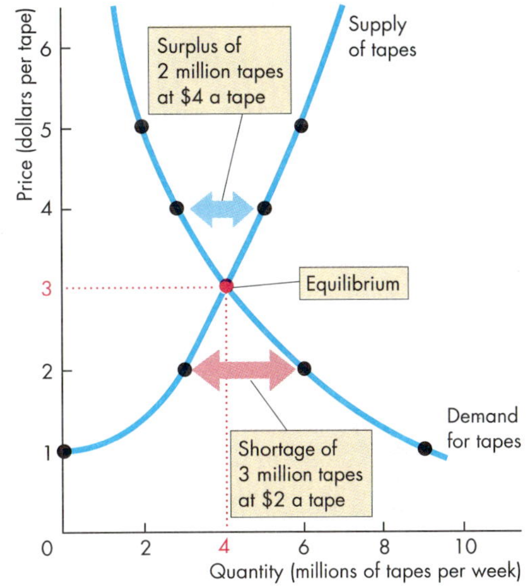

Price (dollars per tape)	Quantity demanded (millions of tapes per week)	Quantity supplied (millions of tapes per week)	Shortage (–) or surplus (+) (millions of tapes per week)
1	9	0	–9
2	6	3	–3
3	4	4	0
4	3	5	+2
5	2	6	+4

The table lists the quantities demanded and quantities supplied as well as the shortage or surplus of tapes at each price. If the price of a tape is $2, 6 million tapes a week are demanded and 3 million are supplied. There is a shortage of 3 million tapes a week, and the price rises. If the price of a tape is $4, 3 million tapes a week are demanded but 5 million are supplied. There is a surplus of 2 million tapes a week, and the price falls. If the price of a tape is $3, 4 million tapes a week are demanded and 4 million are supplied. There is neither a shortage nor a surplus. Neither buyers nor sellers have any incentive to change the price. The price at which the quantity demanded equals the quantity supplied is the equilibrium price.

quantity supplied. The **equilibrium quantity** is the quantity bought and sold at the equilibrium price. To see why equilibrium occurs where the quantity demanded equals the quantity supplied, we need to examine the behavior of buyers and sellers a bit more closely. First, let's look at the behavior of buyers.

The Demand Curve and the Willingness to Pay Suppose the price of a tape is $2. In such a situation, producers plan to sell 3 million tapes a week. Consumers cannot force producers to sell more than they want to sell, so the quantity sold is also 3 million tapes a week. What is the highest price that buyers are willing to pay for the 3 millionth tape each week? The answer can be found on the demand curve in Fig. 4.7—it is $4 a tape.

If the price remains at $2 a tape, the quantity of tapes demanded is 6 million tapes a week—3 million tapes more than are available. In such a situation, the price of a tape does not remain at $2. Because people want more tapes than are available at that price and because they are willing to pay up to $4 a tape, the price rises. If the quantity supplied stays at 3 million tapes a week, the price rises all the way to $4 a tape.

In fact, the price doesn't have to rise by such a large amount because at higher prices, the quantity supplied increases. The price will rise from $2 a tape to $3 a tape. At that price, the quantity supplied is 4 million tapes a week, and $3 a tape is the highest price that consumers are willing to pay. At $3 a tape, buyers are able to make their planned purchases and producers are able to make their planned sales. Therefore no buyer has an incentive to bid the price higher.

The Supply Curve and the Minimum Supply Price Suppose that the price of a tape is $4. In such a situation, the quantity demanded is 3 million tapes a week. Producers cannot force consumers to buy more than they want, so the quantity bought is 3 million tapes a week. Producers are willing to sell 3 million tapes a week for a price lower than $4 a tape. In fact, you can see on the supply curve in Fig. 4.7 that suppliers are willing to sell the 3 millionth tape each week at a price of $2. At $4 a tape, they would like to sell 5 million tapes each week. Because they want to sell more than 3 million tapes a week at $4 a tape, and because they are willing to sell the 3 millionth tape for as little as $2, they will continuously undercut each other to get a bigger share of the market. They will cut their price all the way to $2 a tape if only 3 million tapes a week can be sold.

In fact, producers don't have to cut their price to $2 a tape because the lower price brings forth an increase in the quantity demanded. When the price falls to $3, the quantity demanded is 4 million tapes a week, which is exactly the quantity that producers want to sell at that price. So when the price reaches $3 a tape, producers have no incentive to cut the price any further.

The Best Deal Available for Buyers and Sellers Both situations that we have just examined result in price changes. In the first case, the price starts out at $2 and is bid upward. In the second case, the price starts out at $4 and producers undercut each other. In both cases, prices change until they hit the price of $3 a tape. At that price, the quantity demanded and the quantity supplied are equal, and no one has any incentive to do business at a different price. Consumers are paying the highest acceptable price and producers are selling at the lowest acceptable price.

When people can freely make bids and offers and when they seek to buy at the lowest price and sell at the highest price, the price at which they trade is the equilibrium price—the quantity demanded equals the quantity supplied.

REVIEW

The equilibrium price is the price at which the plans of buyers and sellers match each other —the price at which the quantity demanded equals the quantity supplied. If the price is below equilibrium, the quantity demanded exceeds the quantity supplied, buyers offer higher prices, sellers ask for higher prices, and the price rises. If the price is above equilibrium, the quantity supplied exceeds the quantity demanded, buyers offer lower prices, sellers ask for lower prices, and the price falls. Only when the price is such that the quantity demanded and the quantity supplied are equal are there no forces acting on the price to make it change. Therefore that price is the equilibrium price. At that price, the quantity actually bought and sold is also equal to the quantity demanded and the quantity supplied. ◆

The theory of demand and supply that you have just studied is now a central part of economics. But that was not always so. Only 100 years ago, the best economists of the day were quite confused about these matters, which today even students in introductory courses find relatively easy to get right (see Our Advancing Knowledge on pp. 86–87).

As you'll discover in the rest of this chapter, the theory of demand and supply enables us to understand and make predictions about changes in prices —including the price slides, rockets, and roller coasters described in the chapter opener.

Predicting Changes in Price and Quantity

The theory we have just studied provides us with a powerful way of analyzing influences on prices and the quantities bought and sold. According to the theory, a change in price stems from either a change in demand or a change in supply, or a change in both. Let's look first at the effects of a change in demand.

A Change in Demand

What happens to the price and quantity of tapes if demand for tapes increases? We can answer this question with a specific example. If the price of a Walkman falls from $200 to $50, the demand for tapes will increase as is shown in the table in Fig. 4.8. The original demand schedule and the new one are set out in the first three columns of the table. The table also shows the supply schedule.

The original equilibrium price was $3 a tape. At that price, 4 million tapes a week were demanded and supplied. When demand increases, the price that makes the quantity demanded equal the quantity supplied is $5 a tape. At this price, 6 million tapes are bought and sold each week. When demand increases, both the price and the quantity increase.

We can illustrate these changes in the graph in Fig. 4.8. The graph shows the original demand for and supply of tapes. The original equilibrium price is $3 a tape and the quantity is 4 million tapes a week. When demand increases, the demand curve shifts to the right. The equilibrium price rises to $5 a tape and the quantity supplied increases to 6 million tapes a week, as is highlighted in the figure. There is an increase in the quantity supplied but *no change in supply*.

FIGURE 4.8

The Effect of a Change in Demand

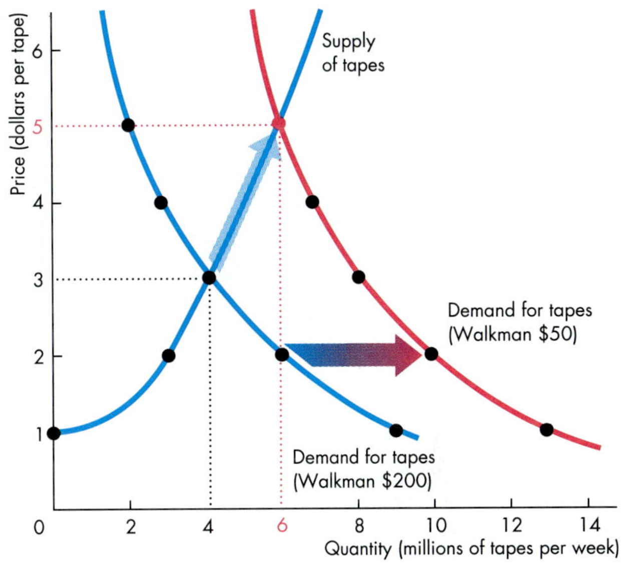

Price (dollars per tape)	Quantity demanded (millions of tapes per week)		Quantity supplied (millions of tapes per week)
	Walkman $200	Walkman $50	
1	9	13	0
2	6	10	3
3	4	8	4
4	3	7	5
5	2	6	6

With the price of a Walkman at $200, the demand for tapes is the blue curve. The equilibrium price is $3 a tape and the equilibrium quantity is 4 million tapes a week. When the price of a Walkman falls from $200 to $50, there is an increase in the demand for tapes and the demand curve shifts to the right—the red curve. At $3 a tape, there is now a shortage of 4 million tapes a week. The quantities of tapes demanded and supplied are equal at a price of $5 a tape. The price rises to this level and the quantity supplied increases. But there is no change in supply. The increase in demand increases the equilibrium price to $5 and increases the equilibrium quantity to 6 million tapes a week.

DISCOVERING the Laws of DEMAND AND SUPPLY

Railroads in the 1850s were as close to the cutting edge of technology as airlines are today. Railroad investment was profitable, but as in the airline industry today, competition was fierce.

The theory of demand and supply was being developed at the same time as the railroads were expanding, and it was their economic problems that gave the newly emerging theory its first practical applications.

In France, Jules Dupuit worked out how to use demand theory to calculate the value of railroad bridges. His work was the forerunner of what is today called *cost-benefit analysis*. Working with the very same principles invented by Dupuit, economists today calculate the costs and benefits of highways, airports, dams, and power stations.

In England, Dionysius Lardner showed railroad companies how they could increase their profits by cutting rates on long-distance business, where competition was fiercest, and raising rates on short-haul business, where they had less to fear from other suppliers. The principles first worked out by Lardner in the 1850s are used by economists working for the major airline companies today to work out the freight rates and passenger fares that will give the airline the largest possible profit. And the rates that result have a lot in common with those railroad rates of the nineteenth century. The airlines have local routes that feed like the spokes of a wheel into a hub on which there is little competition and on which they charge high fares (per mile), and they have long-distance routes between hubs on which they compete fiercely with other airlines and on which fares per mile are lowest.

"When demand and supply are in stable equilibrium, if any accident should move the scale of production from its equilibrium position, there will be instantly brought into play forces tending to push it back to that position; just as, if a stone hanging by a string is displaced from its equilibrium position, the force of gravity will at once tend to bring it back to its equilibrium position."

ALFRED MARSHALL
Principles of Economics

Dupuit used the law of demand to determine whether a bridge or canal would be valued enough by its users to justify the cost of building it, and Lardner first worked out the relationship between the cost of production and supply and used demand and supply theory to explain the costs, prices, and profits of railroad operations and to discover ways of increasing revenue by raising rates on short-haul business and lowering them on long-distance freight.

The Discoverers of The *Laws of Demand and Supply*

Today, using the same principles devised by Dupuit, economists calculate whether the benefits of expanding airports and air traffic control facilities are sufficient to cover their costs, and airline companies use the principles developed by Lardner to set their prices and to decide when to offer "seat sales."

The law of demand was discovered by Antoine-Augustin Cournot (1801–1877), pictured right, professor of mathematics at the University of Lyon, France, and it was he who drew the first demand curve in the 1830s. The first practical application of demand theory, by Jules Dupuit (1804–1866), a French engineer/economist, was the calculation of the benefits from building a bridge—and, given that a bridge had been built, of the correct toll to charge for its use.

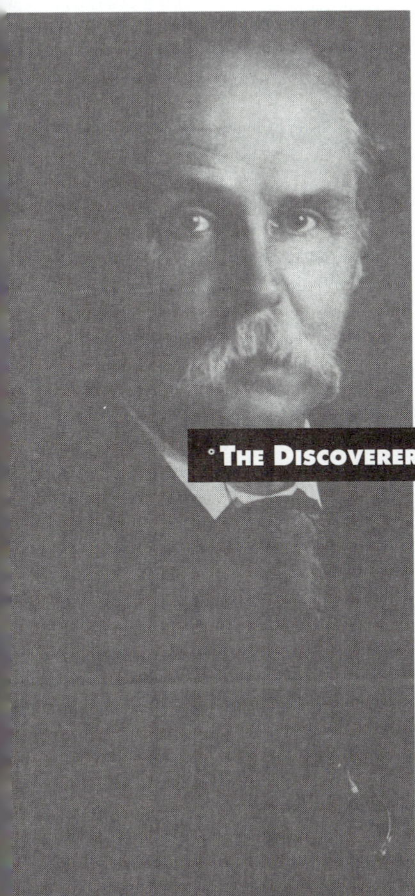

The laws of demand *and* supply and the connection between the costs of production and supply were first worked out by Dionysius Lardner (1793–1859), an Irish professor of philosophy at the University of London. Known satirically among scientists of the day as "Dionysius Diddler," Lardner worked on an amazing range of problems from astronomy to railway engineering to economics. A colorful character, he would have been a regular guest of Arsenio Hall, Phil Donahue, and Oprah Winfrey if their talk shows had been around in the 1850s. He visited the École des Ponts et Chaussées (the School of Bridges and Roads) in Paris and must have learned a great deal from Dupuit, who was doing his major work on economics at the time.

Many others had a hand in refining the theory of demand and supply, but the first thorough and complete statement of the theory as we know it today was that of Alfred Marshall (1842–1924), pictured left, professor of political economy at the University of Cambridge, who, in 1890, published a monumental treatise—*Principles of Economics*—a work that became *the* textbook on economics for almost half a century. Marshall was an outstanding mathematician, but he kept mathematics and even diagrams in the background. His own supply and demand diagram (reproduced here at its original size) appears only in a footnote.

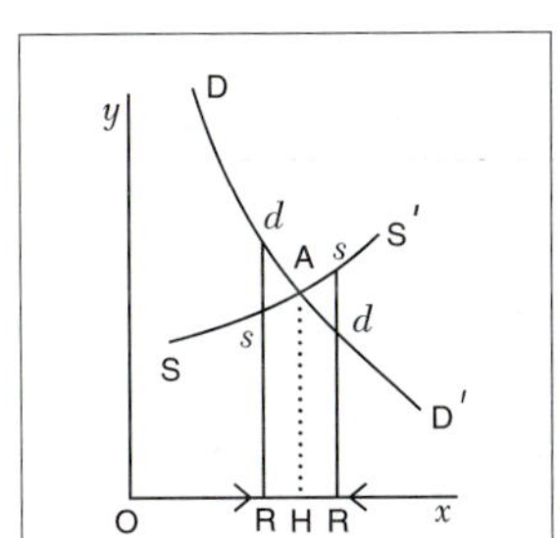

The exercise that we've just conducted can easily be reversed. If we start at a price of $5 a tape, trading 6 million tapes a week, we can then work out what happens if demand falls back to its original level. You can see that the fall in demand decreases the equilibrium price to $3 a tape and decreases the equilibrium quantity to 4 million tapes a week. Such a fall in demand could arise from a decrease in the price of compact discs or of CD players.

We can now make our first two predictions. Holding everything else constant:

- When demand increases, both the price and the quantity increase.
- When demand decreases, both the price and the quantity decrease.

A Change in Supply

Suppose that Sony and 3M have just introduced a new cost-saving technology in their tape-production plants. The new technology changes the supply. The new supply schedule (the same one that was shown in Fig. 4.5) is presented in the table in Fig. 4.9. What is the new equilibrium price and quantity? The answer is highlighted in the table: the price falls to $2 a tape and the quantity rises to 6 million a week. You can see why by looking at the quantities demanded and supplied at the old price of $3 a tape. The quantity supplied at that price is now 8 million tapes a week, and there is a surplus of tapes. The price falls. Only when the price is $2 a tape does the quantity supplied equal the quantity demanded.

Figure 4.9 illustrates the effect of an increase in supply. It shows the demand curve for tapes and the original and new supply curves. The initial equilibrium price is $3 a tape and the original quantity is 4 million tapes a week. When the supply increases, the supply curve shifts to the right. The equilibrium price falls to $2 a tape and the quantity demanded increases to 6 million tapes a week, highlighted in the figure. There is an increase in the quantity demanded but *no change in demand.*

The exercise that we've just conducted can easily be reversed. If we start out at a price of $2 a tape with 6 million tapes a week being bought and sold, we can work out what happens if the supply curve shifts back to its original position. You can see that the fall in supply increases the equilibrium price to $3 a tape and decreases the equilibrium quantity to 4 million tapes a week. Such a fall in supply could arise from an increase in the cost of labor and raw materials.

FIGURE 4.9

The Effect of a Change in Supply

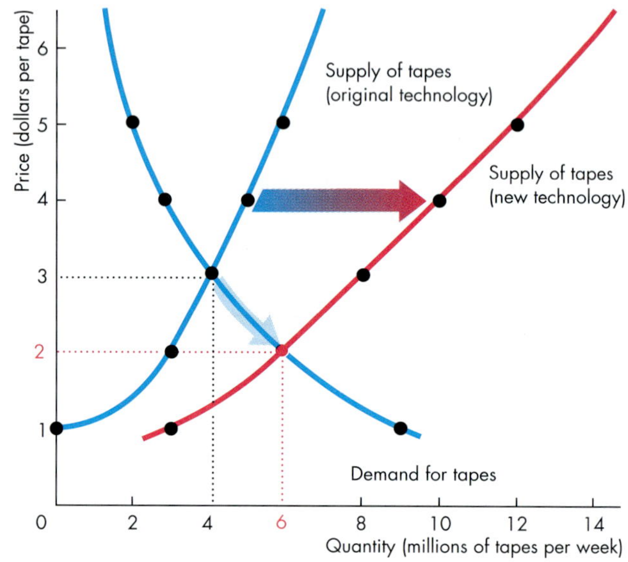

Price (dollars per tape)	Quantity demanded (millions of tapes per week)	Quantity supplied (millions of tapes per week) Original technology	New technology
1	9	0	3
2	6	3	6
3	4	4	8
4	3	5	10
5	2	3	12

With the original technology, the supply of tapes is shown by the blue curve. The equilibrium price is $3 a tape and the equilibrium quantity is 4 million tapes a week. When the new technology is adopted, there is an increase in the supply of tapes. The supply curve shifts to the right—the red curve. At $3 a tape, there is now a surplus of 4 million tapes a week. The quantities of tapes demanded and supplied are equal at a price of $2 a tape. The price falls to this level and the quantity demanded increases. But there is no change in demand. The increase in supply lowers the price of tapes to $2 and increases the quantity to 6 million tapes a week.

We can now make two more predictions. Holding everything else constant:

- When supply increases, the quantity increases and the price falls.
- When supply decreases, the quantity decreases and the price rises.

Reading Between the Lines on pp. 90–91 shows the effects of the floods in the Midwest in the spring and summer of 1993 on the supply of crops.

Changes in Both Supply and Demand

In the above exercises, either demand or supply changed, but only one at a time. If just one of these changes, we can predict the direction of change of the price and the quantity. If both demand and supply change, we cannot always say what will happen to both the price and the quantity. For example, if both demand and supply increase, we know that the quantity increases, but we cannot predict whether the price rises or falls. To make such a prediction, we need to know the relative magnitude of the increase in demand and supply. If demand increases and supply decreases, we know that the price rises, but we cannot predict whether the quantity increases or decreases. Again, to be able to make a prediction about the change in the quantity, we need to know the relative magnitudes of the changes in demand and supply.

As an example of a change in both supply and demand, let's take one final look at the market for tapes. We've seen how demand and supply determine the price and quantity of tapes, how an increase in demand resulting from a fall in the price of a Walkman both raises the price of tapes and increases the quantity bought and sold, and how an increase in the supply of tapes resulting from an improved technology lowers the price of tapes and increases the quantity bought and sold. Let's now examine what happens when both of these changes —a fall in the price of a Walkman (which increases the demand for tapes) and an improved production technology (which increases the supply of tapes)— occur together.

The table in Fig. 4.10 brings together the numbers that describe the original quantities demanded and supplied and the new quantities demanded and supplied after the fall in the price of the Walkman and the improved tape production technology. These same numbers are illustrated in the graph. The original demand and supply curves intersect at a price of $3 a tape and a quantity of 4 million tapes a week.

FIGURE 4.10

The Effect of a Change in Both Demand and Supply

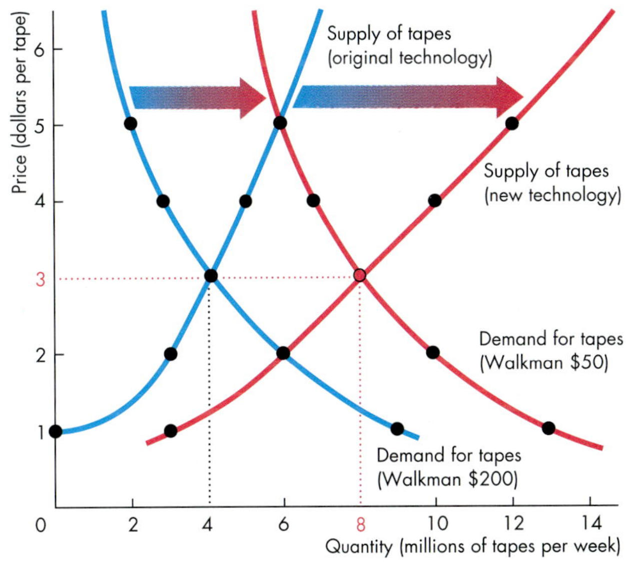

	Original quantities (millions of tapes per week)		New quantities (millions of tapes per week)	
Price (dollars per tape)	Quantity demanded (Walkman $200)	Quantity supplied (original technology)	Quantity demanded (Walkman $50)	Quantity supplied (new technology)
1	9	0	13	3
2	6	3	10	6
3	4	4	8	8
4	3	5	7	10
5	2	6	6	12

When a Walkman costs $200, the price of a tape is $3 and the equilibrium quantity is 4 million tapes a week. A fall in the price of a Walkman increases the demand for tapes, and improved technology increases the supply of tapes. The new technology supply curve intersects the higher demand curve at $3, the same price as before, but the quantity increases to 8 million tapes a week. The increase in both demand and supply increases the quantity but leaves the price unchanged.

Demand and Supply in Action

THE KANSAS CITY STAR, SATURDAY, JULY 10, 1993

Flood Isn't Likely to Jolt Food Prices

By Gene Meyer

So far, the flooding of Midwestern farm fields is not likely to float food prices out of sight, agricultural authorities say.

But if weather hurts crops about three weeks from now, grocery budgets will be in big trouble, the experts warn.

That's because in agriculture, as in other endeavors in life, timing is everything.

For farmers, "the extent of flooding is simply beyond belief," said Mark Bogner, agricultural meteorologist at WeatherData Services Inc. in Wichita.

Rain or floods this spring and summer have devastated crops in much of Kansas, most of northern Missouri, all of Iowa, and a great deal of Minnesota, Wisconsin, and Illinois.

Very simply, this may be the biggest natural calamity farmers in those states have faced since the droughts of 1983 and 1988, Bogner said.

However, federal food price forecasters are sticking by earlier predictions that food prices this year will rise no more than 2 percent to 3 percent, which would be the second smallest increase in about a decade.

Some foods, notably meat, are even apt to drop in price, at least temporarily, said Ralph Parlett of the U.S. Department of Agriculture's Economic Research Service.

That's because when floods or droughts raise prices for livestock feed too sharply, farmers often must sell more cattle or hogs than they might have planned.

"Of course, we pay for it the following year, when meat production drops and prices rise," Parlett said.

Analysts outside government see little reason to dispute the official view.

"Production will be down a bit more than expected and prices will be higher, but you won't see them run up the way they did early in the 1980s," said Sid Love, senior grains analyst with Bill Helming Consulting Services in Lenexa.

. . . The world has changed since the last time widespread meteorological mayhem hit the Midwest.

Economies overseas are shakier, competing farm production is greater, and "the world just does not need as large a U.S. crop as it did 10 or 15 years ago," [Alan] Barkema [a senior economist at the Federal Reserve bank of Kansas City] said.

So, even though some authorities fear that rain and flooding may be a more than $1 billion blow to the national food chain, the price increases consumers will pay because of the flood "will be a few tenths of a percent at most," Barkema estimated. . . .

The Essence of the Story

Rain and floods in the spring and summer of 1993 devastated crops in Kansas, Missouri, Iowa, Minnesota, Wisconsin, and Illinois and created a calamity for farmers in those states.

Despite the floods, food prices were expected to rise by only 2–3 percent in 1993—the second smallest annual increase in a decade.

Meat prices were expected to fall in 1993 and then rise in 1994. The reason is that, when floods raise the prices for livestock feed too sharply, farmers often must sell more cattle or hogs than they might have planned.

Background and Analysis

Figure 1 shows the market for non-meat food in the United States in 1993. The demand curve is D. The world price of non-meat food is P_0. Because large quantities of most food items are available from the rest of the world at the current price, the world supply is S_W. The quantity of non-meat food is Q_0.

Before the floods, the supply of non-meat food by U.S. farmers is the curve labeled S_0 in Fig. 1. The quantity of such food produced in the United States is U_0.

The floods decrease U.S. farm production, and the supply curve shifts leftward to S_1. Food from the rest of the world fills the gap, and the price does not rise. But U.S. farm sales fall to U_1, and farm revenue falls by the amount shown by the red rectangle to the amount shown by the blue rectangle.

Figure 2 shows the market for animal feed. Before the floods, the supply curve is S_0, the price is P_0, and the quantity is Q_0. The floods decrease supply to S_1, and the price rises to P_1.

Figure 3 shows the effects of the change in the price of animal feed on the market for meat. Before the floods, the supply curve is S_0, the price is P_0, and the quantity is Q_0. With higher feed prices, farmers slaughter more animals and the supply of meat increases to S_1. The price of meat falls to P_1. But the following year, with fewer animals, farmers decrease the supply of meat to S_2 and the price rises to P_2.

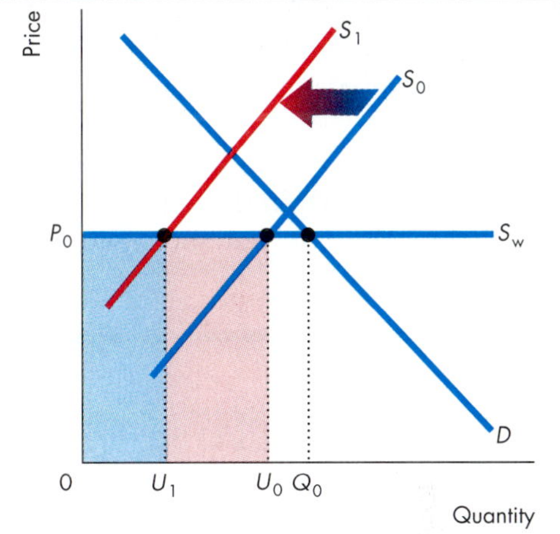

Figure 1

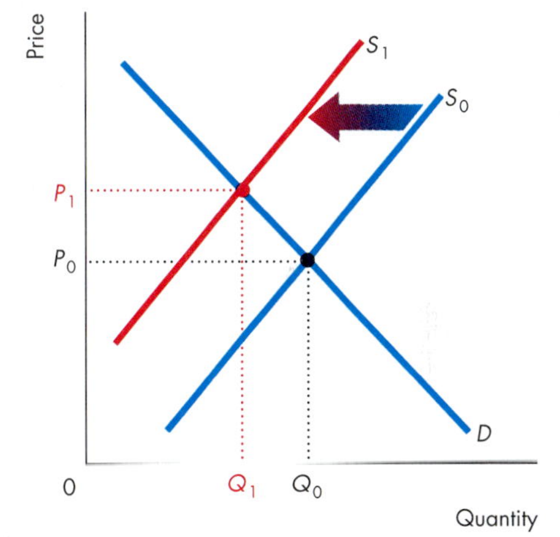

Figure 2

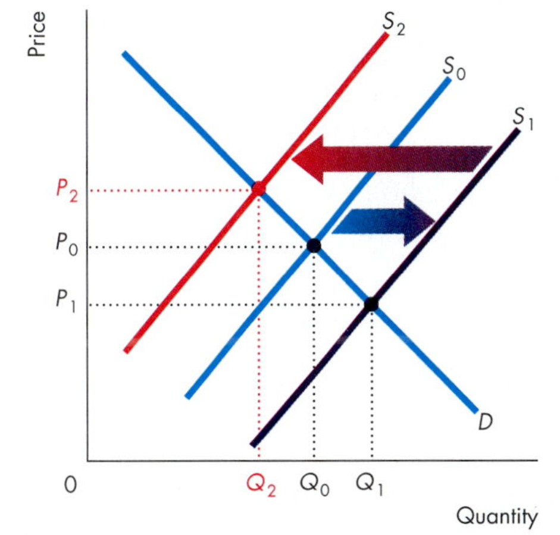

Figure 3

The new supply and demand curves also intersect at a price of \$3 a tape but at a quantity of 8 million tapes a week. In this example, the increases in demand and supply are such that the rise in price brought about by an increase in demand is offset by the fall in price brought about by an increase in supply—so the price does not change. An increase in either demand or supply increases the quantity. Therefore when both demand and supply increase, so does quantity. Note that if demand had increased slightly more than shown in the figure, the price would have risen. If supply had increased by slightly more than shown in the figure, the price would have fallen. But in both cases, the quantity would have increased.

Walkmans, Apartments, and Coffee

At the beginning of this chapter, we looked at some facts about prices and quantities of Walkmans, apartments, and coffee. Let's use the theory of demand and supply to explain the movements in the prices and the quantities of those goods. Figure 4.11 illustrates the analysis.

FIGURE 4.11

More Changes in Supply and Demand

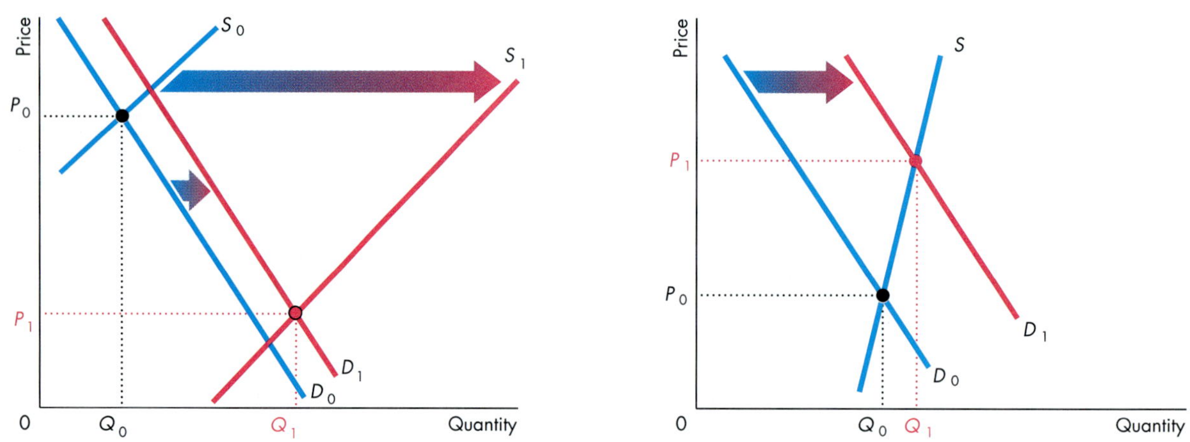

(a) Walkmans **(b) Apartments**

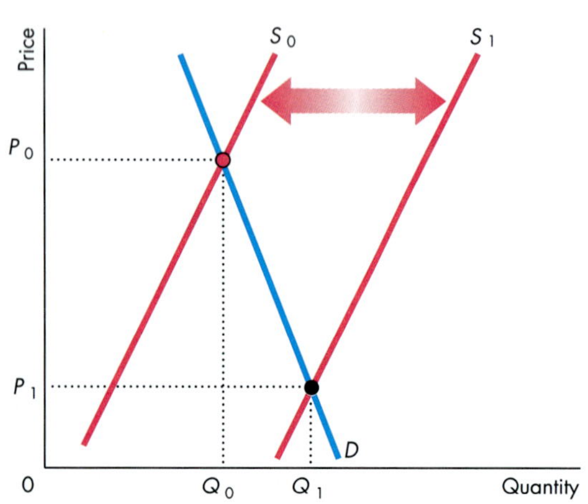

(c) Coffee

A large increase in the supply of Walkmans, from S_0 to S_1, combined with a small increase in demand, from D_0 to D_1, results in a fall in the price of the Walkman, from P_0 to P_1, and an increase in the quantity, from Q_0 to Q_1 (part a). An increase in the demand for apartments produces a large increase in the price, from P_0 to P_1, but only a small increase in the quantity, from Q_0 to Q_1 (part b). Variations in the weather and in growing conditions lead to fluctuations in the supply of coffee, between S_0 and S_1, which produce fluctuations in the price of coffee, between P_0 and P_1, and in the quantity, between Q_0 and Q_1 (part c).

First, let's consider the Walkman, shown in part (a). In 1980, using the original technology, the supply of Walkmans is described by the supply curve S_0. The 1980 demand curve is D_0. The quantities supplied and demanded in 1980 are equal at Q_0, and the price is P_0. Advances in technology and the building of additional production plants increase supply and shift the supply curve from S_0 to S_1. At the same time, increasing incomes increase the demand for Walkmans but not by nearly as much as the increase in supply. The demand curve shifts from D_0 to D_1. With the new demand curve D_1 and supply curve S_1, the equilibrium price is P_1 and the quantity is Q_1. The large increase in supply combined with a smaller increase in demand results in an increase in the quantity of Walkmans and a dramatic fall in their price.

Next, let's consider apartments in the center of the city, as in part (b). The supply of apartments is described by supply curve *S*. The supply curve is steep, reflecting the fact that there is a fixed number of apartment buildings. As the number of young urban professionals increases and the number of two-income families increases, the demand for city apartments increases sharply. The demand curve shifts from D_0 to D_1. As a result, the price increases from P_0 to P_1 and the quantity also increases, but not as much as the price.

Finally, let's consider the market for coffee, shown in part (c). The demand for coffee is described by curve *D*. The supply of coffee fluctuates between S_0 and S_1. When growing conditions are good, the supply curve is S_1. When there are adverse growing conditions such as frost, the supply decreases and the supply curve is S_0. As a consequence of fluctuations in supply, the price of coffee fluctuates between P_0 (the maximum price) and P_1 (the minimum price). The quantity fluctuates between Q_0 and Q_1.

◆ ◆ ◆ ◆ By using the theory of demand and supply, you will be able to explain past fluctuations in prices and quantities and also make predictions about future fluctuations. But you will want to do more than predict whether prices are going to rise or fall. In your study of microeconomics, you will learn to predict *by how much* they will change. In your study of macroeconomics you will learn to explain fluctuations in the economy as a whole. In fact, the theory of demand and supply can help answer almost every economic question.

SUMMARY

Demand

The quantity demanded of a good or service is the amount that consumers plan to buy in a given period of time at a particular price. Demands are different from wants. Wants are unlimited, whereas demands reflect decisions to satisfy specific wants. The quantity that consumers plan to buy of any good depends on:

- The price of the good
- The prices of related goods—substitutes and complements
- Income
- Expected future prices
- Population
- Preferences

Other things being equal, the higher the price of a good, the smaller is the quantity of that good demanded. The relationship between the quantity demanded and price, holding constant all other influences on consumers' planned purchases, is illustrated by the demand schedule or demand curve. A change in the price of a good produces movement along the demand curve for that good. Such a movement is called a change in the quantity demanded.

Changes in all other influences on buying plans are said to change demand. When demand changes, there is a new demand schedule and the demand curve shifts. When there is an increase in demand, the demand curve shifts to the right; when there is a decrease in demand, the demand curve shifts to the left. (pp. 73–78)

Supply

The quantity supplied of a good or service is the amount that producers plan to sell in a given period of time. The quantity that producers plan to sell of any good or service depends on:

- The price of the good
- The prices of factors of production
- The prices of related goods
- Expected future prices
- The number of suppliers
- Technology

Other things being equal, the higher the price of a good, the larger is the quantity of that good supplied. The relationship between the quantity supplied and price, holding constant all other influences on firms' planned sales, is illustrated by the supply schedule or supply curve. A change in the price of a good produces movement along the supply curve for that good. Such a movement is called a change in the quantity supplied.

Changes in all other influences on selling plans are said to change supply. When supply changes, there is a new supply schedule and the supply curve shifts. When there is an increase in supply, the supply curve shifts to the right; when there is a decrease in supply, the supply curve shifts to the left. (pp. 78–82)

Price Determination

Price regulates the quantities supplied and demanded. The higher the price, the greater is the quantity supplied and the smaller is the quantity demanded. At high prices, there is a surplus—an excess of the quantity supplied over the quantity demanded. At low prices, there is a shortage—an excess of the quantity demanded over the quantity supplied. There is one price and only one price at which the quantity demanded equals the quantity supplied. That price is the equilibrium price. At that price, buyers have no incentive to offer a higher price and suppliers have no incentive to sell at a lower price. (pp. 82–84)

Predicting Changes in Price and Quantity

Changes in demand and supply lead to changes in price and in the quantity bought and sold. An increase in demand leads to a rise in price and to an increase in quantity. A decrease in demand leads to a fall in price and to a decrease in quantity. An increase in supply leads to an increase in quantity and to a fall in price. A decrease in supply leads to a decrease in quantity and to a rise in price. A simultaneous increase in demand and supply increases the quantity bought and sold but can raise or lower the price. If the increase in demand is larger than the increase in supply, the price rises. If the increase in demand is smaller than the increase in supply, the price falls. (pp. 85–93)

KEY ELEMENTS

Key Terms

Change in demand, 77
Change in supply, 81
Change in the quantity demanded, 77
Change in the quantity supplied, 81
Complement, 75
Demand, 75
Demand curve, 74
Demand schedule, 74
Equilibrium price, 83
Equilibrium quantity, 84
Inferior good, 75
Normal good, 75
Quantity demanded, 73
Quantity supplied, 78
Substitute, 75
Supply, 79
Supply curve, 79
Supply schedule, 79
Wants, 73

Key Figures and Tables

Figure 4.1 The Demand Curve and the Demand Schedule, 74
Figure 4.3 A Change in Demand versus a Change in the Quantity Demanded, 77

REVIEW QUESTIONS

1 Define the quantity demanded of a good or service.

2 Define the quantity supplied of a good or service.

3 List the more important factors that influence the amount that consumers plan to buy and say whether an increase in each factor increases or decreases consumers' planned purchases.

4 List the more important factors that influence the amount that firms plan to sell and say whether an increase in each factor increases or decreases firms' planned sales.

5 State the law of demand and the law of supply.

6 If a fixed amount of a good is available, what does the demand curve tell us about the price that consumers are willing to pay for that fixed quantity?

7 If consumers are willing to buy only a certain fixed quantity, what does the supply curve tell us about the price at which firms will supply that quantity?

8 Distinguish between:

a A change in demand and a change in the quantity demanded

b A change in supply and a change in the quantity supplied

9 Why is the price at which the quantity demanded equals the quantity supplied the equilibrium price?

10 Describe what happens to the price of a tape and the quantity of tapes sold if:

a The price of CDs increases.

b The price of a Walkman increases.

c The supply of live concerts increases.

d Consumers' incomes increase and firms producing tapes switch to new cost-saving technology.

e The prices of the factors of production used to make tapes increase.

f A new good comes onto the market that makes tapes obsolete.

PROBLEMS

1 Suppose that one of the following events occurs:

a The price of gasoline rises.

b The price of gasoline falls.

c All speed limits on highways are abolished.

d A new fuel-effective engine that runs on cheap alcohol is invented.

e The population doubles.

f Robotic production plants lower the cost of producing cars.

g A law banning car imports from Japan is passed.

h The rates for auto insurance double.

i The minimum age for drivers is increased to 19 years.

j A massive and high-grade oil supply is discovered in Mexico.

k The environmental lobby succeeds in closing down all nuclear power stations.

l The price of cars rises.

m The price of cars falls.

n The summer temperature is 10 degrees lower than normal, and the winter temperature is 10 degrees higher than normal.

State which of the above events will produce:

1 A movement along the demand curve for gasoline
2 A shift of the demand curve for gasoline to the right
3 A shift of the demand curve for gasoline to the left
4 A movement along the supply curve of gasoline
5 A shift of the supply curve of gasoline to the right
6 A shift of the supply curve of gasoline to the left
7 A movement along the demand curve for cars
8 A movement along the supply curve of cars
9 A shift of the demand curve for cars to the right
10 A shift of the demand curve for cars to the left
11 A shift of the supply curve of cars to the right
12 A shift of the supply curve of cars to the left
13 An increase in the price of gasoline
14 A decrease in the quantity of oil bought and sold

2 The demand and supply schedules for gum are as follows:

Price (cents per pack)	Quantity demanded (millions of packs	Quantity supplied per week)
10	200	0
20	180	30
30	160	60
40	140	90
50	120	120
60	100	140
70	80	160
80	60	180
90	40	200

a What is the equilibrium price of gum?
b How much gum is bought and sold each week?

Suppose that a huge fire destroys one half of the gum-producing factories. Supply decreases to one half of the amount shown in the above supply schedule.

c What is the new equilibrium price of gum?
d How much gum is now bought and sold each week?
e Has there been a shift in or a movement along the supply curve of gum?
f Has there been a shift in or a movement along the demand curve for gum?
g As the gum factories destroyed by fire are rebuilt and gradually resume gum production, what will happen to:
  (1) The price of gum
  (2) The quantity of gum bought
  (3) The demand curve for gum
  (4) The supply curve of gum

3 Suppose the demand and supply schedules for gum are those in problem 2. An increase in the teenage population increases the demand for gum by 40 million packs per week.

a Write out the new demand schedule for gum.
b What is the new quantity of gum bought and sold each week?
c What is the new equilibrium price of gum?
d Has there been a shift in or a movement along the demand curve for gum?
e Has there been a shift in or a movement along the supply curve of gum?

4 Suppose the demand and supply schedules for gum are those in problem 2. An increase in the teenage population increases the demand for gum by 40 million packs per week, and simultaneously the fire described in problem 2 occurs, wiping out one half of the gum-producing factories.

a Draw a graph of the original and new demand and supply curves.
b What is the new quantity of gum bought and sold each week?
c What is the new equilibrium price of gum?

PART 2

Introduction to Macroeconomics

Talking with Franco Modigliani

Franco Modigliani was born in Rome, Italy, in 1918. He was an undergraduate in Italy and obtained his B.A. in 1939 as World War II was beginning. He spent the war years in the United States, which has been his professional base ever since. He obtained his Ph.D. in 1944 at the New School for Social Research in New York. He worked at Carnegie-Mellon University in the 1950s and became Professor of Economics and Finance and Institute Professor at the Massachusetts Institute of Technology in 1960. Professor Modigliani was awarded the Nobel Memorial Prize in Economics in 1985 for his pioneering work on consumption and saving—the development of the life-cycle hypothesis—and for his contributions to the theory of finance.

What attracted you to economics?

I studied economics at the University of Rome as part of the requirements for the degree of Doctor in Law. However, the teaching environment under fascism was terrible, and I learned very little, except by studying on my own. I became interested in economics by a fluke: I participated in a national competition in economics and won first prize. I concluded that economics was for me.

What did you study at the New School?

I took advantage of the New School in New York to make up for all that I had not been able to learn in Italy. But my greatest interest was in Keynes and the newly born field of macroeconomics. I also pursued mathematical economics and econometrics—also in its beginning at that time—under the guidance of a great teacher, Jacob Marshack.

"The differences . . . spring . . . from different value judgments about the cost of unemployment or the dangers of allowing the government to have any discretionary power."

You are an "activist" in contrast to a "monetarist," and you've had many notable verbal battles with the monetarists, especially with Milton Friedman. Yet some of your work and some of Friedman's work are remarkably similar—especially the life-cycle hypothesis and the permanent income hypothesis of consumption expenditure. What is it about economics that unites your work and Friedman's, and what is it that divides you and Friedman on policy questions?

I generally agree with Friedman and other reputable economists on basic economic theory. For instance, we agree on the nature of the mechanism through which money affects the economy or on the way consumers choose to allocate their life resources over their lifetime.

The differences arise, typically, at the level of the economic policies we advocate. They spring to an important extent from different value judgments about the cost of unemployment or the dangers of allowing the government to have any discretionary power. Thus Friedman, who profoundly distrusts government, finds that the system is sufficiently stable when left to itself, that we do not need to take the risk of giving government discretionary power, and indeed that discretionary policies, in the hands of an incompetent government, may be destabilizing.

My value judgments and assessment are very different. I believe that instability is extremely costly, and I find that the economy, when left to itself, is not sufficiently stable. I believe that there exist good governments and central banks and that even an average policymaker can successfully contribute to the stabilization of the economy. Thus, in contrast to Friedman, I conclude that the relevant authorities should be given the discretion necessary for a stabilization policy, but with appropriate checks.

You were one of the pioneers of large-scale econometric models. These models are now routinely used for commercial forecasting but don't appear much in the academic journals. How useful are these models?

I have not followed any of the econometric models from the "inside," that is, in terms of model upkeep and testing, since completing work on the model for the Federal Reserve. However, from what I have been able to observe, the leading models, such as DRI, Wharton, and Michigan, have been quite useful. The forecasting record of these models is, of course, far from perfect, and at times it is outright disappointing. Yet there is considerable evidence to suggest that at least these models perform appreciably better than known alternatives. They have also proved useful in testing hypotheses and in working out the short-run effects of alternative policies.

Suppose you were given carte blanche by the president and Congress to fix the American economy and deliver a prosperous closing decade to the twentieth century. What would you recommend?

In my view, the American economy is not in significantly bad shape for the coming years. At the moment, of course, we are in the midst of a slowdown, but it is of modest magnitude, and it should not take long to get over it. For the longer run, the more serious concerns seem to be the slow growth of productivity, the deterioration in the economic welfare of the lowest income and skill classes, and a continuing substantial balance of payments deficit. All these symptoms bear a relation to one underlying cause: the

> "All these symptoms bear a relation to one underlying cause: the great decline in national saving . . ."

great decline in national saving, initiated by the Reagan administration's fiscal deficit policy. It has hardly been corrected by the Bush administration, with the result that national saving has been reduced to about one fourth of what it used to be for many years. The decline in national saving in turn has contributed to the large decline in domestic investment, which in turn contributed to poor productivity performance and to lower incomes of future generations. These future generations will foot the bill for our failure to pay for what we are consuming now.

The decline in investment also very likely accounts for some of the economic deterioration of the lower economic fringe. To be sure, the decline in investment was not as dramatic as that in national saving because the fiscal deficit served to attract foreign capital; but that is precisely what caused the deterioration of the current account and our growing indebtedness to foreigners.

I would therefore give high priority to eliminating the deficit—exclusive of the current social security surplus—preferably by expenditure cuts but if necessary by higher taxes. Americans pay less taxes than most citizens in other industrialized countries and can certainly afford to pay a little more in favor of future generations. The reduction in deficit could be used to expand investment and reduce the foreign deficit. The expansion of investment should include public investments in infrastructures. This expenditure would not add to the deficit if it were classified as an investment, as would be proper, and as is the prevailing practice in other countries. Productivity growth might also be helped by better education, especially at lower levels, even if it is costly.

" **T**he most basic principle in economics is the postulate of rational behavior."

What other counsel would you give the president and Congress for economic policy?

I would stop the current drift toward protectionism and recommend taking a strong lead in opening up economies to international trade. I would also give high priority to a serious policy of environmental protection, despite its costs. On the other hand, I am not a great believer in government industrial policies and would rather trust the economy to the "invisible hand" except in the case of monetary policy, where, as indicated, I believe that some discretion for the monetary authority is essential to the achievement of macroeconomic stability and stable prices.

What are the major principles of economics that you keep returning to and finding the most useful in your work?

The most basic principle in economics is the postulate of rational behavior. Many of the important propositions in economics rest on that principle. However, it must be used with full awareness of its limitations. For instance, I do not necessarily include in rational behavior "rational expectations" as defined and used by the rational expectations school. More generally, I believe that there are circumstances in which agents' behavior is not adequately described by rationality and one must be prepared to formulate alternative hypotheses.

What advice would you give to students starting out in economics today? What other subjects should they study along with economics?

Anyone interested in becoming a professional economist, whether an academic economist or a business one, should acquire a good preparation in the quantitative methods—mathematics, statistics, and econometrics. Without this background, you will miss much of the interesting literature. There are many other subjects that can be useful, depending on one's long-run interests—for instance, social psychology, law, or political science. From my experience, I can say that whatever "extracurricular" subjects I have been exposed to have turned out to be helpful at some point in my career.

CHAPTER 5

INFLATION, UNEMPLOYMENT, CYCLES, AND DEFICITS

After studying this chapter, you will be able to:

- Define inflation and explain its effects
- Define unemployment and explain its costs
- Distinguish among the various types of unemployment
- Define gross domestic product (GDP)
- Distinguish between nominal GDP and real GDP
- Explain the importance of increases and fluctuations in real GDP
- Define the business cycle
- Describe how unemployment, stock prices, and inflation fluctuate over the business cycle
- Define the government budget deficit and the country's international deficit

Shopping Cart Blues

A SHOPPING CART OF GROCERIES THAT TODAY COSTS $100 cost only $20 in 1950. An average hour of work in 1950 earned $1.34. The same average hour earned $11.00 in 1993. Higher prices and higher wages mean that firms need more dollars to pay us and we need more dollars to buy the goods and services that we consume. Does this matter? What are the effects of persistently rising prices? ◆◆ In 1993, for every 13 people with jobs, one other person was looking for work but couldn't find it and an unknown number had become discouraged about their chances of finding jobs and had stopped looking. Why can't everyone who wants a job find one? ◆◆ From 1963 to 1993, the value of goods produced in the United States increased tenfold. How much of that growth in the value of our output is real, and how much of it is an illusion created by inflation? ◆◆ Although output has grown, our economy does not follow a smooth and predictable course. Sometimes, such as from 1982 to 1989, it expands—output grows and unemployment falls. At other times, such as in 1991, output sags and unemployment increases. We call these waves of expansion and contraction business cycles. Are business cycles all alike? Do they occur at predictable intervals? ◆◆ We hear a lot these days about deficits—both the U.S. federal government's deficit and the U.S. international deficit. What are these deficits, and just how big are they? Have they been getting bigger? How can we have a deficit with the rest of the world? How do we make up the difference?

◆ ◆ ◆ ◆ These questions are the subject matter of macroeconomics—the branch of economics that seeks to understand rising prices, unemployment, fluctuating output, and government and international deficits. ◆ ◆ The macroeconomic events through which we are now living are as exciting and tumultuous as any in history. Governments here and around the world face a daily challenge to find policies that will give all of us a smoother macroeconomic ride. ◆ ◆ With what you learn in these chapters, you will be better able to understand these macroeconomic policy challenges. We'll begin by looking at inflation.

Inflation

Inflation is an upward movement in the average level of prices. Its opposite is deflation, a downward movement in the average level of prices. The boundary between inflation and deflation is price stability. Price stability occurs when the average level of prices is moving neither up nor down. The average level of prices is called the **price level**. It is measured by a price index. A **price index** measures the average level of prices in one period as a percentage of their average level in an earlier period called the base period.

U.S. price indexes that go all the way back to 1820 have been compiled, and the story they tell is shown in Fig. 5.1. Over the 173-year period shown in that figure, prices have risen nineteenfold—an average annual rate of increase of 1.76 percent. But prices have not moved upward at a constant and steady pace. In some periods, such as the Civil War, World War I, and World War II, the increase was sharp and pronounced—at times exceeding 20 percent a year. In other periods, such as the 1960s and 1970s, the increase was prolonged and steady. At yet other times there have been periods of falling prices—in the 1840s, following the Civil War, and during the Great Depression.

FIGURE 5.1

The Price Level: 1820–1993

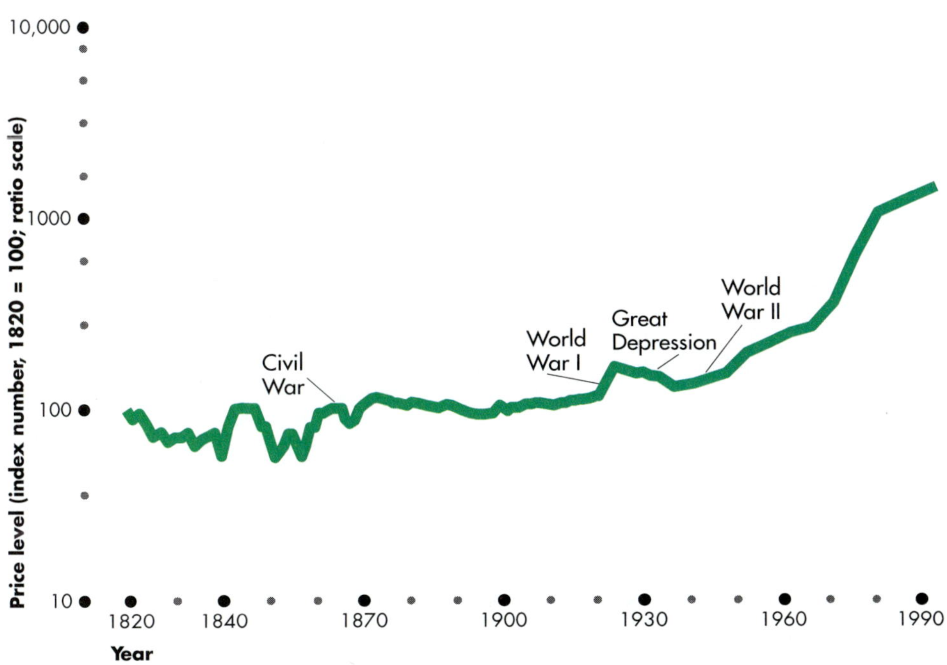

Between 1820 and 1993 prices, on the average, increased nineteenfold. In some periods, such as the Civil War and both world wars, price increases were rapid. In other periods, such as the 1970s, a period of sustained increases occurred. At yet other times, such as the years following the Civil War and during the Great Depression, prices fell.

Sources: Cost-of-living index compiled by the Federal Reserve Bank of New York, *Historical Statistics* (1960), Series E-157, p. 127; Consumer Price Index: *Historical Statistics* (1960), Series E-113, pp. 125–126; and *Economic Report of the President*, 1993.

The Inflation Rate and the Price Level

The **inflation rate** is the percentage change in the price level. The formula for the annual inflation rate is

$$\text{Inflation rate} = \frac{\text{Current year's price level} - \text{Last year's price level}}{\text{Last year's price level}} \times 100.$$

A common way of measuring the price level is to use the *Consumer Price Index,* or simply the CPI. (We'll learn more about the CPI in Chapter 6.) We can illustrate the calculation of the annual inflation rate by using the CPI. In May 1993, the CPI was 144.2. In May 1992, it was 139.7. Substituting these values into the above formula gives the inflation rate for 1993 as

$$\text{Inflation rate} = \frac{144.2 - 139.7}{139.7} \times 100$$

$$= 3.2\%.$$

The Recent Inflation Record

Recent U.S. economic history has seen some dramatic changes in the inflation rate. The inflation rate between 1960 and 1993, as measured by the CPI, is shown in Fig. 5.2.

As you can see, in the early 1960s the inflation rate was low, lying between 1 and 2 percent a year. Its rate began to increase in the late 1960s at the time of the Vietnam War. But the largest increases in inflation occurred in 1974 and again in 1980, years in which the actions of the Organization of Petroleum Exporting Countries (OPEC) resulted in exceptionally large increases in the price of oil. Inflation decreased quickly in the early 1980s at a time when the Federal Reserve chairman, Paul Volcker, pursued a policy of severe monetary restraint, pushing interest rates upward to historically high levels. The inflation rate remained relatively low in the second half of the 1980s, although by the end of the decade, it was beginning to show signs of increasing again.

FIGURE 5.2

Inflation: 1960–1993

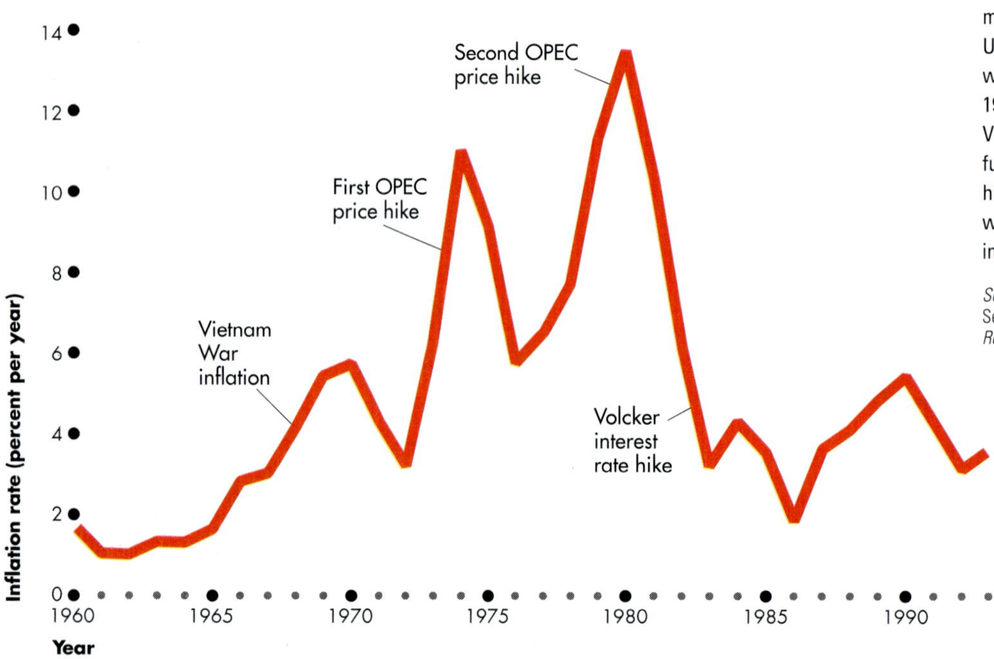

Inflation is a persistent feature of modern economic life in the United States. The inflation rate was low in the first half of the 1960s, but it moved upward in the Vietnam War years. It increased further with the OPEC oil price hikes but eventually declined when the Volcker Fed increased interest rates in the early 1980s.

Sources: Historical Statistics (1960), Series E-113, pp. 125–126; and *Economic Report of the President,* 1993.

The inflation rate rises and falls over the years. But since the 1930s the price level has generally risen (see Fig. 5.1 again). The price level falls only when the inflation rate is negative. Thus even in years such as 1961 and 1986 when the inflation rate was low, the price level was rising.

Inflation and the Value of Money

When inflation is present, money is losing value. The **value of money** is the amount of goods and services that can be bought with a given amount of money. When an economy experiences inflation, the value of money falls—you cannot buy as many groceries with $50 this year as you could last year. The rate at which the value of money falls is equal to the inflation rate. When the inflation rate is high, as it was in 1980, money loses its value at a rapid pace. When inflation is low, as it was in 1961, the value of money falls slowly.

Inflation is a phenomenon that all countries experience. But inflation *rates* vary from one country to another. When inflation rates differ over a prolonged period of time, the result is a change in the foreign exchange value of money. A **foreign exchange rate** is the rate at which one country's money (or currency) exchanges for another country's money. For example, in January 1991, 1 U.S. dollar exchanged for 130 Japanese yen. But in January 1971, you could get 360 yen for a dollar. The value of the U.S. dollar, in terms of the Japanese yen, has gradually fallen over the past 20 years because our inflation rate has been higher than that in Japan. We'll learn more about exchange rates and how they are influenced by inflation in Chapter 19.

Is Inflation a Problem?

Is it a problem if money loses its value and does so at a rate that varies from one year to another? It is, indeed, a problem, but to understand why, we need to distinguish between anticipated and unanticipated inflation. When prices are moving upward, most people are aware of that fact. They also have some notion about the rate at which prices are rising. The rate at which people (on the average) believe that the price level is rising is called the **expected inflation rate**. But expectations may be right or wrong. If they turn out to be right, the actual inflation rate equals the expected inflation rate and inflation is said to be anticipated. That is, an **anticipated inflation** is an inflation rate that has been correctly forecasted (on the average). To the extent that the inflation rate is misforecasted, it is said to be unanticipated. That is, **unanticipated inflation** is the part of the inflation rate that has caught people by surprise.

The problems arising from inflation differ depending on whether its rate is anticipated or unanticipated. Let's begin by looking at the problems arising from unanticipated inflation.

The Problem of Unanticipated Inflation

Unanticipated inflation is a problem because it produces unanticipated changes in the value of money. Money is used as a measuring rod of the value in the transactions that we undertake. Borrowers and lenders, workers and their employers, all make contracts in terms of money. If the value of money varies unexpectedly over time, then the amounts *really* paid and received differ from those that people intended to pay and receive when they signed the contracts. Measuring value with a measuring rod whose units vary is a bit like trying to measure a piece of cloth with an elastic ruler. The size of the cloth depends on how tightly the ruler is stretched.

Let's take a look at the effects of unanticipated inflation by looking at what happens to agreements between borrowers and lenders and between workers and employers.

Borrowers and Lenders People often say that inflation is good for borrowers and bad for lenders. To see how they reach that conclusion—and why it's not always correct—let's consider an example.

Sue is a lender. She lends $5,000 by putting it into a bank deposit for one year at an interest rate of 10 percent. At the end of the year she plans to buy a car that today costs $5,500. She will earn $500 dollars interest on her bank deposit, which she expects will give her just enough to buy the car.

If there is no inflation, Sue can buy her car. But suppose that prices rise during the year and a car that cost $5,500 at the beginning of the year costs $6,000 at the end of the year. Sue can't afford to buy the car at that price. Actually, Sue is as far away from being able to buy the car as she was at the beginning of the year. She's got more money, but everything now costs more. Sue has *really* made no interest income at all, and the bank has *really* paid no interest.

But lenders don't always lose when there is inflation. If Sue and the bank anticipate the inflation, they can adjust the interest rate they agree upon to offset the anticipated fall in the value of money. If the inflation is correctly anticipated, Sue and the bank agree to an interest rate of 20 percent. At the end of the year the bank pays Sue $6,000. Of this amount, $5,000 is the repayment of the initial deposit and $1,000 is interest—at a rate of 20 percent a year. This interest income for Sue consists of $500—the 10 percent rate they agree is appropriate with no inflation—and $500 compensation for the loss in the value of money. Sue *really* receives a 10 percent interest rate, and that's what the bank *really* pays.

If borrowers and lenders correctly anticipate the inflation rate, interest rates are adjusted to cancel out inflation's effect on the interest *really* paid and *really* received. It is only when borrowers and lenders make errors in forecasting the future inflation rate that one of them gains and the other loses. But those gains and losses can go either way. If the inflation rate turns out to be higher than is generally expected, then the borrower gains and the lender loses. Conversely, if the inflation rate turns out to be lower than is generally expected, then the borrower loses and the lender gains.

Thus it is not inflation itself that produces gains and losses for borrowers and lenders. It is an *unanticipated increase* in the *inflation rate* that *benefits borrowers* and hurts lenders. An *unanticipated decrease* in the *inflation rate benefits lenders* and hurts borrowers.

In the United States in the late 1960s and 1970s, the inflation rate kept rising and to some degree the rise was unanticipated, so borrowers tended to gain. In the 1980s, the fall in the inflation rate was also, at least initially, unanticipated and lenders gained. On the international scene, many developing countries, such as Mexico and Brazil, borrowed large amounts of money in the late 1970s and early 1980s at high interest rates in anticipation that an inflation rate above 10 percent a year would persist. But the inflation rate fell. These countries are now stuck with paying the interest on their loans without the extra revenue that they expected to receive from higher prices for their exports.

Workers and Employers Another common belief is that inflation redistributes income between workers and their employers. Some people believe that workers gain at the expense of employers, and others believe the contrary.

The previous discussion concerning borrowers and lenders applies to workers and their employers as well. If inflation increases unexpectedly, then wages will not have been set high enough. Profits will be higher than expected, and wages will buy fewer goods than expected. Employers gain at the expense of workers. Conversely, if the anticipated inflation rate is higher than what the actual inflation rate turns out to be, wages will have been set too high and profits will be squeezed. Workers will be able to buy more with their income than was originally anticipated. In this case, workers gain at the expense of employers.

Large unanticipated changes in the inflation rate that produce fluctuations in the buying power of earnings—fluctuations in the value of paychecks in terms of the goods and services they buy—are not common, but they do occur from time to time. For example, in 1974, when the inflation rate climbed to 10 percent a year, the buying power of earnings fell by 3 percent. In 1980, when the inflation rate rose to 13 percent a year, the buying power of earnings fell by almost 5 percent. These two episodes of higher inflation were largely unanticipated. The *fall* in the inflation rate in 1982 was also to some degree unanticipated and brought a corresponding *rise* in the buying power of earnings.

We've now seen the problems that unanticipated inflation can bring. Let's now turn to anticipated inflation.

The Problem of Anticipated Inflation

At low inflation rates, anticipated inflation is not much of a problem at all. But it becomes more of a problem the higher the anticipated inflation rate is.

At very high inflation rates, people know that money is losing value quickly. The rate at which money is losing value is part of the *opportunity cost* of holding onto money. The higher that opportunity cost, the smaller is the amount of money people want to hold. Instead of having a wallet stuffed with $20 bills and a big checking account balance, people go shopping and spend their incomes as soon as they are received. And the same is true for firms. Instead of hanging onto the money they receive from the sale of their goods and services, they pay it out in wages as quickly as possible.

In Germany, Poland, and Hungary in the 1920s, inflation rates reached extraordinary heights—in excess of 50 percent a month. Such high inflation rates are called *hyperinflations*. At the height of these hyperinflations, firms paid out wages twice a day. As soon as they had been paid, workers rushed off to spend their wages before they lost too much value. To buy a handful of groceries, they needed a shopping cart of currency. People who lingered too long in the coffee shop found that the price of their cup of coffee had increased between the time they placed their order and when the check was presented. Such an anticipated inflation brings economic chaos and disruption.

High and Variable Inflation

Even if inflation is reasonably well anticipated, and even if its rate is not as high as in a hyperinflation, it can still impose very high costs. A high and variable inflation rate causes resources to be diverted from productive activities to forecasting inflation. It becomes more profitable to forecast the inflation rate correctly than to invent a new product. Doctors, lawyers, accountants, farmers—just about everyone—can make themselves better off, not by practicing the profession for which they have been trained, but by becoming amateur economists and inflation forecasters. From a social perspective, this diversion of talent resulting from inflation is like throwing our scarce resources onto the garbage heap. This waste of resources is the main cost of inflation.

Indexing

It is sometimes suggested that the costs of inflation can be avoided by indexing, a technique that links payments made under a contract to the price level. With indexing, Sue and the bank in our example above would not agree to a fixed interest rate; instead, they would agree to an indexing formula for adjusting the interest rate in line with the inflation rate. Similarly, an indexed wage contract does not specify the number of dollars that will be paid to workers; instead, it specifies an indexing formula that takes account of the inflation rate for calculating the number of dollars.

But indexing itself is costly. Reaching agreement on contracts with index clauses is extremely complex, since there are many possible indexes that can be used and the choice of the index has important effects on both parties to a contract.

REVIEW

Inflation is a process in which the average level of prices rises and the value of money falls. The inflation rate is measured as the percentage change in a price index. The inflation rate rises and falls, but, since the 1930s, the *price level* has only risen. The effects of inflation depend on whether it is unanticipated or anticipated. An unanticipated increase in inflation benefits borrowers and hurts lenders; an unanticipated decrease in inflation benefits lenders and hurts borrowers. Anticipated inflation becomes a serious problem when its rate is extremely high. At such times, people spend money as soon as they receive it and there is a severe disruption of economic life. Inflation also becomes a serious problem when its rate is variable because resources get diverted into predicting inflation. Indexing can lower the costs of inflation, but indexing is itself costly. ◆

Unemployment

At many times in the history of the United States, unemployment has been a serious problem. For example, in the recession of 1991, almost 9 million people were seeking jobs. What exactly is unemployment? How is it measured? How has its rate fluctuated? What is full employment? What are the costs of unemployment?

What Is Unemployment?

Unemployment is a state in which there are qualified workers who are available for work at the current wage rate and who do not have jobs. The total number of people who do have jobs—the employed—plus the total number of people who do not have jobs—the unemployed—is called the **labor force**. The **unemployment rate** is the number of people unemployed expressed as a percentage of the labor force.

Measuring Unemployment

Unemployment is measured in the United States every month. The Bureau of Labor Statistics in the U.S. Department of Labor calculates the monthly unemployment figures and publishes them in *Employment and Earnings*. These unemployment figures are based on a survey of households called the Current Population Survey.

To be counted as unemployed in the Current Population Survey, a person must be available for work and must be in one of three categories:

1. Without work, but has made specific efforts to find a job within the previous four weeks
2. Waiting to be called back to a job from which he or she has been laid off
3. Waiting to start a new job within 30 days

Anyone surveyed who satisfies one of these three criteria is counted as unemployed. Part-time workers are counted as being employed.

There are three reasons why the unemployment level as measured by the Current Population Survey may be misleading. Let's examine these.

Unrealistic Wage Expectations If someone is willing to work, but only for a much higher wage than is available, it does not make sense to count that person as unemployed. That is, if someone says that he or she is willing to work at McDonald's, but only for $25 an hour, then that person is not really available for work and, therefore, is not unemployed.

Correcting the unemployment data to take account of wage and job expectations would result in a lower measured unemployment rate. How much lower we do not know. A second factor works in the opposite direction.

Discouraged Workers Many people who still fail to find a suitable job after prolonged and extensive search effort come to believe that there is no work available for them. They become discouraged and stop looking for work. Such people are called discouraged workers. **Discouraged workers** are people who do not have jobs and would like work but have stopped seeking work. Discouraged workers are not counted as unemployed by the Current Population Survey because they have not sought work within the past 30 days. If discouraged workers were added to the unemployment count, the unemployment rate would be higher than what is currently measured.

Part-Time Workers As we have noted, part-time workers are counted as employed. But many part-time workers are available for and seeking full-time work. The measured unemployment rate does not capture this element of part-time unemployment.

The Unemployment Record

The U.S. unemployment record between 1900 and 1993 is set out in Fig. 5.3. The dominant feature of that record is the Great Depression of the early 1930s. During that episode of our history, 25 percent of the labor force was unemployed. Although in recent years we have not experienced anything as devastating as the Great Depression, we have experienced some high unemployment rates. Three such periods are highlighted in the figure—the mid-1970s when oil prices were increased sharply, the early 1980s when the Federal Reserve (under chairman Volcker) increased interest rates sharply, and 1991 when uncertainty and pessimism brought a decrease in spending and recession. The average unemployment rate over this 93-year period was just over 6 percent.

Unemployment is a highly charged topic. We chart the course of the unemployment rate as a measure of U.S. economic health with the intensity with which a physician keeps track of a patient's temperature. What does the unemployment rate tell us? Does all unemployment have the same origin, or are there different types of unemployment? In fact, there are three main sources of variation in unemployment, and they give rise to three types of unemployment. Let's see what they are.

Types of Unemployment

The three types of unemployment are

- Frictional
- Structural
- Cyclical

Frictional Unemployment The unemployment arising from normal labor market turnover is called **frictional unemployment.** Normal labor market turnover arises from two sources. First, people are constantly changing their economic activities—young people are leaving school and joining the labor force; old people are retiring and leaving the labor force; some people are leaving the labor force temporarily, per-

FIGURE 5.3

Unemployment: 1900–1993

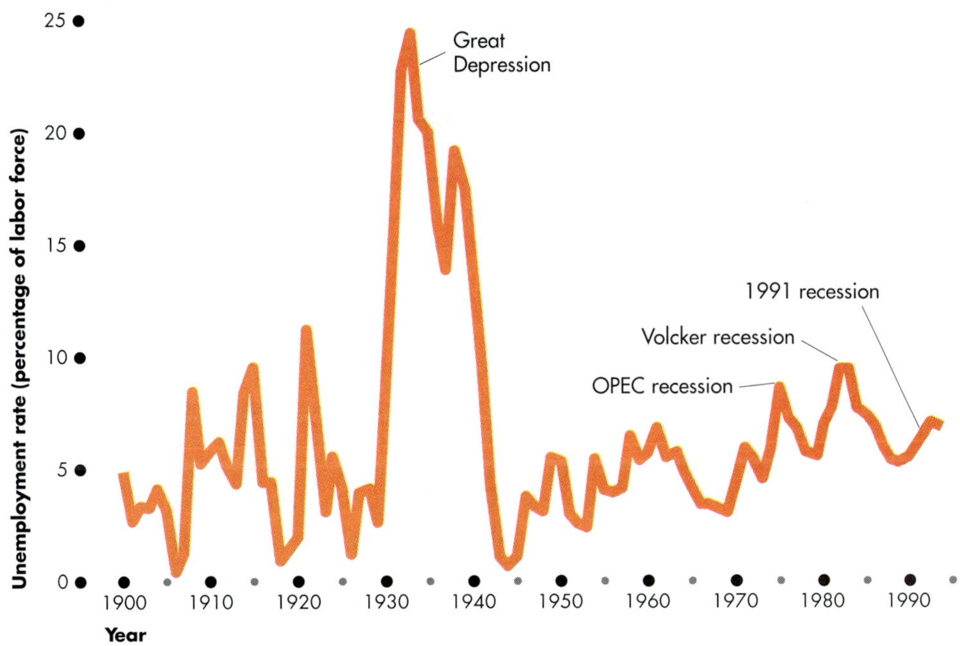

Unemployment is a persistent feature of economic life, but its rate varies considerably. At its worst—during the Great Depression—25 percent of the labor force was unemployed. Even in the recessions following the OPEC price hikes and the Volcker interest rate increases, unemployment climbed toward the 10 percent mark. Between the late 1960s and 1982, there was a general tendency for unemployment to increase. The rate fell between 1983 and 1988 but then increased again through 1992.

Sources: Unemployment, 1900–1946: *Historical Statistics* (1960), Series D-46, p. 73; unemployment, 1946–1988: *Economic Report of the President,* 1993.

haps to raise children or for some other reason, and then rejoining it. Second, the fortunes of businesses are constantly changing—some are closing down and laying off their workers; new firms are starting up and are hiring.

These constant changes result in frictional unemployment. There are always some firms with unfilled vacancies and some people looking for work. Unemployed people don't usually take the first job that comes their way. Instead, they spend time searching out what they believe will be the best job available to them. By doing so, they can match their own skills and interests with the available jobs, finding a satisfying job and income.

It is unlikely that frictional unemployment will ever disappear. The amount of frictional unemployment depends on the rate at which people enter and leave the labor force and on the rate at which jobs are created and destroyed. For example the postwar baby boom of the late 1940s brought a bulge in the number of people entering the labor force in the 1960s and an increase in the amount of frictional unemployment. When a major new shopping mall is built, jobs become available in the mall and a similar number of jobs are lost in the older part of town where shops are struggling to survive. The people who lose jobs aren't always the first to get the new jobs, and while they are between jobs, they are frictionally unemployed.

The length of time that people take to find a job is influenced by unemployment compensation. The more generous the rate of unemployment benefit, the longer is the average time taken in job search and the higher is the rate of frictional unemployment.

Structural Unemployment The unemployment that arises when there is a decline in the number of jobs available in a particular region or industry is called **structural unemployment.** Such a decline might occur because of permanent technological change—for example, the automation of a steel plant. It might also occur because of a permanent change in international competition—for example, the decline of the number of jobs in the U.S. auto industry resulting from Japanese competition.

The distinction between structural and frictional unemployment is not always a sharp one, but some cases are clear. A person who loses a job in a suburban shopping center and gets a job a few weeks later in a new mall has experienced frictional unemployment. An auto worker who loses his or her job and, after a period of retraining and prolonged search, perhaps lasting more than a year, eventually gets a job as an insurance salesperson has experienced structural unemployment.

At some times, the amount of structural unemployment is modest, and at other times it is large. It was especially large during the late 1970s and early 1980s when increases in the price of oil and an increasingly competitive international environment brought a decline in the number of jobs in traditional industries, such as autos and steel, and an increase in the number of jobs in new industries, such as electronics and bio-engineering, as well as in the service industries such as banking and insurance.

Cyclical Unemployment The unemployment arising from a slowdown in the pace of economic expansion is called **cyclical unemployment**. The pace of economic expansion is ever-changing, rapid at some times, slow at others, and even negative on occasion. When the economy is expanding rapidly, cyclical unemployment disappears, and when the economy is expanding slowly or contracting, cyclical unemployment can become extremely high. For example, an auto worker who is laid off because the economy is going through a slow period and who gets rehired some months later when economic activity speeds up has experienced cyclical unemployment.

With frictional and structural unemployment, there are as many job vacancies as there are unemployed workers. The jobs and the workers have simply not found each other. Cyclical unemployment is different. When the level of cyclical unemployment is high, there are fewer job vacancies than unemployed workers. No matter how hard people look for work, they're not all going to find it.

Measuring frictional, structural, and cyclical unemployment and distinguishing one type of unemployment from another are controversial. It is not possible to provide a quantitative breakdown of unemployment among the three types. But we can see the three types in specific real-world situations. Reading Between the Lines on pp. 112–113 gives an example.

Full Employment

At any given time, there are people looking for work and firms looking for people to employ—unemployed people and job vacancies. **Full employment** is a state in which the number of people looking for a job equals the number of job vacancies. Equivalently, full employment occurs when all unemployment is frictional and structural and there is no cyclical unemployment. We've seen that there is always some frictional unemployment and often there is structural unemployment. Thus there is always some unemployment, even at full employment.

The unemployment rate at full employment is called the **natural rate of unemployment**. The natural rate of unemployment fluctuates because of fluctuations in frictional and structural unemployment. But there is controversy about the magnitude of the natural unemployment rate. Some economists believe that the natural rate of unemployment in the United States is between 5 and 6 percent of the labor force. Other economists believe not only that the natural rate of unemployment varies, but that it can be quite high, especially at times when demographic and technological factors point to a high frictional and structural unemployment rate.

What are the costs of unemployment?

The Costs of Unemployment

There are four main costs of unemployment. They are

- Loss of output and income
- Loss of human capital
- Increase in crime
- Loss of human dignity

Loss of Output and Income The most obvious costs of unemployment are the loss of output and the loss of income that the unemployed would have produced if they had jobs. The size of these costs depends on the natural rate of unemployment. If the natural rate of unemployment is between 5 and 6 percent, as economists such as James Tobin of Yale University believe, the lost output from unemployment is enormous.

The late Arthur Okun of the Brookings Institution estimated that for every 1 percentage point rise in the unemployment rate, the nation's output of goods and services falls by 3 percentage points. More recent studies have suggested that each 1 percentage point added to the unemployment rate cuts output by 2 percentage points. If numbers in this range are correct, then the lost output resulting from high unemployment is enormous. One percent of aggregate output in the United States is $55 billion. Thus getting the unemployment rate down from 8 percent to 6 percent raises output between $220 billion and $330 billion. With a U.S. population of 250 million people, the average person could buy additional goods and services each year valued between $880 and $1,320 if this loss could be avoided.

Those economists who believe that the natural rate of unemployment itself varies think that the lost output cost of unemployment is small. They regard the fluctuations in the unemployment rate as arising from fluctuations in structural unemployment. With rapid structural change, people need to find their most productive new jobs. A period of high unemployment is like an investment in the future. It is the price paid today for a larger future income.

Loss of Human Capital A second cost of unemployment is the permanent damage that can be done to an unemployed worker by hindering his or her career development and acquisition of human capital. **Human capital** is the value of a person's education and acquired skills. For example, Jody finishes law school at a time when unemployment is high, and she just can't find a job in a law office. Desperately short of income, she becomes a taxi driver. After a year in this work, she discovers it is impossible to compete with the new crop of law graduates and is stuck with cab driving. Her human capital as a lawyer has been wiped out by high unemployment.

Increase in Crime A high unemployment rate usually leads to a high crime rate. There are two reasons for this relationship. First, when people cannot earn an income from legal work, they sometimes turn to illegal work and the amount of theft increases sharply. Second, with low incomes and increased frustration, family life begins to suffer and there are increases in crimes such as child beating, wife assault, and suicide.

Loss of Human Dignity A final cost that is difficult to quantify, but that is large and very important, is the loss of self-esteem that afflicts many who suffer prolonged periods of unemployment. It is probably this aspect of unemployment that makes it so highly charged with political and social significance.

REVIEW

There have been enormous fluctuations in the unemployment rate, but no matter how low its rate, unemployment never disappears. Some unemployment is frictional, arising from labor market turnover. Some is structural, arising from the decline in certain industries and regions. And some is cyclical, arising from a slowdown in the pace of economic expansion. The natural rate of unemployment is that unemployment rate at which there is a balance between the number of unemployed people and the number of job vacancies. This rate fluctuates with changes in the frictional and structural unemployment rate. The costs of unemployment include lost output and income, loss of human capital, an increase in crime, and a loss of human dignity. ◆

Unemployment is not the only indicator of the state of the nation's economic health. Another is its gross domestic product. Let's now examine that.

Gross Domestic Product

The value of all the final goods and services produced in the economy in a year is called **gross domestic product,** or GDP. **Final goods and services** are goods and services that are not used as inputs in the production of other goods and services but are bought by their final user. Such goods include consumption goods and services and also new durable goods. Examples of final goods are cans of soda and cars. Examples of final services are automobile insurance and haircuts.

Unemployment during "Recovery"

U.S. NEWS & WORLD REPORT, June 28, 1993

White Collar Wasteland

BY DAVID HAGE, LINDA GRANT, AND JIM IMPOCO

Few Americans were so groomed for success as Jim Bennett of New Canaan, Conn. His diplomas read Princeton University and Stanford University Law School. His honors include Phi Beta Kappa. And his résumé boasts such gold-plated employers as General Electric. Yet . . . a budget cut wiped out his job [and] Bennett, 55, hasn't held a steady job since.

. . . For the first time on record, white-collar workers have surpassed blue-collar workers in the nation's unemployment lines, and many of the casualties are still reeling. "Your foundation turns out to be sand," says Bennett. "There's no recovery for people like me."

Jim Bennett is right. The recession officially ended more than two years ago. But white-collar unemployment kept on climbing: from 2.8 million in March 1991, past the 3 million mark, to 3.4 million late last year. And though it has ebbed slightly in recent months, it still stands at 3.1 million today—higher than at the recession's trough. Even in May, when the labor market seemed to shake off its doldrums and created a respectable 209,000 jobs, an additional 15,000 managers and professionals were thrown out of work. . . .

. . . During the 1981–82 downturn, . . . employers kept right on creating office positions, so that the nation's white-collar payrolls rose by a stunning 838,000 jobs *before* the 1983 recovery began. In the 1990–91 recession, on the other hand, white-collar payrolls shrank by 354,000 jobs. . . .

Sadly, the economic recovery can't move into high gear if white-collar workers aren't on board. True, blue-collar workers bear the brunt of most recessions. . . . Even today, their unemployment rate is 9.1 percent, more than twice the rate for white-collar workers. The crucial difference, however, is that blue-collar layoffs often are temporary. . . . But a white-collar worker who loses a job is very likely never to get it back. As a result, permanent separations accounted for 85 percent of job losses in the last recession, compared with 56 percent in four previous downturns. . . .

The Essence of the Story

In mid-1993, the blue-collar unemployment rate was 9.1 percent, more than twice the rate for white-collar workers.

For the first time on record, white-collar workers outnumbered blue-collar workers in the nation's unemployment lines.

White-collar unemployment increased from 2.8 million in March 1991 to 3.4 million in late 1992, before falling to 3.1 million in mid-1993.

In May 1993, the labor market created 209,000 jobs, but 15,000 managerial and professional jobs disappeared.

During the 1981–1982 recession, white-collar jobs increased by 838,000 *before* the 1983 recovery began. In the 1990–1991 recession, white-collar jobs decreased by 354,000.

Blue-collar layoffs often are temporary. In contrast, white-collar unemployment is more likely to be permanent.

Permanent separations accounted for 85 percent of job losses in the 1990–1991 recession, compared with 56 percent in four previous downturns.

Background and Analysis

Unemployment can be frictional, structural, or cyclical.

Frictional unemployment arises mainly from new entrants into the labor force, workers who quit unsuitable jobs, and people who reenter the labor force. The figure shows that these components of unemployment do not fluctuate much.

Structural and cyclical unemployment arise mainly from layoffs and permanent job losses. The figure shows that these two sources of unemployment fluctuate a great deal.

Layoffs affect mainly blue-collar workers. The figure shows that this source of unemployment increased more sharply in the 1981–1982 recession than in the 1990–1991 recession.

Permanent job losses affect both blue-collar and white-collar workers. The figure shows that this source of unemployment represented a much larger percentage of total unemployment in the 1990–1991 recession than in the 1981–1982 recession.

As the unemployment rate fluctuates, the duration of unemployment also fluctuates, as shown in the figure. The duration of unemployment was greater, relative to the unemployment rate, in 1992 than in 1982. But the peak duration of 20 weeks in 1983 was not surpassed.

More economic restructuring that destroyed white-collar jobs occurred in the early 1990s than in the early 1980s. This type of unemployment is *structural*—not cyclical—and will decrease only slowly.

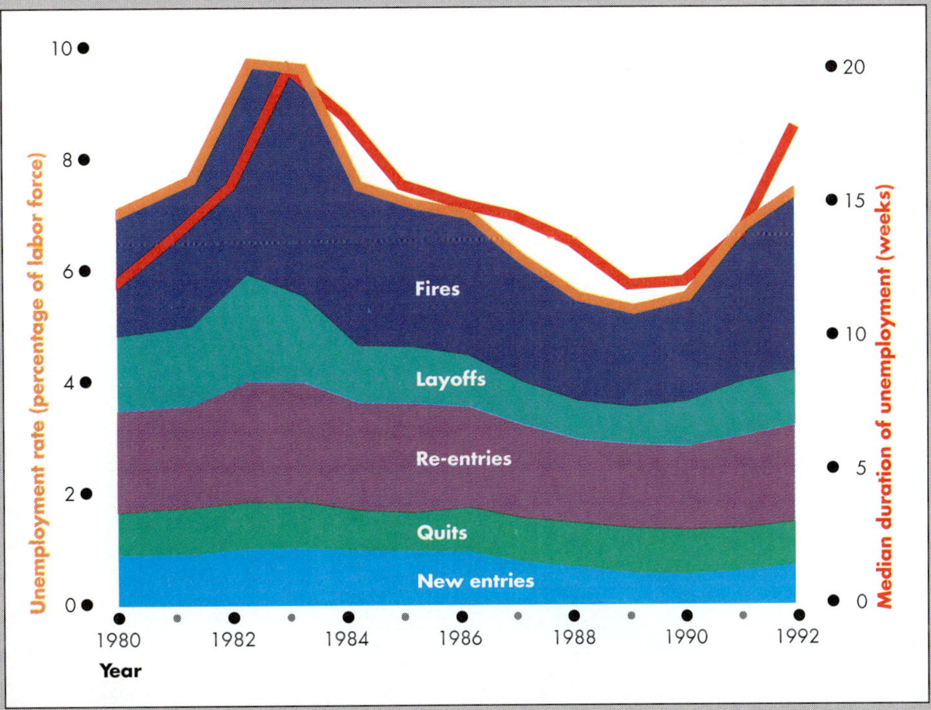

Not all goods and services are "final." Some are intermediate goods and services. **Intermediate goods and services** are those used as inputs into the production process of another good or service. Examples of intermediate goods are the windshields, batteries, and gearboxes used by car producers and the paper and ink used by newspaper manufacturers. Examples of intermediate services are the banking and insurance services bought by car producers and news printers. Whether a good or service is intermediate or final depends on who buys it and for what purpose. For example, electric power purchased by a car producer or a printer is an intermediate good. Electric power bought by you is a final good.

When we measure gross domestic product, we do not include the value of intermediate goods and services produced. If we did, we would be counting the same thing more than once. When someone buys a new car from the local Chrysler dealer, that is a final transaction and the value of the car is counted as part of GDP. But we must not also count as part of GDP the amount the dealer paid to Chrysler for the car or the amount paid by Chrysler to all its suppliers for the car's various parts.

If we want to measure GDP, we somehow have to add together all the *final* goods and services produced. Obviously, we can't achieve a useful measure by simply adding together the number of cars, newspapers, kilowatts of electric power, haircuts, and automobile insurance policies. To determine GDP, we first calculate the dollar *value* of the output of each final good or service. This calculation simply involves multiplying the quantity produced of each final good or service by its price. That is, we measure the output of each good and service in the common unit of dollars. We then add up the dollar values of the outputs of the different goods to arrive at their total value, which is GDP. We measure GDP in dollars, but it is a mixture of real quantities—the numbers of final goods and services produced—and dollar quantities—the prices of the goods and services. A change in GDP, therefore, contains a mixture of the effects of changes in prices and changes in the quantities of final goods and services. For many purposes, it is important to distinguish price changes from quantity changes. To do so, we use the concepts of nominal GDP and real GDP. Let's examine these concepts.

FIGURE 5.4

Gross Domestic Product: 1960–1992

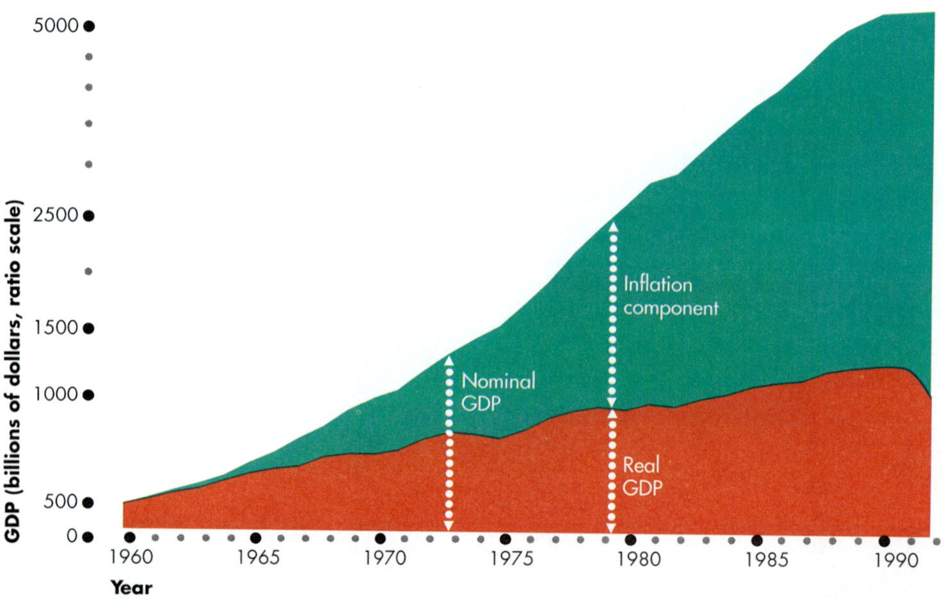

Gross domestic product increased tenfold between 1960 and 1992. But much of that increase was the result of inflation. Real GDP, the increase in GDP attributable to the increase in the volume of goods and services produced, increased but at a more modest pace. The figure shows how real GDP and the inflation component of nominal GDP have evolved. Nominal GDP has increased in every year, but real GDP fell in 1975 and 1982 and again in 1991.

Source: Real and nominal GDP, 1960–1991: *Economic Report of the President,* 1993.

Nominal GDP and Real GDP

Nominal GDP measures the value of the output of final goods and services using *current* prices. It is sometimes called *current dollar GDP.* **Real GDP** measures the value of the output of final goods and services using the prices that prevailed in some base period. An alternative name for real GDP is *constant dollar GDP.*

Comparing real GDP from one year to another enables us to say whether the economy has produced more or fewer goods and services. Comparing nominal GDP from one year to another does not permit us to compare the quantities of goods and services produced in those two years. Nominal GDP may be higher in 1993 than 1992, but that might reflect only higher prices (inflation), not more production. An increase in real GDP means that the production of goods and services expanded.

The importance of the distinction between real GDP and nominal GDP is illustrated in Fig. 5.4. In any year, real GDP is measured by the height of the red area and nominal GDP by the height of the green area. The difference between the height of the green area and the height of the red area shows the inflation component in nominal GDP. In 1960, GDP was $513 billion. By 1992, it had grown to $5,900 billion. But only part of that increase represents an increase in goods and services available—an increase in real GDP. Most of the increase came from inflation. Notice that nominal GDP increases every year in the figure but that real GDP sometimes falls, such as in 1975, 1982, and 1991.

Real GDP—the Record

Estimates of real GDP in the United States go back to 1869. Figure 5.5 illustrates the real GDP record.

FIGURE 5.5

Real GDP: 1869–1992

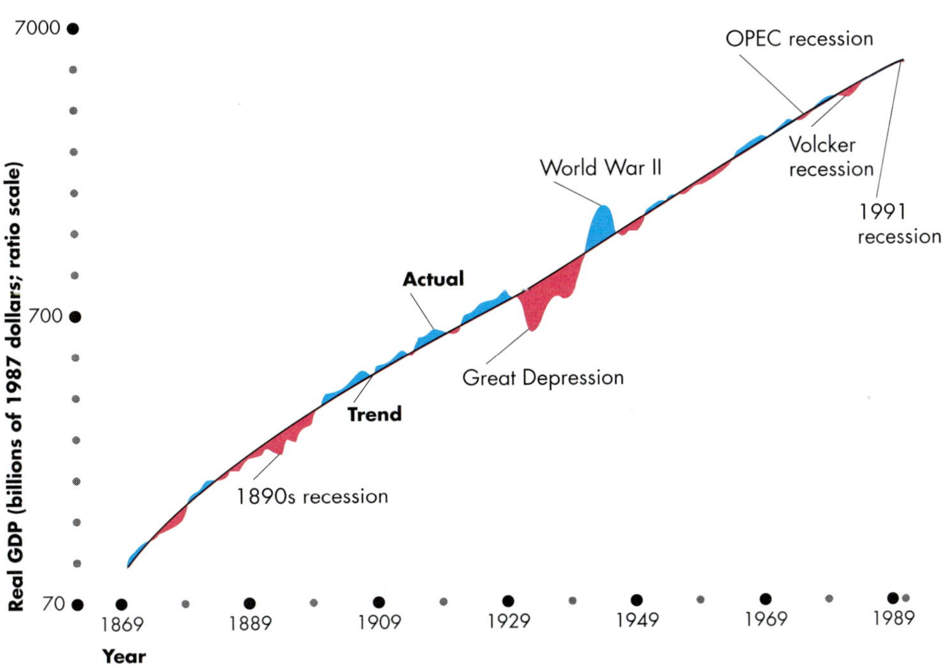

Between 1869 and 1992 real GDP grew at an annual average rate of 3.3 percent. But the growth rate was not the same in each year. In some periods, such as the years during World War II, real GDP expanded quickly. In other periods, such as the Great Depression and, more recently, following the OPEC oil price hikes, the Volcker interest rate increases, and in 1991, real GDP declined. There were several periods of decline in the nineteenth century as well, one of which is marked in the figure.

Source: 1869–1929: Christina D. Romer, "The Prewar Business Cycle Reconsidered: New Estimates of Gross National Product, 1869–1908," *Journal of Political Economy* 97, (1989) 1–37; and Nathan S. Balke and Robert J. Gordon, "The Estimation of Prewar Gross National Product: Methodology and New Evidence," *Journal of Political Economy* 97, (1989) 38–92. The data used are an average of the estimates given in these two sources. 1929–1958: *Economic Report of the President,* 1991. 1959–1992: *Economic Report of the President,* 1993. The data for 1869 to 1958 are GNP and those for 1959 to 1992 are GDP. The difference between these two measures is small and is explained in Chapter 23, pp. 619–620.

Two facts stand out. First, there has been a general tendency for real GDP to increase. Second, the rate of upward movement is not uniform, and sometimes real GDP has actually declined. The most precipitous decline occurred in the early 1930s during the Great Depression. But declines also occurred in recent times during the mid-1970s—the time of the OPEC oil price hikes—during the early 1980s—the time of the Volcker interest rate increases—and in 1991. There were several periods during the nineteenth and early twentieth centuries when real GDP declined, one of which, the 1890s recession, is shown in the figure. There were also periods when real GDP grew extremely quickly—for example, the years during World War II.

In order to obtain a clearer picture of the changes in real GDP, we consider separately the two general tendencies that we've just identified. The first of these tendencies is the general upward movement of real GDP. This feature of real GDP is called trend real GDP. Trend real GDP rises for three reasons:

- Growing population
- Growing stock of capital equipment
- Advances in technology

These forces have produced the general upward tendency that you can see in Fig. 5.5. Trend real GDP is illustrated in Fig. 5.5 as the black thin line passing through the middle of the path followed by real GDP in its meanderings above trend (blue areas) and below trend (red areas).

The second feature of real GDP is its periodic fluctuation around its trend. Real GDP fluctuations are measured as percentage deviations of real GDP from trend. They are illustrated in Fig. 5.6. As you can see, real GDP fluctuations show distinct cycles in economic activity. At times such as during the Great Depression and in the mid-1970s, early 1980s, and 1991, real GDP fluctuates below trend, and during the war years it fluctuates above trend.

The Importance of Real GDP

The upward trend in real GDP is the major source of improvements in living standards. The pace of

FIGURE 5.6

Real GDP Fluctuations: 1869–1992

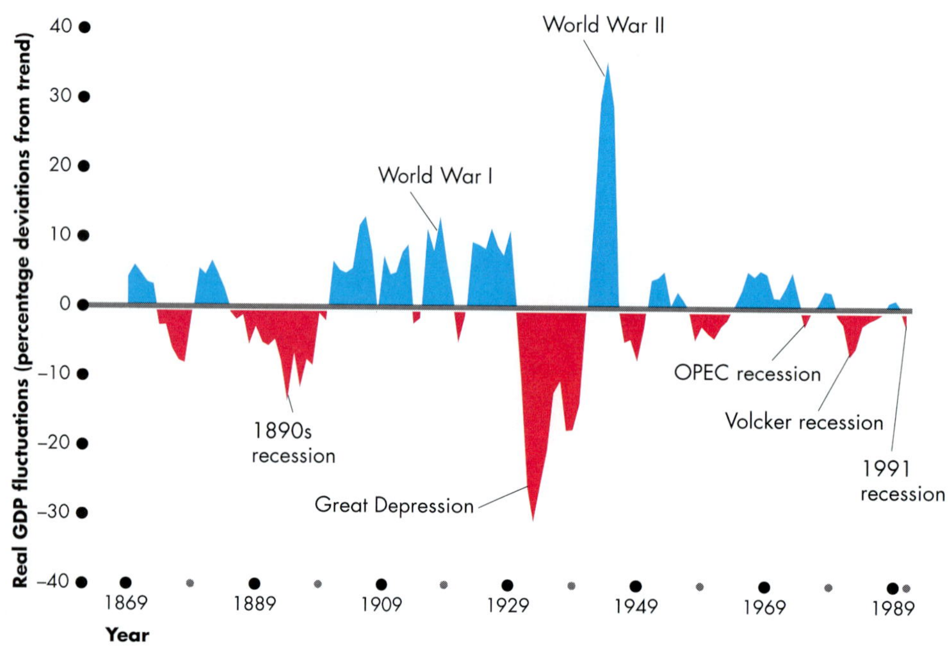

The uneven pace of increase of real GDP is illustrated by tracking its fluctuation measured as the percentage deviation of real GDP from trend. Rapid expansion of real GDP, which occurred during both world wars, puts real GDP above trend. Decreases in real GDP, which occurred during the 1890s recession, the Great Depression, and the three most recent recessions, puts real GDP below trend. The real GDP fluctuations describe the course of the business cycle.

this upward movement has a powerful effect on the standard of living of one generation compared with its predecessor. For example, if real GDP trends upward at 1 percent a year, it takes 70 years for real GDP to double. But a growth trend of 10 percent a year will double real GDP in just 7 years. With an average trend increase of between 2 and 3 percent a year, which is commonly experienced in industrial countries and which has also been the long-term experience of the United States, real GDP doubles approximately every generation (every 25 years or so).

Rapid growth in real GDP brings enormous benefits. It enables us to consume more goods and services of all kinds. It enables us to spend more on health care for the poor and elderly, more on cancer and AIDS research, more on space research and exploration, more on roads, and more on housing. It even enables us to spend more on the environment, cleaning our lakes and protecting our air.

But an upward trend in real GDP has its costs. The more quickly we increase real GDP, the faster are exhaustible resources such as oil and natural gas depleted, and the more severe our environmental and atmospheric pollution problems become. Although we have more to spend on these problems, they become bigger problems requiring higher expenditures. Furthermore, the more quickly real GDP increases, the more we have to accept change, both in what we consume and in the jobs that we do.

The benefits of more rapid growth in real GDP have to be balanced against the costs. The choices that people make to balance these benefits and costs, acting individually and through government institutions, determine the actual pace at which real GDP increases.

As we have seen, real GDP does not increase at an even pace. Are the fluctuations in real GDP important? Economists do not agree on the answer to this question. Some economists believe that real GDP fluctuations are costly. With real GDP below trend, unemployment is above its natural rate and output is lost forever. With real GDP above trend, inflationary bottlenecks and shortages arise. If a downturn can be avoided, average consumption levels can be increased, and if rises above trend can be avoided, inflation can be kept under control.

Other economists believe that fluctuations are the best possible response to the uneven pace and direction of technological change. At some times, technological change is rapid, and at other times it is slow. At some times, new technologies increase the productivity of workers in their existing jobs, and at other times, new technologies increase productivity only after massive structural change has taken place. Real GDP growth fluctuates with the pace of technological change—faster technological change brings faster real GDP growth. But structural change complicates the relationship. Rapid technological and structural changes at first bring structural unemployment and slow real GDP growth. Since we are not able to order the pace and direction of technological change to be smooth, we can smooth the pace of economic growth only by *delaying* the implementation of new technologies. Such delays would result in never-to-be-recovered waste.

Regardless of which position economists take, they all agree that depressions as deep and long as that which occurred in the early 1930s result in extraordinary waste and human suffering. The disagreements concern the more common and gentler ebbs and flows of economic activity that have occurred in the years since World War II, which we saw earlier in Fig. 5.6.

REVIEW

Gross domestic product is the dollar value of all the final goods and services produced in the economy. Nominal GDP measures the value of the output of final goods and services using current prices. Real GDP measures the value of the output using the prices that prevailed in some base period. Nominal GDP rises more quickly than real GDP because of inflation. The general tendency for real GDP to increase is called trend real GDP. Economic fluctuations can be measured by examining departures from trend real GDP. The upward trend in real GDP is the major source of improvements in living standards. However, the upward trend has costs in terms of depletion of exhaustible resources and environmental pollution. ◆

Let's now take a more systematic look at the ebbs and flows of economic activity.

The Business Cycle

The **business cycle** is the periodic but irregular up and down movement in economic activity, measured by fluctuations in real GDP and other macroeconomic variables. As we've just seen, real GDP can be divided into two components:

- Trend real GDP
- Real GDP fluctuations

To identify the business cycle, we focus our attention on the real GDP fluctuations, since this variable gives a direct measure of the uneven pace of economic activity, separate from its underlying trend growth path.

A business cycle is not a regular, predictable, or repeating phenomenon like the swings of the pendulum of a clock. Its timing is random and, to a large degree, unpredictable. A business cycle is identified as a sequence of four phases:

- Contraction
- Trough
- Expansion
- Peak

These four phases are shown in Fig. 5.7. This figure, which is an enlargement of part of Fig. 5.6, shows the business cycle for 1973 to 1991. Notice the four phases of the cycle. A **contraction** is a slowdown in the pace of economic activity, such as occurred between 1979 and 1982. An **expansion** is a speedup in the pace of economic activity, such as occurred between 1983 and 1988. A **trough** is the lower turning point of a business cycle, where a contraction turns into an expansion. A trough occurred in 1982. A **peak** is the upper turning point of a business cycle, where an expansion turns into a contraction. A peak occurred in 1978.

A recession occurs if a contraction is severe enough. A **recession** is a downturn in the level of economic activity in which real GDP declines in two

FIGURE 5.7

The Business Cycle

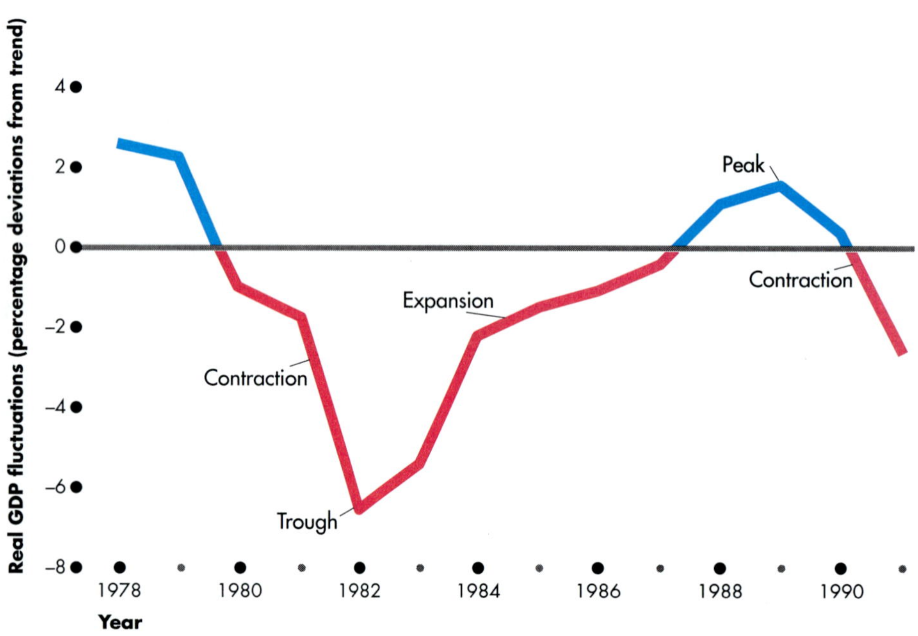

The business cycle has four phases: contraction, trough, expansion, and peak. Our experience in the 1970s and 1980s is used to illustrate these phases. There was a contraction from 1973 to 1975. In 1975, the trough was reached and an expansion began. That expansion reached a peak in 1978, when a new contraction set in that in turn reached a new trough in 1982. From 1982 to 1989, the economy was on a prolonged expansion. In 1989, the expansion reached a peak and a new contraction began.

successive quarters. A deep trough is called a slump or a **depression.**

Unemployment and the Business Cycle

Real GDP is not the only variable that fluctuates over the course of the business cycle. Its fluctuations are matched by related fluctuations in a wide range of other economic variables. One of the most important of these is unemployment. In the contraction phase of a business cycle, unemployment increases; in the expansion phase, unemployment decreases; at the peak, unemployment is at its lowest; at the trough, unemployment is at its highest. This relationship between unemployment and the phases of the business cycle is illustrated in Fig. 5.8.

That figure shows real GDP fluctuations and unemployment in the United States since 1900. The Great Depression, World War II, the OPEC recession, the 1982 recession, and the 1991 recession are highlighted in the figure. The figure also shows the unemployment rate. So that we can see how unemployment lines up with real GDP fluctuations, the unemployment rate has been measured with its scale inverted. That is, as we move down the vertical axis on the right-hand side, the unemployment rate increases. As you can see, fluctuations in unemployment closely follow those in real GDP.

The Stock Market and the Business Cycle

We have defined the business cycle as the ebbs and flows of economic activity and have measured these movements by real GDP fluctuations. We have seen that unemployment fluctuations mirror the business cycle very closely. Another indicator of the state of the economy, and perhaps the most visible of all such indicators, is provided by the stock market. Every weekday evening, newscasts tell us of the day's events on the New York and Tokyo stock exchanges. Movements in share prices attract attention partly for their own sake and also partly for what they may foretell about our *future* economic fortunes.

Do stock prices move in sympathy with fluctuations in real GDP and unemployment? Is a stock

FIGURE 5.8

Unemployment and the Business Cycle

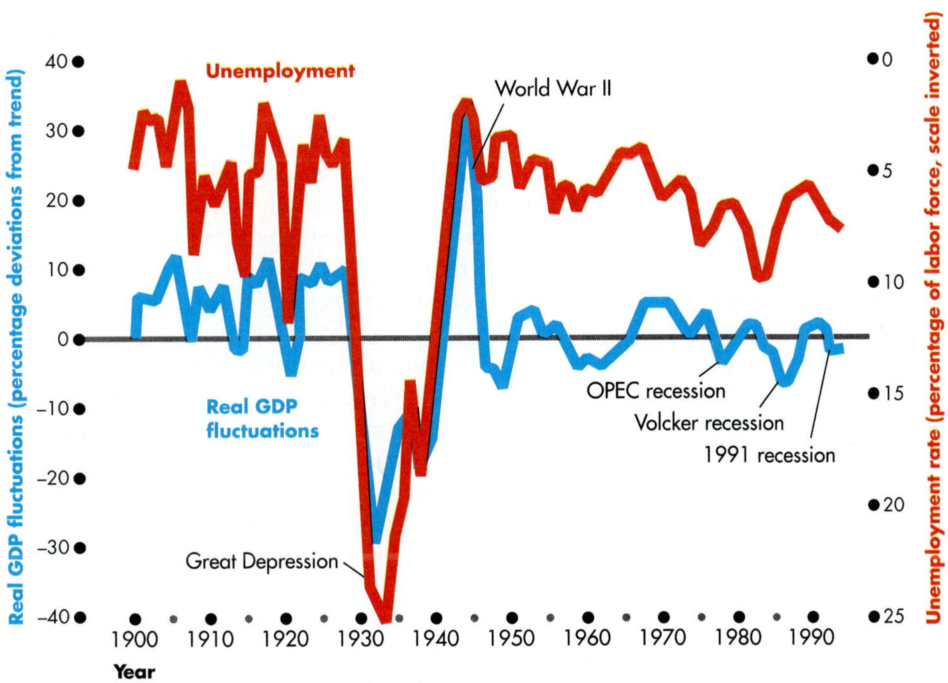

This figure shows the relationship between unemployment and the business cycle. Real GDP fluctuations tell us when the economy is in a contraction or expansion phase. Unemployment is plotted on the same figure but with its scale inverted. The line measuring unemployment is high when unemployment is low, and the line is low when unemployment is high. As you can see, the cycles in real GDP are closely matched by the cycles in unemployment.

FIGURE 5.9

Stock Prices: 1871–1993

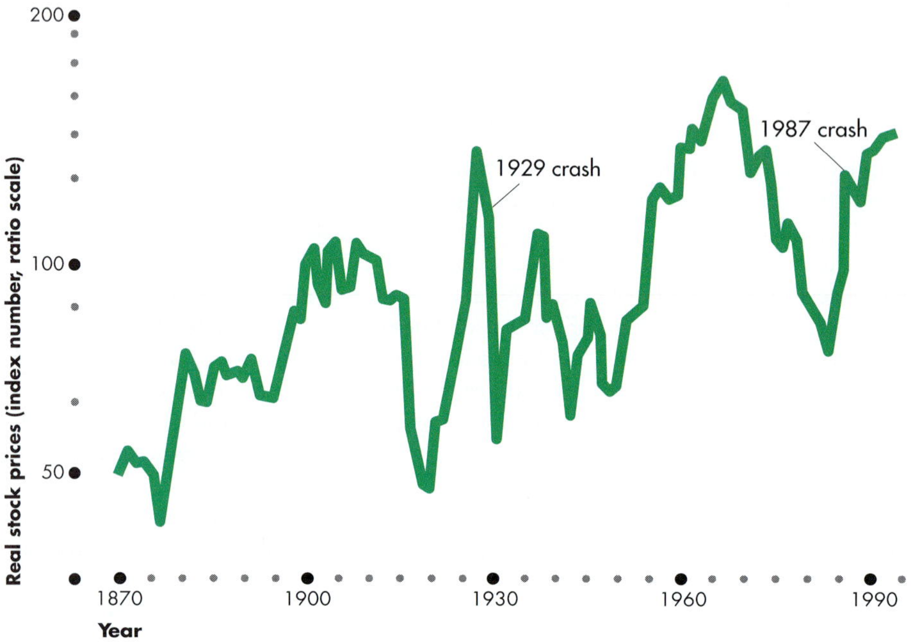

Stock prices are among the most volatile elements of our economy. Here, real stock prices (stock prices measured to take out the effects of changes in the value of money) climbed strongly from 1871 to 1910 but with strong fluctuations. They then fell dramatically through 1920 but increased at a spectacular pace through 1929. Then came the crash that preceded the Great Depression. Stock prices began a new climb after World War II, reaching a peak in 1965. They gradually fell to a trough in 1982, after which they climbed to a new peak before the crash of October 1987. The 1987 crash was short-lived, and real stock prices again increased, even during the 1991 recession.

Sources: 1871–1948: Index of Common Stocks, *Historical Statistics* (1960), Series X-351, p. 657; 1949–1991: The Dow-Jones Industrial Average, *Economic Report of the President,* 1993. The two indexes were linked to form a common index and converted to real terms by using the same price index that converts nominal GDP to real GDP (GNP before 1959). The index is scaled to have an average value between 1871 and 1993 of 100.

price downturn a predictor of economic contraction? Is a stock price boom a predictor of economic expansion? To answer these questions, let's take a look at the behavior of stock prices and see how they relate to the expansions and contractions of economic activity.

Figure 5.9 tracks the course of stock prices from 1871 to 1993. The prices plotted in this figure are inflation-adjusted. Actual stock prices increased much more than indicated here because of inflation, but the purely inflationary parts of the price increases have been removed so that we can see what has "really" been happening to stock prices—that is, the path of real stock prices. The most striking feature of stock prices is their extreme volatility and lack of any obvious cyclical patterns. Two stock price crashes are highlighted in the figure: those of 1929 and 1987. The 1929 crash was a sharp one, and it was followed by two successive years of massive stock price decline. The 1987 crash was much smaller, and the decline in prices was short-lived. There have also been periods of rapid increases in stock prices, the most dramatic being that which preceded the 1929 crash. There were also strong increases in stock prices before the 1987 crash.

How do fluctuations in stock prices correspond with the business cycle? Sometimes they correspond quite closely, and at other times they do not. For example, the movements in stock prices during the Great Depression and the recovery from it suggest that the stock market tells us where the economy is heading. The stock market moved in sympathy with, but slightly ahead of, the contraction and expansion of real GDP and the rise and fall in the unemployment rate.

But do turning points in the stock market always reliably predict the turning points in the economy? The answer is no. In some periods the stock market and real GDP move together, but in others the movements oppose each other. For example, the mini-crash of 1987 occurred at a time when the economy, both in the United States and in the rest of the world, was expanding strongly.

When stock prices collapsed in October 1987, many people drew parallels between that episode and the 1929 stock price crash. In 1930, the economy collapsed. In 1988, the economy continued to grow. Why were the two episodes so different? A key answer—and the key reason for the lack of a strong connection between stock price fluctuations and the business cycle—is our inability to forecast the business cycle. Stock prices are determined by people's expectations about the future profitability of firms. Future profitability, in turn, depends on the state of the economy. Hence stock prices are determined by expectations about the future state of the economy. But those expectations turn out to be wrong about as often as they turn out to be right. Thus the movement in stock prices is not an entirely reliable predictor of the state of the economy.

Inflation and the Business Cycle

We've looked at fluctuations in real variables: real GDP, the unemployment rate, and real stock prices. We've seen that there is a strong and systematic relationship between fluctuations in real GDP and fluctuations in the unemployment rate. We've also seen that there are times when there is a systematic relationship between real stock prices and the business cycle and other times when there isn't. How does inflation behave over the business cycle? Are fluctuations in its rate closely connected with business cycle fluctuations, or does the inflation rate vary independently of the business cycle?

To answer these questions, let's look again at the Great Depression and the two recent recessions and see how inflation varied during those periods. Figure 5.10(a) shows the inflation rate through the Great Depression. The state of the economy is shown by the fluctuations in real GDP. You can see from the figure that as the economy went into the contraction phase of the Great Depression, the inflation rate was also falling. In fact, inflation was negative, so the price level was falling. But the inflation rate reached its low point in 1932, a year before the trough of the business cycle. Thereafter, the inflation rate increased and did so at a much faster pace than the

FIGURE 5.10

Inflation and the Business Cycle

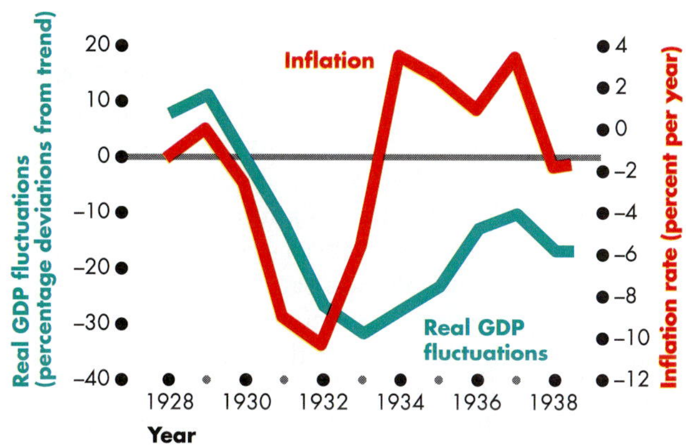

(a) The Great Depression

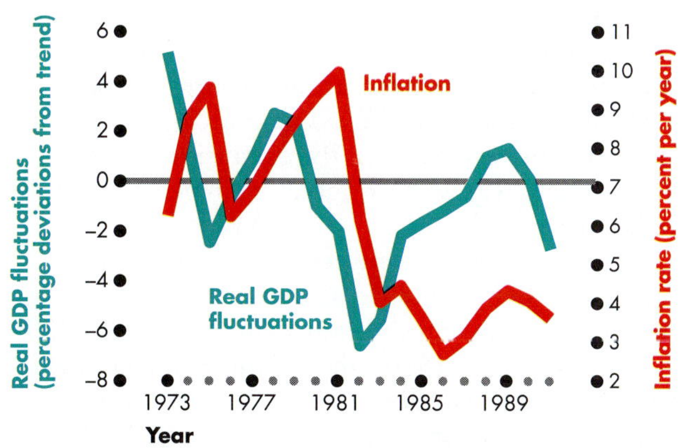

(b) The OPEC, Volcker, and 1991 recessions

Inflation follows the course of the business cycle on some occasions but departs from it on others. As shown in part (a), through the Great Depression, inflation and real GDP moved together during the contraction phase, but in the expansion phase, inflation increased much more strongly than real GDP. As shown in part (b), the inflation rate and real GDP fluctuated together from 1973 to 1982 but with inflation lagging behind real GDP by about a year. From 1982 to 1986, the inflation rate remained moderate as real GDP expanded quickly. From 1986 to 1989, the inflation rate increased as real GDP continued to expand, and after 1989, the inflation rate decreased as real GDP growth slowed down.

real GDP recovery. Thus through this business cycle episode, the inflation rate and the business cycle were in step with each other during the contraction phase, but the inflation rate increased sharply while the economy was still in the depths of the Great Depression.

Part (b) shows the course of inflation and real GDP fluctuations during the years 1973–1991. The cycles in real GDP fluctuations and the inflation rate between 1973 and 1982 look similar, but the inflation cycle lagged behind the real GDP cycle by about a year. After 1982, as the economy went into the expansion phase of the business cycle, the inflation rate remained low. But the inflation rate increased again between 1986 and 1989 as real GDP continued to expand. The inflation rate slowed again as the economy went into recession in 1990–1991.

It is interesting to contrast the course of inflation over these recent cycles with that of the Great Depression. In both cases, there are periods during which the inflation rate fell along with economic contraction and a phase during which the inflation rate increased along with economic expansion. But there are other periods in which the inflation rate and the state of the business cycle went in their own directions. In the recovery from the Great Depression, the inflation rate moved up more quickly than the economy recovered. In the expansion of the 1980s, there was no corresponding increase in the inflation rate.

A further contrast between the two periods is important. During the Great Depression, the average inflation rate was much lower than that of the 1970s and 1980s. In the 1930s, the inflation rate fell from zero to –10 percent per year and then increased to about 3 percent per year. In the 1970s and 1980s, inflation cycled, climbing to a peak of more than 13 percent and then falling to around 2 percent.

These episodes reveal two things about inflation. First, much of the time, inflation moves in sympathy with the business cycle. Second, there are important changes in the inflation rate that are independent of the business cycle—over some cycles the average inflation rate is low, and over others it is high.

REVIEW

The business cycle is the periodic but irregular up and down movement in economic activity. It has four phases: contraction, trough, expansion, and peak. A recession is a contraction in which real GDP declines for at least two quarters. Over the business cycle, real GDP and unemployment fluctuate together. During a contraction, the unemployment rate rises, and during an expansion it falls. Although the stock market sometimes moves in sympathy with the business cycle, it does not reliably predict turning points in the economy. Inflation can also move in sympathy with the business cycle, but there are important fluctuations in the inflation rate that are not related to the business cycle. ◆

We've now studied inflation, unemployment, real GDP fluctuations, and business cycles. Let's turn to our final topic, deficits.

Government Deficit and International Deficit

If you spend more than you earn in a given period, you have a deficit. To cover your deficit, you have to borrow or sell off some of the things that you own. Just as individuals can have deficits, so can governments and so can entire nations. These deficits—the government deficit and the international deficit—have attracted a lot of attention recently.

Government Deficit

The **government deficit** is the total expenditure of the government sector minus the total revenue of that sector in a given period. The government sector is composed of the federal government and the state and local governments. These governments spend on a variety of public and social programs and obtain their revenue from taxes.

Sometimes the government sector is in surplus, and at other times it is in deficit. Occasionally, the deficit is a very large one, as it was in 1975. Since 1980, the government sector has had a persistent deficit, averaging about 3 percent of GDP.

To some degree, the balance of the government budget is related to the business cycle. When the economy is expanding quickly, incomes grow quickly and so do tax receipts. Unemployment decreases, and so do unemployment benefits. The government deficit shrinks through this phase of the business cycle. When the economy is in a contraction phase, tax receipts decline and unemployment benefits increase and the government budget deficit increases. What is significant about the budget deficit in the 1980s is that it persisted despite the fact that the economy experienced strong and prolonged expansion.

We'll study the government deficit more closely and at greater length in Chapter 17. In that chapter, we'll discuss its sources and consequences.

International Deficit

The value of all the goods and services that we sell to other countries (exports) minus the value of all the goods and services that we buy from foreigners (imports) is called our **current account balance.** If we sell more to the rest of the world than we buy from it, we have a current account surplus. If we buy more from the rest of the world than we sell to it, we have a current account deficit.

Most of the time since 1950 we have had a small current account surplus. But in recent years, a current account deficit has emerged. That deficit has been not only persistent but also gradually increasing in magnitude. When we have a current account deficit, we have to borrow from the rest of the world to pay for the goods and services that we are buying in excess of the value of those that we are selling. Mirroring our current account deficit is a current account surplus in some other countries. The most notable country on the opposite side of our international payments balance is Japan. That country has been operating a current account surplus and, in recent years, an increasing surplus. To finance our deficit, we borrow from the rest of the world and the rest of the world lends to us.

The causes of these international surpluses and deficits and their consequences will be discussed at greater length in Chapter 19.

◆ ◆ ◆ ◆ In our study of macroeconomics, we're going to find out what we currently know about the causes of inflation and of variations in its rate; we're also going to discover what we know about the causes of unemployment and business cycle fluctuations. We're going to discover why at certain times the stock market is a good predictor of the state of the economy and at others it is not; we're also going to discover why sometimes inflation and the business cycle move in sympathy with each other and why at times these variables follow separate courses. Finally, we're going to learn more about deficits—the government deficit and the international deficit—and their causes, their importance, and their consequences. ◆ ◆ The next step in our study of macroeconomics is to learn more about macroeconomic measurement—about how we measure GDP, the price level, and inflation.

SUMMARY

Inflation

Inflation is an upward movement in the average level of prices. To measure the average level of prices, we calculate a price index. The inflation rate is the percentage change in the value of a price index.

Inflation is a persistent feature of economic life in the United States, but the rate of inflation fluctuates. In the early 1960s, inflation was between 1 and 2 percent a year. By 1980, its rate exceeded 13 percent a year. There was an upward trend in inflation through the 1960s and 1970s, but inflation has been on a downward trend since 1980.

Inflation is a problem because it brings a fall in the value of money at an unpredictable rate. The more unpredictable the inflation rate, the less useful is money as a measuring rod for conducting transactions. Inflation makes money especially unsuitable for transactions that are spread out over time, such as borrowing and lending or working for an agreed wage rate. A rapid anticipated inflation is a problem because it makes people get rid of money as quickly as possible, disrupting economic life. (pp. 103–107)

Unemployment

Unemployment is a state in which there are qualified workers who are available for work at the current wage rate and who do not have jobs. The labor force is the sum of those who are unemployed and those who are employed. The unemployment rate is the percentage of the labor force that is unemployed. Unemployment is measured each month by a survey of households.

Unemployment in the United States was not regarded as a major problem in the 1960s, when its rate averaged less than 5 percent. Its rate also declined during that decade. Since 1969, unemployment has been on an upward trend and has fluctuated strongly. Its rate reached a peak in 1982 and 1983.

There are three types of unemployment: frictional, structural, and cyclical. Frictional unemployment arises from normal labor market turnover and the fact that people take time to find the job that best matches their skills. Structural unemployment arises when technological change causes a decline in jobs that are concentrated in particular industries or regions. Cyclical unemployment arises when the pace of economic expansion slows down. Full employment is a state in which all unemployment is frictional and structural and the number of job vacancies is equal to the number of unemployed workers. At full employment, the unemployment rate is called the natural rate of unemployment.

The major costs of unemployment are the lost output and earnings that could have been generated if the unemployed had been working. Other major costs include the deterioration of human capital and, when unemployment is prolonged, increased crime and severe social and psychological problems for unemployed workers and their families. (pp. 107–111)

Gross Domestic Product

The nation's total output is measured by gross domestic product (GDP). GDP is the dollar value of all final goods and services produced in the economy in a given time period. Changes in GDP reflect both changes in prices and changes in the quantity of goods and services produced. To separate the effects of prices from real quantities, we distinguish between nominal GDP and real GDP. Nominal GDP is measured by using current prices. Real GDP is measured by using prices for some base year.

Real GDP grows, on average, every year, so the trend of real GDP is upward. But real GDP does not increase at a constant rate. Its rate of expansion fluctuates, so real GDP fluctuates around its trend value. Increases in real GDP bring rising living standards but not without costs. The main costs of fast economic growth are resource depletion, environmental pollution, and the need to face rapid and often costly changes in job type and location. The benefits of higher consumption levels have to be balanced against such costs. (pp. 111–117)

The Business Cycle

The business cycle is the periodic but irregular up and down movement in macroeconomic activity. The cycle has four phases: contraction, trough, expansion, and peak. When real GDP falls for two quarters, the economy is in a recession.

Unemployment fluctuates closely with real GDP fluctuations. When real GDP is above trend, the unemployment rate is low; when real GDP is below trend, the unemployment rate is high. But real stock prices do not fluctuate in a manner similar to business cycle fluctuations. Sometimes a stock market crash precedes a recession, but it does not always do so.

There is no simple relationship between the inflation rate and the business cycle. Sometimes the inflation rate increases in an expansion phase and decreases in a contraction phase. But there are other times when inflation moves independently of the business cycle. Thus there are two types of forces at work generating inflation that have to be investigated—those that are related to the business cycle and those that are not. (pp. 118–122)

Government Deficit and International Deficit

The government deficit is the total expenditure of the government sector minus the total revenue of that sector in a given period. To some degree the government deficit fluctuates over the course of the business cycle. But in the 1980s, the government sector persistently operated with a deficit averaging about 3 percent of GDP while the economy underwent a strong and persistent expansion.

A country's current account balance is the difference between the value of the goods and services that it sells to other countries and the value of the goods and services that it buys from the rest of the world. The United States normally has a current account surplus, but in the 1980s a deficit emerged. Mirroring the U.S. current account deficit is a current account surplus in some other countries. Japan is one of the countries that had a large surplus in the 1980s. (pp. 122–123)

KEY ELEMENTS

Key Terms

Anticipated inflation, 105
Business cycle, 118
Contraction, 118
Current account balance, 123
Cyclical unemployment, 110
Depression, 119
Discouraged workers, 108
Expansion, 118
Expected inflation rate, 105
Final goods and services, 111
Foreign exchange rate, 105
Frictional unemployment, 108
Full employment, 110
Government deficit, 122
Gross domestic product, 111
Human capital, 111
Inflation, 103
Inflation rate, 104
Intermediate goods and services, 114
Labor force, 107
Natural rate of unemployment, 110
Nominal GDP, 115
Peak, 118
Price index, 103
Price level, 103
Real GDP, 115
Recession, 118
Structural unemployment, 109
Trough, 118
Unanticipated inflation, 105
Unemployment, 107
Unemployment rate, 107
Value of money, 105

Key Figures

Figure 5.1 The Price Level: 1820–1993, 103
Figure 5.3 Unemployment: 1900–1993, 109
Figure 5.4 Gross Domestic Product: 1960–1992, 114
Figure 5.5 Real GDP: 1869–1992, 115
Figure 5.6 Real GDP Fluctuations: 1869–1992, 116
Figure 5.7 The Business Cycle, 118
Figure 5.8 Unemployment and the Business Cycle, 119
Figure 5.9 Stock Prices: 1871–1993, 120
Figure 5.10 Inflation and the Business Cycle, 121

REVIEW QUESTIONS

1 What is inflation?

2 What are some of the costs of inflation?

3 What, if any, are the benefits from inflation? If there are none, explain why.

4 Why doesn't inflation always benefit borrowers at the expense of lenders?

5 Why might anticipated inflation be a problem?

6 What is the definition of unemployment?

7 How does the U.S. Department of Labor measure the unemployment rate?

8 Why may the measured unemployment rate understate or overstate the true extent of unemployment?

9 What are the different types of unemployment?

10 What are the main costs of unemployment?

11 What makes GDP grow?

12 What are the costs and benefits of a high average increase in real GDP?

13 What are the costs and benefits of fluctuations in real GDP?

14 What is a business cycle? Describe the four phases of a business cycle. What was the phase of the U.S. business cycle in 1975? In 1980? In 1985? In 1991?

15 When the economy is in a recovery phase, what is happening to the unemployment rate? The stock market?

16 How does the inflation rate fluctuate over the business cycle?

17 Compare the fluctuations in inflation and unemployment.

PROBLEMS

1 At the end of 1992 the price index was 150. At the end of 1991 the price index was 125. Calculate the inflation rate in 1992.

2 In a noninflationary world, Joe and Mary are willing to borrow and lend at 2 percent a year. Joe expects that inflation next year will be 5 percent, and Mary expects that it will be 3 percent. Would Joe and Mary be willing to sign a contract in which one of them borrows from the other? Explain why or why not.

3 Lucy operates the Cone-Heads Ice Cream Parlor. She expects that inflation next year will be 3 percent. The students who work at Cone-Heads expect inflation to be only 2 percent. Will Lucy and the students be able to agree now on a wage rate for next summer? Explain your answer.

4 Obtain data on unemployment in your home state. If your school library has the U.S. Department of Labor publication *Employment and Earnings,* you can get the data from there. Otherwise, you might have to call your local newspaper's business desk for the information. Compare the behavior of unemployment in your home state with that in the United States as a whole. Why do you think your state might have a higher or a lower unemployment rate than the U.S. average?

5 Obtain data on inflation in the United States, Japan, Canada, and Germany since 1980. You will find these data in *International Financial Statistics* in your school library. Draw a graph of the data and answer the following questions:

- **a** Which country had the highest inflation rate?
- **b** Which country had the lowest inflation rate?
- **c** Which country had the fastest-rising inflation rate?
- **d** Which country had the fastest-falling inflation rate?

6 On the basis of your discovery in answering problem 5, what do you expect happened to the foreign exchange rates between the U.S. dollar and the Japanese yen, the Canadian dollar, and the German mark? Check your expectation by finding these exchange rates in the *International Financial Statistics* from which you got the inflation rates.

CHAPTER 6

MEASURING OUTPUT AND THE PRICE LEVEL

After studying this chapter, you will be able to:

- Describe the flows of expenditure and income
- Explain why aggregate expenditure and income are equal to each other
- Explain how gross domestic product (GDP) and gross national product (GNP) are measured
- Describe two measures of the price level—the Consumer Price Index (CPI) and the GDP deflator
- Explain how real GDP is measured
- Distinguish between inflation and changes in relative prices
- Explain why real GDP is not a good measure of economic well-being

Economic Barometers

EVERY THREE MONTHS, THE U.S. DEPARTMENT OF Commerce publishes the latest quarterly estimates of the gross domestic product, or GDP—a barometer of our nation's economy. As soon as it is published, analysts pore over the data, trying to understand the past and peer into the future. But how do government accountants add up all the blooming, buzzing economic activity of the country to arrive at the number called GDP? And what exactly *is* GDP? ◆◆ From economists to homemakers, inflation watchers of all types pay close attention to another economic barometer, the Consumer Price Index, or CPI. The Department of Labor publishes new figures each month, and analysts in newspapers and on TV quickly leap to conclusions. How does the government determine the CPI? How well does it measure the consumer's living costs? ◆◆ The pace of expansion of our economy fluctuates and is occasionally interrupted by a period of contraction. We describe these ebbs and flows of economic activity as the business cycle. But to reveal the business cycle, we must remove the effects of inflation on GDP and assess how GDP has changed not because of changing prices but because of changing production. How do we remove the inflation component of GDP? ◆◆ Some people make a living from crime. Others, although doing work that is legal, try to hide the payment they receive in order to evade taxes or other regulations. Most people undertake some economic activity inside their homes. Fixing meals, laundering shirts, and mowing the lawn are all examples. Are these activities taken into account when we measure GDP? If they are not taken into account, how important are they? And does it matter if they don't show up in GDP?

◆ ◆ ◆ ◆ In this chapter, we're going to learn more about the macroeconomic concepts of GDP and the price level. We'll see how GDP is measured. We'll also see how the real and inflationary components of GDP are separated. We'll learn how to calculate and interpret the CPI. Finally, we'll ask what GDP means: what does it tell us about our standard of living and economic well-being? Let's begin by describing the flows of expenditure and income.

The Circular Flow of Expenditure and Income

The circular flow of expenditure and income provides the conceptual basis for measuring gross domestic product. We'll see some of the key ideas and relationships more clearly if we begin with a model economy that is simpler than the one in which we live. We'll then add some features to make our simplified economy correspond with the real economy.

Circular Flows in a Simplified Economy

Our simplified economy has just two kinds of economic institutions: households and firms.

Households:

- Receive incomes in exchange for the supply of factors of production to firms
- Make expenditures on consumption goods and services bought from firms
- Save some of their incomes

Firms:

- Pay incomes to households in exchange for the factors of production hired (these payments include wages paid for labor, interest paid for capital, rent paid for land, and profits)
- Make investment expenditures—purchases of capital goods from other firms and changes in their inventories
- Receive revenue from the sale of consumption goods and services to households
- Receive revenue from other firms' investment expenditures
- Borrow to finance investment expenditures

The economy has three types of markets:

- Goods (and services) markets
- Factor markets
- Financial markets

Transactions between households and firms take place in these markets. In factor markets, households sell the services of labor, capital, and land to firms. In exchange, firms make income payments to households. These payments are wages for labor services, interest for the use of capital, rent for the use of land, and profits to the owners of firms. These payments for factor services are households' incomes. **Aggregate income** is the amount received by households in payment for the services of factors of production.

In the markets for goods and services, firms sell consumer goods and services—such as popcorn and soda, movies and chocolate bars, microwave ovens and dry cleaning services—to households. In exchange, households make payments to firms. The total payment made by households on consumption goods and services is called **consumption expenditure.**

Firms do not sell all their output to households. Some of what they produce is new capital equipment, and it is sold to other firms. For example, IBM sells a mainframe computer to GM. Also, some of what firms produce might not be sold at all, but added to inventory. For example, if General Motors produces 1,000 cars and sells 950 of them to households, 50 cars remain unsold and GM's inventory of cars increases by 50. When a firm adds unsold output to inventory, we can think of the firm as buying goods from itself. The purchase of new plant, equipment, and buildings and additions to inventories is called **investment.** To finance investment, firms borrow from households in financial markets.

These transactions between households and firms result in flows of income and expenditure, shown in Fig. 6.1. To help you keep track of the different types of flows, they have been color-coded. The blue flow represents aggregate income, which we denote by *Y*. The red flows represent expenditures on goods and services. Consumption expenditure is denoted by *C*. Investment is denoted by *I*. Notice that investment is illustrated in the figure as a flow from firms through the goods markets and back to firms. It is illustrated in this way because some firms produce capital goods and other firms buy them (and firms "buy" inventories from themselves).

FIGURE 6.1

The Circular Flow of Expenditure and Income Between Households and Firms

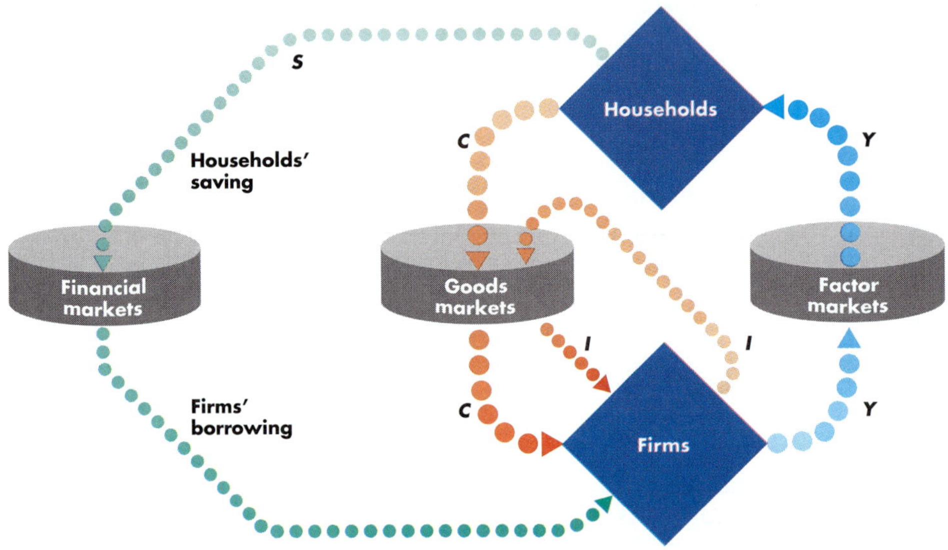

Transactions between households and firms in goods markets and factor markets generate the circular flow of expenditure and income. Households receive factor incomes (*Y*) from firms in exchange for factor services they supply (blue flow). Households purchase consumer goods and services (*C*) from firms, and firms purchase capital goods from other firms and inventories from themselves—investment (*I*)—(red flows).

Outside the circular flow, households save part of their income (*S*) and firms borrow to finance their investment expenditures (green flows). Firms' receipts from the sale of goods and services are paid to households as wages, interest, rent, or profit. Aggregate expenditure (consumption expenditure plus investment) equals aggregate income, which equals GDP.

There are two additional flows in the figure, shown in green. These flows do not represent payments for the services of factors of production or for the purchases of goods and services. They are saving and borrowing. Households do not spend all their income—they save some of it. In this simplified economy, saving is the difference between aggregate income and consumption expenditure and is denoted by *S*. Saving gets channeled through financial markets, in which firms borrow the funds needed to finance their investment.

The most important of the flows illustrated in Fig. 6.1 are aggregate income (the blue flow) and expenditures (the red flows). We're going to discover that the blue flow and the two red flows in aggregate are equal. Let's see why.

Equality of Aggregate Income and Aggregate Expenditure The sum of consumption expenditure (*C*) and investment (*I*) is aggregate expenditure on final goods and services (more briefly, aggregate expenditure). To see the equality of aggregate income and aggregate expenditure, look again at Fig. 6.1 and focus on firms. Notice that there are two red arrows indicating flows of revenue to firms. They are consumption expenditure (*C*) and investment (*I*), or aggregate expenditure. Everything that a firm receives from the sale of its output it also pays out for the services of the factors of production that it hires. To see why, recall that payments for factors of production include not only wages, interest, and rent paid for the services of labor, capital, and land, but also profits. Any difference between the amount received by a firm for the sale of its output and the amount paid to its suppliers of labor, capital, and land is a profit (or loss) for the owner of the firm. The owner of the firm is a household, and the owner receives the firm's profit (or makes good the firm's loss). Thus the total income that each firm pays out to households equals its revenue from the sale of final goods and services. Since this reasoning applies to each and every firm in the economy, then

Aggregate expenditure = Aggregate income.

Gross Domestic Product in the Simplified Economy *Gross domestic product* (GDP) is the value of all the final goods and services produced in the economy. In the simplified economy that we are studying, the final goods and services produced are the consumption goods and services and capital goods produced by firms. There are two ways in which we can value that production. One is to value it on the basis of what buyers have paid. This amount is aggregate expenditure. The other is to value it on the basis of the cost of the factors of production used to produce it. This amount is aggregate income. But we've just discovered that aggregate expenditure equals aggregate income. That is, the total amount spent on the goods and services produced equals the total amount paid for the factors of production used to produce them. Thus GDP equals aggregate expenditure, which in turn equals aggregate income. That is,

GDP = Aggregate expenditure = Aggregate income.

Government and Foreign Sectors In the simplified economy that we've just examined, we focused exclusively on the behavior of households and firms. In real-world economies, there are two other important sectors that add additional flows to the circular flow of expenditure and income: the government and the rest of the world. These sectors do not change the fundamental results that we've just obtained. GDP equals aggregate expenditure or aggregate income, no matter how many sectors we consider and how complicated a range of flows we consider between them. Nevertheless, it is important to add the government and the rest of the world to our model so that we can see the additional expenditure and income flows that they generate.

The government:

- Makes expenditures on goods and services bought from firms
- Receives tax revenue from and makes transfer payments to households and firms
- Borrows to finance the difference between its revenue and its spending

The rest of the world:

- Makes expenditures on goods and services bought from domestic firms and receives revenue from the sale of goods and services to domestic firms
- Lends to (or borrows from) households and firms in the domestic economy

The additional flows arising from the transactions between the government, the rest of the world, and households and firms, along with the original flows that we've already considered, are illustrated in Fig. 6.2.

Let's first focus on the flows involving the government. Government purchases of goods and services from firms are shown as the flow G. This flow is shown in red (like consumption expenditure and investment) to indicate that it is an expenditure on goods and services.

Net taxes are the net flow from households to the government.[1] These net flows are the difference between the taxes paid and transfer payments received. **Transfer payments** are flows of money from the government, such as social security benefits. It is important not to confuse transfer payments with government purchases of goods and services. The term *transfer payments* is designed to remind us that these items are transfers of money and, as such, are similar to taxes except that they flow in the opposite direction—they flow from government to households. Net taxes (T) are illustrated in the figure as a green flow to remind you that this flow does not represent a payment in exchange for goods and services or a factor income. It is simply a transfer of financial resources from households to the government.

[1]The diagram does not show firms paying any taxes. You can think of taxes paid by firms as being paid on behalf of the households that own the firms. For example, a tax on a firm's profit means that the households owning the firm receive less income. It is as if the households receive all the profit and then pay the tax on the profit. This way of looking at taxes simplifies Fig. 6.2 but does not change any conclusions.

FIGURE 6.2

The Circular Flow Including Government and the Rest of the World

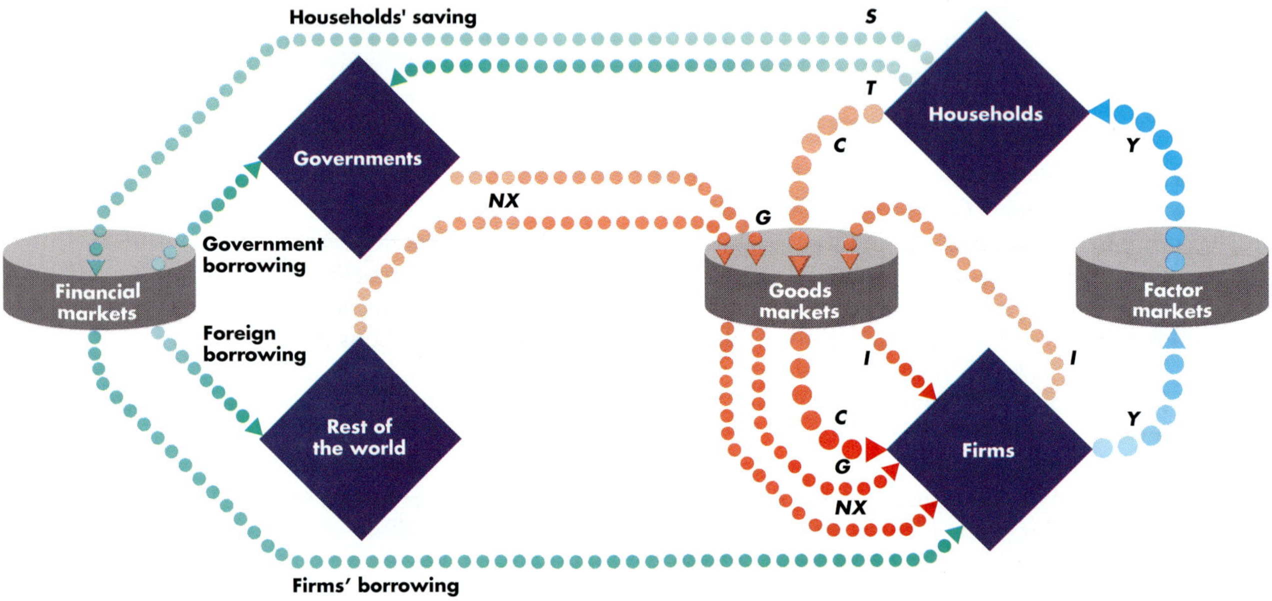

Transactions between households, firms, governments, and the rest of the world in goods markets and factor markets generate the circular flow of expenditure and income. Households receive factor incomes (*Y*) from firms in exchange for factor services they supply (blue flow). Households purchase consumer goods and services (*C*) from firms; firms purchase capital goods from other firms and inventories from themselves (*I*); governments purchase goods and services (*G*); the rest of the world purchases goods and services from firms, and firms purchase goods and services from the rest of the world (*NX*)—(red flows).

Outside the circular flow, households save part of their income (*S*) and pay net taxes (*T*) to governments; firms borrow to finance their investment expenditures; governments borrow to finance their deficits; and the rest of the world borrows (or lends)—(green flows).

Firms' receipts from the sale of goods and services are paid to households as wages, interest, rent, or profit. Aggregate expenditure (consumption expenditure plus investment plus government purchases plus net exports) equals aggregate income, which equals GDP.

The difference between the net taxes received by government and government expenditure on goods and services is the government's budget deficit. The government covers its deficit by borrowing in financial markets. Such borrowing is illustrated by the green flow in the figure.

Next, look at transactions with the rest of the world. The red flow in Fig. 6.2 labeled *NX* is net exports. **Net exports** equals exports of goods and services to the rest of the world minus imports of goods and services from the rest of the world. This flow represents the expenditure by the rest of the world on goods and services produced by domestic firms (exports) minus the expenditure of domestic firms on goods and services produced in the rest of the world (imports).

If exports exceed imports, net exports are positive. There is a net flow into the domestic economy. To finance that net inflow, the rest of the world borrows from the domestic economy in financial markets. This flow is illustrated by the green flow labeled "Foreign borrowing." If imports exceed exports, net exports are negative and there is a flow from domestic firms to the rest of the world. In this case, the domestic economy borrows from the rest of the world in financial markets. To illustrate this case in the figure, we would reverse the directions of the flows of net exports and foreign borrowing.

Now that we have introduced more elements of the real world into our model economy, let's check that aggregate expenditure still equals aggregate income.

Expenditure Equals Income Again Aggregate expenditure equals aggregate income in this more complicated economy just as it does in the economy that has only households and firms. To see this equality, focus on the expenditures on goods and services (the red flows) received by firms and on firms' payments for factor services (the blue flow). We now have four flows representing firms' revenues from the sale of goods and services—consumption expenditure (C), investment (I), government purchases of goods and services (G), and net exports (NX). The sum of these four flows is equal to aggregate expenditure on final goods and services. As before, everything that a firm receives from the sale of its output is paid out as income to the owners of the factors of production that it employs and to the households that have a claim on its profits. The blue factor income flow therefore equals the sum of the red expenditure flows. That is,

$$Y = C + I + G + NX.$$

Thus, as we discovered in the case of the simpler model economy, aggregate income equals aggregate expenditure.

GDP also equals aggregate expenditure, or aggregate income. This equality occurs because we can measure the value of output either as the sum of the incomes paid to the factors of production or as the expenditure on that output.

GDP, Consumption Expenditure, Saving, and Taxes There is an important relationship between GDP, consumption expenditure, saving, and taxes. To see this relationship, look at households in Fig. 6.2. There is one flow into households and three flows out. The flow in is aggregate income (Y), which we've seen is equal to GDP. The flows out are consumption expenditure (C), saving (S), and net taxes (T). Aggregate income minus net taxes (equivalently, GDP minus net taxes) is called **disposable income.** Disposable income is either spent on consumption goods and services or saved. Thus **saving** equals disposable income minus consumption expenditure. Equivalently, everything received by households is either spent on consumption goods and services, saved, or paid in taxes. That is,

$$Y = C + S + T.$$

Income and Expenditure Accounts

We can record the transactions shown in the circular flow diagram in a set of accounts, one for firms and one for households. Table 6.1(a) shows the firm's revenue and expenditure account. The first two sources of revenue are the sale of consumption goods and services to households (C) and the sale of capital goods to other firms (I). In addition, firms now receive revenue from the sale of goods and services to the government (G) and from the sale of goods and services (net of purchases) to the rest of the world (NX). The sum of all their sources of revenue ($C + I + G + NX$) equals the payments made to the owners of factors of production (Y).

The households' income and expenditure account is shown in Table 6.1(b). Households receive income Y in payment for the factors of production supplied and spend that income on consumption goods (C). They also pay net taxes (T), and, as before, the balancing item is household saving (S).

Injections and Leakages The flow of income from firms to households and of consumption expenditure from households to firms is the circular flow of income and expenditure. Investment, government purchases of goods and services, and exports are called **injections** into the circular flow of expenditure and income. Net taxes, saving, and imports are called **leakages** from the circular flow of expenditure and income. Let's take a closer look at these injections and leakages.

We have seen from the firms' accounts that

$$Y = C + I + G + NX.$$

Let's break net exports into its two components, exports of goods and services (EX) and imports of goods and services (IM). That is,

$$NX = EX - IM.$$

Substituting this equation into the previous one, you can see that

$$Y = C + I + G + EX - IM.$$

TABLE 6.1

Firms' and Households' Accounts

(a) Firms

Revenue		Expenditure	
Sale of consumption goods and services	***C***	**Payments to factors of production**	***Y***
Sale of capital goods and changes in inventories	***I***		
Sale of goods and services to government	***G***		
Sale of goods and services to rest of world (*EX*) *less* **Purchases of goods and services from rest of world (*IM*)**	***NX***		
Total	***Y***		***Y***

(b) Households

Income		Expenditure	
Payments for supplies of factors of production	***Y***	**Purchases of consumption goods and services**	***C***
		Taxes paid (*TAX*) *less* **Transfer payments received (*TR*)**	***T***
		Saving	***S***
Total	***Y***		***Y***

Firms, shown in part (a), receive revenue from consumption expenditure (C), investment (I), government purchases of goods and services (G), and net exports (NX). Firms make payments for the services of factors of production (Y). The total income firms pay equals their total revenue: $Y = C + I + G + NX$. Households, shown in part (b), receive an income for the factors of production supplied (Y). They buy consumer goods and services from firms (C) and pay net taxes (taxes minus transfer payments) to the government (T). The part of households' income that is not spent on consumption goods or paid in net taxes is saved (S). Consumption expenditure plus net taxes plus saving is equal to income: $Y = C + T + S$.

We have also seen from the households' accounts that

$$Y = C + S + T.$$

Since the left side of these two equations is the same, it follows that

$$I + G + EX - IM = S + T.$$

If we add IM to both sides of this equation, we get

$$I + G + EX = S + T + IM.$$

The left side shows the injections into the circular flow of expenditure and income, and the right side shows the leakages from the circular flow. *The injections into the circular flow equal the leakages from the circular flow.*

REVIEW

Aggregate expenditure is the sum of consumer expenditure (C), investment (I), government purchases of goods and services (G), and exports of goods and services (EX) minus imports of goods and services (IM). Aggregate expenditure equals the value of the final goods and services produced. It also equals the aggregate income (Y) of the factors of production used to produce these goods and services. That is,

$$Y = C + I + G + EX - IM.$$

Households allocate aggregate income to three activities: consumption expenditure (C), taxes (net of transfer payments) (T), and saving (S). That is,

$$Y = C + S + T.$$

Investment, government purchases, and exports are *injections* into the circular flow of expenditure and income. Saving, net taxes (taxes minus transfer payments), and imports are *leakages* from the circular flow. Injections equal leakages. That is,

$$I + G + EX = S + T + IM.$$

The circular flow of income and expenditure and the income and expenditure accounts of firms and households are our tools for measuring GDP. Let's now see how the accountants at the Department of Commerce use these concepts to measure the GDP of the United States.

U.S. National Income and Product Accounts

The Department of Commerce collects data to measure GDP and publishes its findings in the *National Income and Product Accounts of the United States.* The data are collected by using two approaches:

- Expenditure approach
- Factor incomes approach

Let's look at what is involved in using these two alternative ways of measuring GDP.

The Expenditure Approach

The **expenditure approach** measures GDP by collecting data on consumption expenditure (C), investment (I), government purchases of goods and services (G), and net exports (NX). This approach is illustrated in Table 6.2. The numbers refer to 1992 and are in billions of dollars. The name of the item used in the *National Income and Product Accounts of the United States* (published by the Department of Commerce) appears in the first column, and the symbol we have used in our GDP equations appears in the next column. To measure GDP using the expenditure approach, we add together personal consumption expenditures (C), gross private domestic investment (I), government purchases of goods and services (G), and net exports of goods and services (NX).

TABLE **6.2**

GDP: The Expenditure Approach

Item	Symbol	Amount in 1992 (billions of dollars)	Percentage of GDP
Personal consumption expenditures	***C***	**4,096**	**68.8**
Gross private domestic investment	***I***	**770**	**12.9**
Government purchases of goods and services	***G***	**1,115**	**18.7**
Net exports of goods and services	***NX***	**–30**	**–0.5**
Gross domestic product	***Y***	**5,951**	**100.0**

The expenditure approach measures GDP by adding together personal consumption expenditures, gross private domestic investment, government purchases of goods and services, and net exports. In 1992, GDP measured by the expenditure approach was $5,951 billion. Two thirds of expenditure is on personal consumption goods and services.

Source: U.S. Department of Commerce, *Survey of Current Business* (May 1993).

Personal consumption expenditures are the expenditures on goods and services produced by firms and sold to households. These include goods such as soda, compact discs, books, and magazines, as well as services such as insurance, banking, and legal advice. They do not include the purchase of new residential houses, which is counted as part of investment.

Gross private domestic investment is expenditure on capital equipment by firms and expenditure on new residential houses by households. It also includes the change in firms' inventories. **Inventories** are the stocks of raw materials, semifinished products, and unsold final products held by firms. Inventories are an essential input into the production process. If a firm does not hold inventories of raw materials, its production process can operate only as quickly as the rate at which new raw materials can be delivered. Similarly, if a firm does not have inventories of semifinished goods, processes at later stages of production may become disrupted as a result of breakdowns or accidents at earlier stages. Finally, by holding inventories of finished goods, firms can respond to fluctuations in sales, standing ready to meet an exceptional surge in demand.

The stock of plant, equipment, buildings (including residential housing), and inventories is called the **capital stock**. Additions to the capital stock are investment.

Government purchases of goods and services are the purchases of goods by all levels of government—from Washington to the local town hall. This item of expenditure includes the cost of providing national defense, law and order, street lighting, and garbage collection. It does not include *transfer payments.* As we have seen, such payments do not represent a purchase of goods and services but rather a transfer of money from government to households.

Net exports of goods and services are the difference between the value of exports and the value of imports. When IBM sells a computer to Volkswagen, the German car producer, the value of that computer is part of U.S. exports. When you buy a new Mazda RX7, your expenditure is part of U.S. imports. The difference between what the country earns by selling goods and services to the rest of the world and what it pays for goods and services bought from the rest of the world is the value of net exports.

Table 6.2 shows the relative importance of the four items of aggregate expenditure. As you can see, personal consumption expenditure is by far the largest component of the expenditures that add up to GDP.

The Factor Incomes Approach

The **factor incomes approach** measures GDP by adding together all the incomes paid by firms to households for the services of the factors of production they hire—wages for labor, interest for capital, rent for land, and profits. But this addition, on its own, does not give GDP. Some further adjustments have to be made. Let's see how the factor incomes approach works.

The national income and product accounts divide factor incomes into five components:

- Compensation of employees
- Rental income
- Corporate profits
- Net interest
- Proprietors' income

Compensation of employees is the total payments by firms for labor services. This item includes the net wages and salaries (called take-home pay) that workers receive each week or month, plus taxes withheld on earnings, plus all fringe benefits such as social security and pension fund contributions.

Rental income is the payment for the use of land and other rented inputs. It includes payments for rented housing and imputed rent for owner-occupied housing. (Imputed rent is an estimate of what homeowners would pay to rent the housing they own. By including this item in the national income accounts, we measure the total value of housing services, whether they are owned or rented.)

Corporate profits are the total profits made by corporations. Some of these profits are paid out to households in the form of dividends, and some are retained by the corporations as undistributed profits.

Net interest is the total interest payments received by households on loans made by them minus the interest payments made by households on their own borrowing. This item includes, on the plus side, payments of interest by firms to households on bonds and, on the minus side, households' interest payments on the outstanding balances on their credit cards.

Proprietors' income is a mixture of the elements that we have just reviewed. The proprietor of an owner-operated business supplies labor, capital, and perhaps land and buildings to the business. National income accountants find it difficult to split up the income earned by an owner-operator into its component parts—compensation for labor, payment for the use of capital, rent payments for the use of land or buildings, and profit. As a consequence, the national income accounts lump all these separate factor incomes earned by proprietorships into a single category. **Net domestic income at factor cost** is the sum of all factor incomes. Thus, if we add together the items that we have just reviewed, we arrive at this measure of aggregate income. To measure GDP using the factor incomes approach, we have to make two adjustments to *net domestic income at factor cost.* Let's see what these adjustments are.

Market Price and Factor Cost To calculate GDP using the expenditure approach, we add together expenditures on *final goods and services.* These expenditures are valued at the prices people pay for the various goods and services. The price that people pay for a good or service is called the **market price.**

Another way of valuing a good is factor cost. **Factor cost** is the value of a good measured by adding together the costs of all the factors of production used to produce it. If the only economic transactions were between households and firms, the market price and factor cost methods of measuring value would be identical. But the presence of indirect taxes and subsidies makes these two methods of valuation diverge.

An **indirect tax** is a tax paid by consumers when they purchase goods and services. (In contrast, a *direct* tax is a tax on income.) Examples of indirect taxes are state sales taxes and taxes on alcohol, gasoline, and tobacco products. Indirect taxes result in the consumer paying more than the producer receives for a good. For example, suppose that in your state there is a sales tax of 7 percent. If you buy a $1 chocolate bar, it costs you $1.07. The total cost, including profit, of all the inputs used to produce the chocolate bar is $1. The market price value of the chocolate bar is $1.07. The factor cost value of the chocolate bar is $1.

A **subsidy** is a payment made by the government to producers. Examples are subsidies paid to grain growers and dairy farmers. A subsidy also drives a wedge between the market price value and the factor cost value but in the direction opposite to indirect taxes. A subsidy lowers the market price below the factor cost—consumers pay less for the good than it costs the producer to make the good.

To use the factor incomes approach to measure gross domestic product, we need to add indirect taxes to total factor incomes and to subtract subsidies. Making this adjustment still does not quite get us to GDP. There is one further adjustment needed.

Net Domestic Product and Gross Domestic Product
If we total all the factor incomes and add indirect taxes less subsidies to that total, we arrive at **net domestic product at market prices.** What do the words *gross* and *net* mean, and what is the distinction between the two terms *net domestic product* and *gross domestic product*?

The difference between these two terms is accounted for by the depreciation of capital. **Depreciation** is the decrease in the value of the capital stock that results from wear and tear and the passage of time. We've seen that investment is the purchase of new capital equipment. Depreciation is the opposite—the wearing out or destruction of capital equipment. Part of investment represents the purchase of capital equipment to replace equipment that has worn out. That investment does not add to the capital stock; it simply maintains the capital stock. The other part of investment represents additions to the capital stock—the purchase of new additional plant, equipment, and inventories. Total investment is called gross investment. **Gross investment** is the amount spent on replacing depreciated capital and on making net additions to the capital stock. Gross investment minus depreciation is called **net investment.** Net investment is the net addition to the capital stock. Let's illustrate these ideas with an example.

On January 1, 1994, Swanky, Inc. had a capital stock consisting of three knitting machines that had a market value of $7,500. In 1994, Swanky bought a new machine for $3,000. But during the year the machines owned by Swanky depreciated by a total of $1,000. By December 31, 1994, Swanky's stock of knitting machines was worth $9,500. Swanky's purchase of a new machine for $3,000 is the firm's gross investment. The firm's net investment—the difference between gross investment ($3,000) and

TABLE 6.3

Capital Stock, Investment, and Depreciation for Swanky, Inc.

Capital stock on January 1, 1994 (value of knitting machines owned at beginning of year)		**$7,500**
Gross investment (value of new knitting machine bought in 1994)	**+3,000**	
***less* Depreciation (fall in value of knitting machines during year 1994)**	**–1,000**	
***equals* Net investment**		**2,000**
Capital stock on December 31, 1994 (value of knitting machines owned at end of year)		**$9,500**

Swanky, Inc.'s capital stock at the end of 1994 equals its capital stock at the beginning of the year plus net investment. Net investment is equal to gross investment less depreciation. Gross investment is the value of new machines bought during the year, and depreciation is the fall in the value of Swanky's knitting machines over the year.

TABLE 6.4

GDP: The Factor Incomes Approach

Item	Amount in 1992 (billions of dollars)	Percentage of GDP
Compensation of employees	**3,525**	**59.2**
Rental income	**69**	**1.2**
Corporate profits	**364**	**6.1**
Net interest	**415**	**7.0**
Proprietors' income	**396**	**6.7**
Indirect taxes *less* Subsidies	**529**	**8.9**
Capital consumption (depreciation)	**653**	**11.0**
Gross domestic product	**5,951**	**100.0**

The sum of all factor incomes equals net domestic income at factor cost. GDP equals net domestic income at factor cost plus indirect taxes minus subsidies plus capital consumption (depreciation). In 1992, GDP measured by the factor incomes approach was $5,951 billion. The compensation of employees—labor income—was by far the largest part of total factor incomes.

Source: U.S. Department of Commerce, *Survey of Current Business* (May 1993).

depreciation ($1,000)—is $2,000. These transactions and the relationship between gross investment, net investment, and depreciation are summarized in Table 6.3.

Gross domestic product equals net domestic product plus depreciation. (Depreciation is called *capital consumption* by the national income accountants of the Department of Commerce.) Total expenditure *includes* depreciation—because it includes *gross investment.* Total factor incomes plus indirect taxes less subsidies *excludes* depreciation—because when firms calculate their profit, they make an allowance for depreciation and so subtract from their gross profit their estimate of the decrease in the value of their capital stock. As a result, adding up factor incomes gives a measure of domestic product that is net of the depreciation of the capital stock. To reconcile the factor incomes and expenditure approaches, we must add capital consumption (depreciation) to net domestic product. Table 6.4 summarizes these calculations and shows how the factor incomes approach leads to the same estimate of GDP as the expenditure approach. The table also shows the relative importance of the various factor incomes. As you can see, compensation of employees (wages and salaries) is by far the most important factor income.

Valuing the Output of Firms and Sectors

To value the output of an individual firm or sector of the economy, we calculate the value added by that firm or sector. **Value added** is the value of a firm's output minus the value of *intermediate goods* bought from other firms. Equivalently, it is the sum of the incomes (including profits) paid to the factors of production used by a firm to produce its output. Let's illustrate value added by looking at the production of a loaf of bread.

Figure 6.3 takes you through the brief life of a loaf of bread. It starts with the farmer, who grows the wheat. To do so, the farmer hires labor, capital equipment, and land, paying wages, interest, and rent. The farmer also receives a profit. The entire value of the wheat produced is the farmer's value added. The miller buys wheat from the farmer and turns it into flour. To do so, the miller hires labor and uses capital equipment, paying wages and interest, and receives a profit. The miller has now added some value to the wheat bought from the farmer. The baker buys flour from the miller. The price of the flour includes value added by the farmer and by the miller. The baker adds more value by turning the flour into bread. Wages are paid to bakery workers, interest is paid on the capital used by the baker, and the baker makes a profit. The bread is bought from the baker by the grocery store. The bread now has value added by the farmer, the miller, and the baker. At this stage, the value of the loaf is its *wholesale value*. The grocery store adds further value by making the loaf available in a convenient place at a convenient time. The consumer buys the bread for a price—its *retail price*—that includes the value added by the farmer, the miller, the baker, and the grocery store.

FIGURE 6.3

Value Added in the Life of a Loaf of Bread

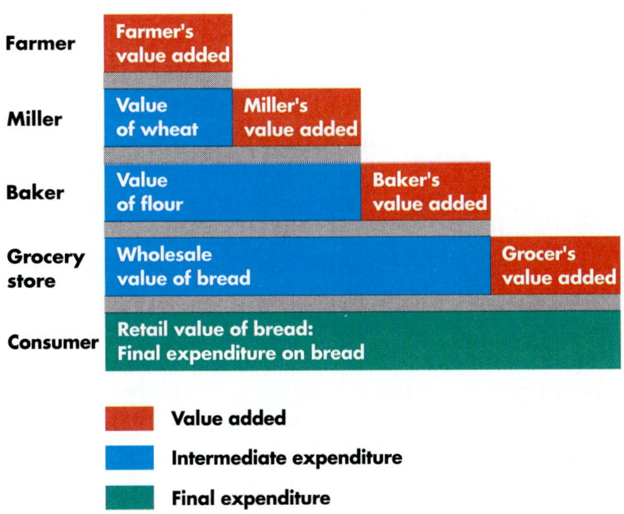

A consumer's expenditure on a loaf of bread is equal to the sum of the value added at each stage in its production. Intermediate expenditure, for example, the purchase of flour by the baker from the miller, already includes the value added by the farmer and the miller. Including intermediate expenditure double counts the value added.

Final Goods and Intermediate Goods In valuing output, we count only *value added.* The sum of the value added at each stage of production equals expenditure on *the final good.* In the above example, the only thing that has been produced and consumed is one loaf of bread. But many transactions occurred in the process of producing the loaf of bread. The miller bought grain from the farmer, the baker bought flour from the miller, and the grocer bought bread from the baker. These transactions were the purchase and sale of *intermediate goods.* To count the expenditure on intermediate goods and services as well as the expenditure on the final good involves counting the same thing twice, or more than twice when there are several intermediate stages, as there are in this example. Counting expenditure on both final goods and intermediate goods is known as **double counting.** Wheat, flour, and even the finished loaf bought by the grocery store are all intermediate goods in the production of a loaf of bread bought by a final consumer.

Many goods are sometimes intermediate goods and sometimes final goods. For example, the electric power used by GM to produce automobiles is an intermediate good, but the electric power that you buy to use in your home is a final good. Whether a good is intermediate or final depends not on what it is, but on what it is used for.

Gross National Product

Until recently, the Department of Commerce focused on a different measure of aggregate economic activity from GDP. This measure is gross national product, or GNP. **Gross national product** is the total value of output *owned by residents* of the United States. Gross *domestic* product measures the value of output *produced in* the United States. The difference between gross *domestic* product and gross *national* product is the net investment income that U.S. residents receive from other parts of the world. For example, Americans own production plants in Japan and Europe. Japanese and European residents own production plants in the United States. Net investment income received from the rest of the world is the total payment of profits and dividends to U.S.

residents on their foreign investments less the payments of interest and dividends to foreigners on their investments in the United States.

Aggregate Expenditure, Income, and GDP

We've now studied the concepts of aggregate expenditure, aggregate income, and the value of output as well as the measurement of these concepts by the Department of Commerce. The equality of the three concepts and the relative importance of their components are illustrated in Fig. 6.4. This figure provides a snapshot summary of the entire description of the national accounting concepts that you've studied in this chapter.

REVIEW

GDP is measured by two methods: the *expenditure approach* (the sum of consumption expenditure, investment, government purchases of goods and services, and exports minus imports) and the *factor incomes approach* (the sum of wages, interest, rent, and profit with adjustments for indirect taxes, subsidies, and depreciation). ◆

FIGURE 6.4

Aggregate Expenditure, Output, and Income

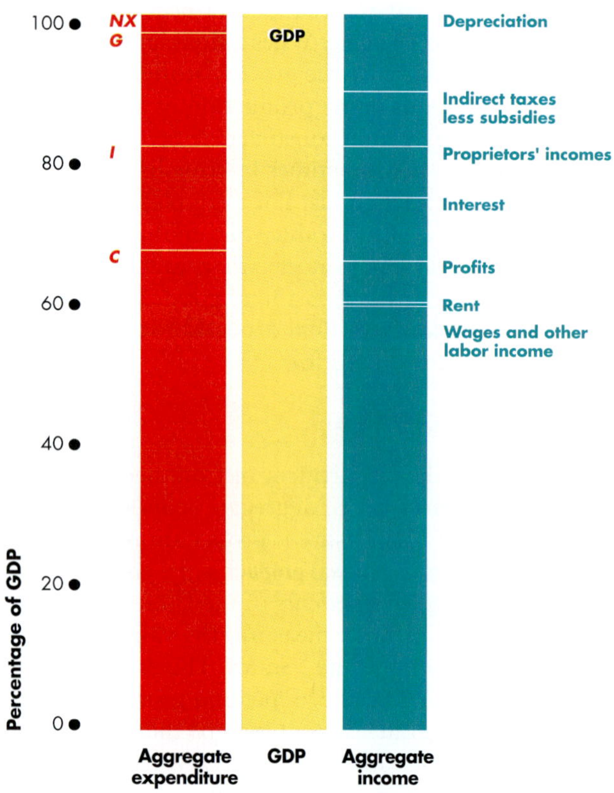

This figure illustrates the relative magnitudes of the main components of aggregate expenditure and aggregate income and also illustrates the equality between aggregate expenditure, aggregate income, and GDP.

So far, in our study of GDP and its measurement, we've been concerned with the dollar value of GDP and its components. But GDP can change either because prices change or because there is a change in the volume of goods and services produced—a change in *real* GDP. Let's now see how we measure the price level and distinguish between price changes and changes in real GDP.

The Price Level and Inflation

The *price level* is the average level of prices measured by a *price index*. To construct a price index, we take a basket of goods and services and calculate its value in the current period and in a base period. The price index is the ratio of its value in the current period to its value in the base period. The price index tells us how much more expensive the basket is in the current period than it was in the base period, expressed as a percentage.

Table 6.5 shows you how to calculate a price index for the basket of goods that Tom buys. His basket is a simple one. It contains four movies and two six-packs of soda. The value of Tom's basket, shown in the table, in 1993 was $30. The same basket in 1994 cost $35.40. Tom's price index is $35.40

TABLE 6.5

Calculating a Price Index

Items in the basket	1993 (base period) Quantity bought	Price	Expenditure	1994 (current period) Price	Expenditure
Movies	4	$6	$24	$6.75	$27.00
Six-packs of soda	2	3	6	4.20	8.40
			$30		$35.40

Price index for 1994 = $\frac{\$35.40}{\$30.00} \times 100 = 118$

A price index for 1994 is calculated in two steps. The first step is to value the goods bought in 1993, the base period, at the prices prevailing in both 1993 and 1994. The second step is to divide the value of those goods in 1994 by their value in 1993 and multiply the result by 100.

expressed as a percentage of $30. That is,

$$\frac{\$35.40}{\$30} \times 100 = 118.$$

Notice that if the current period is also the base period, the price index is 100.

There are two main price indexes used to measure the price level in the United States today: the Consumer Price Index and the GDP deflator. The **Consumer Price Index** (CPI) measures the average level of prices of the goods and services typically consumed by an urban American family. The **GDP deflator** measures the average level of prices of all the goods and services that are included in GDP. We are now going to study the method used for determining these price indexes. In calculating the actual indexes, the Departments of Commerce and Labor process millions of pieces of information. But we can learn the principles involved in those calculations by working through some simple examples and by referring to Reading Between the Lines on pp. 142–143.

Consumer Price Index

The Bureau of Labor Statistics in the U.S. Department of Labor calculates and publishes the *Consumer Price Index* every month. To construct the CPI, the Department of Labor first selects a base period. Currently, the base period is the three-year period from 1982 through 1984. Then, on the basis of surveys of consumer spending patterns, it selects a basket of goods and services—the quantities of approximately 400 different goods and services that were typically consumed by urban households in the base period.

Every month the Department of Labor sends a team of observers to more than 50 urban centers in the United States to record the prices for these 400 items. When all the data are collected, the CPI is calculated by valuing the base-period basket of goods and services at the current month's prices. That value is expressed as a percentage of the value of the same basket in the base period.

To see more precisely how the CPI is calculated, let's work through an example. Table 6.6 summarizes our calculations. Let's suppose that there are only three goods in the typical consumer's basket: oranges, haircuts, and bus rides. The quantities bought and the prices prevailing in the base period are shown in the table. Total expenditure in the base period is also shown: the typical consumer buys 200 bus rides at 70¢ each and so spends $140 on bus rides. Expenditure on oranges and haircuts is worked out in the same way. Total expenditure is the sum of expenditures on the three goods, which is $210.

To calculate the price index for the current period, we need only to discover the prices of the goods

Real GDP Growth and Inflation

The New York Times, July 30, 1993

G.D.P. Gain Is Stronger in Quarter

BY ROBERT D. HERSHEY, JR.

WASHINGTON—In a moderate rebound powered by the spending of consumers and businesses, the economy's growth rate climbed to 1.6 percent in the second quarter as inflation eased, the Commerce Department reported today.

While the rise in gross domestic product—the output of goods and services within American boundaries—was short of most expectations, there was wide agreement among analysts that the 1.6 percent advance was better than it appeared and represented significant improvement from the meager expansion of seven-tenths of a percent for the first three months of the year.

"The actual implication of the report for the economy, going forward, was fine," said William C. Dudley, senior economist at Goldman, Sachs. He cited buoyant consumer spending, which surged 3.8 percent, and continued robust investments by businesses in new equipment. Indeed, the total annualized value of G.D.P. adjusted for inflation in the second quarter exceeded $5 trillion for the first time, reaching $5.019 trillion. . . .

An index published with the G.D.P. data showed prices rose at a 2.7 percent annual rate in the second quarter, down from 3.5 percent in the first three months of the year.

What limited second-quarter growth was a drag from inventories of unsold goods, which had the effect of chopping second-quarter G.D.P. by about two percentage points. All goods produced add to G.D.P., even those that go unsold. Inventories rose only one-fourth as rapidly in the second quarter as in the first, when consumers cut their spending after the holidays and a blizzard disrupted economic life in the East. The effect was that $25.3 billion in inventories was subtracted from second-quarter G.D.P. after $23.7 billion was added in the first quarter. . . .

The Essence of the Story

On July 29, 1993, the Commerce Department reported that the growth rate of real GDP in the second quarter of 1993 was 1.6 percent, up from 0.7 percent for the first quarter.

Consumer spending increased by 3.8 percent, and investment by businesses in new equipment also increased, but investment in business inventories decreased.

An index published with the GDP data showed that prices rose at a 2.7 percent annual rate in the second quarter, down from 3.5 percent in the first three months of the year.

Background and Analysis

The Commerce Department's figures for the second quarter of 1993 published at the end of July were preliminary estimates.

The data reported were compiled by using the expenditure approach and are shown in the table.

The index that is published with the GDP data and that tells us about inflation is the *GDP deflator.*

The main lesson here is that you can't learn much from the data for one quarter. It is more informative to look at the most recent quarter in the context of the past few quarters.

Quarterly data on real GDP growth from mid-1989 to mid-1993 are shown in Fig. 1. Real GDP growth in the second quarter of 1993 (the last observation plotted in the graph) is higher than that in the first quarter of 1993, but down from that in the fourth quarter of 1992.

But the trend of the growth rate is positive since the recession of 1990–1991, when real GDP growth was negative—real GDP shrank.

Figure 2 shows the course of inflation over the same period. Although inflation was down in the second quarter of 1993, in the first quarter it was the highest it had been for seven quarters and in the second quarter it was about where it had been a year earlier.

The news story says that real GDP growth slowed because inventory investment was low. Figure 3 shows inventory investment between mid-1989 and mid-1993. You can see that inventory investment was indeed lower in the second quarter of 1993 than in the first quarter. If consumer spending continued to grow at its second-quarter pace, the change in inventories was predicted to increase in future quarters.

Item	Amount (billions of 1987 dollars)
Personal consumption expenditures	**3,398.1**
Fixed investment	**762.9**
Change in business inventories	**8.2**
Government purchases of goods and services	**920.1**
Net exports	**−69.9**
Gross domestic product	**5,019.5**

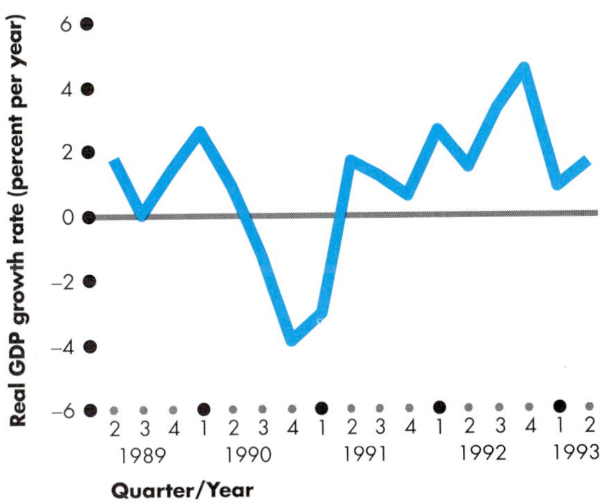

Figure 1

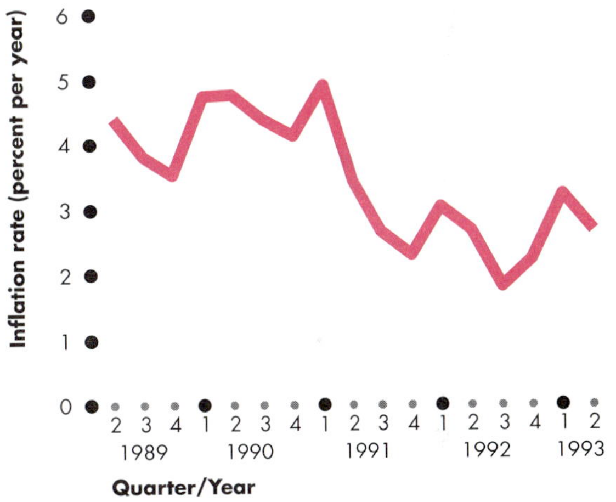

Figure 2

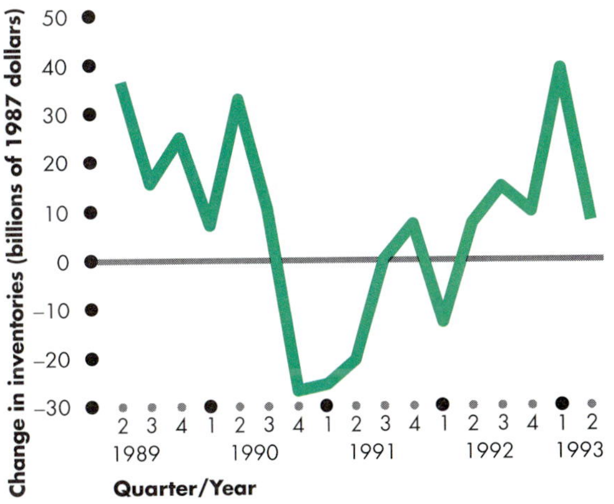

Figure 3

TABLE 6.6

The Consumer Price Index: A Simplified Calculation

Items in the basket	Base period			Current period	
	Quantity	Price	Expenditure	Price	Expenditures on base-period quantities
Oranges	**5 pounds**	**$ 0.80/pound**	**$ 4**	**$ 1.20/pound**	**$ 6**
Haircuts	**6**	**11.00 each**	**66**	**12.50 each**	**75**
Bus rides	**200**	**0.70 each**	**140**	**0.75 each**	**150**
Total expenditure			**$210**		**$231**
CPI		$\frac{\$210.00}{\$210.00} \times 100 = 100$		$\frac{\$231.00}{\$210.00} \times 100 = 110$	

A fixed basket of goods—5 pounds of oranges, 6 haircuts, and 200 bus rides—is valued in the base period at $210. Prices change, and that same basket is valued at $231 in the current period. The CPI is equal to the current-period value of the basket divided by the base-period value of the basket multiplied by 100. In the base period the CPI is 100, and in the current period the CPI is 110.

in the current period. We do not need to know the quantities bought. Let's suppose that the prices are those set out in the table under "Current period." We can now calculate the current period's value of the basket of goods by using the current period's prices. For example, the current price of oranges is $1.20 per pound, so the current period's value of the base-period quantity (5 pounds) is 5 multiplied by $1.20, which is $6. The base-period quantities of haircuts and bus rides are valued at this period's prices in a similar way. The total value in the current period of the base-period basket is $231.

We can now calculate the CPI—the ratio of this period's value of the goods to the base period's value, multiplied by 100. In this example, the CPI for the current period is 110. The CPI for the base period is, by definition, 100.

GDP Deflator

The *GDP deflator* measures the average level of prices of all the goods and services that make up GDP. You can think of GDP as being like a balloon that is being blown up by growing production of goods and services and rising prices. Figure 6.5 illustrates this idea. The purpose of the GDP deflator is to let some air out of the GDP balloon—the contribution of rising prices—so that we can see what has happened to *real* GDP. Real GDP is a measure of the physical volume of output arrived at by valuing the current-period output at prices that prevailed in a *base period.* Currently, the base period for calculating real GDP is 1987. We refer to the units in which real GDP is measured as "1987 dollars." The red balloon for 1987 shows real GDP in that year. The green balloon shows *nominal* GDP in 1994. (We use the term *nominal GDP* because it measures the money value of output.) The red balloon for 1994 shows real GDP for that year. To see real GDP in 1994, we *deflate* nominal GDP using the GDP deflator. Let's see how we calculate real GDP and the GDP deflator.

We are going to learn how to calculate the GDP deflator by studying an imaginary economy. We will calculate nominal GDP and real GDP as well as the GDP deflator. To make our calculations simple, let's imagine an economy that has just three final goods: the consumption good is oranges; the capital good is

FIGURE 6.5

The GDP Balloon

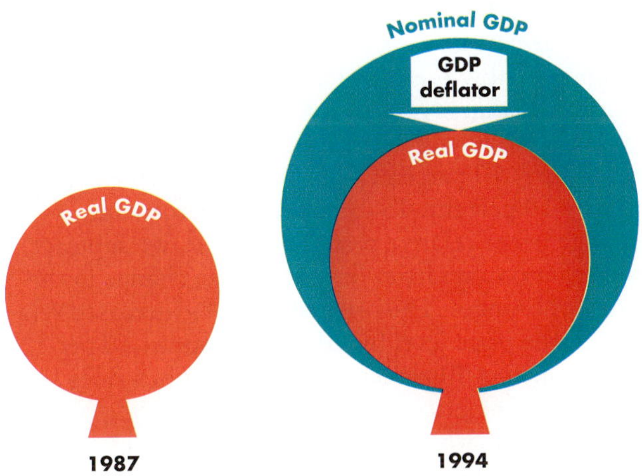

GDP is like a balloon that gets bigger because of growing output and rising prices. The GDP deflator is used to let the air resulting from higher prices out of the balloon so that we can see the extent to which production has grown.

computers; and the government purchases red tape. (Net exports are zero in this example.) Table 6.7 summarizes the calculations of nominal GDP, real GDP, and the GDP deflator in this economy.

Let's focus first on calculating nominal GDP. We'll use the expenditure approach. The table shows the quantities of the final goods and their prices. To calculate nominal GDP, let's work out the expenditure on each good and then total the three expenditures. Consumption expenditure (purchases of oranges) is $4,452, investment (purchases of computers) is $10,500, and government purchases of red tape are $1,060, so nominal GDP is $16,012.

Next, let's calculate real GDP. This is calculated by valuing the current-period quantities at the base-period prices. The table shows the prices for the base period. Real expenditure on oranges for the current period is 4,240 pounds of oranges valued at $1 per pound, which is $4,240. If we perform the same types of calculations for computers and red tape and add up the real expenditures, we arrive at a real GDP of $15,300.

To calculate the GDP deflator for the current period, we divide nominal GDP ($16,012) by real GDP ($15,300) and multiply the result by 100. The GDP deflator that we obtain is 104.7. If the current

TABLE 6.7

Nominal GDP, Real GDP, and the GDP Deflator: Simplified Calculations

	Current period			Base period	
Item	Quantity	Price	Expenditure	Price	Expenditure
Oranges	**4,240 pounds**	**$1.05/pound**	**$ 4,452**	**$1/pound**	**$ 4,240**
Computers	**5**	**$2,100 each**	**10,500**	**$2,000 each**	**$10,000**
Red tape	**1,060 yards**	**$1/yard**	**1,060**	**$1/yard**	**$ 1,060**
		Nominal GDP	**$16,012**	**Real GDP**	**$15,300**

$$\text{GDP deflator} = \frac{\$16{,}012}{\$15{,}300} \times 100 = 104.7$$

An imaginary economy produces only oranges, computers, and red tape. In the current period, nominal GDP is $16,012. If the current-period quantities are valued at the base-period prices, we obtain a measure of real GDP, which is $15,300. The GDP deflator in the current period—which is calculated by dividing nominal GDP by real GDP in that period and multiplying by 100—is 104.7.

period is also the base period, nominal GDP equals real GDP and the GDP deflator is 100. Thus the GDP deflator in the base period is 100, just as for the CPI.

Inflation and Relative Price Changes

The inflation rate is calculated as the percentage increase in the price index. For example, in the case that we studied in Table 6.6, the CPI rose by 10 percent from the base period to the current period. Underlying that change in the CPI are the individual changes in the prices of oranges, haircuts, and bus rides. No individual price rose by 10 percent. The price of oranges rose by 50 percent, the price of haircuts by 13.6 percent, and the price of bus rides by 7.1 percent. This example captures a common feature of the world that we live in: it is rarely the case that all prices change by the same percentage amount. When the prices of goods rise by different percentages, there is a change in relative prices. A **relative price** is the ratio of the price of one good to the price of another good. For example, if the price of oranges is 80¢ per pound and the price of a haircut is $11, the relative price of a haircut is 13¾ pounds of oranges. It costs 13¾ pounds of oranges to buy one haircut.

Prices and inflation mean a great deal to people. But many people are confused by the difference between the inflation rate and relative price changes. Inflation and relative price changes are separate and independent phenomena. To see why this is so, we will work through an example showing that, for the same relative price changes, we can have two entirely different inflation rates.

We will first learn how to calculate a change in relative prices. The percentage change in a relative price is the percentage change in the price of one good minus the percentage change in the price of another good. For example, if the price of oranges increases from 80¢ per pound to 88¢ per pound—an increase of 10 percent—and if the price of a haircut remains constant at $11—an increase of zero percent—the relative price of a haircut falls from 13¾ pounds of oranges to 12½ pounds of oranges—a decrease of (approximately) 10 percent.

For practical calculations of relative price changes, we use the inflation rate—the percentage change in prices on the average—as the reference point. That is, we calculate the rate of change of the price of a good minus the inflation rate. Goods whose prices rise at a higher rate than the inflation rate experience a rising relative price, and goods whose prices rise at a rate below the inflation rate experience a falling relative price.

Let's work out some relative price changes, using again the calculations that we worked through in Table 6.6, now presented in Table 6.8(a). The price of oranges rises from 80¢ to $1.20, or by 50 percent. We have already calculated that the inflation rate is 10 percent. That is, prices on the average rise by 10 percent. To calculate the percentage change in the relative price of oranges, we subtract the inflation rate from the percentage change in the price of oranges. The price of oranges increased relative to the price level by 50 percent minus 10 percent, which is 40 percent. The price of bus rides falls relative to the price level by 2.9 percent.

In Table 6.8(b), we see that relative prices can change without inflation. In fact, part (b) illustrates the same changes in relative prices that occur in part (a) but with no inflation. In this case, the price of oranges increases by 40 percent to $1.12, the price of haircuts increases by 3.6 percent to $11.40, and the price of bus rides falls by 2.9 percent to 68¢. If you calculate the current- and base-period values of the basket in part (b), you will find that consumers spend exactly the same at the new prices as they do at the base-period prices. There is no inflation, even though relative prices have changed.

We've now looked at two cases in which the relative price of oranges increases by 40 percent. In one, inflation is 10 percent; in the other, there is no inflation. Clearly, inflation has not been *caused by* the change in the price of oranges. In the first case, the price of each good increases by 10 percent more than it does in the second case. Singling out the good whose relative price has increased most does not help us explain why all prices are rising by 10 percent more in the first case than in the second case.

Any inflation rate can occur with any behavior of relative prices. Relative prices are determined by supply and demand in the markets for the individual goods and services. The price level and the inflation rate are determined independently of *relative* prices. To explain an increase (or decrease) in the inflation rate, we have to explain why all prices are inflating at a different rate and not why some prices are increasing faster than others.

TABLE 6.8

Relative Price Changes With or Without Inflation

(a) 10 percent inflation

Item	Base-period price	New price	Percentage change in price	Percentage change in relative price
Oranges	**$ 0.80**	**$ 1.20**	**+50.0**	**+40.0**
Haircuts	**11.00**	**12.50**	**+13.6**	**+ 3.6**
Bus rides	**0.70**	**0.75**	**+ 7.1**	**− 2.9**

(b) No inflation

Item	Base-period price	New price	Percentage change in price	Percentage change in relative price
Oranges	**$ 0.80**	**$ 1.12**	**+40.0**	**+40.0**
Haircuts	**11.00**	**11.40**	**+ 3.6**	**+ 3.6**
Bus rides	**0.70**	**0.68**	**−2.9**	**−2.9**

A relative price is the price of one good divided by the price of another good. Relative prices change whenever the price of one good changes by a different percentage than the price of some other good. Relative price changes do not cause inflation. They can occur with or without inflation. In part (a), the price index rises by 10 percent. In part (b), the price index remains constant. In both parts, the relative price of oranges increases by 40 percent and that of haircuts by 3.6 percent, and the relative price of bus rides falls by 2.9 percent. The rise in the price of oranges cannot be regarded as the cause of the rise in the price index in part (a) because that same rise in the price of oranges occurs with no change in the price index in part (b).

The Consumer Price Index and the Cost of Living

Does the Consumer Price Index measure the cost of living? Does a 5 percent increase in the CPI mean that the cost of living has increased by 5 percent? It does not, for three reasons. They are

- Substitution effects
- Arrival of new goods and disappearance of old ones
- Quality improvements

Substitution Effects A change in the CPI measures the percentage change in the price of a *fixed* basket of goods and services. The actual basket of goods and services bought depends on relative prices and on consumers' tastes. Changes in relative prices will lead consumers to economize on goods that have become relatively expensive and to buy more of those goods whose relative prices have fallen. If chicken doubles in price but the price of beef increases by only 5 percent, people will substitute the now relatively less expensive beef for the relatively more expensive chicken. Because consumers make such substitutions, a price index based on a fixed basket will overstate the effects of a given price change on the consumer's cost of living.

Arrival and Disappearance of Goods Discrepancies between the CPI and the cost of living also arise from the disappearance of some commodities and the emergence of new ones. For example, suppose that you want to compare the cost of living in 1994 with that in 1894. Using a price index that has horse feed in it will not work. Though that price featured in people's transportation costs in 1894, it plays no role today. Similarly, a price index with gasoline in it will be of little use, since gasoline, while relevant today, did not feature in people's spending in 1894. Even comparisons between 1994 and 1980 suffer from this same problem. Compact discs and microwave popcorn, which featured in our budgets in 1994, were not available in 1980.

Quality Improvements The Consumer Price Index can overstate a true rise in prices by ignoring quality improvements. Most goods undergo constant quality improvement. Automobiles, computers, CD players, even textbooks, get better year after year. Part of the increase in price of these items reflects the improvement in the quality of the product. Yet the CPI regards such a price change as inflation. Attempts have been made to assess the importance of this factor, and some economists estimate that it contributes as much as 2 percent a year on the average to the measured inflation rate.

Substitution effects, the arrival of new goods and the departure of old ones, and quality changes make the connection between the CPI and the cost of living imprecise. To reduce the problems that arise from this source, the Bureau of Labor Statistics from time to time updates the weights used for calculating the CPI. Even so, the CPI is of limited value for making comparisons of the cost of living over long periods of time. But for the purpose for which it was devised—calculating month-to-month and year-to-year rates of inflation—the CPI does a pretty good job.

REVIEW

The Consumer Price Index is a price index based on the consumption expenditures of a typical urban family. It is calculated as the ratio of the value of a base-period basket in the current period to its value in the base period (multiplied by 100). The GDP deflator is a price index calculated as the ratio of nominal GDP to real GDP (multiplied by 100). Real GDP values the current period's output at base-period prices. ◆◆ A relative price is the price of one good relative to the price of another good. Relative prices are constantly changing but are independent of the inflation rate. Any pattern of relative price changes can take place at any inflation rate. ◆◆ The CPI has limitations as a means of comparing the cost of living over long periods but does a good job of measuring year-to-year changes in the inflation rate. ◆

Now that we've studied the measurement of GDP and the price level and know how *real* GDP is measured, let's take a look at what real GDP tells us about the aggregate value of economic activity, the standard of living, and economic well-being.

Real GDP, Aggregate Economic Activity, and Economic Well-Being

What does real GDP really measure? How good a measure is it? What does it tell us about aggregate economic activity? And what does it tell us about the standard of living and economic welfare? Some of these questions are discussed further in Our Advancing Knowledge on pp. 150–151.

Economic welfare is a comprehensive measure of the general state of well-being and standard of living. Economic welfare depends on the following factors:

1. The quantity and quality of goods and services available
2. The amount of leisure time available
3. The degree of equality among individuals

Real GDP does not accurately measure all the goods and services that we produce, and it provides no information on the amount of leisure time and the degree of economic equality. Its mismeasurement of production has errors in both directions. We'll examine five factors that limit the usefulness of real GDP as a measure of economic welfare. They are

- Underground real GDP
- Household production
- Environmental damage
- Leisure time
- Economic equality

Underground Real GDP

The **underground economy** is all economic activity that is legal but unreported. Underground economic activity is unreported because participants in the underground economy withhold information to evade taxes or regulations. For example, avoiding safety regulations, minimum wage laws, and social security payments are motives for operating in the underground economy. Attempts have been made to assess the scale of the underground economy, and estimates range between 5 and 15 percent of GDP ($300 billion to $900 billion).

Although not usually regarded as part of the underground economy, a great deal of other unreported activity takes place—economic activity that is illegal. In today's economy, various forms of illegal gambling, prostitution, and drug trading are important omitted components of economic activity. It is impossible to measure the scale of illegal activities, but estimates range between 1 and 5 percent of GDP (between $60 billion and $300 billion).

Household Production

An enormous amount of economic activity that no one is obliged to report takes place every day in our own homes. Changing a light bulb, cutting the grass, washing the car, laundering a shirt, painting a door, and teaching a child to catch a ball are all examples of productive activities that do not involve market transactions and that are not counted as part of GDP.

Household production has become much more capital-intensive over the years. As a result, less labor is used in household production than in earlier periods. For example, a microwave meal that takes just a few minutes to prepare uses a great deal of capital and almost no labor. Because we use less labor and more capital in household production, it is not easy to work out whether this type of production has increased or decreased over time. It is likely, however, that it has decreased as more and more people have joined the labor force.

Household production is almost certainly cyclical. When the economy is in recession, household production increases, since households whose members are unemployed buy fewer goods in the marketplace and provide more services for themselves. When the economy is booming, employment outside the home increases and household production decreases.

Environmental Damage

The environment is directly affected by economic activity. The burning of hydrocarbon fuels is the most visible activity that damages our environment. But it is not the only example. The depletion of exhaustible resources, the mass clearing of forests, and the pollution of lakes and rivers are other important environmental consequences of industrial production.

Resources used to protect the environment are valued as part of GDP. For example, the value of catalytic converters that help to protect the atmosphere from automobile emissions is part of GDP. But if we did not use such pieces of equipment and instead polluted the atmosphere, we would not count the deteriorating air that we were breathing as a negative part of GDP.

It is obvious that an industrial society produces more atmospheric pollution than a primitive or agricultural society. But it is not obvious that such pollution increases as we become wealthier. One of the things that wealthy people value is a clean environment, and they devote resources to protecting it. Compare the pollution that was discovered in East Germany in the late 1980s with pollution in the United States. East Germany, a relatively poor country, polluted its rivers, lakes, and atmosphere in a way that is unimaginable in the United States.

Leisure Time

Leisure time is obviously an economic good that adds to our economic welfare. Other things being equal, the more leisure we have, the better off we are. Our time spent working is valued as part of GDP, but our leisure time is not. Yet from the point of view of economic welfare, that leisure time must be at least as valuable to us as the wage that we earn on the last hour worked. If it was not, we would work instead of taking the leisure.

Economic Equality

A country might have a very large real GDP per person, but with a high degree of inequality. A few people might be extremely wealthy, while the vast majority live in abject poverty. Such an economy would generally be regarded as having less economic welfare than one in which the same amount of real GDP was more equally shared. For example, average GDP per person in the oil-rich countries of the

THE Development of ECONOMIC ACCOUNTING

National income was first measured in England by William Petty in 1665. But it was not until the 1930s, when it was needed to test and use the new Keynesian theory of economic fluctuations, that national income measurement became a routine part of the operation of the U.S. Department of Commerce.

With one exception, the national income accounts measure only *market transactions*. The exception is owner-occupied housing. National income includes an estimate of the amount that homeowners would have received (and paid) in rent if they had rented their homes rather than owned them. The idea is that regardless of whether a home is rented or owned, it provides a service, and the rent (actual or implicit) measures the value of that service.

"To express my self in Terms of Number, Weight, or Measure; to use only Arguments of Sense, and to consider only such Causes as have visible Foundations in Nature"

SIR WILLIAM PETTY
Political Arithmetick

But owner-occupied housing is not really so exceptional. We produce lots of services at home that are missed by the national accounts. Watching a video is an example. If you go to the movies, the price you pay for the ticket includes the cost of the movie, the rent of the seat, the cost of heating or cooling the theater, the wages of the theater workers, and the profit (or loss) of the theater owner—the full cost of your entertainment. The price of your ticket is measured as part of national income. But if you watch a home video, only the video rental is counted as part of national income. The rental cost of the television, VCR, armchair, and sitting room (you rent them from yourself so there's no market transaction) is not counted.

The amount of home production has increased over the years. Kitchens equipped with microwaves and dishwashers, automated laundries, and living rooms containing more audio and video equipment than a 1970s TV studio have turned the home into a capital-intensive production center.

Partly because of all this capital equipment, women spend more time outside the home earning a wage and what they earn does get counted as part of national income. But both women and men are more productive in the home than ever before, and the value of this production does not get counted as part of national income.

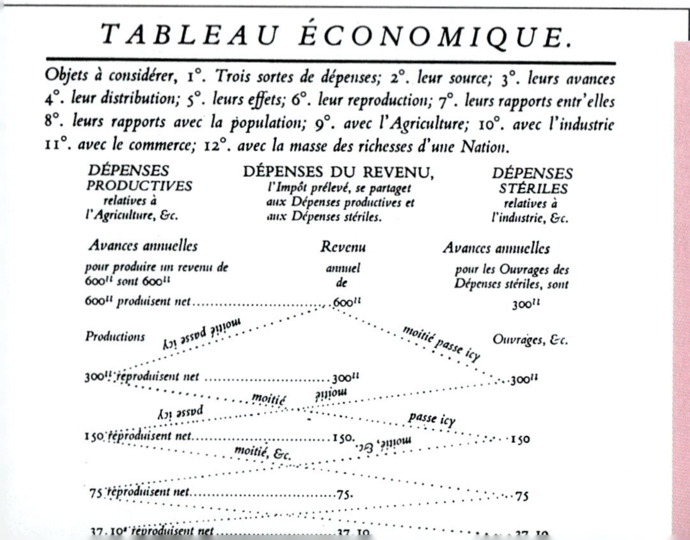

One of the earliest national economic accounts was François Quesnay's *Tableau Économique* used to measure economic activity in France in 1758. One of Quesnay's "disciples" was so impressed with this work that he described it as being worthy of being ranked, along with writing and money, as one of the three greatest inventions of the human race. Quesnay's *Tableau* was praised by Karl Marx, the founder of socialism, and is regarded as the forerunner of the types of input-output tables used in the former Soviet Union to construct annual economic plans. Modern national accounts are less like Quesnay's *Tableau* and more like the income and expenditure accounts of large corporations. They record the incomes of factors of production and the expenditures on final goods and services.

Regardless of the method used to wash an automobile, the output is a clean car. And regardless of whether the factors of production are teenagers, rags, a hose, and a bucket or an automated machine, these factors of production have created a good that is valued. Yet the teenagers' efforts are not measured in the national accounts, while that of the automatic car wash is. As do-it-yourself is replaced by purchasing from specialized producers, part of the apparent increase in the value of national production is just an illusion due to the way the books are kept. To avoid this illusion, it is necessary to develop methods of national income accounting that estimate the value of home production by using a method similar to that used to estimate the rental value of owner-occupied homes.

Sir William Petty: A *Pioneer of Economic Statistics*

William Petty was born in England in 1623. He was a cabin boy on a merchant ship at 13, a student in a Jesuit college in France at 14, a successful doctor of medicine in his early 20s, a professor of anatomy at Oxford University at 27, and a professor of music at 28. As chief medical officer of the British army in Ireland at age 29, he managed a topographical survey of that country, from which he emerged as a substantial owner of Irish land! Petty was also an economic thinker and writer of considerable repute. He was the first person to measure national income and one of the first to propose that a government department be established for the collection of reliable and timely economic statistics. He believed that economic policy could only improve economic performance if it was based on an understanding of cause-and-effect relations discovered by the systematic measurement of economic activity—a process he called "Political Arithmetick."

Middle East is similar to that of several countries in Western Europe but much less equally distributed. Economic welfare is higher in those Western European countries.

Are the Omissions a Problem?

If real GDP increases at the expense of other factors that affect economic welfare, there is no change in economic welfare. But if real GDP increases with no reduction (or even an increase) in the other factors, then economic welfare increases. Whether we get the wrong message from changes (or differences) in real GDP depends on the questions being asked. There are two main types of question:

- Business cycle questions
- Standard of living and economic welfare questions

Business Cycle Questions The fluctuations in economic activity measured by real GDP probably overstate the fluctuations in total production and economic welfare. When there is an economic downturn, household production increases and so does leisure time, but real GDP does not record these changes. When real GDP is growing quickly, leisure time and household production probably decline. Again, this change is not recorded as part of real GDP. But the directions of change of real GDP and economic welfare are likely to be the same.

Standard of Living and Economic Welfare Questions For standard of living comparisons, the factors omitted from real GDP are probably very important. For example, in developing countries the underground economy and the amount of household production are a much higher fraction of economic activity than in developed countries. This fact makes comparisons of GDP between countries such as the United States and Nigeria, for example, unreliable measures of comparative living standards unless the GDP data are supplemented with other information.

Using GDP data to gauge changes in living standards over time is also unreliable. Living standards depend only partly on the value of output. They also depend on the composition of that output. For example, two economies may have the same GDP, but one economy may produce more weapons and the other more music. Consumers will not be indifferent as to which of these two economies they live in.

Other factors affecting living standards include the amount of leisure time available, the quality of the environment, the security of jobs and homes, the safety of city streets, and so on. It is possible to construct broader measures that combine the many factors that contribute to human happiness. Real GDP will be one element in that measure, but it will by no means be the whole of it.

◆ ◆ ◆ ◆ In Chapter 5, we examined the macroeconomic performance of the United States in recent years and over a longer sweep of history. In this chapter, we studied in some detail the methods used for measuring the macroeconomy and in particular the average level of prices and the overall level of real economic activity. In the following chapters, we're going to study some macroeconomic models—models designed to explain and predict the behavior of real GDP, the price level, employment and unemployment, the stock market, and other related phenomena. We start this process in the next chapter by examining a macroeconomic model of demand and supply—a model of *aggregate* demand and *aggregate* supply.

SUMMARY

The Circular Flow of Expenditure and Income

All economic agents—households, firms, government, and the rest of the world—interact in the circular flow of income and expenditure. Households sell factors of production to firms and buy consumption goods and services from firms. Firms hire factors of production from households and pay incomes to households in exchange for factor services. Firms sell consumption goods and services to households and capital goods to other firms. Government collects taxes from households and firms, makes transfer payments under various social programs to households, and buys goods and services from firms. Foreigners buy goods from domestic firms and sell goods to them.

The flow of expenditure on final goods and services winds up as somebody's income. Therefore,

$$\text{Aggregate income} = \text{Aggregate expenditure}.$$

Furthermore, expenditure on final goods and services is a method of valuing the output of the economy. Therefore,

$$\text{GDP} = \text{Aggregate expenditure} = \text{Aggregate income}.$$

From the firm's accounts we know that

$$Y = C + I + G + EX - IM,$$

and from the household's accounts we know that

$$Y = C + S + T.$$

Combining these two equations, we obtain

$$I + G + EX = S + T + IM.$$

This equation tells us that injections into the circular flow (left side) equal the leakages from the circular flow (right side). (pp. 129–135)

U.S. National Income and Product Accounts

Because aggregate expenditure, aggregate income, and the value of output are equal, national income accountants can measure GDP using one of two approaches: the expenditure approach and the factor incomes approach.

The expenditure approach adds together consumption expenditure, investment, government purchases of goods and services, and net exports to arrive at an estimate of GDP.

The factor incomes approach adds together the incomes paid to the various factors of production plus profit paid to the owners of firms. To use the factor incomes approach, it is necessary to make an adjustment from the factor cost value of GDP to the market price value by adding indirect taxes and subtracting subsidies. It is also necessary to add capital consumption in order to arrive at GDP.

To value the output of a firm or sector in the economy, we measure value added. The use of value added avoids double counting. (pp. 135–140)

The Price Level and Inflation

There are two major price indexes that measure the price level and inflation: the Consumer Price Index and the GDP deflator.

The CPI measures the average level of prices of goods and services typically consumed by an urban family in the United States. The CPI is the ratio of the value of a base-period basket of commodities at current-period prices to the same basket valued at base-period prices, multiplied by 100.

The GDP deflator is nominal GDP divided by real GDP, multiplied by 100. Nominal GDP is calculated by valuing current-period quantities produced at current-period prices. Real GDP is calculated by valuing the quantities produced in the current period at the prices that prevailed in the base period.

In interpreting changes in prices, we need to distinguish between inflation and relative price changes. A relative price is the price of one good in terms of another good. Relative prices are constantly changing. We cannot tell anything about the sources of inflation by studying which relative prices have changed most. Any relative price changes can occur with any inflation rate.

Because relative prices are constantly changing and causing consumers to substitute less expensive items for more expensive items, because of the disappearance of some goods and the arrival of new goods, and because of quality changes, the CPI is an imperfect measure of the cost of living, especially when comparisons are made across a long time span. (pp. 140–148)

Real GDP, Aggregate Economic Activity, and Economic Well-Being

Real GDP is not a perfect measure of aggregate economic activity or of economic welfare. It excludes production in the underground economy, household production, environmental damage, and the contribution to economic welfare of equality and leisure. (pp. 148–152)

KEY ELEMENTS

Key Terms

Aggregate income, 129
Capital stock, 136
Consumer Price Index, 141
Consumption expenditure, 129
Depreciation, 137
Disposable income, 133
Double counting, 139
Economic welfare, 148
Expenditure approach, 135
Factor cost, 137
Factor incomes approach, 136
GDP deflator, 141
Gross investment, 137
Gross national product, 139
Indirect tax, 137
Injections, 133
Inventories, 136
Investment, 129
Leakages, 133
Market price, 137
Net domestic income at factor cost, 137
Net domestic product at market prices, 137
Net exports, 132
Net investment, 137
Relative price, 146
Saving, 133
Subsidy, 137
Transfer payments, 131
Underground economy, 149
Value added, 138

Key Figures and Tables

REVIEW QUESTIONS

1 List the components of aggregate expenditure.

2 What are the components of aggregate income?

3 Why does aggregate income equal aggregate expenditure?

4 Why does the value of output (or GDP) equal aggregate income?

5 Distinguish between government purchases of goods and services and transfer payments.

6 What are injections into the circular flow of expenditure and income? What are leakages?

7 Explain why injections into the circular flow of income and expenditure equal leakages from it.

8 How does the Department of Commerce measure GDP?

9 Explain the expenditure approach to measuring GDP.

10 Explain the factor incomes approach to measuring GDP.

11 What is the distinction between expenditure on final goods and expenditure on intermediate goods?

12 What is value added? How is it calculated? What does the sum of value added by all firms equal?

13 What are the two main price indexes used to measure the price level and inflation?

14 How is the Consumer Price Index calculated?

15 How is the basket of goods and services used in constructing the CPI chosen? Is it the same basket in 1992 as it was in 1952? If not, how is it different?

16 How is the GDP deflator calculated?

17 Explain what a relative price change is.

18 How can relative price changes be identified in periods when the inflation rates are different?

19 Is the CPI a good measure to use to compare the cost of living today with that in the 1930s? If not, why not?

20 Is GDP a good measure of economic welfare? If not, why not?

PROBLEMS

1 The following transactions took place in Ecoland last year:

Item	Value of transaction (billions of dollars)
Wages paid to labor	$800,000
Consumption expenditure	600,000
Taxes paid on wages	200,000
Government transfer payments	50,000
Firms' profits	200,000
Investment	250,000
Taxes paid on profits	50,000
Government purchases of goods and services	200,000
Export earnings	300,000
Saving	250,000
Import payments	250,000

a Calculate Ecoland's GDP.

b Did you use the expenditure approach or the factor incomes approach to answer part (a)?

c Does your answer to part (a) value output in terms of market prices or factor cost? Why?

d What extra information do you need in order to calculate net domestic product?

2 Cindy, the owner of The Great Cookie, spends $100 on eggs, $50 on flour, $45 on milk, $10 on utilities, and $60 on wages to produce 200 great cookies. Cindy sells her cookies for $1.50 each. Calculate the value added per cookie at The Great Cookie.

3 A typical family living on Sandy Island consumes only apple juice, bananas, and cloth. Prices in the base year are $4 a gallon for apple juice, $3 a pound for bananas, and $5 a yard for cloth. The typical family spends $40 on apple juice, $45 on bananas, and $25 on cloth. In the current year, apple juice costs $3 a gallon, bananas cost $4 a pound, and cloth costs $7 a yard. Calculate the Consumer Price Index on Sandy Island in the current year and the inflation rate between the base year and the current year.

4 The newspaper on Sandy Island, commenting on the inflation figures that you calculated in problem 3, runs the headline "Inflation Results from Increases in Cloth Prices." Write a letter to the editor pointing out the weakness in the economic reasoning of that paper's business reporter.

5 An economy has the following real GDP and nominal GDP in 1991 and 1992:

Year	Real GDP	Nominal GDP
1990	$1,000 billion	$1,000 billion
1991	$1,050 billion	$1,200 billion
1992	$1,200 billion	$1,500 billion

a What was the GDP deflator in 1991?

b What was the GDP deflator in 1992?

c What is the inflation rate as measured by the GDP deflator between 1991 and 1992?

d What is the percentage increase in the price level between 1990 and 1992 as measured by the GDP deflator?

CHAPTER 7

Aggregate Demand and Aggregate Supply

After studying this chapter, you will be able to:

- Define aggregate demand and explain what determines it
- Explain the sources of growth and fluctuations in aggregate demand
- Define aggregate supply and explain what determines it
- Explain the sources of growth and fluctuations in aggregate supply
- Define macroeconomic equilibrium
- Predict the effects of changes in aggregate demand and aggregate supply on real GDP and the price level
- Explain why real GDP grows and why we have recessions
- Explain why we have inflation and why its rate varies, sometimes exploding as it did in the 1970s

What Makes Our Garden Grow

IN THE 30 YEARS FROM 1964 TO 1994, U.S. real GDP more than doubled. In fact, a doubling of real GDP every 30 years has been routine. What forces drive our economy to grow? ◆ ◆ At the same time as real GDP has been growing, we've experienced persistent inflation. Today, you need $400 to buy what $100 would have bought in 1960. Most of this inflation occurred in the 1970s, when the price level more than doubled. What causes inflation? And why did it explode in the 1970s? ◆ ◆ The U.S. economy doesn't grow at a constant pace. Instead, it ebbs and flows over the business cycle. For example, as the 1990s opened, a recession slowed down real GDP growth. What makes real GDP grow unevenly, sometimes speeding up and sometimes slowing down or even shrinking? ◆ ◆ Sometimes the economy receives a massive shock from some other part of the world. For example, in the summer of 1990 when Saddam Hussein invaded Kuwait, world oil prices increased. But not all the shocks hitting our economy come from abroad. Some are homemade and stem from the actions of the government and the Federal Reserve Board in Washington. How do such foreign and domestic shocks affect prices and production?

◆ ◆ ◆ ◆ To answer questions like these, we need a model—a macroeconomic model. Our first task in this chapter is to build such a model—the *aggregate demand–aggregate supply model*. Our second task is to use the aggregate demand–aggregate supply model to answer the questions we've just posed. You'll discover that this powerful theory of aggregate demand and aggregate supply enables us to analyze and predict many important economic events that have a major impact on our lives.

FIGURE 7.1

The Aggregate Demand Curve and Aggregate Demand Schedule

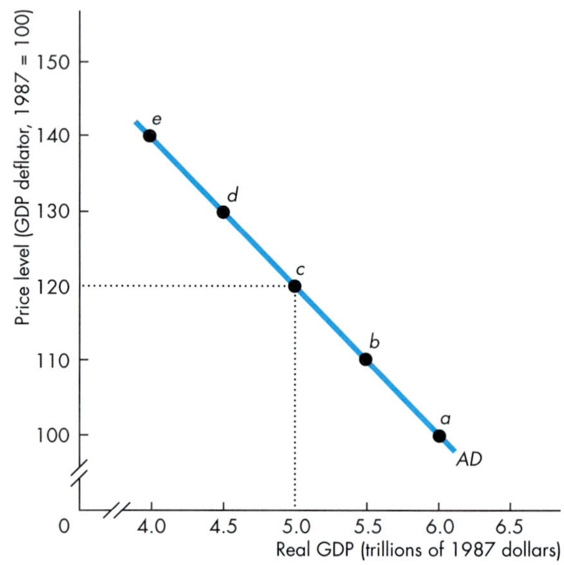

	Price level (GDP deflator)	Real GDP (trillions of 1987 dollars)
a	**100**	**6.0**
b	**110**	**5.5**
c	**120**	**5.0**
d	**130**	**4.5**
e	**140**	**4.0**

The aggregate demand curve (*AD*) traces the quantity of real GDP demanded as the price level varies, holding everything else constant. The aggregate demand curve is derived from the schedule in the table. Each point *a* through *e* on the curve corresponds to the row in the table identified by the same letter. Thus when the price level is 120, the quantity of real GDP demanded is 5.0 trillion 1987 dollars, as illustrated by point *c* in the figure.

Aggregate Demand

The aggregate quantity of goods and services produced is measured as real GDP—GDP valued in constant dollars. The average price of all these goods and services is measured by the GDP deflator. We are going to build a model that determines the values of real GDP and the GDP deflator. The model that we will build is based on the same concepts of demand, supply, and equilibrium that you met in Chapter 4. But here the good is not tapes—it is real GDP—and the price is not the price of tapes—it is the GDP deflator.

The **aggregate quantity of goods and services demanded** is the sum of the quantities of consumption goods and services that households plan to buy, of investment goods that firms plan to buy, of goods and services that governments plan to buy, and of net exports that foreigners plan to buy. Thus the aggregate quantity of goods and services demanded depends on decisions made by households, firms, governments, and foreigners. When we studied the demand for tapes in Chapter 4, we summarized the buying plans of households in a demand schedule and a demand curve. Similarly, when we study the forces influencing aggregate buying plans, we summarize the decisions of households, firms, governments, and foreigners by using an aggregate demand schedule and an aggregate demand curve.

An **aggregate demand schedule** lists the quantity of real GDP demanded at each price level, holding all other influences on buying plans constant. The **aggregate demand curve** plots the quantity of real GDP demanded against the price level. **Aggregate demand** is the entire relationship between the quantity of real GDP demanded and the price level.

Figure 7.1 shows an aggregate demand schedule and an aggregate demand curve. Each row of the table corresponds to a point in the figure. For example, row *c* of the aggregate demand schedule tells us that if the price level (the GDP deflator) is 120, the level of real GDP demanded is 5 trillion 1987 dollars. This row is plotted as point *c* on the aggregate demand curve.

In constructing the aggregate demand schedule and aggregate demand curve, we hold constant all the influences on the quantity of real GDP demanded other than the price level. The effect of a change in the price level is shown as a movement along the aggregate demand curve. A change in any of the other influences on the quantity of real GDP demanded results in a new aggregate demand schedule and a shift in the aggregate demand curve. First, let's concentrate on the effects of a change in the price level on the quantity of real GDP demanded.

You can see from the downward slope of the aggregate demand curve, and from the numbers that describe the aggregate demand schedule, that the higher the price level, the smaller is the quantity of real GDP demanded. Why does the aggregate demand curve slope downward?

Why the Aggregate Demand Curve Slopes Downward

The demand curve for a single good slopes downward because people substitute one good for another as prices change. If the price of Coca-Cola rises, the quantity of Coca-Cola demanded falls because some people switch to drinking Pepsi-Cola and other substitutes. The demand curve for a whole class of goods and services also slopes downward because of substitution effects. If the prices of Coca-Cola, Pepsi-Cola, and all other sodas rise, the quantity of soda demanded falls because some people switch from soda to other substitute drinks and other goods. But why does the demand curve for *all* goods and services slope downward? If the price of all goods increases and people demand less of *all* goods, what do they demand more of? What do they substitute for goods and services?

There are three groups of substitutes for the goods and services that make up current U.S. real GDP. They are

- Money and financial assets
- Goods and services in the future
- Goods and services produced in other countries

People may plan to buy a smaller quantity of the goods and services that make up real GDP and hold a larger quantity of money or other financial assets. They may plan to buy a smaller quantity of goods and services today but a larger quantity at some time in the future. Also, people may decide to buy a smaller quantity of the goods and services made in the United States and buy a larger quantity of the goods and services made in other countries. These decisions are influenced by the price level, and those influences result in the aggregate demand curve sloping downward.

There are three separate effects of the price level on the quantity of real GDP demanded. They are the following:

- Real money balances effect
- Intertemporal substitution effect
- International substitution effect

Real Money Balances Effect The **real money balances effect** is the influence of a change in the quantity of real money on the quantity of real GDP demanded. The **quantity of money** is the quantity of currency, bank deposits, and deposits at other types of financial institutions, such as savings and loan associations and thrift institutions, held by households and firms. **Real money** is a measure of money based on the quantity of goods and services that it will buy. Real money is measured as dollars divided by the price level. For example, suppose that you have $20 in notes and coins in your pocket and $480 in the bank. The quantity of money that you are holding is $500. Suppose that you continue to hold $500 but that the price level increases by 25 percent. Then your real money holdings decrease by 25 percent. That is, the $500 of money that you are holding will now buy what $400 would have bought before the price level increase.

The real money balances effect is the influence of the quantity of real money on the quantity of goods and services bought. Other things being equal, the larger the quantity of real money people are holding, the larger is the quantity of goods and services bought. To understand the real money balances effect, let's think about how the Sony Corporation's spending plans are influenced by its real money holdings.

Suppose that Sony has $20 million in the bank. Furthermore, suppose that Sony has decided that it doesn't want to change the way it's holding its assets. It doesn't want to have less money and more capital equipment in its production and distribution plants. And it doesn't want to sell off some of its productive assets in order to hold more money.

Now suppose that prices fall. Among the prices that fall are those of office buildings, computers, movie studios, and all the other things that Sony owns and operates. The money that Sony is now holding buys more of these and other goods than it would have before. Sony's got *more* real money. But its other equipment is now worth less than before. This fall in the price level has increased Sony's holdings of real money and decreased the value of its holdings of capital equipment. Sony will now take advantage of the fact that it is holding a larger amount of real money to buy some additional capital equipment. But new buildings, plant, and machinery are some of the goods that make up real GDP. Thus Sony's decision to use its extra real money to buy more plant and equipment results in an increase in the quantity of goods and services demanded—an increase in real GDP demanded.

Of course, although Sony is a multinational giant, if only it behaves in this way, real GDP demanded will not increase much. The real money balances effect will be tiny. But if everyone behaves like Sony, the aggregate quantity of goods and services demanded will be larger than before. This increase in the quantity of goods and services demanded results from a fall in the price level.

The real money balances effect is the first reason why the aggregate demand curve slopes downward. A decrease in the price level increases the quantity of real money. The larger the quantity of real money, the larger is the quantity of goods and services demanded.

Intertemporal Substitution Effect The substitution of goods and services now for goods and services later or of goods and services later for goods and services now is called **intertemporal substitution.** An example of intertemporal substitution is your decision to buy a Walkman today instead of waiting until the end of the month. Another example is IBM's decision to speed up its installation of a new computer production plant. Yet another example is your decision to postpone that long-hoped-for vacation.

An important influence on intertemporal substitution is the level of interest rates. Low interest rates encourage people to borrow and change the timing of their spending on capital goods—plant and equipment, houses, and consumer durable goods—shifting some of that spending from the future to the present. High interest rates discourage people from borrowing and change the timing of their spending on goods—shifting some of that spending from the present to the future.

Interest rates, in turn, are influenced by the quantity of real money. We have just seen that the quantity of real money increases if the price level falls. We've also seen that the more real money people have, the larger is the quantity of goods and services they demand. But people do not necessarily have to use all their additional real money to buy other goods. They may lend some of it to others or use some of it to decrease their own borrowing. Some people are borrowers, and others are lenders. Borrowers who have experienced an increase in their real money holdings now need to borrow less and so decrease their demand for loans. Lenders whose real money holdings have increased are now willing to lend even more, and so they increase their supply of loans. A decrease in the demand for loans and an increase in their supply results in a fall in interest rates. And lower interest rates lead to an intertemporal substitution effect—shifting spending plans from the future to the present and increasing the quantity of goods and services demanded.

An increase in the price level decreases the quantity of real money and has the opposite effect on spending plans. With a decrease in the quantity of real money, people to some degree decrease their spending plans (real money balances effect) and decrease their supply of loans or increase their demand for loans. As a consequence, interest rates increase and spending is shifted from the present to the future (intertemporal substitution effect).

This intertemporal substitution effect is the second reason why the aggregate demand curve slopes downward. A lower price level:

- Increases the quantity of real money
- Increases the supply of loans
- Decreases the demand for loans
- Lowers interest rates
- Shifts spending from the future to the present and increases the quantity of goods and services demanded

Let's now look at the third reason why the aggregate demand curve slopes downward.

International Substitution Effect The substitution of domestic goods and services for foreign goods and services, or of foreign goods and services for domestic goods and services, is **international substitution.** An example of international substitution is your decision to buy a Toyota (made in Japan) instead of a General Motors car (made in Detroit). Another example of international substitution is the decision by the British government to equip its armed forces with U.S.-produced weapons rather than weapons made in Great Britain. Yet another example is your decision to take a skiing vacation in the Canadian Rockies instead of Colorado.

If the U.S. price level falls, holding everything else constant, U.S.-made goods become cheaper and therefore more attractive relative to goods made in other countries. Americans will plan to buy more domestically produced goods and fewer imports, and foreigners will plan to buy more U.S.-made goods and fewer of their own domestically produced goods. Thus, at a lower U.S. price level, people and firms will demand a larger quantity of goods and services produced in the United States. International substitution gives us the third reason for the downward slope of the aggregate demand curve.

Changes in the Quantity of Real GDP Demanded

When the price level changes, other things remaining constant, there is a change in the quantity of real GDP demanded. Such a change is illustrated as a movement along the aggregate demand curve. Figure 7.2 illustrates changes in the quantity of real GDP demanded. It also summarizes the three reasons why the aggregate demand curve slopes downward.

REVIEW

The aggregate demand curve traces the effects of a change in the price level—GDP deflator—on the aggregate quantity of goods and services demanded—real GDP demanded. The effect of a change in the price level is shown as a movement along the aggregate demand curve. Other things being equal, the higher the price level, the smaller is the quantity of real GDP demanded—the aggregate demand curve slopes downward. ◆◆ The aggregate demand curve slopes downward for three reasons: money and goods are substitutes (*real money balances effect*); goods today and goods in the future are substitutes (*intertemporal substitution effect*); domestic goods and foreign goods are substitutes (*international substitution effect*). ◆

FIGURE 7.2

Changes in the Quantity of Real GDP Demanded

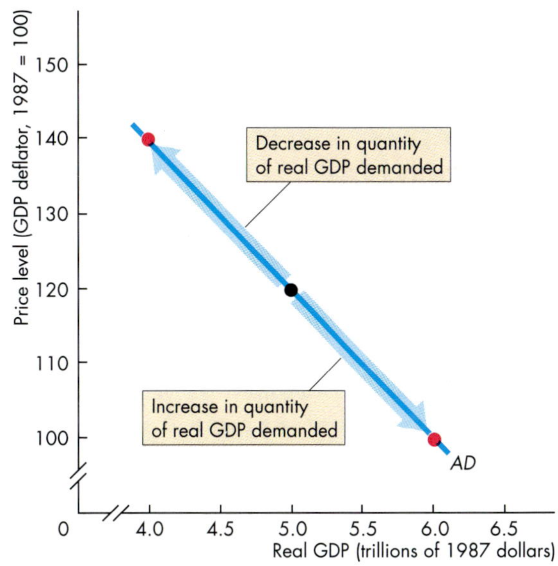

The quantity of real GDP demanded

Decreases if the price level *increases*	*Increases* if the price level *decreases*

because of the:

Real money balances effect

◆ An increase in the price level decreases the real money supply	◆ A decrease in the price level increases the real money supply

Intertemporal substitution effect

◆ An increase in the price level increases interest rates	◆ A decrease in the price level decreases interest rates

International substitution effect

◆ An increase in the price level increases the cost of domestic goods and services relative to foreign goods and services	◆ A decrease in the price level decreases the cost of domestic goods and services relative to foreign goods and services

Changes in Aggregate Demand

The aggregate demand schedule and aggregate demand curve describe aggregate demand at a point in time. But aggregate demand does not remain constant. It frequently changes. As a consequence, the aggregate demand curve frequently shifts. The main influences on aggregate demand that shift the aggregate demand curve are

- Fiscal policy
- Monetary policy
- International factors
- Expectations

Fiscal Policy

The government's decisions about its purchases of goods and services, taxes, and transfer payments have important effects on aggregate demand. The government's attempt to influence the economy using its spending and taxes is called **fiscal policy.**

Government Purchases of Goods and Services The scale of government purchases of goods and services has a direct effect on aggregate demand. If taxes are held constant, the more weapons, highways, schools, and colleges the government demands, the larger are government purchases of goods and services and so the larger is aggregate demand. The most important changes in government purchases of goods and services that influence aggregate demand arise from the state of international tension and conflict. In times of war, government purchases increase dramatically. In this century, increases in government purchases during World War II, the Korean War, and the Vietnam War and decreases following those episodes exerted a large influence on aggregate demand. Compared with these wars, the increased government purchases during the Gulf War of 1991 were small and had a modest effect on aggregate demand.

Taxes and Transfer Payments A decrease in taxes increases aggregate demand. An increase in transfer payments—unemployment benefits, social security benefits, and other welfare payments—also increases aggregate demand. Both of these influences operate by increasing households' *disposable* income. The higher the level of disposable income, the greater is the demand for goods and services. Since lower taxes and higher transfer payments increase disposable income, they also increase aggregate demand.

This source of changes in aggregate demand has been an important one in recent years. Through the late 1960s, there was a large increase in government payments under various social programs, and these led to a sustained increase in aggregate demand. During the 1980s, Reagan's tax cuts increased aggregate demand.

Monetary Policy

Decisions made by the Federal Reserve Board (the Fed) about the money supply and interest rates have important effects on aggregate demand. The Fed's attempt to influence the economy by varying the money supply and interest rates is called **monetary policy.**

Money Supply The money supply is determined by the Fed and the banks (in a process described in Chapters 10 and 11). The greater the *quantity of money,* the greater is the level of aggregate demand. An easy way to see why money affects aggregate demand is to imagine what would happen if the Fed borrowed the Army's helicopters, loaded them with millions of dollars worth of new $10 bills, and sprinkled the bills like confetti across the nation. We would all stop whatever we were doing and rush out to pick up our share of the newly available money. But we wouldn't just put the money we picked up in the bank. We would spend some of it, so our demand for goods and services would increase. Although this story is pretty extreme, it does illustrate that an increase in the quantity of money increases aggregate demand.

In practice, changes in the quantity of money change interest rates and so have an additional influence on aggregate demand by affecting investment and the demand for consumer durables. When the Fed speeds up the rate at which new money is being injected into the economy, there's a tendency for interest rates to fall. When the Fed slows down the pace at which it is creating money, there's a tendency for interest rates to rise. Thus a change in the quantity of money has a second effect on aggregate demand, operating through its effects on interest rates.

Interest Rates Interest rates change for many reasons. We've already seen that they change when the price level changes and that such changes lead to a movement along the aggregate demand curve. But if the Fed takes actions to increase interest rates *at a given price level,* aggregate demand decreases and there is a shift in the aggregate demand curve. Faced with higher interest rates, firms and households cut back on spending, especially investment, to avoid higher interest costs or to take advantage of higher returns on loans.

Fluctuations in the quantity of money and fluctuations in interest rates induced by those fluctuations have been some of the most important sources of changes in aggregate demand. Sustained increases in the quantity of money through the 1970s increased aggregate demand, contributing to the inflation of those years; decreases in the growth rate of the quantity of money slowed aggregate demand growth, contributing to the recessions of 1981 and 1991.

International Factors

There are two main international factors that influence aggregate demand. They are the foreign exchange rate and foreign income.

The Foreign Exchange Rate We've seen that a change in the U.S. price level, other things being equal, leads to a change in the prices of U.S.-produced goods and services relative to the prices of goods and services produced in other countries. Another important influence on the price of U.S.-produced goods and services relative to those produced abroad is the *foreign exchange rate.* The foreign exchange rate affects aggregate demand because it affects the prices that foreigners have to pay for U.S.-produced goods and services and the prices that we have to pay for foreign-produced goods and services.

Suppose that the dollar is worth 125 Japanese yen. You can buy a Toshiba computer (made in Japan) that costs 125,000 yen for $1,000. What if for $900 you can buy a Zenith computer (made in the United States) that is just as good as the Toshiba, which costs 125,000 yen? In such a case, you will buy the Zenith.

But which computer will you buy if the value of the U.S. dollar rises to 150 yen and everything else remains the same? Let's work out the answer. At 150 yen per dollar, you pay only $833.33 to buy the 125,000 yen needed to buy the Toshiba computer. Since the Zenith computer costs $900, the Toshiba is now cheaper and you will substitute the Toshiba computer for the Zenith. The demand for U.S.-made computers falls as the foreign exchange value of the dollar rises. So as the foreign exchange value of the dollar rises, with everything else held constant, aggregate demand decreases.

There have been huge swings in the foreign exchange value of the dollar through the 1980s, leading to large swings in aggregate demand.

Foreign Income The income of foreigners affects the aggregate demand for domestically produced goods and services. For example, an increase in income in Japan and Germany increases the demand by Japanese and German consumers and producers for U.S.-made consumption goods and capital goods. These sources of change in aggregate demand have been important ones since World War II. The rapid economic growth of Japan and Western Europe and of some of the newly industrializing countries of the Pacific Rim, such as Korea and Singapore, has led to a sustained increase in demand for U.S.-made goods and services.

Expectations

Expectations about all aspects of future economic conditions play a crucial role in determining current decisions. But three expectations are especially important. They are expectations about future inflation, future incomes, and future profits.

Expected Future Inflation An increase in the expected inflation rate, other things being equal, leads to an increase in aggregate demand. The higher the expected inflation rate, the higher is the expected price of goods and services in the future and the lower is the expected real value of money and other assets in the future. As a consequence, when people expect a higher inflation rate, they plan to buy more goods and services in the present and hold smaller quantities of money and other financial assets.

There were changes in inflation expectations during the 1980s. At the beginning of the decade, people expected inflation to persist at close to 10 percent a year. But a severe recession in 1982 reduced those inflation expectations. Other things being equal, the effect of this decrease in inflation expectations was to decrease aggregate demand.

Expected Future Incomes An increase in expected future income, other things being equal, increases the amount that households plan to spend on consumption goods and consumer durables. When households expect slow future income growth, or even a decline in income, they scale back their spending plans.

Expectations about future income growth were pessimistic during 1990, and this factor contributed to the decrease in spending that brought on a recession in 1991.

Expected Future Profits A change in expected future profits changes firms' demands for new capital equipment. For example, suppose that there has been a recent wave of technological change that has increased productivity. Firms will expect that by installing new equipment that uses the latest technology, their future profits will rise. This expectation leads to an increase in demand for new plant and equipment and to an increase in aggregate demand.

Profit expectations were pessimistic in 1981 and led to a decrease in aggregate demand. Expectations were optimistic through most of the mid-1980s, leading to sustained increases in aggregate demand.

Now that we've reviewed the factors that influence aggregate demand, let's summarize their effects on the aggregate demand curve.

Shifts of the Aggregate Demand Curve

We illustrate a change in aggregate demand as a shift in the aggregate demand curve. Figure 7.3 illustrates two changes in aggregate demand and summarizes the factors bringing about such changes. Aggregate demand is initially AD_0, the same as in Fig. 7.1.

The aggregate demand curve shifts to the right, from AD_0 to AD_1, when government purchases of goods and services increase, taxes are cut, transfer payments increase, the money supply increases and interest rates fall, the foreign exchange rate falls, income in the rest of the world increases, expected future profits increase, expected future incomes increase, or the expected inflation rate increases.

The aggregate demand curve shifts to the left, from AD_0 to AD_2, when government purchases of goods and services decrease, taxes are increased, transfer payments decrease, the money supply decreases and interest rates rise, the foreign

FIGURE 7.3
Changes in Aggregate Demand

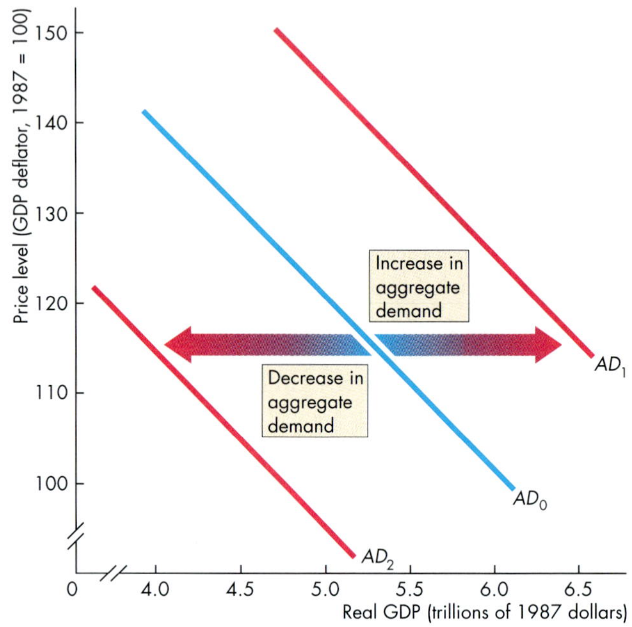

Aggregate demand

Decreases if
- Fiscal policy decreases government spending, increases taxes, or decreases transfer payments
- Monetary policy decreases the money supply or increases interest rates
- The exchange rate increases or foreign income decreases
- Expected inflation, expected income, or expected profits decrease

Increases if
- Fiscal policy increases government spending, decreases taxes, or increases transfer payments
- Monetary policy increases the money supply or decreases interest rates
- The exchange rate decreases or foreign income increases
- Expected inflation, expected income, or expected profits increase

exchange rate rises, income in the rest of the world decreases, expected future profits decrease, expected future incomes decrease, or the expected inflation rate decreases.

Time Lags in Influences on Aggregate Demand

The effects of the influences on aggregate demand that we've considered do not occur instantly. They occur with time lags. A *time lag* is a delay in the response to a stimulus. For example, when you take a pill to cure a headache, the headache doesn't go away immediately—the medication works with a time lag. In a similar way, monetary policy influences aggregate demand with a time lag, one that spreads out over many months. For example, if the Fed increases the money supply, at first there is no change in aggregate demand. A little later, as people reallocate their wealth, there is an increase in the supply of loans and interest rates fall. Later yet, confronted with lower interest rates, households and firms increase their purchases of goods and services. The total effect of the initial change in the quantity of money is spread out over many months.

The next time the Fed takes exactly the same action, there is no guarantee that its effects will take place with exactly the same timing as before. The time lags in the effects of monetary policy on aggregate demand are both spread out and variable and, to a degree, unpredictable.

REVIEW

A change in the price level leads to a change in the aggregate quantity of goods and services demanded. That change is shown as a movement along the aggregate demand curve. A change in any other influence on aggregate demand shifts the aggregate demand curve. These other influences include:

- Fiscal policy
- Monetary policy
- International factors
- Expectations

Aggregate Supply

The **aggregate quantity of goods and services supplied** is the sum of the quantities of all final goods and services produced by all firms in the economy. It is measured as real gross domestic product supplied. In studying aggregate supply, we distinguish between two macroeconomic time frames: the short run and the long run.

Two Macroeconomic Time Frames

The **macroeconomic short-run** is a period during which the prices of goods and services change in response to changes in demand and supply but the prices of factors of production—wage rates and the prices of raw materials—do not change. The short run is an important time frame for two reasons. First, wage rates are determined by labor contracts that run for up to three years. As a result, wage rates change more slowly than prices. Second, the prices of some raw materials, especially oil, are strongly influenced by the actions of a small number of producers that keep the price steady in some periods but change it by a large amount in others.

The **macroeconomic long-run** is a period that is sufficiently long for the prices of all the factors of production—wage rates and other factor prices—to have adjusted to any disturbance so that the quantities demanded and supplied are equal in all markets—goods and services markets, labor markets, and the markets for other factors of production. In the macroeconomic long-run, with wage rates having adjusted to bring equality between the quantities of labor demanded and supplied, there is *full employment*. Equivalently, unemployment is at its *natural rate*.

Short-Run Aggregate Supply

Short-run aggregate supply is the relationship between the aggregate quantity of final goods and services (real GDP) supplied and the price level (the GDP deflator), holding everything else constant. We can represent short-run aggregate supply as either a short-run aggregate supply schedule or a short-run aggregate supply curve. The **short-run aggregate supply schedule** lists the quantity of real GDP supplied at each price level, holding everything else constant. The **short-run aggregate supply curve** plots the relationship between the quantity of real GDP supplied and the price level, holding everything else constant.

Figure 7.4 shows a short-run aggregate supply schedule and the corresponding short-run aggregate supply curve (labeled *SAS*). Part (a) shows the entire curve, and part (b) zooms in on the range of the curve where the economy normally operates. Each row of the aggregate supply schedule corresponds to

FIGURE 7.4

The Aggregate Supply Curves and Aggregate Supply Schedule

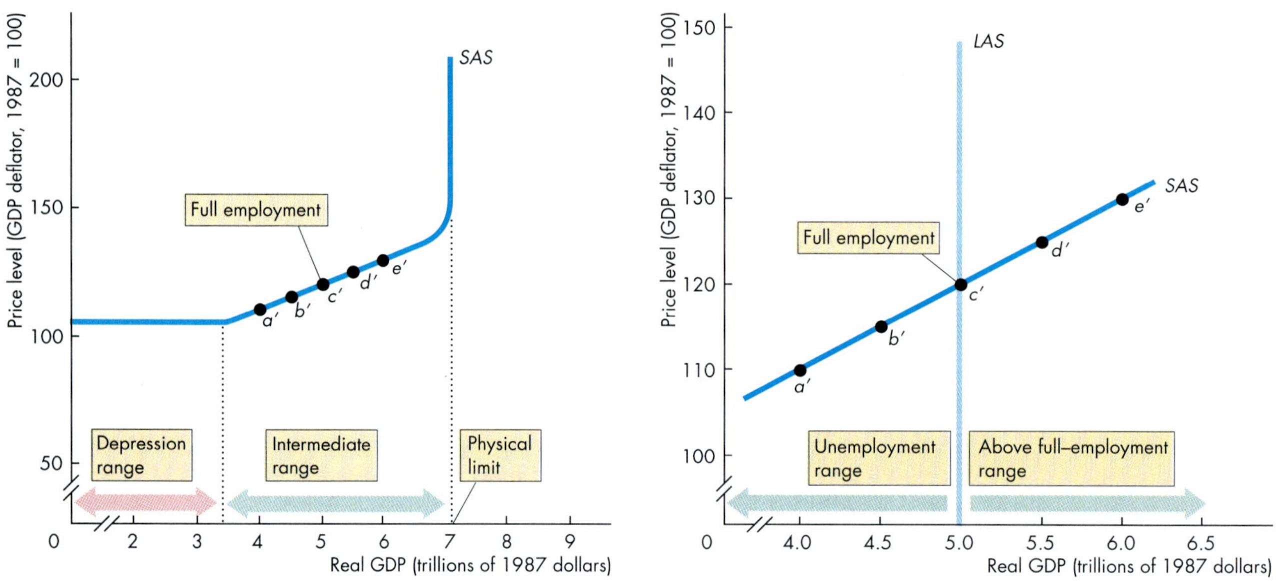

(a) The short-run aggregate supply curve

(b) The short-run and long-run aggregate supply curves

	Price level (GDP deflator)	Real GDP (trillions of 1987 dollars)
Depression range	**105**	**0 to 3.5**
a′	**110**	**4.0**
b′	**115**	**4.5**
c′	**120**	**5.0**
d′	**125**	**5.5**
e′	**130**	**6.0**
Physical limit	**Above 200**	**7.0**

The short-run aggregate supply curve (*SAS*) traces the quantity of real GDP supplied as the price level varies, holding everything else constant. The short-run aggregate supply curves in this figure are derived from the schedule in the table. Part (a) shows the *SAS* curve over its entire range, and part (b) zooms in on the intermediate range. In a depression, firms are willing to increase the quantity sold with no increase in price and the *SAS* curve is horizontal. At its physical limit, the economy can squeeze out no more production and the *SAS* curve becomes vertical. Normally, the economy operates in the upward-sloping intermediate range. In that range, full employment occurs at *c′*, where real GDP is $5.0 trillion.

The long-run aggregate supply curve (*LAS*) shows the relationship between full-employment real GDP and the price level. This level of real GDP is independent of the price level, so the *LAS* curve is vertical as shown in part (b). At levels of real GDP below the long-run level, unemployment is above the natural rate, and at levels of real GDP above the long-run level, unemployment is below the natural rate.

a point in the figure. For example, row *a*' of the short-run aggregate supply schedule and point *a*' on the curve tell us that if the price level is 110 (GDP deflator is 110), the quantity of real GDP supplied is 4.0 trillion 1987 dollars.

Focus first on the entire short-run aggregate supply curve in Fig. 7.4(a). This curve has three ranges. It is horizontal over the depression range, upward sloping over the intermediate range, and vertical at the physical limit of the economy's ability to produce goods and services. Why is the short-run aggregate curve horizontal in the depression range? Why does it slope upward over the intermediate range? And why does it eventually become vertical?

The Depression Range When the economy is severely depressed, firms have lots of excess capacity and are anxious to sell whatever they can at the going price. They would be glad to be able to sell more and willing to offer it for sale with no inducement from a higher price. Thus each firm has a horizontal supply curve. Since each firm has a horizontal supply curve, the aggregate supply curve is also horizontal. The last time the economy was on the depression range of its *SAS* curve was in the 1930s.

The Intermediate Range Normally, the economy operates in the upward-sloping intermediate range of its *SAS* curve. That's why we've zoomed in on this range in Fig. 7.4(b), and it is this part of the *SAS* curve that we'll use in the rest of the book.

To see why the short-run aggregate supply curve slopes upward, think about the supply curve of tapes. When the price of tapes rises and the wages of the workers in the tape factory remain constant, tape producers offer a larger quantity of tapes for sale. There is an increase in the quantity of tapes supplied. What's true for tape factories is also true for Coke bottling plants, auto assembly lines, and firms producing every other good and service. Thus, when prices rise but factor prices remain constant, the aggregate quantity of goods and services supplied—real GDP supplied—increases.

To increase their output in the short run, firms hire additional labor and work their existing labor force for longer hours. Thus a change in the price level, with wage rates held constant, leads to a change in the aggregate quantity of goods and services supplied and to a change in the level of employment and unemployment. The higher the price level, the greater is the aggregate quantity of goods and services supplied, the higher is the level of employment, and the lower is the level of unemployment.

The Physical Limit to Real GDP At some level of real GDP, the short-run aggregate supply curve becomes vertical because there is a physical limit to the output the economy can produce. If prices increase while wages remain constant, each firm increases its output. It does so by working its labor overtime, hiring more labor, and working its plant and equipment at a faster pace. But there is a limit to the amount of overtime workers are willing to accept. There is also a limit below which the unemployment rate cannot be pushed. And there is a limit beyond which firms are not willing to operate their plant and equipment because of the high cost of wear and tear and breakdowns. Once these limits are reached, no more output is produced, no matter how high prices rise relative to wages. At that output, the short-run aggregate supply curve becomes vertical. In the example in Fig. 7.4, when the economy is operating at its physical limit, real GDP is $7 trillion.

Long-Run Aggregate Supply

Long-run aggregate supply is the relationship between the aggregate quantity of final goods and services (real GDP) supplied and the price level (GDP deflator) when there is full employment.

The Long-Run Aggregate Supply Curve Long-run aggregate supply is represented by the long-run aggregate supply curve. The **long-run aggregate supply curve** plots the relationship between the quantity of real GDP supplied and the price level when there is full employment. The long-run aggregate supply curve is vertical and is illustrated in Fig. 7.4(b) as *LAS*. In this example, full employment occurs when real GDP is $5 trillion. If real GDP is below this amount, a smaller quantity of labor is required and unemployment rises above its natural rate. The economy operates in the unemployment range shown in Fig. 7.4(b). If real GDP is greater than $5 trillion, a larger quantity of labor is required and unemployment falls below its natural rate. The economy operates in the above full-employment range shown in Fig. 7.4(b).

Pay special attention to the *position* of the *LAS* curve. It is a vertical line that intersects the short-run aggregate supply curve at point *c*' on its upward-sloping intermediate range. It does not coincide with the vertical part of the *SAS* curve, where the economy is operating at its physical production limit.

Why is the long-run aggregate supply curve vertical? And why is long-run aggregate supply less than the physical limits to production?

Why the Long-Run Aggregate Supply Curve Is Vertical The long-run aggregate supply curve is vertical because there is only one level of real GDP that can be produced at full employment no matter how high the price level is. As we move along the long-run aggregate supply curve, *two* sets of prices vary: the prices of goods and services and the prices of factors of production. And they vary by the same percentage. You can see why the level of output doesn't vary in these circumstances by thinking about the tape factory again. If the price of tapes increases and the cost of producing them also increases by the same percentage, there is no incentive for tape makers to change their output level. What's true for tape producers is true for the producers of all goods and services, so the aggregate quantity supplied does not change.

Why Long-Run Aggregate Supply Is Less Than the Physical Limit of Production Real GDP cannot be increased above its physical limit. But it can be increased above its long-run level by driving unemployment below its natural rate. When this occurs, there are more unfilled job vacancies than there are people looking for work. Firms compete with each other for labor, wages rise faster than prices, and output eventually falls to its long-run level.

REVIEW

The short-run aggregate supply curve shows the relationship between real GDP supplied and the price level, holding everything else constant. With no change in wage rates or other factor prices, an increase in the price level results in an increase in real GDP supplied. The short-run aggregate supply curve is horizontal in a severe depression, upward sloping in the intermediate range, and vertical when the economy is at the physical limit of its productive capacity. ◆◆ The long-run aggregate supply curve shows the relationship between real GDP supplied and the price level when there is full employment. This level of real GDP is independent of the price level, and the long-run aggregate supply curve is vertical. Its position tells us the level of real GDP supplied when the economy is at full employment, which is a lower level of real GDP than the physical production limit. ◆

A change in the price level, with everything else held constant, results in a movement along the short-run aggregate supply curve. A change in the price level, with an accompanying change in wage rates that keeps unemployment at its natural rate, results in a movement along the long-run aggregate supply curve. But there are many other influences on real GDP supplied. These influences result in a change in aggregate supply and shifts in the aggregate supply curves.

Some factors change both short-run aggregate supply and long-run aggregate supply; others affect short-run aggregate supply but leave long-run aggregate supply unchanged. Let's examine these influences on aggregate supply, starting with those that affect only short-run aggregate supply.

Changes in Short-Run Aggregate Supply

The only influences on short-run aggregate supply that do not change long-run aggregate supply are the wage rate and the prices of other factors of production. Factor prices affect short-run aggregate supply through their influence on firms' costs. The higher the level of wage rates and other factor prices, the higher are firms' costs and the lower is the quantity of output that firms want to supply at each price level. Thus an increase in wage rates and other factor prices decreases short-run aggregate supply.

Why do factor prices affect short-run aggregate supply but not long-run aggregate supply? The answer lies in the definition of long-run aggregate supply. Recall that long-run aggregate supply refers to the quantity of real GDP supplied when wages and other factor prices have adjusted by the same percentage amount as the price level has changed.

Faced with the same percentage increase in factor prices and the price of its output, a firm has no incentive to change its output. Thus aggregate output—real GDP—remains constant.

Shift in the Short-Run Aggregate Supply Curve A change in factor prices changes short-run aggregate supply and shifts the short-run aggregate supply curve. Figure 7.5 shows such a shift. The long-run aggregate supply curve is *LAS*, and initially the short-run aggregate supply curve is SAS_0. These curves intersect at the price level 120. Now suppose that labor is the only factor of production and that wage rates increase from \$12 an hour to \$13 an hour. At the original level of wage rates, firms are willing to supply, in total, \$5.0 trillion worth of output at a price level of 120. They will supply that same level of output at the higher wage rate only if prices increase in the same proportion as wages have increased. With wages up from \$12 to \$13, the price level that will keep the quantity supplied constant is 130. Thus the short-run aggregate supply curve shifts to SAS_1. There is a *decrease* in short-run aggregate supply.

FIGURE 7.5

A Decrease in Short-Run Aggregate Supply

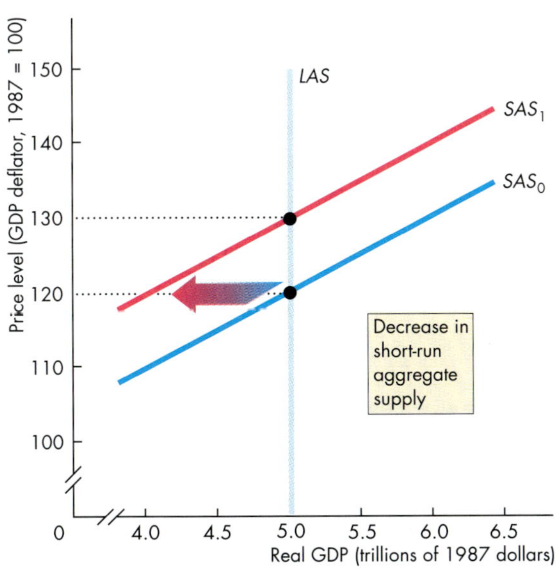

An increase in wage rates or in the prices of other factors of production decreases short-run aggregate supply but does not change long-run aggregate supply. It shifts the short-run aggregate supply curve to the left and leaves the long-run aggregate supply curve unaffected. Such a change is shown here. The original short-run aggregate supply curve is SAS_0, and after the wage rate has increased, the new short-run aggregate supply curve is SAS_1.

Changes in Both Long-Run and Short-Run Aggregate Supply

Four main factors influence both long-run and short-run aggregate supply. They are

- The labor force
- The capital stock
- Technology
- Incentives

The Labor Force The larger the labor force, the larger is the quantity of goods and services produced. Other things being equal, a farm with 10 workers produces more corn than a farm with 1 worker. The same is true for the economy as a whole. With its labor force of more than 125 million people, the United States produces a much larger quantity of goods and services than it would if, everything else remaining the same, it had Canada's labor force of 12.5 million people.

The Capital Stock The larger the stock of plant and equipment, the more productive is the labor force and the greater is the output that it can produce. Also, the larger the stock of *human capital*—the skills that people have acquired in school and through on-the-job training—the greater is the level of output. The capital-rich U.S. economy produces a vastly greater quantity of goods and services than it would if, everything else remaining the same, it had Ethiopia's stock of capital equipment.

Technology Inventing new and better ways of doing things enables firms to produce more from any given amount of inputs. So, even with a constant population and constant capital stock, improvements in technology increase production and increase aggregate supply. Technological advances are by far the most important source of increased production over the past two centuries. As a result of technological advances, in the United States today, one farmer can feed 100 people, and one auto worker can produce almost 14 cars and trucks in a year.

Incentives Aggregate supply is influenced by the incentives that people face. Two examples are unemployment benefits and investment tax credits. In Britain, unemployment benefits are much more generous, relative to wages, than in the United States. There is a greater incentive to find a job in the United States than in Britain. As a result, Britain's natural unemployment rate is higher and its long-run aggregate supply is lower than it would be if Britain had U.S. unemployment compensation arrangements. Investment tax credits are credits that cut business taxes in proportion to the scale of a firm's investment in new plant and equipment. Such credits provide an incentive to greater capital accumulation and, other things being equal, increase aggregate supply.

Shifts in the Short-Run and Long-Run Aggregate Supply Curves If any of the events that change long-run aggregate supply occur, the long-run aggregate supply curve *and the short-run aggregate supply curve* shift. Most of the factors that influence both short-run and long-run aggregate supply bring an *increase* in aggregate supply. This case is summarized in Fig. 7.6.

Initially, the long-run aggregate supply curve is LAS_0 and the short-run aggregate supply curve is SAS_0. These curves intersect at a price level of 120 and a real GDP of 5 trillion 1987 dollars. An increase in productive capacity that increases full-employment real GDP to 6 trillion 1987 dollars shifts the long-run aggregate supply curve to LAS_1 and the short-run aggregate supply curve to SAS_1. Long-run aggregate supply is now 6 trillion 1987 dollars.

FIGURE 7.6

Long-Run Growth in Aggregate Supply

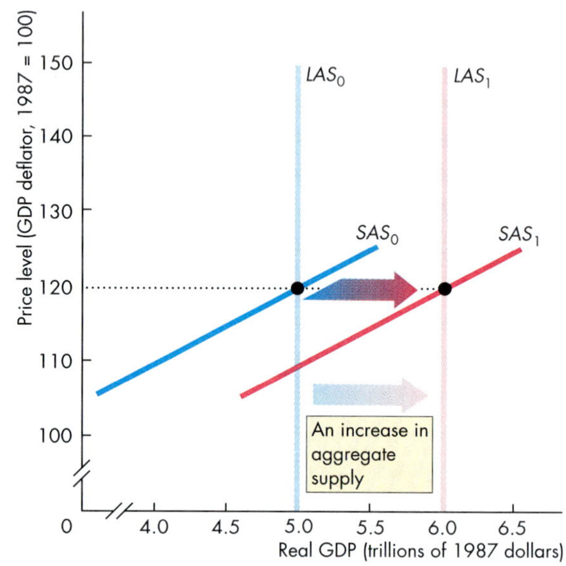

Aggregate supply

Increases in the long run if:

- The labor force increases
- The capital stock increases
- Technological change increases the productivity of labor and capital
- Incentives to work and invest in new plant and equipment are strengthened

Both the long-run and short-run aggregate supply curves shift to the right and do so by the same amount.

REVIEW

A change in wage rates or in other factor prices changes short-run aggregate supply but leaves long-run aggregate supply unchanged. It shifts the short-run aggregate supply curve but does not shift the long-run aggregate supply curve. ◆ ◆ Changes in the size of the labor force and the capital stock, the state of technology, or the incentives households and firms face change both short-run and long-run aggregate supply. Such changes shift both the short-run and long-run aggregate supply curves, and the shifts are in the same direction. ◆

Macroeconomic Equilibrium

The purpose of the aggregate demand–aggregate supply model is to predict changes in real GDP and the price level. To make predictions about real GDP and the price level, we need to combine aggregate demand and aggregate supply and determine macroeconomic equilibrium. **Macroeconomic equilibrium** occurs when the quantity of real GDP demanded equals the quantity of real GDP supplied. Let's see how macroeconomic equilibrium is determined.

Determination of Real GDP and the Price Level

The aggregate demand curve tells us the quantity of real GDP demanded at each price level, and the short-run aggregate supply curve tells us the quantity of real GDP supplied at each price level. There is one and only one price level at which the quantity demanded equals the quantity supplied. Macroeconomic equilibrium occurs at that price level. Figure 7.7 illustrates such an equilibrium at a price level of 120 and a real GDP of 5.0 trillion 1987 dollars (point *c* and *c*').

To see why this position is an equilibrium, let's work out what happens if the price level is something other than 120. Suppose that the price level is 130. In that case, the quantity of real GDP demanded is $4.5 trillion (point *d*), but the quantity of real GDP supplied is $6 trillion (point *e*'). There is an excess of the quantity supplied over the quantity demanded, or a surplus of goods and services. Unable to sell all their output and with inventories piling up, firms cut prices. Prices will be cut until the surplus is eliminated—at a price level of 120.

Next consider what happens if the price level is 110. In this case, the quantity of real GDP that firms supply is $4 trillion worth of goods and services (point *a*') and the quantity of real GDP demanded is $5.5 trillion worth (point *b*). The quantity demanded exceeds the quantity supplied. With inventories running out, firms raise their prices and continue to do so until the quantities demanded and supplied are in balance—again at a price level of 120.

FIGURE 7.7

Macroeconomic Equilibrium

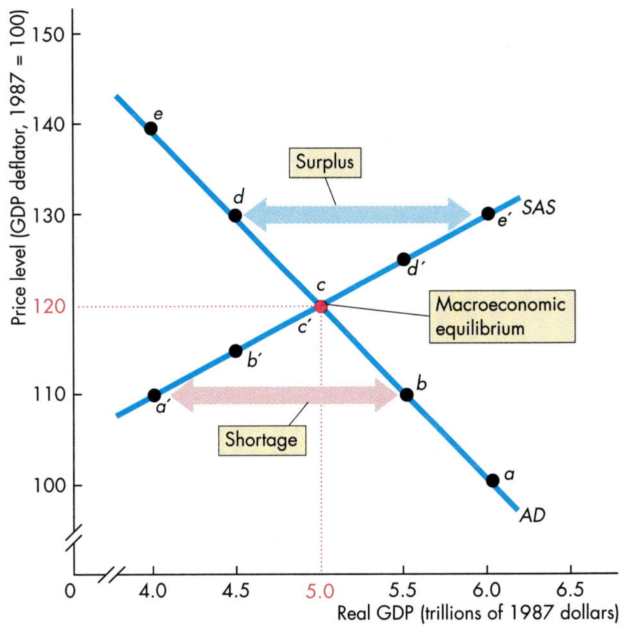

Macroeconomic equilibrium occurs when real GDP demanded equals real GDP supplied. Such an equilibrium is at the intersection of the aggregate demand curve (*AD*) and the short-run aggregate supply curve (*SAS*)—points *c* and *c*′—where the price level is 120 and real GDP is $5.0 trillion 1987 dollars. At price levels above 120, for example, 130, there is an excess of the quantity of goods and services supplied over the quantity demanded—a surplus—and prices fall. At price levels below 120, for example, 110, there is an excess of the quantity of goods and services demanded over the quantity supplied—a shortage—and prices rise. Only when the price level is 120 is the quantity of goods and services demanded equal to the quantity supplied. This is the equilibrium price level.

Macroeconomic Equilibrium and Full Employment

Macroeconomic equilibrium does not necessarily occur at full employment. At full employment, the economy is on its *long-run* aggregate supply curve.

But macroeconomic equilibrium occurs at the intersection of the *short-run* aggregate supply curve and the aggregate demand curve and can occur at, below, or above full employment. We can see this fact most clearly by considering the three possible cases shown in Fig. 7.8.

In Fig. 7.8(a) the fluctuations of real GDP are shown for an imaginary economy over a five-year period. In year 2, real GDP falls below its long-run level to point *b* and there is a recessionary gap. A **recessionary gap** is long-run real GDP minus actual real GDP when actual real GDP is below long-run

FIGURE 7.8

Three Types of Macroeconomic Equilibrium

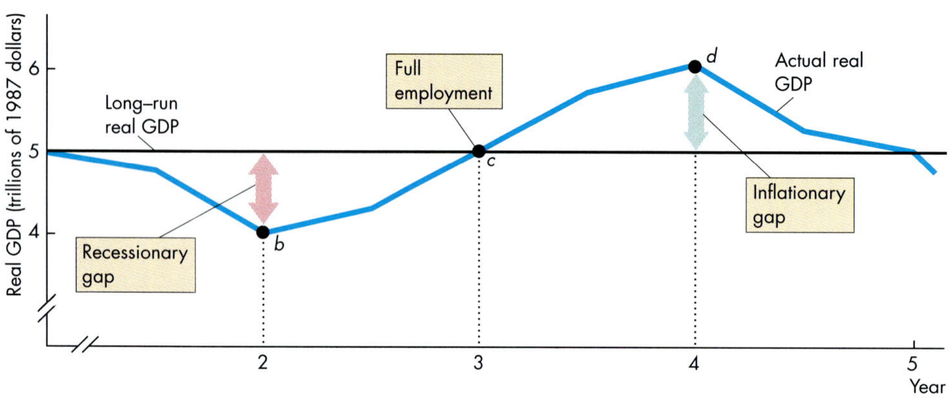

(a) Fluctuations in real GDP

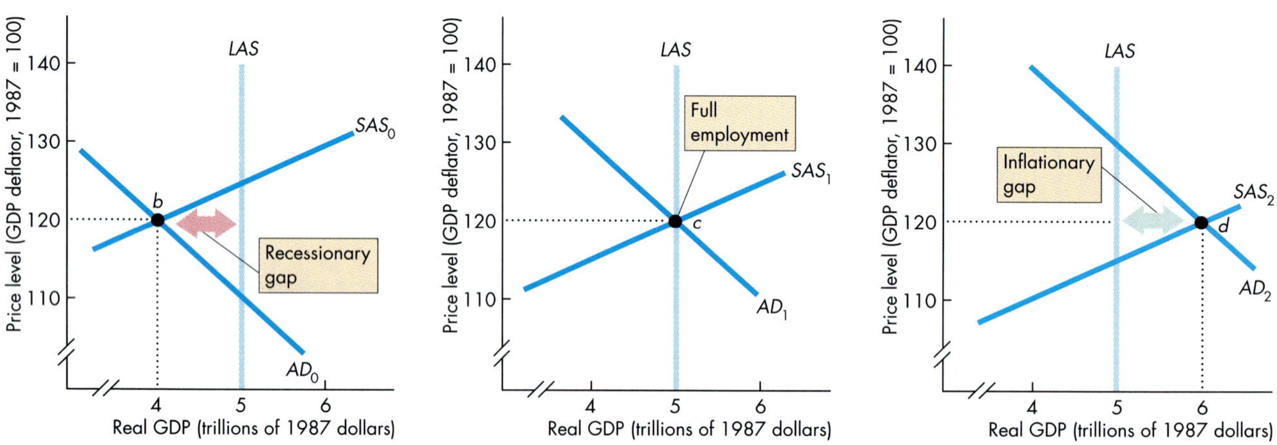

(b) Unemployment equilibrium **(c) Full-employment equilibrium** **(d) Above full-employment equilibrium**

In part (a), real GDP fluctuates around its long-run level. When actual real GDP is below long-run real GDP, there is a recessionary gap (as in year 2). When actual real GDP is above long-run real GDP, there is an inflationary gap (as in year 4). When actual real GDP is equal to long-run real GDP, there is full employment (as in year 3).

In year 2 there is an unemployment equilibrium, as illustrated in part (b). In year 3 there is a full-employment equilibrium, as illustrated in part (c). And in year 4 there is an above full-employment equilibrium, as illustrated in part (d).

real GDP. In year 4, real GDP rises above its long-run level to point *d* and there is an inflationary gap. An **inflationary gap** is actual real GDP minus long-run real GDP when actual real GDP is above long-run real GDP. In year 3, actual real GDP and long-run real GDP are equal and the economy is at full employment, at point *c*.

These situations are illustrated in parts (b), (c), and (d) as the three types of macroeconomic equilibrium. In part (b) there is an unemployment equilibrium. An **unemployment equilibrium** is a situation in which macroeconomic equilibrium occurs at a level of real GDP below long-run GDP. In such an equilibrium, there is a recessionary gap. The unemployment equilibrium illustrated in Fig. 7.8(b) occurs where aggregate demand curve AD_0 intersects short-run aggregate supply curve SAS_0 at a real GDP of 4 trillion 1987 dollars and a price level of 120. There is a recessionary gap of 1 trillion 1987 dollars. The U.S. economy was in a situation similar to that shown in Fig. 7.8(b) in 1982–1983. In those years, unemployment was high and real GDP was substantially below its long-run level.

Figure 7.8(c) is an example of full-employment equilibrium. **Full-employment equilibrium** is a macroeconomic equilibrium in which actual real GDP equals long-run real GDP. In this example, the equilibrium occurs where the aggregate demand curve AD_1 intersects the short-run aggregate supply curve SAS_1 at an actual and long-run real GDP of 5 trillion 1987 dollars. The U.S. economy was in a situation such as that shown in Fig. 7.8(c) in 1987.

Finally, Fig. 7.8(d) illustrates an above full-employment equilibrium. **Above full-employment equilibrium** is a situation in which macroeconomic equilibrium occurs at a level of real GDP above long-run real GDP. In such an equilibrium, there is an inflationary gap. The above full-employment equilibrium illustrated in Fig. 7.8(d) occurs where the aggregate demand curve AD_2 intersects the short-run aggregate supply curve SAS_2 at a real GDP of 6 trillion 1987 dollars and a price level of 120. There is an inflationary gap of 1 trillion 1987 dollars. The U.S. economy was in a situation similar to that depicted in part (d) in 1988–1990.

The economy moves from one type of equilibrium to another as a result of fluctuations in aggregate demand and in short-run aggregate supply. These fluctuations produce fluctuations in real GDP and the price level.

Next, we're going to put the model to work generating macroeconomic fluctuations.

Aggregate Fluctuations and Aggregate Demand Shocks

We're going to work out what happens to real GDP and the price level following a shock to aggregate demand. Let's suppose that the economy starts out at full employment and, as illustrated in Fig. 7.9, is producing $5 trillion worth of goods and services at a price level of 120. The economy is on the aggregate demand curve AD_0, the short-run aggregate

FIGURE 7.9

The Effects of an Increase in Aggregate Demand

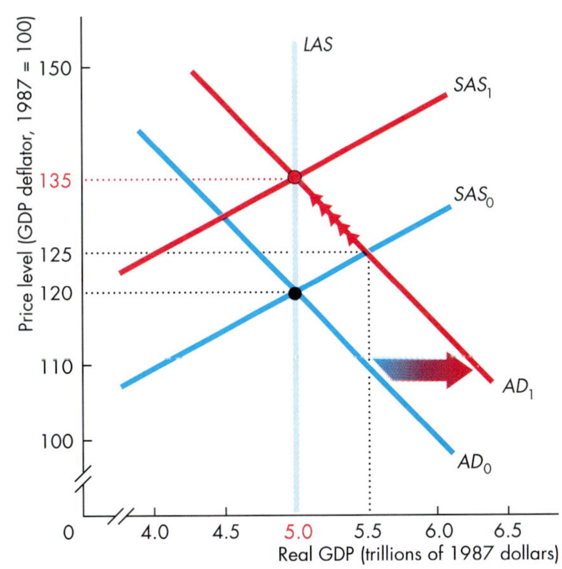

An increase in aggregate demand shifts the aggregate demand curve from AD_0 to AD_1. Real GDP increases from 5.0 trillion to 5.5 trillion 1987 dollars, and the price level increases from 120 to 125. There is an inflationary gap. A higher price level induces higher wage rates, which in turn cause the short-run aggregate supply curve to move leftward. As the *SAS* curve moves leftward from SAS_0 to SAS_1, it intersects the aggregate demand curve AD_1 at higher price levels and lower real GDP levels. Eventually, the price level increases to 135, and real GDP falls back to 5.0 trillion 1987 dollars—its full-employment level.

supply curve SAS_0, and its long-run aggregate supply curve *LAS*.

Now suppose that the Fed takes steps to increase the quantity of money. With more money in the economy, people increase their demand for goods and services—the aggregate demand curve shifts to the right. Suppose that the aggregate demand curve shifts from AD_0 to AD_1 in Fig. 7.9. A new equilibrium occurs where the aggregate demand curve AD_1 intersects the short-run aggregate supply curve SAS_0. Output rises to \$5.5 trillion (1987 dollars), and the price level rises to 125. The economy is now at an above full-employment equilibrium. Real GDP is above its long-run level, and there is an inflationary gap.

The increase in aggregate demand has increased the prices of all goods and services. Faced with higher prices, firms have increased their output rates. At this stage, prices of goods and services have increased but wage rates have not changed. (Recall that as we move along a short-run aggregate supply curve, wage rates are constant.)

The economy cannot stay above its long-run aggregate supply and full-employment levels forever. Why not? What are the forces at work bringing real GDP back to its long-run level and restoring full employment?

If the price level has increased but wage rates have remained constant, workers have experienced a fall in the purchasing power of their wages. Furthermore, firms have experienced a fall in the real cost of labor. In these circumstances, workers demand higher wages, and firms, anxious to maintain their employment and output levels, meet those demands. If firms do not raise wage rates, they either lose workers or have to hire less productive ones.

As wage rates rise, the short-run aggregate supply curve begins to shift leftward. It moves from SAS_0 toward SAS_1. The rise in wages and the shift in the *SAS* curve produce a sequence of new equilibrium positions. At each point on the adjustment path, output falls and the price level rises. Eventually, wages will have risen by so much that the *SAS* curve is SAS_1. At this time, the aggregate demand curve AD_1 intersects SAS_1 at a full-employment equilibrium. The price level has risen to 135, and output is back where it started, at its long-run level. Unemployment is again at its natural rate.

Throughout the adjustment process, higher wage rates raise firms' costs and, with rising costs, firms offer a smaller quantity of goods and services for sale at any given price level. By the time the adjustment is over, firms are producing exactly the same amount as initially produced, but at higher prices and higher costs. The level of costs relative to prices will be the same as it was initially.

We've just worked out the effects of an increase in aggregate demand. A decrease in aggregate demand has similar but opposite effects to those that we've just studied. That is, when aggregate demand falls, real GDP falls below its long-run level and unemployment rises above its natural rate. There is a recessionary gap. The lower price level increases the purchasing power of wages and increases firms' costs relative to their output prices. Eventually, as the slack economy leads to falling wage rates, the short-run aggregate supply curve shifts downward. Real GDP gradually returns to its long-run level, and full employment is restored.

Aggregate Fluctuations and Aggregate Supply Shocks

Let's now work out the effects of a change in aggregate supply on real GDP and the price level. Figure 7.10 illustrates the analysis. Suppose that the economy is initially at full-employment equilibrium. The aggregate demand curve is AD_0, the short-run aggregate supply curve is SAS_0, and the long-run aggregate supply curve is *LAS*. Output is 5 trillion 1987 dollars, and the price level is 120.

Now suppose that the price of oil increases sharply, as it did when OPEC used its market power in 1973–1974 and again in 1979–1980. With a higher price of oil, firms are faced with higher costs and they lower their output. Short-run aggregate supply decreases, and the short-run aggregate supply curves shift leftward to SAS_1.

As a result of this decrease in short-run aggregate supply, the economy moves to a new equilibrium where SAS_1 intersects the aggregate demand curve AD_0. The price level rises to 130, and real GDP falls to 4.5 trillion 1987 dollars. Because real GDP falls, the economy experiences recession. Because the price level increases, the economy experiences inflation. Such a combination of recession and inflation—called *stagflation*—actually occurred in the 1970s and 1980s at the times of the OPEC oil price hikes.

FIGURE 7.10

The Effects of an Increase in the Price of Oil

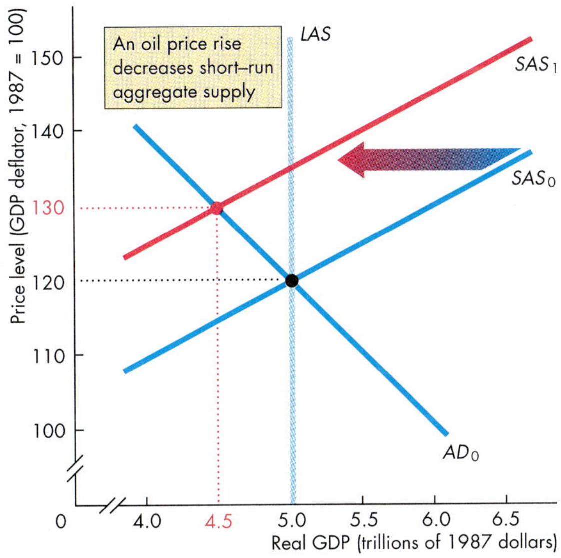

An increase in the price of oil decreases short-run aggregate supply and shifts the short-run aggregate supply curve leftward from SAS_0 to SAS_1. Real GDP falls from 5.0 trillion to 4.5 trillion 1987 dollars, and the price level increases from 120 to 130. The economy experiences both recession and inflation—*stagflation.*

REVIEW

Macroeconomic equilibrium occurs when the quantity of real GDP demanded equals the quantity of real GDP supplied. There are three types of macroeconomic equilibrium—unemployment equilibrium (a situation in which real GDP is below long-run real GDP and there is a recessionary gap), full-employment equilibrium (a situation in which actual real GDP equals long-run real GDP), and above full-employment equilibrium (a situation in which real GDP is above long-run real GDP and there is an inflationary gap). As aggregate demand and aggregate supply fluctuate, the economy moves from one type of macroeconomic equilibrium to another and real GDP and the price level fluctuate. ◆

We've now seen how changes in aggregate demand and aggregate supply influence real GDP and the price level. Let's put our new knowledge to work and see how it helps us understand recent U.S. macroeconomic performance.

Recent Trends and Cycles in the U.S. Economy

We're now going to use our new tools of aggregate demand and aggregate supply to interpret some recent trends and cycles in the U.S. economy. We'll begin by looking at the state of the U.S. economy in 1992–1993.

The Economy in 1992–1993

In 1992, the U.S. economy was recovering from recession. Measured in 1987 dollars, real GDP was \$4.9 trillion but long-run real GDP was \$5.1 trillion. The price level was 121. We can illustrate this state of the U.S. economy by using the aggregate demand–aggregate supply model.

In Fig. 7.11, the aggregate demand curve in 1992 is AD_{92} and the short-run aggregate supply curve in 1992 is SAS_{92}. The point at which these curves intersect determines the price level (121) and real GDP (\$4.9 trillion) in 1992. The long-run aggregate supply curve in 1992 is LAS_{92} at a real GDP of \$5.1 trillion, and there is a recessionary gap—actual real GDP is below long-run real GDP.

Three forces pushed the economy into recession in 1991. One was the price of oil, which increased sharply in the summer of 1990. This force decreased short-run aggregate supply and produced a leftward shift of the *SAS* curve. The second force was monetary policy. During 1989, the Fed had conducted a policy of restraint that increased interest rates and slowed the growth of aggregate demand. The effects of this restraint were still being felt in 1990. The third force was increased uncertainty and pessimism about future profit and income prospects, which lowered spending on new plant and equipment, buildings, and consumer goods. Working in the opposite direction, but with less force than the recessionary forces, was a loosening of fiscal policy. The

FIGURE 7.11

The U.S. Economy in 1992

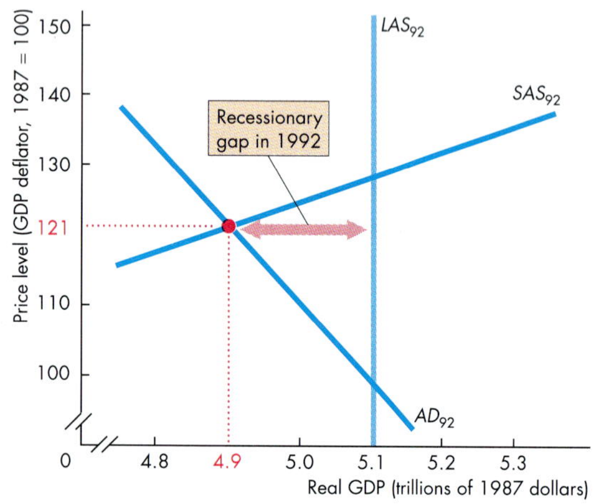

In 1992, the U.S. economy was on the aggregate demand curve AD_{92} and the aggregate supply curve SAS_{92}. The price level was 121, and real GDP was 4.9 trillion 1987 dollars. The long-run aggregate supply curve, LAS_{92}, was at 5.1 trillion 1987 dollars. There was a recessionary gap of 0.2 trillion 1987 dollars.

government's purchases of goods and services increased slightly. The combined effect of these forces led to recession in the winter of 1990–1991.

The economy began to recover from recession in 1991, but extremely slowly, and unemployment remained high throughout the year. The recovery was aided by a decrease in the price of oil. (The price increase of the summer of 1990 proved to be short-lived.) It was also aided by a considerable easing of monetary restraint. The Fed engineered successive decreases in interest rates that led to a gradual increase in aggregate demand. But confidence—business confidence about future profit prospects and consumer confidence about income growth—remained weak, so aggregate demand did not grow quickly.

The recovery continued during 1992, but at a slow pace. As a result, long-run aggregate supply remained above the level of real GDP and a recessionary gap persisted. Even by 1993, the recovery had still not picked up enough steam to lower the unemployment rate back to its pre-recession level. The main debate in 1993, as the Clinton administration came into office, was whether a fiscal stimulus package was needed to speed up the recovery. The consensus was that the recovery would continue without such a stimulus, although it could help—see Reading Between the Lines, pp. 178–179. But there is always a possibility (as portrayed in the cartoon) that aggregate demand might fall again, causing renewed recession.

Growth, Inflation, and Cycles

The economy is continually changing. If you imagine the economy as a video, then Fig. 7.11 is a freeze-frame. We're going to run the video again—an instant replay—but keep our finger on the freeze-frame button, looking at some important parts of the previous action. Let's run the video from 1960.

Figure 7.12 shows the state of the economy in 1960 at the point of intersection of its aggregate demand curve AD_{60} and short-run aggregate supply curve SAS_{60}. Real GDP was \$2 trillion, and the GDP deflator was 26 (less than one quarter of its 1992 level).

By 1992, the economy had reached the point marked by the intersection of aggregate demand curve AD_{92} and short-run aggregate supply curve SAS_{92}. Real GDP was \$4.9 trillion, and the GDP deflator was 121.

There are three important features of the economy's path traced by the blue and red points:

- Growth
- Inflation
- Cycles

"Please stand by for a series of tones. The first indicates the official end of the recession, the second indicates prosperity, and the third the return of the recession."

Growth Over the years, real GDP grows—shown in Fig. 7.12 by the rightward movement of the points. The main force generating this growth is an increase in long-run aggregate supply. Long-run aggregate supply increases because of labor force growth, the accumulation of capital—both physical plant and equipment and human capital—and the advance of technology.

Inflation The price level rises over the years—shown in Fig. 7.12 by the upward movement of the points. The main force generating this persistent increase in the price level is a tendency for aggregate demand to increase at a faster pace than the increase in long-run aggregate supply. All of the factors that increase aggregate demand and shift the aggregate demand curve influence the pace of inflation. But one factor—the quantity of money—is the most important source of *persistent* increases in aggregate demand and persistent inflation.

Cycles Over the years, the economy grows and shrinks in cycles—shown in Fig. 7.12 by the wave-like pattern made by the points, with recessions highlighted in red. The cycles arise because both the expansion of short-run aggregate supply and the growth of aggregate demand do not proceed at a fixed, steady pace.

FIGURE 7.12

Aggregate Demand and Aggregate Supply: 1960 to 1993

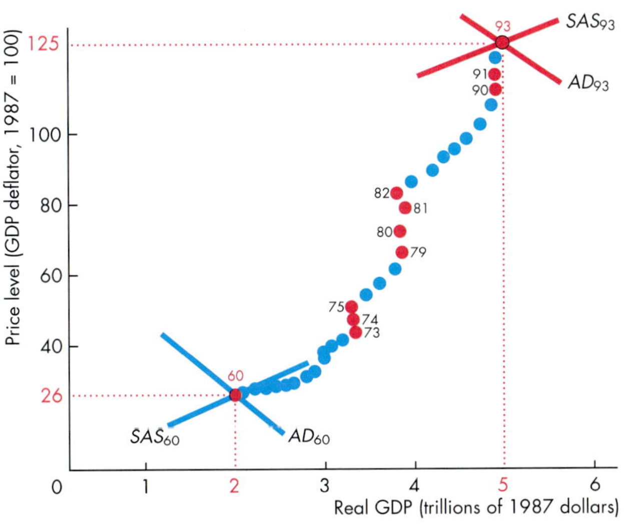

Each point indicates the value of the GDP deflator and real GDP in a given year. In 1960, these variables were determined by the intersection of the aggregate demand curve AD_{60} and the short-run aggregate supply curve SAS_{60}. Each point is generated by the gradual shifting of the *AD* and *SAS* curves. By 1993, the curves were AD_{93} and SAS_{93}. Real GDP grew, and the price level increased. But growth and inflation did not proceed smoothly. Real GDP grew quickly and inflation was moderate in the 1960s; real GDP growth sagged in 1974–1975 and again, more strongly, in 1982. The 1974–1975 slowdown was caused by an unusually sharp increase in oil prices. The 1982 recession was caused by a slowdown in the growth of aggregate demand, which resulted mainly from the Fed's monetary policy. The period from 1982 to 1989 was one of strong, persistent recovery. Inflation was rapid during the 1970s but slowed after the 1982 recession. A recession began in mid-1990.

The Evolving Economy: 1960–1993

During the 1960s, real GDP growth was rapid and inflation was low. This was a period of rapid increases in aggregate supply and of moderate increases in aggregate demand.

The mid-1970s were years of rapid inflation and recession—of stagflation. The major source of these developments was a series of massive oil price increases that shifted the short-run aggregate supply curve leftward and rapid increases in the quantity of money that shifted the aggregate demand curve rightward. Recession occurred because the aggregate supply curve shifted leftward at a faster pace than the aggregate demand curve shifted rightward.

The rest of the 1970s saw high inflation—the price level increased quickly—and only moderate growth in real GDP. This inflation was the product of a battle between OPEC and the Fed. OPEC jacked up the price of oil, and an inflationary recession ensued. Eventually, the Fed gave way and increased the money supply growth rate to stimulate aggregate demand and bring the economy back to full employment. Then OPEC, taking advantage of oil shortages created by a crisis in the relations between the United States and Iran, played a similar hand again, pushing up the price of oil still further. The Fed was faced with a dilemma. Should it stimulate aggregate demand again to restore full employment, notching up the inflation rate yet further, or should it keep the growth of aggregate demand in check?

The answer, delivered by Fed chairman Paul Volcker, was to keep aggregate demand growth in check. You can see the effects of Chairman Volcker's

The Slow 1993 Recovery

FORTUNE, JANUARY 11, 1993

Growth: Slow but Picking Up

BY VIVIAN BROWNSTEIN

Expansion is under way, and America's output of goods and services will continue to grow in real terms during 1993—with or without help from tax incentives or additional government spending programs. Does this prognosis mean that President-elect Clinton should abandon plans for stimulating the economy in the short run? No. If he allows the sense of urgency about the economy to dissipate, making tough policy decisions will become even tougher.

FORTUNE expects the economy to start off 1993 at just under a 3% annual growth rate and to kick up to 4% by the last two quarters. For the year, GDP growth will average 3.1%. The stronger economy will not raise inflation much, only to an average of 3.2%, vs. 3% last year. Employment will remain on the critical list, however, and that should keep the new Administration's attention focused. . . .

Jobs are the core problem. Hiring picked up in November, and claims for unemployment insurance have trended down since August. These developments contributed to an improvement in consumer confidence about finding or holding on to work. But the uptick is slight and confidence could easily fizzle, as it has before in this subnormal recovery.

Total employment is only now getting back to pre-recession levels, and in the meantime 2.5 million more people have entered the labor force looking for work. So the jobless rate is still two percentage points higher than before the recession began. . . .

The Essence of the Story

In January 1993, *Fortune* magazine forecasted a real GDP growth rate of 3.1 percent for the balance of the year but expected the expansion to be running at an annual rate of 4 percent in the second half-year.

The inflation rate was forecasted to increase slightly, from 3 percent in 1992 to 3.2 percent in 1993.

Employment was predicted to grow, but not at a pace fast enough to absorb the growing work force and lower the unemployment rate to its pre-recession level.

Background and Analysis

In 1992, as shown in Fig. 1, the aggregate demand curve was AD_{92}, the short-run aggregate supply curve was SAS_{92}, and real GDP and the price level (the GDP deflator) were determined at the intersection of these curves. Real GDP was $4.9 trillion (in 1987 dollars), and the price level was 121.

Long-run aggregate supply in 1992 was LAS_{92}, and there was a recessionary gap of $0.2 trillion.

Fortune magazine's forecasts for 1993 (made at the end of 1992) are shown in Fig. 2. Aggregate demand was expected to increase because improvements in the job market brought greater consumer confidence and higher consumer spending. Also, the prospect of higher consumer spending brought an increase in business spending on new capital. The effect of these forces is a rightward shift of the aggregate demand curve to AD_{93}.

The growth of the labor force—by an additional 2.5 million people—along with capital accumulation and the ongoing process of technological change that brings productivity gains, was expected to increase aggregate supply and to shift the aggregate supply curves rightward to SAS_{93} and LAS_{93}.

Real GDP was forecasted to be $5.05 trillion, up 3.1 percent from its 1992 level, and the price level was forecasted to be 124.8, up 3.2 percent. These values are determined at the point of intersection of AD_{93} and SAS_{93}.

But long-run aggregate supply growth was expected to keep pace with real GDP growth, and a recessionary gap was expected to persist. This gap is shown in Fig. 2.

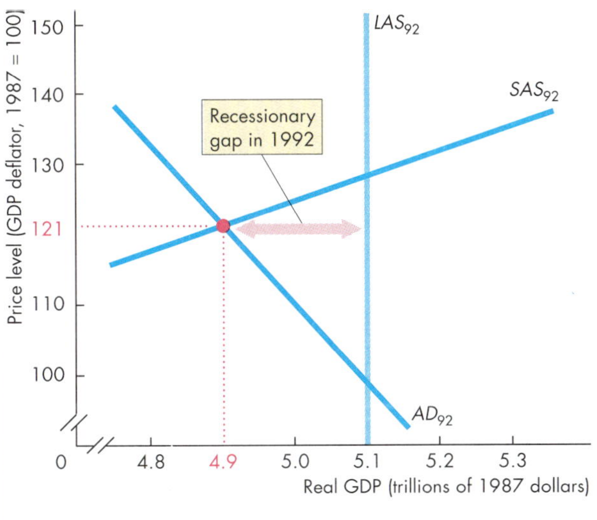

Figure 1

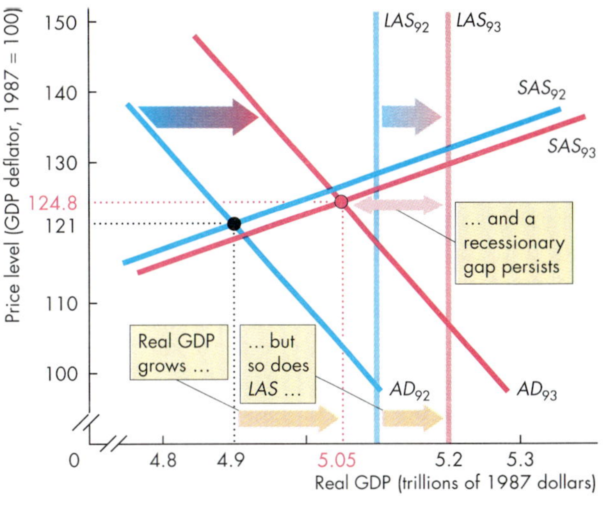

Figure 2

actions in 1979 to 1982. In this period, most people expected high inflation to persist, and wages grew at a rate consistent with those expectations. The short-run aggregate supply curve shifted leftward. Aggregate demand increased, but not at a fast enough rate to create inflation at as fast a pace as most people expected. As a consequence, by 1982 the leftward shift of the short-run aggregate supply curve was so strong relative to the growth of aggregate demand that the economy went into a further deep recession.

During the years 1982 to 1990, capital accumulation and steady technological advance resulted in a sustained rightward shift of the long-run aggregate supply curve. Wage growth was moderate, and the short-run aggregate supply curve also shifted rightward. Aggregate demand growth kept pace with the growth of aggregate supply. Sustained but steady growth in aggregate supply and aggregate demand kept real GDP growing and inflation steady. The economy moved from a recession with real GDP well below its long-run level to above full employment. It was in this condition when the events unfolded (described above) that led to the 1991 recession.

◆ ◆ ◆ ◆ This chapter has provided a model of real GDP and the GDP deflator that can be used to understand the growth, inflation, and cycles that our economy follows. The model is a useful one because it enables us to keep our eye on the big picture—on the broad trends and cycles in inflation and output. But the model lacks detail. It does not tell us as much as we need to know about the components of aggregate demand—consumption, investment, government purchases of goods and services, and exports and imports. It doesn't tell us what determines interest rates or wage rates or even, directly, what determines employment and unemployment. In the following chapters, we're going to start to fill in that detail. ◆ ◆ In some ways, the study of macroeconomics is like doing a large jigsaw puzzle. The aggregate demand–aggregate supply model provides the entire edge of the jigsaw. We know its general shape and size, but we haven't filled in the middle. One block of the jigsaw contains the story of aggregate demand. Another, the story of aggregate supply. And when we place the two together, we place them in the frame of the model developed in this chapter, and the picture is completed.

SUMMARY

Aggregate Demand

Aggregate demand is the relationship between the quantity of real GDP demanded and the price level, holding all other influences constant. Other things held constant, the higher the price level, the smaller is the quantity of real GDP demanded—the aggregate demand curve slopes downward. The aggregate demand curve slopes downward for three reasons: money and goods are substitutes (*real money balances effect*); goods today and goods in the future are substitutes (*intertemporal substitution effect*); domestic goods and foreign goods are substitutes (*international substitution effect*).

The main factors that change aggregate demand—and shift the aggregate demand curve—are fiscal policy (government purchases of goods and services and taxes), monetary policy (the money supply and interest rates), international factors (economic conditions in the rest of the world and the foreign exchange rate), and expectations (especially expectations about future inflation, income, and profits). (pp. 158–165)

Aggregate Supply

Short-run aggregate supply is the relationship between the quantity of real GDP supplied and the price level when wage rates and other factor prices are held constant. The short-run aggregate supply curve is horizontal in a deep depression, vertical at the economy's physical production limit, but generally upward sloping. With factor prices and all other influences on supply held constant, the higher the price level, the more output firms plan to sell.

Long-run aggregate supply is the relationship between the quantity of real GDP supplied and the price level when there is full employment. The long-run aggregate supply curve is vertical—long-run aggregate supply is independent of the price level.

The factors that change short-run aggregate supply shift the short-run aggregate supply curve. The most important of these factors is the average level of wage rates. Factors that change long-run aggregate supply also change short-run aggregate supply. Thus anything that shifts the long-run aggregate supply curve also shifts the short-run aggregate supply curve, and they shift in the same direction. The most important of these factors are the size of the labor force, the capital stock, the state of technology, and incentives. (pp. 165–170)

Macroeconomic Equilibrium

Macroeconomic equilibrium occurs when the quantity of real GDP demanded equals the quantity of real GDP supplied. Macroeconomic equilibrium occurs at the intersection of the aggregate demand curve and the short-run aggregate supply curve. The price level that achieves this equality is the equilibrium price level, and the output level is equilibrium real GDP.

Macroeconomic equilibrium does not always occur at long-run real GDP and full employment—that is, at a point on the long-run aggregate supply curve. Unemployment equilibrium occurs when equilibrium real GDP is less than its long-run level. There is a recessionary gap, and unemployment exceeds its natural rate. When equilibrium real GDP is above its long-run level, there is an inflationary gap and unemployment is below its natural rate.

An increase in aggregate demand shifts the aggregate demand curve to the right and increases both real GDP and the price level. If real GDP is above its long-run level, wage rates begin to increase and, as they do so, the short-run aggregate supply curve shifts to the left. The leftward shift of the short-run aggregate supply curve results in a yet higher price level and a lower real GDP. Eventually, real GDP returns to its long-run level.

An increase in factor prices decreases short-run aggregate supply and shifts the short-run aggregate supply curve to the left. Real GDP decreases, and the price level rises—stagflation occurs. (pp. 171–175)

Recent Trends and Cycles in the U.S. Economy

Growth in the U.S. economy results from labor force growth, capital accumulation, and technological change. Inflation persists in the U.S. economy because of steady increases in aggregate demand largely brought about by increases in the quantity of money. The U.S. economy experiences cycles because the short-run aggregate supply and aggregate demand curves shift at an uneven pace.

Large oil price hikes in 1973 and 1974 resulted in stagflation. Further oil price increases in 1979 intensified the inflationary situation. Restraint in aggregate demand growth in 1980 and 1981 resulted in a severe recession in 1982. This recession resulted in lower output and a lower inflation rate. Moderate increases in wage rates and steady technological advance and capital accumulation resulted in a sustained expansion from 1982 to 1989. But a slowdown in aggregate demand growth brought a recession in mid-1990. (pp. 175–180)

KEY ELEMENTS

Key Terms

Above full-employment equilibrium, 173
Aggregate demand, 158
Aggregate demand curve, 158
Aggregate demand schedule, 158
Aggregate quantity of goods and services demanded, 158
Aggregate quantity of goods and services supplied, 165
Fiscal policy, 162
Full-employment equilibrium, 173
Inflationary gap, 173
International substitution, 161
Intertemporal substitution, 160
Long-run aggregate supply, 167
Long-run aggregate supply curve, 167
Macroeconomic equilibrium, 171
Macroeconomic long-run, 165
Macroeconomic short-run, 165
Monetary policy, 162
Quantity of money, 159

Key Figures

REVIEW QUESTIONS

1 What is aggregate demand?

2 What is the difference between aggregate demand and the aggregate quantity of goods and services demanded?

3 List the main factors that affect aggregate demand. Separate them into those that increase aggregate demand and those that decrease it.

4 Which of the following do not affect aggregate demand?

a Quantity of money
b Interest rates
c Technological change
d Human capital

5 Distinguish between macroeconomic short-run and long-run.

6 What is short-run aggregate supply?

7 What is the difference between short-run aggregate supply and the aggregate quantity of goods and services supplied?

8 Distinguish between short-run aggregate supply and long-run aggregate supply.

9 Consider the following events:

a The labor force increases.
b Technology improves.
c The wage rate increases.
d The quantity of money increases.
e Foreign incomes increase.
f The foreign exchange value of the dollar increases.

Sort these events into the following four categories:

Category A: Those that affect the long-run aggregate supply curve but not the short-run aggregate supply curve.

Category B: Those that affect the short-run aggregate supply curve but not the long-run aggregate supply curve.

Category C: Those that affect both the short-run aggregate supply curve and the long-run aggregate supply curve.

Category D: Those that have no effect on the short-run aggregate supply curve or on the long-run aggregate supply curve.

10 Define macroeconomic equilibrium.

11 Distinguish between an unemployment equilibrium and a full-employment equilibrium.

12 Work out the effect of an increase in the quantity of money on the price level and real GDP.

13 Work out the effect of an increase in the price of oil on the price level and real GDP.

14 What are the main factors generating growth of real GDP in the U.S. economy?

15 What are the main factors generating persistent inflation in the U.S. economy?

16 Why does the U.S. economy experience cycles in aggregate economic activity?

PROBLEMS

1 The economy of Mainland has the following aggregate demand and supply schedules:

Price level (GDP deflator)	Real GDP demanded	Real GDP supplied in the short run
	(trillions of 1987 dollars)	
90	4.5	3.5
100	4.0	4.0
110	3.5	4.5
120	3.0	5.0
130	2.5	5.5
140	2.0	5.5

- **a** Plot the aggregate demand curve and the short-run aggregate supply curve in a figure.
- **b** What is Mainland's real GDP? What is Mainland's price level?
- **c** Mainland's long-run real GDP is 5.0 trillion 1987 dollars. Plot the long-run aggregate supply curve in the same figure with which you answered part (a).
- **d** Is Mainland at, above, or below its natural rate of unemployment?
- **e** What is the physical limit of the economy of Mainland?

2 In problem 1, aggregate demand is increased by 1 trillion 1987 dollars. What is the change in real GDP and the price level?

3 In problem 1, aggregate supply decreases by 1 trillion 1987 dollars. What is the new macroeconomic equilibrium?

4 You are the president's economic advisor, and you are trying to figure out where the U.S. economy is headed next year. You have the following forecasts for the *AD*, *SAS*, and *LAS* curves:

Price level (GDP deflator)	Real GDP demanded	Short-run real GDP supplied	Long-run aggregate supply
	(trillions of 1987 dollars)		
115	6.5	3.5	5.2
120	6.0	4.5	5.2
125	5.5	5.5	5.2
130	5.0	6.5	5.2

This year, real GDP is $5.0 trillion and the price level is 120. The president wants answers to the following questions:

- **a** What is your forecast of next year's real GDP?
- **b** What is your forecast of next year's price level?
- **c** What is your forecast of the inflation rate?
- **d** Will unemployment be above or below its natural rate?
- **e** Will there be a recessionary gap or an inflationary gap? By how much?

5 Carefully draw some figures similar to those in this chapter and use the information in problem 4 to explain:

- **a** What has to be done to aggregate demand to achieve full employment
- **b** What the inflation rate is if aggregate demand is manipulated to achieve full employment

PART 3

AGGREGATE DEMAND FLUCTUATIONS

Talking with Allan Meltzer

Born in Boston, Massachusetts, in 1928, Allan Meltzer is the John M. Olin Professor of Political Economy and Public Policy at Carnegie-Mellon University in Pittsburgh. Professor Meltzer was an undergraduate at Duke University and a graduate student at UCLA, where he obtained his Ph.D. in 1958. Professor Meltzer has made wide-ranging contributions to the theory of money and economic activity and, with the late Karl Brunner, was a co-founder of the Shadow Open Market Committee. More recently, he has been giving some attention to the economic problems of Eastern Europe and the former Soviet Union. Michael Parkin talked with Professor Meltzer about his work as an economist and his views on today's economics problems.

What led you to study economics at UCLA?

I considered graduate school in my last year as an undergraduate majoring in economics, but I wasn't sure that was what I wanted. I started to enroll in Harvard's Ph.D. program but never went through with it. Instead, I moved to California and worked for several different manufacturing companies. After a few years, I realized that I had made the wrong choice and really preferred to study economics. I was married and living in Los Angeles at the time, so I went to UCLA.

What were the earliest economic problems on which you worked?

I was influenced by my teacher at UCLA, Karl Brunner, who had become interested in the money supply while I was a student. My thesis tested money supply theory under conditions of wartime and postwar French inflation. At the time, most of the French economists—and many American economists also—thought money was irrelevant to explaining economic problems. Many economists even considered inflation a non-monetary phenomenon. Soon

> "**A**t the time . . . many American economists . . . thought money was irrelevant to explaining economic problems."

after publishing my work on the French money supply, I began a series of papers on the demand for money in the United States.

You are a co-founder with Karl Brunner of the Shadow Open Market Committee. What is the Shadow Open Market Committee, and what does it do?

Karl and I were disturbed by the trend in economic policy. In the early 1970s, inflation was rising. Activist policymakers shifted from expansive to contractive policies and then back again every few years. This produced rising average unemployment and rising inflation. Several countries, including the United States, experimented with price and wage controls. We thought the trend toward controls, rising unemployment, and inflation was based on mistaken ideas about how the economy worked and what policy could or should do.

Looking for a way to improve public discussion of economic policy, Karl and I started the Shadow Open Market Committee in 1973. The committee brought together economists from universities and businesses who wanted to change policies by creating a public demand for more stable policies and lower inflation. At first we concentrated on monetary policy and inflation. Later we broadened our interest to include issues such as growth of the public sector, tax policy, and restrictions on international trade and capital movements.

You and the other members of the Shadow Open Market Committee are generally regarded as "monetarists." What is a monetarist? And do you agree that you are one?

When Karl Brunner coined the term *monetarism* in 1968, he defined it by stating three propositions: First, monetary impulses are important for changes in output, employment, and prices. Second, money growth is the most reliable measure of the monetary impulse. And third, monetary authorities such as central banks can control money growth in an economy like the United States. If being a monetarist means that I accept these propositions, then yes I am a monetarist because they remain true. However, monetarism has been given many meanings that have no connection to money or monetary economics. These political or journalistic usages are an entirely different matter.

In the past decade, some economists have proposed a "real business cycle" theory based on the idea that monetary disturbances are not very important sources of economic fluctuations. What's your view of the new theory?

Real business cycle theorists worked out the often noticed but undeveloped cyclical implications of changes in aggregate supply. This is an important development for theory, but we should not overstate its practical importance. The largest fluctuations that countries experience still appear to result from changes in monetary conditions. I think of the depression of the early 1930s, the decision by Great Britain to return to the gold standard at an overvalued exchange rate in 1925, the decisions by Britain and France in the 1980s to adopt a fixed exchange rate, the Federal Reserve's decision to double reserve requirement ratios in 1937, and the decisions in many countries to reduce inflation in the early 1980s. Each of these monetary disturbances produced relatively severe recessions. Monetary impulses are also important for some mild recessions or for expansions, but real factors like the oil shocks of the 1970s also affect output. These

"Economists had discussed the problems . . . for years, but Congress, the administration, the press, the public, and the regulators ignored the warnings."

experiences and many others suggest to me that the factors highlighted by real business cycle theories are a supplement to—not a substitute for—monetary impulses in theories of the cycle. It is also important to distinguish between recessions in which the economy departs from and returns to a long-term growth path and real disturbances like the oil shocks that permanently reduce the level of output.

If the president and Congress gave you carte blanche to fix the economy, what would be your recipe?

I would start by introducing five rules, in some cases constitutional rules, for monetary and fiscal policies to increase certainty, improve economic efficiency, and enhance stability of the domestic and international value of money.

First, the share of government spending relative to total spending would be fixed, except in wartime or declared emergency. Second, to provide for countercyclical changes in fiscal policy, tax revenues would be set to equal government spending on a three- or four-year average. As a result, the government budget—properly measured to include many off-budget items—would have a deficit in recessions and a surplus during expansions or booms but would balance over time. Third, a broad-based consumption tax would replace the income tax to reduce the current bias against saving. Fourth, to maintain domestic price level stability, money would grow at a rate equal to the difference between the three-year moving average growth of real output and the three-year moving average growth of monetary velocity. Fifth, to reduce exchange rate fluctuations, I would try to encourage other countries—principally Germany and Japan—to follow a rule similar to the fourth rule. This should not be difficult, since they have followed a similar strategy in the past. Rules 4 and 5 together would permit smaller countries to fix their exchange rates and get the benefit of more stable internal and external values of money. This is a public good.

These proposals would be just a start. Regulation, international trading rules, and many micro policies deserve attention, too.

Your recipe contains a lot of rules. How would you make sure the rules are followed?

There is an old tradition that in a fixed exchange rate regime, a finance minister resigned if the currency had to be devalued. Devaluation was considered a policy failure. I have often suggested a similar procedure for monetary policy. If the central bank does not follow the agreed-upon rule, the bank's officials would have to resign. I would base fiscal rules on known past magnitudes, not forecasts of future values. Failure to follow the rule would require resignation by the chairpersons of the appropriations committees of Congress and the Director of the Budget. Too much attention is now given to processes and promises and too little to outcomes. Congress should be less concerned about who is appointed and how decisions are made and more concerned about the relation of outcomes to announced program or policy.

"To develop economically, Russia must develop financially . . . A properly functioning financial system . . . encourages people to invest their savings at home."

Why is the S&L industry in such a mess?

There is no single reason for the S&L problem. Some of the more important contributing causes were inflation, regulation of interest rates, deposit insurance, and regulatory accounting practices. Inflation imposed real losses on the S&Ls' mortgage portfolio and reduced the equity or net worth of most of these firms. Ceilings on the interest rates that S&Ls could pay caused a loss of their deposit base to less regulated institutions. Deposit insurance encouraged some of them to invest in very risky assets once their net worth had fallen to low levels or even to negative values. An S&L with zero or negative net worth got all of the gain if a risky investment succeeded, but the loss went to the deposit insurance fund—that is to say, the taxpayers.

Bankrupt S&Ls had a lot to gain and nothing much to lose if they took big risks. Many of these wild investments failed, adding to the losses. Government regulators, often prodded by Congress, looked away and even changed accounting rules to hide the losses from public view.

The S&L debacle was a major failure of regulation. Economists had discussed the problems of deposit insurance, risk, and accounting practices for years, but Congress, the administration, the press, the public, and the regulators ignored the warnings. There were many papers and conferences about the problem while it was developing, but bad politics overrode careful economic analysis.

What will it cost to clean up the S&L industry?

A best guess about the cost is $200 billion in present value terms, but it is only an informed guess. We won't know until the assets of the failed S&Ls are sold.

You've been studying Russia and Eastern Europe recently, especially their monetary problems and the problems arising from the freeing of markets. What do you think are the main problems for which *monetary* policy is part of the solution?

Monetary policy can provide a stable price level to help people plan rationally for the long term. To develop economically, Russia must develop financially. Stable money is not just a store of value. It is an efficient means of carrying out exchanges at low or minimum transaction and information costs. Low inflation encourages the development of an efficient financial system. A properly functioning financial system with stable prices, free of controls on currency and financial asset markets, encourages people to invest their savings at home. Inflation and currency controls contribute to capital flight, thereby reducing the resources available for investment. Freedom from controls, greater certainty, and price stability contribute to growth and living standards by reducing costs of transacting and costs of information about prices and values.

If a student in a principles of economics course remembers only a few lessons from the course, what should they be?

Three principles constitute the core of economics. First, all demand curves are downward sloping. Less is demanded at a high price than at a low price. Second, supply curves are upward sloping. More is offered at high prices than at low prices. Third, the longer the run or the greater the period of adjustment, the more varied are the alternatives available and the greater is the opportunity to substitute or change. These principles, when properly applied, will help a student to think through many problems correctly, including many that do not at first seem to be economic problems.

CHAPTER 8

EXPENDITURE DECISIONS AND GDP

After studying this chapter, you will be able to:

- Describe the relative magnitudes of the components of aggregate expenditure and their relative volatility
- Explain how households make consumption and saving decisions
- Explain how firms make investment decisions
- Explain what determines exports, imports, and net exports
- Derive the aggregate expenditure schedule and the aggregate expenditure curve
- Explain how aggregate expenditure is determined

Fear and Trembling in the Shopping Aisles

SOME HEADLINES FROM THE WINTER OF 1991: "AUTO Makers Hobble into the New Year with Little Hope for a Robust Recovery," "Consumer Borrowing Flat," "New Home Sales Down," "Consumer Confidence Slips Again," "Little Christmas Cheer for Retailers." Why all the fear and trembling over what happens in the shopping aisles? Besides a few manufacturers and stores, who really cares whether people buy a lot of gifts for the holidays or whether they buy cars and new homes? How does this affect the rest of us? What makes people decide to spend less and save more? ◆◆ It's not only consumer spending that stirs up hope and fear in the economy. At times, firms' orders for new plant and equipment grow to a flood, and at other times they become a trickle. At some times, government purchases of military hardware grows quickly—as it did in the 1980s and during the Gulf War of 1991—but at other times, it falls—as it did at the end of the Cold War. Our exports to the rest of the world ebb and flow with the changing economic fortunes of Europe and Japan. How do business investment, government purchases, and exports affect us? How much of the country's spending do they make up when compared with consumer spending? Are fluctuations in these components of aggregate expenditure sources of fluctuations in our job prospects and living standards?

◆◆◆◆ The spending that people do in shopping aisles spreads out in waves across the economy, affecting millions of people. In this chapter we study the composition of those waves and see why consumption has a big effect outside the stores. We also study the other components of aggregate expenditure—investment, government purchases of goods and services, and net exports. First, we'll learn about their relative magnitudes and volatility. Second, we'll explain how they are determined. Third, we'll see how the private components of aggregate spending along with government purchases interact to determine aggregate expenditure and GDP. ◆ ◆ Let's begin by looking at the components of aggregate expenditure.

The Components of Aggregate Expenditure

The components of aggregate expenditure are

- Consumption expenditure
- Investment
- Government purchases of goods and services
- Net exports (exports minus imports)

Relative Magnitudes

Figure 8.1 shows the relative magnitudes of the components of aggregate expenditure between 1970 and 1992. By far the biggest portion of aggregate expenditure is consumption expenditure, which ranges between 63 and 69 percent and averages 65 percent of total expenditure. The smallest portion is net exports, whose average value is close to zero. Investment ranges between 14 and 18 percent of GDP and averages 16 percent. Government purchases of goods and services are slightly larger than investment, ranging between 18 and 23 percent of GDP and averaging 21 percent.

FIGURE 8.1

The Components of Aggregate Expenditure: 1970–1992

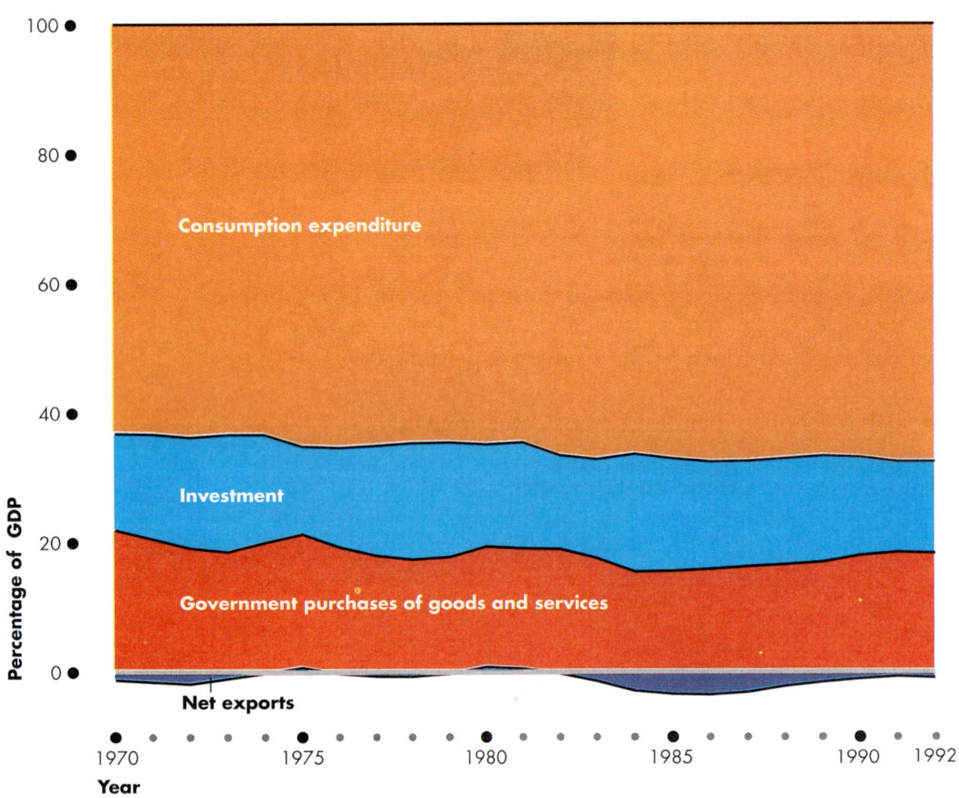

The biggest component of aggregate expenditure is consumption expenditure. It ranges between 63 and 69 percent of GDP and averages 65 percent. Investment averages 16 percent of GDP, fluctuating between 14 and 18 percent. Government expenditure on goods and services ranges between 18 and 23 percent of GDP and averages 21 percent of GDP. The smallest item is net exports and it averages approximately zero.

Relative Volatility

Figure 8.2 shows the relative volatility of the components of aggregate expenditure. The most volatile are investment and net exports. Consumption expenditure and government purchases of goods and services fluctuate much less than these two items.

Notice that although the fluctuations in consumption expenditure have a much smaller range than those in investment, the ups and downs of the two series move in sympathy with each other. Notice also that the three big declines in investment—in 1975, 1982, and 1991—occurred at precisely the time when the economy was in recession (recessions that we saw in Chapter 5, pp. 115–116 and 119, and in Chapter 7, pp. 175–180). Government purchases of goods and services were below trend between 1973 and 1984. But in the second half of the 1980s, they grew quickly and moved above trend. The fluctuations in net exports are similar in magnitude to those in investment, but these two components of aggregate expenditure tend to fluctuate in opposite directions—years of high investment are years of low net exports.

Let's study the choices that determine the size and volatility of the components of aggregate expenditure, beginning with the largest component, consumption expenditure.

FIGURE 8.2

Fluctuations in the Components of Aggregate Expenditure: 1970–1992

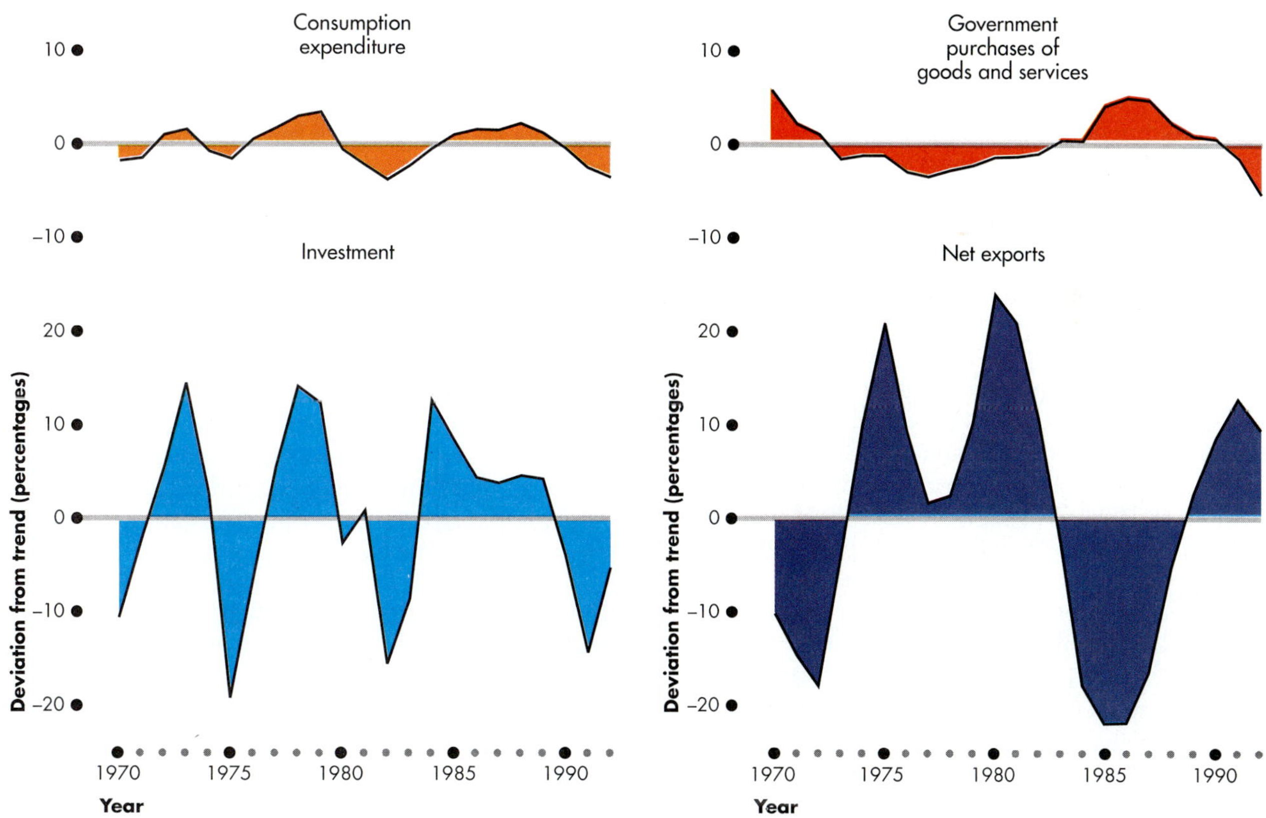

Fluctuations in each component of aggregate expenditure are shown as percentage deviations from trend. Although consumption expenditure is the biggest component of aggregate expenditure, it is the one that fluctuates least in percentage terms. Investment and net exports fluctuate most. Government purchases of goods and services show a strong increase in the 1980s. Net exports fluctuate in the direction opposite to investment.

Consumption Expenditure and Saving

Consumption expenditure is the value of the consumption goods and services bought by households. There are many factors that influence a household's consumption expenditure, but the two most important are

- Disposable income
- Expected future income

1. Disposable Income *Disposable income* is the aggregate income that households receive in exchange for supplying the services of factors of production plus transfers received from the government minus taxes. A household can do only two things with its disposable income: spend it on consumption goods and services or save it.

As a household's disposable income increases, so does its expenditure on food and beverages, clothing, accommodation, transportation, medical care, and most other goods and services. That is, a household's consumption expenditure increases as its income increases.

2. Expected Future Income A household's expected future income depends mainly on the security and income growth prospects of the jobs that its members do. Other things being equal, the higher a household's expected future income, the greater is its current consumption expenditure. That is, if there are two households that have the same disposable income in the current year, the household with the larger expected future income will spend a larger portion of current disposable income on consumption goods and services. Consider, for example, two households whose principal income earner is a senior executive in a large corporation. One executive has just been told of an important promotion that will increase the household's income by 50 percent in the following years. The other has just been told that the firm has been taken over and that there will be no further employment beyond the end of the year. The first household buys a new car and takes an expensive foreign vacation, thereby increasing its current consumption expenditure. The second household sells the family's second car and cancels its winter vacation plans, thereby cutting back on its current consumption expenditure.

The Consumption Function and the Saving Function

The relationship between consumption expenditure and disposable income, other things held constant, is called the **consumption function.** The consumption function has played an important role in macroeconomics over the past 50 years, and the story of its discovery is told in Our Advancing Knowledge on pp. 194–195. The relationship between saving and disposable income, other things held constant, is called the **saving function.** The consumption function and saving function for a typical household—the Polonius household—are shown in Fig. 8.3.

The Consumption Function The Polonius household's consumption function is plotted in Fig. 8.3(a). The horizontal axis measures disposable income, and the vertical axis measures consumption expenditure (both in thousands of dollars). The points labeled *a* through *f* in the figure correspond to the rows having the same letters in the table. For example, point *c* indicates disposable income of \$20,000 and consumption of \$18,000.

The 45° Line Figure 8.3(a) also contains a line labeled "45° line." This line connects the points at which consumption, measured on the vertical axis, equals disposable income, measured on the horizontal axis. When the consumption function is above the 45° line, consumption exceeds disposable income; when the consumption function is below the 45° line, consumption is less than disposable income; and at the point where the consumption function intersects the 45° line, consumption and disposable income are equal.

The Saving Function The saving function is graphed in Fig. 8.3(b). The horizontal axis is exactly the same as that in part (a). The vertical axis measures saving. Again, the points marked *a* through *f* correspond to the rows of the table.

There are two important things to note about the Polonius household's consumption and saving functions. First, even if the Polonius household has no disposable income, it still consumes. It does so by having a negative level of saving. Negative saving is called **dissaving.** Households that consume more than their disposable income do so either by living

FIGURE 8.3

The Polonius Household's Consumption Function and Saving Function

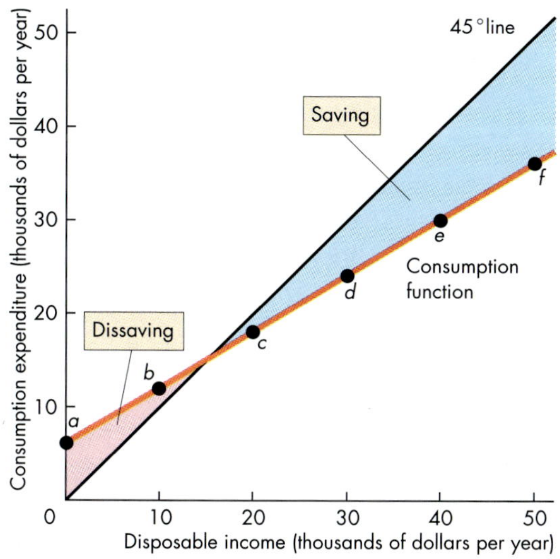

(a) Consumption function

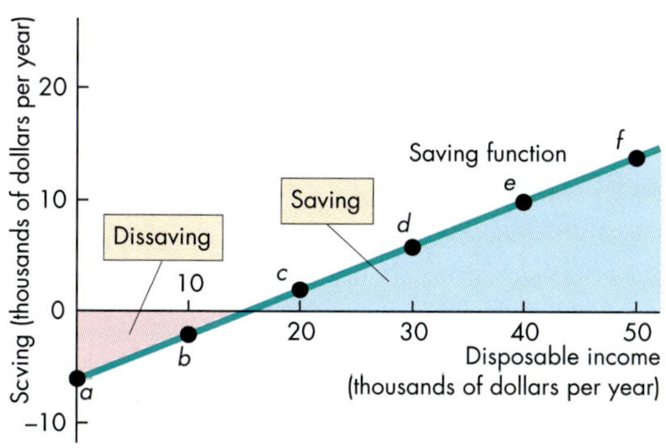

(b) Saving function

	Disposable income	Consumption expenditure	Saving
	(thousands of dollars per year)		
a	0	6	–6
b	10	12	–2
c	20	18	2
d	30	24	6
e	40	30	10
f	50	36	14

The table sets out the consumption and saving plan of the Polonius household at various levels of disposable income. Part (a) of the figure shows the relationship between consumption expenditure and disposable income (the consumption function). Part (b) shows the relationship between saving and disposable income (the saving function). Points *a* through *f* on the consumption and saving functions correspond to the rows in the table.

The 45° line in part (a) is the line of equality between consumption expenditure and disposable income. The Polonius household's consumption expenditure and saving equals its disposable income. When the consumption function is above the 45° line, saving is negative (dissaving occurs) and the saving function is below the horizontal axis. When the consumption function is below the 45° line, saving is positive and the saving function is above the horizontal axis. At the point where the consumption function intersects the 45° line, all disposable income is consumed, saving is zero, and the saving function intersects the horizontal axis.

off assets or by borrowing, a situation that cannot, of course, last forever.

Second, as the Polonius household's disposable income increases, so does the amount that it plans to spend on consumption and the amount that it plans to save. Since a household can only consume or save its disposable income, these two items always add up to disposable income. That is, consumption and saving plans are consistent with disposable income.

This relationship between the consumption function and the saving function can be seen by looking at the two parts of the figure. When the saving function is below the horizontal axis, saving is negative (dissaving) and the consumption function is above the 45° line. When the saving function is above the horizontal axis, saving is positive and the consumption function is below the 45° line. When the saving function intersects the horizontal axis, saving is zero and the consumption function intersects the 45° line.

Other Influences on Consumption Expenditure and Saving Changes in factors other than disposable

DISCOVERING the CONSUMPTION FUNCTION

The theory that consumption is determined by disposable income was proposed by John Maynard Keynes in 1936. With newly available national income data compiled by Simon Kuznets supporting Keynes's theory, it was instantly accepted.

During the 1940s and 1950s, a lot of additional data were collected, some of which revealed shortcomings in Keynes's theory. By the late 1940s, the Keynesian consumption function began to make forecasting errors. The propensity to consume—what Keynes called a "fundamental psychological law"—was revealed to be increasing and to depend on whether a person was young or old, black or white, or from an urban or rural area.

These failings brought forth two new theories—Franco Modigliani's life-cycle hypothesis and Milton Friedman's permanent income hypothesis—based on the proposition that consumption is determined by wealth and wealth depends on current and future income. Other things being equal, the wealthier a person is, the more he or she consumes. But only permanent and previously unexpected changes in income bring changes in wealth and consumption. Temporary changes in income or changes that have been foreseen change wealth by little and bring only small changes in consumption.

The revolution in macroeconomics of the 1970s brought the next reappraisal of consumption and a rational expectations theory of consumption proposed by Robert Hall of Stanford University. Hall started from the same point as Modigliani and Friedman: consumption depends on wealth and wealth depends on future income. But to make consumption decisions, people must form expectations of future income using whatever information is available. Expectations change only as a result of new information, which arrives at random. Therefore people's estimates of how wealthy they are, together with their consumption, change at random. No variable other than current consumption is of any value for predicting future consumption. Consumption and income are correlated, but changes in income do not cause changes in consumption.

"The fundamental psychological law, upon which we are entitled to depend with confidence . . . is that [people] are disposed . . . to increase their consumption as their income increases, but not by as much as the increase in their income."

JOHN MAYNARD KEYNES
General Theory

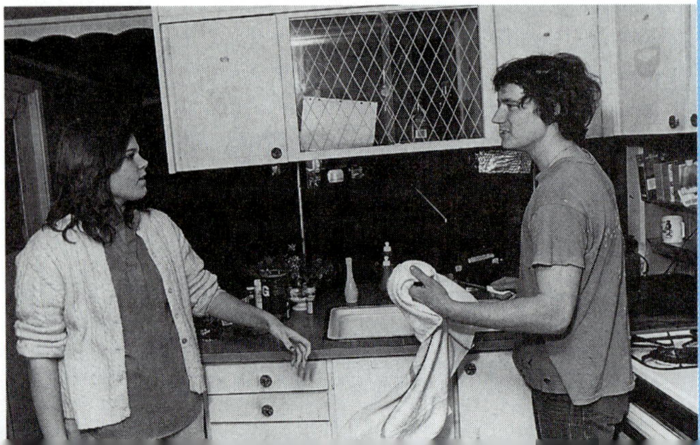

A family whose income is permanently low has a low consumption level. But such a family doesn't always spend all its income every week. Instead, it saves a small amount to smooth its consumption between one year and the next. The amount that such a family saves is influenced by its stage in the life cycle. A young family saves a larger fraction of its income than an older family that has exactly the same level of permanent income. For most low-income families, saving does not mean putting money in the bank or in stocks and bonds. It means buying a home, buying life insurance, and paying social security taxes.

College students usually have low incomes. But they consume at a much higher level than most people whose incomes are similar to theirs. They enjoy a higher standard of housing and consume a much wider range of goods and services—from books and compact discs to athletic facilities and live concerts—than other people with similar incomes. The reason: college students have a high expected future income and, therefore, a high *permanent* income. They sustain a high consumption level by consuming all their income and by taking student loans that enable them to consume beyond their current income level.

John Maynard Keynes: A *Macroeconomic Revolutionary*

When John Maynard Keynes (1883–1946) of Cambridge, England, published his *General Theory of Employment, Interest, and Money* in 1936, he set off a revolution. The centerpieces of Keynes's theory of employment and income were the consumption function and the multiplier. Like all intellectual revolutions, this one was rejected by the older generation and embraced eagerly by the young. Many of Keynes's young adherents were in Cambridge, England (among them Joan Robinson), but many were in Cambridge, Massachusetts.

Keynes was one of the chief architects of the International Monetary Fund and visited the United States to finalize arrangements for the world's new monetary order as World War II was ending. He used the occasion to drop in on the Keynesians of Cambridge, Massachusetts. Asked on his return to England what he thought of his American disciples, he reported that they were far more Keynesian than he!

income that influence consumption expenditure shift both the consumption function and the saving function. For example, an increase in expected future income increases consumption expenditure and decreases saving. In such a case, the consumption function shifts upward and the saving function shifts downward. It is common for shifts like these to occur when the economy begins to recover from a recession. Going into the recession, people expect lower future incomes, but when the recovery begins, they expect higher future incomes. The beginning of the recovery from the 1991 recession was such an occasion—see Reading Between the Lines, pp. 198–199.

The Average Propensities to Consume and to Save

The **average propensity to consume** (*APC*) is consumption expenditure divided by disposable income. Table 8.1(a) shows you how to calculate the average propensity to consume. Let's do a sample calculation. At a disposable income of $20,000, the Polonius household consumes $18,000. Its average propensity to consume is $18,000 divided by $20,000, which equals 0.9.

As you can see from the numbers in the table, the average propensity to consume declines as disposable income rises. At a disposable income of $10,000, the household consumes more than its income, so its average propensity to consume is greater than 1. But at a disposable income of $50,000 the household consumes only $36,000, so its average propensity to consume is $36,000 divided by $50,000, which equals 0.72.

The **average propensity to save** (*APS*) is saving divided by disposable income. Table 8.1(a) shows you how to calculate the average propensity to save. For example, when disposable income is $20,000 the Polonius household saves $2,000, so the average propensity to save is $2,000 divided by $20,000, which equals 0.1. When saving is negative, the average propensity to save is negative. As disposable income increases, the average propensity to save increases.

As disposable income increases, the average propensity to consume falls and the average propensity to save rises. Equivalently, as disposable income increases, the fraction of income saved increases and the fraction of income consumed decreases. These patterns in the average propensities to consume and save reflect the fact that people with very low disposable incomes are so poor that their income is not even sufficient to meet their consumption expenditure. Consumption expenditure exceeds disposable income. As people's incomes increase, they are able to meet their consumption requirements with a lower and lower fraction of their disposable income.

The sum of the average propensity to consume and the average propensity to save is equal to 1. These two average propensities add up to 1 because consumption and saving exhaust disposable income. Each dollar of disposable income is either consumed or saved.

You can see that the two average propensities add up to 1 by using the following equation:

$$C + S = YD.$$

Divide both sides of the equation by disposable income to obtain

$$C/YD + S/YD = 1.$$

C/YD is the *average propensity to consume*, and S/YD is *average propensity to save*. Thus

$$APC + APS = 1.$$

The Marginal Propensities to Consume and to Save

The last dollar of disposable income received is called the marginal dollar. Part of that marginal dollar is consumed, and part of it is saved. The allocation of the marginal dollar between consumption expenditure and saving is determined by the marginal propensities to consume and to save.

The **marginal propensity to consume** (*MPC*) is the fraction of the last dollar of disposable income that is spent on consumption goods and services. It is calculated as the change in consumption expenditure divided by the change in disposable income. The **marginal propensity to save** (*MPS*) is the fraction of the last dollar of disposable income that is saved. The marginal propensity to save is calculated as the change in saving divided by the change in disposable income.

Table 8.1(b) shows the calculation of the Polonius household's marginal propensities to consume and to save. Looking at part (a) of the table, you can see that disposable income increases by $10,000 as we move from one row to the next—

TABLE 8.1

Average and Marginal Propensities to Consume and to Save

(a) Calculating average propensities to consume and to save

Disposable income *(YD)*	Consumption expenditure *(C)*	Saving *(S)*	*APC* *(C/YD)*	*APS* *(S/YD)*
(dollars per year)				
0	**6,000**	**−6,000**	—	—
10,000	**12,000**	**−2,000**	**1.20**	**−0.20**
20,000	**18,000**	**2,000**	**0.90**	**0.10**
30,000	**24,000**	**6,000**	**0.80**	**0.20**
40,000	**30,000**	**10,000**	**0.75**	**0.25**
50,000	**36,000**	**14,000**	**0.72**	**0.28**

(b) Calculating marginal propensities to consume and to save

Change in disposable income	ΔYD	= 10,000
Change in consumption	ΔC	= 6,000
Change in saving	ΔS	= 4,000
Marginal propensity to consume	MPC	= $\Delta C/\Delta YD$ = 0.6
Marginal propensity to save	MPS	= $\Delta S/\Delta YD$ = 0.4

Consumption and saving depend on disposable income. At zero disposable income, some consumption is undertaken and saving is negative (dissaving occurs). As disposable income increases, so do both consumption and saving. The average propensities to consume and to save are calculated in part (a). The average propensity to consume—the ratio of consumption to disposable income—declines as disposable income increases; the average propensity to save—the ratio of saving to disposable income—increases as disposable income increases. These two average propensities sum to 1. Each additional—or *marginal*—dollar of disposable income is either consumed or saved. Part (b) calculates the marginal propensities to consume and to save. The marginal propensity to consume is the change in consumption that results from a $1 change in disposable income. The marginal propensity to save is the change in saving that results from a $1 change in disposable income. The marginal propensities to consume and to save sum to 1.

$10,000 is the change in disposable income. You can also see from part (a) that when disposable income increases by $10,000, consumption increases by $6,000. The marginal propensity to consume—the change in consumption divided by the change in disposable income—is therefore $6,000 divided by $10,000, which equals 0.6. The Polonius household's marginal propensity to consume is constant. It is the same at each level of disposable income. Out of a marginal dollar of disposable income, 60¢ is spent on consumption goods and services.

Part (b) of the table also shows the calculation of the marginal propensity to save. You can see from that part of the table that when disposable income increases by $10,000, saving increases by $4,000. The marginal propensity to save—the change in saving divided by the change in disposable income—is therefore $4,000 divided by $10,000, which equals 0.4. The Polonius household's marginal propensity to save is constant. It is the same at each level of disposable income. Out of the last dollar of disposable income, 40¢ is saved.

The Consumption Function in Action

The New York Times, July 30, 1991

June Gains of 0.5% Posted for Income and Spending

(AP)—Personal income and consumer spending both rose five-tenths of 1 percent in June, the Government said today in a report that analysts saw as a sign that the economy would continue to grow in the third quarter.

"It gives consumer spending quite a bit of momentum going into the third quarter," said Laurence H. Meyer, head of a St. Louis economic forecasting firm. "It's another piece of data that the third quarter is locked in as fairly solid." He added that he thought the recovery would be weaker than normal.

Most analysts are projecting a weaker rebound than the average turnaround in the eight previous recessions since World War II.

Mr. Meyer said there was a significant risk that the economy would slow in the fourth quarter. He said a double-dip recession was possible, although he considered a subdued recovery more likely.

Income growth is needed to continue the economic recovery by providing the resources for consumer spending. Personal consumption represents two-thirds of the nation's economic activity.

Fifth Straight Income Rise

The Commerce Department report said personal income in June totaled $4.80 trillion at a seasonally adjusted annual rate, up from $4.78 trillion a month earlier. It was the fifth straight monthly gain.

At the same time, it said consumer spending totaled $3.83 trillion at an annual rate, up from $3.81 trillion in May. It was the second consecutive gain. . . .

The department reported last week that consumer spending from April through June rose at a 3.6 percent annual rate, the first quarterly increase since the July–September period of 1990.

That helped raise the gross national product by an annual rate of four-tenths of 1 percent, the first advance after two quarters of decline—the generally accepted definition of a recession.

Disposable income—income after taxes—rose five-tenths of 1 percent in June, slightly less than the six-tenths of 1 percent increase a month earlier.

The difference between income and spending meant that the savings rate was the same as in May, at 3.5 percent, but down from 4.1 percent in April.

Wages and salaries rose by $26.6 billion after a $17.2 billion gain in the previous month.

The Essence of the Story

The Commerce Department reported the data in the table for June 1991 and revised data for May 1991.

The Commerce Department also reported the following:

- Personal income had increased for five straight months.
- Consumer spending increased at a 3.6 percent annual rate in the second quarter of 1991, the first quarterly increase since the third quarter of 1990.
- The saving rate of 3.5 percent was down from 4.1 percent rate in April.

The increase in consumer spending helped boost the gross national product at a 0.4 percent annual rate, the first advance after two quarters of decline—the definition of a recession. Because consumer spending represents about two thirds of economic activity, its growth boosted GNP growth and was seen as a sign of recovery from recession.

Background and Analysis

When disposable income increases, consumption expenditure increases by an amount determined by the marginal propensity to consume. Such an increase is shown as a movement along a consumption function.

Consumption expenditure also increases when expected future income increases. Such an increase is shown as an upward shift in the consumption function.

The data reported by the Commerce Department in the news story are consistent with this theory of the consumption function.

The increase in disposable income in June induced an increase in consumption expenditure—there was a movement along the May consumption function shown in the figure.

But consumption expenditure increased by the same amount as the increase in disposable income and by a larger amount than implied by the marginal propensity to consume—there was a shift in the consumption function, as shown in the figure.

This additional increase in consumption expenditure resulted from an increase in expected future income—an expectation of continued recovery from recession.

An increase in income and consumption expenditure (as in June 1991) signals that the economy is recovering from recession.

An increase in consumption expenditure in excess of that implied by the marginal propensity to consume signals an expectation of continued recovery.

Item	May 1991	June 1991
Personal incomes	**\$4.78 trillion**	**\$4.80 trillion**
Consumer spending	**\$3.81 trillion**	**\$3.83 trillion**
Increase in personal incomes	—	**0.5%**
Increase in consumer spending	—	**0.5%**
Increase in disposable incomes	**0.6%**	**0.5%**
Saving rate	**3.5%**	**3.5%**
Increase in wages and salaries	**\$17.2 billion**	**\$26.6 billion**

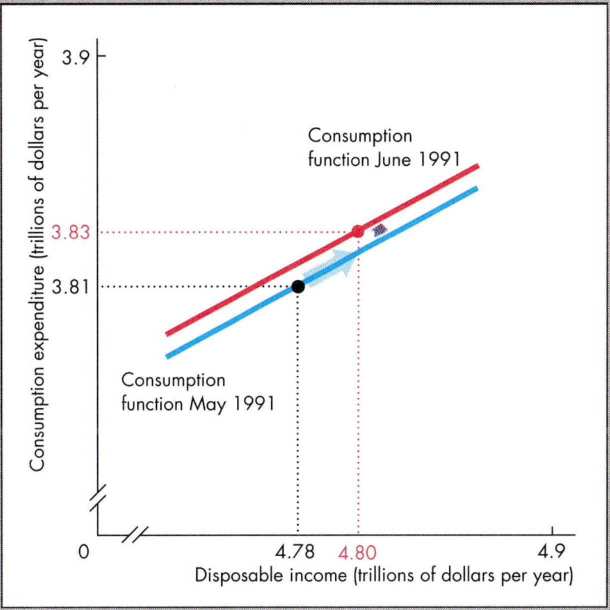

The marginal propensity to consume plus the marginal propensity to save equals 1. Each additional dollar must be either consumed or spent. In this example, when disposable income increases by \$1, 60¢ more is spent and 40¢ more is saved. That is,

$$MPC + MPS = 1.$$

Marginal Propensities and Slopes The marginal propensity to consume is equal to the slope of the consumption function. You can see this equality by looking back at Fig. 8.3. In that figure, the consumption function has a constant slope that can be measured as the change in consumption divided by the change in income. For example, when income increases from \$20,000 to \$30,000—an increase of \$10,000—consumption increases from \$18,000 to \$24,000—an increase of \$6,000. The slope of the consumption function is \$6,000 divided by \$10,000, which equals 0.6—the same value as the marginal propensity to consume that we calculated in Table 8.1.

The marginal propensity to save is equal to the slope of the saving function. You can see this equality by again looking back at Fig. 8.3. In this case, when income increases by \$10,000, saving increases by \$4,000. The slope of the saving function is \$4,000 divided by \$10,000, which equals 0.4—the same value as the marginal propensity to save that we calculated in Table 8.1.

REVIEW

Consumption expenditure is influenced by many factors, but the two most important are disposable income and expected future income. Households allocate their disposable income to either consumption expenditure or saving. The relationship between consumption expenditure and disposable income, other things held constant, is the *consumption function*, and the relationship between saving and disposable income, other things held constant, is the *saving function*. Changes in factors other than disposable income that influence consumption expenditure shift the consumption and saving functions. ◆◆ The change in consumption expenditure divided by the change in disposable income, other things held constant, is the *marginal propensity to consume* (*MPC*), and the change in saving divided by the change in disposable income, other things held constant, is the *marginal propensity to save* (*MPS*). Because consumption expenditure plus saving equals disposable income, *MPC* + *MPS* = 1. ◆

We've studied the consumption function of a household. Let's now look at the U.S. consumption function.

The U.S. Consumption Function

Data for consumption expenditure and disposable income in the United States for the years 1970 to 1992 are shown in Fig. 8.4(a). The vertical axis measures consumption expenditure (in 1987 dollars), and the horizontal axis measures disposable income (also in 1987 dollars). Each point identified by a blue dot represents consumption expenditure and disposable income for a particular year.

The orange line highlights the average relationship between consumption expenditure and disposable income and is an estimate of the U.S. consumption function. It tells us that, on the average, consumption expenditure has been 90 percent of disposable income. The slope of this consumption function—which is also the marginal propensity to consume—is 0.9. The relationship between consumption expenditure and disposable income in any given year does not fall exactly on the orange line. The reason is that the position of the consumption function depends on the other factors that influence consumption expenditure, and as a result the consumption function shifts over time.

Consumption as a Function of GDP Our purpose in developing a theory of the consumption function is to explain the determination of aggregate expenditure and real GDP. To achieve this purpose, we need to establish the relationship between consumption expenditure and real GDP—consumption expenditure as a function of real GDP.

The blue dots in Fig. 8.4(b) show consumption expenditure and real GDP in the United States for each year between 1970 and 1992. The orange line shows consumption expenditure as a function of real GDP. Consumption expenditure is a function of real GDP because disposable income depends on real GDP. Disposable income is real GDP minus net taxes (net taxes are taxes minus transfer payments).

FIGURE 8.4

The U.S. Consumption Function

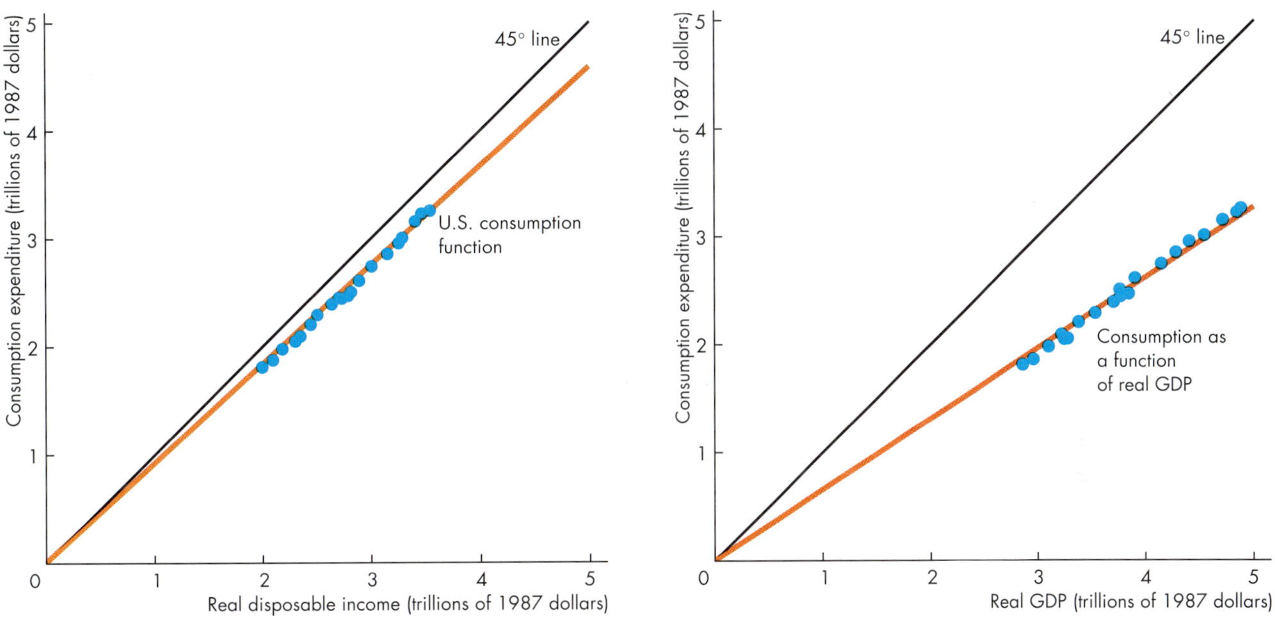

(a) Consumption as a function of disposable income

(b) Consumption as a function of real GDP

Real GDP (Y)	Disposable income ($YD = 0.7Y$)	Consumption expenditure ($C = 0.9YD = 0.63Y$)
	(trillions of 1987 dollars)	
1.0	**0.7**	**0.63**
2.0	**1.4**	**1.26**
3.0	**2.1**	**1.89**
4.0	**2.8**	**2.52**

Part (a) shows the U.S. consumption function—the relationship between real consumption expenditure and real disposable income—for each year between 1970 and 1992. Each blue point in the figure represents real consumption expenditure and real disposable income for a particular year. The orange line shows the average relationship between consumption expenditure and disposable income—an estimate of the U.S. consumption function. This consumption function has a slope and a marginal propensity to consume of 0.9.

Part (b) shows the relationship between consumption expenditure and real GDP. This relationship takes into account the fact that as real GDP increases, so do net taxes. The marginal propensity to consume out of real GDP is approximately 0.63. The connection between consumption as a function of disposable income and consumption as a function of real GDP is shown in the table. The tax rate is 30 percent, so real disposable income is 0.7 times real GDP. The marginal propensity to consume is 0.9. Combining a tax rate of 30 percent with a marginal propensity to consume of 0.9 gives a marginal propensity to consume out of real GDP of 0.63.

But net taxes increase as real GDP increases. Almost all the taxes that we pay—personal taxes, corporate taxes, and social security taxes—increase as our incomes increase. Transfer payments, such as social security and welfare benefits, decrease as our incomes increase. (Social security benefits due to retirement do not vary with income, but aggregate transfer payments do vary with income.) Since taxes increase and transfers decrease, net taxes clearly increase as incomes increase. It turns out that there is a tendency for net taxes to be a fairly stable 30 percent of real GDP. If 30 percent of real GDP is paid in net taxes (taxes minus transfers), 70 percent (or 0.7) of real GDP is available as disposable income.

The table in Fig. 8.4 sets out the relationship between real GDP, disposable income, and consumption expenditure. It incorporates the 0.7 relationship between real GDP and disposable income. For example, if real GDP is $3 trillion, disposable income is 0.7 of that amount, which is $2.1 trillion. The table also shows us the amount of consumption expenditure at various levels of disposable income. We have seen that the marginal propensity to consume is 0.9. Thus, if disposable income is $2.1 trillion, consumption expenditure is 0.9 of that amount, which is $1.89 trillion.

The change in consumption expenditure divided by the change in real GDP is the **marginal propensity to consume out of real GDP.** It is measured by the slope of the orange line in Fig. 8.4(b). Since nine tenths (0.9) of disposable income is consumed and since 70 percent (0.7) of real GDP is available as disposable income, the marginal propensity to consume out of real GDP is 0.63 (0.9 × 0.7, which equals 0.63).

REVIEW

Of all the influences on consumption expenditure, disposable income is the most important. Consumption expenditure in the United States is a function of disposable income. Disposable income is, in turn, related to GDP. Therefore consumption expenditure is a function of GDP. In the United States today, each additional dollar of GDP generates, on the average, an additional 63¢ of consumption expenditure. ◆

The theory of the consumption function has an important implication. Because consumption expenditure is determined mainly by disposable income, most of the changes in consumption expenditure result from changes in income and are not causes of those income changes. It is fluctuations in other components of aggregate expenditure that are the most important sources of fluctuations in income. And the most important of these is investment.

Investment

Gross *investment* is the purchase of new buildings, new plant and equipment, and additions to inventories. It has two components: *net investment*—additions to existing capital—and *replacement investment*—purchases to replace worn out or depreciated capital. As we saw in Fig. 8.2, gross investment is a volatile element of aggregate expenditure. What determines gross investment, and why does it fluctuate so much? The answer lies in the investment decisions of firms—in the answers to questions like these: How does Chrysler decide how much to spend on a new car assembly plant? What determines IBM's outlays on new computer designs? How does AT&T choose what it will spend on fiber-optic communications systems? Let's answer such questions.

Firms' Investment Decisions

The main influences on firms' investment decisions are

- Real interest rates
- Profit expectations
- Existing capital

1. Real Interest Rates The **real interest rate** is the interest rate paid by a borrower and received by a lender after taking into account changes in the value of money resulting from inflation. It is approximately equal to the agreed interest rate (called the *nominal* interest rate) minus the inflation rate. To see why, suppose that prices are rising by 10 percent a year. Each dollar borrowed for one year is repaid at the end of the year with a dollar that is worth only 90¢ today. The borrower gains and the lender loses 10¢ on each dollar. This loss must be subtracted from the agreed interest rate to find the interest *really* paid and received—the real interest rate. If the nominal interest rate is 20 percent a year, the real interest rate is only 10 percent a year.

Firms sometimes pay for capital goods with money they have borrowed, and sometimes they use their own funds—called retained earnings. But regardless of the method of financing an investment project, the real interest rate is part of its *opportunity cost.* The real interest paid on borrowed funds is a direct cost. The real interest cost of using retained earnings arises because these funds could be lent to another firm at the going real interest rate, generating income. The real interest income forgone is the opportunity cost of using retained earnings to finance an investment project.

The lower the real interest rate, the lower is the opportunity cost of any given investment project. Some investment projects that are not profitable at a high real interest rate become profitable at a low real interest rate. The lower the real interest rate, the larger is the number of investment projects that are profitable and, therefore, the greater is the amount of investment.

Let's consider an example. Suppose that Chrysler is contemplating building a new automobile assembly line at a cost of $100 million. The assembly line is expected to produce cars for three years, and then it will be scrapped completely and replaced with a new line that produces an entirely new range of models. Chrysler's expected net revenue is $20 million in each of the first two years and $100 million in the third year. Net revenue is the difference between the total revenue from car sales and the costs of producing those cars. In calculating net revenue, we do not take into account the initial cost of the assembly line or the interest that has to be paid on it. We take separate account of these costs. To build the assembly line, Chrysler plans to borrow the initial $100 million and at the end of each year to use its expected net revenue to pay the interest on the loan outstanding along with as much of the loan as it can. Does it pay Chrysler to invest $100 million in this car assembly line? The answer depends on the real interest rate.

Case 1 in Fig. 8.5 shows what happens if the interest rate is 20 percent per year. (We'll assume the expected inflation rate to be zero, so the expected real interest rate is also 20 percent a year. This is an unlikely high rate but makes the numbers work out easily.) Chrysler borrows $100 million and at the end of the first year has to pay $20 million in interest. It has a net revenue of $20 million and so can just meet this interest payment but cannot reduce the size of its outstanding loan. At the end of the second year, it is in exactly the same situation as at the end of the first. It owes another $20 million on its outstanding loan. Again its revenue just covers the interest payment. At the end of the third year, Chrysler owes another $20 million in interest payments plus the $100 million outstanding loan. Therefore it has to pay $120 million. But net revenue in the third year is only $100 million, so Chrysler has a $20 million loss on this project.

Case 2 in Fig. 8.5 shows what happens if the real interest rate is 10 percent per year. (Again, we'll assume that the expected inflation rate is zero, so the expected real interest rate is also 10 percent a year.) In this case, Chrysler owes $10 million in interest at the end of the first year. Since it has $20 million of revenue, it can make this interest payment and reduce its outstanding loan to $90 million. In the second year, the interest owing on the loan is $9 million (10 percent of $90 million). Again, with revenue of $20 million, Chrysler pays the interest and reduces its outstanding loan by $11 million to $79 million. In the third and final year of the project, the interest on the loan is $7.9 million (10 percent of $79 million), so the total amount owing—the outstanding loan plus the interest—is $86.9 million. Chrysler's revenue in year 3 is $100 million, so it repays the loan, pays the interest, and pockets the balance, a profit of $13.1 million. If Chrysler builds the assembly line, it expects to make a profit of $13.1 million.

You can see that at a real interest rate of 20 percent a year, it does not pay Chrysler to invest in this car assembly plant. At a 10 percent real interest rate, it does pay. The lower the real interest rate, the larger is the number of projects, such as the one considered here, that yield a positive net profit. Thus the lower the real interest rate, the larger is the amount of investment.

2. Profit Expectations The higher the expected profitability of new capital equipment, the greater is the amount of investment. Chrysler's assembly line investment decision illustrates this effect. To decide whether or not to build the assembly line, Chrysler has to work out its net revenue. To perform that calculation, it has to work out the total revenue from car sales, which, in turn, are affected by its expectations of car prices and the share of the market that it can attain. Chrysler also has to figure out its operating costs, which include the wages of its assembly workers and the costs of the products that it buys from other producers. The larger the net revenue

FIGURE 8.5

Investment in an Automobile Assembly Line

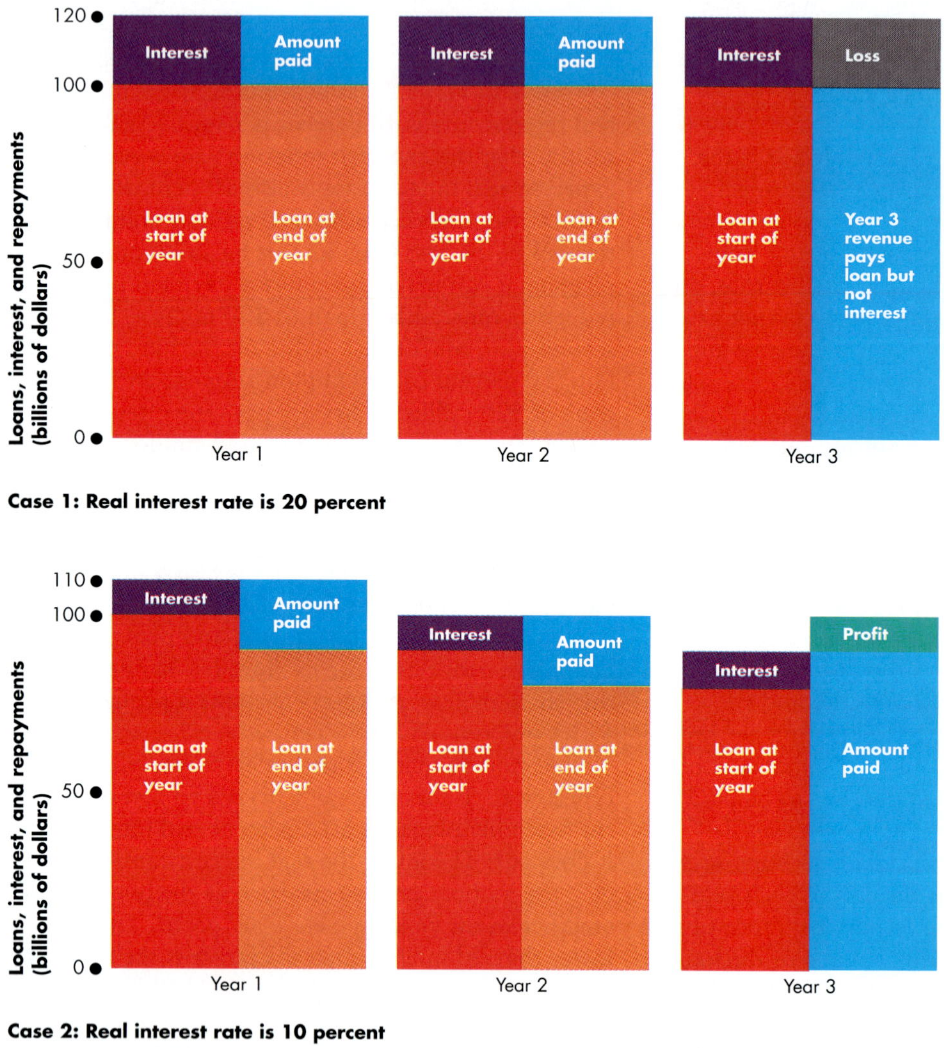

An automobile assembly line costs $100 million to build. It is expected to generate the following revenue:

Year 1	$20 million
Year 2	$20 million
Year 3	$100 million

The line will then be scrapped and replaced by a new one. In case 1, the real interest rate is 20 percent per year. The revenue stream is too low to cover the total expense, and the project is not worth undertaking. In case 2, the real interest rate is 10 percent per year, and the project is profitable. The lower the real interest rate, the larger is the number of projects that are profitable and that are undertaken.

that it anticipates, the more profitable is the investment project that generates those net revenues and the more likely it is that the project will be undertaken.

There are many influences on profit expectations themselves. Among the more important ones are taxes on company profits, the phase of the business cycle through which the economy is passing, and the state of global relations and tensions. For example, the collapse of the Soviet Union and the emergence of the new republics of Eastern Europe are likely to have a large impact on profit expectations in the 1990s—positive in some industries and negative in others.

3. Existing Capital A firm's existing capital influences its investment decisions in two ways. First, the larger the amount of existing capital, other things being equal, the greater is the amount of depreciation and the larger is the amount of replacement investment. But the influence of the amount of existing capital is not a source of volatility in investment.

FIGURE 8.6

Investment Demand Curve and Investment Demand Schedule

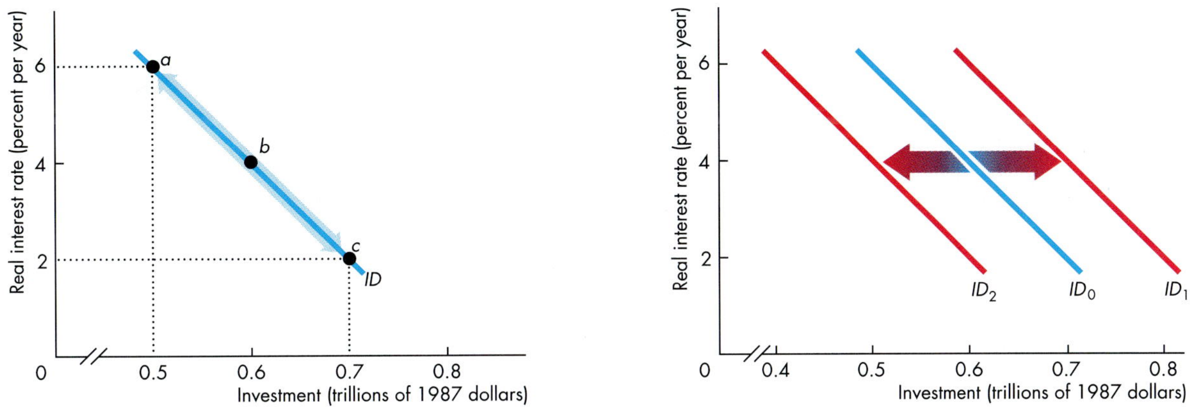

(a) The effect of a change in real interest rate

(b) The effect of a change in profit expectations

	Real interest rate (percent per year)	Investment (trillions of 1987 dollars)		
		Optimistic	Average	Pessimistic
a	**6**	**0.6**	**0.5**	**0.4**
b	**4**	**0.7**	**0.6**	**0.5**
c	**2**	**0.8**	**0.7**	**0.6**

An investment demand schedule lists the quantities of aggregate planned investment at each real interest rate. An investment demand curve graphs an investment demand schedule. The table shows the investment demand schedule when expectations are average, optimistic, and pessimistic. Part (a) shows the investment demand curve for average profit expectations. Along that investment demand curve, as the real interest rate rises from 2 percent to 6 percent, planned investment decreases—there is a movement along the investment demand curve from *c* to *a*. Part (b) shows how the investment demand curve changes when expected future profits change. With average profit expectations, the investment demand curve is ID_0—the same curve as in part (a). With optimistic expectations about future profits, planned investment increases at each real interest rate and the investment demand curve shifts to the right to ID_1. With pessimistic expectations about future profits, planned investment decreases at each real interest rate and the investment demand curve shifts to the left to ID_2.

It is a source of steady investment growth. Second, the higher the degree of utilization of existing capital, the larger is the amount of investment. When capital is underutilized, as in a recession, investment falls off. But when capital is overutilized, as in a boom, investment increases.

Investment Demand

Investment demand is the relationship between the level of planned investment and the real interest rate, holding all other influences on investment constant. The **investment demand schedule** lists the quantity of planned investment at each real interest rate, holding all other influences on investment constant. The **investment demand curve** graphs the relationship between the real interest rate and the level of planned investment, holding everything else constant. Some examples of investment demand schedules and investment demand curves appear in Fig. 8.6. The investment demand schedule and the position of the investment demand curve depend on the other influences on investment—expected profit and the existing capital stock.

Sometimes firms are pessimistic about future profits, sometimes they are optimistic, and sometimes their expectations are average. Fluctuations in profit expectations are the main source of fluctuations in investment demand. The three investment demand schedules in the table in Fig. 8.6 give examples of investment demand under the three types of expectations. In the case of average profit expectations, if the real interest rate is 4 percent a year, investment is \$0.6 trillion. If the real interest rate decreases to 2 percent a year, investment increases to \$0.7 trillion. If the real interest rate increases to 6 percent a year, investment decreases to \$0.5 trillion. In the case of optimistic profit expectations, investment is higher at each interest rate than it is when expectations are average. In the case of pessimistic profit expectations, investment is lower at each interest rate than with average expectations.

The investment demand curve is shown in the figure. In part (a), the investment demand curve (*ID*) is that for average expected profit. Each point (*a* through *c*) corresponds to a row in the table. A change in the real interest rate causes a movement along the investment demand curve. Thus, if the real interest rate is 4 percent a year, planned investment is \$0.6 trillion. If the real interest rate rises to 6 percent a year, there is a movement up the investment demand curve (see blue arrow) and planned investment decreases to \$0.5 trillion. If the real interest rate falls to 2 percent a year, there is a movement down the investment demand curve and planned investment increases to \$0.7 trillion.

The effects of profit expectations are shown in part (b). A change in profit expectations shifts the investment demand curve. The demand curve ID_0 represents average expected profit. When profit expectations become optimistic, the investment demand curve shifts to the right, from ID_0 to ID_1. When profit expectations become pessimistic, the investment demand curve shifts to the left, from ID_0 to ID_2.

The investment demand curve also shifts when there is an increase in the amount of investment to replace depreciated capital. This influence leads to a steady rightward shift in the *ID* curve.

FIGURE 8.7

Gross and Net Investment in the United States

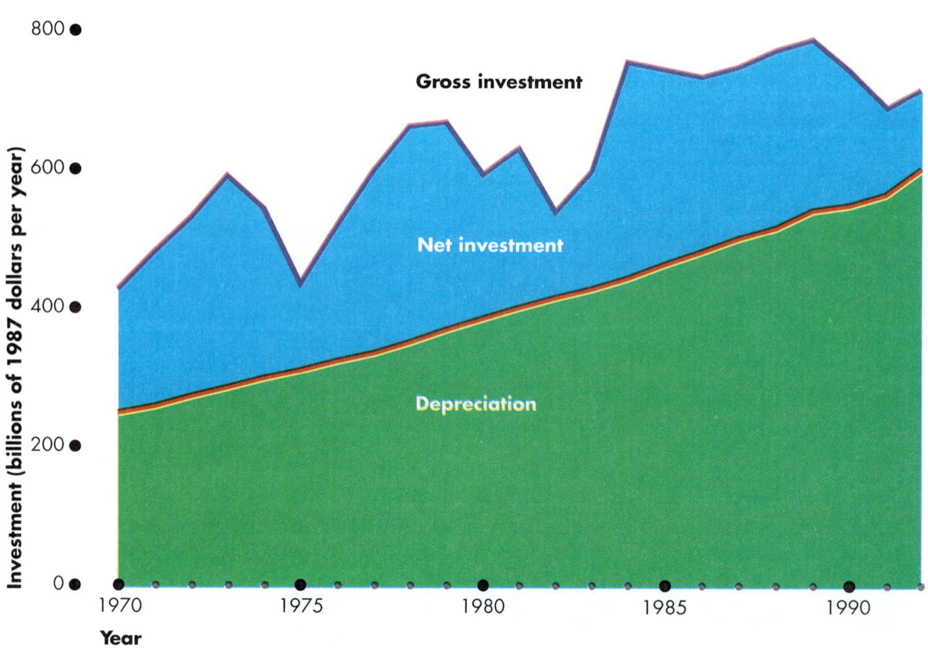

Gross investment is separated into two parts: the replacement of depreciated capital (shaded green) and net investment (shaded blue). Gross investment and depreciation increased steadily between 1970 and 1992. Depreciation follows a very smooth growth path because the capital stock grows steadily and smoothly. Net investment fluctuates.

Source: Economic Report of the President, 1993.

REVIEW

Investment depends on the real interest rate, profit expectations, and the scale of replacement of depreciated capital. Other things held constant, the lower the real interest rate, the larger is the amount of investment. When profit expectations become optimistic, the investment demand curve shifts to the right; when profit expectations become pessimistic, it shifts to the left. Profit expectations are also influenced by taxes, the environment, and the business cycle. When the economy is expanding quickly, profit expectations are optimistic and investment demand is high. When the economy is expanding slowly (or contracting), profit expectations are pessimistic and investment demand is low. Investment to replace depreciated capital grows steadily over time. ◆

We've just studied the *theory* of investment demand. Let's now see how that theory helps us to understand the fluctuations in investment that occur in the U.S. economy.

Investment Demand in the United States

As we saw in Fig. 8.2, investment is one of the most volatile components of aggregate expenditure. In some years, investment is as much as 20 percent below trend, and in others it is more than 10 percent above trend. Let's see how we can interpret these fluctuations in investment with the theory of investment demand we've just been studying.

We'll begin by looking at Fig. 8.7. It shows investment (in billions of 1987 dollars) between 1970 and 1992. It also shows the way in which investment—gross investment—is broken down between net investment and the replacement of depreciated capital—depreciation. As you can see, both depreciation and gross investment increase steadily over time. Depreciation follows a very smooth path. It reflects the fact that the capital stock grows steadily and smoothly. Net investment is the component of investment that fluctuates. You can see that fluctuation as the blue area between gross investment and depreciation.

The theory of investment demand predicts that fluctuations in investment result from fluctuations in the real interest rate and in future profit expectations. What is the relative importance of these two factors? Figure 8.8 answers this question. The points in the figure represent the gross investment and the real interest rate in the United States each year from 1980 to 1992. The figure also shows three U.S. investment demand curves, ID_0, ID_1, and ID_2.

In the early 1980s, the investment demand curve was ID_0. As expected profits increased in 1983 and 1984, the investment demand curve shifted to the right, first to ID_1 and then to ID_2. During the late 1980s, the investment demand curve remained close to ID_2 but began to shift leftward. Then, in 1992,

FIGURE 8.8

The U.S. Investment Demand Curve

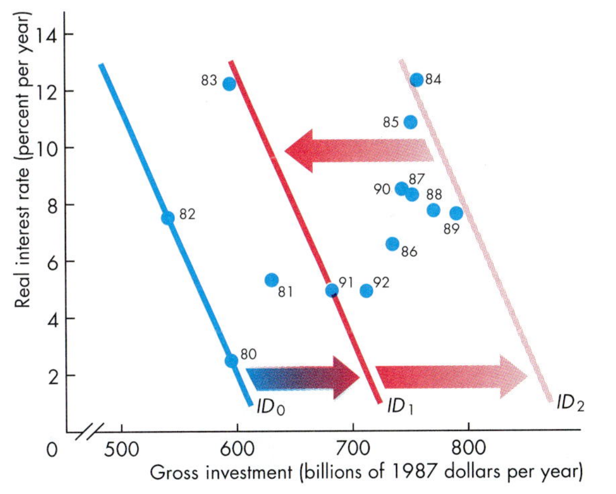

The blue points show the levels of gross investment and the real interest rate in the United States for each year between 1980 and 1992. When expected profits were low in the early 1980s, the investment demand curve was ID_0. As expected profits increased, the investment demand curve shifted rightward. By 1983 it had shifted to ID_1, and by 1984 it had shifted to ID_2. When expected profits declined in 1991, the investment demand curve shifted back to ID_1. Swings in profit expectations are more important than changes in interest rates in creating fluctuations in gross investment.

Source: Economic Report of the President, 1993, and my calculations and assumptions.

expected profits declined as the economy went into recession and the investment demand curve made a large leftward shift to the position it had been in eight years earlier—to ID_1. The fluctuations in investment resulting from changes in expected profits that shift the investment curve are much larger than those resulting from changes in interest rates.

Regardless of whether the fluctuations in investment are generated by shifts in the investment demand curve or movements along it, they have important effects on the economy. We'll learn about some of those effects in Chapter 9.

Let's now turn to the third component of aggregate expenditure, government purchases of goods and services.

Government Purchases of Goods and Services

Government purchases of goods and services cover a wide range of public sector activities. They include goods and services for our national defense, international representation (embassies and delegations in other countries), and domestic programs such as health care, education, and highways.

These expenditures are determined by our political institutions and legislative process. They are influenced by our votes in national, state, and local elections, the views of the members of Congress and state and local legislators we elect, the actions of lobbyists, the political state of the world, and the state of the U.S. and world economies.

Although some components of government purchases do vary with the state of the economy, most do not. Furthermore, government spending decisions are made on a fixed timetable and thus do not respond quickly to the changing economic situation. We will assume, therefore, that government purchases do not vary in a systematic way with the level of GDP. They influence GDP but are not directly influenced by it.

The final component of aggregate expenditure is net exports. Let's now see how they are determined.

Net Exports

Net exports are the expenditure by foreigners on U.S.-made goods and services minus the expenditure by U.S. residents on foreign-made goods and services. That is, net exports are U.S. exports minus U.S. imports. *Exports* are the sale of the goods and services produced in the United States to the rest of the world. *Imports* are the purchase of goods produced in the rest of the world by firms and households in the United States.

Exports

Exports are determined by decisions made in the rest of the world and are influenced by four main factors:

- Real GDP in the rest of the world
- Degree of international specialization
- Prices of U.S.-made goods and services relative to the prices of similar goods and services made in other countries
- Foreign exchange rates

Other things being equal, the higher the level of real GDP in the rest of the world, the greater is the demand by foreigners for U.S.-made goods and services. For example, an economic boom in Japan increases the Japanese demand for U.S.-made goods and services, such as Boeing airplanes, California oranges, Texas beef, and New York investment services, and increases U.S. exports. A recession in Japan cuts the Japanese demand for U.S.-made goods and decreases U.S. exports.

Also, the greater the degree of specialization in the world economy, the larger is the volume of exports, other things being equal. Over time, international specialization has been increasing. For example, the world aircraft industry is now heavily concentrated in the United States. While a small number of transcontinental airliners are built in France, Britain, and Russia, most of the world's major airlines buy their aircraft from either Boeing or McDonnell-Douglas. Also, the United States dominates the world in the manufacture and sale of biotechnology products. But many goods and services, notably in the consumer electronics industry, that were once made in the United States in large quantities are now made almost exclusively in Japan, Hong Kong, and other Asian countries on the Pacific Rim.

Next, other things being equal, the lower the price of U.S.-made goods and services relative to the prices of similar goods and services made in other countries, the greater is the quantity of U.S. exports.

Finally, again other things being equal, the lower the value of the U.S. dollar against other currencies, the larger is the quantity of U.S. exports. For example, as the U.S. dollar fell in value against the German mark and the Japanese yen in 1987, the demand for U.S.-made goods and services by those two countries increased sharply.

Imports

Imports are determined by four main factors:

- U.S. real GDP
- Degree of international specialization
- Prices of foreign-made goods and services relative to the prices of similar goods and services made in the United States
- Foreign exchange rates

Other things being equal, the higher the level of U.S. real GDP, the larger is the quantity of U.S. imports. For example, the long period of sustained income growth in the United States between 1983 and 1987 brought a huge increase in U.S. imports.

Also, the higher the degree of international specialization, the larger is the volume of U.S. imports, other things being equal. For example, there is a high degree of international specialization in the production of VCRs. As a consequence, all the VCRs sold in the United States are now produced in other countries—mainly Japan and Korea.

Finally, again other things being equal, the higher the prices of U.S.-made goods and services relative to the prices of similar foreign-made goods and services, and the higher the value of the U.S. dollar against other currencies, the larger is the quantity of U.S. imports. Though high real GDP growth in the United States in 1985 and 1986 produced an increase in imports, the increase was less severe than it otherwise would have been because of the fall in the value of the U.S. dollar against other currencies. The falling dollar made foreign goods and services more expensive and so slowed down, to some degree, the growth of U.S. imports.

Net Export Function

The **net export function** is the relationship between net exports and U.S. real GDP, holding constant all other influences on U.S. exports and imports. The net export function can also be described by a net export schedule, which lists the level of net exports at each level of real GDP, with everything else held constant. The table in Fig. 8.9 gives an example of a net export schedule.

In the table, exports are a constant \$0.5 trillion—they do not depend on U.S. real GDP. Imports increase by \$0.15 trillion for each \$1.0 trillion increase in U.S. real GDP. Net exports, the difference between exports and imports, are shown in the final column of the table. When real GDP is \$1.0 trillion, net exports are \$0.35 trillion. Net exports decline as real GDP rises. At a real GDP just above \$3 trillion (\$3.33 trillion), net exports are zero; and at real GDP levels higher than that, net exports become increasingly negative (imports exceed exports).

Exports and imports are graphed in Fig. 8.9(a), and the net export function is graphed in Fig. 8.9(b). By comparing part (a) and part (b), you can see that when exports exceed imports, net exports are above zero (there is a surplus), and when imports exceed exports, net exports are below zero (there is a deficit). When real GDP is \$3.33 trillion, there is a balance between exports and imports.

The data in Fig. 8.9 are based on the U.S. economy in 1988. In that year, real GDP was \$4 trillion, exports were \$0.5 trillion, imports were \$0.6 trillion, and net exports were –\$0.1 trillion, highlighted in the figure.

The position of the net export function depends on real GDP in the rest of the world, on the degree of international specialization, and on prices of U.S.-made goods and services compared with the prices of those goods and services made in the rest of the world. If real GDP in the rest of the world increases,

FIGURE 8.9

Net Export Function and Net Export Schedule

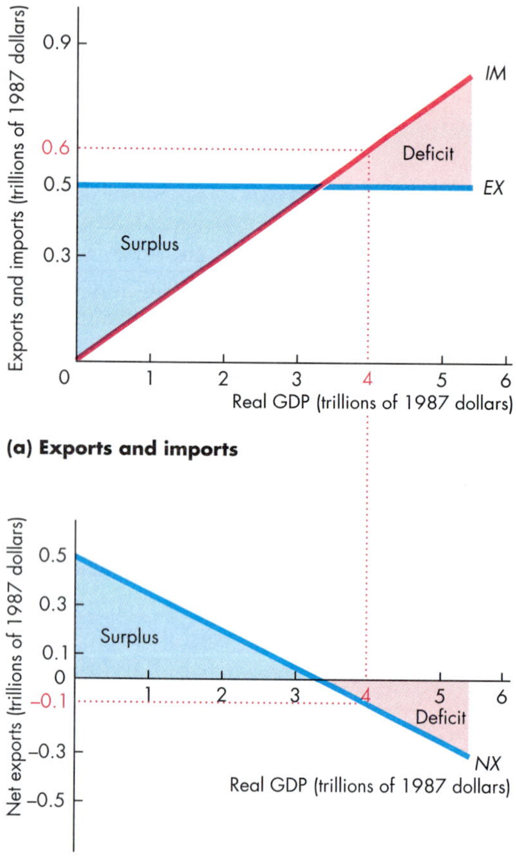

(a) Exports and imports

(b) Net exports

Real GDP (Y)	Exports (EX)	Imports (IM)	Net exports ($EX - IM$)
	(trillions of 1987 dollars)		
0	**0.5**	**0**	**0.5**
1.0	**0.5**	**0.15**	**0.35**
2.0	**0.5**	**0.30**	**0.20**
3.0	**0.5**	**0.45**	**0.05**
4.0	**0.5**	**0.60**	**−0.10**
5.0	**0.5**	**0.75**	**−0.25**

The net export schedule in the table shows the relationship between net exports and real GDP. Net exports are equal to exports (EX) minus imports (IM). Exports are independent of real GDP, but imports rise as real GDP rises. In the table, imports are 15 percent of real GDP. Net exports fall as GDP rises.

Part (a) graphs the export and import schedules. Since exports are independent of real GDP, they are graphed as a horizontal line. Since imports rise as real GDP rises, they appear as an upward-sloping line. The distance between the export curve and the import curve represents net exports. Net exports are graphed in part (b) of the figure. The net export function is downward sloping because the import curve is upward sloping. The real GDP level at which the net export function intersects the horizontal axis in part (b) is the same as that at which the imports curve intersects the exports curve in part (a). That level of real GDP is $3.33 trillion. Below that level of real GDP there is a surplus, and above it there is a deficit. In 1988, when real GDP was $4 trillion, imports exceeded exports and net exports were –$0.1 trillion.

the net export function shifts upward. If U.S.-made goods and services become cheap relative to goods and services made in the rest of the world, the net export function also shifts upward. A change in the degree of international specialization has an ambiguous effect on the position of the net export function. If the United States becomes more specialized in goods and services for which there is an increase in world demand, the net export function shifts upward. If U.S. demand increases for goods and services in which the rest of the world specializes, the net export function shifts downward.

We've now studied the main influences on consumption expenditure, investment, and net exports, and our next task is to see how these components of aggregate expenditure interact with each other and with government purchases of goods and services to determine aggregate expenditure. Our starting point is to establish a relationship between aggregate planned expenditure and real GDP.

Aggregate Expenditure and Real GDP

There is a relationship between aggregate planned expenditure and real GDP. **Aggregate planned expenditure** is the expenditure that economic agents (households, firms, governments, and foreigners) plan to undertake in given circumstances. Aggregate planned expenditure is not necessarily equal to actual aggregate expenditure. We'll see how these two expenditure concepts—planned and actual—differ from each other later in this chapter.

The relationship between aggregate planned expenditure and real GDP may be described by either an aggregate expenditure schedule or an aggregate expenditure curve. The **aggregate expenditure schedule** lists the level of aggregate planned expenditure generated at each level of real GDP. The **aggregate expenditure curve** is a graph of the aggregate expenditure schedule.

Aggregate Expenditure Schedule

The aggregate expenditure schedule is set out in the table in Fig. 8.10. (The data in this figure are examples and do not refer to the real world.) The table shows aggregate planned expenditure as well as its components. To work out the level of aggregate planned expenditure at a given real GDP, we add the various components together. The first column of the table shows real GDP, and the second column shows the consumption expenditure generated by each level of real GDP. When real GDP is $1 trillion, so is consumption expenditure. A $1 trillion increase in real GDP generates a $0.65 trillion increase in consumption expenditure.

The next two columns show investment and government purchases of goods and services. Recall that investment depends on the real interest rate and the state of profit expectations. Suppose that those factors are constant and, at a given point in time, generate a level of investment of $0.5 trillion. This investment level is independent of real GDP. Government purchases of goods and services are also fixed. Their value is $0.7 trillion.

The next three columns show exports, imports, and net exports. Exports are influenced by events in the rest of the world, by our prices compared with prices in other countries, and by the foreign exchange value of our dollar. They are not directly affected by the level of real GDP. In the table, exports appear as a constant $0.45 trillion. In contrast, imports do increase as real GDP increases. In the table, a $1 trillion increase in real GDP generates a $0.15 trillion increase in imports. Net exports—the difference between exports and imports—also vary as real GDP varies. Net exports decrease by $0.15 trillion for each $1 trillion increase in real GDP.

The final column of the table shows aggregate planned expenditure. This amount is the sum of planned consumption expenditure, investment, government purchases of goods and services, and net exports.

Aggregate Expenditure Curve

The aggregate expenditure curve appears in the diagram in Fig. 8.10. Real GDP is shown on the horizontal axis, and aggregate planned expenditure on the vertical axis. The aggregate expenditure curve is the red line labeled *AE*. Points *a* through *f* on that curve correspond to the rows in the table in Fig. 8.10. The *AE* curve is a graph of the last column, "Aggregate planned expenditure," plotted against real GDP.

The figure also shows the components of aggregate expenditure. The constant components—investment, government purchases of goods and services, and exports—are indicated by the horizontal lines in the figure. Consumption is the vertical gap between the line labeled $I + G + EX + C$ and that labeled $I + G + EX$.

To calculate the *AE* curve, we subtract imports from the $I + G + EX + C$ line. Imports are subtracted because they are not expenditure on U.S. real GDP. The purchase of a new car is part of consumption expenditure, but if that car is a Toyota made in Japan, expenditure on it has to be subtracted from consumption expenditure to find out how much is spent on goods and services produced in the United States—on U.S. real GDP. Money paid to Toyota for car imports from Japan does not add to aggregate expenditure in the United States.

FIGURE 8.10

Aggregate Expenditure Curve and Aggregate Expenditure Schedule

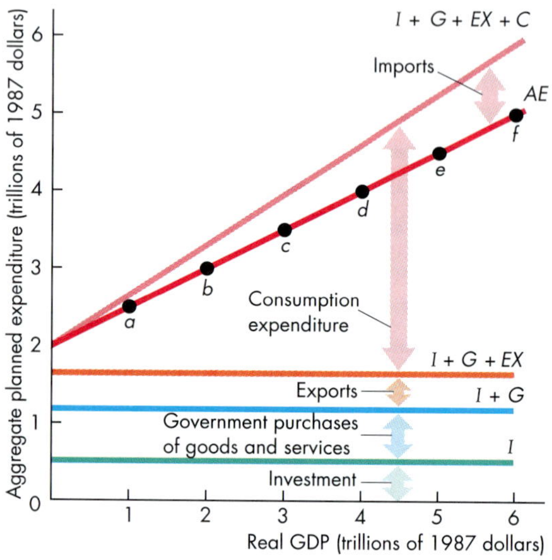

The relationship between aggregate planned expenditure and real GDP may be described by an aggregate expenditure schedule (as shown in the table) or an aggregate expenditure curve (as shown in the diagram). Aggregate planned expenditure is calculated as the sum of planned consumption expenditure, investment, government purchases of goods and services, and net exports. For example, in row *a* of the table, if real GDP is $1.0 trillion, aggregate planned consumption is $1.0 trillion, planned investment is $0.5 trillion, planned government purchases of goods and services are $0.7 trillion, and planned net exports are $0.3 trillion. Thus, when real GDP is $1.0 trillion, aggregate planned expenditure is $2.5 trillion ($1.0 + $0.5 + $0.7 + $0.3). The expenditure plans are graphed in the figure as the aggregate expenditure curve *AE*.

		Planned expenditure						
	Real GDP (Y)	Consumption expenditure (C)	Investment (I)	Government purchases (G)	Exports (EX)	Imports (IM)	Net exports ($NX = EX - IM$)	Aggregate planned expenditure ($AE = C + I + G + NX$)
				(trillions of 1987 dollars)				
a	**1.0**	**1.00**	**0.5**	**0.7**	**0.45**	**0.15**	**0.30**	**2.5**
b	**2.0**	**1.65**	**0.5**	**0.7**	**0.45**	**0.30**	**0.15**	**3.0**
c	**3.0**	**2.30**	**0.5**	**0.7**	**0.45**	**0.45**	**0**	**3.5**
d	**4.0**	**2.95**	**0.5**	**0.7**	**0.45**	**0.60**	**−0.15**	**4.0**
e	**5.0**	**3.60**	**0.5**	**0.7**	**0.45**	**0.75**	**−0.30**	**4.5**
f	**6.0**	**4.25**	**0.5**	**0.7**	**0.45**	**0.90**	**−0.45**	**5.0**

We've now seen how to calculate the aggregate expenditure schedule and aggregate expenditure curve and seen that aggregate planned expenditure increases as real GDP increases. This relationship is summarized in the aggregate expenditure curve. But what determines the point on the aggregate expenditure curve at which the economy operates? We're now going to answer this question.

Equilibrium Expenditure

Equilibrium expenditure occurs when aggregate planned expenditure equals real GDP. At levels of real GDP below equilibrium, planned expenditure exceeds real GDP; at levels of real GDP above equilibrium, planned expenditure falls short of real GDP.

To see how equilibrium expenditure is determined, we need to distinguish between actual expenditure and planned expenditure and understand how actual expenditure, planned expenditure, and real GDP are related.

Actual Expenditure, Planned Expenditure, and Real GDP

Actual aggregate expenditure is always equal to real GDP. (We established this fact in Chapter 6, pp. 131 and 133.) But *planned* expenditure is not necessarily equal to actual expenditure and, therefore, is not necessarily equal to actual real GDP. How can actual expenditure and planned expenditure differ from each other? Why don't people implement their plans? The main reason is that firms may end up with unplanned excess inventories or with an unplanned shortage of inventories. People carry out their consumption expenditure plans, the government implements its planned purchases of goods and services, and net exports are as planned. Firms carry out their plans to invest in buildings, plant, and equipment. One component of investment, however, is the change in firms' inventories of goods that have not yet been sold. Inventories change when aggregate planned expenditure differs from real GDP. If real GDP exceeds planned expenditure, inventories rise, and if real GDP is less than planned expenditure, inventorics fall.

When aggregate planned expenditure is equal to aggregate actual expenditure and equal to real GDP, the economy is in an expenditure equilibrium. When aggregate planned expenditure and aggregate actual expenditure are unequal, a process of convergence toward an equilibrium expenditure occurs. Let's examine equilibrium expenditure and the process that brings it about.

When Planned Expenditure Equals Real GDP

The table in Fig. 8.11 shows different levels of real GDP. Against each level of real GDP, the second column shows aggregate planned expenditure. Only when real GDP equals $4 billion is aggregate planned expenditure equal to real GDP. This level of expenditure is the equilibrium expenditure.

The equilibrium is illustrated in Fig. 8.11(a). The aggregate expenditure curve is *AE*. Since aggregate planned expenditure on the vertical axis and real GDP on the horizontal axis are measured in the same units and on the same scale, a 45° line drawn in Fig. 8.11(a) shows all the points at which aggregate planned expenditure equals real GDP. Where the aggregate expenditure curve intersects the 45° line, at point *d*, equilibrium expenditure is determined.

Convergence to Equilibrium You will get a better idea of why point *d* is the equilibrium if you consider what is happening when the economy is not at point *d*. Suppose that real GDP is $2 trillion. You can see from Fig. 8.11(a) that in this situation, aggregate planned expenditure is $3 trillion (point *b*). Thus aggregate planned expenditure is larger than real GDP. If aggregate expenditure is actually $3 trillion as planned, then real GDP would also be $3 trillion, since every dollar spent by one person is a dollar of income for someone else. But real GDP is $2 trillion. How can real GDP be $2 trillion if people *plan* to spend $3 trillion? The answer is that *actual* spending is less than *planned* spending. If real GDP is $2 trillion, the value of production is also $2 trillion. The only way that people can buy goods and services worth $3 trillion when the value of production is $2 trillion is if firms' inventories fall by $1 trillion (point *b* in Fig. 8.11b). Since changes in inventories are part of investment, actual investment is less than planned investment.

But this is not the end of the story. Firms have target levels for inventories, and when inventories fall below those targets, firms increase production to restore inventories to their target levels. To restore their inventories, firms hire additional labor and increase production. Suppose that they increase production in the next period by enough to replenish their inventories. Real GDP rises by $1.0 trillion to $3.0 trillion. But again, aggregate planned expenditure exceeds real GDP. When real GDP is $3.0 trillion, aggregate planned expenditure is $3.5 trillion (point *c* in Fig. 8.11a). Again, inventories fall, but this time by less than before. With real GDP of $3.0

FIGURE 8.11

Equilibrium Expenditure and Real GDP

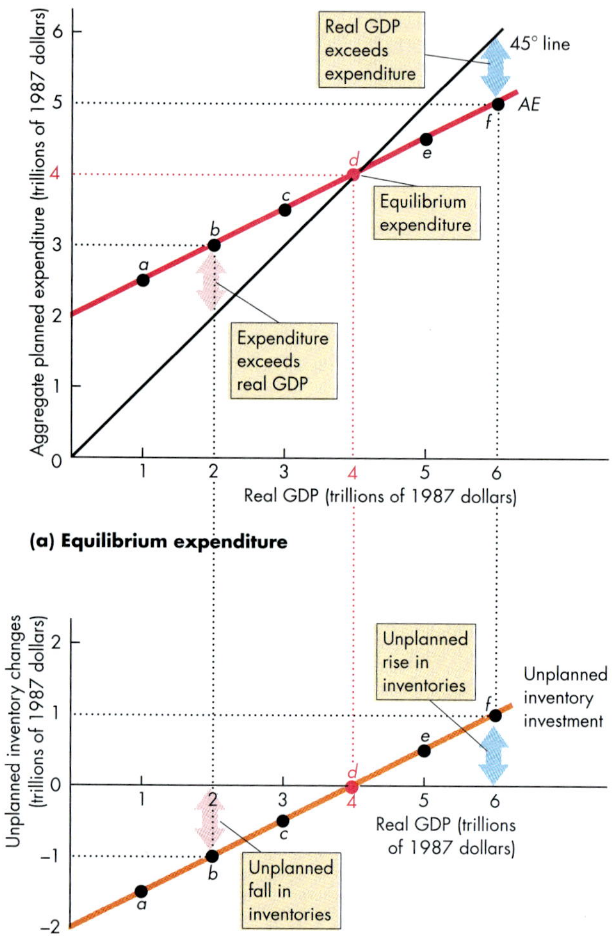

(a) Equilibrium expenditure

(b) Unplanned inventory changes

	Real GDP (Y)	Aggregate planned expenditure (AE)	Unplanned inventory changes ($Y - AE$)
		(trillions of 1987 dollars)	
a	**1.0**	**2.5**	**−1.5**
b	**2.0**	**3.0**	**−1.0**
c	**3.0**	**3.5**	**−0.5**
d	**4.0**	**4.0**	**0**
e	**5.0**	**4.5**	**0.5**
f	**6.0**	**5.0**	**1.0**

The table shows the aggregate expenditure schedule. When real GDP is $4 trillion, aggregate planned expenditure equals real GDP. At real GDP levels below $4 trillion, aggregate planned expenditure exceeds real GDP. At real GDP levels above $4 trillion, aggregate planned expenditure is less than real GDP.

The diagram illustrates equilibrium expenditure in part (a). The 45° line shows those points at which aggregate planned expenditure equals real GDP. The aggregate expenditure curve is *AE*. Actual aggregate expenditure equals real GDP. Equilibrium expenditure and real GDP are $4 trillion. That real GDP level generates planned expenditure that equals real GDP—$4 trillion.

The forces bringing the equilibrium about are illustrated in parts (a) and (b). At real GDP levels below $4 trillion, aggregate planned expenditure exceeds real GDP and inventories fall—for example, point *b* in both parts of the figure. In such cases, firms increase output to restore their inventories and real GDP rises. At real GDP levels higher than $4 trillion, aggregate planned expenditure is less than real GDP and inventories rise—for example, point *f* in both parts of the figure. In such a situation, firms decrease output to work off excess inventories and real GDP falls. Only where the aggregate planned expenditure curve cuts the 45° line is planned expenditure equal to real GDP. This position is the equilibrium. There are no unplanned inventory changes, and output remains constant.

trillion and planned expenditure of $3.5 trillion, inventories fall by only $0.5 trillion (point *c* in Fig. 8.11b). Again, firms hire additional labor, and production increases; real GDP increases yet further.

The process that we have just described—planned expenditure exceeds income, inventories fall, and production rises to restore the unplanned inventory reduction—ends when real GDP has reached $4 trillion. At this level of real GDP, there is an equilibrium. There are no unplanned inventory changes, and firms do not change their production.

Next, let's perform a similar experiment, but one starting with a level of real GDP greater than the equilibrium. Suppose that real GDP is $6.0 trillion.

At this level, aggregate planned expenditure is $5.0 trillion (point *f* in Fig. 8.11a), $1.0 trillion less than real GDP. With aggregate planned expenditure less than real GDP, inventories rise by $1.0 trillion (point *f* in Fig. 8.11b)—there is unplanned investment. With unsold inventories on their hands, firms cut back on production and real GDP falls. If they cut back production by the amount of the unplanned increase in inventories, real GDP falls by $1.0 trillion to $5.0 trillion. At that level of real GDP, aggregate planned expenditure is $4.5 trillion (point *e* in Fig. 8.11a). Again, there is an unplanned increase in inventories, but it is only one half of the previous increase (point *e* in Fig. 8.11b). Again, firms will cut back production and lay off yet more workers, reducing real GDP still further. Real GDP continues to fall whenever unplanned inventories increase. As before, real GDP keeps on changing until it reaches its equilibrium level of $4.0 trillion.

You can see, then, that if real GDP is below equilibrium, aggregate planned expenditure exceeds real GDP, inventories fall, firms increase production to restore their inventories, and real GDP rises. If real GDP is above equilibrium, aggregate planned expenditure is less than real GDP, unsold inventories prompt firms to cut back on production, and real GDP falls.

Only if real GDP equals aggregate planned expenditure are there no unplanned inventory changes and no changes in firms' output plans. In this situation, real GDP remains constant.

REVIEW

Equilibrium expenditure occurs when aggregate planned expenditure equals real GDP. If aggregate planned expenditure exceeds real GDP, inventories fall and firms increase output to replenish inventory levels. Real GDP increases, and so does planned expenditure. If aggregate planned expenditure is below real GDP, inventories accumulate and firms cut output to lower inventory levels. Real GDP and aggregate planned expenditure decline. Only when aggregate planned expenditure equals real GDP are there no unplanned changes in inventories and no changes in output. Real GDP remains constant. ◆

◆ ◆ ◆ ◆ In this chapter, we've studied the factors that influence private expenditure decisions, looking at each item of aggregate expenditure—consumption expenditure, investment, and net exports—in isolation from the others. We've also seen how these private components of expenditure interact with each other and with government purchases of goods and services to determine equilibrium aggregate expenditure. In the next chapter, we'll study the sources of *changes* in the equilibrium. In particular, we'll see how changes in investment, exports, and government fiscal policy actions can change equilibrium aggregate expenditure.

SUMMARY

The Components of Aggregate Expenditure

The components of aggregate expenditure are

- Consumption expenditure
- Investment
- Government purchases of goods and services
- Net exports

The main component of aggregate expenditure is consumption expenditure. On the average, 65 percent of total expenditure comes from consumption. Investment accounts for 16 percent, and government purchases of goods and services account for 21 percent of the total. Net exports on the average are close to zero.

The components of aggregate expenditure that fluctuate most are investment and net exports. (pp. 190–191)

Consumption Expenditure and Saving

Consumption expenditure is influenced by many factors, but the most important are

- Disposable income
- Expected future income

As disposable income increases, so do both consumption expenditure and saving. The relationship between consumption expenditure and disposable income is called the *consumption function.* The relationship between saving and disposable income is called the *saving function.* At low levels of disposable income, consumption expenditure exceeds disposable income, which means that saving is negative (dissaving occurs). As disposable income increases, consumption expenditure increases but by less than the increase in disposable income.

The fraction of each additional dollar of disposable income consumed is called the marginal propensity to consume. The fraction of each additional dollar of disposable income saved is called the marginal propensity to save. All influences on consumption and saving, other than disposable income, shift the consumption and saving functions.

Consumption expenditure is a function of real GDP because disposable income and GDP vary together. (pp. 192–202)

Investment

The amount of investment depends on:

- Real interest rates
- Profit expectations
- Existing capital

The lower the real interest rate, the greater is the amount of investment. The higher the expected profit, the greater is the amount of investment. And the larger the amount of existing capital, the larger is the amount of replacement investment and the smaller is the amount of net investment.

The main influence on investment demand is fluctuations in profit expectations. Swings in the degree of optimism and pessimism about future profits lead to shifts in the investment demand curve. Swings in profit expectations are associated with business cycle fluctuations. When the economy is in an expansion phase, profit expectations are optimistic and investment is high. When the economy is in a contraction phase, profit expectations are pessimistic and investment is low. (pp. 202–208)

Government Purchases of Goods and Services

Government purchases are determined by political processes, and the amount of government purchases is determined largely independently of the current level of real GDP. (p. 208)

Net Exports

Net exports are the difference between exports and imports. Exports are determined by decisions made in the rest of the world and are influenced by real GDP in the rest of the world, the degree of international specialization, the prices of U.S.-made goods and services relative to the prices of similar goods and services made in other countries, and the foreign exchange rate. Imports are determined by U.S. real GDP, the degree of international specialization, the prices of foreign-made goods and services relative to the prices of goods and services produced in the United States, and the foreign exchange rate.

The net export function shows the relationship between net exports and U.S. real GDP, holding constant all the other influences on exports and imports. (pp. 208–210)

Aggregate Expenditure and Real GDP

Aggregate planned expenditure is the sum of planned consumption expenditure, planned investment, planned government purchases of goods and services, and planned net exports. The relationship between aggregate planned expenditure and real GDP can be represented by the aggregate expenditure schedule and the aggregate expenditure curve. (pp. 211–212)

Equilibrium Expenditure

Equilibrium expenditure occurs when aggregate planned expenditure equals real GDP. At real GDP levels above the equilibrium, aggregate planned expenditure is below real GDP, and in such a situation, real GDP falls. At levels of real GDP below the equilibrium, aggregate planned expenditure exceeds real GDP and real GDP rises. Only when real GDP equals aggregate planned expenditure is real GDP constant and in equilibrium. The main influence bringing real GDP and aggregate planned expenditure into equality is the behavior of inventories. When aggregate planned expenditure exceeds real GDP, inventories fall. To restore their inventories, firms increase output, and this action increases real GDP. When planned expenditure is below real GDP, inventories accumulate and firms cut back their output. This action lowers the level of real GDP. Only when there are no unplanned inventory changes do firms keep output constant and so real GDP remains constant. (pp. 212–215)

KEY ELEMENTS

Key Terms

Key Figures and Tables

REVIEW QUESTIONS

1 What are the components of aggregate expenditure?

2 Which component of aggregate expenditure is the largest?

3 Which components of aggregate expenditure fluctuate the most?

4 What is the consumption function?

5 What is the fundamental determinant of consumption?

6 Distinguish between disposable income and GDP.

7 What is the saving function? What is the relationship between the saving function and the consumption function?

8 What is the meaning of the term *marginal propensity to consume*? Why is the marginal propensity to consume less than 1?

9 Explain the relationship between the marginal propensity to consume and the marginal propensity to save.

10 What determines investment? Why does investment increase as the real interest rate falls?

11 What is the effect of each of the following on U.S. net exports?

a An increase in U.S. real GDP
b An increase in real GDP in Japan
c A rise in the price of Japanese-made cars with no change in the price of U.S.-made cars

12 What is the aggregate expenditure schedule? What is the aggregate expenditure curve?

13 How is equilibrium expenditure determined? What would happen if aggregate planned expenditure exceeded real GDP?

PROBLEMS

1 You are given the following information about the Batman family (Batman and Robin):

Disposable income (dollars per year)	Consumption expenditure (dollars per year)
0	5,000
10,000	10,000
20,000	15,000
30,000	20,000
40,000	25,000

- **a** Calculate the Batman family's marginal propensity to consume.
- **b** Calculate the average propensity to consume at each level of disposable income.
- **c** Calculate how much the Batman family saves at each level of disposable income.
- **d** Calculate their marginal propensity to save.
- **e** Calculate their average propensity to save at each level of disposable income.
- **f** Draw a diagram of the consumption function. Calculate its slope.
- **g** Over what range of income does the Batman family dissave?

2 A car assembly plant can be built for $10 million, and it will have a life of three years. At the end of three years, the plant will have a scrap value of $1 million. The firm will have to hire labor at a cost of $1.5 million a year and will have to buy parts and fuel costing another $1.5 million. If the firm builds the plant, it will be able to produce cars that will sell for $7.5 million each year. Will it pay the firm to invest in this new production line at the following interest rates?

- **a** 2 percent a year
- **b** 5 percent a year
- **c** 10 percent a year

3 You are given the following information about the economy of Dreamland: the marginal propensity to consume is 0.75 and taxes net of transfer payments are a quarter of real GDP. What is the marginal propensity to consume out of real GDP in this economy?

4 You are given the following information about the economy of Happy Isle, an isolated economy with no international trade: When disposable income is zero, consumption is $80 billion. The marginal propensity to consume is 0.75. Investment is $400 billion; government purchases of goods and services are $600 billion; taxes are a constant $500 billion and do not vary as income varies. At the expenditure equilibrium, calculate:

- **a** Real GDP
- **b** Consumption
- **c** Saving
- **d** The average and marginal propensities to consume
- **e** The average and marginal propensities to save

CHAPTER 9

Expenditure Fluctuations and Fiscal Policy

After studying this chapter, you will be able to:

- Explain why changes in investment and exports change consumption expenditure and have multiplier effects on aggregate expenditure
- Define and calculate the multiplier
- Explain why changes in government purchases of goods and services have multiplier effects on aggregate expenditure
- Explain why changes in taxes and transfer payments have multiplier effects on aggregate expenditure
- Explain how the government may use fiscal policy in an attempt to stabilize aggregate expenditure
- Explain the relationship between aggregate expenditure and aggregate demand

Economic Amplifier or Shock Absorber

BONNIE RAITT BREATHES INTO A MICROPHONE AT A BARE-ly audible whisper. The electronic signal picked up by the sensitive instrument travels along wires to a huge bank of amplifiers and then through high-fidelity speakers to the ears of 10,000 fans spread out across the Red Rocks Amphitheater near Denver. Moving to a louder passage, Raitt increases the volume of her voice and now, through the magic of electronic amplification, booms across the stadium, drowning out every other sound. ◆◆ Dennis Archer, the mayor of Detroit, is being driven to a business meeting along one of the city's less well-repaired highways. (There are some pretty badly pot-holed highways in Detroit.) He is dictating notes to a secretary, who is taking down the words in impeccable shorthand. The car's wheels are bouncing and vibrating over some of the worst highway in the nation, but its passengers are completely undisturbed, and the shorthand notes are written without a ripple, thanks to the car's efficient shock absorbers. ◆◆ Investment and exports fluctuate like the volume of Bonnie Raitt's voice and the uneven surface of a Detroit highway. How does the economy react to those fluctuations? Does it react like Dennis Archer's limousine, absorbing the shocks and providing a smooth ride for the economy's passengers? Or, does it behave like Bonnie Raitt's amplifier, blowing up the fluctuations and spreading them out to affect the many millions of participants in an economic rock concert? ◆◆ Is the economic machine built to a design that we simply have to live with, or can we modify it, changing its amplification and shock-absorbing powers? And, can the government operate the economic machine in a way that gives us all a smoother ride?

◆ ◆ ◆ ◆ We are now going to explore these questions. We are going to discover that the economy contains an important amplification unit that magnifies the effects of fluctuations in investment and exports, resulting in a larger change in aggregate expenditure than the change in investment or exports that initiated it. We are also going to discover that taxes act as a kind of shock absorber. They don't provide the smooth ride of a Lincoln Continental, but they do a better job than the springs of a stagecoach. Further, we're going to discover that the government can, to some degree, smooth out fluctuations in aggregate expenditure by varying taxes and its purchases of goods and services.

Expenditure Multipliers

We discovered in Chapter 8 that equilibrium expenditure is determined at the point of intersection of the aggregate expenditure curve and the 45° line. We're now going to discover how this equilibrium *changes* when there is a *change* in investment, exports, or government purchases of goods and services. To study the effects of these changes, it is useful to classify the components of aggregate expenditure into two groups:

- Autonomous expenditure
- Induced expenditure

Autonomous Expenditure

The sum of those components of aggregate planned expenditure that are not influenced by real GDP is called **autonomous expenditure.** These components are investment, government purchases of goods and services, exports, and the part of consumption expenditure that does not vary with real GDP. The table in Fig. 9.1 gives an example. In this table, investment is \$0.5 trillion, government purchases are \$0.7 trillion, and exports are \$0.45 trillion. The sum of these items ($I + G + EX$) is \$1.65 trillion. The autonomous part of consumption expenditure (C_A) is \$0.35 trillion. The sum of all these components is autonomous expenditure (A) and is \$2 trillion regardless of the level of real GDP.

Autonomous expenditure is illustrated in both parts of Fig. 9.1 as the point at which the AE curve touches the vertical axis—the level of aggregate planned expenditure when real GDP is zero. In part (b), autonomous expenditure is highlighted by the blue arrow.

Induced Expenditure

The part of aggregate planned expenditure on U.S.-produced goods and services that varies as real GDP varies is called **induced expenditure.** Induced expenditure equals the part of consumption expenditure that varies with real GDP minus imports. In the table in Fig. 9.1, induced expenditure (N) is equal to induced consumption expenditure (C_N) minus imports (IM). An increase in real GDP of \$1 trillion increases consumption expenditure by \$0.65 trillion. This is the induced part of consumption expenditure. But an increase in real GDP of \$1 trillion increases imports by \$0.15 trillion. You can see that as real GDP increases, both consumption expenditure and imports increase, but consumption expenditure increases by more than imports, so induced expenditure also increases. Thus a \$1 trillion increase in real GDP increases aggregate planned expenditure on U.S.-produced goods and services by \$0.5 trillion—\$0.65 additional consumption expenditure minus \$0.15 trillion additional imports. For example, if real GDP increases from \$4 trillion to \$5 trillion—an increase of \$1 trillion—induced expenditure increases from \$2 trillion to \$2.5 trillion—an increase of \$0.5 trillion.

Induced expenditure is illustrated in both parts of Fig. 9.1. In part (a) you can see that as real GDP increases, induced consumption expenditure—the red arrow—increases and imports—the purple arrow—increase, but aggregate planned expenditure also increases. In part (b), induced expenditure is highlighted by the orange arrow.

Slope of the Aggregate Expenditure Curve What determines the slope of the aggregate expenditure curve? The answer is the extent to which expenditure is induced by an increase in real GDP. You can see in Fig. 9.1(b) that if real GDP increases from zero to \$2 trillion, an increase of \$2 trillion, aggregate planned expenditure increases from \$2 trillion to \$3 trillion, an increase of \$1 trillion. The slope of the aggregate expenditure curve equals the increase in aggregate planned expenditure divided by the

FIGURE 9.1

Aggregate Expenditure

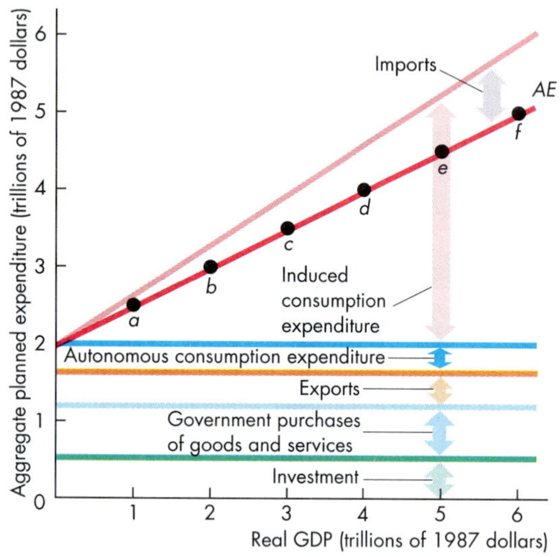

(a) Components of aggregate expenditure

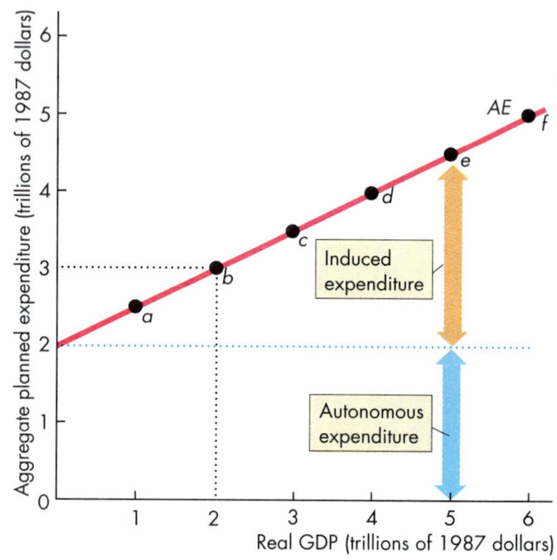

(b) Autonomous and induced expenditure

		Planned expenditure						
	Real GDP (Y)	Investment + government purchases + exports ($I + G + EX$)	Autonomous consumption expenditure (C_A)	Autonomous expenditure ($A = I + G + EX + C_A$)	Induced consumption expenditure (C_N)	Imports (IM)	Induced expenditure ($N = C_N - IM$)	Aggregate planned expenditure ($E = A + N$)
				(trillions of 1987 dollars)				
a	**1.0**	**1.65**	**0.35**	**2.0**	**0.65**	**0.15**	**0.5**	**2.5**
b	**2.0**	**1.65**	**0.35**	**2.0**	**1.30**	**0.30**	**1.0**	**3.0**
c	**3.0**	**1.65**	**0.35**	**2.0**	**1.95**	**0.45**	**1.5**	**3.5**
d	**4.0**	**1.65**	**0.35**	**2.0**	**2.60**	**0.60**	**2.0**	**4.0**
e	**5.0**	**1.65**	**0.35**	**2.0**	**3.25**	**0.75**	**2.5**	**4.5**
f	**6.0**	**1.65**	**0.35**	**2.0**	**3.90**	**0.90**	**3.0**	**5.0**

In the table, autonomous expenditure (A) is \$2 trillion regardless of the level of real GDP. It equals investment plus government purchases plus exports ($I + G + EX$) plus the autonomous part of consumption expenditure (C_A). Autonomous expenditure is the point at which the *AE* curve touches the vertical axis—the level of aggregate planned expenditure when real GDP is zero. It is shown in part (a) by the blue line, and its magnitude is highlighted by the blue arrow in part (b). In the table, induced expenditure (N) is equal to induced consumption expenditure (C_N) minus imports (IM). It increases as real GDP increases. In part (a), induced consumption expenditure is shown by the red arrow and imports by the purple arrow. In part (b), induced expenditure is highlighted by the orange arrow.

increase in real GDP—\$1 trillion divided by \$2 trillion, which equals 0.5.

The increase in induced expenditure is equal to the increase in consumption expenditure minus the increase in imports. Recall that the fraction of the last dollar of real GDP consumed is the *marginal propensity to consume out of real GDP.* In Fig. 9.1, the marginal propensity to consume out of real GDP is 0.65. The fraction of the last dollar of real GDP spent on imports is called the **marginal propensity to import.** In Fig. 9.1, the marginal propensity to import is 0.15. The marginal propensity to consume out of real GDP minus the marginal propensity to import is 0.5 (0.65 – 0.15 = 0.5), which is equal to the slope of the aggregate expenditure curve, *AE*.

A Change in Autonomous Expenditure

There are many possible sources of a change in autonomous expenditure: A fall in the real interest rate might induce firms to increase their planned investment. A major wave of innovation, such as occurred with the spread of computers in the 1980s, might increase expected future profits and lead firms to increase their planned investment. Stiff competition in the auto industry from Japanese and European imports might force GM, Ford, and Chrysler to increase their investment in robotic assembly lines. An economic boom in Western Europe and Japan might lead to a large increase in their expenditure on U.S.-produced goods and services—on U.S. exports. A worsening of international relations might lead the U.S. government to increase its expenditure on armaments—an increase in government purchases of goods and services. These are all examples of increases in autonomous expenditure. What are the effects of such increases on aggregate planned expenditure? And do increases in autonomous expenditure affect consumers? Will they plan to increase their consumption expenditure? Let's answer these questions.

Aggregate planned expenditure is set out in the table in Fig. 9.2. Autonomous expenditure initially is \$2 trillion. For each \$1 trillion increase in real GDP, induced expenditure increases by \$0.5 trillion. Adding induced expenditure and autonomous expenditure together gives aggregate planned expenditure. This aggregate expenditure schedule is shown in the figure as the aggregate expenditure curve AE_0. Initially, equilibrium occurs when real GDP is \$4 trillion. You can see this equilibrium in row *d* of the table and in the figure where the curve AE_0 intersects the 45° line at the point marked *d*.

Now suppose that autonomous expenditure increases by \$0.5 trillion to \$2.5 trillion. What is the new equilibrium? The answer is worked out in the final two columns of the table in Fig. 9.2. When the new level of autonomous expenditure is added to induced expenditure, aggregate planned expenditure increases by \$0.5 trillion at each level of real GDP. The new aggregate expenditure curve is AE_1. The new equilibrium, highlighted in the table (row *e*'), occurs where AE_1 intersects the 45° line and is at \$5 trillion (point *e*'). At this level of real GDP, aggregate planned expenditure is equal to real GDP. Autonomous expenditure is \$2.5 trillion, and induced expenditure is also \$2.5 trillion.

The Multiplier Effect

Notice in Fig. 9.2 that an increase in autonomous expenditure of \$0.5 trillion increases real GDP by \$1 trillion. That is, the change in autonomous expenditure leads, like Bonnie Raitt's music-making equipment, to an amplified change in real GDP. This is the *multiplier effect*—real GDP increases by *more than* the increase in autonomous expenditure. An increase in autonomous expenditure of \$0.5 trillion initially increases aggregate expenditure and real GDP by \$0.5 trillion. But the increase in real GDP *induces* a further increase in aggregate expenditure—an increase in consumption expenditure minus imports. Aggregate expenditure and real GDP increase by the sum of the initial increase on autonomous expenditure and the increase in induced expenditure. In this example, induced expenditure increases by \$0.5 trillion, so real GDP increases by \$1 trillion.

Although we have just analyzed the effects of an *increase* in autonomous expenditure, the same analysis applies to a decrease in autonomous expenditure. If autonomous expenditure is initially \$2.5 trillion, the initial equilibrium real GDP is \$5 trillion. If, in that situation, there is a cut in government purchases, exports, or investment of \$0.5 trillion, then the aggregate expenditure curve shifts downward to AE_0. Equilibrium real GDP decreases from \$5 trillion to \$4 trillion. The decrease in real GDP is larger than the decrease in autonomous expenditure.

FIGURE 9.2

An Increase in Autonomous Expenditure

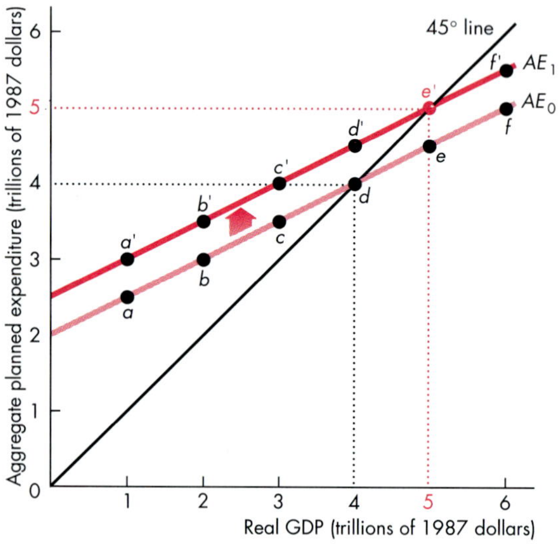

An increase in autonomous expenditure from \$2 trillion to \$2.5 trillion increases aggregate planned expenditure at each level of real GDP by \$0.5 trillion. As shown in the table, the initial equilibrium expenditure of \$4 trillion is no longer the equilibrium. At a real GDP of \$4 trillion, aggregate planned expenditure is now \$4.5 trillion. The new expenditure equilibrium is \$5 trillion, where aggregate planned expenditure equals real GDP. The increase in real GDP is larger than the increase in autonomous expenditure.

The figure illustrates the effect of the increase in autonomous expenditure. At each level of real GDP, aggregate planned expenditure is \$0.5 trillion higher than before. The aggregate planned expenditure curve shifts upward from AE_0 to AE_1. The new AE curve intersects the 45° line at e', where real GDP is \$5 trillion—the new equilibrium.

			Original expenditure			New expenditure	
Real GDP (Y)	Induced expenditure (N)		Autonomous expenditure (A_0)	Aggregate planned expenditure (E_0)		Autonomous expenditure (A_1)	Aggregate planned expenditure (E_1)
			(trillions of 1987 dollars)				
1.0	0.5	*a*	2.0	2.5	*a′*	2.5	3.0
2.0	1.0	*b*	2.0	3.0	*b′*	2.5	3.5
3.0	1.5	*c*	2.0	3.5	*c′*	2.5	4.0
4.0	2.0	*d*	2.0	4.0	*d′*	2.5	4.5
5.0	2.5	*e*	2.0	4.5	*e′*	2.5	5.0
6.0	3.0	*f*	2.0	5.0	*f′*	2.5	5.5

The Paradox of Thrift

One possible source of a decrease in autonomous expenditure is a decrease in autonomous consumption expenditure. For example, if households expect lower *future* incomes, they decrease *current* consumption. Such a decrease is represented by a downward shift in the consumption function and a downward shift in the aggregate expenditure curve.

A decrease in autonomous consumption means an increase in saving—the saving function (described in Chapter 8, pp. 192–196) shifts upward. Another word for saving is thrift. The more a household saves, the thriftier it is. Also, the thriftier a household, the wealthier it becomes. By consuming less than its income, a household can increase its income by lending what it saves and earning interest on it. But what happens if we all become thriftier? Does aggregate income increase? We can work out one answer to this question by using the analysis that we've just performed.

Suppose that initially aggregate expenditure is shown by the curve AE_1 in Fig. 9.2. Real GDP is \$5 trillion. Now suppose that there is an increase in thriftiness. As a result, autonomous expenditure decreases by \$0.5 trillion, and, consequently, the aggregate expenditure curve shifts downward from AE_1 to AE_0. Equilibrium expenditure and real GDP fall to \$4 trillion.

An increase in thriftiness has reduced real GDP. The fall in real GDP caused by an increase in saving is called the **paradox of thrift.** It is a paradox because an increase in thriftiness leads to an increase in income for an individual but to a decrease in aggregate income.

The paradox arises in this model because the increase in saving is *not* associated with an increase in investment. Although people save more, no one buys additional capital goods. This combination of events is an unlikely one in reality, so the paradox of thrift, although logically correct, has little to say about the economy in which we live. In the real world, it is possible that when saving increases, investment will also increase. In such a case there is no fall in aggregate income. An increase in saving shifts the *AE* curve downward, but an increase in investment shifts it upward. If saving and investment change by the same amount, the *AE* curve does not shift. The result is no change in real GDP. But this is a short-run outcome.

There are further and much more important effects of saving and investment. They result in the accumulation of capital that enables incomes, both of individuals and of the economy as a whole, to grow over time. Thus the paradox of thrift is not paradoxical after all. It is a consequence for current income only if increased saving occurs with unchanged investment. In the long run, increased saving results in more capital and a higher level of real GDP.

We have discovered that a change in autonomous expenditure has a multiplier effect on real GDP. But how big is the multiplier effect?

The Size of the Multiplier

Suppose that the economy is recovering from a recession. Profit prospects look good, and firms are making plans for large increases in investment. The world economy is also heading toward recovery, and exports are rising. The question on everyone's lips is: how strong will the recovery be? This is a hard question to answer. But an important ingredient in the answer is working out the size of the multiplier.

The **autonomous expenditure multiplier** (often abbreviated to simply the **multiplier**) is the amount by which a change in autonomous expenditure is multiplied to determine the change in equilibrium expenditure that it generates. To calculate the multiplier, we divide the change in equilibrium real GDP by the change in autonomous expenditure. Let's calculate the multiplier for the example in Fig. 9.3(a). The economy in recession has a real GDP of \$3 trillion. Autonomous expenditure increases from \$1.5 to \$2.5 trillion, and equilibrium real GDP increases from \$3 trillion to \$5 trillion, an increase of \$2 trillion. That is,

- Autonomous expenditure increases by \$1 trillion.
- Real GDP increases by \$2 trillion.

The multiplier is

$$\begin{aligned}\text{Multiplier} &= \frac{\text{Change in equilibrium real GDP}}{\text{Change in autonomous expenditure}}\\ &= \frac{\$2\text{ trillion}}{\$1\text{ trillion}}\\ &= 2.\end{aligned}$$

Thus a change in autonomous expenditure of \$1 trillion produces a change in equilibrium real GDP of \$2 trillion, a change that is twice as big as the initial change in autonomous expenditure.

Next, look at Fig. 9.3(b). Again the economy in recession has a real GDP of \$3 trillion. But now, autonomous expenditure increases from \$1 to \$2 trillion, and equilibrium real GDP increases from \$3 trillion to \$6 trillion, an increase of \$3 trillion. That is,

- Autonomous expenditure increases by \$1 trillion.
- Real GDP increases by \$3 trillion.

The multiplier is

$$\begin{aligned}\text{Multiplier} &= \frac{\text{Change in equilibrium real GDP}}{\text{Change in autonomous expenditure}}\\ &= \frac{\$3\text{ trillion}}{\$1\text{ trillion}}\\ &= 3.\end{aligned}$$

FIGURE 9.3

The Multiplier and the Slope of the *AE* Curve

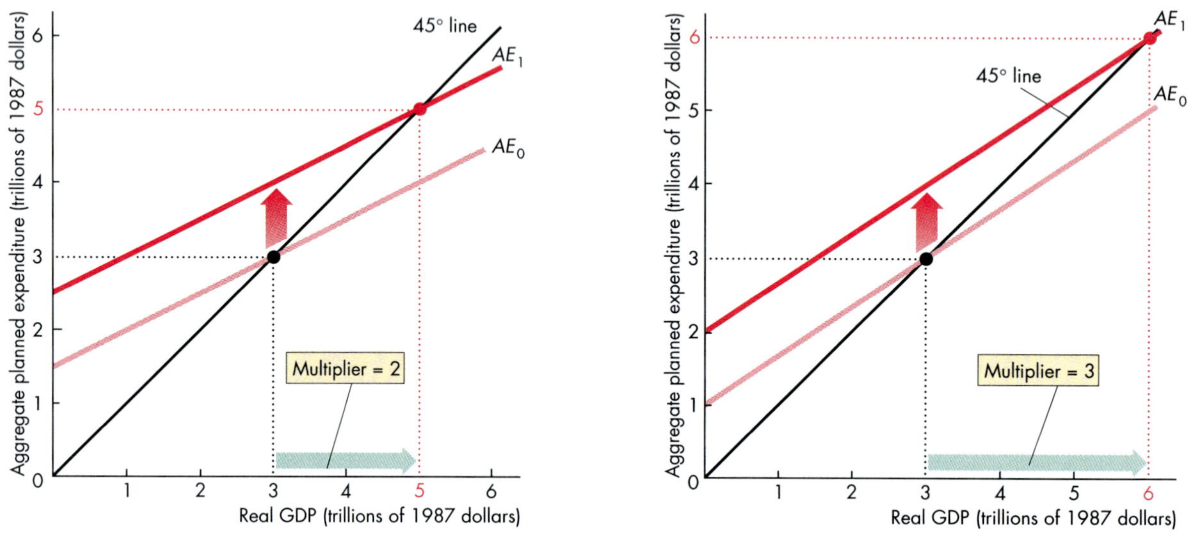

(a) Multiplier is 2

(b) Multiplier is 3

The size of the multiplier depends on the slope of the *AE* curve. The multiplier formula, $1/(1 - g)$, tells us the relationship. If the slope of the *AE* curve (g) is ½, the multiplier is 2. In this case, an increase in autonomous expenditure of $1 trillion shifts the *AE* curve upward from AE_0 to AE_1 in part (a). Real GDP increases from $3 trillion to $5 trillion, twice the increase in autonomous expenditure. If g equals ⅔, the multiplier is 3. In this case, a $1 trillion increase in autonomous expenditure shifts the aggregate expenditure curve upward from AE_0 to AE_1 in part (b). Real GDP increases from $3 trillion to $6 trillion, three times the increase in autonomous expenditure.

Thus a change in autonomous expenditure of $1 trillion produces a change in equilibrium real GDP of $3 trillion, a change that is three times as big as the initial change in autonomous expenditure.

The Multiplier and the Slope of the Aggregate Expenditure Curve

Why is the multiplier in Fig. 9.3(b) bigger than the multiplier in Fig. 9.3(a)? The reason is that the aggregate expenditure curve in part (b) is steeper than that in part (a). The steeper the *AE* curve, the larger is the multiplier. In part (a), the slope of the *AE* curve is ½ and the multiplier is 2. In part (b), the slope of the *AE* curve is ⅔ and the multiplier is 3.

Multiplier Calculations Table 9.1 shows how to calculate the value of the multiplier. Part (a) introduces some definitions. It starts with the change in real GDP, ΔY. Our objective is to calculate the size of this change when there is a given change in autonomous expenditure, ΔA. In the example in Table 9.1, the change in autonomous expenditure is $500 billion. The slope of the aggregate expenditure curve is the marginal propensity to consume out of real GDP minus the marginal propensity to import. Let's call this slope g. In Table 9.1, g is equal to ⅔, the same as in Fig. 9.3(b). The change in aggregate planned expenditure (ΔE) is the sum of the change in autonomous expenditure (ΔA) and the change in induced expenditure (ΔN). Finally, the multiplier is defined as

$$\frac{\Delta Y}{\Delta A}.$$

Part (b) of the table sets out the calculations of the change in real GDP and the multiplier. The change in aggregate planned expenditure (ΔE) is equal to the sum of the change in autonomous

TABLE 9.1
Calculating the Multiplier

	Symbols and formulas*	Numbers
(a) Definitions		
Change in real GDP	ΔY	
Change in autonomous expenditure	ΔA	500
Slope of the *AE* curve	g	⅔
Change in induced expenditure	$\Delta N = g\Delta Y$	$\Delta N = (2/3)\Delta Y$
Change in aggregate planned expenditure	$\Delta E = \Delta A + \Delta N$	
The multiplier (autonomous expenditure multiplier)	$\Delta Y/\Delta A$	
(b) Calculations		
Aggregate planned expenditure	$E = A + gY$	
Change in *AE* curve	$\Delta E = \Delta A + g\Delta Y$	$\Delta E = 500 + (2/3)\Delta Y$
Change in equilibrium expenditure	$\Delta E = \Delta Y$	
Replacing ΔE with ΔY	$\Delta Y = \Delta A + g\Delta Y$	$\Delta Y = 500 + (2/3)\Delta Y$
Subtracting $g\Delta Y$, or $(2/3)\Delta Y$, from both sides and factoring ΔY	$\Delta Y(1 - g) = \Delta A$	$\Delta Y(1 - 2/3) = 500$
Dividing both sides by $(1 - g)$, or $(1 - 2/3)$	$\Delta Y = \frac{1}{1-g}\Delta A$	$\Delta Y = \frac{1}{1-2/3}500$
		or $\Delta Y = \frac{1}{1/3}500$
		or $\Delta Y = 1{,}500$
Dividing both sides by ΔA, or 500, gives the multiplier	$\frac{\Delta Y}{\Delta A} = \frac{1}{1-g}$	$\frac{\Delta Y}{\Delta A} = \frac{1{,}500}{500} = 3$

*The Greek Δ stands for "change in."

expenditure (ΔA) and the change in induced expenditure ($g\Delta Y$). In the example the change in aggregate planned expenditure is equal to \$500 billion plus ⅔ of the change in real GDP. Since in equilibrium the change in aggregate planned expenditure is equal to the change in real GDP, the change in real GDP is

$$\Delta Y = \Delta A + g\Delta Y.$$

Using our numbers,

$$\Delta Y = 500 + (2/3)\Delta Y.$$

This equation has just one unknown, ΔY, and we can find its value as shown in the table. Finally, dividing ΔY by ΔA gives the value of the multiplier, which is:

$$\text{Multiplier} = \frac{1}{(1-g)}.$$

Because g is a fraction—a number lying between 0 and 1—$(1 - g)$ is also a fraction and the multiplier is greater than 1. In the example, g is ⅔, $(1 - g)$ is ⅓, and the multiplier is 3.

You can see that this formula works for the multiplier shown in Fig. 9.3(a). In this case, the slope of the *AE* curve is ½, g is ½, $(1 - g)$ is also ½, and the multiplier is 2.

Why Is the Multiplier Greater Than 1?

The multiplier is greater than 1 because of induced expenditure—an increase in autonomous expenditure *induces* further increases in expenditure. If GM spends \$10 million on a new car assembly line, aggregate expenditure and real GDP immediately increase by \$10 million. But that is not the end of the story. Engineers and construction workers now have more income, and they spend part of the extra income on cars, microwaves, vacations, and a host of other goods and services. Real GDP now rises by the initial \$10 million plus the extra expenditure induced by the \$10 million increase in income. The producers of cars, microwaves, vacations, and other goods now have increased incomes, and they, in turn, also spend part of their increase in income on consumption goods and services. Additional income induces additional expenditure, which creates additional income.

This multiplier process is illustrated in Fig. 9.4. In round 1, there is an increase in autonomous

FIGURE 9.4

The Multiplier Process

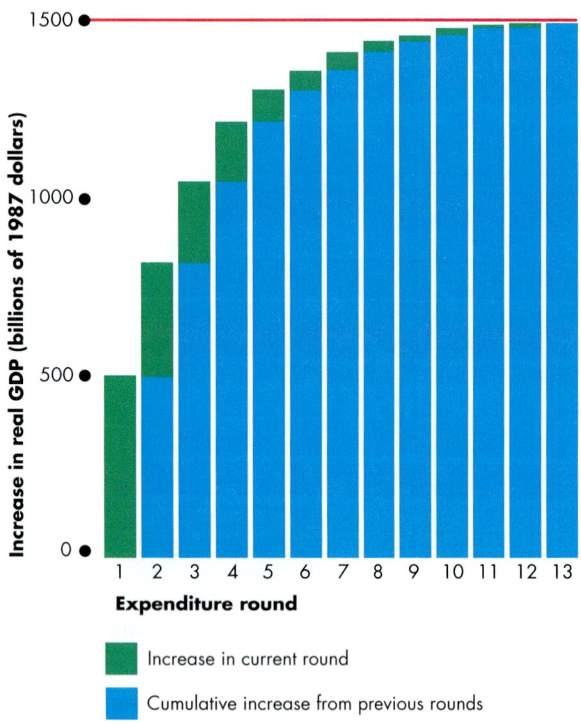

Expenditure round	Increase in aggregate expenditure	Cumulative increase in real GDP
	(billions of 1987 dollars)	
1	500	500
2	333	833
3	222	1,055
4	148	1,203
5	99	1,302
6	66	1,368
7	44	1,412
8	29	1,441
9	20	1,461
10	13	1,474
. . .	. . .	. . .
All others	26	1,500

Autonomous expenditure increases in round 1 by \$500 billion. Real GDP also increases by the same amount. Each additional dollar of real GDP induces an additional two thirds of a dollar of aggregate expenditure—the slope of the aggregate expenditure curve is ⅔. In round 2, the round 1 increase in real GDP induces an increase in expenditure of \$333 billion. At the end of round 2, real GDP has increased by \$833 billion. The extra \$333 billion of real GDP in round 2 induces a further increase in expenditure of \$222 billion in round 3. Real GDP increases yet further to \$1,055 billion. This process continues until real GDP has eventually increased by \$1,500 billion. The table stops counting after round 10, since the extra amounts become smaller and smaller. (Perhaps you would like to run the process further on your pocket calculator. As a matter of interest, after 19 rounds you will be within \$1 of the \$1,500 billion total, and after 30 rounds you will be within 1¢ of that total!) The diagram shows you how quickly the multiplier effect builds up. In this example, the multiplier is 3 because the slope of the *AE* curve is ⅔ (see Table 9.1).

expenditure of $500 billion. At that stage, there is no change in induced expenditure, so aggregate expenditure and real GDP increase by $500 billion. In round 2, the higher real GDP induces higher consumption expenditure. Since, in the example in Fig. 9.4, induced expenditure increases by two thirds the increase in real GDP, the increase in real GDP of $500 billion induces a further increase in expenditure of $333 billion. This change in induced expenditure, when added to the initial change in autonomous expenditure, results in an increase in aggregate expenditure and real GDP of $833 billion. The round 2 increase in real GDP induces a round 3 increase in expenditure. The process repeats through successive rounds recorded in the table. Each increase in real GDP is two thirds the previous increase. The cumulative increase in real GDP gradually approaches $1,500 billion. Even after 10 rounds it has almost reached that level.

It appears, then, that the economy does not operate like the shock absorbers on Dennis Archer's car. The economy's potholes and bumps are changes in autonomous expenditure—mainly brought about by changes in investment and exports. These economic potholes and bumps are not smoothed out, but instead are amplified.

REVIEW

Autonomous expenditure is the part of aggregate expenditure that does not respond to changes in real GDP. Induced expenditure is the part of aggregate expenditure that does respond to changes in real GDP. A change in autonomous expenditure changes equilibrium expenditure and real GDP. The magnitude of the change in real GDP is determined by the multiplier. The multiplier, in turn, is determined by the slope of the aggregate expenditure curve, which equals the marginal propensity to consume out of real GDP minus the marginal propensity to import. The steeper the aggregate expenditure curve, the larger is the multiplier. The multiplier acts like an amplifier. ◆

One of the components of autonomous expenditure that the multiplier amplifies is government purchases of goods and services. Because of this fact, the government can take advantage of the multiplier and attempt to smooth out fluctuations in aggregate expenditure. It can also vary transfer payments and taxes for this purpose. Let's see how.

Fiscal Policy Multipliers

Fiscal policy is the government's attempt to smooth the fluctuations in aggregate expenditure by varying its purchases of goods and services, transfer payments, and taxes. If the government foresees a decline in investment or exports, it may attempt to offset the effects of the decline by increasing its own purchases of goods and services, increasing transfer payments, or cutting taxes. But the government must figure out the size of the increase in purchases or transfers or the size of the tax cut needed to achieve its goal. To make this calculation, the government needs to know the multiplier effects of its own actions. Let's study the multiplier effects of changes in government purchases, transfer payments, and taxes.

Government Purchases Multiplier

The **government purchases multiplier** is the amount by which a change in government purchases of goods and services is multiplied to determine the change in equilibrium expenditure that it generates. Government purchases of goods and services are one component of autonomous expenditure. A change in government purchases has the same effect on aggregate expenditure as a change in any other component of autonomous expenditure. It sets up a multiplier effect exactly like the multiplier effect of a change in investment or exports. That is,

$$\text{Government purchases multiplier} = \frac{1}{(1-g)}.$$

By varying government purchases to offset a change in investment or exports, the government can attempt to keep total autonomous expenditure constant (or growing at a steady rate). Because the government purchases multiplier is the same size as the multiplier effect of a change in investment or exports, stabilization of autonomous expenditure can be achieved by increasing government purchases by \$1 for each \$1 decrease in the other items of autonomous expenditure.

In practice, using variations in government purchases to stabilize aggregate expenditure is not easy because the political decision-making process that changes government purchases of goods and services operates with a long time lag. As a consequence, it is not possible to forecast changes in private expenditure far enough ahead to make this instrument an effective one for macroeconomic stabilization.

A second way in which the government may seek to stabilize aggregate expenditure is by varying transfer payments. Let's see how this type of policy works.

Transfer Payments Multiplier

The **transfer payments multiplier** is the amount by which a change in transfer payments is multiplied to determine the change in equilibrium expenditure that it generates. A change in transfer payments influences aggregate expenditure by changing disposable income, which leads to a change in consumption expenditure. This change in consumption expenditure is a change in autonomous expenditure, and it has a multiplier effect exactly like that of any other change in autonomous expenditure. But how large is the initial change in consumption expenditure? It is equal to the change in transfer payments multiplied by the marginal propensity to consume. If the marginal propensity to consume is b, a \$1 increase in transfer payments initially increases consumption expenditure by \$$b$. For example, if the marginal propensity to consume is 0.9, a \$1 increase in transfer payments initially increases consumption expenditure by 90¢. Therefore the transfer payments multiplier is equal to b times the autonomous expenditure multiplier. That is,

$$\text{Transfer payments multiplier} = \frac{b}{(1-g)}.$$

For example, if the marginal propensity to consume is 0.9 and the slope of the *AE* curve (g) is 0.5, the transfer payments multiplier is 1.8 (0.9/0.5 = 1.8). Notice that the transfer payments multiplier is b times the government purchases multiplier. Because the marginal propensity to consume (b) is less than 1, the transfer payments multiplier is *smaller* than the government purchases multiplier.

The use of variations in transfer payments to stabilize the economy has the same problems as the use of variations in government purchases of goods and services. The political process does not operate on the time scale required for timely changes in transfer payments to offset fluctuations in other components of autonomous expenditure.

Tax Multipliers

A third type of fiscal stabilization policy is to vary taxes. The **tax multiplier** is the amount by which a change in taxes is multiplied to determine the change in equilibrium expenditure that it generates. An *increase* in taxes leads to a *decrease* in disposable income and a decrease in consumption expenditure. The amount by which consumption expenditure decreases initially is determined by the marginal propensity to consume. This initial response of consumption expenditure to a tax increase is exactly the

FIGURE 9.5

The Tax Multiplier

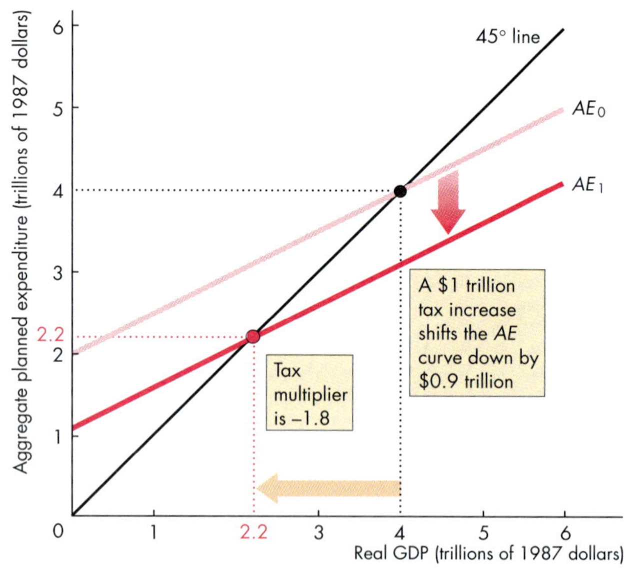

Initially, the aggregate expenditure curve is AE_0, and equilibrium expenditure is \$4 trillion. The slope of the *AE* curve is 0.5. Taxes are increased by \$1 trillion, so disposable income falls by \$1 trillion. The marginal propensity to consume is 0.9, and the aggregate expenditure curve shifts downward by \$0.9 trillion to AE_1. Equilibrium expenditure and real GDP decrease by \$1.8 trillion—the tax multiplier is –1.8.

same as the response of consumption expenditure to a decrease in transfer payments. Thus a tax change works like a change in transfer payments but in the opposite direction, and the tax multiplier equals the negative of the transfer payments multiplier. Because a tax *increase* leads to a *decrease* in equilibrium expenditure, the tax multiplier is *negative*. It is

$$\text{Tax multiplier} = \frac{-b}{(1-g)}.$$

For example, if the marginal propensity to consume (b) is 0.9 and the slope of the AE curve (g) is 0.5, the tax multiplier is –1.8.

Figure 9.5 illustrates the multiplier effect of a tax increase. Initially, the aggregate expenditure curve is AE_0, and equilibrium expenditure is \$4 trillion. The slope of the aggregate expenditure curve AE_0 is 0.5. Taxes increase by \$1 trillion, and disposable income falls by that amount. With a marginal propensity to consume of 0.9, consumption expenditure decreases initially by \$0.9 trillion and the aggregate expenditure curve shifts downward by that amount to AE_1. Equilibrium expenditure and real GDP fall by \$1.8 trillion to \$2.2 trillion. The tax multiplier is –1.8.

Balanced Budget Multiplier

A balanced budget fiscal policy action is one that keeps the government budget deficit or surplus unchanged—both government purchases and taxes change by the same amount. The **balanced budget multiplier** is the amount by which a change in government purchases of goods and services is multiplied to determine the change in expenditure equilibrium when taxes are changed by the same amount as the change in government purchases. What is the multiplier effect of this fiscal policy action?

To answer, we must combine the two multipliers that we have just worked out. We've seen that those two separate multipliers are

$$\text{Government purchases multiplier} = \frac{1}{(1-g)}.$$

$$\text{Tax multiplier} = \frac{-b}{(1-g)}.$$

Adding these two multipliers together gives the balanced budget multiplier, which is

$$\text{Balanced budget multiplier} = \frac{(1-b)}{(1-g)}.$$

Because the marginal propensity to consume (b) is bigger than the slope of the AE curve (g), the balanced budget multiplier is less than 1. For example, if the marginal propensity to consume is 0.9 and the slope of the AE curve is 0.5, the balanced budget multiplier is 0.2 (0.1/0.5 = 0.2).

Figure 9.6 illustrates the balanced budget multiplier. Initially, the aggregate expenditure curve is AE_0, and real GDP is \$4 trillion. A \$1 trillion increase in taxes decreases aggregate planned expenditure by \$0.9 trillion and shifts the aggregate expenditure curve downward to AE_0'. A \$1 trillion increase in government purchases increases aggregate planned expenditure by the entire \$1 trillion and shifts the aggregate expenditure curve upward to AE_1. The net shift in the aggregate expenditure curve is upward by \$0.1 trillion. The new equilibrium occurs at the intersection of AE_1 and the 45° line

FIGURE 9.6

The Balanced Budget Multiplier

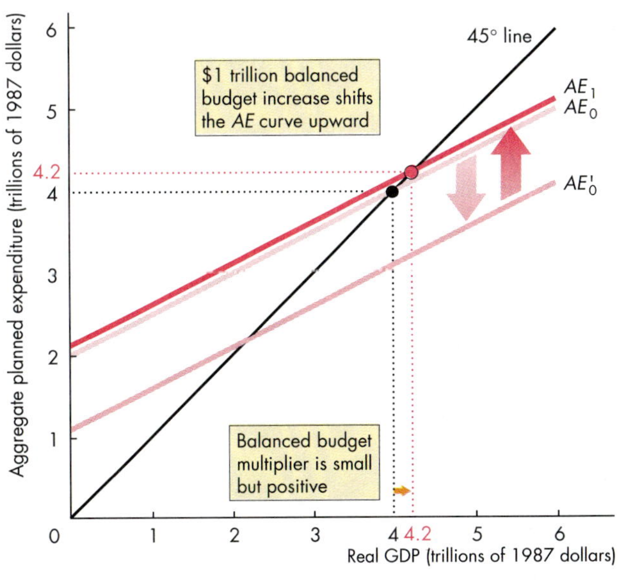

Initially, the aggregate expenditure curve is AE_0. The government increases both taxes and purchases of goods and services by \$1 trillion. The \$1 trillion tax increase shifts the aggregate expenditure curve downward by \$0.9 trillion to AE_0'. The \$1 trillion increase in government purchases shifts the aggregate expenditure curve upward by the entire \$1 trillion to AE_1. Real GDP increases by \$0.2 trillion—the balanced budget multiplier is 0.2.

(highlighted by the red dot). Real GDP increases by \$0.1 trillion times the autonomous expenditure multiplier. Thus the balanced budget multiplier is positive but small. In this example, it is 0.2.

The balanced budget multiplier is important because it means that the government does not have to unbalance its budget and run a deficit in order to stimulate aggregate demand. Reading Between the Lines on pp. 234–235 looks at President Clinton's 1993 budget proposals, intended to simultaneously stimulate investment and lower the deficit.

REVIEW

The government purchases multiplier is equal to the autonomous expenditure multiplier. By varying its purchases of goods and services, the government can try to offset fluctuations in investment and exports. The transfer payments multiplier is equal to the marginal propensity to consume multiplied by the government purchases multiplier. A change in transfer payments works through a change in disposable income. Part of the change in disposable income is spent, and part is saved. Only the part that is spent, that is determined by the marginal propensity to consume, has a multiplier effect. The tax multiplier has the same magnitude as the transfer payments multiplier, but it is negative—a tax *increase* leads to a *decrease* in equilibrium expenditure. An equal change in both purchases of goods and services and taxes has a balanced budget multiplier effect on real GDP. The balanced budget multiplier is small but positive. In practice, fiscal actions are difficult to use to stabilize the economy because of time lags in the legislative process. ◆

Automatic Stabilizers

Income taxes and transfer payments act as automatic stabilizers. An **automatic stabilizer** is a mechanism that decreases the fluctuations in *aggregate* expenditure resulting from fluctuations in a *component* of aggregate expenditure. The automatic stabilizing effects of income taxes and transfer payments mean that they act like an economic shock absorber, making the aggregate effects of fluctuations in investment and exports smaller than they otherwise would be.

To see how income taxes and transfer payments act as an economic shock absorber, let's see how a change in investment or exports affects equilibrium expenditure in two economies: in the first economy there are no income taxes and transfer payments, and in the second there are income taxes and transfer payments similar to those in the United States today.

No Income Taxes and Transfer Payments In an economy with no income taxes and transfer payments, the gap between GDP and disposable income is constant—it does not depend on the level of GDP. If the marginal propensity to consume is 0.9, the marginal propensity to consume out of GDP is also 0.9. That is, each extra dollar of GDP is an extra dollar of disposable income and induces an extra 90¢ of consumption expenditure. Suppose that there are no imports, so not only is the marginal propensity to consume 0.9, but so also is the slope of the *AE* curve.

What is the size of the multiplier in this case? You can answer this question by using the formula

$$\text{Multiplier} = \frac{1}{(1-g)}.$$

The value of g is 0.9, so the value of the multiplier is 10. In this economy, a \$1 million change in autonomous expenditure produces a \$10 million change in equilibrium expenditure. This economy has a very strong amplifier.

Income Taxes and Transfer Payments Contrast the economy that we have just described with one that has income taxes and transfer payments.

The scale of income taxes minus transfer payments is determined by the marginal tax rate. The **marginal tax rate** is the fraction of the last dollar of income paid to the government in net taxes (taxes minus transfer payments).

Let's assume that the marginal tax rate is 0.3. That is, each additional dollar of real GDP generates tax revenue for the government of 30¢ and disposable income of 70¢. If the marginal propensity to consume is 0.9 (the same as in the previous example), a \$1 increase in real GDP increases disposable income by 70¢ and increases consumption expenditure by 63¢ (0.9 of 0.7 equals 0.63). In this economy, the slope of the *AE* curve is 0.63. The value of g is 0.63, so the multiplier is 2.7. The economy still amplifies shocks from changes in exports and investment, but on a much smaller scale than the economy with no income taxes and transfer payments. Thus, to some degree, income taxes and transfer payments absorb the shocks of fluctuations in autonomous expenditure. The higher the marginal tax rate, the greater is the extent to which autonomous expenditure shocks are absorbed.

The existence of taxes and transfer payments that vary with real GDP helps the shock-absorbing capacities of the economy. They don't produce the economic equivalent of the suspension of a Lincoln Continental, but they do produce the economic equivalent of something better than the springs of a stagecoach. As the economy fluctuates, the government's budget fluctuates, absorbing some of the shocks, changing taxes and transfer payments, and smoothing the fluctuations in disposable income and aggregate expenditure.

Let's look at the effects of automatic stabilizers on the government's budget and its deficit.

FIGURE 9.7

The Government Deficit

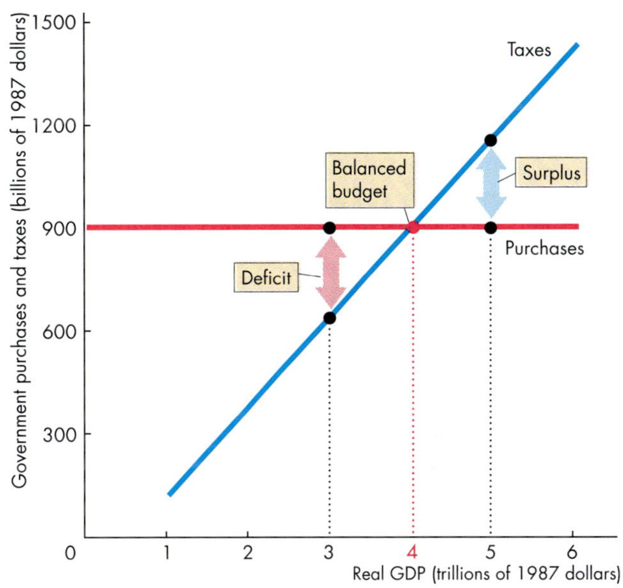

Government purchases (the red line) are independent of the level of real GDP, but income taxes (the blue line) increase as real GDP increases. When real GDP is $4 trillion, the government's budget is balanced. When real GDP is below $4 trillion, there is a deficit, and when real GDP is above $4 trillion, there is a surplus. Fluctuations in taxes act as an automatic stabilizer when the economy is hit by changes in autonomous expenditure.

Automatic Stabilizers and the Government Deficit

Because income taxes and transfer payments fluctuate with real GDP, so does the government's deficit. Figure 9.7 shows how. Government purchases are independent of the level of real GDP. In the figure, they are fixed at $900 billion—shown by the horizontal red line. Income taxes net of transfer payments increase as real GDP increases. In the figure, they are shown by the upward-sloping blue line. There is a particular level of real GDP at which the government's budget is balanced—the deficit is zero. In the figure, that level of real GDP is $4 trillion. When real GDP is below $4 trillion, there is a deficit. And when real GDP is above $4 trillion, there is a surplus.

As investment and exports fluctuate, bringing fluctuations in real GDP, income taxes and the deficit also fluctuate. For example, a large increase in investment increases real GDP, increases income taxes, and reduces the deficit (or creates a surplus). The higher income taxes act as an automatic stabilizer. They decrease disposable income and induce a decrease in consumption expenditure. This decrease dampens the effects of the initial increase in investment and moderates the increase in aggregate expenditure and real GDP.

Conversely, when a large decrease in investment is pushing the economy into recession, income taxes decrease and the deficit increases (or the surplus decreases). The lower income taxes act as an automatic stabilizer. They limit the fall in disposable income and moderate the extent of the decline in aggregate expenditure and real GDP.

REVIEW

The presence of income taxes and transfer payments that vary with real GDP reduces the value of the multiplier and acts as an automatic stabilizer. The higher the marginal tax rate, the smaller are the fluctuations in real GDP resulting from fluctuations in autonomous expenditure. ◆

Clintonomics

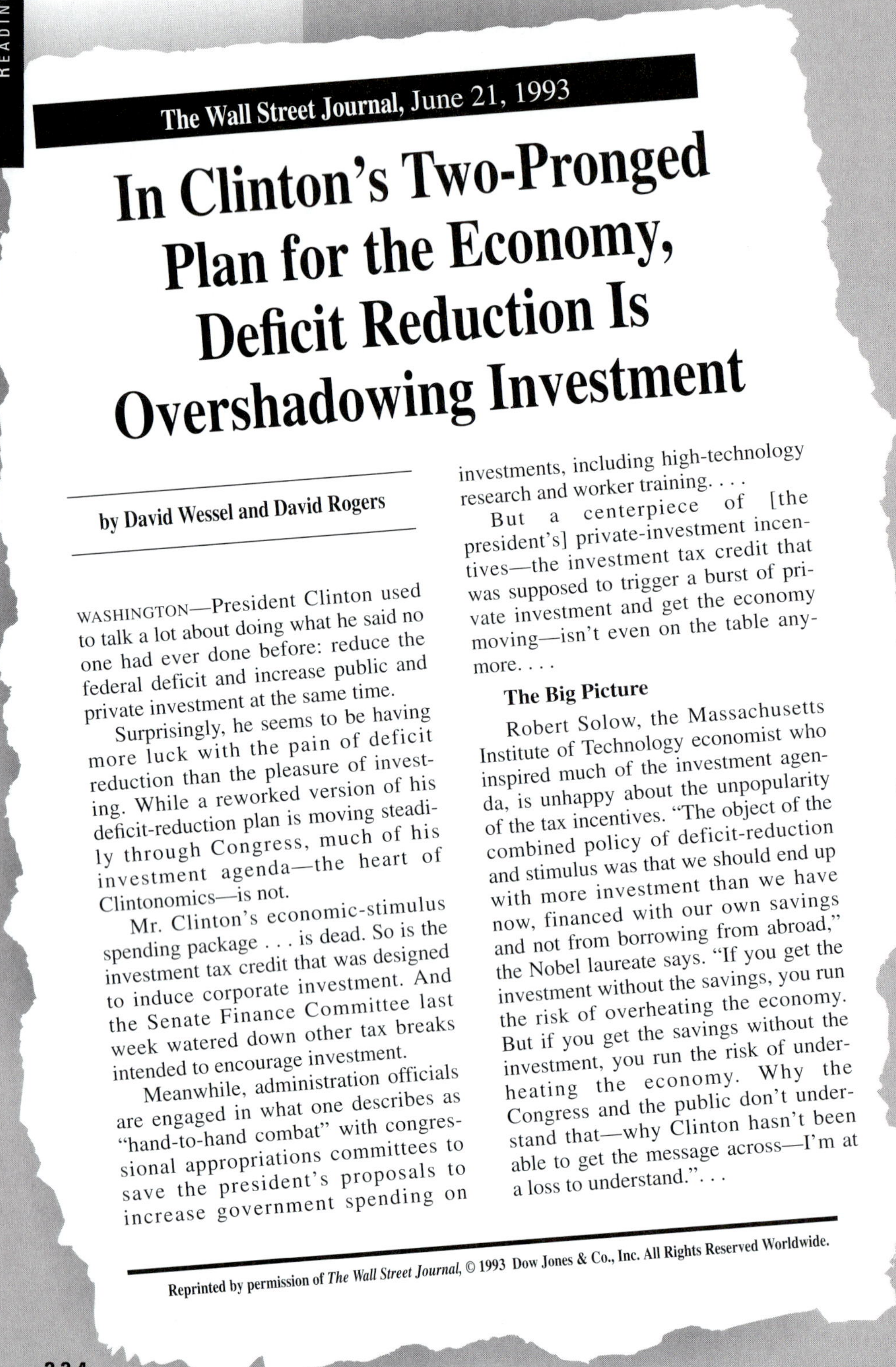
The Wall Street Journal, June 21, 1993

In Clinton's Two-Pronged Plan for the Economy, Deficit Reduction Is Overshadowing Investment

by David Wessel and David Rogers

WASHINGTON—President Clinton used to talk a lot about doing what he said no one had ever done before: reduce the federal deficit and increase public and private investment at the same time.

Surprisingly, he seems to be having more luck with the pain of deficit reduction than the pleasure of investing. While a reworked version of his deficit-reduction plan is moving steadily through Congress, much of his investment agenda—the heart of Clintonomics—is not.

Mr. Clinton's economic-stimulus spending package . . . is dead. So is the investment tax credit that was designed to induce corporate investment. And the Senate Finance Committee last week watered down other tax breaks intended to encourage investment.

Meanwhile, administration officials are engaged in what one describes as "hand-to-hand combat" with congressional appropriations committees to save the president's proposals to increase government spending on investments, including high-technology research and worker training. . . .

But a centerpiece of [the president's] private-investment incentives—the investment tax credit that was supposed to trigger a burst of private investment and get the economy moving—isn't even on the table anymore. . . .

The Big Picture

Robert Solow, the Massachusetts Institute of Technology economist who inspired much of the investment agenda, is unhappy about the unpopularity of the tax incentives. "The object of the combined policy of deficit-reduction and stimulus was that we should end up with more investment than we have now, financed with our own savings and not from borrowing from abroad," the Nobel laureate says. "If you get the investment without the savings, you run the risk of overheating the economy. But if you get the savings without the investment, you run the risk of underheating the economy. Why the Congress and the public don't understand that—why Clinton hasn't been able to get the message across—I'm at a loss to understand.". . .

The Essence of the Story

President Clinton's 1993 budget aimed to reduce the federal deficit and increase both public and private investment.

The president's deficit reduction plan proved more popular with Congress than his investment stimulation proposals were.

An investment tax credit plan and other investment stimulants were either rejected or weakened by Congress.

Economist Robert Solow of MIT explained that, by both cutting the deficit and stimulating investment, we can have more investment financed with our own savings.

Solow also said that increased investment without increased savings might overheat the economy, while increased savings without increased investment might underheat the economy.

Background and Analysis

President Clinton's doomed investment stimulus package was designed to make investment more profitable and to shift the investment demand curve rightward, from ID_0 to ID_1, as shown in Fig. 1.

The effects of this action alone are to increase aggregate planned expenditure and to shift the aggregate expenditure curve upward, from AE_0 to AE_1 in Fig. 2.

The consequence of this single change is what Robert Solow calls "overheating" in the news story. Equilibrium expenditure increases and so does aggregate demand.

A deficit reduction package is a set of tax increases and spending cuts. The effects of these actions are to decrease aggregate planned expenditure and to shift the aggregate expenditure curve downward from AE_0 to AE_2 in Fig. 2.

The consequence of this single change is what Solow calls "underheating" in the news story. Equilibrium expenditure decreases and so does aggregate demand.

By implementing *both* parts of the Clinton budget, Congress could keep aggregate planned expenditure steady at AE_0 and avoid the risks of overheating or underheating.

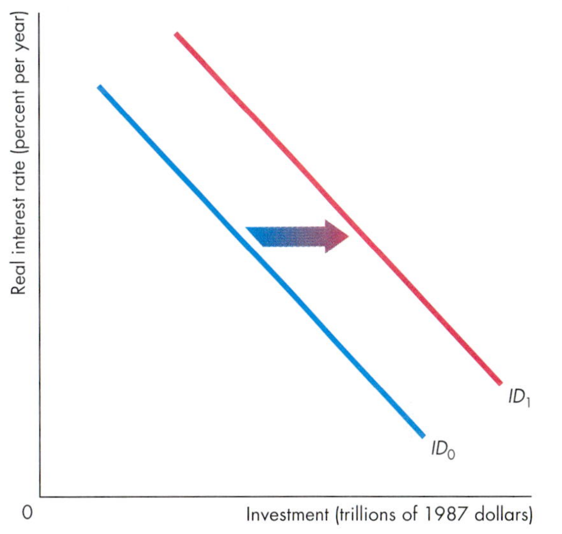

Figure 1

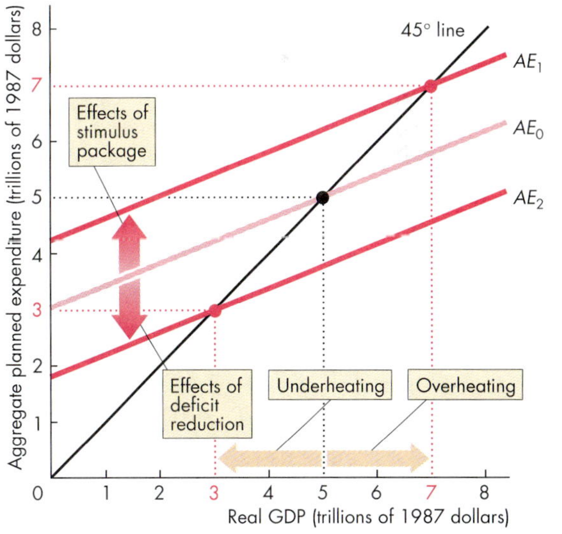

Figure 2

We've now seen what determines the value of the autonomous expenditure multiplier and how the multiplier can be used by the government to influence aggregate planned expenditure by changing government purchases, transfer payments, or taxes. But so far we have studied model economies with hypothetical numbers. Let's now turn to the real world. How big is the multiplier in the U.S. economy?

The Multiplier in the United States

In the model economy that we studied earlier in this chapter, each additional dollar of income induces 50¢ of expenditure. Its multiplier is 2. Let's look at some estimates of the multiplier in the U.S. economy.

The U.S. Multiplier in 1990

In 1990, the marginal propensity to consume in the United States was approximately 0.9 and disposable income was approximately two thirds of GDP. Putting these two pieces of information together, we can calculate that the marginal propensity to consume out of GDP is 0.63 (0.7 of 0.9 equals 0.63). Imports were approximately 15 percent of GDP. Using this percentage as an estimate of the marginal propensity to import gives a value of 0.15; each additional dollar of GDP induces 15¢ of imports. Subtracting the marginal propensity to import from the marginal propensity to consume gives the slope of the *AE* curve, which is 0.48 (that is, 0.63 minus 0.15). The multiplier is 1.92. That is,

$$\text{The multiplier} = \frac{1}{(1 - 0.48)} = \frac{1}{0.42} = 1.92.$$

Thus, on the basis of these estimates, the U.S. multiplier in 1990 was a little under 2.

The Multiplier in Recession and Recovery

Is the multiplier a stable number—a constant—on which we can rely? Does the multiplier take on the same value when the economy is going into a recession as when it is recovering from a recession? Or does its value vary, and if so, does it vary in a systematic way? Answers to questions such as these are important for the design of policies to keep aggregate expenditure steady. How big an increase in government purchases or cut in taxes is needed to avoid a recession? How big a cut in government purchases or increase in taxes is needed to prevent the economy from running into supply bottlenecks?

You can see part of the answers to these questions in Table 9.2, which shows estimates of the value of the U.S. multiplier for selected years between 1960 and 1991. The estimates of the multiplier shown in the table were calculated by dividing the change in real GDP by the change in autonomous expenditure. In these calculations, the change in autonomous expenditure was measured as the change in the sum of investment, government purchases of goods and services, and exports. The

TABLE 9.2

The Multiplier in Selected Years

Period	Change in autonomous expenditure (ΔA)	Change in induced expenditure (ΔN)	Change in real GDP (ΔY)	Multiplier ($\Delta Y/\Delta A$)
	(billions of 1987 dollars)			
1960–1991	**1,255.6**	**1,595.3**	**2,850.8**	**2.27**
1974–1975	**–98.8**	**72.3**	**–26.4**	**0.27**
1981–1982	**–109.6**	**26.8**	**–82.8**	**0.76**
1982–1983	**68.4**	**77.7**	**146.3**	**2.14**
1983–1990*	**560.2**	**436.5**	**996.7**	**1.78**
1990–1991†	**–75.4**	**–3.8**	**–79.3**	**1.05**

*Third quarter of 1990.
†First quarter of 1991.

The average value of the multiplier from 1960 to 1991 was 2.27. In the recessions (shaded red) of 1974–1975 and 1981–1982 the multiplier was less than 1, and in the recession of 1990–1991 the multiplier was close to 1. In the recoveries (shaded blue) of 1982–1983 and 1983–1990 the multiplier was larger than 1. The multiplier was small in recession years because the decrease in income was expected to be temporary. The multiplier was smaller in the 1980s than earlier because the marginal propensity to import increased.

Source: Survey of Current Business, November 1991, pp. 6, 37; and my calculations.

change in induced expenditure is measured as the change in consumption expenditure minus the change in imports.

The first row of the table shows the average value of the multiplier between 1960 and 1991, which is 2.27. The three red rows of the table calculate the multiplier for three recession periods. In 1974–1975, we experienced a sharp cut in investment following the pessimism created by the OPEC oil price hike. In 1981–1982, we experienced a sharp cut in investment caused partly by high interest rates and partly by pessimistic profit expectations. In 1990–1991, investment decreased sharply, mainly because the outlook for profits was bleak. In the first two of these recession periods, despite there being a decrease in autonomous expenditure, induced expenditure increased. As a result, real GDP fell, but by less than the fall in autonomous expenditure. In these two years, the multiplier was less than 1. In the recession of 1991, induced expenditure decreased, but by a tiny amount, and the multiplier was close to 1. The two blue rows of the table calculate the multiplier for recovery periods in the 1980s. As you can see, the multipliers for these periods are larger than the multipliers for the recessions.

Why are multipliers small when the economy goes into recession and larger in recovery? The answer to this question is found in the behavior of the marginal propensity to consume. Consumption expenditure depends on both current disposable income and expected future disposable income. Therefore the effect of a change in current disposable income on consumption expenditure depends on whether the change is expected to be permanent or temporary. A change in current disposable income that is expected to be permanent is larger than the effect of a change that is expected to be temporary. That is, the marginal propensity to consume is larger when there is a permanent change in income than when income changes temporarily. For this reason, the marginal propensity to consume varies and does so in a way that is connected with the business cycle.

At the start of a recovery, income gains are expected to be permanent and the marginal propensity to consume is high. When a business cycle peak is approached and during recessions, income changes are expected to be temporary and the marginal propensity to consume is low. When real GDP fell in 1974–1975 and again in 1981–1982 as the economy went into recession, households expected the income loss they experienced to be temporary. They did not cut their consumption expenditure. Instead, consumption expenditure increased, but by less than it would have done in the absence of the recession. Nevertheless, the increase in consumption expenditure was a rational reaction to events interpreted as a temporary halt to an otherwise ongoing period of economic growth and expansion. Because consumption expenditure did not decline, the recessions were less severe than they otherwise would have been. The multiplier was less than 1, and consumption expenditure acted, to some degree, like a shock absorber.

When a recovery gets under way and real GDP increases, people expect a large part of their increased incomes to be permanent. As a consequence, consumption expenditure increases to reinforce the increase in autonomous expenditure, so the multiplier is larger than 1.

The Declining U.S. Multiplier

Although the multiplier in recovery is larger than that in recession, you can see from the numbers in Table 9.2 that the multiplier has declined over the years. The multiplier is 2.27 for the entire 31 years, 2.14 for the early 1980s, and 1.78 for the late 1980s. Why has the multiplier declined? The answer is the behavior of the *marginal propensity to import.*

We discovered in Chapter 8 that there has been a steady increase in imports as a percentage of GDP over the past 20 years. This steady increase has resulted partly from changes in international relative prices—many goods and services that are produced abroad are produced there at a lower cost than that at which we can produce them in the United States. The increase has also resulted from a steady increase in the degree of international specialization in the production of goods and services. That is, we have become more specialized, increasing our exports, and other countries have also become more specialized, increasing their exports to us. All of these factors have increased the marginal propensity to import. The higher the marginal propensity to import, the lower is the slope of the *AE* curve and the smaller is the multiplier.

We have studied the effects of changes in autonomous expenditure and fiscal policy on real GDP *at a given price level.* We're now going to see how the price level itself responds to changes in autonomous expenditure and fiscal policy. We're also going to see that the autonomous expenditure and fiscal policy multiplier effects on real GDP are smaller when price level changes are taken into account.

Real GDP, the Price Level, and the Multipliers

When firms find unwanted inventories piling up, they cut back on orders and decrease production. They also usually cut prices. Similarly, when firms are having trouble keeping up with sales and their inventories are falling, they increase their orders and step up production. But they also usually increase their prices. So far, we've studied the macroeconomic consequences of firms changing their production levels when their sales change, but we've not looked at the effects of price changes. When firms change their prices, for the economy as a whole the price level changes.

To study the price level, we need to use the *aggregate demand–aggregate supply model*. We also need to work out the relationship between the aggregate demand–aggregate supply model and the aggregate expenditure model that we've used in this chapter. The key to the relationship between these two models is the distinction between the aggregate *expenditure* curve and the aggregate *demand* curve.

Aggregate Expenditure and Aggregate Demand

The aggregate expenditure curve is the relationship between aggregate planned expenditure and real GDP, holding all other influences constant. The aggregate demand curve is the relationship between the aggregate quantity of goods and services demanded and the price level, holding all other influences constant. Let's explore the links between these two relationships.

Aggregate Planned Expenditure and the Price Level

At a given price level, there is a given level of aggregate planned expenditure. But if the price level changes, so does aggregate planned expenditure. Why? There are three main reasons, and they are explained more fully in Chapter 7. They are

- Real money balances effect
- Intertemporal substitution effect
- International substitution effect

A rise in the price level, other things held constant, decreases the real money supply. A lower real money supply decreases aggregate planned expenditure—the *real money balances effect*. A lower real money supply also brings higher interest rates that lead to a decrease in investment—the *intertemporal substitution effect*. A higher price level, other things remaining the same, makes U.S.-produced goods less competitive, increasing imports and decreasing exports—the *international substitution effect*.

All these effects of a higher price level lower aggregate planned expenditure at each level of real GDP. As a result, when the price level rises, the aggregate expenditure curve shifts downward. A decrease in the price level has the opposite effect. When the price level falls, the aggregate expenditure curve shifts upward.

Figure 9.8(a) illustrates these effects. When the price level is 100, the aggregate expenditure curve is AE_0, which intersects the 45° line at point *b*. Equilibrium expenditure and real GDP are \$4 trillion. If the price level increases to 150, the aggregate expenditure curve shifts downward to AE_1, which intersects the 45° line at point *a*. Equilibrium expenditure and real GDP are \$2 trillion. If the price level decreases to 50, the aggregate expenditure curve shifts upward to AE_2, which intersects the 45° line at point *c*. Equilibrium expenditure and real GDP are \$6 trillion.

We've just seen that when the price level changes, other things held constant, the aggregate expenditure curve shifts and a new expenditure equilibrium arises. But when the price level changes, other things held constant, there is a movement along the aggregate demand curve. Figure 9.8(b) illustrates these movements. At a price level of 100, the aggregate quantity of goods and services demanded is \$4 trillion—point *b* on the aggregate demand curve *AD*. If the price level increases to 150, the aggregate quantity of goods and services demanded falls to \$2 trillion. There is a movement along the aggregate demand curve to point *a*. If the price level decreases to 50, the aggregate quantity of goods and services

FIGURE 9.8

Aggregate Expenditure and Aggregate Demand

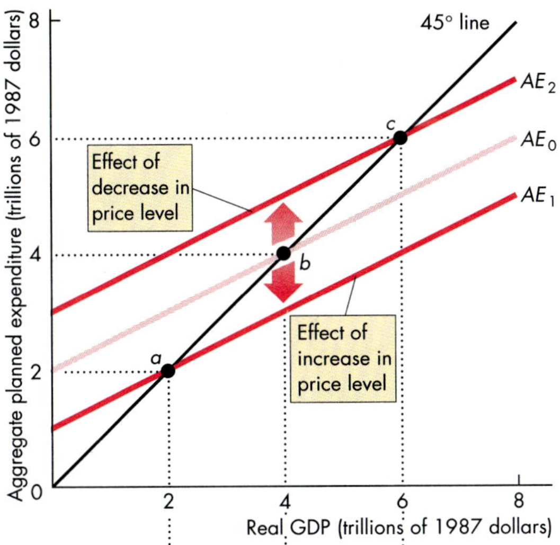

(a) Equilibrium expenditure

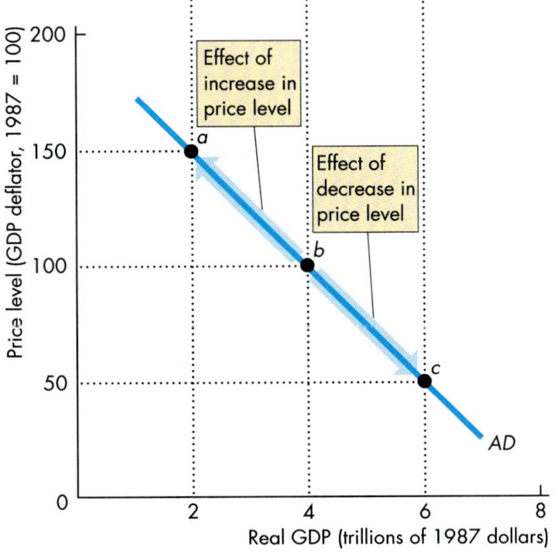

(b) Aggregate demand

The position of the aggregate expenditure curve depends on the price level—a change in the price level shifts the aggregate expenditure curve. When the price level is 100, the aggregate expenditure curve is AE_0, as shown in part (a). Equilibrium occurs where AE_0 intersects the 45° line, at point *b*. The quantity of real GDP demanded is $4 trillion. When the price level increases to 150, the aggregate expenditure curve shifts downward to AE_1, and equilibrium occurs at point *a*, where the quantity of real GDP demanded is $2 trillion. When the price level falls to 50, the *AE* curve shifts upward to AE_2 and the equilibrium occurs at point *c*, where the quantity of real GDP demanded is $6 trillion. Part (b) shows the aggregate demand curve—the relationship between the price level and the quantity of real GDP demanded. A change in the price level shifts the aggregate expenditure curve but results in a movement along the aggregate demand curve. Thus points *a*, *b*, and *c* on the aggregate demand curve correspond to those same equilibrium points in part (a).

demanded rises to $6 trillion. There is a movement along the aggregate demand curve to point *c*. Each point on the aggregate demand curve corresponds to an expenditure equilibrium. The expenditure equilibrium points *a*, *b*, and *c* in Fig. 9.8(a) correspond to the points *a*, *b*, and *c* on the aggregate demand curve in Fig. 9.8(b).

Now that we've seen the relationship between the aggregate demand curve and equilibrium expenditure, let's work out what happens to aggregate demand, the price level, and real GDP when there are changes in autonomous expenditure and changes in fiscal policy. We'll start by looking at the effects on aggregate demand.

Aggregate Demand, Autonomous Expenditure, and Fiscal Policy

We've just seen that the aggregate expenditure curve shifts when the price level changes. But it also shifts for a thousand other reasons. It is these other sources of shifts in the aggregate expenditure curve that we studied earlier in this chapter—for example, a change in investment, exports, and fiscal policy. Any factor other than the price level that shifts the aggregate expenditure curve also shifts the aggregate demand curve. Figure 9.9 illustrates these shifts.

Initially, the aggregate expenditure curve is AE_0 in part (a) and the aggregate demand curve is AD_0 in part (b). The price level is 100. Now suppose that autonomous expenditure increases by $1 trillion. (This increase could result from an increase in investment, exports, or government purchases of goods and services or a tax cut.) At a constant price level of 100, the aggregate expenditure curve shifts upward to AE_1. This curve intersects the 45° line at an equilibrium expenditure of $6 trillion (point *c'*). This amount is the aggregate quantity of goods and services demanded at a price level of 100, as shown by point *c'* in part (b). Point *c'* lies on a new aggregate demand curve. The aggregate demand curve has shifted to the right to AD_1.

The distance by which the aggregate demand curve shifts to the right is determined by the multiplier. The larger the multiplier, the larger is the shift in the aggregate demand curve resulting from a given change in autonomous expenditure. In this example, a $1 trillion increase in autonomous expenditure produces a $2 trillion increase in the aggregate quantity of goods and services demanded at each price level. The multiplier is 2. That is, a $1 trillion increase in autonomous expenditure shifts the aggregate demand curve to the right by $2 trillion.

A decrease in autonomous expenditure shifts the aggregate expenditure curve downward and shifts the aggregate demand curve to the left. You can see these effects by reversing the change that we've just studied. Suppose that the economy initially is on aggregate expenditure curve AE_1 and aggregate demand curve AD_1. There is then a decrease in autonomous expenditure, and the aggregate planned expenditure curve shifts downward to AE_0. The aggregate quantity of goods and services demanded falls to $4 trillion, and the aggregate demand curve shifts leftward to AD_0.

FIGURE 9.9

Changes in Autonomous Expenditure and Aggregate Demand

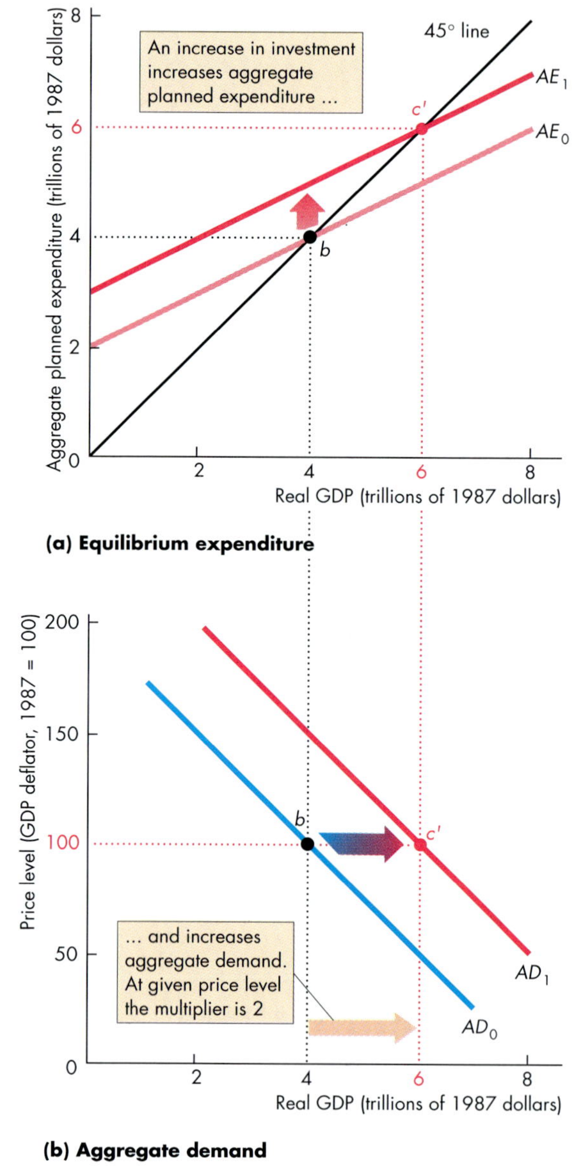

The price level is 100. When the aggregate expenditure curve is AE_0 (part a), the aggregate demand curve is AD_0 (part b). An increase in autonomous expenditure shifts the aggregate expenditure upward to AE_1. In the new equilibrium (at *c'*) real GDP is $6 trillion. Since the quantity of real GDP demanded at a price level of 100 increases to $6 trillion, the aggregate demand curve shifts to the right to AD_1.

We can summarize what we have just discovered in the following way: An increase in autonomous expenditure arising from some source other than a change in the price level shifts the *AE* curve upward and shifts the *AD* curve to the right. The size of the shift of the *AD* curve is determined by the change in autonomous expenditure and the size of the multiplier.

Equilibrium GDP and the Price Level

In Chapter 7, we learned how to determine the equilibrium level of real GDP and the price level as the intersection point of the aggregate demand and short-run aggregate supply curves. We've now put aggregate demand under a more powerful microscope and discovered that changes in autonomous expenditure and fiscal policy shift the aggregate demand curve and that the magnitude of the shift depends on the size of the multiplier. But whether a change in autonomous expenditure results ultimately in a change in real GDP or a change in the price level or some combination of the two depends on aggregate supply. We'll look at two cases. First, we'll see what happens in the short run. Then we'll look at the long run.

An Increase in Aggregate Demand in the Short Run

The economy is described in Fig. 9.10. In part (a), the aggregate expenditure curve is AE_0 and equilibrium expenditure and real GDP are $4 trillion—point *b*. In part (b), aggregate demand is AD_0 and the short-run aggregate supply curve is *SAS*. (Check back to Chapter 7 if you need to refresh your understanding of this curve.) Equilibrium is at point *b*, where the aggregate demand and short-run aggregate supply curves intersect. The price level is 100.

Now suppose there is a tax cut that increases autonomous expenditure by $1 trillion. With the price level held constant at 100, the aggregate expenditure curve shifts upward to AE_1. Equilibrium expenditure and real GDP increase to $6 trillion—point *c'* in part (a). In part (b), the aggregate demand curve shifts to the right by $2 trillion, from AD_0 to AD_1. But with this new aggregate demand curve, the price level does not remain constant. It increases to 125, as determined by the point of intersection of the short-run aggregate supply curve and the new aggregate demand curve—point *d*. And real GDP does not increase to $6 trillion, but to $5 trillion.

FIGURE 9.10

Fiscal Policy, Real GDP, and the Price Level

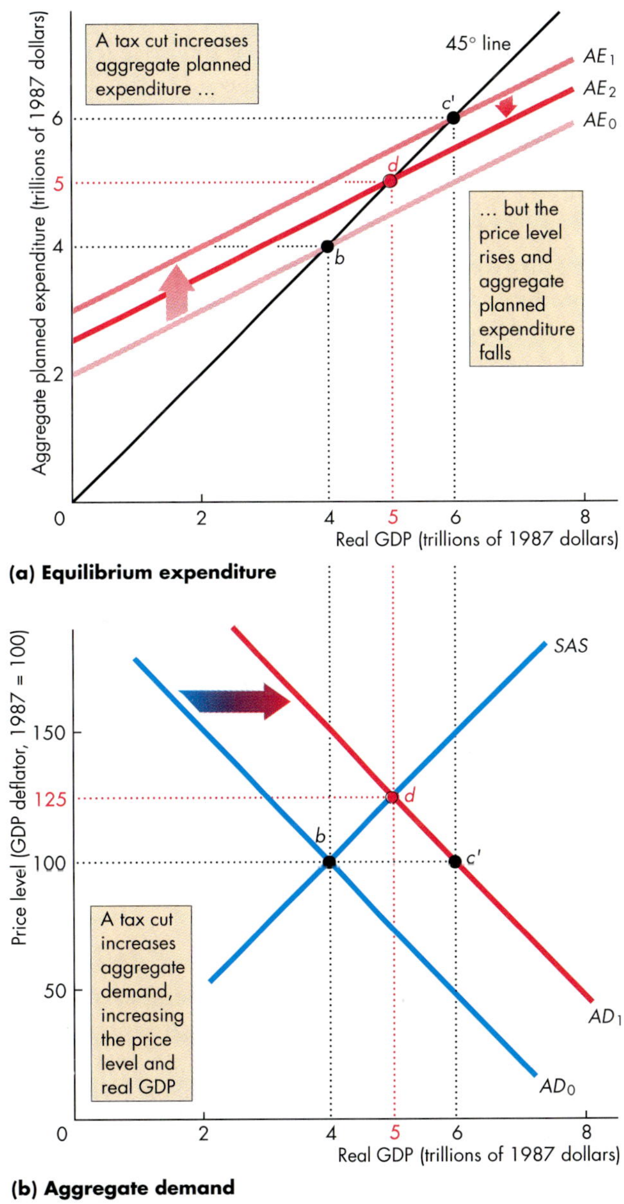

A tax cut shifts the *AE* curve upward from AE_0 to AE_1 (part a). The *AD* curve shifts from AD_0 to AD_1 (part b). The economy moves to point c' (parts a and b), and there is excess demand. The price level rises, and the higher price level shifts the *AE* curve downward to AE_2. The economy moves to point *d* in both parts. The steeper the *SAS* curve, the larger is the price level change and the smaller is the change in real GDP.

At a price level of 125, the aggregate expenditure curve does not remain at AE_1 in part (a). It shifts downward to AE_2, which intersects the 45° line at a level of aggregate expenditure and real GDP of $5 trillion (point *d*).

Taking price level effects into account, the tax cut still has a multiplier effect on real GDP, but the effect is smaller than it would be if the price level remained constant. The steeper the short-run aggregate supply curve, the larger is the increase in the price level and the smaller is the multiplier effect on real GDP.

At a Bottling Plant in Kalamazoo The result that we've just worked out might be easier to understand if you think about what happens in a single factory—a bottling plant in Kalamazoo. When taxes are cut and people have more to spend, part of their extra spending is on bottles of soda. Orders increase at the bottling plant, and it increases production. But costs also increase. To produce more bottles of soda, labor must be hired and the plant must be operated for longer hours. The new labor must be trained, and with longer production hours, less time is available for maintenance, so more plant breakdowns occur. Faced with higher costs, the factory increases prices. Thus the bottling factory responds to an increase in demand partly with an increase in production and partly with higher prices. The higher prices result in a decrease in the quantity of soda demanded, and the eventual increase in production is smaller than it would be if prices held steady. Since all firms respond in a similar way to the bottling plant in Kalamazoo, the macroeconomic outcome is the one described in Fig. 9.10.

An Increase in Aggregate Demand in the Long Run In the long run, the economy is at full-employment equilibrium and on its long-run aggregate supply curve. When the economy is at full employment, an increase in aggregate demand has the same initial effect (short-run effect) as we've just worked out, but its long-run effect is different.

To see the long-run effect, suppose that in Fig. 9.10, long-run aggregate supply is $4 trillion. When aggregate demand increases, shifting the aggregate demand curve from AD_0 to AD_1, the equilibrium *d* is an above full-employment equilibrium. When the labor force is more than fully employed, there are shortages of labor and wages increase. Higher wages bring higher costs and a decrease in aggregate supply. The result is a further increase in the price level and a decrease in real GDP. Eventually, when wage rates and the price level have increased by the same percentage, real GDP is again at its full-employment level. The multiplier in the long run is zero.

Back at the bottling plant in Kalamazoo, production and prices have increased, but there's a severe shortage of labor. Wage rates are rising quickly. The bottling plant, facing ever increasing labor costs, keeps pushing up its prices. Eventually, the wage rate paid by the bottling plant increases by the same percentage as the price of a bottle of soda. In this situation, there is no profit in continuing to produce the higher level of output, so the plant returns to its original production level.

◆ ◆ ◆ ◆ We have now studied the forces that influence the components of aggregate expenditure and have analyzed the way the components interact with each other to determine aggregate expenditure and the position of the aggregate demand curve. Fluctuations in the aggregate expenditure curve and in the aggregate demand curve are caused by fluctuations in autonomous expenditure. An important element of autonomous expenditure is investment, which in turn is determined by, among other things, interest rates. But what determines interest rates? That is the question to which we turn in the next two chapters.

SUMMARY

Expenditure Multipliers

Aggregate expenditure is divided into two components: autonomous expenditure and induced expenditure. Autonomous expenditure is the sum of investment, government purchases, exports, and the part of consumption expenditure that does not vary with income. Induced expenditure is the part of consumption expenditure that does vary with income minus imports.

An increase in autonomous expenditure increases aggregate planned expenditure and shifts the aggregate expenditure curve upward. Equilibrium expenditure and real GDP increase by more than the increase in autonomous expenditure. They do so because the increased autonomous expenditure induces an increase in consumption expenditure. Aggregate expenditure increases by the sum of the initial increase in autonomous expenditure and the increase in induced expenditure.

An increase in saving shifts the aggregate expenditure curve downward and decreases real GDP—the paradox of thrift. The paradox arises because the increase in saving does not automatically bring an increase in investment. If investment and saving increase together, the aggregate expenditure curve does not shift and aggregate income does not fall. In the long run, additional saving enables more capital to be accumulated and makes aggregate income grow more quickly.

The autonomous expenditure multiplier (or simply the multiplier) is the change in equilibrium real GDP divided by the change in autonomous expenditure that brought it about. The size of the multiplier depends on the slope of the *AE* curve (g), and its value is given by the formula

$$\text{Multiplier} = \frac{1}{(1-g)}.$$

Because g is a number between 0 and 1, the multiplier is greater than 1. The larger the value of g, the larger is the multiplier. The multiplier is greater than 1 because of induced expenditure—because an increase in autonomous expenditure induces an increase in consumption expenditure. (pp. 221–229)

Fiscal Policy Multipliers

There are three main fiscal policy multipliers:

- Government purchases multiplier
- Transfer payments multiplier
- Tax multiplier

The government purchases multiplier is the amount by which a change in government purchases of goods and services is multiplied to determine the change in equilibrium expenditure that it generates. Because government purchases of goods and services are one of the components of autonomous expenditure, this multiplier is equal to the autonomous expenditure multiplier. That is,

$$\text{Government purchases multiplier} = \frac{1}{(1-g)}.$$

The transfer payments multiplier is the amount by which a change in transfer payments is multiplied to determine the change in equilibrium expenditure that it generates. Because a change in transfer payments influences aggregate expenditure by changing disposable income, this multiplier is equal to the marginal propensity to consume (b) times the autonomous expenditure multiplier. That is,

$$\text{Transfer payments multiplier} = \frac{b}{(1-g)}.$$

The tax multiplier is the amount by which a change in taxes is multiplied to determine the change in equilibrium expenditure that it generates. A tax increase brings a decrease in equilibrium expenditure. The initial response of consumption expenditure to a tax increase is exactly the same as its response to a decrease in transfer payments. Thus a tax change works like a change in transfer payments, but its multiplier is negative. It is

$$\text{Tax multiplier} = \frac{-b}{(1-g)}.$$

If both government purchases of goods and services and taxes are changed together and by the same amount, there is a balanced budget multiplier that combines the two separate multipliers. The balanced budget multiplier is

$$\text{Balanced budget multiplier} = \frac{(1-b)}{(1-g)}.$$

Because the marginal propensity to consume (b) is bigger than the slope of the *AE* curve (g), the balanced budget multiplier is less than 1.

The tax and transfer payments system acts as an automatic stabilizer—a mechanism that decreases the fluctuations in aggregate expenditure. (pp. 229–236)

The Multiplier in the United States

The multiplier in the United States is close to 2. But it fluctuates over the business cycle, rising during a recovery and falling during a recession. Its value has fallen over time because the marginal propensity to import has increased. (pp. 236–238)

Real GDP, the Price Level, and the Multipliers

The aggregate demand curve is the relationship between the quantity of real GDP demanded and the price level, other things held constant. A change in the price level brings a movement along the aggregate demand curve. The aggregate expenditure curve is the relationship between aggregate planned expenditure and real GDP, other things held constant. At a given price level, there is a given aggregate expenditure curve. A change in the price level changes autonomous expenditure and shifts the aggregate expenditure curve. Thus a movement along the aggregate demand curve is associated with a shift in the aggregate expenditure curve. A change in autonomous expenditure not caused by a change in the price level shifts the aggregate expenditure curve and also shifts the aggregate demand curve. The magnitude of the shift in the aggregate demand curve depends on the size of the multiplier and on the change in autonomous expenditure.

Real GDP and the price level are determined by both aggregate demand and aggregate supply. If an increase in aggregate demand occurs at an unemployment equilibrium, both the price level and real GDP increase. But the increase in real GDP is smaller than the increase in aggregate demand. The steeper the short-run aggregate supply curve, the larger is the change in the price level and the smaller is the change in real GDP. If an increase in aggregate demand occurs at full employment, its long-run effect is entirely on the price level. (pp. 238–242)

KEY ELEMENTS

Key Terms

Key Figures and Tables

REVIEW QUESTIONS

1 The autonomous expenditure multiplier applies to changes in which components of aggregate expenditure?

2 What is the connection between the autonomous expenditure multiplier and the slope of the *AE* curve?

3 Why is the autonomous expenditure multiplier greater than 1?

4 What is the government purchases multiplier? Is its value greater than 1?

5 What is the transfer payments multiplier?

6 What is the tax multiplier? How does it compare with the autonomous expenditure multiplier?

7 How does the transfer payments multiplier compare with the tax multiplier?

8 What is the balanced budget multiplier? Is its value greater than 1?

9 Explain how income taxes and transfer payments act as automatic stabilizers.

10 What is the size of the multiplier in the United States?

11 What is the relationship between the aggregate expenditure curve and the aggregate demand curve?

12 The price level changes, and everything else is held constant. What happens to the aggregate demand curve and the aggregate expenditure curve?

13 A change in autonomous expenditure occurs that is not produced by a change in the price level. What happens to the aggregate expenditure curve and the aggregate demand curve?

PROBLEMS

1 You are given the following information about the economy of Zeeland: Autonomous consumption expenditure is $100 billion, and the marginal propensity to consume is 0.9. Investment is $460 billion, government purchases of goods and services are $400 billion, and taxes are a constant $400 billion—they do not vary with income. Exports are $350 billion, and imports are 10 percent of income. The government of Zeeland makes no transfer payments.

- **a** Calculate the slope of the *AE* curve.
- **b** The government cuts its purchases of goods and services to $300 billion. What is the change in real GDP? What is the government purchases multiplier?
- **c** The government continues to purchase $400 billion worth of goods and services and cuts taxes to $300 billion. What is the change in real GDP? What is the tax multiplier?
- **d** The government simultaneously cuts both its purchases of goods and services and taxes to $300 billion. What is the change in real GDP? What is the name of the multiplier now at work, and what is its value?

2 Everything in Zeeland remains the same as in problem 1 except that the tax laws are changed. Instead of taxes being a constant $400 billion, they become 10 percent of real GDP.

- **a** Calculate the slope of the *AE* curve.
- **b** Government purchases are cut to $300 billion. What is the change in real GDP? What is the government purchases multiplier?
- **c** What is the change in consumption expenditure? Explain why consumption expenditure changes by more than the change in government purchases.
- **d** The government introduces transfer payments of $50 billion. What is the transfer payments multiplier? What is the change in real GDP?

3 You are given three bits of information about the multiplier in the economy of Alphabeta. Its average value is 2, in year A it is 3½, and in year B it is ½.

- **a** Was year A a recovery year or a recession year? Why?
- **b** Was year B a recovery year or a recession year? Why?

4 Suppose that the price level in the economy of Zeeland, as described in problem 1, is 100.

- **a** Find one point on Zeeland's aggregate demand curve.
- **b** If the government of Zeeland increases its purchases of goods and services by $100 billion, what happens to the quantity of real GDP demanded?
- **c** In the short run, does equilibrium real GDP increase by more than, less than, or the same amount as the increase in the quantity of real GDP demanded?
- **d** In the long run, does equilibrium real GDP increase by more than, less than, or the same amount as the increase in the quantity of real GDP demanded?
- **e** In the short run, does the price level in Zeeland rise, fall, or remain unchanged?
- **f** In the long run, does the price level in Zeeland rise, fall, or remain unchanged?

CHAPTER 10

MONEY, BANKING, AND PRICES

After studying this chapter, you will be able to:

- Define money and state its functions
- Describe the different forms of money
- Explain how money is measured in the United States today
- Describe the balance sheets of the main financial intermediaries
- Explain the economic functions of commercial banks and other financial intermediaries
- Describe some of the important financial innovations of the 1980s
- Explain how banks create money
- Explain why the quantity of money is an important economic magnitude
- Explain the quantity theory of money

Money Makes the World Go Around

MONEY, LIKE FIRE AND THE WHEEL, HAS BEEN AROUND for a very long time. No one knows for sure how long or what its origins are. An incredible array of items have served as money—wampum (beads made from shells) was used by North American Indians; cowries (brightly colored shells) were used in India; whales' teeth were used in Fiji; tobacco was used by early American colonists; cigarettes and liquor have been used in more modern times; and even cakes of salt have served as money in Ethiopia, other parts of Africa, and Tibet. What exactly is money? Why has this rich variety of commodities served as money? ◆◆ Today, when we want to buy something, we use coins or bills, write a check, or present a credit card. Are all these things money? When we deposit some coins or bills into a bank or savings and loan association (S&L), is that still money? And what happens when the bank or the S&L lends the money in our deposit account to someone else? How can we get our money back if it's been lent out? Does lending by banks and S&Ls create money—out of thin air? ◆◆ During the 1980s, banks and other financial institutions introduced new types of deposit accounts—NOW accounts and ATS accounts being the most prominent ones. Why were these new kinds of bank accounts introduced? ◆◆ The S&Ls have been in deep trouble in recent years, and in 1989 the federal government came to their rescue with the largest bailout in U.S. history. Why are the S&Ls in trouble? ◆◆ During the 1970s, the quantity of money in existence in the United States increased quickly, but in the 1980s it increased at a slower pace. In China in the late 1940s, Israel in the early 1980s, and some Latin American countries in the late 1980s, the quantity of money increased at an extremely rapid pace. In Switzerland and Germany, the quantity of money has increased at a modest pace. Does the rate of increase in the quantity of money matter? What are the effects of an increasing quantity of money on our economy?

◆ ◆ ◆ ◆ In this chapter, we'll study that useful invention, money. We'll look at its functions, its different forms, and the way it is defined and measured in the United States today. We'll also study commercial banks and other financial institutions and learn how they create money. Finally, we'll examine the relationship between money and prices.

What Is Money?

What do cowrie shells, whales' teeth, nickels, and dimes have in common? Why are they all examples of money? To answer these questions, we need a definition of money.

The Definition of Money

Money is any commodity or token that is generally acceptable as a means of payment for goods and services. The particular commodities and tokens that have served this purpose have varied enormously. We're going to study money and the institutions of monetary exchange that have evolved in the U.S. economy. But first, let's look at the functions of money.

The Functions of Money

Money has four functions:

- Medium of exchange
- Unit of account
- Store of value
- Standard of deferred payment

Medium of Exchange A **medium of exchange** is a commodity or token that is generally accepted in exchange for goods and services. Money acts as such a medium. Without money, it would be necessary to exchange goods and services directly for other goods and services—an exchange known as **barter.** For example, if you wanted to buy a hamburger, you would offer the paperback novel you've just finished reading or half an hour of your labor in the kitchen in exchange for it. Barter can take place only when there is a double coincidence of wants. A **double coincidence of wants** is a situation that occurs when person A wants to buy what person B is selling and person B wants to buy what person A is selling. That is, to get your hamburger, you'd have to find someone who's selling hamburgers and who wants a paperback novel or your work in the kitchen. The occurrence of a double coincidence of wants is sufficiently rare that barter exchange would leave potential gains from specialization and exchange unrealized.

Money guarantees that there is always a double coincidence of wants. People with something to sell will always accept money in exchange for it, and people who want to buy will always offer money. Money acts as a lubricant that smooths the mechanism of exchange. It lowers the costs of making transactions. The evolution of monetary exchange is a consequence of our economizing activity—of getting the most possible out of limited resources.

Unit of Account An agreed measure for stating the prices of goods and services is a **unit of account.** To get the most out of your budget, you have to figure out, among other things, whether seeing one more movie is worth the price you have to pay, not in dollars and cents, but in terms of the number of ice-cream cones, sodas, and cups of coffee that you have to give up. It's not hard to do such calculations when all these goods have prices in terms of dollars and cents (see Table 10.1). If a movie costs \$6 and a six-pack of soda costs \$3, you know right away that seeing one more movie costs you 2 six-packs of soda. If jelly beans are 50¢ a pack, one more movie costs 12 packs of jelly beans. You need only one calculation to figure out the opportunity cost of any pair of goods and services.

But imagine how troublesome it would be if your local movie theater posted its price as 2 six-packs of soda and if the convenience store posted the price of a six-pack of soda as 2 ice-cream cones and if the ice-cream shop posted the price of a cone as 3 packs of jelly beans and if the candy store priced jelly

TABLE 10.1

The Unit of Account Function of Money Simplifies Price Comparisons

Good	Price in money units	Price in units of another good
Movie	**$6.00 each**	**2 six-packs of soda**
Soda	**$3.00 per six-pack**	**2 ice-cream cones**
Ice cream	**$1.50 per cone**	**3 packs of jelly beans**
Jelly beans	**$0.50 per pack**	**2 cups of coffee**
Coffee	**$0.25 a cup**	**1 local phone call**

Money as a unit of account: One movie costs $6 and a cup of coffee costs 25¢, so one movie costs 24 cups of coffee ($6 ÷ 25¢ = 24).

No unit of account: You go to a movie theater and learn that the price of a movie is 2 six-packs of soda. You go to a candy store and learn that a pack of jelly beans costs 2 cups of coffee. But how many cups of coffee does seeing a movie cost you? To answer that question, you go to the convenience store and find that a six-pack of soda costs 2 ice-cream cones. Now you head for the ice-cream store, where an ice-cream cone costs 3 packs of jelly beans. Now you get out your pocket calculator: 1 movie costs 2 six-packs of soda, or 4 ice-cream cones, or 12 packs of jelly beans, or 24 cups of coffee!

beans as 2 cups of coffee! Now how much running around and calculating would you have to do to figure out how much that movie is going to cost you in terms of the soda, ice cream, jelly beans, or coffee that you must give up to see it? You would get the answer for soda right away from the sign posted on the movie theater, but for all the other goods you would have to visit many different stores to establish the price of each commodity in terms of another and then calculate prices in units that are relevant for your own decision. Cover up the column labeled "Price in money units" in Table 10.1 and see how hard it is to figure out the number of local phone calls it costs to see one movie. It's enough to make a person swear off movies! How much simpler it is for everyone to express their prices in terms of dollars and cents.

Store of Value Any commodity or token that can be held and exchanged later for goods and services is called a **store of value.** Money acts as a store of value. If it did not, it would not be acceptable in exchange for goods and services. The more stable the value of a commodity or token, the better it can act as a store of value and the more useful it is as money. There are no stores of value that are completely safe. The value of a physical object such as a house, a car, or a work of art fluctuates over time. The value of a commodity or token used as money also fluctuates, and when there is inflation, its value persistently falls.

Standard of Deferred Payment An agreed measure that enables contracts to be written for future receipts and payments is called a **standard of deferred payment.** If you borrow money to buy a house or if you save money to provide for retirement, your future commitment or future receipt will be agreed to in dollars and cents. Money is used as the standard for a deferred payment.

Using money as a standard of deferred payment is not entirely without risk because, as we saw in Chapter 5, inflation leads to unpredictable changes in the value of money. But, to the extent that borrowers and lenders anticipate inflation, its rate is reflected in the interest rates paid and received. Lenders in effect protect themselves by charging a higher interest rate, and borrowers, anticipating inflation, willingly pay the higher rate.

Different Forms of Money

Money can take four different forms:

- Commodity money
- Convertible paper money
- Fiat money
- Private debt money

Commodity Money A physical commodity that is valued in its own right and also used as a means of payment is **commodity money.** An amazing array of items have served as commodity money at different times and places, several of which were described in the chapter opener. But the most common commodity monies have been coins made from metals such as gold, silver, and copper. The first known coins were made in Lydia, a Greek city-state, at the beginning of the seventh century B.C. These coins were made of electrum, a natural mixture of gold and silver.

Commodity money has considerable advantages but some drawbacks. Let's look first at the advantages.

Advantages of Commodity Money The main advantage of commodity money is that because the commodity is valued for its own sake, its value as money is readily known. This fact provides a guarantee of the value of money. For example, gold may be used to fill teeth and make rings; its value in these uses determines its value as money. Historically, gold and silver were ideal for use as money because they were in limited supply and in constant demand (by those wealthy enough to use them) for ornaments and jewelry. Further, their quality was easily verified, and they were easily divisible into units small enough to facilitate exchange.

Disadvantages of Commodity Money Commodity money has two main disadvantages. First, there is a constant temptation to cheat on the value of the money. Two methods of cheating have been commonly used—clipping and debasement. *Clipping* is reducing the size of coins by an imperceptible amount, thereby lowering their metallic content. *Debasement* is creating a coin having a lower silver or gold content (the balance being made up of some cheaper metal).

This temptation to lower the value of money led to a phenomenon known as Gresham's Law, after the sixteenth-century English financial expert Sir Thomas Gresham. **Gresham's Law** is the tendency for bad money to drive good money out of circulation. Bad money is debased money; good money is money that has not been debased. It's easy to see why Gresham's Law works. Suppose that a person is paid with two coins, one debased and the other not. Each coin has the same value if used as money in exchange for goods. But one of the coins—the one that's not debased—is more valuable as a commodity than as a coin. It will not, therefore, be used as money. Only the debased coin will be used as money. It is in this way that bad money drives good money out of circulation.

A second major disadvantage of commodity money is that the commodity, valued for its own sake, could be used in ways other than as money—it has an opportunity cost. For example, gold and silver used as money cannot be used to make jewelry or ornaments. This opportunity cost creates incentives to find alternatives to the commodity itself for use in the exchange process. One such alternative is a paper claim to commodity money.

Convertible Paper Money When a paper claim to a commodity circulates as a means of payment, that claim is called **convertible paper money.** The first known example of paper money occurred in China during the Ming dynasty (1368–1399 A.D.). This form of money was also used extensively throughout Europe in the Middle Ages.

The inventiveness of goldsmiths and their clients led to the increase and widespread use of convertible paper money. Because gold was valuable, goldsmiths had well-guarded safes in which to keep their own gold. They also rented space to artisans and others who wanted to put their gold in safekeeping. The goldsmiths issued a receipt entitling the owner of the gold to reclaim his or her "deposit" on demand. These receipts were much like the coat check token that you get at a theater or museum.

Suppose that Isabella has a gold receipt indicating that she has 100 ounces of gold deposited with Samuel Goldsmith. She is going to buy a piece of land valued at 100 ounces of gold from Henry. There are two ways that Isabella might undertake the transaction. The first way is to go to Samuel, hand over her receipt and collect her gold, transport the gold to Henry, and take title to the land. Henry now goes back to Samuel with the gold and deposits it there for safekeeping, leaving with his own receipt. The second way of doing this transaction is for Isabella simply to hand over her gold receipt to Henry, completing the transaction by using the gold receipt as money. Obviously, it is much more convenient to complete the transaction in the second way, provided that Henry can trust Samuel. The gold receipt circulating as a means of payment is money. The paper money is *backed* by the gold held by Goldsmith. Also the paper money is *convertible* into commodity money.

Fractional Backing Once the convertible paper money system is operating and people are using their gold receipts rather than gold itself as the means of payment, goldsmiths notice that their vaults are storing a large amount of gold that is never withdrawn. This gives them a brilliant idea. Why not lend people gold receipts? The goldsmith can charge interest on the loan, and the loan is created just by writing on a piece of paper. As long as the number of such receipts created is not too large in relation to the stock of gold in the goldsmith's safe, the goldsmith is in no danger of not being able to honor the promise to convert receipts into gold on demand. The gold in the goldsmith's safe is a *fraction* of the gold receipts in circulation. By this device, *fractionally backed* convertible paper money was invented.

Between 1879 and 1933, the monetary system of the United States was one based on fractionally backed convertible paper. Until 1933, the U.S. dollar had a guaranteed value in terms of gold and could be converted into gold at a fixed value on demand. Between 1933 and 1971, it was illegal for U.S. citizens to hold gold coins or ingots but the U.S. Treasury stood ready to convert dollars into gold at $35 per ounce of gold for foreign central banks and foreign governments. In 1971, the gold convertibility of the U.S. dollar was finally abandoned, the market price of gold having increased far above $35 an ounce.

Even with fractionally backed paper money, valuable commodities that could be used for other productive activities are tied up in the exchange process. There remains an incentive to find a yet more efficient way of facilitating exchange and of freeing up the commodities used to back the paper money. This alternative is fiat money.

Fiat Money The term *fiat* means "let it be done" or "by order of the authority." **Fiat money** is an intrinsically worthless (or almost worthless) commodity that serves the functions of money. Some of the earliest fiat monies were the continental currency issued during the American Revolution and the "greenbacks" issued during the Civil War, which circulated until 1879. Another early issue of fiat money was that of the so-called *assignats* issued during the French Revolution. These early experiments with fiat money ended in rapid inflation because the amount of fiat money created was allowed to increase at a rapid pace, causing the money to lose value.

However, provided that the quantity of fiat money is not allowed to grow too rapidly, it has a reasonably steady value in terms of the goods and services that it will buy. People are willing to accept fiat money in exchange for the goods and services they sell only because they know it will be honored when they go to buy goods and services. The bills and coins that we use in the United States today—collectively known as **currency**—are examples of fiat money. Because of the creation of fiat money, people are willing to accept a piece of paper with a special watermark, printed in green ink, and worth not more than a few cents as a commodity in exchange for $100 worth of goods and services. The small metal alloy disk that we call a quarter is worth almost nothing as a piece of metal, but it pays for a local phone call and many other small commodities. The replacement of commodity money by fiat money enables the commodities themselves to be used productively.

Private Debt Money In the modern world, there is a fourth important type of money—private debt money. **Private debt money** is a loan that the borrower promises to repay in currency on demand. By transferring the entitlement to be repaid from one person to another, such a loan can be used as money. For example, you give me an IOU for $10; I give the IOU to a bookseller to buy a biography of Adam Smith; you pay the holder of the IOU $10—only now it's the bookseller holding the IOU.

The most important example of private debt money is the checkable deposit at commercial banks and other financial institutions. A **checkable deposit** is a loan by a depositor to a bank, the ownership of which can be transferred from one person to another by writing an instruction to the bank—a check—asking the bank to alter its records. We'll have more to say shortly about this type of money. Before doing so, let's look at the different forms of money and their relative magnitudes in the United States today.

Money in the United States Today

There are three official measures of money in current use: **M1**, **M2**, and **M3**. They are defined in Table 10.2, and the terms used to describe the components of the three measures are set out in the compact glossary in Table 10.3.

Are All the Measures of Money Really Money? The items that make up M1 fit the definition of money fairly closely. Currency (both coins and bills of various denominations) and traveler's checks are universally acceptable in payment for goods and services.

TABLE 10.2

The Three Official Measures of Money

M1	◆ Currency held outside banks
	◆ Traveler's checks
	◆ Demand deposits
	◆ Other checkable deposits (OCDs), including NOW accounts and ATS accounts at commercial banks, S&Ls, savings banks, and credit unions
M2	◆ M1
	◆ Savings deposits
	◆ Small time deposits
	◆ Eurodollar deposits, money market mutual fund shares held by individuals, and other M2 deposits
M3	◆ M2
	◆ Large time deposits
	◆ Eurodollar time deposits, money market mutual fund shares held by institutions, and other M3 deposits

M1 consists of currency (pennies, nickels, dimes, and quarters and Federal Reserve bank notes, that is, bills of various denominations) and bank deposits on which a check can be written, including NOW accounts and ATS accounts. The currency component of M1 is only that held outside the banks. Currency held by banks is not part of M1. M2 is M1 plus savings accounts, small time deposits, and other very liquid assets. M3 is M2 plus less liquid assets such as large time deposits and money market mutual fund shares held by institutions.

So also are checkable deposits at commercial banks, S&Ls, savings banks, and credit unions.

The other items that make up M2 and M3 are not quite so clearly money, but they have a high degree of liquidity. **Liquidity** is the degree to which an asset is instantly convertible into money at a known price. Assets vary in their degree of liquidity. Some are not very liquid because some minimum amount of notice has to be given before they can be converted into a means of payment. Others lack liquidity because they are traded on markets and their prices fluctuate, making the amount of money into which they can be converted uncertain. But the savings

TABLE 10.3

A Compact Glossary of the Components of Money

Currency held outside banks

Notes issued by Fed and coins issued by the U.S. Treasury held outside the banking system.

Traveler's check

A bank check convertible into currency on demand.

Checkable deposit

A deposit account on which a check can be written.

Demand deposit

A checkable deposit convertible into currency on demand.

NOW account

Negotiable Order of Withdrawal account—"negotiable order of withdrawal" is another name for a check.

ATS account

Automatic-Transfer Savings account—a checkable deposit the balance on which is maintained at an agreed level by transferring funds to and from a savings account.

Savings deposit

A deposit that technically cannot be withdrawn on demand but in practice can be instantly withdrawn.

Time deposit

A deposit with fixed term to maturity. "Small" deposits are below $100,000; "large" deposits are $100,000 or more.)

Eurodollars

U.S. dollar accounts in banks in other countries, mainly in Europe.

Money market mutual fund

A financial intermediary that obtains funds by issuing shares on which checks may be drawn.

deposits and small time deposits that make up M2 and the large time deposits and other accounts that make up M3 are easily converted into assets that serve as a means of payment. They are highly liquid—or almost money.

The relative magnitudes of the components of the various measures of money are shown in Fig. 10.1. As you can see, the largest components of money in the United States are the deposits in banks and other financial institutions. Even though there is a remarkably large amount of currency in circulation—more than $1,000 per person—currency is only 29 percent of M1. The biggest component of M1 is checkable deposits.

Checkable deposits are money, but the checks people write when they make a payment are not. It is important to understand why.

Checkable Deposits Are Money, but Checks Are Not

The best way to see why checkable deposits are money but checks are not is to consider what happens when someone pays for goods by writing a check. Let's suppose that Barb buys a bike for $200 from Rocky's Mountain Bikes. When Barb goes to Rocky's bike shop, she has $500 in her checkable deposit account at the Laser Bank. Rocky has $1,000 in his checkable deposit account—at the same bank, as it happens. The checkable deposits of these two people total $1,500. On June 11, Barb writes a check for $200. Rocky takes the check to Laser Bank right away and deposits it. Rocky's bank balance rises from $1,000 to $1,200. But the bank not only credits Rocky's account with $200, it also debits Barb's account $200, so her balance falls from $500 to $300. The total checkable deposits of Barb and Rocky are still the same as before, $1,500. Rocky now has $200 more and Barb has $200 less than before. These transactions are summarized in Table 10.4.

This transaction has simply transferred money from one person to another. The check itself was never money. That is, there wasn't an extra $200 worth of money while the check was in circulation. The check simply served as a written instruction to the bank to transfer the money from Barb to Rocky.

In our example, Barb and Rocky use the same bank. Essentially the same story, though with additional steps, describes what happens if Barb and Rocky use different banks. Rocky's bank will credit the check to Rocky's account and then take the check to a check-clearing center. Barb's bank will pay Rocky's bank $200 and then debit Barb's account $200. This process can take a few days, but the principles are the same as when two people use the same bank.

So checks are not money. But what about credit cards? Isn't having a credit card in your wallet and

FIGURE 10.1

The Three Official Measures of Money

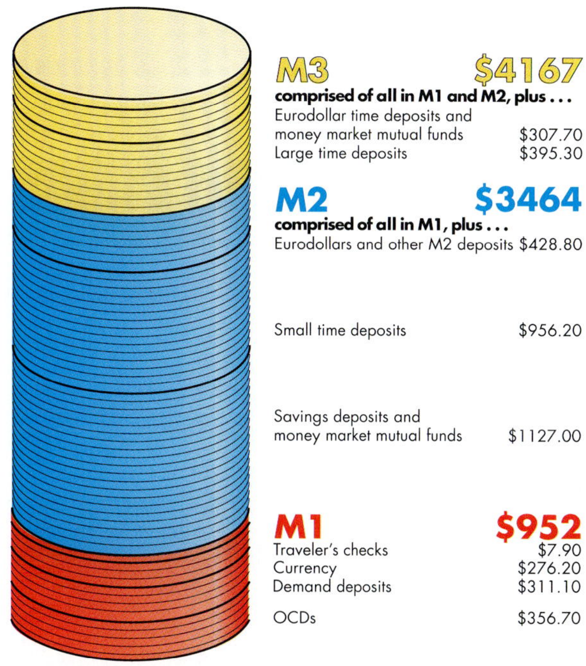

The M1 measure of money consists of all the assets that are a means of payment—currency, traveler's checks, demand deposits, and other checkable deposits. M1 makes up about 27 percent of the M2 measure of the money supply. M2 consists of M1 plus savings deposits and small time deposits as well as money market mutual fund shares held by individuals. M2 constitutes about 83 percent of M3. M3 consists of M2 plus large time deposits, Eurodollar time deposits, and money market mutual fund shares held by institutions.

Source: Economic Report of the President, 1993.

TABLE 10.4

Paying by Check

LASER BANK

137 Dakota Street • Andover, MA 01810 • (508)555–3973

Date	Item	Debit	Credit	Balance
June 1	Opening balance			$500.00 (CR)*
June 11	Rocky's Mountain Bikes	$200.00		$300.00 (CR)

Barb's checkable deposit account

LASER BANK

137 Dakota Street • Andover, MA 01810 • (508)555–3973

Date	Item	Debit	Credit	Balance
June 1	Opening balance			$1,000.00 (CR)
June 11	Barb buys bike		$200.00	$1,200.00 (CR)

Rocky's Mountain Bikes checkable deposit account

*CR means "credit": The bank owes the depositor.

presenting the card to pay for a bike the same thing as using money? Why aren't credit cards somehow valued and counted as part of the quantity of money?

Credit Cards Are Not Money When you pay by check, you are frequently asked to prove your identity by showing your driver's license. It would never occur to you to think of your driver's license as money. Your driver's license is just an ID.

A credit card is also an ID card but one that enables you to borrow money at the instant a purchase is made on the promise of repaying later. When you make a purchase, you sign a credit card sales slip that creates a debt in your name. You are saying: "I agree to pay for these goods when the credit card company bills me." Once you get your statement from the credit card company, you have to make the minimum payment due. To make that payment, you need money—you need to have currency or funds in your checkable deposit so that you can write a check to pay the credit card company. Although you use a credit card to make purchases, it is not money.

REVIEW

Money, a generally acceptable means of payment, has four functions: medium of exchange, unit of account, store of value, and standard of deferred payment. Any durable commodity can serve as money, but modern societies use fiat money and private debt money rather than commodity money. The largest component of money in the United States today is checkable deposits at banks and other financial institutions. Neither checks nor credit cards are money. A check is an instruction to a bank to transfer money from one account to another. Money is the balance in the account itself. A credit card is an ID card that enables a person to borrow at the instant a purchase is made on the promise of repaying later. When repayment is made, money (currency or a checkable deposit) is used for the payment. ◆

We've seen that the most important component of money in the United States is deposits at banks and other financial institutions. Let's take a look at the banking and financial system a bit more closely.

Financial Intermediaries

We are going to study the banking and financial system by first describing the variety of financial intermediaries that operate in the United States today. Then we'll examine the operations of banks and of other financial intermediaries. After describing the main features of financial intermediaries, we'll examine their economic functions, describing what they produce and how they make a profit.

A **financial intermediary** is a firm that takes deposits from households and firms and makes loans to other households and firms. There are five types of financial intermediaries whose deposits are components of the nation's money:

- Commercial banks
- Savings and loan associations
- Savings banks
- Credit unions
- Money market mutual funds

A compact glossary of these financial intermediaries and an indication of their relative size are given in Table 10.5.

Let's begin by examining commercial banks.

Commercial Banks

A **commercial bank** is a private firm, chartered either by the Comptroller of the Currency (in the U.S. Treasury) or by a state agency to receive deposits and make loans. There are close to 13,000 commercial banks in the United States today. The scale and scope of the operations of commercial banks can be seen by examining the balance sheet of the commercial banking sector.

A **balance sheet** is a statement that lists a firm's assets and liabilities. **Assets** are the things of value that a firm owns. **Liabilities** are the things that a firm owes to households and other firms. The liabilities of banks are deposits. Your deposit at a bank is an asset to you but a liability for your bank. The bank has to repay you your deposit (and sometimes interest on it, too) whenever you decide to take your money out of the bank.

The balance sheet for all commercial banks in December 1992 is set out in Table 10.6. The left side—the assets—lists the items *owned* by the banks. The right side—the liabilities—lists the items that the banks *owe* to others. Let's start on the liabilities side. Total liabilities in December 1992 were $3,382 billion. The banks' major liabilities are divided among three types of deposits:

- Checkable deposits
- Savings deposits
- Time deposits

You have met these deposits before in the various definitions of money. The banks' other liabilities

TABLE 10.5

A Compact Glossary of Financial Intermediaries

Type of financial intermediary (approximate number)	Total assets (billions of dollars)	Main functions
Commercial banks (13,000)	**3,380**	**A private firm chartered by either the Comptroller of the Currency (of the U.S. Treasury) or a state agency to receive deposits and make loans.**
Savings and loan associations (2,900)	**1,140**	**Financial institutions that receive savings deposits (sometimes called shares) and checkable deposits and use the funds to make mortgage and other loans.**
Savings banks (500)	**588**	**Financial institutions owned by their depositors that accept deposits and make loans primarily to home buyers.**
Credit unions (13,000)	**197**	**Small cooperative lending institutions often organized in a place of work or by a labor union. They take deposits and make consumer loans.**
Money market mutual funds	**977**	**Financial intermediaries that obtain funds by issuing shares and using the proceeds to buy a portfolio of short-term, liquid assets. Shareholders can write checks on their money market mutual fund share accounts.**

Sources: Federal Reserve Bulletin (May 1993), p. A19; *Federal Reserve Bulletin* (March 1991), pp. A26 and A27; *Economic Report of the President* (1991), p. 364; U.S. Bureau of the Census, *Statistical Abstract of the United States 1991,* 111th edition (Washington, D.C., 1991), p. 499.

TABLE 10.6

The Balance Sheet of All Commercial Banks, December 1992

Assets (billions of dollars)			Liabilities (billions of dollars)	
Reserve assets			**Checkable deposits**	**799**
Reserves with Federal Reserve banks	**29**		**Savings deposits**	**742**
Vault cash	**36**		**Time deposits**	**1,005**
Total reserves		**65**	**Other liabilities**	**836**
Liquid assets		**171**		
Investment securities		**799**		
Loans		**2,281**		
Other assets		**66**		
Total		**3,382**	**Total**	**3,382**

Source: Federal Reserve Bulletin (May 1993), Table 1.25, p. A19.

consist of borrowing by the banks in what is sometimes called the **wholesale deposit market**—the market for deposits among banks and other financial intermediaries.

Why does a bank obligate itself to pay you your money back with interest? Because it wants to use your deposit to make a profit for itself. To achieve this objective, the banks lend the money deposited with them at interest rates higher than the rates they pay for deposits.

The asset side of the balance sheet tells us how the banks do their lending. And the numbers in Table 10.6 tell us what they did with their $3,382 billion worth of borrowed resources in December 1992. The banks kept some of their assets in the form of deposits at Federal Reserve banks and as cash in their vaults. (We'll study the Federal Reserve banks in Chapter 11.) The cash in a bank's vault plus its deposits at Federal Reserve banks are called its **reserves.** You can think of a commercial bank's deposit at the Federal Reserve as being similar to your deposit at your own bank. Commercial banks use these deposits in the same way that you use your bank account. A commercial bank deposits cash into or draws cash out of its account at the Federal Reserve and writes checks on that account to settle debts with other banks.

If the banks kept all their assets in the form of deposits at the Federal Reserve and cash in their vaults, they wouldn't make any profit. But if they didn't keep *some* of their assets as cash in their vaults and as deposits at the Federal Reserve, they wouldn't be able to meet the demands for cash that their customers place on them. Nor would they be able to keep that automatic teller replenished every time you, your friends, and all their other customers raid it for cash for a midnight pizza.

The bulk of a bank's borrowed resources are put to work by making loans. Some of these loans are instantly convertible into cash and with virtually no risk. These are called liquid assets. **Liquid assets,** which take their name from the concept of liquidity, are those assets that are instantly convertible into a means of payment with virtually no uncertainty about the price at which they can be converted. An example of a liquid asset is a U.S. government treasury bond that can be sold at a moment's notice for an almost guaranteed price.

The banks' assets also include investment securities. An **investment security** is a marketable security that a bank can sell at a moment's notice if necessary but at a price that fluctuates. An example of an investment security is a U.S. government long-term bond. Such bonds can be sold instantly, but their prices fluctuate on the bond market. Banks earn a higher interest rate on their investment securities than they do on liquid assets, but investment securities have a higher risk.

Most of the banks' assets are the loans that they have made. A **loan** is a commitment of a fixed amount of money for an agreed period of time. Most of the loans made by banks are used by corporations to finance the purchase of capital equipment and inventories. But banks also make loans to households—personal loans. Such loans are used to buy consumer durable goods such as cars or boats. The outstanding balances on credit card accounts are also bank loans. The interest rates on these balances became a controversial topic in 1991—see Reading Between the Lines, pp. 258–259.

Banks make a profit by earning interest on loans, investment securities, and liquid assets in excess of the interest paid on deposits and other liabilities. Also, banks receive revenue by charging fees for managing accounts.

Money is made up of the various liabilities of the banks. Checkable deposits are an important component of the M1 measure of money—accounting for 70 percent of M1 in 1992. Checkable deposits, savings deposits, and small time deposits are an important part of the M2 measure of money. The commercial banks' total liabilities are an important component of M3. But the deposit liabilities of banks are not the only components of the nation's money. Other financial intermediaries also take deposits that form part—an increasing part—of the nation's money. Let's now examine those financial intermediaries.

Savings and Loan Associations

A **savings and loan association (S&L)** is a financial intermediary that traditionally obtained its funds from savings deposits (called shares) and that made long-term mortgage loans to home buyers. Before 1980, S&Ls were prevented by regulation from offering checking accounts and could make only mortgage loans. Furthermore, the interest rate on these loans was fixed. Many mortgage loans had a term of 30 years, so a large number of mortgages still

High-Cost Card Credit

U.S. NEWS & WORLD REPORT, DECEMBER 2, 1991

How to play your cards

BY EDWARD C. BAIG, WITH FRANCESCA LUNZER KRITZ AND DAVID BOWERMASTER

Consumers may have been disappointed early last week when Congress balked at a bill that would have set a 14 percent ceiling on credit-card interest. The average card rate, after all, has hovered around 19 percent for many months. But that could change—for better and for worse.

The good news: Many card issuers, competing for users, have been lowering rates on their own. AT&T, which ties its Universal Card to the prime, recently dropped the rate for most cardholders to 16.4 percent from 17.4 percent six weeks sooner than it had to. The bad news: the industry's worry over shrinking profits and rising costs. Late payments—and nonpayments—are rising. That trend is making card issuers choosier, especially about which consumers can keep or get lower-rate cards.

Folks who charge often and pay their balances on time might find it easier now to snag lower rates, either from their own bank or from out-of-state institutions. But people who rarely make a due date might find themselves facing a higher rate—or searching for a new card. . . .

Looking low.

Even without pressure from Congress, where there was again a move late last week to push through a cap, creditworthy customers don't seem to be having trouble finding low-interest cards. From January through June, issuers with rates above 18 percent lost about 5 percent of their business, compared with the same period last year. Issuers charging less than 16.5 percent, by contrast, gained 10 percent more new accounts in the same period, according to Ram Research, a credit-card newsletter publisher in Frederick, Md. . . .

Some banks will even waive annual fees for preferred customers who merely ask. You can also inquire about other, less publicized low-rate cards. Citibank's regular cards carry rates of 19.8 percent, but rock-solid customers might qualify for the Bank's 14.9 percent Choice card.

Marginal customers have a better chance of hanging onto their cards if they pay on time and get their finances in order. For example, they might reduce their total available credit by canceling rarely used cards that could conceivably burden them with extra debt. They would have fewer cards in their wallet, but the ones they kept could cost less and let them charge more.

The Essence of the Story

In December 1991, Congress considered but rejected a bill to set a 14 percent ceiling on credit-card interest rates—the average credit-card interest rate had been around 19 percent for many months.

Many credit-card issuers had been lowering interest rates, but a growing incidence of late payments and nonpayments was increasing the costs and shrinking the profits of credit-card issuers.

Banks began to offer regular cards carrying high rates (for example, Citibank's rate was 19.8 percent) and less publicized cards carrying low rates (for example, the rate on Citibank's Choice card, offered only to its "rock-solid customers," was 14.9 percent). Some banks began to waive annual fees for preferred customers.

Card issuers became more careful about which consumers got low-rate cards. People who charge often and pay on time find it easy to get low-rate cards, but those who rarely pay on time face higher interest rates.

Background and Analysis

When a bank or other financial intermediary issues a credit card, it enters into an agreement to make a loan to the card holder up to an agreed limit, to be repaid on an agreed schedule, and at an agreed but variable interest rate.

Borrowing on a credit card is one of several alternative ways of obtaining funds, and, other things being equal, the lower the credit-card interest rate, the greater is the quantity of credit-card loans demanded. The demand curve for credit-card loans is *D* in Fig. 1.

Credit-card issuers obtain their funds from depositors and have alternative uses for those funds. The *opportunity cost* of lending to a credit-card holder is the interest forgone on an alternative type of bank loan. This opportunity cost, assumed to be 10 percent, is illustrated in Fig. 1.

Lending to credit-card holders is costly. Between 2 percent and 3 percent of loans are not repaid. Many more loans that are eventually repaid are costly to collect. Fraud also imposes large costs on card issuers.

The cost of supplying credit-card loans (including the normal rate of economic profit) is equal to the opportunity cost of the funds lent plus these additional costs of credit-card lending. In Fig. 1, these costs make the cost of supplying credit-card loans 19 percent.

The quantity of loans supplied equals the quantity demanded at that interest rate—$250 billion in Fig. 1.

During 1991, most interest rates declined. For example, the prime rate, the rate at which banks lend to their biggest and safest corporate customers, fell from 10 percent to 6.5 percent. This rate decrease lowered the opportunity cost of making loans to credit-card holders—shown in Fig. 2.

Other things being equal, this decline in the prime rate would have lowered the interest rate on credit cards to about 15.5 percent as shown in Fig. 2.

But other things were not equal. In the recession of 1991, the percentage of loans not repaid increased, thus increasing the cost of supplying credit-card loans.

In this situation, credit-card issuers tried to separate their market into high-cost (high-risk) customers and low-cost (low-risk) customers, offering to each group interest rates that reflect their relative costs. Low interest rate business expanded, and high interest rate business declined.

As the news story notes, if Congress puts a cap on the interest rate that card issuers may charge, the trend to weeding out high-cost (high-risk) customers would be intensified, and fewer such customers would be able to obtain credit cards. They would be forced into an even higher-cost segment of the market for loans.

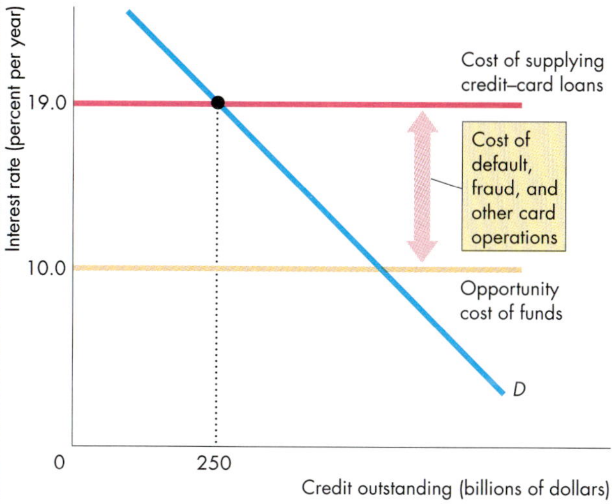

Figure 1

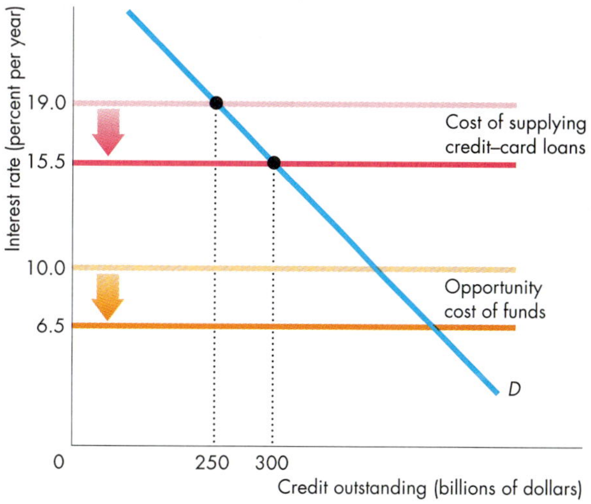

Figure 2

outstanding in the late 1970s had been written in the early 1950s, when the S&Ls were able to borrow at 3 percent a year and lend at 6 percent a year. But by the late 1970s, they had to pay more for deposits than they were making on their older mortgages.

Because of the plight of the S&Ls, Congress loosened the restrictions on them in 1980, permitting them to offer checking accounts and make high-interest consumer and commercial loans. Two years later the Garn–St. Germain Depository Institutions Act loosened the restrictions on the S&Ls yet further, enabling them to invest a larger part of their funds in high-risk commercial real estate ventures. But the way in which they used their greater freedom led the S&Ls to their crisis of the late 1980s.

Savings Banks and Credit Unions

Savings banks are financial intermediaries owned by their depositors that accept savings deposits and make loans, mostly for consumer mortgages. These institutions perform functions similar to those of S&Ls. The key difference is that savings banks, also called *mutual* savings banks, are owned by their depositors. **Credit unions** obtain their funds from checking and savings deposits and make consumer loans. Like savings banks, they are owned by their depositors. The key difference is that credit unions are based on a social or economic group such as a firm's employees.

Money Market Mutual Funds

Money market mutual funds are financial institutions that obtain funds by selling shares and that use these funds to buy highly liquid assets such as U.S. Treasury bills. Money market mutual fund shares act like the deposits at commercial banks and other financial intermediaries. Shareholders can write checks on their money market mutual fund accounts. But there are restrictions on most of these accounts. For example, the minimum deposit accepted might be $2,500, and the smallest check a depositor is permitted to write might be $500.

The Economic Functions of Financial Intermediaries

All financial intermediaries make a profit from a spread between the interest rate they pay on deposits and the interest rate at which they lend. Why can financial intermediaries borrow at a low interest rate and lend at a higher one? What services do they perform that make their depositors willing to put up with a low interest rate and their borrowers willing to pay a higher one?

Financial intermediaries provide four main services:

- Minimizing the cost of obtaining funds
- Minimizing the cost of monitoring borrowers
- Pooling risk
- Creating liquidity

Minimizing the Cost of Obtaining Funds Finding someone from whom to borrow can be a costly business. Imagine how troublesome it would be if there were no financial intermediaries. A firm that was looking for $1 million to buy a new production plant would probably have to hunt around for several dozen people from whom to borrow in order to acquire enough funds for its capital project. Financial intermediaries lower those costs. The firm needing $1 million can go to a single financial intermediary to obtain those funds. The financial intermediary has to borrow from a large number of people, but it's not doing that just for this one firm and the million dollars it wants to borrow. The financial intermediary can establish an organization capable of raising funds from a large number of depositors and can spread the cost of this activity over a large number of borrowers.

Minimizing the Cost of Monitoring Borrowers Lending money is a risky business. There's always a danger that the borrower might not repay. Most of the money lent gets used by firms to invest in projects that they hope will return a profit. But sometimes those hopes are not fulfilled. Checking up on the activities of a borrower and ensuring that the best possible decisions are being made for making a profit and avoiding a loss are costly and specialized activities. Imagine how costly it would be if each and every household that lent money to a firm had to incur the costs of monitoring that firm directly. By depositing funds with a financial intermediary, households avoid those costs. The financial intermediary performs the monitoring activity by using specialized resources that have a much lower cost than what each household would incur if it had to undertake the activity individually.

Pooling Risk As we noted above, lending money is risky. There is always a chance of not being repaid—of default. The risk of default can be reduced by lending to a large number of different individuals. In such a situation, if one person defaults on a loan, it is a nuisance but not a disaster. In contrast, if only one person borrows and that person defaults on the loan, the entire loan is a write-off. Financial intermediaries enable people to pool risk in an efficient way. Thousands of people lend money to any one financial intermediary, and, in turn, the financial intermediary re-lends the money to hundreds, perhaps thousands, of individual firms. If any one firm defaults on its loan, that default is spread across all the depositors with the intermediary and no individual depositor is left exposed to a high degree of risk.

Creating Liquidity Financial intermediaries create liquidity. We defined liquidity earlier as the ease and certainty with which an asset can be converted into money. Some of the liabilities of financial intermediaries are themselves money; others are highly liquid assets that are easily converted into money.

Financial intermediaries create liquidity by borrowing short and lending long. Borrowing short means taking deposits but standing ready to repay them on short notice (and on even no notice in the case of checkable deposits). Lending long means making loan commitments for a prearranged, and often quite long, period of time. For example, when a person makes a deposit with a savings and loan association, that deposit can be withdrawn at any time. But the S&L makes a lending commitment for perhaps more than 20 years to a homebuyer.

REVIEW

Most of the nation's money is made up of deposits in financial intermediaries. Those financial intermediaries are commercial banks, savings and loan associations, savings banks, credit unions, and money market mutual funds. The main economic functions of financial intermediaries are minimizing the cost of obtaining funds, minimizing the cost of monitoring borrowers, pooling risk, and creating liquidity. ◆

Financial Regulation, Deregulation, and Innovation

Financial intermediaries are highly regulated institutions. But regulation is not static, and in the 1980s some important changes in their regulation as well as deregulation took place. Also, the institutions are not static. In their pursuit of profit, they are constantly seeking lower-cost ways of obtaining funds, monitoring borrowers, pooling risk, and creating liquidity. They also are inventive in seeking ways of avoiding the costs imposed on them by financial regulation. Let's take a look at regulation, deregulation, and innovation in the financial sector in recent years.

Financial Regulation

Financial regulation imposes two types of restrictions on financial intermediaries:

- Deposit insurance
- Balance sheet rules

Deposit Insurance The deposits of banks and S&Ls are insured by the Federal Deposit Insurance Corporation (FDIC). The FDIC is a federal agency that receives its income from compulsory insurance premiums paid by commercial banks and other financial intermediaries. The FDIC operates two separate insurance funds, the Bank Insurance Fund (BIF), which insures deposits in commercial banks, and the Saving Association Insurance Fund (SAIF), which insures the deposits of S&Ls. Each of these funds insures deposits of up to $100,000 per depositor.

The existence of deposit insurance provides protection for depositors in the event that a financial intermediary fails. But it also limits the incentive for the owner of a financial intermediary to make safe investments and loans. Some economists believe that deposit insurance played an important role in worsening the problems faced by S&Ls in the 1980s. Savers, knowing that their deposits were being used to make high-risk loans, did not remove their deposits from S&Ls because they knew they had the security of deposit insurance. The S&L owners making high-risk loans knew they were making a one-way bet. If their loans paid off, they made a high rate of return. If they failed and could not meet their obligations to the depositors, the insurance fund would step in. Bad loans were good business!

Because of this type of problem, all financial intermediaries face regulation of their balance sheets.

Balance Sheet Rules The most important balance sheet regulations are

- Capital requirements
- Reserve requirements
- Lending rules

Capital requirements are the minimum amount of an owner's own financial resources that must be put into an intermediary. This amount must be sufficiently large to discourage owners from making loans that are too risky. *Reserve requirements* are rules setting out the minimum percentages of deposits that must be held in currency or other safe, liquid assets. These minimum percentages vary across the different types of intermediaries and deposits; they are largest for checkable deposits and smallest for long-term savings deposits. *Lending rules* are restrictions on the proportions of different types of loans that an intermediary may make. It is these rules that created the sharpest distinctions between the various institutions. Before 1980, commercial banks were the only intermediaries permitted to make commercial loans, and S&Ls and savings banks were restricted to making mortgage loans to home buyers.

To enable S&Ls and savings banks to compete with commercial banks for funds, a ceiling was imposed on the interest rates that could be paid on deposits. This interest ceiling regulation was known as *Regulation Q*. Also, banks were not permitted to pay interest on checkable deposits.

Deregulation in the 1980s

In 1980, Congress passed the Depository Institutions' Deregulation and Monetary Control Act. This legislation removed many of the distinctions between commercial banks and other financial intermediaries. It permitted nonbank financial intermediaries to compete with commercial banks in a wider range of lending business. At the same time it permitted the payment of interest on checkable deposits so that NOW accounts and ATS accounts could be offered by all deposit-taking institutions—banks and nonbanks.

The ability of S&Ls and savings banks to compete for lending business with commercial banks was further strengthened in 1982 with the passage of the Garn–St. Germain Depository Institutions Act. This legislation further eased restrictions on the scale of commercial lending that S&Ls and savings banks could undertake.

Another important regulatory change occurred in 1986—the abolition of Regulation Q. With the abolition of Regulation Q, a fiercely competitive environment was created. In this environment, there was rapid innovation in the types of deposits offered and rapid growth in money market mutual funds.

Financial Innovation

The development of new financial products—of new ways of borrowing and lending—is called **financial innovation.** The aim of financial innovation is to lower the cost of borrowing or to increase the return from lending or, more simply, to increase the profit from financial intermediation. There are three main influences on financial innovation. They are

- Economic environment
- Technology
- Regulation

The pace of financial innovation was remarkable in the 1980s, and all three of these forces played a role.

Economic Environment Some of the innovation of the 1980s was a response to high inflation and high interest rates. An important example is the development of adjustable interest rate mortgages. Traditionally, house purchases have been financed on mortgage loans at a guaranteed interest rate. Rising interest rates brought rising borrowing costs for S&Ls, and since they were committed to fixed interest rates on their mortgages, the industry incurred severe losses. The creation of adjustable interest rate mortgages has taken some of the risk out of long-term lending for house purchases.

Technology Other financial innovations resulted from technological change, most notably that associated with the decreased cost of computing and long-distance communication. The spread of the use of credit cards and the development of international financial markets—for example, the increased importance of Eurodollars—are consequences of technological change.

Regulation A good deal of financial innovation takes place to avoid regulation. The development of NOW accounts and ATS accounts is an example. Regulation that prevented banks from paying interest on checking accounts gave the impetus to devising these new types of deposit accounts, thereby getting around the regulation.

Deregulation, Innovation, and the Money Supply

Deregulation and financial innovation that have led to the development of new types of deposit accounts have brought important changes in the composition of the nation's money. In 1960, M1 consisted of only currency and demand deposits. In the 1980s, other checkable deposits expanded while demand deposits declined. Similar dramatic changes took place in the composition of M2. Savings deposits declined while time deposits, money market mutual fund shares of individuals, and Eurodollar deposits expanded quickly. There have been less dramatic but important changes involving M3. In 1960, M2 and M3 were almost the same concept, but the growth of large time deposits and other types of time deposits included in M3 has gradually expanded.

REVIEW

Financial intermediaries insure their deposits, and their lending is regulated. The 1980s saw a wave of financial deregulation that blurred the distinction between commercial banks and other financial institutions. Financial intermediaries are constantly seeking new ways of making a profit by reacting to the changing economic environment, adopting new technologies, and avoiding the adverse effects of regulations on their activities. Deregulation and innovation in the 1980s brought a whole range of new types of deposit accounts that led to important changes in the composition of the nation's stock of money. ◆

Because financial intermediaries are able to create liquidity and to create assets that are a means of payment—money—they occupy a unique place in our economy and exert an important influence on the quantity of money in existence. Let's see how money gets created.

How Banks Create Money

Money is created by the activities of commercial banks and other financial intermediaries—by all those institutions whose deposits circulate as a means of payment. In this section, we'll use the term *banks* to refer to all these depository institutions.

Actual and Required Reserves

As we saw in Table 10.6, banks don't have \$100 in bills for every \$100 that people have deposited with them. In fact, a typical bank today has \$1.25 in currency and another \$1.15 on deposit at a Federal Reserve bank for every \$100 deposited in it. No need for panic. Banks have learned, from experience, that these reserve levels are adequate for ordinary business needs. The fraction of a bank's total deposits that are held in reserves is called the **reserve ratio**. The value of the reserve ratio is influenced by the actions of a bank's depositors. If a depositor withdraws currency from a bank, the reserve ratio falls. If a depositor puts currency into a bank, the reserve ratio increases.

The **required reserve ratio** is the ratio of reserves to deposits that banks are required, by regulation, to hold. A bank's **required reserves** are equal to its deposits multiplied by the required reserve ratio. Actual reserves minus required reserves are **excess reserves.** Whenever banks have excess reserves, they are able to create money. When we say that banks create money, we don't mean that they have smoke-filled back rooms in which counterfeiters are busily working. Remember, most money is deposits, not currency. What banks create is deposits, and they do so by making loans. To see how banks create money, we are going to look at a model of the banking system.

Creating Deposits by Making Loans

Let's suppose that the banks have a required reserve ratio of 25 percent. That is, for each dollar deposited, they want to keep 25¢ in the form of reserves. Al, a customer of the Golden Nugget Bank, decides to reduce his holdings of currency and put $100 in his deposit account at the bank. Suddenly, the Golden Nugget Bank has $100 of new deposits and $100 of additional reserves. But with $100 of new deposits the Golden Nugget Bank doesn't want to hold onto $100 of additional reserves. It has excess reserves. Its required reserve ratio is 25 percent, so it plans to lend $75 of the additional $100 to another customer. Amy, a customer at the same bank, borrows $75. At this point, the Golden Nugget Bank has new deposits of $100, new loans of $75, and new reserves of $25. As far as Golden Nugget is concerned, that is the end of the matter. No money has been created. Al has reduced his holdings of currency by $100 and increased his bank deposit by $100, but the total amount of money has remained constant. Although that's the end of the story for the Golden Nugget Bank, it is not the end of the story for the entire banking system. What happens next?

Amy uses the $75 loan to buy a jacket from Barb. To undertake this transaction, she writes a check on her account with the Golden Nugget, and Barb deposits the check in the Laser Bank. The Laser Bank now has new deposits of $75 and an additional $75 of reserves. The total amount of money supply is now $75 higher than before.

The Laser Bank doesn't need to hang on to the entire $75 as reserves: it needs only a quarter of that amount—$18.75. The Laser Bank lends the additional amount, $56.25, to Bob, who buys some used stereo equipment from Carl. Bob writes a check on his account at the Laser Bank, which Carl deposits in his account at the Apollo Bank. The Apollo Bank now has new deposits of $56.25, so the amount of money has increased by a total of $131.25 (the $75 lent to Amy and paid to Barb plus the $56.25 lent to Bob and paid to Carl).

The transactions that we've just described are summarized in Table 10.7. But the story is still incomplete. The process that we're describing continues through the remaining banks and their depositors and borrowers, all the way down the list in that table. By the time we get down to the Pirates Bank, Ken has paid Len $5.63 for a box of computer disks, and so the Pirates Bank has new deposits of $5.63 and additional reserves of that same amount. Since it needs only $1.41 of additional reserves, it makes a loan of $4.22 to Lee, who in turn spends the money. By this time, the total amount of money has increased by $283.11, the new deposits at each stage of the process listed in the first column of numbers in the table less Al's deposit of $100. Remember that when Al made his deposit, he also reduced his holding of currency, so his new deposit did not increase the total amount of money.

This process continues but with amounts that are now getting so tiny that we will not bother to keep track of them. All the remaining stages in the process taken together add up to the numbers in the second to last row of the table. The final tallies appear as the totals at the bottom of the table. Deposits have increased by $400, loans by $300, and reserves by $100. The banks have created money by making loans. The quantity of money created is $300—the same amount as the additional loans made. It's true that deposits have increased by $400, but $100 of that increase is Al's original deposit. That increase in deposits does not increase the quantity of money. The currency that Al deposited was already money. It is only the new deposits created by the lending activity of the banks that have increased the quantity of money in existence.

The Simple Money Multiplier

The ability of banks to create money does not mean that they can create an indefinite amount of money.

TABLE 10.7

Creating Money by Making Loans: Many Banks

Bank	Depositor	Borrower	New deposits	New loans	New reserves	Increase in money	Cumulative increase in money
Golden Nugget	Al	Amy	$100.00	$ 75.00	$ 25.00	$ 0.00	
Laser	Barb	Bob	75.00	56.25	18.75	75.00	$ 75.00
Apollo	Carl	Con	56.25	42.19	14.06	56.25	131.25
Monty Python	Di	Dan	42.19	31.64	10.55	42.19	173.44
Plato	Ed	Eve	31.64	23.73	7.91	31.64	205.08
J. R. Ewing	Fran	Fred	23.73	17.80	5.93	23.73	228.81
1st Madonna	Gus	Gail	17.80	13.35	4.45	17.80	246.61
Rambo	Holly	Hal	13.35	10.01	3.34	13.35	259.96
Trump	Jim	Jan	10.01	7.51	2.50	10.01	269.97
Disney	Kym	Ken	7.51	5.63	1.88	7.51	277.48
Pirates	Len	Lee	5.63	4.22	1.41	5.63	283.11
			⋮	⋮	⋮	⋮	⋮
All others			16.89	12.67	4.22	16.89	
Total banking system			$400.00	$300.00	$100.00	$300.00	$300.00

The amount that they can create depends on the size of their reserves and on the required reserve ratio. In this example, in which the required reserve ratio is 25 percent, bank deposits have increased by four times the level of reserves.

The **simple money multiplier** is the amount by which an increase in bank reserves is multiplied to calculate the effect of the increase in reserves on total bank deposits. The simple money multiplier is

$$\text{Simple money multiplier} = \frac{\text{Change in deposits}}{\text{Change in reserves}}.$$

In the example we've just worked through, the simple money multiplier is 4—a $100 increase in reserves created the $400 increase in deposits.

The simple money multiplier is related to the required reserve ratio. In our example, that ratio is 25 percent (or ¼). That is,

$$\text{Required reserves} = (1/4)\text{Deposits}.$$

Whenever required reserves exceed actual reserves (a situation of negative excess reserves), the banks call in loans. When required reserves are below actual reserves (a situation of positive excess reserves), the banks make additional loans. By adjusting their loans, the banks bring their actual reserves into line with their required reserves, eliminating excess reserves. Thus, when banks have changed their loans and reserves to make actual reserves equal required reserves,

$$\text{Actual reserves} = (1/4)\text{Deposits}.$$

If we divide both sides of this equation by ¼, we obtain

$$\text{Deposits} = (1/\tfrac{1}{4})\text{Actual reserves}.$$

When the banks receive new deposits, actual reserves increase. If the increase in reserves occurs when required reserves and actual reserves are equal, the banks have excess reserves. They lend these excess reserves until bank deposits have increased by enough to increase required reserves by the same amount as the increase in actual reserves. A decrease in deposits lowers reserves and forces the banks to call in some loans. The end result of this process is a decrease in deposits by an amount that decreases required reserves by the same amount as the decrease in actual reserves. When deposits have changed by enough to have eliminated excess reserves, the following change in deposits has taken place:

$$\text{Change in deposits} = (1/\tfrac{1}{4})\text{Change in reserves.}$$

By definition, $(1/\tfrac{1}{4})$ is the simple money multiplier. It is the amount by which the change in reserves is multiplied to calculate the change in deposits. In our example, this multiplier equals 4. The relationship between the simple money multiplier and the required reserve ratio is

$$\text{Simple money multiplier} = \frac{1}{\text{Required reserve ratio}}.$$

Real-World Money Multipliers The money multiplier in the real world differs from the simple money multiplier that we have just calculated for two reasons. First, the required reserve ratio of real-world banks is much smaller than the 25 percent we used here. Second, in the real world, not all the loans made by banks return to the banks in the form of reserves. Some of them remain outside the banks in the form of currency in circulation. These two differences between the real-world money multiplier and the simple money multiplier we've just calculated work in opposing directions. The smaller required reserve ratio of real-world banks makes the real-world multiplier larger than the above numerical example. The fact that some currency remains in circulation outside the banks makes the real-world multiplier smaller. We study the actual values of real-world money multipliers in the next chapter.

REVIEW

Banks create money by making loans. The amount that they can lend is determined by their reserves and the required reserve ratio. Each time they make a loan, deposits increase and so do required reserves. When deposits are at a level that makes required reserves equal to actual reserves, the banks cannot increase their lending or deposits any further. An initial change in deposits that changes reserves brings about an eventual change in deposits equal to the change in reserves multiplied by the simple money multiplier. ◆

Concern over the supply of money arises because money has a powerful effect on our economy. Our next task in this chapter is to examine some of these effects.

Money, Real GDP, and the Price Level

We now know what money *is*. We also know that in a modern economy such as that of the United States today, most of the money is made up of deposits at banks and other financial intermediaries. We've seen that these institutions can actually create money by making loans. Does the quantity of money created by the banking and financial system matter? What effects does it have? Does it matter whether the quantity increases quickly or slowly?

We're going to address these questions first by using the aggregate demand–aggregate supply model. Then we're going to consider a special theory of money and prices—the quantity theory of money. Finally, we'll look at some historical and international evidence on the relationship between money and prices. Also, Our Advancing Knowledge on pp. 268–269 looks at the evolution of our understanding of the effects of changes in the quantity of money.

Money in the *AD-AS* Model

Figure 10.2 illustrates the aggregate demand–aggregate supply model. In part (a) there is unemployment, and in part (b) there is full employment. In both parts, the long-run aggregate supply curve is *LAS*.

An Increase in the Money Supply with Unemployment Initially, the aggregate demand curve is AD_0, and the short-run aggregate supply curve is *SAS* (in part a). Equilibrium occurs where the aggregate demand curve AD_0 intersects the short-run aggregate supply curve. The price level is 90, and real GDP is \$4.4 trillion. Now suppose there is an increase in the quantity of money. The increase occurs as a result of the process that we've just studied. Banks, flush with excess reserves, make loans, and the loans create money. With more money in their bank accounts, people increase their expenditure, and aggregate demand increases. The aggregate demand curve shifts to the right to become AD_1. The new equilibrium is at the intersection point of AD_1 and *SAS*. The price level rises to 100, and real GDP increases to \$4.5 trillion. The economy is now on its long-run aggregate supply curve, and there is full employment. A smaller increase in the money supply would not shift the aggregate demand curve as far to the right, and the economy would remain in an unemployment equilibrium. But the general effect is the same—an increase in both real GDP and the price level.

An Increase in the Money Supply at Full Employment Initially, the aggregate demand curve is AD_1, and the short-run aggregate supply curve is SAS_1 (in part b). Equilibrium occurs where the aggregate demand curve AD_1 intersects the short-run aggregate supply curve SAS_1. The price level is 100 and real GDP is \$4.5 trillion. The economy is on its long-run aggregate supply curve and is in full-employment equilibrium. Now suppose there is an increase in the quantity of money that increases aggregate demand and shifts the aggregate demand curve to AD_2. The new equilibrium is at the intersection point of AD_2 and SAS_1. The price level rises to 110, and real GDP increases to \$4.6 trillion. But this is the short-run effect. The economy is now at an above full-employment equilibrium, and wages start to increase. As they do so, the short-run aggregate supply curve shifts upward. The price level increases, and real GDP falls. Wages continue to increase until full employment is restored. By this time, the short-run aggregate supply curve is SAS_2 and the price level is 120.

Thus between one full-employment equilibrium and another, an increase in the quantity of money results in an increase in the price level and no change in real GDP. It is this relationship between

FIGURE 10.2

Aggregate Demand, Aggregate Supply, and the Quantity of Money

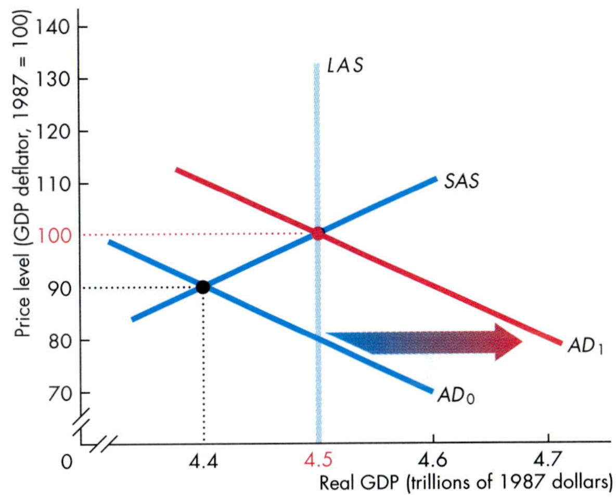

(a) Money supply increase with unemployment

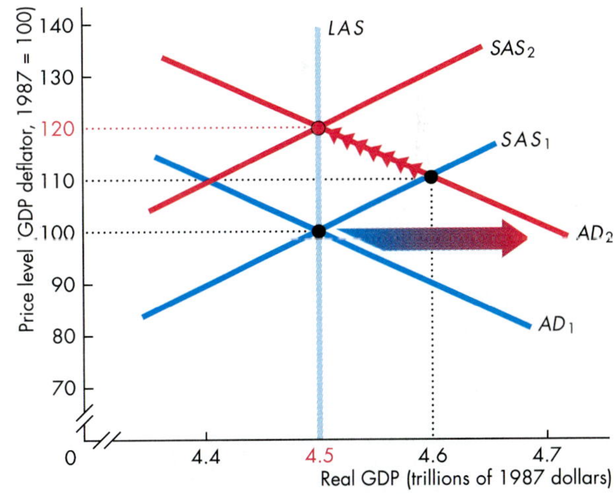

(b) Money supply increase at full employment

In part (a), an increase in the money supply shifts the aggregate demand curve from AD_0 to AD_1, and the price level rises to 100 and real GDP increases to \$4.5 trillion, its full-employment level. In part (b), an increase in the quantity of money shifts the aggregate demand curve from AD_1 to AD_2. The price level rises to 110, and real GDP increases to \$4.6 trillion. The economy is at an above full-employment equilibrium. Wages rise, and the short-run aggregate supply curve shifts upward to SAS_2. Real GDP falls back to its initial level, and the price level increases to 120.

UNDERSTANDING the Causes of INFLATION

The combination of history and economics has taught us a great deal about the causes of inflation.

Severe inflation—hyperinflation—arises from a breakdown of the normal fiscal policy processes at times of war and political upheaval. Tax revenues fall short of government spending, and the gap between them is filled by printing money. As inflation increases, there is a *shortage* of money, so its rate of creation is increased yet further and prices rise even faster. Eventually, the monetary system collapses. Such was the experience of Germany in the 1920s, and Russia is heading in this direction today.

In earlier times, when commodities were used as money, inflation resulted from the discovery of new sources of money. The most recent occurrence of this type of inflation was in the nineteenth century when gold, then used as money, was discovered in California and Australia.

In modern times, inflation has resulted from increases in the money supply that have accommodated increases in costs. The most dramatic such inflations occurred during the 1970s when oil price increases were accommodated by the Fed and other central banks around the world.

To avoid inflation, money supply growth must be held in check. But at times of severe cost pressure, central banks feel a strong tug in the direction of avoiding recession and accommodating the cost pressure. Yet some countries have avoided inflation more effectively than others. A key source of success is central bank independence. In low-inflation countries, such as Germany and Japan, the central bank decides how much money to create and at what level to set interest rates and does not take instructions from the government. In high-inflation countries, such as the United Kingdom and Italy, the central bank takes direct orders from the government about interest rates and money supply growth. This connection between central bank independence and inflation has been noticed by the architects of a new monetary system for the European Community who are modeling the European Central Bank on Germany's Bundesbank, not on the Bank of England.

"Inflation is always and everywhere a monetary phenomenon."

MILTON FRIEDMAN
The Counter-Revolution in Monetary Theory

When inflation is especially rapid, as it was in Germany in 1923, money becomes almost worthless. In Germany at that time, bank notes were more valuable as kindling than as money, and the sight of people burning Reichmarks was a common one. Because no one wanted to hold money for too long, wages were paid and spent twice a day. Banks took deposits and made loans, but at interest rates that compensated depositors and the bank for the falling value of money—rates that could exceed 100 percent a day. The price of a dinner might double during the course of an evening, making lingering over coffee a very expensive pastime.

Hyperinflation has never occurred in a computer-age economy. But imagine the scene if hyperinflation—an inflation rate of 50 percent a month—did break out. ATMs would have to be refilled several times an hour, and the volume of paper (both money and receipts) they would spew out would grow to astronomical proportions. But most of us would try to avoid using money. Instead, we would buy as much as possible using credit cards. And we'd be eager to pay off our card balances quickly because the interest rate on unpaid balances would be 70 percent a month. Only at such a high interest rate would it pay banks to lend to cardholders, since banks themselves would be paying interest rates of more than 50 percent a month to induce people to deposit their money.

DAVID HUME AND THE *Quantity Theory of Money*

Born in Edinburgh, Scotland, in 1711 and a close friend of Adam Smith, David Hume was a philosopher, historian, and economist of extraordinary breadth. His first book, by his own description, "fell dead-born from the press." But his essays—on topics ranging from love and marriage and the immortality of the soul to money, interest, and the balance of payments—were widely read and earned him a considerable fortune.

Hume gave the first clear statement of the quantity theory of money—the theory that an increase in the quantity of money brings a proportional increase in the price level. And his account of the way in which an increase in the quantity of money brings an increase in prices anticipated the discovery, some 220 years later, of the Phillips curve and the Keynesian theory of aggregate demand.

the money supply and the price level at full employment that gives rise to the quantity theory of money.

The Quantity Theory of Money

The **quantity theory of money** is the proposition that an increase in the quantity of money leads to an equal percentage increase in the price level. The original basis of the quantity theory of money is a concept known as the velocity of circulation and an equation called the equation of exchange. The **velocity of circulation** is the average number of times a dollar of money is used annually to buy the goods and services that make up GDP. GDP is equal to the price level (P) multiplied by real GDP (Y). That is,

$$\text{GDP} = PY.$$

Call the quantity of money M. The velocity of circulation, V, is determined by the equation

$$V = PY/M.$$

For example, if GDP is $5 trillion and if the quantity of money is $2 trillion, the velocity of circulation is 2.5. On the average, each dollar of money circulates 2.5 times in its use to purchase the final goods and services that make up GDP.

The **equation of exchange** states that the quantity of money (M) multiplied by the velocity of circulation (V) equals GDP, or

$$MV = PY.$$

Given the definition of the velocity of circulation, this equation is always true—it is true by definition. With M equal to $2 trillion and V equal to 2.5, MV is equal to $5 trillion, the value of GDP.

The equation of exchange becomes the quantity theory of money by making two propositions:

- The velocity of circulation is a constant.
- Real GDP is not influenced by the quantity of money.

If these two propositions are true, the equation of exchange tells us that a given percentage change in the quantity of money brings about an equal percentage change in the price level. You can see why by solving the equation of exchange for the price level. Dividing both sides of the equation by real GDP (Y) gives

$$P = (V/Y)M.$$

Because V and Y are constant, the relationship between the change in the price level (ΔP) and the change in the money supply (ΔM) is

$$\Delta P = (V/Y)\Delta M.$$

Dividing this equation by the previous one gives the quantity theory proposition, namely that the percentage increase in the price level ($\Delta P/P$) equals the percentage increase in the money supply ($\Delta M/M$), that is,

$$\Delta P/P = \Delta M/M.$$

The Quantity Theory and the *AD-AS* Model

The quantity theory of money can be interpreted in terms of the aggregate demand–aggregate supply model. The aggregate demand curve is a relationship between the quantity of real GDP demanded (Y) and the price level (P), other things remaining constant. We can obtain such a relationship from the equation of exchange,

$$MV = PY.$$

Dividing both sides of this equation by real GDP (Y) gives

$$P = MV/Y.$$

This equation may be interpreted as describing an aggregate demand curve. For a given money supply (M) and a given velocity of circulation (V), the higher the price level (P), the lower is the quantity of real GDP demanded (Y).

In general, when the quantity of money changes, the velocity of circulation might also change. But the quantity theory asserts that velocity is a constant. If velocity is constant, an increase in the quantity of money increases aggregate demand and shifts the aggregate demand curve upward by the same amount as the percentage change in the quantity of money. For example, in Fig. 10.2(b), the shift in the aggregate demand curve from AD_1 to AD_2, measured by the vertical distance between the two demand curves, is 20 percent. With a given velocity of circulation, this shift is brought about by a 20 percent increase in the quantity of money.

The quantity theory of money also asserts that real GDP is not affected by the money supply. This assertion is true in the aggregate demand–aggregate supply model only at full-employment equilibrium.

As we saw in Fig. 10.2(a), starting out with unemployment, an increase in the quantity of money increases real GDP. In this case, the price level increases by a smaller percentage than the percentage increase in aggregate demand and the money supply. But Fig. 10.2(b) shows what happens at full employment. Here, from the initial full-employment equilibrium to the new one, a 20 percent increase in the quantity of money increases the price level by 20 percent.

According to the aggregate demand–aggregate supply model, the relationship between the quantity of money and the price level is a much looser one than that implied by the quantity theory. First, the aggregate demand–aggregate supply model takes account of influences of the money supply on the velocity of circulation that the quantity theory ignores. We discuss these influences in the next chapter. Second, the aggregate demand–aggregate supply model predicts that changes in the quantity of money change real GDP, an influence that the quantity theory asserts does not occur.

Which theory of the relationship between the quantity of money and the price level is correct? Is the relationship as precise as implied by the quantity theory, or is it a looser relationship as implied by the aggregate demand–aggregate supply model? Let's look at the relationship between money and the price level, both historically and internationally.

Historical Evidence on the Quantity Theory of Money

The quantity theory of money can be tested on the historical data of the United States by looking at the relationship between the growth rate of the quantity of money and the inflation rate. Figure 10.3 shows this relationship for the years between 1875 and

FIGURE 10.3

Money Growth and Inflation in the United States

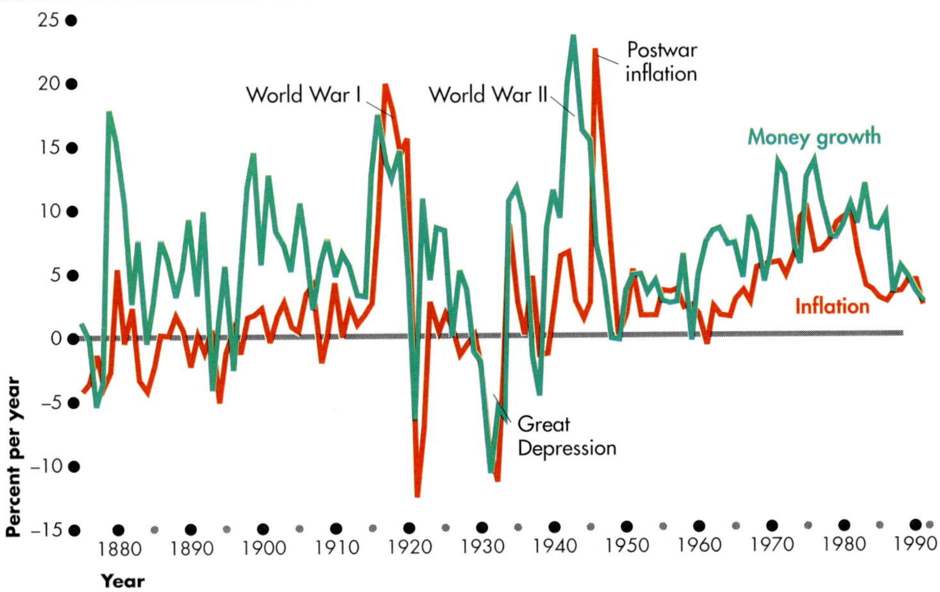

Year-to-year percentage changes in the price level—inflation—and the quantity of money—money growth—are plotted for each year between 1875 and 1993. The figure shows that (1) on the average, money growth exceeds inflation; (2) variations in inflation are correlated with variations in money growth; (3) during World War I, inflation and money growth surged upward together, but during World War II and its aftermath there was a break in the relationship; (4) during the years before 1915 and after 1950, inflation was less volatile than money growth.

Sources: Quantity of money (M2): 1875–1960, Milton Friedman and Anna J. Schwartz, *A Monetary History of the United States* (Princeton, N.J.: Princeton University Press, 1963); 1961–1991, *Economic Report of the President*, 1992. Price level and inflation (GDP deflator): 1875–1929, Nathan S. Balke and Robert J. Gordon, "The Estimation of Prewar Gross National Product: Methodology and New Evidence," *Journal of Political Economy* 97 (February 1989); 1930–1991, *Economic Report of the President*, 1993.

1993. The figure reveals four features of the relationship between money supply growth—measured by M2—and inflation. They are

1. On the average, the quantity of money grows at a rate that exceeds the inflation rate.
2. Variations in the growth rate of the quantity of money are correlated with variations in the inflation rate.
3. During World War I, there was a strong relationship between money growth and inflation, but during World War II and its aftermath, there was a break in that relationship.
4. There is a general tendency, especially clear before 1915 and after 1950, for fluctuations in the inflation rate to be smaller than those in the money growth rate.

1. Average Money Growth and Inflation You can see that the money growth rate is larger than the inflation rate, on the average, by looking at the two lines in Fig. 10.3. Most of the time the money growth line is above the inflation line. The difference in the averages is accounted for by the fact that the economy expands with real GDP growing. Money growth that matches real GDP growth does not add to inflation.

2. Correlation Between Money Growth and Inflation The correlation between money growth and inflation is most evident in the data for the years 1915 to 1940. For example, the massive buildup of inflation between 1915 and 1920 was accompanied by a huge increase in the growth rate of the quantity of money. The falling prices of the early 1920s and the Great Depression were associated with a decrease in the quantity of money. Although the correlation in the post–World War II years has been weak, you can see that the steadily increasing money growth rate through the 1960s and 1970s was associated with steadily rising inflation through those decades.

3. The Effects of Wars During World War I, there was a large increase in the money growth rate and in the inflation rate. There was also a large increase in the money growth rate during World War II. But during World War II, there was no corresponding increase in the inflation rate. Inflation was suppressed by a program of price controls and rationing, but when these measures were lifted at the end of World War II, inflation temporarily exploded even though money growth was, by then, moderate.

4. Relative Volatility of Money Growth and Inflation The quantity theory predicts a closer correlation between money growth and inflation than that visible in the data. In particular, it does not predict the generally observed fact that money growth is more volatile than inflation. You can see this relative volatility both in the years before 1915 and since 1950. This tendency for money growth to fluctuate more than inflation, although not consistent with the quantity theory, is predicted by the aggregate demand–aggregate supply model. The phenomenon arises from fluctuations in real GDP that accompany fluctuations in the quantity of money and from changes in the velocity of circulation.

The year-to-year fluctuations in money supply growth and inflation look very different from the predictions of the quantity theory. But the longer-term fluctuations in money supply growth and inflation are similar to the predictions of the quantity theory.

International Evidence on the Quantity Theory of Money

The international evidence on the quantity theory of money is summarized in Fig. 10.4, which shows the inflation rate and the money growth rate for 60 countries. There is an unmistakable tendency for high money growth to be associated with high inflation.

But like the historical evidence for the United States, these international data also tell us that money supply growth is not the only influence on inflation. Some countries have an inflation rate that exceeds the money supply growth rate, while others have an inflation rate that falls short of the money supply growth rate.

Correlation and Causation

The fact that money growth and inflation are correlated does not mean that we can determine, from that correlation, the direction of causation. Money growth might cause inflation; inflation might cause money growth; or some third variable might simultaneously cause inflation and money growth. In the quantity theory and in the aggregate demand–aggregate supply model, causation runs from money growth to inflation. But neither theory denies the possibility that, at different times and places, causa-

FIGURE 10.4

Money Growth and Inflation in the World Economy

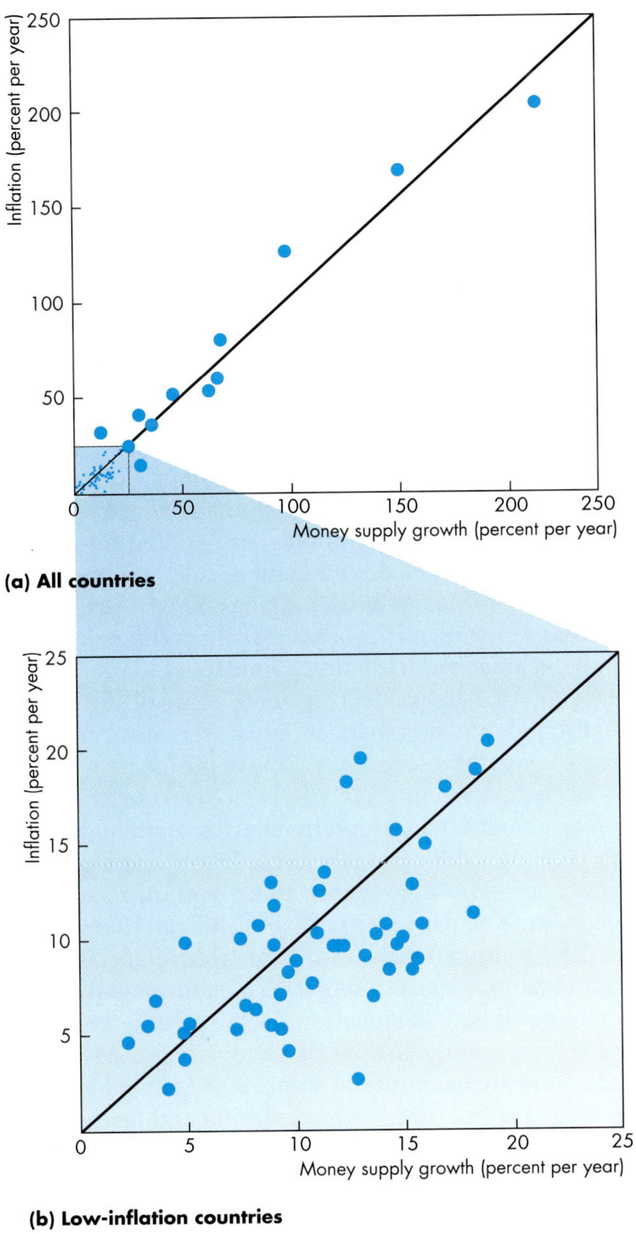

Inflation and money growth in 60 countries (in part a) and low-inflation countries (in part b) show that money growth is an important influence, though not the only influence, on inflation.

Source: Federal Reserve Bank of St. Louis, *Review* (May/June 1988): 15.

tion might run in the other direction or that some third factor, such as a government budget deficit, might be the root cause of both rapid money growth and inflation.

There are some occasions, however, that give us an opportunity to test our assumptions about causation. One of these is World War II and the years immediately following it. Rapid money supply growth during the war years accompanied by price controls almost certainly caused the postwar inflation. The inflationary consequences of the money growth were delayed by the controls but not removed. It is inconceivable that this was an example of reverse causation—of postwar inflation causing wartime money growth.

REVIEW

The quantity of money exerts an important influence on the price level. An increase in the quantity of money increases aggregate demand. In the short run, an increase in aggregate demand increases both the price level and real GDP. But on the average, real GDP fluctuates around its full-employment level and increases in the quantity of money bring increases in the price level. The quantity theory of money predicts that an increase in the quantity of money produces an equivalent percentage increase in the price level. The historical and international evidence on the relationship between the quantity of money and the price level provides broad support for the quantity theory of money as a proposition about long-run tendencies but also reveals important changes in the price level that occur independently of changes in the quantity of money. ◆

◆ ◆ ◆ ◆ In this chapter, we have studied the institutions that make up our banking and financial system. We've seen how the deposit liabilities of commercial banks and other financial institutions comprise our means of payment—our money. Banks and other financial institutions create money by making loans. The quantity of money in existence has important effects on the economy and, in particular, on the price level. ◆ ◆ In the next chapter, we're going to see how the quantity of money is regulated and influenced by the actions of the Federal Reserve System. We're also going to discover how, by its influence on the money supply, the Fed is able to influence interest rates, thereby affecting the level of aggregate demand. It is through its effects on the money supply and interest rates and their wider ramifications that the Fed is able to help steer the course of the economy.

SUMMARY

What Is Money?

Money has four functions. It is a medium of exchange, a unit of account, a standard of deferred payment, and a store of value. The earliest forms of money were commodities. In the modern world, we use a fiat money system. The biggest component of money is private debt money.

There are three official measures of money in the United States today: M1, M2, and M3. M1 consists of currency held outside banks, traveler's checks, demand deposits, and other checkable deposits. M2 includes M1 plus savings deposits, small time deposits, Eurodollar deposits, money market mutual fund shares held by individuals, and other M2 deposits. M3 adds to M2 large time deposits, Eurodollar time deposits, money market mutual fund shares held by institutions, and other M3 deposits. M1 serves the function of the means of payment, but the additional items in M2 and M3 are easily converted into M1 assets—assets that are highly liquid. Checkable deposits are money, but checks and credit cards are not. (pp. 248–255)

Financial Intermediaries

The main financial intermediaries whose liabilities serve as money are commercial banks, savings and loan associations, savings banks, credit unions, and money market mutual funds. These institutions take in deposits, hold cash reserves to ensure that they can meet their depositors' demands for currency, and use the rest of their financial resources either to buy securities or to make loans. Financial intermediaries make a profit by borrowing at a lower interest rate than that at which they lend. All financial intermediaries provide four main economic services: they minimize the cost of obtaining funds, minimize the cost of monitoring borrowers, pool risks, and create liquidity. (pp. 255–261)

Financial Regulation, Deregulation, and Innovation

Financial intermediaries are regulated to protect depositors. Deposits are insured by the FDIC, owners of intermediaries are required to put a certain minimum amount of their own financial resources into the institution, minimum cash and liquid assets reserves are specified, and lending rules are imposed.

Before 1980, S&Ls and savings banks were permitted to make only mortgage loans to home buyers and excluded from making commercial loans. Interest rates on savings deposits were controlled by Regulation Q, and commercial banks were not permitted to pay interest on checkable deposits.

Deregulation in the 1980s removed restrictions on nonbank financial intermediaries, enabling them to compete with commercial banks for lending business and permitting interest to be paid on checkable deposits. Regulation Q was abolished in 1986.

The continual search for profitable financial opportunities leads to financial innovation—to the creation of new financial products such as new types of deposits and loans. NOW accounts and ATS accounts are examples of some of the new financial products of the 1980s. Deregulation and financial innovation have brought important changes in the composition of the nation's money. (pp. 261–263)

How Banks Create Money

Banks create money by making loans. When a loan is made to one person and the amount lent is spent, much of it ends up as someone else's deposit. The total quantity of deposits that can be supported by a given amount of reserves (the simple money multiplier) is equal to 1 divided by the required reserve ratio. (pp. 263–266)

Money, Real GDP, and the Price Level

The quantity of money affects aggregate demand. An increase in the quantity of money increases aggregate demand and, in the short run, increases both the price level and real GDP. Over the long run, real GDP grows and fluctuates around its full-employment level, and increases in the quantity of money bring increases in the price level. The quantity theory of money predicts that an increase in the quantity of money increases the price level by the same percentage amount and leaves real GDP undisturbed. Both historical and international evidence suggests that the quantity theory of money is correct only in a broad average sense. The quantity of money does exert an important influence on the price level but also on real GDP. There are other important influences on the price level. Further, the correlation between money growth and inflation does not tell us the direction of causation. (pp. 266–273)

KEY ELEMENTS

Key Terms

Asset, 255
Balance sheet, 255
Barter, 248
Checkable deposit, 251
Commercial bank, 255
Commodity money, 249
Convertible paper money, 250
Credit union, 260
Currency, 251
Double coincidence of wants, 248
Equation of exchange, 270
Excess reserves, 264
Fiat money, 251
Financial innovation, 262
Financial intermediary, 255
Gresham's Law, 250
Investment security, 257
Liability, 255
Liquid asset, 257
Liquidity, 252
Loan, 257
M1, 251
M2, 251
M3, 251
Medium of exchange, 248
Money, 248
Money market mutual fund, 260
Private debt money, 251
Quantity theory of money, 270
Required reserve ratio, 264
Required reserves, 264
Reserve ratio, 263
Reserves, 257
Savings and loan association, 257
Savings bank, 260
Simple money multiplier, 265
Standard of deferred payment, 249
Store of value, 249
Unit of account, 248
Velocity of circulation, 270
Wholesale deposit market, 257

Key Figures and Tables

REVIEW QUESTIONS

1 What is money? What are its functions?

2 What are the different forms of money?

3 What are the three official measures of money in the United States today?

4 Are checks and credit cards money? Explain your answer.

5 What are financial intermediaries? What are the types of financial intermediaries in the United States? What are the main institutions other than commercial banks that take deposits?

6 What are the main items in the balance sheet of a commercial bank?

7 What are the economic functions of financial intermediaries?

8 How do banks make a profit, and how do they create money?

9 Define the simple money multiplier. Explain why it equals 1 divided by the required reserve ratio.

10 Explain why real-world money multipliers are smaller than the simple money multiplier.

11 What does the aggregate demand–aggregate supply model predict about the effects of a change in the quantity of money on the price level and real GDP?

12 What is the equation of exchange? What is the velocity of circulation? What assumptions are necessary to make the equation of exchange the quantity theory of money?

13 What is the historical and international evidence on the quantity theory of money?

PROBLEMS

1 In the United States today, money includes which of the following items?

- **a** Federal Reserve banknotes in the Bank of America's cash machines
- **b** Your Visa card
- **c** The quarters inside public phones
- **d** Federal Reserve banknotes in your wallet
- **e** The check you have just written to pay for your rent
- **f** The loan you took out last August to pay for your school fees

2 Which of the following items are fiat money? Which are private debt money?

- **a** Checkable deposits at Citicorp
- **b** Shares of IBM stock held by individuals
- **c** Gold bars held by banks
- **d** The Susan B. Anthony dollar
- **e** U.S. government securities
- **f** NOW accounts

3 Sara withdraws $1,000 from her savings deposit at the Lucky S&L, keeps $50 in cash, and deposits the balance in her checkable account, which is a demand deposit at Bank of America. What are the immediate changes in M1, M2, and M3?

4 The commercial banks in Desertland have the following assets and liabilities:

Total reserves	$250 million
Loans	$1,000 million
Deposits	$2,000 million
Total assets	$2,500 million

- **a** Construct the commercial banks' balance sheet. If you are missing any assets, call them "other assets"; if you are missing any liabilities, call them "other liabilities."
- **b** Calculate the commercial banks' reserve ratio.

c If the reserve ratio in part (b) is equal to the commercial banks' desired reserve ratio, calculate the simple money multiplier.

5 An immigrant arrives in New Transylvania with $1,200. The $1,200 is put into a bank deposit. All the banks in New Transylvania have a required reserve ratio of 10 percent.

a What is the initial increase in the quantity of money of New Transylvania?

b What is the initial increase in the quantity of bank deposits when the immigrant arrives?

c How much does the immigrant's bank lend out?

d Using a format similar to that in Table 10.7, calculate the amount lent and the amount of deposits created at each "round," assuming that all the funds lent are returned to the banking system in the form of deposits.

e By how much has the quantity of money increased after 20 rounds of lending?

f What are the ultimate increases in the quantity of money, bank loans, and bank deposits?

6 Quantecon is a country in which the quantity theory of money operates. The country has a constant population, capital stock, and technology. In year 1, real GDP was $400 million, the price level was 200, and the velocity of circulation of money was 20. In year 2, the quantity of money was 20 percent higher than in year 1.

a What was the quantity of money in Quantecon in year 1?

b What was the quantity of money in Quantecon in year 2?

c What was the price level in Quantecon in year 2?

d What was the level of real GDP in Quantecon in year 2?

e What was the velocity of circulation in Quantecon in year 2?

CHAPTER 11

THE FEDERAL RESERVE, MONEY, AND INTEREST RATES

After studying this chapter, you will be able to:

- Describe the structure of the Federal Reserve System (the Fed)
- Describe the tools used by the Fed to influence the money supply and interest rates
- Explain what an open market operation is and how it works
- Explain how an open market operation changes the money supply
- Distinguish between the nominal money supply and the real money supply
- Explain what determines the demand for money
- Explain the effects of financial innovations on the demand for money in the 1980s
- Explain how interest rates are determined
- Explain how the Fed influences interest rates

Fiddling with the Knobs

THE YEAR IS 1983. A YOUNG COUPLE THINKING OF buying a first home has found the perfect place. But mortgage rates are 16 percent a year. Amid much gnashing of teeth, they put off their purchase until interest rates decline, making a home affordable. What determines interest rates? Are they determined by forces of nature? Or is somebody fiddling with the knobs somewhere? ◆◆ You suspect that someone is indeed fiddling with the knobs. You've just read in your newspaper: "Fed nudging interest rates down to spark recovery." And a few months earlier, you read: "The Fed doesn't plan to push interest rates higher unless it sees further rebound of inflation." What is "the Fed"? Why would the Fed want to change interest rates? And how can the Fed influence interest rates? ◆◆ There is enough currency—coins and Federal Reserve bills—circulating in the United States for every single individual to have a wallet stuffed with more than $1,000. There are enough checking deposits in banks and other financial institutions for everyone to have almost $2,500 in these accounts. Of course, not many people hold as much currency and checkable deposits as these averages. But these *are* the averages. Therefore, if most people don't hold this much, some people must be holding a great deal more. What determines the quantity of money that people hold? ◆◆ The 1980s saw a revolution in our banking and financial sector. There was an explosion in the use of credit cards, and many people stopped using cash to buy gasoline, restaurant meals, and many other commonly purchased items. But you can't buy everything with a credit card. For example, you feel like a midnight snack, but your favorite spot doesn't accept credit cards and you're out of cash.

No problem! You head straight for the automatic teller and withdraw what you need tonight and for the next few days as well. While walking out, you wonder to yourself: How much cash would I need to hold if I didn't have quick access to an automatic teller machine? How did people get cash for midnight pizza before such machines existed? How have credit cards and computers affected the amount of money that we hold?

◆ ◆ ◆ ◆ In this chapter, we are going to discover how interest rates are determined by the demand for and supply of money. We are also going to study the Federal Reserve System and learn how the Fed influences the quantity of money and interest rates in an attempt to smooth the business cycle and keep inflation in check.

The Federal Reserve System

The **Federal Reserve System** is the central bank of the United States. A **central bank** is a public authority charged with regulating and controlling a country's monetary and financial institutions and markets. The Fed is also responsible for the nation's monetary policy. *Monetary policy* is the attempt to control inflation and moderate the business cycle by changing the quantity of money in circulation and adjusting interest rates. We are going to study the tools available to the Fed in its conduct of monetary policy and also work out the effects of the Fed's actions on interest rates. But first we'll examine the origins and structure of the Fed.

The Origins of the Federal Reserve System

The Fed was created by the Federal Reserve Act of 1913. Thus, for more than 100 years of our history, we had no central bank. Central banking and a deep hostility to central power—visible in the checks and balances built into our Constitution—just did not seem to mix. As a consequence, we tried to get along without a central bank for the first 137 years of our history. During this period, there was a series of severe national bank panics. In 1907, bank failures and depositors' losses were so severe that the need for a central bank became clear to almost everyone. It was the serious financial turmoil of 1907 that led to the emergence of a consensus on the need for a central bank. That consensus finally found expression in the Federal Reserve Act of 1913.

By the time the Fed was created, most other countries already had a central bank. The first such banks were established in Sweden and England in the seventeenth century. But their origins were very different from that of the Fed. They were set up as private banks designed to solve the financial problems of monarchs. These banks gradually evolved into modern central banks, eventually becoming publicly owned corporations. Central banks, as their name suggests, concentrate the power to control and influence the banking system in a single center. In setting up the Federal Reserve System, care was taken to design a central bank that diffused and decentralized, as far as possible, responsibility for monetary policy. The result was a central bank with a unique structure, unlike all other central banks. Let's examine that structure.

The Structure of the Federal Reserve System

There are three key elements in the structure of the Federal Reserve System:

- Board of Governors
- Regional Federal Reserve banks
- Federal Open Market Committee

Board of Governors The Board of Governors of the Federal Reserve System consists of seven members appointed by the President of the United States and confirmed by the Senate. The board is located in Washington, D.C. Each member is appointed for a 14-year term, and the terms are staggered so that one place on the board becomes vacant every two years. One of the members of the board is named chairman. The length of the term of the chairman is four years.

Regional Federal Reserve Banks There are 12 Federal Reserve banks, one for each of 12 Federal Reserve districts (see Fig. 11.1). Each Federal

FIGURE 11.1

The Federal Reserve System

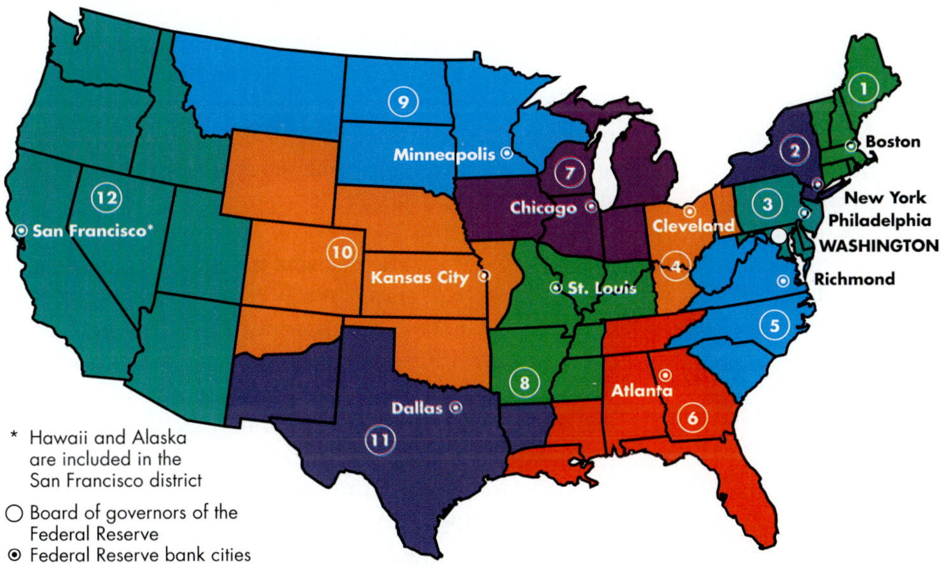

The nation is divided into 12 Federal Reserve districts, each having a Federal Reserve bank. (Some of the larger districts also have branch banks.) The Board of Governors of the Federal Reserve System is located in Washington, D.C.

Source: Federal Reserve Bulletin, published monthly.

Reserve bank has nine directors, three of whom are appointed by the Board of Governors and six of whom are elected by the commercial banks in the Federal Reserve district. The directors of the regional Federal Reserve banks appoint the bank's president and other senior officers.

The Federal Reserve Bank of New York (or the New York Fed as it is often called) occupies a special place in the Federal Reserve System. It is the New York Fed that implements some of the Fed's most important policy decisions.

Federal Open Market Committee The **Federal Open Market Committee** (FOMC) is the main policy-making organ of the Federal Reserve System. The FOMC consists of the following members:

- The chairman of the Board of Governors
- The other six members of the Board of Governors
- The president of the Federal Reserve Bank of New York
- The presidents of four other regional Federal Reserve banks elected to the board on a rotating basis

The FOMC meets once a month to review the state of the economy and to formulate detailed policy actions to be carried out by the New York Fed.

The Fed's Power Center

A description of the formal structure of the Fed gives the impression that power in the Fed resides with the Board of Governors. In practice, it is the chairman of the Board of Governors who has the largest influence on the Fed's monetary policy actions. This position has been held by some remarkable individuals. The current chairman is Alan Greenspan, who was appointed by President Reagan in 1987 and reappointed by President Bush in 1991. His predecessor was Paul Volcker, who was appointed in 1979 by President Carter and reappointed in 1983 by President Reagan.

The chairman's power and influence stem in an important way from his ability to control the agenda at and to dominate the meetings of the FOMC. His influence is yet further enhanced by virtue of his day-to-day contact with and control of a sizable staff of economists and other technical experts who provide the chairman, the Board of Governors, and the FOMC with the detailed background briefings necessary to formulate monetary policy.

The Fed's Policy Tools

The Federal Reserve System has many responsibilities, but we'll examine its single most important one—regulating the amount of money floating around in the United States. How does the Fed control the money supply? It does so by adjusting the reserves of the banking system. It is also by adjusting the reserves of the banking system and by standing ready to make loans to banks that the Fed is able to prevent banking panics and bank failures. The Fed uses three main policy tools to achieve its objectives:

- Required reserve ratios
- Discount rate
- Open market operations

Required Reserve Ratios All depository institutions in the United States are required to hold a minimum percentage of deposits as reserves. This minimum percentage is known as a *required reserve ratio.* The Fed determines a required reserve ratio for each type of deposit, and the ratios in force in 1993 are set out in Table 11.1.

TABLE 11.1

Required Reserve Ratios

Type of deposit	Minimum reserve required (percentage of deposits)
Transactions accounts— $0–46.8 million*	**3**
Transactions accounts— more than $46.8 million	**10**
Nonpersonal time deposits	**0**
Eurodollar deposits	**0**

*Transactions accounts include demand deposits and other checkable deposits.

Source: Federal Reserve Bulletin (May 1993).

By increasing required reserve ratios, the Fed can create a shortage of reserves for the banking system, reducing the amount of bank lending. Reduced lending lowers the money supply by a process similar to that described in Chapter 10. We'll look at this process later in this chapter (see pp. 286–289).

Although changes in required reserve ratios can have an important influence on the money supply, the Fed does not use this policy tool very often. That is, the Fed does not vary required reserve ratios as an active tool for achieving *variations* in the money supply.

Discount Rate The **discount rate** is the interest rate at which the Fed stands ready to lend reserves to commercial banks. The discount rate is proposed by the 12 Federal Reserve banks and determined with the approval of the Board of Governors. By increasing the discount rate, the Fed can make it more costly for banks to borrow reserves, thereby encouraging them to cut back their lending, which reduces the money supply. By lowering the discount rate, the Fed can encourage banks to borrow more reserves, thereby stimulating bank lending, which increases the money supply.

The discount rate can be an effective tool of Federal Reserve policy only if the banking system is short of reserves and needs to borrow some reserves from the Fed. If the banks are not borrowing from the Fed, the level of the discount rate has no immediate impact on the banks' behavior. But the Fed can determine whether or not the banking system has a shortage or a surplus of reserves. It does so by using open market operations.

Open Market Operations An **open market operation** is the purchase or sale of U.S. government securities—U.S. Treasury bills and bonds—by the Federal Reserve System designed to influence the money supply. Decisions to buy or sell government securities are made by the FOMC. They are carried out by the Federal Reserve Bank of New York. When the Fed sells government securities, they are paid for with bank reserves, and tighter monetary and credit conditions are created. With lower reserves, the banks cut their lending, and the money supply decreases. When the Fed buys government securities, the Fed's payment for them puts additional reserves in the hands of the banks and loosens credit conditions. With extra reserves, the banks increase their lending, and the money supply increases.

FIGURE 11.2
The Fed: Structure and Tools

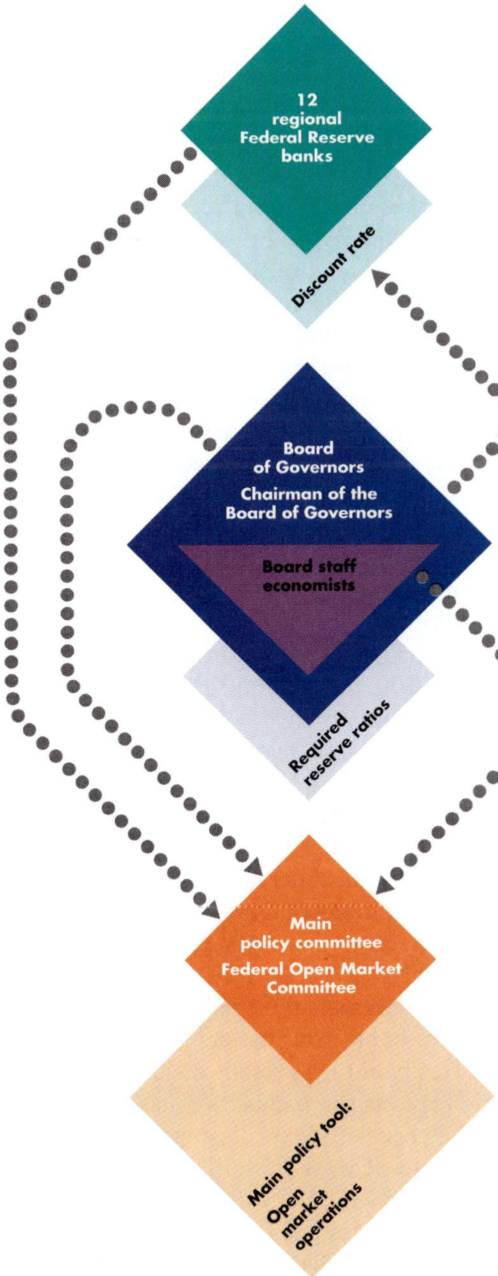

The main organs of the Federal Reserve System are the Board of Governors, the 12 regional Federal Reserve banks, and the Federal Open Market Committee. The Fed's policy tools are required reserve ratios, the discount rate, and open market operations.

The structure and policy tools of the Federal Reserve System are summarized in Fig. 11.2. The most important and powerful of the Fed's policy tools are its open market operations. In order to understand the Fed's open market operations, we first need to examine the structure of the Fed's balance sheet.

The Fed's Balance Sheet

The balance sheet of the Federal Reserve System for December 1992 is set out in Table 11.2. The assets on the left side are what the Fed owns, and the liabilities on the right side are what it owes. Most of the Fed's assets are U.S. government securities. In addition, the Fed holds some gold and foreign exchange—foreign central banks' liabilities. The most important aspect of the Fed's balance sheet is on the liabilities side.

The largest liability of the Fed is Federal Reserve notes in circulation. These are the bank notes that we use in our daily transactions. Some of these bank notes are in circulation with the public, and others are in the tills and vaults of banks and other financial institutions.

You might be wondering why Federal Reserve notes are considered a liability of the Fed. When notes were invented, they gave their owner a claim on the gold reserves of the issuing bank. Such notes were *convertible paper money.* The holder of such a note could convert the note on demand into gold (or some other commodity such as silver) at a guaranteed price. Thus when a bank issued a note, it was holding itself liable to convert that note into a commodity. Modern bank notes are nonconvertible. A **nonconvertible note** is a bank note that is not convertible into any commodity and that obtains its value by government fiat—hence the term fiat money. Such bank notes are considered the legal liability of the bank that issues them, but they are backed not by commodity reserves but by holdings of securities and loans. Federal Reserve notes are backed by the Fed's holdings of U.S. government securities.

The other important liability of the Fed is the deposits held there by banks. We saw these deposits as an asset in the balance sheets of the banks. The remaining liability of the Fed consists of items such as U.S. Treasury deposits (federal government bank accounts at the Fed) and accounts held by foreign central banks (such as the Bank of England and the Bank of Canada).

TABLE 11.2

The Balance Sheet for the Federal Reserve System, December 1992

Assets (billions of dollars)		Liabilities (billions of dollars)	
Gold and foreign exchange	19	**Federal Reserve notes in circulation**	314
U.S. government securities	300	**Banks' deposits**	32
		Monetary base	346
Other assets	42	**Other liabilities**	15
Total	361	**Total**	361

Source: Federal Reserve Bulletin (May 1993), Table 1.18, p. A11.

The two largest items on the liability side of the Fed's balance sheet are Federal Reserve notes in circulation and banks' deposits at the Fed. These two items, together with coins in circulation (coins are issued by the Treasury and are not liabilities of the Fed) are the **monetary base.** The monetary base is so called because it acts like a base that supports the nation's money supply.

By buying or selling government securities, the Fed can directly determine the scale of its own liabilities and change the monetary base. Such purchases and sales of government securities are the Fed's open market operations, its main method of controlling the money supply.

Controlling the Money Supply

The money supply is determined by the actions of the Fed. Let's see how. We begin by looking at what happens when the Fed conducts an open market operation.

How Open Market Operations Work

When the Fed conducts an open market operation in which it buys U.S. government securities, it increases the reserves of the banking system. When it conducts an open market operation in which it sells U.S. government securities, it decreases the reserves of the banking system. Let's study the effects of an open market operation by working out what happens when the Fed buys $100 million of U.S. government securities.

Open market operations affect the balance sheets of the Fed, the banks, and the rest of the economy. Table 11.3 keeps track of the changes in these balance sheets. When the Fed buys securities, there are two possible sellers: the banks or other agents in the economy. Part (a) of the table works out what happens when banks sell the securities that the Fed buys.

When the Fed buys securities from the banks, the Fed pays for the securities by crediting the banks' deposit accounts at the Fed. The changes in the Fed's balance sheet are that its assets increase by $100 million (the additional U.S. government securities bought) and its liabilities also increase by $100 million (the additional bank deposits). The banks' total assets remain constant, but their deposits at the Fed increase by $100 million and their securities decrease by $100 million.

Part (b) of the table deals with the case in which the banks do not sell any securities and the Fed buys securities from agents in the rest of the economy other than the banks. The Fed's holdings of U.S. government securities increase by $100 million, and other agents' holdings of U.S. government securities go down by $100 million. The Fed pays for the securities by giving checks drawn on itself to the sellers. The sellers take the checks to the banks and deposit them. Bank deposits increase by $100 million. The banks in turn present the checks to the Fed, which credits the banks' accounts with the value of the checks. Banks' deposits with the Fed—reserves—increase by $100 million.

Regardless of which of the two cases takes place, by conducting an open market purchase of securities the Fed increases the banks' deposits with itself—increases the banks' reserves.

If the Fed conducts an open market *sale* of securities, the events that we have just traced occur in reverse. The Fed's assets and liabilities will decrease in value, and so will the reserves of the banks.

The effects of an open market operation on the

TABLE 11.3
An Open Market Operation

(a) BANKS SELL THE SECURITIES BOUGHT BY THE FED

Effects on the balance sheet of the Fed (millions of dollars)

Change in assets		Change in liabilities	
U.S. government securities	**+100**	**Banks' deposits (reserves)**	**+100**

Effects on the balance sheet of the banks (millions of dollars)

Change in assets		Change in liabilities	
Banks' deposits (reserves)	**+100**		
U.S. government securities	**–100**		

(b) AGENTS OTHER THAN BANKS SELL THE SECURITIES BOUGHT BY THE FED

Effects on the balance sheet of the Fed (millions of dollars)

Change in assets		Change in liabilities	
U.S. government securities	**+100**	**Banks' deposits (reserves)**	**+100**

Effects on the balance sheet of the banks (millions of dollars)

Change in assets		Change in liabilities	
Banks' deposits (reserves)	**+100**	**Deposits**	**+100**

Effects on the balance sheet of the other agents (millions of dollars)

Change in assets		Change in liabilities	
Deposits	**+100**		
U.S. government securities	**–100**		

balance sheets of the Fed and the banks that we've traced in Table 11.3 are not the end of the story—they are just the beginning. With an increase in their reserves, the banks are now able to make more loans, and by making loans they create money. We studied this money creation process in Chapter 10, where we learned that the change in the money supply is a multiple of the change in reserves that brings it about. We'll look again at this process. But now that you understand the basic idea, we'll add an element of realism we ignored in Chapter 10: the distinction between the monetary base and bank reserves.

Monetary Base and Bank Reserves

We've defined the *monetary base* as the sum of Federal Reserve notes, coins, and banks' deposits at the Fed. The monetary base is held either by banks as *reserves* or outside the banks as currency in circulation. When the monetary base increases, both bank reserves and currency in circulation increase. Only the increase in bank reserves can be used by banks to make loans and create additional money. An increase in currency held outside the banks is called a **currency drain.** A currency drain reduces the amount of additional money that can be created from a given increase in the monetary base.

The **money multiplier** is the amount by which a change in the monetary base is multiplied to determine the resulting change in the quantity of money. It differs from the simple money multiplier that we studied in Chapter 10. The *simple money multiplier* is the amount by which a change in bank reserves is multiplied to determine the change in the quantity of bank deposits. Since the Fed influences the monetary base (not bank reserves), it is the *money multiplier* that is relevant for determining the effects of the Fed's actions on the money supply.

Let's now look at the money multiplier.

The Multiplier Effect of an Open Market Operation

We'll work out the multiplier effect of an open market operation in which the Fed buys securities from the banks. In this case, although the open market operation increases the banks' reserves, it has no immediate effect on the quantity of money. The banks are holding additional reserves and fewer U.S. government securities. But they have excess reserves. When the banks have excess reserves, the sequence of events shown in Fig. 11.3 takes place. These events are

FIGURE 11.3

A Round in the Multiplier Process Following an Open Market Operation

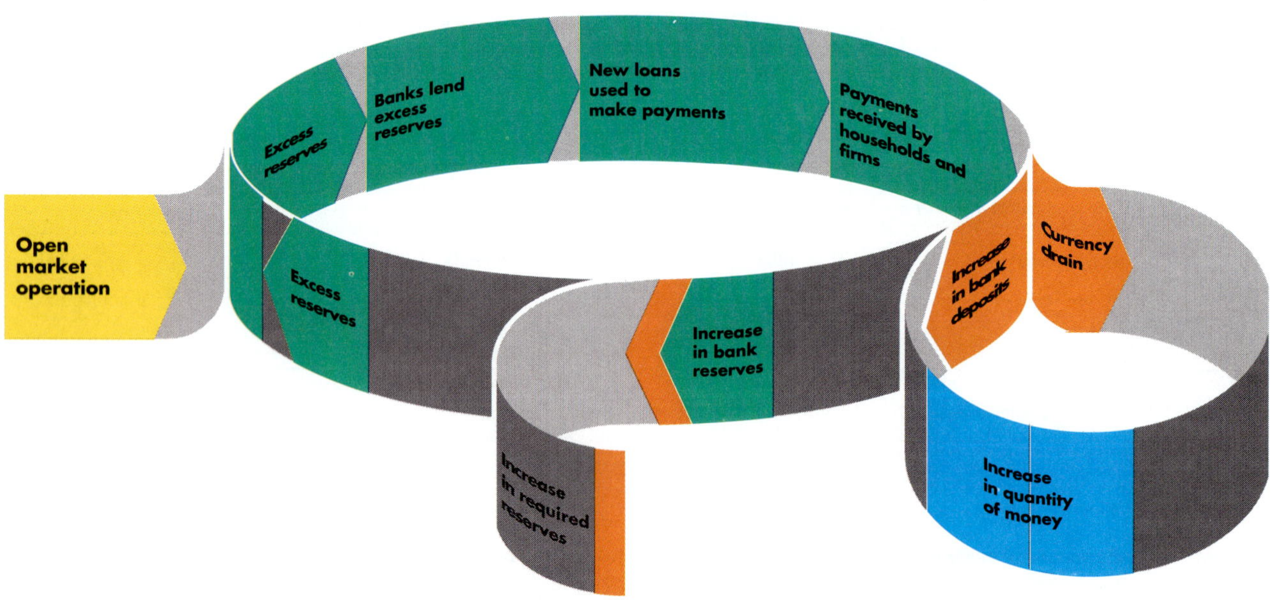

An open market purchase of U.S. government securities increases bank reserves and creates excess reserves. Banks lend the excess reserves, and new loans are used to make payments. Households and firms receiving payments keep some of the receipts in the form of currency—a currency drain—and place the rest on deposit in banks. The increase in bank deposits increases banks' reserves but also increases banks' required reserves. Required reserves increase by less than actual reserves, so the banks still have some excess reserves, though less than before. The process repeats until excess reserves have been eliminated. There are two components to the increase in the quantity of money: the currency drain and the increase in deposits.

- Banks lend excess reserves.
- New loans are used to make payments.
- Households and firms receive payments from new loans.
- Part of the receipts are held as currency—a *currency drain.*
- Part of the receipts are deposited in banks.
- Bank reserves increase (by the same amount as the increase in deposits).
- Required reserves increase (by a fraction—the required reserve ratio—of the increase in deposits).
- Excess reserves decrease but remain positive.
- The quantity of money increases by the amount of the currency drain and the increase in bank deposits.

The sequence just described is similar to the one we studied in Chapter 10 except that there we ignored the currency drain. As before, the sequence repeats in a series of rounds, but each round begins with a smaller quantity of excess reserves than did the previous one. The process continues until excess reserves have finally been eliminated.

Figure 11.4 illustrates the accumulated increase in the quantity of money and in its components, bank

FIGURE 11.4

The Multiplier Effect of an Open Market Operation

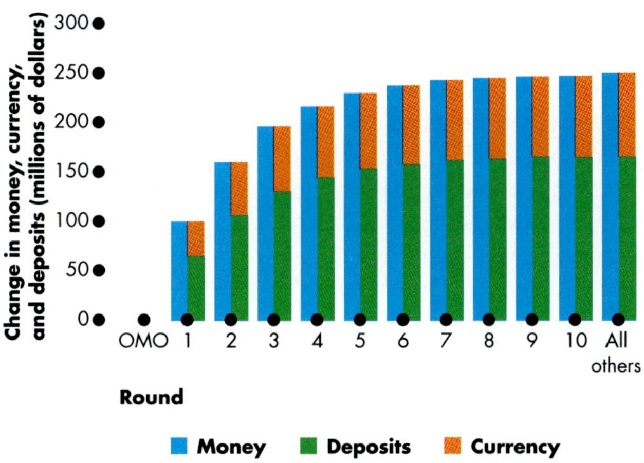

An open market operation (OMO) in which the Fed buys $100 million of government securities from the banks has no immediate effect on the money supply but creates excess reserves in the banking system. When loans are made with these reserves, bank deposits and currency holdings increase. Each time a new loan is made, part of the loan drains out from the banks and is held as currency and part of the loan stays in the banking system in the form of additional deposits and additional reserves. Banks continue to increase their lending until excess reserves have been eliminated. The effects for the first five rounds of lending and money creation are described in the table and the process is illustrated in the figure. The magnitude of the ultimate increase in the money supply is determined by the money multiplier.

Round	Excess reserves at start of round	New loans	Change in deposits	Currency drain	Change in reserves	Change in required reserves	Excess reserves at end of round	Change in quantity of money
	(millions of dollars)							
1	**100.00**	**100.00**	**66.67**	**33.33**	**66.67**	**6.67**	**60.00**	**100.00**
2	**60.00**	**60.00**	**40.00**	**20.00**	**40.00**	**4.00**	**36.00**	**60.00**
3	**36.00**	**36.00**	**24.00**	**12.00**	**24.00**	**2.40**	**21.60**	**36.00**
4	**21.60**	**21.60**	**14.40**	**7.20**	**14.40**	**1.44**	**12.96**	**21.60**
5	**12.96**	**12.96**	**8.64**	**4.32**	**8.64**	**0.86**	**7.78**	**12.96**
	⋮	⋮	⋮	⋮	⋮	⋮	⋮	⋮
All others		**19.44**	**12.96**	**6.48**		**9.63**		**19.44**
Total		**250.00**	**166.67**	**83.33**		**25.00**		**250.00**

deposits and currency, resulting from an open market operation of $100 million. In this figure, the *currency drain* is one third and the *required reserve ratio* is 10 percent. As you can see, when the open market operation takes place (labeled OMO in the figure), there is no initial change in either the quantity of money or its components. Then, after the first round of bank lending, the quantity of money increases by $100 million—the size of the open market operation. In successive rounds, the quantity of money and its components—currency and bank deposits—continue to increase but by successively smaller amounts until, after 10 rounds, the quantities of currency and deposits and their sum, the quantity of money, have almost reached the values to which they are ultimately heading.

The table in Fig. 11.4 keeps track of the magnitudes of new loans, the currency drain, the increases in deposits and reserves, the increase in required reserves, and the change in excess reserves. The initial open market operation increases the banks' reserves, but since deposits do not change, there is no change in required reserves. The banks have excess reserves of $100 million. They lend those reserves. When the money borrowed from the banks is spent, two thirds of it returns as additional deposits and one third drains off as currency. Thus when the banks lend the initial $100 million of excess reserves, $66.67 million comes back to them in the form of deposits and $33.33 million drains off and is held outside the banks as currency. The quantity of money has now increased by $100 million—the increase in deposits plus the increase in currency holdings.

The increased bank deposits of $66.67 million generate an increase in required reserves of 10 percent of that amount, which is $6.67 million. But actual reserves have increased by the same amount as the increase in deposits—$66.67 million. Therefore, the banks now have excess reserves of $60 million. At this stage we have completed round 1. We have gone once around the circle shown in Fig. 11.3. The banks still have excess reserves, but the level has fallen from $100 million at the beginning of the round to $60 million at the end of the round. Round 2 now begins.

The process keeps on repeating. The table in Fig. 11.4 shows the first five rounds and collapses all the remaining ones into the next to last row of the table. At the end of the process, the quantity of money has increased by $250 million.

The U.S. Money Multiplier

The money multiplier is calculated as the ratio of the change in the quantity of money to the change in the monetary base. That is,

$$\text{Money multiplier} = \frac{\text{Change in the quantity of money}}{\text{Change in the monetary base}}.$$

The money multiplier in 1991 (for M1) was 2.9. Its average value between 1960 and 1991 was approximately 2.5. What determines the size of the money multiplier, and what makes it fluctuate?

The size of the money multiplier is determined by two ratios that fluctuate over time. They are

- The ratio of banks' reserves to bank deposits
- The ratio of currency holdings of households and firms to bank deposits

Table 11.4 shows how the money multiplier depends on these two ratios. It also provides numbers that illustrate the M1 money multiplier on the average between 1960 and 1991. Over that period the currency holdings of households and firms were 50 percent (0.5) of the bank deposits that make up M1. Equivalently, currency makes up one third of M1, and deposits make up two thirds. Reserve holdings were approximately 10 percent (0.1) of the deposits in M1. Combining these ratios in the formula derived in the table shows that the M1 money multiplier is 2.5.

Fluctuations in the size of the money multiplier occur because of fluctuations in the two ratios. But it is the currency to deposits ratio that fluctuates most. In determining the effects of its open market operations on the money supply, the Fed must constantly monitor the ratios that determine the money multiplier and adjust the scale of its operations to take into account changes in the size of the multiplier.

Other Policy Tools

The Fed's other policy tools—the required reserve ratio and the discount rate—also affect the quantity of money by changing the excess reserves of the banking system. An increase in the required reserve ratio increases the reserves that the banks must hold at a given level of deposits. With no change in actual reserves, excess reserves fall. An increase in the discount rate also increases the reserves that the banks

TABLE 11.4

Calculating the Money Multiplier

	In general	Numbers
1. The variables		
Reserves	$= R$	
Currency	$= C$	
Monetary base	$= MB$	
Deposits	$= D$	
Quantity of money	$= M$	
Money multiplier	$= mm$	
2. Definitions		
The monetary base is the sum of reserves and currency	$MB = R + C$	
The quantity of money is the sum of deposits and currency	$M = D + C$	
The money multiplier is the ratio of the change in the quantity of money to the change in the monetary base	$mm = \Delta M/\Delta MB$	
3. Ratios		
Change in reserves to change in deposits	$\Delta R/\Delta D$	0.1
Change in currency to change in deposits	$\Delta C/\Delta D$	0.5
4. Calculations		
Begin with the definition	$mm = \Delta M/\Delta MB$	
Use the definitions of *M* and *MB* to give	$mm = \dfrac{\Delta D + \Delta C}{\Delta R + \Delta C}$	
Divide top and bottom by ΔD to give	$mm = \dfrac{1 + \Delta C/\Delta D}{\Delta R/\Delta D + \Delta C/\Delta D}$	$= \dfrac{1 + 0.5}{0.1 + 0.5}$
		$= \dfrac{1.5}{0.6}$
		$= 2.5$

plan to hold. When it costs more to borrow reserves, the banks want to run less risk of being in that position and so plan to hold a larger quantity of reserves to reduce the likelihood of having to borrow from the Fed.

Whatever the source of a change in excess reserves, once it is present, it sets up a chain of events similar to those described earlier, following an open market operation. Thus the Fed's minor policy instruments work in a similar way to its open market operations. By changing excess reserves, they change the amount of bank lending and the quantity of money in circulation.

But required reserve ratios and the discount rate also affect the size of the money multiplier. As we've seen, the required reserve ratio is one of the elements in the money multiplier. The higher the banks' reserve ratio, the smaller is the money multiplier. But because these policy tools are not often used, changes in the money multiplier resulting from these instruments do not often occur.

REVIEW

The Federal Reserve System is the nation's central bank. The Fed influences the quantity of money in circulation by changing the excess reserves of the banking system. It has three instruments at its disposal: changing the required reserve ratio, changing the discount rate, and conducting open market operations. The last of these is the most important and most frequently used. Open market operations not only change the excess reserves of the banking system but also set up a multiplier effect. When excess reserves are lent, some of the loans drain out of the banking system, but others come back in the form of new deposits. The banks continue to lend until the currency drain and the increase in their required reserves have eliminated excess reserves. The multiplier effect of an open market operation depends on the scale of the currency drain and the size of the banks' required reserve ratio. ◆

The Fed's objective in conducting open market operations or taking other actions that influence the quantity of money in circulation is not simply to affect the money supply for its own sake. Its objective is to influence the course of the economy—especially the level of output, employment, and prices. But these effects are indirect. The Fed's immediate objective is to move interest rates up or down. To work out the effects of the Fed's actions on interest rates, we need to work out how and why interest rates change when the quantity of money changes. We'll discover the answer to these questions by studying the demand for money.

The Demand for Money

The amount of money that we *receive* each week in payment for our labor is income—a flow. The amount of money that we hold in our wallet or in a deposit account at the bank is an inventory—a stock. There is no limit to how much income—or flow—we would like to receive each week. But there is a limit to how big an inventory of money each of us would like to hold, on the average.

The Motives for Holding Money

Why do people hold an inventory of money? Why do you carry coins and bills in your wallet, and why do you keep money in a deposit account at your neighborhood bank?

There are three main motives for holding money:

- Transactions motive
- Precautionary motive
- Speculative motive

Transactions Motive The main motive for holding money is to be able to undertake transactions and to minimize the cost of transactions. By carrying an inventory of currency, you are able to undertake small transactions such as buying your lunch at the college cafeteria. If you didn't carry an inventory of currency, you'd have to go to the bank every lunchtime in order to withdraw enough cash. The opportunity cost of these transactions, in terms of your own lost studying or leisure time, would be considerable. You avoid those transactions costs by keeping an inventory of currency large enough to make your normal purchases over a period of perhaps a week in length.

You also keep an inventory of money in the form of deposits at the bank to make transactions such as paying the rent on your apartment or paying your college bookstore bill. Instead of having an inventory of bank deposits for these purposes, you might put all your assets into the stock or bond market—buying IBM stock or U.S. government securities. But if you did that, you would have to call your broker and sell some stocks and bonds each time you needed to pay the rent or the bookstore. Again, you'd have to pay the opportunity cost of such transactions. Instead, those costs can be avoided by holding larger inventories of bank deposits.

Individual holdings of money for transactions purposes fluctuate during any week or month. But aggregate money balances held for transactions purposes do not fluctuate much because what one person is spending, someone else is receiving.

Firms' money holdings are at their peak just before the moment they pay their employees' wages. Households' money holdings are at a peak just after wages have been paid. As households spend their incomes, their money holdings decline and firms' holdings of money increase. Firms' holdings of money are actually quite large, and it is this fact that makes average money holdings appear to be so large. Average money holdings of households are much lower than the economy-wide averages presented in the chapter opener.

Precautionary Motive Money is held as a precaution against unforeseen events that require unplanned purchases to be made. For example, on an out-of-town trip you carry some extra money in case your car breaks down and has to be fixed. Or if you are shopping in the January sales, you take with you more money than you are planning on spending in case you come across a real bargain that you just can't pass up.

Speculative Motive The final motive for holding money is to avoid losses from holding stocks or bonds that are expected to fall in value. Suppose, for example, that a week before the stock market crashes, you predict the crash. On the Friday afternoon before the markets close, you sell all your stocks and put the proceeds into your bank deposit account for the weekend. This temporary holding of money persists until stock prices have fallen. Only then do you reduce your bank deposit and buy stocks again.

The Influences on Money Holding

What determines the quantity of money that households and firms choose to hold? There are three important influences on this quantity:

- Prices
- Real expenditure
- The opportunity cost of holding money

The higher the level of prices, other things being equal, the larger is the quantity of money that people will want to hold. The higher the level of real expenditure, other things being equal, the larger is the quantity of money that people plan to hold. The higher the opportunity cost of holding money, the smaller is the quantity of money that people plan to hold.

These influences on individual decisions about money holding translate into three macroeconomic variables that influence the aggregate quantity of money demanded:

- The price level
- Real GDP
- The interest rate

Price Level and the Quantity of Money Demanded The quantity of money measured in current dollars is called the quantity of **nominal money.** The quantity of nominal money demanded is proportional to the price level. That is, other things being equal, if the price level (GDP deflator) increases by 10 percent, people will want to hold 10 percent more nominal money than before. What matters to people is not the number of dollars that they hold but the buying power of those dollars. Suppose, for example, that to undertake your weekly expenditure on movies and soda, you carry an average of $20 in your wallet. If your income and the prices of movies and soda increased by 10 percent, you would increase your average cash holdings by 10 percent to $22.

The quantity of money measured in constant dollars (for example, in 1987 dollars) is called *real money*. Real money is equal to nominal money divided by the price level. The quantity of real money demanded is independent of the price level. In the above example, you held $20, on the average, at the original price level. When the price level increased by 10 percent, you increased your average cash holding by 10 percent, keeping your *real* cash holding constant. Your $22 at the new price level is the same quantity of *real money* as your $20 at the original price level.

Real GDP and the Quantity of Money Demanded An important determinant of the quantity of money demanded is the level of real income—for the aggregate economy, real GDP. As you know, real GDP and real aggregate expenditure are two sides of the same transaction. The amount of money that households and firms demand depends on the amount that they are spending. The higher the expenditure—the higher the income—the larger is the quantity of money demanded. Again, suppose that you hold an average of $20 to finance your weekly purchases of movies and soda. Now imagine that prices remain constant but that your income increases. As a consequence, you now spend more, and you also keep a larger amount of money on hand to finance your higher volume of expenditure.

The Interest Rate and the Quantity of Money Demanded

You already know the fundamental principle that as the opportunity cost of something rises, people try to find substitutes for it. Money is no exception to this principle. The higher the opportunity cost of holding money, other things being equal, the lower is the quantity of real money demanded. But what is the opportunity cost of holding money?

The opportunity cost of holding money is the interest rate. To see why, recall that the opportunity cost of any activity is the value of the best alternative forgone. What is the best alternative to holding money, and what is the value forgone? The best alternative to holding money is holding an interest-earning financial asset such as a savings bond or treasury bill. By holding money instead of such an asset, you forgo the interest that you otherwise would have received. This forgone interest is the opportunity cost of holding money. The higher the interest rate, the higher is the opportunity cost of holding money and the smaller is the amount of money held. At the same time, the quantity of interest-earning assets held increases. Interest-earning assets are substituted for money.

Money loses value because of inflation. Why isn't the inflation rate part of the cost of holding money? It is; other things being equal, the higher the expected inflation rate, the higher are interest rates and the higher, therefore, is the opportunity cost of holding money.

The Demand for Real Money

The **demand for real money** is the relationship between the quantity of real money demanded and the interest rate, holding constant all other influences on the amount of money that people wish to hold. To make the demand for real money more concrete, let's consider an example. A household's demand for real money can be represented as a demand schedule for real money. Such a schedule sets out the quantity of real money that a person wants to hold at a given level of real income for different levels of the interest rate.

FIGURE 11.5

The Polonius Household's Demand for Real Money

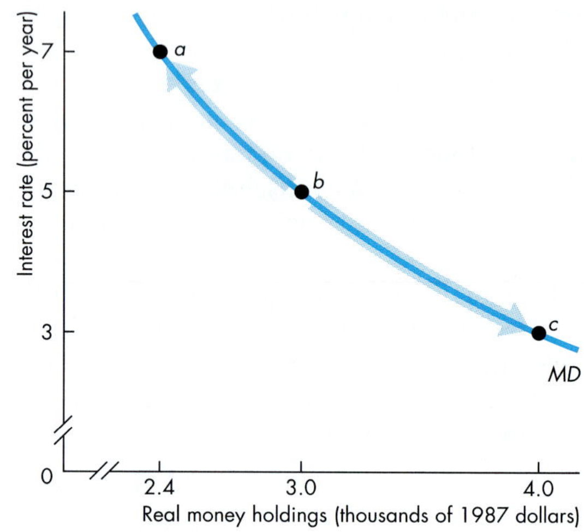

Polonius household's real income is $20,000; price level is 1

	Interest rate (percent per year)	Real money holdings (thousands of 1987 dollars)
a	**7**	**2.4**
b	**5**	**3.0**
c	**3**	**4.0**

The table shows the Polonius household's demand schedule for real money. The lower the interest rate, the larger is the quantity of real money that the household plans to hold. The graph shows the household's demand curve for real money (*MD*). Points *a, b,* and *c* on the curve correspond to the rows in the table. A change in the interest rate leads to a movement along the demand curve. The demand curve for real money slopes downward because the interest rate is the opportunity cost of holding money. The higher the interest rate, the larger is the interest forgone on holding another asset.

Figure 11.5 sets out some numbers for the Polonius household. The household's real income is $20,000 a year. The price level is 1, or the GDP deflator is equal to 100, so the quantity of money is the same whether we measure it in nominal terms or real terms. The table tells us how the quantity of real money demanded by the Polonius household changes as the interest rate changes. For example, in row *a*, when the interest rate is 7 percent a year, the Polonius household holds $2,400 of money, on the average. When the interest rate is 5 percent a year, real money holdings increase to $3,000, and when the interest rate falls to 3 percent a year, real money holdings increase to $4,000.

The figure also graphs the Polonius household's demand curve for real money (*MD*). If the interest rate increases from 5 percent to 7 percent, there is a rise in the opportunity cost of holding money and a decrease in the quantity of real money demanded—illustrated by an upward movement along the demand curve in Fig. 11.5. If the interest rate decreases from 5 percent to 3 percent, there is a fall in the opportunity cost of holding money and an increase in the quantity of real money demanded—illustrated by a downward movement along the demand curve in Fig. 11.5.

Shifts in the Demand Curve for Real Money

The demand curve for real money shifts when:

- Real income changes
- Financial innovation occurs

Changes in Real Income An increase in real income shifts the demand curve for real money to the right, and a decrease shifts it to the left. The effect of real income on the demand curve for real money is shown in Fig. 11.6. The table shows the effects of a change in real income on the quantity of real money demanded when the interest rate is constant at 5 percent. Look first at row *b* of the table. It tells us that when the interest rate is 5 percent and real income is $20,000, the quantity of real money demanded by the Polonius household is $3,000. This row corresponds to point *b* on the demand curve for real money MD_0. If we hold the interest rate constant and real income falls to $12,000, the quantity of real money held falls to $2,400. Thus the demand curve for real money shifts from MD_0 to MD_1 in Fig. 11.6. If the Polonius household's real income increases to $28,000, the quantity of real money held by the household increases to $3,600. In this case, the demand curve shifts to the right from MD_0 to MD_2.

Financial Innovation Financial innovation also results in a change in the demand for real money and a shift in the demand curve for real money. The most important such innovation in recent years has been the development of highly liquid deposits with banks and other financial institutions that makes it possible for people to quickly and easily convert

FIGURE 11.6

Changes in the Polonius Household's Demand for Real Money

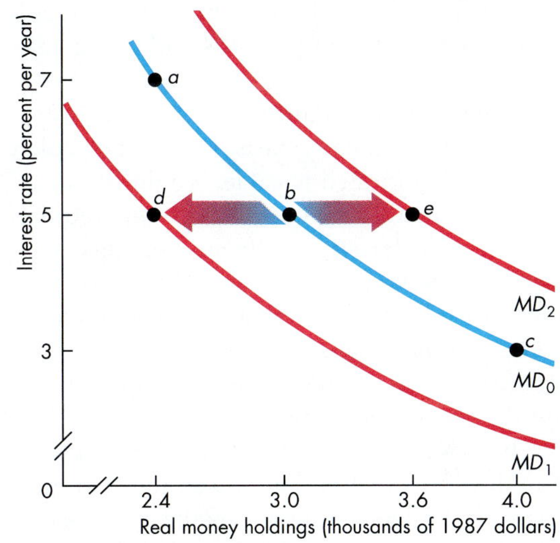

Interest rate is 5 percent; price level is 1

	Real income (thousands of 1987 dollars)	Real money holdings (thousands of 1987 dollars)
d	12	2.4
b	20	3.0
e	28	3.6

A change in real income leads to a change in the demand for real money. The table shows the quantity of real money held by the Polonius household at three different levels of real income when the interest rate is constant at 5 percent. The graph shows the effects of a change in real income on the demand curve for real money. When real income is $20,000 and the interest rate is 5 percent, the household is at point *b* on the demand curve for real money MD_0. When real income falls to $12,000, the demand curve shifts to MD_1, and, at a 5 percent interest rate, the household is at point *d*. When real income rises to $28,000, the demand curve shifts to MD_2. With an interest rate of 5 percent, the household is at point *e*.

such deposits into a medium of exchange—into money. These innovations have been brought about partly as a result of deregulation of the financial sector (see Chapter 10, pp. 262–263) and partly by the availability of low-cost computing power.

Computers are an important part of the story of financial innovation because they have dramatically lowered the cost of keeping records and doing calculations. Interest-bearing checking accounts, for example, have to have balances and interest payments calculated on a daily basis. Doing such calculations by hand, although feasible, would be very costly. Arrangements such as ATS accounts require that funds be transferred to or from a savings account when the balance on a checking account rises above or falls below a certain pre-agreed level. Again, keeping the records that make such bank accounts feasible would have been prohibitively costly in the precomputer age.

Now that banks have access to a vast amount of extremely low-cost computing power, they can offer a wide variety of deposit arrangements that make it convenient to convert non–medium of exchange assets into medium of exchange assets at extremely low cost. The development of these arrangements has led to a decrease in the demand for money—a leftward shift in the demand curve for money.

The availability of low-cost computing power in the financial sector is also responsible, in large degree, for the widespread use of credit cards. Again, keeping the records and calculating the interest and outstanding debt required to operate a credit card system is feasible by hand but too costly to undertake. No one would find it worthwhile to use plastic cards, shuffle sales slips, and keep records if all the calculations had to be done by hand (or even by pre-electronic mechanical calculating machines). This innovation—low-cost computing power—has also lowered the demand for money. By using a credit card to make purchases, people can operate with a much smaller inventory of money. Instead of holding money for transactions purposes through the month, people can charge purchases to a credit card and pay the credit card bill a day or two after payday. As a consequence the average holding of money throughout the month is much smaller.

The financial innovations that we have just considered affect the demand for money. Some financial innovations have changed the composition of our money holdings but not their total amount. One of these is the automatic teller machine. On the average, we can now function efficiently with smaller currency holdings than before, simply because we can easily obtain currency at almost any time or place. Although this innovation has decreased the demand for currency and increased the demand for deposits, it has probably not affected the overall demand for real money.

REVIEW

The quantity of money demanded depends on the price level, real GDP, and the interest rate. The quantity of nominal money demanded is proportional to the price level. Real money is the quantity of nominal money divided by the price level. The quantity of real money demanded increases as real GDP increases. The opportunity cost of holding money is the interest rate. The benefit from holding money is the avoidance of frequent transactions. The higher the interest rate, the smaller is the quantity of real money demanded. ◆◆ The demand curve for real money shows how the quantity of real money demanded varies as the interest rate varies. When the interest rate changes, there is a movement along the demand curve for real money. Other influences on the quantity of real money demanded shift the demand curve for real money. An increase in real income shifts the demand curve to the right; financial innovations that develop convenient near-money deposits shift the demand curve to the left. ◆

Now that we have studied the theory of the demand for real money, let's look at the facts about money holdings in the United States and see how they relate to real income and the interest rate.

The Demand for Money in the United States

We've just seen that the demand curve for real money, which shows how the quantity of real money demanded varies as the interest rate varies, shifts whenever there is a change in real GDP or when there is a financial innovation influencing money holding. Because these factors that shift the demand curve for real money frequently change, it is not easy to "see" the demand curve for real money in a real-world economy.

Instead of examining the demand for money, we'll look at something closely related to it, the *velocity of circulation.* The velocity of circulation is defined as

$$V = PY \div M.$$

Equivalently, it is

$$V = Y \div (M/P),$$

or real GDP divided by the real quantity of money. If the quantity of money demanded equals the quantity supplied, we can study the demand for money by studying the behavior of the velocity of circulation. When the quantity of money demanded falls relative to GDP, the velocity of circulation rises, and when the quantity of money demanded rises relative to GDP, the velocity of circulation falls.

The theory of the demand for money predicts that the higher the interest rate, the lower is the quantity of real money demanded and, therefore, the higher is the velocity of circulation. By examining the velocity of circulation and comparing it with movements in the interest rate, we can check whether the theory of the demand for real money provides a good description of money holding in the United States.

Figure 11.7 shows the relationship between the interest rate and the velocity of circulation of M1 and M2. The interest rate is measured on the left vertical scale of each part of the figure, and the velocity of circulation on the right scale. As you can see, there is a distinct relationship between the interest rate and the velocity of circulation of M1 and M2. The relationship is more pronounced in the case of the velocity of circulation of M2 in part (b). The velocity of circulation of M1 in part (a) is less closely related to the movements in the interest rate than is the velocity of circulation of M2. In fact, the main feature of the velocity of circulation of M1 is its steady increase from 1960 to 1980. Even when interest rates fell, as they did in 1971 and 1972 and again in 1975 and 1976, the velocity of circulation of M1 continued to increase. But the fall in interest rates after 1980 was associated with a decrease in the velocity of circulation of M1 through 1986. And as interest rates fluctuated after 1986, M1 velocity also fluctuated in the same direction.

The fact that the velocities of circulation of M1 and M2 fluctuate in sympathy with fluctuations in interest rates means that the U.S. economy has a demand curve for real money that is similar to that of the Polonius household. As interest rates rise, the economy slides up its demand curve for real money and the quantity of real money demanded decreases, *other things held constant.* But in the real world, other things are not constant. Steadily growing real income has brought an increase in the demand for real money—shifting the demand curve for real money to the right. Financial innovations have slowed that increase.

There is another aspect of the velocities of circulation of M1 and M2 that is interesting and should be noted. It concerns the range of variation in the velocities. The velocity of circulation of M2 is a remarkably stable number. Look at the range of values on the right scale of Fig. 11.7(b). As you can see, the lowest value of the M2 velocity is 1.5, the highest value is 1.7, and the average value is around 1.6. The fact that the M2 velocity varies by only a small amount means that the demand curve for M2 is very steep. Large changes in interest rates bring about only a small change in the quantity of M2 demanded and in its velocity of circulation. In contrast, the variation in the velocity of circulation of M1 is much larger. It ranges from less than 4 to 7. This fact means that the slope of the demand curve for M1 is much less steep than that for M2. An increase in the interest rate produces a much larger decrease in the quantity of M1 demanded and a much larger increase in the velocity of circulation of M1 than it does in the quantity of M2 demanded and the velocity of circulation of M2.

Why does an increase in the interest rate produce a larger decrease in the quantity of M1 demanded than in the quantity of M2 demanded? It is because currency and most of the checkable deposits that make up M1 do not earn interest, while the deposits that are added to M1 to make up M2 do earn interest. There is a tendency for interest rates to vary together. Thus when interest rates in general increase, the interest rate on savings deposits also increases. This increase in interest rates on the deposits in M2 means that people have less incentive to decrease their holdings of such deposits when interest rates in general increase. In contrast, M1, most of which earns no interest, becomes more expensive to hold—its opportunity cost increases—so the quantity of M1 held decreases.

We have now studied the factors that determine the demand for money and discovered that an important determinant of the quantity of real money

FIGURE 11.7

The Interest Rate and the Velocity of Circulation of M1 and M2

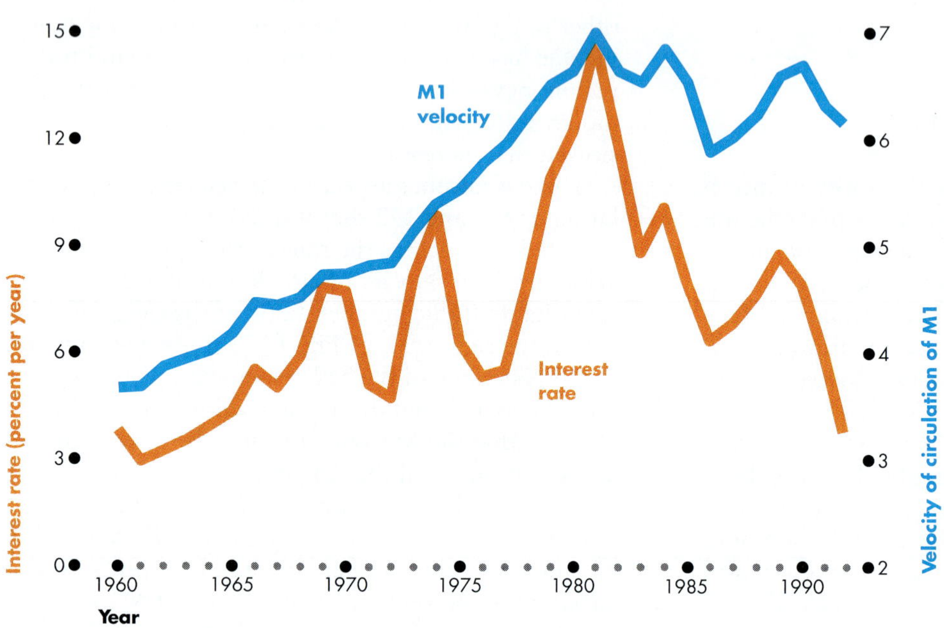

(a) M1 velocity and the interest rate

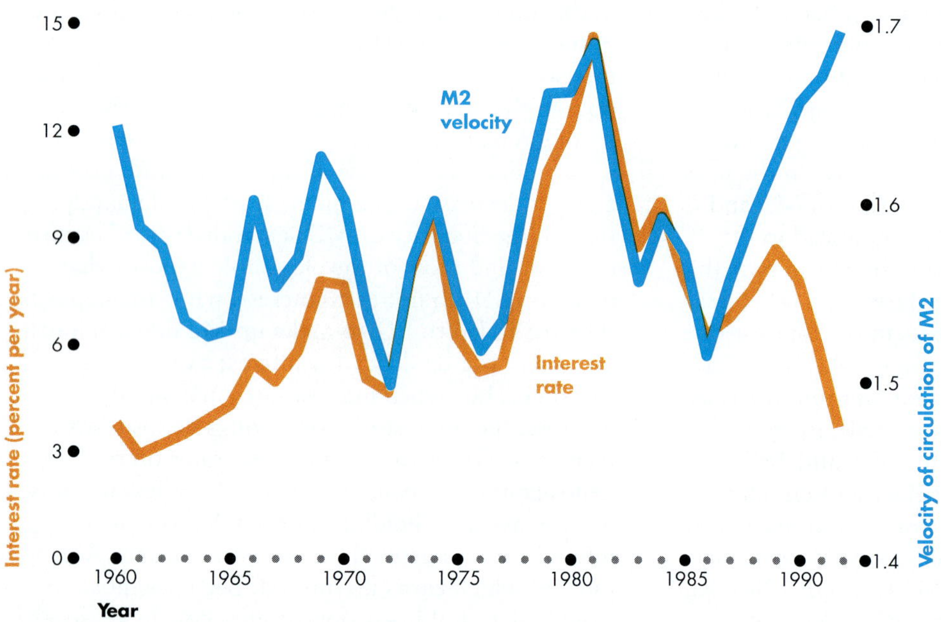

(b) M2 velocity and the interest rate

In part (a), the velocity of circulation of M1 is measured on the right scale and interest rates on the left scale. Both the velocity of circulation of M1 and interest rates increased until 1980 and declined through the 1980s. M1 velocity is much smoother than interest rates and does not have the pronounced cycles visible in interest rates in the 1970s. The two series follow similar trends. In part (b), the velocity of circulation of M2 is measured on the right scale and interest rates on the left scale. These two variables fluctuate remarkably closely together. But the range of variation in the velocity of circulation of M2 is much lower than the range of variation in interest rates (or in the range of variation of the velocity of M1, as seen in part a).

Source: Economic Report of the President, 1993.

demanded is the opportunity cost of holding it—the interest rate. We've also studied the way in which the Fed can influence the quantity of money supplied. We're now going to combine our models of the demand side and the supply side of the money market to see how the interest rate is determined.

Interest Rate Determination

An interest rate is the percentage yield on a financial security such as a *bond* or a *stock*. There is an important relationship between the interest rate and the price of a financial asset. Let's spend a moment studying that relationship before analyzing the forces that determine interest rates.

Interest Rates and Asset Prices

A bond is a promise to make a sequence of future payments. There are many different possible sequences, but the simplest one, for our purposes, is the case of a bond called a perpetuity. A **perpetuity** is a bond that promises to pay a certain fixed amount of money each year forever. The issuer of such a bond will never buy the bond back (redeem it); the bond will remain outstanding forever and will earn a fixed dollar payment each year. The fixed dollar payment is called the *coupon*. Since the coupon is a fixed dollar amount, the interest rate on the bond varies as the price of the bond varies. Table 11.5 illustrates this fact.

First, the table shows the formula for calculating the interest rate on a bond. The interest rate (r) is the coupon (c) divided by the price of the bond (p), all multiplied by 100 to convert it into a percentage. The table goes on to show some numerical examples for a bond whose coupon is $10 a year. If the bond costs $100 (row *b* of Table 11.5), the interest rate is 10 percent per year. That is, the holder of $100 worth of bonds receives $10 a year.

Rows *a* and *c* of Table 11.5 show two other cases. In row *a*, the price of the bond is $50. With the coupon at $10, this price produces an interest rate of 20 percent—$10 returned on a $50 bond

TABLE 11.5

The Interest Rate and the Price of a Bond

Formula for interest rate

r = interest rate, c = coupon, p = price of bond

$$r = \frac{c}{p} \times 100$$

Examples

	Price of bond	Coupon	Interest rate (percent per year)
a	$ 50	$10	20
b	100	10	10
c	200	10	5

holding is an interest rate of 20 percent. In row *c*, the bond costs $200 and the interest rate is 5 percent—which gives $10 return on a $200 bond holding.

There is an inverse relationship between the price of a bond and the interest rate earned on the bond. As a bond price rises, the bond's interest rate declines. Understanding this relationship will make it easier for you to understand the process whereby the interest rate is determined. Let's now turn to studying how interest rates are determined.

Money Market Equilibrium

The interest rate is determined at each point in time by equilibrium in the markets for financial assets. We can study that equilibrium in the market for money. We've already studied the determination of the supply of money and the demand for money. We've seen that money is a stock. When the stock of money supplied equals the stock of money demanded, the money market is in equilibrium. *Stock equilibrium* in the money market contrasts with *flow equilibrium* in the markets for goods and services. A **stock equilibrium** is a situation in which the available stock of an asset is willingly held. That is, regardless of what the available stock is, conditions are such that people actually want to hold precisely that stock and neither more nor less. A **flow equilibrium** is a situation in which the quantity of goods or services supplied per unit of time equals the quantity demanded per unit of time. The equilibrium expenditure that we studied in Chapter 9 is an example of a flow equilibrium. So is the equality of aggregate real GDP demanded and supplied.

The quantity of nominal money supplied is determined by the policy decisions of the Fed and by the lending actions of banks and other financial intermediaries. The real quantity of money supplied is equal to the nominal quantity supplied divided by the price level. At a given moment in time, there is a particular price level, and so the quantity of real money supplied is a fixed amount.

The demand curve for real money depends on the level of real GDP. And on any given day, the level of real GDP may be treated as fixed. But the interest rate is not fixed. The interest rate adjusts to achieve stock equilibrium in the money market. If the interest rate is too high, people will try to hold less money than is available. If the interest rate is too low, people will try to hold more than the stock that is available. When the interest rate is such that people want to hold exactly the amount of money that is available, then a stock equilibrium prevails.

Figure 11.8 illustrates an equilibrium in the money market. The quantity of real money supplied is $3 trillion. This amount is independent of the interest rate, so the money supply curve (*MS*) is vertical. The table sets out the quantity of real money demanded at three different interest rates when real GDP and the price level are constant. These quantities are graphed as the demand curve for real money (*MD*) in the figure.

The equilibrium interest rate is 5 percent, the rate at which the quantity demanded equals the quantity supplied. If the interest rate is above 5 percent, people will want to hold less money than is available. At an interest rate below 5 percent, people will want to hold more money than is available. At a 5 percent interest rate, the amount of money available is willingly held.

How does money market equilibrium come about? To answer this question, let's perform a thought experiment. First, imagine that the interest rate is temporarily at 7 percent. In this situation, people will want to hold only $2 trillion in real money even though $3 trillion exists. But since $3

FIGURE 11.8

Money Market Equilibrium

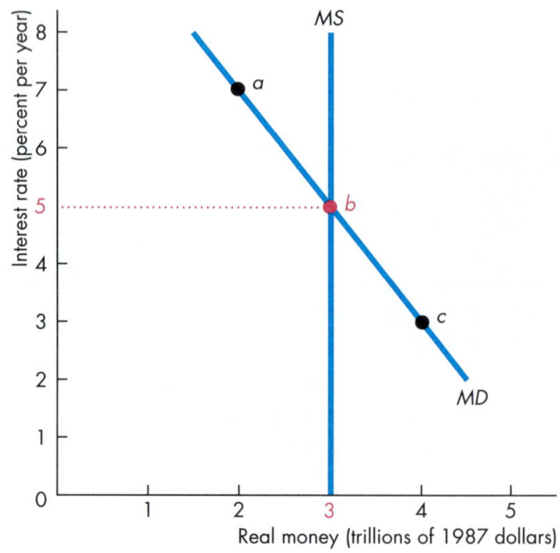

Real GDP is $4 trillion; price level is 1

	Interest rate (percent per year)	Quantity of real money demanded (trillions of 1987 dollars)	Quantity of real money supplied (trillions of 1987 dollars)
a	**7**	**2**	**3**
b	**5**	**3**	**3**
c	**3**	**4**	**3**

The demand for real money is given by the schedule in the table and the curve *MD*. The supply of real money, shown in the table and by the curve *MS* is $3 trillion. Adjustments in the interest rate achieve money market equilibrium. Here, equilibrium occurs in row *b* of the table (point *b* in the figure) at an interest rate of 5 percent. At interest rates above 5 percent, the quantity of real money demanded is less than the quantity supplied, so the interest rate falls. At interest rates below 5 percent, the quantity of real money demanded exceeds the quantity supplied, so the interest rate rises. Only at 5 percent is the quantity of real money in existence willingly held.

trillion exists, people must be holding it. That is, people are holding more money than they want to. In such a situation, they will try to get rid of some of their money. Each individual will try to reorganize his or her affairs in order to lower the amount of money held and take advantage of the 7 percent interest rate by buying more financial assets. But everybody will be trying to buy financial assets, and nobody will be trying to sell them at a 7 percent interest rate. There is an excess demand for financial assets such as bonds. When there is an excess demand for anything, its price rises. So with an excess demand for financial assets, the prices of financial assets will rise. We saw earlier that there is an inverse relationship between the price of a financial asset and its interest rate. As the price of a financial asset rises, its interest rate falls.

As long as anyone is holding money in excess of the quantity demanded, that person will try to lower his or her money holdings by buying additional financial assets. Financial asset prices will continue to rise, and interest rates will continue to fall. Only when the interest rate has moved down to 5 percent will the amount of money in existence be held willingly. That is, people's attempts to get rid of unwanted excess money do not result in reducing the amount of money held in aggregate. Instead, those efforts result in a change in the interest rate that makes the amount of money available willingly held.

The thought experiment that we have just conducted can be performed in reverse by supposing that the interest rate is 3 percent. In this situation, people want to hold $4 trillion even though only $3 trillion is available. To acquire more money, people will sell financial assets. There will be an excess supply of financial assets, so their prices will fall. As the prices of financial assets fall, the yield on them—the interest rate—rises. People will continue to sell financial assets and try to acquire money until the interest rate has risen to 5 percent, at which point the amount of money available is the amount that they want to hold.

Changing the Interest Rate

Imagine that the economy is slowing down and the Fed wants to encourage additional aggregate demand and spending. To do so, it wants to lower interest rates and encourage more borrowing and more expenditure on goods and services. What does the Fed do? How does it fiddle with the knobs to achieve lower interest rates?

The Fed undertakes an open market operation, buying government securities from banks, households, and firms. As a consequence, the monetary base increases, and banks start making additional loans. The money supply increases.

Suppose that the Fed undertakes open market operations on a sufficiently large scale to increase the money supply from $3 trillion to $4 trillion. As a consequence, the supply curve of real money shifts to the right, as shown in Fig. 11.9(a), from MS_0 to MS_1, and the thought experiment that we conducted earlier now becomes a real-world event. The interest rate falls as people use some of their new money to buy financial assets. When the interest rate has fallen to 3 percent, people are willing to hold the higher $4 trillion stock of real money that the Fed and the banking system have created.

Conversely, suppose that the economy is overheating and the Fed fears inflation. The Fed decides to take action to slow down spending and cuts the money supply. In this case, the Fed undertakes an open market sale of securities. As it does so, it mops up bank reserves and induces the banks to cut down the scale of their lending. The banks make a smaller quantity of new loans each day until the stock of loans outstanding has fallen to a level consistent with the new lower level of reserves. Suppose that the Fed undertakes an open market sale of securities on a scale big enough to cut the real money supply to $2 trillion. Now the supply of real money curve shifts to the left, as shown in Fig. 11.9(b), from MS_0 to MS_2. With less money available, people attempt to acquire additional money by selling interest-earning assets. As they do so, asset prices fall and interest rates rise. Equilibrium occurs when the interest rate has risen to 7 percent, at which point the new lower real money stock of $2 trillion is willingly held.

The Fed in Action

All this sounds nice in theory, but does it really happen? Indeed, it does happen, sometimes with dramatic effect. Let's look at two episodes in the life of the Fed, one from the turbulent years of the early 1980s and the other from the period since the stock market crash of 1987.

FIGURE 11.9

The Fed Changes Interest Rates

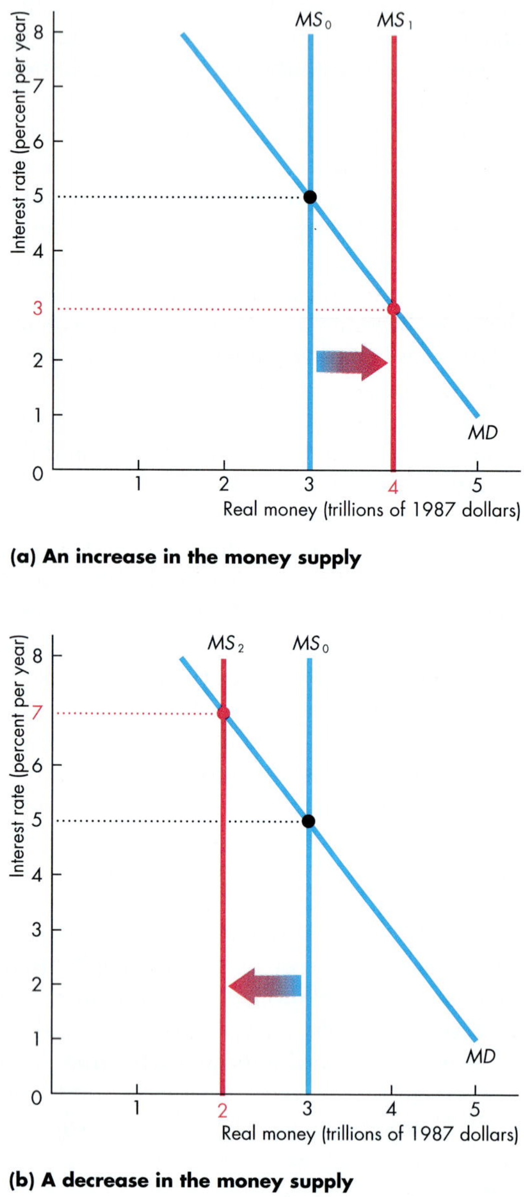

In part (a), the Fed conducts an open market purchase of securities, increasing the money supply to $4 trillion. The real money supply shifts to the right. The new equilibrium interest rate is 3 percent. In part (b), the Fed conducts an open market sale of securities, decreasing the real money supply to $2 trillion. The money supply curve shifts to the left, and the interest rate rises to 7 percent. By changing the money supply, at a given real GDP and price level, the Fed can adjust interest rates daily or weekly.

Paul Volcker's Fed At the start of Paul Volcker's term of office as chairman of the Fed, which began in August 1979, the United States was locked in the grip of double-digit inflation. Volcker ended that inflation. He did so by forcing interest rates sharply upward from 1979 through 1981. This increase in interest rates resulted from the Fed using open market operations and increases in the discount rate to keep the banks short of reserves, which in turn held back the growth in the supply of loans and of money relative to the growth in their demand.

As we saw in Fig. 11.9(b), to increase interest rates, the Fed has to cut the real money supply. In practice, because the economy is growing and because prices are rising, a *slowdown* in nominal money supply growth is enough to increase interest rates. It is not necessary to actually *cut* the nominal money supply.

When Volcker became chairman of the Fed, the money supply was growing at more than 8 percent a year. Volcker slowed down that money supply growth to 6.5 percent in 1981. As a result, interest rates increased. The treasury bill rate—the rate at which the government borrows—increased from 10 percent to 14 percent. The rate at which big corporations borrow increased from 9 percent to 14 percent. Mortgage rates—the rates at which home buyers borrow—increased from 11 percent to 15 percent. The economy went into recession. The money supply growth slowdown and interest rate hike cut back the growth rate of aggregate demand. Real GDP fell, and the inflation rate slowed down.

Alan Greenspan's Fed Alan Greenspan became chairman of the Fed in August 1987. In the two preceding years the money supply had grown at a rapid pace, interest rates had tumbled, and the stock market had boomed. Then, suddenly and with no warning, stock prices fell, bringing fears of economic calamity and recession. This was Greenspan's first test as Fed chairman.

The Fed's immediate reaction to the new situation was to emphasize the flexibility and sensitivity of the financial system and to make reserves plentiful to avoid any fear of a banking crisis. But as the months passed, it became increasingly clear that the economy was not heading for any kind of a recession. Unemployment continued to fall, income growth continued to be strong, and the fears that emerged were of inflation, not recession.

Seeking to avoid a serious upturn in inflation, the Fed slowed money growth and, just as Paul Volcker had done eight years earlier, forced interest rates sharply upward. Open market operations were targeted toward creating a shortage of reserves in the banking system to slow down the growth rate of the money supply. As a consequence, during the year from May 1988 to May 1989 the M1 measure of the money supply was virtually constant and the M2 measure grew by only 2.4 percent, both down from growth rates of around 5 percent a year earlier and down from around 10 percent a year before the stock market crash. The slowdown in money supply growth had the effect implied by the model that you have been studying in this chapter. Interest rates increased throughout 1988. The interest rate on U.S. government three-month treasury bills increased from less than 6 percent a year at the start of 1988 to almost 9 percent a year by early 1989.

As 1989 advanced, concern about inflation remained, but renewed fears of recession returned as an increasing number of signs of a slowing economy emerged. Interest rates were gradually lowered, and the money supply was permitted to grow more quickly. By 1990, recession had become a reality. At first, the Fed's reaction was to adopt a neutral position, waiting for signs of recovery from an increase in investment and consumption expenditure. But as the months passed and recovery seemed elusive, the Fed eventually began to act vigorously to stimulate spending with a series of interest rate cuts. During 1991, interest rates declined by 3 percentage points as the Fed tried to encourage an increase in borrowing and spending.

Profiting by Predicting the Fed

Every day, the Fed influences interest rates by its open market operations. By buying securities and increasing the money supply, the Fed can lower interest rates; by selling securities and lowering the money supply, the Fed can increase interest rates. Sometimes such actions are taken to offset other influences and keep interest rates steady. At other times the Fed moves interest rates up or down. The higher the interest rate, the lower is the price of a bond; the lower the interest rate, the higher is the price of a bond. Thus predicting interest rates is the same as predicting bond prices. Predicting that interest rates are going to fall is the same as predicting that bond prices are going to rise—a good time to buy bonds. Predicting that interest rates are going to rise is the same as predicting that bond prices are going to fall—a good time to sell bonds.

Because the Fed is the major player whose actions influence interest rates and bond prices, predicting the Fed is profitable and a good deal of effort goes into that activity. (An example is the news story in Reading Between the Lines on pp. 302–303.) But people who anticipate that the Fed is about to increase the money supply buy bonds right away, pushing their prices upward and pushing interest rates downward *before* the Fed acts. Similarly, people who anticipate that the Fed is about to decrease the money supply sell bonds right away, pushing their prices downward and pushing interest rates upward before the Fed acts. In other words, bond prices and interest rates change as soon as the Fed's actions are foreseen. By the time the Fed actually takes its actions, if those actions are correctly foreseen, they have no effect. The effects occur in anticipation of the Fed's actions. Only changes in the money supply that are not foreseen change the interest rate at the time that those changes occur.

REVIEW

At any given moment, the interest rate is determined by the demand for and the supply of money. The interest rate makes the quantity of money demanded equal to the quantity of money supplied. Changes in the interest rate occur as a result of changes in the money supply. When the money supply change is unanticipated, interest rates change at the same time as the change in the money supply. When the money supply change is anticipated, interest rates might change ahead of the change in the money supply. ◆

◆ ◆ ◆ ◆ In this chapter, we've studied the determination of interest rates and discovered how the Fed can "fiddle with the knobs" to influence interest rates by its open market operations that change the quantity of money. In Chapters 8 and 9 we discovered that the interest rate has an important influence on investment, aggregate expenditure, and real GDP. In the next chapter, we're going to bring these two aspects of the macroeconomy together and study the wider effects of the Fed's actions—effects on investment and aggregate demand.

The Fed in Action

The New York Times, June 23, 1993

A Nudging Up of Rates Is Considered by the Fed

BY LOUIS UCHITELLE

After rising unexpectedly in the beginning of the year, inflation seemed to have abated in May, but the Federal Reserve remains haunted by its specter.

Another inflationary spike this year strikes most economists as unlikely in an economy that remains subdued. But the Fed's policy makers say they are toying with the notion of nudging up interest rates anyway to make doubly sure that inflation does not return.

"The logic is impeccable that inflation should not be a problem," said David W. Mullins Jr., the Federal Reserve's vice chairman. "But it has risen in recent months anyway, when it should not have. If inflation were to become re-established in the minds of the markets, with no timely response from the Fed, that could be damaging to the economy."

For the Fed, a "timely response" means an increase in rates before the end of the summer—a possibility that Mr. Mullins and other Fed policy makers are for the first time discussing openly, in effect calling the strategy a pre-emptive strike against resurgent inflation. At least one high Administration official, declining to be named, said the Administration was prepared to accept a mild rate increase.

"At this point, a one-quarter of a percentage point rise in interest rates would have more of a psychological impact than an economic one," the Treasury Department official said.

The surge in inflation early this year led many economists to speculate that the Fed would respond by raising interest rates. At a policy meeting in May, Fed officials reportedly passed a resolution that in effect expressed a greater willingness to raise rates than to lower them, but the minutes from the meeting will not be made public until next month. Only now are Fed officials beginning to speak openly of raising rates soon—as if preparing the American public for the change after nearly four years of pushing rates down. . . .

The Essence of the Story

- Inflation was not expected to be a problem in 1993.
- But if inflation did increase, the Fed was ready to act quickly with an increase in interest rates.
- The Fed made this decision at a policy meeting held in May, and some Fed officials went public with their views in June.
- A small rise in interest rates was not expected to have a damaging effect on the economy.

Background and Analysis

The policy meeting referred to in the news story is the monthly meeting of the Federal Open Market Committee (FOMC).

During 1992 and the first half of 1993, the annual inflation rate—the change in the Consumer Price Index (CPI) over the preceding 12 months—was almost constant at 3 percent (the green line in Fig. 1).

During the same period, the quarterly inflation rate—the change in the CPI over the preceding 3 months—fluctuated and was rising during the first quarter of 1993 (the purple line in Fig. 1).

Short-term interest rates fell during 1992 and the first half of 1993. By the end of 1992, *real* short-term interest rates were negative—the interest rate was less than the inflation rate. Interest rates fell because, as shown in Fig. 2, the money supply increased (the shift from MS_{92} to MS_{93}) by more than the demand for money increased (the shift from MD_{92} to MD_{93}).

To increase interest rates, the Fed could conduct an open market sale of securities that would decrease the money supply from MS_0 to MS_1 in Fig. 3. With a decrease in the money supply, interest rates would increase.

A small increase in interest rates might signal the Fed's readiness to act against inflation without causing a fall in investment and a slowdown in the growth of aggregate demand.

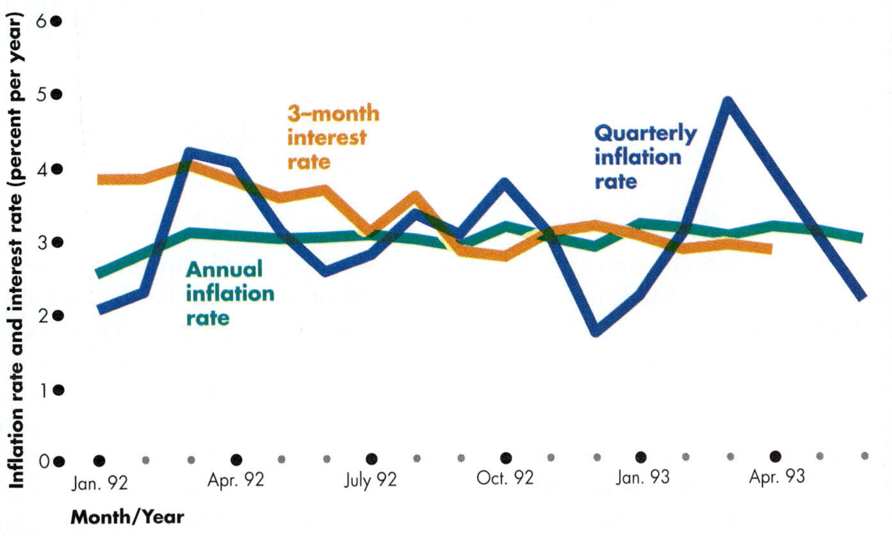

Figure 1

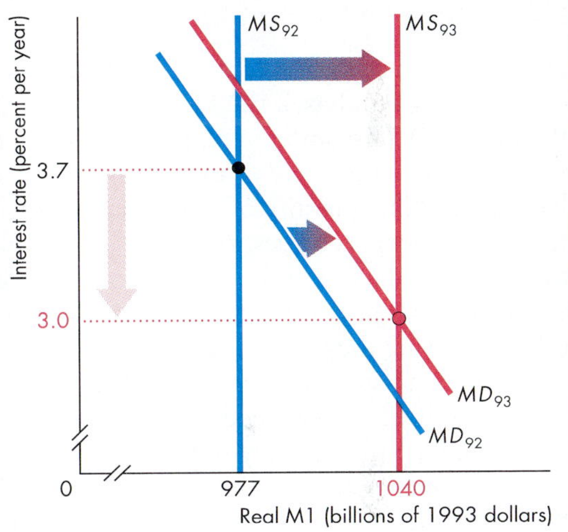

Figure 2

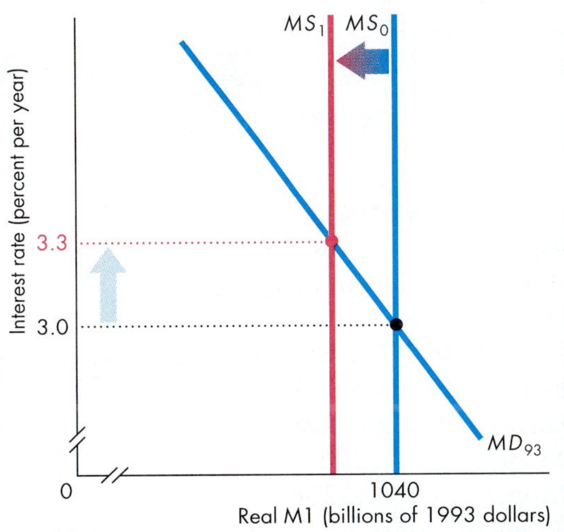

Figure 3

SUMMARY

The Federal Reserve System

The Federal Reserve System is the central bank of the United States. The Fed consists of the Board of Governors and 12 regional Federal Reserve banks. The main policy-making committee is the Federal Open Market Committee. The Fed influences the economy by setting the required reserve ratio for banks and other deposit-taking institutions, by setting the discount rate—the interest rate at which it is willing to lend reserves to the banking system—and by open market operations. (pp. 280–284)

Controlling the Money Supply

By buying government securities in the market (an open market purchase), the Fed is able to increase the monetary base and the reserves available to banks. As a result, there is an expansion of bank lending and the quantity of money increases. By selling government securities, the Fed is able to decrease the monetary base and the reserves of banks and other financial institutions, thereby curtailing loans and decreasing the quantity of money. The overall effect of a change in the monetary base on the money supply is determined by the money multiplier. The value of the money multiplier depends on the ratio of currency to deposits held by households and firms and the ratio of reserves to deposits held by banks and other financial institutions. (pp. 284–290)

The Demand for Money

The quantity of money demanded is the amount of currency, checkable deposits, and other deposits that people hold on the average. The quantity of nominal money demanded is proportional to the price level, and the quantity of real money demanded depends on the interest rate and real GDP. A higher interest rate induces a smaller quantity of real money demanded—a movement along the demand curve for real money. A higher level of real GDP induces a larger demand for real money—a shift in the demand curve for real money. Technological changes in the financial sector also change the demand for money and shift the demand curve for real money. (pp. 290–297)

Interest Rate Determination

Changes in interest rates achieve equilibrium in the markets for money and financial assets. There is an inverse relationship between the interest rate and the price of a financial asset. The higher the interest rate, the lower is the price of a financial asset. Money market equilibrium achieves an interest rate that makes the quantity of real money available willingly held. If the quantity of real money is increased by the actions of the Fed, the interest rate falls and the prices of financial assets rise. (pp. 297–301)

KEY ELEMENTS

Key Terms

Key Figures and Tables

REVIEW QUESTIONS

1 What are the three main elements in the structure of the Federal Reserve System?

2 What are the three policy tools of the Fed? Which of these is the Fed's main tool?

3 If the Fed wants to cut the quantity of money, does it buy or sell U.S. government securities in the open market?

4 Describe the events that take place when banks have excess reserves.

5 Explain the motives for holding money.

6 What is the money multiplier?

7 What determines the size of the money multiplier, and why has its value changed in the United States in recent years?

8 Distinguish between nominal money and real money.

9 What do we mean by the demand for money?

10 What determines the demand for real money?

11 What is the opportunity cost of holding money?

12 What happens to the interest rate on a bond if the price of the bond increases?

13 How does equilibrium come about in the money market?

14 What happens to the interest rate if real GDP and price level are constant and the money supply increases?

15 Explain why it pays people to try to predict the Fed's actions.

PROBLEMS

1 You are given the following information about the economy of Nocoin: The banks have deposits of $300 billion. Their reserves are $15 billion, two thirds of which is in deposits with the central bank. There is $30 billion in currency outside the banks. There are no coins in Nocoin!

a Calculate the monetary base.

b Calculate the currency drain.

c Calculate the money supply.

d Calculate the money multiplier.

2 Suppose that the Bank of Nocoin, the central bank, undertakes a $0.5 million open market purchase of securities. What happens to the money supply? Explain why the change in the money supply is not equal to the change in the monetary base.

3 You are given the following information about the economy of Miniland: For each $1 increase in real GDP, the demand for real money increases by one quarter of a dollar, other things being equal. Also, if the interest rate increases by 1 percentage point (for example, from 4 percent to 5 percent), the quantity of real money demanded falls by $50. If real GDP is $4,000 and the price level is 1:

a At what interest rate is no money held?

b How much real money is held at an interest rate of 10 percent?

c Draw a graph of the demand for real money.

4 Given the demand for real money in Miniland, if the price level is 1, real GDP is $4,000, and the real money supply is $750, what is the equilibrium in the money market?

5 Suppose that the Bank of Miniland, the central bank, wants to lower the interest rate by 1 percentage point. By how much would it have to change the real money supply to achieve that objective?

CHAPTER 12

FISCAL AND MONETARY INFLUENCES ON AGGREGATE DEMAND

After studying this chapter, you will be able to:

- Explain how fiscal policy—a change in government purchases or taxes—influences interest rates and aggregate demand
- Explain how monetary policy—a change in the money supply—influences interest rates and aggregate demand
- Explain what determines the relative effectiveness of fiscal and monetary policy on aggregate demand
- Describe the Keynesian-monetarist controversy about the influence of fiscal and monetary policy on aggregate demand
- Explain how the mix of fiscal and monetary policy influences the composition of aggregate expenditure
- Explain how fiscal and monetary policy influence real GDP and the price level in both the short run and the long run

Congress, the Fed, and the White House

EACH YEAR, CONGRESS AND THE STATE LEGISLATURES approve budgets that determine the level of government purchases of goods and services, the transfer payments associated with social programs, and the taxes that pay for this spending. By 1991, these spending and tax levels were close to $2 trillion—almost two fifths of GDP. Government purchases, transfer payments, and taxes are the levers of fiscal policy. How do these levers influence the economy? In particular, how do they affect aggregate demand? How do they affect other variables that influence aggregate demand, such as interest rates and the exchange rate? ◆◆ Five city blocks from the White House is the home of the Board of Governors of the Federal Reserve System. Here the Fed pulls the nation's monetary policy levers. Sometimes, such as in 1989, the Fed uses those levers to slow down the economy—slowing money growth, increasing interest rates, and slowing the growth of aggregate demand. At other times, such as in 1991, the Fed uses its monetary policy levers to speed up the economy—speeding up money growth, lowering interest rates, and increasing aggregate demand. We've seen how the Fed's policy levers influence interest rates. But how do the effects of the Fed's actions ripple through from interest rates to the rest of the economy? How do they affect aggregate demand? ◆◆ In the Executive Office Building—part of the White House complex—is the home of the President's Council of Economic Advisors. This council, established by the Employment Act of 1946, monitors both the fiscal policy actions of the Congress and the monetary policy actions of the Fed. It also attempts to keep the president and Cabinet informed about the actions and plans of each branch of macroeconomic policy making and of their likely effects. Both fiscal actions taken by the Congress and monetary actions taken by the Fed can increase or decrease aggregate demand. Are these methods of changing aggregate demand equivalent to each other? Does it matter whether a recession is avoided by having the Fed loosen up its monetary policy or by getting Congress to implement a tax cut? Do changes in taxes and government purchases and changes in the money supply always reinforce each other, or do they sometimes offset each other? For example, when the Fed under Alan Greenspan slowed down money growth and increased interest rates in 1989 to keep the lid on inflation in 1990, could Congress have offset the Fed's actions by taking actions of its own—for example, cutting taxes or increasing government purchases? Or, alternatively, if Congress cuts government purchases, creating fears of recession, could the Fed increase the money supply and keep GDP up, thereby avoiding recession?

◆ ◆ ◆ ◆ We are going to answer these important questions in this chapter. You already know that the effects of fiscal and monetary policy are determined by the interaction of aggregate demand and aggregate supply. And you already know quite a lot about these two concepts. But this chapter gives you an even deeper understanding of aggregate demand and the way it is affected by the monetary policy actions of the Fed and the fiscal policy actions of the federal government.

Money, Interest, and Aggregate Demand

Our goal is to understand how fiscal and monetary policy influence real GDP and the price level (as well as unemployment and inflation). Real GDP and the price level are determined by the interaction of aggregate demand and aggregate supply, as described in Chapter 7. But the main effects of fiscal and monetary policy are on aggregate *demand*. Thus we focus our attention initially on these effects.

To study the effects of fiscal and monetary policy on aggregate demand, we use the aggregate expenditure model of Chapters 8 and 9. This model determines equilibrium expenditure *at a given price level*. Such an equilibrium corresponds to a point on the aggregate demand curve (see Fig. 9.8). When equilibrium expenditure changes, the aggregate demand curve shifts and by the amount of the change in equilibrium expenditure.

The aggregate expenditure model freezes the price level and asks questions about the directions and magnitudes of the shifts of the aggregate demand curve at a given price level. But the price level is not actually fixed. It is determined by aggregate demand and aggregate supply.

We begin our study of fiscal and monetary policy by discovering an important interaction among aggregate expenditure decisions, the interest rate, and the supply of money.

Spending Decisions, Interest, and Money

We discovered in Chapter 9 (pp. 223–224) that equilibrium expenditure depends on the level of autonomous expenditure. We also discovered that one of the components of autonomous expenditure—investment—varies with the interest rate. The higher the interest rate, other things held constant, the lower is investment and hence the lower is autonomous expenditure and the lower is equilibrium expenditure. Therefore equilibrium expenditure and real GDP depend on the interest rate.

In Chapter 11 (pp. 297–299), we saw how the interest rate is determined by equilibrium in the money market. We also saw that the demand for money depends on both real GDP and the interest rate. The higher the level of real GDP, other things held constant, the greater is the demand for money and the higher is the interest rate. Therefore the interest rate depends on real GDP.

We're now going to see how *both* real GDP and the interest rate are determined simultaneously. We'll then go on to see how the Fed's monetary policy and the government's fiscal policy affect both real GDP and the interest rate at a given price level.

Equilibrium Expenditure and the Interest Rate

Let's see how we can link together the money market, in which the interest rate is determined, and the market for goods and services, in which equilibrium expenditure is determined. Figure 12.1 illustrates the

FIGURE 12.1
Equilibrium Interest Rate and Real GDP

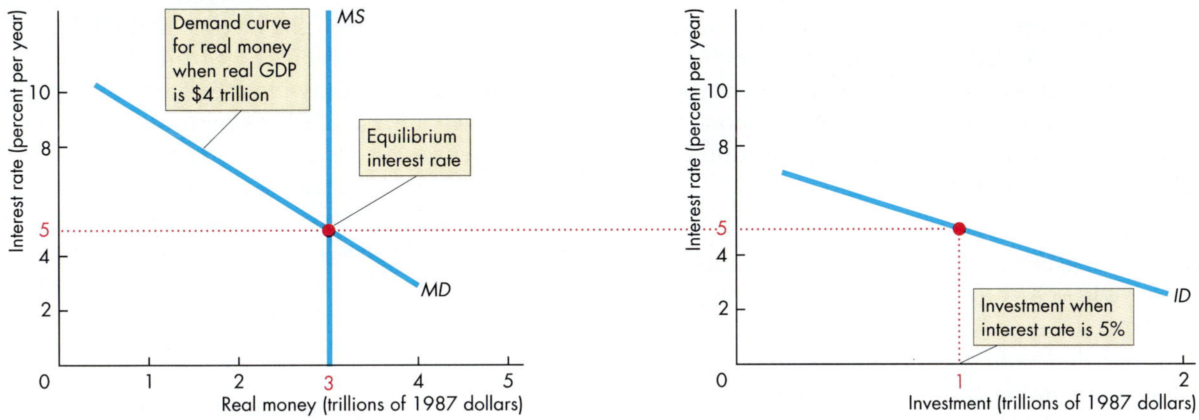

(a) Money and the interest rate

(b) Investment and the interest rate

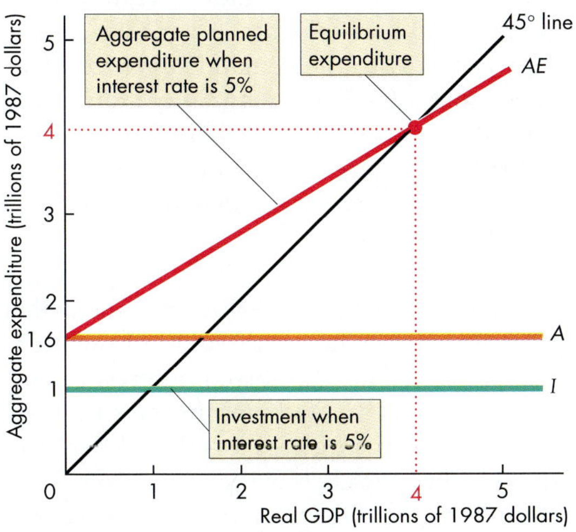

(c) Expenditure and real GDP

Equilibrium in the money market (part a) determines the interest rate. The money supply curve is *MS*, and the demand curve for real money is *MD*. The position of the *MD* curve is determined by real GDP and the curve shown is for a real GDP of $4 trillion. The investment demand curve (*ID*) in part (b) determines investment at the equilibrium interest rate determined in the money market. Investment is part of autonomous expenditure, and its level determines the position of the aggregate expenditure curve (*AE*) shown in part (c). Equilibrium expenditure and real GDP are determined at the point at which the aggregate expenditure curve intersects the 45° line. In equilibrium, real GDP and the interest rate are such that the quantity of real money demanded equals the quantity of real money supplied and aggregate planned expenditure equals real GDP.

determination of equilibrium expenditure and the interest rate. The figure has three parts: part (a) illustrates the money market; part (b) shows investment demand; and part (c) shows aggregate planned expenditure and the determination of equilibrium expenditure. Let's begin in part (a).

The Money Market The curve labeled *MD* is the demand for real money. The position of this curve depends on the level of real GDP. For a given level of real GDP, there is a given demand curve for real money. Suppose that the demand curve shown in the figure describes the demand for real money when real GDP is $4 trillion. If real GDP is higher than $4 trillion, the demand curve for real money is to the right of the one shown; if real GDP is below $4 trillion, the demand curve for real money is to the left of the one shown.

The curve labeled *MS* is the supply curve of real money. Its position is determined by the monetary policy actions of the Fed, the behavior of the banking system, and the price level. At a given point in time, all these influences determine a quantity of money supplied that is independent of the interest rate. Hence the supply curve for real money is vertical.

The interest rate adjusts to achieve equilibrium in the money market—equality between the quantity of real money demanded and the quantity supplied. This equilibrium occurs at the point of intersection of the demand and supply curves of real money. In the economy illustrated in Fig. 12.1, the equilibrium interest rate is 5 percent.

Investment and Interest Rate Next, let's look at part (b), where investment is determined. The investment demand curve is *ID*. The position of the investment demand curve is determined by profit expectations, and as those expectations change, the investment demand curve shifts. For given expectations, there is a given investment demand curve. This curve tells us the level of planned investment at each level of the interest rate. We already know the interest rate from equilibrium in the money market. When the investment demand curve is *ID* and the interest rate is 5 percent, the level of planned investment is $1 trillion.

Equilibrium Expenditure Part (c) shows the determination of equilibrium expenditure. This diagram is similar to the one that you studied in Chapter 8 (Fig. 8.11a). The aggregate expenditure curve (*AE*) tells us aggregate planned expenditure at each level of real GDP. Aggregate planned expenditure is made up of autonomous expenditure and induced expenditure. Investment is part of autonomous expenditure. In this example, investment is $1 trillion and the other components of autonomous expenditure are $0.6 trillion, so autonomous expenditure is $1.6 trillion. These amounts of investment *I* and autonomous expenditure *A* are shown by the horizontal lines in part (c). Induced expenditure is the induced part of consumption expenditure minus imports. In this example, the slope of the *AE* curve is 0.6; therefore induced expenditure equals 0.6 multiplied by real GDP.

Equilibrium expenditure is determined at the point of intersection of the *AE* curve and the 45° line. Equilibrium expenditure occurs when aggregate planned expenditure and real GDP are $4 trillion each. That is, the level of aggregate demand is $4 trillion.

The Money Market Again Recall that the demand curve *MD*, in part (a), is the demand curve for real money when real GDP is $4 trillion. We've just determined in part (c) that when aggregate expenditure is at its equilibrium level, real GDP is $4 trillion. What happens if the level of real GDP that we discover in part (c) is different from the value that we assumed when drawing the demand curve for real money in part (a)? Let's perform a thought experiment to answer this question.

Suppose, when drawing the demand curve for real money, we assume that real GDP is $3 trillion. In this case, the demand curve for real money is to the left of the *MD* curve in part (a). The equilibrium interest rate is lower than 5 percent. With an interest rate below 5 percent, investment is not $1 trillion as determined in part (b), but a larger amount. If investment is larger than $1 trillion, autonomous expenditure is larger and the *AE* curve lies above the one shown in part (c). If the aggregate expenditure curve is above the *AE* curve shown, equilibrium expenditure and real GDP are larger than $4 trillion. Thus if we start with the demand curve for real money for a real GDP less than $4 trillion, equilibrium expenditure occurs at a real GDP that is greater than $4 trillion. There is an inconsistency. The real GDP assumed in drawing the demand curve for real money is too low.

Next, let's reverse the experiment. Assume a level of real GDP of $5 trillion. In this case, the demand curve for real money lies to the right of the *MD* curve in part (a). The equilibrium interest rate is higher than 5 percent. With an interest rate higher than 5 percent, investment is less than $1 trillion and the *AE* curve lies below the one shown in part (c). In this case, equilibrium expenditure occurs at a real GDP that is less than $4 trillion. Again, there is an inconsistency, but now the real GDP assumed in drawing the demand curve for real money is too high.

We've just seen that for a given money supply, money market equilibrium determines an interest rate that varies with real GDP. The higher the level of real GDP, the higher is the equilibrium interest rate. But the interest rate determines investment, which in turn determines equilibrium expenditure. The higher the interest rate, the lower is investment and therefore the lower is equilibrium real GDP.

There is one particular level of both the interest rate and real GDP that simultaneously gives money market equilibrium and equilibrium expenditure. In the example we are studying, that interest rate is 5 percent and real GDP is \$4 trillion. Only if we use a real GDP of \$4 trillion to determine the position of the demand curve for real money do we get a consistent story in the three parts of this figure. If the demand curve for real money is based on a real GDP of \$4 trillion, the interest rate determined (5 percent) delivers investment of \$1 trillion, which, in turn, generates equilibrium expenditure at the same level of real GDP that determines the position of the demand curve for real money.

Let's now turn to an examination of the effects of fiscal policy on aggregate demand.

FIGURE 12.2

First Round Effects of an Expansionary Fiscal Policy

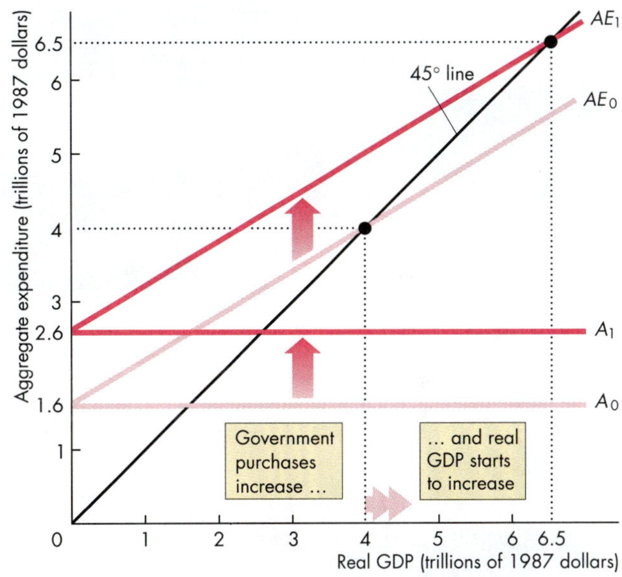

Initially, autonomous expenditure is A_0, the aggregate expenditure curve is AE_0, and real GDP is \$4 trillion. An increase in government purchases of goods and services increases autonomous expenditure to A_1. The aggregate expenditure curve shifts upward to AE_1, and equilibrium expenditure increases to \$6.5 trillion. A multiplier process is set off in which real GDP starts to increase. These are the first round effects of an expansionary fiscal policy.

Fiscal Policy and Aggregate Demand

The government is concerned that the economy is slowing down and that a recession looks likely. To head off the recession, the government decides to stimulate aggregate demand by using fiscal policy, increasing its purchases of goods and services by \$1 trillion. A fiscal policy that increases aggregate demand is called an *expansionary fiscal policy.*

The effects of the government's actions are similar to those of throwing a pebble into a pond. There's an initial splash followed by a series of ever smaller ripples. The initial splash is the "first round effect" of the fiscal policy action. The ripples are the "second round effects." Let's start by looking at the first round effects of the government's fiscal policy action.

First Round Effects of Fiscal Policy

The economy starts out in the situation shown in Fig. 12.1. The interest rate is 5 percent, investment is \$1 trillion, and real GDP is \$4 trillion. In this situation, the government increases its purchases of goods and services by \$1 trillion.

The first round effects of this action are shown in Fig. 12.2. The increase in government purchases increases autonomous expenditure. This increase is shown in Fig. 12.2 by the shift of the line A_0 to A_1. The increase in autonomous expenditure increases aggregate planned expenditure and shifts the *AE* curve upward from AE_0 to AE_1. Equilibrium expenditure increases to \$6.5 trillion. This increase in aggregate planned expenditure and equilibrium expenditure sets off a multiplier process that starts real GDP increasing. We described this process in Chapter 9, pp. 223–226. These are the first round effects of an expansionary fiscal policy, and they are summarized in Fig. 12.3(a).

Second Round Effects of Fiscal Policy

At the end of the first round that we've just studied, real GDP is rising. The increase in real GDP increases the demand for money. The increase in the

FIGURE 12.3

How the Economy Adjusts to an Expansionary Fiscal Policy

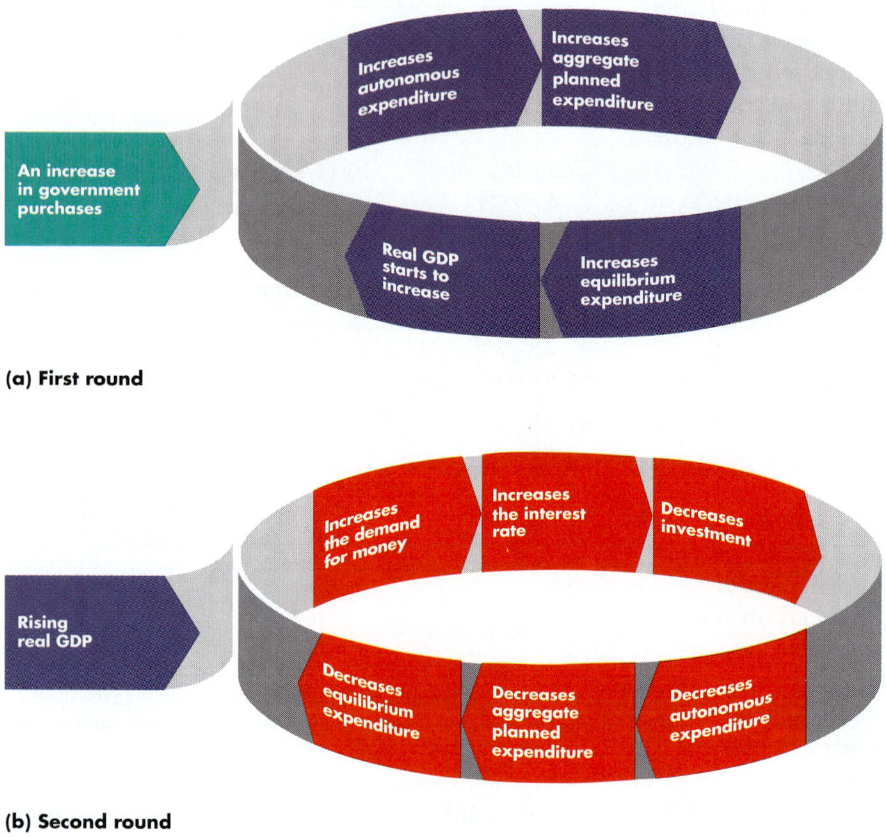

In the first round (part a), an increase in government purchases increases autonomous expenditure. Aggregate planned expenditure and equilibrium expenditure increase. A multiplier process is set off that starts real GDP increasing. In the second round (part b), the rising real GDP increases the demand for money and interest rates rise. The rising interest rate decreases investment, decreases autonomous expenditure, and decreases aggregate planned expenditure and equilibrium expenditure. The second round effects work in the opposite direction to the first round effects but are smaller in magnitude. The outcome of an increase in government purchases is an increase in real GDP, a rise in the interest rate, and a decrease in investment.

demand for money raises the interest rate. The rise in the interest rate decreases investment, and autonomous expenditure decreases. The decrease in autonomous expenditure decreases aggregate planned expenditure, which in turn decreases equilibrium expenditure. These second round effects are summarized in Fig. 12.3(b). These effects go in the opposite direction to the first round effects, but they are smaller. They diminish the magnitude of the first round effects but do not change the direction of the outcome of the fiscal policy action. That outcome is an increase in real GDP, an increase in the interest rate, and a decrease in investment.

When a new equilibrium is arrived at, the new higher real GDP and higher interest rate give simultaneous money market equilibrium and equilibrium expenditure, similar to the situation in Fig. 12.1. This equilibrium is shown in Fig. 12.4. The demand for real money has increased to MD_1, and the interest rate has risen to 6 percent in part (a). The higher interest rate has decreased investment in part (b). The increase in autonomous expenditure is \$0.6 trillion, which is equal to the initial increase in government purchases of \$1 trillion minus the decrease in investment of \$0.4 trillion, shown in part (c). Finally, aggregate planned expenditure has increased to AE_2, and the new equilibrium expenditure is at a real GDP of \$5.5 trillion (also shown in part c).

FIGURE 12.4

The Effects of a Change in Government Purchases

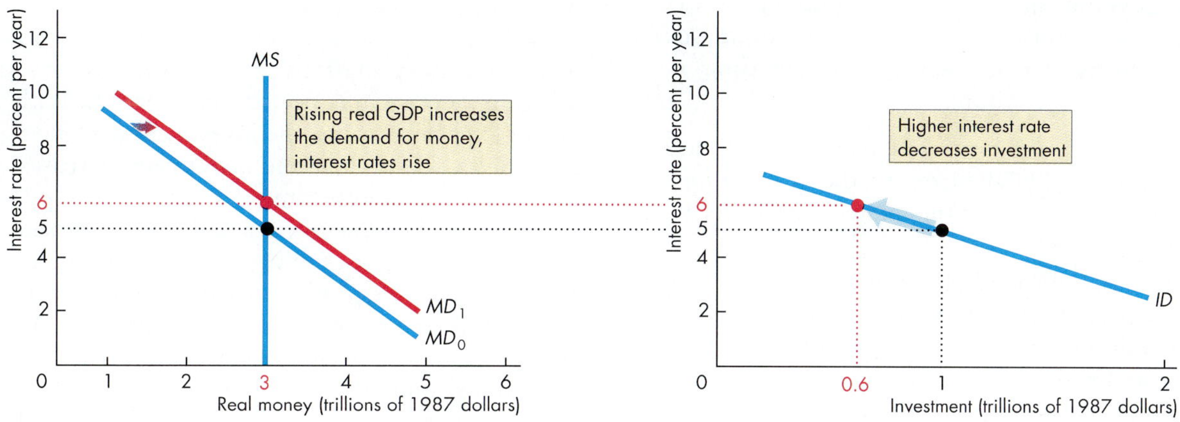

(a) Increase in the demand for money

(b) Decrease in investment

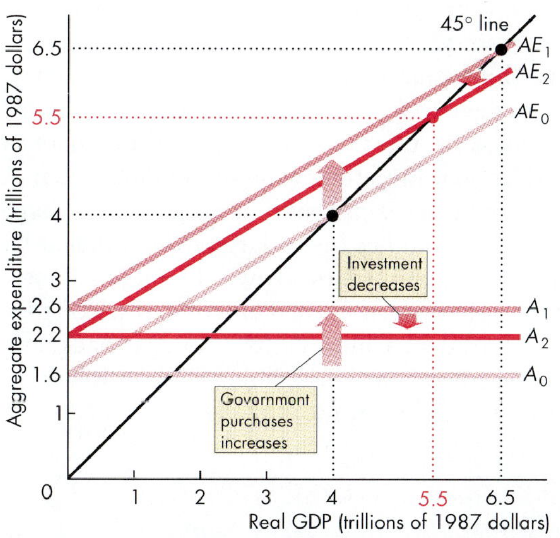

(c) Expenditure and real GDP

Initially, the demand curve for real money is MD_0, the real money supply is *MS*, and the interest rate is 5 percent (part a). With an interest rate of 5 percent, investment is $1 trillion on the investment demand curve *ID* (part b). The aggregate expenditure curve is AE_0, autonomous expenditure is A_0, and equilibrium expenditure and real GDP are $4 trillion (part c). A $1 trillion increase in government purchases increases autonomous expenditure (part c). Real GDP increases, which leads to an increase in the the demand for money. The demand curve for real money shifts rightward to MD_1, raising the interest rate (part a). The higher interest rate decreases investment (part b). Autonomous expenditure decreases to A_2, and aggregate planned expenditure decreases to AE_2 (part c). The new equilibrium expenditure occurs at real GDP of $5.5 trillion.

Other Fiscal Policies A change in government purchases is only one possible fiscal policy action. Others are a change in transfer payments, such as an increase in unemployment compensation or an increase in social security benefits, and a change in taxes. All fiscal policy actions work by changing autonomous expenditure. The magnitude of the change in autonomous expenditure differs for different fiscal actions. But fiscal policy actions that change autonomous expenditure by a given amount and in a given direction have similar effects on equilibrium real GDP and the interest rate regardless of whether they involve changes in purchases of goods and services, transfer payments, or taxes.

REVIEW

An expansionary fiscal policy—an increase in government purchases of goods and services or an increase in transfer payments or a decrease in taxes—affects aggregate demand by increasing autonomous expenditure.

- In the first round, aggregate planned expenditure increases, real GDP increases, the demand for money increases, and the interest rate starts to rise.
- In the second round, the rising interest rate decreases investment, decreases autonomous expenditure, and decreases equilibrium expenditure and real GDP.

The second round effects go in the opposite direction to the first round effects but are smaller. An expansionary fiscal policy increases real GDP, increases the interest rate, and decreases investment. ◆

We've seen that an expansionary fiscal policy raises interest rates and decreases investment. Let's take a closer look at this effect of fiscal policy.

Crowding Out and Crowding In

The tendency for an expansionary fiscal policy to increase interest rates and decrease investment is called **crowding out.** Crowding out may be partial or complete. Partial crowding out occurs when the decrease in investment is less than the increase in government purchases. This is the normal case—and the case we've just seen. Increased government purchases of goods and services increase real GDP, which increases the demand for real money, and so interest rates rise. Higher interest rates decrease investment. However, the effect on investment is smaller than the initial change in government purchases.

Complete crowding out occurs if the decrease in investment equals the initial increase in government purchases. For complete crowding out to occur, a small change in the demand for real money must lead to a large change in the interest rate, and the change in the interest rate must lead to a large change in investment.

Another influence of government purchases on investment that we haven't considered so far works in the opposite direction to the crowding out effect and is called "crowding in." **Crowding in** is the tendency for an expansionary fiscal policy to *increase* investment. This effect works in three ways.

First, in a recession, an expansionary fiscal policy might create expectations of a speedier recovery and bring an increase in expected future profits. With higher expected profits, the investment demand curve shifts to the right and investment increases despite higher interest rates.

The second source of crowding in is increased government purchases of capital. Such expenditure might increase the profitability of privately owned capital and lead to an increase in investment. For example, suppose the government increased its expenditure and built a new highway that cut the cost of transporting a farmer's produce to a market that previously was too costly to serve. The farmer might now purchase a new fleet of refrigerated trucks to take advantage of the newly available profit opportunity.

The third source of crowding in is decreased taxes. If the expansionary fiscal policy cuts the taxes on business profits, firms' after-tax profits increase and additional investment might be undertaken.

Crowding out is probably more common than crowding in, and because a large federal deficit has persisted for many years, crowding out is a continuing focus of concern in the United States. For this reason, President Clinton's 1993 budget package focused on investment, as you can see in Reading Between the Lines on pp. 318–319.

The Exchange Rate and International Crowding Out

We've seen that an expansionary fiscal policy leads to higher interest rates. But a change in interest rates also affects the exchange rate. Higher interest rates make the dollar rise in value against other currencies. With interest rates higher in the United States than in the rest of the world, funds flow into the United States and people around the world demand more U.S. dollars. As the dollar rises in value, foreigners find U.S.-produced goods and services more expensive and Americans find imports less expensive. Exports fall and imports rise—net exports fall. The tendency for an expansionary fiscal policy to decrease net exports is called **international crowding**

out. The decrease in net exports offsets to some degree the initial increase in aggregate expenditure brought about by an expansionary fiscal policy.

REVIEW

Crowding out is the tendency for an expansionary fiscal policy to increase interest rates, thereby reducing investment. Crowding out can be partial or complete. The normal case is partial crowding out—the decrease in investment is less than the initial increase in autonomous expenditure resulting from the fiscal action. ◆◆ Crowding in is the tendency for an expansionary fiscal policy to *increase* investment. Crowding in might occur in a recession if fiscal stimulation brings expectations of higher future profits, if the government purchases of capital hasten economic recovery, or if tax cuts stimulate investment. ◆◆ International crowding out is the tendency for an expansionary fiscal policy to decrease net exports. International crowding out occurs because fiscal expansion increases interest rates and makes the dollar rise in value against other currencies. A higher dollar increases imports and decreases exports. ◆

Let's now turn to an examination of the effects of monetary policy on aggregate demand.

Monetary Policy and Aggregate Demand

The Fed is concerned that the economy is overheating and that inflation is about to take off. To slow down the economy, the Fed decides to reduce aggregate demand by decreasing the money supply. To work out the consequences of this monetary policy action, we divide its effects into first round and second round effects (just as we did with fiscal policy). Let's look at the first round effects of the Fed's monetary policy action.

First Round Effects of a Change in the Money Supply

The economy is in the situation that we studied in Fig. 12.1. The interest rate is 5 percent, investment is \$1 trillion, and real GDP is \$4 trillion. The Fed now decreases the real money supply by \$1 trillion, from \$3 trillion to \$2 trillion. The first round effects of this action are shown in Fig. 12.5. The immediate effect is shown in part (a). The real money supply curve shifts leftward from MS_0 to MS_1, and the interest rate rises from 5 percent to 7 percent. The effect of the higher interest rate is shown in part (b). Investment decreases from \$1 trillion to \$0.2 trillion—a movement along the investment demand curve. The effect of lower investment is shown in part (c). The fall in investment lowers aggregate planned expenditure—a downward shift in the *AE* curve from AE_0 to AE_1. The fall in aggregate planned expenditure lowers equilibrium expenditure, and real GDP starts to decrease. That is, a multiplier process begins in which real GDP gradually falls toward its equilibrium level. We described such a process in Chapter 9 (pp. 240–242).

We've just described the first round effects of a decrease in the money supply: the interest rate rises, investment decreases, and real GDP starts to decrease. These effects are illustrated in Fig. 12.6(a).

Second Round Effects of a Change in the Money Supply

At the end of the first round that we've just studied, real GDP is decreasing. Decreasing real GDP sets off the second round, which is illustrated in Fig. 12.6(b). A lower real GDP decreases the demand for real money, and the interest rate falls. The lower interest rate brings an increase in investment and an increase in aggregate planned expenditure. With aggregate planned expenditure increasing, equilibrium expenditure is also increasing.

These second round effects go in the opposite direction to the first round effects, but they are smaller. They diminish the magnitude of the first round effects, but they do not change the direction of the outcome of the monetary policy action. That outcome is a decrease in real GDP and an increase in the interest rate. In the new equilibrium, the lower real GDP and higher interest rate give simultaneous money market equilibrium and equilibrium expenditure, similar to the situation shown in Fig. 12.1.

FIGURE 12.5

First Round Effects of a Decrease in the Money Supply

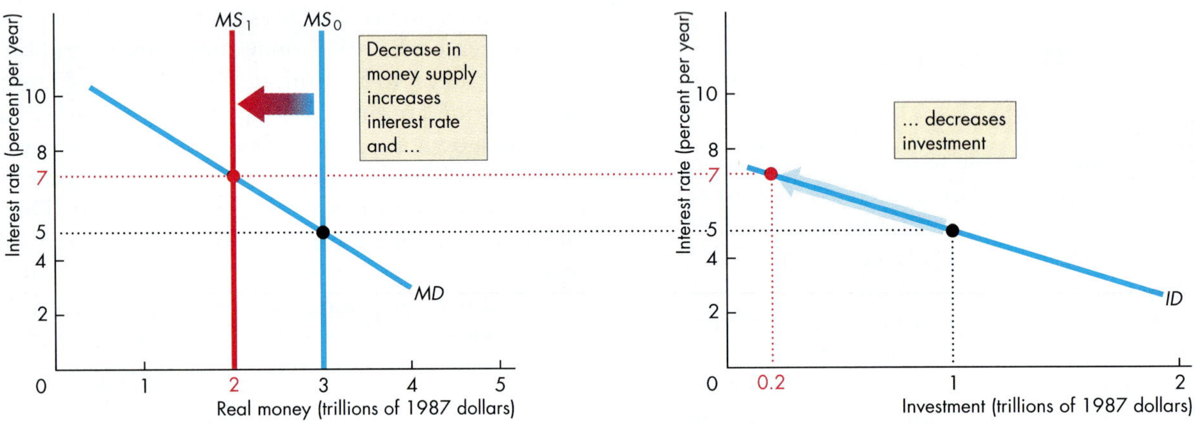

(a) Change in money supply

(b) Change in investment

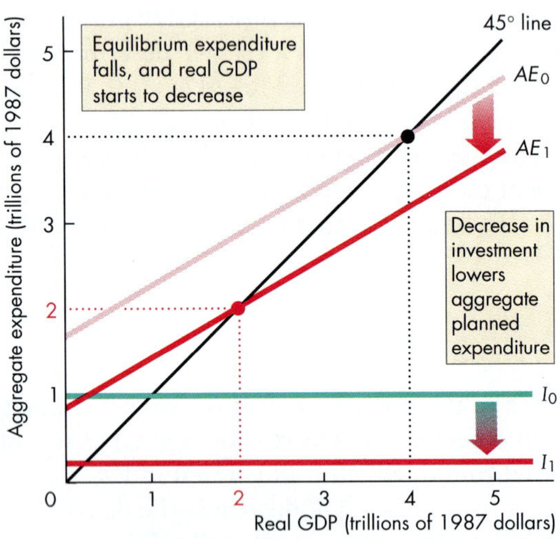

(c) Change in expenditure and real GDP

A decrease in the money supply shifts the supply curve of real money from MS_0 to MS_1 (part a). Equilibrium in the money market is achieved by an increase in the interest rate from 5 percent to 7 percent. At the higher interest rate, investment decreases (part b). The decrease in investment decreases both autonomous expenditure and aggregate planned expenditure (part c). The *AE* curve shifts downward from AE_0 to AE_1. Equilibrium real GDP falls from $4 trillion to $2 trillion. And a multiplier process is set up in which real GDP decreases.

REVIEW

A decrease in the money supply sets up the following sequence of events:

- In the first round, the interest rate increases, investment decreases, and real GDP starts to decrease.
- In the second round, falling real GDP decreases the demand for money, lowers the interest rate, increases investment, and increases equilibrium expenditure.

The second round effects go in the opposite direction to the first round effects but are smaller. A decrease in the money supply decreases real GDP and increases the interest rate.

FIGURE 12.6

How the Economy Adjusts to a Decrease in the Money Supply

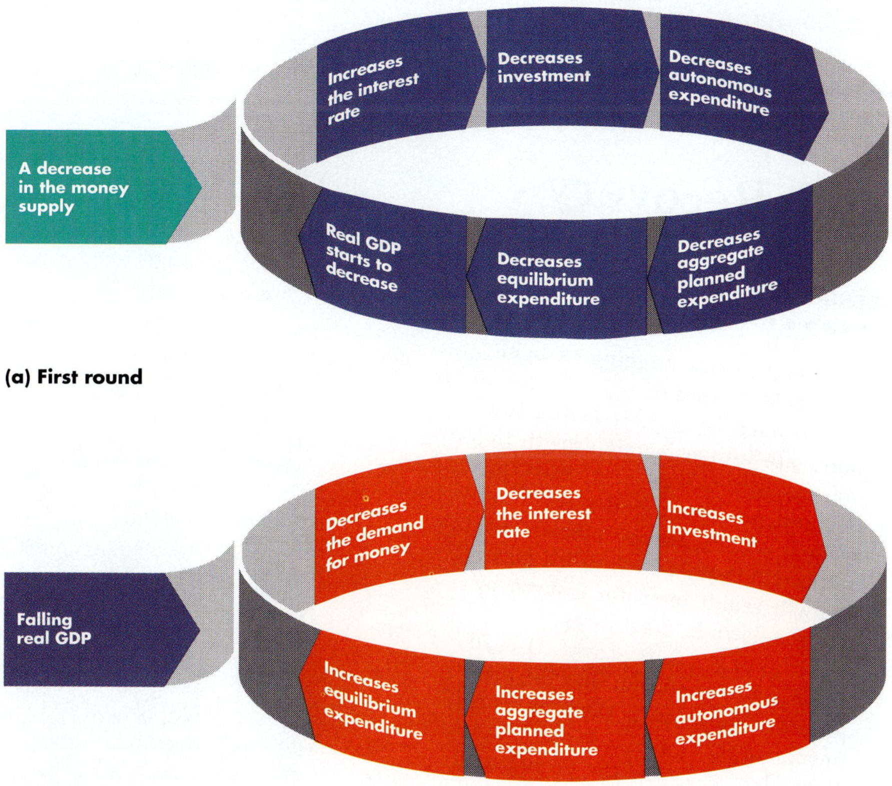

(a) First round

(b) Second round

In the first round (part a), a decrease in the money supply increases the interest rate, decreases investment, autonomous expenditure, aggregate planned expenditure, and equilibrium expenditure, and makes real GDP start to decrease. In the second round (part b), the decreasing real GDP decreases the demand for money, the interest rate falls, and investment increases. The increase in investment increases autonomous expenditure, aggregate planned expenditure, and equilibrium expenditure. The second round effects work in the opposite direction to the first round effects but are smaller in magnitude. The outcome of a decrease in the money supply is a decrease in real GDP and a rise in the interest rate.

So far, we have looked at the effects of monetary policy on the interest rate and investment. There is another important effect—on the foreign exchange rate and exports.

The Exchange Rate and Exports

A decrease in the money supply increases the interest rate. If the interest rate rises in the United States but does not rise in Japan and Western Europe, international investors buy the now higher-yielding U.S. assets and sell the relatively lower-yielding foreign assets. As they undertake these transactions, they buy U.S. dollars and sell foreign currency. These actions increase the demand for U.S. dollars and decrease the demand for foreign currencies. The result is a higher value of the U.S. dollar against other currencies. (This mechanism is discussed in greater detail in Chapter 19, pp. 515–519.)

With the U.S. dollar worth more, foreigners face higher prices for U.S.-produced goods and services and Americans face lower prices for foreign-produced goods and services. Foreigners cut their imports from the United States, and Americans increase their imports from the rest of the world. The result is a net decrease in the demand for U.S.-produced goods and services. The effects of a decrease in net exports are similar to the effects of a decrease in investment that we've described above.

Fiscal Stimulus or Restraint?

The New York Times, July 12, 1993

Protecting a Fragile Recovery

BY STEVEN GREENHOUSE

WASHINGTON—Discouraged by recent weak economic reports, Administration officials are nervous that President Clinton's deficit-reduction plan could slow the economy further. But they see no need for an emergency stimulus package because they are confident that growth will pick up in the second half of this year. . . .

Administration officials said they would urge House and Senate negotiators, when hammering out a compromise budget plan, to pay attention to how leaving in or lopping out certain provisions, like investment incentives, would affect growth.

"I would hope that in the process of reconciliation some thought would be given to the signals the economy is giving out," Laura D'Andrea Tyson, chairwoman of the President's Council of Economic Advisers, said in an interview. . . .

She said that once President Clinton's budget package wins Congressional approval, growth should accelerate because most of the uncertainties nagging at business would disappear. . . .

Historically, deficit-reduction plans bite into economic growth by increasing taxes and cutting Government spending. But this time around, Administration officials are optimistic that Mr. Clinton's package will result in faster growth by pushing down interest rates.

Treasury Secretary Lloyd Bentsen has often said that the drop in long-term interest rates of a full percentage point since last November will give the economy a stimulus equivalent to that of $100 billion in extra Government spending.

Ms. Tyson said most of the benefits of lower rates had still not percolated through the economy. Some of the Administration's economic models show that only 30 percent of the benefits of falling interest rates are felt in the first year, with the remaining 70 percent felt in the subsequent years. . . .

The Essence of the Story

In mid-1993, Clinton administration officials believed that economic growth would increase in the second half of the year and that no fiscal stimulus package was needed.

However, they were nervous that the president's deficit reduction plan could slow the economy, and they urged legislators to pay attention to details such as investment incentives.

In the past, deficit reduction plans have cut economic growth by increasing taxes and cutting government spending. But administration officials believed that President Clinton's package would push interest rates down and stimulate growth.

Treasury Secretary Lloyd Bentsen said that the drop in long-term interest rates of a full percentage point since November 1992 would give the economy a stimulus equivalent to that of $100 billion in extra government spending.

Council of Economic Advisers chairwoman Laura D'Andrea Tyson said that some economic models show that only 30 percent of the effects of falling interest rates are felt in the first year, with 70 percent felt in subsequent years.

Background and Analysis

Long-term interest rates fell by 1 percentage point between November 1992 and mid-1993. The first-year effects of the lower interest rates are shown in Fig. 1. The curve labeled *IDS* is the investment demand curve in the *short run.* This curve is steep—investment demand is not highly responsive to a change in the interest rate in the short run. The fall in the real interest rate from r_0 to r_1 increases investment from I_0 to I_1.

Over a longer term, investment is more responsive to a change in the interest rate, and the investment demand curve in the *long run* is *IDL* in Fig. 1. If the real interest rate remains at r_1, investment will eventually increase to I_2.

Figure 1 reflects the assumption stated by Laura D'Andrea Tyson that only 30 percent of the effects of lower interest rates are felt in the first year. If the further assumption stated by Lloyd Bentsen is correct—that an interest rate decrease of 1 percent is equivalent to a $100 billion increase in government purchases—the increase in investment from I_0 to I_2 is equal to $100 billion.

The effects on aggregate expenditure are shown in Fig. 2. The first-year effect of the lower interest rate is about 30 percent, so the aggregate expenditure curve shifts from AE_0 to AE_1, and in the subsequent years the effects take the aggregate expenditure curve to AE_2. The quantity of real GDP demanded (at a given price level) increases to Y_1 in the first year and to Y_2 in subsequent years.

Everything else remaining the same, rising real GDP brings an increase in the demand for money, a higher interest rate, and a decrease in investment. To keep interest rates and investment steady, the Fed must keep the quantity of money increasing in line with the growth of real GDP.

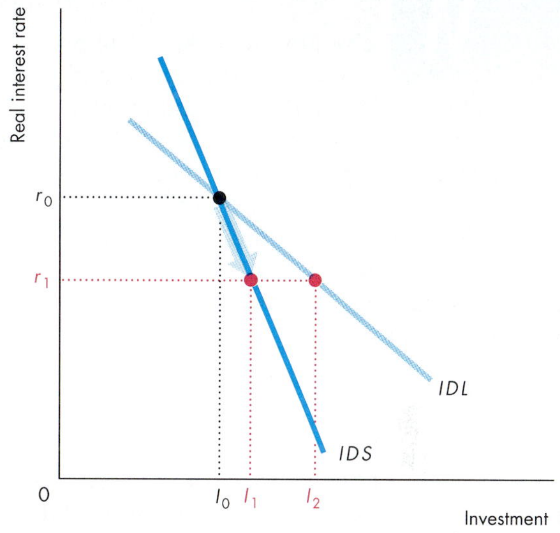

Figure 1

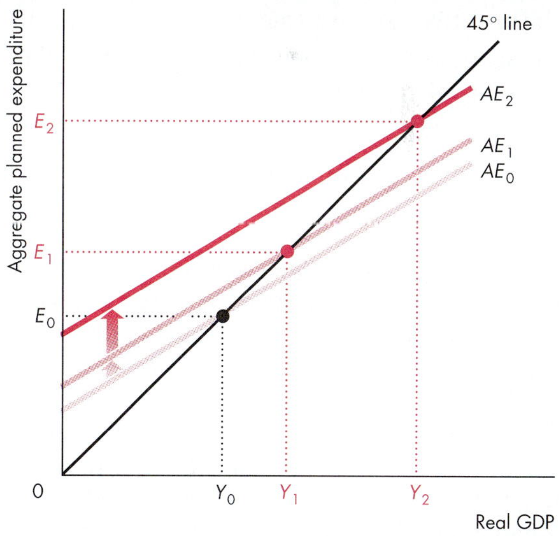

Figure 2

The Relative Effectiveness of Fiscal and Monetary Policy

We've now seen that equilibrium aggregate expenditure and real GDP are influenced by both fiscal and monetary policy. But which policy is the more potent? Which has the larger "bang per buck"? This question was once at the center of a controversy among macroeconomists, and later in this section we'll look at that controversy and see how it was settled. Let's begin by discovering what determines the relative effectiveness of fiscal and monetary policy.

The Effectiveness of Fiscal Policy

The effectiveness of fiscal policy is measured by the magnitude of the increase in equilibrium real GDP resulting from a given increase in government purchases of goods and services (or decrease in taxes). The effectiveness of fiscal policy depends on two key factors:

- The sensitivity of investment to the interest rate
- The sensitivity of the quantity of money demanded to the interest rate

We're going to discover how these two factors influence the effectiveness of fiscal policy by studying Fig. 12.7.

Fiscal Policy Effectiveness and Investment Demand

Other things being equal, the more sensitive investment is to the interest rate, the smaller is the effect of a change in fiscal policy on equilibrium real GDP. Figure 12.7(a) shows why.

The figure shows two investment demand curves, ID_A and ID_B. Investment is more sensitive to a change in the interest rate along the demand curve ID_A than along the demand curve ID_B. An increase in government purchases increases real GDP and increases the demand for money. The demand curve for real money shifts from MD_0 to MD_1. This increase in the demand for money increases the interest rate from 5 percent to 6 percent. If the investment demand curve is ID_A, investment decreases from \$1 trillion to \$0.6 trillion. Contrast this outcome with what happens if the investment demand curve is ID_B. The same increase in the interest rate decreases investment from \$1 trillion to \$0.8 trillion.

The decrease in investment decreases autonomous expenditure, offsetting to some degree the increase in government purchases. Therefore the larger the decrease in investment, the smaller is the increase in equilibrium real GDP resulting from a given increase in government purchases. Thus fiscal policy is less effective with the investment demand curve ID_A than with the investment demand curve ID_B.

Fiscal Policy Effectiveness and the Demand for Money

Other things being equal, the more sensitive the quantity of money demanded is to the interest rate, the bigger is the effect of fiscal policy on equilibrium real GDP. Figure 12.7(b) shows why.

The figure shows two alternative initial (blue) demand curves for real money, MD_{A0} and MD_{B0}. The quantity of money demanded is less sensitive to a change in the interest rate along the demand curve MD_A than along the demand curve MD_B.

An increase in government purchases increases real GDP and increases the demand for money, shifting the demand curve for real money to the right. If the initial curve is MD_{A0}, the new curve is MD_{A1}; if the initial curve is MD_{B0}, the new curve is MD_{B1}. Notice that the size of the rightward shift is the same in each case. In the case of MD_A, the increase in the demand for real money increases the interest rate from 5 percent to 6 percent and investment decreases from \$1 trillion to \$0.6 trillion. In the case of MD_B, the increase in the demand for real money increases the interest rate from 5 percent to 5.5 percent and investment decreases from \$1 trillion to \$0.8 trillion.

A decrease in investment decreases autonomous expenditure, offsetting to some degree the increase in government purchases. Therefore the smaller the decrease in investment, the larger is the increase in equilibrium real GDP resulting from a given increase in government purchases. Thus fiscal policy is less effective with the demand for real money curve MD_A than with the demand for real money curve MD_B.

The Effectiveness of Monetary Policy

The effectiveness of monetary policy is measured by the magnitude of the increase in equilibrium real GDP resulting from a given increase in the money

FIGURE 12.7

The Effectiveness of Fiscal Policy

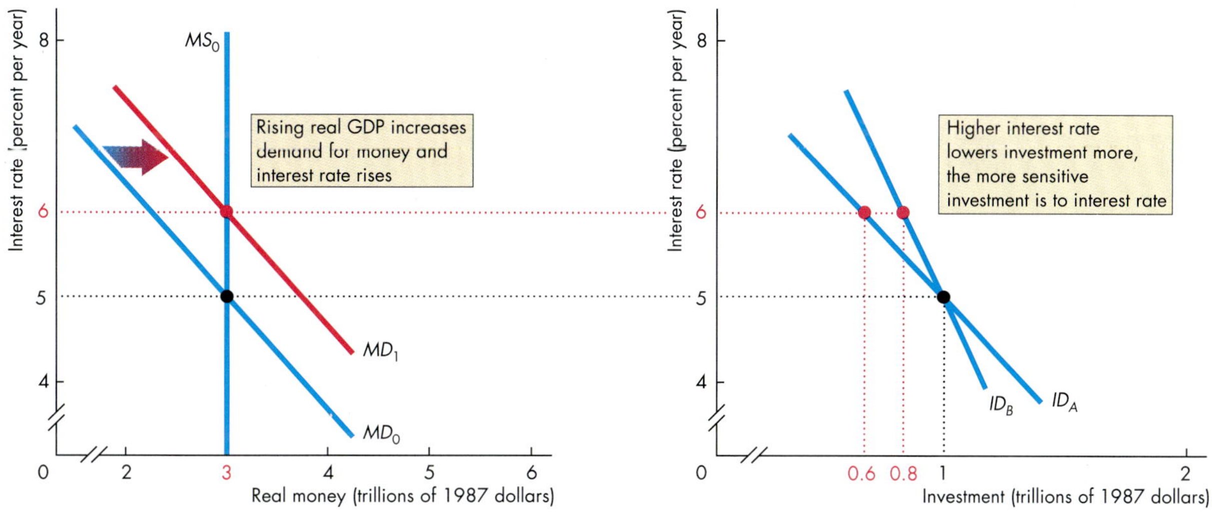

(a) Effectiveness and investment demand

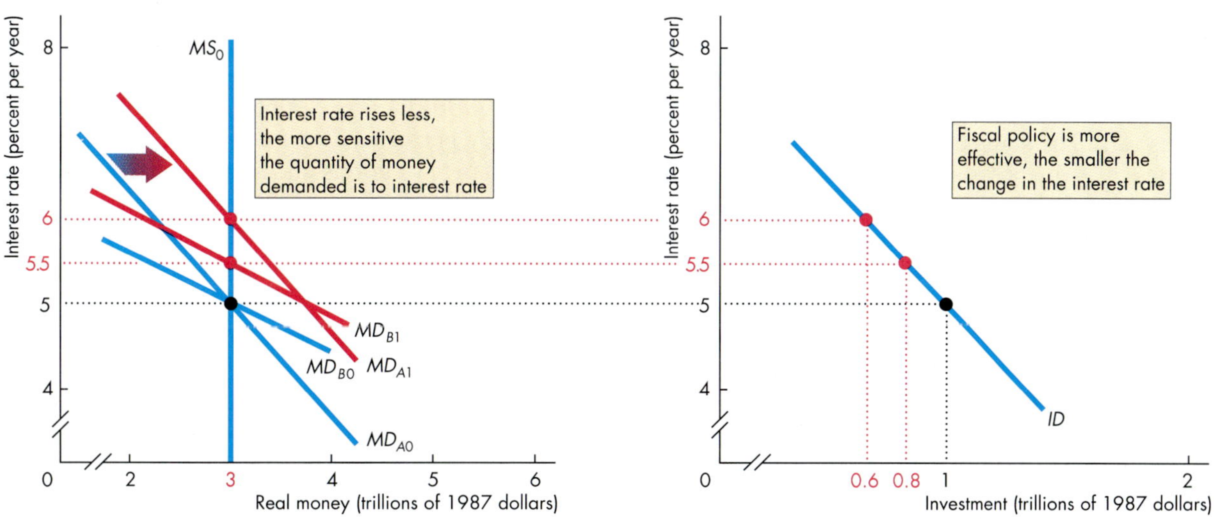

(b) Effectiveness and the demand for money

In part (a), the level of planned investment is more sensitive to a change in the interest rate along ID_A than along ID_B. An increase in government purchases increases real GDP and shifts the demand curve for real money from MD_0 to MD_1, raising the interest rate from 5 percent to 6 percent. With investment demand curve ID_A, investment decreases from \$1 trillion to \$0.6 trillion, but with demand curve ID_B, investment decreases to only \$0.8 trillion. So fiscal policy is less effective with investment demand curve ID_A than with ID_B.

In part (b), the quantity of money demanded is less sensitive to a change in the interest rate along MD_{A0} than along MD_{B0}. An increase in government purchases increases real GDP, and the demand curve for real money shifts to the right—MD_{A0} shifts to MD_{A1} and MD_{B0} shifts to MD_{B1}. The size of the rightward shift is the same in each case. In the case of MD_A, the interest rate rises from 5 percent to 6 percent and investment decreases from \$1 trillion to \$0.6 trillion. In the case of MD_B, the interest rate rises to 5.5 percent and investment decreases to only \$0.8 trillion. So fiscal policy is less effective with the demand curve for real money MD_A than with MD_B.

supply. The effectiveness of monetary policy depends on the same two factors as the effectiveness of fiscal policy:

- The sensitivity of investment to the interest rate
- The sensitivity of the quantity of money demanded to the interest rate

But other things being equal, the more effective is fiscal policy, the less effective is monetary policy. Let's see why by studying Fig. 12.8.

Monetary Policy Effectiveness and Investment Demand Other things being equal, the more sensitive investment is to the interest rate, the bigger is the effect of a change in the money supply on equilibrium real GDP. Figure 12.8(a) shows why.

The figure shows two investment demand curves, ID_A and ID_B. Investment is more sensitive to a change in the interest rate along the demand curve ID_A than along the demand curve ID_B.

With the demand curve for real money *MD*, an increase in the money supply that shifts the real money supply curve from MS_0 to MS_1 decreases the interest rate from 5 percent to 3 percent. If the investment demand curve is ID_A, investment increases from $1 trillion to $1.8 trillion. Contrast this outcome with what happens if the investment demand curve is ID_B. The same decrease in the interest rate increases investment from $1 trillion to $1.4 trillion.

The larger the increase in investment, the larger is the resulting increase in equilibrium real GDP. Thus with the investment demand curve ID_A, monetary policy is more effective than with the investment demand curve ID_B.

Monetary Policy Effectiveness and the Demand for Money Other things being equal, the less sensitive the quantity of money demanded is to the interest rate, the bigger is the effect of a change in the money supply on equilibrium real GDP. Figure 12.8(b) shows why.

The figure shows two demand curves for real money, MD_A and MD_B. The quantity of money demanded is less sensitive to a change in the interest rate along the demand curve MD_A than along the demand curve MD_B.

If the demand curve for real money is MD_A, an increase in the money supply that shifts the real money supply curve from MS_0 to MS_1 decreases the interest rate from 5 percent to 3 percent. Investment increases from $1 trillion to $1.8 trillion. Contrast this outcome with what happens if the demand curve for real money is MD_B. In this case, the same increase in the money supply lowers the interest rate from 5 percent to only 4 percent and investment increases to only $1.4 trillion.

The larger the increase in investment, the larger is the resulting increase in equilibrium real GDP. Thus with the demand curve for real money MD_A, monetary policy is more effective than with the demand curve for real money MD_B.

Interest Sensitivity of Investment and the Quantity of Money Demanded

What determines the degree of sensitivity of investment and the quantity of money demanded to interest rates? The answer is the degree of substitutability between capital and other factors of production and the degree of substitutability between money and other financial assets.

Investment is the purchase of capital—of productive buildings, plant, and equipment. The amount of capital used, and the amount of investment undertaken, decreases as the interest rate increases. The degree to which a change in the interest rate brings a change in investment depends on how easily other factors of production can be substituted for capital.

Money performs a unique function—it facilitates the exchange of goods and services. Therefore money and other financial assets are imperfect substitutes. Holding money has an opportunity cost, which is the interest forgone by not holding other financial assets. The amount of money that we hold decreases as its opportunity cost—the interest rate—increases. The degree to which a change in the interest rate brings a change in the quantity of money held depends on how easily other financial assets can be substituted for money.

The analysis that we have presented in this chapter of the effects of fiscal and monetary policy on aggregate expenditure was for several years in the 1950s and 1960s extremely controversial. It was at the heart of what was called the Keynesian-monetarist controversy. The controversy of today is different from that of the 1950s and 1960s, and we'll consider today's controversy—a controversy about how labor markets work—in Chapter 13. But the Keynesian-monetarist controversy was an interesting and important episode in the development of modern macroeconomics. Let's take a look at the essentials of the dispute and see how it was resolved.

FIGURE 12.8

The Effectiveness of Monetary Policy

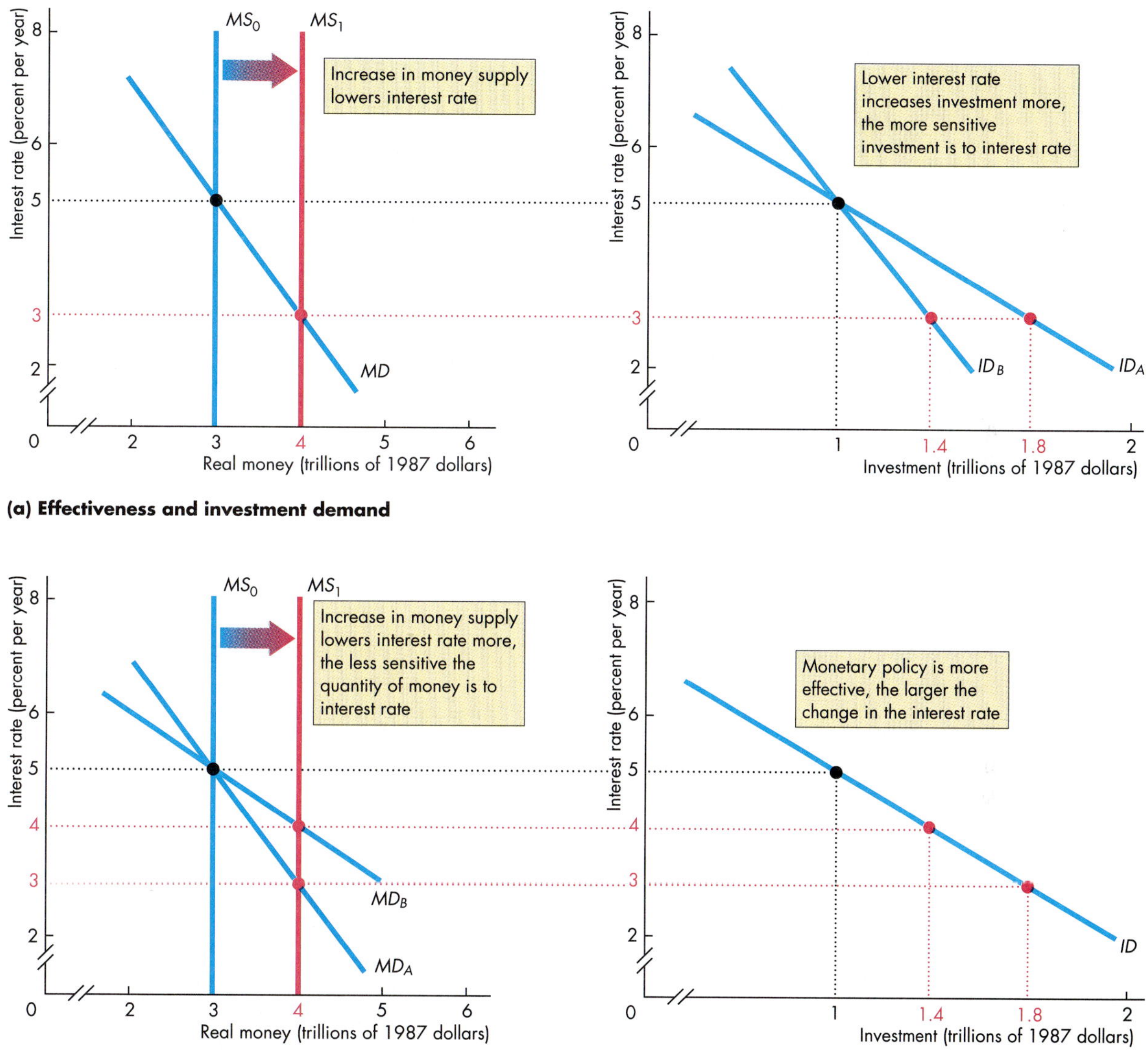

(a) Effectiveness and investment demand

(b) Effectiveness and the demand for money

In part (a), planned investment is more sensitive to a change in the interest rate along the investment demand curve ID_A than along the demand curve ID_B. With the demand curve for real money *MD*, a shift in the real money supply curve from MS_0 to MS_1 lowers the interest rate from 5 percent to 3 percent. With investment demand curve ID_A, investment increases from \$1 trillion to \$1.8 trillion, but with investment demand curve ID_B, investment increases to only \$1.4 trillion. The larger the increase in investment, the larger is the resulting increase in equilibrium real GDP. So monetary policy is more effective with investment demand curve ID_A than with ID_B.

In part (b), the quantity of money demanded is less sensitive to a change in the interest rate along MD_A than along MD_B. With the demand curve MD_A, an increase in the money supply that shifts the real money supply curve from MS_0 to MS_1 lowers the interest rate from 5 percent to 3 percent and increases investment from \$1 trillion to \$1.8 trillion. With demand curve MD_B, the same increase in the money supply lowers the interest rate to only 4 percent and increases investment to only \$1.4 trillion. The larger the increase in investment, the larger is the resulting increase in equilibrium real GDP. So monetary policy is more effective with demand curve MD_A than with MD_B.

The Keynesian-Monetarist Controversy

The Keynesian-monetarist controversy was a dispute in macroeconomics between two broad groups of economists. Keynesians are macroeconomists whose views about the functioning of the economy represent an extension of the theories of John Maynard Keynes, published in his *General Theory* (see Our Advancing Knowledge, pp. 194–195). **Keynesians** regard the economy as being inherently unstable and as requiring active government intervention to achieve stability. They assign a low degree of importance to monetary policy and a high degree of importance to fiscal policy. **Monetarists** are macroeconomists who assign a high degree of importance to variations in the quantity of money as the main determinant of aggregate demand and who regard the economy as inherently stable. The founder of modern monetarism is Milton Friedman (see Our Advancing Knowledge, pp. 438–439).

The Keynesian-monetarist debate in the 1950s and 1960s was a debate about the relative effectiveness of fiscal policy and monetary policy in changing aggregate demand. We can see the essence of that debate by distinguishing three views:

- Extreme Keynesianism
- Extreme monetarism
- Intermediate position

Extreme Keynesianism The extreme Keynesian hypothesis is that a change in the money supply has no effect on the level of aggregate demand and a change in government purchases of goods and services or in taxes has a large effect on aggregate demand.

There are two circumstances in which a change in the money supply has no effect on aggregate demand. They are

- A vertical investment demand curve
- A horizontal demand curve for real money

If the investment demand curve is vertical, investment is completely insensitive to interest rates. In this situation, a change in the money supply changes interest rates but those changes do not affect aggregate planned expenditure. Monetary policy is impotent.

A horizontal demand curve for real money means that people are willing to hold any quantity of money at a given interest rate—a situation called a **liquidity trap.** With a liquidity trap, a change in the money supply affects only the quantity of money held. It does not affect interest rates. With an unchanged interest rate, investment remains constant. Monetary policy is impotent.

Extreme Keynesians assume that both of these conditions prevail. Notice that either one of these circumstances on its own is sufficient for monetary policy to be impotent, but extreme Keynesians suppose that both situations exist in reality.

Extreme Monetarism The extreme monetarist hypothesis is that a change in government purchases of goods and services or in taxes has no effect on aggregate demand and that a change in the money supply has a large effect on aggregate demand. There are two circumstances giving rise to these predictions:

- A horizontal investment demand curve
- A vertical demand curve for real money

If an increase in government purchases of goods and services induces an increase in interest rates that is sufficiently large to reduce investment by the same amount as the initial increase in government purchases, then fiscal policy has no effect on aggregate demand. This outcome is complete crowding out, which we described earlier in this chapter. For this result to occur, either the demand curve for real money must be vertical—a fixed quantity of money is demanded regardless of the interest rate—or the investment demand curve must be horizontal—any amount of investment will be undertaken at a given interest rate.

The Intermediate Position The intermediate position is that both fiscal and monetary policy affect aggregate demand. Crowding out is not complete, so fiscal policy does have an effect. There is no liquidity trap and investment responds to interest rates, so monetary policy does indeed affect aggregate demand. This position is the one that now appears to be correct and is the one that we've spent most of this chapter exploring. Let's see how economists came to this conclusion.

Sorting Out the Competing Claims The dispute between monetarists, Keynesians, and those taking an intermediate position was essentially a disagreement about the magnitudes of two economic parameters:

- The sensitivity of investment to interest rates
- The sensitivity of the quantity of money demanded to interest rates

If investment is highly sensitive to interest rates or the quantity of money demanded is hardly sensitive at all, then monetary policy is powerful and fiscal policy is relatively ineffective. In this case, the world looks similar to the claims of extreme monetarists. If investment is very insensitive to interest rates or the quantity of money demanded is highly sensitive, then fiscal policy is powerful and monetary policy is relatively ineffective. In this case, the world looks similar to the claims of the extreme Keynesians.

By using statistical methods to study the demand for real money and investment demand and by using data from a wide variety of historical and national experiences, economists were able to settle this dispute. Neither extreme position turned out to be supported by the evidence, and the intermediate position won. The demand curve for real money slopes downward. So does the investment demand curve. Neither curve is vertical or horizontal, so the extreme Keynesian and extreme monetarist hypotheses are rejected.

This particular controversy in macroeconomics is now behind us, but other controversies are still around. One concerns the relative magnitudes of the multiplier effects of fiscal and monetary policy. Another concerns the time lags of those effects. But the major unresolved issue that divides economists today concerns the working of the labor market, a controversy that we'll meet in the next chapter.

REVIEW

The relative effectiveness of fiscal and monetary policy depends on the sensitivity to interest rates of investment and the quantity of money demanded. Other things being equal, the more sensitive investment is to interest rates or the less sensitive the quantity of money demanded is, the smaller is the effect of a change in government purchases and the greater is the effect of a change in the money supply on equilibrium expenditure. The less sensitive investment is to interest rates or the more sensitive the quantity of money demanded is, the larger is the effect of a change in government purchases and the smaller is the effect of a change in the money supply on equilibrium expenditure. In the extreme case in which investment is completely insensitive to the interest rate or the quantity of money demanded is infinitely sensitive, fiscal policy is effective and monetary policy is completely ineffective. In the opposite extreme case, in which investment is infinitely sensitive to the interest rate or the quantity of money demanded is completely insensitive, monetary policy is effective and fiscal policy is ineffective. These extremes do not occur in reality. ◆

Influencing the Composition of Aggregate Expenditure

Aggregate expenditure can be increased by either an expansionary fiscal policy or an increase in the money supply. An expansionary fiscal policy increases aggregate expenditure and raises interest rates. Increased expenditure increases income and consumption expenditure, but higher interest rates decrease investment. Hence if aggregate expenditure is increased by an expansionary fiscal policy, consumption expenditure increases and investment decreases. In contrast, an increase in the money supply increases aggregate expenditure and *lowers* interest rates. Again, increased expenditure increases income and consumption expenditure, but in this case lower interest rates also increase investment. Hence if aggregate expenditure is increased by an increase in the money supply, both consumption expenditure and investment increase. Thus the method whereby aggregate expenditure is increased has an important effect on the *composition* of expenditure.

Fiscal Policy and Clintonomics

An expansionary fiscal policy can lead to a decrease in investment and slow the long-term growth of the economy. Because fiscal stimulus tends to decrease investment, the government must seek ways of boosting investment. Two fiscal policy proposals for increasing investment form the core of Clintonomics.

The first proposal gives tax breaks to businesses that invest. An increase in the after-tax profitability of investment causes the investment demand curve to shift rightward. The higher level of investment increases aggregate expenditure and sets off a multiplier effect of increased consumer spending. The second proposal is for the government to purchase more productive capital such as highways—the economy's infrastructure—and to spend more on education and health care that increase human capital.

With an unchanged monetary policy, a fiscal stimulus package always increases the interest rate, and the higher interest rate in turn dampens the growth of investment. With upward pressure on the interest rate, the Clinton administration might want to see the Fed loosen its grip on the money supply and keep interest rates steady. But the Fed is more likely to be ready to accommodate an expanding economy if the federal government is keeping the overall budget deficit under control. For this reason, another important part of Clintonomics is to adopt a fiscal policy that will achieve a substantial deficit reduction over the next five years.

Real GDP and the Price Level

We've now studied the effects of fiscal and monetary policy on equilibrium expenditure and real GDP at a given price level. But the effects that we've worked out occur at each and every price level. Thus the fiscal and monetary policy effects that we've studied tell us about changes in aggregate demand and shifts in the aggregate demand curve.

When aggregate demand changes, both real GDP and the price level change. To determine the amounts by which each changes, we need to look at both aggregate demand and aggregate supply. Let's now do this, starting with the short-run effects of fiscal and monetary policy.

The Short-Run Effects on Real GDP and the Price Level

When aggregate demand changes and the aggregate demand curve shifts, there is a movement along the short-run aggregate supply curve and both real GDP and the price level change. Figure 12.9 illustrates the changes in real GDP and the price level that result from an increase in aggregate demand. Initially, the aggregate demand curve is AD_0, and the short-run aggregate supply curve is *SAS*. Real GDP is \$4 trillion, and the GDP deflator is 130.

Now suppose that changes in fiscal and monetary policy increase aggregate demand, shifting the aggregate demand curve to AD_1. At the initial price level (GDP deflator equal to 130), the quantity of real GDP demanded increases to \$5.5 trillion. This increase is the one we studied earlier in this chapter. But real GDP does not actually increase to this level.

FIGURE 12.9

Policy-Induced Changes in Real GDP and the Price Level

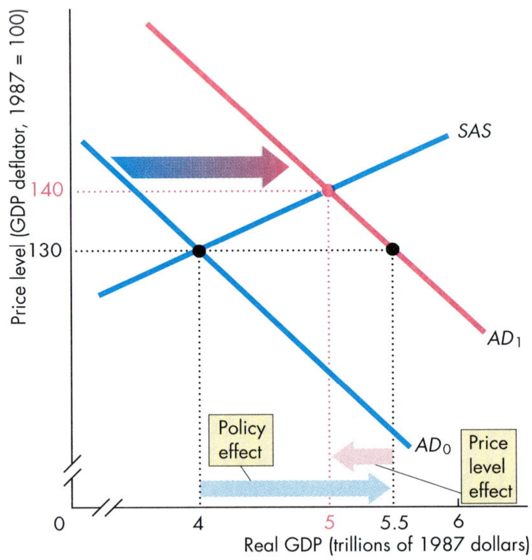

Initially, aggregate demand is AD_0, and the short-run aggregate supply curve is *SAS*. Real GDP is \$4 trillion, and the GDP deflator is 130. Fiscal and monetary policy changes shift the aggregate demand curve to AD_1. At the initial price level (GDP deflator equal to 130), real GDP rises to \$5.5 trillion. But the price level increases, bringing a decrease in the real money supply. The decrease in the real money supply increases the interest rate, decreases investment, and decreases equilibrium expenditure and real GDP. The increase in real GDP from \$4 trillion to \$5.5 trillion is the result of the initial policy-induced increase in aggregate demand at a given price level. The decrease in real GDP from \$5.5 trillion to \$5 trillion is the result of the decrease in the real money supply induced by the higher price level.

The reason is that the price level increases, bringing a decrease in the quantity of real GDP demanded. The higher level of aggregate demand puts upward pressure on the prices of all goods and services, and the GDP deflator rises to 140. At the higher price level, the real money supply decreases.

A decrease in the real money supply resulting from a rise in the price level has exactly the same effects on real GDP (and the interest rate) as a decrease in the real money supply resulting from a decrease in the *nominal* money supply brought about by the Fed's monetary policy. We've already seen what these effects are. A decrease in the real money supply increases the interest rate, decreases investment, and decreases equilibrium expenditure and real GDP.

The increase in real GDP from \$4 trillion to \$5.5 trillion is the result of the initial policy-induced increase in aggregate demand at a given price level; and the decrease in real GDP from \$5.5 trillion to \$5 trillion is the result of the decrease in the real money supply induced by the higher price level.

The exercise that we've just conducted for an increase in aggregate demand can be reversed to see what happens when there is a policy-induced decrease in aggregate demand. In this case, real GDP decreases and the price level falls.

The effects that we've just worked out are short-run effects. Let's now look at the long-run effects of fiscal and monetary policy.

The Long-Run Effects on Real GDP and the Price Level

The long-run effects of fiscal and monetary policy depend on the state of the economy when the policy action is taken. Again, we'll concentrate on the case of an *increase* in aggregate demand. If initially unemployment is above its natural rate and real GDP is below its long-run level, fiscal and monetary policy can be used to restore full employment. We can use the example in Fig. 12.9 to illustrate this case.

Suppose, in Fig. 12.9, that long-run aggregate supply is \$5 trillion. The increase in aggregate demand moves the economy from below full employment to full employment, and that is the end of the story. The short-run and long-run adjustments are the same. For example, the tax cuts and expansionary monetary policy of 1982 and 1983 were policy actions used to move the U.S. economy out of a serious recession into a period of sustained expansion.

In contrast, suppose that a policy-induced increase in aggregate demand occurs when the economy is already at full employment with real GDP at its long-run level. The U.S. economy was in such a situation in the late 1960s when spending on social programs and the Vietnam War increased. What then are the long-run effects?

We can see the answers in Fig. 12.10. The long-run aggregate supply curve is *LAS*. Initially, the aggregate demand curve is AD_0, and the short-run aggregate supply curve is SAS_0. Real GDP is \$5 trillion, and the GDP deflator is 130.

FIGURE 12.10

The Long-Run Effects of Policy-Induced Changes in Real GDP and the Price Level

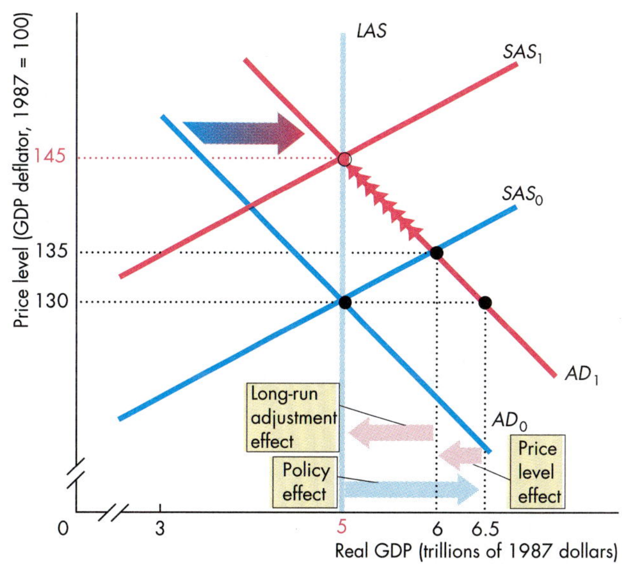

The long-run aggregate supply curve is *LAS*, and initially the aggregate demand curve is AD_0 and the short-run aggregate supply curve is SAS_0. Real GDP is \$5 trillion, and the GDP deflator is 130. Fiscal and monetary policy changes shift the aggregate demand curve to AD_1. At the new short-run equilibrium, real GDP is \$6 trillion and the GDP deflator is 135. Because real GDP is above its long-run level, wages increase and the short-run aggregate supply curve begins to shift upward to SAS_1. At the new long-run equilibrium, the GDP deflator is 145 and real GDP is back at its original level.

Suppose that changes in fiscal and monetary policy increase aggregate demand, shifting the aggregate demand curve to AD_1. At the initial price level (GDP deflator equal to 130), the quantity of real GDP demanded increases to $6.5 trillion—the policy effect. But, as we've just seen, real GDP does not actually increase to this level. The higher price level decreases the real money supply and raises the interest rate. As a result, investment, equilibrium expenditure, and real GDP decrease—the price level effect. The new short-run equilibrium occurs at a real GDP of $6 trillion and a GDP deflator of 135.

But real GDP is now above its long-run level, and unemployment is below its natural rate. There is an inflationary gap. A shortage of labor puts upward pressure on wages. And as wages increase, the short-run aggregate supply curve begins to shift to the left. It keeps shifting until it reaches SAS_1. The GDP deflator increases to 145, and real GDP returns to its long-run level—the long-run adjustment effect.

Thus the long-run effect of an expansionary fiscal and monetary policy at full employment brings a rising price level but no change in real GDP. The rising price level during the late 1960s was the result of the increased government spending on social programs and the Vietnam War.

REVIEW

A policy-induced change in aggregate demand changes both real GDP and the price level. The amount by which each changes depends on aggregate supply. In the short run, both real GDP and the price level increase. In the long run, the effects of policy depend on the state of the economy when the policy action is taken. Starting from below long-run real GDP, expansionary policy increases both real GDP and the price level and restores full employment. But starting from full employment, an expansionary policy brings a rise in the price level and no change in real GDP. ◆

◆ ◆ ◆ ◆ We have now studied the effects of fiscal and monetary policy on real GDP, interest rates, and the price level. But we've seen that the effects of these policies on real GDP and the price level depend not only on the behavior of aggregate demand but also on aggregate supply. Our next task is to study the determination of long-run and short-run aggregate supply.

SUMMARY

Money, Interest, and Aggregate Demand

Real GDP and the price level are determined by the interaction of *aggregate demand* and *aggregate supply* (Chapter 7). Fiscal and monetary policy influence *aggregate demand.*

One component of autonomous expenditure, investment, varies with the interest rate. The higher the interest rate, other things held constant, the lower is investment and hence the lower is the quantity of real GDP demanded.

The interest rate is determined by equilibrium in the money market. The demand for real money depends on both real GDP and the interest rate. The higher is real GDP, other things held constant, the greater is the demand for real money and the higher is the interest rate. Therefore the interest rate depends on real GDP.

Real GDP and the interest rate are determined simultaneously. Equilibrium real GDP and the interest rate are such that the money market is in equilibrium and aggregate planned expenditure equals real GDP. (pp. 308–311)

Fiscal Policy and Aggregate Demand

A change in government purchases of goods and services or transfer payments or taxes influences aggregate demand by changing autonomous expenditure. An expansionary fiscal policy increases autonomous expenditure and increases aggregate planned expenditure. The increase in aggregate planned expenditure increases equilibrium expenditure and sets up a multiplier effect that increases real GDP. These are the first round effects. The rising real GDP sets up a second round. The increasing real GDP increases the demand for money, and the interest rate rises. With a rise in the interest rate, investment decreases. A decrease in investment decreases autonomous expenditure and decreases aggregate planned expenditure. These second round effects work in the opposite direction to the first round effects but are smaller in magnitude. The outcome of an increase in government purchases is an increase in real GDP, a rise in the interest rates, and a decrease in investment.

The effect of higher interest rates on investment—the crowding out effect—might, in an extreme situation, be complete. That is, the decrease in investment might be sufficient to offset the initial increase in government purchases. In practice, complete crowding out does not occur. An opposing effect is crowding in, an increase in investment resulting from an increase in government purchases of goods and services. Such an effect may occur in a recession if fiscal stimulation brings expectations of economic recovery and higher future profits, if the government purchases capital that strengthens the economy, or if tax cuts stimulate investment.

Fiscal policy also influences aggregate demand through the foreign exchange rate. An increase in government purchases or a cut in taxes tends to increase interest rates and to make the value of the dollar rise against other currencies. When the dollar strengthens, Americans buy more imports and foreigners buy fewer U.S.-produced goods, so U.S. net exports decline. (pp. 311–315)

Monetary Policy and Aggregate Demand

Monetary policy influences aggregate demand by changing the interest rate. A decrease in the money supply increases the interest rate. The higher interest rate decreases investment, and lower investment reduces aggregate planned expenditure. A decrease in aggregate planned expenditure sets up a multiplier effect in which real GDP starts to decrease. This is the first round effect. Decreasing real GDP sets up a second round effect in which the demand for money decreases and the interest rate falls. A fall in the interest rate increases investment and increases aggregate planned expenditure. The second round effect works in the opposite direction to the first round effect but is smaller in magnitude. The outcome of a decrease in the money supply is a decrease in real GDP and a rise in the interest rate.

Monetary policy also influences aggregate demand through the foreign exchange rate. A decrease in the money supply increases the interest rate and makes the value of the dollar rise against other currencies. When the dollar strengthens, Americans buy more imports and foreigners buy fewer U.S.-produced goods and services, so U.S. net exports decline. (pp. 315–319)

The Relative Effectiveness of Fiscal and Monetary Policy

The relative effectiveness of fiscal and monetary policy depends on two factors: the sensitivity of investment to the interest rate and the sensitivity of the quantity of money demanded to the interest rate. The less sensitive investment is to the interest rate or the more sensitive the quantity of money demanded is to the interest rate, the larger is the effect of a fiscal policy change on aggregate demand. The more sensitive investment is to the interest rate or the less sensitive the quantity of money demanded is to the interest rate, the larger is the effect of a change in the money supply on aggregate demand.

The Keynesian-monetarist controversy concerns the relative effectiveness of fiscal and monetary actions in influencing aggregate demand. The extreme Keynesian position is that only fiscal policy affects aggregate demand and monetary policy is impotent. The extreme monetarist position is the converse—that only monetary policy affects aggregate demand and that fiscal policy is impotent. This controversy was the central one in macroeconomics in the 1950s and 1960s. As a result of statistical investigations, we now know that neither of these extreme positions is correct. The demand curve for real money and the investment demand curve both slope downward, and both fiscal and monetary policy influence aggregate demand.

The mix of fiscal and monetary policy influences the composition of aggregate demand. If aggregate demand increases as a result of an increase in government purchases of goods and services, interest rates rise and investment falls. If aggregate demand increases as a result of an increase in the money supply, interest rates fall and investment increases. These different effects of fiscal and monetary policy on aggregate demand create some political tensions. To keep aggregate demand in check and interest rates moderate, there must be a high enough level of taxes to support the level of government purchases. (pp. 320–326)

Real GDP and the Price Level

When aggregate demand changes, both real GDP and the price level change by amounts determined by both aggregate demand and aggregate supply. A policy-induced increase in aggregate demand shifts the aggregate demand curve to the right. The magnitude of the shift of the aggregate demand curve is equal to the effect of the policy change on aggregate demand at a given price level. In the short run, real GDP and the price level increase. The rise in the price level decreases the real money supply. The decrease in the real money supply increases the interest rate, decreases investment, and decreases real GDP.

The long-run effects of fiscal and monetary policy depend on the state of the economy when the policy action is taken. Starting out with unemployment above its natural rate and real GDP below its long-run level, expansionary fiscal and monetary policy increases real GDP and the price level and restores full employment. But starting out from full employment with real GDP at its long-run level, a policy-induced increase in aggregate demand increases the price level and leaves real GDP unchanged. (pp. 326–328)

KEY ELEMENTS

Key Terms

Key Figures

REVIEW QUESTIONS

1 Explain the link between the money market and the market for goods and services.

2 What are the first round effects of an increase in government purchases of goods and services?

3 What are the second round effects of an increase in government purchases of goods and services?

4 What is the outcome of an increase in government purchases of goods and services?

5 What role does the foreign exchange rate play in influencing aggregate demand when there is an expansionary fiscal policy?

6 What are crowding out, crowding in, and international crowding out? Explain how each occurs.

7 What are the first round effects of a decrease in the money supply?

8 What are the second round effects of a decrease in the money supply?

9 What is the outcome of a decrease in the money supply?

10 What role does the foreign exchange rate play in influencing aggregate demand when there is a change in the money supply?

11 What factors determine the effectiveness of fiscal policy and monetary policy?

12 Under what conditions is fiscal policy more effective than monetary policy in stimulating aggregate demand?

13 Distinguish between the hypotheses of extreme Keynesians and extreme monetarists.

14 Explain the Keynesian-monetarist controversy about the influence of monetary policy and fiscal policy on aggregate demand.

15 Explain how the Keynesian-monetarist controversy in question 14 was settled.

16 Explain how fiscal policy and monetary policy influence the composition of aggregate demand.

17 Explain the effect of an increase in the money supply or an expansionary fiscal policy on the price level and real GDP. Be careful to distinguish between the short-run and long-run effect.

PROBLEMS

1 In the economy described in Fig. 12.1, suppose the government decreases its purchases of goods and services by $1 trillion.

- **a** Work out the first round effects.
- **b** Explain how real GDP and the interest rate change.
- **c** Explain the second round effects that take the economy to a new equilibrium.

2 In the economy described in Fig. 12.1, suppose the Fed increases the money supply by $1 trillion.

- **a** Work out the first round effects.
- **b** Explain how real GDP and the interest rate change.
- **c** Explain the second round effects that take the economy to a new equilibrium.

3 The economies of two countries, Alpha and Beta, are identical in every way except the following: In Alpha, a change in the interest rate of 1 percentage point (for example, from 5 percent to 6 percent) results in a $1 trillion change in the quantity of real money demanded. In Beta, a change in the interest rate of 1 percentage point results in a $0.1 trillion change in the quantity of real money demanded.

- **a** In which economy does an increase in government purchases of goods and services have a larger effect on real GDP?
- **b** In which economy is the crowding out effect weaker?
- **c** In which economy does a change in the money supply have a larger effect on equilibrium real GDP?

4 The economy is in a recession, and the government wants to increase aggregate demand, stimulate exports, and increase investment. It has three policy options: increase government purchases of goods and services, decrease taxes, and increase the money supply.

- **a** Explain the mechanisms at work under each alternative policy.
- **b** What is the effect of each policy on the composition of aggregate demand?
- **c** What are the short-run effects of each policy on real GDP and the price level?
- **d** Which policy would you recommend that the government adopt?

5 The economy is at full employment, but the government is disappointed with the growth rate of real GDP. It wants to stimulate investment and at the same time avoid an increase in the price level. Suggest a combination of fiscal and monetary policies that will achieve the government's objective.

PART 4

AGGREGATE SUPPLY, INFLATION, AND RECESSION

Talking with Edmund Phelps

Edmund S. Phelps was born in Evanston, Illinois, in 1933 and is McVickar Professor of Political Economy at Columbia University. Professor Phelps was an undergraduate at Amherst College and obtained his Ph.D. from Yale in 1959. He was one of the initiators of New Macroeconomics—macroeconomics built on microeconomic foundations—and was the first to formalize the idea of the "natural rate of unemployment." Professor Phelps is a theorist—but a theorist who is driven by the desire to understand and explain the facts of unemployment and inflation and business cycles.

Why did you first study economics?

When I was going into my sophomore year at Amherst, my father prevailed on me to try a course in economics. I had guessed it was a dull subject that didn't get much beyond balance sheets or profit-and-loss statements, but I couldn't refuse my father's sole request. To my surprise, I took to the subject right away. The teacher and the textbook were part of the explanation. My professor, Jim Nelson, had a breezy style and was good at devising brain teasers for the weekly quizzes, and the textbook, by Paul Samuelson, was written in a brilliant style. I did very well, too, which was a reinforcement.

The other important point for me and a lot of students, I think, is that you are vaguely aware that you don't really have down how the various parts of the subject fit together. So you keep deciding to take one more course—until one day you find you've got a Ph.D.

What were the first questions that attracted your attention?

Even as a sophomore, I noticed that the microeconomics chapter on the theory of the firm talked

"... the New Classical models failed one empirical test after another. There are two possible reasons for these failures. The first is that expectations are not generally rational."

about employment levels and relative prices in various industries being determined by supply and demand, while the macroeconomics chapter talked about employment as determined by aggregate demand plus some "story" about rigidity or stickiness of wages and prices. It turned out I spent a big chunk of my career working on that "story."

From thinking about that fundamental theoretical question, I started asking questions about the more applied areas of monetary and fiscal policy and public finance: What difference does it make what kind of inflation targets the monetary authorities adopt? Similarly, what difference does it make what fiscal policy is chosen? Or what tax rate structure is legislated?

These questions appealed to my interest, which went way back, in notions of the just state and the good society or, in economic terms, the optimum economy. The idea of economic justice, of just rewards for contributions to the output of the economy, is a flickering passion of mine. But there are very few economists around who respond to it as I do. It's a minority taste, I guess. Like opera.

How did you hit on the idea that there is a natural rate of unemployment—an equilibrium unemployment rate—that is independent of the inflation rate? Were you driven by the internal logic of the theory or by your observations of events?

I had read enough of earlier scholars—like Lerner and Fellner—to know that the idea of an equilibrium rate of unemployment that is not influenced by inflation had to be good economics. The problem was to develop, or at least sketch, the rudiments of a theory of how the natural rate is actually determined. Then I could develop a concrete, specific explanation of why steady inflation wouldn't affect the equilibrium rate.

How do you rate the predictive power of the natural rate theory?

I kept looking over my shoulder at each month's inflation rate in 1966 and 1967 when the unemployment rate had gotten pretty low. The inflation rate rose so slowly that I worried. Fortunately, the model looked better and better as we got to 1970, and statistical studies over subsequent years have given it mounting support.

The so-called "New Classical" approach of the 1970s in many ways followed your earlier work on wages in a setting of incomplete information. What is your evaluation of the contribution of the New Classicals?

On the one hand, I admired them very much for deriving such beautiful results so clearly. But I was a bit shocked that they accepted the idea of rational expectations so uncritically. And, like a lot of others, I was repelled by the imperious attitude that to be scientific, economics had to be done their way—that you don't question the faith.

Anyway, the New Classical models failed one empirical test after another. For example, they couldn't explain in a plausible way why the economy tends to come out of even short recessions as gradually as it does—what's called the "persistence problem." Also, they couldn't explain why changes in the money supply that are perfectly anticipated by people have about as much effect on output and employment as money supply changes that are presumably unforeseen. There are two possible reasons for these failures. The first is that expectations are not generally rational. The second

is that wages and prices are not all reset simultaneously every month or quarter-year, contrary to the New Classical theory.

You are regarded as one of the founders of the New Keynesian school of macroeconomics. What is New Keynesian macroeconomics, and why do you find it attractive?

The New Keynesian school proposes that prices and wages are *not* all adjusted at the same time. When you introduce that possibility into your model, the average price level can adjust only gradually to monetary and real shocks to the economy. In other words, the effects of a shock are spread out over a long period of time. And even correctly foreseen shocks to the money supply are not offset by anticipatory changes in wages and prices.

At this time the New Keynesian model is still the model of choice for me and many others.

What is your evaluation of the real business cycle school?

The hope was that this school would show how the underlying equilibrium path of employment and output was disturbed by fundamental non-monetary factors. It would be the final achievement rounding out macroeconomic theory.

But it has not gotten as far as it could have because of its insistence on so many of the fetishes of neoclassical theory plus some new self-inflicted constraints.

For example, they can't let go of the neoclassical feature of their models that all unemployment, or nonemployment, is basically voluntary because prices and wages are all market clearing. With only a little exaggeration, you can say that the natural rate of unemployment in their models is zero. Their only way of explaining fluctuations in employment is by explaining fluctuations in the length of the workweek that workers are willing to work.

"The result is a labor market equilibrium in which not all workers can get the jobs they want and meet the qualifications . . ."

"**A**ny analysis of the consequences of an economic disturbance that focuses just on the short-run or on the long-run . . . runs a big risk of being wrong."

It's a shame, really. Here are these technical wizards who have for some reason decided to turn their backs on the most important development within economic theory of the twentieth century. That is the rise of a modern theory of economic equilibrium based on asymmetric information, or private information. This theory explains that employees inflict damage on their employers, abusing their relationship by quitting frivolously or shirking unconscionably or arriving shamelessly unfit to work. Just about the only thing firms can do about it is to offer any new worker hired a better rate of pay to induce better behavior. But this makes labor too expensive and hence causes some people not to be able to get jobs who otherwise could have. The result is a labor market equilibrium in which not all workers can get the jobs they want and meet the qualifications for because there is no way they can provide convincing information to a firm that they would not quit or shirk or be absent with the same frequency as the firm's existing employees—or be worse if the pay was worse.

What key principle of economics do you keep returning to in your own work?

Well, when I am wondering what economics suggests will be the consequences of some event or other, I keep rediscovering the importance of distinguishing between near-term and far-term effects. In trying to figure out the short-term or medium-term effects, I sooner or later realize I had better focus on the long-run effect first and then work backward to try to see what sort of short-run or medium-term scenario could lead to that long-run outcome. I guess the main principle is that the short term and the long term are distinct, though the one flows into the other. Any analysis of the consequences of an economic disturbance that focuses just on the short run or on the long run is apt to be misleading. And, being incomplete, it runs a big risk of also being wrong.

CHAPTER 13

PRODUCTIVITY, WAGES, AND UNEMPLOYMENT

After studying this chapter, you will be able to:

- Explain why productivity and real GDP grow
- Explain how firms decide how much labor to employ
- Explain how households decide how much labor to supply
- Explain how wages, employment, and unemployment are determined if wages are flexible
- Explain how wages, employment, and unemployment are determined if wages are "sticky"
- Derive the short-run and long-run aggregate supply curves
- Explain what makes aggregate supply and unemployment fluctuate

Incomes and Jobs

OVER THE YEARS, WE BECOME MORE PRODUCTIVE. AS A result, our economy expands and our incomes grow. On the average, in 1992, each hour of work earned us 60 percent more than it did in 1960. But Japanese and German wages have grown even more quickly than our own. What makes our productivity and wages grow over the years, and why do wages in some countries grow faster than those in the United States? ◆◆ Our economy does not expand along a smooth path. It ebbs and flows through the business cycle, sometimes growing quickly and sometimes contracting. As it does so, employment and unemployment and real GDP march in close step with each other. Sometimes the U.S. economy is in a state of recession—as it was in 1991. The official unemployment rate in that recession was close to 7 percent, up from 5.4 percent a year earlier. Add to the official unemployment rate an allowance for part-time workers who want a full-time job and "discouraged workers"—those who want jobs but have stopped looking—and the rate climbs to more than 10 percent. One third of the unemployed had been without jobs for only four weeks or less, but one third had been without jobs for between one and three months, and one out of six had not worked for more than six months. Why does unemployment occur? And what makes its rate rise and fall? ◆◆ In the eighteen months between the start of a recession in July 1990 and December 1991, 1.9 million jobs were lost in the United States. Three big employers alone—General Motors, Xerox, and IBM—eliminated more than 100,000 jobs. Why, instead of firing workers, didn't these companies cut back on everybody's hours and negotiate pay cuts?

◆ ◆ ◆ ◆ In this chapter we'll take a close look at productivity, wages, and the U.S. labor market. We'll discover what makes our productivity and wages grow, why the unemployment rate is sometimes unusually high, and what brings high unemployment rates down. We'll also take a close look at the major disagreement among macroeconomists—a disagreement about how flexible the labor market is in bringing about changes in wages to keep the quantity of labor supplied equal to the quantity demanded. ◆ ◆ Our study of productivity growth and the labor market completes a further block in the macroeconomic jigsaw puzzle—the aggregate supply block. We'll return to the long-run and short-run aggregate supply curves that you met in Chapter 7 and see how those curves are related to the labor market. We'll also see what makes aggregate supply grow and at a pace that fluctuates, bringing cycles in employment, incomes, and unemployment. ◆ ◆ Let's begin by looking at labor productivity and income growth.

Productivity and Income Growth

When we talk about *productivity,* we usually mean labor productivity—although we can measure the productivity of any factor of production. **Labor productivity** is measured as total output per person employed. To study the growth of labor productivity and its effects on wages, employment, and unemployment, we use the concept of the production function. A **production function** shows how output varies as the employment of inputs is varied. A **short-run production function** shows how output varies when the quantity of labor employed varies, holding constant the quantity of capital and the state of technology. Production functions exist for every kind of economic activity—building dams and highways or baking loaves of bread. But the production function that tells us about the relationship between *aggregate* employment and *aggregate* output is the short-run *aggregate* production function. The **short-run aggregate production function** shows how real GDP varies as the quantity of labor employed is varied, holding constant all other inputs including the capital stock and state of technology.

The table in Fig. 13.1 records part of an economy's short-run aggregate production function. In that table, we look at the aggregate quantity of labor, measured in billions of hours a year, over the range 135 billion to 155 billion. Through that range of employment, real GDP varies between $4.35 trillion and $4.53 trillion a year (measured in 1987 dollars). The short-run aggregate production function (*PF*) is illustrated in the graph in Fig. 13.1. The labor input is measured on the horizontal axis, and real GDP is measured on the vertical axis. The short-run production function slopes upward, indicating that more labor input produces more real GDP.

The Marginal Product of Labor

The **marginal product of labor** is the additional real GDP produced by one additional hour of labor input, holding all other inputs and technology constant. We calculate the marginal product of labor as the change in real GDP divided by the change in the quantity of labor employed. Let's do such a calculation, using Fig. 13.1.

When the labor input increases from 135 to 145 billion hours, real GDP increases from $4.35 trillion to $4.46 trillion—an increase of $0.11 trillion, or $110 billion. The marginal product of labor over this range is $11 an hour ($110 billion divided by 10 billion hours). Next, look at what happens at a higher level of labor input. When the labor input increases by the same 10 billion hours but from 145 billion to 155 billion hours, real GDP increases, but by less than in the previous case—by only $0.07 trillion, or $70 billion. Now the marginal product of labor is $7 an hour ($70 billion divided by 10 billion hours).

The marginal product of labor is measured by the slope of the production function. Figure 13.1 highlights this fact. The slope of the production function at point *b* is $11 an hour. This slope is calculated as $110 billion—the change in real GDP from $4.35 trillion to $4.46 trillion—divided by 10 billion hours—the change in employment from 135 billion hours to 145 billion hours. Similarly, the slope of the production function at point *d* is $7 an hour.

FIGURE 13.1

The Short-Run Aggregate Production Function

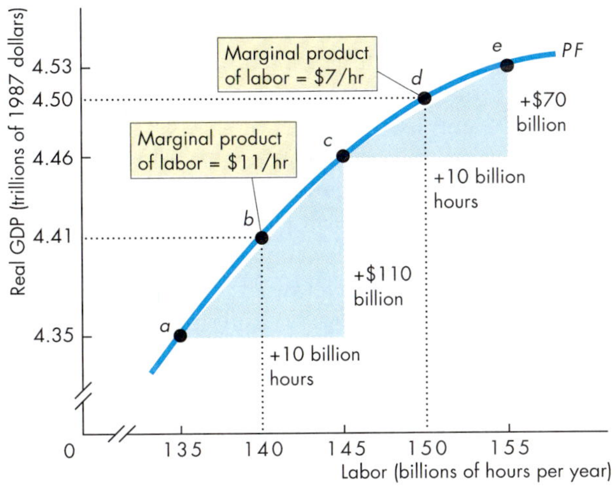

	Labor (billions of hours per year)	Real GDP (trillions of 1987 dollars per year)
a	135	4.35
b	140	4.41
c	145	4.46
d	150	4.50
e	155	4.53

The short-run aggregate production function shows the level of real GDP at each quantity of labor input, holding all other inputs constant. The table lists five points on a short-run aggregate production function. Each row tells us the amount of real GDP that can be produced by a given labor input. Points *a* through *e* in the graph correspond to the rows in the table. The curve passing through these points traces the economy's short-run aggregate production function. The marginal product of labor is highlighted in the diagram. As the labor input increases, real GDP increases but by successively smaller amounts. For example, a 10 billion hour increase in labor from 135 to 145 billion increases real GDP by $0.11 trillion—a marginal product of $11 an hour. But the same 10 billion hour increase in labor from 145 to 155 billion hours increases real GDP by only $0.07 trillion—a marginal product of $7 an hour.

Diminishing Marginal Product of Labor

The most important fact about the marginal product of labor is that it declines as the labor input increases. This phenomenon, apparent from the calculations we've just performed and visible in the figure, is called the diminishing marginal product of labor. The **diminishing marginal product of labor** is the tendency for the marginal product of labor to decline as the labor input increases, holding everything else constant.

Diminishing marginal product of labor arises because we are dealing with a *short-run* production function. As the quantity of labor employed is varied, all other inputs are held constant. Thus, although more labor can produce more output, a larger labor force operates the same capital equipment—machines and tools—as does a smaller labor force. As more people are hired, the capital equipment is worked closer and closer to its physical limits, more breakdowns occur, and bottlenecks arise. As a result, output does not increase in proportion to the amount of labor employed. The marginal product of labor declines as more labor is hired. This feature is present in almost all production processes and also in the relationship between aggregate employment and aggregate output—real GDP.

The fact that the marginal product of labor diminishes has an important influence on the demand for labor, as we shall see shortly. But first, let's look at some of the things that make the production function shift.

Economic Growth and Technological Change

Economic growth is the expansion of the economy's productive capacity. Every year, some of the economy's resources are devoted to developing new technologies to achieve greater output from a given amount of labor input. Also, resources are devoted to building new capital equipment that incorporates the most productive technologies available. Capital accumulation and technology advances shift the short-run aggregate production function upward over time. Figure 13.2 illustrates such a shift. The curve labeled PF_{94} is the same as the production function in Fig. 13.1. During 1994, capital accumulates and new technologies are incorporated into the

FIGURE 13.2

The Growth of Output

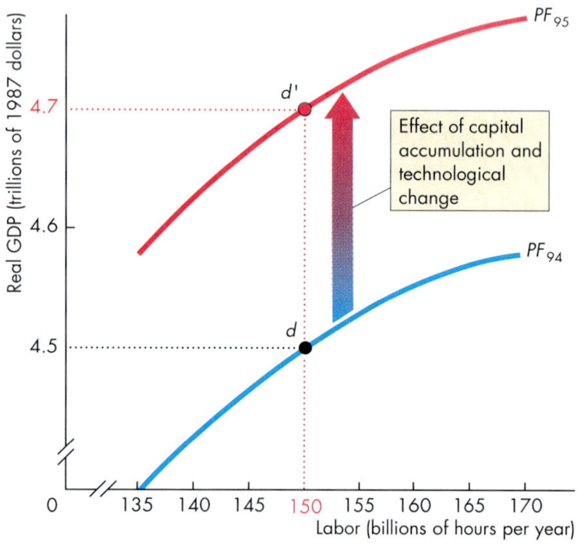

Output grows over time. The accumulation of capital and the adoption of more productive technologies make it possible to achieve a higher level of real GDP for any given labor input. For example, between 1994 and 1995 the production function shifts upward from PF_{94} to PF_{95}. A labor input of 150 billion hours produces $4.5 trillion of real GDP in 1994 (point *d*) and $4.7 trillion in 1995 (point *d'*).

new, more productive capital equipment. Some old, less productive capital wears out and is retired to the scrap heap. The net result is an increase in the productivity of the economy that results in an upward movement of the short-run aggregate production function to PF_{95}. When 150 billion hours of labor are employed, the economy can produce a real GDP of $4.5 trillion in 1994 (point *d*). By 1995, that same quantity of labor can produce $4.7 trillion (point *d'*). Each level of labor input can produce more output in 1995 than in 1994.

Variable Growth Rates

Capital accumulation and technological change do not proceed at a constant pace. In some years, the level of investment is high and the capital stock grows quickly. In other years—recession years—investment decreases and the capital stock grows slowly. Also, there are fluctuations in the pace of technological change. Technological change has two stages, invention and innovation. **Invention** is the discovery of a new technique; **innovation** is the act of putting a new technique to work. At some times, lots of new things are being discovered but not being put to use—invention is rapid but innovation is slow. It is the pace of innovation that influences the growth rate of productivity. Although the short-run aggregate production function shifts upward over time, occasionally it shifts downward—productivity decreases. Negative influences, or shocks, that make the aggregate production function shift downward are widespread droughts, major disruptions to international trade, civil unrest, or war. A serious disruption of international trade occurred in 1974 when the Organization of Petroleum Exporting Countries (OPEC) placed an embargo on oil exports. This deprived the industrialized world of one of its most crucial raw materials. Firms could not obtain all the fuel they needed, and as a result the labor force was not able to produce as much output as normal. As a consequence, the short-run aggregate production function shifted downward in 1974.

Let's take a closer look at the short-run aggregate production function in the United States and see what it tells about our productivity growth.

U.S. Productivity Growth

We can examine productivity growth in the United States by looking at the U.S. short-run aggregate production function shown in Fig. 13.3. Concentrate first on the blue dots in this figure. There is a dot for each year between 1960 and 1992, and each one represents aggregate employment and real GDP for a particular year. For example, the dot for 1960 tells us that in 1960 labor hours were 136 billion and real GDP was $2 trillion; in 1992, labor hours were 214 billion and real GDP was $4.9 trillion.

These two dots together with the other dots in the figure do not all lie on the same short-run aggregate production function. Instead, each dot lies on its own short-run aggregate production function. Each year the stock of capital equipment and the state of technology change, so the economy's productive potential usually is higher than in the year before. The production function for 1960 is PF_{60}, and that for 1992 is PF_{92}.

The 1992 short-run aggregate production function is 90 percent higher than the 1960 short-run aggregate production function. This fact means that

FIGURE 13.3

The U.S. Short-Run Aggregate Production Function

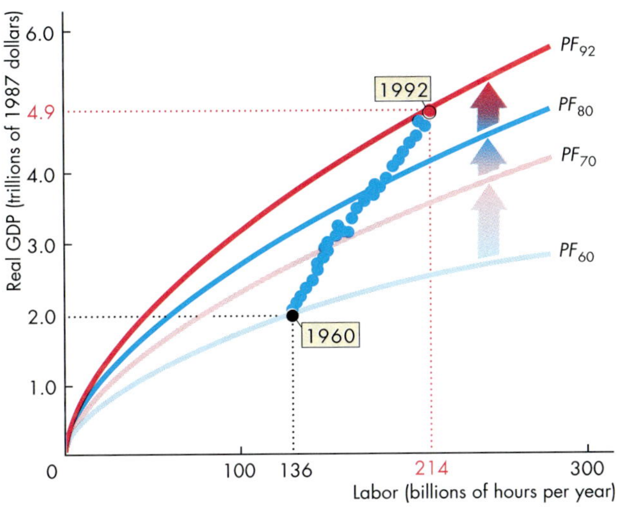

The dots in the figure show real GDP and aggregate hours of labor employed in the United States for each year between 1960 and 1992. For example, in 1960, labor input was 136 billion hours and real GDP was \$2 trillion. In 1992, labor input was 214 billion hours and real GDP was \$4.9 trillion. The dots do not lie on one short-run aggregate production function. Instead, the short-run aggregate production function shifts from year to year as capital accumulates and technologies change. The figure shows the short-run aggregate production functions for 1960 and 1992—PF_{60} and PF_{92}. The 1992 production function is 90 percent higher than that for 1960. For example, the 136 billion hours of labor that produced \$2 trillion of real GDP in 1960 would have produced \$3.7 trillion of real GDP in 1992. Similarly, the 214 billion hours of labor that produced \$4.9 trillion of real GDP in 1992 would have produced approximately \$2.6 trillion of real GDP in 1960.

if employment in 1992 had been the same as it was in 1960, real GDP in 1992 would have been \$3.7 trillion. Equivalently, if employment in 1960 had been the same as it was in 1992, real GDP in 1960 would have been \$2.6 trillion.

The Productivity Slowdown

The short-run production function shifts upward over time because we become more productive—a given amount of labor produces an increased amount of output. But labor productivity does not grow at an even pace, and during the 1970s we experienced a productivity slowdown. You can see this slowdown in Fig. 13.3. In addition to the production functions for 1960 and 1992 that we've just discussed, the figure shows the production functions for 1970 (PF_{70}) and 1980 (PF_{80}). You can see that there was a large shift in the production function between 1960 and 1970. During that decade, productivity increased by 36 percent. But between 1970 and 1980, the production function shift was smaller. During the 1970s, productivity increased by only 17 percent. Productivity growth increased during the 1980s, but it did not get back to its 1960s performance.

There are several reasons for the slowdown in U.S. productivity growth during the 1970s. Two of the most important are energy price shocks and changes in the composition of output. First, energy prices quadrupled in 1973–1974 and increased sharply again in 1979–1980, forcing firms to find energy-saving, labor-using, and capital-using methods of production. Second, as our economy expanded, the composition of output changed. Agriculture and manufacturing contracted, and services expanded. Productivity growth is the fastest in agriculture and manufacturing and slowest in services; so as the composition of output changed toward a greater emphasis on services, average productivity growth slowed down. Other possible sources of slow productivity growth in the United States compared with some other countries and some possible solutions to the problem are examined in Reading Between the Lines on pp. 342–343.

REVIEW

A production function tells us how the output that can be produced varies as inputs are varied. A short-run production function tells us how the output that can be produced varies as the employment of labor varies, holding everything else constant. The short-run aggregate production function tells us how real GDP varies as total labor hours vary. The marginal product of labor—the increase in real GDP resulting from a one-hour increase of labor input—diminishes as the labor input increases. ◆◆ The short-run production function usually shifts upward from year to year,

The Productivity Slowdown

The New York Times, February 9, 1992

Attention America! Snap Out of It!

BY STEVEN GREENHOUSE

After years of watching Japan increase its manufacturing might, Americans have awakened to the dangers of losing the industrial base that long made their nation the envy of the world. At long last, Americans of all stripes, Democrat and Republican, white collar and blue, are groping for ways to close the competitiveness gap that has allowed Japan to muscle into the lead in such key industries as cars and computer chips.

Some . . . experts say the Federal Reserve should pump $25 billion into the nation's hobbled banks by purchasing their shares, which would enable them to lend some $250 billion to American companies for modernization.

. . . Other experts say the country should adopt the German job-training system in which many high school students spend time in factories learning to master modern technologies and solve problems in teams.

Some say Washington should allow banks to own shares in industrial companies, as they do in Germany and Japan. . . .

A New Cottage Industry

These are just a few of the ideas being churned out by a new cottage industry in which hundreds of economists, think tanks, professors, politicians, columnists, and management consultants ruminate full time on how to improve America's competitiveness.

To a surprising degree, these deep thinkers . . . have reached a consensus on many prescriptions for America's economic ills. They generally agree that the nation needs to take the following steps.

- Increase savings to provide business with more money to invest in buildings and machines that increase productivity. . . .
- Step up efforts to train American workers so they can adapt to the technologies and more flexible factories of tomorrow.
- Get companies to think long-term so they will make the strategic investments in equipment, training, and research. . . .
- Rein in health-care spending, which puts a heavy burden on American industry. . . .
- Spend more on research and development so that industry not only maintains its lead in innovation but also improves its ability to turn ideas into hot-selling products.
- Invest more in public structures like highways, bridges, railways, and airports. . . .

The Essence of the Story

A consensus has emerged on the country's competitiveness problem. It has the following elements:

- Increase saving and invest more in buildings and machines.
- Improve training of American workers.
- Encourage companies to think long-term.
- Cut health care costs.
- Spend more on research and development.
- Invest more in public structures (highways, bridges, railways, and airports).

More controversial proposed solutions are

- Inject Federal Reserve money into banks.
- Put more high school students into factories where they can learn to master modern technologies and solve problems in teams.
- Allow banks to own shares in industrial companies.

Background and Analysis

Between 1960 and 1991, income per person grew in the United States by 82 percent, in Germany by 138 percent, and in Japan by 441 percent.

These *apparently* diverging income levels are shown in Fig. 1.

But in 1960, income per person in the United States was $7,400, in Germany it was $5,200, and in Japan it was $2,200. (These amounts are based on U.S. dollars valued at 1980 prices.)

Because in 1960 the U.S. income level was much higher than Germany's and Japan's, the faster income growth in Germany and Japan has enabled them to close the gap on the United States.

But, as Fig. 2 shows, these countries have not *overtaken* the United States.

During the years 1989–1991, income per person in the United States decreased, while in Germany and Japan it continued to increase.

The U.S. slowdown in 1989–1991 looks more like a business cycle slowdown—similar to that in 1982 (see Fig. 2)—than a permanent change in trend.

The U.S. productivity slowdown is real, but the reactions of the "experts" and their proposed solutions need careful evaluation.

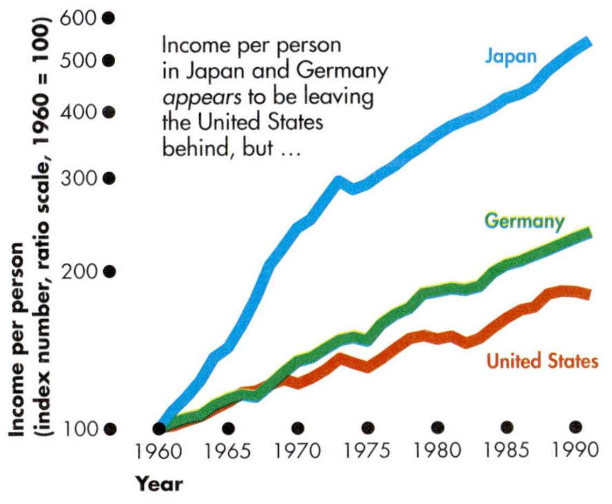

Figure 1

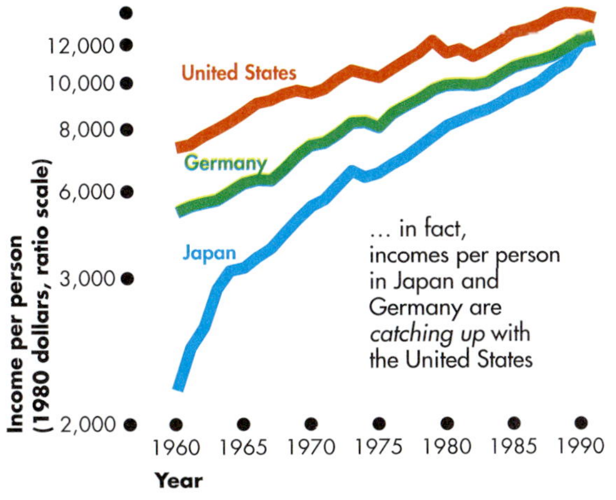

Figure 2

Increasing saving and investment, improving the training of American workers, "thinking long-term," spending more on research and development, and investing more in public structures will pay off only if each individual action passes the market test of delivering a rate of return that is greater than or equal to the next best alternative.

Cutting health care costs is fine if that does not mean cutting health care. But one of the benefits of a high income is a high standard of health care, and, to some degree, high costs in the United States reflect a high standard of care.

The proposal that the Fed pump $25 billion into the banks would increase aggregate *demand*, but it is not clear that aggregate *supply* would increase by much.

The proposal that the banks buy shares in industrial companies would increase the riskiness of the banks, imposing a cost that needs to be weighed against any possible benefits.

but on occasion it shifts downward. Capital accumulation and technological advances shift the short-run aggregate production function upward. Shocks such as droughts, disruptions of international trade, or civil and political unrest shift the production function downward. The short-run aggregate production function in the United States shifted upward by 90 percent between 1960 and 1992. ◆

We've seen that output in any year depends on the position of the short-run aggregate production function and on the quantity of labor employed. Even if the short-run aggregate production function shifts upward, it is still possible for output to fall because of a fall in employment. For example, in 1991, employment and real GDP fell as the economy went into recession. To determine the level of output, we need to understand not only the influences on the short-run aggregate production function but also those on the level of employment. To determine the level of employment, we need to study the demand for and supply of labor and how the market allocates labor to jobs. We'll begin by studying the demand for labor.

The Demand for Labor

The **quantity of labor demanded** is the number of labor hours hired by all the firms in an economy. The **demand for labor** is the quantity of labor demanded at each real wage rate. The **real wage rate** is the wage per hour expressed in constant dollars—for example, the wage per hour expressed in 1987 dollars. The wage rate expressed in *current dollars* is called the **money wage rate.** A real wage rate expressed in 1987 dollars tells us what today's money wage rate would buy if prices today were the same as in 1987. We calculate the real wage rate by dividing the money wage rate by the GDP deflator and multiplying by 100. For example, if the money wage rate is $7 an hour and the GDP deflator is 140, the real wage rate is $5 ($7 divided by 140 and multiplied by 100 equals $5).

We can represent the demand for labor as a schedule or a curve. The table in Fig. 13.4 sets out an example of a demand for labor schedule. Row *b* tells us that at a real wage rate of $11 an hour, 140 billion hours of labor (per year) are demanded. The other rows of the table are read in a similar way. The demand for labor schedule is graphed as the demand for labor curve (*LD*). Each point on the curve corresponds to the row identified by the same letter in the table.

Why is the quantity of labor demanded influenced by the *real* wage rate? Why isn't it the *money* wage rate that affects the quantity of labor demanded? Also, why does the quantity of labor demanded increase as the real wage rate decreases? That is, why does the demand for labor curve slope downward? We're now going to answer these questions.

Diminishing Marginal Product and the Demand for Labor

Firms are in business to maximize profits. Each worker that a firm hires adds to its costs and increases its output. Up to a point, the extra output produced by the worker is worth more to the firm than the wages the firm has to pay. But each additional hour of labor hired produces less output than the previous hour—the marginal product of labor diminishes. As the amount of labor employed increases and the capital equipment employed is constant, more workers have to use the same machines and the plant operates closer and closer to its physical limits. Output increases, but it does not increase in proportion to the increase in labor input. As the firm hires more workers, it eventually reaches the point at which the revenue from selling the extra output produced by an additional hour of labor equals the hourly wage rate. If the firm hires even one more hour of labor, the extra cost incurred will exceed the revenue brought in from selling the extra output. The firm will not employ that additional hour of labor. It hires the quantity of labor such that the revenue brought in by the last hour of labor input equals the money wage rate.

To see why it is the *real* wage rate, rather than the money wage rate, that affects the quantity of labor demanded, let's consider an example.

FIGURE 13.4

Demand for Labor

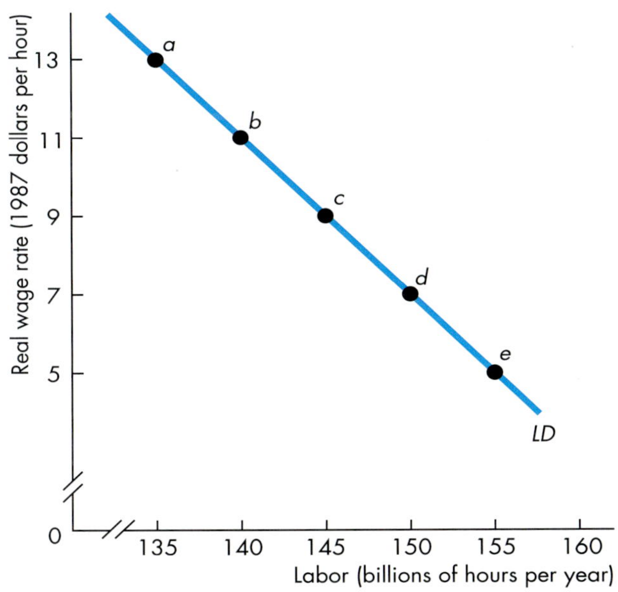

	Real wage rate (1987 dollars per hour)	Quantity of labor demanded (billions of hours per year)
a	**13**	**135**
b	**11**	**140**
c	**9**	**145**
d	**7**	**150**
e	**5**	**155**

The quantity of labor demanded increases as the real wage rate decreases, as illustrated by the labor demand schedule in the table and the demand for labor curve (*LD*). Each row in the table tells us the quantity of labor demanded at a given real wage rate and corresponds to a point on the labor demand curve. For example, when the real wage rate is $7 an hour, the quantity of labor demanded is 150 billion hours a year (point *d*). The demand for labor curve slopes downward because it pays firms to hire labor as long as the firm's marginal product of labor is greater than or equal to the real wage rate. The lower the real wage rate, the larger is the number of workers whose marginal product exceeds that real wage rate.

The Demand for Labor in a Soda Factory

A soda factory employs 400 hours of labor. The additional output produced by the last hour hired is 11 bottles of soda. That is, the marginal product of labor is 11 bottles of soda per hour. Soda sells for 50¢ a bottle, so the revenue brought in from selling these 11 bottles is $5.50. The money wage rate is also $5.50 an hour. This last hour of labor hired brings in as much revenue as the wages paid out, so it just pays the firm to hire that hour of labor. The firm is paying a real wage rate that is exactly the same as the marginal product of labor—11 bottles of soda. That is, the firm's real wage rate is equal to the money wage rate of $5.50 an hour divided by the price of soda, 50¢ a bottle.

A Change in the Real Wage Rate Let's work out what happens when the real wage rate changes. Suppose the money wage rate increases to $11 an hour while the price of soda remains constant at 50¢ a bottle. The real wage rate has now increased to 22 bottles of soda—equal to the money wage of $11 an hour divided by 50¢ a bottle, the price of a bottle of soda. The last hour of labor hired now costs $11 but brings in only $5.50 of extra revenue. It does not pay the firm to hire this hour of labor. The firm decreases the quantity of labor employed until the marginal product of labor brings in $11 of revenue. This occurs when the marginal product of labor is 22 bottles of soda—that is, 22 bottles at 50¢ a bottle sell for $11. The marginal product of labor is again equal to the real wage rate. But to make the marginal product of labor equal to the real wage rate, the firm has to decrease the quantity of labor employed. Thus, when the real wage rate increases, the quantity of labor demanded decreases.

In the example we've just worked through, the real wage rate increased because the money wage rate increased with a constant output price. But the same outcome occurs if the money wage rate remains constant and the output price decreases. For example, if the wage rate remains at $5.50 an hour while the price of soda falls to 25¢ a bottle, the real wage rate is 22 bottles of soda and the soda bottling factory hires the amount of labor that makes the marginal product of labor equal to 22 bottles.

A Change in the Money Wage Rate with a Constant Real Wage To see why the money wage rate does not affect the quantity of labor demanded, suppose that the money wage rate and all prices double. The money wage rate increases to $11 an hour, and the price of soda increases to $1 a bottle. The soda factory is in the same real situation as before. It pays $11 for the last hour of labor employed and sells the output produced by that labor for $11. The money wage rate has doubled from $5.50 to $11 an hour, but nothing *real* has changed. The real wage rate is still 11 bottles of soda. As far as the firm is concerned, 400 hours is still the right quantity of labor to hire. The money wage rate has changed, but the real wage rate and the quantity of labor demanded have remained constant.

The Demand for Labor in the Economy

The demand for labor in the economy as a whole is determined in the same way as in the soda factory. Thus the quantity of labor demanded depends on the real wage rate, not the money wage rate, and the higher the real wage rate, the smaller is the quantity of labor demanded.

We now know why the quantity of labor demanded depends on the real wage rate and why the demand for labor curve slopes downward, but what makes it shift?

Changes in the Demand for Labor

When the marginal product of each hour of labor changes, the demand for labor changes and the demand for labor curve shifts. The accumulation of capital and the development of new technologies are constantly increasing the marginal product of each hour of labor. We've already seen one effect of such changes. They shift the short-run aggregate production function upward, as shown in Fig. 13.2. At the same time, they make the short-run aggregate production function *steeper.* Anything that makes the short-run production function steeper increases the marginal product of each hour of labor—increases the extra output obtained from one additional hour of labor. At a given real wage rate, firms will increase the amount of labor they hire until the revenue brought in from selling the extra output produced by the last hour of labor input equals the hourly wage. Thus as the short-run aggregate production function shifts upward, the demand for labor curve also shifts to the right.

In general, the demand for labor curve shifts to the right over time. But there are fluctuations in the pace at which the demand for labor curve shifts that match the fluctuations in the short-run aggregate production function. Let's look at the demand for labor in the United States and see how it has changed over the period since 1960.

The U.S. Demand for Labor

Figure 13.5 shows the average real wage rate and the quantity of labor employed in each year between 1960 and 1992. For example, in 1992 the real wage was $15.05 an hour (in 1987 dollars) and 214 billion hours of labor were employed.

FIGURE 13.5

The U.S. Demand for Labor

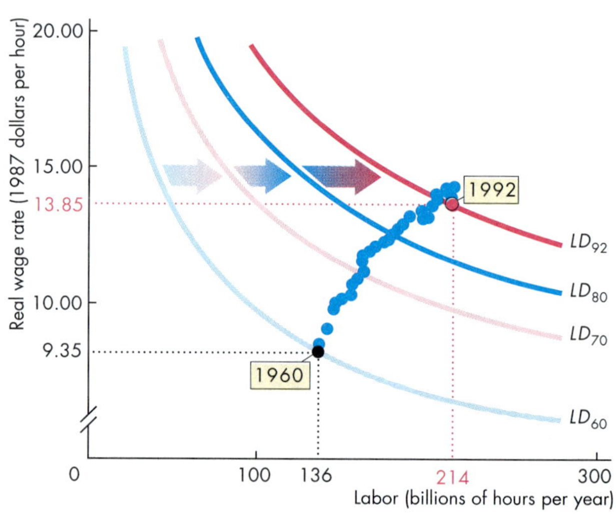

The figure shows the quantity of labor employed and the average real wage rate in the United States from 1960 to 1992. For example, in 1960 the real wage rate was $9.35 an hour and 136 billion hours of labor were employed. In 1992 the real wage rate was $15.05 an hour and 214 billion hours of labor were employed. These two points (and the dots for the years between them) do not lie on a single demand for labor curve. The demand for labor curve has shifted as a result of shifts in the short-run aggregate production function. The figure shows the demand curves for 1960 and 1992—LD_{60} and LD_{92}. Over time, the demand for labor curve has shifted to the right.

The figure shows four demand for labor curves, for 1960, 1970, 1980, and 1992. Between 1960 and 1992, the short-run aggregate production function shifted upward and the marginal product of labor increased. If the quantity of labor employed in 1992 had been the same as in 1960 (136 billion hours), the real wage rate would have been $18.02 per hour. If the quantity of labor employed in 1960 had been as high as that in 1992 (214 billion hours), the real wage rate in that year would have been only $7.80 per hour.

Another View of the Productivity Slowdown

Figure 13.5 also gives another view of the productivity slowdown of the 1970s and 1980s. The demand for labor curve is also the marginal product of labor curve. Thus shifts in the demand curve reflect changes in the marginal productivity of labor. You can see that the productivity of labor increased much more during the 1960s than it did during the two subsequent decades. The demand curve shifted farther between 1960 (LD_{60}) and 1970 (LD_{70}) than it did between and 1970 (LD_{70}) and 1980 (LD_{80}).

REVIEW

The quantity of labor demanded is the quantity of labor hours hired by all firms in the economy. It depends on the real wage rate. For an individual firm, the real wage rate is the money wage rate paid to the worker divided by the price for which the firm's output sells. For the economy as a whole, the real wage rate is the money wage rate divided by the price level. The lower the real wage rate, the greater is the quantity of labor demanded. The demand for labor curve slopes downward. ◆◆ The demand for labor curve shifts because of shifts in the short-run aggregate production function. An increase in the capital stock or advances in technology embodied in the capital stock shift the short-run aggregate production function upward and increase the marginal product of labor. The demand for labor curve shifts to the right, but at an uneven pace. ◆

Let's now turn to the other side of the labor market and see how the supply of labor is determined.

The Supply of Labor

The **quantity of labor supplied** is the number of hours of labor services that households supply to firms. The **supply of labor** is the quantity of labor supplied at each real wage rate.

We can represent the supply of labor as a schedule or a curve. The table in Fig. 13.6 shows a supply of labor schedule. For example, row *b* tells us that at a real wage rate of $3 an hour, 140 billion hours of labor (per year) are supplied. The other rows of the table are read in a similar way. The supply of labor schedule is graphed as the supply of labor curve (*LS*). Each point on the *LS* curve represents the row identified by the same letter in the table. As the real wage rate increases, the quantity of labor supplied increases. The supply of labor curve slopes upward.

But why does the quantity of labor supplied increase when the real wage rate increases? There are two reasons:

- Hours per worker increase.
- The labor force participation rate increases.

The Determination of Hours per Worker

In choosing how many hours to work, a household has to decide how to allocate its time between work and other activities. If a household chooses not to work for an hour, it does not get paid for that hour. The opportunity cost of not working an hour is what the household really gives up by not working. It is all the goods and services that the household could buy with the hourly money wage. So the opportunity cost of an hour of time spent not working is the real hourly wage rate.

What happens to people's willingness to work if the real wage rate increases? Such a change has two opposing effects:

- A substitution effect
- An income effect

Substitution Effect The substitution effect of a change in the real wage rate works in exactly the

FIGURE 13.6

The Supply of Labor

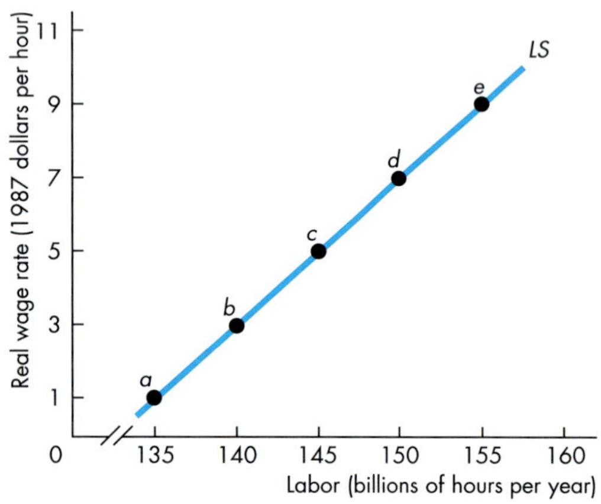

	Real wage rate (1987 dollars per hour)	Quantity of labor demanded (billions of hours per year)
a	1	135
b	3	140
c	5	145
d	7	150
e	9	155

The quantity of labor supplied increases as the real wage rate increases, as illustrated by the labor supply schedule in the table and the supply of labor curve (*LS*). Each row of the table tells us the quantity of labor supplied at a given real wage rate and corresponds to a point on the labor supply curve. For example, when the real wage rate is $7 an hour, the quantity of labor supplied is 150 billion hours a year (point *d*). The supply of labor curve slopes upward because households work longer hours, on the average, at higher real wage rates and more households participate in the labor force. These responses are reinforced by intertemporal substitution—the retiming of work to take advantage of temporarily high wages.

same way that a change in the price of tapes affects the quantity of tapes demanded. Just as tapes have a price, so does time. As we've just noted, the real hourly wage rate is the opportunity cost of an hour spent not working. A higher real wage rate increases the opportunity cost of time and makes time itself a more valuable commodity. This higher opportunity cost of not working encourages people to reduce their nonwork time and increase the time spent working. Thus as the real wage rate increases, more hours of work are supplied.

Income Effect But a higher real wage rate also increases people's incomes. The higher a person's income, the greater is his or her demand for all the different types of goods and services. One such "good" is leisure—the time to do pleasurable things that don't generate an income. Thus a higher real wage rate also makes people want to enjoy longer leisure hours and supply fewer hours of work.

Which of these two effects dominates depends on each individual's attitude toward work and also on the real wage rate. Attitudes toward work, though varying across individuals, do not change much, on the average, over time. But the real wage rate does change and brings changes in the quantity of labor supplied. At a very low real wage rate, the substitution effect is stronger than the income effect. That is, as the real wage rate increases, the inducement to substitute working time for leisure time is stronger than the inducement to spend part of a larger income on more leisure hours. As a consequence, as the real wage rate increases, the quantity of labor supplied increases.

At a high enough real wage rate, the income effect becomes stronger than the substitution effect. As the real wage increases, the inducement to spend more of the additional income on leisure time is stronger than the inducement to economize on leisure time.

Some people undoubtedly receive such a high real wage rate that a further increase would cause them to reduce their hours of work. But for most of us a higher real wage rate coaxes us to work more. Thus, on the average, the higher the real wage rate, the more hours each person works.

The Participation Rate

The **labor force participation rate** is the proportion of the working age population that is either employed or unemployed (but seeking employment). For a variety of reasons, people differ in their willingness to work. Some people have more productive opportunities at home and so need a bigger inducement to quit those activities and work for someone else.

Other individuals place a very high value on leisure, and they require a high real wage to induce them to do any work at all. These considerations suggest each person has a reservation wage. A **reservation wage** is the lowest wage at which a person will supply any labor. Below that wage, a person will not work.

Those people who have a reservation wage below or equal to the actual real wage will be in the labor force, and those who have a reservation wage above the real wage will not be in the labor force. The higher the real wage rate, the larger is the number of people whose reservation wage falls below the real wage rate and hence the larger is the labor force participation rate.

Reinforcing and strengthening the increase in hours worked per household and the labor force participation rate is an intertemporal substitution effect on the quantity of labor supplied.

Intertemporal Substitution

Households have to decide not only whether to work but also *when* to work. This decision is based not just on the current real wage but also on the current real wage relative to expected future real wages.

Suppose that the real wage rate is higher today than it is expected to be later on. How does this fact affect a person's labor supply decision? It encourages more work today and less in the future. Thus the higher is today's real wage rate relative to what is expected in the future (other things being constant), the larger is the supply of labor.

Temporarily high real wages are similar to a high rate of return. If real wages are temporarily high, people can obtain a higher rate of return on their work effort by enjoying a smaller amount of leisure and supplying more labor in such a period. By investing in some work now and taking the return in more leisure time later, they can obtain a higher overall level of consumption of goods and services and of leisure.

REVIEW

The opportunity cost of time is the real wage rate—the goods and services that can be bought with the income from an hour of work. An increase in the real wage rate, other things being equal, increases the supply of hours per worker and increases the labor force participation rate. A higher *current* real wage relative to the expected future real wage encourages people to supply more labor today and less in the future. ◆

We've now seen why, as the real wage rate increases, the quantity of labor supplied increases—why the supply of labor curve slopes upward. Let's next bring the two sides of the labor market together and study the determination of wages and employment.

Wages and Employment

We've discovered that as the real wage rate increases, the quantity of labor demanded declines and the quantity of labor supplied increases. We now want to study how the two sides of the labor market interact to determine the real wage rate, employment, and unemployment.

There is disagreement about how the labor market works, and this disagreement is the main source of current controversy in macroeconomics.

There are two leading theories about the labor market:

- Flexible wage theory
- Sticky wage theory

The flexible wage theory is built on the assumption that the labor market operates in a similar way to the markets for goods and services, with the real wage rate continuously and freely adjusting to keep the quantity demanded equal to the quantity supplied. The sticky wage theory is based on the assumption that wage contracts *fix* the money wage rate—hence the name sticky wages. If the money wage rate is sticky, the real wage rate does not continuously adjust to keep the quantity of labor demanded equal to the quantity supplied. Let's look at these two theories, beginning with the flexible wage theory.

The Flexible Wage Theory

Most people's wages—*money wages*—are determined by wage contracts that run for at least one year and often for two or three years. Doesn't this fact mean that money wages are not flexible? Not necessarily. Money wage rates, even those that are fixed by wage contracts, can and do adjust upward or downward. For example, some workers receive bonus payments in good times and lose those bonuses in bad times. Some workers get overtime at high rates of pay in good times but only get work at the normal hourly wage rate in bad times. Workers often get unusually rapid promotion to jobs with a higher wage rate in good times and get stuck on a lower rung of the promotion ladder in bad times. Thus fluctuations in bonuses, overtime pay, and the pace of promotion result in changes in the average wage rate even when wage rate schedules do not change.

The flexible wage theory of the labor market assumes that these sources of wage adjustment are sufficient to achieve a continuous balance between the quantities of labor supplied and demanded. The economy remains at full employment.

Figure 13.7 illustrates the theory. The demand for labor curve is *LD*, and the supply of labor curve is *LS*. This market determines an equilibrium real wage rate of $7 an hour and a quantity of labor employed of 150 billion hours. If the real wage rate is below its equilibrium level of $7 an hour, the quantity of labor demanded exceeds the quantity supplied. In such a situation, the real wage rate will rise, since firms are willing to offer higher and higher wages in order to overcome their labor shortages. The real wage rate will continue to rise until it reaches $7 an hour, at which point there will be no shortage of labor.

If the real wage rate is higher than its equilibrium level of $7 an hour, the quantity of labor supplied exceeds the quantity demanded. In this situation, households are not able to get all the work they want and firms find it easy to hire labor. Firms will have an incentive to cut the wage, and households will accept the lower wage to get a job. The real wage rate will fall until it reaches $7 an hour, at which point every household is satisfied with the quantity of labor it is supplying.

Changes in Wages and Employment The flexible wage theory makes predictions about wages and employment that are identical to the predictions of the demand and supply model we studied in Chapter 4. An increase in the demand for labor shifts the demand for labor curve to the right and increases both the real wage rate and the quantity of labor employed. A decrease in the demand for labor shifts the demand for labor curve to the left and decreases both the real wage rate and the quantity of labor employed. An increase in the supply of labor shifts the supply of labor curve to the right, lowering the real wage rate and increasing employment. A decrease in the supply of labor shifts the supply of labor curve to the left, raising the real wage rate and decreasing employment.

The demand for labor increases over time because capital accumulation and technological change increase the marginal product of labor. The supply of labor increases over time because the working age population is steadily increasing. Rightward shifts in

FIGURE 13.7

Equilibrium with Flexible Wages

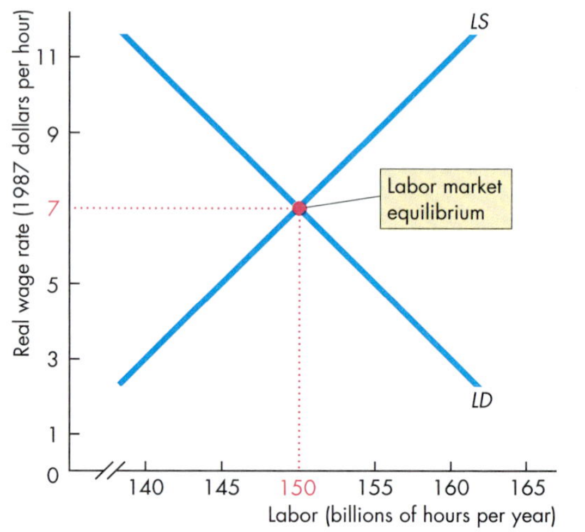

Equilibrium occurs when the real wage rate makes the quantity of labor demanded equal to the quantity supplied. This equilibrium occurs at a real wage rate of $7 an hour. At that real wage rate, 150 billion hours of labor are employed. At real wage rates below $7 an hour, the quantity of labor demanded exceeds the quantity supplied and the real wage rate rises. At real wage rates above $7 an hour, the quantity of labor supplied exceeds the quantity of labor demanded and the real wage rate falls.

the demand for labor curve have generally been larger than shifts in the supply of labor curve, so, over time, both the quantity of labor employed and the real wage rate have increased.

Aggregate Supply with Flexible Wages

The flexible wage theory of the labor market has a remarkable implication for the aggregate supply of goods and services—of real GDP. The quantity of real GDP supplied is independent of the price level.

Recall the definitions of the short-run aggregate supply curve and the long-run aggregate supply curve (Chapter 7, pp. 165–166). The short-run aggregate supply curve tells us how the quantity of real GDP supplied varies as the price level varies, holding everything else constant. The long-run aggregate supply curve tells us how the quantity of real GDP varies as the price level varies when wages change along with the price level to achieve full employment.

According to the flexible wage theory of the labor market, the money wage rate *always* adjusts to determine a real wage rate that brings equality between the quantity of labor demanded and quantity supplied. That is, as the price level changes, the money wage rate adjusts so as to keep the real wage rate constant. The labor market remains in equilibrium—at full employment. The aggregate supply curve generated by the flexible wage model of the labor market is the same as the long-run aggregate supply curve. It is vertical. Let's see why.

Figure 13.8 illustrates the derivation of the long-run aggregate supply curve. Part (a) shows the aggregate labor market. The demand and supply curves shown are exactly the same as those in Fig. 13.7. The equilibrium, a real wage of $7 an hour and employment of 150 billion hours, is exactly the same equilibrium that was determined in that figure.

Figure 13.8(b) shows the short-run aggregate production function. This production function is the one shown in Fig. 13.1. We know from the labor market (part a) that 150 billion hours of labor are employed. Part (b) tells us that when 150 billion hours of labor are employed, real GDP is $4.5 trillion.

Figure 13.8(c) shows the long-run aggregate supply curve. That curve tells us that real GDP is $4.5 trillion regardless of the price level. To see why, look at what happens to real GDP when the price level changes.

Start with a GDP deflator of 100. In this case, the economy is at point *j* in part (c) of the figure. That is, the GDP deflator is 100, and real GDP is $4.5 trillion. We've determined, in part (a), that the real wage rate is $7. With a GDP deflator of 100, the money wage rate (the wage rate in current dollars) is also $7 an hour.

What happens to real GDP if the GDP deflator falls from 100 to 80 (a 20 percent decrease in the price level)? If the money wage rate remains at $7 an hour, the real wage rate rises and the quantity of labor supplied exceeds the quantity demanded. In such a situation, the money wage rate will fall. It falls to $5.60 an hour. With a money wage rate of $5.60 and a GDP deflator of 80, the real wage rate is still $7 ($5.60 divided by 80 and multiplied by 100 equals $7). With the lower money wage rate but a constant real wage rate, employment remains at 150 billion hours (full employment) and real GDP is constant at $4.5 trillion. The economy is at point *k* in Fig. 13.8(c).

What happens to real GDP if the GDP deflator rises from 100 to 120 (a 20 percent increase in the price level)? If the money wage rate stays at $7 an hour, the real wage rate falls and the quantity of labor demanded exceeds the quantity supplied. In such a situation, the money wage rate rises. It will keep rising until it reaches $8.40 an hour. At that money wage rate, the real wage rate is $7 ($8.40 divided by 120 and multiplied by 100 equals $7) and the quantity of labor demanded equals the quantity supplied. Employment remains at 150 billion hours (full employment), and real GDP remains at $4.5 trillion. The economy is at point *l* in Fig. 13.8(c).

Points *j*, *k*, and *l* in part (c) all lie on the long-run aggregate supply curve. We have considered only three price levels. We could have considered any price level, and we would have reached the same conclusion: a change in the price level generates a proportionate change in the money wage rate and leaves the real wage rate unchanged. Employment and real GDP are also unchanged. The long-run aggregate supply curve is vertical.

Fluctuations in Real GDP In the flexible wage theory of the labor market, fluctuations in real GDP arise from shifts in the long-run aggregate supply curve. Technological change and capital accumulation shift the short-run aggregate production function upward and also shift the demand for labor

FIGURE 13.8

Aggregate Supply with Flexible Wages

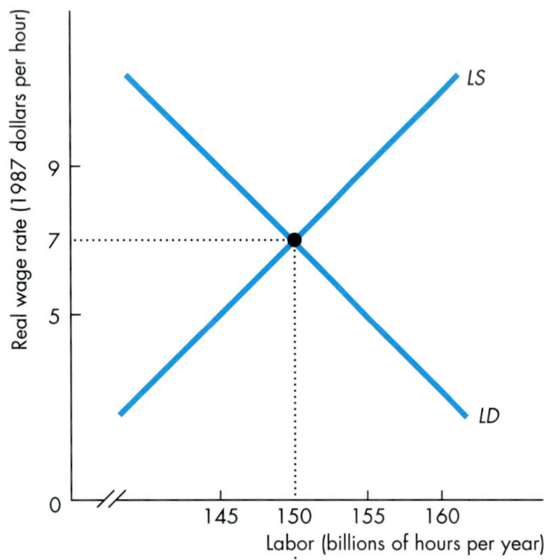

(a) Labor market

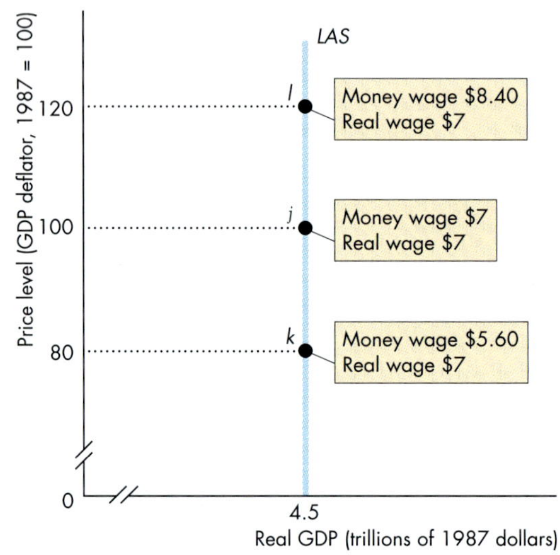

(c) Long-run aggregate supply curve

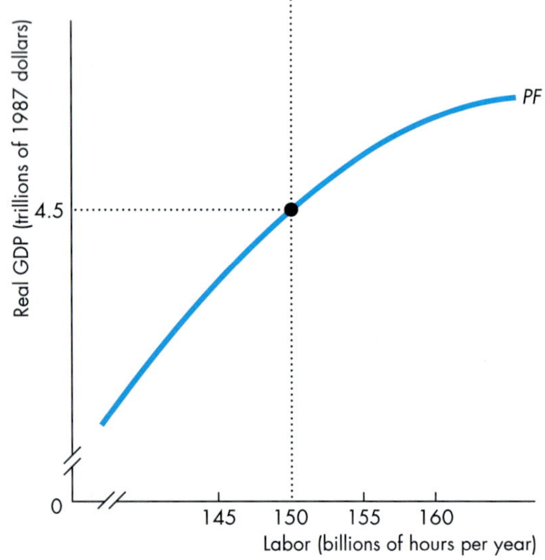

(b) Short-run aggregate production function

Labor market equilibrium determines the real wage rate and employment. The demand for labor curve (*LD*) intersects the supply of labor curve (*LS*) at a real wage rate of $7 an hour and 150 billion hours of employment (part a). The short-run aggregate production function (*PF*) and employment of 150 billion hours determine real GDP at $4.5 trillion (part b). Real GDP supplied is $4.5 trillion regardless of the price level. The long-run aggregate supply curve is the vertical line (*LAS*) in part (c). If the GDP deflator is 100, the economy is at point *j*. If the GDP deflator is 120, the money wage rate rises to keep the real wage rate constant at $7 an hour, employment remains at 150 billion hours, and real GDP is $4.5 trillion. The economy is at point *l*. If the GDP deflator is 80, the money wage rate falls to keep the real wage rate constant at $7 an hour, employment remains at 150 billion hours, and real GDP is $4.5 trillion. The economy is at point *k*.

curve to the right. Growth of the working age population shifts the supply of labor curve to the right. These changes in economic conditions change equilibrium employment and full-employment real GDP and also shift the long-run aggregate supply curve. Most of the time these changes result in the long-run aggregate supply curve moving to the right—increasing real GDP. But the pace at which the long-run aggregate supply curve shifts to the right varies, leading to fluctuations in the growth rate of real

GDP. Occasionally, the short-run aggregate production function shifts downward. When it does so, the demand for labor curve shifts to the left, employment falls, and the long-run aggregate supply curve shifts to the left, decreasing real GDP.

REVIEW

The flexible wage theory of the labor market maintains that the money wage rate adjusts sufficiently freely to maintain continuous equality between the quantity of labor demanded and the quantity of labor supplied. In such an economy, the real wage rate and employment are constant. Therefore as the price level varies, full-employment real GDP remains steady. There is only one aggregate supply curve—the vertical long-run aggregate supply curve. Fluctuations in employment, real wages, and real GDP occur because of fluctuations in the supply of labor and in the short-run aggregate production function that, in turn, bring fluctuations in the demand for labor. The most important source of fluctuations is the uneven pace of technological change, but there are other occasional negative influences on the short-run aggregate production function. ◆

Let's now examine the sticky wage theory of the labor market.

The Sticky Wage Theory

Most economists, while recognizing the scope for flexibility in wages from bonuses and overtime wage rates, believe that these sources of flexibility are insufficient to keep the quantity of labor supplied equal to the quantity demanded. Basic money wage rates rarely adjust more frequently than once a year, so money wage rates are fairly rigid—sticky. Real wage rates change more frequently than do money wage rates because of changes in the price level, but according to the sticky wage theory these adjustments do not make real wages sufficiently flexible to achieve continuous full employment.

The starting point for the sticky wage theory of the labor market is a theory of the determination of the money wage rate.

Money Wage Determination Firms, naturally, like to pay as low a wage as possible. Workers like as high a wage as possible. But workers want to get hired, and firms want to be able to find labor. Firms recognize that if they offer too low a wage, there will be a labor shortage. Workers recognize that if they try to achieve too high a wage, there will be a shortage of jobs—excessive unemployment. The wage that balances these opposing forces is the equilibrium wage—the wage that makes the quantity of labor demanded equal to the quantity supplied. But if money wages are going to be set for a year or more ahead, it will be impossible to achieve a continuous balance between the quantity of labor demanded and the quantity supplied. In such a situation, how is the money wage rate determined? It is set at a level designed to achieve an expectation or belief that, on the average, the quantity of labor demanded will equal the quantity supplied. Let's work out what that money wage rate is.

If the labor demand and supply curves are the same as those we used in Fig. 13.7, the real wage rate that achieves equality between the quantity demanded and quantity supplied is $7 an hour, as shown in Fig. 13.9. The money wage rate that this real wage rate translates into depends on the price level. But when firms and workers agree on a money wage rate for a future contract, they do not know what the price level is going to be. All they can do is base the contract on their best forecast of the future price level. Let's suppose that firms and their workers all have the same expectations about the future. Suppose that they *expect* the GDP deflator for the coming year to be 100. That being the case, firms and workers will be ready to agree to a money wage rate of $7 an hour. That is, with an expected GDP deflator of 100, a money wage rate of $7 an hour translates into an expected real wage rate of $7 an hour.

Real Wage Determination The real wage rate that actually emerges depends on the *actual* price level. If the GDP deflator turns out to be 100, as expected, then the real wage rate is $7 an hour, as expected. But many other outcomes are possible. Let's consider two of them, one in which the price level turns out to be higher than expected and one in which it turns out to be lower than expected.

First, suppose that the GDP deflator turns out to be 140. In this case, the real wage rate is $5 an hour.

FIGURE 13.9

A Labor Market with Sticky Money Wages

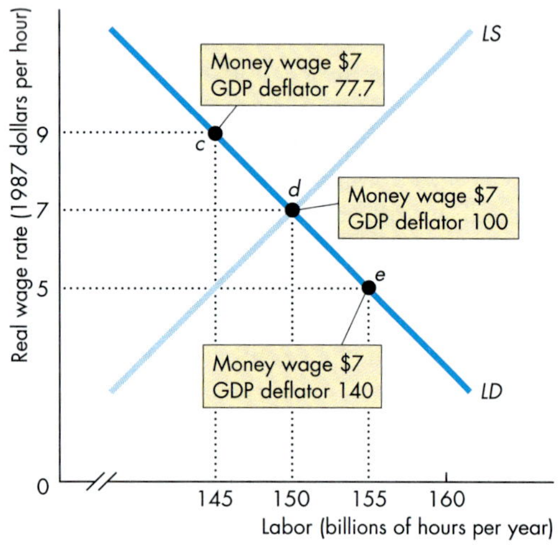

The labor demand curve is *LD* and the labor supply curve is *LS*. The money wage rate is set to achieve an expected balance between the quantity of labor demanded and the quantity supplied. If the GDP deflator is expected to be 100, the money wage rate is set at $7 an hour. The labor market is expected to be at point *d*. The quantity of labor employed is determined by the demand for labor. If the GDP deflator turns out to be 100, then the real wage rate is equal to $7 and the quantity of labor employed is 150 billion hours of labor. The economy operates at point *d*. If the GDP deflator turns out to be 77.7, then the real wage rate is $9 an hour and the quantity of labor employed falls to 145 billion hours. The economy operates at point *c*. If the GDP deflator is 140, then the real wage rate is $5 an hour and the quantity of labor employed increases to 155 billion hours. The economy operates at point *e*.

That is, a money wage rate of $7 an hour and a GDP deflator of 140 enables people to buy the same goods and services that a money wage rate of $5 an hour buys when the GDP deflator is 100. Next, suppose that the GDP deflator turns out to be 77.7 instead of 100. In this case, the real wage rate is $9 an hour. A money wage rate of $7 an hour with a GDP deflator of 77.7 buys the same quantity of goods and services that a money wage rate of $9 an hour buys when the GDP deflator is 100. The three points *c*, *d*, and *e* in Fig. 13.9 illustrate the relationship between the price level, the money wage rate, and the real wage rate. The money wage rate is constant at $7 an hour, and the higher the price level, the lower is the real wage rate. But as the real wage rate varies, what determines the quantity of labor employed?

Employment with Sticky Wages The sticky wage theory assumes that firms determine the level of employment. Provided that firms pay the agreed money wage rate, households supply whatever labor firms demand. These assumptions imply that the level of employment is determined by the demand curve for labor and that households are willing to be "off" their supply curves.

In Fig. 13.9, the money wage rate is $7 an hour. If the GDP deflator turns out to be 100 as expected, the real wage rate is $7 an hour and 150 billion hours of labor are employed (point *d* in the figure). If the GDP deflator turns out to be 77.7, the real wage rate is $9 an hour and the quantity of labor demanded and employed is 145 billion hours (point *c* in the figure). Households supply less labor than they would like to. If the GDP deflator turns out to be 140, the real wage rate is $5 an hour and the quantity of labor demanded and employed is 155 billion hours (point *e* in the figure). In this case, households supply more labor than they would like to.

It is easy to understand why a household might supply less labor, but why would it supply *more* labor than it would like to? In the long run, it would not. But for the duration of the existing contract, the household agrees to supply whatever quantity of labor the firm demands in exchange for a guaranteed money wage rate.

Aggregate Supply with Sticky Wages

When money wages are sticky, the short-run aggregate supply curve slopes upward. Figure 13.10 illustrates why this is so. Let's start by looking at part (a), which describes the labor market. The three equilibrium levels of real wages and employment we discovered in Fig. 13.9 are shown again here. The money wage rate is fixed at $7 an hour. If the price level is 100, the real wage rate is also $7 an hour and 150 billion hours of labor are employed—point *d*. If the price level is 77.7, the real wage rate is $9

FIGURE 13.10

Aggregate Supply with Sticky Wages

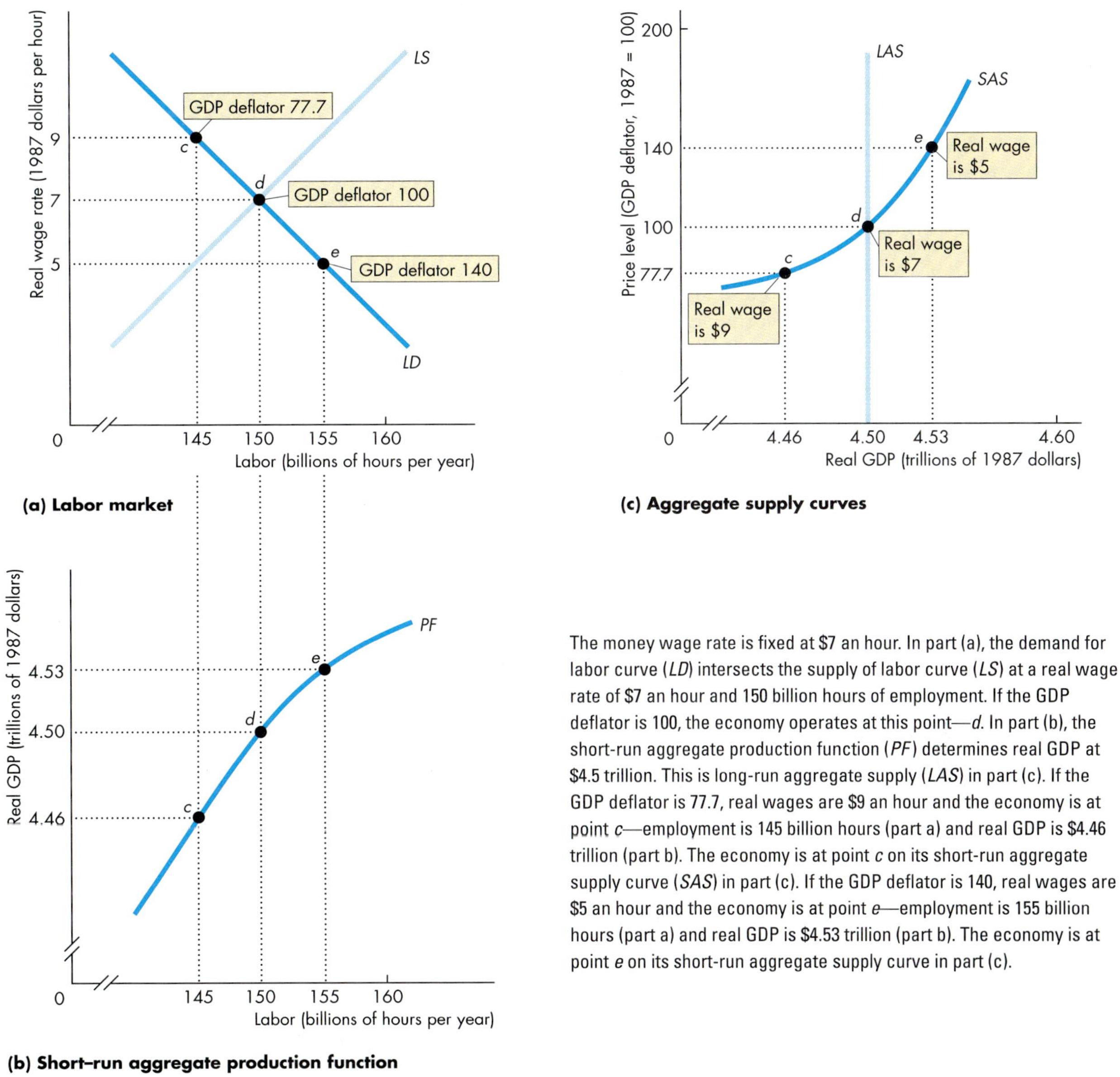

The money wage rate is fixed at $7 an hour. In part (a), the demand for labor curve (*LD*) intersects the supply of labor curve (*LS*) at a real wage rate of $7 an hour and 150 billion hours of employment. If the GDP deflator is 100, the economy operates at this point—*d*. In part (b), the short-run aggregate production function (*PF*) determines real GDP at $4.5 trillion. This is long-run aggregate supply (*LAS*) in part (c). If the GDP deflator is 77.7, real wages are $9 an hour and the economy is at point *c*—employment is 145 billion hours (part a) and real GDP is $4.46 trillion (part b). The economy is at point *c* on its short-run aggregate supply curve (*SAS*) in part (c). If the GDP deflator is 140, real wages are $5 an hour and the economy is at point *e*—employment is 155 billion hours (part a) and real GDP is $4.53 trillion (part b). The economy is at point *e* on its short-run aggregate supply curve in part (c).

an hour and employment is only 145 billion hours—point *c*. If the price level is 140, the real wage rate is $5 an hour and employment is 155 billion hours—point *e*.

Figure 13.10(b) shows the short-run aggregate production function. We know from the labor market (part a) that at different price levels, different quantities of labor are employed. Part (b) tells us how these employment levels translate into real GDP. For example, when employment is 145 billion hours, real GDP is $4.46 trillion—point *c*. When employment is 150 billion hours, real GDP is $4.5

trillion—point *d*—and when employment is 155 billion hours, real GDP is $4.53 trillion—point *e*.

Figure 13.10(c) shows the aggregate supply curves. The long-run aggregate supply curve, *LAS*, is the one we've already derived in Fig. 13.8. The short-run aggregate supply curve, *SAS*, is derived from the labor market and production function we've just examined. To see why, first focus on point *c* in all three parts of the figure. At point *c*, the price level is 77.7. From the labor market (part a), we know that in this situation the real wage is $9 an hour and 145 billion hours of labor are employed. At this employment level we know from the production function (part b) that real GDP is $4.46 trillion. That's what point *c* in part (c) is telling us—when the price level is 77.7, real GDP supplied is $4.46 trillion. The other two points, *d* and *e*, are interpreted in the same way. At point *e*, the price level is 140 so the real wage rate is $5 an hour and 155 billion hours of labor are employed (part a). This employment level produces a real GDP of $4.53 trillion. Points *c*, *d*, and *e* are all points on the short-run aggregate supply curve. Notice that this curve, like the one in Chapter 7, is *curved*. As the price level rises, real GDP increases but the increments in real GDP become successively smaller. The straight-line *SAS* curve we are using is an approximation to this curve.

The short-run aggregate supply curve intersects the long-run aggregate supply curve at the expected price level—where the GDP deflator is 100. At price levels higher than that expected, the quantity of real GDP supplied exceeds its long-run level, and at price levels lower than that expected, the quantity of real GDP supplied falls short of its long-run level.

Fluctuations in Real GDP All the factors that lead to fluctuations in long-run aggregate supply in the flexible wage theory apply to the long-run aggregate supply curve of the sticky wage theory. They lead to changes in short-run aggregate supply and to shifts in the short-run aggregate supply curve. But in addition, employment and real GDP can fluctuate because of movements along the short-run aggregate supply curve. These movements occur because of changes in real wages. The real wage rate changes in the sticky wage theory when the price level moves, but the contractually determined money wage rate stays constant.

REVIEW

The sticky wage theory assumes that the money wage rate is set on the basis of expectations about the price level over the course of the wage contract to make the expected quantities of labor demanded and supplied equal. The level of employment is determined by the demand for labor and the real wage rate. If the price level equals the expected price level, the quantity of labor demanded equals the quantity supplied. If the price level is lower than expected, the real wage is higher than expected and the quantity of labor demanded decreases. If the price level is higher than expected, the real wage is lower than expected and the quantity of labor demanded increases. Changes in the price level that bring changes in the level of employment result in changes in real GDP—movements along the short-run aggregate supply curve. ◆

So far, although we have been examining models of the labor market, we have used those models to determine the level of employment and wages but have ignored unemployment. How is unemployment determined?

Unemployment

We discovered in Chapter 5 that unemployment is an ever present feature of economic life and that the unemployment rate sometimes rises to a level that poses a massive problem for millions of families (see pp. 107–111). Yet the labor market models that we have just been studying seem to ignore this important phenomenon. They determine the real wage rate and aggregate hours of labor employed, but they don't say anything about *who* supplies the hours. Unemployment arises when some people in the labor force are working zero hours but are seeking work. Why does unemployment exist? Why does its rate vary?

There are four main reasons why unemployment arises.

- To vary employment, it pays firms to vary the number of workers employed rather than the number of hours per worker.
- Firms have imperfect information about people looking for work.
- Households have incomplete information about available jobs.
- Wage contracts prevent the wage adjustments that would be needed to keep the quantity of labor demanded equal to the quantity supplied.

The flexible wage theory places emphasis on the first three of these sources of unemployment. The sticky wage theory acknowledges the importance of these factors but regards the fourth factor as the most significant cause of unemployment and of variations in its rate. First, we'll examine the sources of unemployment that are present regardless of whether wages are flexible or sticky. Then we'll see how wage stickiness generates yet more unemployment.

Indivisible Labor

If it were profitable to do so, firms would vary the amount of labor they employ by varying the hours worked by each person on their payrolls. For example, suppose that a firm employs 400 hours of labor each week and has 10 workers, each working 40 hours. If the firm decides to cut back its production and reduce employment to 360 hours, it might either lay off one worker or cut the hours of each of its 10 workers to 36 hours a week. In most production processes, the profitable reaction for the firm is to lay off one worker and keep the remaining workers' hours constant. There is an optimum or efficient number of hours for each worker. Work hours in excess of the optimum level result in decreased output per hour as workers become tired. Employing a large number of workers for a small number of hours each also lowers output per hour, since workers take time to get started up and there are disruptions to the production process caused by workers leaving and arriving. It is for these reasons that labor is an economically indivisible factor of production. That is, taking account of the output produced per hour, it pays firms to hire labor in indivisible lumps. As a consequence, when the demand for labor changes, the number of people employed changes rather than the number of hours per worker.

Being fired or laid off would not be important if an equally good job could be found right away. But finding a job takes time and effort—it has an opportunity cost. Firms are not fully informed about all the potential workers available to them, and households are not fully informed about all the potential jobs available to them. As a consequence, both firms and workers have to search for a profitable match. Let's examine this source of unemployment.

Job Search and Unemployment

Because households are incompletely informed about available jobs, they find it efficient to devote resources to searching for the best available job. Time spent searching for a job is part of unemployment. Let's take a closer look at this source of unemployment by examining the labor market decisions that people make and the flows that arise from those decisions. Figure 13.11 provides a schematic summary of this discussion.

The working age population is divided into two groups: those in the labor force and those not in the labor force. Those not in the labor force are full-time students, homemakers, and retirees. The labor force consists of two groups: the employed and the unemployed.

Decisions made by the demanders of labor and the suppliers of labor result in five types of flows that change the numbers of people employed and unemployed. The flows resulting from these decisions are shown by the arrows in the figure. Let's look at these decisions and see how the flows that result from them affect the amount of employment and unemployment.

First, there is a flow into the labor force as full-time students decide to quit school and homemakers decide to enter or re-enter the labor force. Initially, when such people enter the labor force, they are unemployed. These decisions result in an increase in the labor force and an increase in unemployment.

Second, there is a flow from employment to unemployment resulting from employers deciding to lay off workers temporarily or fire workers and from workers deciding to quit their current job to

FIGURE 13.11

Labor Market Flows

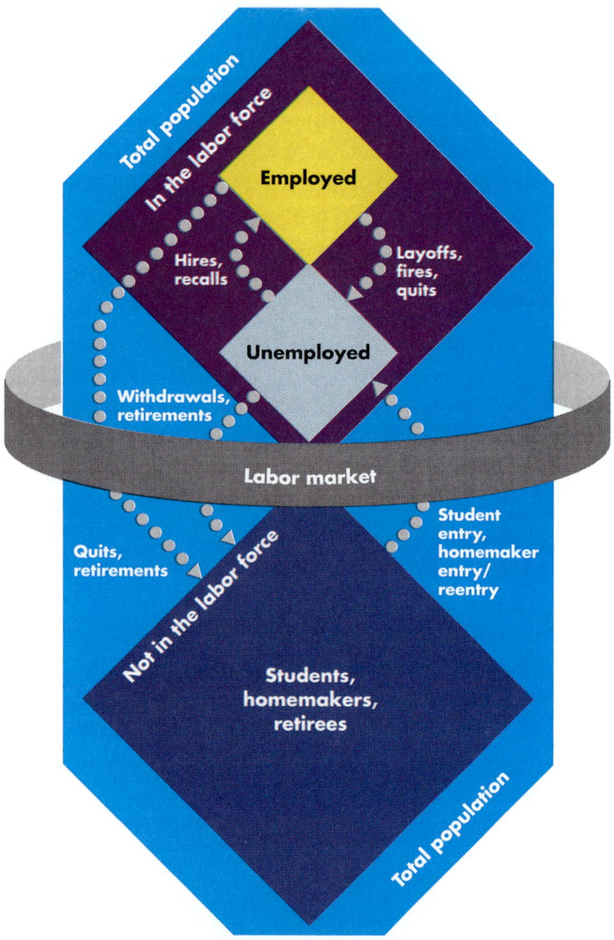

The working age population is divided into two groups: those in the labor force and those not in the labor force. The labor force is comprised of the employed and the unemployed. Flows into and out of the labor force and between employment and unemployment determine the number of people unemployed. New entrants from full-time schooling and re-entrants flow into unemployment. Flows from employment to unemployment result from fires, layoffs, and quits. Flows from unemployment to employment result from hires and recalls. Flows from the labor force occur as people decide to become homemakers, go back to school, or retire. Flows from the labor force also occur as unemployed people get discouraged by their failure to find a job.

find a better one. These decisions result in a decrease in employment and an increase in unemployment, but no change in the labor force.

Third, there is a flow from the labor force as employed people decide to quit their jobs to become homemakers, go back to school, or retire. These decisions result in a decrease in employment and a decrease in the labor force, but no change in unemployment.

Fourth, there is a flow from the labor force as unemployed people give up the search for a job. These people are *discouraged workers* whose job search efforts have been repeatedly unsuccessful. These decisions to leave the labor force result in a decrease in unemployment and a decrease in the labor force.

Fifth, there is a flow from unemployment to employment as firms recall temporarily laid-off workers and hire new workers. These decisions result in an increase in employment, a decrease in unemployment, and no change in the labor force.

At any one moment, there is a stock of employment and unemployment. Over any given period, there are flows into and out of the labor force and between employment and unemployment. In December 1992, for example, there were 129 million people in the labor force—66 percent of the working age population. Of these, 9 million (7 percent of the labor force) were unemployed and 120 million (93 percent of the labor force) were employed. Of the 9 million unemployed, 56 percent had been fired from their previous job or laid off, 24 percent had re-entered the labor force after a period of specializing in household production, 10 percent had voluntarily quit their previous job to seek a better one, and 9 percent were new entrants.

Unemployment with Flexible Wages

According to the flexible wage model of the labor market, all the unemployment that exists arises from the sources we've just reviewed. The unemployment rate is always equal to the natural rate of unemployment. There is a balance between the quantity of labor demanded and the quantity of labor supplied. But the quantity of labor supplied is the number of hours available for work at a given moment without further search for a better job. And the quantity of labor demanded is the number of hours that firms

FIGURE 13.12

Unemployment with Flexible Wages

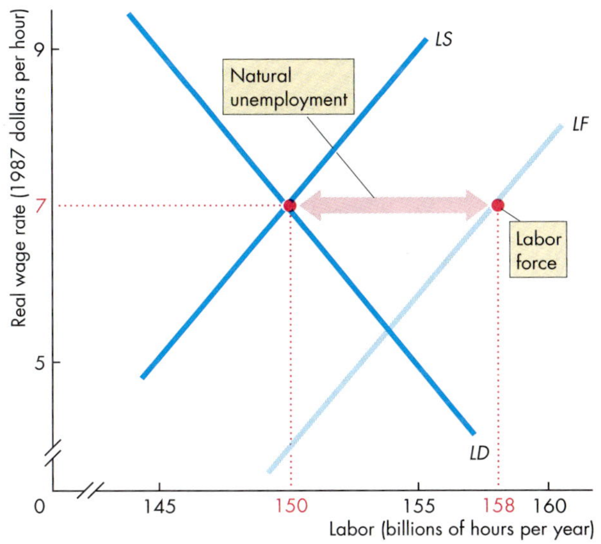

Some members of the labor force are immediately available for work at a given real wage rate, and this amount determines the supply of labor (*LS*). Other members of the labor force are searching for the best available job. Adding this quantity to the supply of labor gives the labor force curve (*LF*). Equilibrium occurs at the real wage rate that makes the quantity of labor supplied equal to the quantity demanded. The economy is at full employment, and unemployment is at its natural rate.

wish to hire at a given moment in time, given their knowledge of the individual skills and talents available. In addition to supplying hours for work, households also supply time for job search. Those people that devote no time to working and specialize in job search are the ones who are unemployed.

Figure 13.12 illustrates such a situation. The labor force—everyone who has a job and all those who are looking for one—is larger than the supply of labor. The supply curve of labor (*LS*) tells us about the quantity of labor available with no further job search. The labor force curve (*LF*) tells us about the quantity of labor available with no further job search plus the quantity of job search. In the figure, the quantity of labor supplied and the labor force increase as the real wage rate increases. But the quantity of job search, measured by the horizontal distance between the *LS* and *LF* curves, is constant. (This is an assumption. In real labor markets, the supply of job search may also increase as the real wage rate increases.)

Equilibrium occurs at the real wage rate that makes the quantity of labor supplied—not the labor force—equal to the quantity of labor demanded. Unemployment arises from the fact that information about jobs and workers is costly and it takes time for people without work to find an acceptable job. Such unemployment is called "natural" because it arises from the normal functioning of the labor market.

According to the flexible wage theory, fluctuations in unemployment are caused by fluctuations in labor market flows that arise on both the supply side and the demand side of the labor market. Changes in these flows lead to shifts in the *LS* and *LF* curves that increase and decrease the natural rate of unemployment.

Supply-Side Events The supply side of the labor market is influenced by the age distribution of the population. A large increase in the proportion of the population of working age brings an increase in the rate of entry into the labor force and a corresponding increase in the unemployment rate as the new entrants take time to find the best available jobs. This factor has been important in the U.S. labor market in recent years. A bulge in the birth rate occurred in the late 1940s and early 1950s, following World War II. This bulge resulted in an increase in the proportion of new entrants into the labor force during the 1970s. It resulted in a rightward shift in the *LS* curve, an even greater rightward shift in the *LF* curve, and an increase in the unemployment rate.

As the birth rate declined, the bulge moved to higher age groups, and the proportion of new entrants into the labor force declined during the 1980s. During this period, the rightward shift in the *LS* curve was larger than the shift in the *LF* curve and the unemployment rate declined.

Demand-Side Events Cycles in unemployment arise from the fact that the scale of hiring, firing, and job quitting ebbs and flows with fluctuations in real GDP—with the business cycle. These labor market flows and the resulting unemployment are also strongly influenced by the pace and direction of technological change. When some firms and sectors of the economy are expanding quickly and others are contracting quickly, labor turnover increases. This means large flows between employment and unemployment, and the pool of those temporarily unemployed increases at such a time. The relative decline of industries in the so-called "Rust Belt" and the rapid expansion of industries in the so-called "Sun Belt" are an important source of large flows of labor and of the rise in unemployment that occurred during the 1970s and early 1980s.

Job Creation and Destruction

The importance of changes in labor market flows can be seen by looking at some newly available data compiled by Steve Davis of the University of Chicago Business School and John Haltiwanger of the University of Maryland. Using data from individual plants in the manufacturing sector of the U.S. economy, they have painted a remarkable picture of the changing U.S. job scene. This picture is shown in Fig. 13.13.

Look first at part (a), which shows the amount of job creation and destruction. On the average, about 5 percent of all jobs disappear each year and a similar number of new jobs are created. Adding together the jobs destroyed and created gives a measure of the total amount of turnover in the labor market arising from this process—shown as the curve labeled "Sum" in the figure. Subtracting jobs destroyed from jobs created gives the change in the number of jobs—shown as the curve labeled "Net" in the figure. As you can see, the scale of job turnover is large and fluctuates a great deal. Part (b) shows how the fluctuations in job creation and destruction correspond with fluctuations in the unemployment rate.

Whether fluctuations in the job creation and destruction rate cause fluctuations in the unemployment rate or whether fluctuations in both the job creation and destruction rate and the unemployment rate have a common cause is not known. According to the sticky wage theory of the labor market, they do have a common cause, which is fluctuations in aggregate demand. Let's see why.

FIGURE 13.13

Job Creation, Job Destruction, and Unemployment

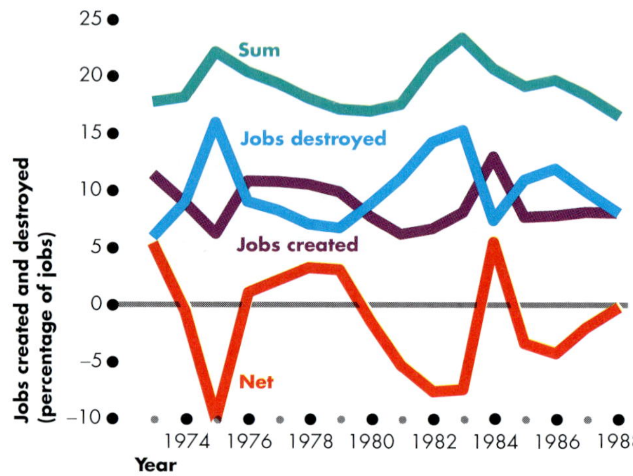

(a) Job creation and destruction rates

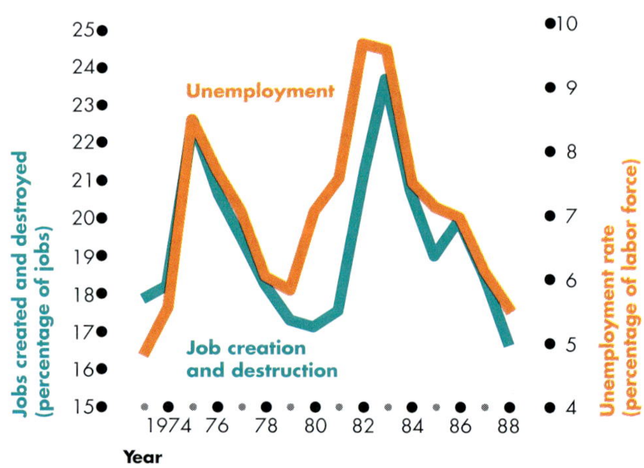

(b) Job creation and destruction and unemployment

On the average, 5 percent of existing jobs disappear each year (the curve labeled "Jobs destroyed" in part a) and a similar number of new jobs are created. The total amount of job creation and destruction (the curve labeled "Sum") and the rate of job creation minus the rate of job destruction (the curve labeled "Net") fluctuate. Those fluctuations follow a similar cycle to that in the unemployment rate (part b).

Source: Job Creation and Destruction in U.S. Manufacturing by Steven J. Davis, John Haltiwanger, and Scott Schuh. Data kindly provided by Steve Davis and John Haltiwanger.

Unemployment with Sticky Wages

With sticky money wages, unemployment might rise above or fall below the natural rate. If the real wage rate is above its full-employment level, the quantity of labor employed is less than the quantity supplied and unemployment is above its natural rate. Such a situation is shown in Fig. 13.14. The *LS* and *LF* curves are the same as those in Fig. 13.12, and the amount of natural unemployment is measured by the horizontal distance between those two curves.

The money wage rate is $7 an hour. If the GDP deflator is 87.5, the real wage rate is $8 an hour and the quantity of labor demanded is 147 billion hours. Unemployment is above its natural rate. If the GDP deflator is 116.6, the real wage rate is $6 an hour and the quantity of labor demanded is 153 billion hours. Unemployment is below its natural rate.

Fluctuations in aggregate demand bring fluctuations in the price level. These fluctuations move the economy (upward and downward) along its demand for labor curve. At the same time, unemployment fluctuates around its natural rate. According to the sticky wage theory, fluctuations in unemployment arise primarily from the mechanism just described. Changes in the real wage rate arising from a sticky money wage rate and a changing price level result in movements along the labor demand curve and movements along the short-run aggregate supply curve. The rates of job creation and destruction also fluctuate (as shown in Fig. 13.13), but those fluctuations are the result of aggregate demand fluctuations.

Those economists who emphasize the role of sticky wages in generating fluctuations in unemployment usually regard the natural rate of unemployment as constant—or slowly changing. Fluctuations in the actual unemployment rate are fluctuations around the natural rate. Notice that this interpretation of fluctuations in unemployment contrasts with that of the flexible wage theory. A flexible wage model predicts that *all* changes in unemployment are fluctuations in the natural rate of unemployment.

If most of the fluctuations in unemployment *do* arise from sticky wages, aggregate demand management can moderate those fluctuations in unemployment. If aggregate demand is kept steady so that the price level stays close to its expected level, the economy can be kept close to full employment.

FIGURE 13.14

Unemployment with Sticky Money Wages

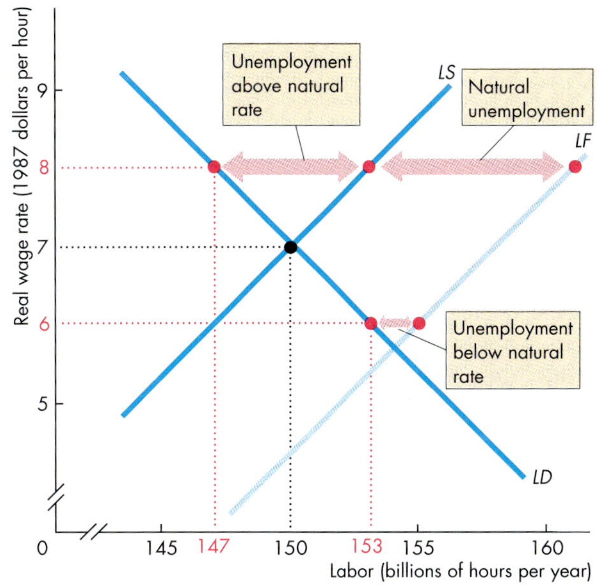

The money wage rate is $7 an hour. If the GDP deflator turns out to be 87.5, the real wage rate is $8 an hour. At this higher real wage rate, the quantity of labor demanded falls short of the quantity of labor supplied and unemployment is above its natural rate. If the GDP deflator turns out to be 116.6, the real wage rate is $6 an hour. At this lower real wage rate, the quantity of labor demanded exceeds the quantity of labor supplied and unemployment is below its natural rate. Fluctuations in the price level, with sticky money wages, cause fluctuations in the level of unemployment.

◆ ◆ ◆ ◆ We have now studied the labor market and the determination of long-run and short-run aggregate supply, employment, wages, and unemployment. We've examined the forces that change aggregate supply, shifting the long-run and short-run aggregate supply curves. We've also examined the sources of productivity growth in the U.S. economy. Our next task is to bring together the aggregate demand and aggregate supply sides of the economy again and see how they interact to determine inflation and business cycles. We are going to pursue these tasks in the next two chapters.

Summary

Productivity and Income Growth

The short-run aggregate production function tells us how real GDP varies as the aggregate quantity of labor employed varies with a given stock of capital equipment and given state of technology. As the labor input increases, real GDP increases but by diminishing marginal amounts. Capital accumulation and technological change lead to productivity growth that causes the short-run aggregate production function to shift upward over time. Occasionally, the production function shifts downward because of negative influences such as restrictions on international trade. The U.S. short-run aggregate production function shifted upward by 88 percent between 1960 and 1991. (pp. 338–344)

The Demand for Labor

Firms choose how much labor to demand. The lower the real wage rate, the larger is the quantity of labor hours demanded. In choosing how much labor to hire, firms aim to maximize their profits. They achieve this objective by ensuring that the revenue brought in by an additional hour of labor equals the hourly wage rate. The more hours of labor that are employed, the lower is the revenue brought in by the last hour of labor. Firms can be induced to increase the quantity of labor hours demanded, either by a decrease in the wage rate or by an increase in the revenue brought in—by an increase in the price of output. Both a decrease in the wage rate and an increase in prices result in a lower real wage rate. Thus the lower the real wage rate, the greater is the quantity of labor demanded.

The relationship between the real wage rate and the quantity of labor demanded is summarized in the demand for labor curve, which slopes downward. The demand for labor curve shifts as a result of shifts in the short-run aggregate production function. (pp. 344–347)

The Supply of Labor

Households choose how much labor to supply. They also choose the timing of their labor supply. A higher real wage rate encourages the substitution of work for leisure—the substitution effect—and encourages the taking of more leisure—the income effect. The substitution effect dominates the income effect, so the higher the real wage rate, the more hours each worker supplies. Also, the higher the real wage rate, the higher is the labor force participation rate. A higher *current* wage relative to the expected future wage encourages more work in the present and less in the future—the intertemporal substitution effect. Taking all these forces together, the higher the real wage rate, the greater is the quantity of labor supplied.

The relationship between the real wage rate and the quantity of labor supplied is summarized in the supply of labor curve, which slopes upward. (pp. 347–349)

Wages and Employment

There are two theories of labor market equilibrium, one based on the assumption that wages are flexible and the other based on the assumption that they are sticky. Under the flexible wage theory, the real wage rate adjusts to ensure that the quantity of labor supplied equals the quantity demanded.

With flexible wages, the aggregate supply curve is vertical—the long-run aggregate supply curve. The quantity of real GDP supplied is independent of the price level. The long-run aggregate supply curve shifts as a result of shifts in the supply of labor curve and shifts in the short-run aggregate production function that lead to shifts in the demand for labor curve.

With sticky money wages, real wages do not adjust to balance the quantity of labor supplied and the quantity demanded. The money wage rate is set to make the expected quantity of labor demanded equal to the expected quantity supplied. The real wage rate depends on the contracted money wage rate and the price level. The level of employment is determined by the demand for labor, with households agreeing to supply the quantity demanded. Fluctuations in the price level relative to what was expected generate fluctuations in the quantity of labor demanded and in employment and real GDP. The higher the price level relative to what was expected, the lower is the real wage rate. The lower the real wage rate, the greater is the quantity of labor demanded, the greater is employment, and the greater is real GDP.

With sticky money wages, the aggregate supply curve slopes upward—the short-run aggregate supply curve. The higher the price level, the higher is the quantity of real GDP supplied. (pp. 349–356)

Unemployment

The labor market is in a constant state of change or labor turnover. Labor turnover creates unemployment. New entrants to the labor force and workers re-entering after a period of household production must take time to find a job. Some people quit an existing job to seek a better one. Some are laid off, and others are fired and forced to find another job. The pace of labor turnover is not constant. When technological change is expanding one sector and leading to a contraction of another sector, labor turnover increases. Finding new jobs takes time, and the process of adjustment may create overtime and unfilled vacancies in the expanding sector but unemployment in the contracting sector.

Even if wages are flexible, unemployment arising from labor-market turnover cannot be avoided. The unemployment rate arising from this source is the natural rate of unemployment. In labor markets with flexible wages, all fluctuations in unemployment are fluctuations in the natural rate arising from changes in the rate of labor turnover. The scale and cycles in the rates of job creation and job destruction are consistent with the flexible wage theory.

If wages are sticky, unemployment arises for all the same reasons as in the case of flexible wages and for one additional reason. With sticky wages the real wage might not move quickly enough to keep the quantity of labor demanded equal to the quantity supplied. In such a case, an increase in the real wage rate can result in unemployment rising above its natural rate and a decrease in real wages can result in unemployment falling below its natural rate. (pp. 356–361)

KEY ELEMENTS

Key Terms

Demand for labor, 344
Diminishing marginal product of labor, 339
Innovation, 340
Invention, 340
Labor force participation rate, 348
Labor productivity, 338
Marginal product of labor, 338
Money wage rate, 344
Production function, 338
Quantity of labor demanded, 344
Quantity of labor supplied, 347
Real wage rate, 344
Reservation wage, 349
Short-run aggregate production function, 338
Short-run production function, 338
Supply of labor, 347

Key Figures

Figure 13.1	The Short-Run Aggregate Production Function, 339
Figure 13.2	The Growth of Output, 340
Figure 13.7	Equilibrium with Flexible Wages, 350
Figure 13.8	Aggregate Supply with Flexible Wages, 352
Figure 13.9	A Labor Market with Sticky Money Wages, 354
Figure 13.10	Aggregate Supply with Sticky Wages, 355
Figure 13.12	Unemployment with Flexible Wages, 359
Figure 13.14	Unemployment with Sticky Money Wages, 361

REVIEW QUESTIONS

1 What is the relationship between output and labor input in the short run? Why does the marginal product of labor diminish?

2 If the short-run production function shifts from 1992 to 1993 by the amount shown in Fig. 13.2, what happens to the marginal product of labor between 1992 and 1993?

3 Explain why the demand for labor curve slopes downward.

4 Given your answer to question 2, does the demand for labor curve shift between 1992 and 1993? If so, in what direction and by how much?

5 Why does the labor force participation rate rise as the real wage rate rises?

6 How is the quantity of labor currently supplied influenced by the wage rate today relative to those expected in the future?

7 Explain what happens in a labor market with flexible wages when technological change increases the marginal product of labor for each unit of labor input.

8 In question 7, explain what happens to the long-run aggregate supply curve.

9 What are sticky wages?

10 Explain what happens in a labor market with sticky wages when technological change increases the marginal product of labor for each unit of labor input.

11 In question 10, explain what happens to the short-run aggregate supply curve.

12 Explain how unemployment can arise if wages are flexible.

13 Describe the main facts about the rates of job creation and job destruction.

14 Explain how unemployment fluctuates around its natural rate.

PROBLEMS

Use the following information about an economy to answer problems 1 through 7. The economy's short-run production function is

Labor (billions of hours per year)	Real GDP (billions of 1987 dollars per year)
1	38
2	54
3	68
4	80
5	90
6	98
7	104
8	108

Its demand and supply schedules for labor are

Real wage rate (1987 dollars per hour)	Quantity of labor demanded (billions of hours per year)	Quantity of labor supplied (billions of hours per year)
3	8	4
5	7	5
7	6	6
9	5	7
11	4	8
13	3	9
15	2	10
17	1	11

1 If real wages are flexible, how much labor is employed, and what is the real wage rate?

2 If the GDP deflator is 120, what is the money wage rate?

3 If the real wage rate is flexible, calculate the aggregate supply curve in this economy.

4 If money wages are sticky and the GDP deflator is expected to be 100, what is the money wage rate in this economy?

5 Find three points on the economy's short-run aggregate supply curve when the money wage rate is at the level determined in problem 4.

6 Calculate the real wage rate at each of the points you used in answering problem 5.

7 At what price level and level of employment do the short-run and long-run aggregate supply curves intersect?

8 There are two economies, each with a *constant* unemployment rate but with a great deal of labor market turnover. In economy A, there is a rapid pace of technological change. Twenty percent of the labor force either is fired or quits its job every year, and 20 percent is hired every year. In economy B, only 5 percent is fired or quits and 5 percent is hired. Which economy has the higher unemployment rate? Why?

9 There are two economies, Flexiland and Fixland. These economies are identical in every way except that in Flexiland, real wages are flexible and maintain equality between the quantities of labor demanded and supplied. In Fixland, wages are sticky but the money wage rate is set so that, *on the average,* the quantity of labor demanded equals the quantity supplied.

a Explain which economy has the higher average unemployment rate.

b Explain which economy has the largest fluctuations in unemployment.

CHAPTER 14

INFLATION

After studying this chapter, you will be able to:

- Explain why inflation is a problem
- Explain how increasing aggregate demand generates a price-wage inflation spiral
- Explain how decreasing aggregate supply generates a cost-price inflation spiral
- Explain why it pays to anticipate inflation accurately
- Explain how inflation expectations are made
- Explain how inflation expectations affect *actual* inflation
- Explain the relationship between inflation and interest rates
- Explain the relationship between inflation and unemployment

From Rome to Russia

At the end of the third century A.D., during the fading years of the Roman Empire, Emperor Diocletian struggled to contain rampant inflation. Prices increased at a rate of more than 300 percent a year. At the end of the twentieth century, during the years of transition from the Soviet Union's planned economy to a market economy, Boris Yeltsin grappled with a similarly high inflation rate. And Boris Yeltsin was not alone. High inflation rates also occurred in other Eastern European countries, such as Ukraine and Poland, as well as in many Latin American countries. Inflation has never been severe in the United States, but even here, the inflation rate was uncomfortably high during the 1970s and early 1980s. But today in the United States, and in most other rich industrial countries, inflation has moderated. What causes inflation? Why does inflation sometimes increase and at other times subside?

To make good decisions, we need good forecasts of inflation, and not for just next year but for many years into the future. How do people try to anticipate inflation? And how do expectations of inflation influence the economy? As the inflation rate rises and falls, the unemployment rate and interest rates also fluctuate. What is the connection between inflation and unemployment and between inflation and interest rates? Do we have to "buy" low unemployment by paying the price of high inflation? Or does high inflation cause high unemployment? And how do interest rates respond to inflation? Does high inflation mean that lenders lose and borrowers gain, or do interest rates rise and fall to keep in step with the inflation rate?

◆◆ The forces that determine inflation (and real GDP growth) are studied by using the aggregate demand–aggregate supply model. In that model, inflation—a rising price level—can result from increasing aggregate demand, decreasing aggregate supply, or a combination of the two. Before embarking on a study of the causes of inflation, let's remind ourselves of what inflation is and why it is a problem.

Why Inflation Is a Problem

The inflation rate is the percentage rise in the price level. That is,

$$\text{Inflation rate} = \frac{\text{Current year's price level} - \text{Last year's price level}}{\text{Last year's price level}} \times 100.$$

Let's write this equation in symbols. We'll call this year's price level P_1 and last year's price level P_0, so

$$\text{Inflation rate} = \frac{P_1 - P_0}{P_0} \times 100.$$

This equation shows the connection between the inflation rate and the price level. For a given price level last year, the higher the price level in the current year, the higher is the inflation rate.

The inflation rate is a measure of the rate at which money is losing value, and this fact is the source of the inflation problem. But the nature of the problem depends on whether the inflation is *anticipated* or *unanticipated*.

Anticipated Inflation

If money loses value at a rapid but anticipated rate, it does not function well as a medium of exchange. In such a situation, people try to avoid holding onto money. They spend their incomes as soon as they receive them, and firms pay out incomes—wages and dividends—as soon as they receive revenue from their sales. During the 1920s, when inflation in Germany reached *hyperinflation* levels, rates in excess of 50 percent a month, wages were paid and spent twice in a single day! Also, at high anticipated inflation rates, people seek alternatives to money as a means of payment (for example, cigarettes or foreign currency). During the 1980s, when inflation in Israel reached 1,000 percent a year, the U.S dollar became an important component of that country's money supply. Also, in times of anticipated inflation, barter becomes more common.

The activities that are encouraged by a high anticipated inflation rate use valuable time and other resources. Instead of people concentrating on the activities at which they have a comparative advantage, they find it more profitable to search for ways of avoiding the losses that inflation inflicts.

Anticipated inflation becomes a serious problem only at very high inflation rates. But there are many examples of costly anticipated inflations around the world, especially in South American countries such as Argentina, Bolivia, and Brazil. The closest the United States has come to such a situation was in the late 1970s and early 1980s, when the inflation rate exceeded 10 percent a year.

Unanticipated Inflation

Unanticipated inflation is a problem even at low inflation rates. It redistributes wealth between borrowers and lenders and income between employers and employees. An unanticipated increase in inflation transfers real buying power from lenders to borrowers, and an unanticipated decrease in inflation transfers resources in the opposite direction. An unanticipated increase in inflation also decreases real wages and increases real GDP and employment, while an unanticipated decrease in inflation increases real wages and decreases real GDP and employment. Unanticipated fluctuations in inflation produce fluctuations in the economy—fluctuations in real GDP, employment, and unemployment. Much of this chapter explains why unanticipated inflation has these effects. Let's begin by looking at the unanticipated inflation that results from an increase in aggregate demand.

Demand-Pull Inflation

The inflation resulting from an increase in aggregate demand is called **demand-pull inflation.** Such an inflation may arise from any individual factor that increases aggregate demand. Although there are several such factors, the most important that generate *ongoing* increases in aggregate demand are

- Increases in the money supply
- Increases in government purchases

When aggregate demand increases, the aggregate demand curve shifts to the right. Let's trace the effects of such an increase.

Inflation Effect of an Increase in Aggregate Demand

Suppose that last year the GDP deflator was 120 and real GDP was \$5 trillion. Long-run real GDP was also \$5 trillion. This situation is shown in Fig. 14.1(a). The aggregate demand curve is AD_0, the short-run aggregate supply curve is SAS_0, and the long-run aggregate supply curve is *LAS*.

In the current year, aggregate demand increases to AD_1. Such a situation arises if, for example, the Fed loosens its grip on the money supply or the government increases its purchases of goods and services. The economy moves to the point where the aggregate demand curve AD_1 intersects the short-run aggregate supply curve SAS_0. The GDP deflator increases to 125, and real GDP increases to \$5.5 trillion. The economy experiences 4.2 percent inflation (a GDP deflator of 125 compared with 120 in the previous year) and a rapid expansion of real GDP.

FIGURE 14.1

Demand-Pull Inflation

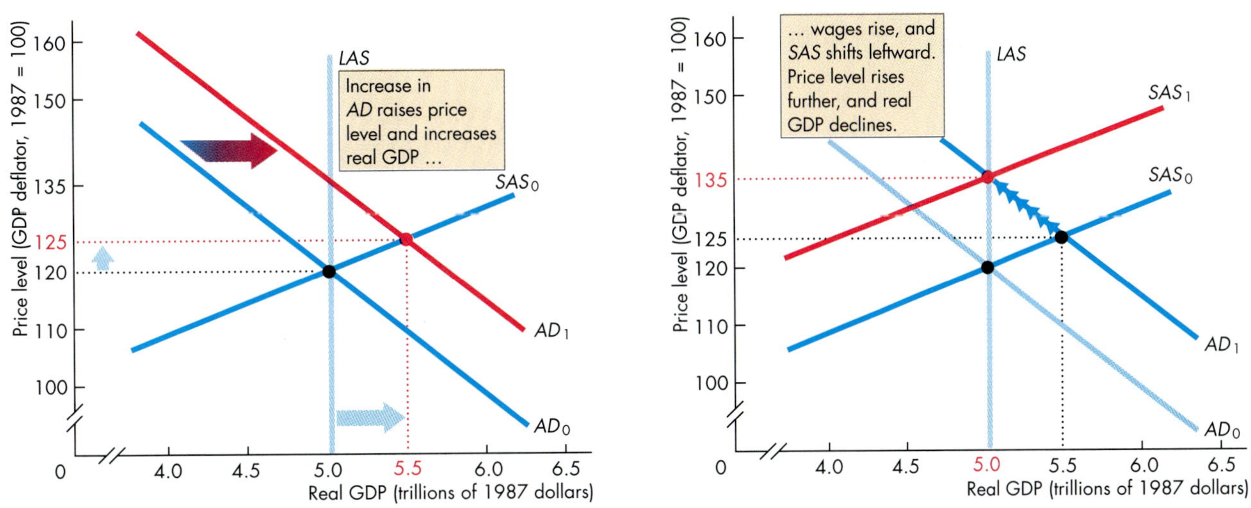

(a) Initial effect

In part (a), the aggregate demand curve is AD_0, the short-run aggregate supply curve is SAS_0, and the long-run aggregate supply curve is *LAS*. The GDP deflator is 120, and real GDP is \$5 trillion, its long-run level. Aggregate demand increases to AD_1 (because the Fed increases the money supply or the government increases its purchases of goods and services). The new equilibrium occurs where AD_1 intersects SAS_0.

(b) Wages adjust

The economy experiences inflation (the GDP deflator rises to 125), and real GDP increases to \$5.5 trillion. In part (b), starting from above full employment, wages begin to rise and the short-run aggregate supply curve shifts to the left toward SAS_1. The price level rises further, and real GDP returns to its long-run level.

The situation that developed in the U.S. economy toward the end of the 1960s is a good example of the process we have just analyzed. In those years, a large increase in government purchases on the Vietnam War and an increase in spending on social programs, together with an increase in the growth rate of the money supply, increased aggregate demand. As a consequence, the aggregate demand curve shifted rightward, the price level increased quickly, and real GDP moved above its long-run or full-employment level. But eventually, wages began to rise to catch up with the rising price level. Let's see why.

Wage Response

The economy cannot produce an above full-employment level of real GDP forever. With unemployment below its natural rate, there is a shortage of labor. Wages begin to increase, and the short-run aggregate supply curve starts to shift to the left. Prices rise further, and real GDP begins to fall. With no further change in aggregate demand—the aggregate demand curve remains at AD_1—this process comes to an end when the short-run aggregate supply curve has moved to SAS_1 in Fig. 14.1(b). At this time, the GDP deflator has increased to 135 and real GDP has returned to its long-run level, the level from which it started.

A Price-Wage Inflation Spiral

The inflation process we've just studied eventually comes to an end when, for a given increase in aggregate demand, wages have adjusted enough to restore the real wage rate to its full-employment level. But suppose that the initial increase in aggregate demand resulted from a large government budget deficit financed by creating more and more money. If such a policy remains in place, aggregate demand will continue to increase year after year. The aggregate demand curve will keep shifting to the right, putting continual upward pressure on the price level. The economy will experience perpetual demand-pull inflation.

Figure 14.2 illustrates a perpetual demand-pull inflation. The starting point is the same as that shown in Fig. 14.1. The aggregate demand curve is AD_0, the short-run aggregate supply curve is SAS_0, and the long-run aggregate supply curve is *LAS*. Real GDP is $5 trillion, and the GDP deflator is 120. Aggregate demand increases, shifting the aggregate demand curve to AD_1. Real GDP increases to $5.5 trillion, and the GDP deflator rises to 125. The economy is at an above full-employment equilibrium. There is a shortage of labor, and the wage rate rises, shifting the short-run aggregate supply curve to SAS_1. The GDP deflator increases to 135, and real GDP returns to its long-run level.

But the money supply increases again by the same percentage as before, and aggregate demand continues to increase. The aggregate demand curve shifts

FIGURE 14.2

A Price-Wage Inflation Spiral

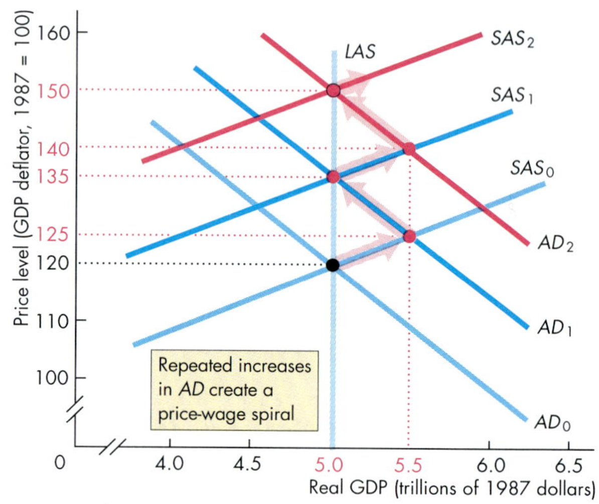

The aggregate demand curve is AD_0, the short-run aggregate supply curve is SAS_0, and the long-run aggregate supply curve is *LAS*. Real GDP is $5 trillion, and the GDP deflator is 120. Aggregate demand increases, shifting the aggregate demand curve to AD_1. Real GDP increases to $5.5 trillion, and the GDP deflator rises to 125. With the economy operating above full employment, the wage rate begins to rise, shifting the short-run aggregate supply curve leftward to SAS_1. The GDP deflator increases to 135, and real GDP returns to its long-run level. As aggregate demand continues to increase, the aggregate demand curve shifts to AD_2. The GDP deflator increases further, real GDP exceeds its long-run level, and the wage rate continues to rise. As the short-run aggregate supply curve shifts leftward to SAS_2, the GDP deflator increases to 150. As aggregate demand continues to increase, the price level rises, generating a perpetual demand-pull inflation. Real GDP fluctuates between $5 trillion and $5.5 trillion. But if aggregate demand increases *at the same time* as wages increase, real GDP remains at $5.5 trillion as the demand-pull inflation occurs.

rightward to AD_2. The GDP deflator increases further, real GDP exceeds its long-run level, and the wage rate continues to rise. As the *SAS* curve shifts to SAS_2, the GDP deflator increases further to 150. As aggregate demand continues to increase, the price level rises continuously, generating a perpetual demand-pull inflation and a price-wage inflation spiral. Real GDP fluctuates between $5 trillion and $5.5 trillion.

In the price-wage inflation spiral that we've just described, aggregate demand increases and wage increases alternate—first aggregate demand increases, then wages, then aggregate demand, and so on. If, after the initial increase in aggregate demand that took real GDP to $5.5 trillion, aggregate demand continues to increase *at the same time* as the wage rate increases, real GDP remains above its long-run level at $5.5 trillion as the demand-pull inflation proceeds.

Demand-Pull Inflation in Kalamazoo You may better understand the inflation process that we've just described by considering what is going on in an individual part of the economy, such as a Kalamazoo soda bottling plant. Initially, when aggregate demand increases, the demand for soda increases and the price of soda rises. Faced with a higher price, the soda plant works overtime and increases production. Conditions are good for workers in Kalamazoo, and the soda factory finds it hard to hang onto its best people. To do so, it has to offer higher wages. As wages increase, so do the costs of the soda factory.

What happens next depends on what happens to aggregate demand. If aggregate demand remains constant (as in Fig. 14.1b), the firm's costs are increasing but the price of soda is not increasing as quickly as its costs. Production is scaled back. Eventually, wages and costs increase by the same amount as the price of soda. In real terms, the soda factory is in the same situation as initially—before the increase in aggregate demand. The bottling plant produces the same amount of soda and employs the same amount of labor.

But if aggregate demand continues to increase, so does the demand for soda, and the price of soda rises at the same rate as wages. The soda factory continues to operate above full employment, and there is a persistent shortage of labor. Prices and wages chase each other upward in an unending price-wage spiral.

REVIEW

Demand-pull inflation results from any initial factor that increases aggregate demand. The most important such factors are an increase in the money supply and an increase in government purchases of goods and services. Initially, the increase in aggregate demand increases the price level and real GDP. With the economy operating at above full employment, the wage rate rises, decreasing short-run aggregate supply. If aggregate demand remains constant at its new level, the price level rises further and real GDP returns to its long-run level. If aggregate demand continues to increase, wages chase prices in an unending price-wage inflation spiral. ◆

Next, let's look at how shocks to aggregate supply can create inflation.

Supply Inflation and Stagflation

Inflation can result from a decrease in aggregate supply. Let's look at the main reasons why aggregate supply might decrease.

Sources of Decreasing Aggregate Supply

There are two main sources of a decrease in aggregate supply. They are

- An increase in wage rates
- An increase in the prices of raw materials

These sources of a decrease in aggregate supply operate by increasing costs, and such an inflation is called **cost-push inflation.** Other things remaining the same, the higher the cost of production, the smaller is the amount produced. At a given price level, rising wage rates or rising prices of raw materials such as oil lead firms to decrease the quantity of labor employed and to cut production. This decrease in short-run aggregate supply shifts the short-run aggregate supply curve to the left. Let's see what that does to the price level.

Inflation Effect of a Decrease in Aggregate Supply

Suppose that last year the GDP deflator was 120 and real GDP was \$5 trillion. Long-run real GDP was also \$5 trillion. This situation is shown in Fig. 14.3. The aggregate demand curve was AD_0, the short-run aggregate supply curve was SAS_0, and the long-run aggregate supply curve was *LAS*. In the current year, a sharp increase in world oil prices decreases short-run aggregate supply. The short-run aggregate supply curve shifts leftward to SAS_1. The GDP deflator increases to 130, and real GDP decreases to \$4.5 trillion. The economy experiences 8.3 percent inflation (a GDP deflator of 130 compared with 120 in the previous year) and a contraction of real GDP—*stagflation*.

The situation that developed in the U.S. economy in 1974 was similar to what we've just described. At that time, a fourfold increase in oil prices decreased aggregate supply, bringing a sharp increase in inflation and a decrease in real GDP.

Aggregate Demand Response

When the economy is stuck at an unemployment equilibrium such as that shown in Fig. 14.3, there is often an outcry of concern and a call for action to restore full employment. Such action can include an increase in government purchases of goods and services or a tax cut, but the most likely is a response from the Fed that increases the money supply. If the Fed does respond in this way, aggregate demand increases and the aggregate demand curve shifts rightward. Figure 14.4 shows an increase in aggregate demand that shifts the aggregate demand curve

FIGURE 14.3

Cost-Push Inflation

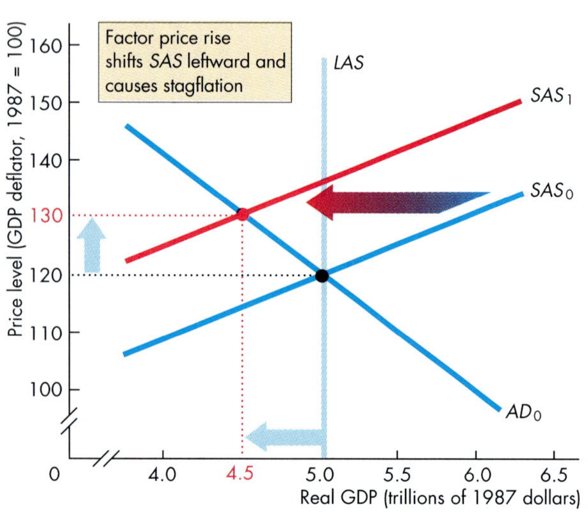

Initially, the aggregate demand curve is AD_0, the short-run aggregate supply curve is SAS_0, and the long-run aggregate supply curve is *LAS*. A decrease in aggregate supply (for example, resulting from an increase in the world price of oil) shifts the short-run aggregate supply curve to SAS_1. The economy moves to the point where the short-run aggregate supply curve SAS_1 intersects the aggregate demand curve AD_0. The GDP deflator increases to 130, and real GDP decreases to \$4.5 trillion. The economy experiences inflation and a contraction of real GDP—*stagflation*.

FIGURE 14.4

Aggregate Demand Response to Cost Push

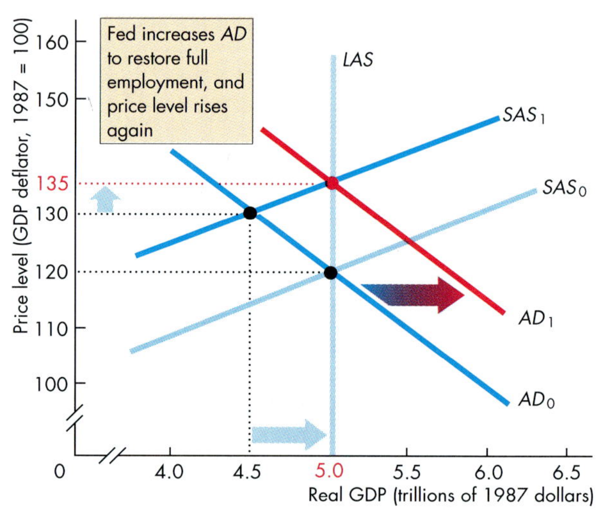

Initially, the aggregate demand curve is AD_0, the short-run aggregate supply curve is SAS_0, and the long-run aggregate supply curve is *LAS*. A decrease in aggregate supply shifts the short-run aggregate supply curve leftward to SAS_1. The GDP deflator rises from 120 to 130, and real GDP decreases from \$5 trillion to \$4.5 trillion. The economy experiences stagflation. It is stuck at an unemployment equilibrium. If the Fed responds by increasing aggregate demand to restore full employment, the aggregate demand curve shifts to the right to AD_1. The economy returns to full employment, but at the expense of higher inflation. The price level rises to 135.

to AD_1 and restores full employment. But this happens at the expense of a yet higher price level. The price level rises to 135, a 12.5 percent increase over the original price level.

A Cost-Price Inflation Spiral

Suppose now that the oil producers, seeing the prices of everything that they buy increase by 12.5 percent, decide to increase the price of oil yet again. Figure 14.5 continues the story. The short-run aggregate supply curve now shifts to SAS_2, and another bout of stagflation ensues. The price level rises further to 145, and real GDP falls to $4.5 trillion. Unemployment increases above its natural rate. If the Fed responds yet again with an increase in the money supply, aggregate demand increases and the aggregate demand curve shifts to AD_2. The price level rises even higher—to 150—and full employment is again restored. A cost-price inflation spiral results. But if the Fed does not respond, the economy remains below full employment until the initial price increase that triggered the stagflation is reversed.

You can see that the Fed has a dilemma. If it increases the money supply to restore full employment, it invites another oil price hike that will call forth yet a further increase in the money supply. Inflation will rage along at a rate decided by the oil-exporting nations. If the Fed keeps the lid on money supply growth, the economy operates with a high level of unemployment. The Fed faced such a dilemma in 1980 when OPEC again pushed oil prices higher. On that occasion the Fed decided not to respond to the oil price hike with an increase in the money supply. The result was a massive recession but also, eventually, a fall in inflation.

Cost-Push Inflation in Kalamazoo What is going on in the Kalamazoo soda bottling plant when the economy is experiencing cost-push inflation? When the oil price increases, so do the costs of bottling soda. These higher costs decrease the supply of soda, increasing its price and decreasing the quantity produced. The soda plant lays off some workers. This situation will persist until either the Fed increases aggregate demand or the price of oil falls. If the Fed increases aggregate demand, as it did in the mid-1970s, the demand for soda increases and so does its price. The higher price of soda brings higher profits, and the bottling plant increases its production. The soda factory rehires the laid-off workers.

FIGURE 14.5

A Cost-Price Inflation Spiral

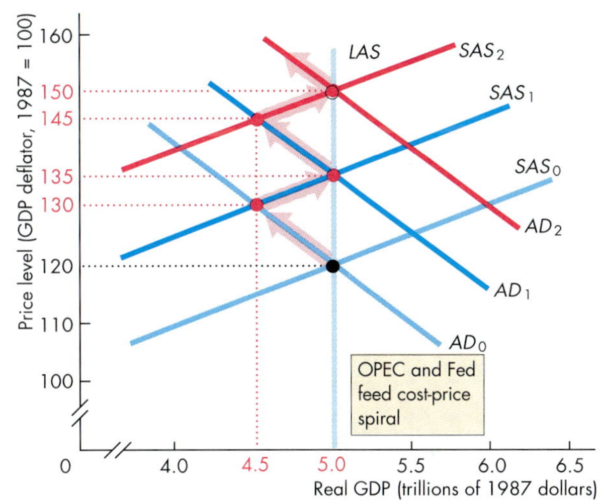

When a cost increase (for example, an increase in the world oil price) decreases short-run aggregate supply from SAS_0 to SAS_1, the GDP deflator rises to 130 and real GDP decreases to $4.5 trillion. The Fed responds with an increase in the money supply that shifts the aggregate demand curve from AD_0 to AD_1. The GDP deflator rises again to 135, and real GDP returns to $5 trillion. The cost increase is applied again, shifting the short-run aggregate supply curve to SAS_2. Stagflation is repeated, and the GDP deflator now rises to 145. The Fed responds again, and the cost-price inflation spiral continues.

REVIEW

Cost-push inflation results from any initial factor, such as an increase in the wage rate or an increase in the price of a raw material, that decreases aggregate supply. The initial effect of a decrease in aggregate supply is an increase in the price level and a decrease in real GDP—*stagflation.* If monetary or fiscal policy increases aggregate demand to restore full employment, the price level rises further. If aggregate demand remains constant, the economy stays below full employment until the initial price rise is reversed. If the response to stagflation is always an increase in aggregate demand, a freewheeling cost-push inflation takes place at a rate determined by the speed with which costs are pushed upward.

Inflation Expectations

With demand-pull inflation, a persistent increase in the money supply increases aggregate demand and creates a price-wage inflation spiral. With cost-push inflation, a persistent increase in factor prices accommodated by persistent increases in the money supply creates a cost-price inflation spiral. Regardless of whether the inflation is demand pull or cost push, the failure to correctly *anticipate* inflation imposes costs. And these costs create an incentive for people to try to anticipate the inflation.

Let's examine the costs of not anticipating inflation correctly.

The Cost of Wrong Inflation Forecasts

Our inability to know the future combined with our need to make forecasts about it inevitably imposes costs on us. The more wrong we are in assessing the future price level, the more expensive our mistake will be. To see why errors in forecasting inflation are costly, let's review what we've just discovered about the process of unanticipated inflation. And let's do this by returning to the soda bottling plant in Kalamazoo.

Wages When we looked at the effects of demand-pull inflation, we saw that initially the price of soda and of other goods increases but the wage rate doesn't change. The real wage rate falls, and the bottling plant increases production. Workers begin to quit the bottling plant to find jobs that pay a higher real wage rate, one closer to that prevailing before the outburst of inflation. This outcome imposes costs on both the firm and the workers. The firm operates its plant at a high output rate and incurs overtime costs and higher plant maintenance and parts replacement costs. The workers wind up feeling cheated. They have worked overtime to produce the extra output, and when they come to spend their wages, they discover that the prices have increased, so, in reality, their wages buy a smaller quantity of goods and services than was originally anticipated.

Contrast this outcome with what might have happened if the burst of inflation had been correctly anticipated. In this case, the wage rate at the bottling plant increases at the same rate as prices—the price of soda and the price level. The real wage rate, employment, and output remain constant. Anticipated inflation is virtually costless.

Interest Rates Just as firms and workers incur costs from wrong forecasts of the price level, so do borrowers and lenders. Interest rates are agreed upon on the basis of some expectation of the future value of money—which, in turn, depends on the future course of the price level. If inflation turns out to be unexpectedly high, borrowers gain and lenders lose. But neither borrowers nor lenders are as happy as they would have been in the absence of unanticipated inflation. Borrowers would like to have borrowed more and lenders would like to have lent less; so both groups feel that opportunities for extra gain have been lost.

If inflation turns out to be lower than expected, lenders gain and borrowers lose. But again, what lenders gain is less than what borrowers lose. In this case, borrowers would like to have borrowed less and lenders would like to have lent more. Again, both groups feel that they could have made better decisions with greater foresight.

Costs occur regardless of whether inflation expectations turn out to be wrong on the up side or the down side. Wrong expectations impose costs on firms and households, and the larger the forecasting error, the larger are those costs. The costs of wrong forecasts, like any other costs, are something to be minimized. These costs arise from scarcity in the same way that all other costs arise from scarcity. In this case, what is scarce is information about the future. Nevertheless, although the costs of wrong forecasts cannot be entirely avoided, they can be made as small as possible.

Minimizing the Losses from Wrong Forecasts

Lacking crystal balls, people cannot be right about the future all the time. But they can use all the relevant information available to them to make their forecasting errors as small as possible. That is, they can form a rational expectation. A **rational expectation** is a forecast based on all the available relevant information. A rational expectation has two features:

- The expected forecast error is zero.
- The range of the forecast error is as small as possible.

With an expected forecast error of zero, a rational expectation is right *on the average*. But it is not an accurate forecast. There is the same chance that the forecast will be too high as there is that it will be too low. By making a forecast that consciously errs on one side or the other, people avoid being wrong in one direction. But the cost of that is being more wrong in the other direction. Since the costs of wrong forecasts occur regardless of whether expectations are too high or too low, the best that can be done is to make a forecast that has an equal chance of being too high or too low. In making the range of forecast error as small as possible, information has been put to its best possible use. Information is a scarce resource, and none of it has been wasted.

Do people actually forecast by forming rational expectations? Let's see how people in the real world make their forecasts.

How People Forecast in the Real World

People devote different amounts of time and effort to forecasting. Some people specialize in forecasting and even make a living by selling their forecasts. For example, investment advisors forecast the future prices of stocks and bonds. Banks, large stock and commodity brokers, government agencies, and private forecasting firms make macroeconomic forecasts about inflation.

Specialist forecasters stand to lose a great deal from wrong forecasts. They have a strong incentive, therefore, to make their forecasts as accurate as possible—minimizing the range of error and at least making them correct on the average. Furthermore, organizations that stand to lose by having wrong forecasts invest a good deal of effort in checking the forecasts of the professionals. For example, all the large banks, the major labor unions, government departments, and most large private-sector producers of goods and services devote a lot of effort to making their own forecasts and comparing them with the forecasts of others. Specialist forecasters use vast amounts of data, which they analyze with the help of statistical models of the economy. The models they use are based on (but are more detailed than) the aggregate demand–aggregate supply model that you are studying in this book.

In contrast to the specialists, most people devote little time and effort to forecasting. Instead, they either buy their forecasts from specialists or mimic the people who appear to have been successful.

How do economists explain the forecasts that people make?

How Economists Predict People's Forecasts

Economics tries to predict the choices that people make. Because these choices are influenced by people's forecasts of phenomena such as inflation, to predict their choices we must also predict their forecasts. How do economists go about that task?

They assume that people are as rational in their use of information when forming expectations as they are in all their other economic actions. This idea leads economists to the rational expectations hypothesis. The **rational expectations hypothesis** is the proposition that the forecasts that people make are the same as the forecasts made by an economist using the relevant economic theory together with all the information available at the time the forecast is made. For example, to predict people's expectations of the price of orange juice, economists use the economic model of demand and supply together with all the available information about the positions of the demand and supply curves for orange juice. To make a prediction about people's expectations of the price level and inflation, economists use the economic model of aggregate demand and aggregate supply.

Let's see how we can use the model of aggregate demand and aggregate supply to work out the rational expectation of the price level.

A Rational Expectation of Inflation

To form a rational expectation of inflation, we use the model of aggregate demand and aggregate supply to forecast the state of the economy in much the same way that meteorologists use a model of the atmosphere to forecast the weather. But there is an important difference between the meteorologist's model of the atmosphere and the economist's model of aggregate demand and aggregate supply.

Tomorrow's weather will not be affected by our forecast of it. We may forecast a sunny day or a torrential downpour, but the outcome is independent of that forecast. But the consensus forecast of the price level might affect the actual price level. We must take this possibility into account when working out a rational expectation of the price level.

We're going to work out the rational expectation of the price level, using Fig. 14.6 to guide our analysis. The aggregate demand–aggregate supply model predicts that the price level is at the point of intersection of the aggregate demand and short-run aggregate supply curves. To forecast the price level, therefore, we have to forecast the positions of these curves.

Let's begin with aggregate demand. To forecast the position of the aggregate demand curve, we must forecast all the variables that influence aggregate demand. Suppose that we have done this and come up with the forecast of aggregate demand given by the curve *EAD*, the *expected* aggregate demand curve.

Our next task is to forecast the position of the short-run aggregate supply curve, but here we have a problem. We know that the position of the short-run aggregate supply curve is determined by two things:

- Long-run aggregate supply
- The wage rate

The short-run aggregate supply curve intersects the long-run aggregate supply curve at the full-employment price level. So we need a forecast of the position of the long-run aggregate supply curve. To

FIGURE 14.6

Rational Expectation of the Price Level

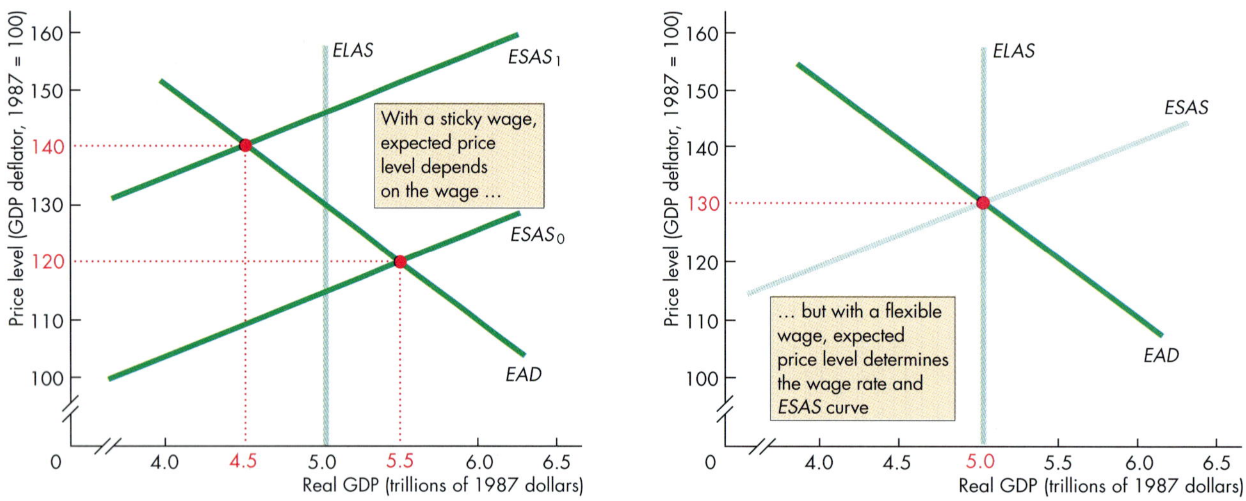

(a) Sticky wages

(b) Flexible wages

The rational expectation of the price level is the best available forecast. That forecast is constructed by forecasting the expected aggregate demand curve (*EAD*) and the expected short-run aggregate supply curve (*ESAS*). The rational expectation of the price level occurs at the point of intersection of curves *EAD* and *ESAS*. To forecast the position of *ESAS*, forecasts of the long-run aggregate supply curve *ELAS* and the wage rate are needed. In part (a), wages are sticky and do not respond to price level expectations, so the position of the expected short-run aggregate supply curve depends on *ELAS* and the fixed wage rate. With a low wage rate, the expected short-run aggregate supply curve is $ESAS_0$, and the rational expectation of the price level is 120. With a high wage rate, the expected short-run aggregate supply curve is $ESAS_1$, and the rational expectation of the price level is 140. In part (b), wages are flexible and respond to the expected price level. The rational expectation of the price level is at the point of intersection of *EAD* and *ELAS*. The wage rate is determined by this expected price level, and the expected short-run aggregate supply curve is *ESAS*.

make such a forecast, we must forecast all the factors that determine long-run aggregate supply. Suppose that we have made the best forecast we can of long-run real GDP and that we expect long-run aggregate supply to be $5 trillion. The *expected* long-run aggregate supply curve is *ELAS* in Fig. 14.6.

The final ingredient we need is a forecast of the wage rate. Armed with this information, we have a forecast of the point on the *ELAS* curve at which the short-run aggregate supply intersects it. The forecast of the wage rate depends on the degree of wage flexibility, and we need to look at two cases:

- Sticky wages
- Flexible wages

Rational Expectation with Sticky Wages

With sticky wages the position of the short-run aggregate supply curve is determined by the known and fixed wage rate. Given that fixed wage rate and given the expected long-run aggregate supply curve *ELAS*, there is an expected short-run aggregate supply curve. Figure 14.6(a) illustrates such a curve as $ESAS_0$.

The rational expectation of the price level is the point of intersection of *EAD* and $ESAS_0$, a price level of 120. The rational expectation of inflation is calculated as the percentage amount by which the forecasted future price level exceeds the current price level. For example, if the current price level is 110 and next year's forecasted price level is 120, the expected inflation rate over the year is 9 percent.

There is also a rational expectation of real GDP. Given the wage rate and the expected short-run aggregate supply curve $ESAS_0$, the rational expectation is that real GDP will be $5.5 trillion and the economy will be at an above full-employment equilibrium.

Figure 14.6(a) shows another case—one in which the expected short-run aggregate supply curve is $ESAS_1$. Here, the wage rate is higher. The rational expectation of the price level is determined at the point of intersection of *EAD* and $ESAS_1$, an expected price level of 140. With a current price level of 110, the expected inflation rate over the year is 27 percent. The economy is expected to be at an unemployment equilibrium, with a real GDP of $4.5 trillion.

Rational Expectation with Flexible Wages

When wages are flexible, it is harder to forecast the position of the short-run aggregate supply curve because the wage rate must also be forecasted. Furthermore, the wage rate depends on the expected price level, the variable we are trying to forecast. There seems to be a big problem: to forecast the price level, we need a forecast of the wage rate; and to forecast the wage rate, we need a forecast of the price level.

The problem is solved by finding a forecast of the price level that makes the expected aggregate demand curve and the expected short-run aggregate supply curve intersect at a price level that is the same as the forecasted price level. There is only one such price level. It is the one at which the expected aggregate demand curve intersects the expected long-run aggregate supply curve. This case is shown in Fig. 14.6(b). The wage rate adjusts in response to changes in the expected price level until the expected short-run aggregate supply curve is *ESAS* in Fig. 14.6(b). We forecast the position of the short-run aggregate supply curve and the price level at the same time, and the two forecasts are consistent with each other. Our forecast of the price level is a GDP deflator of 130, and *ESAS* is our forecast of the short-run aggregate supply curve.

Theory and Reality

The analysis we've just conducted shows how economists work out a rational expectation. But do real people form expectations of the price level by using that same analysis? We can imagine that graduates of economics might, but it seems unrealistic to attribute such calculations to most people. Does this make the whole idea of rational expectations invalid?

The answer is no! In performing our calculations, we have been building an economic model. That model does not seek to describe the thought processes of real people. Its goal is to make predictions about *choices,* not mental processes. The *rational expectations hypothesis* states that the forecasts that people make, regardless of how they make them, are on the average the same as those forecasts that an economist makes using the relevant economic theory.

REVIEW

Decisions to produce, work, borrow, and lend are based on forecasts of inflation, but the returns to firms, workers, borrowers, and lenders depend on actual inflation. Wrong inflation forecasts impose costs on firms, workers, borrowers, and lenders. To minimize forecasting errors, people use all available information and form a *rational expectation*. Real-world specialist forecasters use data and statistical models to generate expectations. Others either buy forecasts from specialists or copy people who seem to be successful. Economists use the rational expectations hypothesis to predict people's forecasts. A rational expectation of inflation is the forecast of the future price level made by using the aggregate demand–aggregate supply model. ◆

Now that we know what rational expectations are and how rational expectations of inflation are calculated, let's go on to see how actual real GDP and the actual inflation rate are determined. Let's also compare actual real GDP and actual inflation with people's rational expectations of these variables.

Rational Expectations Equilibrium

So far in this chapter we've studied the process of *unanticipated* inflation and the determination of inflation expectations—the way people try to *anticipate* inflation. Our next task is to bring these two things together and see what happens when there are disturbances to aggregate demand or aggregate supply *and at the same time* people do the best they can to anticipate the consequences of those changes. Such a situation is called a rational expectations equilibrium. A **rational expectations equilibrium** is a macroeconomic equilibrium based on expectations that are the best available forecasts.

Let's look at such situations and see how they come about, using Fig. 14.7. The figure has three parts. Part (a) contains people's *forecasts* of the economy, and parts (b) and (c) show two alternative *outcomes* that differ from the forecast. The forecast in part (a) is exactly the same as that seen in Fig. 14.6(b). The forecasted price level is 130, and real GDP is forecasted to be at its long-run level of $5 trillion.

If the outcome is exactly what was forecasted, then part (a) also describes that outcome. The actual price level is 130, real GDP is $5 trillion, and there is full employment.

Figure 14.7(b) shows what happens when aggregate demand turns out to be less than expected but aggregate supply is the same as expected. The aggregate supply curves (*LAS* and *SAS*) in part (b) are identical to the expected aggregate supply curves (*ELAS* and *ESAS*) in part (a). But the aggregate demand curve (*AD*) is farther to the left in part (b) than the expected aggregate demand curve (*EAD*) in part (a). Such an outcome might arise from an *unexpected* slowdown in the rate at which the Fed is creating money, an *unexpected* fall in foreign demand for U.S. exports, an *unexpected* tax increase, or an *unexpected* reduction in government purchases of goods and services.

Equilibrium is determined where the actual aggregate demand curve intersects the short-run aggregate supply curve. The GDP deflator is 125, and real GDP is $4.5 trillion. With actual aggregate demand less than expected, the price level is lower than expected and real GDP is below its long-run level. There is an unemployment equilibrium.

You can work out, using Fig. 14.7(b), what happens if aggregate demand turns out to be higher than expected. In such a case, the price level is higher than expected and so is real GDP.

Figure 14.7(c) shows what happens when aggregate supply turns out to be less than expected but aggregate demand is the same as expected. The aggregate demand curve (*AD*) in part (c) is identical to the expected aggregate demand curve (*EAD*) in part (a). But the aggregate supply curves (*LAS* and *SAS*) are farther to the left in part (c) than the expected aggregate supply curves (*ELAS* and *ESAS*) in part (a). Such a situation might arise from an *unexpected* slowdown in the pace of technological change or capital accumulation.

Again, the equilibrium occurs where the aggregate demand curve intersects the short-run aggregate supply curve. In this case, the GDP deflator is 135 and real GDP is $4.75 trillion. The actual price level

FIGURE 14.7

Rational Expectations Equilibrium

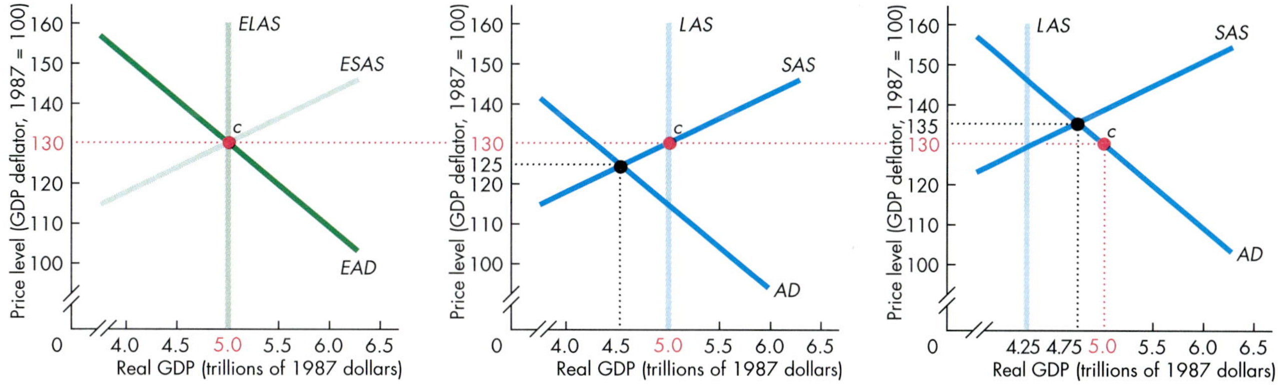

(a) Forecast: full employment

(b) Outcome: unexpected fall in aggregate demand

(c) Outcome: unexpected fall in aggregate supply

The rational expectation of the price level is calculated in part (a). It occurs at the intersection of curves *EAD* and *ELAS* (point *c*). If long-run aggregate supply turns out to be as expected but aggregate demand is lower than expected, as in part (b), real GDP decreases below its long-run level and the price level falls below that expected. If aggregate demand turns out to be as expected but long-run aggregate supply is lower than expected, as in part (c), the price level rises above its expected level and real GDP decreases.

is higher than expected because short-run aggregate supply is lower than expected. With the price level higher than expected, real GDP is above its long-run level. In this particular case, long-run real GDP has decreased compared with its expected value, and real GDP itself has also decreased but by less than long-run real GDP.

You can work out, using Fig. 14.7(c), what happens if aggregate supply turns out to be higher than expected. In such a case the price level is lower than expected and real GDP is higher than expected.

The outcomes that we've just looked at do not depend on whether wages are sticky or flexible. Even if wages are flexible, they cannot respond to what is not known and not expected. Thus flexible wages do not deliver full employment. In the examples of rational expectations equilibrium that we've just studied, there is unemployment or above full employment.

Individuals in a Rational Expectations Equilibrium

The key characteristic of any economic equilibrium is that all the people in the economy have reached a situation in which they cannot make a reallocation of their resources that they regard as superior to the one they have chosen.

Each household and firm sees itself as a small part of the overall economy. Those firms and households that have sufficient market power to influence prices have exerted that influence to their maximum possible advantage. But most households and firms are not able to exert a significant effect on the prices that they face. Instead, each household and firm does its best to forecast those prices relevant to its own actions.

Armed with its best forecasts, each household works out how many chickens, microwaves, and suits to buy, how much to spend on cars and plumbing, how much money to have in the bank, and how many hours a week to work. These decisions are expressed not as fixed quantities but as demand and supply schedules.

On the other side of the markets, each firm, also armed with its best forecasts, determines how much new capital equipment to install (investment), how much output to supply, and how much labor to demand. Like households, firms don't express their decisions as fixed quantities. Instead, they express them as demand schedules for factors of production and supply schedules of output.

Prices, wages, and interest rates are determined in the markets for goods and services, labor, and money at levels that ensure the mutual consistency of the plans of all the individual households and firms trading in these markets. The quantities demanded and supplied in each market balance.

In a rational expectations equilibrium, each person is satisfied that there is no better action that he or she could currently take. But such an equilibrium is not static. The economy is constantly changing. You could imagine the economy at each point that we observe as a frozen frame in a video: in the frame, the supply and demand curves in the markets for all the different goods, services, and factors of production all intersect, determining their prices and quantities at that moment. Economists try to understand what is happening by stopping the video to take a closer look at it.

We've now seen how unexpected changes in aggregate demand and aggregate supply affect both the price level and real GDP, even when people are doing their best to anticipate these changes. Let's next see how things work out when forecasts are correct—when people get lucky and correctly anticipate the future.

Anticipated Inflation

If people could correctly anticipate the future course of inflation, they would never agree to a wage contract in which the wage rate was fixed. Wages would change in line with prices. We'll study anticipated inflation, therefore, using the flexible wage model only.

Let's suppose that last year the GDP deflator was 120 and real GDP was \$5 trillion. Let's also suppose that the economy was at full employment and its long-run real GDP last year was \$5 trillion. Figure 14.8 illustrates the economy last year. The aggregate demand curve last year was AD_0, the aggregate supply curve was SAS_0, and the long-run aggregate supply curve was *LAS*. Since the economy was in equilibrium at long-run real GDP, the actual price level equaled the expected price level.

To simplify our analysis, let's suppose that at the end of last year, long-run real GDP was not expected to change, so this year's expected long-run aggregate supply is the same as last year's. Let's also suppose that aggregate demand was expected to increase, so

FIGURE 14.8

Anticipated Inflation

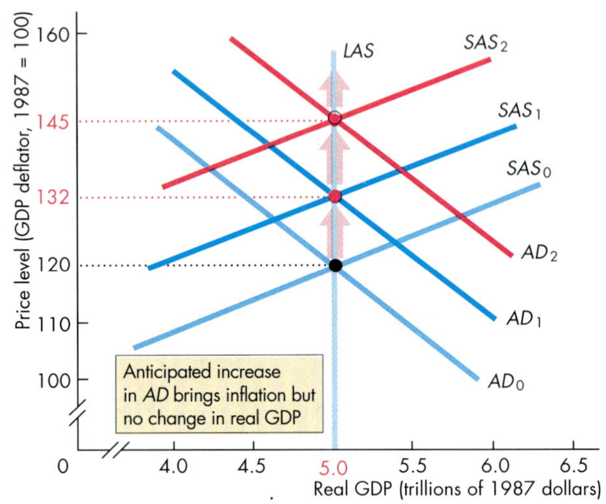

The actual and expected long-run aggregate supply curve (*LAS*) is at a real GDP of \$5 trillion. Last year, aggregate demand was AD_0, and the short-run aggregate supply curve was SAS_0. The actual price level was the same as that expected—a GDP deflator of 120. This year, aggregate demand is expected to rise to AD_1. The rational expectation of the GDP deflator changes from 120 to 132. As a result, the short-run aggregate supply curve shifts up to SAS_1. If aggregate demand actually increases as expected, the actual aggregate demand curve AD_1 is the same as the expected aggregate demand curve. Equilibrium occurs at a real GDP of \$5 trillion and an actual GDP deflator of 132. The inflation is correctly anticipated. Next year, the process continues with aggregate demand increasing as expected to AD_2 and wages rising to shift the short-run aggregate supply curve to SAS_2. Again, real GDP remains at \$5 trillion and the GDP deflator rises, as anticipated, to 145.

the expected aggregate demand curve for this year is AD_1. We can now calculate the rational expectation of the price level for this year. It is a GDP deflator of 132, the price level at which the new expected aggregate demand curve intersects the expected long-run aggregate supply curve. The expected inflation rate is 10 percent, the percentage change in the price level from 120 to 132.

Wages increase as a result of the expected inflation, and the short-run aggregate supply curve also shifts to the left. In particular, given that expected inflation is 10 percent, the short-run aggregate supply curve for next year (SAS_1) shifts upward by that same percentage amount (10 percent) and passes through the long-run aggregate supply curve (*LAS*) at the expected price level.

If aggregate demand turns out to be the same as expected, the actual aggregate demand curve is AD_1. The intersection point of AD_1 and SAS_1 determines the actual price level—where the GDP deflator is 132. Between last year and this year, the GDP deflator increased from 120 to 132 and the economy experienced an inflation rate of 10 percent, the same as the inflation rate that was anticipated.

What caused the inflation? The immediate answer is the anticipated and actual increase in aggregate demand. Because aggregate demand was *expected* to increase from AD_0 to AD_1, the short-run aggregate supply curve shifted up from SAS_0 to SAS_1. Because aggregate demand actually did increase by the amount that was expected, the actual aggregate demand curve shifted from AD_0 to AD_1. The combination of the anticipated and actual shifts of the aggregate demand curve to the right produced an increase in the price level that was anticipated.

Only if aggregate demand growth is correctly forecasted does the economy follow the course described in Fig. 14.8. If the expected growth rate of aggregate demand is different from its actual growth rate, the expected aggregate demand curve shifts by an amount different from the actual aggregate demand curve. The inflation rate departs from its expected level, and, to some extent, there is unanticipated inflation. It is this type of inflation that we studied in the first part of this chapter.

Anticipated inflations can be very stubborn and hard to stop. The monetary and fiscal policy that creates inflation also creates expectations of inflation that reinforce the inflationary effects of the policy. Also, people don't like to have their expectations disappointed—so if they anticipate a high inflation rate, they want a high inflation rate. Such was the situation in the United States in the late 1970s and early 1980s. And such is the situation in Brazil today, as you can see in Reading Between the Lines on pp. 382–383.

REVIEW

A *rational expectations equilibrium* is a macroeconomic equilibrium based on expectations that are the best available forecasts. A rational expectations equilibrium describes how real GDP and the price level are determined when people are doing the best they can to anticipate the levels of aggregate demand and aggregate supply. ◆◆ In a rational expectations equilibrium, if aggregate demand is lower than expected, real GDP and the price level are lower than expected. If long-run aggregate supply is lower than expected, the price level is higher and real GDP is lower than expected. These outcomes do not depend on whether wages are sticky or flexible. Even flexible wages cannot respond to the unknown and unexpected, and a rational expectations equilibrium is not always a full-employment equilibrium. ◆◆ If people do correctly anticipate changes in aggregate demand and aggregate supply, the result is anticipated inflation. The price level changes at an anticipated rate, and real GDP and unemployment are unchanged. ◆

Inflation lowers the value of money and changes the real value of amounts borrowed and repaid. Because of this, interest rates are influenced by inflation. Let's see how.

Interest Rates and Inflation

There have been massive fluctuations in interest rates in the U.S. economy in recent years: In the early 1960s, corporations could borrow to finance long-term capital projects at interest rates of 4.5 to 5 percent a year. By the end of the 1960s, that interest rate had almost doubled and stood at 8 percent a year. During the 1970s, the interest rates paid by firms for long-term loans fluctuated between 7.5 and 10.5 percent. In 1981, interest rates hit the high teens. They fell during the rest of the 1980s and by 1991 had returned to the levels of the late 1960s. Why have interest rates fluctuated so much, and why were they so high in the late 1970s and early 1980s?

To answer these questions, it is necessary to distinguish between nominal interest rates and real interest rates. **Nominal interest rates** are those actually paid and received in the marketplace. *Real* interest

Intractable Anticipated Inflation

The Wall Street Journal, March 29, 1991

Brazil's Battle to Curb Inflation Faces Hurdle: A Lot of People Like It

by Thomas Kamm

On March 15, 1990, a new president took office in Brazil and immediately shocked his countrymen with a harsh economic program. President Fernando Collor de Mello's target was wild inflation, long an albatross burdening the country's economy and then soaring at 1,764% a year.

Mr. Collor's radical, enough-is-enough decree seemed finally to be medicine as tough as the disease. He froze about half the money then circulating in the economy, created a new currency and froze all prices.

Yet less than one year later, what was Mr. Collor doing? On Jan. 31 [1991], he was imposing still *another* anti-inflation program for Brazil.

What is it in the economy of this nation—a nation whose economic health deeply concerns its legions of U.S. creditors—that makes runaway inflation so intractable? Why didn't it yield to the recession that was set off by the 1990 program and might have been expected to moderate price increases?

The answer seems to lie, at least partly, in a kind of inflation culture in Brazil. It is a set of expectations that even some of those who call inflation a menace and a curse find curiously comforting.

Consider the experience of Gil Pace. An economist and former government official, he worries that Brazil is "entering chaos as a result of the persistence" of inflation. But as a private citizen, Mr. Pace offers a different view. Inflation allowed him to buy an apartment in Rio's swanky Lagoa district "almost for free."

It worked like this: When Mr. Pace first started making mortgage payments in 1975, both his salary and the mortgage were adjusted annually for inflation, then 30% a year. The state lender continued adjusting the mortgage once a year, but before long inflation was so bad that his employer began raising his salary every month. With inflation totaling more than one million percent between 1985 and 1990, by the time he paid off the mortgage last year, the lagging adjustment on his loan had practically wiped out the debt.

By the end, he was paying the equivalent of a mere $6.50 a month. "It was costing them more than that to send me the mortgage bill," Mr. Pace says. His conclusion: "I'm against inflation, but here, you have to defend inflation." . . .

The Essence of the Story

In March 1990, Brazil's inflation rate was 1,764 percent a year.

The country's new president, Fernando Collor de Mello, froze about half the money then circulating in the economy, created a new currency, and froze all prices.

In January 1991, President Collor introduced another anti-inflation program for Brazil.

Inflation is intractable in Brazil and does not yield to recession, at least partly because people expect inflation and some people, like Gil Pace, gain a great deal from it.

Background and Analysis

Throughout the 1980s, Brazil's inflation rate exceeded 100 percent a year.

By the end of the decade, the rate began to accelerate, reaching 6,000 percent a year in the final quarter of 1989—see the figure.

The government of Brazil persistently spends more than it collects in taxes—has a budget deficit—on a scale that exceeds 10 percent of GDP.

To pay for its deficit, the government of Brazil borrows from the central bank and the money supply grows at a rapid rate.

Brazil's inflation results from this persistent government budget deficit and rapid money supply growth rate. These forces bring a rapid rate of increase in aggregate demand.

The increase in aggregate demand is anticipated, hence wages also increase rapidly, and the inflation is not accompanied by a rise in real GDP.

Also, the inflation is anticipated, so interest rates adjust to compensate lenders for the loss in the value of money—see the figure.

The inflation of the 1980s was *not anticipated* in the 1970s. Hence people (like Gil Pace in the article) borrowed at an interest rate that did not keep up with the inflation of the 1980s and gained from the inflation.

Stopping a persistent and expected inflation is very difficult. Aggregate demand growth must be slowed, and people must *expect* its growth to be slowed.

To achieve this end in Brazil's case, the government budget deficit—which is the source of the rapid money supply growth rate—must be brought under control.

The Collor program did not tackle this cause of inflation. Instead, it tackled the symptom of inflation—rising prices. Without a change in the underlying cause, the symptoms broke out again.

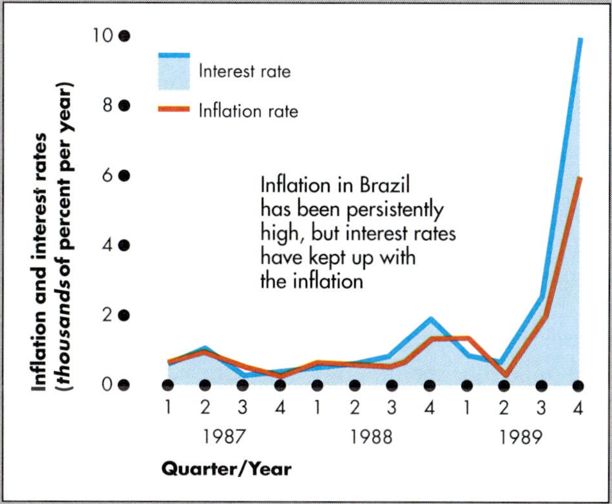

rates are the rates that nominal interest rates translate into when the effects of inflation are taken into account. If the nominal interest rate is 15 percent a year and prices are rising by 10 percent a year, the real interest rate is only 5 percent a year. If you made a loan of $100 on January 1, 1994, it's true you'd have $115 to spend on January 1, 1995. But you'd need $110 to buy the same goods that $100 would have bought a year earlier. All you've really made is $5—the difference between the $110 you need to buy $100 worth of goods and the $115 that you've got.

When we studied the determination interest rates in Chapter 11, we analyzed an economy in which the price level was constant. In such an economy, there is no difference between the nominal and real interest rates. But in the real world, the price level is rarely constant, and most of the time it increases. What are the effects on interest rates of a rising price level and of expectations of the price level continuing to rise?

Expectations of Inflation and Interest Rates

Imagine two economies that are identical in every way except for one: the first economy has no inflation and none is expected; the second economy has an inflation rate of 10 percent a year that is correctly anticipated. In both economies, the real interest rate is 5 percent. What is the difference in the nominal interest rates in these two economies?

In the zero-inflation economy the nominal interest rate is 5 percent a year—the same as the real interest rate. In the second economy the nominal interest rate is 15.5 percent a year. Why?

Lenders in the economy that is inflating at a rate of 10 percent a year recognize that the value of the money that they have lent is falling at a rate of 10 percent a year. They protect themselves against this loss in the value of money by asking for a higher nominal interest rate on the loans that they make. Borrowers in this economy recognize that the money they use to repay their loans is worth 10 percent a year less than money they borrowed. They willingly agree to a higher nominal interest rate. In recognition of the falling value of money, borrowers and lenders agree to add 10 percentage points a year to the interest rate. In addition, they agree to add 10 percent of the interest because they recognize that even the interest buys 10 percent less at the end of the year than at the beginning of the year. Since the real interest rate is 5 percent a year, 10 percent of the interest rate is half a percentage point. So the total amount that borrowers and lenders agree to add to the real interest rate of 5 percent a year is 10.5 percentage points, and the nominal interest rate is 15.5 percent a year.

We've seen that, other things being equal, the higher the expected inflation rate, the higher is the nominal interest rate. Usually, an economy with a high expected inflation rate is one actually experiencing a high inflation rate. We would expect, therefore, that interest rates and inflation rates move up and down together. Let's see if they do.

Inflation and Interest Rates in the United States

The relationship between inflation and nominal interest rates in the United States is illustrated in Fig. 14.9. The interest rate measured on the vertical axis is that paid by large corporations on short-term (6-month) loans. Each point on the graph represents a year in recent U.S. macroeconomic history between 1960 and 1992. The blue line shows the relationship between the nominal interest rate and the inflation rate if the real interest rate is constant at 2.2 percent a year, its actual average value in this period. As you can see, there is a clear relationship between the inflation rate and the interest rate, but it is not exact. As we have just seen, it is only *anticipated* inflation that influences interest rates. Thus only to the extent that a higher inflation rate is anticipated does it result in higher interest rates.

During the 1960s, both actual and expected inflation were moderate and so were nominal interest rates. In the early 1970s, inflation began to increase but it was not expected to increase much and certainly not to persist. As a result, nominal interest rates did not rise very much at that time. By the mid-1970s, there was a burst of unexpectedly high inflation. Interest rates increased somewhat but not by nearly as much as the inflation rate. During the late 1970s and early 1980s, inflation of close to 10 percent a year came to be expected as an ongoing and highly persistent phenomenon. As a result, nominal interest rates increased to around 15 percent a year. Then in 1984 and 1985, the inflation rate

FIGURE 14.9

Inflation and the Interest Rate

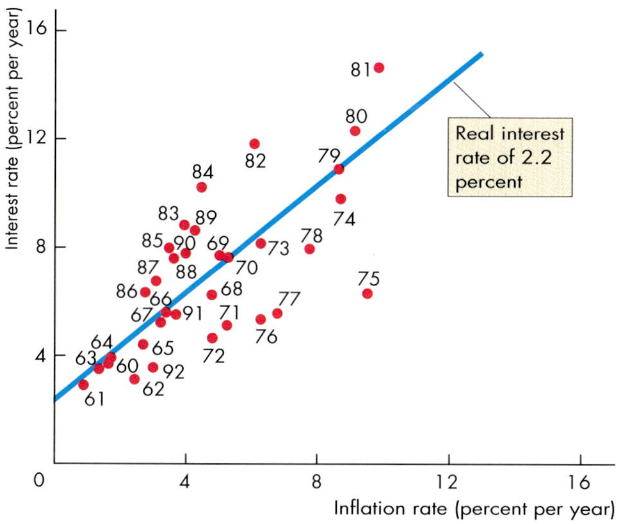

Other things being equal, the higher the expected inflation rate, the higher is the interest rate. A graph showing the relationship between interest rates and the actual inflation rate reveals that the influence of inflation on interest rates is a powerful one. Here, the interest rate is that paid by large corporations on short-term loans (the 6-month commercial paper rate) and the inflation rate is the percentage change in the GDP deflator. Each point represents a year in U.S. macroeconomic history between 1960 and 1992.

Source: Economic Report of the President, 1993.

fell—at first unexpectedly. Interest rates began to fall but not nearly as quickly as the inflation rate. Short-term interest rates fell more quickly than long-term interest rates because, at that time, it was expected that inflation would be lower in the short term but not as low in the longer term.

The relationship between inflation and interest rates is even more dramatically illustrated by international experience. For example, in recent years, Chile has experienced an inflation rate of around 30 percent with nominal interest rates of about 40 percent. Brazil has experienced inflation rates of more than 200 percent a year with nominal interest rates also above 200 percent a year. At the other extreme, such countries as Japan and Belgium have had low inflation and low nominal interest rates.

Money Supply and Interest Rates We have seen that high nominal interest rates and high expected inflation rates go together. We have also seen that high expected inflation is the product of a high anticipated money supply growth rate. Thus a high anticipated growth rate of the money supply brings not only a high anticipated inflation rate but also high nominal interest rates.

In Chapter 11, when we studied the effects of the Fed's actions on interest rates, we concluded that an increase in the quantity of money *lowers* nominal interest rates. How can both of these conclusions be correct? How can an increase in the anticipated growth rate of the money supply increase interest rates while an increase in the quantity of money lowers them?

The answer lies in the time it takes interest rates to adjust to a change in the money supply. If the Fed takes an unexpected action that increases the quantity of money, the immediate effect is lower nominal interest rates. Lower interest rates are needed to make the quantity of money demanded equal the quantity supplied. But if the Fed continues to increase the money supply and keeps on increasing it year after year at a faster pace than real GDP is growing, people come to expect that increase in the money supply and the inflation that goes with it.

In these circumstances, with low interest rates and a high expected inflation rate, people increase their borrowing and increase their spending on goods and services. The inflation rate speeds up and overtakes the growth rate of the money supply. With inflation proceeding at a faster pace than money supply growth, the quantity of real money declines. That is, the fact that the Fed is increasing the money supply but prices are rising even more quickly means that the real money supply is decreasing. The Fed controls the *nominal* money supply but doesn't control the *real* money supply.

Lower quantity of real money brings higher interest rates. Only when interest rates have increased by enough to compensate for the anticipated falling value of money is a long-run equilibrium restored.

Thus an unanticipated increase in the money supply brings a fall in interest rates. An anticipated and ongoing increase in the money supply increases interest rates. The decrease in interest rates following an increase in the money supply is an immediate but temporary response. The increase in interest rates associated with an increase in the growth rate of the money supply is a long-run response.

REVIEW

The nominal interest rate is the rate actually paid and received in the marketplace. The real interest rate is the rate *really* paid and received when the effects of inflation are taken into account. The nominal interest rate is approximately equal to the real interest rate plus the expected inflation rate. The nominal interest rate is also the interest rate that makes the quantity of money demanded equal to the quantity of money supplied. ◆

Inflation over the Business Cycle: The Phillips Curve

We've seen that a speedup in aggregate demand growth that is not fully anticipated increases both inflation and real GDP growth. It also decreases unemployment. Similarly, a slowdown in the growth rate of aggregate demand that is not fully anticipated slows down both inflation and real GDP growth and increases unemployment. We've also seen that a fully anticipated change in the growth rate of aggregate demand changes the inflation rate and has no effect on real GDP or unemployment. Finally, we've seen that a decrease in aggregate supply increases inflation and decreases real GDP growth. In this case, unemployment increases.

The aggregate demand–aggregate supply model that we have used to obtain these results gives predictions about the level of real GDP and the price level. Given these predictions, we can work out how unemployment and inflation have changed. But the aggregate demand–aggregate supply model does not place inflation and unemployment at center stage.

An alternative way of studying inflation and unemployment focuses directly on their joint movements and uses a relationship known as the Phillips curve. The Phillips curve is so named because it was popularized by New Zealand economist A. W. Phillips when working at the London School of Economics in the 1950s. A **Phillips curve** is a curve showing the relationship between inflation and unemployment. There are two time frames for Phillips curves:

- The short run
- The long run

The Phillips Curve in the Short Run

The **short-run Phillips curve** is a curve showing the relationship between inflation and unemployment, holding constant:

1. The expected inflation rate
2. The natural rate of unemployment

Figure 14.10 shows a short-run Phillips curve *SRPC*. Suppose that the expected inflation rate is 10 percent a year and the natural rate of unemployment is 6 percent, point *a* in the figure. The short-run

FIGURE 14.10
The Short-Run Phillips Curve

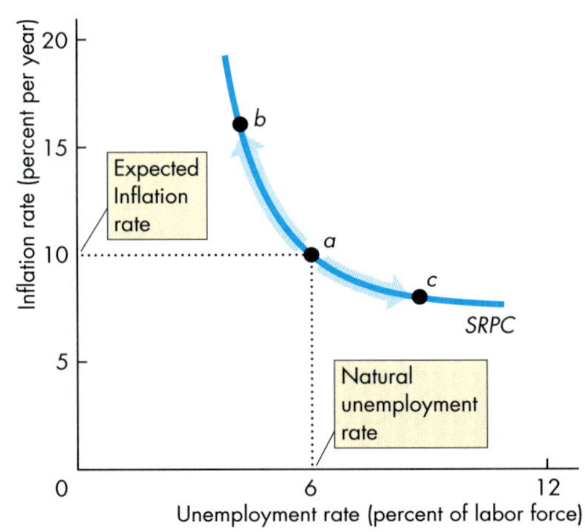

The short-run Phillips curve *SRPC* shows the relationship between inflation and unemployment at a given expected inflation rate and given natural rate of unemployment. With an expected inflation rate of 10 percent a year and a natural rate of unemployment of 6 percent, the short-run Phillips curve passes through point *a*. An unanticipated increase in aggregate demand lowers unemployment and increases inflation—a movement up the short-run Phillips curve. An unanticipated decrease in aggregate demand increases unemployment and lowers inflation—a movement down the short-run Phillips curve.

Phillips curve passes through this point. If the unemployment rate falls below its natural rate, inflation rises above its expected rate. This joint movement in the inflation rate and the unemployment rate is illustrated as a movement up the short-run Phillips curve from point *a* to point *b* in the figure. Similarly, if unemployment rises above the natural rate, inflation falls below its expected rate. In this case, there is movement down the short-run Phillips curve from point *a* to point *c*.

This negative relationship between inflation and unemployment along the short-run Phillips curve is explained by the aggregate demand–aggregate supply model. Suppose that, initially, inflation is anticipated to be 10 percent a year and unemployment is at its natural rate. This situation is illustrated by the aggregate demand–aggregate supply model in Fig. 14.8 and by the Phillips curve approach as point *a* in Fig. 14.10. Suppose that now an unanticipated increase in the growth of aggregate demand occurs. In Fig. 14.8 the aggregate demand curve shifts to the right more quickly than expected. Real GDP increases, the unemployment rate decreases, and the price level starts to increase at a faster rate than expected. There has been a movement from point *a* to point *b* in Fig. 14.10. If the unanticipated increase in aggregate demand is temporary, aggregate demand growth slows to its previous level. When it does so, the process is reversed and the economy moves back to point *a* in Fig. 14.10.

A similar story can be told to illustrate the effects of an unanticipated decrease in the growth of aggregate demand. In this case, an unanticipated slowdown in the growth of aggregate demand reduces inflation, slows real GDP growth, and increases unemployment. There is a movement down the short-run Phillips curve from point *a* to point *c*.

The Phillips Curve in the Long Run

The **long-run Phillips curve** is a curve showing the relationship between inflation and unemployment when the actual inflation rate equals the expected inflation rate. The long-run Phillips curve is vertical at the natural rate of unemployment—the **natural rate hypothesis.** The natural rate hypothesis was proposed independently in the mid-1960s by Edmund Phelps (now at Columbia University but then a young professor at the University of Pennsylvania—see Talking with Edmund Phelps on pp. 332–335) and by Milton Friedman. Sometimes the natural rate hypothesis is given the alternative name the *Phelps-Friedman hypothesis*.

A long-run Phillips curve is shown in Fig. 14.11 as the vertical line *LRPC*. If the expected inflation rate is 10 percent a year, the short-run Phillips curve is $SRPC_0$. If the expected inflation rate falls to 8 percent a year, the short-run Phillips curve shifts downward to $SRPC_1$. At points *a* and *d*, inflation is equal to its expected rate and unemployment is equal to its natural rate. The distance by which the short-run Phillips curve shifts downward when the expected inflation rate falls is equal to the change in the expected inflation rate. Points *a* and *d* lie on the long-run Phillips curve *LRPC*. This curve tells us

FIGURE 14.11

The Short-Run and Long-Run Phillips Curves

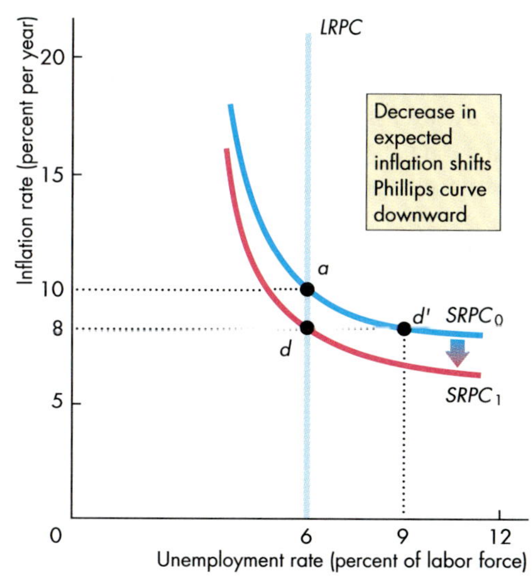

The long-run Phillips curve is *LRPC*, a vertical line at the natural rate of unemployment. A decrease in inflation expectations shifts the short-run Phillips curve down by the amount of the fall in the expected inflation rate. Here, when expected inflation falls from 10 percent a year to 8 percent a year, the short-run Phillips curve shifts from $SRPC_0$ to $SRPC_1$. The new short-run Phillips curve intersects the long-run Phillips curve at the new expected inflation rate at point *d*. With the original expected inflation rate (of 10 percent), an inflation rate of 8 percent a year would occur at an unemployment rate of 9 percent, at point *d'*.

that any inflation rate is possible at the natural rate of unemployment.

To see why the short-run Phillips curve shifts when the expected inflation rate changes, let's do an experiment. The economy is at full employment, and a fully anticipated inflation is raging at 10 percent a year. Now suppose that the Fed and the government begin a permanent attack on inflation by slowing money supply growth and cutting the deficit. Aggregate demand growth slows down, and the inflation rate falls to 8 percent a year. At first, this decrease in inflation is unanticipated, so wages continue to rise at their original rate, shifting the short-run aggregate supply curve to the left at the same pace as before. Real GDP falls, and unemployment increases. In Fig. 14.11, the economy moves from point *a* to point *d'* on the short-run Phillips curve $SRPC_0$.

If the actual inflation rate remains steady at 8 percent a year, eventually this rate will come to be expected. As this happens, wage growth slows down and the short-run aggregate supply curve moves leftward less quickly. Eventually, it shifts to the left at the same pace at which the aggregate demand curve is shifting to the right. When this occurs, the actual inflation rate equals the expected inflation rate and full employment is restored. Unemployment is back at its natural rate. In Fig. 14.11, the short-run Phillips curve has shifted from $SRPC_0$ to $SRPC_1$ and the economy is at point *d*.

FIGURE 14.12

A Change in the Natural Rate of Unemployment

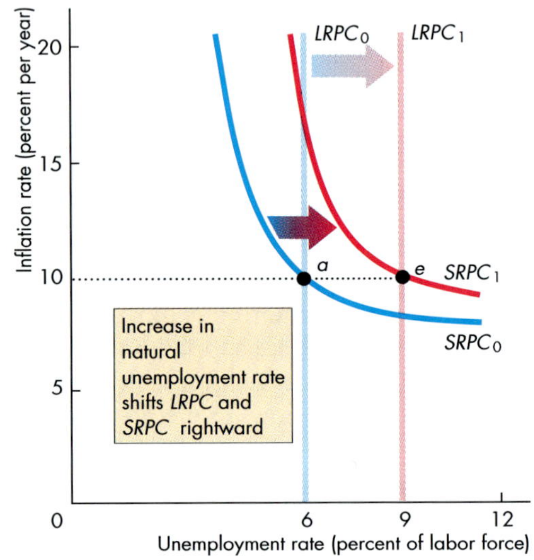

A change in the natural rate of unemployment shifts both the short-run and long-run Phillips curves. Here, the natural rate of unemployment increases from 6 percent to 9 percent, and the two Phillips curves shift right to $SRPC_1$ and $LRPC_1$. The new long-run Phillips curve intersects the new short-run Phillips curve at the expected inflation rate—point *e*

Variable Natural Rate of Unemployment

Until the 1970s, the natural rate of unemployment was regarded as a constant. In recent years, however, it has become clear that the natural rate of unemployment varies. Some of these variations arise from changes in the amount of labor market turnover resulting from technological change, which leads to job switching from firm to firm, sector to sector, and region to region. A change in the natural rate of unemployment shifts both the short-run and long-run Phillips curves. Such shifts are illustrated in Fig. 14.12. If the natural rate of unemployment increases from 6 percent to 9 percent, the long-run Phillips curve shifts from $LRPC_0$ to $LRPC_1$, and if expected inflation is constant at 10 percent a year, the short-run Phillips curve shifts from $SRPC_0$ to $SRPC_1$. Because the expected inflation rate is constant, the short-run Phillips curve $SRPC_1$ intersects the long-run curve $LRPC_1$ (point *e*) at the same inflation rate as that at which the short-run Phillips curve $SRPC_0$ intersects the long-run curve $LRPC_0$ (point *a*).

The Phillips Curve in the United States

Figure 14.13 shows the relationship between inflation and unemployment in the United States. Begin by looking at part (a), a scatter diagram of inflation and unemployment since 1960. Each dot in the figure represents the combination of inflation and unemployment for a particular year. As you can see, there does not appear to be any clear relationship between inflation and unemployment. We certainly cannot see a Phillips curve similar to that shown in Fig. 14.10.

But we can interpret the data in terms of a shifting short-run Phillips curve. Figure 14.13(b) provides such an interpretation. Four short-run Phillips curves appear in the figure. The short-run Phillips curve of the 1960s (discovered by Paul Samuelson and Robert Solow of MIT—see Talking with Robert Solow, pp. 1–4) is $SRPC_0$. At that time, the expected inflation rate was 2 percent a year and the natural rate of unemployment was 5 percent.

The short-run Phillips curve of the early 1970s and late 1980s is $SRPC_1$. These two periods have a natural rate of unemployment similar to that of the 1960s but an expected inflation rate that is much higher. The short-run Phillips curve of the late 1970s is $SRPC_2$. This period followed the large increase in oil prices that disrupted the economy and had profound effects on both the natural rate of unemployment, which increased to 8 percent, and the expected inflation rate, which increased to around 6 percent a year. The short-run Phillips curve of the early 1980s (and also of 1975) is $SRPC_3$. In these years, both the expected inflation rate and the natural rate of unemployment were high.

Although in the late 1980s the economy was on the same short-run Phillips curve as in the early 1970s ($SRPC_1$), there is an important difference between these two periods. In the early 1970s, the natural rate of unemployment was around 5 percent and the expected inflation rate was around 6 percent a year, while in the late 1980s, the natural rate of unemployment was probably around 6 percent with expected inflation at about 4 percent a year. Thus, although the short-run Phillips curves for these two periods are similar, a different combination of expected inflation and natural rate of unemployment underlies the two curves.

FIGURE 14.13

Phillips Curves in the United States

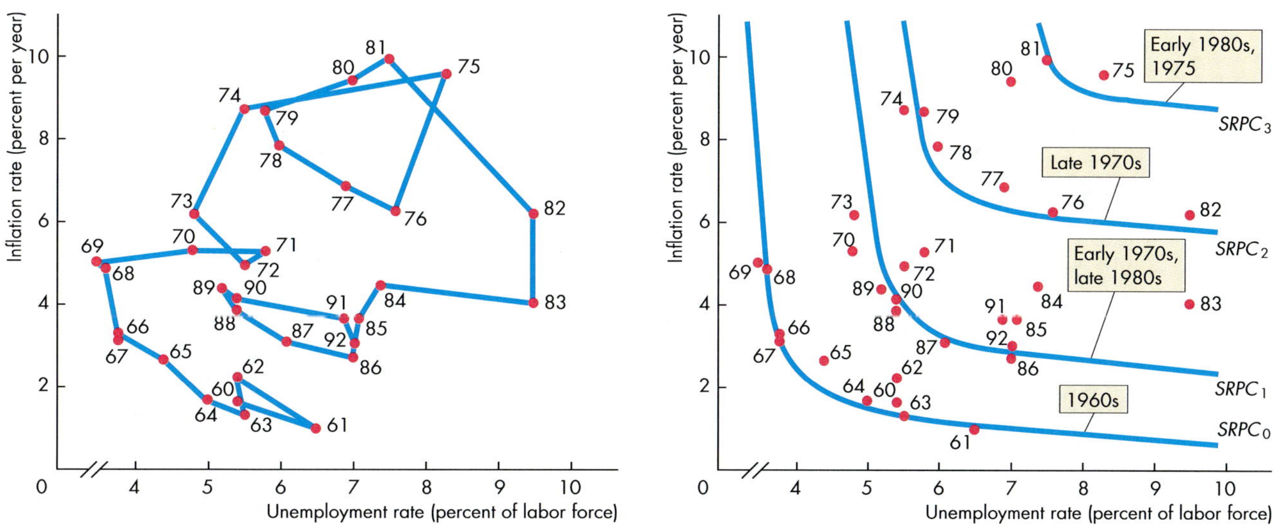

(a) The time sequence

(b) Four Phillips curves

In part (a), each dot represents the combination of inflation and unemployment for a particular year in the United States. There is no clear relationship between the two variables. Part (b) interprets the data in terms of a shifting short-run Phillips curve. The short-run Phillips curve of the 1960s, when the expected inflation rate was 2 percent a year and the natural rate of unemployment was 5 percent, is $SRPC_0$. The short-run Phillips curve of the early 1970s and late 1980s is $SRPC_1$. These two periods have a natural rate of unemployment similar to that of the 1960s but a higher expected inflation rate. The short-run Phillips curve of the late 1970s, when oil price hikes increased both the natural rate of unemployment and the expected inflation rate, is $SRPC_2$. In 1975 and the early 1980s, when oil price increases had their maximum impact on inflation expectations, the short-run Phillips curve is $SRPC_3$.

Source: Economic Report of the President, 1993.

REVIEW

The short-run Phillips curve shows the relationship between inflation and unemployment at a given expected inflation rate and natural rate of unemployment. An unanticipated burst of aggregate demand growth increases inflation and decreases unemployment—a movement up the short-run Phillips curve. An unanticipated slowdown in aggregate demand growth reduces inflation and increases unemployment—a movement down the short-run Phillips curve. ◆◆ The long-run Phillips curve, the relationship between inflation and unemployment when the actual inflation rate equals the expected inflation rate, is vertical at the natural rate of unemployment—the natural rate hypothesis. A change in the expected inflation rate shifts the short-run Phillips curve (up for an increase in inflation and down for a decrease) by an amount equal to the change in the expected inflation rate. ◆◆ A change in the natural rate of unemployment shifts both the short-run and the long-run Phillips curve to the right for an increase in the natural rate and to the left for a decrease. ◆◆ The relationship between inflation and unemployment in the United States can be interpreted in terms of a shifting short-run Phillips curve. ◆

◆◆◆◆ We have now completed our study of inflation and the relationships between the inflation rate, the interest rate, and the unemployment rate. Our next task, which we'll pursue in Chapter 15, is to see how the aggregate demand–aggregate supply model that we have used to study inflation also helps us to explore and interpret fluctuations in real GDP and explain recessions and depressions.

SUMMARY

Why Inflation Is a Problem

Inflation is a problem because it results in a fall in the value of money. The nature of the problem depends on whether inflation is *anticipated* or *unanticipated.* Anticipated inflation reduces the effectiveness of money as a medium of exchange. Unanticipated inflation is a problem because it redistributes wealth between borrowers and lenders and income between employers and employees. Unanticipated fluctuations in the inflation rate produce fluctuations in real GDP, employment, and unemployment. (p. 368)

Demand-Pull Inflation

Demand-pull inflation arises from increasing aggregate demand. Its origin can be any of the factors that shift the aggregate demand curve to the right. The most important of these factors are an increasing money supply and increasing government purchases of goods and services. When the aggregate demand curve shifts to the right, other things remaining the same, both real GDP and the GDP deflator increase and unemployment falls. With a shortage of labor, wages begin to increase and the short-run aggregate supply curve shifts to the left, raising the GDP deflator still more and decreasing real GDP.

If aggregate demand continues to increase, the aggregate demand curve keeps shifting to the right and the price level keeps on rising. Wages respond, aggregate demand increases again, and a price-wage inflation spiral ensues. (pp. 369–371)

Supply Inflation and Stagflation

Cost-push inflation can result from any factor that decreases aggregate supply, but the most important of these are increasing wage rates and increasing prices of raw materials. These sources of a decreasing aggregate supply bring increasing costs that shift the short-run aggregate supply curve to the left. Firms decrease the quantity of labor employed and cut back production. Real GDP declines, and the price level rises. If no action is taken to increase aggregate demand, the economy remains below full employment until the initial price increase that triggered the stagflation is reversed.

Action by the Fed or the government to restore full employment (an increase in the money supply or in government purchases of goods and services or a tax cut) increases aggregate demand and shifts the aggregate demand curve to the right, resulting in a yet higher price level and higher real GDP. If the original source of cost-push inflation is still present, costs rise again and the short-run aggregate supply curve shifts to the left again. If the Fed or the government responds again with a further increase in aggregate demand, the price level rises even higher. Inflation proceeds at a rate determined by the cost-push forces. (pp. 371–373)

Inflation Expectations

The decisions made by firms and households to produce and work and to borrow and lend are based on forecasts of inflation. But the real wages and real interest rates they actually pay and receive depend on actual inflation. Errors in forecasting inflation are costly, and people use all available information to minimize these errors.

Specialist forecasters use data and statistical models to generate expectations. Others either buy forecasts from specialists or copy people who are successful. Economists predict people's forecasts by using the rational expectations hypothesis—the hypothesis that inflation forecasts are made by using the aggregate demand–aggregate supply model together with all the available information on the positions of the aggregate demand and aggregate supply curves. (pp. 374–378)

Rational Expectations Equilibrium

A rational expectations equilibrium is a macroeconomic equilibrium based on expectations that are the best available forecasts. The rational expectations equilibrium occurs at the intersection of the aggregate demand and short-run aggregate supply curves. A rational expectations equilibrium might be a full-employment equilibrium, but other possibilities can occur. Aggregate demand and aggregate supply may be higher or lower than expected. The combination of these possibilities means that output may be above or below its long-run level and the price level may be higher or lower than expected. Regardless of which of these states the economy is experiencing, in a rational expectations equilibrium no one would have acted differently, given the state of affairs in which they made their choices.

When changes in aggregate demand and aggregate supply are correctly anticipated, their only effects are on the price level—inflation is anticipated. (pp. 378–381)

Interest Rates and Inflation

Expectations of inflation affect nominal interest rates. The higher the expected inflation rate, the higher is the nominal interest rate. Borrowers will willingly pay more and lenders will successfully demand more as the anticipated inflation rate rises. Borrowing and lending and asset-holding plans are made consistent with each other by adjustments in the real interest rate—the difference between the nominal interest rate and the expected inflation rate. (pp. 381–386)

Inflation over the Business Cycle: The Phillips Curve

Phillips curves describe the relationships between inflation and unemployment. The short-run Phillips curve shows the relationship between inflation and unemployment, holding constant the expected inflation rate and the natural rate of unemployment. The long-run Phillips curve shows the relationship between inflation and unemployment when the actual inflation rate equals the expected inflation rate. The short-run Phillips curve slopes downward—the lower the unemployment rate, the higher is the inflation rate, other things remaining the same. The long-run Phillips curve is vertical at the natural rate of unemployment—the natural rate hypothesis.

Changes in aggregate demand with a constant expected inflation rate and natural rate of unemployment bring movements along the short-run Phillips curve. Changes in expected inflation bring shifts in the short-run Phillips curve. Changes in the natural rate of unemployment bring shifts in both the short-run and long-run Phillips curves.

There is no clear relationship between inflation and unemployment in the United States, but the joint movements in those variables can be interpreted in terms of a shifting short-run Phillips curve. (pp. 386–390)

KEY ELEMENTS

Key Terms

Cost-push inflation, 371
Demand-pull inflation, 369
Long-run Phillips curve, 387
Natural rate hypothesis, 387
Nominal interest rate, 381
Phillips curve, 386
Rational expectation, 374
Rational expectations equilibrium, 378
Rational expectations hypothesis, 375
Short-run Phillips curve, 386

Key Figures

REVIEW QUESTIONS

1 Distinguish between the price level and the inflation rate.

2 Distinguish between anticipated and unanticipated inflation.

3 Distinguish between demand-pull inflation and cost-push inflation.

4 Explain how a price-wage inflation spiral occurs.

5 Explain how a cost-price inflation spiral occurs.

6 Why are wrong inflation expectations costly? Suggest some of the losses that an individual would suffer in labor markets as well as in asset markets.

7 Explain why wrong expectations do more than redistribute between employers and workers and between borrowers and lenders.

8 What is a rational expectation? Explain the two features of a rational expectation.

9 Explain the rational expectations hypothesis.

10 What is the rational expectation of the price in each of the following situations?

a Wages are sticky.
b Wages are flexible.

11 What is a rational expectations equilibrium? Draw three figures to show a rational expectations equilibrium when there is

a Unemployment
b Full employment
c Above full employment

12 Explain how anticipated inflation arises.

13 What are the main factors leading to changes in aggregate demand that produce ongoing and persistent inflation?

14 What is the connection between expected inflation and nominal interest rates?

15 What does the short-run Phillips curve show?

16 What does the long-run Phillips curve show?

17 What were the main shifts in the U.S. short-run Phillips curve during the 1970s and 1980s?

PROBLEMS

1 Work out the effects on the price level of the following unexpected events:

- **a** An increase in the money supply
- **b** An increase in government purchases of goods and services
- **c** An increase in income taxes
- **d** An increase in investment demand
- **e** An increase in the wage rate
- **f** An increase in labor productivity

2 Work out the effects on the price level of the events listed in problem 1 when they are correctly anticipated.

3 An economy in which wages are flexible has a long-run aggregate supply of $3.5 trillion. It has the following expected aggregate demand curve:

Price level (GDP deflator)	Expected GDP demanded (trillions of 1987 dollars)
80	5.0
90	4.5
100	4.0
110	3.5
120	3.0
130	2.5
140	2.0

- **a** What is the expected price level?
- **b** What is expected real GDP?

4 In the economy of problem 3, the expected price level increases to 120.

- **a** What is the new *SAS* curve?
- **b** What would the new *SAS* curve be if wages were sticky?

5 In 1992, the expected aggregate demand schedule for 1993 is as follows:

Price level (GDP deflator)	Expected real GDP demanded (trillions of 1987 dollars)
120	4.0
121	3.9
122	3.8
123	3.7
124	3.6

In 1992, the long-run real GDP is $3.8 trillion, the price level is 110, and the real GDP expected for 1993 is $3.9 trillion. Calculate the 1992 rational expectation of the price level for 1993 if wages are flexible.

6 The economy in problem 5 has the following actual aggregate demand schedule and short-run aggregate supply schedule in 1993:

Price level (GDP deflator)	Real GDP demanded (trillions of 1987 dollars)	Real GDP supplied (trillions of 1987 dollars)
120	4.4	3.2
121	4.3	3.5
122	4.2	3.8
123	4.1	4.1
124	4.0	4.4

- **a** Calculate the actual and expected inflation rate.
- **b** Calculate the level of real GDP.
- **c** Is the economy above or below full employment?

7 An economy has a natural rate of unemployment of 4 percent when its expected inflation is 6 percent. Its inflation and unemployment history is

Inflation rate (percent per year)	Unemployment rate (percent)
8	3
6	4
4	5

- **a** Draw a diagram of this economy's short-run and long-run Phillips curves.
- **b** If the actual inflation rate rises from 6 percent a year to 8 percent a year, what is the change in the unemployment rate? Explain why it occurs.
- **c** Show on your diagram the shifts in the long-run and short-run Phillips curves from:
  - **(1)** A rise in the natural rate of unemployment to 5 percent
  - **(2)** A fall in the expected inflation rate to 4 percent

  Explain these shifts.

CHAPTER 15

RECESSIONS AND DEPRESSIONS

After studying this chapter, you will be able to:

- Describe the origins of the 1991 recession and other recessions of the 1970s and 1980s
- Describe the course of money, interest rates, and expenditure as the economy contracts
- Describe the labor market in recession
- Compare and contrast the flexible and sticky wage theories of the labor market in recession
- Describe the onset of the Great Depression in 1929
- Describe the economy in the depths of the Great Depression between 1929 and 1933
- Compare the economy of the 1930s with that of today and assess the likelihood of another Great Depression

What Goes Up Must Come Down

THE 1920S WERE YEARS OF UNPRECEDENTED PROSPERITY for Americans. After the horrors of World War I, the economic machine was back at work, producing such technological marvels as cars and airplanes, telephones and vacuum cleaners. Houses and apartments were being built at a frantic pace. ◆◆ Then, almost without warning, in October 1929, came an unprecedented stock market crash. Overnight, the values of stocks and shares trading on Wall Street fell by 30 percent. In the four succeeding years, there followed the most severe economic contraction in recorded history. By 1933, real GDP had fallen by 30 percent; unemployment had increased to 25 percent of the labor force; employment was down 20 percent; and prices were down 25 percent. ◆◆ The cost of the Great Depression, in terms of human suffering, will never be fully known. Families were unclothed, hungry, and homeless. But the cost went far beyond the hardship faced by those having no jobs. Social tensions and crime increased, and a polarization of political attitudes occurred that was to dominate the world for the next 50 years. What caused the Great Depression? ◆◆ In October 1987, stock markets in the United States and throughout the world crashed. The crash was so steep and so widespread that it has been dubbed a stock market "meltdown"—conjuring up images of Three Mile Island and Chernobyl. This severe and widespread stock market crash has caused some commentators to draw parallels between 1987 and 1929—the eve of the greatest economic depression in history. Are there similar forces at work in the U.S. and world economies today that might bring about a Great Depression of the 1990s? ◆◆ Although they are not in the same league as the Great Depression, we have experienced three recessions in recent history. The worst of these, and the most severe recession since the Great Depression, occurred in 1982, a year in which real GDP fell by 2.5 percent and unemployment increased to almost 11 percent. Eight years earlier, in 1974–1975, real GDP fell by 1.8 percent over two years and unemployment almost doubled to 8.5 percent. The most recent recession began in 1990. In the final quarter of that year, real GDP fell at a 2 percent annual rate and unemployment climbed to 6 percent. Throughout 1991, unemployment continued to climb, ending the year at close to 7 percent. What caused these recessions? Are all recessions triggered in the same way, or is there a variety of causes?

◆ ◆ ◆ ◆ In this chapter, we're going to use the macroeconomic tools that we studied in the previous chapters to explain economic contractions. We're going to unravel some of the mysteries of recession and depression and assess the likelihood of a serious depression such as that of the 1930s occurring again. We're going to begin by examining the three most recent recessions in U.S. economic history.

Three Recent Recessions

The three most recent recessions in the United States occurred in 1974–1975, 1982, and 1990–1991. We're going to compare and contrast the origins and mechanisms at work during these episodes of U.S. macroeconomic history. We'll pay special attention to the labor market and to the central disagreement among economists about how the labor market works during an economic contraction. Let's begin with their origins.

The Origins of Recent Recessions

Recessions can be triggered by a variety of forces. Some have their origins in shocks to aggregate supply, some in shocks to aggregate demand, and some in a combination of these shocks. The three recent recessions provide examples of all three cases.

The OPEC Recession In the early 1970s, the U.S. economy was progressing in an unremarkable manner. Real GDP was close to its trend value and growing at a rate similar to its long-run average growth rate. Unemployment ranged between 5 and 6 percent, and inflation ranged between 3 and 6 percent a year. More and more people were enjoying and sharing in the benefits of sustained economic expansion.

Then, toward the end of 1973, the economy was dealt a devastating blow. The price of a barrel of oil, which had cost $2.60 on January 1, 1973, was increased to $11.65 by January 1, 1974. This massive 348 percent increase in the price of crude oil was engineered by OPEC (the Organization of Petroleum Exporting Countries), which controlled 68 percent of world oil production (outside the communist countries). The price hike had dramatic macroeconomic effects. For the next two years, the U.S. economy went into a severe recession. The severity of the recession and its immediate cause can be seen in Fig. 15.1. Before the oil price shock, the aggregate demand and short-run aggregate supply curves were AD_{73} and SAS_{73}. Real GDP was $3.3 trillion, and the GDP deflator was 41. Through the subsequent two years, aggregate demand continued to increase at roughly the same steady pace as it had increased in the previous few years. The aggregate demand curve shifted to the right to AD_{75}. If the prices of inputs—labor and raw materials—had also continued to increase at their normal pace, the short-run aggregate supply curve would have shifted to SAS_n. By 1975, the economy would have moved to point *a*. Inflation would have been about 3 percent a year, and real GDP would have continued to grow at a similar pace.

But that's not how things turned out. When OPEC producers increased the price of crude oil, the prices of other fuels as well as the prices of many other raw materials also increased. The index of all commodity prices excluding fuel (published by the International Monetary Fund) increased by 63 percent in 1973 and 24 percent in 1974. Labor costs also started to increase more quickly. As a result, the short-run aggregate supply curve shifted all the way to SAS_{75}. This shift in the short-run aggregate supply curve, triggered by the oil price increase, was the single most important event producing the OPEC recession. Real GDP fell to $3.2 trillion, and the GDP deflator increased to 49—an almost 20 percent increase in the price level over the two years of

FIGURE 15.1

The OPEC Recession

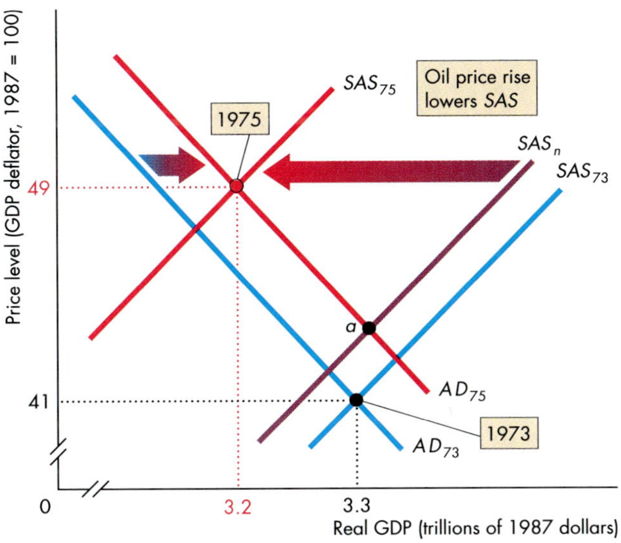

In 1973, the economy was on its aggregate demand curve AD_{73} and its short-run aggregate supply curve SAS_{73}, with real GDP at $3.3 trillion and a GDP deflator of 41. Between 1973 and 1975, aggregate demand continued to increase at a moderate pace and the aggregate demand curve shifted to AD_{75}. In the normal course of events, input prices would have increased at a moderate rate, shifting the short-run aggregate supply curve to SAS_n. The economy would have settled down at point *a* with an increase in real GDP and a continuation of moderate inflation. But in 1974, OPEC increased the price of oil by 348 percent. Other input prices and wages moved up more quickly than in a normal year. The short-run aggregate supply curve shifted to SAS_{75}. The large shift of the *SAS* curve combined with the moderate shift of the *AD* curve led to stagflation—a fall in real GDP and an acceleration of inflation.

recession. Thus during the OPEC recession, real GDP fell but the inflation rate increased. This combination of events gave rise to a new word, *stagflation*, a combination of falling real GDP and rising inflation.

The Volcker Recession The years 1979 to 1981 were not outstanding ones for the U.S. economy. To begin with, the economy had to endure a further series of increases in the price of oil in 1979—to $15 in April, to $19 in June, and finally to $26 by the year's end. Oil prices went on increasing through 1980 and 1981, and by October 1981, crude oil cost $37 a barrel. These large and continued increases in the price of oil put great strain on the U.S. economy. Energy-intensive production activities declined, and research efforts were devoted to finding more energy-efficient methods of production, transportation, and home heating.

Running alongside these energy shocks was a massive revolution in the electronics sector of the economy. Microprocessors of all kinds became cheaper, and affordable computing power found more widespread applications.

The combination of these two forces—continued increases in the price of energy and expanded applications for microprocessors—generated an unusually large reallocation of resources in the U.S. economy. Traditionally strong sectors began to grow more slowly or even to decline, and new sectors emerged with rapid growth. What came to be called the Rust Belt was the scene of relative decline, and the Sun Belt, Silicon Valley, and other areas specializing in electronics and related products (for example, Minneapolis and Massachusetts) became focal points for expansion and growth.

The years 1979 through 1981 were also times of high inflation. The price level increased by close to 10 percent during each of these years. There was a widely held belief that inflation was so entrenched that it could be anticipated to continue at this level into the foreseeable future. This, then, was the scene for the 1982 recession.

The origin of that recession and its magnitude are illustrated in Fig. 15.2. Aggregate demand and short-run aggregate supply in 1980 are shown by AD_{80} and SAS_{80}. Real GDP was $3.80 trillion, and the GDP deflator was 74. Over the next two years to 1982, with a widespread expectation that inflation was going to continue at 10 percent a year, wages and other input prices increased, shifting the short-run aggregate supply curve to SAS_{82}. Aggregate demand was expected to continue increasing at the same pace as in the late 1970s. If it had done so, by 1982 the aggregate demand curve would have shifted to the right to EAD_{82}. The economy would have been at point *a*, with real GDP continuing to grow at its trend rate and inflation remaining at around 10 percent a year.

But events did not turn out like that. Anxious to bring inflation under control, the Federal Reserve Board, under Chairman Paul Volcker, applied a

FIGURE 15.2

The Volcker Recession

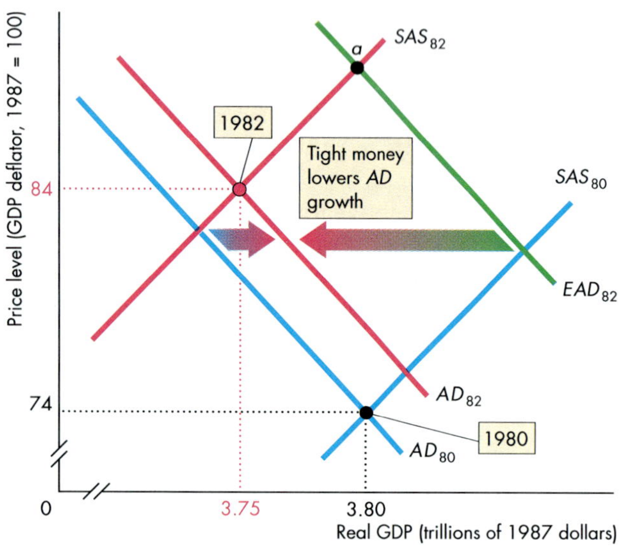

In 1980, the economy was on its aggregate demand curve AD_{80} and its short-run aggregate supply curve SAS_{80}, with real GDP at \$3.80 trillion and a GDP deflator of 74. Inflation was raging, and wages and other input prices were increasing at a rapid rate because of strong inflationary expectations. The aggregate supply curve shifted to SAS_{82}. Aggregate demand was expected to increase at the pace of the late 1970s, and the aggregate demand curve was expected to shift to EAD_{82}. The expected equilibrium was point *a*, with inflation at around 10 percent per year. But in 1982, the Fed slowed down money growth and forced interest rates up. The aggregate demand curve shifted to AD_{82}. The combination of continuing high inflation expectations and a slowdown of aggregate demand growth put the economy into recession. Real GDP fell, and inflation moderated.

severe dose of monetary restraint. The Fed forced interest rates up, which slowed the pace of investment. As a result, the aggregate demand curve did not shift to EAD_{82} but to AD_{82}. By slowing the growth of aggregate demand down to below the pace at which the short-run aggregate supply curve was shifting, the Fed put the economy into recession. Real GDP fell to \$3.75 trillion, and the inflation rate began to fall.

The 1990–1991 Recession At the beginning of 1990, the economy was at full employment. The unemployment rate was just above 5 percent, and inflation was steady at 4 percent a year. But the events of 1990 disturbed this situation and brought an end to the longest sustained recovery in U.S. history.

The dominant events of that year were the Persian Gulf crisis and the ensuing Gulf War triggered by Saddam Hussein's invasion of Kuwait. The course of the economy was influenced by these events. The Gulf crisis brought shocks to both aggregate demand and aggregate supply. The aggregate demand shocks went in both directions. First, fiscal policy became less restrained as government purchases increased to handle the military consequences of the crisis. The Gulf situation also increased uncertainty and lowered profit expectations, bringing lower investment. With lower investment, aggregate demand decreased. Although fiscal policy was working in the opposite direction, it was not strong enough to prevent aggregate demand from falling.

On the supply side, the Gulf crisis put the world energy markets into turmoil yet again. Between April 1990 and October 1990, the price of crude oil more than doubled. This oil price increase operated in a similar way to that of the 1970s, lowering short-run aggregate supply.

The combined effects of these forces and the onset of the 1990–1991 recession are illustrated in Fig. 15.3. In mid-1990, the economy was on aggregate demand curve AD_{90} and short-run aggregate supply curve SAS_{90} with real GDP at \$4.9 trillion and the GDP deflator at 113. By mid-1991, the short-run aggregate supply curve had shifted to SAS_{91}, and investment uncertainty had shifted the aggregate demand curve to AD_{91}. Real GDP had fallen to \$4.8 trillion, and inflation had slowed slightly, the GDP deflator having increased to 117, which is an inflation rate of only 3.5 percent over the year.

Origins Compared The OPEC recession was caused by an unexpectedly large increase in the price of oil that shifted the short-run aggregate supply curve to the left. This large shift in the aggregate supply curve, combined with a moderate increase in aggregate demand, lowered real GDP and increased the inflation rate—stagflation.

The Volcker recession was triggered by an unexpectedly sharp slowdown in the pace at which the Fed permitted aggregate demand to grow. Aggregate demand increased by less than expected, leading to a fall in real GDP and a lower inflation rate.

FIGURE 15.3

The 1990–1991 Recession

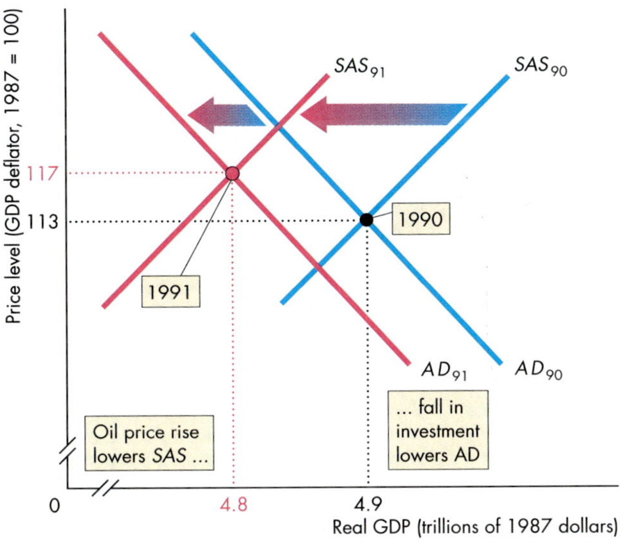

In 1990, the economy was on its aggregate demand curve AD_{90} and its short-run aggregate supply curve, SAS_{90}, with real GDP at \$4.9 trillion and a GDP deflator of 113. A large increase in oil prices decreased aggregate supply and shifted the short-run aggregate supply curve to SAS_{91}. Uncertainty surrounding the world economy lowered profit expectations, leading to a fall in investment and a decrease in aggregate demand. The aggregate demand curve shifted to AD_{91}. The combination of a decrease in both aggregate supply and aggregate demand put the economy into recession.

The 1990–1991 recession had the ingredients of *both* of these earlier recessions. Oil price increases again operated to lower aggregate supply, and increased uncertainty about future profits lowered investment, bringing lower aggregate demand. On this occasion, real GDP fell and the inflation rate slowed slightly.

Although recessions have different origins that produce different impacts on inflation, they have some common features. Let's take a look at them, starting with the behavior of interest rates.

Money and Interest Rates in Recession

At the onset of a recession, interest rates may either rise, fall, or remain steady. In both the OPEC and Volcker recessions they increased, and in the 1990–1991 recession they were steady. But once a recession is underway, interest rates begin to fall. By the time real GDP has reached its trough, interest rates have fallen, often to levels lower than those at the onset of the recession. Why do interest rates behave in this way? To find out, let's study the money market in the three recent recessions. Figure 15.4 contains the relevant analysis.

OPEC Recession The OPEC recession is illustrated in Fig. 15.4(a). In 1973, the *real money supply* (M1) was \$637 billion. The demand curve for real money in 1973 was MD_{73}, supply curve of real money was MS_{73}, and interest rate was 8 percent.

In 1974, the *real money supply* decreased by about 5 percent, and the supply curve of real money shifted from MS_{73} to MS_{74}. This decrease in the supply of real money occurred because the GDP deflator increased by an amount larger than the increase in the *nominal money supply.* The demand for real money fell in 1974 but only slightly. It fell because real GDP fell. (Recall that the demand for real money depends on real GDP. An increase in real GDP shifts the demand curve for real money to the right, and a decrease in real GDP shifts that curve to the left.) Because real GDP fell only slightly in 1974, the demand curve for real money shifted only slightly to the left. The supply of money curve shifted farther to the left than the demand for money curve. As a consequence, the interest rate increased. In 1974, the interest rate was 10 percent—at the point of intersection of MS_{74} and MD_{74}.

Between 1974 and 1975, the *nominal* money supply continued to increase but at a much slower pace than the price level was rising. As a result, the real money supply continued to decline, shifting the supply curve to MS_{75}. But by 1975, the economy was at the depth of recession. The large fall in real GDP reduced the demand for money. The demand curve shifted to the left to MD_{75}. The interest rate fell to 6 percent a year.

Volcker Recession The money market during the Volcker recession years is illustrated in Fig. 15.4(b). In 1980, interest rates were just over 12 percent a year, at the point of intersection of MS_{80} and MD_{80}.

During 1981, the GDP deflator continued to increase at around 10 percent a year. The Fed slowed the growth rate of the nominal money supply, permitting the quantity of money to increase by only 7 percent. As a consequence, the real money

FIGURE 15.4

Interest Rates and Money in Recession

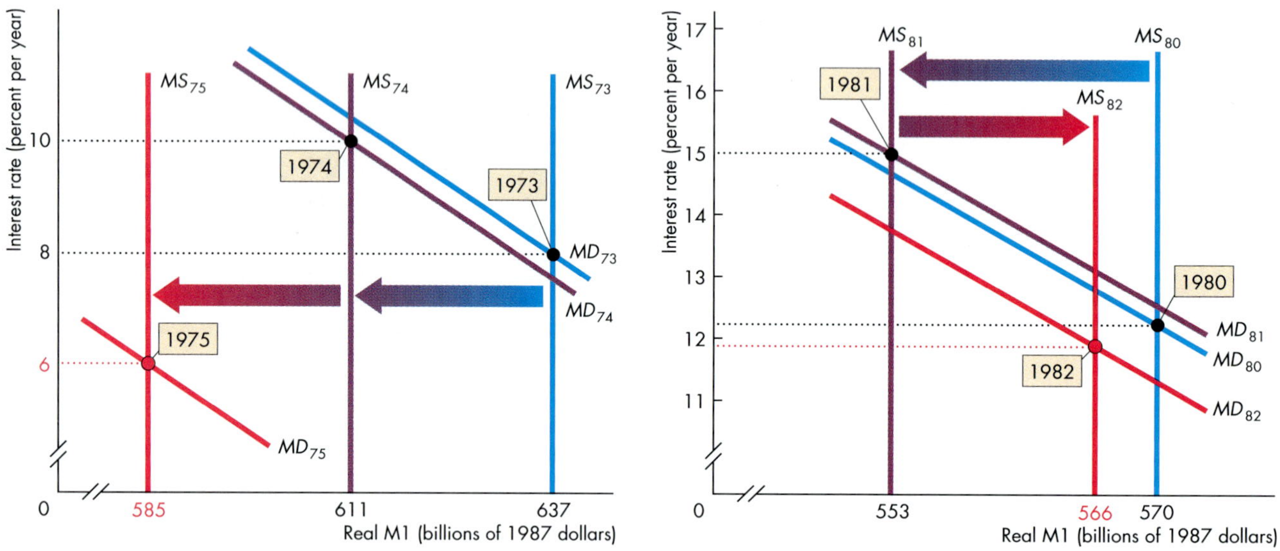

(a) The OPEC recession

(b) The Volcker recession

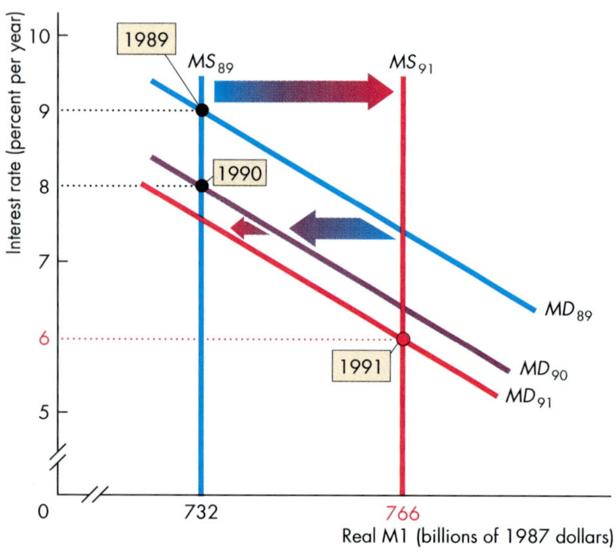

(c) The 1990–1991 recession

In 1973, the interest rate was 8 percent (part a). In 1974, the real money supply decreased, shifting the supply curve to MS_{74}, which, with the demand curve MD_{74}, increased the interest rate to 10 percent. As the recession deepened, the demand for money decreased (to MD_{75}), which, with the supply curve MS_{75}, lowered the interest rate to 6 percent.

In 1980, the interest rate was just above 12 percent (part b). In 1981, the real money supply decreased to MS_{81}, which, with the demand curve MD_{81}, increased the interest rate to 15 percent. As the recession deepened, the demand for money decreased (to MD_{82}), which, with money supply curve MS_{82}, lowered the interest rate to just below 12 percent.

In 1989, the interest rate was 9 percent (part c). In 1990, as the recession deepened, the demand for money decreased to MD_{90}, which, with the supply curve MS_{90}, lowered the interest rate to 8 percent. In 1991, the deepening recession decreased the demand for money further to MD_{91}. At the same time the Fed increased the money supply growth rate above the inflation rate, and the real money supply increased to MD_{91}. Interest rates declined to 6 percent.

supply fell. The fall in the real money supply shifted the supply curve from MS_{80} to MS_{81}. During the same year, real GDP continued to increase. As a result, the demand for real money increased and the demand curve shifted to the right to MD_{81}. The combination of an increased demand for real money and a decreased supply of real money pushed interest rates up to 15 percent a year. These high interest rates began to slow down spending and pushed the economy into its recession.

In 1982, real GDP fell to a level below that of 1980. As a result of the fall in real GDP, the demand for real money decreased and the demand curve shifted to the left to MD_{82}. At the same time, the inflation rate was slowing down. The slowdown in inflation combined with growth in the money supply was sufficient to increase the quantity of real money supplied in 1982, shifting the supply curve to MS_{82}. Money market equilibrium in 1982 occurred at an interest rate of slightly below 12 percent a year.

1990–1991 Recession The money market in the 1990–1991 recession is illustrated in Fig. 15.4(c). In 1989, interest rates were 9 percent a year, at the point of intersection of MS_{89} and MD_{89}.

During 1990, the GDP deflator increased by 4 percent and the Fed kept the growth rate of the nominal money supply close to this rate, holding the real money supply steady. As a consequence, in 1990 the supply curve remained at MS_{89}. At the same time, real GDP growth slowed and real GDP fell in the final quarter of the year. As a result, the demand for real money decreased and the demand curve shifted to the left to MD_{90}. Interest rates fell to 8 percent a year.

During 1991, real GDP continued to fall and the demand for real money decreased further. The demand curve shifted leftward to MD_{91}. At the same time, the Fed increased the money supply quickly in an attempt to get the economy to start a recovery. The real money supply increased to $766 billion, and the money supply curve shifted rightward to MS_{91}. Interest rates declined, and, on the average, during 1991 short-term rates were 6 percent, as shown in Fig. 15.4(c).

Comparing Recessions Comparing the events in the money market in the three recessions reveals some common features. In the first two recessions the interest rate followed a similar path. In both recessions, interest rates rose at first and then declined. But the source of those interest rate movements is different in each case. In the OPEC recession, interest rates increased because a sharp rise in the price level cut the real money supply. Interest rates subsequently fell because of the depth of the recession and the effects of the lower real GDP on the demand for real money. Because of continued strong inflation, the supply of real money continued to decrease through 1975. In the Volcker recession, the initial increase in interest rates was directly induced by Fed policy. Subsequent downward pressure on interest rates came from a fall in the demand for real money, just as in the OPEC recession. In addition, however, the real money supply increased in 1982 and reinforced the effects of the decrease in the demand for real money on interest rates.

Why did the real money supply continue to fall through 1975 but begin to increase in 1982? The key reason is the behavior of the price level in the two recessions. In 1975, inflation continued to be high, higher than the growth rate of the nominal money supply. In 1982, the inflation rate fell substantially below the growth rate of the nominal money supply.

In the 1990–1991 recession, interest rates did not increase initially because the Fed kept the supply of money growing in line with the growth in the demand for money. But interest rates fell, just as they had done in the two earlier recessions, as the economy contracted. And the reason they fell was the same: lower real GDP decreased the demand for money.

Changes in interest rates produce the next step in the recession mechanism—changes in aggregate expenditure.

Expenditure in Recession

When the economy is in a recession, real GDP falls and real aggregate expenditure also falls. (Recall that real GDP and real aggregate expenditure are equal to each other.) But the main component of aggregate expenditure that falls is investment. Investment falls for two reasons. First, interest rates increase. Second, profit expectations worsen.

During the OPEC recession, investment (in 1987 dollars) fell from $592 billion in 1973 to $438 billion by 1975. During the Volcker recession, investment fell from $594 billion in 1980 to $541 billion in 1982. During the 1990–1991 recession, investment fell from $800 billion in 1989 to $656 billion by mid-1991. Such decreases in investment have two effects. First, they decrease aggregate expenditure and aggregate demand. Second, they result in the capital stock growing less quickly, which slows down the pace of innovation of new technologies. This aspect of the investment slowdown feeds back to slow down the growth of aggregate supply. But the effect of decreased investment on aggregate demand dominates.

One of the main reasons people fear recession is because it is associated with a high unemployment rate. What happens in the labor market during a recession? Why does unemployment increase during a recession? Let's now examine these questions.

The Labor Market in Recession

For illustrative purposes, we'll examine the labor market in just one of the three recent recessions—the OPEC recession. Figure 15.5 provides a summary and analysis of the main events.

The starting point to understanding what happens in the labor market during a recession is an examination of the short-run aggregate production function. (Recall that we studied the short-run aggregate production function in Chapter 13.) The short-run aggregate production function, which shows the maximum real GDP that can be produced for a given labor input, is shown in Fig. 15.5(a). Curve PF_{73} is the short-run aggregate production function for 1973, just prior to the OPEC recession. In that year, 164 billion hours of labor produced \$3.3 trillion of real GDP. The effect of the OPEC oil price increase was to shift the short-run production function downward from PF_{73} to PF_{75}. Why did this happen?

There are two aspects of the oil price increase that resulted in the downward shift of the production function. First, to enforce the massive price increase, OPEC severely restricted the output of crude oil. It placed an embargo on oil exports for a period. This disruption of international trade in oil had the direct effect of lowering the availability of a key productive resource. But there was a second and perhaps even more important effect. With such an enormous increase in the price of energy, energy users of all kinds sought ways to economize on their use of this now more expensive commodity. Activities that were intensive in their use of energy were cut back, and other activities were expanded. For example, the cars and airplanes designed with engines that were highly suitable for the cheap fuel that prevailed in the 1960s were scrapped at a much more rapid pace than they otherwise would have been. Research and design efforts were put into making cars, planes, and all kinds of transportation and heating equipment that were more energy-efficient. This redirection of economic activity from fuel-intensive production and consumption to fuel-saving production and consumption created a severe

FIGURE 15.5

Sticky Wages in Recession

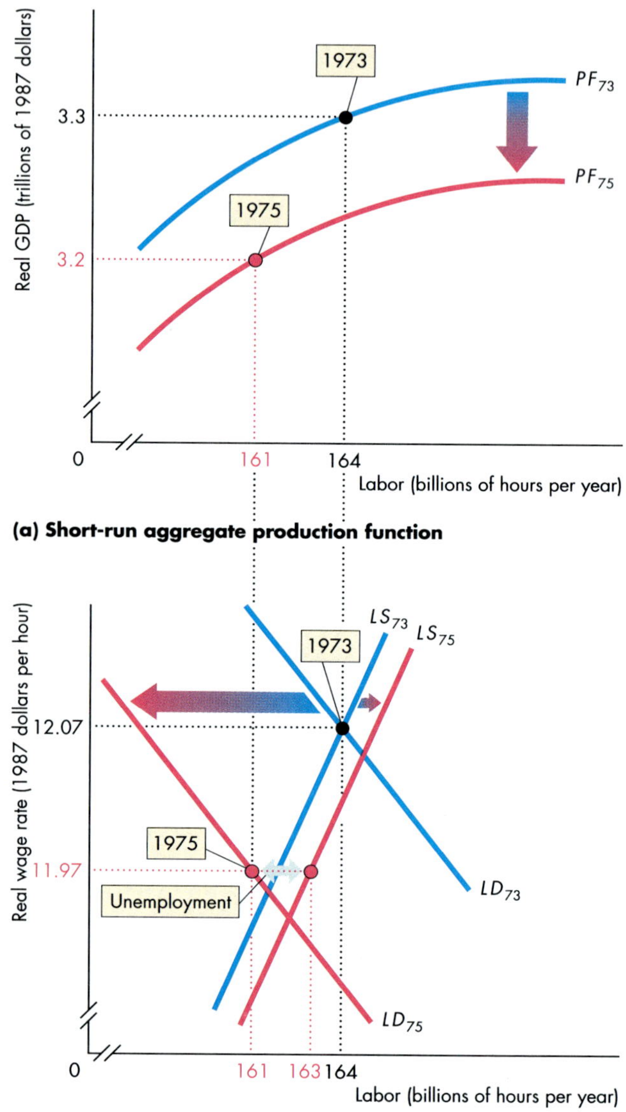

(a) Short-run aggregate production function

(b) The labor market

The OPEC price hike and embargo lowered the short-run aggregate production function from PF_{73} to PF_{75} in part (a). The marginal product of labor fell, so the demand for labor curve shifted from LD_{73} to LD_{75} in part (b). Assuming quantity of labor demanded equaled quantity supplied in 1973, the real wage rate of \$12.07 and employment of 164 billion hours are at the point of intersection of LD_{73} and LS_{73}. An increase in the labor force shifted the supply curve from LS_{73} to LS_{75}. Real wages fell but not by enough to bring equality to the quantities of labor supplied and demanded. The quantity demanded was 161 billion hours, but the quantity supplied was 163 billion hours. Unemployment increased.

mismatch of people and jobs. More of the labor force, even if it remained employed, had to devote its efforts to retraining and other activities that did not directly, at least initially, produce real GDP. As a consequence of these two related factors, the production function shifted downward as shown in Fig. 15.5(a).

Not only did the production function shift downward, but also the level of employment declined. The economy moved to the point highlighted in Fig. 15.5(a), at which employment was 161 billion hours and real GDP was $3.2 trillion. To see why employment declined, we need to study the labor market.

The downward shift of the production function lowered the marginal product of labor. As we discovered in Chapter 13, the quantity of labor demanded depends on its marginal product. With a lower marginal product of labor, the demand for labor curve shifts to the left. That shift is shown in Fig. 15.5(b) as the shift from LD_{73} to LD_{75}.

Sticky Wage Theory

There is not too much controversy in macroeconomics about the demand side of the labor market. But there is considerable disagreement about the supply side of the labor market and the ability of the labor market to act as a coordination mechanism, bringing about equality of the quantities of labor demanded and supplied. One theory, the sticky wage theory, is that the supply of labor is not very sensitive to changes in real wages and that money wages are sticky—they do not adjust quickly enough to maintain a continuous balance between the quantities of labor demanded and supplied. Let's interpret the labor market in the OPEC recession by using the sticky wage theory.

In 1973, the real wage was $12.07 an hour and 164 billion hours of labor were employed. Let's assume that the actual unemployment rate in 1973 was also the natural rate of unemployment for that year. (This is an assumption, not a fact.) Given this assumption, the real wage rate and employment rate in that year were at the point of intersection of the labor demand and labor supply curves. We'll assume that the supply of labor curve was LS_{73} and the demand for labor curve was LD_{73} in Fig. 15.5(b).

Through 1974 and 1975, the labor force increased, and as a result, the supply of labor curve shifted to the right from LS_{73} to LS_{75}. Money wages continued to increase through the recession but at a slower pace than that at which the price level was rising. As a result, real wages decreased. By 1975, real wages had fallen to $11.97 an hour. But that fall in real wages was insufficient to maintain equality between the quantity of labor supplied and the quantity demanded. The level of employment fell to 161 billion hours—the quantity of labor demanded. That is, at a real wage rate of $11.97 and with the demand for labor curve LD_{75}, the amount of labor that firms wished to hire (to maximize their profits) was 161 billion hours.

Given the assumptions made about the supply of labor curve, the quantity of labor supplied was 163 billion hours. The difference between the amount of labor supplied and the amount employed (and demanded) was unemployment. According to the sticky wage theory of the labor market, this increase in unemployment represents an addition to the natural unemployment that prevailed before the recession's onset.

Flexible Wage Theory

There is an alternative interpretation of the labor market in recession to the one that we have just presented—the flexible wage theory. According to this theory, the supply of labor is highly responsive to a change in real wages, and money wages *do* adjust to maintain equality between the quantity of labor demanded and the quantity supplied. Fluctuations in unemployment are fluctuations in the natural rate of unemployment. Let's examine the OPEC recession again and interpret it in terms of this alternative theory.

Recall that the labor market effects of recession that we've just analyzed are based on an *assumption* about the supply of labor curve. In Fig. 15.5 the labor supply curves LS_{73} and LS_{75} are fairly steep, indicating that a large change in the real wage rate evokes only a small change in the quantity of labor supplied. We are uncertain about the slope of the labor supply curve, but we're reasonably sure that the curve shifted to the right by the amount shown because we know exactly the amount by which the labor force increased over the relevant period. Suppose that the supply of labor curve is less steep than those shown in Fig. 15.5. In particular, suppose that the supply of labor for 1973 and that for 1975 are represented by the curves shown in Fig. 15.6.

Figure 15.6 is identical to Fig. 15.5(b) except that the labor supply curves do not slope upward as

FIGURE 15.6

The Labor Market in Recession: Flexible Wage Theory

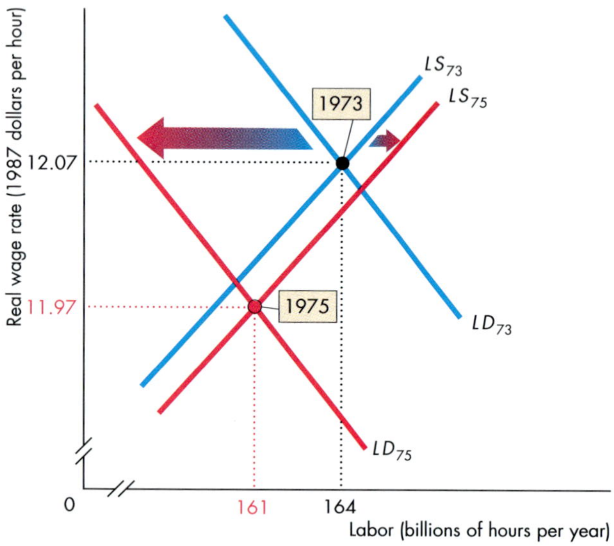

During the OPEC recession, real wages fell from $12.07 an hour to $11.97 an hour and employment fell from 164 billion hours to 161 billion hours. These movements of real wages and employment are consistent with the flexible wage theory if the quantity of labor supplied is highly responsive to a change in the real wage as shown by the labor supply curves LS_{73} and LS_{75}. According to the flexible wage theory, the increase in unemployment that occurred between 1973 and 1975 is interpreted as a temporary increase in the natural rate of unemployment.

steeply. Again, the labor market in 1973 is depicted as a situation in which the quantity of labor demanded equals the quantity supplied, so unemployment is at the natural rate. When this supply of labor curve shifts to the right, it moves to LS_{75}. The magnitude of the shift from LS_{73} to LS_{75} is identical in this figure to the magnitude of the shift in Fig. 15.5(b). The demand for labor curve shifts from LD_{73} to LD_{75}. In 1975, the demand for labor curve and the supply of labor curve intersect at a real wage rate of $11.97 and employment of 161 billion hours, exactly the values that prevailed in 1975. The labor market shown in Fig. 15.6 agrees with the assumptions of the flexible wage theory. Wages fall and employment falls.

But what happens to unemployment? The flexible wage theory of unemployment is that all unemployment arises from job market turnover. During a recession, job market turnover increases because some sectors of the economy decline quickly while others continue to expand. An increase in the amount of labor force reallocation—from the declining sectors to the expanding sectors—results in an increased amount of labor turnover and a temporarily higher natural rate of unemployment. During the 1975 recession, the declining sectors were those sectors that relied heavily on oil and other high-cost energy sources; the expanding sectors were those sectors associated with developing energy-saving technologies.

Which Theory of the Labor Market Is Correct? What exactly do economists agree and disagree about concerning the labor market and why? The essence of the controversy is summarized in Figs. 15.5(b) and 15.6. First, everyone agrees about the facts. Real wages in 1973 were $12.07 an hour, on the average. In 1975, they had fallen to $11.97, on the average. Employment in 1973 was 164 billion hours, and it fell to 161 billion hours in 1975.

In addition, there is not much disagreement about the demand for labor. Most economists agree that the quantity of labor actually employed is determined by the profit-maximizing decisions of firms. That quantity depends on the real wage. This means that the level of employment and the real wage in any particular year are a point on the demand for labor curve. If we agree that the employment level and real wage are a point on the demand for labor curve, we can figure out where the demand for labor curve is and work out what makes it shift. Thus there is not much disagreement among economists about the slope and position of the demand for labor curve.

But economists disagree about the supply of labor. Because a large amount of labor is supplied on long-term contracts and on wages and other terms that remain fixed for the duration of the contract, most economists believe that households are not normally operating on their supply of labor curve. Sometimes they are, but much of the time they are not. Furthermore, many economists believe that on the basis of evidence from variations in hours of work and wages, the quantity of labor supplied does not respond much to changes in real wages. In other words, they believe that the supply of labor curve is steep like those shown in Fig. 15.5(b).

Other economists believe that the combination of the real wage rate and the level of employment represents not only a point on the demand for labor curve but also a point on the supply of labor curve. From this assumption they infer that the quantity of labor supplied is highly responsive to wages and that the supply of labor curve looks like those in Fig. 15.6.

No one has yet suggested a test that is sufficiently clear for all economists to agree on. The controversy will be settled only when economists can agree on, and implement, a test of their competing views about the responsiveness of the quantity of labor supplied to a change in real wages. Once such a test has been implemented, we shall be able to put this controversy (like the controversy about monetary and fiscal influences on aggregate demand that you met in Chapter 12) behind us. But until then, economists and students of economics have to live with the fact that we remain ignorant about an important issue at the heart of macroeconomics. This controversy is featured in Our Advancing Knowledge on pp. 412–413.

Determining which of these two theories is correct is not just a matter of academic curiosity. It is a matter of enormous importance in designing an appropriate antirecessionary policy. If the flexible wage theory is correct, there is only one aggregate supply curve—the vertical long-run aggregate supply curve. This fact means that any attempt to bring the economy out of recession by increasing aggregate demand—for example, by lowering interest rates and increasing the money supply or by fiscal policy measures—is doomed to failure and can result only in a higher price level (more inflation). Conversely, if the sticky wage theory is correct, then the short-run aggregate supply curve slopes upward. An increase in aggregate demand, although increasing the price level somewhat, increases real GDP and will bring the economy out of a recession.

From the viewpoint of the unemployed, it matters little whether their unemployment is the result of sticky wages or very costly labor market restructuring with flexible wages. Unemployment is painful, as you can see in Reading Between the Lines on pp. 406–407.

Another Great Depression?

Following the Volcker recession, the U.S. economy moved into a period of long sustained recovery. In fact, that recovery was the longest and strongest on record. Its end was repeatedly (and wrongly) foreseen, and by the fall of 1987 there was widespread fear that the good times were coming to an end, at least for a while. In October 1987, these fears were strengthened by the biggest stock market crash to hit the U.S. economy (and, indeed, the world economy) since that of 1929, which had heralded the Great Depression. The magnitude of the 1987 crash was almost identical to that of the 1929 crash—the range between the high and the low was 34 percent. This similarity was so striking that many commentators concluded that the closing years of the 1980s and the early 1990s would resemble the Great Depression of the early 1930s. But the recovery kept going until the middle of 1990. And when it did end, the recession that followed, although a relatively long one, was not deep.

Yet the question remains: is there going to be another Great Depression? Of course, the answer to this question is that no one knows. But we can try to assess the likelihood of such an event. Let's begin by first asking some questions. What was the Great Depression like? Just how bad did things get in the early 1930s? What would the U.S. economy look like in 1999 if the events of 70 years earlier were to recur? Once we've charted the broad anatomy of the Great Depression, we'll examine why it happened and consider the question of whether it could happen again and how likely such an event would be.

What the Great Depression Was Like

At the beginning of 1929, the U.S. economy was operating at full employment and with only 3.2 percent of the labor force unemployed. But as that eventful year unfolded, increasing signs of economic weakness began to appear. The most dramatic events occurred in October, when the stock market collapsed, losing more than one third of its value in

Unemployment in Recession

The New York Times, July 28, 1991

For Forlorn Millions, the Recession Goes On

BY PETER T. KILBORN

The experts say the economy is growing again after a year in a recession, but tell that to Charles Moreira. A despairing 22-year-old waiting for yet another job counseling session in the New Bedford office of the Massachusetts state employment agency, Mr. Moreira is his family's sole wage earner because his wife stays home with their 3-year-old child.

Mr. Moreira, a mechanic, lost a $6.75-an-hour job in an automobile dealership last December and has been looking fruitlessly for work since. His $170 a week in unemployment benefits has run out. He is vying with scores of similarly strapped contenders for a warehouse job that pays $6 an hour.

"I'm kind of disgusted," he said. "I'm losing all my ambition. I wanted to be the greatest." What about going to a boom town somewhere? "I don't have the money," he said.

Fewer Jobs, Worse Jobs

Nearly nine million people are out of work and looking for jobs. The government does not count several million more among the unemployed because they have given up looking. For all the unemployed, the recession is still going strong. Worse, more of the jobs that are now being offered are inferior to the old ones.

As recessions end, some disappointment is predictable. On getting wind of an improving economy, people who have dropped out of the labor force start looking again. Others look more earnestly with the end of their unemployment benefits, which are often more than $1,000 a month and usually last six months. That makes it harder for all to find jobs.

At the same time, employers put off hiring while they wait to be sure business is truly improving. Instead, they ask the workers whom they have kept on board to work longer and harder.

Mostly for those reasons, economists say, the unemployment rate rose only slightly in June, from 6.9 percent to 7 percent, even as most other gauges of the economy were gaining. In 1983, a whole year after the last, longer and harsher recession ended, the rate was 9.6 percent, hardly different from the high point of 9.7 percent in 1982. . . .

The Essence of the Story

In the summer of 1991, as the economy recovered from a year of recession, unemployment was still rising.

Nearly nine million people were out of work and looking for jobs, and several million more without jobs had given up looking.

As a recession ends, people who have dropped out of the labor force start looking again for work and those whose unemployment benefits have run out search harder for jobs, making it harder for everyone to find jobs.

Employers ask the workers whom they have kept on board to work longer and harder and put off hiring until they are sure business is improving.

Background and Analysis

When real GDP falls in a recession, unemployment increases.

When recovery from a recession begins and real GDP increases, unemployment continues to increase for a while.

You can see this feature of the change in unemployment in the figure.

During the recovery from the OPEC recession, unemployment was still increasing in the second quarter of 1975 (the dot marked 752 in part a of the figure) even though real GDP was increasing at an annual rate of 5 percent.

During the recovery from the Volcker recession, real GDP began to increase in the second quarter of 1982 (the dot marked 822 in part b) but unemployment did not begin to decrease until the first quarter of 1983 (the dot marked 831 in part b).

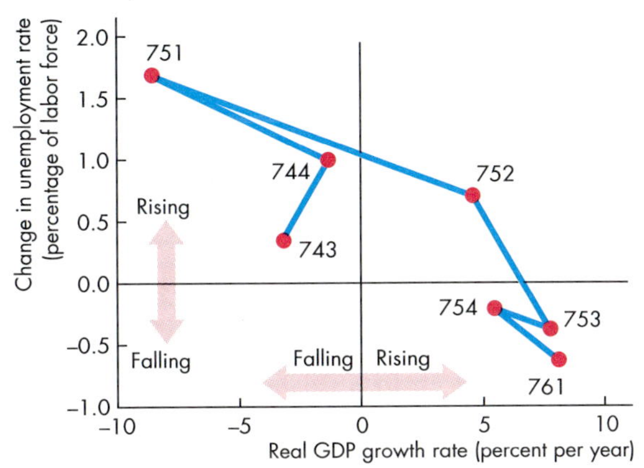

(a) OPEC recession and recovery

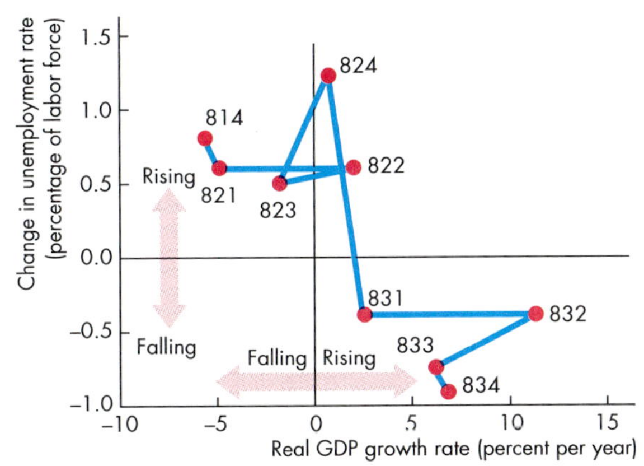

(b) Volcker recession and recovery

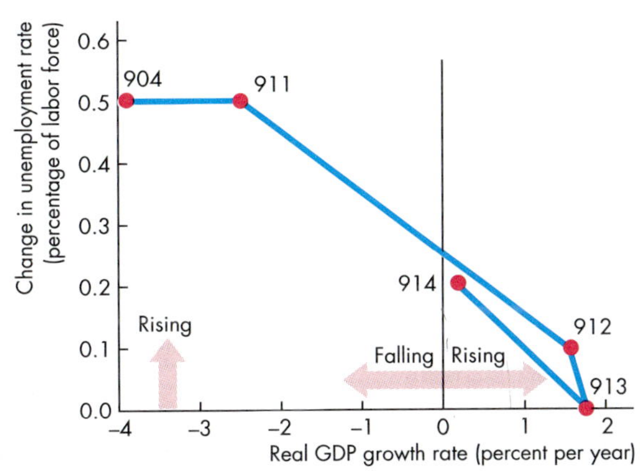

(c) 1991 recession and recovery

During the recovery from the 1991 recession, unemployment was still increasing in the fourth quarter of 1991 (marked 914 in part c), even though real GDP had been growing for three quarters.

Unemployment lags behind real GDP growth for the reasons identified in the article: in the early stages of recovery, firms work their existing labor forces harder, previously discouraged workers start looking for jobs, and workers whose unemployment benefits have run out intensify their job search.

two weeks. The four years that followed were years of monstrous economic depression—depression so severe that it came to be called the Great Depression.

The dimensions of the Great Depression can be seen in Fig. 15.7. That figure shows the situation on the eve of the Great Depression in 1929 when the economy was on its aggregate demand curve AD_{29} and short-run aggregate supply curve SAS_{29}. Real GDP was $835 billion and the GDP deflator was 18. (Real GDP in 1991 was almost 6 times its 1929 level, and the GDP deflator was more than 8 times its 1929 level.)

In 1930, there was widespread expectation that prices would fall, and wages fell. With lower wages, the short-run aggregate supply curve shifted from SAS_{29} to SAS_{30}. But increased pessimism and uncertainty resulted in a drop in investment and in the demand for durables. Aggregate demand fell, by a larger amount than expected, to AD_{30}. In 1930, the economy went into recession as real GDP fell by about 7 percent. The price level also fell by a similar amount. (It was not unusual at that time for prices occasionally to fall.) When the price level is falling, the economy is experiencing *deflation*.

If the normal course of events had ensued in 1930, the economy might have remained in its depressed state for several months and then started a recovery. But 1930 was not a normal year. In 1930 and the next two years, the economy was further bombarded with huge negative demand shocks (the sources of which we'll look at in a moment). The aggregate demand curve shifted to the left all the way to AD_{33}. With a depressed economy, the price level was expected to fall, and wages fell in line with those expectations. The money wage fell from 55¢ an hour in 1930 to 44¢ an hour by 1933. As a result of lower wages, the aggregate supply curve shifted from SAS_{30} to SAS_{33}. But the size of the shift of the short-run aggregate supply curve was much less than the decrease in aggregate demand. As a result, the aggregate demand curve and the short-run aggregate supply curve intersected in 1933 at a real GDP of $600 billion and a GDP deflator of 13. Real GDP had fallen by almost 30 percent from its 1929 level, and the price level had fallen by more than 25 percent.

Although the Great Depression brought enormous hardship, the distribution of that hardship was very uneven. A quarter of the work force had no jobs at all. Also, at that time there were virtually no organized social security and unemployment programs in place. So for many families there was virtually no income. But the pocketbooks of those who kept their jobs barely noticed the Great Depression. It's true that wages fell (from 57¢ an hour in 1929 to 44¢ an hour in 1933). But at the same time, the price level fell by just about exactly the same percentage amount as the fall in wages. Hence real wages remained constant. Thus those who had jobs continued to be paid a wage rate that had roughly the same buying power at the end of the Great Depression as in 1929.

You can begin to appreciate the magnitude of the Great Depression if you compare it with the three recessions we studied earlier in this chapter. Between

FIGURE 15.7

The Great Depression

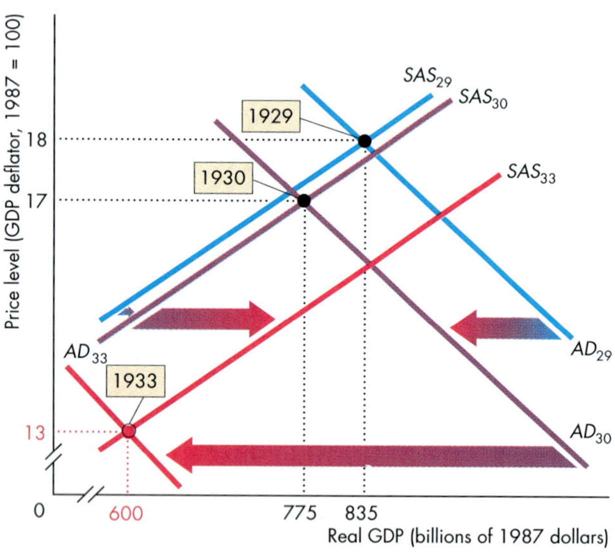

In 1929, real GDP was $835 billion and the GDP deflator was 18—at the intersection of AD_{29} and SAS_{29}. Increased pessimism and uncertainty resulted in a drop in investment, resulting in a decrease in aggregate demand to AD_{30}. To some degree, this decrease was anticipated and wages fell, so the short-run aggregate supply curve shifted to SAS_{30}. Real GDP and the price level fell. In the next three years, decreases in the money supply and investment lowered aggregate demand, shifting the aggregate demand curve to AD_{33}. Again, to some degree, the decrease in aggregate demand was anticipated, so wages fell and the short-run aggregate supply curve shifted to SAS_{33}. By 1933, real GDP had fallen to $600 billion (about 70 percent of its 1929 level) and the GDP deflator had fallen to 13 (73 percent of its 1929 level).

1973 and 1975, real GDP fell by 1.75 percent. From 1981 to 1982, it fell by 2.5 percent. From mid-1990 to mid-1991, it fell by 1.6 percent. In comparison, in 1930 real GDP fell by more than 7 percent, and from 1929 to 1933 it fell by close to 30 percent. A 1999 Great Depression of the same magnitude would lower income per person to its level of more than 20 years earlier.

Why the Great Depression Happened

The late 1920s were years of economic boom. New houses and apartments were built on an unprecedented scale, new firms were created, and the capital stock of the nation expanded. But these were also years of increasing uncertainty. The main source of increased uncertainty was international. The world economy was going through tumultuous times. The patterns of world trade were changing as Britain, the traditional economic powerhouse of the world, began its period of relative economic decline and new economic powers such as Japan began to emerge. International currency fluctuations and the introduction of restrictive trade policies by many countries (see Chapter 18) further increased the uncertainty faced by firms. There was also domestic uncertainty arising from the fact that there had been such a strong boom in recent years, especially in the capital goods sector and housing. No one believed that this boom could continue, but there was great uncertainty as to when it would end and how the pattern of demand would change.

This environment of uncertainty led to a slowdown in consumer spending, especially on new homes and household appliances. By the fall of 1929, the uncertainty had reached a critical level and contributed to the stock market crash. The stock market crash, in turn, heightened people's fears about economic prospects in the foreseeable future. Fear fed fear. Investment collapsed. The building industry almost disappeared. An industry that had been operating flat out just two years earlier was now building virtually no new houses and apartments. It was this drop in investment and a drop in consumer spending on durables that led to the initial leftward shift of the aggregate demand curve from AD_{29} to AD_{30} in Fig. 15.7.

At this stage, what became the Great Depression was no worse than many previous recessions had been. What distinguishes the Great Depression from previous recessions are the events that followed between 1930 and 1933. But economists, even to this day, have not come to agreement on how to interpret those events. One view, argued by Peter Temin, is that spending continued to fall for a wide variety of reasons—including a continuation of increasing pessimism and uncertainty.[1] According to Temin, the continued contraction resulted from a leftward shift in the investment demand curve and a fall in autonomous expenditure. Milton Friedman and Anna J. Schwartz have argued that the continuation of the contraction was almost exclusively the result of the subsequent worsening of financial and monetary conditions.[2] According to Friedman and Schwartz, it was a severe cut in the money supply that lowered aggregate demand, prolonging the contraction and deepening the depression.

Although there is disagreement about the causes of the contraction phase of the Great Depression, the disagreement is not about the elements at work but about the degree of importance attached to each. Everyone agrees that increased pessimism and uncertainty lowered investment demand, and everyone agrees that there was a massive contraction of the real money supply. Temin and his supporters assign primary importance to the fall in autonomous expenditure and secondary importance to the fall in the money supply. Friedman and Schwartz and their supporters assign primary responsibility to the money supply and regard the other factors as being of limited importance.

Let's look at the contraction of aggregate demand a bit more closely. Between 1930 and 1933, there was a massive 20 percent contraction in the nominal money supply. This fall in the money supply was not directly induced by the Fed's actions. The *monetary base* (currency in circulation and bank reserves) hardly fell at all. But the bank deposits component of the money supply suffered an enormous collapse. It did so primarily because a large number of banks failed. The primary source of bank failure was unsound lending during the boom preceding the onset of the Great Depression. Fueled by increasing stock prices and booming business conditions, bank loans expanded. But after the stock market crash

[1]Peter Temin, *Did Monetary Forces Cause the Great Depression?* (New York: W. W. Norton, 1976).

[2]This explanation was developed by Milton Friedman and Anna J. Schwartz in *A Monetary History of the United States 1867–1960* (Princeton, N.J.: Princeton University Press, 1963), Ch. 7.

and the downturn, many borrowers found themselves in hard economic times. They could not pay the interest on their loans, and they could not meet the agreed repayment schedules. Banks had deposits that exceeded the realistic value of the loans that they had made. When depositors withdrew funds from the banks, the banks lost reserves and many of them simply couldn't meet their depositors' demands to be repaid.

Bank failures feed on themselves and create additional failures. Seeing banks fail, people become anxious to protect themselves and so take their money out of the banks. Such were the events of 1930. The quantity of notes and coins in circulation increased, and the volume of bank deposits declined. But the very action of taking money out of the bank to protect one's wealth accentuated the process of banking failure. Banks were increasingly short of cash and unable to meet their obligations.

Bank failure and the massive contraction of the money supply had two effects on the economy. First, the bank failures themselves brought financial hardship to many producers, increasing the business failure rate throughout the economy. At the same time, a sharp drop in the money supply kept interest rates high. Not only did nominal interest rates stay high, but with falling prices, real interest rates increased sharply. The real interest rate is (approximately) the difference between the nominal interest rate and the expected inflation rate. During the Great Depression, inflation was negative—the price level was falling. Thus the real interest rate equaled the nominal interest rate plus the expected rate of deflation. With high real interest rates, investment remained low.

What role did the stock market crash of 1929 play in producing the Great Depression? It certainly created an atmosphere of fear and panic and probably also contributed to the overall air of uncertainty that dampened investment spending. It also reduced the wealth of stockholders, encouraging them to cut back on their consumption spending. But the direct effect of the stock market crash on consumption, although a contributory factor to the Great Depression, was not the major source of the drop in aggregate demand. It was the collapse in investment arising from increased uncertainty that brought the 1930 decline in aggregate demand.

But the stock market crash was a predictor of severe recession. It reflected the expectations of stockholders concerning future profit prospects. As those expectations became pessimistic, the prices of stocks were bid lower and lower (i.e., the behavior of the stock market was a consequence of expectations about future profitability, and those expectations were lowered as a result of increased uncertainty).

Can It Happen Again?

Since, even today, we have an incomplete understanding of the causes of the Great Depression, we are not able to predict such an event or to be sure that it cannot occur again. But there are some important differences between the economy of the 1990s and that of the 1930s that make a severe depression much less likely today than it was 60 years ago. The most important features of the economy that make severe depression less likely today are as follows:

- Bank deposit insurance
- The Fed's role as lender of last resort
- Taxes and government spending
- Multi-income families

Let's examine these in turn.

Bank Deposit Insurance As a result of the Great Depression, the federal government established, in the 1930s, the Federal Deposit Insurance Corporation (FDIC). The FDIC insures bank deposits for up to $100,000 per depositor so that most depositors need no longer fear bank failure. If a bank fails, the FDIC pays the deposit holders. With federally insured bank deposits, the key event that turned a fairly ordinary recession into the Great Depression is most unlikely to occur. It was the fear of bank failure that caused people to withdraw their deposits from banks. The aggregate consequence of these individually rational acts was to cause the very bank failures that were feared. With deposit insurance, most depositors have nothing to lose if a bank fails and so have no incentive to take actions that are likely to give rise to that failure.

Some recent events reinforce this conclusion. With massive failures of S&Ls in the 1980s and with bank failures in New England in 1990 and 1991, there was no tendency for depositors to panic and withdraw their funds in a self-reinforcing run on similar institutions.

Lender of Last Resort The Fed is the lender of last resort in the U.S. economy. If a single bank is short of reserves, it can borrow reserves from other banks. If the entire banking system is short of reserves, banks can borrow from the Fed. By making reserves available (at a suitable interest rate), the Fed is able to make the quantity of reserves in the banking system respond flexibly to the demand for those reserves. Bank failure can be prevented or at least contained to cases in which bad management practices are the source of the problem. Widespread failures of the type that occurred in the Great Depression can be prevented.

But the Fed was around in the Great Depression and was acting as lender of last resort throughout that episode. Why did it not make sufficient bank reserves available? The Fed in fact kept the level of the monetary base roughly constant. And it thought that by so doing it was making an appropriate contribution to economic stability. It was only long after the event, when Friedman and Schwartz examined the contraction years of the Great Depression, that economists came to realize that the Fed would have had to *increase* the monetary base by a sizable amount to have prevented the intensification of the contraction. Now that this lesson has been learned, there is at least some chance that the mistake will not be repeated.

It is interesting to note, in this regard, that during the weeks following the October 1987 stock market crash, Fed Chairman Alan Greenspan used every opportunity available to remind the American banking and financial community of the Fed's ability and readiness to maintain calm financial conditions.

Taxes and Government Spending The government sector was a much less important part of the economy in 1929 than it has become today. On the eve of that earlier recession, government purchases of goods and services were less than 9 percent of GDP. In contrast, today they are more than 20 percent. Government transfer payments were less than 6 percent of GDP in 1929. These items have grown to more than 15 percent of GDP at the present time.

A larger level of government purchases of goods and services means that when recession hits, a large component of aggregate demand does not decline. It is government transfer payments, however, that is the most important economic stabilizer. When the economy goes into recession and depression, more people qualify for unemployment compensation and social security. As a consequence, although disposable income decreases, the extent of the decrease is moderated by the existence of such programs. Consumption expenditure, in turn, does not decline by as much as it would in the absence of such government programs. The limited decline in consumption spending further limits the overall decrease in aggregate expenditure, thereby limiting the magnitude of an economic downturn.

Multi-income Families At the time of the Great Depression, families with more than one wage earner were much less common than they are today. The labor force participation rate in 1929 was around 55 percent. Today, it is 66 percent. Thus, even if the unemployment rate increased to around 25 percent today, close to 50 percent of the adult population would actually have jobs. During the Great Depression, less than 40 percent of the adult population had work. Multi-income families have greater security than single-income families. The chance of both (or all) income earners in a family losing their jobs simultaneously is much lower than the chance of a single earner losing work. With greater family income security, family consumption is likely to be less sensitive to fluctuations in family income that are seen as temporary. Thus when aggregate income falls, it does not induce a cut in consumption. For example, during the OPEC and Volcker recessions, personal consumption expenditure increased.

For the four reasons we have just reviewed, it appears that the economy has better shock-absorbing characteristics today than it had in the 1920s and 1930s. Even if there is a collapse of confidence leading to a fall in investment, the recession mechanism that is now in place will not translate that initial shock into the large and prolonged fall in real GDP and rise in unemployment that occurred more than 60 years ago.

Because the economy is now more immune to severe recession than it was in the 1930s, even a stock market crash of the magnitude that occurred in 1987 had barely noticeable effects on spending. A crash of a similar magnitude in 1929 resulted in the near collapse of housing investment and consumer durable purchases. In the period following the 1987 stock market crash, investment and spending on durable goods hardly changed.

None of this is to say that there might not be a deep recession or even a Great Depression in the 1990s (or beyond). But it would take a very severe shock to trigger one.

UNDERSTANDING Business CYCLES

Economic activity has fluctuated between boom and bust for as long as we've had records, and the range of fluctuations became especially pronounced during the nineteenth and early twentieth centuries. Understanding the sources of economic fluctuations has turned out to be difficult for two reasons.

First, there are no simple patterns. Every new episode of the business cycle is different from its predecessor in some important way. Some cycles are long and some short, some are mild and some severe, some begin in the United States and some abroad. We never know with any certainty when the next turning point (down or up) is coming or what will cause it.

Second, resources are scarce even in a recession or a depression. But at such times, large quantities of scarce resources go unemployed. A satisfactory theory of the business cycle must explain this fact. Why don't scarce resources *always* get fully employed?

There are plenty of simple, but wrong, theories of the business cycle. And when these theories are used to justify policies, they can create severe problems. For example, during the 1960s, recessions were believed to result from insufficient aggregate demand. The solution: increase government spending, cut taxes, and cut interest rates. Countries that pursued such policies most vigorously, such as the United Kingdom, found their economic growth rates sagging, unemployment rising, and inflation accelerating.

Today's new theory—real business cycle theory—predicts that fluctuations in aggregate demand have *no* effect on output and employment and change only the price level and inflation rate. But this theory ignores the *real* effects of financial collapse of the type that occurred in the 1930s. If banks fail on a large scale and people lose their wealth, other firms also begin to fail and jobs are destroyed. Unemployed people cut their spending, and output falls yet further. Demand stimulation may not be called for, but action to ensure that sound banks survive certainly is.

"We don't want to manage the U.S. economy. And we don't think anybody else should take the job either."

ROBERT E. LUCAS, JR.
Personal Interview

"All the News That's Fit to Print."
The New York Times.
LATE CITY EDITION
ROOSEVELT ORDERS 4-DAY BANK HOLIDAY, PUTS EMBARGO ON GOLD, CALLS CONGRESS
HITLER BLOC WINS A REICH MAJORITY; RULES IN PRUSSIA
JAPANESE PUSH ON IN FIERCE FIGHTING; CHINA CLOSES WALL
BANKS HERE ACT AT ONCE
City Scrip to Be Ready Today or Tomorrow to Replace Currency.
The President's Bank Proclamation
USE OF SCRIP AUTHORIZED
President Takes Steps Under Sweeping Law of War Time.

What happens to the economy when people lose confidence in banks? They withdraw their funds. These withdrawals feed on themselves, creating a snowball of withdrawals and, eventually, panic. Short of funds with which to repay depositors, banks call in loans, and previously sound businesses are faced with financial distress. They close down and lay off workers. Recession deepens and turns into depression. Bank failures and the resulting decline in the nation's supply of money and credit were a significant factor in deepening and prolonging the Great Depression. But they taught us the importance of stable financial institutions and gave rise to the establishment of federal deposit insurance to prevent such financial collapse.

How can it be that a building designed as a store has no better use than to be boarded up and left empty? Not enough aggregate demand, say the Keynesians. Not so, say the real business cycle theorists. Technological change has reduced the building's current productivity as a store to zero. But its expected future productivity is sufficiently high that it is not efficient to refit the building for some other purpose. All unemployment—whether of buildings or people—can be explained in a similar way. For example, how can it be that a person trained as a store clerk is without work during a recession? Not enough aggregate demand is one answer. Another is that the current productivity of store clerks is low, but their expected future productivity is sufficiently high that it does not pay an unemployed clerk to retrain for a job that is currently available.

Robert E. Lucas, Jr.: Today's *Macroeconomic Revolutionary*

Many economists, past and present, have advanced our understanding of business cycles. But one contemporary economist stands out. He is Robert E. Lucas, Jr., of the University of Chicago. In 1970, as a 32-year-old professor at Carnegie-Mellon University, Lucas challenged the Keynesian theories of economic fluctuations and launched a macroeconomic revolution based on two principles: rational expectations and equilibrium. Like all scientific revolutions, the one touched off by Lucas was controversial. Twenty years later, rational expectations (whether right or wrong) is accepted by most economists. But the idea that the business cycle and unemployment can be understood as equilibria remains controversial and, for some economists, even distasteful. Lucas believes that we still know too little about the causes of the business cycle to be able to stabilize the economy.

◆ ◆ ◆ ◆ We have now completed our study of the working of the macroeconomy. We've studied the macroeconomic model of aggregate demand and aggregate supply, and we've learned a great deal about the workings of the markets for goods and services, labor, and money and financial assets. We have applied our knowledge to explain and understand the problems of unemployment, inflation, and business cycle fluctuations. ◆ ◆ In the next part of the book we will study two aspects of macroeconomic policy—the monetary and fiscal policies that governments can take to stabilize the economy and the policy problems posed by the government's budget deficit.

SUMMARY

Three Recent Recessions

The three most recent recessions in U.S. history occurred in 1974–1975, 1982, and 1990–1991. The first recession was caused by the actions of OPEC. At the end of 1973 and the beginning of 1974, OPEC increased the price of oil and, for a period, placed an embargo on the export of oil. These events resulted in a severe decrease in aggregate supply. Aggregate demand also decreased but not by as much as aggregate supply. As a consequence, real GDP fell and the price level increased at an accelerating pace. The phenomenon gave rise to a new economic term—stagflation.

The Volcker recession of 1982 resulted from a fall in the growth of aggregate demand triggered by the monetary policy of the Federal Reserve. In its attempt to beat inflation, the Fed unexpectedly slowed the growth of aggregate demand. Wages increased on the presumption that inflation would continue at close to 10 percent a year, and those wage changes decreased aggregate supply. But the fall in aggregate supply was smaller than the fall in aggregate demand. As a consequence, real GDP declined but the inflation rate moderated.

The 1990–1991 recession resulted from the Persian Gulf crisis, which increased the price of oil—a decrease in aggregate supply—and increased uncertainty, bringing lower investment—a decrease in aggregate demand. The result was a fall in real GDP with a slight moderation in the inflation rate.

In all recessions, interest rates eventually decline as the lower level of real GDP decreases the demand for money.

There is controversy about the behavior of the labor market during a recession. According to the sticky wage theory, the quantity of labor supplied is not very responsive to changes in real wages and wages themselves do not fall much in a recession. As a result, when the economy goes into recession, the quantity of labor supplied exceeds the quantity demanded. According to the flexible wage theory, the quantity of labor supplied is highly responsive to changes in real wages. When the economy goes into recession, real wages fall a little, by enough to keep the quantity of labor demanded equal to the quantity supplied. Unemployment increases, but the increase arises from increased job search activity associated with a higher degree of labor turnover.

Macroeconomists have not yet found the acid test that enables them to resolve their uncertainty about the labor market mechanism in recession. (pp. 396–405)

Another Great Depression?

The Great Depression that began in 1929 lasted longer and was more severe than any before it or since. The Great Depression started with increased uncertainty and pessimism, which brought a fall in investment (especially in housing) and spending on consumer durables. Increased uncertainty and pessimism also brought on the stock market crash. The crash added to the pessimistic outlook, and further spending cuts occurred. There then followed a near total collapse of the financial system. Banks failed and the money supply fell, resulting in a continued fall in aggregate demand. Expectations of falling prices led to falling wages, but the fall in aggregate demand continued to exceed expectations and real GDP continued to decline.

The Great Depression itself produced a series of reforms that make a repeat of such a depression much less likely. The most important of these were the Fed's willingness to act as lender of last resort and the introduction of federal bank deposit insurance, both of which reduced the risk of bank failure and financial collapse. Higher taxes and government spending have given the economy greater resistance against depression, and an increased labor force participation rate provides a greater measure of security, especially for families with more than one wage earner. For these reasons, an initial change in either aggregate demand or aggregate supply is much less likely to translate into an accumulative depression, as it did in the early 1930s. Thus even a stock market crash as severe as the one that occurred in 1987 did not lead to a collapse in aggregate demand. (pp. 405–413)

KEY ELEMENTS

Key Figures

REVIEW QUESTIONS

1 When did the Great Depression, the OPEC recession, and the Volcker recession occur?

2 What triggered each of the following?

a The OPEC recession
b The Volcker recession
c The 1990–1991 recession

3 Which of the three recessions in question 2 was a period of stagflation?

4 Compare the movements in interest rates in the three recessions in question 2.

5 Describe the changes in employment and real wages in the OPEC recession. What is the sticky wage theory of these changes? What is the flexible wage theory of these changes?

6 Describe the changes in real GDP, employment and unemployment, and the price level that occurred during the Great Depression years of 1929 to 1933.

7 What were the main causes of the onset of the Great Depression in 1929?

8 What events in 1931 and 1932 led to the continuation and increasing severity of the fall in real GDP and the rise in employment?

9 What four features of today's economy make it less likely now than in 1929 that a Great Depression will occur? Why do they make it less likely?

PROBLEMS

1 During the OPEC recession, real wages fell from $12.07 an hour to $11.97 an hour. Employment fell from 164 billion hours to 161 billion hours. Illustrate these changes in the labor market by drawing demand and supply curves for labor in 1973 and 1975. Draw two diagrams, one that illustrates these changes in wages and employment if the flexible wage theory is true and one that illustrates these changes if the sticky wage theory is true.

2 Analyze the changes in the interest rate during the Volcker recession by drawing a diagram of the money market showing shifts in the demand and supply curves for real money. What policy changes could have prevented interest rates from rising? What would the effects of such actions have been on real GDP and the price level?

3 During the Volcker recession, real wages did not fall. They held steady at $12.60 an hour. Employment fell from 184 to 180 billion hours. How can these events be explained by the sticky wage theory? By the flexible wage theory?

4 Analyze the changes in the interest rate during the 1990–1991 recession by drawing a diagram of the money market showing shifts in the demand and supply curves for real money. What policy changes could have prevented the recession?

5 During the 1990–1991 recession, real wages increased from $13.78 in 1990 to $13.86 in 1991 and employment decreased from 212 billion hours in 1990 to 209 billion hours in 1991. How can these changes be explained by the sticky and flexible wage theories?

6 Compare and contrast the recessions of 1974–1975, 1982, and 1990–1991. In what ways are they similar, and in what ways do they differ?

7 List all of the features of the U.S. economy today that you can think of that are consistent with a pessimistic outlook for the mid-1990s.

8 List all of the features of the U.S. economy today that you can think of that are consistent with an optimistic outlook for the mid-1990s.

9 How do you think the U.S. economy is going to evolve over the next year or two? Explain your predictions, drawing on the pessimistic and optimistic factors that you listed in the previous two problems and on your knowledge of macroeconomic theory.

PART 5

MACROECONOMIC POLICY

Talking with Andrew F. Brimmer

Born September 13, 1926, in Newellton, Louisiana, Andrew F. Brimmer is now President of Brimmer & Company, Inc., a Washington, D.C.–based economic and financial consulting firm. He holds an additional appointment as Wilmer D. Barrett Professor of Economics at the University of Massachusetts–Amherst. Dr. Brimmer is a former member of the Board of Governors of the Federal Reserve System. He is also a member of the boards of directors of several major corporations. Author of several books in the areas of monetary policy, banking, and international finance, he has also published numerous articles in professional journals. Dr. Brimmer has served as vice-president of the American Economic Association and president of the Eastern Economic Association. He has been on the faculties of Harvard University, Michigan State University, and the University of Pennsylvania. He earned his Ph.D. in economics at Harvard.

How did you first become interested in economics?

I was introduced to economics during my second year at the University of Washington. I began my college work as a journalism major, and a survey course in economics was part of the required curriculum. In taking that course, I had a very good teacher. I found that the subject matter dealt with contemporary issues such as the tradeoffs between depression versus prosperity, inflation versus stagnation, and free trade versus protection. I was immediately attracted to the orderly and systematic thinking that lies at the core of economics. At the end of my junior year, I switched my major to economics.

How would you grade the Fed's conduct of monetary policy over the past few years?

I would assign a grade of A–. The main task confronting the Federal Reserve Board until the summer of 1990 was to prevent the resurgence of inflation. To that end, the Federal Reserve adopted a restrictive monetary policy in the spring of 1989. The threat of accelerating inflation became even more pressing after Iraq invaded Kuwait in August 1990, which led to a sharp spurt in oil prices. To limit the spread of these inflationary pressures through the rest of the economy, the Federal Reserve exerted even more restraint on the availability of money and credit. This posture was maintained until the closing months of 1990. By that time, the 1990–91 recession was underway. Although the evidence of declining output was widespread, the Federal Reserve System was reluctant to relax restraint on the growth of bank reserves in order to reduce interest rates. Because of this error in timing the shift to a stimulative monetary policy, the Federal Reserve should get less than a perfect grade.

However, as the recession deepened, the stimulative policy was pursued vigorously. Because the recovery during 1991–92 was exceptionally weak when compared with the record since the end of World War II, the Federal Reserve was generous in supplying bank reserves, and interest rates—particularly short-term rates—remained quite low. This phase of monetary management deserves a grade of A.

Is the Fed doing enough to stimulate full recovery from the 1990–91 recession and to ensure sustained growth in the years ahead?

Yes. The contribution the Fed can make is to supply bank reserves, which will increase liquidity. The latter, in turn, will enable banks to expand loans and purchases of securities. The increased supply of money and credit will lead to a decline in interest rates and a rise in business investment and consumer spending.

The Federal Reserve has pursued these objectives. For example, in 1989, when a restrictive monetary policy was in force, total reserves decreased by 0.8 percent. Monetary restraint continued well into 1990, and total reserves rose by only 2.6 percent for the year. However, as the recession become more evident, a stimulative policy was adopted, and reserves expanded by 5.5 percent in 1991. During 1992, total reserves were projected to increase by 12.9 percent. Reflecting these changes in monetary policy, interest rates decreased appreciably. For instance, the federal funds rate declined from an average of 9.22 percent in 1989 to 8.10 percent in 1990, to 5.69 percent in 1991, and to a projected 4.25 percent in 1992. Parallel—though less dramatic—reductions occurred in the case of long-term interest rates. Yields on 30-year U.S. government bonds decreased from 8.45 percent in 1989 to 8.61 percent in 1990, to 8.14 percent in 1991, and to a projected 7.95 percent in 1992.

In your experience, what are the most effective macroeconomic stabilization policies?

That depends on the nature of the problems the economy is facing at any particular time. There are essentially two types of policies available: (1) fiscal policy and (2) monetary policy. The former focuses on variations in the net position of the federal budget—that is, whether it is in surplus or deficit. The latter focuses on bank reserves and interest rates.

In the simplest case, if the economy is drifting into a recession, the objective should be to stimulate aggregate demand. To achieve this goal, government revenue should decrease while expenditures increase—causing the budget to shift into deficit, or an existing deficit should become larger. The Federal Reserve should expand bank reserves and reduce interest rates. In the opposite case—when excess aggregate demand is pushing the economy toward inflation—both fiscal and monetary policy should become restrictive.

The more difficult problem arises when the economy is suffering from "stagflation"—a mixture of slow growth, a large budget deficit, and inflationary pressures. Under these circumstances, fiscal policy should be restrictive. Perhaps even a budget surplus should be sought. Monetary policy should be less restrictive—which would permit somewhat lower interest rates to promote investment. The fundamental challenges in these more complex cases are to find the right combination of policies and to shift the degree of stimulation and restraint in a timely fashion.

Some people believe that the Fed is too independent and that some of its independence should be removed. What is your opinion?

The Federal Reserve System is an independent agency *within* the federal government, but it is *outside* the executive branch. The Federal Reserve exercises—on delegated authority—the power that the U.S. Constitution vested in Congress "to coin money and determine the value thereof." Congress, in turn, has delegated that authority to the Federal Reserve Board. On four occasions in our history, Congress has debated delegating the "money power" to the president and each time decided against taking that step. Instead, it has tried four different arrangements: the First Bank of the United States (1790), the Second Bank of the United States (1816), the National Banking System (1863), and the Federal Reserve System (1913). In each case, the Congress delegated its authority to control money to an agency outside the executive branch of the government. These were wise decisions.

If the president had control over the power to create money, there would be a strong temptation to use that power to finance the federal budget deficit. This would give the federal government control over goods and services in excess of the tax revenue collected. It would contribute to inflation in the long run.

We occasionally hear reports indicating that the deliberations of the Federal Open Market Committee—the Fed's policymaking arm—get quite heated, with the members of the committee disagreeing with each other concerning the appropriate direction for policy. Are these reports accurate? If so, how does the committee ultimately decide monetary policy?

The appropriate course for monetary policy under different economic conditions is debated vigorously at the periodic meetings of the Federal Open Market Committee (FOMC). However, the discussion is always calm and courteous. Of course, some members are more vocal than others. Yet on most occasions, the chairman can lead the committee to a broadly based consensus that is supported unanimously. Ultimately, the twelve members of the FOMC, which consists of seven Federal Reserve board members and five Federal Reserve bank presidents—four of whom serve on a rotating basis—vote on each proposed change in policy. Dissents are rare; when they do occur, only one or two negative votes are typically cast.

What do you consider the most pressing economic problem facing the United States today?

"The result is a labor market equilibrium in which not all workers can get the jobs they want and meet the qualifications . . ."

The large and persistent federal budget deficit is a matter of great concern. However, the anemic recovery from the 1990–91 recession and the prospect of sub-par growth over the next several years constitute the most pressing problems facing this country. Consequently, the most urgent task is to stimulate investment in the private sector. Measured in real terms, we have suffered a significant decline in spending for plant and equipment and R&D in relation to gross domestic product. We are also lagging significantly in public investment for infrastructure—such as urban transit and water supply systems. Ultimately, these kinds of outlays must be financed by the federal government, and we should press ahead to do it at this time.

Why should we be concerned about the sustained increase in the nation's debt?

There are several reasons why we should be seriously concerned. In the first place, the debt represents the accumulated federal budget deficit incurred in the past. To service the outstanding debt and to cover the new deficits, the federal government has to borrow in the money and capital markets both at home and abroad. Thus the government absorbs savings that would otherwise be available to the private sector. The added competition for funds exerts upward pressure on interest rates. Moreover, an increasing share of the national debt is owned by foreign investors. The amount of interest paid to them provides foreigners with a growing command over U.S. resources and income.

What economic problems await us as we approach the twenty-first century?

Aside from the lag in investment already mentioned, we need to upgrade the nation's labor force. Over the next decade, women, blacks, and members of other minority groups will provide most of the net increase in the civilian labor force. Many of the people from these segments of the population do not have the skills that will be needed to compete successfully in the labor market in the years ahead. Therefore we must substantially increase our investment in education to equip them to undertake the more sophisticated production and management tasks they will be required to perform.

The decline in the competitive position of American industry also has to be reversed. The United States has suffered serious erosion in its world market share in a number of manufactured products for which we once had a significant comparative advantage. Not only are we losing out to advanced industrial countries such as Germany and Japan, but we are also losing market share to a number of the newly industrialized nations such as Hong Kong, South Korea, Singapore, Taiwan, and Thailand. Moreover, imports have taken a sizable share of the U.S. domestic market. Many foreign manufacturers are increasingly able to produce and deliver high-quality products to American consumers at prices below what U.S. firms would require. To counter these trends, U.S. manufacturers will have to increase the productivity of American workers and raise the quality of domestic products.

"Many foreign manufacturers are increasingly able to produce and deliver high-quality products to American consumers at prices below what U.S. firms would require."

What professional activity provides you with the most satisfaction?

Today, I work primarily as an economic and financial consultant. I spend most of my time preparing analyses and forecasts of interest rates and other developments in money and capital markets at home and abroad. Based on these assessments, I provide advice to clients—who consist mainly of banks, portfolio managers, and other financial institutions. In addition, I serve as a director of several corporations and teach economics on a part-time basis—mainly to graduate students through seminars and workshops. I also write a column for the monthly magazine *Black Enterprise.* All of these activities provide considerable satisfaction.

In your opinion, what is the most important message that college students should take away from a principles of economics course?

Students should take away several important lessons. First, you need to understand the basic tasks that any economy must perform, such as: (1) Given the scarcity of resources, how are decisions made with respect to what is to be produced and by what method of organization? (2) How is the income that is generated from economic activity to be distributed? (3) What is the role of supply and demand in allocating goods and services in the context of a market system?

Also, you need to remember that economics provides citizens with help in making choices among competing claims and the allocation of scarce resources but that economics cannot dictate which choices are to be selected. For example, economics can help to determine the costs and benefits of pollution abatement, but it cannot decide whether a policy of abatement should be adopted. Likewise, economic analysis can show the expected effect of airline deregulation on the volume of air travel, but it cannot decide whether the airline industry should be deregulated.

CHAPTER 16

Stabilizing the Economy

After studying this chapter, you will be able to:

- Describe the goals of macroeconomic stabilization policy
- Explain how the economy influences government popularity
- Describe the main features of fiscal policy since 1960
- Describe the main features of monetary policy since 1960
- Distinguish between fixed-rule and feedback-rule stabilization policies
- Explain how the economy responds to aggregate demand and aggregate supply shocks under fixed-rule and feedback-rule policies
- Explain why lowering inflation usually brings recession

Who's in Charge?

PEOPLE PANIC WHEN TIMES ARE HARD AND TURN TO their political leaders for action. Thus it was in the depths of the Great Depression that our grandparents turned to Franklin Delano Roosevelt to deliver them from that economic holocaust. Sixty-four years later, with George Bush in the White House, the situation was remarkably similar. The economic ills of 1992 were not as severe as those of 1929, but the economy was again in recession, and for many there was no relief in sight. And so again the cry went out—"Who's in charge?" Who *is* in charge of the U.S. economy? When recession strikes, what can the government do about it? ◆◆ With employment and incomes growing slowly, the 1992 presidential election campaign was dominated by a single issue—the economy. Rightly or wrongly, the electorate blamed incumbent George Bush for the nation's economic ills and gave the victory to challenger Bill Clinton, who promised to get America working again. A similar thing happened some years earlier, in 1976, when Ronald Reagan displaced an economically shell-shocked Jimmy Carter. How important is the economy in determining election outcomes? And what aspects of the economy do voters worry about most—unemployment or inflation or both? ◆◆ The second half of the 1980s was a period of unimagined prosperity and macroeconomic stability. The early 1990s, in contrast, were years of slow income growth, high unemployment, and recession. How were the stability and prosperity of the 1980s achieved? And what can be done to achieve a similar degree of success in the 1990s?

◆ ◆ ◆ ◆ In this chapter, we're going to study the problems of stabilizing the U.S. economy—of avoiding inflation, high unemployment, and wildly fluctuating growth rates of real GDP. At the end of the chapter, you will have a clearer and deeper understanding of the macroeconomic policy problems facing the United States today and of the political debate that surrounds us concerning those problems.

The Stabilization Problem

The stabilization problem is to deliver a macroeconomic performance that is as smooth and predictable as possible. Solving this problem involves specifying targets to be achieved and then devising policies to achieve them. There are two main macroeconomic stabilization policy targets. They are

- Real GDP growth
- Inflation

Real GDP Growth

When real GDP grows less quickly than the economy's ability to produce, output is lost. When real GDP grows more quickly than the economy's ability to produce, bottlenecks arise. Keeping real GDP growth steady and equal to long-run aggregate supply growth avoids these problems.

Fluctuations in real GDP growth also bring fluctuations in unemployment. When unemployment rises above its natural rate, productive labor is wasted and there is a slowdown in the accumulation of human capital. If such unemployment persists, serious psychological and social problems arise for the unemployed workers and their families. When unemployment falls below its natural rate, expanding industries are held back by labor shortages. Keeping real GDP growth steady helps keep unemployment at its natural rate and avoids the waste and shortage of labor.

Fluctuations in real GDP growth contribute to fluctuations in our international trade balance. An international trade deficit enables us to purchase more goods and services than we have produced. But to do so, we must borrow from the rest of the world and pay interest on our borrowing. An international trade surplus enables us to lend to the rest of the world and earn interest. But to do so, we must purchase fewer goods and services than we have produced. Keeping real GDP growth steady helps keep our balance of trade with the rest of the world steady and enables us to consume what we have produced and avoid a buildup of international debt interest.

Inflation

When inflation fluctuates unpredictably, money becomes less useful as a measuring rod for conducting transactions. Borrowers and lenders and employers and workers must take on extra risks. Keeping the inflation rate steady and predictable avoids these problems.

Keeping inflation steady also helps keep the value of the dollar abroad steady. Other things being equal, if the inflation rate goes up by 1 percentage point, the dollar loses 1 percent of its value against the currencies of other countries. Large and unpredictable fluctuations in the foreign exchange rate—the value of the dollar against other currencies—make international trade and international borrowing and lending less profitable and limit the gains from international specialization and exchange. Keeping inflation low and predictable helps avoid such fluctuations in the exchange rate and enables international transactions to be undertaken at minimum risk and on the desired scale.

Policy performance, judged by the two policy targets—real GDP growth and inflation—is shown in Fig. 16.1. Here the red line is real GDP growth, and the green shaded area is inflation. As you can see, our performance has fallen far short of stabilizing the economy. Why has the economy been so unstable? And can policy do better, making the next thirty years more stable than what is shown in Fig. 16.1? Answering these questions will occupy most of the rest of this chapter. Let's begin by identifying the key players and the policy actions they have taken.

FIGURE 16.1

Macroeconomic Performance: Real GDP and Inflation

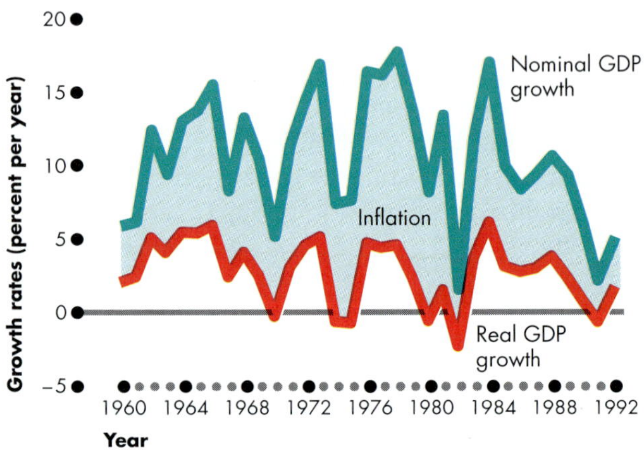

Real GDP growth and inflation fluctuate a great deal. During the 1970s, inflation mushroomed (the green shaded area). This macroeconomic performance falls far short of the goals of a stable real GDP growth rate and moderate and predictable inflation.

Source: Economic Report of the President, 1993.

Players and Policies

There are three key players that formulate and execute macroeconomic stabilization policy:

- Congress
- The Board of Governors of the Federal Reserve System
- The administration

Congress

The House of Representatives and the Senate and various committees of Congress implement the nation's fiscal policy, summarized in the federal budget. The **federal budget** is a statement of the federal government's financial plan, itemizing programs and their costs, tax revenues, and the proposed budget deficit or surplus.

The timetable for the federal budget process is fairly rigid. The U.S. fiscal year runs from October 1 to September 30. Most of the high-profile political action surrounding the budget takes place in the fall, as Congress and the president attempt to agree on a budget. But the process begins in January when Congress receives the president's proposed budget for the following year. The Congressional Budget Office studies the president's proposals and prepares a report on them for Congress. Then follows a series of long committee sessions and reports. Eventually, the Senate and the House develop a concurrent resolution describing a budget package that both houses are willing to approve. Because of this timetable, fiscal policy, while having an important effect on macroeconomic performance, is not used as a means of fine-tuning the economy.

Fiscal policy has three elements:

- Spending plans
- Tax laws
- Deficit

Spending Plans The expenditure side of the budget is a list of programs with the amount that the government plans to spend on each program and a forecast of the total amount of government expenditure. Some expenditure items in the federal budget are directly controlled by government departments. Others arise from decisions to fund particular programs, the total cost of which depends on actions that Congress can forecast but not directly control. For example, social security expenditure depends on the state of the economy and on how many people qualify for support. Farm subsidies depend on farm costs and prices.

Tax Laws Congress makes decisions about government revenue by enacting tax laws. As in the case of some important items of government expenditure, Congress cannot control with precision the amount of tax revenue it will receive. The amount of tax paid is determined by the actions of the millions of people and firms that make their own choices about how much to work, spend, and save.

Deficit The difference between government spending and taxes is the government deficit. Every year since 1969, the federal government has had a deficit, and in the early 1980s the deficit became unusually large.

The persistence of a federal government deficit has caused alarm and led to a variety of creative ideas on the part of Congress to keep spending in check or to increase revenue. One idea, proposed by Senators Gramm, Rudman, and Hollings and incorporated into the Gramm-Rudman-Hollings Act of 1985, is to impose automatic spending cuts if the deficit does not follow a predetermined path that will ultimately result in a balanced budget by 1993.

Another way of balancing the federal budget is to increase government revenue. But there is disagreement and two competing views about how this objective might be achieved. One, supported by former President Ronald Reagan, is that tax reform and lower tax rates will increase revenue by stimulating economic activity. The incomes on which taxes are paid will increase by enough to ensure that lower tax rates bring in higher revenue. The other view is that revenue can be increased only by increasing tax rates and introducing new taxes.

The Federal Reserve Board

The Federal Reserve System is the nation's central bank. The main features of the Federal Reserve System are described in Chapter 11. Monetary policy actions are formulated and monitored by the Federal Open Market Committee (FOMC) (see p. 281). Each month, the FOMC meets to formulate detailed guidelines for the conduct of monetary policy in the coming month. The minutes of the FOMC are confidential until enough time has elapsed for the actions based on the decisions taken to have already occurred. This confidentiality is regarded as an important means of preventing anyone from benefiting from inside knowledge of the Fed's forthcoming actions.

The Fed influences the economy by trading in markets in which it is one of the major participants. The two most important groups of such markets are those for government debt and for foreign currency. The Fed's decisions to buy and sell in these markets influence interest rates, the value of the dollar in terms of foreign currencies, and the amount of money in the economy. These variables that the Fed can directly influence in turn affect the conditions on which the millions of firms and households in the economy undertake their own economic actions.

Because the Fed's policymaking committee, the FOMC, meets frequently and because the Fed operates daily in financial markets, monetary policy is used in an attempt to fine-tune the economy.

The Administration

The role of the administration in formulating and implementing macroeconomic stabilization policy is to give advice and attempt to persuade. Even the president of the United States has severely limited powers when it comes to stabilizing the economy.

Persuading the Fed The president can attempt to influence the chairman and members of the Board of Governors of the Federal Reserve System, persuading them to take whatever stabilization policy actions the administration deems appropriate. And the president carries some important carrots and sticks that enhance his influence. For example, the president appoints the chairman (for four years) and members of the Federal Reserve Board (for fourteen years). But once they have been appointed, the president cannot remove them until their term of office is complete. This fact means that a president often has to live with a Federal Reserve Board appointed largely by previous presidents.

Influencing Congress The president can also try to influence Congress and the outcome of congressional debates. One source of this influence is the president's power of veto. But in the case of government spending bills, the president has the power only to take the entire bill or to leave it. He does not have a line-item veto as do many state governors. That is, the president cannot decide to veto certain items in a budget proposed by Congress. He either approves the entire package or rejects the entire package. In practical terms, this means that the president does not have a veto on financial bills. To veto a half-billion-dollar dam project would require also vetoing the entire defense budget.

The Economic Report of the President Each year, the president prepares an economic report that reviews the state of the economy and sets out his goals and ambitions for the future. The report is accompanied by the annual report of the president's Council of Economic Advisers. Established in the

Employment Act of 1946, the council consists of a small group of economists who work closely with the president, keeping him informed and advised of economic developments and of policy developments in the Fed and Congress. The Council of Economic Advisers, together with the president, takes a position on the appropriate combination of monetary and fiscal policy actions. It also offers opinions on the actions of the two branches of policymaking, paying special attention to consistency of policies.

At the head of the Council of Economic Advisers is its chairperson. Almost always the chairperson is a highly distinguished economist, often with an academic background. The current chairwoman is Laura D'Andrea Tyson, on leave from her regular job as a professor of economics and business administration at the University of California at Berkeley. Usually, the Council of Economic Advisers and its chairperson operate quietly in the background. Occasionally, however, the chairperson becomes embroiled in public debate. The most notable such occasion arose in 1984 when Ronald Reagan's Council of Economic Advisers chairman, Martin Feldstein, a Harvard professor, vocally and publicly expressed his concern about the administration's attitude toward the large, and seemingly permanent, federal deficit. But such public disagreements are rare, and most of the time the Council of Economic Advisers works in close harmony with the president.

We've described the key players in the policymaking game. Let's now turn our attention to the policies they have pursued.

Fiscal and Monetary Policy Performance

Macroeconomic stabilization policy is strongly influenced by the constraints on Congress, the Fed, and the president. And the most important constraint is that arising from the effects of economic performance on voters in congressional and presidential elections. To ensure adequate voter support to get re-elected, macroeconomic policy must deliver a macroeconomic performance acceptable to the electorate. What is an acceptable macroeconomic performance?

Macroeconomic Performance and Voter Behavior

The effects of economic performance on voter behavior have been studied most thoroughly by Ray Fair of Yale University. By studying the outcome of all the presidential elections between 1916 and 1984, Fair discovered the following formula:

- For each 1 percentage point *increase* in the real GDP growth rate, the incumbent political party gets a 1 percentage point *increase* in voter share.
- For each 3 percentage point *increase* in the inflation rate, the incumbent political party gets a 1 percentage point *decrease* in voter share.

We can use Fair's discovery to calculate the predicted change in popularity (the change in the percentage of votes that the incumbent is expected to receive in the next election) as follows:

$$\begin{aligned}\text{Percentage of votes} = {} & \text{Real GDP growth} \\ & - \tfrac{1}{3} \times \text{Inflation rate} \\ & + \text{Other influences.}\end{aligned}$$

Politicians take actions that they believe will get them re-elected. That is, they take actions designed to increase the percentage of votes they receive. Among these actions are macroeconomic stabilization policies that increase real GDP growth and lower inflation. But a 1 percentage point increase in real GDP growth brings in as many additional votes as a 3 percentage point decrease in the inflation rate. Therefore politicians tend to favor policies that increase real GDP growth over those that decrease inflation.

Popularity and Economic Performance since 1960

The macroeconomic performance of the United States since 1960, as measured by its predicted effects on the popularity of the incumbent party (but with other influences ignored), is shown in Fig.16.2. The figure also gives information about the timing of presidential elections and the outcomes of those elections, winners in red and losers in black.

You can see that between 1961 and 1966, economic performance contributed to political popularity. But economic performance then deteriorated through 1971. There followed, through the 1970s and early 1980s, a series of large swings in performance and popularity.

But look closely at the timing of the swings. In every election year except one, the economy was improving and increasing the popularity of the incumbent administration in the year of the election. Only in one year, 1980, did the president (Jimmy

FIGURE 16.2

Election Outcomes and the Economy

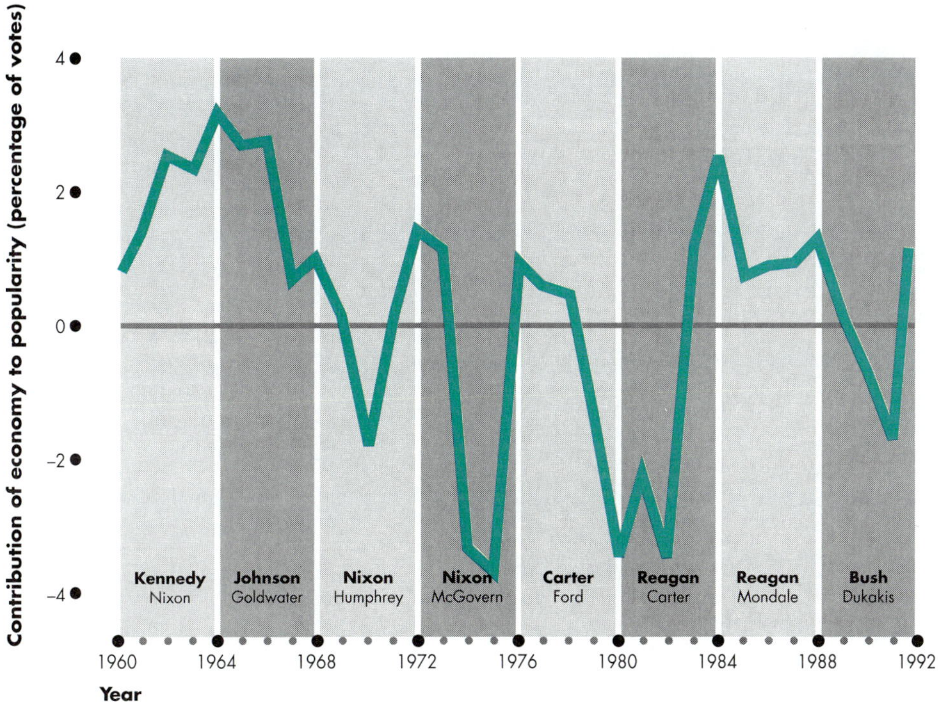

Presidential elections are won or lost depending on the state of the economy. Faster real GDP growth and slower inflation increase the popularity of the incumbent party. Usually, real GDP growth slows after an election and speeds up just before an election, enabling the incumbent to win. Two exceptions are 1976, when the speedup in growth came too late, and 1980, when real GDP growth slowed in the election year.

Source: Economic Report of the President, 1993, and my calculations based on the work of Ray Fair described in the text. The "predicted popularity" variable is the growth rate of real GDP minus one third of the inflation rate.

Carter) go into an election with a negative economic performance. And, predictably, he lost. Other incumbent administrations that lost were Johnson/Humphrey in 1968 (Johnson withdrew from the race and Humphrey ran as the presidential candidate), Ford in 1976, and Bush in 1992. In all three cases, economic performance was improving in the election year. But in neither case was economic performance strong enough to get the incumbent party re-elected.

Figure 16.2 shows convincingly that economic performance has been linked to presidential elections, so much so that the cycle has been called a political business cycle. A **political business cycle** is a business cycle whose origins are fluctuations in aggregate demand brought about by policies designed to improve the chance of an administration being re-elected. Is the U.S. business cycle to some extent a political business cycle? And if it is, which policies have caused it, fiscal or monetary? To answer these questions, let's look at fiscal and monetary policy over the years since 1960.

Fiscal Policy since 1960 A broad summary of fiscal policy since 1960 is contained in Fig. 16.3. Here you can see the levels of government spending, taxes, and the deficit (each as a percentage of GDP). You can also see the election years and names of the incumbent presidents.

Fiscal policy was mildly expansionary during the Kennedy years and strongly expansionary during the later Johnson years, with the Vietnam war buildup. During Nixon's presidency, spending growth was kept moderate. But under the pressure of the first OPEC oil shock, spending soared under Ford. The Carter years were a period of spending cuts, and the first Reagan term was a period of spending growth. The Bush administration worked hard to keep spending in check and was initially committed to "no new taxes" but in mid-term favored a tax increase. As the 1991 recession intensified and the 1992 election drew closer, tax cuts became the rage, especially in Congress (see Reading Between the Lines, pp. 428–429).

Fiscal Policy in Action

TIME, NOVEMBER 4, 1991

Is It a Treat or a Trick?

BY JOHN GREENWALD WITH MICHAEL DUFFY AND HAYS GOREY

What Washington politicians were singing last week sounded like the chorus of a wistful Beach Boys song. Wouldn't it be nice, they all sang, if we could cut taxes? Wouldn't that make voters happy in 1992 and lift the economy too? . . .

Lawmakers hastily crafted programs to appeal to everyone from the super-rich to the working poor. Texas Democrat Lloyd Bentsen, who chairs the U.S. Senate Finance Committee, stirred the most talk by proposing a $72.5 billion tax cut aimed squarely at the middle class. . . . Bentsen would pay for the cuts by reducing defense spending. . . .

Politicians rushed forward with nearly a dozen rival plans, including a move by Democratic Senator Daniel Patrick Moynihan of New York to revive his long-standing proposal to cut Social Security taxes. Not to be outdone by the Democrats, Senate Republican Phil Gramm of Texas and House minority whip Newt Gingrich of Georgia introduced wide-ranging legislation that repeated the Bush Administration's cherished call for reduced capital gains taxes. . . .

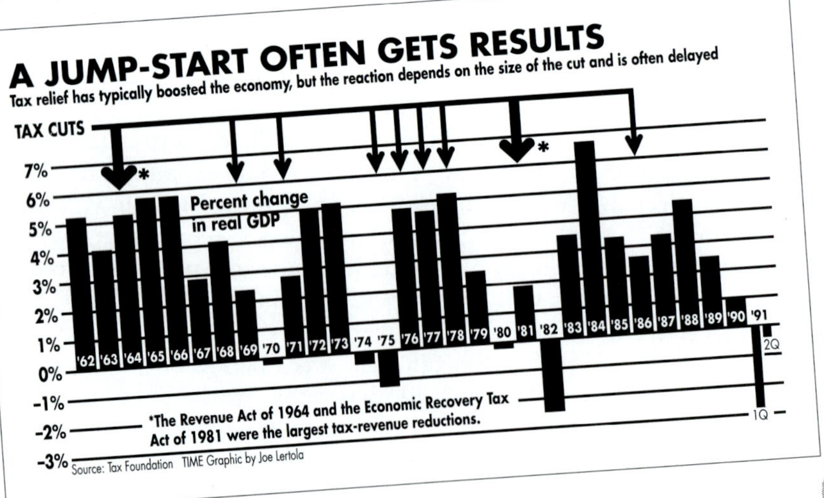

The Essence of the Story

In October 1991, politicians were anxious to speed economic recovery and boost their popularity. They proposed tax cuts aimed at the rich, the middle class, and the poor.

Senator Lloyd Bentsen (Texas Democrat who chairs the U.S. Senate Finance Committee) proposed a $72.5 billion tax cut for the middle class to be paid for by lower defense spending.

Senator Daniel Patrick Moynihan (New York Democrat) proposed a social security tax cut—a proposal he has repeatedly made.

Senator Phil Gramm (Texas Republican) and Representative Newt Gingrich (Georgia Republican and House minority whip) proposed capital gains tax cuts—proposals favored by President Bush.

Background and Analysis

In October 1991, the Commerce Department reported that orders for steel, machinery, aircraft, and other durable goods had fallen by 4.1 percent in August and 3.2 percent in September—the economy appeared stagnant.

In such a situation, feedback fiscal policy can take two forms: automatic or active.

Automatic stabilization occurs because:

- Tax revenues fall as wage and profit incomes fall.
- Transfer payments rise as more people receive unemployment and other benefits.

Active stabilization occurs if Congress passes laws that cut taxes or increase expenditures on programs.

In the 1991 recession, the automatic stabilizers added almost $40 billion to the deficits of the federal, state, and local governments—shown in Fig. 1. But during 1991 the automatic stabilizers began to lose their effect before the economy had recovered. The reason is that corporate taxes began to rise in mid-1991—shown in Fig. 2.

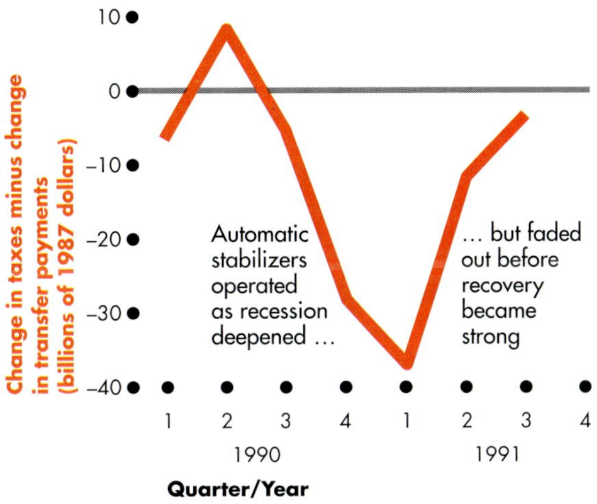

Figure 1

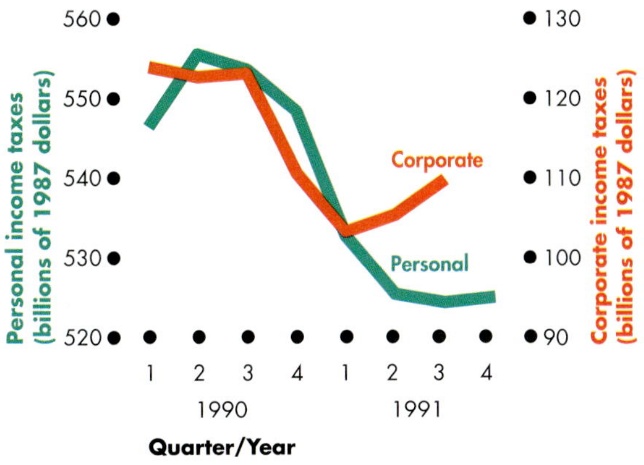

Figure 2

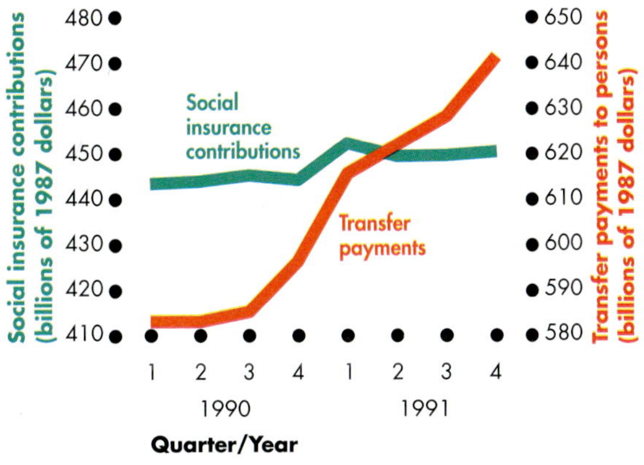

Figure 3

Figure 3 shows an increase in social insurance contributions at the beginning of 1991. (This was not part of stabilization policy, but it had an effect on the economy.) This figure also shows that transfer payments continued to rise during 1991, a sign of continuing high unemployment.

With the economy remaining weak and the steam having gone from the automatic stabilizers, there was a case for additional active stimulus at the beginning of 1992. But some of the proposals in the news article would cut taxes *and* cut spending by the same amount. Such a *balanced budget change* would not be expansionary (see Chapter 9, pp. 231–232). Lower defense spending would decrease aggregate demand by a larger amount than the increase in aggregate demand coming from an equal size tax cut.

The effects of active tax cuts between 1960 and 1991 is mixed, as the chart in the news article makes clear. The Kennedy tax cuts of the early 1960s and the Reagan tax cuts in 1986 were followed by strong economic growth, but for other tax cuts the record is mixed.

FIGURE 16.3

The Fiscal Policy Record: A Summary

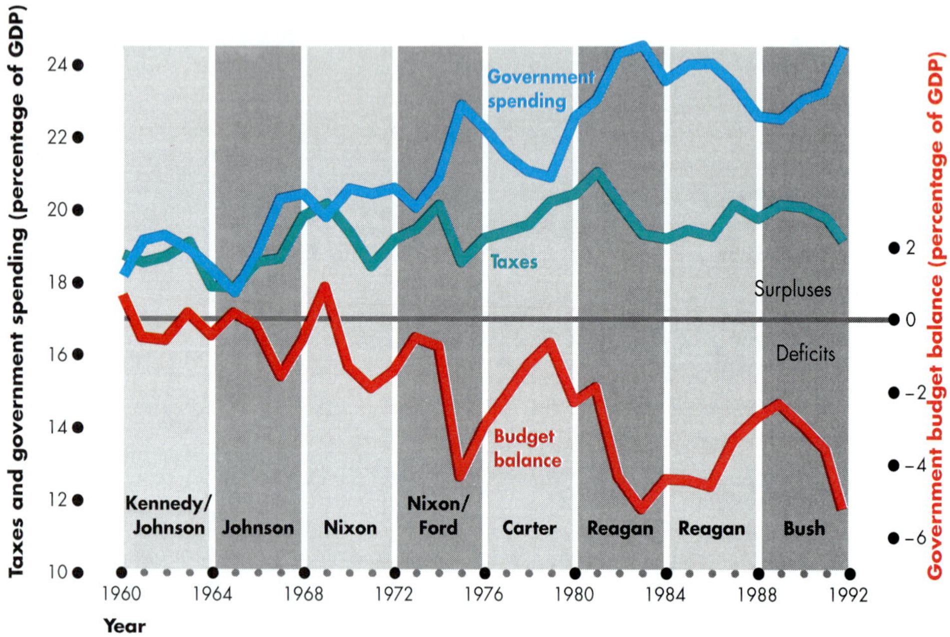

Fiscal policy is summarized here by the performance of government spending, taxes, and the deficit. Both spending and taxes have been on an upward trend, but spending has increased more than taxes, with a deficit emerging. Cycles in spending and taxes have resulted in cycles in the deficit that often have been expansionary in the year before an election and contractionary in the year following an election.

Source: Economic Report of the President, 1993, and my calculations.

The deficit tells an interesting story. During the terms of Johnson, Nixon, and Ford and the first Reagan term, the deficit decreased in the immediate post-election year and increased as the next election approached. This pattern is consistent with the political business cycle theory. Jimmy Carter broke the pattern. He inherited a large deficit, brought it under control, and did *not* permit it to increase during his last year in office. Perhaps as a result, the economy failed to expand during 1980—the main reason Carter lost the election that year. The pattern was also broken by George Bush, who saw the deficit increase during each of his last three years in office. Bill Clinton is currently promising to break the pattern as well, by attacking the deficit with a $500 billion reduction package.

Fiscal policy, then, has followed a cycle that has contributed to the political business cycle. But so has monetary policy.

Monetary Policy since 1960 A broad measure of the influence of monetary policy is the growth rate of the money supply. Figure 16.4 shows such a measure, the growth rate of M2. It also identifies the election years, the presidents, and the Fed chairmen. Notice the remarkable tendency for the money supply growth rate to decrease immediately following an election and to increase as the next election approaches. Also notice the only important break in that pattern during the term of Jimmy Carter. Usually, monetary policy has been expansionary a full year before an election, enabling the policy to be effective in the election year.

The performance of monetary policy shown in this figure suggests that the administration is well able to bring sufficient pressure to bear on the independent Fed to ensure that its independence does not get in the way of electoral success too often.

Alternative Stabilization Policies

We've seen that the stabilization policies actually pursued have not brought macroeconomic stability. How might the economy be stabilized? Many different fiscal and monetary policies can be pursued, but they all fall into two broad categories:

- Fixed rules
- Feedback rules

Fixed Rules A **fixed rule** specifies an action to be pursued independently of the state of the economy. There are many examples of fixed rules in everyday

FIGURE 16.4

The Monetary Policy Record: A Summary

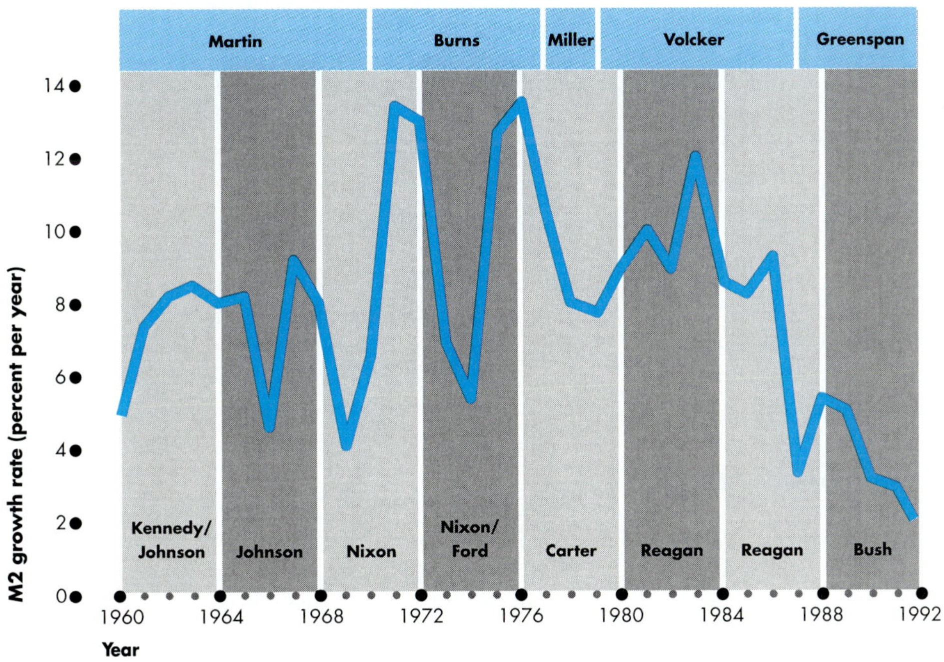

The monetary policy record is summarized here by the growth rate of M2. Fluctuations in M2 growth have coincided with elections, the growth rate usually increasing in the year before an election. An important exception is 1979–1980, when monetary policy did not become expansionary and the incumbent president lost the election.

Source: Economic Report of the President, 1993.

life. Perhaps the best-known one is the rule that keeps the traffic flowing by having us all stick to the right. The best-known fixed rule for stabilization policy is one that has long been advocated by Milton Friedman. He proposes setting the quantity of money growing at a constant rate year in and year out, regardless of the state of the economy. Inflation persists because continual increases in the money supply increase aggregate demand. Friedman proposes allowing the money supply to grow at a rate that keeps the *average* inflation rate at zero.

Feedback Rules A **feedback rule** specifies how policy actions respond to changes in the state of the economy. An everyday example of a feedback rule is that governing your actions in choosing what to wear and whether to carry an umbrella. You base those actions on the best available forecast of the day's temperature and rainfall. (With a fixed rule, you either always or never carry an umbrella.) A stabilization policy feedback rule is one that changes policy instruments such as the money supply, interest rates, or even taxes, in response to the state of the economy. For example, the Fed pursues a feedback rule if an increase in unemployment causes it to engage in an open market operation aimed at increasing the money supply growth rate and lowering interest rates. The Fed also pursues a feedback rule if an increase in the inflation rate triggers an open market operation aimed at cutting the money supply growth rate and raising interest rates.

REVIEW

Fiscal policy conducted by Congress and the administration and monetary policy conducted by the Fed have generally been cyclical. Policy has usually been restrained following an election and expansionary as another election approaches. Alternative policies based on either fixed rules or feedback rules may be used to stabilize the economy. ◆

We'll study the effects of a fixed rule and a feedback rule for the conduct of stabilization policy by examining how real GDP growth and inflation behave under two alternative rules. We'll begin by studying demand shocks.

Stabilization Policy and Aggregate Demand Shocks

We'll study an economy that starts out at full employment and has no inflation. Figure 16.5 illustrates this situation. The economy is on aggregate demand curve AD_0 and short-run aggregate supply curve *SAS*. These curves intersect at a point on the long-run aggregate supply curve *LAS*. The GDP deflator is 100, and real GDP is $5 trillion. Now suppose that there is an unexpected and temporary fall in aggregate demand. Let's see what happens.

Perhaps investment falls because of a wave of pessimism about the future, or perhaps exports fall because of a recession in the rest of the world. Regardless of the origin of the fall in aggregate demand, the aggregate demand curve shifts to the left, to AD_1 in the figure. Because the fall in aggregate demand is unanticipated, expected aggregate demand remains at AD_0, so the expected GDP deflator remains at 100. The short-run aggregate supply curve stays at *SAS*. Aggregate demand curve AD_1 intersects the short-run aggregate supply curve *SAS* at a GDP deflator of 90 and a real GDP of $4 trillion. The economy is in a depressed state. Real GDP is below its long-run level, and unemployment is above its natural rate.

Recall that we are assuming the fall in aggregate demand from AD_0 to AD_1 to be temporary. As confidence in the future improves, firms' investment picks up, or as economic recovery proceeds in the rest of the world, exports gradually rise. As a result, the aggregate demand curve gradually returns to AD_0, but it takes some time to do so.

We are going to work out how the economy responds during the period in which aggregate demand gradually increases to its original level. To do so, we'll consider two alternative policy rules: a fixed rule and a feedback rule.

FIGURE 16.5

A Fall in Aggregate Demand

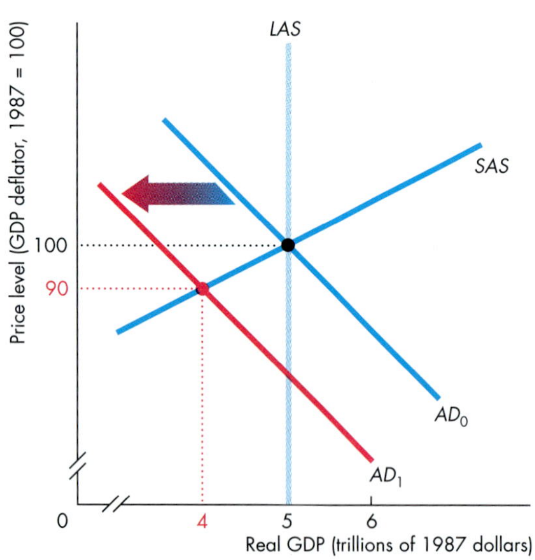

The economy starts out at full employment on aggregate demand curve AD_0 and short-run aggregate supply curve *SAS*, with the two curves intersecting on the long-run aggregate supply curve *LAS*. Real GDP is $5 trillion, and the GDP deflator is 100. A fall in aggregate demand (due to pessimism about future profits, for example) unexpectedly shifts the aggregate demand curve to AD_1. Real GDP falls to $4 trillion, and the GDP deflator falls to 90. The economy is in a recession.

Aggregate Demand Shock with a Fixed Rule

The fixed rule that we'll study here is one in which government purchases of goods and services, taxes, and the deficit remain constant and the money supply remains constant. Neither fiscal policy nor monetary policy responds to the depressed economy.

The response of the economy under this fixed-rule policy is shown in Fig. 16.6(a). When aggregate demand falls to AD_1, no policy measures are taken to bring the economy back to full employment. But recall that we are assuming that the decrease in aggregate demand is temporary and that it gradually increases to AD_0. As it does so, real GDP and the

GDP deflator gradually increase. The GDP deflator gradually returns to 100 and real GDP to its long-run level of $5 trillion. Throughout this process, the economy experiences more rapid growth than usual but beginning from a state of excess capacity. Unemployment remains high until the aggregate demand curve has returned to AD_0.

Let's contrast this adjustment with what occurs under a feedback-rule policy.

Aggregate Demand Shock with a Feedback Rule

The feedback rule that we'll study is one in which government purchases of goods and services increase, taxes decrease, the deficit increases, and the money supply increases when real GDP falls below its long-run level. In other words, both fiscal policy and monetary policy become expansionary when real GDP falls below long-run real GDP. When real GDP rises above its long-run level, both policies operate in reverse, becoming contractionary.

The response of the economy under this feedback-rule policy is shown in Fig. 16.6(b). When aggregate demand falls to AD_1, the expansionary fiscal and monetary policies increase aggregate demand, shifting the aggregate demand curve to AD_0. As the other forces that increase aggregate demand kick in, the fiscal and monetary policies become contractionary, holding the aggregate demand curve steady at AD_0. Real GDP jumps back to its full-employment level, and the GDP deflator jumps back to 100.

FIGURE 16.6

Two Stabilization Policies: Aggregate Demand Shocks

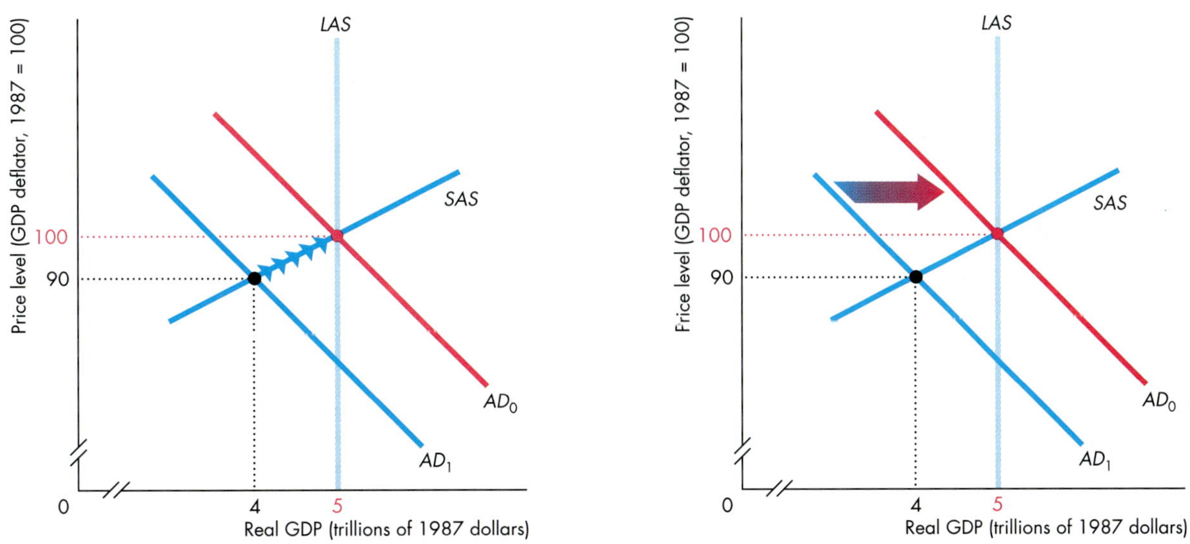

(a) Fixed rule

(b) Feedback rule

The economy is in a depressed state with a GDP deflator of 90 and real GDP of \$4 trillion. The short-run aggregate supply curve is *SAS*. A fixed-rule stabilization policy (part a) leaves aggregate demand initially at AD_1, so the GDP deflator remains at 90 and real GDP at \$4 trillion. As other influences on aggregate demand gradually increase, the aggregate demand curve shifts back to AD_0. As it does, real GDP rises back to \$5 trillion and the GDP deflator increases to 100. Part (b) shows a feedback-rule stabilization policy. Expansionary fiscal and monetary policy increases aggregate demand, shifting the aggregate demand curve from AD_1 to AD_0. Real GDP returns to \$5 trillion, and the GDP deflator returns to 100. Fiscal and monetary policy becomes contractionary as the other influences on aggregate demand increase its level. As a result, the aggregate demand curve is kept steady at AD_0 and real GDP stays at \$5 trillion.

The Two Rules Compared

Under a fixed-rule policy, the economy goes into a recession and stays there for as long as it takes for aggregate demand to increase again under its own steam. Only gradually does the recession come to an end and the aggregate demand curve return to its original position.

Under a feedback-rule policy, the economy is pulled out of its recession by the policy action. Once back at its long-run level, real GDP is held there by a gradual, policy-induced decrease in aggregate demand that exactly offsets the increase in aggregate demand coming from private spending decisions.

The price level and real GDP fall and rise by exactly the same amounts under the two policies, but real GDP stays below its long-run level for longer with a fixed rule than it does with a feedback rule.

So Feedback Rules Are Better? Isn't it obvious that a feedback rule is better than a fixed rule? Can't the government and the Fed use feedback rules to keep the economy close to full employment with a stable price level? Of course, unforecasted events—such as a collapse in business confidence—will hit the economy from time to time. But by responding with a change in tax rates, spending, and money supply, can't the government and the Fed minimize the damage from such a shock? It appears to be so from our analysis.

Despite the apparent superiority of a feedback rule, many economists remain convinced that a fixed rule stabilizes aggregate demand more effectively than a feedback rule. These economists assert that fixed rules are better than feedback rules because:

- Full-employment real GDP is not known.
- Policy lags are longer than the forecast horizon.
- Feedback-rule policies are less predictable than fixed-rule policies.

Let's look at these assertions.

Knowledge of Full-Employment Real GDP

To decide whether a feedback-rule policy needs to stimulate aggregate demand or retard it, it is necessary to determine whether real GDP is currently above or below its full-employment level. But full-employment real GDP is not known with certainty. It depends on a large number of factors, one of which is the level of employment when unemployment is at its natural rate. But there is uncertainty and disagreement about how the labor market works, so we can only estimate the natural rate of unemployment. As a result there is uncertainty about the *direction* in which a feedback-rule policy should be pushing the level of aggregate demand.

Policy Lags and the Forecast Horizon

The effects of policy actions taken today are spread out over the following two years. But no one is able to forecast that far ahead. The forecast horizon of the policymakers is usually less than one year. Further, it is not possible to predict the precise timing and magnitude of the effects of policy itself. Thus feedback-rule policies that react to today's economy might be inappropriate for the state of the economy at that uncertain future date when the policy's effects are felt.

For example, suppose that today the economy is in recession. The Fed reacts with an increase in the money supply growth rate. When the Fed puts on the monetary accelerator, the first reaction is a fall in interest rates. Some time later, lower interest rates produce an increase in investment and the purchases of consumer durable goods. Some time still later, this rise in expenditure increases income, which in turn induces higher consumption expenditure. Later yet, the higher expenditure increases the demand for labor, and eventually wages and prices rise. The sectors in which the spending increases occur vary, and so does the impact on employment. It can take anywhere from nine months to two years for an initial action by the Fed to cause a change in real GDP, employment, and the inflation rate.

By the time the Fed's actions are having their maximum effect, the economy has moved on to a new situation. Perhaps a world economic slowdown has added a new negative effect on aggregate demand that is offsetting the Fed's expansionary actions. Or perhaps a boost in business confidence has increased aggregate demand yet further, adding to the Fed's own expansionary policy. Whatever the situation, the Fed can take the appropriate actions today only if it can forecast those future shocks to aggregate demand.

Thus to smooth the fluctuations in aggregate demand, the Fed needs to take actions today based on a forecast of what will be happening over a period stretching up to two years into the future. It is no use taking actions a year from today to influence the situation that then prevails. It's too late.

If the Fed is good at economic forecasting and bases its policy actions on its forecasts, then the Fed can deliver the type of aggregate demand–smoothing performance that we assumed in the model economy we studied earlier in this chapter. But if the Fed takes policy actions that are based on today's economy rather than based on a forecast of the state of the economy a year in the future, then those actions will often be inappropriate ones.

When unemployment is high and the Fed puts its foot on the accelerator, it speeds the economy back to full employment. But the Fed cannot see far enough ahead to know when to ease off the accelerator and gently tap the brake, holding the economy at its full-employment point. Usually, it keeps its foot on the accelerator for too long, and after the Fed has taken its foot off the accelerator pedal, the economy races through the full-employment point and starts to experience shortages and inflationary pressures. Eventually, when inflation increases and unemployment falls below its natural rate, the Fed steps on the brake, pushing the economy back below full employment.

The Fed's own reaction to the current state of the economy has become one of the major sources of fluctuations in aggregate demand and the major factor that people have to forecast in order to make their own economic choices.

The problems for fiscal policy feedback rules are similar to those for monetary policy but are even more severe because of the lags in the implementation of fiscal policy. The Fed can take actions relatively quickly. But before a fiscal policy action can be taken, the entire legislative process must be completed. Thus even before a fiscal policy action is implemented, the economy may have moved on to a new situation that calls for a different feedback from the one that is in the legislative pipeline.

Predictability of Policies

To make decisions about long-term contracts for employment (wage contracts) and for borrowing and lending, people have to anticipate the future course of prices—the future inflation rate. To forecast the inflation rate, it is necessary to forecast aggregate demand. And to forecast aggregate demand, it is necessary to forecast the policy actions of the government and the Fed.

If the government and the Fed stick to rock-steady, fixed rules for tax rates, spending programs, and money supply growth, then policy itself cannot be a contributor to unexpected fluctuations in aggregate demand.

In contrast, when a feedback rule is being pursued, there is more scope for the policy actions to be unpredictable. The main reason is that feedback rules are not written down for all to see. Rather, they have to be inferred from the behavior of the government and the Fed.

Thus with a feedback-rule policy it is necessary to predict the variables to which the government and Fed react and the extent to which they react. Consequently, a feedback rule for fiscal and monetary policies can create more unpredictable fluctuations in aggregate demand than a fixed rule.

Economists disagree whether those bigger fluctuations offset the potential stabilizing influence of the predictable changes the Fed makes. No agreed measurements have been made to settle this dispute. Nevertheless, the unpredictability of the Fed in its pursuit of feedback-rule policies is an important fact of economic life. And the Fed does not always go out of its way to make its reactions clear. Even in congressional testimony, Federal Reserve Board chairmen are reluctant to make the Fed's actions and intentions entirely plain. (It has been suggested that two former chairmen of the Federal Reserve Board, the pipe-puffing Arthur Burns and the cigar-puffing Paul Volcker, carried their own smokescreens around with them as if to exemplify the mysteriousness and unpredictability of the Fed.)

It is not surprising that the Fed seeks to keep some of its actions behind a smokescreen. First, the Fed wants to maintain as much freedom of action as possible and so does not want to state with too great a precision the feedback rules that it will follow in any given circumstances. Second, the Fed is part of a political process, and, although legally independent of the federal government, it is not immune to subtle influence. For at least these two reasons, the Fed does not specify feedback rules as precisely as the one we've analyzed in this chapter. As a result, the Fed cannot deliver an economic performance that has the stability we generated in the model economy.

To the extent that the Fed's actions are unpredictable, they lead to unpredictable fluctuations in aggregate demand. These fluctuations, in turn, produce fluctuations in real GDP, employment, and unemployment.

If it is difficult for the Fed to pursue a predictable feedback stabilization policy, it is probably impossible for Congress. The stabilization policy of Congress is formulated in terms of spending programs and tax laws. Since these programs and laws are the outcome of a political process that is constrained only by the Constitution, there can be no effective way in which a predictable feedback fiscal policy can be adhered to.

REVIEW

Fixed-rule policies keep fiscal and monetary policy set steady and independent of the state of the economy. Feedback-rule policies cut taxes, increase spending, and speed up money supply growth when the economy is in recession and reverse these measures when the economy is overheating. Feedback rules apparently do a better job, but we are not sure that is the case. Their successful use requires a good knowledge of the current state of the economy, an ability to forecast as far ahead as the policy actions have effects, and clarity and openness about the feedback rules being used. ◆

We have reviewed three reasons why feedback rules might not be more effective than fixed rules in controlling aggregate demand. The evolution of views about aggregate demand stimulation is featured in Our Advancing Knowledge on pp. 438–439. But there is a fourth reason why fixed rules are preferred by some economists—not all shocks to the economy are on the demand side. Advocates of feedback rules believe that most fluctuations do come from aggregate demand. Advocates of fixed rules believe that aggregate supply fluctuations are the dominant ones. Let's now see how aggregate supply fluctuations affect the economy under a fixed rule and a feedback rule. We will also see why those economists who believe that aggregate supply fluctuations are the dominant ones also favor a fixed rather than a feedback rule.

Stabilization Policy and Aggregate Supply Shocks

There are two reasons why aggregate supply fluctuations can cause problems for a stabilization feedback rule:

- Cost-push inflation
- Slowdown in productivity growth

In either of these situations, the economy experiences *stagflation*. Let's study the effects of alternative policies to deal with this problem.

Cost-Push Inflation

Cost-push inflation is inflation that has its origins in cost increases. The two most important potential sources of cost-push inflation are wage increases and increases in raw material prices (such as the increases in the price of oil that occurred in the 1970s and the early 1980s). To proceed, a cost-push inflation must be accommodated by an increase in the money supply—which in turn increases aggregate demand. A monetary policy feedback rule makes cost-push inflation possible. A fixed rule makes such inflation impossible. Let's see why.

Consider the economy that is shown in Fig. 16.7. Aggregate demand is AD_0, short-run aggregate supply is SAS_0, and long-run aggregate supply is LAS. Real GDP is $5 trillion, and the GDP deflator is 100.

Now suppose that a number of labor unions or the key suppliers of an important raw material such as oil try to gain a temporary advantage by increasing the price at which they are willing to sell their services—by increasing wages or by increasing the price of the raw material. To make the exercise interesting, let's suppose that the people in question control a significant portion of the economy. As a consequence, when they increase the wage rate or the price of oil, the short-run aggregate supply curve shifts leftward from SAS_0 to SAS_1.

Fixed Rule Figure 16.7(a) shows what happens if the Fed follows a fixed rule for monetary policy and the government follows a fixed rule for fiscal policy.

FIGURE **16.7**

Stabilization Policy and Aggregate Supply: A Factor Price Increase

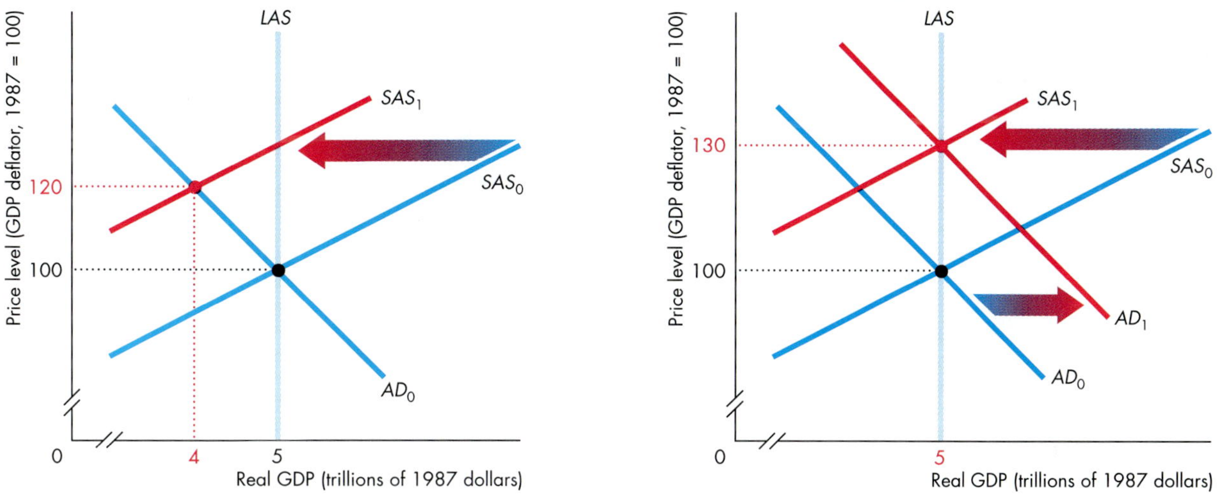

(a) Fixed rule

(b) Feedback rule

The economy starts out on AD_0 and SAS_0, with a GDP deflator of 100 and real GDP of $5 trillion. A labor union (or a key supplier of raw materials) forces up the wage rate (or the price of a raw material), shifting the short-run aggregate supply curve to SAS_1. Real GDP falls to $4 trillion and the GDP deflator increases to 120. With a fixed-rule stabilization policy (part a), the Fed and Congress make no change to aggregate demand. The economy stays depressed until wages (or raw material prices) fall again and the economy returns to its original position. With a feedback rule (part b), the Fed injects additional money and/or Congress cuts taxes or increases spending, increasing aggregate demand to AD_1. Real GDP returns to $5 trillion (full employment), but the GDP deflator increases to 130. The economy is set for another round of cost-push inflation.

Suppose that the fixed rule is for zero money growth and no change in taxes or government purchases of goods and services. With these fixed rules, the Fed and the government pay no attention to the fact that there has been an increase in wages or raw material prices. No policy actions are taken. The short-run aggregate supply curve has shifted to SAS_1, but the aggregate demand curve remains at AD_0. The GDP deflator rises to 120, and real GDP falls to $4 trillion. The economy is experiencing stagflation. Until wages or raw material prices fall, the economy will be depressed and will remain depressed. This decrease in wages or raw material prices may take a long time to come about. Eventually, however, the low level of real GDP will bring lower oil prices and wages—those very prices and wages whose increase caused the initial problem. Eventually, the short-run aggregate supply curve will shift back to SAS_0. The GDP deflator will fall to 100, and real GDP will increase to $5 trillion.

Feedback Rule Figure 16.7(b) shows what happens if the Fed and the government operate monetary and fiscal policy feedback rules. The starting point is the same as before—the economy is on SAS_0 and AD_0 with a GDP deflator of 100 and real GDP of $5 trillion. Wages or raw material prices increase, and the short-run aggregate supply curve shifts to SAS_1. The economy goes into a recession with real GDP falling to $4 trillion and the price level increasing to 120. The monetary feedback rule is to increase the money supply growth rate when real GDP is below its long-run level. And the fiscal feedback rule is to cut taxes and increase government purchases when real GDP is below its long-run level. So, with real GDP at $4 trillion, the Fed pumps up

EVOLVING Approaches TO ECONOMIC STABILIZATION

When it comes to stabilizing the economy, people differ in their opinions about what's best. But there was a time when you would have been hard pressed to find an economist who did not believe that active measures taken by a well-informed government could make the market economy function more smoothly. That time was the early 1960s, when President John F. Kennedy was in the White House.

Using the expenditure multiplier model (of Chapter 9), economists believed that setting the levels of government purchases and taxes at the appropriate levels would allow continuous full employment, and steady economic expansion could be maintained indefinitely.

The practice of active stabilization policy worked well until the mid-1960s, but then inflation began to creep upward. Advocates of activist policies blame the Vietnam War and President Lyndon Johnson's unwillingness to finance the war with tax increases. Opponents of activism blame the activist policies themselves, claiming that once an activist policy is anticipated, its effects on output are weak and its main effects are on inflation.

Whichever view is correct, activist policies came into official disrepute during the 1970s, when oil price hikes left no doubt that the main problem (at least for the time being) was not demand fluctuations, but supply shocks. Distrust of activist stabilization became particularly strong during President Ronald Reagan's administration when the prevailing view was that government should set the rules of the game and leave the private sector to get on with the creation of jobs and wealth.

The recession of 1991 saw a return to a more pragmatic approach with attempts to stimulate demand by lowering interest rates, but not too aggressively, especially with such a large and persistent federal deficit. If and when the deficit subsides, there is likely to be renewed enthusiasm for more ambitious fiscal policies to stimulate demand during recessions.

"You have to find a real crackpot to get an economist who doesn't accept the principle of government intervention in the business cycle."

KENNETH ARROW
Time, March 3, 1961

The accumulation of economic data and the development of statistical models of the economy gave a strong boost of confidence to President Kennedy's economic advisors—Kermit Gordon, James Tobin, and Walter Heller. Said Heller, "We simply know a whole lot more about where we are than we ever did before." Using their models and best judgments about where the economy was and where it was heading, Kennedy's economists worked out a program of tax cuts and spending changes designed to keep the economy expanding but with low inflation and high employment.

Today, even in a recession, there is little talk of cutting taxes and increasing spending to lift the economy back to full employment. Instead, people worry about the scale of the deficit. When Budget Director Richard Darman testifies before the Senate, a graph showing the projected decline of the deficit has become a mandatory part of the presentation. But in contrast to the optimism of the projections, the deficit persists, limiting the range of maneuver for fiscal policy. Tax increases and spending cuts would lower the deficit but might intensify the recession. Tax cuts or spending increases would make the deficit higher but might not bring economic recovery. Instead, with a larger deficit, interest rates might rise—bringing a decline in investment.

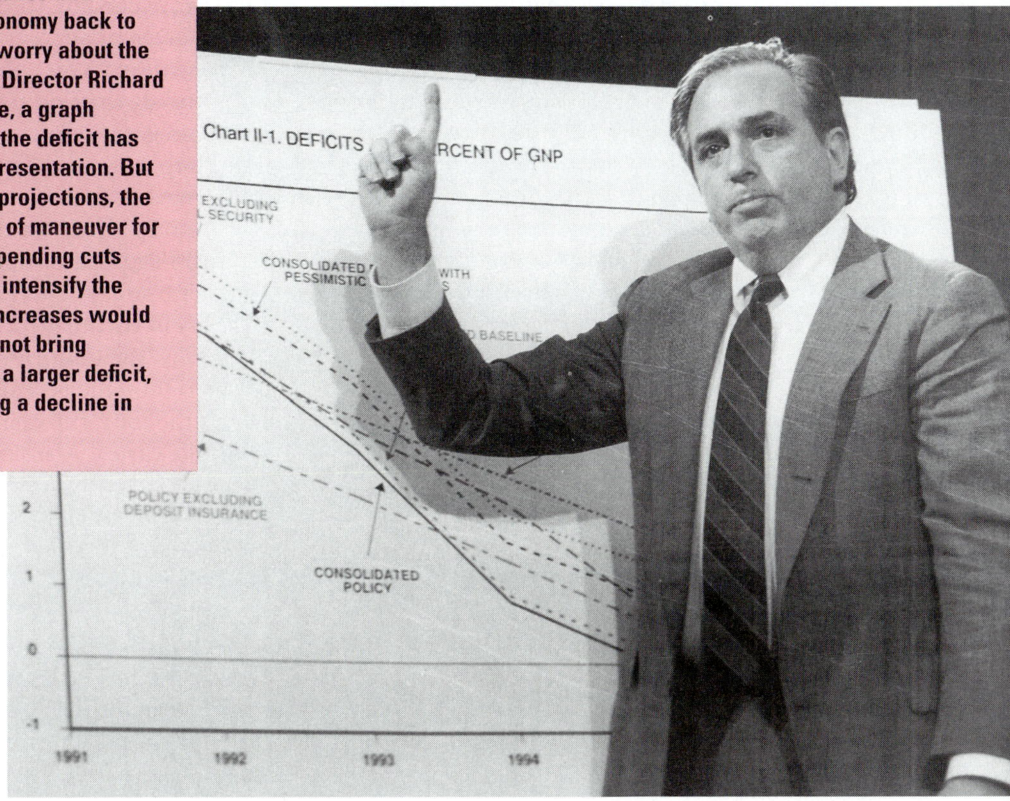

Milton Friedman Versus the Keynesians: The *Rise and Fall of Fine-Tuning*

From 1946 to 1983, Milton Friedman, now a Senior Fellow at the Hoover Institution at Stanford University, was one of the leading members of the Chicago School. This approach to economics was developed at the University of Chicago and based on the views that free markets allocate resources efficiently and that stable and low money supply growth delivers macroeconomic stability. In the early 1960s, these views were in a distinct minority, and many economists placed them in the "crackpot" category. By reasoning from basic economic principles, Friedman predicted that persistent demand stimulation would not increase output but would cause inflation. When output growth slowed and inflation broke out in the 1970s, Friedman seemed like a prophet, and for a time, his policy prescription—known as monetarism—was embraced around the world.

the money supply growth rate, Congress passes a tax cut bill and a series of bills that increase spending, and the aggregate demand curve shifts to AD_1. The price level increases to 130, and real GDP returns to $5 trillion. The economy moves back to full employment but at a higher price level.

The unionized workers or the raw material suppliers, who saw an advantage in forcing up their wages or prices before, see the same advantage again. Thus the short-run aggregate supply curve shifts up once more, and the Fed and the government chase it with increases in aggregate demand. The economy is in a freewheeling inflation.

Incentives to Push Up Factor Prices You can see that there are no checks on the incentives to push up factor prices if the Fed pursues a feedback rule of the type that we've just analyzed. If some group sees a temporary gain from pushing up the price at which it is selling its resources and if the Fed and the government always accommodate to prevent unemployment and slack business conditions from emerging, then cost-push elements will have a free rein.

But when the Fed and the government pursue fixed-rule policies, the incentive to attempt to steal a temporary advantage by increasing wages or prices is severely weakened. The cost of higher unemployment and lower output is a consequence that each group will have to face and recognize.

Thus a fixed rule is capable of delivering a steady inflation rate (or even zero inflation), while a feedback rule, in the face of cost-push pressures, will leave the inflation rate free to rise and fall at the whim of whichever group believes a temporary advantage to be available from pushing up its wage or price.

Slowdown in Productivity Growth

Some economists believe that fluctuations in real GDP (and in employment and unemployment) are caused by fluctuations in productivity growth. These economists have developed a new theory of aggregate fluctuations called real business cycle theory. **Real business cycle theory** is a theory of aggregate fluctuations based on flexible wages and random shocks to the economy's aggregate production function. The word *real* draws attention to the idea that it is real things—random shocks to the economy's real production possibilities—rather than nominal things—the money supply and its rate of growth—that are, according to that theory, the most important sources of aggregate fluctuations.

According to real business cycle theory, there is no useful distinction to be made between the long-run aggregate supply curve and the short-run aggregate supply curve. Because wages are flexible, the labor market is always in equilibrium and unemployment is always at its natural rate. The vertical long-run aggregate supply curve is also the short-run aggregate supply curve. Fluctuations occur because of shifts in the long-run aggregate supply curve. Normally, the long-run aggregate supply curve shifts to the right—the economy expands. But the pace at which the long-run aggregate supply curve shifts to the right varies. Also, on occasion, the long-run aggregate supply curve shifts to the left, bringing a decrease in aggregate supply and a fall in real GDP.

Economic policy that influences aggregate demand has no effect on real GDP. But it does affect the price level. However, if a feedback-rule policy is used to increase aggregate demand every time real GDP falls, and if the real business cycle theory is correct, the feedback-rule policy will make price level fluctuations more severe than they otherwise would be. To see why, consider Fig. 16.8.

Imagine that the economy starts out on aggregate demand curve AD_0 and long-run aggregate supply curve LAS_0 at a GDP deflator of 100 and with real GDP equal to $5 trillion. Now suppose that the long-run aggregate supply curve shifts to LAS_1. An actual decrease in long-run aggregate supply can occur as a result of a severe drought or other natural catastrophe or perhaps as the result of a disruption of international trade such as the OPEC embargo of the 1970s.

Fixed Rule With a fixed rule, the fall in long-run aggregate supply has no effect on the Fed or the government and no effect on aggregate demand. The aggregate demand curve remains AD_0. Real GDP falls to $4 trillion, and the GDP deflator increases to 120.

Feedback Rule Now suppose that the Fed and the government use feedback rules. In particular, suppose that when real GDP falls, the Fed increases the money supply and Congress enacts a tax cut to increase aggregate demand. In this example, the money supply and tax cut shift the aggregate demand curve to AD_1. The policy goal is to bring

FIGURE 16.8

Stabilization Policy and Aggregate Supply: A Decrease in Productivity

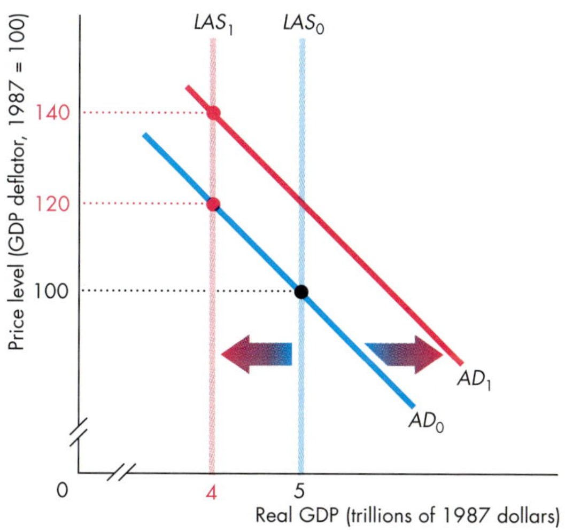

A decrease in productivity shifts the long-run aggregate supply curve from LAS_0 to LAS_1. Real GDP falls to $4 trillion, and the GDP deflator rises to 120. With a fixed rule, there is no change in the money supply, taxes, or government spending, so aggregate demand stays at AD_0, and that is the end of the matter. With a feedback rule, the Fed increases the money supply and/or Congress cuts taxes or increases spending, intending to increase real GDP. Aggregate demand moves to AD_1, but the long-run result is an increase in the price level—the GDP deflator rises to 140—with no change in real GDP.

real GDP back to $5 trillion. But the long-run aggregate supply curve has shifted, and so long-run real GDP has decreased to $4 trillion. The increase in aggregate demand cannot bring forth an increase in output if the economy does not have the capacity to produce that output. So real GDP stays at $4 trillion, but the price level rises still further—the GDP deflator goes to 140. You can see that in this case the attempt to stabilize real GDP by using a feedback-rule policy has no effect on real GDP but generates a substantial price level increase.

We've now seen some of the shortcomings of using feedback rules for stabilization policy. Some economists believe that these shortcomings are serious and want to constrain Congress and the Fed so that they use fixed rules. Others, regarding the potential advantages of feedback rules as greater than their costs, advocate the continued use of such policies but with an important modification that we'll now look at.

Nominal GDP Targeting

Attempting to keep the growth rate of nominal GDP steady is called **nominal GDP targeting.** James Tobin of Yale University and John Taylor of Stanford University have suggested that nominal GDP targeting is a useful operating goal for macroeconomic policy.

The nominal GDP growth equals the real GDP growth rate plus the inflation rate. When nominal GDP grows quickly, it is usually because the inflation rate is high. When nominal GDP grows slowly, it is usually because real GDP growth is negative—the economy is in recession. Thus if nominal GDP growth is kept steady, the excesses of both inflation and recession might be avoided.

Nominal GDP targeting uses feedback rules. Expansionary fiscal and/or monetary actions increase aggregate demand when nominal GDP is below target, and contractionary fiscal and/or monetary actions decrease aggregate demand when nominal GDP is above target. The main problem with nominal GDP targeting is that there are long and variable time lags between the identification of a need to change aggregate demand and the effects of the policy actions taken.

Macroeconomists are still debating the merits of the alternative policies for achieving stability. But they are gradually arriving at a new consensus about what can be achieved.

Taming Inflation

So far, we've concentrated on stabilizing real GDP either directly or indirectly and *avoiding* inflation. But often the problem is not to avoid inflation but to tame it. How can inflation, once it has set in, be cured? Let's look at some alternative ways.

A Surprise Inflation Reduction

To study the problem of lowering inflation, we'll use two equivalent approaches, aggregate demand–aggregate supply and the Phillips curve. You met the Phillips curve in Chapter 14 (pp. 386–389), and it enables us to keep track of what is happening to both inflation and unemployment.

The economy is shown in Fig. 16.9. In part (a), it is on aggregate demand curve AD_0 and short-run aggregate supply curve SAS_0 with real GDP at $5 trillion and the GDP deflator at 100. With real GDP at its long-run level (on the *LAS* curve), there is full employment. Equivalently, in part (b), the economy is on its long-run Phillips curve *LRPC* and short-run Phillips curve $SRPC_0$. Inflation is raging at 10 percent a year, and unemployment is at its natural rate.

Next year, aggregate demand is *expected* to increase, shifting the aggregate demand curve in Fig. 16.9(a) to AD_1. Expecting this increase in aggregate demand, wages increase to shift the short-run aggregate supply curve to SAS_1. If expectations are fulfilled, the GDP deflator rises to 110 (10 percent inflation), real GDP remains at its long-run level, and unemployment remains at its natural rate.

But suppose the Fed tries to slow down inflation to 4 percent a year. If it simply slows down the growth of aggregate demand, the aggregate demand curve (in part a) shifts to AD_2. With no slowdown in the expected inflation rate, wage increases shift the short-run aggregate supply curve to SAS_1. Real GDP decreases to $4 trillion, and the GDP deflator rises to 108—an inflation rate of 8 percent a year. In Fig. 16.9(b), there is a movement along the short-run

FIGURE 16.9

Lowering Inflation

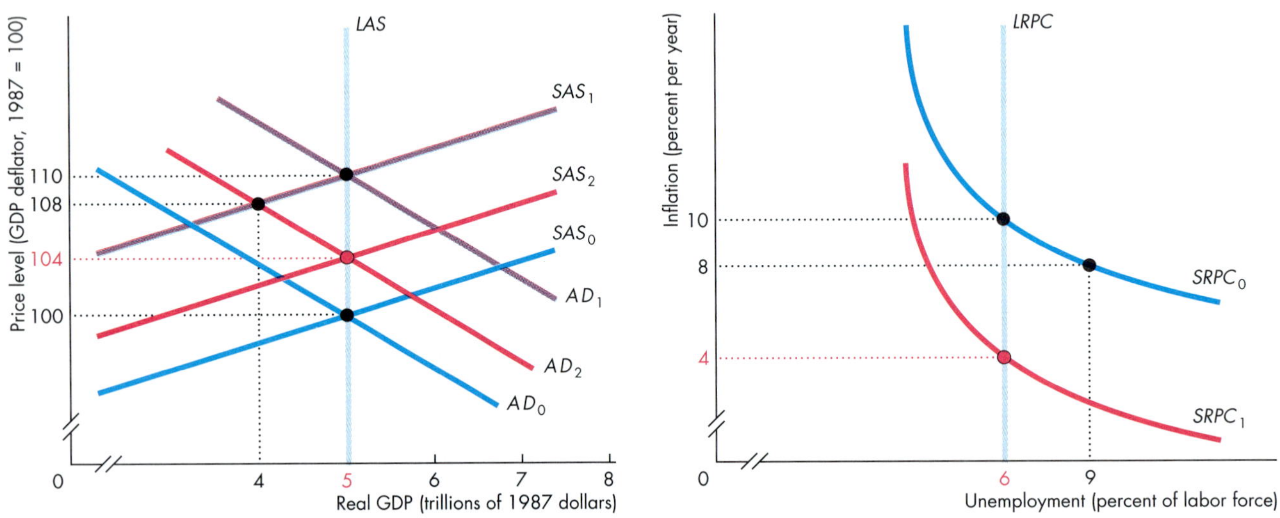

(a) Aggregate demand and aggregate supply

(b) Phillips curves

Initially, aggregate demand is AD_0, and short-run aggregate supply is SAS_0. Real GDP is $5 trillion (its full-employment level on the long-run aggregate supply curve *LAS*). Inflation is proceeding at 10 percent a year. If it continues to do so, the aggregate demand curve shifts to AD_1 and the short-run aggregate supply curve shifts to SAS_1. The GDP deflator rises to 110. This same situation is shown in part (b) with the economy on the short-run Phillips curve $SRPC_0$.

With an unexpected slowdown in aggregate demand growth, the aggregate demand curve (part a) shifts to AD_2, real GDP falls to $4 trillion, and inflation slows to 8 percent (a GDP deflator of 108). In part (b), unemployment rises to 9 percent as the economy slides down $SRPC_0$.

If a credibly announced slowdown in aggregate demand growth occurs, the short-run aggregate supply curve (part a) shifts to SAS_2, the short-run Phillips curve (part b) shifts to $SRPC_1$, inflation slows to 4 percent, real GDP remains at $5 trillion, and unemployment remains at its natural rate of 6 percent.

Phillips curve $SRPC_0$ as unemployment rises to 9 percent and inflation falls to 8 percent a year. The policy has succeeded in slowing inflation but by less than desired and at a cost of recession. Real GDP is below its long-run level, and unemployment is above its natural rate.

A Credibly Announced Inflation Reduction

Suppose that instead of simply slowing down the growth of aggregate demand, the Fed announced its intention ahead of its action and in a credible and convincing way so that its announcement was believed. The lower level of aggregate demand becomes expected. In this case, wages increase at a pace consistent with the lower level of aggregate demand, and the short-run aggregate supply curve (in Fig. 16.9a) shifts to SAS_2. When aggregate demand increases, shifting the aggregate demand curve to AD_2, the GDP deflator rises to 104—an inflation rate of 4 percent a year—and real GDP remains at its full-employment level.

In Fig. 16.9(b), the lower expected inflation rate shifts the short-run Phillips curve downward to $SRPC_1$, and inflation falls to 4 percent a year while unemployment remains at its natural rate.

Inflation Reduction in Practice

When the Fed in fact slowed down inflation in 1981, we all paid a very high price. The Fed's monetary policy action was unpredicted. As a result, it occurred in the face of wages that had been set at too high a level to be consistent with the growth of aggregate demand that the Fed subsequently allowed. The consequence was recession—a decrease in real GDP and a rise in unemployment. Couldn't the Fed have lowered inflation without causing recession by telling people far enough ahead of time that it did indeed plan to slow down the growth rate of aggregate demand?

The answer appears to be no. The main reason is that people form their expectation of the Fed's action (as they form expectations about anyone's actions) on the basis of actual behavior, not on the basis of stated intentions. How many times have you told yourself that it is your firm intention to take off ten unwanted pounds or to keep within the budget and put a few dollars away for a rainy day, only to discover that, despite your very best intentions, your old habits win out in the end?

Forming expectations about the Fed's behavior is no different except, of course, it is more complex than forecasting your own behavior. To form expectations of the Fed's actions, people look at the Fed's past *actions,* not its stated intentions. On the basis of such observations—called Fed-watching—they try to work out what the Fed's policy is, to forecast its future actions, and to forecast the effects of those actions on aggregate demand and inflation.

A Truly Independent Fed

One suggestion for dealing with inflation is to make the Fed more independent and to charge it with the single responsibility of achieving and maintaining price level stability. Some central banks are more independent than the Fed. The German and Swiss central banks are the best examples. Another example is the New Zealand central bank. All these central banks have the responsibility of stabilizing prices but not real GDP and of doing so without interference from the government.

If an arrangement could be devised for making the Fed take a longer-term view concentrated only on inflation, it is possible that inflation could be lowered and kept low at a low cost.

REVIEW

Usually, when inflation is tamed, a recession results. The reason is that people form their expectation about policy on the basis of past policy actions. A more independent Fed pursuing only price stability could possibly achieve price stability with greater credibility and at lower cost. ◆

◆ ◆ ◆ ◆ We've now examined the main issues of stabilization policy. We've looked at the goals of stabilization policy, at the effects of the economy on political popularity, and at the fiscal and monetary policies pursued. We've seen how fixed and feedback rules operate under differing assumptions about the behavior of the economy and why economists take different views on using these rules. We've also seen why lowering inflation usually is accompanied by recession. ◆ ◆ In the next chapter, we examine what many people believe is our economy's single most serious policy problem—the government's budget deficit.

SUMMARY

The Stabilization Problem

The stabilization problem is to keep the growth rate of real GDP steady and keep inflation low and predictable. (pp. 423–424)

Players and Policies

The key macroeconomic policy players are Congress, the Federal Reserve Board, and the administration.

Macroeconomic policy is influenced by the effects of macroeconomic performance on votes in congressional and presidential elections. Both fiscal policy and monetary policy have a cycle that creates a political business cycle.

Fixed-rule policies (such as a constant growth rate of the money supply) are those that do not respond to the state of the economy. Feedback-rule policies do respond to the state of the economy, stimulating activity in recession and holding activity in check in time of inflation. (pp. 424–431)

Stabilization Policy and Aggregate Demand Shocks

In the face of an aggregate demand shock, a fixed-rule policy takes no action to counter the shock. It permits aggregate demand to fluctuate as a result of all the independent forces that influence it. As a result, there are fluctuations in real GDP and the price level. A feedback-rule policy adjusts taxes, government purchases, or the money supply to offset the effects of other influences on aggregate demand. An ideal feedback rule keeps the economy at full employment with stable prices.

Some economists argue that feedback rules make the economy less stable because they require greater knowledge of the state of the economy than we have, operate with time lags that extend beyond the forecast horizon, and introduce unpredictability about policy reactions. (pp. 432–436)

Stabilization Policy and Aggregate Supply Shocks

Two main aggregate supply shocks generate stabilization problems: cost-push inflation and a slowdown in productivity growth. A fixed rule minimizes the threat of and the problems associated with cost-push inflation. A feedback rule reinforces cost-push inflation and leaves the price level and inflation rate free to move to wherever they are pushed. If productivity growth slows down, a fixed rule results in lower output (and higher unemployment) and a higher price level. A feedback rule that increases the money supply or cuts taxes to stimulate aggregate demand results in an even higher price level and higher inflation. Output (and unemployment) follows the same course as with a fixed rule. (pp. 436–441)

Taming Inflation

Inflation can be tamed, at little or no cost in terms of lost output or excessive unemployment, by slowing the growth of aggregate demand in a credible and predictable way. But usually, when inflation is slowed down, a recession occurs. The reason is that people form their expectation about policy on the basis of actual behavior, by looking at past actions, not by believing announced intentions. (pp. 441–443)

KEY ELEMENTS

Key Terms

Federal budget, 424
Feedback rule, 431
Fixed rule, 430
Nominal GDP targeting, 441
Political business cycle, 427
Real business cycle theory, 440

Key Figures

REVIEW QUESTIONS

1 What are the goals of macroeconomic stabilization policy?

2 Describe the key players that formulate and execute macroeconomic policy. Explain the interaction between these players.

3 What is a political business cycle? Explain the evidence for a political business cycle in the United States since 1960.

4 Explain the distinction between a fixed-rule policy and a feedback-rule policy.

5 Analyze the effects of a temporary decrease in aggregate demand if a fixed rule is employed.

6 Analyze the behavior of real GDP and the price level in the face of a permanent decrease in aggregate demand under:

a A fixed rule
b A feedback rule

7 Why do economists disagree with each other on the appropriateness of fixed and feedback rules?

8 Explain the main problems in using fiscal policy for stabilizing the economy.

9 Analyze the effects of a rise in the price of oil on real GDP and the price level if the Fed employs:

a A fixed monetary rule
b A feedback monetary rule

10 Explain nominal GDP targeting and why it reduces real GDP fluctuations and inflation.

11 Explain why the Fed's credibility affects the cost of lowering inflation.

PROBLEMS

1 The economy is experiencing 10 percent inflation and 7 percent unemployment. Set out policies for the Fed and Congress to pursue that will lower both inflation and unemployment. Explain how and why your proposed policies will work.

2 The economy is booming, and inflation is beginning to rise, but it is widely agreed that a massive recession is just around the corner. Weigh the advantages and disadvantages of Congress pursuing a fixed-rule and a feedback-rule fiscal policy.

3 The economy is in a recession, and inflation is falling. It is widely agreed that a strong recovery is just around the corner. Weigh the advantages and disadvantages of the Fed pursuing a fixed-rule and a feedback-rule monetary policy.

4 You have been hired by the president to draw up an economic plan that will maximize the chance of his being re-elected.

a What are the macroeconomic stabilization policy elements in that plan?
b What do you have to make the economy do in an election year?
c What policy actions would help the president achieve his objectives?

(In dealing with this problem, be careful to take into account the effects of your proposed policy on expectations and the effects of those expectations on actual economic performance.)

CHAPTER 17

THE DEFICIT

After studying this chapter, you will be able to:

- Explain why, during the past decade, the federal government spent more each year than it raised in taxes
- Distinguish between debt and the deficit
- Distinguish between the *nominal* deficit and the *real* deficit
- Explain why the deficit appears to be larger than it really is
- Describe the different means available for financing the deficit
- Explain why the deficit makes the Fed's job harder
- Explain why a deficit can cause inflation
- Explain why a deficit can be a burden on future generations
- Describe the measures that are being taken to eliminate the deficit

Spendthrift Uncle Sam

EVERY SINGLE YEAR SINCE 1970, THE FEDERAL government has spent more than it collected in taxes. In 1992, its deficit was $300 billion. In 1983, the total debt of the federal government was just over $1 trillion. Ten years later it stood at $3 trillion. Why does the federal government have a deficit and growing debt? Is the deficit really as large as it appears? How can we gauge the size of the deficit when the value of money is steadily falling because of inflation? ◆◆ Some countries, such as Bolivia, Chile, Brazil, and Israel, have had large government deficits and runaway inflation. Do these experiences mean that the United States will eventually be the victim of rapid inflation? Does the deficit somehow make it harder, or even impossible, for the Fed to control the money supply and keep inflation in check? ◆◆ When we incur a personal debt, we accept a self-imposed obligation. When the nation incurs a debt, it imposes an obligation on its taxpayers. But the obligation does not end with the current taxpayers. It is passed on to their children and grandchildren. Does a government deficit impose a burden on future generations? ◆◆ There are two ways in which we can approach any problem: pretend it doesn't exist or try to identify its nature and solve it. How are we approaching the deficit? Are we sticking our heads in the sand like ostriches, or are we taking steps that are likely to eliminate the deficit? What are the prospects for the future of the deficit?

◆ ◆ ◆ ◆ In this chapter, we're going to study what became perhaps the hottest economic topic of the 1980s and remains a hot topic today. We're going to examine the origins of the deficit, gauge its true scale, and explain why deficits are feared and why they constitute a problem. We'll also discuss some of the measures that are being taken to eliminate the deficit. Because the deficit is a hot economic and political topic, the public debate on it has generated more heat and smoke than light. In this chapter, we'll clear away some of the rhetorical smoke, lower the temperature, and try to answer the questions posed above. By the time you're through with this chapter, you'll be able to explain what the deficit is all about.

The Sources of the Deficit

What exactly is the deficit? The federal government's **budget balance** is equal to its total tax revenue minus its total expenditure in a given period of time (normally a year). Thus the government's budget balance is

$$\text{Budget balance} = \text{Revenue} - \text{Expenditure}.$$

The government's revenue consists of various types of taxes. Its expenditure is the sum of government purchases of goods and services, transfer payments, and interest on debt. If revenue exceeds expenditure, the budget balance is positive and the federal government has a **budget surplus.** If expenditure exceeds revenue, the budget balance is negative and the federal government has a **budget deficit.** If the budget balance is zero, in other words, if tax revenue and expenditure are equal, the government has a **balanced budget.**

Government debt is the total amount of borrowing that the government has undertaken and the total amount that it owes to households, firms, and foreigners. Government debt is a stock. It is the accumulation of all the past deficits minus all the past surpluses. Thus if the government has a deficit, its debt is increasing. If the government has a surplus, its debt is decreasing. If the government has a balanced budget, its debt is constant.

The Federal Budget since 1975

Figure 17.1 shows the federal government's revenue, expenditure, and deficit since 1975. As the figure

FIGURE 17.1

The Deficit

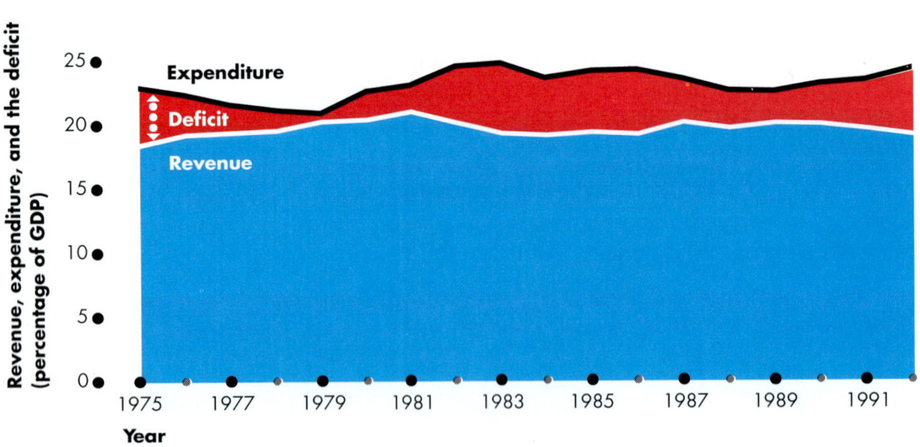

The figure records revenue, expenditure, and the deficit from 1975 to 1992. The deficit was small and falling in the 1970s but became large and persistent during the 1980s. The deficit arose from a combination of a decline in revenue and an increase in spending.

Source: Economic Report of the President, 1993.

illustrates, throughout this period the U.S. federal government had a budget deficit. The deficit was small and falling between 1975 and 1979, and in 1979 the budget was almost balanced. The deficit then climbed to a peak of 5.3 percent of GDP in 1983. It declined from 1983 through 1989 but averaged more than 3½ percent of GDP through the entire decade. The deficit climbed again in the 1991 recession and kept rising in 1992.

The effect of the deficit on the government's debt is shown in Fig. 17.2. So that you can see the government's debt over a slightly longer perspective, this figure begins in 1960. As you can see, federal government debt declined as a percentage of GDP through 1974. The ratio of debt to GDP in this year stood at its lowest point since World War II. The debt-to-GDP ratio increased slightly in the late 1970s and dramatically between 1981 and 1986. In the late 1980s, its growth continued but at a more moderate rate. It grew quickly again in the 1991 recession.

Why did the government deficit grow in the early 1980s and remain high? The immediate answer is that expenditure increased and revenue declined. But which components of expenditure increased and which sources of revenue decreased? Let's answer these questions by looking at revenue and expenditure in a bit more detail.

FIGURE **17.2**

The Government Debt

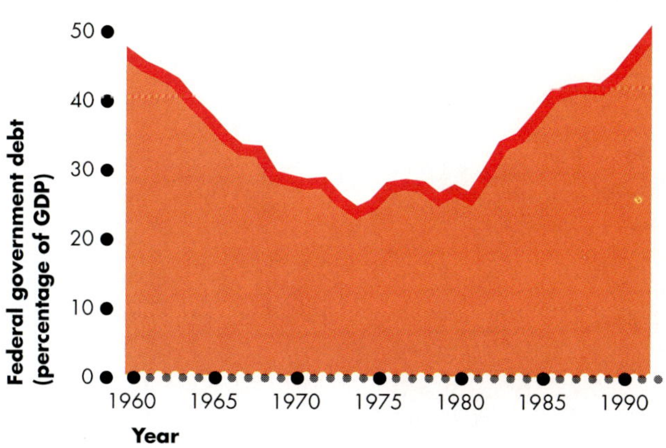

Government debt (the accumulation of past deficits less past surpluses) declined through 1974 but then started to move upward. After a further brief decline in the late 1970s, it exploded in the 1980s.

Source: Economic Report of the President, 1993.

Federal Government Revenue There are four broad categories of federal government revenue:

- Personal income taxes
- Corporate income taxes
- Indirect taxes
- Social insurance contributions

Personal income taxes are the taxes paid by individuals on their labor and capital incomes. Corporate income taxes are the taxes that companies pay on their profits. Indirect taxes are taxes on the goods and services that we buy and include the customs duties that we pay when we import goods from other countries. Social insurance contributions are the taxes paid by employees and employers to finance social security programs such as Medicare and unemployment insurance.

Figure 17.3(a) shows the levels and fluctuations in these taxes and in total taxes between 1975 and 1992. As you can see, total taxes increased as a percentage of GDP between 1975 and 1981 but then declined through 1986. Most of the decline was in corporate and personal income taxes and resulted from the Economic Recovery Tax Act of 1981. Indirect taxes and social insurance contributions remained relatively stable as percentages of GDP.

Federal Government Expenditure We will examine federal government expenditure by dividing it into three categories:

- Purchases of goods and services
- Transfer payments
- Debt interest payments

The main item in the federal government's shopping basket is the purchase of goods and services for national defense. Other purchases of goods and services include items such as law and order and interstate highways. Transfer payments include payments of social security and welfare benefits to households and subsidies to farms and other producers. Debt interest payments are the amounts paid by the government to the holders of its bonds—its outstanding debt.

FIGURE 17.3

Federal Government Revenue and Expenditure

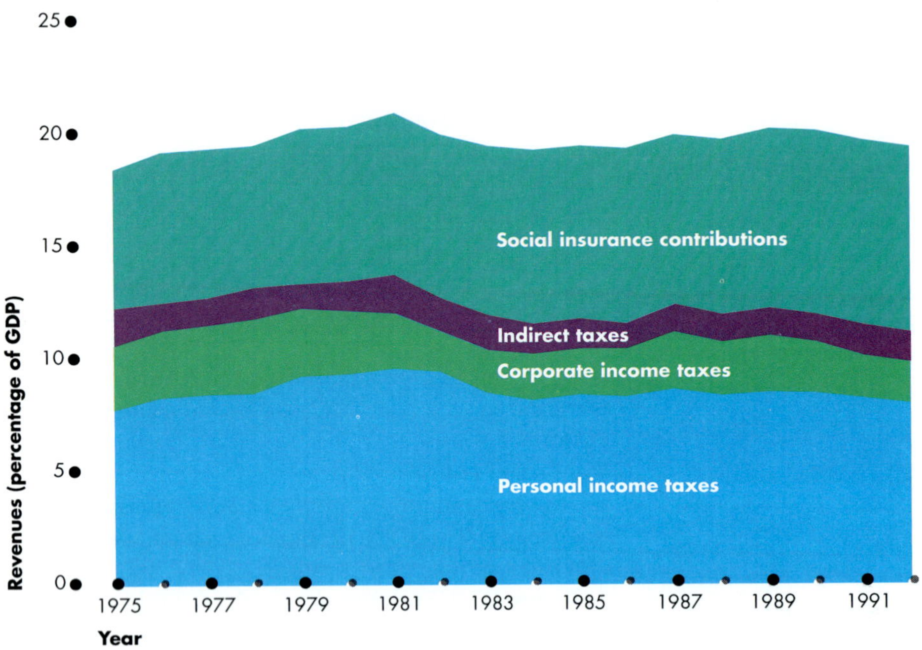

(a) Revenues

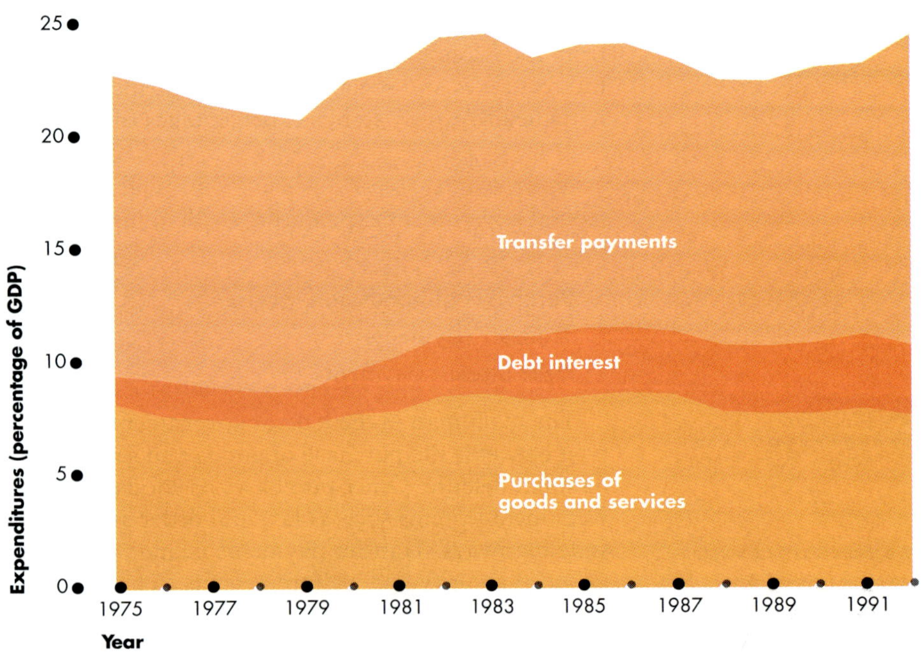

(b) Expenditures

The four categories of federal government revenue shown in part (a) are personal income taxes, corporate income taxes, indirect taxes, and social insurance contributions. Personal and corporate income taxes declined during the early 1980s. The other two revenue components remained steady.

The three categories of federal government expenditure shown in part (b) are purchases of goods and services, debt interest, and transfer payments. Purchases of goods and services have fluctuated but not increased. Transfer payments have fluctuated most and increased especially in the early 1980s. Debt interest has increased steadily as the deficit has fed on itself.

Source: Economic Report of the President, 1993.

Figure 17.3(b) shows the levels and fluctuations in these components of expenditure and in total expenditure between 1975 and 1992. As you can see, total expenditure decreased between 1975 and 1979 but increased between 1979 and 1983. It then declined slightly through 1989 before increasing again. Both the purchase of goods and services and transfer payments fluctuated. But the item that increased most persistently was debt interest. Once a persistent deficit had emerged, that deficit began to feed on itself. The deficit led to increased borrowing; increased borrowing led to higher interest payments; and higher interest payments led to a larger deficit. That is the story of the rising deficit of the 1980s.

A Personal Analogy Perhaps you will see more clearly why the deficit feeds on itself if you think in more personal terms. Suppose that each year you spend more than you earn. Suppose that you keep on doing this. Your debt, let's say at the bank, rises each year. Therefore, you owe the bank more in interest each year as a result of having a bigger debt outstanding. The government is in exactly the same situation. But the government doesn't just borrow from banks. It borrows from anyone who buys the bonds that it issues—households, firms, the Fed, and foreigners. The government has been running a large deficit throughout the 1980s and early 1990s so its outstanding debt has been rising and the interest payments on that debt have also been rising.

The Deficit and the Business Cycle

There is an important relationship between the size of the deficit and the stage of the business cycle through which the economy is passing. This relationship is illustrated in Fig. 17.4. This figure tracks the deficit against the business cycle—measured as the percentage deviations of real GDP from trend. As you can see, the deficit follows the business cycle. The years in which the deficit is especially large are years of severe recession—the OPEC recession of 1975, the Volcker recession of 1981 to 1982, and the 1990–1991 recession.

FIGURE 17.4

The Business Cycle and the Deficit

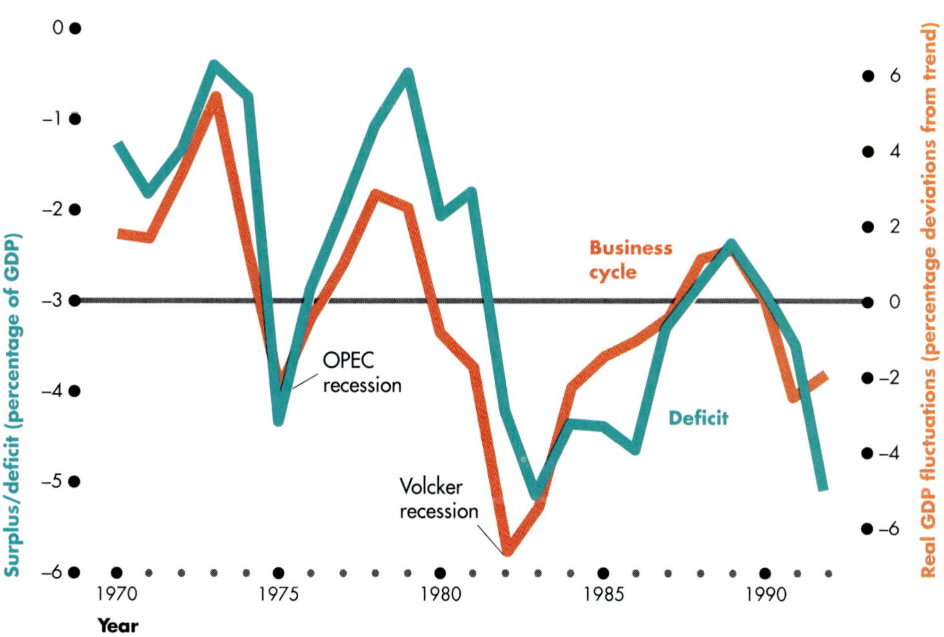

The business cycle—real GDP fluctuations—and the deficit move together. A recession leads to lower taxes, higher transfer payments, and a higher deficit. A recovery leads to higher taxes, lower transfer payments, and a lower deficit.

Source: Economic Report of the President, 1993.

Why does the deficit become larger when the economy goes into recession? Part of the answer lies on the expenditure side and part on the tax revenue side of the government's account. The scale of government expenditure and tax revenue depends on the state of the economy. The government passes tax laws defining tax *rates*, not *dollars* to be paid in taxes. As a consequence, the tax revenue that the government collects depends on the level of income: if the economy is in a recovery phase of the business cycle, tax collections rise; if the economy is in a recession phase of the business cycle, tax collections fall.

Spending programs behave similarly. Many government programs are related to the state of well-being of individual citizens and firms. For example, when the economy is in a recession, unemployment is high, economic hardship from poverty increases, and a larger number of firms and farms experience hard times. Government transfer payments increase to respond to the increased economic hardship. When the economy experiences boom conditions, expenditure on programs to compensate for economic hardship declines.

In light of both of these factors, the deficit rises when the economy is in a depressed state and falls when the economy is in a state of boom. In order to take into account these facts, economists have developed a modified deficit concept called the cyclically adjusted deficit. The **cyclically adjusted deficit** is the deficit that would occur if the economy were at full employment. To measure the cyclically adjusted deficit, we calculate what tax revenue and expenditures would be if the economy were at full employment.

The formula established by the Department of Commerce for determining the effect of the business cycle on the deficit has two key elements:[1]

- Each 1 percentage point increase in the unemployment rate increases the federal deficit by $30 billion.
- Each $100 billion decrease in current GDP increases the deficit by $35 billion.

[1]Thomas M. Holloway, "The Economy in the Federal Budget: Guides to the Automatic Effects," *Survey of Current Business* 64, 7 (July 1984): 102–5.

The Deficit in Recovery From 1982 to 1989, the economy was in a prolonged and strong recovery. According to the formula for calculating the effect of the business cycle on the deficit, the deficit should have fallen dramatically through these years. But it did not. It persisted at around 3 percent of GDP, and the persistence of a large deficit, even in the face of strong economic recovery, led some observers to express grave concern about the potential effects of an ongoing deficit on the long-term health of the economy.

The Deficit in the 1991 Recession During the 1991 recession, the deficit predictably increased as the growth of tax revenues slowed and spending on unemployment benefits and social programs increased. The deficit climbed from 2½ percent of GDP in 1989 to 3 percent of GDP in 1990 and 3½ percent of GDP in 1991.

Reading Between the Lines on pp. 454–455 looks at President Clinton's actions to reduce the deficit and highlights the role of continued economic expansion in generating the revenues needed to achieve the president's deficit reduction targets.

REVIEW

The federal deficit grew in the early 1980s because expenditure increased and tax revenue decreased. Because the deficit persisted, debt and interest increased and the deficit fed on itself. A higher deficit led to higher debt, which in turn led to higher interest payments and a yet higher deficit. The deficit is related to the business cycle. Other things being equal, the stronger the economy, the lower is the deficit. When the economy went into recession in 1991, the deficit climbed to 3½ percent of GDP. ◆

We've seen when and how the deficit emerged and how it relates to the business cycle. We've also seen that the deficit is not only large but persistent. But is the deficit really as bad as it looks? Can it really be true that in eight years government debt increased by more than in the entire previous history of the nation? These are important questions to which we'll now turn our attention.

The Real Deficit

Inflation distorts many things, not least of which is the deficit. To remove the inflationary distortion from the measured deficit, we need a concept of the real deficit. The **real deficit** is the change in the real value of outstanding government debt. The real value of outstanding government debt is equal to the market value of the debt divided by the price level. We are going to see how we can calculate the real deficit and how such a calculation changes our view of the size of the government's deficit. But before we do that, let's consider real deficits in more personal terms by examining the real deficit of a family.

The Real Deficit of a Family

In 1960, a young couple (perhaps your parents) ran a deficit to buy a new house. The deficit took the form of a mortgage. The amount borrowed to cover the deficit—the difference between the cost of the house and what the family had available to put down as a deposit—was $30,000. Today, the children of that couple are buying their first house. To do so, they also are incurring a deficit. But they're borrowing $120,000 to buy their first house. Is the $120,000 deficit (mortgage) of the 1990 house-buyer really four times as big as the deficit (mortgage) of the 1960 house-buyer? In dollar terms, the 1990 borrowing is indeed four times as big as the 1960 borrowing. But in terms of what money will buy, these two debts are almost equivalent. Inflation in the years between 1960 and 1990 has raised the prices of most things to about four times what they were in 1960. Thus a mortgage of $120,000 in 1990 is really the same as a mortgage of $30,000 in 1960.

When a family buys a new home and finances it on a mortgage, the family has a deficit in the year in which it buys the home. But in all the following years, until the debt has been paid off, the family has a surplus. That is, each year the family pays to the lender a sum of money, part of which covers the interest on the outstanding debt but part of which *reduces* the outstanding debt. The reduction in the outstanding debt is the household's surplus. Inflation has another important effect here. Because inflation brings higher prices, it also brings a lower real value of outstanding debts. Thus the real value of the mortgage declines by the amount paid off each year plus the amount wiped out by inflation. Other things being equal, the higher the inflation rate, the faster is the mortgage really paid off and the larger is the household's real surplus.

The Government's Real Deficit

This line of reasoning applies with equal force to the government. Because of inflation, the government's deficit is not *really* as big as it appears. To see how we can measure the deficit and correct for the distortion of inflation, we'll work through a concrete numerical example. First, look at Case A in Table 17.1—a situation in which there is no inflation. Government expenditure, excluding debt interest, is $17 billion and tax revenue is $20 billion. Thus if the government didn't have interest to pay, it would have a surplus of $3 billion. But the government has outstanding debt of $50 billion, and interest rates are running at 4 percent. Thus the government must pay $2 billion of debt interest (4 percent on $50 billion). When we add the $2 billion of debt interest to the government's other spending, we see that the government's total expenditure is $19 billion, so the government has a $1 billion surplus. The government's debt falls to $49 billion—the $50 billion outstanding at the beginning of the year is reduced by the surplus that the government has run. Ignore the last two rows of Table 17.1 for the moment.

Next, let's look at this same economy with exactly the same expenditure, tax revenue, and debt but in a situation in which there is a 10 percent *anticipated* inflation rate—Case B in Table 17.1. With 10 percent inflation that is anticipated, the market interest rate will not be 4 percent, but 14 percent. The reason why the interest rate is higher by 10 percentage points is that the real value of outstanding debt declines by 10 percent a year. Lenders—the households, firms, and foreigners that are buying government debt—know that the money they'll receive in repayment of the loans they make to the government will be worth less than the money they

Clinton's Deficit Reduction Package

The Wall Street Journal, August 9, 1993

With Signature, President Will Erase Reagan's Legacy

by Jackie Calmes

WASHINGTON—Clintonomics is coming.

After the Senate's high-drama 51–50 approval Friday, President Clinton's economic program will become law with his signature this week, six months after its unveiling.

The measure will raise taxes on the wealthy and corporations to upend the tax-cut policies of the Reagan era. And it will trim defense, Medicare and other programs to achieve $496 billion in deficit reduction over five years. At the same time, the measure will provide billions of dollars in tax incentives for businesses and the poor. . . .

According to congressional analysts, the bill will increase taxes by a net $241 billion over five years, and cut spending by $255 billion. Counted as spending cuts are $102 billion that will be saved by freezing spending, mostly on defense; nearly $56 billion in reductions from projected Medicare increases over the next five years; $7.1 billion from Medicaid; and $65 billion that otherwise would be paid as interest on debt if the deficit went unrestrained. . . .

At the end of the fifth year, in fiscal 1998, the deficit will be a projected $213 billion. Without action, it was estimated to be $361 billion.

. . . Polls showed that two-thirds of the public believes the middle class will bear the burden of the package through tax increases; in fact, the middle class will see only a 1% increase in its taxes on average, mainly because of the gasoline tax rise.

Workers making less than $30,000 a year are in line for a tax cut, thanks to a major expansion of the earned-income tax credit that will cost about $21 billion over five years. The credit would be available not only to workers with children but also to individuals without children.

In contrast, people earning more than $200,000 annually will pay an average of 17.4% more in taxes. The top marginal rate will rise to 36% from 31% for couples making more than $140,000 in taxable income ($115,000 for individuals), and to 39.6% for those making more than $250,000 annually. . . .

The Essence of the Story

On August 6, 1993, the Senate approved President Clinton's economic program by 51 to 50 votes.

The measures will bring a net increase in taxes of $241 billion over five years and will hold spending at $255 billion below what it would otherwise have been.

The spending cuts include $102 billion on defense, $56 billion on Medicare, $7.1 billion on Medicaid, and $65 billion in interest on the debt.

The projected deficit for fiscal 1998 is $213 billion rather than the $361 billion it would be with no policy changes.

People earning less than $30,000 a year will pay $21 billion less in taxes over five years.

Middle-class Americans will pay a 1 percent increase in taxes on average because of a gasoline tax rise.

People earning more than $200,000 annually will pay an average of 17.4 percent more in taxes, and the top marginal tax rate will rise from 31 percent to 36 percent for couples making more than $140,000 in taxable income ($115,000 for individuals) and to 39.6 percent for those making more than $250,000 annually.

Background and Analysis

In 1993, the federal government received \$800 billion, spent \$1,200 billion, and had a deficit of \$400 billion (in round numbers).

With no policy changes, the budget outcome projected for 1998 was a deficit of \$360 billion.

The Clinton deficit reduction package of 1993 was designed to cut the federal deficit in 1998 to \$210 billion (again in round numbers). To achieve this outcome, taxes in 1998 will be \$100 billion a year higher than with no policy change, and spending will be held to \$100 billion below what it would have been with an unchanged policy.

For the Clinton package to achieve its 1998 budget target, the economy must grow fast enough to generate some additional tax revenues, as shown in the figure. The line G_0 shows government expenditures in 1993, and the line T_0 shows tax receipts in that year. In 1993, GDP was \$6 trillion and the deficit was the vertical distance between G_0 and T_0.

With no policy change, taxes would increase along the line T_0 and by 1998, with GDP at \$7.5 trillion, would be \$1,000 billion. But spending would also increase, and government expenditures would increase to G_1.

The Clinton plan is to cut spending so that in 1998 government expenditures are G_2 and to increase taxes so that in 1998 taxes are T_1. With these policy changes and provided the economy continues to expand, the deficit will decrease to \$210 billion.

Supporters of Reaganomics and critics of the Clinton plan believe that higher taxes on high-income groups have disincentive effects that slow the pace of economic growth and put the deficit reduction plan in jeopardy.

Supporters of Clintonomics believe that cutting the deficit will end uncertainty and boost investment, bringing faster economic growth that will help reduce the deficit.

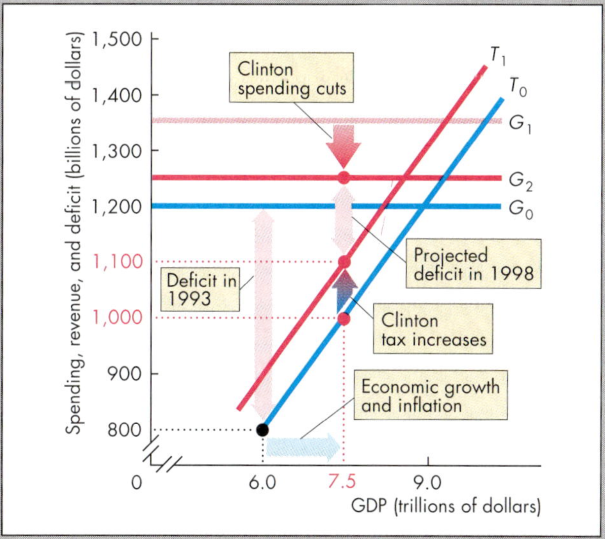

TABLE 17.1

How Inflation Distorts the Deficit

	Case A	Case B
Government expenditure (excluding debt interest)	**$17 billion**	**$17 billion**
Tax revenue	**$20 billion**	**$20 billion**
Government debt	**$50 billion**	**$50 billion**
Market interest rate	**4 percent**	**4 percent**
Inflation rate	**0 percent**	**10 percent**
Real interest rate	**4 percent**	**14 percent**
Debt interest paid	**$ 2 billion**	**$ 7 billion**
Surplus (+) or deficit (–)	**+$ 1 billion**	**–$ 4 billion**
Government debt at end of year	**$49 billion**	**$54 billion**
Real government debt at end of year	**$49 billion**	**$49 billion**
Real surplus (+) or deficit (–)	**+$ 1 billion**	**+$ 1 billion**

Inflation distorts the measured deficit by distorting the debt interest payments made by the government. In this example, the real interest rate is 4 percent and government debt is $50 billion, so debt interest in real terms is $2 billion. With no inflation, Case A, the actual debt interest paid is also $2 billion. At 10 percent inflation, Case B, interest rates rise to 14 percent (in order to preserve a real interest rate of 4 percent) and debt interest increases to $7 billion. The deficit increases by $5 billion from a surplus of $1 billion to a deficit of $4 billion. This deficit is apparent, not real. With 10 percent inflation, the real value of the government's debt falls by $5 billion, offsetting the deficit of $4 billion and resulting in a $1 billion real surplus.

lend out. The government also recognizes that the money it will use to repay its debt will have a lower value than the money it borrows. Thus the government and the people from whom it borrows readily agree to a higher interest rate that compensates for these foreseen changes in the value of money. So with a 14 percent interest rate, the government has to pay $7 billion in debt interest—14 percent of $50 billion. When the $7 billion of debt interest is added to the government's other spending, total expenditure is $24 billion, $4 billion more than tax revenue. Therefore the government has a deficit of $4 billion. At the end of the year, the government's debt will have increased from $50 billion to $54 billion.

The difference between the two situations we've just described is a 10 percent inflation rate. Nothing else is different. Real expenditure by the government and real tax revenue are the same, and the real interest rate is the same in the two cases. But at the end of one year, government debt has increased to $54 billion in Case B and has fallen to $49 billion in Case A. Nevertheless, the real debt is the same in the two cases. You can see this equality by keeping in mind that although government debt increases to $54 billion in Case B, the prices of all things have increased by 10 percent. If we deflate the government debt in Case B to express the debt in constant dollars instead of current dollars, we see that real government debt has actually fallen in Case B to $49 billion. ($54 billion divided by 1.1—1 plus the proportionate inflation rate—equals $49 billion.) Thus even in Case B, the real situation is that there is a surplus of $1 billion. Inflation makes it appear that there is a $4 billion deficit when really there is a $1 billion surplus.

The numbers in Table 17.1 are, of course, hypothetical. They deal with two imaginary situations. But the calculations that we've just done provide us with a method of adjusting the U.S. government deficit to eliminate the effects of inflation and reveal the real deficit. How important is it to adjust the U.S. deficit for inflation in order to obtain an inflation-free view of the deficit?

The Real and Nominal Deficit in the United States

Figure 17.5 provides an answer to the above question. It plots the nominal and real deficits of the United States alongside each other. As you can see, the real deficit has not been as large as the nominal deficit, especially during the 1970s. The reason is that inflation was high during those years. Only when inflation declined in the mid-1980s did a large and persistent real deficit emerge.

You can see, then, that the distinction between the real and nominal deficit is an important practical distinction only when the inflation rate is high. Taking the distinction into account changes our view of the scale and seriousness of the deficit during the 1970s. But it does not change the story much in the second half of the 1980s and the 1990s because by then inflation had subsided.

FIGURE 17.5

The Real Deficit and the Nominal Deficit

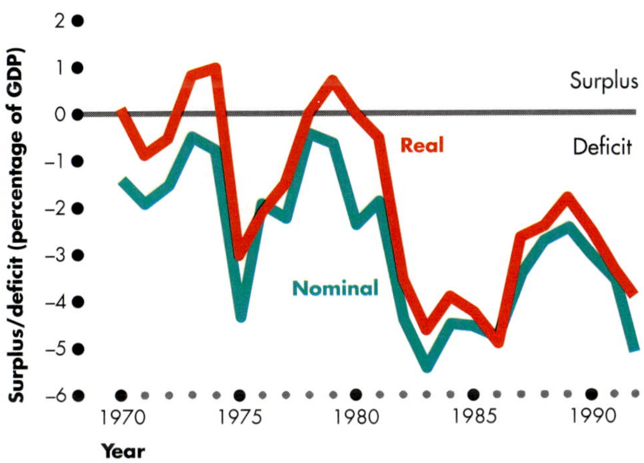

The real deficit removes the effects of inflation from interest rates and from the outstanding value of government debt. The real deficit and the nominal deficit follow a similar path, but the real deficit is smaller than the nominal deficit. Only when inflation declined in the 1980s did the two deficit measures move close together.

Source: Economic Report of the President, 1993, and my calculations.

Deficits and Inflation

Many people fear government deficits because they believe deficits lead to inflation. Do deficits cause inflation? That depends on how the deficit is financed.

Financing the Deficit

To finance its deficit, the government sells bonds. But the effect of bond sales depends on who buys the bonds. If they are bought by the Fed, they bring an increase in the money supply. But if they are bought by anyone other than the Fed, they do not bring a change in the money supply.

When the Fed buys government bonds, it pays for them by creating new money (see Chapter 11, pp. 284–289). We call such financing of the deficit money financing. **Money financing** is the financing of the government deficit by the sale of bonds to the Federal Reserve System, which results in the creation of additional money. All other financing of the government's deficit is called debt financing. **Debt financing** is the financing of the government deficit by selling bonds to anyone (household, firm, or foreigner) other than the Federal Reserve System.

Let's look at the consequences of these two ways of financing the deficit, starting with debt financing.

Debt Financing First, suppose that the government borrows money by selling treasury bonds to households and firms. In order to sell a bond, the government must offer the potential buyer a sufficiently attractive deal. In other words, the government must offer a high enough rate of return to convince people to lend their money.

Let's suppose that the going interest rate is 10 percent a year. In order to sell a bond worth \$100 and cover its deficit of \$100, the government must promise not only to pay back the \$100 at the end of the year but also to pay the interest of \$10 accumulated on that debt. Thus to finance a deficit of \$100 today, the government must pay \$110 a year from today. In one year's time, in order simply to stand still, the government would have to borrow \$110 to cover the cost of repaying, with interest, the bond that it sold a year earlier. Two years from today, the government will have to pay \$121—the \$110 borrowed plus the 10 percent interest (\$11) on that \$110. The process continues, with the total amount of debt and total interest payments mushrooming year after year.

Money Financing Next, consider what happens if instead of selling bonds to households and firms, the government sells treasury bonds to the Fed. There are two important differences in this case compared with the case of debt financing. First, the government winds up paying no interest on these bonds; second, additional money gets created.

The government ends up paying no interest on bonds bought by the Fed because the Fed, although an independent agency, pays any profit it makes to the government. Thus, other things being equal, if the Fed receives an extra million dollars from the government in interest payments on government bonds held by the Fed, the Fed's profits increase by that same million dollars and flow back to the government. Second, when the Fed buys bonds from the government, it uses newly created money to do so. This newly created money flows into the banking system in the form of an increase in the monetary base and enables the banks to create yet additional money by making additional loans. (See Chapter 10 and Chapter 11.)

As we studied in Chapter 7 and Chapter 14, an increase in the money supply causes an increase in aggregate demand. And higher aggregate demand eventually brings a higher price level. Persistent money financing leads to a continuously increasing aggregate demand and to inflation.

Debt Financing versus Money Financing In comparing these two methods of financing the deficit, it is clear that debt financing leaves the government with an ongoing obligation to pay interest—an obligation that gets bigger each year if the government keeps running deficits. When the government uses money financing, it pays its bills and that is the end of the matter. (The government pays interest to the Fed, but the Fed pays its profit to the government, so the government has no ongoing interest obligation.) Thus there is a clear advantage, from the government's point of view, to covering its deficit by money financing rather than by debt financing. Unfortunately, this solution causes inflationary problems for everybody else.

But the alternative, debt financing, is not problem-free. Financing the deficit through bond sales to households, firms, and foreigners causes a mushrooming scale of debt and interest payments. The larger the scale of debt and interest payments, the bigger the deficit problem becomes and the greater is the temptation to end the process of debt financing. Thus the temptation increases to finance the deficit by selling bonds to the Fed—money financing. This ever-present temptation is what leads many to fear that deficits are inflationary even when they are not immediately money financed.

Unpleasant Arithmetic

Some economists have argued that debt financing can be even more inflationary than money financing. Because debt financing creates more debt and a bigger interest burden, the amount of money eventually created is greater, the longer the debt financing persists. Anticipating such an outcome, rational people start to dump money—decreasing the demand for money. At the same time they increase the demand for goods, putting upward pressure on prices. Inflation takes off even though no money financing has yet begun.

Thomas Sargent (of the University of Chicago and the Hoover Institution at Stanford University) and Neil Wallace (of the University of Minnesota) first showed this possibility and called their conclusion "unpleasant monetarist arithmetic." It is *unpleasant* arithmetic because postponing money creation worsens the inflation that ensues. It is unpleasant *monetarist* arithmetic because it attacks the central proposition of monetarism—that inflation is caused purely by the growth rate of the money supply. According to monetarism, if the money supply growth rate is contained, inflation will not erupt. According to unpleasant monetarist arithmetic, even if the money supply growth rate is contained, inflation will erupt if the deficit is large enough to create an expectation of its eventual financing by newly created money.

The cure for inflation in an economy with a large and persistent deficit is not merely a slowing in the pace of money creation. The deficit must also be brought under control. Slowing money growth is a necessary part of the process of slowing inflation, but rapid money growth is not the fundamental source of the inflation, and hence it is not the solution.

But for the deficit to have the unpleasant arithmetic effects it must be a persistent phenomenon. A deficit that is large and that lasts even for a decade does not inevitably bring inflation. If the deficit is actually going to be brought under control and the expectation is that it will be brought under control, its presence does not lead to inflation.

International Evidence

We have a large amount of experience from a wide variety of countries on the relationship between inflation and deficits. What does that experience tell us? Are deficits, in fact, inflationary?

This question is answered in Fig. 17.6. It contains data on inflation and deficits for 67 countries covering the 1980s. The countries are in three groups: Latin America (part a), Western Europe (part b), and 48 others (part c). The 67 countries are the only

FIGURE 17.6

Deficits and Inflation

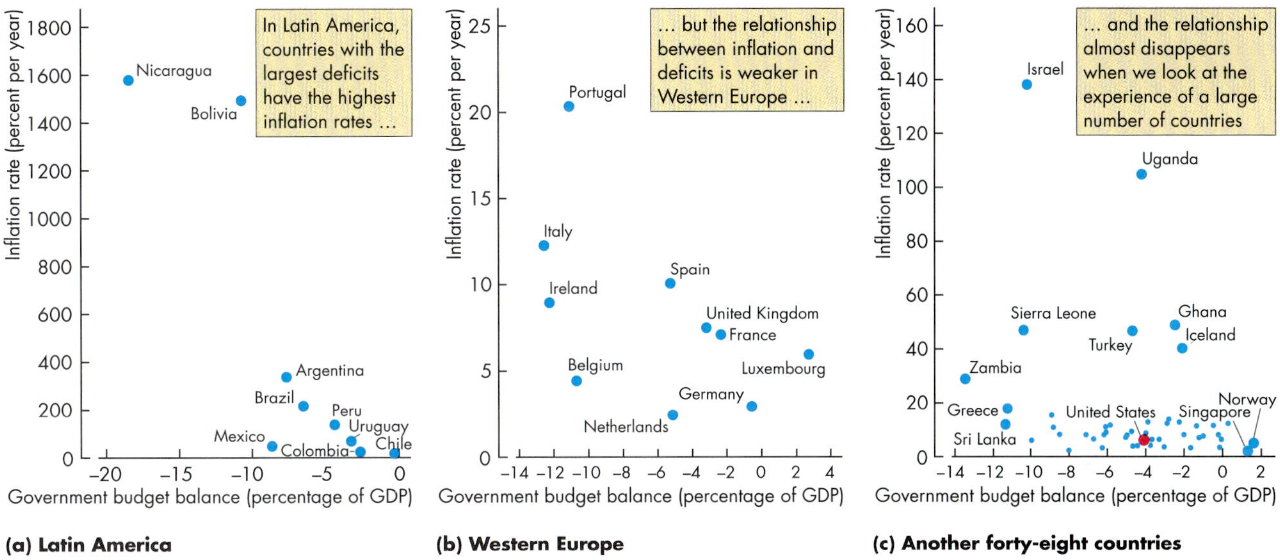

The relationship between the deficit and inflation is shown for 9 Latin American countries (part a), 10 countries in Western Europe (part b), and 48 other countries—including the United States (part c). There is a tendency for large deficit countries to be high inflation countries, but the correlation is weak.

Source: International Financial Statistics Yearbook, 1990. For each country, the dot shows its deficit (as a percentage of GDP) and inflation (GDP deflator) for the 1980s (or part decade where the full decade is not available).

ones for which there are data on both inflation and the deficit for most of the 1980s.

First, notice the tremendous range of experience. The highest inflation rate was almost 1600 percent per year—in Nicaragua (part a). The lowest inflation rate was less than 3 percent—in the Netherlands (part b). The largest deficit was almost 20 percent of GDP—again in Nicaragua. The smallest deficit (actually a surplus) was more than 2 percent of GDP—in Luxembourg.

Second, look at the relationships between deficits and inflation. In the Latin American countries (part a), there is a clear tendency for these two variables to be correlated. The countries with the largest deficits (Nicaragua and Bolivia) have the highest inflation rates. The countries with the smallest deficits (Chile, Colombia, and Uruguay) have the lowest inflation rates. And countries with deficits between these have inflation rates that are intermediate as well (Argentina and Brazil). Only Mexico does not fit the pattern. Its inflation rate is lower than that in countries with much smaller deficits. In Western Europe (part b), there is a similar, although somewhat weaker, relationship between deficits and inflation. And the relationship, although still present, is very loose for the countries shown in part (c).

Third, notice the position of the United States. Its deficit is in the middle of the pack, but its inflation rate is among the lowest.

We have now reviewed the relationship between deficits and inflation. Deficits are not inevitably inflationary. But there is a correlation between deficits and inflation. And the larger the deficit and the longer it persists, the greater are the inflationary pressures.

Another common view about the deficit is that it places a burden on future generations. Let's now examine that view.

A Burden on Future Generations?

It is a common and popular cry that "we owe it to our children to control the deficit." Is this popular view correct? How would the deficit place a burden on future generations?

We've already examined one burden that the deficit might place on future generations—the burden of inflation. But when people talk about the deficit as a burden on future generations, they usually mean something other than inflation. For example, somebody has to pay the interest on the huge national debt that the deficit creates. The government will pay the interest with money it takes from the people as taxes. Taxes will have to be raised. Won't those taxes burden future generations?

Wait, though. Doesn't the interest paid each year get financed with taxes collected each year? So how can the deficit be a burden to *future* generations? It might be a burden to some members of the future generation, but it must be a benefit to others, so in the aggregate it evens out.

Although in the aggregate the interest paid equals the tax revenue collected, there may be important redistribution effects. For example, one feature of our present deficit is that some government debt is being bought not by Americans but by European and Japanese investors. So part of the future burden of the current deficit is that future American taxpayers will have to provide the resources with which to pay interest to foreign holders of U.S. government debt.

There's another way in which today's deficit can make people poorer tomorrow: by slowing today's pace of investment and reducing the stock of productive capital equipment available for future generations. This phenomenon is called crowding out.

Crowding Out

Crowding out is the tendency for an increase in government purchases of goods and services to bring a decrease in investment (see Chapter 12, p. 314). If crowding out does occur, and if government purchases of goods and services are financed by government debt, the economy will have a larger stock of government debt and a smaller stock of capital—plant and equipment. Unproductive government debt replaces productive capital.

Crowding out does *not* occur if:

1. There is unemployment.
2. The deficit arises from the government's purchases of capital on which the return equals (or exceeds) that on privately purchased capital.

Crowding out *does* occur if:

1. There is full employment.
2. The government purchases consumption goods and services or capital on which the return is less than that on privately purchased capital.

The Level of Employment If there is full employment, increased government purchases of goods and services (and an increased deficit) must result in a decrease in the purchases of other goods and services. But if there is unemployment, it is possible that an increase in government purchases (and increased deficit) could result in a decrease in unemployment and an increase in output. In such a case the deficit does not completely crowd out other expenditure. This possibility can occur only for short periods and when the economy is in recession.

Productive Government Purchases Much of what the government purchases is productive capital. Highways, dams, airports, schools, and universities are some obvious examples. But there are some not so obvious examples. Education and health care are investments in productive human capital. Defense expenditure protects our physical and human capital resources and is productive capital expenditure. To the extent that the deficit results from our acquisition of such assets, it does not crowd out productive capital. On the contrary, it contributes to it.

But it is possible for government purchases of consumption goods and services to crowd out productive capital. Let's see how.

How Crowding Out Occurs For crowding out to occur, a deficit must result in less investment, with the consequence that future generations have a smaller capital stock than they otherwise would have had. This drop in the capital stock will lower their income and, in a sense, be a burden to them. (They will still be richer than they were, but not as rich as they would have been if they had had a larger stock of productive machines.)

The scale of investment depends on its opportunity cost. That opportunity cost is the real interest rate. Other things being equal, the higher the real interest rate, the less firms will want to invest in new plant and equipment. For a government deficit to crowd out investment, the deficit must cause real interest rates to rise.

Some people believe that a deficit does increase interest rates because the government's own borrowing represents an increase in the demand for loans with no corresponding increase in the supply of loans. Figure 17.7 shows what happens in this case. Part (a) shows the demand and supply curves for loans. Initially, the demand for loans is D_0, and the supply of loans is S_0. The real interest rate is 3 percent, and the quantity of loans made is $1 trillion. Part (b) shows investment. At a real interest rate of 3 percent, investment is $0.8 trillion. Now suppose that the government runs a deficit. To finance its deficit, the government borrows. The demand for loans increases, and the demand curve for loans shifts from D_0 to D_1. There is no change in the supply of loans, so the real interest rate increases to 4 percent and the quantity of loans increases to $1.2 trillion. Notice that the increase in the quantity of loans made is smaller than the increase in the demand for loans. That is, the demand curve shifts to the right by a larger amount than the increase in loans that actually occurs. The higher interest rate decreases investment and brings a smaller capital stock. Thus the increased stock of government debt crowds out some productive capital.

FIGURE 17.7

The Deficit, Borrowing, and Crowding Out

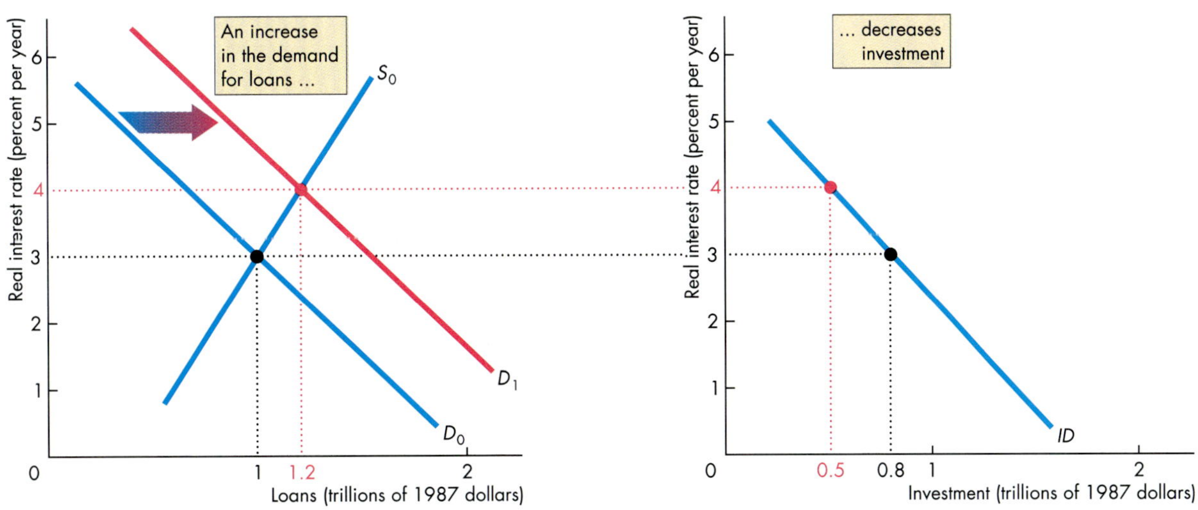

(a) The market for loans

(b) Investment

Part (a) shows the market for loans. The demand for loans is D_0, and the supply is S_0. The quantity of loans made is $1 trillion, and the real interest rate is 3 percent. Part (b) shows the determination of investment. At an interest rate of 3 percent, investment is $0.8 trillion. The government runs a deficit and finances the deficit by borrowing. The government's increase in demand for loans shifts the demand curve to D_1. The interest rate rises to 4 percent, and the equilibrium quantity of loans increases to $1.2 trillion. The higher interest rate leads to a decrease in investment in part (b). The government deficit crowds out capital accumulation.

Does a deficit make real interest rates rise as shown in Fig. 17.7? Many economists believe so, and they have some pretty strong evidence to point to. Real interest rates in the United States in the last decade, in precisely the years in which we have had a large real deficit, have been higher than at any time in history. Furthermore, there is a general tendency for real interest rates and the real deficit to fluctuate in sympathy with each other.

It is this relationship in the data that leads some economists to predict that a higher real deficit means higher real interest rates, lower investment, and a smaller scale of capital accumulation—government debt crowds out productive capital. As a consequence, future output will be lower than it otherwise would have been, and so the deficit burdens future generations.

FIGURE 17.8

Ricardian Equivalence

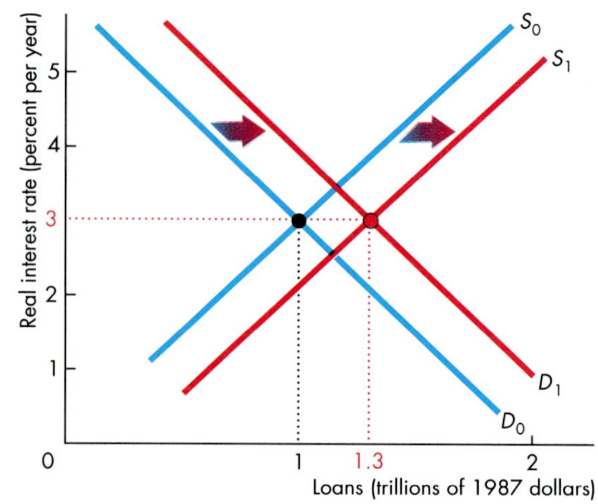

Initially, the demand for loans is D_0, and the supply of loans is S_0. The equilibrium quantity of loans is $1 trillion, and the real interest rate is 3 percent a year. An increase in the government deficit, financed by borrowing, increases the demand for loans, shifting the demand curve to D_1. Households, recognizing that the increased government deficit will bring increased future taxes to pay the additional interest charges, cut their consumption and increase their saving. The supply curve of loans shifts to the right to S_1. The equilibrium quantity of loans increases to $1.3 trillion, but the real interest rate stays constant at 3 percent a year. There is no crowding out of investment.

Ricardian Equivalence

Some economists do not believe that deficits crowd out capital accumulation. On the contrary, they argue, debt financing and paying for government spending with taxes are equivalent. The level of purchases of goods and services matters, but not the way in which it is financed.

The first economist to advance this idea (known as Ricardian equivalence) was the great English economist David Ricardo. Recently, Ricardo's idea has been given a forceful restatement by Robert Barro of Harvard University. Barro argues as follows: If the government increases its purchases of goods and services but does not increase taxes, people are smart enough to recognize that the government will increase taxes later in order to cover the increased spending and interest payments on the debt being issued today. In recognition of having to pay higher taxes later, people will cut their consumption now and save more. They'll increase their saving so that when the higher taxes are finally levied, sufficient wealth has been accumulated to meet those tax liabilities without a further cut in consumption. The scale of increased saving matches the scale of increased government spending.

Figure 17.8 illustrates this case. Initially, the demand for loans is D_0, and the supply of loans is S_0. The real interest rate is 3 percent, and the quantity of loans made is $1 trillion. The government runs a deficit and finances that deficit by borrowing. The demand curve for loans shifts to the right to D_1. At the same time, using the reasoning of Ricardo and Barro, there is a decrease in consumption and an increase in saving. The supply of loans increases, shifting the supply curve to the right to S_1. The quantity of loans increases from $1 trillion to $1.3 trillion, and the real interest rate stays constant at 3 percent. With no change in the real interest rate, there is no crowding out of investment.

Some economists argue that Ricardian equivalence breaks down because people take into account only the future tax liabilities that will be borne by themselves and not by their children and their grandchildren. Proponents of the Ricardian equivalence proposition argue that it makes no difference whether future tax liabilities are going to be borne by those currently alive or by their descendants. If the taxes are going to be borne by children and grandchildren, the current generation takes account of those future taxes and adjusts its own consumption so that it can make bequests on a large enough scale to enable those taxes to be paid.

Laying out the assumptions necessary for Ricardian equivalence leaves most economists convinced that the Ricardian equivalence proposition cannot apply to the real world. Yet there is a surprising amount of evidence in its support. In order to interpret the evidence, it is important to be clear that Ricardian equivalence does *not* imply that real interest rates are not affected by the level of government purchases. A high level of government purchases, other things being equal, brings a higher real interest rate. The Ricardian equivalence proposition implies that real interest rates are not affected by the way in which a given level of government purchases is financed. Regardless of whether government purchases are financed by taxes or by borrowing, real interest rates will be the same.

Whether it is the deficit or the level of government purchases of goods and services that affects real interest rates remains unclear. If people do take into account future tax burdens (and not just their own but their children's and grandchildren's future tax burdens), then saving will respond to offset the deficit. The deficit itself will have little or no effect on real interest rates and capital accumulation. If people ignore the implications of the deficit for their own and their descendants' future consumption possibilities, the deficit will indeed increase real interest rates. The jury remains out on this question.

Eliminating the Deficit

Measures to eliminate the deficit can attack either the revenue side or the expenditure side of the government's budget. That is, there are two ways to eliminate the deficit:

- Reducing expenditure
- Increasing revenue

Reducing Expenditure

Throughout the modern history of most countries, government expenditure has increased as a percentage of GDP. The federal government of the United States has contained the growth of government expenditure more effectively than most governments. In most European countries, governments spend close to 50 percent of GDP, and in the Netherlands, expenditure was more that 53 percent of GDP at its peak in 1983.

Many components of government expenditure have a built-in tendency to increase at a faster pace than GDP. Two such components are education and health care. Even when these items are purchased privately, people spend a larger fraction of their incomes on them as incomes increase. When the government plays a significant role in the provision of these two goods, voter pressure for better provision of services is irresistible and the government has little choice but to increase its expenditures to meet the voter demands. Only by privatizing these activities can the government's share of GDP be prevented from increasing.

In many European countries the government is privatizing a variety of manufacturing operations. The Thatcher government in Britain (in the 1980s) even tried to limit its involvement in health care and health insurance. But there is much less scope for such privatization in the United States. In fact, the political debate appears to be leaning in the direction of expanding the scope of government in the health care insurance business. A major theme in the 1992 presidential campaign was a debate about the desirability of introducing a comprehensive and universal health insurance program similar to that of Canada.

In the early 1990s, one factor working against the tide of ever larger government expenditure is the "peace dividend"—the reduction in defense spending resulting from the end of the Cold War. It is possible that the peace dividend will finance enhanced health and other social programs without an increase in the overall level of government spending. But this dividend is likely to be short-lived. In the long run, growing incomes will bring higher expenditure.

Faced with the general tendency for government spending to increase, there are four main proposals for attempting to keep federal government expenditure under control:

- Cutting revenue to force spending cuts
- Line-item veto
- Budget Enforcement Act of 1990
- Balanced budget amendment

Cutting Revenue to Force Spending Cuts The approach adopted by the Reagan administration toward the deficit, and advocated by Milton Friedman, is based on the view that Congress behaves like an undisciplined child. The child wants more candy. Give the child a dollar, and the child will buy more candy. Take a dollar away from the child, and the child will scream but will eventually find a way of managing without candy. Revenue was certainly reduced in the 1980s. As you can see by looking back at Fig. 17.3, tax revenue as a percentage of GDP declined each year from 1981 through 1984. It increased (again as a percentage of GDP) in subsequent years but did not return to its 1981 peak level. It is impossible to say what the exact effects of these revenue cuts were on spending. It does seem likely, however, that the revenue decrease was in part responsible for keeping the lid on the growth of expenditure and social programs through the 1980s. But, as we have seen, it has not reduced spending to the level of tax revenue. If this method works, it works in a time frame that is more drawn out than most people regard as sensible.

Line-Item Veto In order to give the administration more power to help bring spending under control, it has been suggested that the president be given a line-item veto. A **line-item veto** is a veto power vested in the executive branch to eliminate any specific item in a budget. Many state governors have a line-item veto, but the President of the United States does not. When Congress passes a bill calling for expenditures and taxes, the president must either sign the bill into law in its entirety or veto it in its entirety. He cannot eliminate particular items.

Some people believe that giving the president this power would bring a sharper and more precise scalpel to bear on the process of cutting spending. But it has to be borne in mind that the budget itself emerges as a result of compromise and is Congress's own best attempt to balance competing claims on public resources. If the president had such a veto power, there would likely be an increase in lobbying effort directed at the executive branch itself and there would be no guarantee that the president would be tougher on spending than Congress is.

Budget Enforcement Act of 1990 In an attempt to impose budget discipline on itself, Congress has passed legislation designed to keep total spending growth below the growth of revenue. Its most recent attempt to do this is the Budget Enforcement Act of 1990. This act contains provisions intended to lower the federal budget deficit by more than $0.5 trillion by 1995.

The act contains spending caps and pay-as-you-go rules to prevent new programs from increasing total federal spending. Any spending increase in one program must be offset by a spending decrease in other programs, and if this requirement is violated, across-the-board spending cuts must be made to remain within the cap.

The 1990 act also permits automatic stabilization through an increased deficit during an economic downturn. To facilitate the operation of countercyclical fiscal policy, the law specifies procedures for adjusting the target deficit in light of the state of the economy.

Balanced Budget Amendment Many people want to go further than a congressional self-imposed balanced budget strategy such as the 1990 legislation. They want to amend the Constitution of the United States to include a formula for requiring the federal government to balance its budget. Many economists, including Nobel laureates Milton Friedman and James Buchanan, advocate a balanced budget amendment to the Constitution.

Those favoring a balanced budget amendment argue two things. First, the process of debating and achieving the amendment would itself increase the level of awareness of the importance of financial discipline on the federal government. Second, once such an amendment were in place, Congress would have a cast-iron excuse for not satisfying all the many claims and demands imposed upon it and would, in effect, be able to take refuge behind the balanced budget law. Those who argue against such an amendment argue that it is difficult, if not impossible, to frame the law in such a way as to make it effective.

Because of the difficulty of making significant reductions in government spending, many people take the view that the only way to eliminate the deficit is to increase government revenue. Let's now examine that option.

Increasing Revenue

Two approaches to increasing revenue have been proposed:

- Increase tax rates
- Decrease tax rates

Sound paradoxical? Not really, when you remember that what the government wants to do is to increase its tax *revenue*. *Tax revenue* is the product of the tax rate and the tax base. A **tax rate** is the percentage rate of tax levied on a particular activity. The **tax base** is the activity on which a tax is levied. For example, the tax base for personal income tax is earned income minus some specified allowances. The tax rates on personal income are 15 percent, 28 percent, and 31 percent (depending on income level).

There is ambiguity and disagreement about whether an increase in tax rates increases or decreases tax revenues. The source of the disagreement is something called the Laffer curve. The **Laffer curve** (named after Arthur Laffer, who first proposed it) is a curve that relates tax revenue to the tax rate. Figure 17.9 illustrates a hypothetical Laffer curve. The tax rate ranges between 0 percent and 100 percent on the vertical axis. Tax revenue, measured in billions of dollars, is shown on the horizontal axis. If the tax rate is zero, then no tax revenue is raised. That is why the curve begins at the origin. As the tax rate increases, tax revenue also increases, but only up to some maximum. In this example, once the tax rate has reached 40 percent, tax revenue is at its maximum—point *m* in the figure. If the tax rate increases above 40 percent, tax revenue falls. Why does this happen?

Revenue falls because there is a fall in the scale of the activity that is being taxed. Suppose that the item in question is gasoline. With no tax, lots of people drive gas-guzzling cars and consume billions of gallons a week. If gasoline is taxed, its price increases and the quantity bought declines. At first, the quantity bought decreases by a smaller percentage than the percentage increase in tax, and tax revenue rises. But there comes a point at which the decrease in the quantity demanded rises by a bigger percentage than the rise in taxes. At that point, tax revenue begins to decline. People sell their gas-guzzlers, buy smaller cars, join car pools, and use public transportation. The tax rate goes up, but the tax base goes down and tax revenue declines.

You can now see that whether a cut in the *tax rate* increases or decreases *tax revenue* depends on where we are on the Laffer curve. If we're at a point such as *a* in Fig. 17.9, a decrease in the tax rate results in an increase in tax revenue. But if we're at point *b*, a decrease in the tax rate results in a decrease in tax revenue. To increase tax revenue from point *b*, we have to increase the tax rate.

FIGURE 17.9

The Laffer Curve

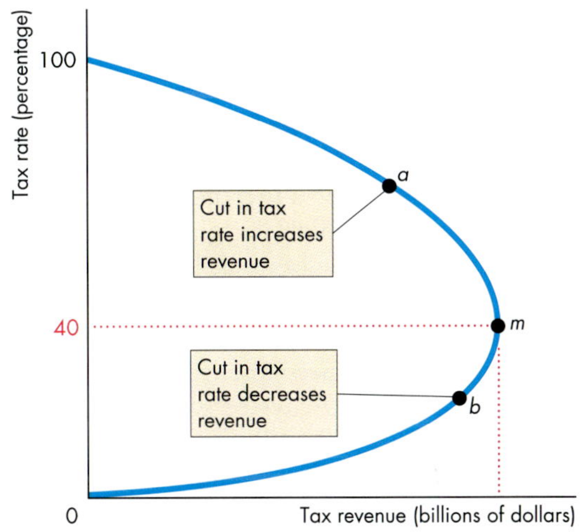

The Laffer curve shows the relationship between a tax rate and tax revenue. If the tax rate is 0 percent, the government collects no tax revenue. As the tax rate increases, the government's tax revenue also increases, but only up to some maximum (point *m*). As the tax rate continues to increase, tax revenue declines. At a tax rate of 100 percent, the government collects no revenue. Higher taxes act as a disincentive. The more heavily taxed is an activity, the less that activity is undertaken. When the percentage decrease in the activity is less than the percentage increase in the tax rate, we are at a point such as *b* and tax revenue rises. When the percentage decrease in the activity exceeds the percentage increase in the tax rate, we are at a point such as *a* and tax revenue decreases.

Economists and other observers argue about where we are on the Laffer curve for each of the various taxes. Some people suspect that for very highly taxed commodities, such as gasoline, tobacco products, and alcohol, we are on the backward-bending part of the Laffer curve, so an increase in the tax rate would decrease tax revenue. But hardly anyone believes this to be the case for personal income taxes and sales taxes. It is much more likely, in the case of those taxes, that an increase in tax rates would increase tax revenue.

The second approach to increasing revenue is to reform taxes, lowering high marginal tax rates and perhaps introducing new taxes at low rates on activities not previously taxed.

The search for changes in taxes that will bring higher tax revenue is a permanent feature of our economic life and will always be with us, regardless of whether there is a deficit. But in a deficit situation, that search takes on a much greater urgency.

◆ ◆ ◆ ◆ We have now completed our study of macroeconomics and of the challenges and problems of stabilizing the economy. In this study, our main focus has been the economy of the United States. Occasionally, we have taken into account the linkages between the United States and the rest of the world, but international economic relations have not been our main concern. In the remaining chapters we are going to shift our focus and study some vital international issues. First, in Chapter 18, we examine the international exchange of goods and services. Second, in Chapter 19, we study the financing of international trade and the determination of the value of our dollar in terms of other currencies. Third, in Chapter 20, we turn our attention to the problems of the poor developing countries of the Third World. Fourth and finally, in Chapter 21, we examine economic systems that are different from our own, such as those employed in the former Soviet Union and China.

SUMMARY

The Sources of the Deficit

The U.S. federal government deficit grew in the early 1980s because the percentage of GDP spent by the federal government grew and the percentage collected in taxes declined. The deficit, although fluctuating, has tended to get larger. The main items of spending that have increased are transfer payments and debt interest. But the main persistent source of the increasing deficit in the 1980s was the increase in debt interest.

The deficit fluctuates in sympathy with the business cycle. When the economy is in a recovery, tax revenue increases and transfer payments decrease as a percentage of GDP. The deficit declines. When the economy goes into recession, tax revenue decreases and transfer payments increase as a percentage of GDP, and so the deficit increases.

Adjusting the deficit for the effects of the business cycle results in the cyclically adjusted deficit. After cyclical adjustment, the deficit remained large through the expansion of the 1980s. And the deficit increased again in the 1991 recession. (pp. 448–452)

The Real Deficit

Inflation distorts the deficit by overstating the real interest burden carried by the government. Adjusting the deficit for this fact and measuring the real deficit lower the deficit in the 1970s but make little difference in the later 1980s. The cycles in the deficit remain the same, whether measured in real or current dollar terms. (pp. 453–457)

Deficits and Inflation

If deficits are money financed, they cause inflation. If they are debt financed, whether or not they cause inflation depends on how permanent they are. A temporary debt-financed deficit will have no inflationary effects. A permanent debt-financed deficit leads to inflation. It does so because the buildup of debt leads to a buildup of interest payments and a yet higher deficit. At some future date, the deficit will be money financed and the amount of money created will be larger, the longer the deficit persists and the more debt is issued. Fear of future inflation leads to a demand here and now for less government debt and less money. As a consequence, both interest rates and inflation increase in anticipation of a future (and perhaps the distant future) increase in money creation to finance the deficit. (pp. 457–459)

A Burden on Future Generations?

Whether the deficit is a burden on future generations is a controversial issue. Some economists believe that the deficit causes real interest rates to rise, thereby crowding out investment and reducing the amount of capital that we accumulate. As a consequence, future output will be lower than it otherwise would have been and future generations will be burdened with the effects of the deficit.

Other economists argue that government expenditure affects interest rates but the way in which that expenditure is financed does not. They suggest that if government spending is financed by borrowing, people will recognize that future taxes will have to increase to cover both the spending and the interest from the accumulated debt. And in anticipation of those higher future taxes, saving will increase and consumption will decrease in the present. Thus the burden of increased government expenditure—not the burden of the deficit—is spread across all generations. (pp. 460–463)

Eliminating the Deficit

The deficit can be eliminated by reducing expenditure, by increasing revenue, or by a combination of the two. There are four main proposals for reducing expenditure: cut revenue and wait for Congress to gradually bring spending into line; give the president a line-item veto; pursue target spending cuts such as those proposed in the 1990 Budget Enforcement Act; introduce a constitutional amendment requiring Congress to balance the federal budget. Increasing revenue could result from either increasing tax rates (if we are on the upward-sloping part of the Laffer curve) or decreasing tax rates (if we are on the backward-bending part of the Laffer curve). (pp. 463–466)

KEY ELEMENTS

Key Terms

Balanced budget, 448
Budget balance, 448
Budget deficit, 448
Budget surplus, 448
Cyclically adjusted deficit, 452
Debt financing, 457
Government debt, 448
Laffer curve, 465
Line-item veto, 464
Money financing, 457
Real deficit, 453
Tax base, 465
Tax rate, 465

Key Figures

Figure 17.1 The Deficit, 448
Figure 17.4 The Business Cycle and the Deficit, 451
Figure 17.5 The Real Deficit and the Nominal Deficit, 457
Figure 17.9 The Laffer Curve, 465

REVIEW QUESTIONS

1 List the main changes in taxes and government spending that are associated with the emergence of the federal government's deficit.

2 Trace the events between 1980 and 1983 that resulted in an increase in the federal government's deficit.

3 What is meant by the cyclically adjusted deficit?

4 Distinguish between the real deficit and the nominal deficit.

5 In calculating the real deficit, which of the following would you do?

- **a** Value the interest payments in real terms and take into account the change in the real value of government debt
- **b** Calculate the interest payments in nominal terms and take into account the change in the real value of government debt
- **c** Calculate the interest payments in real terms but ignore the change in the real value of outstanding government debt

6 Explain how debt financing of a deficit results in mushrooming interest payments.

7 Explain how the government finances its deficit by creating money.

8 Review the ways in which the deficit can be a burden on future generations.

9 Why do some economists argue that taxes and government debt are equivalent to each other and so the deficit does not matter?

10 What are the four main proposals for reducing government expenditure?

11 Why do some economists think that government revenue can be increased by cutting tax rates?

PROBLEMS

1 You are given the following information about the economy of Spendland. When unemployment is at its natural rate, which is 5.5 percent, government spending and tax revenue are each 10 percent of GDP. There is no inflation. For each 1 percentage point increase in the unemployment rate, government spending increases by 1 percentage point of GDP and tax revenue falls by 1 percentage point of GDP. Suppose that Spendland experiences a cycle in which the unemployment rate takes the following values:

Year	1	2	3	4	5	6	7
Unemployment rate	5	6	7	6	5	4	5

- **a** Calculate the actual deficit (as a percentage of GDP) for each year.
- **b** Calculate Spendland's cyclically adjusted deficit.

2 Government expenditure, excluding debt interest, on Day Dream Island is \$8.5 billion. Taxes are \$10 billion. The government has a \$25 billion outstanding debt. Interest rates are 24 percent, and there is a 20 percent inflation rate. Calculate the following:

- **a** The debt interest that the government pays
- **b** The government's budget surplus or deficit
- **c** The value of the government debt outstanding at the end of the year
- **d** The government's real deficit
- **e** The real value of the government's debt outstanding at the end of the year

3 The rate of return on private capital is 5 percent. The government is planning an increase in public health and welfare programs at an annual cost of \$100 billion. These programs are expected to improve health and labor productivity, resulting in an increase in GDP of \$50 billion a year. There is full employment.

- **a** What is the opportunity cost of the government program?
- **b** Does it make any difference to the opportunity cost if the program is financed by current taxes, borrowing, or money creation?
- **c** Will the program be a burden or a benefit to future generations if it is financed by borrowing?

PART 6

INTERNATIONAL ECONOMICS

Talking with Laura D'Andrea Tyson

Laura D'Andrea Tyson was born in New Jersey in 1947. She was an undergraduate at Smith College and obtained her Ph.D. in economics from MIT in 1974. Dr. Tyson is Professor of Economics and Business Administration at the University of California at Berkeley and chairwoman of President Clinton's Council of Economic Advisers. Her central area of work has been on the competitiveness and trade performance of the United States.

Professor Tyson, how did you get into economics?

I was immediately taken with economics when I first studied it as a sophomore in college. I was fascinated by both the international and public policy aspects: that is to say, how different countries try to solve their basic economic problems and how both the problems and countries relate to one another. I was also looking for a way to combine my analytic instincts with a public policy discipline, and economics was a wonderful match.

Most economists are free traders. But some, perhaps an increasing number, believe some measure of protectionism can help a developing country get off the ground. Where do you stand in the free trade versus protection debate for developing countries?

Like most economists, I consider myself to be a free trader. I believe that GATT has provided significant benefits to the world by breaking down many formal trade barriers. I'd like to see even more free trade. My studies of how countries interact suggest that free trade as an ideal does

not exist; we're actually quite far from it. Countries have to push very hard for change at the international level. At the same time, they have to use the domestic policies they have at their disposal to compensate for the fact that free trade doesn't exist.

Trade is of critical importance for bringing developing countries greater prosperity. Developing countries can't depend on aid or investment to the same extent they could in the past. They depend on trading in the world economy to increase their prosperity. They've become extremely dependent on their ability to find markets for their products.

Trade between poor and rich countries is likely to be based on different resource endowments, resulting in differences in comparative advantage. This is the kind of trade that traditional trade theory explains and the kind of trade that benefits both sides. When there exist big differences in development level and resource endowments, countries on both sides of the trading relationship stand to benefit by exploiting these differences and specializing in things that they are good at—their comparative advantage. So you have a powerful argument in favor of freer trade between developed and developing countries.

What about trade between developed countries such as Japan and the United States?

Much of the trade among the developed nations is not based on simple comparative advantage, because all of them are quite similar in underlying resource endowments and technological capabilities. Instead, such trade is often based on differences in product quality, design, reliability, and other non-price characteristics. Such trade takes place in imperfectly competitive markets in which competitive advantage and trade patterns can be manipulated by the market power of individual firms and the policy interventions of individual governments.

For informed national policymaking in such markets, the real choices are not simple choices between free trade and protection but choices about the appropriate combination of liberalization and government intervention that will improve national economic welfare while sustaining an open, international trading system.

GATT must be overhauled to address the sources of trade friction among the developed countries. Rules about traditional border policies like tariffs and quotas are no longer enough. Deep interdependence among nations requires deep integration—the harmonization of significant national differences and the development of enforceable multilateral rules regulating such nonborder policies as intellectual property protection, competition policy, and industrial targeting.

There appears to be an increasing tendency toward large regional trading blocs—the European Community and the North American Free Trade Area being the two most important. What are the benefits of large regional trading blocs such as these?

I think the benefits of trading blocs really are twofold. First, because of the benefits of freer trade and specialization, countries within a trading bloc are likely to grow faster. More rapid growth and increased prosperity within the bloc will, in turn, encourage imports from outside the bloc. This is called the "trade creation effect"—there will be new trade opportunities, even for countries that are not members of the bloc itself. Everybody benefits.

Second, a trading bloc can be a model for creating systemic change and establishing new multilateral rules. The politics of forming a free trade area are very complicated. If, over the course of decades, a group of countries such as those in Europe slowly develop a common set of rules and institutions, what they learn "[among the developed countries] Rules about traditional border policies like tariffs and quotas are no longer enough."

in the process can be a rich source of lessons and education for the rest of the world.

What are the dangers that result from the creation of these large regional blocs?

The possible costs of blocs are also, I think, twofold. First of all, there is what economists call "trade diversion," as opposed to trade creation. Trade diversion always occurs when a bloc is formed, because blocs are inherently discriminatory. The bloc by definition breaks down barriers within the bloc nations but not between them and the rest of the world. As a result, the formation of a bloc changes the incentives to trade, encouraging trade among the members of the bloc at the expense of trade between them and the rest of the world. For example, when France and Germany eliminate a barrier to trade between them, they have an incentive to trade more with one another and less with other countries like the United States, with whom trade barriers persist. This is the trade diversion effect.

The trade diversion effect works in conflict with the trade creation effect. On the one hand, the United States will be helped by the trade creation effect—if all of Europe grows faster, there will be a bigger market for the United States. On the other hand, the United States will be hurt by the trade diversion effect because an advantage it had before has now been diminished. Countries forming a bloc can mitigate the diversion effect or make it worse, depending on whether they raise or reduce the common barriers to trade with non-bloc members.

The second basic drawback to the creation of regional trading blocs is what might be called "attention diversion." Countries may expend so much energy and political capital working on their own bloc that they don't have any left to work on the GATT system. The collective effort of the United States, Europe, and Japan is required to improve GATT. But if the Europeans are so heavily engaged in attending to their own regional development, they may not have the political will or energy to commit to the collective problem-solving process.

What will trade barriers between Europe and the rest of the world look like over the next ten years?

That's an open question at this point. There's a big conflict in Europe between the liberalizers who want to see these barriers come down and those who really want to protect Europe for Europeans. It's not clear how that conflict will resolve, but it will be very sensitive to what happens to the world economy. If the world economy stays in a slow growth phase, it's more likely that we will see a protectionist outcome in Europe, as the Europeans strive to keep employment and production at home.

What are the challenges and opportunities created by the emerging new nations of Eastern Europe?

There are three major challenges. The first is macroeconomic stabilization. These economies must be rebuilt on a sound macroeconomic foundation. Fiscal deficits must be controlled, monetary and credit policies must contain inflationary pressure, and outstanding foreign debts must be repaid on a timely basis. Otherwise, macroeconomic crises will undermine the transition, as they have undermined the efforts of developing countries in other parts of the world to build prosperous market economies. The second challenge is restructuring the composition of the economic base. Because the Eastern European countries were inward looking and traded primarily with one another, they have inherited an industrial base that is not competitive by international standards. Many industries have to be scaled back dramatically and some closed down altogether because they simply do not meet the demands of the international marketplace. Additionally, many things must be put into place, such as the appropriate infrastructure of financial services and transportation services that do not exist. These countries do not have a whole series of industries and activities that support modern industrial economies. The last challenge is one of economic reform itself. By that I mean changing the institutions and policy environment in which individ-

"**W**hen perfect markets don't exist, there may be a role for government intervention, since free trade does not always produce welfare-enhancing outcomes."

ual consumers and producers make their decisions. Distinct from the challenge of economic restructuring, which changes the composition of the economy, this third challenge involves changing the basic institutions of the economy—for example, privatizing state-run institutions.

We now see after two years of economic reforms that the process itself is very slow. One can deal with macroeconomic crises rather quickly, although with considerable political risk because of the pain and austerity necessitated by macroeconomic stabilization. Reform and privatization, however, are not changes that can happen quickly. The problems are just too big and the solutions too few.

Now let's consider the opportunities. Many of the Eastern European countries are not that poor by international development standards. It sounds ridiculous when you think about the suffering going on there, but you have to contrast it with the suffering in other parts of the world. Their relative prosperity may permit the Eastern European countries to make a very difficult transition without getting derailed politically. Their second advantage is their location. Trade flows are still disproportionately the greatest between countries that are near one another. Therefore, the Eastern European countries benefit from being near Western Europe, which will shortly become the largest developed market in the world. Finally, these countries have highly educated work forces and are starting out with very high levels of skills. The ability of their workers to learn new skills quickly is enhanced by their high levels of educational achievement.

What are the key principles of economics that you find most useful in your work as an international economist?

I would start with comparative advantage. Students need to understand the benefits of specialization. They need to understand how differences in resource endowments and technologies can lead to differences in cost. Further, they need to recognize that not all countries can do everything well and that countries should specialize in those things they do relatively well.

I would go a step further because I'm a policy-oriented economist and say comparative advantage is to some extent inherited and to some extent created. The trick for national policymakers is to undertake policies that will either enhance the nation's comparative advantage or create new advantage by creating new skills in the work force and new technologies.

It is also important for students and policymakers to understand the role of imperfect competition. Traditional comparative advantage theory is based on the notion of perfectly functioning markets, but almost all of the industries critical to trade among the developed countries have some of the features of imperfectly competitive markets. When perfect markets don't exist, there may be a role for government intervention, since free trade does not always produce welfare-enhancing outcomes.

How would you advise a student who is setting out on the study of economics and is interested in a career that emphasizes the international aspects of our subject?

I would advise students to study comparative economics as well as international economics because it's important to understand how national economies are organized and how they interact with one another. Since how countries organize to solve their economic problems is influenced by their politics, I would also suggest that students take a course or two in political science. They should also regularly read an international economics journal, like *The Economist* or the *Financial Times*. Finally, I strongly recommend that they either work or study abroad sometime during their college career. Studying at home is an imperfect substitute for living abroad when it comes to developing a real feel for differences among nations.

CHAPTER 18

Trading with the World

After studying this chapter, you will be able to:

- Describe the patterns and trends in international trade
- Explain comparative advantage
- Explain why all countries can gain from international trade
- Explain how prices adjust to bring about balanced trade
- Explain how economies of scale and diversity of taste lead to gains from international trade
- Explain why trade restrictions lower the volume of imports and exports and lower our consumption possibilities
- Explain why we have trade restrictions even though they lower our consumption possibilities

Silk Routes and Rust Belts

Since ancient times, people have striven to expand their trading as far as technology allowed. Roman coins have been found in the ruins of ancient Indian cities, and Marco Polo opened up the silk route between Europe and China in the thirteenth century. Today, container ships laden with cars and machines and Boeing 747s stuffed with farm-fresh foods ply sea and air routes, carrying billions of dollars worth of goods. Why do people go to such great lengths to trade with those in other nations? ◆◆ In recent years, a massive increase in the penetration of the foreign car industry into the United States has brought about a severe contraction of our own car industry. Jobs in Detroit and other car-producing cities have disappeared, creating what has come to be called the Rust Belt. Do the benefits of international trade make up for the cost of jobs displaced by foreign competition? Could we, as politicians often claim, improve our economy by restricting imports? ◆◆ The wages earned by the workers in the textile and electronics factories of Singapore, Taiwan, and Hong Kong are low compared with wages in the United States. Obviously, these countries can make manufactured goods much more cheaply than we can. How can we possibly compete with countries that pay their workers a fraction of U.S. wages? Are there any industries, besides perhaps the Hollywood movie industry, in which we have an advantage? ◆◆ In the 1930s, Congress passed the Smoot-Hawley Act, an act that increased taxes on imports to 60 percent, provoking widespread retaliation from the world's major trading countries. In contrast, after World War II, a process of trade liberalization brought about the creation of the General Agreement on Tariffs and Trade

(GATT) and a gradual reduction of taxes on imports. What are the effects of taxes on international trade? Why don't we have completely unrestricted international trade?

◆ ◆ ◆ ◆ In this chapter, we're going to learn about international trade. We'll discover how *all* nations can gain by specializing in producing the goods and services at which they have an advantage compared with other countries and by exchanging some of their output with each other. We'll discover that all countries can compete, no matter how high their wages. We will also explain why, despite the fact that international trade brings benefits to all, countries restrict trade. We'll discover who suffers and who benefits when international trade is restricted.

TABLE 18.1

U.S. Exports and Imports in 1992

Category	Exports	Imports	Balance
	(billions of dollars)		
Agricultural products	43.9	27.9	16.0
Industrial supplies and materials (excluding agricultural)	109.6	139.8	−30.2
Manufactured goods	285.8	367.8	−82.0
Services	178.5	123.4	55.1
Total	617.8	658.9	−41.1

Source: Survey of Current Business (May 1993), vol. 73.

Patterns and Trends in International Trade

The goods and services that we buy from people in other countries are called **imports**. The goods and services that we sell to people in other countries are called **exports**. What are the most important things that we import and export? Most people would probably guess that a rich nation such as the United States imports raw materials and exports manufactured goods. While that is one feature of U.S. international trade, it is not its most important feature. The vast bulk of our exports *and* imports is manufactured goods. We sell earth-moving equipment, airplanes, supercomputers, and scientific equipment, and we buy TVs, VCRs, blue jeans, and T-shirts. Also, we are a major exporter and importer of agricultural products and raw materials. We also import and export a huge volume of services. Let's look at the international trade of the United States in a recent year.

U.S. International Trade

Table 18.1 classifies U.S. international trade in four major categories of goods—agricultural products, industrial supplies and materials, manufactured goods, and services. The second column gives the value of U.S. exports, and the third column gives the value of U.S. imports. The fourth column tells us the balance of trade in the various categories. The **balance of trade** is the value of exports minus the value of imports. If the balance is positive, then the value of exports exceeds the value of imports and the United States is a **net exporter**. But if the balance is negative, the value of imports exceeds the value of exports and the United States is a **net importer**.

Trade in Goods About 80 percent of U.S. international trade is trade in goods, and 20 percent is trade in services. Of the categories of goods traded, by far the most important is manufactured goods. But the total value of exports of manufactured goods is less than that of imports—the United States is a net importer of manufactured goods. The United States is also a net importer of industrial supplies. It is a net exporter of agricultural products and services.

Table 18.2 highlights some of the major items of U.S. imports and exports of goods. The country's biggest net exports are aircraft, machinery, grains, and chemicals. The country's largest net imports are manufactured consumer goods, fuel, and automobiles (including auto parts).

TABLE 18.2

U.S. Exports and Imports of Goods in 1990: Some Large Individual Items

Item	Exports	Imports	Balance
	(billions of dollars)		
Aircraft	32.3	10.7	21.6
Machinery	119.8	104.6	15.2
Grains	14.9	—	14.9
Chemicals	28.4	14.3	14.1
Automobiles	37.4	87.3	−49.9
Fuels	14.0	65.7	−51.7
Manufactured consumer goods	43.3	105.7	−62.4

Source: *Survey of Current Business* (December 1991), vol. 71.

TABLE 18.3

U.S. Trade in Services in 1990

Category	Exports	Imports	Balance
	(billions of dollars)		
Travel and transportation	75.2	71.1	4.1
Other services	48.2	18.7	29.5
Military services	9.9	17.1	−7.2
Total	133.3	106.9	26.4

Source: *Survey of Current Business* (December 1991), vol. 71.

Trade in Services One fifth of U.S. international trade is not of goods but of services. You might be wondering how a country can "export" and "import" services. Let's look at some examples.

Suppose that you decided to vacation in France, traveling there on an Air France flight from New York. What you buy from Air France is not a good, but a transportation service. Although the concept might sound odd at first, in economic terms you are importing that service from France. Since you pay U.S. money to a French company in exchange for a service, it doesn't matter that most of your flight time is over the Atlantic Ocean. For that matter, the money you spend in France on hotel bills, restaurant meals, and other things is also classified as the import of services. Similarly, the vacation taken by a French student in the United States counts as an export of services to France.

When we import TV sets from South Korea, the owner of the ship that carries those TV sets might be Greek and the company that insures the cargo might be British. The payments that we make for the transportation and insurance to the Greek and British companies are also payments for the import of services. Similarly, when an American shipping company transports California wine to Tokyo, the transportation cost is an export of a service to Japan.

The importance of the various components of trade in services is set out in Table 18.3. As you can see, transportation and travel are the largest items—accounting for more than 50 percent of exports and almost 70 percent of imports.

Geographical Patterns The United States has important trading links with almost every part of the world except for Eastern Europe, where trade is almost nonexistent. As you can see from Table 18.4, our biggest trading partners are Canada and the European Community. Our *imports* from Japan and the newly industrializing countries of Asia such as Hong Kong, Singapore, South Korea, and Taiwan are also very large. Our international trade deficit is almost exclusively with this group of countries.

Trends in Trade

International trade has become an increasingly important part of our economic life. In 1950, we exported less than 5 percent of total output and imported only 4 percent of the goods and services that we consumed ourselves. Over the years since then, that percentage has steadily increased, and today it is more than double its level of 1950.

On the export side, all the major commodity categories have shared in the increased volume of international trade. Machinery, food, and raw materials have remained the most important components of

TABLE 18.4

U.S. Exports and Imports of Goods in 1992: Geographical Patterns

Country or region	Exports	Imports	Balance
	(billions of dollars)		
Canada	90.4	100.7	−10.3
Japan	46.9	96.9	−50.0
European Community	100.6	94.0	6.6
Latin America	75.3	69.1	6.2
Other Western Europe	13.8	17.4	−3.6
Eastern Europe	5.6	2.0	3.6
Other Asia and Africa	98.0	151.7	−53.7
Australia, New Zealand, and South Africa	8.7	3.7	5.0
Total	439.3	535.5	−96.2

Source: Survey of Current Business (March 1993), vol. 73.

FIGURE 18.1

The U.S. Balance of Trade

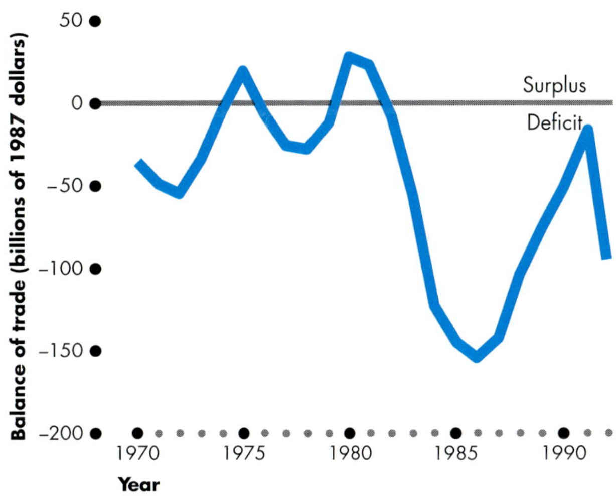

The balance of trade has fluctuated around zero, but since 1982, imports have been higher than exports and a deficit has emerged.

Source: Economic Report of the President, 1993.

exports and have roughly maintained their share in total exports.

But there have been dramatic changes in the composition of imports. Food and raw material imports have declined steadily. Imports of fuel increased dramatically in the 1970s but declined in the 1980s. Imports of machinery of all kinds, after being a fairly stable percentage of total imports until the middle 1980s, now approach 50 percent of total imports.

There have been important trends in the overall balance in U.S. international trade in recent years. That overall *balance of trade* (of goods and services) is shown in Fig. 18.1. As you can see, the balance fluctuates around zero, but in the years since 1982 there has been a large excess of imports over exports (a negative balance of trade).

Balance of Trade and International Borrowing

When people buy more than they sell, they have to finance the difference by borrowing. When they sell more than they buy, they can use the surplus to make loans to others. This simple principle that governs the income and expenditure and borrowing and lending of individuals and firms is also a feature of our balance of trade. If we import more than we export, we have to finance the difference by borrowing from foreigners. When we export more than we import, we make loans to foreigners to enable them to buy goods in excess of the value of the goods they have sold to us.

This chapter does *not* cover the factors that determine the balance of trade and the scale of the international borrowing and lending that finance that balance. It is concerned with understanding the volume, pattern, and directions of international trade rather than its balance. So that we can keep our focus on these topics, we'll build a model in which there is no international borrowing and lending—just international trade in goods and services. We'll find that we are able to understand what determines the volume, pattern, and direction of international trade and also establish its benefits and the costs of trade restrictions within this framework. This model can be expanded to include international borrowing and lending, but such an extension does not change the conclusions that we'll reach here about the factors that determine the volume, pattern, and directions of international trade.

Let's now begin to study those factors.

Opportunity Cost and Comparative Advantage

Let's apply the lessons that we learned in Chapter 3 about the gains from trade between Jane and Joe to the trade between nations. We'll begin by recalling how we can use the production possibility frontier to measure opportunity cost.

Opportunity Cost in Pioneerland

Pioneerland (a fictitious country) can produce grain and cars at any point inside or along the production possibility frontier shown in Fig. 18.2. (We're holding constant the output of all the other goods that Pioneerland produces.) The Pioneers (the people of Pioneerland) are consuming all the grain and cars that they produce, and they are operating at point *a* in the figure. That is, Pioneerland is producing and consuming 15 billion bushels of grain and 8 million cars each year. What is the opportunity cost of a car in Pioneerland?

We can answer that question by calculating the slope of the production possibility frontier at point *a*. As we discovered in Chapter 3 (pp. 54–56), the slope of the frontier measures the opportunity cost of one good in terms of the other. To measure the slope of the frontier at point *a*, place a straight line tangential to the frontier at point *a* and calculate the slope of that straight line. Recall that the formula for the slope of a line is the change in the value of the variable measured on the *y*-axis divided by the change in the value of the variable measured on the *x*-axis as we move along the line. Here, the variable measured on the *y*-axis is billions of bushels of grain, and the variable measured on the *x*-axis is millions of cars. So the slope (opportunity cost) is

FIGURE 18.2

Opportunity Cost in Pioneerland

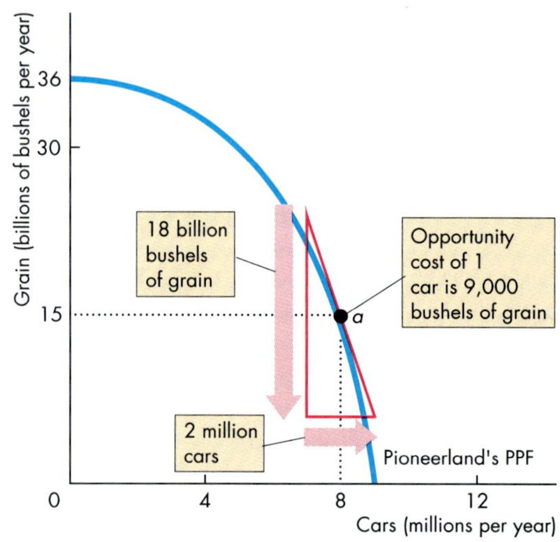

Pioneerland produces and consumes 15 billion bushels of grain and 8 million cars a year. That is, it produces and consumes at point *a* on its production possibility frontier. Opportunity cost is measured as the slope of the production possibility frontier. At point *a*, 2 million cars cost 18 billion bushels of grain. Equivalently, 1 car costs 9,000 bushels of grain or 9,000 bushels cost 1 car.

the change in the number of bushels of grain divided by the change in the number of cars. As you can see from the red triangle at point *a* in the figure, if the number of cars produced increases by 2 million, grain production decreases by 18 billion bushels. Therefore the slope is 18 billion divided by 2 million, which equals 9,000. To get one more car, the people of Pioneerland must give up 9,000 bushels of grain. Thus the opportunity cost of 1 car is 9,000 bushels of grain. Equivalently, 9,000 bushels of grain cost 1 car.

Opportunity Cost in Magic Empire

Now consider the production possibility frontier in Magic Empire (another fictitious country and the only other country in our model world). Figure 18.3 illustrates its production possibility frontier. Like the Pioneers, the Magicians (the people in Magic Empire) consume all the grain and cars that they produce. Magic Empire consumes 18 billion bushels of grain a year and 4 million cars, at point *a*'.

FIGURE 18.3

Opportunity Cost in Magic Empire

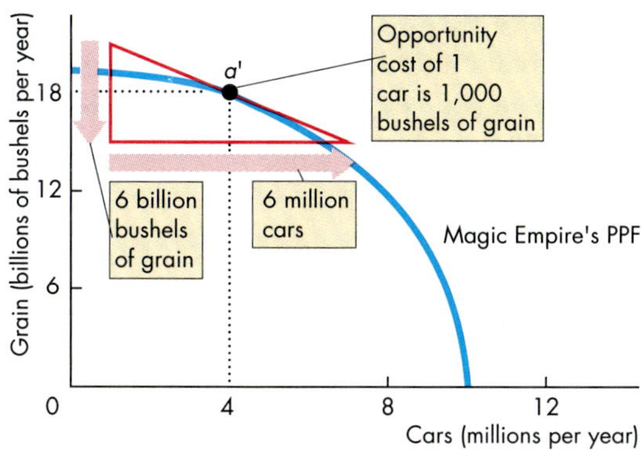

Magic Empire produces and consumes 18 billion bushels of grain and 4 million cars a year. That is, it produces and consumes at point *a'* on its production possibility frontier. Opportunity cost is measured as the slope of the production possibility frontier. At point *a'*, 6 million cars cost 6 billion bushels of grain. Equivalently, 1 car costs 1,000 bushels of grain or 1,000 bushels cost 1 car.

We can do the same kind of calculation of opportunity cost for Magic Empire as we have just done for Pioneerland. At point *a'*, 1 car costs 1,000 bushels of grain, or, equivalently, 1,000 bushels of grain costs 1 car.

Comparative Advantage

Cars are cheaper in Magic Empire than in Pioneerland. One car costs 9,000 bushels of grain in Pioneerland but only 1,000 bushels of grain in Magic Empire. But grain is cheaper in Pioneerland than in Magic Empire—9,000 bushels of grain cost only 1 car in Pioneerland, while that same amount of grain costs 9 cars in Magic Empire.

Magic Empire has a comparative advantage in car production. Pioneerland has a comparative advantage in grain production. A country has a **comparative advantage** in producing a good if it can produce that good at a lower opportunity cost than any other country can. Let's see how opportunity cost differences and comparative advantage generate gains from international trade.

The Gains from Trade

If Magic Empire bought grain for what it costs Pioneerland to produce it, then Magic Empire could buy 9,000 bushels of grain for 1 car. That is much lower than the cost of growing grain in Magic Empire, since there it costs 9 cars to produce 9,000 bushels of grain. If the Magicians buy at the low Pioneerland price, they will reap some gains.

If the Pioneers buy cars for what it costs Magic Empire to produce them, they will be able to obtain a car for 1,000 bushels of grain. Since it costs 9,000 bushels of grain to produce a car in Pioneerland, the Pioneers would gain from such an activity.

In this situation, it makes sense for Magicians to buy their grain from Pioneers and for Pioneers to buy their cars from Magicians. Let's see how such profitable international trade comes about.

Reaping the Gains from Trade

We've seen that the Pioneers would like to buy their cars from the Magicians and that the Magicians would like to buy their grain from the Pioneers. Let's see how the two groups do business with each other, concentrating attention on the international market for cars.

Figure 18.4 illustrates such a market. The quantity of cars traded internationally is measured on the horizontal axis. On the vertical axis we measure the price of a car, but it is expressed as its opportunity cost—the number of bushels of grain that a car costs. If no international trade takes place, that price in Pioneerland is 9,000 bushels of grain, indicated by point *a* in the figure. Again, if no trade takes place, that price is 1,000 bushels of grain in Magic Empire, indicated by point *a'* in the figure.

The points *a* and *a'* in Fig. 18.4 correspond to the points identified by those same letters in Figs. 18.2 and 18.3. The lower the price of a car (in terms of bushels of grain), the greater is the quantity of cars that the Pioneers import from the Magicians. This fact is illustrated in the downward-sloping curve that shows Pioneerland's import demand for cars.

FIGURE 18.4

International Trade in Cars

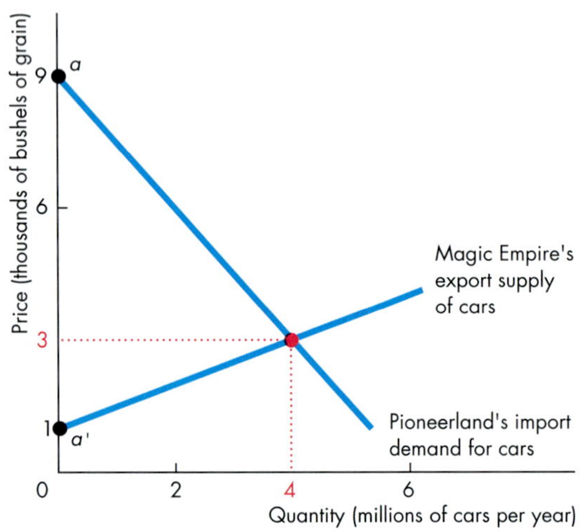

As the price of a car decreases, the quantity of imports demanded by Pioneerland increases—Pioneerland's import demand curve for cars is downward-sloping. As the price of a car increases, the quantity of cars supplied by Magic Empire for export increases—Magic Empire's export supply curve of cars is upward-sloping. Without international trade, the price of a car is 9,000 bushels of grain in Pioneerland (point *a*) and 1,000 bushels of grain in Magic Empire (point *a'*). With free international trade, the price of a car is determined where the export supply curve intersects the import demand curve—a price of 3,000 bushels of grain. At that price, 4 million cars a year are imported by Pioneerland and exported by Magic Empire. The value of grain exported by Pioneerland and imported by Magic Empire is 12 billion bushels a year, the quantity required to pay for the cars imported.

The Magicians respond in the opposite direction. The higher the price of cars (in terms of bushels of grain), the greater is the quantity of cars that Magicians export to Pioneers. This fact is reflected in Magic Empire's export supply of cars—the upward-sloping line in the figure.

The international market in cars determines the equilibrium price and quantity traded. This equilibrium occurs where the import demand curve intersects the export supply curve. In this case, the equilibrium price of a car is 3,000 bushels of grain. Four million cars a year are exported by Magic Empire and imported by Pioneerland. Notice that the price at which cars are traded is lower than the initial price in Pioneerland but higher than the initial price in Magic Empire.

Balanced Trade

Notice that the number of cars exported by Magic Empire—4 million a year—is exactly equal to the number of cars imported by Pioneerland. How does Pioneerland pay for its cars? By exporting grain. How much grain does Pioneerland export? You can find the answer by noticing that for 1 car, Pioneerland has to pay 3,000 bushels of grain. Hence for 4 million cars they have to pay 12 billion bushels of grain. Thus Pioneerland's exports of grain are 12 billion bushels a year. Magic Empire imports this same quantity of grain.

Magic Empire is exchanging 4 million cars for 12 billion bushels of grain each year, and Pioneerland is doing the opposite, exchanging 12 billion bushels of grain for 4 million cars. Trade is balanced between these two countries. The value received from exports equals the value paid out for imports.

Changes in Production and Consumption

We've seen that international trade makes it possible for Pioneers to buy cars at a lower price than that at which they can produce them for themselves. It also enables Magicians to sell their cars for a higher price, which is equivalent to saying that Magicians can buy grain for a lower price. Thus everybody seems to gain. Magicians buy grain at a lower price, and Pioneers buy cars at a lower price. How is it possible for everyone to gain? What are the changes in production and consumption that accompany these gains?

An economy that does not trade with other economies has identical production and consumption possibilities. Without trade, the economy can consume only what it produces. But with international trade, an economy can consume different quantities of goods from those that it produces. The production possibility frontier describes the limit of what a country can produce, but it does not describe the limits to what it can consume. Figure 18.5 will help you to see the distinction between production possibilities and consumption possibilities when a country trades with other countries.

First of all, notice that the figure has two parts, part (a) for Pioneerland and part (b) for Magic Empire. The production possibility frontiers that you saw in Figs. 18.2 and 18.3 are reproduced here. The slopes of the two black lines in the figure represent the opportunity costs in the two countries when

FIGURE 18.5

Expanding Consumption Possibilities

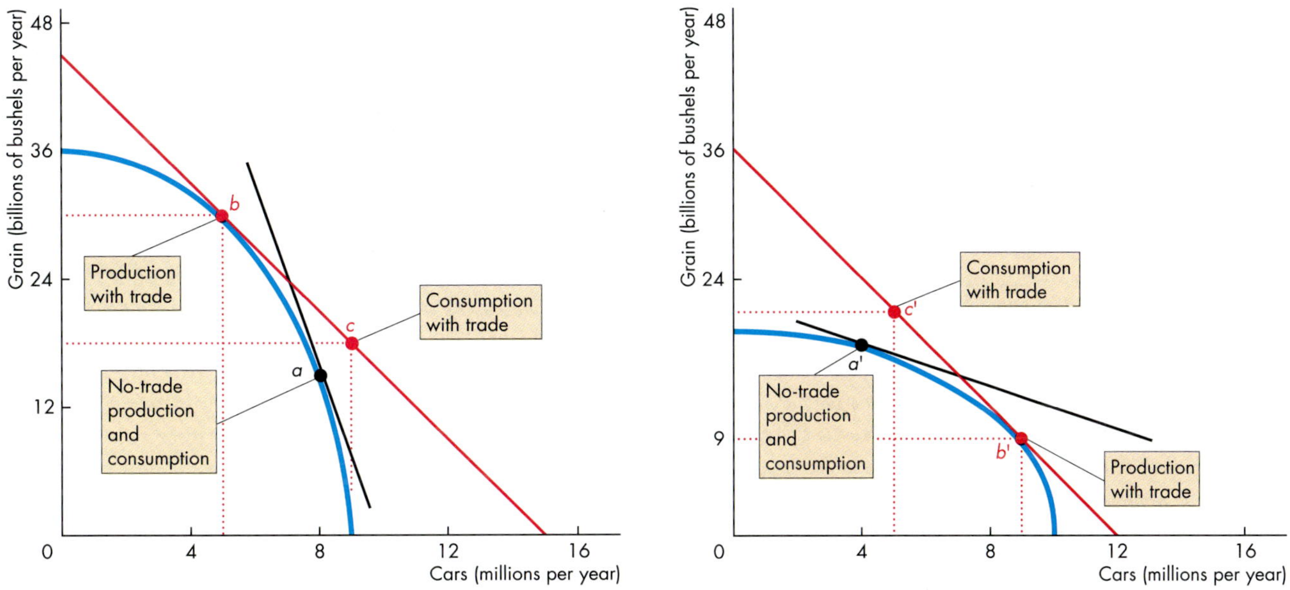

(a) Pioneerland **(b) Magic Empire**

With no international trade, the Pioneers produce and consume at point *a* and the opportunity cost of a car is 9,000 bushels of grain (the slope of the black line in part a). Also, with no international trade, the Magicians produce and consume at point *a*' and the opportunity cost of 1,000 bushels of grain is 1 car (the slope of the black line in part b).

Goods can be exchanged internationally at a price of 3,000 bushels of grain for 1 car along the red line. In part (a), Pioneerland decreases its production of cars and increases its production of grain, moving from *a* to *b*. It exports grain and imports cars, and it consumes at point *c*. The Pioneers have more of both cars and grain than they would if they produced all their own consumption goods—at point *a*. In part (b), Magic Empire increases car production and decreases grain production, moving from *a*' to *b*'. Magic Empire exports cars and imports grain, and it consumes at point *c*'. The Magicians have more of both cars and grain than they would if they produced all their own consumption goods—at point *a*'.

there is no international trade. Pioneerland produces and consumes at point *a*, and Magic Empire produces and consumes at *a*'. Cars cost 9,000 bushels of grain in Pioneerland and 1,000 bushels of grain in Magic Empire.

Consumption Possibilities The countries' consumption possibilities with international trade are shown by the two red lines in Fig. 18.5. These lines in both parts of the figure have the same slope, and that slope is the opportunity cost of a car in terms of grain on the world market—3,000 bushels per car. The *slope* of the consumption possibilities line is common to both countries because it is determined by the *world* price. But the position of a country's consumption possibilities line depends on its production possibilities. A country cannot produce outside its production possibility curve, so its consumption possibilities curve touches its production possibility curve. Thus Pioneerland could choose to consume what it produces, at point *b*, and not trade internationally or to trade internationally and consume at a point on its red consumption possibilities line.

Free Trade Equilibrium With international trade, the producers of cars in Magic Empire can get a higher price for their output. As a result, they increase the quantity of car production. At the same time, grain producers in Magic Empire are getting a lower price for their grain and so they reduce production. Producers in Magic Empire adjust their output until the opportunity cost in Magic Empire equals the opportunity cost in the world market. This situation arises when Magic Empire is producing at point *b*' in Fig. 18.5(b).

But the Magicians do not consume at point *b*'. That is, they do not increase their consumption of cars and decrease their consumption of grain. They sell some of the cars they produce to Pioneerland in exchange for some of Pioneerland's grain. But to see how that works out, we first need to check in with Pioneerland to see what's happening there.

In Pioneerland, cars are now less expensive and grain more expensive than before. As a consequence, producers in Pioneerland decrease car production and increase grain production. They do so until the opportunity cost of a car in terms of grain equals the cost on the world market. They move to point *b* in part (a). But the Pioneers do not consume at point *b*. They exchange some of the additional grain they produce for the now cheaper cars from Magic Empire.

The figure shows us the quantities consumed in the two countries. We saw in Fig. 18.4 that Magic Empire exports 4 million cars a year and Pioneerland imports those cars. We also saw that Pioneerland exports 12 billion bushels of grain a year and Magic Empire imports that grain. Thus Pioneerland's consumption of grain is 12 billion bushels a year less than it produces, and its consumption of cars is 4 million a year more than it produces. Pioneerland consumes at point *c* in Fig. 18.5(a).

Similarly, we know that Magic Empire consumes 12 billion bushels of grain more than it produces and 4 million cars fewer than it produces. Thus Magic Empire consumes at *c*' in Fig. 18.5(b).

Calculating the Gains from Trade

You can now literally "see" the gains from trade in Fig. 18.5. Without trade, Pioneers produce and consume at *a* (part a)—a point on Pioneerland's production possibility frontier. With international trade, Pioneers consume at point *c* in part (a)—a point *outside* the production possibility frontier. At point *c*, Pioneers are consuming 3 billion bushels of grain a year and 1 million cars a year more than before. These increases in consumption of cars and grain, beyond the limits of the production possibility frontier, are the gains from international trade.

But Magicians also gain. Without trade, they consume at point *a*' in part (b)—a point on Magic Empire's production possibility frontier. With international trade, they consume at point *c*'—a point outside the production possibility frontier. With international trade, Magic Empire consumes 3 billion bushels of grain a year and 1 million cars a year more than without trade. These are the gains from international trade for Magic Empire.

Gains for All

When Pioneers and Magicians trade with each other, potentially everyone can gain. Domestic sellers add the net demand of foreigners to their domestic demand, and so their market expands. Buyers are faced with domestic supply plus net foreign supply and so have a larger total supply available to them. As you know, prices increase when there is an increase in demand and they decrease when there is an increase in supply. Thus the increased demand (from foreigners) for exports increases their price and the increased supply (from foreigners) of imports decreases their price. Gains in one country do not bring losses in another. Everyone, in this example, gains from international trade.

Absolute Advantage

Suppose that in Magic Empire, fewer workers are needed to produce any given output of either grain or cars than in Pioneerland—productivity is higher in Magic Empire than in Pioneerland. In this situation, Magic Empire has an *absolute advantage* over Pioneerland. We defined absolute advantage in Chapter 3 in terms of an individual. If one person has greater productivity than another in the production of all goods, that person is said to have an absolute advantage. A country has an absolute advantage if it has greater productivity than another country in the production of all goods. With an absolute advantage, isn't it the case that Magic Empire can outsell Pioneerland in all markets? Why, if Magic Kingdom has greater productivity than Pioneerland, does it pay Magic Empire to buy *anything* from Pioneerland?

The answer is that the cost of production in terms of the factors of production employed is irrelevant for determining the gains from trade. It does not matter how much labor, land, and capital are required to produce 1,000 bushels of grain or a car.

What matters is how many cars must be given up to produce more grain or how much grain must be given up to produce more cars. That is, what matters is the opportunity cost of one good in terms of the other good. Magic Empire may have an absolute advantage in the production of all things, but it cannot have a comparative advantage in the production of all goods. The statement that the opportunity cost of cars in Magic Empire is lower than in Pioneerland is identical to the statement that the opportunity cost of grain is higher in Magic Empire than that in Pioneerland. Thus *whenever opportunity costs diverge, everyone has a comparative advantage in something*. All countries can potentially gain from international trade.

The story of the discovery of the logic of the gains from international trade is presented in Our Advancing Knowledge on pp. 484–485.

REVIEW

When countries have divergent opportunity costs, they can gain from international trade. Each country can buy goods and services from another country at a lower opportunity cost than that at which it can produce them for itself. Gains arise when each country increases its production of those goods and services in which it has a comparative advantage (of goods and services that it can produce at an opportunity cost that is lower than that of other countries) and exchanges some of its production for that of other countries. All countries gain from international trade. Everyone has a comparative advantage at something. ◆

Gains from Trade in Reality

The gains from trade that we have just studied between Pioneerland and Magic Empire in grain and cars are taking place in a model economy—in an economy that we have imagined. But these same phenomena are occurring every minute of every day in real-world economies. We buy cars made in Japan, and American producers of grain and lumber sell large parts of their output to Japanese households and firms. We buy cars and machinery from European producers and sell airplanes and computers to Europeans in return. We buy shirts and fashion goods from the people of Hong Kong and sell them machinery in return. We buy TV sets and VCRs from South Korea and Taiwan and sell them financial and other services as well as manufactured goods in return.

Thus much of the international trade that we see in the real world takes precisely the form of the trade that we have studied in our model of the world economy. But as we discovered earlier in this chapter, a great deal of world trade is heavily concentrated among industrial countries and primarily involves the international exchange of manufactured goods. Thus the type of trade that we have just analyzed—exchanging cars for grain—although an important and clearly profitable type of trade, is not the most prominent type. Why do countries exchange manufactured goods with each other? Can our model of international trade explain such exchange?

Trade in Similar Goods

At first thought, it seems puzzling that countries would trade manufactured goods. Consider, for example, America's trade in automobiles and auto parts. Why does it make sense for the United States to produce automobiles for export and at the same time to import large quantities of them from Canada, Japan, Korea, and Western Europe? Wouldn't it make more sense to produce all the cars that we buy here in the United States? After all, we have access to the best technology available for producing cars. Auto workers in the United States are surely as productive as their fellow workers in Canada, Western Europe, and the Pacific countries. Capital equipment, production lines, robots, and the like used in the manufacture of cars are as available to American car producers as they are to any others. This line of reasoning leaves a puzzle concerning the sources of international exchange of similar commodities produced by similar people using similar equipment. Why does it happen?

Diversity of Taste The first part of the answer to the puzzle is that people have a tremendous diversity of taste. Let's stick with the example of cars. Some people prefer a sports car, some prefer a limousine, some prefer a regular, full-size car, and some prefer a compact. In addition to size and type of car, there are many other dimensions on which cars vary.

Our Advancing Knowledge

UNDERSTANDING the Gains from INTERNATIONAL TRADE

Until the mid-eighteenth century, it was generally believed that the purpose of international trade was to keep exports above imports and pile up gold. If gold was accumulated, it was believed, the nation would prosper; and if gold was lost through an international deficit, the nation would be drained of money and be impoverished. These beliefs are called *mercantilism,* and the *mercantilists* were pamphleteers who advocated with missionary fervor the pursuit of an international surplus. If exports did not exceed imports, the mercantilists wanted imports restricted.

In the 1740s, David Hume explained that as the quantity of money (gold) changes, so also does the price level, and the nation's *real* wealth is unaffected. In the 1770s, Adam Smith explained that restricting imports lowers the gains from specialization and makes a nation poorer. Mercantilism was intellectually bankrupt.

Gradually, through the nineteenth century, the mercantilists' influence waned, and North America and Western Europe prospered in an environment of increasingly free international trade. But despite remarkable advances in economic understanding, mercantilism never quite died. It had a brief and devastating revival in the 1920s and 1930s, when tariff hikes brought about the collapse of international trade and accentuated the Great Depression. It subsided again after World War II with the establishment of the General Agreement on Tariffs and Trade (GATT).

But mercantilism lingers on. The often expressed view that the United States should restrict Japanese imports and reduce its deficit with Japan is a modern manifestation of mercantilism. It would be interesting to have Hume and Smith commenting on these views. But we know what they would say—the same things that they said to the eighteenth-century mercantilists. And they would still be right.

"Free trade, one of the greatest blessings which a government can confer on a people, is in almost every country unpopular."

Thomas Macaulay
Essay on Mitford's History of Greece

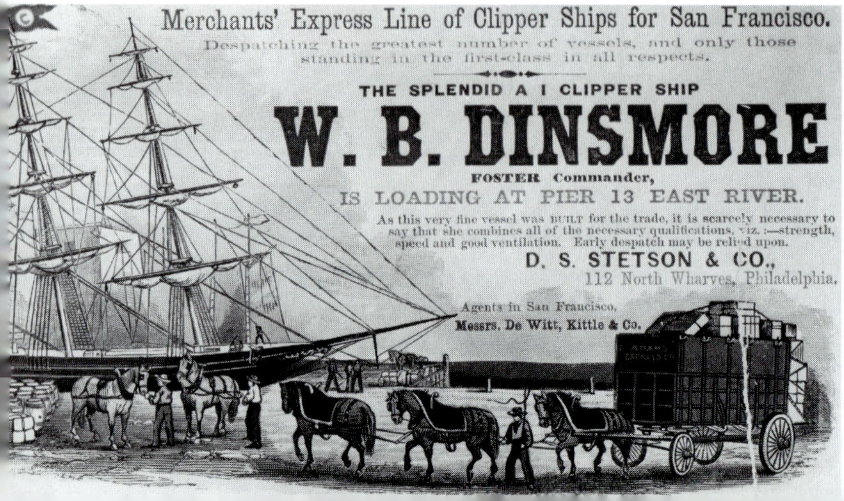

In the eighteenth century, when mercantilists and economists were debating the pros and cons of free international exchange, the transportation technology available severely limited the gains from international trade. Sailing ships with tiny cargo holds took close to a month to cross the Atlantic Ocean. But the potential gains were large and so was the incentive to cut shipping costs. By the 1850s, the clipper ship had been developed, cutting the time for the journey from Boston to Liverpool to only 12¼ days. Half a century later, 10,000-ton steamships were sailing between America and England in just 4 days. As sailing times and costs declined, the gains from international trade increased and the volume of trade expanded.

The container ship and the Boeing 747 have revolutionized international trade and contributed to its continued expansion. Today, most goods cross the oceans in containers—metal boxes—packed into and piled on top of ships like the one shown here. Container technology has cut the cost of ocean shipping by economizing on handling and by making cargoes harder to steal, which lowers insurance costs. It is unlikely that there would be much international trade in goods such as television sets and VCRs without this technology. High-value and perishable cargoes such as flowers and fresh foods, as well as urgently needed items, travel by air. Every day, dozens of cargo-laden 747s fly between all major U.S. cities and destinations across the Atlantic and Pacific Oceans.

FROM SMITH & RICARDO TO GATT

David Ricardo (1772–1832) was a highly successful 27-year-old stockbroker when he stumbled on a copy of Adam Smith's *Wealth of Nations* on a weekend visit to the country. He was immediately hooked and went on to become the most celebrated economist of his age and one of the greatest economists of all time. One of his many contributions was to develop the principle of comparative advantage, the foundation on which the modern theory of international trade is built. The example he used to illustrate this principle was the trade between England and Portugal in cloth and wine.

The General Agreement on Tariffs and Trade (GATT) was established as a reaction against the devastation wrought by beggar-my-neighbor tariffs imposed during the 1920s. But it is also a triumph for the logic first worked out by Smith and Ricardo.

Some have low fuel consumption, some have high performance, some are spacious and comfortable, some have a large trunk, some have four-wheel drive, some have front-wheel drive, some have manual transmission, some have automatic transmission, some are durable, some are flashy, some have a radiator grill that looks like a Greek temple, others look like a wedge. People's preferences across these many dimensions vary.

The tremendous diversity in tastes for cars means that people would be dissatisfied if they were forced to consume from a limited range of standardized cars. People value variety and are willing to pay for it in the marketplace.

Economies of Scale The second part of the answer to the puzzle is economies of scale. *Economies of scale* are the tendency, present in many production processes, for the average cost of production to be lower, the larger the scale of production. In such situations, larger and larger production runs lead to ever lower average production costs. Many manufactured goods, including cars, experience economies of scale. For example, if a car producer makes only a few hundred (or perhaps a few thousand) cars of a particular type and design, the producer has to use production techniques that are much more labor-intensive and much less automated than those actually employed to make hundreds of thousands of cars in a particular model. With low production runs and labor-intensive production techniques, costs are high. With very large production runs and automated assembly lines, production costs are much lower. But to obtain lower costs, the automated assembly lines have to produce a large number of cars.

It is the combination of diversity of taste and economies of scale that produces such a large amount of international trade in similar commodities. Diversity of taste and the willingness to pay for variety do not guarantee that variety will be available. It could simply be too expensive to provide a highly diversified range of different types of cars, for example. If every car bought in the United States today was made in the United States and if the present range of diversity and variety was available, production runs would be remarkably short. Car producers would not be able to reap economies of scale. Although the current variety of cars could be made available, it would be at a very high price, perhaps at a price that no one would be willing to pay.

But with international trade, each manufacturer of cars has the whole world market to serve. Each producer specializes in a limited range of products and then sells its output to the entire world market. This arrangement enables large production runs on the most popular cars and feasible production runs even on the most customized cars demanded by only a handful of people.

The situation in the market for cars is also present in many other industries, especially those producing specialized machinery and specialized machine tools. Thus international exchange of similar but slightly differentiated manufactured products is a highly profitable activity.

This type of trade can be understood with exactly the same model of international trade that we studied earlier. Although we normally think of cars as a single commodity, we simply have to think of sports cars, sedans, and so on as different goods. Different countries, by specializing in a few of these "goods," are able to enjoy economies of scale and, therefore, a comparative advantage in their production.

You can see that comparative advantage and international trade bring gains regardless of the goods being traded. When the rich countries of the European Community, Japan, and the United States import raw materials from the Third World and from Australia and Canada, the rich importing countries gain and so do the exporting countries. When we buy cheap TV sets, VCRs, shirts, and other goods from low-wage countries, both we and the exporters gain from the exchange. It's true that if we increase our imports of cars and produce fewer cars ourselves, jobs in our car industry disappear. But jobs in other industries, industries in which we have a comparative advantage and supply to other nations, expand. After the adjustment is completed, people whose jobs have been lost find employment in the expanding industries. They buy goods produced in other countries at even lower prices than those at which the goods were available before. The gains from international trade are not gains for some at the expense of losses for others.

But changes in comparative advantage that lead to changes in international trade patterns can take a long time to adjust to. For example, the increase in automobile imports and the corresponding relative decline in domestic car production have not brought increased wealth for displaced auto workers. Good new jobs take time to find, and often people go through a period of prolonged search, putting up with inferior jobs and lower wages than they had before. Thus only in the long run does everyone potentially gain from international specialization and exchange. Short-run adjustment costs that can be large and relatively prolonged are borne by the people who have lost their comparative advantage. Some of the people who lose their jobs may be too old for it to be worth their while to make the move to another region of the country or industry, and so they never share in the gains.

Partly because of the costs of adjustment to changing international trade patterns, but partly also for other reasons, governments intervene in international trade, restricting its volume. Let's examine what happens when governments restrict international trade. We'll contrast restricted trade with free trade. We'll see that free trade brings the greatest possible benefits. We'll also see why, in spite of the benefits of free trade, governments sometimes restrict trade.

Trade Restrictions

Governments restrict international trade in order to protect domestic industries from foreign competition. The restriction of international trade is called **protectionism.** There are two main protectionist methods employed by governments:

- Tariffs
- Nontariff barriers

A **tariff** is a tax that is imposed by the importing country when a good crosses an international boundary. A **nontariff barrier** is any action other than a tariff that restricts international trade. Examples of nontariff barriers are quantitative restrictions and licensing regulations limiting imports. We'll consider nontariff barriers in more detail below. First, let's look at tariffs.

The History of Tariffs

Average tariff levels in the United States today are quite modest compared with their historical levels. As you can see from Fig. 18.6, tariff levels averaged around 40 percent before World War II. During the 1930s, with the passage of the Smoot-Hawley Act, they reached 60 percent. Today, average tariffs are only 4 percent of total imports and 6 percent of the value of those imports that are subject to a tariff.

The reduction in tariffs followed the establishment of the General Agreement on Tariffs and Trade (GATT). The **General Agreement on Tariffs and Trade** is an international agreement designed to limit government intervention to restrict international trade. It was negotiated immediately following World War II and was signed in October 1947. Its goal is to liberalize trading activity and to provide an organization to administer more liberal trading arrangements. GATT itself is a small organization located in Geneva, Switzerland.

Since the formation of GATT, several rounds of negotiations have taken place that have resulted in general tariff reductions. One of these, the Kennedy Round, which began in the early 1960s, resulted in large tariff cuts in the late 1960s. Yet further tariff cuts resulted from the Tokyo Round, which took place between 1973 and 1979, and the Uruguay Round of the late 1980s and early 1990s.

In addition to the agreements under the GATT, the United States is a party to several important trade agreements with individual countries. One of these is the Canada–United States free trade agreement that became effective on January 1, 1989. Under this agreement, barriers to international trade between Canada and the United States will be virtually eliminated after a ten-year phasing-in period. Another important development is an attempt to work out a free trade deal with Mexico that could create a large North American free trade area embracing Mexico, Canada, and the United States. Within Western Europe, trade barriers among the member countries of the European Community were virtually eliminated by 1992, creating the largest unified tariff-free market in the world.

The benefits of free trade, both in theory and in the recent experience of the countries of the European Community, have given impetus to a series of talks among the countries of Central and South America aimed at creating a series of free-trade

FIGURE 18.6

U.S. Tariffs: 1900–1990

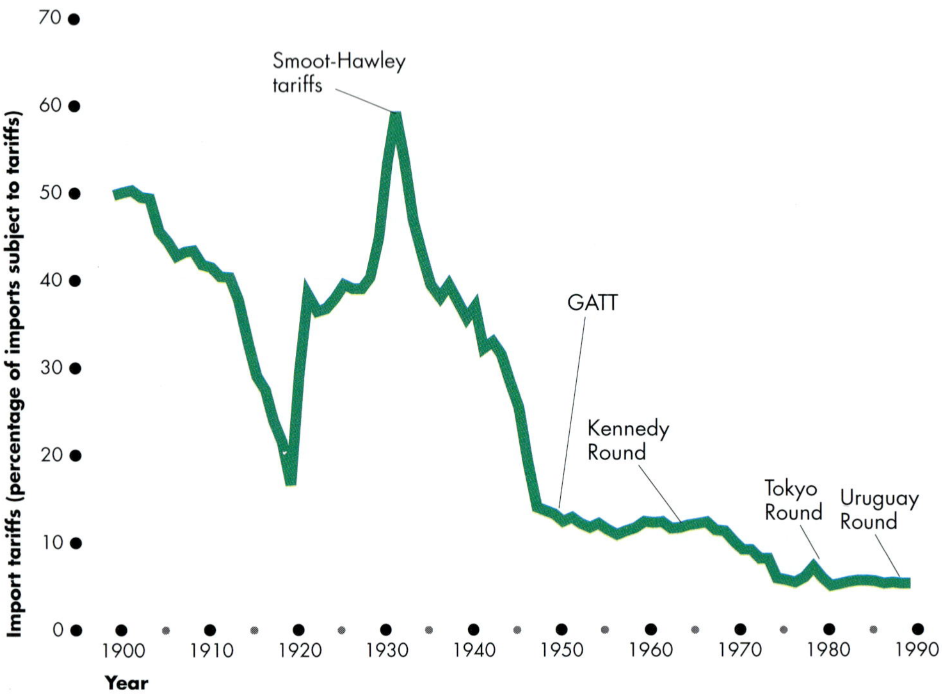

Tariffs in the United States averaged around 40 percent before World War II. In the early 1930s, they increased to 60 percent with the passage of the Smoot-Hawley Act. Since the establishment of GATT following World War II, tariffs have steadily declined in a series of negotiating rounds and are now at the lowest level they have ever been.

Sources: U.S. Bureau of the Census, *Historical Statistics of the United States, Colonial Times to 1970, Bicentennial Edition, Part 1* (Washington D.C.: 1975); Series U-212: *Statistical Abstract of the United States: 1986,* 106th edition (Washington, D.C.: 1985); and *Statistical Abstract of the United States: 1992,* 112th edition (Washington, D.C.: 1992).

agreements among these countries and, even more ambitiously, free-trade American continents. This movement is discussed in Reading Between the Lines on pp. 490–491.

The talks taking place among the countries of North and South America underline the fact that despite a steady process of tariff reductions, trade among some countries and trade in some goods are still subject to extremely high tariffs. The highest tariffs faced by U.S. buyers are those on textiles and footwear. A tariff of more than 10 percent (on the average) is imposed on almost all our imports of textiles and footwear. For example, when you buy a pair of blue jeans for $20, you pay about $5 more than you would if there were no tariffs on textiles. Other goods protected by tariffs are agricultural products, automobiles, energy and chemicals, minerals, and metals. Almost all the meat and cheese that you consume costs significantly more because of protection than it would with free international trade.

The temptation for governments to impose tariffs is a strong one. First, tariffs provide revenue to the government. Second, they enable the government to satisfy special interest groups in import-competing industries. But, as we'll see, free international trade brings enormous benefits that are reduced when tariffs are imposed. Let's see how.

How Tariffs Work

To analyze how tariffs work, let's return to the example of trade between Pioneerland and Magic Empire. Suppose that these two countries are trading cars and grain in exactly the same way that we analyzed before. Magic Empire exports cars, and Pioneerland exports grain. The volume of car imports into Pioneerland is 4 million a year, and cars are selling on the world market for 3,000 bushels of grain. Let's suppose that grain costs $1 a bushel, so, equivalently, cars are selling for $3,000. Figure 18.7 illustrates this situation. The volume of trade in cars and their price are determined at the point of intersection of Magic Empire's export supply curve of cars and Pioneerland's import demand curve for cars.

Now suppose that the government of Pioneerland, perhaps under pressure from car producers, decides to impose a tariff on imported cars. In particular, suppose that a tariff of $4,000 per car is imposed. (This is a huge tariff, but the car producers of Pioneerland are pretty fed up with competition from Magic Empire.) What happens?

The first part of the answer is obtained by studying the effects on the supply of cars in Pioneerland. Cars are no longer going to be available at the Magic Empire export supply price. The tariff of $4,000 must be added to that price—the amount paid to the government of Pioneerland on each car imported. As a consequence, the supply curve in Pioneerland shifts upward as shown in Fig. 18.7. The new supply curve becomes that labeled "Magic Empire's export supply of cars plus tariff." The vertical distance between Magic Empire's export supply curve and the new supply curve is the tariff imposed by the government of Pioneerland.

The next part of the answer is found by determining the new equilibrium. Imposing a tariff has no effect on the demand for cars in Pioneerland and so has no effect on Pioneerland's import demand for cars. The new equilibrium occurs where the new supply curve intersects Pioneerland's import demand curve for cars. That equilibrium is at a price of $6,000 a car with 2 million cars a year being imported. Imports fall from 4 million to 2 million cars a year. At the higher price of $6,000 a car, domestic car producers increase their production. Domestic grain production decreases to free up the resources for the expanded car industry.

The total expenditure on imported cars by the Pioneers is $6,000 a car multiplied by the 2 million cars imported ($12 billion). But not all of that money goes to the Magicians. They receive $2,000 a car, or $4 billion for the 2 million cars. The difference—$4,000 a car, or a total of $8 billion for the 2 million cars—is collected by the government of Pioneerland as tariff revenue.

Obviously, the government of Pioneerland is happy with this situation. It is now collecting $8 billion that it didn't have before. But what about the Pioneers? How do they view the new situation? The demand curve tells us the maximum price that a buyer is willing to pay for one more unit of a good. As you can see from Pioneerland's import demand curve for cars, if one more car could be imported, someone would be willing to pay almost $6,000 for it. Magic Empire's export supply curve of cars tells us the minimum price at which additional cars are available. As you can see, one additional car would be supplied by Magic Empire for a price only slightly more than $2,000. Thus, since someone is willing to pay almost $6,000 for a car and someone is willing to supply one for little more than $2,000, there is obviously a gain to be had from trading an extra car. In fact, there are gains to be had—willingness to pay exceeds the minimum supply price—all the way up to 4 million cars a year. Only when 4 million cars are being traded is the maximum price that a Pioneer is willing to pay equal to the minimum price that is acceptable to a Magician. Thus restricting

FIGURE 18.7

The Effects of a Tariff

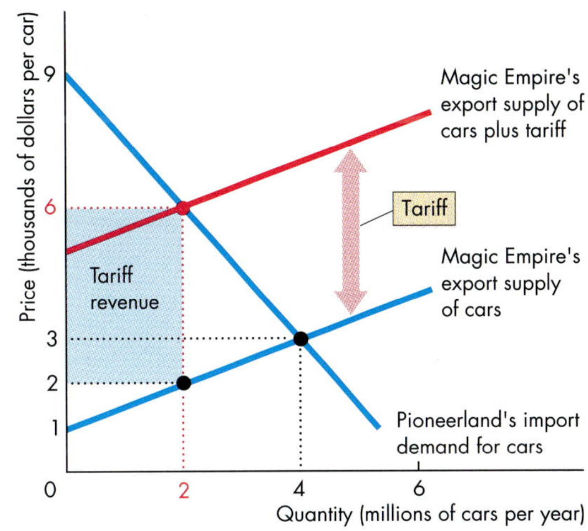

Pioneerland imposes a tariff on car imports from Magic Empire. The tariff increases the price that Pioneers have to pay for cars. It shifts the supply curve of cars in Pioneerland upward. The distance between the original supply curve and the new one is the amount of the tariff. The price of cars in Pioneerland increases, and the quantity of cars imported decreases. The government of Pioneerland collects a tariff revenue of $4,000 per car—a total of $8 billion on the 2 million cars imported. Pioneerland's exports of grain decrease, since Magic Empire now has a lower income from its exports of cars.

The Gains from Trade in Action

THE ECONOMIST, JANUARY 4, 1992

Free-trade free-for-all

Having spent the 1950s and 1960s building the non-communist world's most impenetrable trade barriers, Latin America is pulling them down as fast as it can . . ., preparing the way for a single Latin American trade block. In fact the dream of most Latin American countries is to join, together or alone, with a North American Free-Trade Area of Mexico, Canada and the United States. . . .

The first pillar in this ambitious and hurried edifice is this month's free-trade pact between Venezuela, Colombia and Bolivia. Peru and Ecuador will join the pact in six months' time. . . .

[A] . . . free-trade agreement [is] being forged by Argentina, Brazil, Uruguay and Paraguay. Called Mercosur, it originated in 1988 as a free-trade pact between Brazil and Argentina and was expanded to embrace Uruguay and Paraguay last March. By the end of 1994 it is supposed to enshrine a completely free market in goods, services and labour for Argentina and Brazil, with Uruguay and Paraguay following a year later. . . .

Two other pacts are in the offing. Central America is trying to revive its common market, which was set up in the 1960s. It collapsed in 1969, when war broke out between Honduras and El Salvador. . . .

Lastly, there is the customs union that . . . the English-speaking Caribbean countries under the auspices of the Caribbean Community (Caricom) [are attempting to establish]. . . .

The real prize is . . . the establishment of a pan-American free-trade area. . . . Since 1987 the United States has signed 16 "framework" agreements with Latin American countries. In theory these are agreements merely to talk about trade. In practice, they are paving the way for a trade block embracing all the Americas.

Achieving such a goal depends almost entirely upon success of the free-trade agreement that the United States is negotiating with Mexico. Once this is approved by Congress, other Latin American governments might accede to it, just as new members join the EC. A stampede to join is expected. . . .

The Essence of the Story

Among Latin American countries, trade barriers are high, but a movement is underway to lower them.

Four agreements are being forged:

- The Andean Pact between Bolivia, Colombia, Ecuador, Peru, and Venezuela
- Mercosur, a free-trade area embracing Argentina, Brazil, Uruguay, and Paraguay
- The Central American common market embracing Costa Rica, El Salvador, Guatemala, Honduras, and Nicaragua
- Caricom, a customs union among the English-speaking Caribbean countries

Since 1987 the United States has signed 16 "framework" agreements to talk about trade with Latin American countries. These agreements are paving the way for a trade block embracing all the Americas.

Achieving such a goal depends crucially on the success of the United States–Mexico free-trade agreement. Once this agreement is approved by Congress, there could be a stampede of other Latin American governments seeking to join the group—just like countries joining the European Community.

Background and Analysis

With the exception of the Caricom countries, international trade plays a much smaller part in the nations of North and South America than it does in Western Europe—see Fig. 1.

The move to open up the countries of the Americas to greater international competition will bring increased specialization as countries seek to gain from exporting the goods and services in which they have a comparative advantage.

The evidence from Western Europe is that lower trade barriers bring a larger amount of international trade and more rapidly growing real incomes—see Fig. 2.

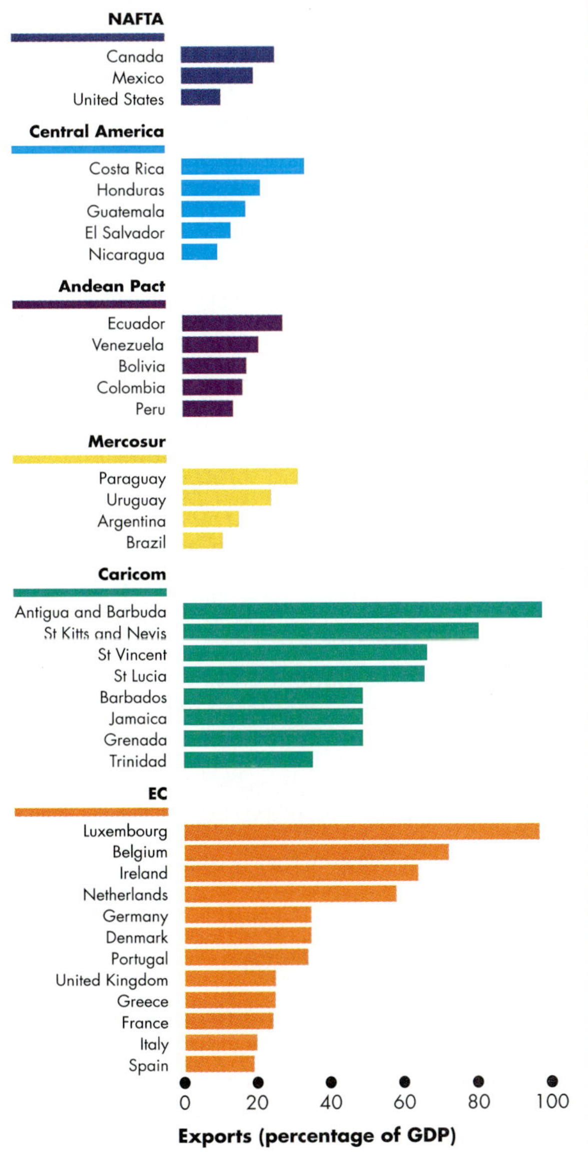

Figure 1

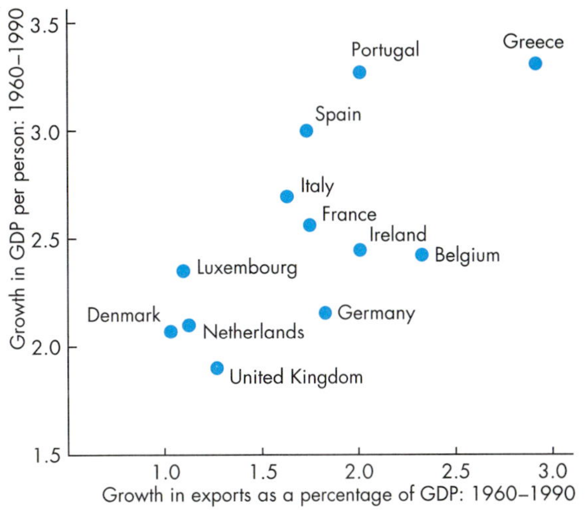

Figure 2

international trade reduces the gains from international trade.

It is easy to see that the tariff has lowered Pioneerland's total import bill. With free trade, Pioneerland was paying $3,000 a car and buying 4 million cars a year from Magic Empire. Thus the total import bill was $12 billion a year. With a tariff, Pioneerland's imports have been cut to 2 million cars a year and the price paid to Magic Empire has also been cut to only $2,000 a car. Thus the import bill has been cut to $4 billion a year. Doesn't this fact mean that Pioneerland's balance of trade has changed? Is Pioneerland now importing less than it is exporting?

To answer that question, we need to figure out what's happening in Magic Empire. We've just seen that the price that Magic Empire receives for cars has fallen from $3,000 to $2,000 a car. Thus the price of cars in Magic Empire has fallen. But if the price of cars has fallen, the price of grain has increased. With free trade, the Magicians could buy 3,000 bushels of grain for one car. Now they can buy only 2,000 bushels for a car. With a higher price of grain, the quantity demanded by the Magicians decreases. As a result, Magic Empire's import of grain declines. But so does Pioneerland's export of grain. In fact, Pioneerland's grain industry suffers from two sources. First, there is a decrease in the quantity of grain sold to Magic Empire. Second, there is increased competition for inputs from the now expanded car industry. Thus the tariff leads to a contraction in the scale of the grain industry in Pioneerland.

It seems paradoxical at first that a country imposing a tariff on cars would hurt its own export industry, lowering its exports of grain. It might help to think of it this way: Foreigners buy grain with the money they make from exporting cars. If they export fewer cars, they cannot afford to buy as much grain. In fact, in the absence of any international borrowing and lending, Magic Empire has to cut its imports of grain by exactly the same amount as the loss in revenue from its export of cars. Grain imports into Magic Empire will be cut back to a value of $4 billion, the amount that can be paid for by the new lower revenue from Magic Empire's car exports. Thus trade is still balanced in this post-tariff situation. Although the tariff has cut imports, it has also cut exports, and the cut in the value of exports is exactly equal to the cut in the value of imports. The tariff, therefore, has no effect on the balance of trade—it reduces the volume of trade.

The result that we have just derived is perhaps one of the most misunderstood aspects of international economics. On countless occasions, politicians and others have called for tariffs in order to remove a balance of trade deficit or have argued that lowering tariffs would produce a balance of trade deficit. They reach this conclusion by failing to work out all the implications of a tariff. Because a tariff raises the price of imports and cuts imports, the easy conclusion is that the tariff strengthens the balance of trade. But the tariff also changes the *volume* of exports. The equilibrium effects of a tariff are to reduce the volume of trade in both directions and by the same value on each side of the equation. The balance of trade itself is left unaffected.

Learning the Hard Way Although the analysis that we have just worked through leads to the clear conclusion that tariffs cut both imports and exports and make everyone worse off, we have not found that conclusion easy to accept. Time and again in our history, we have imposed high tariff barriers on international trade (as Fig. 18.6 illustrates). Whenever tariff barriers are increased, trade collapses. The most vivid historical example of this interaction of tariffs and trade occurred during the Great Depression years of the early 1930s when, in the wake of the Smoot-Hawley tariff increases and the retaliatory tariff changes that other countries introduced as a consequence, world trade almost dried up.

Let's now turn our attention to the other range of protectionist weapons—nontariff barriers.

Nontariff Barriers

There are two important forms of nontariff barriers:

- Quotas
- Voluntary export restraints

A **quota** is a quantitative restriction on the import of a particular good. It specifies the maximum amount of the good that may be imported in a given period of time. A **voluntary export restraint** is an agreement between two governments in which the government of the exporting country agrees to restrain the volume of its own exports. Voluntary export restraints are often called VERs.

Nontariff barriers have become important features of international trading arrangements in the period since World War II, and there is now general agreement that nontariff barriers are a more severe impediment to international trade than tariffs.

It is difficult to quantify the effects of nontariff barriers in a way that makes them easy to compare with tariffs, but some studies have attempted to do just that. Such studies attempt to assess the tariff rate that would restrict trade by the same amount as the nontariff barriers do. With such calculations, nontariff barriers and tariffs can be added together to assess the total amount of protection. When we add nontariff barriers to tariffs for the United States, the overall amount of protection increases more than threefold. Even so, the United States is the least protectionist country in the world. Total protection is higher in the European Community and higher still in other developed countries and Japan. The less developed countries and the so-called newly industrializing countries have the highest protection rates.

Quotas are especially important in the textile industries, in which there exists an international agreement called the Multifiber Agreement, which establishes quotas on a wide range of textile products. Agriculture is also subject to extensive quotas. Voluntary export restraints are particularly important in regulating the international trade in cars between Japan and the United States.

FIGURE 18.8

The Effects of a Quota

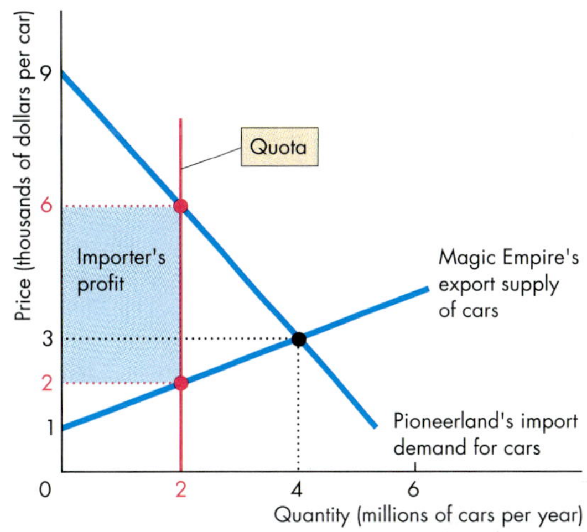

Pioneerland imposes a quota of 2 million cars a year on car imports from Magic Empire. That quantity appears as the vertical line labeled "Quota." Since the quantity of cars supplied by Magic Empire is restricted to 2 million, the price at which those cars will be traded increases to $6,000. Importing cars is profitable, since Magic Empire is willing to supply cars at $2,000 each. There is competition for import quotas—rent seeking.

How Quotas and VERs Work

To understand how nontariff barriers affect international trade, let's return to the example of trade between Pioneerland and Magic Empire. Suppose that Pioneerland imposes a quota on car imports. Specifically, suppose that the quota restricts imports to not more than 2 million cars a year. What are the effects of this action?

The answer is found in Fig. 18.8. The quota is shown by the vertical red line at 2 million cars a year. Since it is illegal to import more than that number of cars, car importers buy only that quantity from Magic Empire producers. They pay $2,000 a car to the Magic Empire producer. But what do they sell their cars for? The answer is $6,000 each. Since the import supply of cars is restricted to 2 million cars a year, people with cars for sale will be able to get $6,000 each for them. The quantity of cars imported equals the quantity determined by the quota.

Importing cars is now obviously a profitable business. An importer gets $6,000 for an item that costs only $2,000. Thus there is severe competition among car importers for the available quotas. The pursuit of the profits from quotas is called "rent seeking."

The value of imports—the amount paid to Magic Empire—declines to $4 billion, exactly the same as in the case of the tariff. Thus with lower incomes from car exports and with a higher price of grain, Magicians cut back on their imports of grain in exactly the same way they did under a tariff.

The key difference between a quota and a tariff lies in who gets the profit represented by the difference between the import supply price and the domestic selling price. In the case of a tariff, that difference goes to the government. In the case of a quota, that difference goes to the person who has the right to import under the import-quota regulations.

A voluntary export restraint is like a quota arrangement in which quotas are allocated to each exporting country. The effects of voluntary export restraints are similar to those of quotas but differ from them in that the gap between the domestic price and the export price is captured not by domestic importers but by the foreign exporter. The government of the exporting country has to establish procedures for allocating the restricted volume of exports among its producers.

Paying with Your Shirt! Two of the most heavily protected industries in the United States today are apparel and textiles. It has been estimated that the total protection on these industries, most of which takes the form of quotas, costs the average American family between $200 and $400 a year. Despite this fact, the House of Representatives passed a new act (the Textile and Apparel Trade Act) in 1975 that, if it had become law, would have increased protection in those industries even further, adding $300 to $400 a year in additional costs for the average household.[1] Taking all protection together, it has been estimated that the cost per year to an individual U.S. family is more than $1,000.[2]

Another way of looking at the cost of protection is to calculate the cost per job saved. It has been estimated, for example, that to protect one job in the textile industry costs $46,000 a year; one job in the footwear industry costs close to $80,000 a year; and one job in the carbon, steel, and auto industries costs more than $80,000 a year. In all these cases, it costs many times more to save a job through international trade barriers than the wages of the workers involved.[3]

[1]For more on this topic, see "Expanding Trade and Avoiding Protectionism," *Economic Report of the President* (1988), pp. 127–162.

[2]Murray Weidenbaum and N. Munger, "Protection at Any Price?" *Regulation* (July/August 1983): 14–18.

[3]Keith E. Maskus, "Rising Protectionism and U.S. International Trade Policy," *Economic Review of the Federal Reserve Bank of Kansas City* (July/August 1984): 3–17.

REVIEW

When a country opens itself up to international trade and trades freely at world market prices, it expands its consumption possibilities. When trade is restricted, some of the gains from trade are lost. A country may be better off with restricted trade than with no trade but not as well off as it could be if it engaged in free trade. A tariff reduces the volume of imports, but it also reduces the volume of exports. Under both free trade and restricted trade (and without international borrowing and lending), the value of imports equals the value of exports. With restricted trade, both the total value of exports and the total value of imports are lower than under free trade, but trade is still balanced. ◆

Why Quotas and VERs Might Be Preferred to Tariffs

At first sight, it seems puzzling that countries would ever want to use quotas and even more puzzling that they would want to use voluntary export restraints. We have seen that the same domestic price and the same quantity of imports can be achieved by using any of the three devices for restricting trade. However, a tariff provides the government with a source of revenue; a quota provides domestic importers with a profit; and a voluntary export restraint provides the foreigner with a profit. Why, then, would a country use a quota or a voluntary export restraint rather than a tariff?

There are three possible reasons. First, a government can use quotas to reward its political supporters. Under a quota, licenses to import become tremendously profitable. So the government bestows riches on the people to whom it gives licenses to import.

Second, quotas are more precise instruments for holding down imports. As demand fluctuates, the domestic price of the good fluctuates but not the quantity of imports. You can see this implication of a quota by going back to Fig. 18.8. Suppose that the demand for imports fluctuates. With a quota, these demand fluctuations simply produce fluctuations in the domestic price of the import but no change in the volume of imports. With a tariff, fluctuations in demand lead to no change in the domestic price but to large changes in the volume of imports. Thus if for some reason the government wants to control the quantity of imports and does not care about fluctuations in the domestic price, it will use a quota.

Third, different branches of government have jurisdiction over different aspects of international trade restriction. Congress has the power to impose tariffs. The administration has the power to impose nontariff barriers. Thus changing tariffs is a slow and cumbersome matter requiring the passage of an act of Congress. In contrast, nontariff barriers can be changed quickly, provided that the administration is persuaded of the need for the change.

Why would a government use voluntary export restraints rather than a tariff or quota? The government might want to avoid a tariff or quota war with another country. If one country imposes a tariff or a quota, that might encourage another country to impose a similar tariff or quota on the exports of the first country. Such a tariff or quota war would result in a much smaller volume of trade and a much worse outcome for both countries. A voluntary export restraint can be viewed as a way of achieving trade restrictions to protect domestic industries but with some kind of compensation to encourage the foreign country to accept that situation and not retaliate with its own restrictions. Finally, VERs are often the only form of trade restriction that can be legally entered into under the terms of the General Agreement on Tariffs and Trade.

Dumping and Countervailing Duties

Dumping is the selling of a good in a foreign market for a lower price than in the domestic market or for a lower price than its cost of production. Such a practice can arise from a discriminating monopoly seeking to maximize profit. An example of alleged dumping has occurred with Japanese sales of pickup trucks to the United States. Under current U.S. law and under GATT, dumping is illegal and antidumping duties may be imposed on foreign producers if U.S. producers can show that they have been injured by dumping.

Countervailing duties are tariffs that are imposed to enable domestic producers to compete with subsidized foreign producers. Often, foreign governments subsidize some of their domestic industries. Two examples are the Canadian pork and lumber industries. Under current U.S. law, if American producers can show that a foreign subsidy has damaged their market, a countervailing duty may be imposed.

Why Is International Trade Restricted?

There are many reasons why international trade is restricted. We've just seen two reasons—to offset the effects of dumping and of foreign subsidies. Even in these cases, it does not obviously benefit a country to protect itself from cheap foreign imports. However, more generally, we've seen that international trade benefits a country by raising its consumption possibilities. Why do we restrict international trade when such restrictions lower our consumption possibilities?

The key reason is that consumption possibilities increase *on the average* but not everyone shares in the gain and some people even lose. Free trade brings benefits to some and costs to others, with total benefits exceeding total costs. It is the uneven distribution of costs and benefits that is the principal source of impediment to achieving more liberal international trade.

Returning to our example of international trade in cars and grain between Pioneerland and Magic Empire, the benefits from free trade accrue to all the producers of grain and to those producers of cars who would not have to bear the costs of adjusting to a smaller car industry. The costs of free trade are borne by those car producers and their employees who have to move and become grain producers. The number of people who gain will, in general, be enormous compared with the number who lose. The gain per person will, therefore, be rather small. The loss per person to those who bear the loss will be large. Since the loss that falls on those who bear it is large, it will pay those people to incur considerable expense in order to lobby against free trade. On the other hand, it will not pay those who gain to organize to achieve free trade. The gain from trade for any one individual is too small for that individual to spend much time or money on a political organization to achieve free trade. The loss from free trade will be seen as being so great by those bearing that loss that they *will* find it profitable to join a political organization to prevent free trade. Each group is optimizing—weighing benefits against costs and choosing the best action for themselves. The anti–free-trade group will, however, undertake a larger quantity of political lobbying than the pro–free-trade group.

Compensating Losers

If, in total, the gains from free international trade exceed the losses, why don't those who gain compensate those who lose so that everyone is in favor of free trade? To some degree, such compensation does take place. It also takes place indirectly as a consequence of unemployment compensation arrangements. But, as a rule, only limited attempts are made to compensate those who lose from free international trade. The main reason why full compensation is not attempted is that the costs of identifying the losers would be enormous. Also, it would never be clear whether a person who has fallen on hard times is suffering because of free trade or for other reasons, perhaps reasons largely under the control of the individual. Furthermore, some people who look like losers at one point in time may, in fact, wind up gaining. The young auto worker who loses his job in Michigan and becomes an insurance salesperson in Chicago resents the loss of work and the need to move. But a year or two later, looking back on events, he counts himself fortunate. He's made a move that has increased his income and given him greater job security.

It is because we do not, in general, compensate the losers from free international trade that protectionism is such a popular and permanent feature of our national economic and political life.

Political Outcome

The political outcome that emerges from this activity is one in which a modest amount of restriction on international trade occurs and is maintained. Politicians react to constituencies pressing for protection and find it necessary, in order to get re-elected, to support legislative programs that protect those constituencies. The producers of protected goods are far more vocal and much more sensitive swing-voters than the consumers of those goods. The political outcome, therefore, leans in the direction of maintaining protection.

The politics of trade can be seen easily today. The United States restricts imports of sugar by quota. Who profits from the quotas? Not the foreign exporters. Whereas voluntary export restraints give exporters like Toyota and Honda big profits, quotas do not help foreign producers. In this case, the quotas have brought real economic and political suffering to Central American and Caribbean countries that produce sugar. The U.S. sugar growers, on the other hand, who benefit from the quotas, are extremely active in their support for politicians who can see their point of view. Similarly, the auto producers and unions are extremely active in their attempts to further limit the intrusion of Japanese imports.

◆ ◆ ◆ ◆ You've now seen how free international trade enables everyone to gain from increased specialization and exchange. By producing goods in which we have a comparative advantage and exchanging some of our own production for that of others, we expand our consumption possibilities. Placing impediments on that exchange when it crosses national borders restricts the extent to which we can gain from specialization and exchange. When we open our country up to free international trade, the market for the things that we sell expands and the price rises. The market for the things that we buy also expands, and the price falls. All countries gain from free international trade. As a consequence of price adjustments, and in the absence of international borrowing and lending, the value of imports adjusts to equal the value of exports. ◆ ◆ In the next chapter, we're going to study the ways in which international trade is financed and also learn why the international borrowing and lending that permits unbalanced international trade arises. We'll discover the forces that determine the U.S. balance of payments and the value, in terms of foreign currency, of our dollar.

SUMMARY

Patterns and Trends in International Trade

Large flows of trade take place between rich and poor countries. Resource-rich countries exchange natural resources for manufactured goods, and resource-poor countries import their resources in exchange for their own manufactured goods. However, by far the biggest volume of trade is in manufactured goods exchanged among the rich industrialized countries. The biggest single U.S. export item is machinery. However, the biggest single U.S. net export is grain. Trade in services has grown in recent years. Total trade has also grown over the years. The U.S. balance of trade fluctuates around zero, but since 1982 the United States has had a balance of trade deficit. (pp. 475–478)

Opportunity Cost and Comparative Advantage

When opportunity costs differ between countries, the country with the lowest opportunity cost of producing a good is said to have a comparative advantage in that good. Comparative advantage is the source of the gains from international trade. A country can have an absolute advantage, but not a comparative advantage, in the production of all goods. Every country has a comparative advantage in something. (pp. 478–479)

The Gains from Trade

Countries can gain from trade if their opportunity costs differ. Through trade, each country can obtain goods at a lower opportunity cost than it could if it produced all goods at home. International trade allows a country to consume outside its production possibilities. By specializing in producing the good in which it has a comparative advantage and then trading some of that good for imports, a country can consume at points outside its production possibility frontier. Each country can consume at such a point.

In the absence of international borrowing and lending, trade is balanced as prices adjust to reflect the international supply of and demand for goods. The world price is established at the level that balances the production and consumption plans of the trading parties. At the equilibrium price, trade is balanced and domestic consumption plans exactly match a combination of domestic production and international trade.

Comparative advantage explains the enormous volume and diversity of international trade that takes place in the world. But much trade takes the form of exchanging similar goods for each other—one type of car for another. Such trade arises because of economies of scale in the face of diversified tastes. By specializing in producing a few goods, having long production runs, and then trading those goods internationally, consumers in all countries can enjoy greater diversity of products at lower prices. (pp. 479–487)

Trade Restrictions

A country can restrict international trade by imposing tariffs or nontariff barriers—quotas and voluntary export restraints. All trade restrictions raise the domestic price of imported goods, lower the volume of imports, and reduce the total value of imports. They also reduce the total value of exports by the same amount as the reduction in the value of imports.

All trade restrictions create a gap between the domestic price and the foreign supply price of an import. In the case of a tariff, that gap is the tariff revenue collected by the government. But the government raises no revenue from a quota. Instead, domestic importers who have a license to import increase their profit. A voluntary export restraint resembles a quota except that a higher price is received by the foreign exporter.

Governments restrict trade because restrictions help the producers of the protected commodity and the workers employed by those producers. Because their gain is sufficiently large and the loss per consumer is sufficiently small, the political equilibrium favors restricted trade. Politicians pay more attention to the vocal concerns of the few who stand to lose than to the less strongly expressed views of the many who stand to gain. (pp. 487–496)

KEY ELEMENTS

Key Terms

Key Figures

REVIEW QUESTIONS

1 What are the main exports and imports of the United States?

2 How does the United States trade services internationally?

3 Which items of international trade have been growing the most quickly in recent years?

4 What is comparative advantage? Why does it lead to gains from international trade?

5 Explain why international trade brings gains to all countries.

6 Distinguish between comparative advantage and absolute advantage.

7 Explain why all countries have a comparative advantage in something.

8 Explain why we import and export such large quantities of certain goods that are similar—for example, cars.

9 What are the main ways in which we restrict international trade?

10 What are the effects of a tariff?

11 What are the effects of a quota?

12 What are the effects of a voluntary export restraint?

13 Describe the main trends in tariffs and nontariff barriers.

14 Which countries have the largest restrictions on their international trade?

15 Why do countries restrict international trade?

PROBLEMS

1 Using Fig. 18.2, calculate the opportunity cost of cars in Pioneerland at the point on the production possibility frontier at which 4 million cars are produced.

2 Using Fig. 18.3, calculate the opportunity cost of a car in Magic Empire when it produces 8 million cars.

3 With no trade, Pioneerland produces 4 million cars and Magic Empire produces 8 million cars. Which country has a comparative advantage in the production of cars?

4 If there is no trade between Pioneerland and Magic Empire, how much grain is consumed and how many cars are bought in each country?

5 Suppose that the two countries in problems 1–4 trade freely.

- **a** Which country exports grain?
- **b** What adjustments will be made to the amount of each good produced by each country?
- **c** What adjustment will be made to the amount of each good consumed by each country?
- **d** What can you say about the price of a car under free trade?

6 Compare the total production of each good produced in problems 1–5.

7 Compare the situation in problems 1–5 with that analyzed in this chapter (pp. 478–482). Why does Magic Empire export cars in the chapter but import them in problem 5?

8 The following figure depicts the international market for soybeans (there are only two countries in the world).

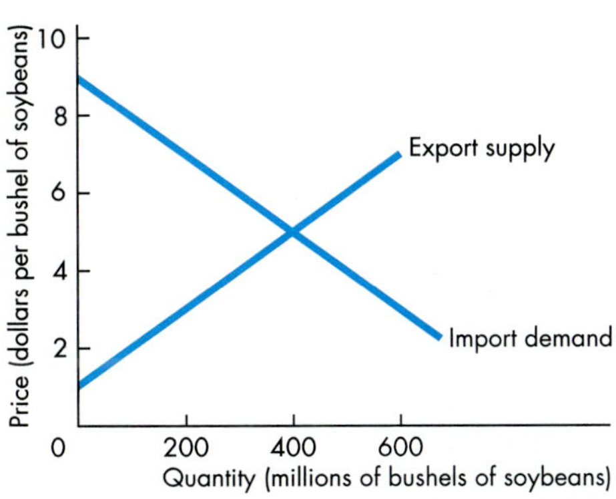

- **a** What is the world price of soybeans if there is free trade between these countries?
- **b** If the country that imports soybeans imposes a tariff of $2 per bushel, what is the world price of soybeans and what quantity of soybeans gets traded internationally? What is the price of soybeans in the importing country? Calculate the tariff revenue.

9 If the importing country in problem 8(a) imposes a quota of 300 million bushels, what is the price of soybeans in the importing country? What is the revenue from the quota, and who gets this revenue?

10 If the exporting country in problem 8(a) imposes a VER of 300 million bushels of soybeans, what is the world price of soybeans? What is the revenue of soybean growers in the exporting country? Which country gains from the VER?

11 Suppose that the exporting country in problem 8(a) subsidizes production by paying its farmers $1 a bushel for soybeans harvested.

- **a** What is the price of soybeans in the importing country?
- **b** What action might soybean growers in the importing country take? Why?

CHAPTER 19

THE BALANCE OF PAYMENTS AND THE DOLLAR

After studying this chapter, you will be able to:

- Explain how international trade is financed
- Describe a country's balance of payments accounts
- Explain what determines the amount of international borrowing and lending
- Explain why the United States changed from being a lender to being a borrower in the mid-1980s
- Explain how the foreign exchange value of the dollar is determined
- Explain why the foreign exchange value of the dollar fluctuated in the 1980s
- Explain the effects of changes in the exchange rate
- Explain what determines interest rates and why they vary so much from one country to another

For Sale: America

FOREIGN ENTREPRENEURS ARE ROAMING THE UNITED States with a giant shopping cart and loading it up with everything in sight, from high-rise buildings in Manhattan to movie studios in Los Angeles. The Rockefeller Center and Columbia Pictures are just two small examples of an enormous buying spree. What is causing this foreign invasion of the United States? Why are foreigners finding U.S. real estate and businesses such attractive investments? ◆◆ In 1971, one U.S. dollar was enough to buy 360 Japanese yen. By mid-1993, that same dollar bought only 108 yen. But the slide from 360 to 108 yen was not a smooth one. At some times, the dollar held its own or even rose in value against the Japanese currency, as it did, for example, in 1982. But at other times, the dollar's slide was precipitous, as in the period between 1985 and 1988. The dollar has fallen in value not only against the Japanese currency. It has fallen against the German mark and the Swiss franc. But the dollar has gained in value in terms of the Canadian dollar, the British pound, and the French franc. What makes our dollar fluctuate in value against other currencies? Why have the fluctuations been particularly extreme in recent years? Is there anything we can do to stabilize the value of the dollar?

◆◆ The world capital market is becoming ever more integrated. As the Wall Street stock market rises and falls, so also do the stock markets around the globe—such as those in London, Paris, Tokyo, and Toronto. But despite the fact that the world is getting smaller, there are enormous differences in the interest rates at which people borrow and lend around the world. For example, in early

1992, the U.S. government was paying just under 8 percent a year on its long-term borrowing. At that same time, governments in Australia, Italy, and Spain were paying more than 10 percent. In Japan, the government was borrowing for only 5½ percent. How can interest rates diverge so widely? Why don't loans dry up in low-interest-rate countries with all the money flooding to countries where interest rates are high? Why aren't interest rates made the same everywhere by the force of such movements?

◆ ◆ ◆ ◆ During the 1980s, the issues of international economics became important matters for almost every American. We're going to study these issues in this chapter. We're going to discover why the U.S. economy has become such an attractive target for foreign investors, why the dollar fluctuates against the values of other currencies, and why interest rates vary from country to country.

Financing International Trade

When 47th Street Photo in New York City imports Minolta cameras, it does not pay for those cameras with U.S. dollars—it uses Japanese yen. When Saks Fifth Avenue imports Fila track suits, it pays for them using Italian lire. And when a French construction company buys an earth mover from Caterpillar, Inc., it uses U.S. dollars. Whenever we buy things from another country, we use the currency of that country in order to make the transaction. It doesn't make any difference what the item being traded is—it might be a consumer good or a capital good, a building, or even a firm.

We're going to study the markets in which transactions in money—in different types of currency—take place. But first we're going to look at the scale of international trading and borrowing and lending and at the way in which we keep our records of these transactions. Such records are called the balance of payments accounts.

Balance of Payments Accounts

A country's **balance of payments accounts** records its international trading, borrowing, and lending. There are in fact three balance of payments accounts:

- Current account
- Capital account
- Official settlements account

The **current account** records the receipts from the sale of goods and services to foreigners, the payments for goods and services bought from foreigners, and gifts and other transfers (such as foreign aid

TABLE 19.1

U.S. Balance of Payments Accounts in 1992

	Billions of dollars
Current account	
Import of goods and services	**–658.9**
Export of goods and services	**617.8**
Net factor incomes	**10.1**
Net transfers	**–31.4**
Current account balance	**–62.4**
Capital account	
Foreign investment in the United States	**120.4**
U.S. investment abroad	**–48.9**
Statistical discrepancy	**–13.0**
Capital account balance	**58.5**
Official settlements account	
Decrease (+) in official U.S. reserves	**3.9**

Source: Survey of Current Business (March 1993), vol. 73.

FIGURE 19.1

The Balance of Payments

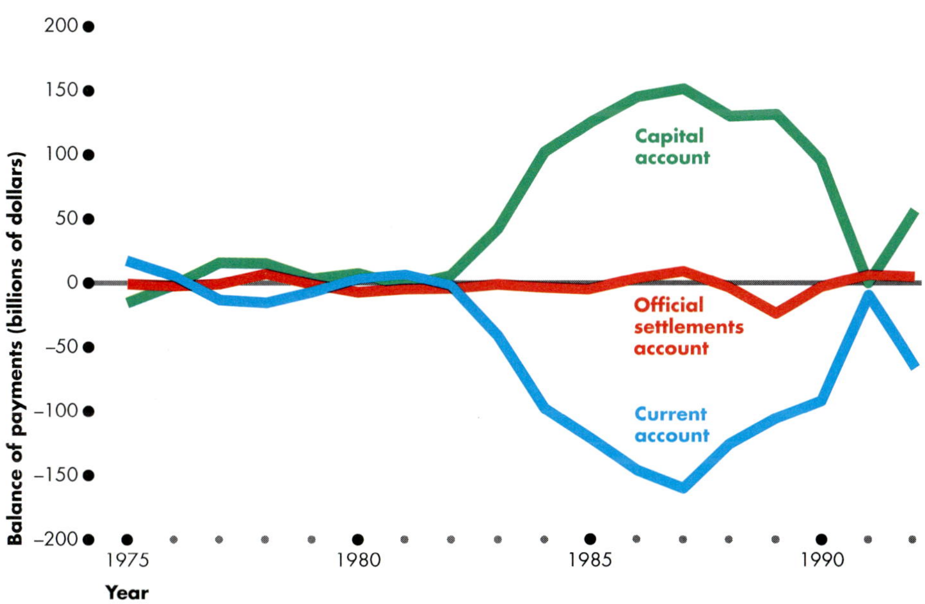

During the 1970s, fluctuations in the balance of payments were small. In the 1980s, an enormous current account deficit arose. The capital account balance mirrors the current account balance. When the current account balance is positive, the capital account balance is negative—we lend to the rest of the world—and when the current account balance is negative, the capital account balance is positive—we borrow from the rest of the world. Fluctuations in the official settlements balance are small compared with fluctuations in the current account balance and the capital account balance.

Source: Economic Report of the President, 1993.

payments) received from and paid to foreigners. By far the largest items in the current account are the receipts from the sale of goods and services to foreigners (the value of exports) and the payments made for goods and services bought from foreigners (the value of imports). Net transfers are relatively small items. The **capital account** records all the international borrowing and lending transactions. The capital account balance records the difference between the amounts that a country lends to and borrows from the rest of the world. The **official settlements account** shows the net increase or decrease in a country's holdings of foreign currency.

Table 19.1 shows the U.S. balance of payments accounts in 1992. As you can see from the table, the United States had a current account deficit of $62.4 billion in 1992. How do we pay for our current account deficit? That is, how do we pay for imports that exceed the value of our exports? We pay by borrowing from abroad. The capital account tells us by how much. We borrowed $120.4 billion but made loans of $48.9 billion. Thus our identified net foreign borrowing was $71.5 billion. There is also a statistical discrepancy in the capital account of –$13 billion.[1] Actually, this discrepancy represents a combination of capital and current account transactions such as unidentified borrowing from abroad, illegal international trade—for example, the import of illegal drugs—and transactions not reported in order to illegally evade tariffs or other international trade protection measures.

Our net borrowing from abroad minus our current account deficit is the change in U.S. official reserves. **Official reserves** are the government's holdings of foreign currency. In 1992, those reserves decreased by $3.9 billion (net borrowing from foreigners was $58.5 billion, the current account deficit was $62.4 billion, and the difference, $3.9 billion, was the decrease in official reserves).

The numbers in Table 19.1 give a snapshot of the balance of payments accounts in 1992. Figure 19.1 puts that snapshot into perspective by showing the

[1]The statistical discrepancy in 1992 was not particularly large. Sometimes it is much larger than this.

balance of payments between 1975 and 1992. As you can see, the current account balance is almost a mirror image of the capital account balance, and the official settlements balance is very small compared with the balances on these other two accounts. A large current account deficit (and capital account surplus) emerged during the 1980s but was declining after 1987.

You will perhaps obtain a better understanding of the balance of payments accounts and the way in which they are linked together if you consider the income and expenditure, borrowing and lending, and bank account of an individual.

Individual Analogy An individual's current account records the income from supplying the services of factors of production and the expenditure on goods and services. Consider, for example, Joanne. She earned an income in 1994 of $25,000. Joanne has $10,000 worth of investments that earned her an income of $1,000. Joanne's current account shows an income of $26,000. Joanne spent $18,000 buying goods and services for consumption. She also bought a new house, which cost her $60,000. So Joanne's total expenditure was $78,000. The difference between her expenditure and income is $52,000 ($78,000 minus $26,000). This amount is Joanne's current account deficit.

To pay for expenditure of $52,000 in excess of her income, Joanne has to either use the money that she has in the bank or take out a loan. In fact, Joanne took a mortgage of $50,000 to help buy her house. This was the only borrowing that Joanne did, so her capital account surplus was $50,000. With a current account deficit of $52,000 and a capital account surplus of $50,000, Joanne is still $2,000 short. She got that $2,000 from her own bank account. Her cash holdings decreased by $2,000.

Joanne's supply of factors of production is analogous to a country's supply of exports. Her purchases of goods and services, including her purchase of a house, are analogous to a country's imports. Joanne's mortgage—borrowing from someone else—is analogous to a country's foreign borrowing. Joanne's purchase of the house is analogous to a country's foreign investment. The change in her own bank account is analogous to the change in the country's official reserves.

Later in this chapter, we will study the factors that influence the official settlements balance, but for now we'll concentrate on the current account and the capital account.

Borrowers and Lenders, Debtors and Creditors

A country that is borrowing more from the rest of the world than it is lending to it is called a **net borrower.** Similarly, a **net lender** is a country that is lending more to the rest of the world than it is borrowing from it. A net borrower might be going deeper into debt or might simply be reducing its net assets held in the rest of the world. The total stock of foreign investment determines whether a country is a debtor or a creditor. A **debtor nation** is a country that, during its entire history, has borrowed more from the rest of the world than it has lent to it. It has a stock of outstanding debt to the rest of the world that exceeds the stock of its own claims on the rest of the world. The United States became a debtor nation in the mid-1980s. A **creditor nation** is a country that has invested more in the rest of the world than other countries have invested in it. The largest creditor nation is Japan. A creditor nation is one whose net receipts of interest on debt are positive—payments made to it exceed the payments that it makes.

At the heart of the distinction between a net borrower/net lender and a debtor/creditor nation is the distinction between flows and stocks. Borrowing and lending are flows. They are amounts borrowed or lent per unit of time. Debts are stocks. They are amounts owed at a point in time. The flow of borrowing and lending changes the stock of debt. But the outstanding stock of debt depends mainly on past flows of borrowing and lending, not on the current period's flows. The current period's flows determine the *change* in the stock of debt outstanding.

The United States is a newcomer to the ranks of net borrower nations. Throughout the 1960s and most of the 1970s, it had a surplus on its current account and a deficit on its capital account. Thus the country was a net lender to the rest of the world. It was not until 1983 that it became a significant net borrower. Since then, borrowing has increased each year and, by the end of the 1980s, exceeded $100 billion a year. The United States is not only a net borrower nation. It is also a debtor nation. That is, its total stock of borrowing from the rest of the world exceeds its lending to the rest of the world.

The largest debtor nations are the capital-hungry developing countries. The international debt of these countries grew from less than a third to more than a half of their gross domestic product during the 1980s, giving rise to what has been called the "Third World debt crisis."

The majority of countries are net borrowers. But a small number of countries are huge net lenders. Examples of net lenders are the oil-rich countries, such as Kuwait and Venezuela, and successful developed economies, such as Japan and Germany.

Should the United States be concerned about the switch from being a net lender to being a net borrower? The answer to this question depends mainly on what the net borrower is doing with the borrowed money. If borrowing is financing investment that in turn is generating economic growth and higher income, borrowing is not a problem. If the borrowed money is being used to finance consumption, then higher interest payments are being incurred, and, as a consequence, consumption will eventually have to be reduced. The more the borrowing and the longer it goes on, the greater is the reduction in consumption that will eventually be necessary. We'll explore whether the United States is borrowing for investment or for consumption.

Current Account Balance

What determines the current account balance and the scale of a country's net foreign borrowing or lending?

To answer that question, we need to begin by recalling and using some of the things that we learned about the national income accounts. Table 19.2 is going to refresh your memory and summarize the necessary calculations for you. Part (a) lists the national income variables that are needed, with their symbols. Their values in the United States in 1990 are also shown.

Part (b) presents two key national income equations. First, equation (1) reminds us that aggregate expenditure is the sum of consumption expenditure, investment, government purchases of goods and services, and net exports (the difference between exports and imports). Equation (2) reminds us that aggregate income is used in three different ways. It can be consumed, saved, or paid to the government in the form of taxes (net of transfer payments). Equation (1) tells us how our expenditure generates our income. Equation (2) tells us how we dispose of that income.

Part (c) of the table takes you into some new territory. It examines surpluses and deficits. We'll look at three surpluses/deficits—those of the current account, the government's budget, and the private sector. To get at these surpluses and deficits, first subtract equation (2) from equation (1) in Table 19.2. The result is equation (3). By rearranging equation (3), we obtain a relationship for the current account—exports minus imports—that appears as equation (4) in the table.[2]

Notice that the current account, in equation (4), is made up of two components. The first is taxes minus government spending, and the second is saving minus investment. These items are the surpluses/deficits of the government and private sectors. Taxes (net of transfer payments) minus government purchases of goods and services equals the budget surplus or deficit. If that number is positive, the government's budget is a surplus, and if the number is negative, it is a deficit. The **private sector surplus or deficit** is the difference between saving and investment. If saving exceeds investment, the private sector has a surplus to lend to other sectors. If investment exceeds saving, the private sector has a deficit that has to be financed by borrowing from other sectors. As you can see from our calculations, the current account deficit is equal to the sum of the other two deficits—the government's budget deficit and the private sector deficit. In the United States in 1990, the most important of these other two deficits was the government budget deficit. The private sector was almost in balance, and the $95 billion current account deficit was accounted for almost exclusively by the $104 billion government budget deficit.

Part (d) of Table 19.2 shows you how investment is financed. To increase investment, either private saving, the government surplus, or the current account deficit must increase.

The calculations that we've just performed are really nothing more than bookkeeping. We've manipulated the national income accounts and dis-

[2]In the national income accounts, the difference between exports and imports is called *net exports*. There are some slight differences in the way these numbers are calculated in the national income accounts and the balance of payments accounts, but for most purposes you can regard net exports and the current account balance as meaning the same thing.

TABLE 19.2

The Current Account Balance, Net Foreign Borrowing, and the Financing of Investment

	Symbols and equations	U.S. values in 1992 (billions of dollars)
(a) Variables		
Gross domestic product (GDP)	Y	5,951
Consumption expenditure	C	4,096
Investment	I	770
Government purchases of goods and services	G	1,115
Exports of goods and services	EX	636
Imports of goods and services	IM	668
Saving	S	1,021
Taxes, net of transfer payments	T	832
(b) Domestic income and expenditure		
Aggregate expenditure	(1) $Y = C + I + G + EX - IM$	
Uses of income	(2) $Y = C + S + T$	
Subtracting (1) from (2)	(3) $0 = I - S + G - T + EX - IM$	
(c) Surpluses and deficits		
Current account	(4) $EX - IM = (T - G) + (S - I)$	636 – 668 = –32
Government budget	(5) $T - G$	832 – 1,115 = –283
Private sector	(6) $S - I$	1,021 – 770 = 251
(d) Financing investment		
Investment is financed by		
the sum of private saving,	S,	1,021
net government saving,	$T - G$,	–283
and net foreign saving,	$IM - EX$,	32
that is:	(7) $I = S + (T - G) + (IM - EX)$	770 = 1,021 – 283 + 32

Source: Survey of Current Business May 1993, vol. 73.

covered that the current account deficit is just the sum of the deficits of the government and private sectors. But these calculations do reveal a fundamental fact—our international balance of payments can change only if either our government budget balance changes or our private sector financial balance changes. This fact is often lost sight of in popular discussions of our international deficit—see Reading Between the Lines, pp. 508–509.

We've seen that our international deficit is equal to the sum of the government deficit and the private sector deficit. But what determines those two deficits? Why isn't the private sector in a surplus equal to the government's budget deficit so that the current account deficit is zero? Does an increase in the government budget deficit bring an increase in the current account deficit?

The Twin Deficits

You can see the answer to this question by looking at Fig. 19.2. In that figure, the government sector (federal, state, and local governments) budget balance is plotted alongside the current account balance. As you can see, these two balances moved in close sympathy with each other during the 1980s. This tendency for the two deficits to move together has given rise to the term *twin deficits*. The **twin deficits** are the government budget deficit and current account deficit. But the twin deficits are not identical. There are independent variations in the two deficits that are accommodated by variations in the private sector deficit. Let's see why.

Effects of Government Deficit on Private Surplus

As we've just seen, the private sector surplus/deficit is the gap between saving and investment. One of the main influences on the level of saving is disposable income. Anything that increases disposable income, other things being equal, increases saving and increases the private sector surplus. The main influences on investment are the interest rate and expectations of future profits. Other things being equal, anything that lowers interest rates or increases expected future profits increases investment and decreases the private sector surplus.

Changes in taxes or government spending change the budget deficit and influence income and interest rates. These changes, in turn, influence private sector saving and investment and hence change the private sector surplus/deficit. An increase in government purchases of goods and services or a tax cut—either

FIGURE 19.2

The Twin Deficits

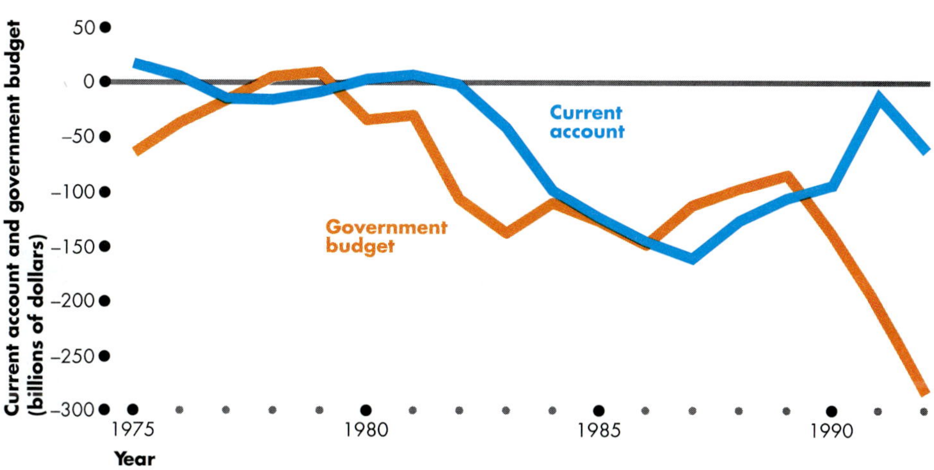

The twin deficits are the current account deficit and the government budget deficit, which sometimes move in sympathy with each other. As the government budget deficit grew larger during the 1980s, so did the current account deficit. More recently, the two deficits have diverged.

Source: Survey of Current Business (May 1993), vol. 73.

The U.S.-Japan Trade Gap

THE ECONOMIST, JANUARY 11, 1992

A poor match in Tokyo

The president arrived in Japan on January 7th hoping to depart three days later with a list of goodies that would help him get re-elected in November. . . .

. . . With 8.5 million Americans out of work, and America's trade deficit with Japan nosing back towards $42 billion, this was, his advisers advised, the time to get tough. Bashing Japan for not buying enough goods made in America should, it was argued, go down well in Detroit. . . .

What have the Americans gained? Two dozen Japanese companies have been bullied into buying more manufactured goods from abroad. . . .The Japanese may or may not chip in something towards an $8.25 billion atom-smashing machine that American scientists want to build in Texas. Nine Japanese car manufacturers have outlined plans for buying $19 billion-worth of components from America by 1994. . . .

Though they are already widely known, the import targets for American cars ($6.4 billion worth by 1994) have not been put in the plan. No one in Japan wants to be blamed for breaking a written promise—as happened when the Semi-conductor Accord of 1986 recklessly guaranteed American chip makers 20% of the Japanese market. Mr Miyazawa has also offered to relax import-inspection standards that have irked the Americans on more than 50 items. . . .

The Americans will gain access to $5 billion-worth of trade insurance covering the next five years. The cash is for underwriting Japanese overseas projects in which American firms take part, such as building power stations in Latin America and drilling for oil in Siberia. The scheme came into effect last May and has so far provided some $700 million of Japanese government insurance for six overseas projects—helping American firms export $2 billion-worth of goods.

On the tricky issue of rice, the Americans have been urging Japan to accept GATT proposals for replacing import restrictions on agricultural products with tariffs. This would help bring the Uruguay round of multilateral trade talks to a successful conclusion. But the ruling Liberal Democrats are afraid of offending Japan's farmers before July's election. . . .

When they are added up, the measures announced this week will buy few jobs for Americans. They may even backfire on Mr Bush in the months ahead. Expectations have been rising in Washington that Japan's latest market-opening measures are somehow different from the dozens that have gone before. All have helped, bit by bit, to make the Japanese market more accessible to foreigners, but none has allowed Japan's trading partners to eliminate their deficits. Mr Bush's efforts will be no different.

. . .

The Essence of the Story

With a recession in the United States (8.5 million unemployed), a trade deficit with Japan ($42 billion), and an upcoming election (in November 1992), President Bush visited Tokyo in January 1992 hoping to return with agreements that would boost U.S. exports to Japan and limit Japanese imports into the United States.

The outcome:

- Two dozen Japanese companies agreed to buy more manufactured goods from abroad.
- The Japanese agreed to consider making a contribution toward the cost of the $8.25 billion supercollider to be built in Texas.
- Nine Japanese car manufacturers outlined plans for buying components from U.S. auto makers ($19 billion worth by 1994).
- Import inspection standards on more than 50 items were to be relaxed.
- $5 billion worth of trade insurance underwriting was to be bought from U.S. companies over a five-year period.
- There was to be no relaxation of restrictions on rice imports into Japan.

The bottom line: few jobs for Americans and little change in the U.S. trade deficit with Japan.

Background and Analysis

In 1991, U.S. exports of goods and services were 10 percent of GDP, and imports were 11 percent of GDP. Japan's exports of goods and services were 11 percent of GDP, and its imports were 10 percent of GDP.

A large part of the U.S. deficit was in its trade with Japan.

To decrease the U.S. trade deficit with Japan, a number of measures have been proposed to limit U.S. imports of specific Japanese manufacturers and to increase U.S. exports of specific goods and services to Japan. The measures have not worked.

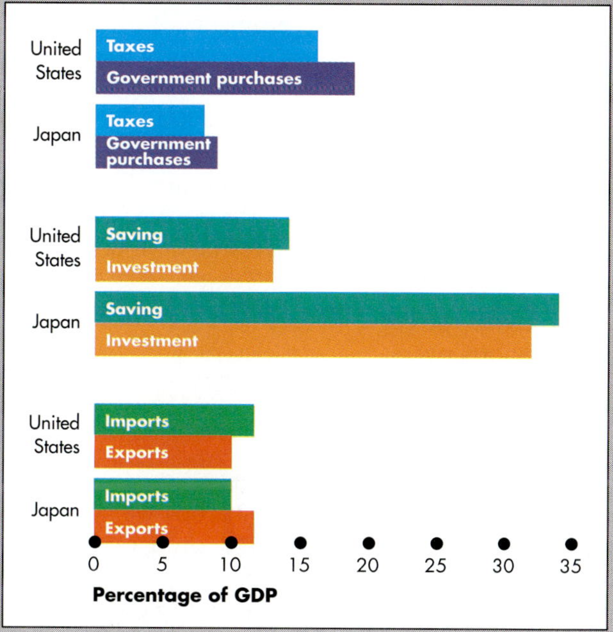

It is not surprising that the measures have not worked. A decrease in Japanese car exports to the United States does not necessarily lower the U.S.-Japan trade deficit. It could lower Japanese imports from the United States or increase U.S. imports of other Japanese manufactures.

Net exports NX are linked to the government and private sector surpluses by the equation

$$NX = (T - G) + (S - I).$$

The main difference between the United States and Japan is in the levels of taxes, government purchases, saving, and investment—shown in the figure. Japan has smaller government purchases and larger saving and investment than the United States.

Only if U.S. saving or taxes increase or government purchases or investment decreases can U.S. net exports increase.

Measures that boost U.S. saving, other things being equal, will increase U.S. net exports. Measures aimed at changing the volume of trade in specific goods and services will increase net exports only if they also change the level of saving in the United States.

of which increases the budget deficit—tends to increase GDP and the interest rate. The higher GDP stimulates additional saving, and the higher interest rate dampens investment plans. Thus, to some degree, an increased government budget deficit induces an increased private sector surplus.

For an increase in the government budget deficit to lead to an increase in the private sector surplus, the government's actions must stimulate higher income and/or induce higher interest rates. There are two factors that tend to limit these channels of influence. First, when the economy is operating close to full employment, as it is much of the time, a higher budget deficit does not produce a higher level of real GDP. Second, internationally mobile capital lessens the effect of increased government spending on interest rates. Thus the two mechanisms by which an increase in the budget deficit increases the private sector surplus can be weak.

Effects of Government Deficit on Current Account Deficit

Since the three deficits—the government budget deficit, the current account deficit, and the private sector deficit—add up to zero, any change in the government budget deficit that does not influence the private sector deficit must affect the current account deficit. But how does this effect come about? The easiest way of seeing the effect is to consider what happens when there is full employment. An increase in government purchases of goods and services or a tax cut leads to an increase in aggregate demand. But with the economy at full employment there is no spare capacity to generate a comparable increase in output. Part of the increased aggregate demand, therefore, spills over into the rest of the world, and imports increase. Also, part of the domestic production going for export is diverted to satisfy domestic demand. Exports decrease. The rise in imports and the fall in exports increase the current account deficit. The excess of imports over exports leads to a net increase in borrowing from the rest of the world.

Of course, the economy is not always at full employment. Nor does foreign capital flow in at a fixed interest rate. Thus the link between government budget deficit and the current account deficit is not a mechanical one. It is, nevertheless, a remarkably strong relationship, as we saw in Fig. 19.2.

Is U.S. Borrowing for Consumption or Investment?

We noted above that whether international borrowing is a problem or not depends on what that borrowing is used for. You've seen that in recent years the United States has borrowed internationally to finance the purchase of goods and services provided by the government. Private sector saving has been sufficient to pay for investment in plant and equipment, but it has not been sufficient to pay for the spending by the government in excess of its tax revenue. Does the fact that the government deficit has been similar to the amount of foreign borrowing mean that we're borrowing to consume?

It probably does not. There is no sure way to determine the extent to which government spending is consumption or investment. Some items, such as the purchase of improved highways, are investment. But what about expenditure on education and health care? Are these expenditures consumption or investment? A good case can be made that they are investment—investment in human capital—and that they earn a rate of return at least equal to the interest rate that we pay on our foreign debt.

Another reason for believing that most foreign lending is used to finance productive investment in the United States is that foreign investors do not buy a large volume of government bonds. In fact, in 1992, less than a third of the government's deficit was *directly* financed by foreigners buying U.S. government securities. Most of the foreign investment in the United States is in the private sector and is undertaken in the pursuit of the highest available profit. Foreigners diversify their lending to spread their risk. We do the same. Some of our saving is used to finance investment in U.S. firms, some is lent to the government, and some is used to finance U.S. investment in other countries.

REVIEW

When we buy goods from the rest of the world or invest in the rest of the world, we use foreign currency. When foreigners buy goods from us or invest in the United States, they use U.S. currency.

We record international transactions in the balance of payments accounts. The current account shows our exports and imports of goods and services and net transfers to the rest of the world. The capital account shows our net foreign borrowing or lending. The official settlements account shows the change in the country's holdings of a foreign currency. In the late 1980s, the U.S. current account moved into a large deficit, and the capital account moved into a large surplus—the country became a net borrower. The current account deficit is equal to the sum of the government budget deficit and the private sector deficit. During the 1980s, the U.S. current account deficit fluctuated in a similar way to the government budget deficit—the phenomenon of the twin deficits. We borrow from the rest of the world to purchase goods and services provided by the government in excess of the taxes that we pay. ◆

Foreign Exchange and the Dollar

When we buy foreign goods or invest in another country, we have to obtain some of that country's currency to make the transaction. When foreigners buy U.S.-produced goods or invest in the United States, they have to obtain some U.S. dollars. We get foreign currency, and foreigners get U.S. dollars in the foreign exchange market. The **foreign exchange market** is the market in which the currency of one country is exchanged for the currency of another. The foreign exchange market is not a place like a downtown flea market or produce market. The market is made up of thousands of people—importers and exporters, banks, and specialists in the buying and selling of foreign exchange called foreign exchange brokers. The foreign exchange market opens on Monday morning in Hong Kong, which is still Sunday evening in New York. As the day advances, markets open in Singapore, Tokyo, Bahrain, Frankfurt, London, New York, Chicago, and San Francisco. As the West Coast markets close, Hong Kong is only an hour away from opening for the next day of business. As Fig. 19.3 shows, the sun barely sets on the foreign exchange market. Dealers around the world are continually in contact by telephone, and on any given day, billions of dollars change hands.

The price at which one currency exchanges for another is called a **foreign exchange rate.** For example, in July 1993, 1 U.S. dollar bought 97 Japanese yen. The exchange rate between the U.S. dollar and the Japanese yen was 108 yen per dollar. Exchange rates can be expressed either way. We've just expressed the exchange rate between the yen and the dollar as a number of yen per dollar. Equivalently, we could express the exchange rate in terms of dollars per yen. That exchange rate in July 1993 was $0.0093 per yen. (In other words, a yen was worth about a penny.)

The actions of the foreign exchange brokers make the foreign exchange market highly efficient. Exchange rates are almost identical no matter where in the world the transaction is taking place. If U.S. dollars were cheap in London and expensive in Tokyo, within a flash someone would have placed a buy order in London and a sell order in Tokyo, thereby increasing the demand in one place and increasing the supply in another, moving the prices to equality.

Foreign Exchange Regimes

Foreign exchange rates are of critical importance for millions of people. They affect the costs of our foreign vacations and our imported cars. They affect the number of dollars that we end up getting for the oranges and beef that we sell to Japan. Because of its importance, governments pay a great deal of attention to what is happening in foreign exchange markets and, more than that, take actions designed to achieve what they regard as desirable movements in exchange rates. There are three ways in which the government can operate the foreign exchange market—three regimes. They are

- Fixed exchange rate
- Flexible exchange rate
- Managed exchange rate

A **fixed exchange rate** is an exchange rate the value of which is held steady by the country's central bank. For example, the U.S. government could adopt a fixed exchange rate by defining the U.S.

FIGURE 19.3

The Global Foreign Exchange Market

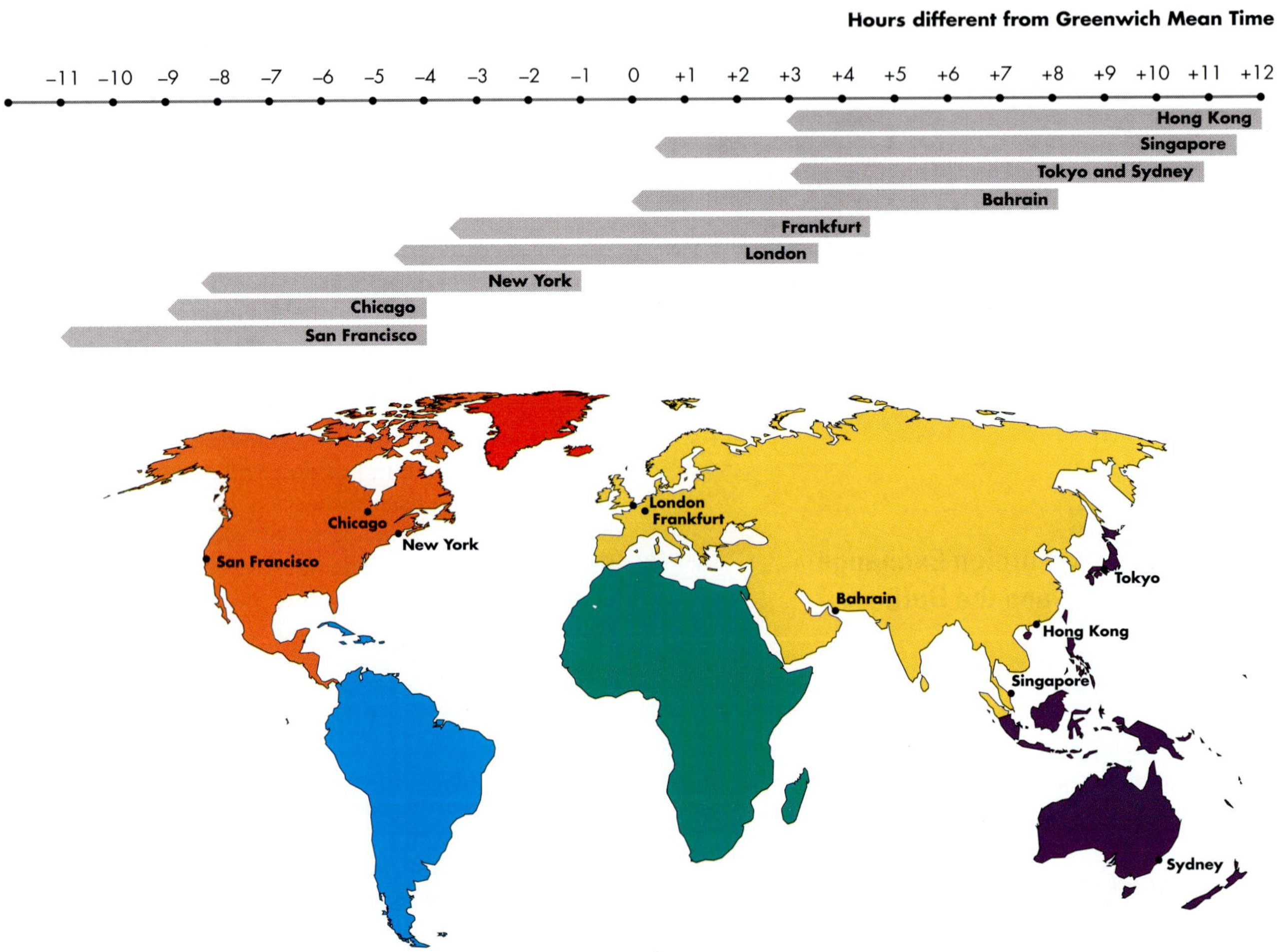

The foreign exchange market barely closes. The day begins in Hong Kong, and as the globe spins, markets open up in Singapore, Tokyo, Sydney, Bahrain, Zurich, Frankfurt, London, New York, Chicago, and San Francisco. By the time the West Coast markets close, Hong Kong is almost ready to begin another day.

Source: Based on a similar map in Steven Husted and Michael Melvin, *International Economics* (New York: Harper & Row, 1989), and data from *Euromoney*, April 1979, p. 14.

dollar to be worth a certain number of units of some other currency and having the Fed take actions designed to maintain that announced value. We'll study what those actions are below.

A **flexible exchange rate** is an exchange rate the value of which is determined by market forces in the absence of central bank intervention. A **managed exchange rate** is an exchange rate the value of which

FIGURE 19.4

Exchange Rates

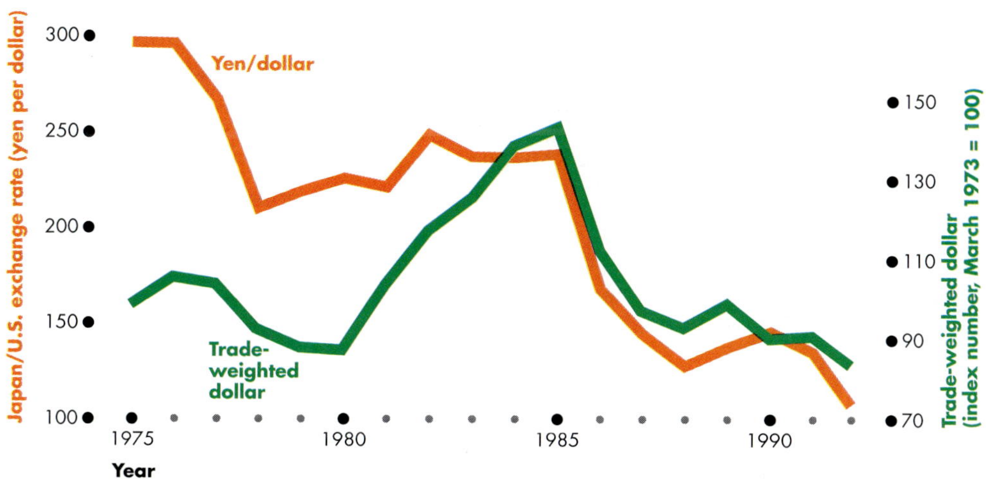

The exchange rate is the price at which two currencies can be traded. The yen-dollar exchange rate, expressed as yen per dollar, shows that the dollar has fallen in value—depreciated—against the yen. An index of the value of the U.S. dollar against all currencies shows that the U.S. dollar appreciated on the average against all currencies between 1980 and 1985 and depreciated between 1985 and 1990.

Source: Economic Report of the President, 1993.

is influenced by central bank intervention in the foreign exchange market. Under a managed exchange rate regime, the central bank's intervention does not seek to keep the exchange rate fixed at a preannounced level.

Recent Exchange Rate History

At the end of World War II, the major countries of the world set up the International Monetary Fund (IMF). The **International Monetary Fund** is an international organization that monitors balance of payments and exchange rate activities. The IMF is located in Washington, D.C. It came into being as a result of negotiations between the United States and the United Kingdom during World War II. In July 1944, at Bretton Woods, New Hampshire, 44 countries signed the Articles of Agreement of the IMF. At the centerpiece of those agreements was the establishment of a worldwide system of fixed exchange rates between currencies. The anchor for this fixed exchange rate system was gold. One ounce of gold was defined to be worth 35 U.S. dollars. All other currencies were pegged to the U.S. dollar at a fixed exchange rate. For example, the Japanese yen was set at 360 yen per dollar; the British pound was set to be worth $4.80. Although the fixed exchange rate system established in 1944 served the world well during the 1950s and early 1960s, it came under increasing strain in the late 1960s, and by 1971 the order had almost collapsed. In the period since 1971, the world has operated a variety of flexible and managed exchange rate arrangements. Some currencies have increased in value, and others have declined. The U.S. dollar is among the currencies that have declined. The Japanese yen is the currency that has had the most spectacular increase in value.

Figure 19.4 shows what happened to the exchange rate of the U.S. dollar between 1975 and 1992. The orange line shows the value of the dollar against the Japanese yen. As you can see, the value of the dollar has fallen against the yen—the dollar has depreciated. **Currency depreciation** is the fall in the value of one currency in terms of another currency.

Although the dollar has depreciated in terms of the Japanese yen, it has not depreciated, on the average, in terms of all other currencies. To calculate the value of the U.S. dollar in terms of other currencies on the average, a trade-weighted index is calculated. The **trade-weighted index** is the value of a basket of currencies when the weight placed on each currency is related to its importance in U.S. international trade. An example of the calculation of the trade-weighted index is set out in Table 19.3. In this example, we suppose that the United States trades with only three countries: Canada, Japan, and Great Britain. Fifty percent of the trade is with Canada, 30 percent with Japan, and 20 percent with Great Britain. In year 1, the U.S. dollar is worth either 1.25 Canadian dollars, 100 Japanese yen, or 0.50 British pound. Imagine putting these three currencies into a "basket" worth 100 U.S. dollars, in which 50 percent of the value of the basket is in Canadian dollars, 30 percent in Japanese yen, and 20 percent in British pounds. In year 1, the index number for the basket is 100. Suppose that in year 2, the exchange rates change in the way shown in the table. The Canadian dollar stays constant; the Japanese yen goes up in value, so only 90 Japanese yen can be bought for 1 U.S. dollar; and the British pound goes down in value, so 1 U.S. dollar buys 0.55 British pound. What is the change in the value of the basket? The percentage changes in the value of the U.S. dollar against each currency are calculated in the table. The dollar goes down against the Japanese yen by 10 percent and up against the British pound by 10 percent. Applying the trade weights to these percentage changes, we can calculate the weighted average change in the value of the U.S. dollar. Since the weight on the Japanese yen is 0.3 and that on the British pound is 0.2, the yen is more important than the pound. That is, a larger fraction of the basket's value consists of yen than of pounds. The weighted average value of the basket falls by 1 percent. The trade-weighted index declines by 1 percent and is 99. In this example, the U.S. dollar has depreciated on the average against the other three currencies.

The calculations that we have just worked through used hypothetical numbers. How the U.S. dollar has actually fluctuated against other currencies on the average in the period 1975 to 1992 is shown in Fig. 19.4. As you can see, during the 1970s the value of the U.S. dollar fluctuated but on the average remained steady against other currencies; from 1980 to 1985 it appreciated very strongly; and after 1985 it depreciated almost equally strongly.

TABLE 19.3

Trade-Weighted Index Calculation

Currency	Trade weights	Exchange rates (units of foreign currency per U.S. dollar)		Percentage changes	
		Year 1	Year 2	Unweighted	Weighted
Canadian dollar	**0.5**	**1.25**	**1.25**	**0**	**0**
Japanese yen	**0.3**	**100**	**90**	**–10**	**–3**
British pound	**0.2**	**0.50**	**0.55**	**+10**	**+2**
Total	**1.0**				**–1**

Trade-weighted index: year 1 = 100
year 2 = 99

Exchange Rate Determination

What determines the foreign currency value of the dollar? The foreign exchange value of the dollar is a price and, like any other price, is determined by demand and supply. But what exactly do we mean by the demand for and supply of dollars? And what is the quantity of dollars?

The Quantity of U.S. Dollar Assets

The **quantity of U.S. dollar assets** (which we'll call the **quantity of dollars**) is the *stock* of financial assets denominated in U.S. dollars minus the *stock* of financial liabilities denominated in U.S. dollars. In other words, it is the *stock of net financial assets denominated in U.S. dollars*. There are three things about the quantity of dollars that need to be emphasized and explained a bit more fully.

First, the quantity of dollars is a *stock*, not a *flow*. People make decisions about the quantity of dollars to hold and about the quantities to buy or sell. But it is the decision about how many dollars to hold that determines whether people plan to buy or sell dollars.

Second, the quantity of dollars is a stock *denominated in U.S. dollars*. The denomination of an asset defines the units in which a debt must be repaid. It is possible to make a loan using any currency of denomination. The U.S. government could borrow Japanese yen. If it did borrow in yen, it would issue a bond denominated in yen. Such a bond would be a promise to pay an agreed number of yen on an agreed date. It would not be a dollar debt and, even though issued by the U.S. government, would not be part of the supply of dollars. Many governments actually do issue bonds in currencies other than their own. The Canadian government, for example, issues bonds denominated in U.S. dollars, British pounds, German marks, and Swiss francs.

Third, the supply of dollars is a *net* supply—the quantity of assets *minus* the quantity of liabilities. This fact means that the quantity of dollars supplied does not include dollar assets created by private households, firms, financial institutions, or foreigners. The reason is that when a private debt is created, there is both an asset (for the holder) and a liability (for the issuer), so the *net* financial asset is zero. The quantity of dollars includes only the dollar liabilities of the federal government *plus* those of the Fed. This quantity is equal to the government debt held outside the Fed plus the dollar liabilities of the Fed—the monetary base (see p. 286). That is,

Quantity of dollars = Government debt held outside the Fed + Monetary base.

Changes in the Quantity of Dollar Assets

There are two ways in which the quantity of dollar assets can change:

- The federal government has a deficit or surplus.
- The Fed buys or sells assets denominated in foreign currency.

When the federal government has a deficit, it borrows by issuing bonds. These bonds, denominated in U.S. dollars, are held by households, firms, financial institutions, foreigners, and the Fed. Bonds bought by the Fed are not part of the stock of dollar assets. But to buy the bonds, the Fed creates additional monetary base, and this equivalent amount *is* part of the quantity of dollar assets. Thus when the Fed buys U.S. government debt, there is no change in the quantity of dollar assets, just a change in its composition.

The Fed can increase the quantity of dollars by buying assets denominated in foreign currency. If the Fed buys Japanese yen in the foreign exchange market, the monetary base increases by the amount paid for the yen.

We've now seen what dollar assets are and how their quantity can change. Let's now study the demand for these assets.

The Demand for Dollar Assets

The law of demand applies to dollar assets just as it does to anything else that people value. The quantity of dollar assets demanded increases when the price of dollars in terms of foreign currency falls and decreases when the price of dollars in terms of foreign currency rises. There are two separate reasons why the law of demand applies to dollars.

First, there is a transactions demand. The lower the value of the dollar, the larger is the demand for U.S. exports and the lower is our demand for imports, so the larger also is the amount of trade financed by dollars. Foreigners demand more dollars to buy U.S. exports, and we demand fewer units of foreign currency and more dollars as we switch from importing to buying U.S.-produced goods.

Second, there is a demand arising from expected capital gains. Other things being equal, the lower the value of the dollar today, the higher is its expected rate of appreciation (or the lower is its expected rate of depreciation), so the higher is the expected gain from holding dollar assets relative to the expected gain from holding foreign currency assets. Suppose that you expect the dollar to be worth 110 Japanese yen at the end of one year. If today the dollar is worth 120 yen, you're expecting the dollar to depreciate by 10 yen.

Other things being equal, you will not plan to hold dollar assets in this situation. Instead, you will plan to hold yen assets. But if today's value of the dollar is 100 yen, then you're expecting the dollar to appreciate by 10 yen. In this situation, you will plan to hold dollar assets and take advantage of the expected rise in their value. Holding assets in a particular currency in anticipation of a gain in their value arising from a change in the exchange rate is one of the most important influences on the quantity demanded of dollar assets and of foreign currency assets. The more a currency is expected to appreciate, the greater is the quantity of assets in that currency that people want to hold.

Figure 19.5 shows the relationship between the price of the U.S. dollar in yen and the quantity of dollar assets demanded—the demand curve for dollar assets. When the foreign exchange rate changes, other things being equal, there is a movement along the demand curve.

Any other influence on the quantity of dollar assets that people want to hold results in a shift in the demand curve. Demand either increases or decreases. These other influences are

- The volume of dollar-financed trade
- The interest rates on dollar assets
- The interest rates on foreign currency assets
- The expected future value of the dollar

Table 19.4 summarizes the above discussion of the influences on the quantity of dollar assets that people demand.

FIGURE 19.5

The Demand for Dollar Assets

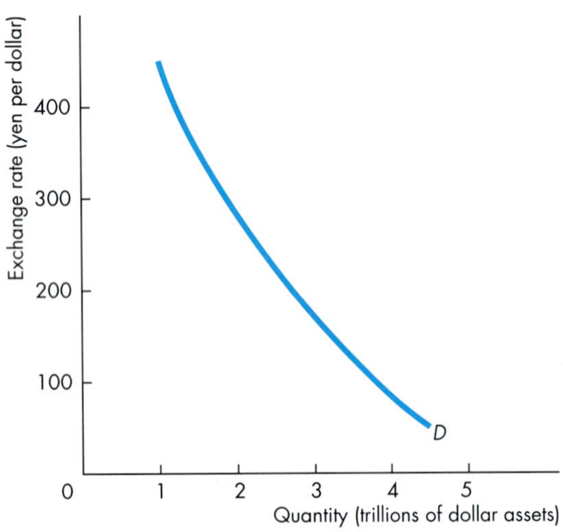

The quantity of dollar assets that people demand, other things held constant, depends on the exchange rate. The lower the exchange rate (the smaller the number of yen per dollar), the larger is the quantity of dollar assets demanded. The increased quantity demanded arises from an increase in the volume of dollar trade (the Japanese buy more American goods and we buy fewer Japanese goods) and an increase in the expected appreciation (or decrease in the expected depreciation) of dollar assets.

TABLE 19.4

The Demand for Dollar Assets

The law of demand	
The quantity of dollar assets demanded	
Increases if:	***Decreases if:***
The foreign currency value of the dollar falls	**The foreign currency value of the dollar rises**
Changes in demand	
The demand for dollar assets	
Increases if:	***Decreases if:***
Dollar-financed trade increases	**Dollar-financed trade decreases**
Interest rates on dollar assets rise	**Interest rates on dollar assets fall**
Interest rates on foreign currency assets fall	**Interest rates on foreign currency assets rise**
The dollar is expected to appreciate	**The dollar is expected to depreciate**

The Supply of Dollar Assets

The supply of dollar assets is determined by the actions of the government and the Federal Reserve. We've seen that the quantity of dollars is equal to government debt plus the monetary base. Of these two items, the monetary base is by far the smallest. But it plays a crucial role in determining the supply of dollars, since the behavior of the monetary base itself depends crucially on the foreign exchange rate regime in operation.

Under a fixed exchange rate regime, the supply curve of dollar assets is horizontal at the chosen exchange rate. The Fed stands ready to supply whatever quantity of dollar assets is demanded at the fixed exchange rate. Under a managed exchange rate regime, the government wants to smooth fluctuations in the exchange rate, so the supply curve of dollar assets is upward-sloping. The higher the foreign exchange rate, the larger is the quantity of dollar assets supplied. Under a flexible exchange rate regime, a fixed quantity of dollar assets is supplied, regardless of their price. As a consequence, under a flexible exchange rate regime, the supply curve of dollar assets is vertical.

The supply of dollar assets changes over time as a result of the following:

- The government's budget
- The Fed's monetary policy

If the government has a budget deficit, the supply of dollar assets increases. If the government has a budget surplus, the supply of dollar assets decreases. The supply of dollar assets increases whenever the Fed increases the monetary base and decreases whenever the Fed reduces the monetary base.

The above discussion of the influences on the supply of dollar assets is summarized in Table 19.5.

The Market for Dollar Assets

Let's now bring the demand and supply sides of the market for dollar assets together and determine the exchange rate. Figure 19.6 illustrates the analysis.

Fixed Exchange Rate First, consider a fixed exchange rate regime such as that from 1944 to 1971. This case is illustrated in Fig. 19.6(a). The supply curve of dollars is horizontal at the fixed exchange rate of 200 yen per dollar. If the demand curve is D_0, the quantity of dollar assets is Q_0. An increase in demand to D_1 results in an increase in the quantity of dollar assets from Q_0 to Q_1 but no change in the yen price of dollars.

Flexible Exchange Rate Next look at Fig. 19.6(b), which shows what happens under a flexible exchange rate regime. In this case, the quantity of dollar assets supplied is fixed at Q_0, so the supply curve of dollar assets is vertical. If the demand curve for dollars is D_0, the exchange rate is 200 yen per dollar. If the demand for dollars increases from D_0 to D_1, the exchange rate increases to 300 yen per dollar.

Managed Exchange Rate Finally, consider a managed exchange rate regime, which appears in Fig. 19.6(c). Here, the supply curve is upward-sloping. When the demand curve is D_0, the exchange rate is 200 yen per dollar. If demand increases to D_1, the yen value of the dollar rises, but only to 225 yen per dollar. Compared with the flexible exchange rate case, the same increase in demand results in a smaller increase in the exchange rate when it is managed.

TABLE 19.5

The Supply of Dollar Assets

Supply

Fixed exchange rate regime

The supply curve of dollar assets is horizontal at the fixed exchange rate.

Managed exchange rate regime

In order to smooth fluctuations in the price of the dollar, the quantity of dollar assets supplied by the Fed increases if the foreign currency price of the dollar rises and decreases if the foreign currency price of the dollar falls. The supply curve of dollar assets is upward-sloping.

Flexible exchange rate

The supply curve of dollar assets is vertical.

Changes in supply

The supply of dollar assets

Increases if:	***Decreases if:***
The U.S. government has a deficit	**The U.S. government has a surplus**
The Fed increases the monetary base	**The Fed decreases the monetary base**

FIGURE 19.6

Three Exchange Rate Regimes

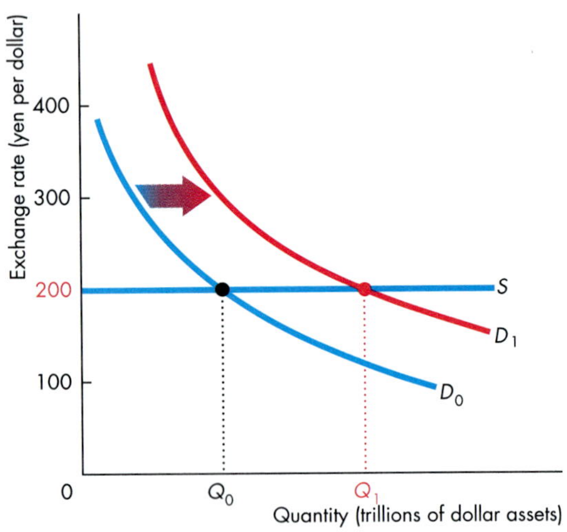

(a) Fixed exchange rate

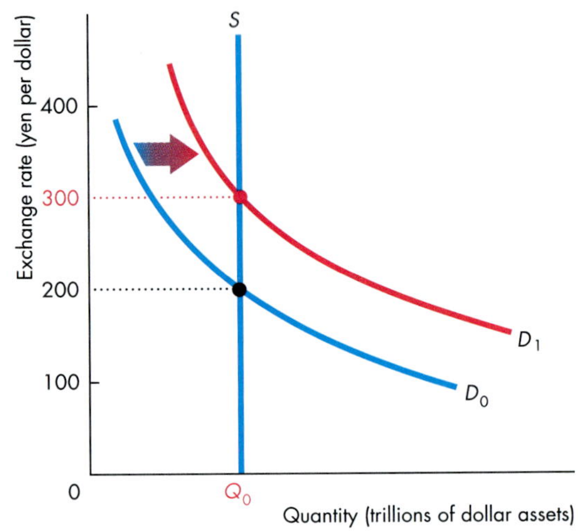

(b) Flexible exchange rate

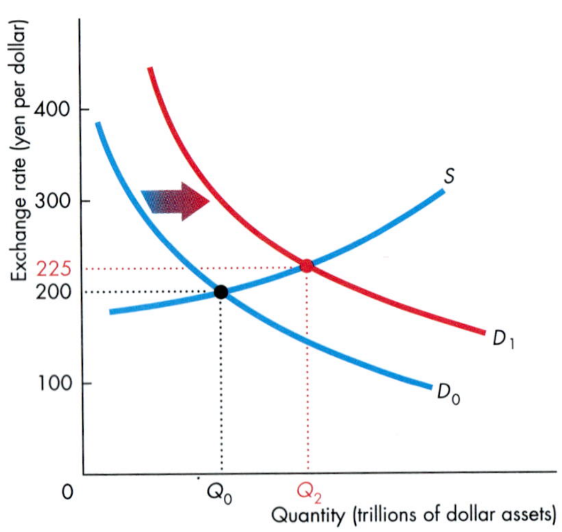

(c) Managed exchange rate

Under a fixed exchange rate regime (part a), the Fed stands ready to supply dollar assets or to take dollar assets off the market (supplying foreign currency in exchange) at a fixed exchange rate. The supply curve for dollar assets is horizontal. Fluctuations in demand lead to fluctuations in the quantity of dollar assets outstanding and to fluctuations in the nation's official holdings of foreign exchange. If demand increases from D_0 to D_1, the quantity of dollar assets increases from Q_0 to Q_1. Under a flexible exchange rate regime (part b), the Fed fixes the quantity of dollar assets so that their supply curve is vertical. An increase in the demand for dollar assets from D_0 to D_1 results only in an increase in the value of the dollar—the exchange rate rises from 200 to 300 yen per dollar. The quantity of dollar assets remains constant at Q_0. Under a managed exchange rate regime (part c), the Fed has an upward-sloping supply curve of dollar assets, so if demand increases from D_0 to D_1, the dollar appreciates but the quantity of dollar assets supplied also increases—from Q_0 to Q_2. The increase in the quantity of dollar assets supplied moderates the rise in the value of the dollar but does not completely prevent it as in the case of fixed exchange rates.

The reason for this is that the quantity supplied increases in the managed exchange rate case.

Exchange Rate Regime and Official Settlements Balance There is an important connection between the foreign exchange rate regime and the balance of payments. The official settlements account of the balance of payments records the change in the country's official holdings (by the government and the Fed) of foreign currency. Under fixed exchange rates (as shown in Fig. 19.6a), every time there is a change in the demand for dollar assets, the Fed must change the quantity of dollar assets supplied to match it. When the Fed has to increase the quantity of dollar assets supplied, it does so by offering dollar assets (bank deposits) in exchange for foreign currency (foreign bank deposits). In this case, the official holdings of foreign exchange increase. If the demand for dollar assets decreases, the Fed has to decrease the quantity of dollar assets supplied. The Fed does so by buying dollars back, using its foreign exchange holdings to do so. In this case, official holdings of foreign exchange decrease. Thus with a fixed exchange rate, fluctuations in the demand for dollar assets result in fluctuations in official holdings of foreign exchange.

Under a flexible exchange rate regime, there is no government or Fed intervention in the foreign exchange market. Regardless of what happens to the demand for dollars, no action is taken to change the quantity of dollars supplied. Therefore there are no changes in the country's official holdings of foreign exchange. In this case, the official settlements balance is zero.

With a managed exchange rate, official holdings of foreign exchange have to be adjusted to meet fluctuations in demand but in a less extreme manner than under fixed exchange rates. As a consequence, fluctuations in the official settlements balance are smaller under a managed floating regime than in a fixed exchange rate regime.

Up to 1970, the United States operated a fixed exchange rate, but so did all the other countries in the world. Furthermore, the United States was the largest country in the system. The task of keeping exchange rates fixed under that system was left to the individual smaller countries. Thus it was the Japanese government and the Bank of Japan that were charged with the responsibility of maintaining the yen-dollar exchange rate; the British government and the Bank of England were charged with maintaining the exchange rate of the British pound. Since 1971, the United States has been on a managed exchange rate regime, but on occasion it has come close to having a flexible exchange rate.

Why Is the Exchange Rate So Volatile?

We've seen times, especially recently, when the dollar-yen exchange rate has moved dramatically. On most of these occasions, the dollar has depreciated spectacularly, but on some occasions it has appreciated strongly.

The main reason why the exchange rate fluctuates so remarkably is that fluctuations in supply and demand are not always independent of each other. Sometimes a change in supply will trigger a change in demand that reinforces the effect of the change in supply. Let's look at two episodes to see how these effects work.

1981 to 1982 Between 1981 and 1982, the dollar appreciated against the yen, rising from 220 to 250 yen per dollar. Figure 19.7(a) explains why this happened. In 1981, the demand and supply curves were those labeled D_{81} and S_{81}. The foreign exchange value of the dollar was 220 yen—where these supply and demand curves intersect. The period between 1981 and 1982 was one of severe recession. This recession was brought about in part by the Fed pursuing a very restrictive monetary policy. The Fed permitted interest rates to rise sharply, cutting back on the monetary base and thus on the supply of dollar assets. The direct effect was a shift in the supply curve from S_{81} to S_{82}—a decrease in the supply of dollars. But higher U.S. interest rates induced an increase in demand for dollars to take advantage of the higher interest rates. As a result, the demand curve shifted from D_{81} to D_{82}. These two shifts reinforced each other, increasing the yen price of the dollar to 250 yen.

1985 to 1986 There was a spectacular depreciation of the dollar in terms of yen from 240 yen per dollar in 1985 to 170 yen per dollar in 1986. This fall came about in the following way. First, in 1985, the demand and supply curves were those labeled D_{85} and S_{85} in Fig. 19.7(b). The yen price of the dollar—the price at which these two curves intersect—was 240 yen per dollar. From 1982 to 1985, the U.S. economy had been on a recovery. But it was a recovery through which a budget deficit of increasing severity was emerging. Thus with a large government deficit, the supply of dollar assets was increasing. The Fed was also loosening up its monetary policy, permitting money supply growth rates to be rapid enough to keep the recovery going. The direct effect of these actions was an increase in the supply of dollar assets from S_{85} to S_{86}. But interest rates in the United States began to fall, and expectations of future declines in the value of the dollar also became widely held. As a consequence, the demand for dollar assets decreased from D_{85} to D_{86}. The result of this combined increase in supply and decrease in demand was a dramatic fall in the value of the dollar to 170 yen in 1986.

FIGURE 19.7

Why the Exchange Rate Is So Volatile

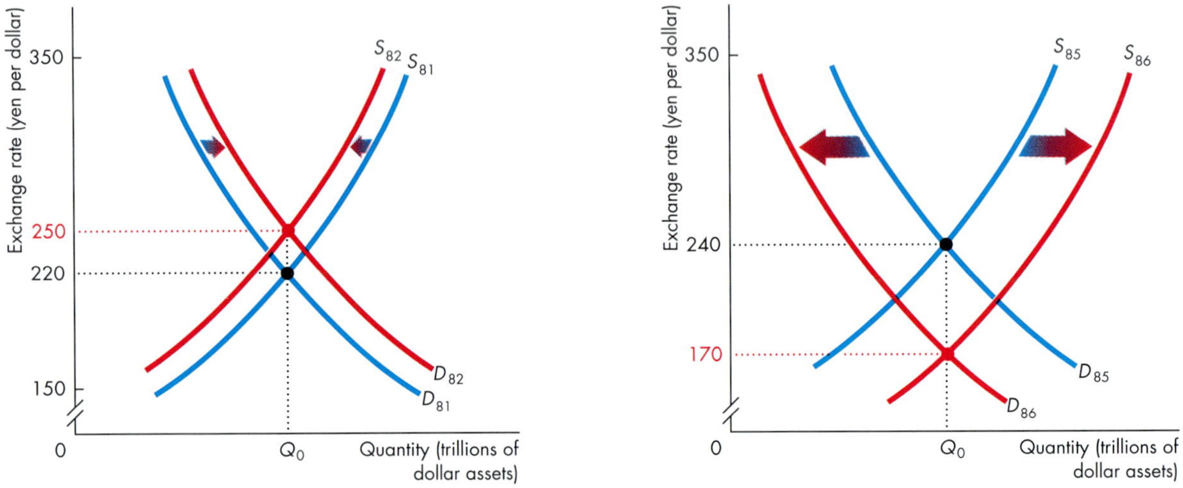

(a) 1981 to 1982

The exchange rate is volatile because shifts in the demand and supply curves for dollar assets are not independent of each other. Between 1981 and 1982 (part a), the dollar appreciated from 220 to 250 yen per dollar. This appreciation arose because the supply curve of dollar assets shifted to the left and higher interest rates induced an increase in demand for dollar assets, shifting the demand curve to the right. The result was a large increase in the foreign exchange value of the dollar.

(b) 1985 to 1986

Between 1985 and 1986 (in part b), the Fed permitted the quantity of dollar assets to increase to sustain the long economic recovery. The supply curve shifted to the right. At the same time, interest rates decreased and expectations of further declines in the value of the dollar shifted the demand curve to the left. The result was a steep fall in the exchange rate, from 240 yen to 170 yen per dollar between 1985 and 1986.

REVIEW

There are three possible foreign exchange rate regimes: fixed, flexible, and managed. Under a fixed exchange rate regime, the government and the Fed hold the exchange rate steady but the official settlements account of the balance of payments has to carry the burden of holding the exchange rate constant. A decrease in the demand for U.S. dollar assets is met by lowering the country's official holdings of foreign currency. Under a flexible exchange rate regime, the government and the Fed do not intervene in the foreign exchange markets. The official settlements balance is zero, and the country's official holdings of foreign currency remain constant. Under a managed exchanged rate regime, the Fed smooths exchange rate fluctuations to a degree but less strongly than under fixed exchange rates. Under a flexible or managed exchange rate regime, the exchange rate is determined by the demand for and supply of dollar assets. Fluctuations in supply often induce reinforcing fluctuations in demand, bringing severe fluctuations in the exchange rate. ◆

Arbitrage, Prices, and Interest Rates

Arbitrage is the activity of buying low and selling high in order to make a profit on the margin between the two prices.

Arbitrage has important effects on exchange rates, prices, and interest rates. An increase in the quantity of purchases forces the buying price up. An increase in the quantity of sales forces the selling price down. The prices move until they are equal and there is no arbitrage profit available. An implication of arbitrage is the law of one price. The **law of one price** states that any given commodity will be available at a single price.

The law of one price has no respect for national borders or currencies. If the same commodity is being bought and sold on either side of the Detroit River, it doesn't matter that one of these transactions is being undertaken in Canada and the other in the United States and that one is using U.S. dollars and the other Canadian dollars. The forces of arbitrage bring about one price. Let's see how.

Arbitrage

Consider the price of a floppy disk that can be bought in either the United States or Canada. We will ignore taxes, tariffs, and transportation costs in order to keep the calculations simple, since these factors do not affect the fundamental issue.

Suppose that we can buy floppy disks in the United States for US$10 a box. Suppose that this same box of disks is available in Canada for C$15 a box. (The symbol US$ stands for the U.S. dollar and C$ for the Canadian dollar.) Where would it pay to buy disks—in Canada or in the United States? The answer depends on the relative costs of Canadian and U.S. money. If a U.S. dollar costs C$1.50, then it is clear that the price of the disks is the same in both countries. Americans can buy a box of disks in the United States for US$10, or they can use US$10 to buy C$15 and then buy the disks in Canada. The cost will be the same either way. The same is true for Canadians. Canadians can use C$15 to buy a box of disks in Canada, or they can use C$15 to buy US$10 and then buy the disks in the United States. Again, there is no difference in the price of the disks.

Suppose, however, that a U.S. dollar is less valuable than in the above example. In particular, suppose that a U.S. dollar costs C$1.40. In this case, it will pay to buy the disks in the United States. Canadians can buy US$10 for C$14 and therefore can buy the disks in the United States for C$14 a box compared with C$15 in Canada. The same comparison holds for Americans. Americans can use US$10 to buy C$14, but that would not be enough to buy the disks in Canada since the disks cost C$15 there. It therefore pays Americans also to buy the disks in the United States.

If the situation described above did prevail, there would be an advantage in switching the purchases of disks from Canada to the United States. Canadians would cross the border to buy their disks in the United States and keep on doing so until the Canadian price had fallen to C$14. Once that had happened, Canadians would be indifferent between buying their disks in Canada and in the United States. Arbitrage would have eliminated the difference in prices in the two countries.

Perhaps you are thinking that this is a pretty crazy example, since Canadians don't rush down to the United States every time they want to buy a box of floppy disks. But the fact that there is a profit to be made means that it would pay someone to organize the importing of disks into Canada from the United States, thereby increasing the number of disks available there and lowering their price. The incentive to undertake such a move would be present as long as disks were selling for a higher price in Canada than in the United States.

Purchasing Power Parity

Purchasing power parity occurs when money has equal value across countries. (The word *parity* simply means equality. The phrase *purchasing power* refers to the *value of money.* Thus *purchasing power parity* directly translates to *equal value of money.*) Purchasing power parity is an implication of arbitrage and of the law of one price. In the floppy disk example, when US$1 is worth C$1.40, US$10 will buy the same box of floppy disks that C$14 will buy. The value of money, when converted to common prices, is the same in both countries. Purchasing power parity thus prevails in that situation.

Purchasing power parity theory predicts that purchasing power parity applies to all goods and to price indexes, not just to a single good such as the floppy disk that we considered above. That is, if any goods are cheaper in one country than in another, it will pay to convert money into the currency of that country, buy the goods in that country, and sell them in another. By such an arbitrage process, all prices are brought to equality.

One test of the purchasing power parity theory that has been proposed is to calculate the prices of goods in different countries converted to a common currency. One such good that has been used is the Big Mac, sold by McDonald's in all the major countries. It is claimed that if purchasing power parity holds, the Big Mac will cost the same everywhere. In fact, the Big Mac is more expensive in Tokyo than in Toronto and more expensive in Toronto than in Buenos Aires. These facts have led some people to conclude that purchasing power parity does not hold.

There is an important problem with this test of purchasing power parity. Big Macs are not easily traded internationally. In fact, they are not even easily traded across cities within the United States. For example, it's lunch time in Provo, you are hungry, and Big Macs are your thing. You don't have much choice but to buy your Big Mac right there. You can't take advantage of the fact that Big Macs are cheaper in Houston and begin an arbitrage operation. Big Macs are examples of nontraded goods. A **nontraded good** is one that cannot be traded over long distances. Sometimes it is technically possible to undertake such a trade but prohibitively costly. In other cases, it is simply not possible to undertake the trade.

There are many examples of nontraded goods. Almost all the public services provided by the government are nontraded. You can't buy cheap street-sweeping services in Seoul and sell them at a profit in San Francisco. Location-specific services, such as fast food, are also in this category. When goods cannot be traded over long distances, the goods are strictly different goods. A Big Mac in Provo is as different from a Big Mac in Houston as it is from a pancake across the street.

"On the foreign-exchange markets today, the dollar fell against all major currencies and the doughnut."

Arbitrage operates to bring about equality in prices of identical goods, not different goods. It does not operate to bring about equality between prices of similar-looking goods in widely differing locations. For this reason, tests of the purchasing power parity theory based on the prices of nontraded goods are faulty. In fact, for nontraded goods to have identical prices in different countries, every time the exchange rate changes, the prices of all goods will also have to change—the dollar will have to fall against all currencies, the Big Mac, and the doughnut!

Arbitrage does not occur only in markets for goods and services. It also occurs in markets for assets. As a result, it brings about another important equality or parity—interest rate parity.

Interest Rate Parity

Interest rate parity occurs when interest rates are equal across countries once the differences in risk are taken into account. Interest rate parity is a condition brought about by arbitrage in the markets for assets—markets in which borrowers and lenders operate.

At the beginning of this chapter, we noted that there are large differences in the interest rates at which people borrow and lend in different countries. For example, in the United States, interest rates are much lower than in England. Suppose that it is possible to borrow in New York at an interest rate of 6 percent a year and lend in London at an interest rate of 12 percent a year. Isn't it possible, in this situation, to make a huge profit on such a transaction? In fact, it is not. Interest rates in New York and London are actually equal—interest rate parity prevails.

The key to understanding why the interest rates are equal is to realize that when you borrow in New York, you borrow *dollars,* and when you lend money in England—such as by placing it on deposit in a bank—you are lending *pounds.* You are obliged to repay *dollars,* but you will be repaid in *pounds.* It's a bit like borrowing apples and lending oranges. But if you're borrowing apples and lending oranges, you've got to convert the apples to oranges. When the loans become due, you've got to convert oranges back into apples. The prices at which you do these transactions affect the interest rates that you pay and receive. How many dollars you get for your pounds depends on the exchange rate when the loan is repaid. If the pound has fallen in value, you'll get fewer dollars per pound than you paid in the first place.

The difference between the interest rates in New York and London reflects the change in the exchange rate between the dollar and the pound that, on the average, people are expecting. In this example, the average expectation is that the pound will fall against the dollar by 6 percent a year. So when you sell pounds to repay your dollar loan, you can expect to get 6 percent fewer dollars than you needed by buy the pounds. This 6 percent foreign exchange loss must be subtracted from the 12 percent interest income you earn in London. Thus your return from lending in London, when you convert your money back into dollars, is the same 6 percent that you must pay for the funds in New York. Your profit is zero. Actually, you would incur a loss because you would pay commissions on your foreign exchange transactions.

In the situation that we've just described, interest rate parity prevails. The interest rate in New York, when the expected change in the price of the dollar is taken into account, is almost identical to that in London. If interest rate parity did *not* prevail, it would be possible to profit, without risk, by borrowing at low interest rates and lending at high interest rates. Such *arbitrage* actions would increase the demand for loans in countries with low interest rates, and their interest rates would rise. And these actions would increase the supply of loans in countries with high interest rates, and their interest rates would fall. Such movements would restore interest rate parity very quickly.

A World Market

Arbitrage in asset markets operates on a worldwide scale and keeps the world capital markets linked in a single global market. This market is an enormous one. It involves borrowing and lending through banks, in bond markets, and in stock markets. The scale of this international business has been estimated by Salomon Brothers, an investment bank, at more than $1 trillion. It is because of international arbitrage in asset markets that the fortunes of the stock markets around the world are so closely linked. A stock market crash in New York makes its new low-priced stocks look attractive compared with high-priced stocks in Tokyo, Hong Kong, Zurich, Frankfurt, and London. As a consequence, investors make plans to sell high in these other markets and buy low in New York. But before many such transactions can be put through, the prices in the other markets fall to match the fall in New York. Conversely, if the Tokyo market experiences rapid price increases and markets in the rest of the world stay constant, investors seek to sell high in Tokyo and buy low in the rest of the world. Again, these trading plans will induce movements in the prices in the other markets to bring them into line with the Tokyo market. The action of selling high in Tokyo will lower the prices there, and the action of buying low in Frankfurt, London, and New York will raise the prices there.

◆ ◆ ◆ ◆ You've now discovered what determines a country's current account balance and the value of its currency. The most important influence on the current account balance is the government budget deficit. A country in which taxes are less than government spending is likely to be one that has a deficit in its trade with the rest of the world. The value of a country's currency is determined by the demand for and supply of that currency and is strongly influenced by monetary actions. A rapid increase in the supply of a currency will result in a decline in its value relative to other currencies. ◆ ◆ You've also learned how international arbitrage links prices and interest rates together in different countries. International arbitrage does not occur in markets for nontraded goods. But arbitrage operates in markets for traded goods and is especially powerful in markets for assets. Arbitrage in asset markets keeps interest rates equal around the world. Differences in national interest rates reflect the expectations of changes in exchange rates. Once these differences in exchange rates are taken into account, interest rates are equal across countries. ◆ ◆ In the final two chapters, we're going to look at some further global economic issues. First, in Chapter 20, we'll examine the problems faced by developing countries as they seek to grow. Then, in Chapter 21, we'll look at the countries of Eastern Europe and China as they make the transition from planned economies to market economies.

SUMMARY

Financing International Trade

International trade, borrowing, and lending are financed by using foreign currency. A country's international transactions are recorded in its balance of payments accounts. The current account records receipts and expenditures connected with the sale and purchase of goods and services, as well as net transfers to the rest of the world; the capital account records international borrowing and lending transactions; the official settlements account shows the increase or decrease in the country's foreign currency holdings.

Historically, the United States has been a net lender to the rest of the world, but in the mid-1980s that situation changed and it became a huge net borrower and a net debtor. Nevertheless, the stock of U.S. investment in the rest of the world exceeds foreign investment here.

The current account deficit is equal to the government budget deficit plus the private sector deficit. The private sector deficit is small, and fluctuations in the trade balance arise mainly from fluctuations in the government's budget. As the government budget deficit has grown, so the trade deficit has also grown. (pp. 502–511)

Foreign Exchange and the Dollar

Foreign currency is obtained in exchange for domestic currency in the foreign exchange market. There are three types of foreign exchange rate regimes: fixed, flexible, and managed. When the exchange rate is fixed, the government declares a value for the currency in terms of some other currency and the Fed takes actions to ensure that that price is maintained. To fix the exchange rate, the Fed has to stand ready to supply dollars and take in foreign currency or to remove dollars from circulation in exchange for foreign currency. The country's reserves of foreign currency fluctuate to maintain the fixed exchange rate.

A flexible exchange rate is one in which the central bank takes no actions to influence the value of its currency in the foreign exchange market. The country's holdings of foreign currencies remain constant, and fluctuations in demand and supply lead to fluctuations in the exchange rate.

A managed exchange rate is one in which the central bank takes actions to smooth fluctuations that would otherwise arise but does so less strongly than under a fixed exchange rate regime.

In a flexible or managed exchange rate regime, the exchange rate is determined by the demand for and supply of dollars. The demand for dollars depends on the volume of dollar trade financed, the interest rates on dollar assets, the interest rates on foreign currency assets, and expected changes in the value of the dollar.

The supply of dollars depends on the exchange rate regime. Under fixed exchange rates, the supply curve is horizontal; under flexible exchange rates, the supply curve is vertical; under managed exchange rates, the supply curve is upward-sloping. The position of the supply curve depends on the government's budget and the Fed's monetary policy. The larger the budget deficit or the more rapidly the Fed permits the monetary base to grow, the further to the right the supply curve moves. Fluctuations in the exchange rate occur because of fluctuations in demand and supply, and sometimes these fluctuations are large. Large fluctuations arise from interlinked changes in demand and supply. A shift in the supply curve often produces an induced change in the demand curve that reinforces the effect on the exchange rate. (pp. 511–520)

Arbitrage, Prices, and Interest Rates

Arbitrage—buying low and selling high—keeps the prices of goods and services that are traded internationally close to equality across all countries. Arbitrage also keeps the different interest rates in line with each other.

Interest rates around the world look unequal, but the appearance arises from the fact that loans are contracted in different currencies in different countries. To compare interest rates across countries, we have to take into account changes in the values of currencies. Countries whose currencies are appreciating have low interest rates; countries whose currencies are depreciating have high interest rates. If the rate of currency depreciation is taken into account, interest rates are nearly equal. (pp. 520–523)

KEY ELEMENTS

Key Terms

Arbitrage, 520
Balance of payments accounts, 502
Capital account, 503
Creditor nation, 504
Currency depreciation, 514
Current account, 502
Debtor nation, 504
Fixed exchange rate, 511
Flexible exchange rate, 512
Foreign exchange market, 511
Foreign exchange rate, 511
Interest rate parity, 522
International Monetary Fund, 513
Law of one price, 521
Managed exchange rate, 512
Net borrower, 504
Net lender, 504
Nontraded good, 522
Official reserves, 503
Official settlements account, 503
Private sector surplus or deficit, 505
Purchasing power parity, 521
Quantity of U.S. dollar assets (quantity of dollars), 515
Trade-weighted index, 514
Twin deficits, 507

Key Figures and Tables

REVIEW QUESTIONS

1 What are the transactions recorded in a country's current account, capital account, and official settlements account?

2 What is the relationship between the balance on the current account, the capital account, and the official settlements account?

3 Distinguish between a country that is a net borrower and one that is a creditor. Are net borrowers always creditors? Are creditors always net borrowers?

4 What is the connection between a country's current account balance, the government's budget deficit, and the private sector deficit?

5 Why do fluctuations in the government budget balance lead to fluctuations in the current account balance?

6 Distinguish among the three exchange rate regimes: fixed, flexible, and managed.

7 Review the main influences on the quantity of dollars that people demand.

8 Review the influences on the supply of dollars.

9 How does the supply curve of dollars differ under the three exchange rate regimes?

10 Why does the dollar fluctuate so much?

11 What is arbitrage?

12 How does arbitrage lead to purchasing power parity?

13 What is interest rate parity?

14 How does interest rate parity come about?

PROBLEMS

1 The citizens of Silecon, whose currency is the grain, conducted the following transactions in 1990:

	Billions of grains
Imports of goods and services	350
Exports of goods and services	500
Borrowing from the rest of the world	60
Lending to the rest of the world	200
Increase in official holdings of foreign currency	10

a Set out the three balance of payments accounts for Silecon.
b Does Silecon have a flexible exchange rate?

2 You are told the following about Ecflex, a country with a flexible exchange rate whose currency is the band:

	Billions of bands
GDP	100
Consumption expenditure	60
Government purchases of goods and services	24
Investment	22
Exports of goods and services	20
Government budget deficit	4

Calculate the following for Ecflex:
a Imports of goods and services
b Current account balance
c Capital account balance
d Taxes (net of transfer payments)
e Private sector deficit or surplus

3 A country's currency appreciates, and its official holdings of foreign currency increase. What can you say about the following?
a The exchange rate regime being pursued by the country
b The country's current account
c The country's official settlements account

4 The average annual interest rate in Japan is 4 percent; in the United States it is 6 percent; in Germany it is 9 percent; and in England it is 13 percent. What is the expected percentage change over the coming year in each of the following?
a The U.S. dollar against the Japanese yen
b The British pound against the German mark
c The U.S. dollar against the British pound
d The Japanese yen against the German mark
e The U.S. dollar against the German mark

PART 7

GROWTH, DEVELOPMENT, AND REFORM

Talking with Jeffrey Sachs

Jeffrey Sachs was born in Detroit in 1954 and has spent his entire university career at Harvard, first as an undergraduate and eventually as a professor. Today, however, Professor Sachs spends most of his time on airplanes or in Eastern Europe. He first began advising foreign governments on economic policy by helping Bolivia with hyperinflation in 1985. His name burst before the public with his work on Poland, but now he is increasingly associated with the economic reforms of Boris Yeltsin and the Russian Federation.

How did you get drawn into the Eastern European reform area?

I started my work in Eastern Europe in Poland at the time that Solidarity was legalized in the spring of 1989. I had been invited by the Communist government to give advice to them about their financial troubles. Events obviously went very fast because soon after legalization there was an election, which Solidarity won overwhelmingly. From that point on, I became an economic advisor to believers in Solidarity and helped them draft an outline of a radical economic reform program. Soon after that, a Solidarity government actually came to power, and I began to work on the implementation of economic reforms, which were widely viewed as the first and most comprehensive reforms in Eastern Europe. From there, I got to know reformers in all of the countries in the region and began to work closely with some Russian economists who are now senior members of the Yeltsin government. As democratization proceeded in Russia, these people invited me to help them develop their reform strategy.

Your name has been associated with the "big bang" or "cold turkey" approach to reform. Can you describe that approach and explain why you favor it over a more gradual and tentative one?

The basic idea is to start with the goal of the reform, such as to put in place a working capitalist system. Of course, it'll be a capitalist system that reflects the particular culture, history, tradition, and resources of the country. It is an attempt not to find a so-called "third way in" between the old system and the new system but to go fully toward the working capitalist model. In the case of Eastern Europe, the goal is even more explicit: to implement reforms that will make these countries harmonize with the economies of Western Europe so that in a short period of time—within a decade is their hope—they can actually become members of the European Community.

The essence of "big bang" is that it's important to move comprehensively and quickly toward the goal of a working capitalist economy because various aspects of the market economy are all interrelated. If one does just a piece of the reform but leaves much of the old system intact, the conflicts of the old and the new are likely to make things considerably worse rather than better.

What are the major pieces of the radical reform strategy that you're recommending to governments in Eastern Europe?

The reform strategy comes down to four components. The first is macroeconomic stabilization, because usually these countries start out in a deep macroeconomic crisis characterized by high inflation and intense shortages. Second is economic liberalization, which means ending central planning, trade quotas, and other barriers that cut the country off from the world market. The third part of the reform is privatization, which is the transfer of state property back to private owners. Those private owners could be individuals or they could be, as in the West, financial intermediaries like mutual funds or banks or pension funds that are in turn owned by individuals. When I say privatization, I use the word "transfer" rather than "sell" because selling state property is only one way to privatize. There are other ways, such as giving away the state property to workers, managers, or the public. The Eastern European countries are privatizing through a mix of sales and direct giveaways. The fourth part of the radical reform is the introduction of social safety nets, which provide protection for the most vulnerable parts of the society that are perhaps hardest hit by the reform or are already suffering even irrespective of the reform. That means putting in place unemployment benefits, an adequate retirement system and health care system, job training, public works spending, and so forth. Those are the four main pillars.

It's called "big bang" because you must move quickly on this. Probably the most dramatic part of all is the stabilization and liberalization phase, where subsidies are cut very quickly and price controls are eliminated. The result is usually a very dramatic one-time jump in prices. That starts off the reform.

How long does the reform process generally take?

Certain things can be done quickly, and others take more time. Stabilization and liberalization can be accomplished fast, or most parts of them. Freeing price controls, eliminating trade barriers, and cutting subsidies, for example, can all be done on the first day of the program, which is why it's sometimes called "shock therapy" or "cold turkey." Privatization, though, takes much longer. Some aspects of the fourth component of the reform strategy, the social safety net, can be done quickly. For example, pensions of retirees can be protected through budgetary allocation. An unemployment insurance system was started up very quickly in Poland, and it has worked adequately. Other parts of the social safety net, for instance, real reform of the health care system, are very complex and take a considerable amount of time to effect.

Even if the reforms go very quickly, the process of change that those reforms set loose will take years or even decades to work themselves out. What do I mean? The socialist system wasn't just messed up in terms of the organization of production and the ways that prices were set. It was also systematically misusing resources by putting tremendous overemphasis on heavy industrial production while neglecting other important parts of the economy, such as services and wholesale and retail trade. When you free up market forces, the market doesn't demand all the heavy industrial production that was built up in the past. This leads to unemployment, a drop in demand, and people voluntarily quitting those industries to move into areas that were starved for people, resources, and capital in the past. You get a great boom in retail trade, for example, with tens of thousands of new shops opening up. The reforms set loose that process, but the corresponding shift of resources could take five, ten, fifteen, even twenty years to adjust.

Even within a big bang approach, presumably you can't literally do everything at once. What are the highest priorities?

The highest priority is to avoid real financial chaos. Poland, Yugoslavia, and Russia all fell into hyperinflation at the end of the Communist system. That meant that the new democratic governments' highest priority was to end the underlying conditions that were feeding the hyperinflation. If you can accomplish the financial stability, then I think the next highest priority is to have the rudiments of the private property system in place, such as a commercial code and laws for corporate enterprises, contracts, and protection of private property. Then the next priority is rapid privatization because until the enterprises are with real owners facing proper incentives, one has to be skeptical that they'll be managed in an efficient and sensible way.

What are the earliest indicators of whether the reforms are beginning to take hold?

Of course, different things happen at different times. The first thing one looks for if an economy is trying to emerge from hyperinflation is stability of prices. After freeing prices and experiencing a significant one-time jump in the price level, this should not turn into ongoing high inflation but rather be followed by price stability.

Can the countries of Eastern Europe and the former Soviet Union evolve into democratic nations with market economies without economic aid from the West?

The whole history of radical economic change underscores the importance of financial assistance during the first critical years of reform. It takes many years for the real fruits of the reform to be widely evident in the society. Certain costs of the reform, however, such as closing down old inefficient enterprises, can become evident very quickly. It's during that crucial period between the introduction of the reforms and the time when they really are bearing fruit that lie the greatest dangers and also the greatest need for international assistance to help provide a cushion to living standards and a bolstering of the reform effort until the reforms really take hold.

The foreign assistance does not actually pay for the reconstruction of the country. It's never big enough. The Marshall Plan was not enough to really rebuild Europe, but what the Marshall Plan did was to give the new democratic postwar governments time to put in place market-based policies so that they could take hold.

Whether it's postwar Germany or Japan, Mexico's turnaround in the 1980s, or Poland at the beginning of the 1990s, countries on the path to economic and political reform need help at the beginning. For Russia and the other states of the former Soviet Union, it will be the same. They will definitely need some years of Western and foreign help to keep their reforms on track and to make the living conditions tolerable.

What form will that aid take? Free-trading opportunities? Private investment? Government loans?

The form of aid has to be linked to the timetable of the reform process. At the beginning, say in the first year, the aid is inevitably of two sorts. First, humanitarian emergency assistance to make sure that food is getting to the table and that medical supplies are available. Second, stabilization assistance, or various kinds of financial support to help make the currency strong and to increase the flow of basic imports, which are needed just to keep the economy functioning. Russia has suffered a sharp decline in its own capacity to buy imports because its export earnings have fallen sharply in the past few years. They need help just to keep basic imports going, and by doing that you help strengthen the currency.

In later years, you want to get away from that kind of emergency stabilization support and put much more attention on project financing to get new enterprises going. One hopes these will become the major engine of economic growth in the future. Private investment, of course, is to be desired, but it will take many years to attract. Private investors first want to know the market, and then they wait to see signs that the reforms are working and that political stability is being achieved. The official support from government has to come first. Then the private money will flow in.

What are the economic principles that you find most valuable in dealing with the acute problems of Russia today?

The starting point for me is to recognize that all of the successful economies in the world have a shared core set of institutions. There are, of course, major differences across countries, but all of the advanced industrial economies share certain features—such as a currency that trades, that can be used to buy goods without facing fixed prices or shortages, and that is convertible internationally; an open trading system in which, with some exceptions, goods can be bought and sold from abroad on normal market terms; an economy based on private ownership not state ownership; a legal infrastructure that supports private ownership so that property rights are clearly defined and defensible. Things like that. It's that core of institutions that is so important to put into place.

What are the undergraduates studying economics in Russia today actually studying? Are they learning about demand and supply, competition and monopoly, aggregate demand and aggregate supply, and the role of money in creating inflation?

Of course, things are changing very fast. It was only a few years ago that ideas like market economy and private property were unfamiliar. What one sees now is incredible hunger to study and analyze the basic properties of market economies. There is no doubt, I think, in the minds of virtually everybody that the old system was a terrible failure and that what Russia should have is a normal economy like that which is in place in Western Europe, the United States, and Japan. The curricula are being revised with incredible speed to teach the standard economics that we also learn. Of course, students' attention is focused not just on the well-functioning system but also on the problems of transitions.

What do you see as the major obstacles to economic development in Eastern Europe?

The major obstacle is that this is a time of great upheaval. The collapse of communism occurred, in part, because the old system had failed so thoroughly and people were in economic misery. So all this transformation is starting in the midst of a real economic crisis—a crisis that breeds confusion, fear, and anxiety. That confusion, fear, and anxiety can lead a whole country astray from its basic path of building up democratic market institutions. There are politicians waiting with messages attacking democracy, trying to take advantage of the anxieties of the people to win power. This could derail the reforms. If the new governments cannot deliver economic improvement, then I think risks to democracy will certainly exist. And once there is doubt about the basic direction of these changes, then things become unpredictable, but very hazardous results are possible. I don't think that's the likely outcome, but it's one of the reasons why I underscored the need for support, understanding, and a financial cushion from the West during this very critical and complicated stage of implementing the reforms.

Assuming that Russia does develop rapidly and solves its economic problems in the decade ahead, what are the major implications for the United States?

The overwhelming implication is that the chance for us to live in a peaceful world is enormously improved. We should not underestimate the difference that will mean to our own quality of life. The success of Russian democracy will make a huge difference to our security and, in financial terms, to our ability to divert our own resources from military spending to civilian use. Now, Russia's success with democracy depends a great deal on its success in overcoming this economic crisis. We know all too well that economic instability is one of the great dangers to a young democracy.

There are many, many other implications. The whole world will change, and I think vastly for the better. There will be a huge trading and investment opportunity when a country that covers one sixth of the world's land mass, spanning over eleven time zones, becomes closely integrated with the rest of the world economy after having been cut off for seventy-five years. There will be important changes in trade patterns, investment opportunities, and global cooperation.

CHAPTER 20

GROWTH AND DEVELOPMENT

After studying this chapter, you will be able to:

- Describe the international distribution of income
- Explain the importance of economic growth
- Explain how the accumulation of capital and technological progress bring higher per capita incomes
- Describe the obstacles to economic growth in poor countries
- Explain the possible effects of population control, foreign aid, free trade, and demand stimulation on economic growth and development
- Evaluate policies designed to stimulate economic growth and development

Feed the World

MOST COUNTRIES OF AFRICA, ASIA, AND CENTRAL America have much lower living standards than our own. Some countries, such as Ethiopia, are so poor that people die from an inadequate diet. Why are some countries, like Ethiopia, chained to poverty? Why are there such differences in income between the poorest and richest countries? In 1946, as World War II ended, Hong Kong emerged from occupation by the Japanese as a poor colony of Britain. Occupying a cluster of overcrowded rocky islands, Hong Kong today is a city of vibrant, hardworking, and increasingly wealthy people. A similar story can be told of Singapore. Two and a half million people crowded into an island city-nation have, by their dynamism, transformed their economy, increasing their average income more than sixfold since 1960. How do some countries manage to unshackle themselves from poverty? What do they have that other poor countries lack? Can their lessons be applied elsewhere? ◆◆ The world's population has passed 5 billion inhabitants. These billions of people are unevenly distributed over the earth's surface. More than 4 billion live in the world's poor countries, and only 1 billion live in the rich industrial countries. It is estimated that by the year 2020, world population will exceed 8 billion, with close to 7 billion living in the poor countries and only 1.4 billion in the industrial countries. Why is the population growth rate so rapid in poor countries? What are the effects of rapid population growth on economic growth and development? ◆◆ In a typical year in the 1980s, $85 billion worth of aid was given by rich countries to developing countries. The United States provided more than a third of this aid. Does foreign aid help poor countries? Why hasn't it alleviated their poverty? ◆◆ Some poor countries try to encourage growth and development by protecting their industries from international trade and foreign competition. Other countries are outward-looking and engage in free trade with the rest of the world. What kind of international trade policy gives a developing country the best chance of rapid and sustained economic growth?

◆◆◆◆ In this chapter, we'll study the questions just posed. They are all aspects of one of the big economic questions posed in Chapter 1: what causes differences in wealth among nations, making the people in some countries rich and those in others poor? We don't fully understand the answer to this question. But there are some things that we do know. We'll review that knowledge in this chapter. We'll also review some of the ideas people have advanced about what can be done to speed up the growth of poor countries. Some strategies truly help poor countries, but others have mixed results and may even hurt their development.

The International Distribution of Income

When we studied the distribution of U.S. income, we discovered that there is a great deal of inequality. As we will see, the differences in income within a country, large though they are, look insignificant when compared with the differences among the nations. Let's see how income is distributed among the nations of the world.

Poorest Countries

The poorest countries are sometimes called underdeveloped countries. An **underdeveloped country** is a country in which there is little industrialization, limited mechanization of the agricultural sector, very little capital equipment, and low per capita income. In many underdeveloped countries, large numbers of people live on the edge of starvation. Such people devote their time to producing the supplies of food and clothing required for themselves and their families. They have no surplus to trade with others or to invest in new tools and capital equipment. One of the most publicized of the poor countries is Ethiopia, where thousands of people spend their lives trekking across parched landscapes in search of meager food supplies.

Just how poor are the poorest countries? Twenty-seven percent of the world's population lives in countries whose per capita incomes range between 4 and 9 percent of those in the United States. Although these countries contain 27 percent of the world's people, they earn only 6 percent of world income. These poorest of countries are located mainly in Africa.

Developing Countries

A **developing country** is one that is poor but is accumulating capital and developing an industrial and commercial base. The developing countries have a large and growing urban population and have steadily growing incomes. The per capita income level in such countries ranges between 10 and 30 percent of that in the United States. These countries are located in all parts of the world, but many are found in Asia, the Middle East, and Central America. Seventeen percent of the world's people live in these countries and earn 11 percent of world income.

Newly Industrialized Countries

Newly industrialized countries (often called NICs) are countries in which there is a rapidly developing broad industrial base and per capita income is growing quickly. Today their per capita income levels approach 50 percent of those in the United States. Examples of such countries are Trinidad, Israel, and South Korea. Three percent of the world's people live in the newly industrialized countries and earn 3 percent of world income.

Industrial Countries

Industrial countries are countries that have a large amount of capital equipment and in which people undertake highly specialized activities, enabling them to earn high per capita incomes. These are the countries of Western Europe, the United States and Canada, Japan, and Australia and New Zealand. Seventeen percent of the world's people live in these countries, and they earn 49 percent of world income.

Oil-Rich Countries

A small number of oil-rich countries have very high per capita incomes despite the fact that they are, in most other respects, similar to the poorest countries or developing countries. These countries have little industry, and indeed little of anything of value to sell to the world, except oil. Four percent of the world's people live in these countries, and they earn 4 percent of world income. But that income is very unequally distributed within the countries: most of the people in these countries have incomes similar to those in the poorest countries, but a small number of people are extremely rich—indeed, among the richest people in the world.

Communist and Former Communist Countries

Close to 33 percent of the world's people live in communist countries or in countries that were formerly communist and are now making a transition toward capitalism. These countries earn 28 percent of world income. A **communist country** is a country in which there is limited private ownership of productive capital and of firms, there is limited reliance on the market as a means of allocating resources, and government agencies plan and direct the production and distribution of most goods and services. Rapid changes are taking place in many of these countries at the present time. We describe the economies of these countries, and the changes that are taking place as they move toward market economies, in Chapter 21.

Per capita incomes in these countries vary enormously. In China, per capita income is around 15 percent of that in the United States. China is a developing country. Per capita income in the former East Germany—now part of a reunited Germany—is almost 70 percent of that of the United States. Other countries in this category are Czechoslovakia, Poland, Hungary, and the former Soviet Union. Some formerly communist countries, such as Rumania, Yugoslavia, and Bulgaria, have per capita incomes similar to those of the newly industrialized countries. Thus within the communist and formerly communist countries, there is a great deal of variety in income levels and the degree of economic development.

The World Lorenz Curve

A **Lorenz curve** plots the cumulative percentage of income against the cumulative percentage of population. If income is equally distributed, the Lorenz curve is a 45° line running from the origin. The degree of inequality is indicated by the extent to which the Lorenz curve departs from the 45° line of equality. Figure 20.1 shows two Lorenz curves: one curve depicts the distribution of income among families in the United States, and the other depicts the distribution of average per capita income across countries.

FIGURE 20.1
The World Lorenz Curve, 1985

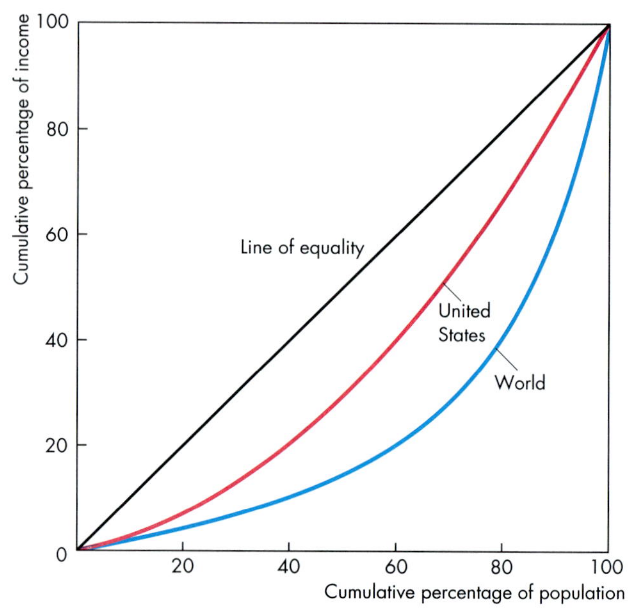

The cumulative percentage of income is plotted against the cumulative percentage of population. If income were distributed equally across countries, the Lorenz curve would be a straight diagonal line. The distribution of per capita income across countries is even more unequal than the distribution of income among families in the United States.

Source: Robert Summers and Alan Heston, "A New Set of International Comparisons of Real Product and Price Levels; Estimates for 130 Countries, 1950–1985," *Review of Income and Wealth,* Series 34 (1988): 207–262; and *Current Population Reports, Consumer Income,* Series P-60, Nos. 167 and 168 (Washington, D.C.: U.S. Department of Commerce, Bureau of the Census, 1990).

As you can see, the distribution of income among countries is more unequal than the distribution of income among families within the United States. Forty percent of the world's people live in countries whose incomes account for less than 10 percent of the world's total. The richest 20 percent of the world's people live in countries whose incomes account for 55 percent of the world's total income. Inequality in income is even more severe than that apparent in Fig. 20.1, because the world Lorenz curve tells us only how unequal average incomes are among countries. Inequality within countries is not revealed by the world Lorenz curve.

Such numbers provide a statistical description of the enormity of the world's poverty problem. And they are *real* numbers. That is, the effects of differences in prices have been removed. To better appreciate the severity of the problem, imagine that your family has an income of 30 cents a day for each person. That 30 cents has to buy housing, food, clothing, transportation, and all the other things consumed. Such is the lot of more than a quarter of the world's people.

Although there are many poor people in the world, there are also many whose lives are undergoing dramatic change. They live in countries in which rapid economic growth is taking place. As a result of economic growth and development, millions of people now enjoy living standards undreamt of by their parents and inconceivable to their grandparents. Let's look at the connection between income levels and the rate of economic growth.

Growth Rates and Income Levels

Poor countries can and do grow into rich countries. Poor countries become rich countries by achieving high growth rates of real per capita income over prolonged periods of time. Over the years, a small increase in the growth rate, like compound interest, pays large dividends. A slowdown in the growth rate, maintained over a number of years, can result in a huge loss of real income.

The importance of economic growth and its effects on income levels are vividly illustrated by our own recent experience. In the United States in the early 1960s, aggregate income, measured by real GDP, was growing at around 4 percent a year. After 1965, GDP growth slowed down. The path actually followed by U.S. GDP growth is shown in Fig. 20.2(a). The path that would have been followed if the pre-1965 growth trend had been maintained is also shown in that figure. By 1991, U.S. real GDP was approximately $2 trillion below—40 percent below—what it would have been if the 1965 growth rate had been maintained.

When poor countries have a slow growth rate and rich countries have a fast growth rate, the gap between the rich and the poor widens. Figure 20.2(b) shows how the gap between the United States and many poor countries, such as Ethiopia, has widened over the years.

For a poor country to catch up to a rich country, it is necessary for its growth rate to exceed that of the rich country. In 1980, per capita income in China was 14 percent of that in the United States. In the 1980s, the United States experienced an average per capita income growth rate of 1.5 percent a year. If that growth rate is maintained and if per capita income in China also grows at 1.5 percent a year, China will remain at 14 percent of U.S. income levels forever. The gap will remain constant. If per capita income in the United States were to grow at 1.5 percent and if China could maintain a per capita income growth rate at twice that level—3 percent per year—China would catch up to the United States in per capita income levels in the first part of the *twenty-second* century, around 2115. If China could do even twice as well as that—maintaining a 6 percent per year growth rate in per capita incomes—the people of China would have income levels as high as those in the United States within your own lifetime—in the mid-2030s. If China could pull off a miracle and make per capita income grow at 12 percent a year, it would take just 20 years to catch up to the United States.

Growth rates as high as 10 or 12 percent are not unknown. Japan's per capita income grew in excess of 10 percent a year, on the average, for almost 20 years following World War II. Recently, China has indeed experienced per capita income growth of 12 percent a year, a rate that, if sustained, doubles per capita income every six years. Even the poorest

FIGURE 20.2

Growth Rates and Income Levels

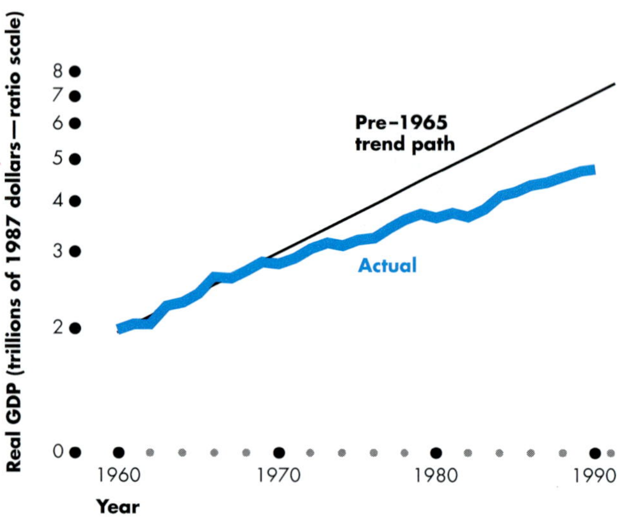

(a) U.S. output loss from growth slowdown

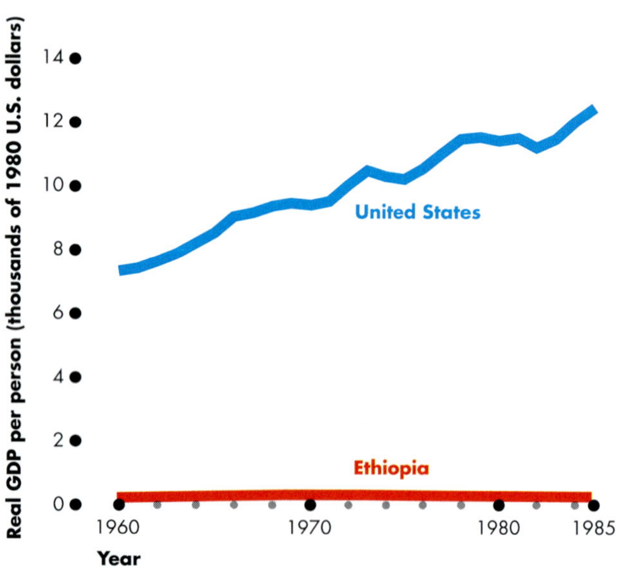

(b) The gap widens between rich and poor

A fall in the U.S. growth rate after 1965 (part a) has resulted in real GDP being some $2 trillion (40 percent) below its pre-1965 trend path. But with almost no growth, Ethiopia has fallen further behind the United States (part b).

Source: Robert Summers and Alan Heston, "A New Set of International Comparisons of Real Product and Price Levels; Estimates for 130 Countries, 1950–1985," *Review of Income and Wealth,* Series 34 (1988): 207–262; and *Economic Report of the President,* 1992.

countries in the world—those with per capita incomes of only 4 percent of those of the United States—would catch up to the United States in a matter of 30 or 40 years if they could achieve and maintain growth rates of this level.

The key, then, to achieving high per capita income is to attain and maintain a high rate of economic growth. That is how today's rich countries attained their high living standards. The poor countries of today will join the rich countries of tomorrow only if they can find ways of attaining and maintaining rapid growth.

Clearly, the question of what determines a country's economic growth rate is a vital one. What does determine a country's economic growth rate? Let's turn to an examination of this crucial question.

Resources, Technological Progress, and Economic Growth

In the aggregate, income equals the value of output. Thus to increase average income, a country has to increase its output. A country's output depends on its resources and the techniques it employs for transforming these resources into outputs. This relationship between resources and outputs is the *production function.* There are three types of resource:

- Land
- Labor
- Capital

Land includes all the natural, nonproduced resources such as land itself, the minerals under it, and all other nonproduced inputs. The quantity of these resources is determined by nature, and countries have no choice but to put up with whatever natural resources they happen to have. Countries cannot achieve rapid and sustained economic growth by increasing their stock of natural resources. But countries can and do experience fluctuations in income as a result of fluctuations in the prices of their natural resources. Furthermore, there are times when those prices are rising quickly, and such periods bring temporary income growth. The late 1970s is an example of a period in which resource-rich countries experienced rapid income growth as a result of rising commodity prices. But to achieve long-run, sustained income growth, countries have to look beyond their natural resources.

One such source of increased output is a sustained increase in *labor* resources. That is, a country can produce more output over the years simply because its population of workers grows. But for each successively larger generation of workers to have a higher *per capita* income than the previous generation, per capita output must increase. Population growth, on its own, does not lead to higher per capita output.

The resource most responsible for rapid and sustained economic growth is capital. There are two broad types of capital—physical and human. *Physical capital* includes such things as highways and railways, dams and irrigation systems, tractors and plows, factories, trucks and cars, and buildings of all kinds. *Human capital* is the accumulated knowledge and skills of the working population. As individuals accumulate more capital, their incomes grow. As nations accumulate more capital per worker, labor productivity and output per capita grow.

To study the behavior of per capita output, we use the per capita production function. The **per capita production function** shows how per capita output varies as the per capita stock of capital varies in a given state of knowledge about alternative technologies. Figure 20.3 illustrates the per capita production function. Per capita output is measured on the vertical axis, and the per capita stock of capital is measured on the horizontal axis. Curve *PF* shows how per capita output varies as the amount of per capita capital varies. A rich country such as the United States has a large amount of per capita capital and a large per capita output. A poor country such as Ethiopia has hardly any capital and a very low per capita output.

FIGURE 20.3

The Per Capita Production Function

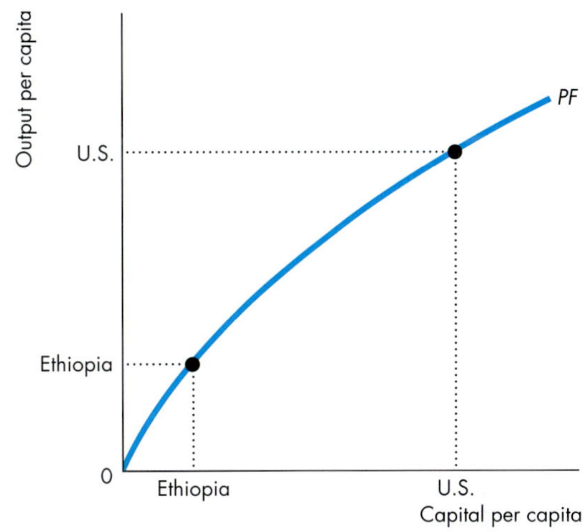

The per capita production function (*PF*) traces how per capita output varies as the stock of per capita capital varies. If two countries use the same technology but one country has a larger capital stock, that country will also have a higher per capita income level. For example, suppose that Ethiopia and the United States use the same technology. Ethiopia has a low per capita capital stock and low level of output per capita. The United States has a large per capita capital stock and a large per capita output rate.

Capital Accumulation

By accumulating capital, a country can grow and move along its per capita production function. The greater the amount of capital (per capita), the greater is output (per capita). But the fundamental *law of diminishing returns* applies to the per capita production function. That is, as capital per capita increases, output per capita also increases but by decreasing increments. Thus there is a limit to the extent to which a country can grow merely by accumulating capital. Eventually, the country reaches the point at which the extra output from extra capital is simply not worth the effort of accumulating more capital. At such a point, it pays the country to consume rather than to increase its capital stock.

But no country has yet reached such a point because the per capita production function is constantly shifting upward as a result of improvements in technology. Let's see how technological change affects output and growth.

Technological Change

Although rich countries have much more capital per capita than poor countries, that is not the only difference between them. Typically, rich countries use more productive technologies than do poor countries. That is, even if they have the same per capita capital, the rich country produces more output than the poor country. For example, a farmer in a rich

FIGURE 20.4

Technological Change

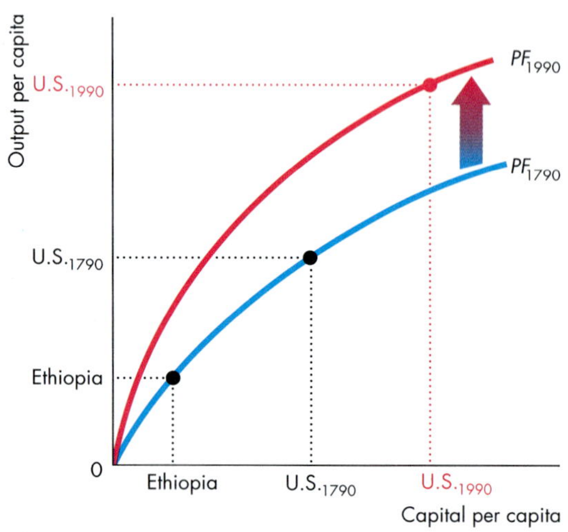

In 1790, the United States and Ethiopia have the same production function, PF_{1790}. By 1990, technological change has shifted the production function upward in the United States to PF_{1990}. Per capita income in the United States has increased from U.S.$_{1790}$ to U.S.$_{1990}$, partly because of an increase in the per capita capital stock and partly because of an increase in productivity arising from the adoption of better technology.

country might use a ten-horsepower tractor, whereas a farmer in a poor country might literally use ten horses. Each has the same amount of "horsepower," but the output achieved by using the tractor is considerably more than that produced by using ten horses. The combination of better technology and more per capita capital accentuates still further the difference between the rich and poor countries.

Figure 20.4 illustrates the importance of the difference that technological progress makes. Imagine that the year is 1790 and both the United States and Ethiopia (then called Abyssinia) use the same techniques of production and have the same per capita production function, PF_{1790}. With a larger per capita stock of capital, the United States produces a higher level of per capita output in 1790 than does Ethiopia. By 1990, technological advances adopted in the United States, but not in Ethiopia, enable the United States to produce more output from given inputs. The per capita production function in the United States shifts upward to PF_{1990}. Output per capita in the United States in 1990 is much higher than it was in 1790 for two reasons. First, the per capita stock of capital equipment has increased dramatically; second, the techniques of production have improved, resulting in an upward shift in the production function.

The faster the pace of technological progress, the faster the production function shifts upward. The faster the pace of capital accumulation, the more quickly a country moves along its production function. Both of these forces lead to increased per capita output. A poor country becomes a rich country partly by moving along its production function and partly by adopting better technology, thereby shifting its production function upward.

The importance of the connection between capital accumulation and output growth is illustrated in Fig. 20.5. Capital accumulation is measured by the percentage of output represented by investment. (Recall that investment is the purchase of new capital equipment.) The figure shows what has been happening to investment over time in developing countries and industrial countries and in the two extreme cases of Singapore and Ethiopia. As you can see in part (a), the percentage of income invested by developing countries increased through 1981 and then began to decline. In the industrial countries, the percentage of income invested has persistently declined, the fall being especially sharp in 1975. Fast-growing Singapore invests more than 40 percent of its income. Slow-growing Ethiopia invests less than 15 percent of its income. The source of Singapore's dramatic growth and of Ethiopia's almost static income level can be seen in part (b).

REVIEW

There is enormous inequality in the world. The poorest people in the poorest countries live on the edge of starvation. The poorest fifth of the world's people consume less than one twentieth of total output, and the richest fifth consume more than half of total output. Nations become rich by establishing and maintaining high rates of economic growth over prolonged periods. Economic growth results from the accumulation of capital and the adoption of increasingly efficient technologies. The more rapidly capital is accumulated and the more rapid is the pace of technological change, the higher

FIGURE 20.5

Investment Trends

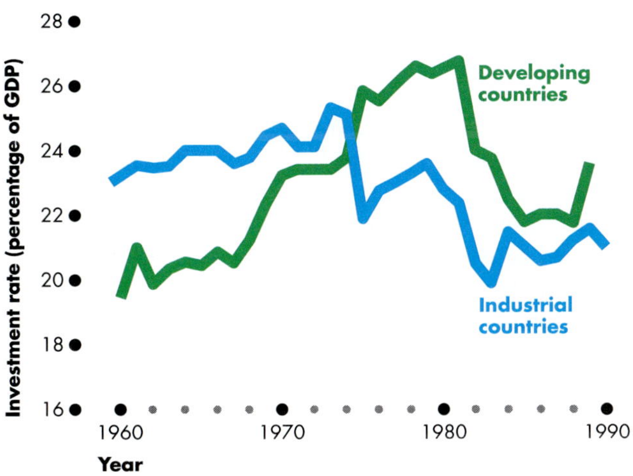

(a) Investment rates in developing and industrial countries

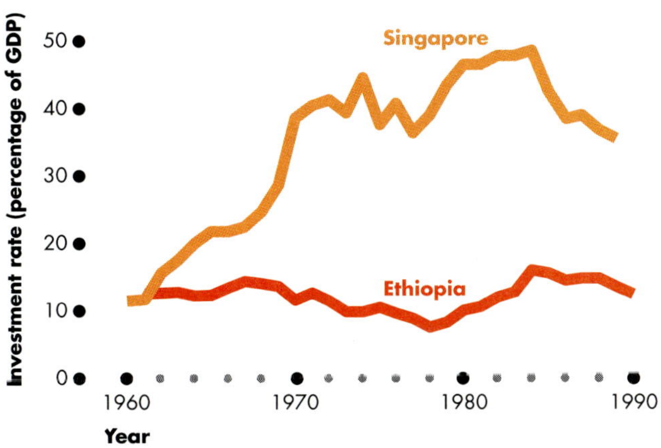

(b) Investment rates in Singapore and Ethiopia

The rate of investment in developing countries increased from 1960 to 1981 and subsequently decreased. Investment in industrial countries was steady during the 1960s and early 1970s but fell after 1974 (part a). Investment in Singapore has increased dramatically, while that in Ethiopia has been almost constant (part b). High investment in Singapore has led to rapid growth, while low investment in Ethiopia has led to low growth.

Source: International Monetary Fund, *International Financial Statistics Yearbook,* 1991.

is the rate of growth of output. Small changes in growth rates maintained over a long period of time make large differences in income levels. ◆

Obstacles to Economic Growth

The prescription for economic growth seems straightforward: poor countries can become wealthy by accumulating capital and adopting the most productive technologies. But if the cure for abject poverty is so simple, why haven't more poor countries become rich? Why are there so many poor people in the world today?

We do not know the answers to these questions. If we did, we would be able to solve the problem of economic underdevelopment and there wouldn't be any poor countries. But we do understand some of the reasons for poverty and underdevelopment. Let's see what they are.

Population Growth

One of the obstacles to economic development and rapid and sustained growth in per capita income is rapid population growth. In the past 20 years, world population has been growing at an average rate of 2 percent per year. At a population growth rate this high, world population doubles every 37 years. That population is now more than 5 billion. But the pattern of population growth is uneven. Rich industrial countries have relatively low population growth rates—often less than half a percent a year—while the poor, underdeveloped countries have high population growth rates—in some cases exceeding 3 percent a year.

Why is fast population growth an impediment to economic growth and development? Doesn't a larger population give a country more productive resources and permit more specialization, more division of labor, and therefore yet greater output? These benefits do indeed stem from a large population. But when the population is growing at a rapid rate and a country is poor, there are two negative effects on economic growth and development that outweigh the benefits of a larger population. They are

- An increase in the proportion of dependents to workers
- An increase in the amount of capital devoted to supporting the population rather than producing goods and services

Some facts about the relationship between the number of dependents and population growth are shown in Fig. 20.6. The number of dependents is measured on the vertical axis as the percentage of the population under 15 years of age. As you can see, the higher the population growth rate, the larger is the percentage of the population under 15. In countries such as the United States, where the population growth rate is less than 1 percent per year, about one person in five (20 percent) is under the age of 15. In countries such as Ethiopia that have rapid population growth rates (3 percent per year or higher), close to one half (50 percent) of the population is under the age of 15.

Let's see why there is a connection between the population growth rate and the percentage of young people in the population. A country might have a steady population because it has a high birth rate and an equally high death rate. But the same steady population growth could occur with a low birth rate and a low death rate. Population growth rates increase when either the birth rate increases or the death rate decreases. Historically, it is a fall in the death rate with a relatively constant birth rate that has led to population explosions. The fall in the death rate mainly takes the form of a fall in the infant mortality rate, and it is this phenomenon that results in an enormous increase in the proportion of young people in the population.

In a country with a large number of young people, capital resources are directed toward providing schools, hospitals, roads, and housing rather than irrigation schemes and industrial capital projects. Such a use of scarce capital resources is obviously not wasteful and does bring great benefits, but it does not add to the economy's capacity to produce goods and services out of which yet additional capital accumulation can be provided.

FIGURE 20.6

Population Growth and Number of Dependents

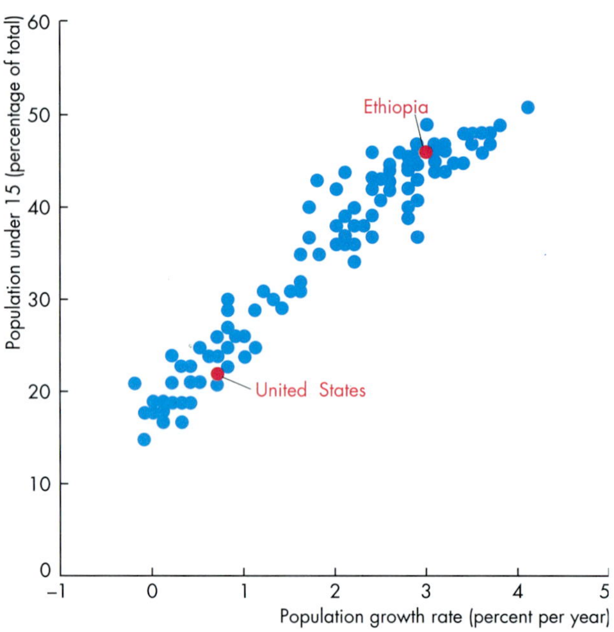

Each point represents a country. It shows the percentage of the population that is under 15 years of age (measured on the vertical axis) and the population growth rate (measured on the horizontal axis). The number of young people in the population is strongly influenced by the population growth rate. In slow-growing countries such as the United States, about a fifth of the population is under the age of 15, while in fast-growing countries such as Ethiopia, more than 40 percent of the population is under the age of 15.

Source: Population Reference Bureau Inc., *World Population Data Sheet* (Washington, D.C.: 1988).

Low Saving Rate

There is a further obstacle to rapid and sustained economic growth and development. It is the fact that poor people have such a low level of income that they consume most of it, undertaking a tiny volume of saving. Saving is the source of finance for capital accumulation, and, as we have seen, capital accumulation is itself one of the main engines of economic growth. Let's investigate the connection between capital accumulation and saving.

There are just three things that people can do with their income: consume it, save it, or pay it in taxes. That is,

$$\text{Income} = \text{Consumption} + \text{Saving} + \text{Taxes}.$$

An economy's output consists of consumption goods, capital goods, goods and services bought by the government, and net exports (exports minus imports). Expenditure on capital goods is investment, and expenditure on goods and services bought by the government is called government purchases of goods and services. Thus,

$$\text{Income} = \text{Consumption} + \text{Investment} + \text{Government purchases} + \text{Net exports.}$$

The first of the above equations tells us that income minus consumption is equal to saving plus taxes. The second equation tells us that income minus consumption is equal to the value of investment plus government purchases plus net exports. Using these two equations, then, we see that

$$\text{Saving} + \text{Taxes} = \text{Investment} + \text{Government purchases} + \text{Net exports.}$$

The difference between government purchases and taxes is the government budget deficit. Net exports are the balance of payments current account surplus—known more simply as the current account surplus. We can rearrange the last equation, therefore, as

$$\text{Investment} = \text{Saving} - \text{Current account surplus} - \text{Government budget deficit.}$$

There are three influences on the pace at which a country can accumulate capital (can invest): saving, the government budget, and the current account surplus. Other things being equal, the larger the volume of saving, the smaller the government budget deficit (the larger the government budget surplus), and the smaller the current account surplus (the larger the current account deficit), the faster is the pace of capital accumulation.

The fraction of income that people save depends on the income level. Very poor people save nothing. As income rises, some part of income is saved. The higher the income level, the higher is the proportion of income saved. These patterns in the relationship between income and saving crucially affect the pace at which a country can grow.

Saving is by far the most important component in the sources of financing investment. But, in general, the larger the amount of saving, the larger also is the amount of resources available from the rest of the world through the country's current account deficit. Furthermore, the countries with the least resources are those in which the government runs a deficit, thereby restricting yet further the amount available for capital accumulation through investment.

Let's now look at a third obstacle to rapid growth and development, the burden of international debt.

International Debt

Poor countries often go into debt with the rest of the world. Loans have to be repaid, and interest has to be paid on the loans outstanding. To make debt repayments and interest payments, poor countries need a net export surplus. That is, a country needs a current account surplus. As we have just seen, when a country has a current account deficit, that deficit provides additional financial resources to domestic saving, enabling the country to accumulate capital at a faster pace than would otherwise be possible. A country that has a current account surplus is one that is accumulating capital at a slower pace than its domestic saving permits. Such a country uses part of its saving to accumulate capital—and thereby increases productivity—and uses the other part to pay interest on or repay loans from the rest of the world.

A poor country that borrows heavily from the rest of the world and uses the borrowing to invest in productive capital will not become overburdened by debt, provided that the growth rate of income exceeds the interest rate on the debt. In such a situation, debt interest can be paid out of the higher income and there is still some additional income leftover for additional domestic consumption or capital accumulation. Countries that borrow from the rest of the world and use the resources for consumption or invest in projects that have a low rate of return—lower than the interest rate on the debt—are the ones that become overburdened by debt.

The burden of international debt became particularly onerous for many developing countries during the 1980s. For example, the Latin American countries have accumulated external debts of almost half a trillion dollars. Many of these debts were incurred during the 1970s when raw material prices were rising quickly. From 1973 to 1980, the prices of most raw materials increased on the average by close to 20 percent per year—a rate much higher than the interest rates on the foreign debt being accumulated. In such a situation, countries producing raw materials, hungry for capital, borrowed on an enormous scale. In the 1980s, raw material prices collapsed. Huge debts had been incurred, but the revenue with which to repay those debts was not coming in. To add a further burden, interest rates increased sharply during the 1980s. Today, because of the combination of sagging raw material prices and higher interest rates, many poor countries have a crippling burden of international debt.

The Underdevelopment Trap

The obstacles to economic development are so severe that some economists have suggested that there is a kind of poverty trap that applies to countries—the underdevelopment trap. The **underdevelopment trap** is a situation in which a country is locked into a low per capita income situation that reinforces itself. A low level of capital per worker (both physical and human capital) results in low output per worker. Low productivity in turn produces low per capita income. Low per capita income results in low saving. With low saving, there is a low rate of capital accumulation. Capital accumulation can barely keep up with population growth, so the stock of capital per worker remains low and the cycle repeats itself.

Overcoming the Obstacles to Economic Development

A variety of ways of breaking out of the underdevelopment trap have been suggested. They are

- Population control
- Foreign aid
- Removal of trade restrictions
- Aggregate demand stimulation

Let's look at each of these in turn.

Population Control

Almost all developing countries use population control methods as part of their attempt to break out of the underdevelopment trap. Population control programs have two key elements: the provision of low-cost birth control facilities and the provision of incentives encouraging people to have a small number of children. These methods meet with some, but limited, success. One of the most highly publicized programs of population control is that employed in China. In that country, families are strongly discouraged from having more than one child. Despite this policy, the population of China continues to grow, and forecasts suggest that by the year 2000 the population will have grown above its target level by an amount equal to one half of the entire population of the United States.

Thus important though they are, population control methods are not the most likely to yield success in the fight against underdevelopment and poverty.

Foreign Aid

The idea that foreign aid helps economic development arises from a simple consideration. If a poor country is poor because it has too little capital, then by obtaining aid, it can accumulate more capital and achieve a higher per capita output. Repeated applications of foreign aid year after year can enable a country to grow much more quickly than it could if it had to rely exclusively on its own domestic saving. By this line of reasoning, the greater the flow of foreign aid to a country, the faster it will grow.

Some economists suggest that foreign aid will not necessarily make a country grow faster. They argue that such aid consolidates the position of corrupt and/or incompetent politicians and that these politicians and their policies are two of the main impediments to economic development. Most people who administer foreign aid do not take this view. The consensus is that foreign aid does indeed help economic development. But it is also agreed that foreign aid is not a major factor in influencing the pace of development of poor countries. Its scale is simply too small to make a decisive difference.

A factor that has made a decisive difference in many countries is international trade policy. Let's now turn to an examination of the effects of international trade on growth and development.

Removal of Trade Restrictions

There is steady political pressure in the rich countries in support of protection from imports produced with "cheap labor" in the underdeveloped countries. Some people also complain that buying from underdeveloped countries exploits low-wage workers. As a consequence, countries introduce tariffs, quotas, and voluntary restrictions on trade (see Chapter 18). How do such restrictions affect underdeveloped countries, and how does the removal of such restrictions affect their growth and development? To

FIGURE 20.7

International Trade and Economic Development

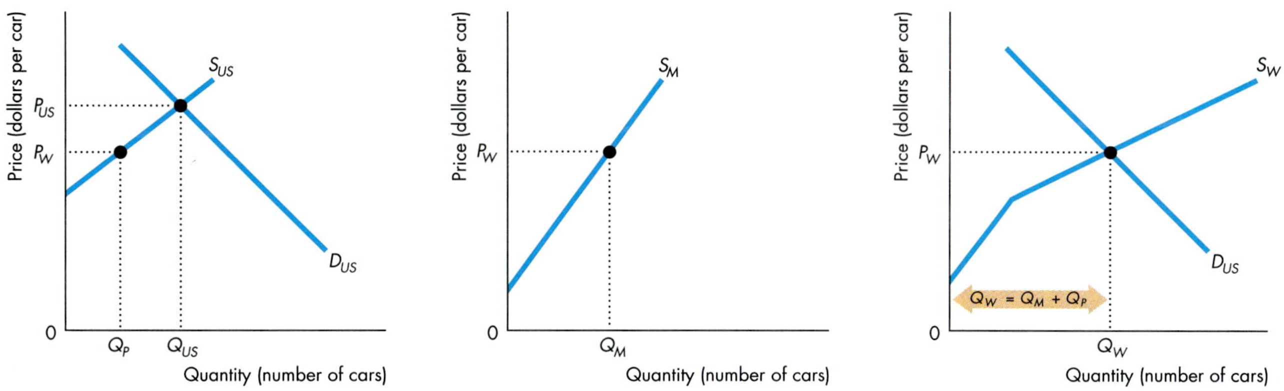

(a) U.S. production and demand **(b) Mexican production** **(c) U.S. car market with free trade**

The market for cars in the United States (part a) has demand curve D_{US} and supply curve S_{US}. The price of cars is P_{US} and the quantity produced and bought is Q_{US}. Mazda builds an automobile plant in Mexico, and the supply curve of cars from that plant is S_M (part b). If the United States prohibits the import of cars from Mexico, the U.S. automobile market remains unchanged and Mexican output is zero. If the United States permits free international trade in cars with Mexico, the price in the U.S. market is P_W (part c) and the total quantity of cars bought in the United States is Q_W (*W* stands for "with trade"). Parts (a) and (b) show that at price P_W, Q_M cars are produced in Mexico and Q_P (*P* stands for "production") in the United States. Free international trade permits poor countries to sell their output for a price higher than they would otherwise receive and rich countries to buy goods for a price lower than they would otherwise pay.

answer this question, consider the following example (which is illustrated in Fig. 20.7). Imagine a situation (such as that prevailing in the 1950s) in which the United States produces virtually all its cars. The automobile market in the United States is shown in part (a). The demand for cars is shown by curve D_{US}, and the supply is shown by curve S_{US}. The price of cars is P_{US}, and the quantity produced and bought is Q_{US}.

Suppose that Mazda builds an automobile production plant in Mexico. The supply curve of cars produced in Mexico is shown in Fig. 20.7(b) as the curve S_M. What happens in the United States depends on U.S. international trade policy.

First, suppose that the United States restricts the import of cars from Mexico. To make things as clear as possible, let's suppose that there is a complete ban on such imports. In this case, Mexico produces no cars for export to the United States. The price of cars in the United States remains at P_{US}, and the quantity traded remains at Q_{US}.

In contrast, let's see what happens if the United States engages in free trade with Mexico. (A trade accord between the United States and Mexico has, in fact, recently been negotiated.) To determine the price of cars, the quantities produced and consumed in the United States, and the quantity produced in Mexico for export to the United States, we need to consider Fig. 20.7(c). The demand curve for cars in the United States remains D_{US}, but the supply curve becomes S_W. This supply curve is made up of the sum of the quantities supplied in both the United States and Mexico at each price. Equilibrium is achieved in the U.S. market at a price of P_W and a quantity traded of Q_W. To see where these cars are produced, go back to parts (a) and (b) of the figure. Mexico produces Q_M, the United States produces Q_P, and these two production levels sum to Q_W.

Mazda's Mexican plant increases its output of cars, and its workers generate an income. The output of cars is decreased in the United States. By permitting unrestricted trade with underdeveloped countries, rich countries gain by being able to consume goods that are imported at lower prices than would be possible if only domestic supplies were available. Developing countries gain by being able to sell their output for a higher price than would prevail if they had only the domestic market available to them.

Some of the most dramatic economic growth and development success stories have been based on reaping the gains from relatively unrestricted international trade. Countries such as Hong Kong and Singapore have opened their economies to free trade with the rest of the world and dramatically increased their living standards by specializing and producing goods and services at which they have a *comparative advantage*—which they can produce at a lower opportunity cost than other countries. The potential economic development that can result from specialization and trade is discussed further in Reading Between the Lines on pp. 544–545.

Aggregate Demand Stimulation

It is often suggested that growth and development can be stimulated by expanding aggregate demand. The suggestion takes two forms. Sometimes it is suggested that if the rich countries stimulate their own aggregate demand, their economies will grow more quickly, and, as a consequence, commodity prices will remain high. High commodity prices help poor countries and so stimulate their income growth and economic development. It is also often suggested that poor countries can make themselves grow faster by stimulating their own level of aggregate demand.

Can stimulating aggregate demand in the rich countries help the poor countries? Can aggregate demand stimulation in poor countries help them grow? The answers to both of these questions are almost certainly no, but let's see why. As we discovered when we studied the theory of aggregate demand and aggregate supply in Chapter 7, changes in aggregate income can occur as a result of either a change in aggregate demand or a change in aggregate supply. But aggregate demand changes affect output and income in the short run only. That is, when wages and other input prices are fixed, a change in aggregate demand changes both output and the price level. But in the long run, a change in aggregate demand leads to a change in the prices of goods and services and of factors of production. Once input prices have adjusted in response to a change in aggregate demand, income returns to its long-run level. Changes in per capita long-run aggregate supply can be brought about only by changes in per capita productivity—which in turn are brought about by changes in the stock of per capita capital and in the state of technology.

This macroeconomic model of aggregate demand and aggregate supply applies to all countries, rich and poor alike. If rich countries stimulate aggregate demand by persistently permitting aggregate demand to grow at a pace faster than the growth rate of long-run aggregate supply, they will generate inflation. If they permit aggregate demand to grow at a pace similar to the growth rate of long-run aggregate supply, prices will be stable. In recent history, we have seen rich countries generating rapid inflation and moderate inflation. The 1970s were a decade of rapid inflation. During that decade, commodity prices also increased quickly, enabling many developing countries to increase the pace of capital accumulation and income growth. The 1980s were a decade of moderate inflation. It is this decade that brought falling raw material prices and the burden of large international debt to many developing countries.

Don't the facts of the 1970s and 1980s support the conclusion that rapid aggregate demand growth and inflation in the rich countries help the poor countries? They do not. Rather, they provide an example of what can happen, over a limited time period, when there is a previously unexpected increase or decrease in the growth rate of aggregate demand. In the 1970s, there was an unexpectedly rapid increase in aggregate demand. As a consequence, many countries experienced increasing inflation and increasing output growth. In the 1980s, there was an unexpectedly severe contraction of aggregate demand in the rich countries, notably in the United States, resulting in falling inflation and a slowdown in output growth (and in some countries, including the United States, a fall in output). Unexpected fluctuations in the inflation rate can produce fluctuations in output growth—precisely what happened in the 1970s and 1980s. But sustained aggregate demand growth and sustained steady inflation are not capable of producing sustained growth in output.

FIGURE 20.8

Inflation and Economic Growth

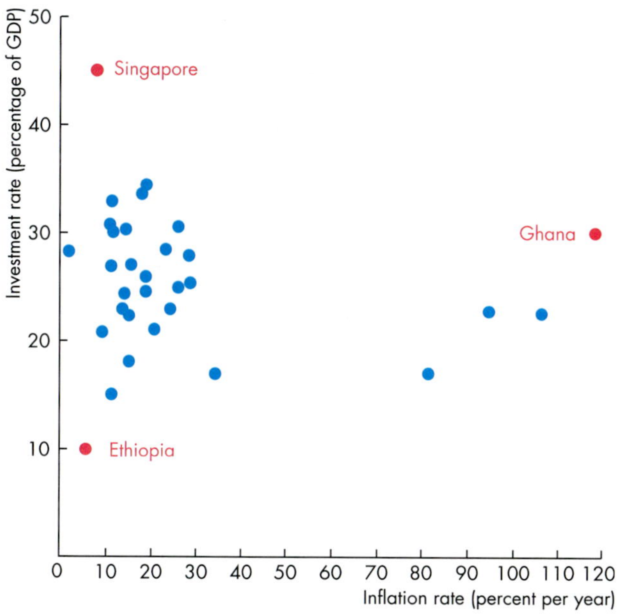

Each point in the figure represents a country. It shows the country's investment level (as a percentage of GDP) plotted against the annual inflation rate. The data are for 1960 to 1990. There is no discernible connection between a country's inflation rate and its pace of investment and economic growth. Fast-growing Singapore has a low inflation rate, as does slow-growing Ethiopia. Medium-growth Ghana has the highest inflation rate in the developing world.

Source: International Monetary Fund, *International Financial Statistics,* 1991.

Developing countries can make aggregate demand grow at a rapid or a moderate rate. The more rapidly aggregate demand grows, relative to the growth of long-run aggregate supply, the higher is the inflation rate. Some developing countries inflate quickly, and others inflate slowly. But there is virtually no connection between the pace of their development and the rate of inflation. As Fig. 20.8 illustrates, fast-growing Singapore, which invests more than 40 percent of its income in capital equipment each year, has a moderate inflation rate, while average-growing Ghana has the highest inflation rate of the developing countries—a rate in excess of 100 percent a year. Slow-growing Ethiopia, which invests only 10 percent of its income, has a moderate inflation rate. Each blue dot in the figure shows the investment percentage and inflation rate in a developing country. As you can see, the dots do not form a clear relationship between these variables. Thus the pace at which a developing country stimulates aggregate demand, while affecting its inflation rate, has no appreciable effect on the growth rate of real income or the pace of economic development.

We've seen that to grow quickly, a country must accumulate capital at a rapid pace. To do so, it must achieve a high saving rate and undertake foreign borrowing that is used in high-return activities. The most rapidly growing developing countries have a high pace of capital accumulation and obtain a high return on their capital by pursuing a free trade policy, thereby ensuring that they produce those goods and services in which they have a comparative advantage.

SUMMARY

The International Distribution of Income

There is enormous inequality in the international distribution of income. The poorest countries have average per capita income levels of 4 percent to 9 percent of that in the United States. Half of the world's population earns only 15 percent of world income, and the richest 20 percent of the world's population earns 55 percent of world income. (pp. 533–535)

Growth Rates and Income Levels

Poor countries become rich by achieving and maintaining for prolonged periods high rates of per capita income growth. Rich countries grow at about 1.5 percent per year. Poor countries that have a growth rate lower than 1.5 percent fall further behind. Poor countries that achieve a growth rate higher than 1.5 percent close the gap on the rich countries. High and sustained growth makes a dramatic difference in a

Capital, Trade, and Economic Development

THE ECONOMIST, March 21, 1992

Hard sell

The names hardly trip off the tongue. But if all goes as planned, by the end of the 1990s the sleepy backwaters of Najin in North Korea, Hunchun in China and Posyet in Russia's far east will be the whirring hub of a larger circle of prosperity that will stretch from Vladivostok down to North Korea's Chongjin and west to Yanji in China's north-eastern Jilin province.

The plan is for a huge duty-free shipping and processing zone, on the Tumen River close to the point where the borders of Russia, China and North Korea meet. These three plus South Korea, Japan and Mongolia are the unlikely partners in the venture, which calls for an unaccustomed degree of co-operation and, for now, improbable amounts of cash: the necessary roads, railways, ports and airports are expected to cost at least $30 billion over 15–20 years. The United Nations Development Programme has promised the $2m–3m needed for the feasibility study. The planners next meet in Beijing in April.

The economies of the region could complement one another. Japan and South Korea have the capital to invest, along with modern industrial technologies and management and marketing skills. North Korea and China can provide the labour. Between them the three closest neighbours, North Korea, China and Russia, have the coal, timber, minerals and other raw materials to supply new manufacturing industries.

There is flat land for building and fresh water in abundance. There is also biting winter cold, with temperatures plunging to the minus-30s. For industrialists wanting to take a look there is an arduous day-or-more-long train journey from Harbin, the nearest Chinese metropolis worthy of the name. . . .

Hence the importance of all those new transport links. Once in place they would greatly facilitate trade across the Sea of Japan and dramatically improve prospects for the neglected eastern reaches of both China and Russia. At present China's Japan-bound cargoes sail from the more southerly port of Dalian and around the Korean peninsula. Russian and Chinese trade with South Korea could be done directly, rather than via intermediaries. And all this bustle, it is hoped, will help tempt hermit-like North Korea out of its economic isolation. With extra rail links, distant, land-locked Mongolia, desperate to win new outlets for its minerals, wool and livestock, would benefit from quicker access to ports. . . .

The Essence of the Story

Russia, China, North Korea, South Korea, Japan, and Mongolia are the partners in a planned venture that, if implemented, will create a huge duty-free shipping and processing zone on the Tumen River close to the point where the borders of Russia, China, and North Korea meet.

The area has abundant flat land and fresh water and is ideally situated to open up trade links with the landlocked regions of eastern Russia, China, and Mongolia and to speed and ease the flow of trade across the Sea of Japan.

But the region has extreme winters and is currently almost inaccessible. A priority, therefore, is establishing communication links. The cost of the necessary roads, railways, ports, and airports is expected to be at least $30 billion over 15–20 years.

Background and Analysis

The economies of the region complement one another. Japan and South Korea have capital, modern technologies, and management and marketing skills. North Korea and China have labor. North Korea, China, and Russia (between them) have the coal, timber, minerals, and other raw materials.

If the plan succeeds, by the end of the 1990s a large region that currently has almost no economic activity will become a prosperous industrial and commercial region.

Economic development occurs in a variety of ways, but there are two essential ingredients of any development project likely to succeed:

- Capital
- Specialization and exchange

The Tumen River project in northeast Asia (see the maps) is an outstanding example of the applications of these ingredients.

The capital required for this project includes:

- Transportation infrastructure—roads, railroads, airports, and seaports (estimated cost $30 billion)
- Buildings, plant, and equipment for hundreds (perhaps thousands) of factories, processing plants, warehouses, and offices
- Housing, schools, hospitals, and retail and commercial buildings

The financing of this huge amount of investment will likely come from the capital markets of Japan, Europe, and North America, together with some government funding from the countries involved.

The project also requires human capital—the skills of technicians, managers, and marketers. These will likely come, initially, from Japan and South Korea.

This massive accumulation of capital will push the *production possibility frontier* for the region outward and bring higher living standards.

But the most crucial ingredient in this project is the removal of political barriers to economic activity, specialization, and exchange. By creating a *duty-free* shipping and processing zone, the countries involved in this project are creating (albeit on a limited scale) *free trade* in a wide range of goods and services.

By permitting individuals and firms in the six countries involved to specialize in the activities at which they have a comparative advantage and freely exchange their products, the Tumen River project will allow all the countries in the region to share in the gains from trade.

This aspect of the project will enable the people of the region to consume at a point outside their new expanded production possibility frontier and bring even greater prosperity both to the region and to the people who trade with it.

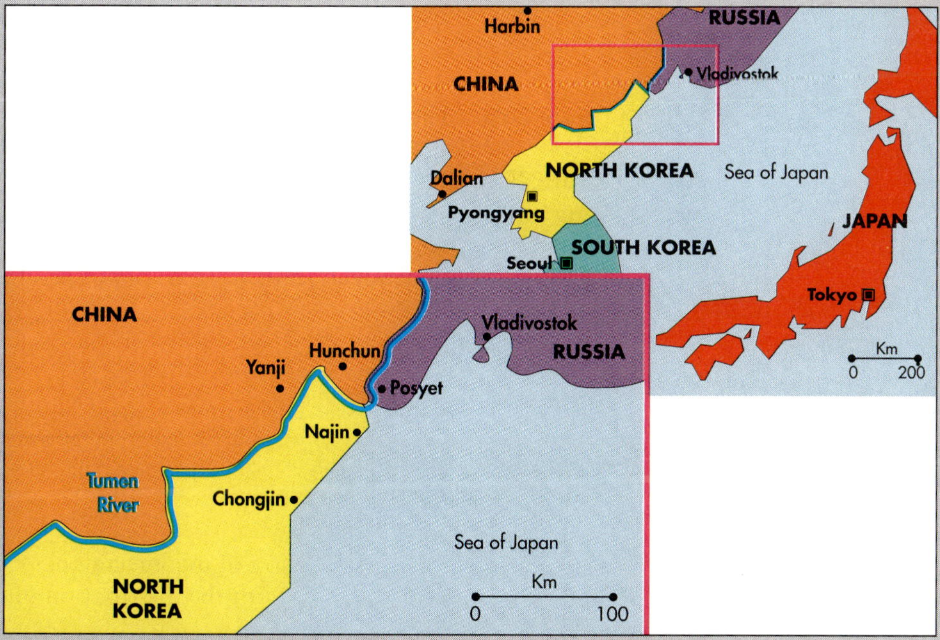

short time span. If China can achieve and maintain a per capita income growth rate of 6 percent per year, the per capita income of China will catch up with that of the United States by the mid-2030s. (pp. 535–536)

Resources, Technological Progress, and Economic Growth

Per capita income growth results from growth in per capita capital and technological change. The greater the fraction of income invested in new capital equipment and the faster the pace of technological change, the higher is the rate of economic growth. (pp. 536–539)

Obstacles to Economic Growth

There are three major obstacles to sustained economic growth and development: rapid population growth, a low saving rate, and an international debt burden. Rapid population growth results in there being a large proportion of young dependents in the population. A low saving rate results in a low rate of capital accumulation. A large international debt burden results in some saving having to be used to pay debt interest rather than to accumulate capital and improve productivity.

Low income results in low saving, which in turn results in low investment and thus low income growth. Many poor countries are caught in what appears to be an underdevelopment trap. (pp. 539–542)

Overcoming the Obstacles to Economic Development

The main techniques for overcoming the obstacles to economic development are the implementation of population control measures, foreign aid, and the removal of trade restrictions. Of these, the most dramatic success stories have almost always involved rapid expansion of international trade.

The stimulation of aggregate demand, by either rich or poor countries, cannot contribute, in the long run, to economic growth and development. If aggregate demand grows at the same rate as long-run aggregate supply, prices are stable; if aggregate demand grows at a faster rate than long-run aggregate supply, prices rise—there is inflation. The rate of inflation does not appear to have a major influence on the rate of economic growth and development. (pp. 542–547)

KEY ELEMENTS

Key Terms

Key Figures

REVIEW QUESTIONS

1 Describe the main differences between the richest and poorest countries.

2 Compare the distribution of income among families in the United States with the distribution of income among countries in the world. Which distribution is more unequal?

3 What determines a country's per capita income level? What makes the per capita income level change?

4 Give an example of a country in which rapid economic growth has occurred and one in which slow economic growth has occurred. Which country has the higher investment rate?

5 Review the obstacles to economic growth.

6 Why is rapid population growth an obstacle to economic growth?

7 Describe the underdevelopment trap.

8 What are the main ways in which poor countries try to overcome their poverty?

9 Why does free trade stimulate economic growth and development?

10 Why does demand stimulation not improve a country's rate of economic growth and its development?

PROBLEMS

1 A poor country has 10 percent of the income of a rich country. The poor country achieves a growth rate of 10 percent per year. The rich country is growing at 5 percent per year. How many years will it take income in the poor country to catch up with that in the rich country?

2 Silecon is a poor country with no natural resources except sand. Per capita income is $500 a year, and this entire income is consumed. Per capita income is constant—there is no economic growth. The government has a balanced budget, and there are no exports or imports. Then, one day, the price of silicon increases, and Silecon is able to export sand at a huge profit. Exports soar from zero to $400 (per capita). Per capita income increases to $1,000 a year, and per capita consumption increases to $600 a year. There are still no imports, and Silecon has a balance of payments current account surplus of $400 per capita.

- **a** What happens to investment and the growth rate in Silecon?
- **b** If Silecon imports capital goods equal in value to its exports, what will be its investment?
- **c** What will be Silecon's current account balance?
- **d** If the government of Silecon runs a budget deficit of $100 (per capita), what will be its investment?

3 The per capita production function in Machecon is illustrated in the figure, and in year 1, Machecon has 1 machine per person.

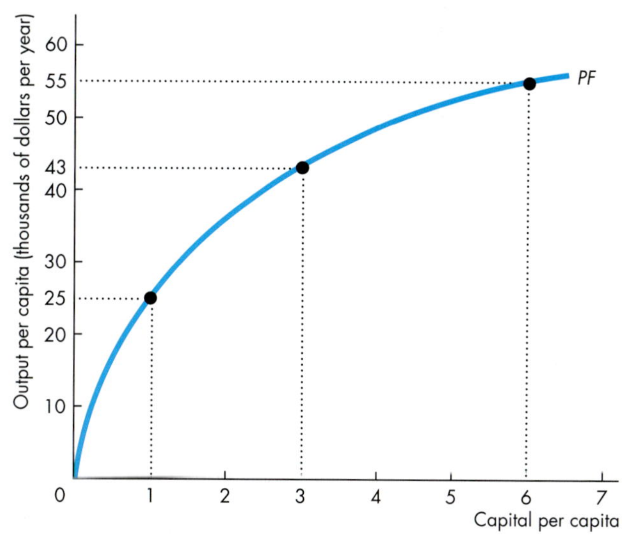

- **a** What is per capita output in Machecon?
- **b** If Machecon adds 1 machine per person to its capital stock during year 2, what is its new level of output and what is its output growth rate in year 2?
- **c** In year 3, Machecon adds 1 more machine per person to its capital stock. What now is its output, and what is its growth rate in year 3?
- **d** If in year 4 Machecon adds no new machines to its capital stock, but a new technology becomes available that increases the productivity of each machine by 20 percent, what is the level of output in Machecon in year 4?

CHAPTER 21

ECONOMIC SYSTEMS IN TRANSITION

After studying this chapter, you will be able to:

- Describe the fundamental economic problem that confronts all nations
- Describe the alternative systems that have been used to solve the economic problem
- Describe the Soviet-style system of central planning
- Describe the economic problems confronting the former Soviet Union
- Describe the economic problems of Eastern European countries
- Describe the process of economic change in China
- Describe and evaluate the alternative strategies for making the transition from a centrally planned economy to a market economy

The Market Bandwagon

EXTRAORDINARY EVENTS HAVE TAKEN PLACE IN EASTERN Europe. The Berlin Wall has fallen, and Germany is reunited. The centrally planned economy of East Germany has been replaced by the market economic system of West Germany. Poland, Hungary, the Czech Republic, Slovakia, Bulgaria, and Rumania have embraced democratic political institutions and are creating market economies. The Soviet Union has disintegrated. Some of its former republics are now independent nations, and the others are loosely linked in a Commonwealth of Independent States. These nations have abandoned central economic planning and are moving toward a market economy. And the process of adopting the market economic system does not end with Eastern Europe. The People's Republic of China, although remaining a communist dictatorship, is undergoing massive economic change, gradually replacing its system of central planning with the market. ◆◆ Why are so many countries abandoning central economic planning and jumping on the market bandwagon? What are the problems that a country faces as it makes the transition to a market economy?

◆◆◆◆ This chapter brings you full circle. In Chapter 1 you studied the fundamental economic problem of scarcity and considered the alternative ways in which people attempt to solve that problem. In the rest of the book you studied the way in which our own economy (and the similar economies of Western Europe, Japan, and most of the world) solves the economic problem. But a significant number of countries, in which more than a quarter of the human population lives, have employed an economic system that relies on the state to direct the economy through a central planning system. We are going to look at this alternative system and also at the extraordinary—perhaps revolutionary—process of change that is taking place during the 1990s as the centrally planned economies make the transition toward market economies.

FIGURE 21.1
The Fundamental Economic Problem

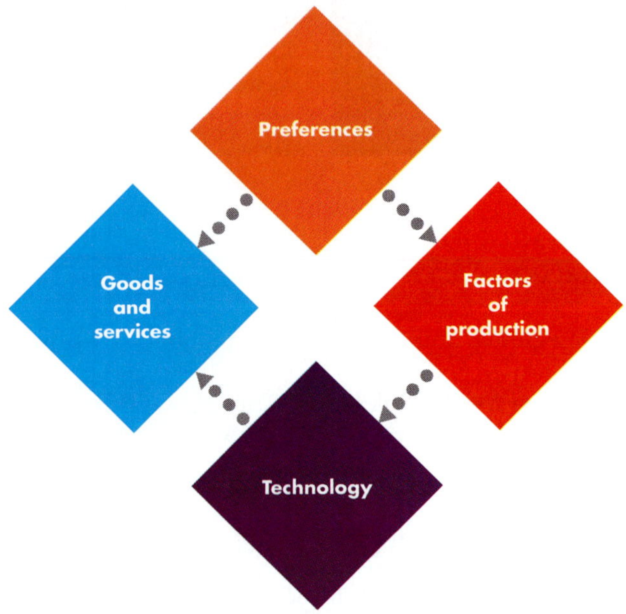

People have preferences about goods and services and the use of factors of production. Technologies are available for transforming factors of production into goods and services. People want to consume more goods and services than can be produced with the available factors of production and technology. The fundamental economic problem is to choose *what* goods and services to produce, *how* to produce them, and *for whom* to produce them. Different economic systems deliver different solutions to this problem.

The Economic Problem and Its Alternative Solutions

The economic problem is the universal fact of scarcity—we want to consume more goods and services than the available resources make possible. The economic problem is illustrated in Fig. 21.1. People have preferences about the goods and services they would like to consume and about how they would like to use the factors of production that they own or control. Techniques of production—technologies—convert factors of production into goods and services. The economic problem is to choose the quantities of goods and services to produce—*what*—the ways to produce them—*how*—and the distribution of goods and services to each individual—*for whom.*

The production of goods and services is the objective of the economic system. But *what, how,* and *for whom* goods and services are produced depend on the way the economy is organized—on who makes which decisions. Different systems deliver different outcomes. Let's look at the main alternatives that have been used.

Alternative Economic Systems

Economic systems vary in two dimensions:

- Ownership of capital and land
- Incentive structure

Ownership of Capital and Land Capital and land may be owned entirely by individuals, entirely by the state, or by a mixture of the two. The private ownership of capital and land enables individuals to create and operate their own firms. It also enables them to buy and sell capital, land, and firms freely at their going market prices. State ownership of capital and land enables individuals to control the use of these resources in state-owned firms but does not permit this control to be passed to others in a market transaction.

In practice, no economy has pure private ownership or pure and exclusive state ownership. For example, in an economy with widespread private ownership, the freedom to buy and sell firms is modified by the antitrust laws. Also, national defense or the public interest may be invoked to limit private ownership. Such limitations operate to restrict the private ownership of beaches and areas of natural scenic beauty.

In an economy that has predominantly state ownership, individuals sometimes own small plots of land and their homes. Also, in many economies, private ownership and state ownership exist side by side. In such cases, the state acts like a private individual and buys capital, land, or even a production enterprise from its existing owner.

Incentive Structure An **incentive structure** is a set of arrangements that induce people to take certain actions. Incentives may be created by market prices, by administered prices and administrative sanctions, or by a mixture of the two.

An incentive system based on market prices is one in which people respond to the price signals they receive and the price signals themselves respond to people's actions. For example, suppose a severe frost wipes out the Florida orange crop one year. The supply of orange juice falls. As a result, the price of orange juice rises. Faced with the higher price, people have an *incentive* to economize on orange juice and they decrease the quantity demanded. At the same time, the higher price of orange juice induces an increase in the demand for apple juice, a substitute for orange juice. As a result, the price of apple juice also rises. With higher prices for orange juice and apple juice, orange and apple growers in other parts of the country and in other countries have an *incentive* to increase the quantity supplied.

An incentive system based on administered prices is one in which administrators set prices to achieve their own objectives. For example, a government might want everyone to have access to low-cost bread. As a result, bread might be priced at, say, a penny a loaf. Under these circumstances, people have an *incentive* to buy lots of bread. Poor children might even use stale loaves as footballs! (This use of bread apparently did actually occur in the former Soviet Union.) An incentive system based on administrative sanctions is one in which people are rewarded or punished in a variety of non-monetary ways to induce them to take particular actions. For example, a manager might reward a salesperson for achieving a sales goal with more rapid promotion or with a bigger office. Alternatively, a salesperson might be punished for failing to achieve a sales goal by being moved to a less desirable sales district. When an entire economy is operated on administrative incentives, everyone, from the highest political authority to the lowest rank of workers, faces non-monetary rewards and punishments from immediate superiors.

Types of Economic System Economic systems differ in the ways in which they combine ownership and incentive arrangements. The range of alternatives is illustrated in Fig. 21.2. One type of economic

FIGURE 21.2

Alternative Economic Systems

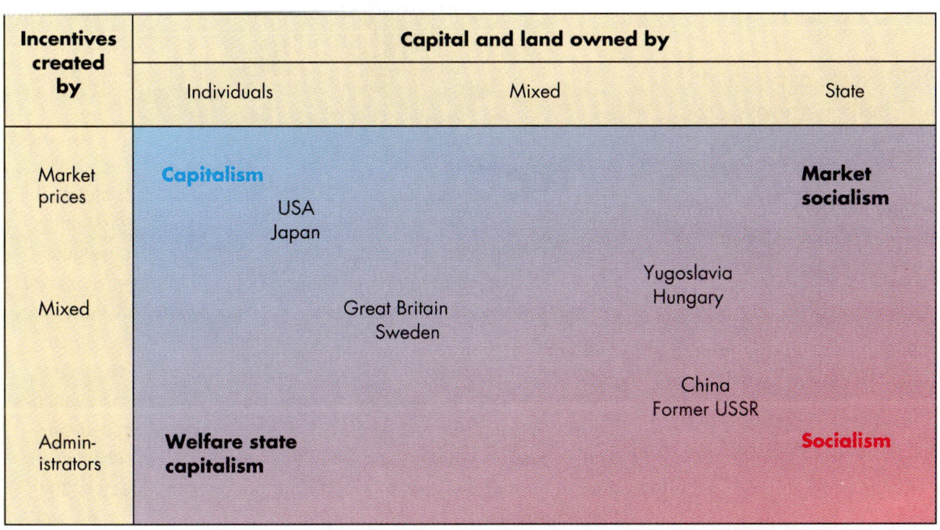

Under capitalism, individuals own capital—farms and factories, plant and equipment—and incentives are created by market prices. Under socialism, the state owns capital, and incentives are created by administrated prices and administrative sanctions. Market socialism combines state ownership of capital with incentives based on market prices. Welfare state capitalism combines private capital ownership with a high degree of state intervention in the incentive structure.

system is **capitalism,** a system based on the private ownership of capital and land and on an incentive system based on market prices. Another type of economic system is **socialism,** a system based on state ownership of capital and land and on an incentive system based on administered prices or sanctions arising from a central economic plan. **Central planning** is a method of allocating resources *by command.* A central plan for action is drawn up, and the plan is implemented by creating a set of sanctions and rewards that ensure that the commands are carried out.

No country has used an economic system that precisely corresponds to one of these extreme types, but the United States and Japan come closest to being capitalist economies and the former Soviet Union and China before the 1980s came closest to being socialist economies. Socialism evolved from the ideas of Karl Marx (see Our Advancing Knowledge on pp. 558–559).

Some countries combine private ownership with state ownership, and some combine market price incentives with administrative incentives and central planning. **Market socialism** (also called **decentralized planning**) is an economic system that combines state ownership of capital and land with incentives based on a mixture of market and administered prices. Hungary and Yugoslavia have had market socialist economies. In such economies, planners set the prices at which the various production and distribution organizations are able to buy and sell and then leave those organizations free to choose the quantities of inputs and outputs. But the prices set by the planners responded to the forces of demand and supply.

Another combination is welfare state capitalism. **Welfare state capitalism** combines the private ownership of capital and land with state intervention in markets that change the price signals that people respond to. Sweden, Great Britain, and other Western European countries are examples of such economies.

Alternative Systems Compared

Since all economic systems are made up of a combination of the two extreme special cases—capitalism and socialism—let's examine these two extreme types a bit more closely.

Capitalism Figure 21.3 shows how capitalism solves the economic problem of scarcity. Households

FIGURE 21.3

Capitalism's Solution to the Economic Problem

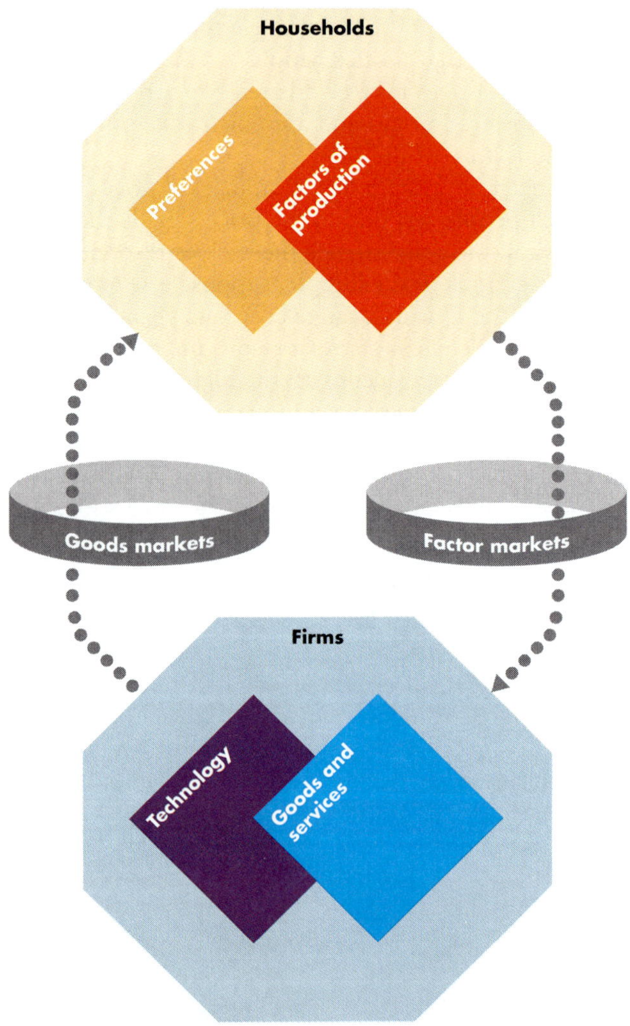

Under capitalism, the preferences of individual households dictate the choices that are made. Households own all the factors of production and sell the services of those factors in factor markets. Households decide which goods and services to consume and buy them in markets for goods and services. Firms decide which goods and services to produce and which factors of production to employ, selling their output and buying their inputs in the goods and factor markets. The markets determine the prices that bring the quantities demanded and quantities supplied into equality for each factor of production and good or service. Capitalism economizes on information because households and firms need to know only the prices of various goods and factors that they buy and sell.

own the factors of production and are free to use those factors, and the incomes they receive from the sale of their services, in any way they choose. These choices are governed by their preferences. The preferences of households are all-powerful in a capitalist economy.

Households choose the quantity of each factor of production to sell, and firms, which organize production, choose the quantity of each factor to buy. These choices respond to the prices prevailing in the factor markets. An increase in a factor price gives households an incentive to increase the quantity supplied and gives firms an incentive to decrease the quantity demanded. Factor prices adjust to bring the quantity of each factor supplied into equality with the quantity of each factor demanded.

Households choose the quantity of each good or service to buy, and firms choose the quantity of each to produce and sell. These choices respond to the prices confronting households and firms in the goods markets. An increase in the price of a good gives firms an incentive to increase the quantity supplied of that good and gives households an incentive to decrease the quantity demanded. Prices adjust to bring the quantities demanded and supplied into equality with each other.

Resources and goods and services flow in a clockwise direction from households to firms and back to households through the factors and goods markets. *What* is produced, *how* it is produced, and *for whom* it is produced are determined by the preferences of the households, the resources that they own, and the technologies available to the firms.

Nobody *plans* the capitalist economy. Doctors perform nearly miraculous life-saving surgery by using sophisticated computer-controlled equipment. The equipment is designed by medical and electronic engineers, programmed by mathematicians, financed by insurance companies and banks, and bought and installed by hospital administrators. Each individual household and firm involved in this process allocates the resources that it controls in the way that seems best for it. The firms try to maximize profit, and the households try to maximize utility. And these plans are coordinated in the markets for health care equipment, computers, engineers, computer programmers, insurance, hospital services, nurses, doctors, and hundreds of other items that range from anaesthetic chemicals to apple juice.

When a surgeon performs an operation, an incredible amount of information is used. Yet no one possesses this information. It is not centralized in one place. The capitalist economic system economizes on information. Each household or firm needs to know very little about the other households and firms with which it does business. The reason is that *prices convey most of the information it needs.* By comparing the prices of factors of production, households choose the quantity of each factor to supply. And by comparing the prices of goods and services, they choose the quantity of each to buy. Similarly, by comparing the prices of factors of production, firms choose the quantity of each factor to use, and by comparing the prices of goods and services, they choose the quantity of each to supply.

Socialism Figure 21.4 shows how socialism solves the economic problem of scarcity. In this case the planners' preferences carry the most weight. Those preferences dictate the activities of the production enterprises. The planners control capital and natural resources, directing them to the uses that satisfy their priorities. The planners also decide what types of jobs will be available, and the state plays a large role in the allocation of the only factor of production owned by households—labor.

The central plan is communicated to state-owned enterprises, which use the factors of production and the available technologies to produce goods and services. These goods and services are supplied to households in accordance with the central plan. The purchases by each household are determined by household preferences, but the total amount available is determined by the central planners.

A centrally planned economy has prices, but prices do not adjust to make quantity demanded and quantity supplied equal. Instead, they are set to achieve social objectives. For example, the prices of staple food products are set at low levels so that even the poorest families can afford an adequate basic diet. The effect of setting such prices at low levels is chronic shortages. The incentives that people respond to are the penalties and rewards that superiors can impose on and give to their subordinates.

REVIEW

The economic problem—*what, how,* and *for whom* to produce the various goods and

FIGURE 21.4

Socialism's Solution to the Economic Problem

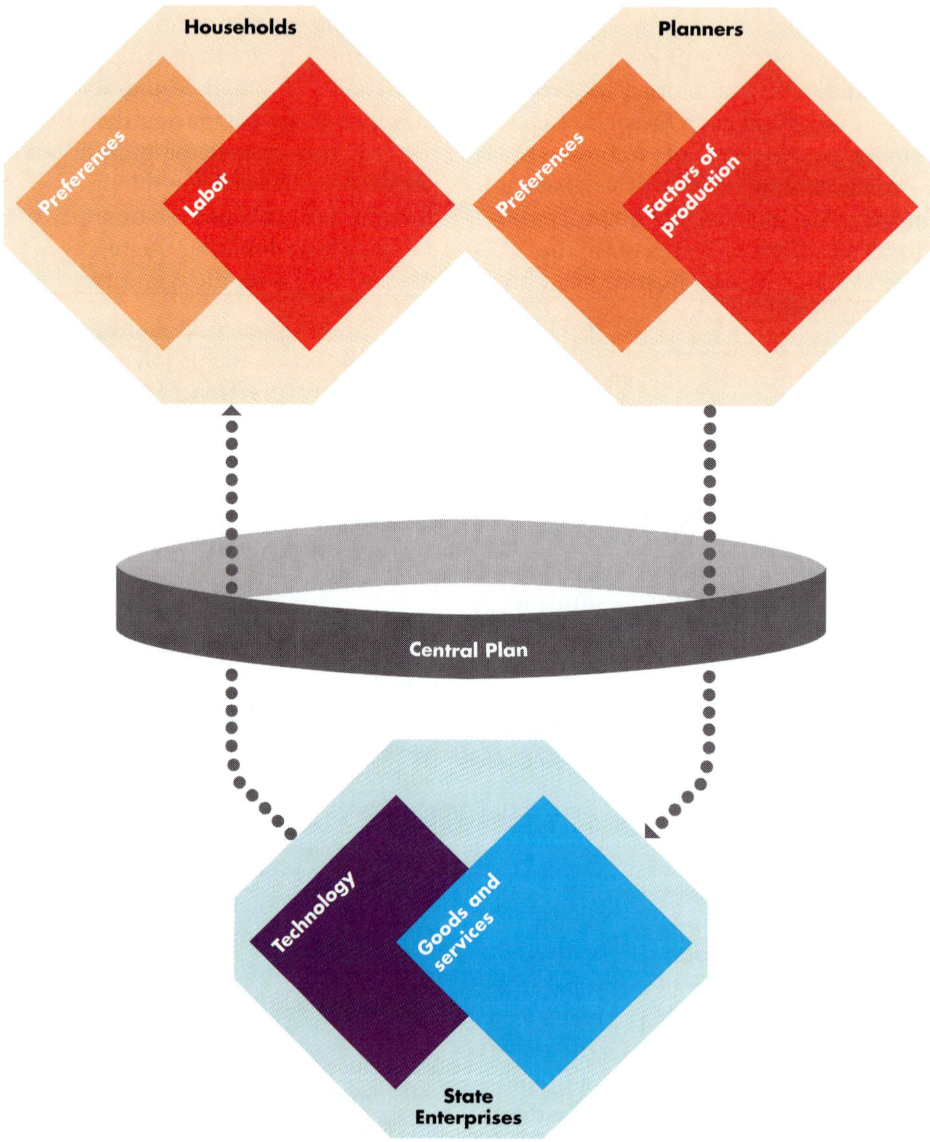

Under socialism, the preferences of the planners dictate the choices that are made. The planners control all the capital and natural resources owned by the state. They draw up plans and issue orders that determine how these resources will be used in the production of goods and services. Households decide which goods and services to consume and buy them from state-owned shops. State enterprises produce the goods and services and employ the factors of production required by the central plan. The output of state enterprises is shipped to other enterprises in accordance with the plan or sold in the state-owned shops. Prices are set by the planners to achieve social objectives and bear no relation to the quantities demanded and quantities supplied. Prices set at low levels for social reasons—as in the case of basic food products—result in chronic shortages.

services—is solved in different ways by different economic systems. Capitalism solves it by permitting households and firms to exchange factors of production and goods and services in markets. Firms produce the items that maximize their profits, households buy the goods that maximize their utility, and markets adjust prices to make buying and selling plans compatible. Socialism solves the economic problem by setting up a central planning system. The planners decide what will be produced and communicate their plans to state-owned enterprises. Incentives to fulfill the plan are created by a series of non-monetary rewards and sanctions. Each household decides what it wants to buy, but the total amount available is determined by the planners. Shortages, especially of basic staple food products, frequently arise. ◆

Let's now take a closer look at some socialist economies. We'll begin with the country that invented central planning and "exported" its system to the other socialist countries, the former Soviet Union.

Economic Change in the Former Soviet Union

The Soviet Union, or the Union of Soviet Socialist Republics (USSR), was founded in 1917 following the Bolshevik revolution led by Vladimir Ilyich Lenin. The union collapsed and was replaced by the Commonwealth of Independent States (CIS) in 1991. The republics that make up the Commonwealth are resource-rich and diverse. Their land area is three times that of the United States; their population is approaching 300 million, 20 percent larger than the United States; they have vast reserves of coal, oil, iron ore, natural gas, timber, and almost every other mineral resource. They are republics of enormous ethnic diversity with Russians making up 50 percent of the population and many European, Asian, and Arabic ethnic groups making up the other 50 percent.

Economic History of the Soviet Union

A compact economic history of the Soviet Union appears in Table 21.1. Although the nation was founded in 1917, its economic management system was not put in place until the 1930s. The architect of this system was Joseph Stalin. The financial,

TABLE 21.1

A Compact Summary of Key Periods in the Economic History of the Soviet Union

Period	Main economic events/characteristics
1917–1921 (Lenin)	◆ **Bolshevik Revolution** ◆ **Nationalization of banking, industry, and transportation** ◆ **Forced requisitioning of agricultural output**
1921–1924 (Lenin)	◆ **New Economic Policy (NEP), 1921** ◆ **Market allocation of most resources**
1928–1953 (Stalin)	◆ **Abolition of market** ◆ **Introduction of command planning and five-year plans** ◆ **Collectivization of farms** ◆ **Emphasis on capital goods and economic growth** ◆ **Harsh conditions**
1953–1970 (Khrushchev to Brezhnev)	◆ **Steady growth** ◆ **Increased emphasis on consumer goods**
1970–1985 (Brezhnev to Chernenko)	◆ **Deteriorating productivity in agriculture and industry** ◆ **Slowdown in growth**
1985–1991 (Gorbachev)	◆ **Perestroika—reforms based on increased accountability**
1991	◆ **Breakup of the Soviet Union**
1992	◆ **Creation of the Commonwealth of Independent States**

OUR ADVANCING KNOWLEDGE

UNDERSTANDING the Limits of CENTRAL PLANNING

Our economy is a highly planned one. But it is not *centrally* planned. The planning takes place inside corporations—some of them huge. General Motors, for example, is bigger than many countries. If it makes sense to plan GM's economy, why doesn't it make sense to plan a national economy?

This question has puzzled and divided economists for many years. The answer given by Friedrich von Hayek is that an economy produces billions of different goods and services, while a corporation, even a very large one, produces only a limited range of items. As a consequence, central planning requires the centralization of vast amounts of information that it is extremely costly to collect. The market economizes on this information. Each household or firm needs to know only the prices of the range of goods and services that it buys and sells. No household or firm needs to know every price. And none needs to know the technologies for producing anything beyond its area of specialization. Markets find the prices that make the plans of producers and consumers consistent.

"The more complicated the whole, the more dependent we become on that division of knowledge between individuals whose separate efforts are coordinated by the impersonal . . . price system."

FRIEDRICH VON HAYEK
The Road to Serfdom

But Hayek's answer leaves open another question. Why does GM plan? Why isn't the market used to allocate resources inside GM? This question was answered by Ronald H. Coase. Planning, he explained, economizes on transactions costs, while the market economizes on information costs. There is an optimal size of the planning unit (firm) and an optimal extent of the market for each activity.

The poor economic performance of the former Soviet Union, the communist countries of Eastern Europe, and China before 1978 suggests that planning was taken too far in those countries and that the scope of the market was too restricted. These countries were run like big firms, but the firms were too big.

Before 1978, the farms of China were operated as part of the national economic plan. The planners decided what would be produced and how the food would be distributed. Peasant farmers received an allocation of food, but their rewards were unrelated to their efforts. Food production and living standards were low. In 1978, Deng Xiaoping reformed the farms. Families were permitted to take long-term leases on their land and to decide what to produce and where to sell it. The result was a massive increase in food production and a rapid increase in the standard of living. By 1984, the farms had become so productive that China became an *exporter* of grain.

Deng Xiaoping's 1978 :onomic reforms have had dramatic effects on ·ina's large cities and urban population. New ws that permitted the creation of private firms sulted in massive numbers of new private ·terprises springing up—manufacturing a wide nge of consumer goods and providing employ- ent for people who were no longer needed on e increasingly efficient farms. By 1990, real come per person had increased to 2½ times its 78 level. Between 1982 and 1988, real income r person grew at a staggering 9.7 percent a ar, almost doubling in six years. Many of the w private firms sell on world markets, and ·ina's exports grew at a much faster rate than P during the 1980s. By 1990, they stood at 17 rcent of GDP.

KARL MARX: AN *Alternative Economic Vision*

Karl Marx (1818–1883) was a social scientist (political scientist, sociologist, and economist) of extraordinary breadth and influence. Born in Germany, he spend most of his adult life in London, using the British Museum as his workplace. With little income, life was harsh for Marx and his wife (his childhood sweetheart to whom he was devoted). Marx's major work in economics was *Das Kapital,* in which he argued that capitalism was self-destructive and would be replaced by a system in which private property was abolished and a central plan replaced the market—a system he called "communism." Events have rejected Marx's theory, and his lasting contribution to modern economics is negligible. But his contribution to modern politics is substantial. Marxism, a political creed based on his ideas, thrives throughout much of the world today.

manufacturing, and transportation sectors of the economy had been taken under state ownership and control by Lenin. Stalin added the farms to this list. He abolished the market and introduced a command planning mechanism, initiating a series of five-year plans that placed their major emphasis on setting and attaining goals for the production of capital goods. The production of consumer goods was given a secondary place, and personal economic conditions were harsh. With emphasis on the production of capital goods, the Soviet economy grew quickly.

By the 1950s, after Stalin's death, steady economic growth continued, but the emphasis in economic planning gradually shifted away from capital goods production toward consumer goods production. In the 1960s, the growth rate began to sag, and by the 1970s and early 1980s, the Soviet economy was running into serious problems. Productivity was actually declining, especially in agriculture but also in industry. Growth slowed, and, by some estimates, per capita income in the Soviet Union began to fall. It was in this situation that Mikhail Gorbachev came to power with plans to restructure the Soviet economy, based on the idea of increased individual accountability and rewards based on performance.

As a unified political entity, the Soviet Union effectively disintegrated following an unsuccessful coup to topple former President Gorbachev in August 1991. What emerged from that coup in 1992 was a more loosely federated Commonwealth of Independent States. Political freedoms began to be enjoyed in the late 1980s under President Gorbachev's programs of *perestroika* (restructuring) and *glasnost* (openness). These political freedoms released nationalist and ethnic feelings that had been held in check for 50 years and created a virtual explosion of political activity. At the same time, the economies of the now independent republics underwent tumultuous change.

We are going to look at that change. But you will better appreciate the severity and nature of the problems posed by economic change if we first look at the way the Soviet Union operated before it abandoned its central planning system.

Soviet-Style Central Planning

Soviet-style central planning is a method of economic planning and control that has four key elements:

- Administrative hierarchy
- Iterative planning process
- Legally binding commands
- Taut and inflexible plans

Administrative Hierarchy A large and complex hierarchy implements and controls the central economic plan that determines almost every aspect of economic activity. A **hierarchy** is an organization arranged in ranks, each rank being subordinate to the one above it. At the top of an economic planning hierarchy is the highest *political* authority. Immediately below it is the economic planning ministry, the senior of a large number of ministries. Below the planning ministry are a large number of ministries that are responsible for the detailed aspects of production. For example, one ministry deals with engineering production, another with fruit and vegetables, and another with railroad transportation. Responsibility for production processes is divided and subdivided yet further down to the level of the individual factories that carry out the production processes. For example, engineering is divided into light, heavy, electrical, and civil divisions. Light engineering is divided into departments that deal with individual product groups, such as ball bearings. And finally, ball bearings are manufactured in a number of factories. At each level of the hierarchy, there are superiors and subordinates. Superiors have absolute and arbitrary power over their subordinates.

Iterative Planning Process Central planning is an iterative planning process. An iterative process is a repetitive series of calculations that get closer and closer to a solution. A plan is proposed, and adjustments are repeatedly made until all the elements of the plan are consistent with each other. But a plan is not arrived at as the result of a set of neat calculations performed on a computer. Rather, the process involves a repeated sequence of communications of proposals and reactions down and up the administrative hierarchy.

The process begins with the issue of a big picture set of objectives or directives by the highest political authority. These directives are translated into targets by the planning ministry and retranslated into ever more detailed targets as they are passed down the hierarchy. Tens of millions of raw materials and intermediate goods featured in the detailed plans of the Soviet Union, which filled 70 volumes, or 12,000 pages, each year.

When the targets are specified as production plans for individual products, the factories react with their own assessments of what is feasible. Reactions as to feasibility are passed back up the hierarchy, and the central planning ministry makes the targets and reports of feasibility consistent. A good deal of bargaining takes place in this process, the superiors demanding the impossible and subordinates claiming requests to be infeasible.

Legally Binding Commands Once a consistent (even if infeasible) plan has been determined by the planning ministry, the plan is given the force of law in a set of binding commands from the political authority. The commands are translated into increasing detail as they pass down the chain of command and are implemented by the production units in a way that most nearly satisfies the superiors of each level.

Taut and Inflexible Plans In the Soviet Union, the targets set by superiors for their subordinates were infeasible. The idea was that in the attempt to do the impossible, more would be achieved than if an easily attained task was set. The outcome of this planning process was a set of taut and inflexible plans. A taut plan is one that has no slack built into it. If one unit fails to meet its planned targets, all the other units that rely on the output of the first unit will fail to meet their targets also. An inflexible plan is one that has no capacity for reactions to changing circumstances.

Faced with impossible targets, factories produced a combination of products that enabled their superiors to report plan fulfillment, but the individual items produced did not meet the needs of the other parts of the economy. No factory received exactly the quantity and types of inputs needed, and the economy was unable to respond to changes in circumstances. In practice, the plan for the current year was the outcome of the previous year plus a wished for but unattainable increment.

The Market Sector

Although the economy of the Soviet Union was a planned one, a substantial amount of economic activity took place outside the planning and command economy. The most important component of the market sector was in agriculture. It has been estimated that during the 1980s there were 35 million private plots worked by rural households in the Soviet Union. These private plots constituted less than 3 percent of the agricultural land of the Soviet Union but produced close to 25 percent of total agricultural output and a third of all the meat and milk. Some estimates suggested that the productivity on private plots was 40 times that of state enterprise farms and collective farms. Other economic activities undertaken by Soviet citizens outside the planning system were illegal.

Money in the Soviet Union

Money played a minor role in the economy of the Soviet Union. It was used in the market sector and in the state sector to pay wages and buy consumer goods and services. But all the transactions among state enterprises and between state enterprises and government took place as part of the *physical* plan, and money was used only as a means of keeping records. International trade was undertaken by the direct exchange of goods for goods—barter.

Soviet Economic Decline

Table 21.2 describes the growth performance of the Soviet economy between 1928 and 1990. The economy performed extraordinarily well before 1970. Growth rates of output in excess of 5 percent a year were achieved on the average for the entire period between 1928 and 1970, bringing an eightfold increase in aggregate output over these years. Then the growth rate began to fall. During the 1970s, output expanded by 3.2 percent a year, and in the 1980s, growth collapsed to 2 percent a year between 1980 and 1986 and then to only 1 percent a year between 1986 and 1990. In 1990, the economy shrank by 4 percent.

Why did the economy perform well before 1970 and then begin to deliver successively slower growth rates? What brought the decline of the Soviet economy during the 1980s? The combination and interaction of three features were responsible. They are

- Transition from investment to consumption economy
- External shocks
- Taut and inflexible plans

TABLE 21.2

Economic Growth Rates in the Soviet Union

Years	Growth rates (percent per year)
1928–1937	**5.4**
1940–1960	**5.7**
1960–1970	**5.1**
1970–1979	**3.2**
1980–1986	**2.0**
1987	**1.6**
1988	**4.4**
1989	**2.5**
1990	**−4.0**

Economic growth in the Soviet Union was rapid between 1928 and 1970. During the 1970s, growth began to slow down, and the growth rate became successively lower until the early 1990s, when the economy began to contract.

Sources: Paul R. Gregory and Robert C. Stuart, *Soviet Economic Structure and Performance*, 2nd edition (New York: Harper and Row, 1981); U.S. Central Intelligence Agency, *USSR: Measures of Economic Growth and Development, 1950–1980,* U.S. Congress, Joint Economic Committee (Washington, D.C.: U.S. Government Printing Office, 1982); U.S. Central Intelligence Agency, "Gorbachev's Economic Program," Report to U.S. Congress, Subcommittee on National Security Economics, April 13, 1989 (Washington, D.C.: U.S. Government Printing Office, 1989); and The World Bank, *The Economy of the USSR* (Washington, D.C.: 1990).

Transition from Investment to Consumption Economy Before 1960, the Soviet economic planners concentrated on producing capital goods and maintaining a rapid rate of investment in new buildings, plant, and equipment. They ran the Soviet economy like a large corporation intent on rapid growth that puts all its profits into yet more growth. The central planning system is at its best when implementing such a strategy. The planners know exactly which types of capital they need to remove or reduce bottlenecks and can achieve a high rate of growth.

During the 1960s, the orientation of the Soviet economy began to change with a relative increase in the production of consumer goods and services. By the 1970s and 1980s, this process had gone much further. A centrally planned economy does a very bad job of handling the complexities of producing a large variety of types, sizes, colors, designs, and styles of consumer goods. The planners need to collect and take into account more information than their computers can handle.

As a result, the planners order the wrong goods to be produced, creating surpluses of some and chronic shortages of others. Easy-to-produce plain white bread is available in excessive quantities at give-away prices, and hard-to-produce blueberry muffins can't be found at any price. Surplus goods get wasted or used inefficiently, and increasing amounts of the resources that could be used to add to the economy's productive capital get diverted to meeting ever more desperate consumer demands. Gradually, economic growth vanishes.

External Shocks As the world's largest producer of crude oil, the Soviet Union benefited enormously, during the 1970s, from the massive oil price increases. The extra revenue obtained from oil exports helped, during those years, to mask the problems just described. But the 1980s brought *falling* oil prices and exposed the problems of the Soviet Union in a sharp light.

During the late 1980s, the countries of Eastern Europe that had been the Soviet Union's traditional trading partners embarked on their own transitions to market economies and began to look to the West for trading opportunities. As a consequence, the Soviet Union's sources of international trade collapsed.

Taut and Inflexible Plans A flexible economic system might have been able to deal with the switch to consumption goods production and the consequences of a changing world economic environment. But the Soviet economy was not flexible. On the contrary, with its system of taut planning and its unresponsive command structure, it was only able to attempt to produce the same bundle of goods as it had produced in the previous year. With less revenue from oil and other raw material exports, fewer imported inputs could be obtained. Imbalances in the central plan rippled through the entire economy, disrupting the production of all goods and putting the system itself under enormous strain.

Living Standards in the Late 1980s

The problems of the Soviet economy are put in sharp focus in Fig. 21.5. In this figure, the productivity and consumption levels of the Soviet Union in the mid-1980s are compared with those of the United States, Western Europe (Germany, France, and Italy), Japan, and Portugal. As you can see from the figure, average worker productivity in the Soviet Union, measured by GDP per worker, was less than 40 percent of real GDP per worker in the United States and lagged considerably behind that in the other Western European countries and Japan. A similar picture is painted by comparing consumption per worker and consumption per person. The capitalist country whose level of productivity and consumption was most similar to that of the Soviet Union was Portugal.

FIGURE 21.5

GDP and Consumption in the Soviet Union and Other Countries

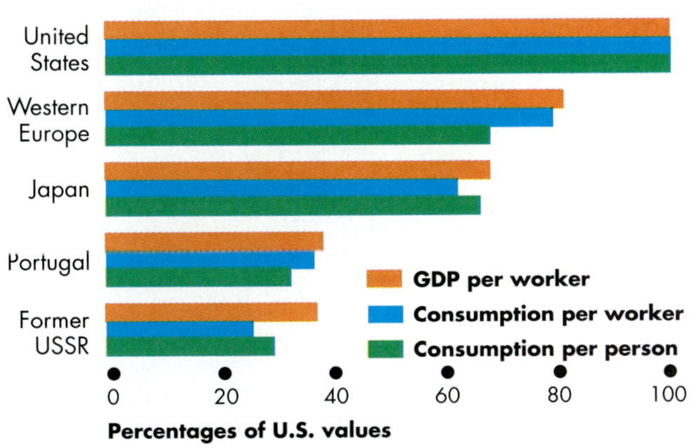

GDP per worker in the Soviet Union in the mid-1980s was less than 40 percent of its level in the United States and similar to the level in Portugal. Consumption per worker and consumption per person were even lower at less than 30 percent of the U.S. level. The Soviet Union lagged considerably behind Western Europe and Japan in GDP and consumption level.

Source: Abram Bergson, "The USSR Before the Fall: How Poor and Why," *Journal of Economic Perspectives* 5, 4 (Fall 1991): 29–44.

Market Economy Reforms

By the end of the 1980s, there was widespread dissatisfaction throughout the Soviet Union with the economic planning system, and a process of transition toward a market economy began. This process had three main elements:

1. Relaxing central plan enforcement
2. Deregulating prices
3. Permitting limited private ownership of firms

The transition in all three areas was one of gradual change. But the relaxation of central plan enforcement was the fastest and most far-reaching element of the transition. The idea was that by relaxing central control over the annual plan and permitting the managers of state enterprises greater freedom to act like the managers of private firms, enterprises would be able to respond to changing circumstances without having to wait for orders from the center.

Price deregulation was gradual and covered a limited range of products. Here, the idea was that with the removal of price controls, the price mechanism would allocate scarce resources to their highest-value uses. Shortages would disappear and be replaced by available but sometimes expensive goods and services. High prices would strengthen the inducement for producers to increase the quantities supplied. The move toward private ownership of firms was extremely gradual. The idea here was that enterprising individuals would move quickly to seize profit opportunities by responding to price signals much more rapidly than the replaced planning system could respond to shortages and bottlenecks.

But the transition process ran into problems. One of these problems was that of unlearning the old methods of the centrally planned economy. Reading Between the Lines on pp. 564–565 looks at an example of this problem in the Moscow market for bread. But deeper transition problems arose from the nature of the system being replaced.

Transition Problems

There are three major problems confronting the republics of the former Soviet Union that complicate

The Market Comes to Moscow

The Wall Street Journal, January 21, 1992

Moscow's 'Capitalists' Decide the Best Price Is a Firmly Fixed One

by Laurie Hays and Adi Ignatius

Late last month, on the eve of Russia's historic plunge into a market economy, Vladimir Grechanik, the top financial planner of Moscow's Bread Factory No. 14, went into a panic.

After 70 years of government control of everything from the cost of raw materials to salaries, the factory suddenly would be able to set its own prices. He and his fellow producers anxiously tried to calculate how much flour would cost, how much transportation might rise and what consumers would be willing to pay.

Just before prices were freed Jan. 2, Mr. Grechanik and executives from Moscow's other bread factories were called to a meeting at the Moscow Bread Consortium, the de facto ministry of bread. They eyed one another nervously, suspicious that, after years of mandated equality, the system might make rivals of former comrades. The bread consortium suggested raising the free-market bread price to 3½ times the old price, but not a kopeck more. The factory men were confused. In the old days, such a "suggestion" carried the full weight of a decree. But there were no certainties anymore. The new freedom was unbearable.

An Old Reflex

Left to his own devices, Mr. Grechanik returned to his office and got on the phone. For the next two days he and the other factory directors discussed their fears. Finally, they came to a decision: If the state was no longer to set prices, the factories themselves would jointly fix them—to ensure their mutual survival.

"We all agreed on a single price," says Mr. Grechanik, as he walks past huge vats of flour on the factory floor. Lowering his voice, he confides, "I've heard that Bread Factory No. 26 is charging a little less, but I hope it's just a rumor." . . .

The Essence of the Story

In Russia, the prices of many items, including bread, were deregulated on January 2, 1992.

In December 1991, in preparation for this event, the executives of Moscow's bread factories attended a meeting at the Moscow Bread Consortium (the de facto ministry of bread).

The consortium suggested that producers increase the price of bread to 3½ times the old price. This "suggestion" did not, as in the formerly planned economy, have the force of law.

The bread producers were confused, anxious, nervous, and suspicious.

For two days the factory directors discussed their fears by telephone and eventually decided to jointly fix the price of bread.

There was a rumor that one bread factory (No. 26) was charging a lower price.

Background and Analysis

When the central planning system operated, the price and quantity of bread were determined by the planners.

Figure 1 illustrates this situation. The plan quantity is Q_0, and the plan price is 0.50 ruble (50 kopecks). The average cost of producing bread was higher than this price, and bread factories were subsidized. In this example (the numbers are hypothetical) the subsidy is 50 kopecks per loaf.

The move toward the market economy that began in January 1992 resulted in:

- The removal of the subsidy to bread producers
- Increased cost of flour and other raw materials and salaries

Increases in incomes (increases in ruble incomes, not increases in real incomes) and increases in other prices also led to an increase in the demand for bread.

The combination of these changes is illustrated in Fig. 2. There was uncertainty in the minds of the executives of the bread factories about the magnitude of these changes.

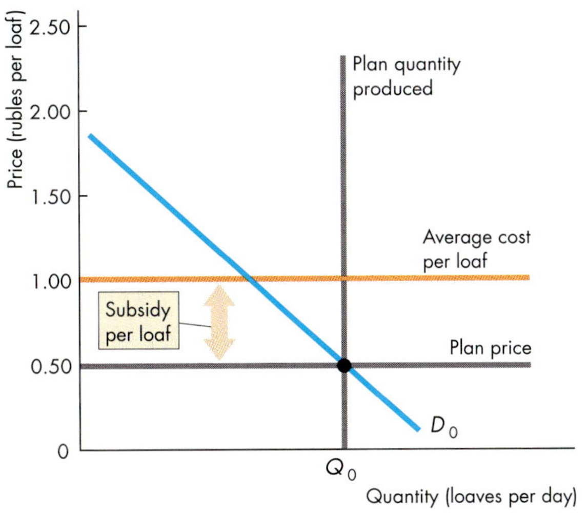

Figure 1

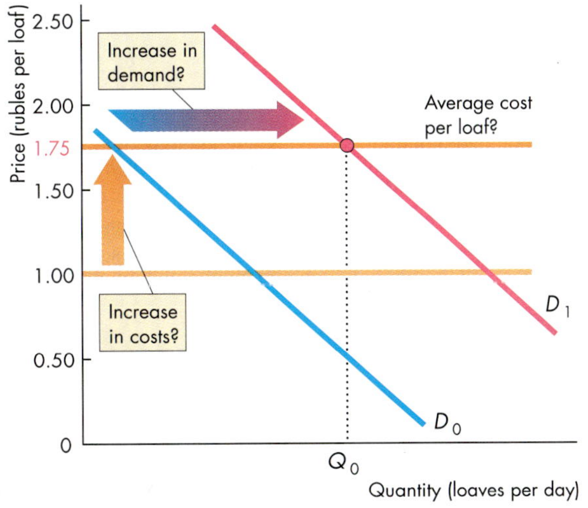

Figure 2

Adding to these uncertainties, each producer was uncertain about the prices that the other producers would charge for bread.

To remove the last-mentioned uncertainty, the producers pooled their information and fixed a single price. This price is based on the assumption that the costs of production—the opportunity cost of bread—would increase to 1.75 rubles a loaf.

If the demand for bread increased to D_1, the quantity produced would remain at its previous level of Q_0.

If the bread producers overestimated the opportunity cost of producing bread, the free market would result in new firms entering to compete with them and the price would fall below the level they had fixed.

If the bread producers underestimated the opportunity cost of bread, some of them would begin to incur losses and might eventually go out of business. In this event, the supply of bread would decrease and its price would rise until it covered its opportunity cost.

their transition to the capitalist market economic system. They are

- Value and legal systems alien to capitalism
- Collapse of traditional trade flows
- Fiscal crisis

Value and Legal Systems More than 60 years of socialist dictatorship have left a legacy of values and memories alien to the rapid and successful establishment of a capitalist, market economy. The political leaders and people of the former Soviet Union have no personal memories of free political institutions and markets. And they have been educated, both formally and informally, to believe in a political creed in which traders and speculators are not just shady characters, but criminals. Unlearning these values will be a slow and perhaps painful process.

The legal system is also unsuited to the needs of a market economy in two ways. First, there are no well-established property rights and methods of protecting those rights. Second, and more important, there is no tradition of government behaving like individuals and firms before the rule of law. In the Soviet system, the government *was* the law. Its economic plan and the arbitrary decisions made by superiors at each level in the hierarchy were the only law that counted. Rational, self-promoting actions taken outside the plan were illegal. It will take a long time to establish a legal system based on private property rights and the rule of law.

Collapse of Traditional Trade Flows A centrally administered empire has collapsed, and its constituent republics have decided to create a loose federation. Such a political reorganization can have devastating economic consequences. The most serious of these is the collapse of traditional trade flows. The Soviet Union was a highly interdependent grouping of republics organized on a wheel-hub basis with Moscow (and to a lesser degree Leningrad—now St. Petersburg) at its center. This view of the Soviet economy is shown in Fig. 21.6. The figure also shows the magnitude of the flows of goods from the republics through the Moscow hub.

The most heavily dependent republic, Belorussia, delivered 70 percent of its output to other republics and received a similar value of goods from the other republics. Even the least dependent republic, Kazakhstan, traded 30 percent of its production with the other republics. The vast amount of inter-republic trade, managed by the central planners and channeled through the Moscow hub, meant that individual enterprise managers had (and still have) little knowledge of where their products end up being used or their inputs originate.

With the collapse of the central plan, managers must search for supplies and for markets. Until they have built new networks of information, shortages of raw materials and other material inputs will be

FIGURE 21.6
The Wheel-Hub Economy of the Soviet Union

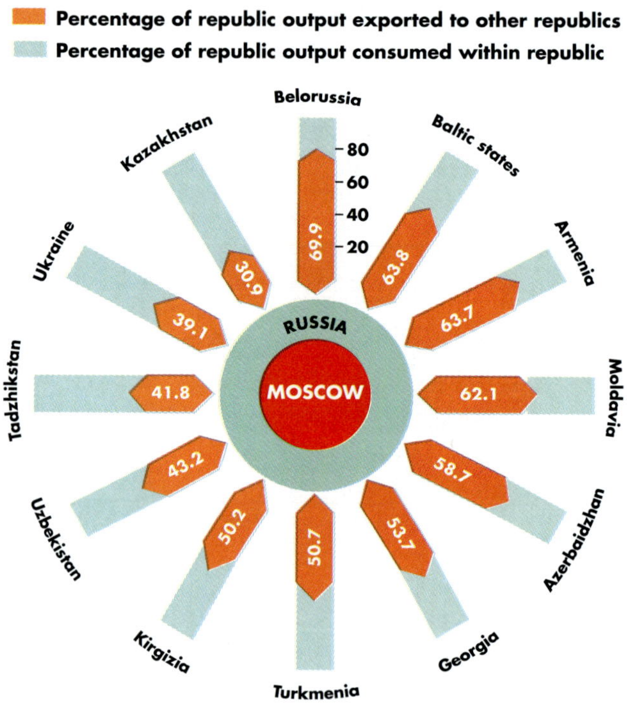

The Soviet economy was organized on a wheel-hub model. Vast amounts of goods and services were traded among the republics but mainly through the Moscow hub. The percentages of production in each republic exported to other republics are shown along the spokes of the wheel.

Source: The World Bank, *The Economy of the USSR* (Washington, D.C.: 1990), p. 51.

Note: The names of the republics in this figure are the ones used in the former Soviet Union. With the breakup of the Soviet Union, Belorussia became Belarus, Moldavia became Moldova, Turkmenia became Turkmenistan, Kirgizia became Kyrgyzstan, and Talzhikstan became Tajikistan.

common and a lack of markets will stunt production. This problem can be solved by the activities of specialist traders and speculators, but the emergence of this class of economic agent is likely to be slow because of political attitudes toward this activity.

The collapse of an economic empire does not inevitably lead to a collapse of traditional trade flows and an associated decline in production. But it usually has done so. The most similar collapse this century was that of the Austro-Hungarian Empire in 1919. Like the Soviet Union, the Austro-Hungarian Empire was a centralized economic system organized with Vienna and Budapest as its hubs with a single currency and free trade. The empire was a great economic success, achieving rapid improvements in living standards for its people. Following the collapse of the empire, tariffs were introduced, each country established its own currency, trade flows dried up, and economic growth declined.

Fiscal Crisis Under the central planning system of the Soviet Union, the central government collected taxes in an arbitrary way. One source of revenue was a tax on consumer goods. But the major source of revenue was the profits of the state enterprises. Since the state owned these enterprises, it also received the profits. Money played virtually no role in the centrally planned system. Workers received their wages in currency and used it to purchase consumer goods and services. But for the state enterprises and the government, money was just a unit for keeping records.

With the collapse of central planning, money has become more important, especially for the government. With the loss of its traditional sources of revenue and with little change in its spending, the government has a large budget deficit. It covers this deficit by printing money, and the result is inflation. The inflation rate during the final six months of the life of the Soviet Union—the first half of 1991—reached close to 200 percent and was on a rising path.

Inflation is not an inevitable accompaniment of the collapse of an economic empire, but like the collapse of trade flows, it has happened before. The rates of growth of the newly created currencies of Austria, Hungary, Poland, Rumania, and Yugoslavia following the disintegration of the Austro-Hungarian Empire were extremely rapid and led to hyperinflation. In Poland, the hyperinflation reached an annual rate of 250 million percent.

Review

The Soviet Union's system of central economic planning and state ownership was established in the 1930s. Under this system, a hierarchical administrative structure engaged in an iterative planning process to arrive at a consistent economic plan. The plan was implemented by the political authority issuing legally binding commands that were translated into ever greater detail as they were passed down the chain of command. In practice, the plans were infeasible and inflexible. The system performed well before 1970 but became steadily less effective during the 1970s and 1980s. The system's inflexibility could not cope with the transition from an investment to a consumption economy and with a series of external shocks. As a result, its growth rate slowed, and eventually output began to decrease. A market reform process was begun that deregulated prices, permitted limited private ownership of firms, and relaxed the enforcement of the central plan. But the value and legal systems, the collapse of traditional trade flows, the loss of tax revenue, and inflation are making the transition extremely costly. ◆

Economic Transition in Eastern Europe

The formerly planned economies of Eastern Europe—Czechoslovakia, East Germany, Hungary, and Poland—are also making transitions to market economies. The processes being followed and the problems faced are similar to those of the former Soviet Union. But their problems, although severe, take different forms from those of the Soviet Union. The major differences arise from political factors. Let's take a brief look at the transition process in these countries.

East Germany

For East Germany, the transition from a centrally planned economy has been the most dramatic and the most complete. On October 3, 1990, East

Germany united with West Germany. East Germany was a country with 16 million people, 26 percent of the population of West Germany, and with a GDP per person of less than 80 percent of that of West Germany. Even before the formal reunification of the two parts of Germany, East Germany had begun to dismantle its Soviet-style planning system and replace it with a market economy.

The former East Germany adopted the monetary system of West Germany, deregulated its prices, and opened itself up to free trade with its western partner. State enterprises were permitted to fail in the competition with western private firms, private firms were permitted to open up in the former East Germany, and a massive sell-off of state enterprises was embarked upon.

The process of selling state enterprises began by the creation of a state corporation called Treuhandanstalt (which roughly translates as "Trust Corporation") that took over the assets of the almost 11,000 state enterprises. The idea was to then sell off these enterprises in an orderly way over a few years. By November 1991, Treuhandanstalt had disposed of more than 4,000 firms. Most of these firms had been sold to the private sector, but about 900 firms were closed down or merged with other firms.

The loss of jobs resulting from this rapid shakeout of state enterprises was large. Even by July 1990, before the two Germanies were reunited, unemployment in East Germany had reached one third of the labor force. The unemployment rate in the east will remain high for some years, but the safety net of the West German social security system will cushion the blow to individual workers and their families.

East Germany has no fiscal policy crisis and no inflation problem. It has adopted the West German taxation and monetary systems and has assured financial stability. But the transition for East Germany will last for several years, even though it will be the most rapid transition imaginable.

Czech Republic, Slovakia, Hungary, and Poland

The problems facing the Czech Republic, Slovakia, Hungary, and Poland differ in important ways but share some common features. And these common features are similar to some of the problems faced by the former Soviet Union that we've already seen. The most severe of these are the collapse of traditional trade flows and the loss of traditional sources of government revenue.

Czech Republic and Slovakia The Czech Republic and Slovakia (formerly Czechoslovakia) removed their communist government in what has been called the "Velvet Revolution" in November 1989 and almost immediately embarked on a program of economic reforms aimed at replacing a centrally planned economy with a market system.

The first step in the transition was the freeing of wages, prices, and interest rates. This step was accomplished quickly, but the emergence of well-functioning markets did not immediately follow. Financial markets were especially nervous, and a shortage of liquidity created a financial crisis.

The second step in the transition was privatization. Czechoslovakia pursued a so-called two-track policy of "little privatization" and "big privatization." "Little privatization" is the sale or, where possible, the return to their former owners of small businesses and shops. "Big privatization" is the sale of shares in the large industrial enterprises. One feature of this privatization process is the issue of vouchers to citizens that may be used to buy shares in formerly state-owned enterprises.

Czechoslovakia's transition was slowed down by the decision of its people to divide the country into two parts. It has not yet reached the point of a positive economic payoff.

Hungary Hungary has been in a long transition toward a capitalist, market economy. The process began in the 1960s when central planning was replaced by decentralized planning based on a price system. Hungary has also established a taxation system similar to that in the market economies. But the privatization of large-scale industry began only in the 1990s and is proceeding slowly.

Because of its extreme gradualism, Hungary's transition is much less disruptive than those in the other countries. But it is feeling the repercussions of the economic restructuring of the other Eastern European countries with which it has traditionally had the strongest trade links, so its rate of economic expansion has slowed substantially in recent years.

Poland Severe shortages, black markets, and inflation were the jumping off point for Poland's journey toward a market economy. This journey began in September 1989 when a non-communist government that included members of the trade union Solidarity took office. The new government has deregulated prices, and black markets have disappeared. It has also pursued a policy of extreme financial restraint, bringing the state budget and inflation under control.

Privatization has also been put on a fast track in Poland. In mid-1991, the government announced its Mass Privatization Scheme. Under this scheme, the shares of 400 state enterprises were to be transferred to a Privatization Fund, the shares in which were to be distributed freely to the entire adult population. This method of privatization is like creating a giant insurance company that owns most of the production enterprises and that is in turn owned by private shareholders.

Although the transition to the market economy is the most dynamic in Eastern Europe and the former Soviet Union, it has been going on for longer and has had more dramatic effects on living standards in China. Let's now look at this country.

Economic Transition in China

China is the world's largest nation. In 1990, its population was 1.2 billion—almost a quarter of the world's population. Chinese civilization is ancient and has a splendid history, but the modern nation—the People's Republic of China—dates only from 1949. A compact summary of key periods in the economic history of the People's Republic is presented in Table 21.3.

Modern China began when a revolutionary Communist movement, led by Mao Zedong, captured control of China, forcing the country's previous leader, Chiang Kai-shek (Jiang Jie-shi) onto the island of Formosa—now Taiwan. Like the Soviet Union, China is a socialist country. But unlike the Soviet Union, China is largely nonindustrialized—it is a developing country.

During the early years of the People's Republic, the country followed the Soviet model of economic planning and command. Urban manufacturing industry was taken over and operated by the state, and the farms were collectivized. Also, following the Stalin model of the 1930s, primary emphasis was placed on the production of capital equipment.

TABLE 21.3

A Compact Summary of Key Periods in the Economic History of the People's Republic of China

Period	Main economic events/characteristics
1949	◆ **People's Republic of China established under Mao Zedong**
1949–1952	◆ **Economy centralized under a new communist government**
	◆ **Emphasis on heavy industry and "socialist transformation"**
1952–1957	◆ **First five-year plan**
1958–1960	◆ **The Great Leap Forward: an economic reform plan based on labor-intensive production methods**
	◆ **Massive failure**
1966	◆ **Cultural Revolution: revolutionary zealots**
1976	◆ **Death of Mao Zedong**
1978	◆ **Deng's reforms: under leadership of Deng Xiaoping, liberalization of agriculture and introduction of individual incentives**
	◆ **Growth rates accelerated**
1989	◆ **Democracy movement, government crackdown**

The Great Leap Forward

In 1958, Mao Zedong set the Chinese economy on a sharply divergent path from that which the Soviet Union had followed. Mao called his new path the Great Leap Forward. The **Great Leap Forward** was an economic plan based on small-scale, labor-intensive production. The Great Leap Forward paid little or no attention to linking individual pay to individual effort. Instead, a revolutionary commitment to the success of collective plans was relied upon. The Great Leap Forward was an economic failure. Productivity increased, but so slowly that living standards hardly changed. In the agricultural sector, massive injections of modern high-yield seeds, improved irrigation, and chemical fertilizers were insufficient to enable China to feed its population. The country became the largest importer of grains, edible vegetable oils, and even raw cotton.

The popular explanation within China for poor performance, especially in agriculture, was that the country had reached the limits of its arable land and that its population explosion was so enormous that agriculture was being forced to use substandard areas for farming. But the key problem was that the revolutionary and ideological motivation for the Great Leap Forward degenerated into what came to be called the Cultural Revolution. Revolutionary zealots denounced productive managers, engineers, scientists, and scholars and banished them to the life of the peasant. Schools and universities were closed, and the accumulation of human capital was severely disrupted.

The 1978 Reforms

By 1978, two years after the death of Mao Zedong, the new Chinese leader, Deng Xiaoping, proclaimed major economic reforms. Collectivized agriculture was abolished. Agricultural land was distributed among households on long-term leases. In exchange for a lease, a household agreed to pay a fixed tax and contracted to sell part of its output to the state. But the household made its own decisions on cropping patterns and the quantity and types of fertilizers and other inputs to use, and it also hired its own workers. Private farm markets were liberalized, and farmers received a higher price for their produce. Also, the state increased the price that it paid to farmers, especially for cotton and other nongrain crops.

The results of the reforms of Deng Xiaoping were astounding. Annual growth rates of output of cotton and oil-bearing crops increased a staggering fourteenfold. Soybean production, which had been declining at an annual rate of 1 percent between 1957 and 1978, started to grow at 4 percent a year. Growth rates of yields per acre also increased dramatically. By 1984, a country that six years earlier had been the world's largest importer of agricultural products became a food exporter!

The reforms led to more than a massive expansion in the agricultural sector. Increased rural incomes brought an expanding rural industrial sector that, by the mid-1980s, was employing a fifth of the rural population.

China has gone even further and is encouraging foreign investment and joint ventures. In addition, China is experimenting with formal capital markets and now has a stock market.

Motivated partly by political considerations, China is proclaiming the virtues of what it calls the "one country, two systems" approach to economic management. The political source of this movement is the existence of two capitalist enclaves in which China has a close interest—Taiwan and Hong Kong. China claims sovereignty over Taiwan and wants to create an atmosphere in which it becomes possible for China to be "reunified" at some future date. Hong Kong, a British crown colony, is currently leased by Britain from China, and that lease terminates in 1997. When the lease expires, Hong Kong will become part of China. Anxious not to damage the economic prosperity of Hong Kong, China is proposing to continue operating Hong Kong as a capitalist economy. With Hong Kong and Taiwan as part of the People's Republic of China, the stage will be set for the creation of other capitalist "islands" in such dynamic cities as Shanghai.

The results of this move toward capitalism in China are dramatically summarized in the country's real GDP growth statistics. Between 1978 and 1990, real GDP per person grew at an average rate of 7.2 percent a year—a 2.3-fold increase in income per person over the twelve-year period. Between 1982 and 1988, real GDP per person grew at a staggering 9.7 percent a year, almost doubling in a six-year period. To see how staggering these growth rates are, look at Fig. 21.7. It shows the consequences of China and the United States maintaining their post-1978 average growth rates of real GDP per person. For the United States, that growth rate was a little over 1 percent a year, and for China it was almost 8 percent a year. If they maintain these growth rates, China will catch up with the United States in a single generation, by 2010. Even if China's growth slackens off to 5 percent a year, with no change in the U.S. growth rate, China will catch up by 2030.

China is not only experiencing rapid growth of real income per person but is also increasing its international competitiveness. Its exports have grown during the 1980s at a much faster rate than GDP and, by 1990, stood at 17 percent of GDP.

How has China achieved this dramatic success?

FIGURE 21.7

Economic Growth in China

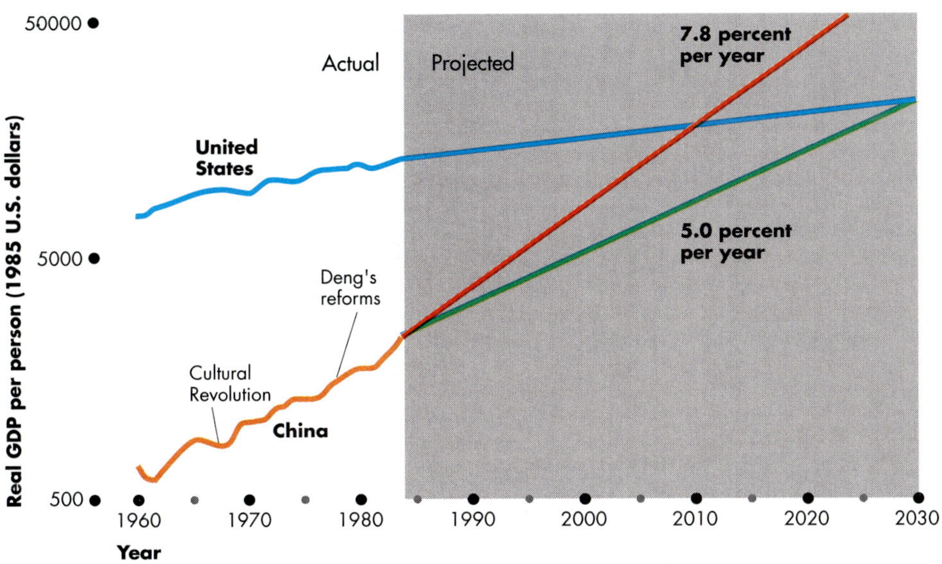

Source: Alan Heston and Robert Summers, "A New Set of International Comparisons of Real Product and Price Levels: Estimates for 130 Countries, 1950–1985," *Review of Income and Wealth,* series 34, vol. 1, 1988, pp. 1–25, Appendix B.

The growth of per capita income in China has been strongly influenced by the economic system. During the Cultural Revolution, per capita income fell. Under a central planning and command mechanism in the early 1970s, per capita income grew at a moderate pace. Under capitalist methods of production in agriculture following the 1978 reforms, per capita income growth increased dramatically. If China continues to grow at the pace it has achieved since 1978, and if the United States also maintains its post-1978 growth rate, China will catch up with the United States in 2010. Even if China slows to a 5 percent growth rate, it will catch up with the United States in 2030.

China's Success

China's success in achieving a high rate of economic growth has resulted from four features of its reforms.[1] They are

- Massive rate of entry of new non-state firms
- Increases in the productivity and profitability of state firms
- An efficient taxation system
- Gradual price deregulation

Entry of Non-State Firms The most rapidly growing sector of the Chinese economy during the 1980s was non-state industrial firms located typically in rural areas. This sector grew at an annual rate of 17½ percent between 1978 and 1990. In 1978 this sector produced 22 percent of the nation's industrial output. By 1990 it was producing 45 percent of total industrial output. By contrast, the state-owned firms—the firms organized by the state under its national plan—shrank (relatively) from producing 78 percent of total output in 1978 to 55 percent in 1990.

The entry of new firms created a dramatic increase in competition both among the new firms and between the new firms and the state firms. This competition spurred both non-state and state firms into greater efficiency and productivity.

Increases in the Productivity and Profitability of State Firms China has not privatized its economy by selling off state firms. Instead, privatization has come from the entry of new firms. The state firms have continued to operate. But the government has a strong incentive to ensure that the state firms are profitable. If state firms make no profit, the government collects no taxes from them.

To achieve the greatest possible level of profit and tax revenue, the Chinese economic planners have changed the incentives faced by the managers of

[1]This section is based on John McMillan and Barry Naughton, *How to Reform a Planned Economy: Lessons from China,* Graduate School of International Relations and Pacific Studies, University of California, San Diego, 1991.

state enterprises to resemble those of the market incentives faced by the non-state sector. Managers of state-owned firms are paid according to the firm's performance—similar to managers in private firms.

The Chinese system gives incentives for managers of state enterprises to be extremely enterprising and productive. As a result of this new system the Chinese government is now able to auction off top management jobs. Potential managers bid for the right to be manager. The manager offering the best promise of performance is the one who gets the job.

Efficient Taxation System Firms (both private and state firms) are taxed, but the tax system is unusual and different from that in our own economy. Firms are required to pay a fixed amount of profit to the government. Once that fixed amount of tax has been paid, the firm keeps any additional profit beyond that point. In contrast, the U.S. corporate tax system requires firms to pay a fixed percentage of their profits in tax. Thus in the United States, more profit means higher taxes, while in China, taxes are set independently of a firm's profit level. The Chinese system creates much stronger incentives than does our own system for firms to seek out and pursue profitable ventures.

Gradual Price Deregulation China has not abandoned planning its prices. The socialist planning system keeps the prices of manufactured goods fairly high and keeps domestic prices higher than world prices. This pricing arrangement makes private enterprise production in China extremely profitable. In 1978, when the non-state sector was small, the profit rate in that sector was almost 40 percent—for every dollar invested, 40¢ a year was earned. With such high profits there was a tremendous incentive for enterprising people to find niches and engage in creative and productive activity. The forces of competition have gradually lowered prices; by 1990, rates of return had fallen to 10 percent. But the price movements were gradual. There was no "big bang" adjustment of prices—no abandonment of the planning mechanism and introduction of a rip-roaring free market system.

Growing Out of the Plan

As a result of the reforms adopted in the 1970s and pursued vigorously since that time, the Chinese economy has gradually become a much more market-oriented economy and is, in effect, growing out of its central plan.[2] The proportion of the economy accounted for by private enterprise and market-influenced prices has gradually increased, and the proportion accounted for by state enterprises and planned and regulated prices has gradually decreased.

To sustain this process, changes in fiscal policy and monetary policy have been necessary. The reform of the economy has entailed the redesigning of the tax system. In a centrally planned economy the government's tax revenues come directly through its pricing policy. Also, the government, as the controller of all financial institutions, receives all of the nation's saving. When the central planning system is replaced by the market, the government must establish a tax collection agency similar to the Internal Revenue Service of the United States. Also, it must establish financial markets so that the savings of households can be channeled into the growing private firms to finance their investment in new buildings, plant, and equipment.

Despite the reform of its tax system, the government of China spends more than it receives in tax revenue and covers its deficit by the creation of money. The result is a steady rate of inflation. But the inflation in China is not out of control, as it is in the former Soviet Union, because the rapidly growing level of economic activity absorbs a great deal of the new money.

Whether China has found a way of making the transition from socialism to capitalism in a relatively painless way is a controversial issue. The violent suppression of the democracy movement in Tiananmen Square in the summer of 1989 suggests that China might have bought economic gains at the expense of political freedoms. Because China has retained a strong central government and only gradually changed its system, its experience is not directly useful to the struggling countries of Eastern Europe. But the experiment in comparative *economic* systems currently going on in China is one of the most exciting that the world has seen. Economists of all political shades of opinion will closely watch its outcome, and its lessons will be of enormous value for future generations—whatever those lessons turn out to be.

---

[2]Barry Naughton, *Growing Out of the Plan: Chinese Economic Reform, 1978–90,* Graduate School of International Relations and Pacific Studies, University of California, San Diego, 1992.

The Transition from Central Plan to Market

As the countries of Eastern Europe and China abandon their central planning systems, they must make a series of important choices. The key ones are these:

- The style of market economy to adopt
- The sequencing of reforms
- The speed of reforms

Styles of Market Economy

There is no unique type of market economy, and countries that formerly relied on central planning must choose from an array of possible models. The three main ones are

1. U.S.-style capitalism
2. Japanese-style capitalism
3. Welfare state capitalism

U.S.-Style Capitalism No country relies on a pure, unregulated market mechanism to solve its economic problem. But the United States comes closer than any other country to doing so. In this country, individuals own the factors of production and decide how to use their factors to earn an income. They decide how much of their incomes to save to add to their capital resources and how much to spend, and on which goods and services. These decisions by more than 250 million individuals are coordinated in markets. Governments (federal, state, and local) regulate these markets, provide public goods and services, and tax income and expenditure. Command mechanisms similar in kind to those used in the centrally planned economies are used in the government sector and by firms in their internal planning processes.

The other types of capitalism depart from the U.S. model mainly in the degree and nature of state intervention in the economy. But there are two distinct styles.

Japanese-Style Capitalism Japan's economic performance since World War II has been called the "Japanese economic miracle." Emerging from war with an average income per person that was less than one fifth of that in the United States, Japan has transformed itself into an economic giant whose income per person now approaches our own. The most spectacular growth period occurred in the 25 years from 1945 to 1970, when per capita income increased eightfold. Today, Japan has a dominant position in world markets for cars and computers, audio and video equipment, and a whole range of high-tech commodities. The Japanese tourist is now as common a sight in London, Paris, and Rome as the U.S. tourist. And there are more Japanese visitors to the United States than U.S. visitors to Japan. What has led to this transformation of Japan into one of the world's most powerful and richest economies?

Three features of the Japanese economy have contributed to its dramatic success: reliance on free-market, capitalist methods; the small scale of government; and pro-business government intervention.

The economic system in Japan is like that in the United States. People are free to pursue their ideas, to own firms, to hire labor and other inputs, and to sell their outputs in relatively free markets.

The Japanese government is the smallest in the capitalist world. Average taxes and government spending account for slightly less than one fifth of GDP. This contrasts with close to 30 percent in the United States and more than 40 percent in some Western European capitalist countries. A small scale of government means that taxes are low and therefore do not constitute a discouragement to work and to saving and accumulating capital.

But the Japanese government does intervene in the economy, and its intervention is pro-business. The main vehicle for intervention is the Ministry of International Trade and Industry (MITI)—a government agency responsible for stimulating Japanese industrial development and international trade. In the years immediately following World War II, MITI encouraged the development of basic industries such as coal, electric power, shipbuilding, and steel. It used tariffs and quotas to protect these industries in their early stages of development, subsidized them, and ensured that capital resources were abundantly available for them. MITI is almost entrepreneurial in its activities. During the 1960s, with the basic industries in place, MITI turned its attention to helping the chemical and lighter manufacturing industries. In the 1980s, it helped Japanese industry dominate the world computer market.

MITI not only fosters the growth and development of industries. It also helps speed the decline of those industries that are not contributing to rapid income growth. For example, in the mid-1970s, when the price of oil increased dramatically, the smelting of bauxite to create aluminum became inefficient in Japan. Within two years, Japan's bauxite-smelting industry had been closed down, and Japan was importing all its aluminum from Australia. By identifying industries for profitable growth and those for profitable decline, MITI helps speed the adjustment process in reallocating resources to take maximum advantage of technological change and trends in prices.

The result of Japan's economic system and government economic intervention has been a high rate of capital accumulation. There has also been a high rate of accumulation of human capital, especially in the applied sciences. Going along with a high rate of capital accumulation—both physical and human—has been a high rate of technological advance with no inhibitions about using the best technologies available, wherever in the world they might have been developed.

Welfare State Capitalism Capitalism in Western Europe is more heavily tinged with socialism than in either the United States or Japan. It is welfare state capitalism. The countries of Western Europe, many of which now belong to the European Community, are basically capitalist market economies in the sense that most productive resources are owned by private individuals and most resources are allocated by individuals trading freely in markets for both goods and services and factors of production. But the scale of government and the degree and direction of government intervention are much larger in these countries than in the United States and Japan.

Government expenditure and taxes range between 40 and 50 percent of GDP in European countries. Tax rates this high create disincentives that result, other things being equal, in less effort and lower saving rates than in countries with lower taxes. The European countries also have a large, nationalized industry sector. A **nationalized industry** is an industry owned and operated by a publicly owned authority that is directly responsible to the government. Railways, airlines, gas, electricity, telephones, radio and television broadcasting, coal, steel, banking and finance, and even automobiles are among the industries that are either wholly or partly publicly owned in some European countries. Nationalized industries are often managed on a command rather than a market principle and usually are less efficient than privately owned, competitive firms.

Increasingly in recent years, European governments have been selling state-owned enterprises. The process of selling state-owned enterprises is called **privatization**. There has also been a retreat, in some countries, from very high tax rates. European countries, impressed by the economic success of Japan and the United States, have reached the conclusion that the greater reliance on capitalism in those economies is, in part, responsible for their economic success, and they are seeking to emulate the more successful economies.

The Sequence of Reform

We've seen that socialism and capitalism differ along two dimensions: the ownership of capital and land and the incentive structure. The features of a capitalist economy that must be adopted by a socialist economy if it is to make the transition are

- Private ownership of capital and natural resources
- Market-determined prices

In making the transition from socialism to capitalism, a country must choose the order in which to adopt these capitalist features.

By placing firms in private ownership, a formerly socialist economy gets the benefits of strengthened incentives to put resources to work at their most profitable uses. Also, by permitting the free entry of new firms, the economy is able to reap the benefits of increased competition. Both the existing firms and new firms become more efficient. At the same time, the state loses its major source of revenue—the profits of state enterprises. Thus, as industry is privatized, a taxation system must be set up to enable the state to raise the revenue needed to provide public goods and services.

By freeing markets and allowing prices to be determined by supply and demand, a formerly socialist economy gets the benefits of price signals that reflect the relative scarcity of different goods and services. These signals get translated into changes in production. Those items whose prices rise most become highly profitable, so their production increases fastest.

But often, the prices that rise the fastest are those on such basic staples as bread and milk. Because food items such as these are a very important part of the budget of the poorest families, when their prices increase sharply, there is great hardship. There is also likely to be political opposition to the reform process.

The Speed of Reform

Since reform brings turmoil, there is a case for doing it slowly—gradualism—and a case for doing it quickly—in a "big bang." The case for gradualism is that the adverse effects of reform are minimized and the transition can be managed and made smooth. The case for a big bang is that the socialist economy is a complete organism and that it cannot function unless it is left intact. Remove one piece of the system and the rest ceases to function.

◆ ◆ ◆ ◆ The countries that we've studied in this chapter—the former Soviet Union, the countries of Eastern Europe, and China—are undergoing enormous political and economic change. These changes will have repercussions throughout the world economy of the 1990s of historical proportions. No one can foresee what the world economy of the mid-1990s will look like. ◆ ◆ But the world has seen change of historical proportions before. The transformation of the economies of formerly war-torn Germany and Japan into the economic powerhouses of today is one example. Throughout all this change—past and present—our knowledge and understanding of the economic forces that produce the change and are unleashed by it have been gradually getting better. There remains a great deal that we do not understand. But we have made a great deal of progress. The economic principles presented in this book summarize this progress and the current state of knowledge. As the world continues to change, you will need a compass to guide you into unknown terrain. The principles of economics are that compass!

SUMMARY

The Economic Problem and Its Alternative Solutions

The economic problem is the universal fact of scarcity. Different economic systems deliver different solutions to the economic problem of determining *what*, *how*, and *for whom* goods and services are produced. Alternative economic systems vary in two dimensions: ownership of capital and land and the incentives people face. Capital and land may be owned by individuals, by the state, or by a mixture of the two. Incentives may be created by market prices, by administered prices and administrative sanctions, or by a mixture of the two. Economic systems differ in the ways in which they combine ownership and incentive arrangements. Capitalism is based on the private ownership of capital and land and on market price incentives. Socialism is based on state ownership of capital and land and on administrative incentives and a central economic plan. Market socialism combines state ownership of capital and land with incentives based on a mixture of market and administered prices. Welfare state capitalism combines the private ownership of capital and land with state intervention in markets that change the price signals that people respond to. (pp. 552–557)

Economic Change in the Former Soviet Union

The Soviet Union was founded in 1917 and collapsed in 1991. The economy of the Soviet Union was based on a system of central planning that had four key elements: an administrative hierarchy, an iterative planning process, legally binding commands, and taut and inflexible plans. The Soviet Union had a market sector in which a substantial amount of economic activity took place, especially in agriculture. Money played only a minor role in the economy of the Soviet Union.

The Soviet economy grew extraordinarily quickly before 1970—in excess of 5 percent a year—but during the 1970s, and more especially during the 1980s, output growth declined. By the early 1990s, the economy was shrinking. A combination of three features of the Soviet economy caused this deterioration in economic performance: the economy made a transition from being an investment economy to being a consumption economy; the economy was hit by serious external shocks; and its taut and inflexible planning system was incapable of coping with these events.

By the end of the 1980s, the Soviet Union began a process of transition toward a market economy. This process had three main elements: the relaxation of central plan enforcement, the deregulation of prices, and the introduction of limited private ownership of firms. The transition was a process of gradual change, but it ran into severe problems. The most important were value and legal systems alien to capitalism, the collapse of traditional trade flows, and the emergence of a large state budget deficit and inflation. (pp. 557–567)

Economic Transition in Eastern Europe

The formerly planned economies of East Germany, Czechoslovakia, Hungary, and Poland are also making transitions to market economies. East Germany's transition has been the most dramatic and the most complete. It has taken the form of a reunification of the two Germanies and the adoption by the former East Germany of West Germany's monetary and taxation system. Price deregulation and privatization have been rapid. Czechoslovakia has deregulated wages, prices, and interest rates and is privatizing its industry by returning small businesses and shops to their former owners and by issuing vouchers to its citizens that they may use to buy shares in formerly state-owned enterprises. Hungary began the process of moving toward a market economy during the 1960s when central planning was replaced by decentralized planning. Hungary has established a taxation system similar to that in the market economies. But the privatization of large-scale industry began only in the 1990s and is proceeding slowly. Poland has deregulated prices, pursued a policy of financial restraint that has brought inflation under control, and put privatization on a fast track. (pp. 567–569)

Economic Transition in China

Since the foundation of the People's Republic of China, economic management has been through turbulent changes. At first, China used the Soviet system of central planning. It then introduced the Great Leap Forward, which in turn degenerated into the Cultural Revolution. China at first grew quickly with heavy reliance on state planning and capital accumulation, but growth slowed, and, at times, per capita income actually fell. In 1978, China revolutionized its economic management, placing greater emphasis on private incentives and markets. As a consequence, productivity grew at a rapid rate and per capita income increased.

China's success in achieving a high rate of economic growth has resulted from four features of its reforms: a massive rate of entry of new non-state firms, large increases in the productivity and profitability of state firms, an efficient taxation system, and gradual price deregulation. Whether China has found a way of making the transition from socialism to capitalism in a relatively painless way is a controversial issue. (pp. 569–572)

The Transition from Central Plan to Market

In the transition from central planning to the market economy, three important choices must be made: the style of market economy to adopt, the sequencing of reforms, and the speed of reforms.

There are three main types of market economy to choose from: U.S.-style capitalism, Japanese-style capitalism, and welfare state capitalism. Two features of Japanese capitalism distinguish it from U.S. capitalism: its smaller scale of government and its pro-business government intervention. The capitalism of Western Europe, welfare state capitalism, is more heavily tinged with socialism than is that of either the United States or Japan. Government expenditure and taxes are much higher there—between 40 and 50 percent of GDP—and more of the manufacturing sector is state-owned, or nationalized.

The main issue in the sequencing of reform is the order in which to privatize the ownership of capital and land and to deregulate prices. The main issue concerning the speed of reform is whether to go slowly—gradualism—or quickly—in a "big bang." (pp. 573–575)

KEY ELEMENTS

Key Terms

Capitalism, 554
Central planning, 554
Decentralized planning, 554
Great Leap Forward, 569
Hierarchy, 560
Incentive structure, 553
Market socialism, 554
Nationalized industry, 574
Privatization, 574
Socialism, 554
Welfare state capitalism, 554

Key Figures and Tables

REVIEW QUESTIONS

1 What is the fundamental economic problem that any economic system must solve?

2 What are the main economic systems? Set out the key features of each.

3 Give examples of countries that are capitalist, socialist, market socialist, and welfare state capitalist. (Name some countries other than those in Fig. 21.2.)

4 How does capitalism solve the economic problem? What determines how much of each good to produce?

5 How does socialism solve the economic problem? What determines how much of each good to produce?

6 How does market socialism determine the price and quantity of each good?

7 Why did the Soviet economy begin to fail in the 1980s?

8 What are the main features of the transition program in the former Soviet Union?

9 What are the main problems faced by the republics of the former Soviet Union?

10 What are the problems faced by the Eastern European countries as they make the transition to a market economy?

11 Review the main episodes in China's economic management since 1949.

12 Compare the economic growth performance of the United States and China. What do we learn from this comparison?

13 What are the lessons of the economic experiment that is going on in China?

GLOSSARY

Above full-employment equilibrium A situation in which macroeconomic equilibrium occurs at a level of real GDP above long-run real GDP.

Absolute advantage A person has an absolute advantage in production if that person has greater productivity than anyone else in the production of all goods. A country has an absolute advantage if its output per unit of inputs of all goods is larger than that of another country.

Aggregate demand The relationship between the aggregate quantity of goods and services demanded—real GDP demanded—and the price level—the GDP deflator—holding everything else constant.

Aggregate demand curve A curve showing real GDP demanded at each price level, holding everything else constant.

Aggregate demand schedule A list showing the quantity of real GDP demanded at each price level, holding everything else constant.

Aggregate expenditure curve A graph of the aggregate expenditure schedule.

Aggregate expenditure schedule A list of the level of aggregate planned expenditure generated at each level of real GDP.

Aggregate income The amount received by households in payment for the services of factors of production.

Aggregate planned expenditure The expenditure that economic agents (households, firms, governments, and foreigners) plan to undertake in given circumstances.

Aggregate quantity of goods and services demanded The sum of the quantities of consumption goods and services that households plan to buy, of investment goods that firms plan to buy, of goods and services that governments plan to buy, and of net exports that foreigners plan to buy.

Aggregate quantity of goods and services supplied The sum of the quantities of all final goods and services produced by all firms in the economy.

Anticipated inflation An inflation rate that has been correctly forecasted (on the average).

Arbitrage The activity of buying low and selling high in order to make a profit on the margin between the two prices.

Asset Anything of value that a household, firm, or government owns.

Assumptions The foundation on which a model is built.

Automatic stabilizer A mechanism that decreases the fluctuations in aggregate expenditure resulting from fluctuations in a component of aggregate expenditure.

Autonomous expenditure The sum of those components of aggregate planned expenditure that are not influenced by real GDP.

Autonomous expenditure multiplier The amount by which a change in autonomous expenditure is multiplied to determine the change in equilibrium expenditure that it generates.

Average propensity to consume The ratio of consumption expenditure to disposable income.

Average propensity to save The ratio of saving to disposable income.

Axes The scale lines on a graph.

Balanced budget A government budget in which tax revenue and expenditure are equal.

Balanced budget multiplier The amount by which a change in government purchases of goods and services is multiplied to determine the change in expenditure equilibrium when taxes are changed by the same amount as the change in government purchases.

Balance of payments accounts A country's record of international trading, borrowing, and lending.

Balance of trade The value of exports minus the value of imports.

Balance sheet A list of assets and liabilities.

Barter The direct exchange of goods and services for other goods and services.

Budget balance Total tax revenue minus the government's total expenditure in a given period of time (normally a year).

Budget deficit A government's budget balance that is negative—expenditure exceeds tax revenue.

Budget surplus A government's budget balance that is positive—tax revenue exceeds expenditure.

Business cycle The periodic but irregular up-and-down movement in economic activity, measured by fluctuations in real GDP and other macroeconomic variables.

Capital The real assets—the equipment, buildings, tools, and other manufactured goods used in production—owned by a household, firm, or government.

Capital account A record of a country's international borrowing and lending transactions.

Capital accumulation The growth of capital resources.

Capital goods Goods that are added to our capital resources.

Capital stock The stock of plant, equipment, buildings (including residential housing), and inventories.

Capitalism An economic system that permits private ownership of capital and land used in production and market allocation of resources.

Central bank A public authority charged with regulating and controlling a country's monetary and financial institutions and markets.

Central planning A method of allocating resources by command.

Ceteris paribus Other things being equal, or other things remaining constant.

Change in demand A shift of the entire demand curve that occurs when some influence on buyers' plans, other than the price of the good, changes.

Change in quantity demanded A movement along a demand curve that results from a change in the price of the good.

Change in quantity supplied A movement along a supply curve that results from a change in the price of the good.

Change in supply A shift of the entire supply curve that occurs when some influence on producers' plans, other than the price of the good, changes.

Checkable deposit A loan by a depositor to a bank, the ownership of which can be transferred from one person to another by writing an instruction to the bank—a check—asking the bank to alter its records.

Closed economy An economy that has no links with any other economy.

Command economy An economy that relies on a command mechanism.

Command mechanism A method of determining *what*, *how*, and *for whom* goods and services are produced, based on the authority of a ruler or ruling body.

Commercial bank A private firm, chartered either by the Comptroller of the Currency (in the U.S. Treasury) or by a state agency to receive deposits and make loans.

Commodity money A physical commodity valued in its own right and also used as a means of payment.

Communist country A country in which there is limited private ownership of productive capital and of firms, there is limited reliance on the market as a means of allocating resources, and government agencies plan and direct the production and distribution of most goods and services.

Comparative advantage A person has a comparative advantage in producing a good if he or she can produce that good at a lower opportunity cost than anyone else. A country has a comparative advantage in producing a good if it can produce that good at a lower opportunity cost than any other country.

Competition A contest for command over scarce resources.

Complement A good that is used in conjunction with another good.

Consumer Price Index An index that measures the average level of prices of the goods and services typically consumed by an urban American family.

Consumption The process of using up goods and services.

Consumption expenditure The total payment made by households on consumption goods and services.

Consumption function The relationship between consumption expenditure and disposable income, other things held constant.

Consumption goods Goods that are used up as soon as they are produced.

Contraction A business cycle phase in which there is a slowdown in the pace of economic activity.

Convertible paper money A paper claim to a commodity (such as gold) that circulates as a means of payment.

Cooperation People working with others to achieve a common end.

Coordinates Lines running from a point on a graph perpendicularly to the axes.

Cost-push inflation Inflation that results from a decrease in aggregate supply, which increases costs.

Countervailing duty A tariff that is imposed to enable domestic producers to compete with subsidized foreign producers.

Credit union A financial intermediary based on a social or economic group that obtains its funds from checking and savings deposits and makes consumer loans.

Creditor nation A country that has invested more in the rest of the world than other countries have invested in it.

Crowding in The tendency for an expansionary fiscal policy to increase investment.

Crowding out The tendency for an expansionary fiscal policy to increase interest rates, thereby reducing—crowding out—investment.

Currency The bills and coins that we use today.

Currency appreciation The increase in the value of one currency in terms of another currency.

Currency depreciation The fall in the value of one currency in terms of another currency.

Currency drain The tendency for some of the funds lent by banks and financial institutions to remain outside the banking system and circulate as currency in the hands of the public.

Current account A record of receipts from the sale of goods and services to foreigners, the payments for goods and services bought from foreigners, and gifts and other transfers (such as foreign aid payments) received from and paid to foreigners.

Current account balance The value of all the goods and services that we sell to other countries minus the value of goods and services that we buy from foreigners.

Curve Any relationship between two variables plotted on a graph, even a linear relationship.

Cyclical unemployment The unemployment arising from the slowdown in the pace of economic expansion.

Cyclically adjusted deficit The deficit that would occur if the economy were at full employment.

Debt financing The financing of the government deficit by selling bonds to anyone (household, firm, or foreigner) other than the Federal Reserve System.

Debtor nation A country that, during its entire history, has borrowed more from the rest of the world than it has lent to it. It has a stock of outstanding debt to the rest of the world that exceeds the stock of its own claims on the rest of the world.

Decentralized planning An economic system that combines state ownership of capital and land with incentives based on a mixture of market and administered prices.

Demand The entire relationship between the quantity demanded of a good and its price.

Demand curve A graph showing the relationship between the quantity demanded of a good and its price, holding everything else constant.

Demand for labor The quantity of labor demanded at each level of the real wage rate.

Demand for real money The relationship between the quantity of real money demanded and the interest rate, holding constant all other influences on the amount of money that people wish to hold.

Demand-pull inflation Inflation that results from an increase in aggregate demand.

Demand schedule A list of the quantities demanded at different prices, holding everything else constant.

Depreciation The decrease in the value of capital stock or the value of a durable input that results from wear and tear and the passage of time.

Depression A deep business cycle trough.

Developing country A country that is poor but is accumulating capital and developing an industrial and commercial base.

Diminishing marginal product of labor The tendency for the marginal product of labor to decline as the labor input increases, holding everything else constant.

Discount rate The interest rate at which the Fed stands ready to lend reserves to commercial banks.

Discouraged workers People who do not have jobs and would like to work but have stopped seeking work.

Disposable income Income plus transfer payments minus taxes.

Dissaving Negative saving; a situation in which consumption expenditure exceeds disposable income.

Double coincidence of wants A situation that occurs when person A wants to buy what person B is selling and person B wants to buy what person A is selling.

Double counting Counting the expenditure on both the final good and the intermediate goods and services used in its production.

Dumping The sale of a good in a foreign market for a lower price than in the domestic market or for a lower price than its cost of production.

Economic activity What people do to cope with scarcity.

Economic growth The expansion of our production possibilities.

Economic theory A rule or principle that enables us to understand and predict economic choices.

Economic welfare A comprehensive measure of the general state of well-being and standard of living.

Economics The study of how people use their limited resources to try to satisfy unlimited wants.

Economizing Making the best use of scarce resources.

Economy A mechanism that allocates scarce resources among competing uses.

Endowment The resources that people have.

Equation of exchange An equation that states that the quantity of money multiplied by the velocity of circulation of money equals GDP—the price level multiplied by real GDP.

Equilibrium A situation in which everyone has economized—that is, all individuals have made the best possible choices in the light of their own preferences and given their endowments, technologies, and information—and in which those choices have been coordinated and made compatible with the choices of everyone else. Equilibrium is the solution or outcome of an economic model.

Equilibrium expenditure The level of aggregate planned expenditure that equals real GDP.

Equilibrium price The price at which the quantity demanded equals the quantity supplied.

Equilibrium quantity The quantity bought and sold at the equilibrium price.

Excess reserves A bank's actual reserves minus its required reserves.

Expansion A business cycle phase in which there is a speedup in the pace of economic activity.

Expected inflation rate The rate at which people, on the average, believe that the price level is rising.

Expenditure approach A measure of GDP obtained by adding together consumption expenditure, investment, government purchases of goods and services, and net exports.

Exports The goods and services that we sell to people in other countries.

Factor cost The value of a good measured by adding together the costs of all the factors of production used to produce it.

Factor incomes approach A measure of GDP obtained by adding together all the incomes paid by firms to households for the services of the factors of production they hire—wages, interest, rent, and profits.

Factor market A market in which the factors of production are bought and sold.

Factors of production The economy's productive resources—land, labor, and capital.

Federal budget A statement of the federal government's financial plan, itemizing programs and their costs, tax revenues, and the proposed deficit or surplus.

Federal Open Market Committee The main policymaking organ of the Federal Reserve System.

Federal Reserve System The central bank of the United States.

Feedback rule A rule that states how policy actions respond to changes in the state of the economy.

Fiat money An intrinsically worthless (or almost worthless) commodity that serves the functions of money.

Final goods and services Goods and services that are not used as inputs in the production of other goods and services but are bought by their final user.

Financial innovation The development of new financial products—of new ways of borrowing and lending.

Financial intermediary A firm that takes deposits from households and firms and makes loans to other households and firms.

Firm An institution that buys or hires factors of production and organizes them to produce and sell goods and services.

Fiscal policy The government's attempt to influence the economy by varying its purchases of goods and services and taxes to smooth the fluctuations in aggregate expenditure.

Fixed exchange rate An exchange rate, the value of which is held steady by the country's central bank.

Fixed rule A rule that specifies an action to be pursued independently of the state of the economy.

Flexible exchange rate An exchange rate, the value of which is determined by market forces in the absence of central bank intervention.

Flow equilibrium A situation in which the quantity of goods or services supplied per unit of time equals the quantity demanded per unit of time.

Foreign exchange market The market in which the currency of one country is exchanged for the currency of another.

Foreign exchange rate The rate at which one country's money (or currency) exchanges for another country's money.

Frictional unemployment Unemployment arising from normal labor turnover—new entrants are constantly coming into the labor market, and firms are constantly laying off workers and hiring new workers.

Full employment A situation in which the number of people looking for a job equals the number of job vacancies.

Full-employment equilibrium A macroeconomic equilibrium in which real GDP equals long-run real GDP.

GDP deflator A price index that measures the average level of the prices of all the goods and services that make up GDP.

General Agreement on Tariffs and Trade An international agreement that limits government intervention to restrict international trade.

Goods and services All the valuable things that people produce. Goods are tangible, and services are intangible.

Goods market A market in which goods and services are bought and sold.

Government An organization that provides goods and services to households and firms and redistributes income and wealth.

Government debt The total amount of borrowing that the government has undertaken and the total amount that it owes to households, firms, and foreigners.

Government deficit The total expenditure of the government sector less the total revenue of that sector in a given period.

Government purchases multiplier The amount by which a change in government purchases of goods and services is multiplied to determine the change in equilibrium expenditure that it generates.

Great Leap Forward An economic plan for postrevolutionary China based on small-scale, labor-intensive production.

Gresham's Law The tendency for bad money to drive good money out of circulation.

Gross domestic product The value of all final goods and services produced in the economy in a year.

Gross investment The amount spent on replacing depreciated capital and on net additions to the capital stock.

Gross national product The total value of output owned by residents of the United States.

Hierarchy An organization arranged in ranks, each rank being subordinate to the one above.

Household Any group of people living together as a decision-making unit.

Human capital The accumulated skill and knowledge of human beings; the value of a person's education and acquired skills.

Implications The outcome of a model that follows logically from its assumptions.

Imports The goods and services that we buy from people in other countries.

Incentive structure A set of arrangements that induce people to take certain actions.

Indirect tax A tax paid by consumers when they purchase goods and services.

Induced expenditure The part of aggregate planned expenditure on U.S.-produced goods and services that varies as real GDP varies.

Industrial country A country that has a large amount of capital equipment and in which people undertake highly specialized activities, enabling them to earn high per capita incomes.

Inferior good A good the demand for which decreases when income increases.

Inflation An upward movement in the average level of prices.

Inflation rate The percentage change in the price level.

Inflationary gap Actual real GDP minus long-run real GDP when actual real GDP is above long-run real GDP.

Injections Expenditures that add to the circular flow of expenditure and income—investment, government purchases of goods and services, and exports.

Innovation The act of putting a new technique to work.

Intellectual property The intangible product of creative effort, protected by copyrights and patents. This type of property includes books, music, computer programs, and inventions of all kinds.

Interest rate parity A situation in which interest rates are equal across all countries once the differences in risk are taken into account.

Intermediate goods and services Goods and services that are used as inputs into the production process of another good or service.

International crowding out The tendency for an expansionary fiscal policy to decrease net exports.

International Monetary Fund An international organization that monitors the balance of payments and exchange rate activities.

International substitution The substitution of domestic goods and services for foreign goods and services or of foreign goods and services for domestic goods and services.

Intertemporal substitution The substitution of goods and services now for goods and services later or of goods and services later for goods and services now.

Invention The discovery of a new technique.

Inventories The stocks of raw materials, semifinished products, and unsold final goods held by firms.

Investment The purchase of new plant, equipment, and buildings and additions to inventories.

Investment demand The relationship between the level of planned investment and the real interest rate, holding all other influences on investment constant.

Investment demand curve A curve showing the relationship between the real interest rate and the level of planned investment, holding everything else constant.

Investment demand schedule The list showing the quantity of planned investment at each real interest rate, holding everything else constant.

Investment security A marketable security that a bank can sell at a moment's notice if necessary but at a price that fluctuates.

Keynesian A macroeconomist who regards the economy as being inherently unstable and as requiring active government intervention to achieve stability.

Labor The brain power and muscle power of human beings.

Labor force The total number of employed and unemployed workers.

Labor force participation rate The proportion of the working age population that is either employed or unemployed (but seeking employment).

Labor productivity Total output per person employed.

Laffer curve A curve that relates tax revenue to the tax rate.

Land Natural resources of all kinds.

Law of one price A law stating that any given commodity will be available at a single price.

Leakages Income that is not spent on domestically produced goods and services—saving, taxes (net of transfer payments), and imports.

Liability A debt—something that a household, firm, or government owes.

Line-item veto A veto power vested in the executive branch of the government to eliminate any specific item in a budget.

Linear relationship The relationship between two variables depicted by a straight line on a graph.

Liquid asset An asset that is instantly convertible into a means of payment with virtually no uncertainty about the price at which it can be converted.

Liquidity The degree to which an asset is instantly convertible into cash at a known price.

Liquidity trap A situation in which people are willing to hold any amount of money at a given interest rate—the demand curve for real money is horizontal.

Loan A commitment of a fixed amount of money for an agreed period of time.

Long-run aggregate supply The relationship between the aggregate quantity of final goods and services (GDP) supplied and the price level (GDP deflator) when there is full employment.

Long-run aggregate supply curve A curve showing the quantity of real GDP supplied and the price level when there is full employment.

Long-run Phillips curve A curve showing the relationship between inflation and unemployment when the actual inflation rate equals the expected inflation rate.

Lorenz curve A curve that shows the cumulative percentage of income or wealth against the cumulative percentage of families or population.

M1 A measure of money that sums currency held outside banks, traveler's checks, demand deposits, and other checkable deposits such as NOW and ATS accounts.

M2 A measure of money that sums M1, savings deposits, small time deposits, Eurodollar deposits, money market mutual fund shares held by individuals, and other M2 deposits.

M3 A measure of money that sums M2, large time deposits, Eurodollar time deposits, institutional money market mutual fund shares, and other M3 deposits.

Macroeconomic equilibrium A situation in which the quantity of real GDP demanded equals the quantity of real GDP supplied.

Macroeconomic long-run A period that is sufficiently long for the prices of all the factors of production to have adjusted to any disturbance.

Macroeconomic short-run A period during which the prices of goods and services change in response to changes in demand and supply but the prices of factors of production do not change.

Macroeconomics The branch of economics that studies the economy as a whole. Macroeconomics is concerned with the overall level of economic activity rather than with detailed individual choices.

Managed exchange rate An exchange rate, the value of which is influenced by bank intervention in the foreign exchange market.

Marginal product of labor The change in total product (output) resulting from a one-unit increase in the quantity of labor employed, holding the quantity of all other inputs constant.

Marginal propensity to consume The fraction of the last dollar of disposable income that is spent on consumption goods and services.

Marginal propensity to consume out of real GDP The change in consumption expenditure divided by the change in real GDP.

Marginal propensity to import The fraction of the last dollar of real GDP spent on imports.

Marginal propensity to save The fraction of the last dollar of disposable income that is saved.

Marginal tax rate The fraction of the last dollar of income paid to the government in net taxes (taxes minus transfer payments).

Market Any arrangement that facilitates buying and selling of a good, service, factor of production, or future commitment.

Market economy An economy that determines *what*, *how*, and *for whom* goods and services are produced by coordinating individual choices through markets.

Market price The price that people pay for a good or service.

Market socialism An economic system that combines state ownership of capital and land with incentives based on a mixture of market and administered prices.

Medium of exchange Anything that is generally acceptable in exchange for goods and services.

Microeconomics The branch of economics that studies the decisions of individual households and firms and the way in which individual markets work. Microeconomics also studies the way in which taxes and government regulation affect our economic choices.

Mixed economy An economy that relies partly on markets and partly on a command mechanism to coordinate economic activity.

Monetarist A macroeconomist who assigns a high degree of importance to variations in the quantity of money as the main determinant of aggregate demand and who regards the economy as inherently stable.

Monetary base The sum of the Federal Reserve notes in circulation, banks' deposits at the Fed, and coins in circulation.

Monetary exchange A system in which some commodity or token serves as the medium of exchange.

Monetary policy The Fed's attempt to influence the economy by varying the money supply and interest rates.

Money Any commodity or token that is generally acceptable as a means of payment for goods and services.

Money financing The financing of the government deficit by the sale of bonds to the Federal Reserve System, which results in the creation of additional money.

Money market mutual fund A financial institution that obtains funds by selling shares and that uses the funds to buy highly liquid assets such as U.S. Treasury bills.

Money multiplier The amount by which a change in the monetary base is multiplied to determine the resulting change in the quantity of money.

Money wage rate The wage rate expressed in current dollars.

Multiplier The change in equilibrium real GDP divided by the change in autonomous expenditure.

Nationalized industry An industry owned and operated by a publicly owned authority that is directly responsible to the government.

Natural rate hypothesis The proposition that the long-run Phillips curve is vertical at the natural rate of unemployment.

Natural rate of unemployment The unemployment rate when the economy is at full employment.

Negative relationship A relationship between two variables that move in opposite directions.

Net borrower A country that is borrowing more from the rest of the world than it is lending to it.

Net domestic income at factor cost The sum of all factor incomes.

Net domestic product at market prices The sum of all factor income plus indirect taxes less subsidies.

Net export function The relationship between net exports and U.S. real GDP, holding constant all other influences on U.S. exports and imports.

Net exporter A country whose value of exports exceeds its value of imports—its balance of trade is positive.

Net exports The expenditure by foreigners on U.S.-produced goods minus the expenditure by U.S. residents on foreign-produced goods—exports minus imports.

Net importer A country whose value of imports exceeds its value of exports—its balance of trade is negative.

Net investment Net additions to the capital stock—gross investment minus depreciation.

Net lender A country that is lending more to the rest of the world than it is borrowing from it.

Newly industrialized country A country in which there is a rapidly developing broad industrial base and per capita income is growing quickly.

Nominal GDP The output of final goods and services valued at current prices.

Nominal GDP targeting The attempt to keep the growth of nominal GDP steady.

Nominal interest rate The interest rate actually paid and received in the marketplace.

Nominal money The quantity of money measured in current dollars.

Nonconvertible note A bank note that is not convertible into any commodity and that obtains its value by government fiat.

Nontariff barriers Any action other than a tariff that restricts international trade.

Nontraded good A good that cannot be traded over long distances.

Normal good A good the demand for which increases when income increases.

Normative statement A statement about what *ought* to be. An expression of an opinion that cannot be verified by observation.

Official reserves The government's holdings of foreign currency.

Official settlements account An account showing the net increase or decrease in a country's holdings of foreign currency.

Open economy An economy that has economic links with other economies.

Open market operation The purchase or sale of government securities by the Federal Reserve System designed to influence the money supply.

Opportunity cost The best forgone alternative.

Optimizing The process of balancing benefits against costs and doing the best within the limits of what is possible.

Origin The zero point that is common to both axes on a graph.

Paradox of thrift The fact that an increase in thriftiness leads to an increase in the income of an individual but to a decrease in aggregate income. The paradox arises because an increase in saving occurs with no increase in investment.

Peak The upper turning point of a business cycle, where an expansion turns into a contraction.

Per capita production function A curve showing how per capita output varies as the per capita stock of capital varies in a given state of knowledge about alternative technology.

Perpetuity A bond that promises to pay a certain fixed amount of money each year forever.

Phillips curve A curve showing the relationship between inflation and unemployment.

Political business cycle A business cycle whose origins are fluctuations in aggregate demand brought about by policies designed to improve the chance of the government being re-elected.

Positive relationship A relationship between two variables that move in the same direction.

Positive statement A statement about what *is*. Something that can be verified by careful observation.

Preferences People's likes and dislikes and the intensity of those likes and dislikes.

Price index A measure of the average level of prices in one period as a percentage of their level in an earlier period.

Price level The average level of prices as measured by a price index.

Private debt money A loan that the borrower promises to repay in currency on demand.

Private enterprise An economic system that permits individuals to decide on their own economic activities.

Private sector surplus or deficit The difference between saving and investment.

Privatization The process of selling state-owned enterprises to private individuals and firms.

Production The conversion of natural, human, and capital resources into goods and services.

Production function A relationship showing how output varies as the employment of inputs is varied.

Production possibility frontier The boundary between attainable and unattainable levels of production.

Productivity The amount of output produced per unit of inputs used to produce it.

Property Anything of value that is owned.

Property rights Social arrangements that govern the ownership, use, and disposal of economic resources.

Protectionism The restriction of international trade.

Purchasing power parity A situation that occurs when money has equal value across countries.

Quantity demanded The amount of a good or service that consumers plan to buy in a given period of time at a particular price.

Quantity of labor demanded The number of labor hours hired by all the firms in an economy.

Quantity of labor supplied The number of hours of labor services that households supply to firms.

Quantity of money The quantity of currency, bank deposits, and deposits at other types of financial institutions such as savings and loan associations and thrift institutions held by households and firms.

Quantity of U.S. dollar assets The stock of financial assets denominated in U.S. dollars minus the stock of financial liabilities denominated in U.S. dollars.

Quantity supplied The amount of a good or service that producers plan to sell in a given period of time at a particular price.

Quantity theory of money The proposition that an increase in the quantity of money leads to an equal percentage increase in the price level.

Quota A restriction on the quantity of a good that a firm is permitted to produce or that a country is permitted to import.

Rational choice The choice that, among all possible choices, best achieves the goals.

Rational expectation A forecast that uses all of the relevant information available about past and present events and that has the least possible error.

Rational expectations equilibrium A macroeconomic equilibrium based on expectations that are the best available forecasts.

Rational expectations hypothesis The proposition that the forecasts people make, regardless of how they make them, are the same as the forecasts made by an economist using the relevant economic theory together with all information available at the time the forecast is made.

Real business cycle theory A theory of aggregate fluctuations based on flexible wages and random shocks to the economy's aggregate production function.

Real deficit The change in the real value of outstanding government debt.

Real GDP The output of final goods and services valued at prices prevailing in the base period.

Real interest rate The interest rate paid by a borrower and received by a lender after taking into account the change in the value of money resulting from inflation.

Real money A measure of money based on the quantity of goods and services it will buy.

Real money balances effect The influence of a change in the quantity of real money on the quantity of real GDP demanded.

Real wage rate The wage rate per hour expressed in constant dollars.

Recession A downturn in the level of economic activity in which real GDP falls in two successive quarters.

Recessionary gap Long-run real GDP minus actual real GDP when actual real GDP is below long-run real GDP.

Relative price The ratio of the price of one good to the price of another.

Required reserve ratio The ratio of reserves to deposits that banks are required, by regulation, to hold.

Required reserves The minimum reserves that a bank is permitted to hold—its deposits multiplied by the required reserve ratio.

Reservation wage The lowest wage rate at which a person or household will supply labor to the market. Below that wage, a person will not work.

Reserve ratio The fraction of a bank's total deposits that are held in reserves.

Reserves Cash in a bank's vault plus the bank's deposits with the Federal Reserve banks.

Saving Income minus consumption. Saving is measured in the national income accounts as disposable income (income less taxes) minus consumption expenditure.

Saving function The relationship between saving and disposable income, other things held constant.

Savings and loan association A financial intermediary that traditionally obtained its funds from savings deposits and that made long-term mortgage loans to home buyers.

Savings bank A financial intermediary owned by its depositors that accepts deposits and makes loans, mostly for consumer mortgages.

Scarcity The universal state in which wants exceed resources.

Scatter diagram A diagram that plots the value of one economic variable associated with the value of another.

Self-sufficiency A state that occurs when people produce only enough for their own consumption.

Short-run aggregate production function The relationship showing how real GDP varies as the quantity of labor employed varies, holding constant the inputs, including the capital stock and state of technology.

Short-run aggregate supply The relationship between the aggregate quantity of goods and services (real GDP) supplied and the price level (the GDP deflator), holding everything else constant.

Short-run aggregate supply curve A curve showing the relationship between the quantity of real GDP supplied and the price level, holding everything else constant.

Short-run aggregate supply schedule A list showing the quantity of real GDP supplied at each price level, holding everything else constant.

Short-run Phillips curve A curve showing the relationship between inflation and unemployment, holding constant the expected inflation rate and the natural rate of unemployment.

Short-run production function The relationship showing how output varies when the quantity of labor employed varies, holding constant the quantity of capital and the state of technology.

Simple money multiplier The amount by which an increase in bank reserves is multiplied to calculate the effect of the increase in reserves on total bank deposits when there are no losses of currency from the banking system.

Slope The change in the value of the variable measured on the *y*-axis divided by the change in the value of the variable measured on the *x*-axis.

Socialism An economic system based on state ownership of capital and land and on an incentive system based on administered prices or sanctions arising from a central economic plan.

Specialization The production of only one good or a few goods.

Standard of deferred payment An agreed measure that enables contracts to be written for future receipts and payments.

Stock equilibrium A situation in which the available stock of an asset is willingly held.

Store of value Any commodity or token that can be held and exchanged later for goods and services.

Structural unemployment The unemployment that arises when there is a decline in the number of jobs available in a particular region or industry.

Subsidy A payment made by the government to producers that depends on the level of output.

Substitute A good that may be used in place of another good.

Supply The entire relationship between the quantity supplied of a good and its price.

Supply curve A graph showing the relationship between the quantity supplied and the price of a good, holding everything else constant.

Supply of labor The quantity of labor supplied at each real wage rate.

Supply schedule A list of quantities supplied at different prices, holding everything else constant.

Tariff A tax on an import by the government of the importing country.

Tax base The activity on which a tax is levied.

Tax multiplier The amount by which a change in taxes is multiplied to determine the change in equilibrium expenditure that it generates.

Tax rate The percentage rate at which a tax is levied on a particular activity.

Technological progress The development of new and better ways of producing goods and services.

Technology The method for converting resources into goods and services.

Time-series graph A graph showing the value of a variable on the *y*-axis plotted against time on the *x*-axis.

Trade-weighted index The value of a basket of currencies when the weight placed on each currency is related to its importance in U.S. international trade.

Transfer payments Payments made by the government to households under social programs.

Transfer payments multiplier The amount by which a change in transfer payments is multiplied to determine the change in equilibrium expenditure that it generates.

Trend A general tendency for a variable to rise or fall.

Trough The lower turning point of a business cycle, where a contraction turns into an expansion.

Twin deficits The government budget deficit and the current account deficit.

Unanticipated inflation Inflation that catches people by surprise.

Underdeveloped country A country in which there is little industrialization, limited mechanization of the agricultural sector, very little capital equipment, and low per capita income.

Underdevelopment trap A situation in which a country is locked into a low per capita income situation that reinforces itself.

Underground economy All economic activity that is legal but unreported.

Unemployment A state in which there are qualified workers who are available for work at the current wage rate and who do not have jobs.

Unemployment equilibrium A situation in which macroeconomic equilibrium occurs at a level of real GDP below long-run real GDP.

Unemployment rate The number of people unemployed expressed as a percentage of the labor force.

Unit elastic demand An elasticity of demand of 1; the quantity demanded of a good and its price change in equal proportions.

Unit of account An agreed measure for stating the prices of goods and services.

Value added The value of a firm's output minus the value of the intermediate goods bought from other firms.

Value of money The amount of goods and services that can be bought with a given amount of money.

Velocity of circulation The average number of times a dollar of money is used annually to buy the goods and services that make up GDP.

Voluntary export restraint A self-imposed restriction by an exporting country on the volume of its exports of a particular good. Voluntary export restraints are often called VERs.

Wants The unlimited desires or wishes that people have for goods and services.

Welfare state capitalism An economic system that combines the private ownership of capital and land with state interventions in markets that change the price signals that people respond to.

Wholesale deposit market The market for deposits among banks and other financial institutions.

***x*-axis** The horizontal scale on a graph.

***x*-coordinate** A line running from a point on a graph horizontally to the *y*-axis. It is called the *x*-coordinate because its length is the same as the value marked off on the *x*-axis.

***y*-axis** The vertical scale on a graph.

***y*-coordinate** A line running from a point on a graph vertically to the *x*-axis. It is called the *y*-coordinate because its length is the same as the value marked off on the *y*-axis.

INDEX

Key concepts and pages on which they are defined appear in boldface.

Macroeconomic data for the United States: 1959–1992

Year	Gross domestic product (*Y*)	Personal consumption expenditures (*C*)	Gross private domestic investment (*I*)	Government purchases of goods and services (*G*)	Net exports (*NX*)	Unemployment rate (percentage of all workers)	GDP deflator (1987 = 100)	M1	M2
	(billions of 1987 dollars)							(billions of dollars)	
1959	1,931.3	1,178.9	296.4	477.8	–21.8	5.3	25.6	140.0	297.8
1960	1,973.2	1,210.8	290.8	479.2	–7.7	5.4	26.0	140.7	312.4
1961	2,025.6	1,238.4	289.4	503.3	–5.4	6.5	26.3	145.2	335.5
1962	2,129.8	1,293.3	321.2	525.9	–10.5	5.4	26.8	147.9	362.7
1963	2,218.0	1,341.9	343.3	538.7	0.1	5.5	27.2	153.4	393.3
1964	2,343.3	1,417.2	371.8	551.7	2.5	5.0	27.7	160.4	424.8
1965	2,473.5	1,497.0	413.0	569.9	–6.4	4.4	28.4	167.9	459.4
1966	2,622.3	1,573.8	438.0	628.5	–18.0	3.7	29.4	172.1	480.0
1967	2,690.3	1,622.4	418.6	673.0	–23.7	3.7	30.3	183.3	524.4
1968	2,801.0	1,707.5	440.1	691.0	–37.5	3.5	31.7	197.5	566.4
1969	2,877.1	1,771.2	461.3	686.1	–41.4	3.4	33.3	204.0	589.6
1970	2,875.8	1,813.5	429.7	667.8	–35.1	4.8	35.1	214.5	628.1
1971	2,965.1	1,873.7	481.5	655.8	–45.9	5.8	37.0	228.4	712.7
1972	3,107.1	1,978.4	532.2	653.0	–56.5	5.5	38.8	249.3	805.2
1973	3,268.6	2,066.7	591.7	644.2	–34.1	4.8	41.3	262.9	861.0
1974	3,248.1	2,053.8	543.0	655.4	–4.0	5.5	44.9	274.4	908.6
1975	3,221.7	2,097.5	437.6	663.5	23.1	8.3	49.2	287.6	1,023.3
1976	3,380.8	2,207.3	520.6	659.2	–6.3	7.6	52.3	306.4	1,163.7
1977	3,533.2	2,296.6	600.4	664.1	–27.8	6.9	55.9	331.3	1,286.6
1978	3,703.5	2,391.8	664.6	677.0	–29.9	6.0	60.3	358.4	1,388.7
1979	3,796.8	2,448.4	669.7	689.3	–10.6	5.8	65.5	382.8	1,496.7
1980	3,776.3	2,447.1	594.4	704.2	30.6	7.0	71.7	408.8	1,629.5
1981	3,843.1	2,476.9	631.1	713.2	22.0	7.5	78.9	436.5	1,792.9
1982	3,760.3	2,503.7	540.5	723.6	–7.4	9.5	83.8	474.6	1,951.9
1983	3,906.6	2,619.4	599.5	743.8	–56.2	9.5	87.2	521.4	2,186.1
1984	4,148.5	2,746.1	757.5	766.9	–122.0	7.4	91.0	552.5	2,374.3
1985	4,279.8	2,865.8	745.9	813.4	–145.4	7.1	94.4	620.2	2,569.4
1986	4,404.5	2,969.1	735.1	855.4	–155.1	6.9	96.9	724.6	2,811.1
1987	4,540.0	3,052.2	749.3	881.5	–143.1	6.1	100.0	750.0	2,910.8
1988	4,718.6	3,162.4	773.4	886.8	–104.1	5.4	103.9	786.9	3,071.1
1989	4,838.0	3,223.3	784.0	904.4	–73.7	5.2	108.4	794.1	3,227.3
1990	4,877.5	3,260.4	739.1	929.9	–51.8	5.4	112.9	826.1	3,339.0
1991	4,821.0	3,240.8	661.1	941.0	–21.8	6.6	117.8	898.1	3,439.8
1992	4,892.4	3,228.5	713.6	934.2	–43.9	7.4	120.6	1,019.0	3,507.5

Sources: GDP: 1959–1992, *Economic Report of the President, 1993,* Table B-2; unemployment: 1959–1992, *Economic Report of the President, 1993,* Table B-37; GDP deflator: 1959–1992, *Economic Report of the President, 1993,* Table B-3; Consumer Price Index: 1959–1992, *Economic Report of the President, 1993,* Table B-58; money supply: *Economic Report of the President, 1993,* Table B-65.

Federal, state, and local government receipts and expenditures / **Bond yields and interest rates**

Year	Receipts (billions of dollars)	Expenditures (billions of dollars)	Surplus or deficit (–) (billions of dollars)	U.S. treasury bills (percent per year)	Corporate bonds (percent per year)
1959	128.8	131.9	–3.1	3.4	4.4
1960	138.8	135.2	3.6	2.9	4.4
1961	144.1	147.1	–3.0	2.4	4.4
1962	155.8	158.7	–2.9	2.8	4.3
1963	167.5	165.9	1.6	3.2	4.3
1964	172.9	174.5	–1.6	3.5	4.4
1965	187.0	185.8	1.2	4.0	4.5
1966	210.7	211.6	–1.0	4.9	5.1
1967	226.4	240.2	–13.7	4.3	5.5
1968	260.9	265.5	–4.6	5.3	6.2
1969	294.0	284.0	10.0	6.7	7.0
1970	299.8	311.2	–11.5	6.5	8.0
1971	318.9	338.1	–19.2	4.3	7.4
1972	364.2	368.1	–3.9	4.1	7.2
1973	408.5	401.6	6.9	7.0	7.4
1974	450.7	455.2	–4.5	7.9	8.6
1975	465.8	530.6	–64.8	5.8	8.8
1976	532.6	570.9	–38.3	5.0	8.4
1977	598.4	615.2	–16.8	5.3	8.0
1978	673.2	670.3	2.9	7.2	8.7
1979	754.7	745.3	9.4	10.0	9.6
1980	825.7	861.0	–35.3	11.5	11.9
1981	941.9	972.3	–30.3	14.0	14.2
1982	960.5	1,069.1	–108.6	10.7	13.8
1983	1,016.4	1,156.2	–139.8	8.6	12.0
1984	1,123.6	1,232.4	–108.8	9.6	12.7
1985	1,217.0	1,342.2	–125.3	7.5	11.4
1986	1,290.8	1,437.5	–146.8	6.0	9.0
1987	1,405.2	1,516.9	–111.7	5.8	9.4
1988	1,492.4	1,590.7	–98.3	6.7	9.7
1989	1,622.6	1,700.1	–77.5	8.1	9.3
1990	1,704.4	1,840.5	–136.1	7.5	9.3
1991	1,746.8	1,940.1	–193.3	5.4	8.8
1992	1,809.6	2,094.9	–285.2	3.5	8.1

Sources: Economic Report of the President, 1993, Tables B-69 and B-77.